The Cook's Companion

A Rutledge Book
Crown Publishers, Inc.
New York

EDITORIAL
Fred R. Sammis
John Sammis
Beverlee Galli
Jay Hyams
Jeremy Friedlander

ART DIRECTION
Allan Mogel

PRODUCTION
Lori Stein

Prepared and produced by Rutledge Books, Inc., 25 West 43
Street, New York, N.Y. 10036.

Published in 1978 by Crown Publishers, Inc., One Park Avenue,
New York, N.Y. 10016.

Library of Congress Cataloging in Publication Data
Townsend, Doris McFerran.
   The cook's companion.
   "A Rutledge book."
   1. Cookery—Dictionaries.   2. Food—Dictionaries.
I. Title.
TX349.T65   641.3′003   78–14792
ISBN 0–517–53199–2

Printed in the United States of America
First Printing 1978

For the information they supplied, for the cheerful cooperation
they gave, thanks are due to: Alabama Peanut Producers
Association; American Dairy Association; American Egg Board;
American National Metric Council; American Spice Trade
Association; California Avocado Growers Association; California
Beef Council; California Dried Fig Advisory Board; California Egg
Industry; California Foods Research Institute; California Milk
Advisory Board; California Prune Advisory Board; California
Strawberry Advisory Board; Canned Salmon Institute; Durum
Wheat Institute; Economic Research Service; General Nutrition
Corporation; International Apple Institute; Lamb Education Center;
National Canners Association, Home Economics-Consumer
Services; National Dairy Council; National Live Stock and Meat
Board; National Macaroni Institute; New Hampshire Maple
Producers Association; North Dakota State University,
Cooperative Extension Service; Pear Growers League; Potato
Board; Rice Council of America; Sugar Information, Inc.; United
Fresh Fruit and Vegetable Association; United States Department
of Agriculture; United States Department of Health, Education and
Welfare, Office of Consumer Affairs; United States Department of
the Interior, Fish and Wildlife Service; United States Food and
Drug Administration, and *FDA Consumer;* University of California,
Division of Agricultural Science.

INTRODUCTION

According to the USDA, the average American family eats about 2.5 tons of food a year, including 694 pounds of meat and fish, 598 pounds of fruit, 1,136 pounds of dairy products, 1,154 pounds of vegetables, 592 pounds of grain products, and 394 pounds of poultry. Small wonder that women constantly hone their skills for ventures into new culinary territories, that men and even children are attending cooking schools as never before and bringing the expertise they acquire into their homes to help cope with that vast tonnage.

In my own coping with it, I have been singularly fortunate in the large number of food-oriented people with whom, from time to time, I have shared a kitchen. My grandmother's succession of Swedish "hired girls" who put up with my being constantly under foot when I was a child. My aunt Hazel, totally deaf and almost blind, a spectacular cook who taught me all she knew. Helga Swenson, the sorority house cook, who whipped up luncheons for thirty-five and dinner for a hundred without turning a hair, but was made very nervous by the fact that I enjoyed helping her rather than playing bridge or gossiping with the other girls. Dr. Anna Augusta von Helmholtz-Phelan, formidable professor of literature, who wrote excellent poetry with one hand and turned out magnificent soufflés with the other. My four sisters-in-law, who teamed with me to cook for many huge family reunions. Assorted home economists, of temperament serene to crotchety, with whom I have worked, including Hyla O'Connor, who introduced me to the joys and woes of cooking for color photography. And Bill, my husband, who enjoys helping, who cheerfully peels and slices, chops and grinds—and doles out large measures of encouragement.

I've been lucky, too, in the people I've fed over the years; they have exhibited what I like to think of as taste and discernment in offering heady praise of my efforts. Among them have been editors and publishers who liked what I wrote as much as they liked what I put on the table—liked it well enough to publish it.

But even with such support and companionship, I could not have written the present monster book if I were not by nature a pack rat. All along, I've been filing away bits and pieces of food information against the day when someone would say to me, "Why don't you write a big book about all the many kinds of food?"

Someone finally did, and this is it.

It wasn't easy. A large number of areas about which I had no filed-away information had to be researched. Art has to be considered and ordered. I ran through uncounted amounts of paper and numbers of typewriter ribbons, and three excellent typists—Juanita Smith, Elizabeth Nipperus, and Fay Wells—ruffled my own generally serene feathers on numerous occasions, and upped my swearing quota by a considerable figure.

But it was fun. And it was worthwhile to me, as I hope it will prove to be to you.

Doris McFerran Townsend
San Diego, California
March 12, 1978

CONTENTS

HOW TO USE THIS BOOK

Everything to do with food itself is listed alphabetically. Find whatever food item you want to know about, from "a la" to zwieback, under its initial letter; if that particular food is a part of a larger subject, you'll find a cross reference to guide you. Locate the pages for each letter of the alphabet in the listing. For additional information on a subject, cross references in capital letters often appear within an article.

Those subjects that are not food per se but have to do with food are treated separately, as special features. These occur between letters of the alphabet. Often an alphabetical listing will refer you to one of the special features for related information. These special features, too, are listed.

ALPHABETICAL LISTINGS

SPECIAL FEATURES

metrication is coming, sure as sunrise—it behooves us all to learn the new terms, new ways to weigh and measure

whatever you buy, whatever you use, one of Uncle Sam's watchdogs has graded, inspected, or otherwise regulated it

We may live without poetry, music and art;
We may live without conscience and live without heart;
We may live without friends, we may live without books;
But civilized man cannot live without cooks.
He may live without books—what is knowledge but
grieving?
He may live without hope—what is hope but deceiving?
He may live without love—what is passion but pining?
But where is the man who can live without dining?
—Edward Robert Bulwer Lytton

A LA: see page 450

ABALONE: see SHELLFISH

ABBREVIATIONS IN RECIPES

It is the fashion in many recently published cookbooks to spell in full everything that would once have been abbreviated—pounds, ounces, cups, tablespoons, teaspoons, and all the rest. A good idea, this, because the abbreviations used were often difficult to tell apart, and although some quantities don't matter all that much, others—especially in baking—count for a great deal. The margin for error between a teaspoon and a tablespoon of salt can make the difference between an agreeable dish and an unpalatable one, a teaspoon and a tablespoon of baking powder the difference between success and disaster.

In older cookbooks, and often in new ones in which space is a critical factor, abbreviations are still to be found. Some of the common ones are: t or tsp. or teasp. = teaspoon; T or tbs. or tbsp. = tablespoon; c = cup; oz. = ounce; lb. = pound; pkg. = package; pkt. = packet; env. = envelope.

Now that metric is imminent, there are some new abbreviations for home cooks to learn: cm = centimeter; ml = milliliter; g = gram; k = kilogram. For more about how metric will affect your buying and cooking, see the special feature: MEASURING UP TO METRIC.

It's a good idea to read a recipe through carefully before starting to cook, not only to be certain you have all the ingredients on hand, but also from the point of view of logic. Does it sound sensible? Will the size pan called for accommodate the finished product? Is anything missing? (Editors and printers, being human, make mistakes.) Do the proportions, in relation to one another, seem reasonable? A cup of salt and ½ teaspoon of sugar in the list of ingredients of a cake recipe would certainly make the recipe suspect. When you're sure you understand—and approve—assemble the ingredients and go to work.

ACIDOPHILUS: see MILK

ACIDS: see ADDITIVES AND PRESERVATIVES

ACORN SQUASH: see SQUASH

ADDITIVES AND PRESERVATIVES

In 1958, an amendment to the Food, Drug and Cosmetic Act defined an additive as "any substance the intended use of which results or may reasonably be expected to result directly or indirectly in its becoming a component or otherwise affecting the characteristic of any food." The controversial "Delaney clause" in the same amendment stated that "no additive shall be deemed safe if it is found to induce cancer when ingested by man or animal, or if it is found, after tests which are appropriate for the evaluation of the safety of food additives, to induce cancer in man or animal."

The Food and Drug Administration (FDA) is the government agency that regulates the use of food additives under the amendment. To begin its work, the FDA sent to nutritionists, chemists, physicians, and many other authorities concerned with food and its effects on the body a list of food additives, asking for an evaluation of the safety of each. Those considered unsafe or of doubtful safety were tested at once. The others, given passing marks, formed the FDA's GRAS list—substances Generally Recognized As Safe.

Taking up the cudgels. Since it was first formulated, the GRAS list has been subject to a number of changes, and has kindled countless controversies. Because we tend to be a people who opt for all or nothing, "Ban chemicals in food!" became the battle cry of many people who didn't know any better and a large number of people who should have known better but somehow got carried away. If you ban chemicals in food, you ban food—all food, in simplistic terms, is a combination of chemicals. Your body does not care whether you give it steak or salad or ice cream or whatever, it simply goes busily to work breaking down whatever is offered into component parts, putting some immediately to work, storing others, discarding others to be excreted. If you feed it sensibly, it works well. If you starve it, its functions are impaired. If you feed it something toxic, you become ill, and if the toxicity is too great for the body's defenses to cope with, you die. Simple but complex—and inclined to be hair-raising.

Nature is very big on additives, including some that can be poisonous in large quantities. There is arsenic in shrimp, for example. Potatoes contain solanine—enough in the amount of potatoes eaten by the average person over a year's time to send that average person to his eternal rest if ingested in a single dose. But the point is academic, because no one eats 119 pounds of potatoes (yes, that's the national average) at one time. So the controversy over additives becomes, as you can see, not only one of quality, but also of quantity.

Food processors—fortunately or unfortunately, depending on the point of view—are also very big on additives. They add chemicals to strengthen flavors, to improve keeping qualities, to enhance appearance, to fortify nutritional value. It's the FDA's job to police these additions to our food, to evaluate their worth. Since additives have proliferated so greatly since the 1958 amendment, the burden of proof has been shifted to the food processor—he must test each new additive and prove to the FDA's satisfaction that it is safe in the quantity he wishes to use.

Benefit versus risk. Often the decision whether or not to ban an additive is an easy one. If it is found to be harmful, particularly if it is a carcinogen—a cancer-producing agent—there seems to be no rational choice other than to ban it. Certain ingredients of food that induce cancer in laboratory animals are banned even though there is no real evidence of their effect on human beings. Cyclamate is a case in point. When diet sodas were sweetened with cyclamates, a 12-ounce bottle contained from a quarter of a gram to a full gram of the artificial sweetener. In order to ingest a quantity sufficient to cause cancer in laboratory animals, an adult would have had to drink between 138 and 552 bottles of diet soda every day. Nevertheless, cyclamates were banned. They could be harmful, and they had no discernible benefit.

Sometimes, however, the risk must be balanced against the benefit, and a Solomon-like decision arrived at. Nitrites are an example. Under certain conditions, nitrites form nitrosamines, which are known—also under certain conditions—to produce cancer. On the other hand, nitrites prevent or retard the growth of the deadly *botulinum* toxin. Added, in small amounts, to cured meats such as frankfurters, bacon, and sausage, nitrites are the most effective means of controlling botulism, which is often fatal. In such cases, the question becomes one of acceptable risk. If the additive offers risk but no clear benefit, it is no problem to ban it. If it does offer benefit, is the risk offset by the benefit? In other words, is the game worth the candle?

The cook as chemist. "All those chemicals listed as ingredients on the labels of the foods I buy!" today's housewife exclaims, shaking her head. "There ought to be a law!" There is. Until present labeling laws were passed, many of those chemicals were in the foods, but you didn't know it. And before the Pure Food and Drug laws, there were many others, too—some of them exceedingly harmful—that have since been removed from the foods you buy.

The whole picture of the benefits/risks of additives and preservatives comes somewhat more sensibly into focus when we consider that in our home cooking we constantly employ additives and preservatives. Preparing peaches for a dessert dish, you dip the slices in acid—lemon juice, which contains citric acid—to keep them from turning brown. Citric acid is an antioxidant (it is the effect of oxygen that turns the peaches brown) and a preservative as well. Canning pears, you prevent discoloration by adding ascorbic acid—vitamin C—to the syrup. Present in fresh green foods and citrus fruits, ascorbic acid also prevents scurvy. Cooking vegetables, you automatically add a little sodium chloride—table salt—to alleviate the flat taste, and if it's iodized salt, you're throwing in a little iodide for good measure. (And it is good measure—since the introduction of iodized salt, the incidence of goiter has dropped amazingly.) Making a batch of good old homestyle biscuits, you add sodium bicarbonate, sodium aluminum sulfate, calcium sulphate, calcium acid phosphate, and calcium silicate, all ingredients in double-acting baking powder. Putting up pickles, you add the acetic acid of vinegar to enhance taste, and also as a preservative.

Sometimes there may be serendipitous benefits concealed in food additives. Antioxidants added to various kinds of food to preserve freshness may be one such class of additive, according to continuing studies in many places, including the Cleveland Clinic and the University of Nebraska School of Medicine. One investigation is exploring the likelihood that antioxidants, which prevent rancidity in fats, are responsible for the pronounced decline in the incidence of stomach cancer in the United States. Another supports the theory that antioxidants, vitamin E in particular, improve the body's immunity system and retard aging. So it seems we must, as in so many things, refrain from condemning additives as all bad or hailing them as all good, but pursue a middle-of-the-road course, waiting until all the results are in before passing final judgment.

Sorting out the additives. Below, in alphabetical order and grouped according to the contribution they make to the food to which they're added, are the kinds of additives whose names you're likely to encounter on labels.

acids and alkalis: Added to give foods a tart flavor or to bring into line their pH (acid-base) balance. In canned fruits and juices and in jams and jellies, citric, lactic, or tartaric acid adds tartness and/or retards spoilage. For the same purpose, acetic acid is added to pickles and relishes and to canned salad-type products. Fizzing beverages do so because of their carbonic acid additive. Alkalis (bases) are used in baking powder—sodium bicarbonate and carbonate and potassium carbonate.

antioxidants: When fats combine with oxygen they become rancid. Not only does this produce an off-putting flavor but, even more serious, the product of such a union is peroxide—useful as a mild antiseptic and essential to many ladies blonde by choice rather than by nature, but toxic when ingested. Antioxidants—vitamins C (ascorbic acid) and E (tocopherols) are natural, BHA, BHT, and propyl gallate are synthetic—prevent this union, preserving the fresh taste of all fats, oils, polyunsaturated fatty acids, and fat-soluble vitamins.

artificial sweeteners: The FDA proposed to ban saccharin early in 1977; to make it available only by prescription for those, such as diabetics, who must restrict their intake of sugar for the purpose of keeping their disease under control. Congress, reacting to constituents' outcries, postponed the ban, and at the time this is written, the controversy still rages. Cyclamates have been banned as possible carcinogens, and a third sweetener, aspartame, is still being tested and may or may not, when final test results are evaluated, be placed on the market. Frutilose, a natural sweetener twice as sweet as sugar, is also being tested. (See SACCHARIN.)

coloring agents: This is one of the very iffy areas of the additives question. There are a few natural coloring agents, such as yellow-orange carotene, often used to give naturally pale margarine a butter color. But the vast majority of colors used are artificial and, more important, have no nutritional or other useful value in their favor (such as preventing spoilage, for example). Nevertheless, they are widely employed because we, the consumers, demand them, whether or not we are aware that we're making the demand. They are used because we tend not to buy colorless products, and many foods lose their natural color when processed. We expect a product that normally contains eggs to be a nice, yellow eggy color, a chocolate-flavored product to be a rich chocolate brown. We expect cherries to be red, bananas to be pale golden. Worse, if the food we choose isn't the "right" color, we tend to feel it doesn't have the "right" taste, either—even if it is, indeed, the unenhanced natural flavor.

flavor enhancers: These are different from flavoring agents (below) in that they have no flavor of their own, but are used to make stronger or otherwise more appealing the flavor the food already has. MSG (monosodium glutamate) is the one with which consumers are most familiar. Another, maltol, brings out the flavors of fruit, vanilla, and chocolate. GMP (disodium guanylate) enhances the meaty flavor of processed meats; so does IMP (inositate). These additives impart little or no flavor of their own, but they beef up the taste already present.

flavoring agents: These do have a taste of their own—and, again, are one of the iffy areas of the additives. There are considerably more than a thousand flavoring agents available to food processors, some of them natural, some synthetic. Of the synthetic ones it is the scientific point of view,

as with coloring agents, that they offer no benefit and some of them may have toxic effects. Food processors reply that there simply are not enough natural flavors available to go around, and that consumers aren't all that fond of many of the natural ones, anyway. See ARTIFICIAL FLAVORS for a broader discussion of this.

fortifiers and enrichers: These, generally, are nutrients added to products to replace nutrients lost in processing or to make the product even more nutritionally valuable than in the natural state. Iron and the B vitamins are added to white flour to replace those lost in the milling, giving us the "enriched flour" we see listed as a chief ingredient on the label of the bread we buy. Vitamin D, lost in pasteurization, is returned to milk. In other cases, nutrients beyond those found in the natural ingredients are added, as in the case of some dry cereals into which, for each serving, the U.S. Recommended Daily Allowance (a day's total requirements for adequate nutrition) of eight or more essential vitamins and minerals are incorporated. Thus, if you are fond of dry cereal and if you choose the right brand, you can pop a serving for breakfast instead of popping a vitamin pill.

"improvers": This is a mixed bag of miscellaneous substances that do something to change in some way (for the better, the users contend) the foods we buy. They include such agents as hydrogen peroxide used to bleach white flour truly white, instead of the pale yellow-tan it is in the unbleached state. Also in this group are additives to keep salt and other powdered substances from caking, agents to make such items as whipped toppings foam and, conversely, others to keep foods from foaming, and humectants to fight off the humidity that turns crisp foods limp. In this group, too, are tenderizers, as well as glazes that add shine to candy and baked goods.

preservatives: Bacteria, fungi, and various molds go forth and multiply in foods to an alarming (and, in many cases, health-threatening or even life-threatening) extent. And old age descends on other foods when they are in their relative childhood. To prevent these two unpleasant happenings, preservatives are added to a multitude of the foods we buy to prevent spoilage and prolong useful life. Sorbic acid, benzoic acid, acetic acid, lactic acid, sodium diacetate, sulfur dioxide, monocalcium phosphate, sulphite, sodium propionate, calcium propionate—these are among the substances you'll find listed on food labels; all are preservatives.

stabilizers, emulsifiers, and gels: In margarine, the oil and water tend to separate. In salad dressings, the oil and vinegar do the same. In peanut butter, the oil parts from the mass of crushed peanuts and rises to the top of the jar. Without help, some jellies and other similar products won't gel or won't stay gelled. Along the way between manufacturer and consumer, ice cream comes "uncreamed." At least, all these unhappy occurrences come about unless the food processor has had what he, at least, considers the foresight to prevent them through the use of additives. Such jaw-breaking terms as sodium triphosphate, disodium pyrophosphate, polysorbate, sorbitan monostearate, mono- and diglycerides, and methylcellulose on the label of the food you buy tell you that the manufacturer has used an additive to prevent what you might consider, on opening the package, to be a catastrophe. Other stabilizers, emulsifiers, and gelling agents are rather more familiar—pectin (our jelly-making friend in the kitchen), alginate (made from algae), various vegetable gums, and agar. (See GUM.)

All in all, it pays to be wary about additives, but don't condemn them out of hand. Without many of the additives and preservatives used in the foods we buy, we'd all be out in the kitchen making everything from scratch. The shelves at the market would be almost as bare as Mother Hubbard's cupboard, and most of the items still in the store would carry mind-boggling price tags. Many of the prepared foods we rely on wouldn't ever have gotten off the drawing board. True, dry cereals and TV dinners may not have notably enriched the lives of many of us, but to each his own. And where would the kids be without that ubiquitous bottle of catsup?

ADULTERANTS: see FOOD ADULTERANTS

AGNEAU: see page 451

AKEES: see EXOTIC FRUIT

AL DENTE: see page 451

ALBACORE: see TUNA, CANNED

ALBONDIGAS: see page 451

ALE

Dionysius, the Greeks say, left Mesopotamia in a huff because the people there were addicted to ale in preference to his own favorite libation. Sumerians made nineteen varieties of ale, eight from barley, eight from wheat, and three from a mixture of grains, and Sumerian temple workers were given a ration of a little more than a quart a day—not enough to impair their functioning, probably, but sufficient to keep things around the temple moving harmoniously, at a brisk pace.

A fermented beverage, cousin to beer, ale is brewed from malt, cereals, and hops (although fermented cereals alone produced these early brews—the bitter hops weren't added until the end of the Middle Ages). Present-day ale has a more pronounced flavor of hops than beer, because the "top fermentation" process, at a temperature higher than that used for beer, causes the yeast to rise to the top of the brew.

Our term for the beverage comes from the Saxon word *eale*. Saxons of all ages drank ale because, although it may

not have been particularly tasty by present standards, it was at least safe—and the water was not. Indeed, ale was the beverage of choice, if not of necessity, in most northern countries where grapes for wine-making could not be successfully cultivated.

Colonial Americans were fond of ale, particularly of an ale flip, very warming on a cold night. Ale, rum, and molasses were combined in proportions to suit the taste of the imbiber, then heated by plunging a red-hot poker into the mixture. A refinement called for ale, eggs, sugar, nutmeg, and cloves to be heated over an open fire until the eggs thickened the beverage.

Porter and stout, variations of ale, are more popular— perhaps because they are more widely available—in Great Britain than in the United States. Both are sweeter and darker than the regular ale, and stout is the sweeter and darker brown of the two. Regular ale also falls into two groups in Britain; they are called "mild" and "bitter" and are often ordered in pubs in a half-and-half combination known as, quite logically, a mild-and-bitter. Another combination is a black and tan, which is half ale, half porter. Half champagne and half stout results in black velvet. A mixture of ale and ginger beer is a shandy gaff.

Buying ale, serving ale. Available in cans or bottles, ale contains about 13 calories per ounce. Not much can be said for it from a nutritional point of view. An ounce offers a little more than 1 gram of carbohydrate and only about .1 of a gram of protein, 2 milligrams of calcium, 9 of phosphorus, 2 of sodium, and 8 of potassium, and trace amounts of other minerals and vitamins. Like beer, ale is about 4.5 percent alcohol by volume, and is about 92 percent water.

Experts say that ale should be served chilled, but not as cold as beer—between 40 and 50° F., a temperature it will reach in almost any home refrigerator in about 4 hours. And they caution that the glass in which it is served must be clean, preferably washed in detergent rather than with soap, as the slightest speck of grease will kill the foam. As with beer, pour ale gently down the side of the slightly tilted glass to control foaming and to produce a head about one inch deep.

Ale is used in cooking a wide variety of dishes, and may be used, measure for measure, as a substitute in any recipe that calls for beer. Cheese dishes are particularly flavorful when this substitution is made, and pork develops better flavor when cooked with ale rather than beer.

ALESSANDRI: see SAUSAGES

ALFALFA SPROUTS: see SPROUTS

ALKALIS: see ADDITIVES AND PRESERVATIVES

ALLERGIES, FOOD

You sneeze, your eyes water, your nose runs, you break out

in a rash or develop hives—and you say, "I must be allergic to something." Perhaps you are. And, if you are, unless the episode is minor and fleeting, the diagnosis is not properly yours to make, and certainly not the business of a book like this one. Rather, it is a matter on which you should seek professional help.

Allergies are caused by all manner of things such as dust, animal dander, feathers, and dozens of other allergens in the air, in our homes, in the clothes we wear, the things we touch. And, quite often, by things we eat—eggs, wheat, nuts, many other foods. An allergy is a reaction to one or another (or several) of these substances unlike the effect produced by such a substance on the average person. The reaction may be slight, or serious—even to the point of anaphylactic shock. In any case, the decision as to which substance or substances is causing the trouble and what should be done about it should be made by your doctor, who may undertake treatment himself or recommend an allergist, a specialist in the field.

ALLIGATOR PEARS: see AVOCADOS

ALL-PURPOSE FLOUR: see FLOUR

ALLSPICE: see SPICES

ALMOND EXTRACT: see FLAVORING EXTRACTS

ALMOND PASTE

A flavor and consistency that most people either love or hate, almond paste is a dense preparation of blanched almonds, finely ground or pounded in a mortar, sugar, and a liquid—water or, less often, rose water or orange-flower water. Almond extract is sometimes added as well, to intensify the flavor.

If you are very much into from-scratch cooking, you can make almond paste at home, but the prepared product is widely available in cans or packages at specialty food shops or in baking or gourmet-food sections of supermarkets, and is of a better consistency and flavor than the homemade.

Commercial almond paste can be had in 8-ounce packages and 8-ounce and 1-, 3-, and 5-pound cans. The 8-ounce size is sufficient for most recipes, unless, for example, you are going on a macaroon-making binge for the holidays. Store the can in a cool place before opening and tightly covered in the refrigerator after opening. Canned almond paste keeps well, both before and after opening, if properly stored. If you purchase the packaged variety (generally imported from Denmark or one of the other Scandinavian countries), check it before buying—the paste should be firm, but slightly pliable. If it is rock-hard, or if the package looks as if it had seen better days, pass it by. It may be old, in which case it will have substituted an unpleasant, stale/rancid taste for the good almond flavor.

Almond macaroons, fillings for danish pastries and coffeecakes, and marzipan—those delightful, colorful little fruit- or vegetable-shaped confections—are the chief uses for almond paste. The paste must be softened and worked before you attempt to mix it with other ingredients. Grate on a coarse grater or simply crumble with those best of kitchen tools, your fingers. See also MARZIPAN.

ALMONDS

Elegantly shaped, decked in beautiful flowers of a heavenly scent, producing a crisply delectable seed of almost limitless versatility—what more could one expect of this relative of the peach tree? That it once was thought to be the father of all life, because it blossomed earlier than any other tree. That it was considered a symbol of fertility in ancient Greece, the sign of hope of heaven to early Moslems. That the tree itself and its blossoms and fruit were essential to certain early Hebrew rituals. That the kernel of the pit inside its leathery fruit is used in all sorts of dishes of many cuisines, as well as in balms, drugs, oils, and cosmetics. That its kernel, encased in flavored sugar, has been for many years—and still is—offered as a token of rejoicing on the occasion of marriage and birth in France as well as in many Mediterranean, Middle Eastern, and North African countries. All those things, and more, are true of the almond.

ALMONDS IN YOUR KITCHEN

In this country, almonds are available the year around in many forms. They are grown in California, having been brought there by priests from Spain, where the almond has long been cultivated. Harvested in the fall, the heaviest supply of nuts in the shell occurs in November, in time for the holiday season. It is easiest of the nuts to crack, a light tap will open the shell to reveal the brown-skinned white kernel. Paper-shell varieties can be cracked with the fingers.

yields: Purchased in the shell, ½ pound of almonds will yield about ½ cup of meats; ½ pound shelled and blanched whole almonds will yield about 1½ cups ground almonds. A cup of whole shelled almonds weighs approximately 5½ ounces— good to know, because many delightful European recipes specify almonds by weight rather than by volume.

how to buy: When you buy the nuts in the shell, be sure that the shells are clean, without cracks or holes, and fresh-looking. They can be purchased by the pound in bulk, or in 1-pound plastic bags or 6-ounce cans. Shelled nuts should be plump, crisp, and fresh-looking—pass by any that are shriveled or limp.

how to store: In the shells, keep in a cool, dry place. Shelled, store in the original container until opened, then in the refrigerator in an airtight container. If you are going to keep the unopened kind for any time, they too are better off in the refrigerator.

11

nutritive value: One cup of whole shelled almonds contains about 850 calories—a little over 26 grams of protein, 77 grams of fat, 27.7 grams of carbohydrate. Almonds have no vitamin A, only a trace of vitamin C, and small amounts of the B vitamins. They are high in calcium and contain appreciable amounts of other minerals.

Tips on preparing, cooking. For eating out of hand, and for cooking as well, almonds can be used with the brown skin left in place or blanched—with the skin removed.

to blanch almonds: Cover shelled almonds with boiling water and let stand about 3 minutes. At this point, the brown skins should slip off easily between the fingers. Remove from the water one at a time, slip off skins, dry on absorbent paper.

To slice or sliver the nuts (blanched or not), use a very sharp knife and keep a sharp eye on your fingers. Or, more conveniently, buy the almonds already cut. To chop, use the blender or a nut chopper. To grate, use a small drum-type grater made especially for nuts and dry cheese.

Salted, spiced, or smoked (all may be purchased that way), almonds are eaten as confections or as nibblers with drinks. Whole, ground (used to replace part or all of the flour in many recipes), chopped, sliced, or slivered, the nuts have a place in all sorts of cookies, candies, and various other kinds of sweets—cakes, pies, puddings—as well as in casseroles and skillet dishes, to top vegetables (as in green beans amandine), and to garnish many kinds of foods.

to toast almonds: Spread the chopped or slivered nuts on a baking sheet, bake at 350°F. until they are a shade of brown that suits you, stirring frequently.

Freezing almonds. If you wish to keep almonds fresh and flavorful for any length of time, freeze them, airtight, in closely covered containers. Thaw at room temperature; spread out on absorbent paper. Allow to dry well before using.

Other ways, other forms. Almonds are available on grocery shelves in 6-ounce cans or 1- or 2-ounce plastic bags, in a wide variety of forms. The canned ones are more likely to be fresher when you buy them, and they keep much longer unopened.

whole natural: Shelled, unroasted, with their brown skins still in place.

whole blanched: Shelled, unroasted, with their skins removed.

sliced natural: Skins still in place, thin-sliced the long way.

blanched slivered: Blanched, halved, then sliced lengthwise.

chopped: Skins still in place, but in irregular chunks.

roasted, salted diced: Finely chopped, with their skins still in place—lightly roasted, lightly salted.

In addition, whole almonds can be purchased salted (blanched or not), roasted, dry roasted (without fat), onion/ garlic-, cheese-, barbecue-, and smoke-flavored, as well as spiced, curried, and sugared (burnt almonds). See also JORDAN ALMONDS.

For a discussion of almond oil, see OILS, SALAD AND COOKING.

ALPINO: see SAUSAGES

ALUMINUM FOIL

This is one of those kitchen helpers we wonder how we ever managed without before it was invented. Now that we do have it, we use it in dozens of household ways—as a wrap for cooked and uncooked foods stored in the refrigerator, as a freezer wrap, as a cover for casseroles and other baking dishes not fitted with covers of their own, as a pouch for cooking *en papillote,* as a liner for shelves and ovens, and even, in a pinch, as a decorative gift wrap.

What's it made of? Aluminum, and nothing else. A block of pure aluminum is rolled, much in the way pie crust is rolled, until it becomes a long, thin, pliable sheet. In the rolling process, the side of the sheet in contact with the heavy roller becomes brightly polished, the other side remains less shiny. Which side is up? It doesn't matter. Whether you use the shiny or the dull side next to food, the results will be the same.

Weight, length, width. You can buy aluminum foil in regular and heavy-duty weights, in several widths and lengths. Generally, as with anything that doesn't spoil, the "large economy size" is a better buy—in this case, the longer rolls. A roll of regular foil of 200 square feet (66⅔ yards long, 12 inches wide) or heavy-duty foil of 100 square feet (22⅓ yards long, 18 inches wide) gives you more foil for the money than shorter rolls of 25 and 75 square feet for the regular weight, 23⅓ and 37½ square feet for the heavy-duty.

Use the regular foil to wrap food or to cover containers for refrigerator storage, to wrap sandwiches, to package cookies to be mailed, for short-term freezing. The heavy-duty weight is for lining—broiler pan (but not the rack), outdoor grill, roasting and baking pans—and wrapping—foods to be baked, foods to be frozen—and for any purpose where you want to keep liquid enclosed without leakage.

Foil on KP duty. If you are not a dedicated pot-and-pan scrubber, which few of us are, foil is a blessing. A foil-lined broiling, baking, or roasting pan is easily cleaned, because all the drips and grease and baked-on crusts can be thrown out with the foil liner. Foil is a lifesaver liner for the outdoor grill, one of the least appealing of all clean-up jobs. A piece of foil on the oven shelf below the shelf on which a boil-over is likely to occur, as with fruit pies and full-to-the-brim casseroles and such, catches the drippage and saves a lot of oven cleaning —and there are, according to the last census, *no* dedicated oven-cleaners among us. Don't cover the entire shelf, however. That prevents proper heat circulation.

If you like, carpet the floor of the oven with foil, but it must be done properly. In electric ranges, the rod that carries the current is just above the oven floor. Lift the rod and slip a sheet of foil underneath, smoothing the foil so that it lies flat. In gas ranges, the oven burner is beneath the floor of the oven. Place foil on the bottom of the oven, but do not block the openings through which the heat passes; cut holes in the foil to conform with those openings, or make the foil liner small enough so that you don't cover them.

As well as protecting the bottom of the oven from crumbs and drips, foil reflects heat upward and helps baking food to brown on the bottom.

Cautionary notes. Foil of both weights can be fairly easily punctured or torn, so be gentle. If you're wrapping meat with sharp bones, for either cooking or freezing, pad the ends of the bones with extra wads of foil before wrapping.

Although foil will not catch fire, fat certainly will. Simply lining your broiler pan or any other pan you're going to use for broiling with foil, and then placing the food on the foil, won't prevent fire. The food must be placed on a rack so that melted fat can run off into the bottom of the pan. (Obviously, if you also cover the rack with foil you are simply compounding the problem.)

Some foods cause a slight discoloration of the foil. It's akin to the tarnish that forms on silver, and it's harmless. Also, some acid or very salty foods may cause the foil to pit and perforate—tomato sauces, salted meats, and salads are examples. Again, no harm done. Chicken and turkey skin has a gelatinous quality that sometimes causes it to stick to foil or, for that matter, almost anything else. Prevent this by shimming the foil with pieces of vegetable—carrot, onion, celery—in the places where it would otherwise touch the poultry skin, or by brushing the bird with soft fat.

ALUMINUM POTS, PANS, KITCHEN UTENSILS:
see special feature: YOU CAN'T WORK
WITHOUT TOOLS

AMANDINE: see page 451

AMINO ACIDS: see special feature:
NUTRITION NOTEBOOK

AMORINI: see PASTA

ANCHOVIES

Anchovies are small fish of the herring family, no more than 5 inches long, with a big mouth—a sort of gill-to-gill smile. They are caught in the spring and summer on dark moonless nights, attracted by the thousands to the nets by artificial lights flashed by the fishermen. Available canned, usually in 2-ounce tins, as flat fillets or as fillets rolled around capers, anchovies are packed in oil or brine or (these generally come from the Scandinavian countries) in wine or a flavored wine sauce. Anchovy paste, in tubes or (a richer, heavier variety) in small jars, is also widely distributed. Dried, salt-packed anchovies are not as readily available.

As with many other delicious foods, a little anchovy goes a long way. Our Colonial ancestors used anchovies—salt-packed then, rather than canned—as flavor-enhancers and often in place of salt, which was scarce and expensive, in dishes such as stews and meat pies. Nowadays the best anchovies come from the Mediterranean countries, where they have been relished since the time of the Romans, one of many facets of the cuisine of that era passed on to us in *The Roman Cookery Book* of Apicius—who, having squandered a huge fortune on extravagant foods, committed suicide in A.D. 37.

Used with restraint, anchovies add zip to sauces and to many bland foods. A light spreading of anchovy paste or a fillet or two gives personality to a hard-cooked egg sandwich, a nutritious food unlikely, without some such embellishment, to appeal to many over the age of five. An inch or so of anchovy paste, or the equivalent in mashed fillets, gives zest to cream sauce or cheese sauce for vegetables, and perks up meat gravy. The little fish have a particular affinity for eggs, cheese, tomatoes, and pimientos. A casserole of potatoes and anchovies, intriguingly named Jansson's Temptation (and intriguingly spelled Jansen, Janson, and several other ways, depending on which cookbook you consult), is staple Swedish fare, and very good indeed. Salad dressings, homemade or bottled, profit by the addition of a little anchovy paste or several mashed fillets. But it is in appetizers that anchovies shine. An antipasto without them is hardly worthy of the name.

Five drained anchovy fillets contain 35 calories, offer 3.8 grams of protein, 2.1 grams of fat, .1 gram of carbohydrate, 34 milligrams of calcium, and 42 milligrams of phosphorus.

ANGEL FOOD CAKES: see CAKES

ANISE: see SEEDS AND SPICES

ANTELOPE: see GAME

ANTIOXIDANTS: see ADDITIVES AND PRESERVATIVES

ANTIPASTO

This is the traditional Italian appetizer, an attractively arranged platter (for communal or individual service) of delicious tidbits chosen for their highly individual flavors and interesting and contrasting colors and textures.

Actually, the only thing truly traditional about antipasto is that it exists. From there, almost anything goes—at least, almost anything tasty, spicy, and appetite provoking. It can be as quintessentially simple as whisper-thin slices of rosy *prosciutto crudo* wrapped around or draped over wedges of melon at its perfection of ripeness. Or it can be a glorious mish-mash of many meat, fish, cheese, and vegetable appetizers, a sort of nosher's heaven. Or a flavorful mixed dish such as *caponatina,* a combination of eggplant, onions, tomato sauce, capers, olives, and pignola (pine nuts), well seasoned and served cold.

The antipasto goodies are generally placed in a handsome pattern on a bed of shredded or torn salad greens. Such a platter might be centered with tunafish masked with mayonnaise and sprinkled with capers. In an agreeable mosaic around the tuna, arrange any number of (or even, for true antipasto nuts, all of them) separate piles of chick-peas in olive oil, hard-cooked egg halves, salami rolled into cones, pickled baby eggplants and okra and tiny hot peppers, mushrooms with lemon and olive oil, slices of provolone, drained pimientos crisscrossed with anchovy fillets, chunks of finocchio, rings of green peppers, basil-sprinkled tomato slices, marinated artichoke hearts or bottoms, pickled beets and onions (an American specialty that has somehow elbowed its way in), marinated raw cauliflower, a salad of baby clams and squid and mussels, roasted peppers, ripe figs wrapped with prosciutto, garlicky white bean salad, sardines with lemon. Whatever comes to mind that is highly flavored and appetite whetting can be added. Always, olives in profusion. And, on the side, a cruet of olive oil, another of red wine vinegar, salt, and pepper in a mill to be freshly ground over all. Obviously, antipasto is fork, not finger, food and if served on a large platter, individual plates should be provided. See also APPETIZERS.

APERITIF: see page 451

APHRODISIAC FOODS

Since time beyond recorded history, man (woman too, but, perhaps because of her anatomical construction, she hasn't been as single-mindedly devoted to the subject) has searched for substances to promote, increase, or restore sexual potency. The list of edibles thought at one time or another to have aphrodisiac qualities is staggering and sounds, in the listing, rather like the recipe for a witches' brew: snout and foot of hippopotamus, eyes of hyena, horn of rhinoceros, mandrake and ginseng roots, nettle seed, wormwood, shark's fins. You name it and some ambitious lover, somewhere at some time, has tried it.

Early Greeks favored carrots and leeks, early Romans honey, garden herbs, eggs, and pine nuts—more appetizing if not more efficacious than the animal's testicles and intestines of birds and fish recommended by Roman authorities a few centuries later. An Oriental scholar espoused asparagus, first boiled, then sautéed, served with a sauce of well-seasoned egg yolk (sounds quite inviting, doesn't it?) eaten every day (it now begins to sound less inviting) as a sure-fire "stimulant for amorous desires."

Dr. Van de Velde, a Dutchman, whose book *Ideal Marriage* was not all that long ago about the only nonpornographic sex manual available—times do change—recommended asparagus also, as well as artichokes and celery. Brillat-Savarin opted in favor of truffles. As for seafood, it has had universal appeal through the ages. Oysters in particular appear high on practically all lists of aphrodisiac foods.

The final word on aphrodisiac foods: there aren't any. Truly. Good health, bolstered by a nutritionally sound diet, is the basis for a satisfactory sex life. Beyond that, it's a matter of attitude, upbringing, and genes.

However—and, the human intellect being the interesting and sometimes playful instrument that it is, this is a big however—if you truly and wholeheartedly believe that a substance will act as an aphrodisiac, it probably will. Any substance at all, from a cold boiled potato on up. It is, as they say, all in the mind, and mind-over-mattering can be a formidable pastime.

APPETIZERS

There is an increasing trend toward lumping together under one heading, "starters," all those foods we nibble—or, sometimes, fall on like a hoard of locusts—before the meal or at the meal's beginning. Nevertheless, it's useful to sort them out under more descriptive terms. (Besides, "starters" is an ugly nonfood word, conjuring up pictures of a heavy-handed Someone holding back the hungry mob while preparing to fire a pistol or yell, "One, two, three—*go!*")

"Appetizer" is one of Alice's portmanteau words, covering all of those things that we serve at our ever-present cocktail parties or the less structured "drop in for a drink" gatherings. We have appetizers, the Scandinavians have smörgasbord, the Spanish tapas, the Italians antipasto, the Russians zakuska, the French hors d'oeuvres, and undoubtedly there's a word for it in every language, including that of cannibals. Whatever the term, it's a collection of savory delights to keep body and soul together while waiting for the main part of the meal.

Appetizers are generally finger foods or, at most, savory little somethings to be speared with a food pick—that is, a fork, and certainly not a knife, isn't necessary to cope with them. However, kindly hostesses should provide napkins, and if drippy appetizers such as tiny meatballs in a sauce, or fairly large-sized ones, such as deviled eggs, are served, little plates should be available as well.

Here is a sorting out of kinds of appetizers, admittedly arbitrary in some cases, because they tend to overlap.

canapés: Whatever the savory substance that is the star of this mouthful, it is seated on something—a cracker, a piece of bread or toast, a pastry shape, a slice of firm vegetable such as raw zucchini. Usually, the cracker or toast or whatever is spread with a dressing, such as mayonnaise or a mayonnaise-lemon juice-mustard combination, or with a savory butter (butter combined with anchovy paste, curry, chutney, chives, or any of a dozen other flavorful additions) before being topped with the canapé's chief attraction. The topper might be as simple as a slice of cheese or a shrimp sprinkled with chopped fresh dill, or a little more elaborate, such as a combination of crabmeat, slivered almonds, and chopped celery bound with lemon mayonnaise and decorated with a tiny sprig of watercress.

Canapés can be hot (quite often, the hot ones are broiled) or cold. Sets of small cutters are available to shape bread for canapés—it can then be toasted or, even better, lightly sautéed in butter—and even smaller cutters for attractive garnishes to provide the finishing touch. Or simply cut the bread into small squares or diamonds with a sharp knife. Bread for canapés should be a day old and firm-textured. If you top the bread, toast, or crackers with a salad or other damp mixture, do it shortly before serving or the canapés will be soggy.

crudités: These are fresh raw vegetables cut into pieces of a size easy to handle. Generally they are accompanied by a dip—more often than not a light one, for crudités are the appetizer of choice for those who are dieting, although they are so delicious they're welcomed by one and all. Plain yogurt, seasoned with chives, curry powder, chili powder, chopped dill (or dill pickle) or parsley or tarragon makes a most acceptable dip for crudités. As for the vegetables themselves, they can be any combination of carrot or celery sticks, cucumber or zucchini fingers, small radishes, little green onions, small button mushrooms, thin slices of turnip or jicama, strips of green pepper, flowers of young broccoli, young and tender green beans—almost any vegetable as long as it's raw, fresh, and icy cold. Provide a shaker of salt and another of seasoned salt for those purists who prefer their vegetables minus the dip. Prepare crudités as long as 24 hours in advance; refrigerate until serving time.

skewered appetizers: These call for small skewers or food picks. They can be plastic for cold skewered appetizers, but for hot ones choose those made of wood—metal can burn the fingers of the partaker, and plastic has a nasty tendency to melt. Any two or three or four foods of complementary flavor can be strung on picks to provide an appetizer much more attractive and interesting than those same foods offered separately.

Try a cube of cheese sandwiched between two squares of salami or two pickled onions for a simple cold appetizer. Or for a hot one, a stuffed olive or half a cooked chicken liver or a water chestnut or an oyster wrapped in bacon, secured with a pick, and broiled until the bacon is crisp. There are dozens of possible combinations, all as good to eat as to look at. All can be prepared 4 or 5 hours in advance and refrigerated until serving or cooking time.

stuffed appetizers: Almost anything that has an indentation in it or can have one made, or anything that can be rolled around something else, can be stuffed and be the better for it. Mushroom caps, raw or briefly sautéed before filling or broiled or baked after filling, are a good example. A savory minced liver or fish mixture, or one made simply with the chopped mushroom stems sautéed with bread crumbs and nicely seasoned, stuff mushrooms well. Chunks or small whole stalks of celery, or blades of belgian endive take kindly

15

to being filled with seasoned cheese mixtures—bleu cheese with walnuts, cheddar with bacon bits, whipped cream cheese with chives or dill. Large sections of cucumber or zucchini can be hollowed with an apple corer, stuffed, chilled, and sliced before serving. Try the same thing with hollowed out small-diameter french bread or sourdough rolls. Spread thin slices of high-flavor meat—sausage, dried beef, corned beef, pastrami—with a cheese or other complementary mixture, roll like a jelly roll, serve whole or cut in chunks. Give smoked salmon the same treatment. Make up to 24 hours in advance; refrigerate.

dips and dunks: Well-flavored mixtures, of a texture suitable to being hand-scooped with crackers or chips or other reasonably sturdy foods, dips and dunks may be hot or cold, although "dip" is most often used for the cold ones, "dunk" reserved for the hot. Both dips and dunks are often cheese based. Dips (including the tasty but too-often-served California dip made with onion soup mix) can also be made with sour cream or yogurt as a base, be flavored with minced clams, snipped chives, mustard, finely chopped chutney, horseradish—the list is endless. A half-and-half mixture of honey and lime juice is great for dipping raw fruit. Serve dips well chilled or at room temperature in attractive bowls or in hollowed-out vegetables or fruits such as eggplant, cabbage, grapefruit, pineapple. Guacamole—seasoned mashed avocado with lemon juice, onion juice or chopped green onions, often with chopped tomato—is a favorite dip, particularly good with corn chips or pieces of tortilla. Serve it in the avocado half shells.

Examples of hot dunks are rarebit-type mixtures (particularly good made with beer or ale), beef broth with soy sauce for dunking chunks of rare beef, mashed kidney or other red beans with chili and/or bits of bacon, sweet-sour sauce for shrimp. Keep dunks hot over candle warmers or serve in fondue pots or chafing dishes.

As for dippers and dunkers, their name is legion—all manner of crackers, toasts, chips, pretzels; chunks of raw or cooked fruits or vegetables; cubes of meat, poultry, fish, or cheese; cocktail-size sausages; little meatballs; whole shrimp; tiny whole mushrooms.

Both dips and dunks should be of a not-too-thin consistency in order to minimize drippage on clothes and carpets. Nearby napkins are a must. Make dips and dunks in advance and refrigerate—don't store guacamole more than 4 hours.

spreads: Of a texture firmer than dips or dunks, these are meant to be spread (small knives or spreaders must be furnished) on accompanying crackers, toast shapes, or cocktail breads. Potted meats or fish or shellfish, pastes of the same ingredients, savory gelatin molds, smooth blends of various kinds of livers, cheese mixtures—these are the most usual spread offerings. Almost anything good as a dip or dunk, mixed to a firmer texture, is also good as a spread. Make in advance and refrigerate.

nibblers: These are emergency-shelf appetizers, requiring only the opening of a bag or package or jar. Among them are olives (ripe or green—pitted, please—plain or stuffed with bits of pimiento, pickled onions, almonds, or anchovy—to be found in gourmet-food sections), chips, pretzels, nuts (all kinds, salted or spiced, smoked or seasoned with garlic or curry or the like), any of the packaged crisp nibbles such as pork rinds, corn nuts, salted sunflower seeds and soybeans, and so on.

cocktails: Eaten, not imbibed, these cocktails are fork (sometimes spoon) food, most often served at the table as the start of the meal. They are set out in small glass or china bowls, sherbet dishes, or the handsome servers made especially for the purpose that consist of a container to be filled with cracked or shaved ice, in which rests a smaller container for the cocktail.

Seafood tops the list of cocktail ingredients—crabmeat, lobster meat, shrimp, oysters, or a combination. But melon balls make a handsome and delicious cocktail, and so does almost any other fruit, cut into bite-size pieces. Mixed vegetable cocktails—the vegetables raw or cooked—are not as common, but very good indeed. This kind of cocktail is always served well chilled. There is almost always a complementary sauce, served over the cocktail or passed separately. Prepare in advance; refrigerate.

hors d'oeuvres: These, too, are served-at-the-table foods, to be eaten from plates with a fork. Salads of rare beef or sausage, of various kinds of poultry or fish, come under this heading. So do oysters or clams on the half shell, and snails and mussels. So do barquettes—small hot tarts filled with a savory mixture of meat, fish, or cheese—or little pastry turnovers similarly filled, or wedges of quiche. So do stuffed avocados, or other stuffed fruits. Eggs à la russe or in aspic or other foods in aspic are delightful hors d'oeuvres. A slice of ineluctable pâté, homemade or purchased, is an hors d'oeuvre difficult to better. Herring bits in wine, or in sour cream with onion rings, come under this heading, as does ratatouille served cold or hot, and mushrooms or other vegetables à la grecque, asparagus vinaigrette, and artichokes, stuffed or simply served with lemon butter. Indeed, almost anything you like that is piquant, that is not sweet, can be offered as an hors d'oeuvre, including a mixed green salad, served first rather than with or after the main course, in the California fashion that is rapidly spreading east. Most of these can be prepared in advance and refrigerated; add sauce or dressing just before serving.

caviar: Hardly your everyday appetizer, considering its price, caviar is in a class by itself. The gray-black pearls are, unfortunately, as habit forming as any drug—and as costly a habit to support.

Roe of sturgeon, lightly salted, caviar is categorized by the size of the eggs. Gray-to-black beluga has the biggest eggs—sometimes as large as peas—and is the most costly. Osetra, gray or gray-green, is next in both size and price. Sevruga is next in size but not always in price—one sevruga sturgeon in thousands has roe that is golden instead of gray, an exceedingly rare and commensurately costly delicacy, reserved when come upon in Iran exclusively for the table of the Shah. Still smaller are sterlet and ship caviars.

Lesser roes than those of the sturgeon are also called caviar—no match, aficionados insist, for the real thing. Various cod roes and lumpfish caviar are black or gray (either by nature or through processing). Salmon roe has large eggs, is oily, and is orange-red in color; it is sold in jars labeled "salmon caviar." There is also tarama, which is orange carp roe. These may seem expensive if you've never purchased the real thing, cheap if you have; they are delicious if you are not a fan of, or can't afford, the real thing, not worth the effort of eating if you are. Whatever your preference, these are excellent ingredients for canapés and spreads, and—especially the salmon caviar—may be served with pride and pleasure in the same manner as the real thing.

Exceedingly perishable, fresh caviar must be refrigerated from the moment it is taken from the sturgeon until the moment it is eaten. Salted (malossol) or pasteurized caviar, and acid-treated pressed caviar are less perishable, but may also require refrigeration—the label will tell you.

Serve fresh caviar in its original container sunk into a bowl of crushed ice or a hollowed-out block of ice. Count on an ounce to two ounces per serving. If you're a purist, you'll offer only buttered toast and lemon wedges as accompaniments, but chopped raw onion, chopped egg whites and sieved egg yolks, sour cream, and thinly sliced pumpernickel with unsalted butter are all acceptable. See also ANTIPASTO, DIPS, KABOBS, and PATES.

APPLE-PIE SPICE: see SPICES

APPLES

When Adam said, "Hey, I'm hungry—what's to eat?" and Eve replied, "I've got just the thing for you!" it probably was not an apple that she handed him. More likely, some scholars say, it was a peach or an apricot. But even if the apple didn't get its start in the Garden of Eden, it very soon made its presence felt, for the fruit is often mentioned in both myth and history.

Apples were known and used by primitive man. Carbonized remains of the fruit have been found in the prehistoric Iron Age lake dwellings in Switzerland, and there is evidence that they were eaten, and also preserved by sun drying, in Stone-Age Europe. Earliest recorded history in China, Egypt, and Babylonia mentions apples, telling us that man understood the arts of budding and grafting twenty centuries ago.

When Caesar's Roman legions invaded Britain, they brought the apple with them, and it has grown in the British Isles ever since. The Roman Cato wrote of seven varieties of apples in the third century B.C.; three centuries later, Pliny named thirty-six varieties—obviously, pomology (the science of apple-growing) was flourishing.

The apple that launched a thousand ships. Again and again in myth and legend, the apple plays a starring role. One of Hercules' labors was to obtain the golden apples of the Hesperides, prized because they gave immortality to their possessors. Fleet Atalanta lost her race with mortal Hippomenes because she greedily stopped to retrieve the golden apples he dropped. Loki, god of mischief, stole the Scandinavian gods' apple tree, the fruit of which kept them young. They grew old and enfeebled, and everything in the world went awry until they luckily retrieved their miraculous tree.

An apple was the cause of the Trojan War. Eris, goddess of discord, in a huff at not being invited to a wedding, tossed a golden apple inscribed "To the Fairest" among the guests. Three goddesses claimed it, and Paris was called in to judge what was probably the first beauty contest. Aphrodite offered Paris the fairest of all women, Helen of Troy, as his wife if he awarded her the apple. What man could refuse? Unfortunately, Helen already had a husband, King Menelaus, who resented this intrusion into his domestic arrangements. Paris abducted Helen, Menelaus took issue, and the ten-year war was on.

In the new land. The Pilgrims brought apple seeds with them on the Mayflower, and the settlers at Jamestown counted apple seeds among the provisions they carried to the colony. In a manner of speaking, all the apples we know today come from those first orchards in Massachusetts and Virginia. New Amsterdam's Governor Stuyvesant imported a grafted apple tree from Holland and planted it on what is now the corner of Third Avenue and 13th Street in New York City. There it remained until a horse-drawn dray knocked it down 200 years later, in 1866.

In Flushing, Long Island, the first commercial apple tree nursery was established in 1730. Those excellent Virginia farmers and students of horticulture, George Washington and Thomas Jefferson, were both well-known apple growers in their day. In Pennsylvania, the German colonists known as the Pennsylvania Dutch became adept at producing schnitz, dried sliced apples that made fine pies and sauce and were the basis of a robust dish, Schnitz und Knepp—apples stewed with ham and topped with fluffy dumplings, as delicious today as the day it was invented. The Pennsylvania Amish and Mennonites also made—and still make—particularly tasty apple cider.

Moving west. An important part of the cargo of the west-going wagon trains was apple trees and "scion wood" for grafting. (Apples do not grow true to type from seeds.) Treasured and protected throughout the long journey, the trees became the foundation for orchards from the far side of the

Appalachians to the west coast. Indians, traders, and missionaries carried apples far beyond the settlements, and the seeds of those apples were often carefully planted and lovingly nurtured.

John Chapman, who came to be known as Johnny Appleseed, was one of those missionaries. Friend of both white man and Indian, he traveled throughout the Ohio valley country—often barefoot both summer and winter—spreading the word of his Swedenborgian faith and planting and tending apple trees and distributing seeds. He died in 1845 in Fort Wayne, Indiana, where a memorial park now commemorates his life and work.

An apple a day. In great-grandmother's day, a barrel of apples in the cellar to "winter over" was an important staple, along with the stored cabbages and root vegetables that supplied virtually the only fresh foods available during the long cold season. Those thrifty forefathers of ours knew very well that one bad apple can spoil a barrel, so they constantly used the apples that were beginning to wither—and so, unhappily, seldom had a truly good apple to eat.

Apples are still stored to winter over, but under such conditions that we can buy and use good crisp, juicy apples all year around. Low temperature—32°F.—and high humidity —85 percent or higher—constitute those optimum conditions. Until 1940, apples in baskets or boxes were kept in centrally located "cold storage" warehouses and moved to market as needed. Then increasing demand, and the fact that loss was high because often too much time elapsed between picking and refrigerated storage, led to the building of "fresh pack" storage warehouses on the growers' own property, so that the apples could be refrigerated shortly after picking. From these storage areas, the apples were packed "fresh on order" as required, with spoiled apples culled before packing.

Unfortunately a good deal of culling was required even under those improved conditions, and in the 1950s a still better method, Controlled Atmosphere storage—commonly called CA storage—was developed. This takes advantage of the natural process of respiration of all living things, including apples. Just as humans and animals do, apples use oxygen and give off carbon dioxide—in other words, they are alive and, being alive, they "breathe." CA storage combines low temperature with a reduced supply of oxygen and an increase in carbon dioxide to slow down the rate of the apple's metabolism and greatly prolong its life in storage and extend its retail season.

Apple trees are planted 27 to 500 trees per acre, depending on the size of the trees at maturity. An acre of trees yields up to 1,000—in some cases even 2,000—bushels per acre. An apple tree's productive life is from 6 years after planting until it is 35 to 40 years old.

APPLES IN YOUR KITCHEN

As with all fresh fruit, you are buying the best quality for the lowest price when you buy in peak season. Apples are sold by the piece, the pound, or in multiple-piece packages in markets, and in larger units—bushels and half-bushels—at farmers' markets and by producers/wholesalers who also sell at retail.

However, buy only what you need, what you can eat within a reasonable time. It doesn't pay to buy perishable fruit in quantity only because the price is lower, if part of that quantity will spoil before you put it to good use.

Varieties, uses. See The Wise Apple Buyer chart, adjacent page.

how to buy: All apples are graded by United States Department of Agriculture standards for fresh fruit and vegetables. U.S. Extra Fancy, U.S. Fancy, U.S. No. 1, and combinations of these grades yield firm, crisp apples acceptable for eating and cooking. U.S. No. 2 is a less desirable grade. Grading is based on maturity, appearance, quality, waste, and the use to which the apple will be put. Grade marks appear on original containers in which apples are shipped, but not in most cases on packages of fruit that you buy in the market.

Your eyes, nose, and fingers—and common sense—are your best guides when you purchase fruit. Apples should be firm, crisp, well-colored, should look bright and fresh. They should smell fresh, lightly winy but not deeply so, and never musty. Their skins should be clean, and there should be no cuts, punctures, abrasions, bruises, or soft spots, no appearance of shriveling, no blemishes of any description. Like all fresh fruit, apples are perishable, and a blemished fruit will spoil much more rapidly than an unblemished one. Also, an outward blemish may signal interior damage that you can't see. Overripe apples yield to a slight pressure on the skin; the flesh will be soft and mealy.

You are your own best judge of quality, so take the time to buy carefully. Preferably, buy by the piece or pound rather than the package, if the package conceals any part of the apples. If you must buy by the package, examine it carefully for damp spots that might indicate hidden spoilage. Finally, buy apples of a variety suited to the use you are going to make of them, for eating out of hand, for sauce, for baking, or for other cooking purposes.

As with all other fresh produce, handle apples carefully in the market. Someone must pay for fruit lost by careless handling—in the long run, it will be you.

When you buy by the pound, you'll get 2 to 4 apples per pound, depending on size. One pound of apples will make about 2 cups of applesauce, or will yield about 3 cups of raw sliced or diced apples.

how to store: If you buy in quantity, store in a cool, dark

THE WISE APPLE BUYER

Each apple has a flavor and texture slightly different from all of the others—whatever your taste, whatever the use to which you want to put it, there is an apple to suit your purpose. The following are the most common apples in wide distribution throughout the United States. Quantities should be great during the larger part of the season indicated, more limited at the beginning and end. Best uses are shown, but use need not be confined to the suggestions below.

variety	season	availability	appearance, flavor	use for	worth knowing
baldwin	Nov.–April	Eastern U.S.	Dull red, sometimes with russet marks; tart	Baking, sauce, all kinds of cooking; not usually eaten raw	Marketed mostly in N.Y. and New England states; bulk of crop commercially processed
cortland	Sept.–April	Eastern and central states	Two-tone red and green, red having a purplish undertone; flesh snow white; juicy, tender, somewhat tart	Baking, sauce, all kinds of cooking; also salads, fruit cups	Very tender—bakes and cooks more rapidly than many other varieties
golden delicious	Sept.–June	Throughout the U.S.	Yellow-green to bright yellow, sometimes burnished or russeted; sweet and juicy	The all-purpose apple for out-of-hand eating, for salads, and for all kinds of cooking	This is the most universally used all-purpose apple in this country
red delicious	Sept.–June	Throughout the U.S.	Bright red; sweet	Out-of-hand eating, salads, fruit cups; not for cooking	Most universally available, universally used eating (raw) apple in this country
gravenstein	Aug.–Oct.	Eastern and western U.S.	Red striped or with red blush; tart, spicy, juicy	Sauce and all cooking uses except whole baked apples; not for out-of-hand eating	Limited availability except in California; most of crop commercially processed
grimes Golden	Sept.–Feb.	Eastern and central U.S.	Yellow-green to golden yellow; flavorful, slightly tart	Out-of-hand eating, salads, cups, all cooking uses	Old favorite now declining in supply; most of crop commercially processed
jonathan	Sept.–April	Throughout the U.S.	Bright red; slightly tart; juicy; rich flavor	Out-of-hand eating, salads, cups, all cooking uses	Less generally available in Northeast and Southwest at beginning and end of season
mcintosh	Sept.–June	Throughout the U.S.	Two-tone red and green; slightly tart; juicy; tender; sprightly flavor, good aroma	All uses, raw and cooked, except whole baked apples	Less generally available in western and southern U.S. except at height of season
newtown pippin	Oct.–May	Western states only	Green to yellow-green; slightly tart; more mealy than juicy	Salads, cooking, baking	Limited supply also available in Virginia; most of crop commercially processed
northern spy	Nov.–May	Eastern and central U.S.	Two-tone red and green; fairly tart; crisp; juicy; rich flavor	All uses, raw and cooked	Like golden delicious, a fine all-purpose apple; supplies declining; most of crop commercially processed
rhode island greening	Oct.–April	Eastern and central U.S.	Green to yellow-green; slightly tart	Baking, sauce, all kinds of cooking	Limited fresh distribution; most of crop commercially processed

variety	season	availability	appearance, flavor	use for	worth knowing
rome beauty	Oct.–June	Throughout the U.S.	Bright red, sometimes yellow striped; very slightly tart	Baking, sauce, all kinds of cooking	Excellent for cooking, not often eaten raw
spartan	Oct.–April	Eastern, central, western states	Bright red; slightly tart; crisp, juicy	Out-of-hand eating, salads, cups; fine dessert apple; not choice for cooking	Cross between mcintosh and yellow newtown; somewhat limited distribution and availability
wealthy	Aug.–Oct.	Eastern and central states	Two-tone red and green, often striped; tart, spicy	All cooking uses except whole baked apples; not often eaten raw	Production is declining; most of crop commercially processed
winesap	Nov.–July	Throughout the U.S.	Dark red; rich, winelike flavor; juicy, moderately tart	Out-of-hand eating, salads, cups, all kinds of cooking	Production and distribution of this late season apple declining

In addition, numerous local varieties of summer and early-fall apples are available from July through September; none of these is widely distributed. Most of these apples are better for cooking—other than as whole baked apples—than for eating raw. Imported apples are available as well, particularly the Australian granny smith, which arrives here in summer (Australia's winter), when local varieties are in short supply and often far below their best in flavor and texture.

place; sort regularly and remove any apples that show signs of spoilage. For average home use, buy only the amount you can use in 1 to 2 weeks; place in plastic bags (prevents shriveling and transfer of odor) and store in refrigerator.

Properly prepared for freezing, apples can be stored in the frozen-food section of the refrigerator about 2 months, in a separate freezer, at 0°F. or below, for 1 year.

Store canned and bottled apple products at room temperature until opened, up to 1 year. After opening, refrigerate, tightly covered, up to 5 days.

nutritive value: Although an apple a day may not truly keep the doctor away, apples are nevertheless an excellent food. An apple 3 inches in diameter (there are approximately 2½ such apples in a pound) contains 96 calories, is about 84 percent water, and offers:

protein	.3	gram
fat	1	gram
carbohydrate	24	grams
calcium	12	milligrams
phosphorus	17	milligrams
iron	.5	milligram
sodium	2	milligrams
potassium	182	milligrams
thiamin	.05	milligram
riboflavin	.03	milligram
niacin	.2	milligram
ascorbic acid	7	milligrams
vitamin A	150	international units

Unsweetened applesauce contains about 100 calories per cup; sweetened applesauce, about 185 calories per cup; apple juice, 126 calories per cup.

Tips on preparing, cooking, serving. Apples to be served raw should be washed well—wash just before serving, rather than before storing, for longer storage life. Raw apples make a fine snack for adults and children alike, and an excellent dessert, particularly with cheese.

Although many people prefer to peel apples before eating them, the apple peel is edible and supplies food fiber—old-fashioned "roughage"—that helps to maintain functional regularity of the body (the cellulose in the meat of the apple offers the same benefit).

Sliced or diced, apples are a staple ingredient of fruit cups and salads, particularly in the winter when there is not a great variety of fresh fruit available. If cut apples must stand for a time, dip the pieces in lemon, orange, grapefruit, or lime juice, or drop them into a half-and-half combination of lemon juice and water to prevent browning. The vinegar and/or lemon juice in salad dressings will generally prevent discoloration of apples used in salads. Red delicious, golden delicious, and cortlands are slow to discolor—use them in salads and fruit cups.

When you cook apples, if you wish to maintain the shape of whole apples or of slices, add sugar at the start of cooking. If shape isn't a factor, as in making applesauce, add sugar after the cooking is completed.

Freezing apples. Whole apples—perfect fruit, tree-ripened and firm of flesh—can be frozen. So can dry packed apple slices and slices in syrup. (See special feature: PUTTING FOOD BY.) Applesauce, baked apples, and apple juice also freeze well, as do homemade baked goods containing apples—pies, strudels, kuchen, and so on.

Other ways, other forms. In your market, you'll find apples available in many ways other than fresh.

on grocery shelves, in cans, jars, or bottles: Sliced apples, sweetened or not; apple-pie filling (slices, sweetened and slightly thickened, sometimes spiced); applesauce, sweetened or unsweetened, sometimes lightly flavored with cinnamon; apple-combination sauces; baby food applesauce, apple puddings; apple jelly and apple butter; apple juice; apple cider; cider vinegar; baked apples (sweetened, sometimes spiced); chutneys and other apple-combination relishes.

on grocery shelves, in packages: Dried apples, in 8-ounce packages or in smaller, snack-size bags; to be reconstituted for pies or sauce, or eaten out of hand.

in grocery frozen-food section: Bake-and-serve or heat-and-serve apple dumplings, turnovers, pies, cobblers, strudels, coffeecakes; apple juice concentrate; apple cider; not in wide distribution, applesauce and apple slices.

Some perfect partners. Sautéed apple slices are a tasty accompaniment for pork or poultry dishes; sprinkle them lightly with cinnamon-sugar. Apple fritters serve the same good purpose. Chutney and other relishes often use apples as a chief ingredient. Chopped apples make an interesting addition to stuffing for poultry—good with chicken or turkey, particularly good with duck or goose. Wedges of raw apple are an excellent, unusual addition to the tray of "dunkers" to serve with a cocktail dip. Chopped apples make a good lamb curry better. Sweet breads and cookies profit from the addition of chopped apples, too. Use apples in salads, in fruit cocktails to start a meal and fruit compotes to end one. Apple desserts are legion, from the simple baked apple (try filling the hollow with a combination of dates, nuts, and honey) to dumplings, charlotte, strudel, brown betty, pandowdy, apple tapioca, and many others. Foremost is America's favorite, apple pie, served hot or cold, plain or with ice cream, lemon sauce, or a wedge of sharp cheddar. And what would autumn be without candied apples on a stick?

Apples are with us almost daily, not only in our meals and snacks, but in our language. It was once most desirable to curry favor with teacher by taking her a nicely polished red apple, although that homey habit seems to have fallen out of fashion. But we still tidy things up by putting them "in apple-pie order," say of a little girl that she is "the apple of her daddy's eye," and aver that a statement is true "as sure as God made little green apples." Bombastic politicians refer to themselves coyly as "American as apple pie." Singers of nostalgic songs implore a departed loved one not to "sit under the apple tree with anyone else but me." Poets employ apples in imagery—speaking of lovers reunited, Yeats says that together they will pick "the silver apples of the moon, the golden apples of the sun." And in Solomon's Song of Songs—depending upon your point of view, another book of the Bible to be treated as gospel, or some of the most gloriously sensual poetry ever written—appears the verse, "Stay me with flagons, comfort me with apples, for I am sick of love."

Like them or not, eat them or not, apples are an everyday part of our lives. In regular cold storage and CA storage, more than 75 million bushels of apples are "wintered over" today. The full yearly apple crop, for fresh use, storage, and commercial packing of various sorts, comes close to 200 million bushels (bushels average 42 pounds), or about 90 apples per person. See also CRAB APPLES.

APPLIANCES: see special feature: YOU CAN'T WORK WITHOUT TOOLS

APRICOTS

For the most part, fresh fruit is one of the few remaining seasonal foods. Because of improved techniques of shipping and storage, even some fruits know no season—apples, oranges, lemons, grapefruit, and melons, among others, are to be had virtually all year long. But apricots are indeed seasonal. Nearly 95 percent of the fresh apricots are in the markets in June and July, and there are virtually none to be had the rest of the year. Those shipped in from the Mediterranean countries where apricots grow so bountifully account for most of the other 5 percent, which appear in gourmet food markets—at gourmet prices—during December and January. A few from Mexico reach western markets in the spring.

A relative of the peach, the smaller apricot is a pale golden-yellow, with deeper orange-gold flesh surrounding an oval pit smaller and smoother than that of the peach. The tree, which puts out pink blossoms of great beauty and entrancing odor before the leaves appear, will grow only in areas where there is no frost.

Native to Asia, where it still grows wild, the apricot was cultivated in China more than 2,000 years ago. From there, the tree was carried west by explorers and soldiers. It is thought that Alexander the Great brought it to Greece. The Crusaders carried the tree home to England, where it still grows, espaliered on garden walls in the warmer, more protected parts of the country. Now the apricot is grown commercially in all the Mediterranean countries and, courtesy of the Spanish missionaries in the 1700s, in California. Pacific coast orchards and some in Utah account for virtually all the apricots that reach markets in the United States today.

Apricots are very perishable. They bruise easily and, because they develop their flavor and sweetness best on the tree, they should not be picked green to ripen in shipment, in the market, or in the buyer's home, as works very well for a number of fruits. Consequently, their life from tree to buyer is necessarily a short one.

APRICOTS IN YOUR KITCHEN

Because they are delightfully sweet when ripe—and for greatest enjoyment they should not be purchased any other way—and because they have a delicate, not-too-assertive flavor (subtle and somewhat exotic, but don't bother to tell the kids that), apricots make a perfect snack food, to be eaten out of hand. And a neat snack. They are not overly juicy, to the point of dribbling, and because their skins are tender and flavorful, they need not be peeled.

how to buy: Select fruit that is plump, reasonably firm, and of a uniform yellow-gold color. A ripe apricot yields to gentle pressure. As with all fruit, test by pressing between the palms of your hands rather than by pinching. With fruit, as with people, a pinch leaves a bruise, and the more delicate the fruit (or the person) the more damaging the bruise. In picking out fruit, avoid apricots that look dull, that are soft and mushy (overripe), or that are pale or greenish-yellow (underripe).

Apricots are generally sold loose, by the pound, although you may also find them in plastic-wrapped cardboard or plastic trays. As with all fruit packaged this way, take time to inspect the package and the fruit carefully, with a sharp eye for dark spots and for tray stains that may indicate the beginning of spoilage.

Depending on size, there are eight to twelve apricots in a pound.

how to store: Refrigerate, without washing, in a covered container or a perforated plastic bag. Slightly green apricots will improve somewhat in flavor when stored at room temperature, although they will never reach the flavor perfection of the tree-ripened variety. Refrigerator life is 3 to 5 days. Wash before serving, or peel if you prefer. Apricots resist peeling, but a small sharp knife, plus patience, should do the trick. If not, give them the treatment that assists peach peeling—dip briefly in and out of hot water, then into cold water, although a truly ripe apricot should not require this.

nutritive value: Apricots are high in natural sugars, and are an excellent source of vitamin A. Three whole raw apricots, not peeled, contain 55 calories, are about 85 percent water and offer:

protein	1.1	grams
fat	.2	gram
carbohydrate	13.7	grams
calcium	18	milligrams
phosphorus	25	milligrams
iron	.5	milligram
sodium	1	milligram
potassium	301	milligrams
thiamin	.03	milligram
riboflavin	.04	milligram
niacin	.6	milligram
ascorbic acid	11	milligrams
vitamin A	2,890	international units

Canned apricots generally have, in addition to the values above, a bonus of extra ascorbic acid (vitamin C) added during the processing to prevent the fruit from darkening.

Tips on preparing, cooking, serving. Fresh apricots are at their best eaten raw, out of hand as a snack food. (Some people like to bruise them all over just before eating for added sweetness and juiciness.) Or serve in a salad alone or with other fruits or with cottage cheese (try flavoring it with grated orange peel and chopped fresh mint for a salad that tastes like the essence of summer). Or offer them for dessert with a mild cheese such as cream or brie. Or try them puréed and marbleized through vanilla ice cream. Or slice them into the bottom of tart shells, top with a cooked custard, and sprinkle with toasted almonds.

Fresh apricots can be cooked, of course. They can be gently poached, halved and pitted or whole, in water or a combination of water and white wine with a few whole cloves or an inch of stick cinnamon for a delicious fruit sauce to serve at breakfast or for dessert. Or bake them in a pie with a streusel topping. A favorite dish of ancient Romans was a stew of diced pork shoulder with shallots and apricots, and it is worth repeating today.

Freezing apricots. Halves, peeled or not, may be frozen in heavy syrup with ascorbic acid or citric acid added to prevent discoloration, or dry-sugar packed, in which case the addition of one or the other acid is not necessary. (See special feature: PUTTING FOOD BY.) Freezer life, at 0°F. or below, is 1 year, or in the frozen-food compartment of a refrigerator, about 2 months.

Other ways, other forms. Unlike many other fruits, apricots when canned or dried or frozen retain very little of the flavor of the fresh fruit. Fortunately, they take on a delicious, if quite different, taste that is often preferred by those who aren't all that fond of fresh apricots.

on grocery shelves, in cans, jars, or bottles: Canned apricots are available peeled or unpeeled, whole (pitted or not), or as halves or slices. They are packed in syrup, in juice, or in water. Apricot preserve, used as a glaze in many delectable desserts as well as a spread for bread or toast, is available in jars of several sizes. Strained or chopped, they are to be had in small jars as baby food. You will also find apricot syrup in bottles and apricot nectar in cans or bottles on your grocer's shelves.

All of these items can be stored in your kitchen, unopened, for as long as 2 years. Opened and stored in the refrigerator, tightly covered, they will keep 2 to 4 days.

Use canned apricots in fruit cups and salads, in meat dishes as an integral part of the dish or as a delicious edible garnish, and in desserts such as upside-down cake, bavarian cream, various puddings and pies, and hot or cold soufflés. Apricot nectar can be served as a breakfast juice, a simple appetizer before dinner, and alone or mixed with other fruit juices as a refreshing (alcoholic or nonalcoholic) beverage or punch; it can also form the basis of a delicious gelatin salad or dessert. Apricot baby food is useful—for nonbabies—as a sauce for ice cream or cake—particularly if lightly spiced, combined with chopped nuts, or simply flavored with a few drops of almond extract.

on grocery shelves, in packages: Dried apricots are pitted apricot halves with a large amount of the moisture removed; they are treated with sulfur dioxide to preserve their color. Sometimes sold in bulk, they can more usually be found in moistureproof packages or in plastic bags, and they often form a part of dried fruit mixtures. A pound of dried apricots will yield about 5 cups before cooking. Store unopened packages on kitchen shelves. One large dried apricot half contains 12 to 14 calories.

They are fine to eat out of hand, as a snack (candy-sweet but, because their sweetness comes from concentrated natural sugars, they are not nearly as likely to cause tooth decay as candy, so see if you can get your children hooked on them), or stewed, or used in combination with other fruits in hot compotes. They can be reconstituted by simmering in water to cover until tender, about 15 minutes, and—sweetened or not—used as canned apricots are with meats and in desserts such as pies and puddings, in fruit salads (try them stuffed with nutted cream cheese), and as a sauce for ice cream or plain cake.

But best of all, seek out apricots—not a great quantity reaches any one market—in their brief season, to enjoy raw, eaten out of hand, while dreaming of sun-bright, faraway places.

ARABIC BREADS: see POCKET BREADS

ARLES: see SAUSAGES

ARROWROOT

This is a thickening agent for sauces, puddings, and the like, used more often in Victorian times than ours. Victorian ladies, you will recall, were very delicate indeed, subject to fainting fits and attacks of the vapors at the drop of a suggestion. Delicacy of digestion went hand in hand with this delicacy of sensibilities, and called for gentle measures in the kitchen. Arrowroot, more readily digestible than wheat flour—and therefore, by extension more ladylike—was one of those measures. (See FLOUR.)

A starch leached from the tubers of several kinds of tropical plants, then refined, arrowroot is still a remarkably good thickening agent to use in place of wheat flour or cornstarch. It is particularly useful in thickening acid fruits, for it remains more stable than flour in the presence of acid. Cooked, it becomes clear—as cornstarch does—to produce a sparkling, unclouded mixture that retains the true color of the fruit, but it does not impart the unpleasantly chalky-starchy taste that improperly cooked cornstarch does. Delicate puddings—grandma's blancmange, for example—and soups and sauces profit from the use of arrowroot as a thickener because of its lightness and lack of flavor. It is ideal for use in baby foods, in bland and other invalid diets.

A soft, fine white powder, arrowroot is generally shelved with or close to the spices in markets. Use 1½ teaspoons of arrowroot to replace each tablespoon of flour a recipe calls for. Mix with cold liquid, being sure the result is free of lumps, before heating or adding to hot mixtures. One of its useful properties is that it can cook at a lower temperature for a shorter time than other starch thickeners, making it ideal for mixtures that, because they contain eggs, should not boil, such as custards and egg-enriched sauces.

ARTICHOKES, GLOBE

The buds of a plant of the thistle family, artichokes are a love 'em or leave 'em sort of vegetable, known—and adored or reviled, but seldom accepted without comment—for many centuries. In the Rome of the second century A.D. they were the highest-priced vegetable obtainable, in spite of the fact that Pliny (who had visited Africa, where artichokes, or at least the eating of them, are supposed to have originated) observed that four-footed creatures shunned the vegetable, leaving the diner to draw his own conclusions.

By the eighteenth century artichokes were known throughout Europe and had begun to travel to the New World, notably to Louisiana with the French and to California with the Spanish.

The bulk of the artichokes that come to market today are grown in California's central coastal area. They will grow wherever the climate is cool but frost-free, and they seem to enjoy fog.

The "common artichoke." This misnomer is often applied to a vegetable that is actually exceedingly uncommon in looks, in taste, and in the manner in which it is served. The flavor cannot be compared with any other; it leaves a slight puckery sensation in the mouth, a sweetness in the throat.

Even the most rigid authorities on table manners agree that it is impossible to eat a whole globe artichoke except with the fingers. The leaves are broken off one by one, dipped into melted butter or some savory sauce; the bottom part of the leaf is drawn through the teeth to remove the flavorful soft part, and the remainder of the leaf discarded. (Indeed, there seems to be more left over after eating an artichoke than there was before you started.) Then the choke is removed, if a kindly cook has not already done the chore for you, and the heart and bottom attacked with knife and fork. If all this sounds like damning with faint praise, it is not meant to be. An artichoke is truly a gustatory delight, a pleasure not to be missed.

ARTICHOKES IN YOUR KITCHEN

Common in Italian and French cuisines and only slightly less so in Spanish, the artichoke is today gaining commendably wider acceptance. It can be found now in supermarkets and greengroceries almost everywhere at the height of its season, rather than having to be sought out in ethnic markets.

how to buy: Fresh artichokes are available the year around, but the peak season is the months of March, April, and May. There is virtually no relationship between size and quality, so choose a size suitable for your purpose. Select solid, heavy-for-their-size artichokes without any loose or spread or discolored leaves—signs that old age is setting in. They should be a pleasant deep green. Pass by any that are pale, or that have extensive purplish-brown blemishes.

One large globe artichoke makes one serving—remember that one of an artichoke's least lovable features is the amount of garbage it engenders. If you are going to use only the hearts—the cluster of small, pale leaves in the center, plus the smooth, mealy artichoke bottom—count on four to six hearts to make a serving. If you are going to use only the bottoms, you'll want to choose very large artichokes. Two bottoms—they are generally offered filled with some savory preparation—will serve one person, or one such filled bottom if it is used as an edible garnish rather than an integral part of the meal.

how to store: Preferably, don't buy artichokes until the day, or at most the day before, you are going to cook them. Store in the refrigerator in a plastic bag or covered container until just before cooking. They prefer a cool, moist atmosphere. If you must, keep them this way up to 4 days, but they may not be at their best by the time you get around to them.

nutritive value: One large globe artichoke—of which about 60 percent is waste—may offer a calorie range of from 12 to 65 or slightly more, depending on whether the vegetable is freshly harvested or has been stored before being put on the market. In a freshly harvested artichoke most of the carbohydrate occurs as inulin, generally not used by the body. An older artichoke has converted its inulin to sugar, of which the body will make use, and its calorie count is higher.

A large globe artichoke, which is nearly 87 percent water, contains:

protein	4.3	grams
fat	.3	gram
carbohydrate	15	grams
calcium	78	milligrams
phosphorus	105	milligrams
iron	1.7	milligrams
sodium	46	milligrams
potassium	458	milligrams
thiamin	.11	milligram
riboflavin	.06	milligram
niacin	1.1	milligrams
ascorbic acid	12	milligrams
vitamin A	230	international units

Not by any means a nutritionist's dream of the ideal food, artichokes are eaten more for gustatory pleasure (and sometimes for their snob appeal) than for food value.

Tips on preparing, cooking, serving. The first time around, artichokes seem to be something of a nuisance to work on, but a rhythm is quickly established. To wash, hold the artichoke by its stem and plunge it in and out of cold water several times. Pull off the outside row of leaves at the bottom, and any bruised or discolored leaves beyond that point. With a sharp knife, cut off the stem flush with the base of the vegetable. Switching to scissors, trim off the thorn-tipped top of each leaf. Drop into acidulated water if you are preparing several at a time. (Because they begin to discolor almost immediately after they are cut, artichokes should be dropped into an acidulated bath—3 tablespoons of lemon juice or vinegar to each quart of water.) Cook, uncovered, in boiling salted and acidulated water, until a center leaf pulls out easily and the base tests tender when pierced with a fork, anywhere from 15 to 45 minutes, depending on the size and the variety. Turn upside down on absorbent paper to drain. If you're an artichoke nut, peel and cook the stems, too—they have the delicious flavor of the heart.

You're not through. Gently separate the leaves—they'll separate easily now, if the artichoke was cooked a proper length of time. Seize the bunch of small, pale leaves at the center and pull them out. Underneath is the grayish, fuzzy choke; remove this with a small spoon, making certain to get all of it. If you are serving the vegetables plain, you can leave the choke-removing chore to each diner if you like, but if you're stuffing them you should do it yourself, or the artichoke lover may get a nasty surprise.

Serve hot or cold. Melted butter or butter and lemon juice or hollandaise are traditional accompaniments for hot artichokes, mayonnaise or vinaigrette or seasoned sour cream for the cold ones. Incidentally, each of those pale leaves you pulled out to get at the choke has attached to it a tiny bit of the meat of the bottom—a nice bonus for the cook who's a dedicated artichoke buff. And don't forget the stems, while you're treating yourself so royally.

To cook hearts only, pull off and discard all but the tender inner leaves. Trim base and tops of remaining leaves. Remove the choke—this is much easier to do if you cut the heart in half vertically, and the heart shows off its handsome shape better that way. Cook as above, 10 to 15 minutes.

To cook bottoms only, you still have some trimming left to do. Prepare as for hearts, but remove even the tops of the tender inner leaves, leaving only half an inch attached to the base. Take out the choke. Cook as above, whole or sliced.

Whole artichokes are delicious plain or stuffed. Give them their due and serve them as a separate course, either as an appetizer (hot or cold) or in place of a salad (cold). Hearts may be served hot—sauced or buttered—as a vegetable (fork food, this way), or cold in (or as) a salad, or marinated as an appetizer. They team well with seafood in a casserole or in a lightly garlicky tomato sauce as a filling for an omelet. Sauté bottoms briefly (after regular cooking) or fill with a vegetable such as tiny green peas or tomato-sauced

diced eggplant, or use them in salads, particularly in fish or seafood combinations.

Freezing artichokes. Whole artichokes, hearts, and bottoms can all be successfully frozen at home. They must be scalded in boiling acidulated water for roughly half the time they would take to cook. Properly prepared, they can be kept at 0°F. or below for about 1 year, or in a refrigerator's frozen food compartment for about a month. (See special feature: PUTTING FOOD BY.)

Other ways, other forms. Food processors have been making the serving of artichoke hearts and bottoms painless for years. Unfortunately, if you want to serve the vegetable whole, you'll have to be a do-it-yourselfer.

on grocery shelves, in cans or jars: Hearts come packed in water or brine, or in a seasoned, olive oil-based dressing, in cans or jars. Bottoms are usually water-packed, sometimes stacked in tall, narrow glass jars. These are a luxury item.

in grocery frozen-food section: Artichoke hearts come in 10-ounce packages. Follow the package directions for cooking. If they are overcooked, they lose flavor and become flabby.

ARTICHOKES, JERUSALEM

Nobody seems to know why these tubers, which look vaguely like a somewhat wartier ginger root, were named "artichokes." They don't come from the same (thistle) family as globe artichokes, nor do they really taste like them, although some people find a resemblance in the two flavors. One brand of jerusalem artichoke is marketed under the name "sunchoke," a much better choice, because the vegetable is the rootlike tuber of a kind of sunflower.

We do know, however, where the jerusalem part of the name came from. It was conferred by someone with a tin ear for language, who corrupted the Italian *giarasole,* meaning "turn to the sun," in the manner of a sunflower. Indeed, jerusalem artichokes are sometimes labeled "girasoles" in markets working on the principle that obfuscation is the better part of salesmanship.

A western hemisphere vegetable, jerusalem artichokes were taken in the early seventeenth century to Europe from their native eastern Canada by travelers interested in finding new foods as a benefit incidental to exploring new lands. They appeared more often on tables in the United States a generation ago than they do today, but they are regaining popularity, along with some other "forgotten" vegetables such as salsify and kale.

Cooking, serving. To serve raw (in a salad or as part of an appetizer tray of raw vegetables, to be served with a dip), wash well, peel or not as you like, cut into very thin slices, and drop into acidulated water or dip into lemon juice. Very crisp when raw, jerusalem artichokes become tender on cooking, but toughen if overcooked. Test whole vegetables at 15 minutes, continue cooking if not tender. Sliced or diced, they will cook in a shorter time, depending on the size of the pieces. They are easier to peel after cooking than before, an excellent reason for cooking them whole. Salt the cooking water lightly, and add lemon juice, mild vinegar or, if you like, white wine, to acidulate it, which prevents discoloration. A teaspoon to a tablespoon is sufficient, depending on the amount of water. One or two jerusalem artichokes will serve one person. After cooking, they may be mashed, creamed, served with a cheese sauce, or become a part of a vegetable medley. Or simply dress with butter, pepper, and a little lemon juice.

Jerusalem artichokes can be found in produce markets, loose (sold by the pound) or in plastic bags. They are not available canned or frozen.

ARTIFICIAL FLAVORS

Over the years, chemists have developed a broad spectrum of flavorings for use in canned, condensed, dried, frozen, and otherwise processed foods. Many are scientific marvels that reproduce a taste almost indistinguishable from the real flavor they imitate. Others are what might be called more real than real—they strive to improve on nature to produce taste and appearance better than what the tree, bush, and field have to offer. An example is a breakfast beverage that is sweeter, smoother, "orangier" than orange juice, one that turns out to be more acceptable to many palates than the tart, rather acid flavor characteristic of the fruit itself—particularly to those who have grown up since the time when there was no way to put orange juice on the breakfast table other than by squeezing the fruit at home.

When nature offers such a wide range of interesting, delightful flavors, why bother even to attempt to duplicate them chemically? One reason is economy; artificial flavors, in many cases, cost the food processor much less than the real thing. Artificial vanilla is an example—it's relatively cheap compared to an extract of vanilla beans or the even more costly beans themselves.

Looks can kill. Appearance of the product influences the manufacturer, too. Those costly vanilla beans leave small, dark pepperlike flecks in the food, immediately suspect by people who don't understand that these specks are a concomitant of a product with a true vanilla-bean flavor. Many an ice cream manufacturer has put out—with pride and satisfaction, and in anticipation of shouts of joy from a grateful public —a delicious, true vanilla ice cream, only to find that nobody wants dessert with little bits of "dirt" in it. It tastes good, the not-so-grateful public admits, but it looks awful.

Fresh strawberry ice cream meets with the reverse of that opinion. The consensus is that it looks nice, with all those chunks of fresh strawberry in it, but it tastes terrible. Actually,

"it tastes artificial" is what taste-test panel members say of it. So many manufacturers add strawberries for the sake of appearance along with the artificial strawberry flavor that the general public has come to want and expect.

Another reason for the use of these chemical flavoring substances is stability. Time takes an unfortunate toll of many natural flavors. They fade to the point of being imperceptible or, worse, undergo such a change that what once was delicious in time becomes unpalatable.

Sometimes the best isn't good enough. But perhaps the reason most important to the manufacturer is acceptance —which he created, and now (happily, from his point of view) is stuck with. Many people find fresh pineapple juice not nearly as good as canned because they've become accustomed to the slightly metallic flavor the juice takes from its container. There's a whole segment of the population that considers homemade bread bland, heavy, totally undesirable compared with the bread on the supermarket shelf. Many breakfast cereals barely hold their own, or have gone off the market entirely, because they taste like real wheat, real oats, real bran, real rice. Fresh, real flavors have become unfamiliar, and the unfamiliar is more often than not also the unacceptable. See also ADDITIVES AND PRESERVATIVES.

ARTIFICIAL SWEETENERS: see
   ADDITIVES AND PRESERVATIVES,
   SACCHARIN, and XYLITOL

ASIAGO: see CHEESE

ASPARAGUS

The Greeks ate asparagus, so did the Romans. It grew wild throughout the Mediterranean area (and still does, in many places), migrated north, and was—as it still is—considered throughout Europe the height of vegetable elegance. (For some reason, the English preferred it raw for a time, but that eccentricity seems to have gone out of style.) Across the ocean, Thomas Jefferson grew asparagus in his Monticello greenhouses, New England housewives cut the first stalks and thanked their stars that winter was over. Travelers west took the roots with them and established beds that made their new homes seem more comfortably like their old ones.

Today, when the first fresh asparagus goes on sale, usually in February, women take the tender green stalks home for a tastes-like-spring meal, often with the first fresh strawberries, providentially brought to market at the same time, for dessert.

26

The fresh asparagus season lasts from February—the California crop is the earliest—through June, when the New Jersey crop runs out. The peak of the season begins in April and lasts through May.

Incidentally, if you're a language purist, asparagus is plural. But you'd be hard put to it to find a home cook who refers to asparagus as "them," and we'll go along with the tide.

ASPARAGUS IN YOUR KITCHEN

Although there are a number of varieties of asparagus, we generally tend to think of the vegetable only in terms of the two colors, green or white. Green asparagus is the more familiar here, although the white—produced in small hills of mulch so that the stalks, deprived of sun, do not turn green—is considered the greater delicacy in European markets. Some fresh white asparagus is offered for sale here, particularly in recent years, but lovers of the white variety generally must find their favorite in gourmet markets, or be content with the sort found in glass jars on grocers' shelves.

how to buy: Look for fresh-appearing, crisp stalks and tightly closed heads. Wrinkled or twisted stalks and/or open heads indicate overmaturity and mean that the vegetable will be tough, stringy, and lacking in the fresh flavor that is so delicious. Avoid asparagus that is excessively sandy. The sand works its way insidiously into the heads and scales, is exceedingly difficult to wash out, and is the bane of the dedicated asparagus eater.

Asparagus is sold loose, by the pound, or in bunches that generally weigh in the neighborhood of a little over two pounds. Two pounds will serve four to six. Bunches are held together prosaically with rubber bands or sometimes with red tape—a convenience, surely, rather than a commentary? Medium-size asparagus averages between sixteen and twenty stalks per pound. As is true of all fresh foods, asparagus is most expensive at the beginning and end of the five-month season, least expensive at the season's peak.

how to store: Preferably, buy asparagus the day you're going to cook it. Store it unwashed in the refrigerator, in a covered container or plastic bag. It will keep up to four days, but lose a little of its *joie de vivre* with each passing day.

nutritive value: Vitamin A is the chief contribution of asparagus to a balanced diet—it offers about .1 of the U.S. RDA, as well as appreciable amounts of vitamin C, phosphorus, and potassium. Four medium spears of cooked asparagus contain only 12 calories—a pleasure to calorie-counters—and are low in carbohydrates, too, if you're a carbohydrate-watcher. Four spears offer:

protein	1.3	grams
fat	.1	gram
carbohydrate	2.2	grams
calcium	13	milligrams
phosphorus	30	milligrams
iron	.4	milligram
sodium	1	milligram
potassium	183	milligrams
thiamin	.1	milligram
riboflavin	.11	milligram
niacin	.8	milligram
ascorbic acid	16	milligrams
vitamin A	540	international units

This is as good a time as any to make a point for all home cooks interested in nutrition to ponder. Sodium values given in this list, and in any other list of nutrients in this book, are for the unseasoned product. If you add salt to the water in which the food is cooked, or to the cooked food at the table, the amount of sodium goes up.

Tips on preparing, cooking. In washing asparagus, be thorough. Dunk in and out of tepid water a number of times, or wash head-side up under running tepid-to-cold water. If the vegetable seems at all sandy, peel the scales off the stems with a vegetable peeler. Some cooks prefer to peel the entire stem, but this is really being over-nice—and, like throwing the baby out with the bath water, tosses perfectly good flavor and nutritive value into the garbage. Do it only if the asparagus is old and tough, in which case broccoli would have been a wiser buy.

To prepare the green variety, snap off the bottoms of the stalks—they will obligingly come off at the point where the tough part begins. In very young asparagus, there is virtually no tough end to the stem. White asparagus must be peeled.

In cooking asparagus, be brief. There are three basic ways to do it. An asparagus steamer is made especially for this purpose. It consists of a tall pan with holes in the bottom that fits snugly into another, slightly taller—and solid-bottomed—pan, with a cover that tops the whole works. Stand the asparagus up in the inner pan. Place water in the outer one to the point where it will just cover the bottoms of the stalks. Bring to a boil, put the inner pan and the cover in position; cook until just barely tender, 10 to 12 minutes—even 15 to 20 minutes if the vegetable has reached that certain age.

In an asparagus steamer, the bottoms of the stalks are cooked in water, the upper stalks and the heads are steamed. To achieve this desirable result without a steamer, place the stalks upright (tie in a bundle, if necessary) in about ½ cup of boiling water in the bottom part of a double boiler. Turn the top of the double boiler upside down and use as a cover.

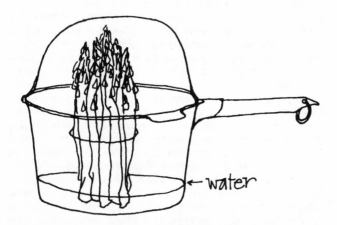

Alternatively, prepare a large, deep, covered skillet by placing three or four flattish wads of aluminum foil in the bottom. Over this lay a 4-inch-wide strip of doubled foil long enough to hang over the pan on both sides. With a kitchen

fork, punch a dozen holes in the foil strip. Pour ½ inch of water into the pan; bring to a boil. Lay the asparagus flat on the foil strip, cover, and cook as above. When the vegetable is done, drain by picking up the two long ends of the foil. (Never lose your head and dump the asparagus spears into a colander to drain, or they'll lose theirs.)

Freezing asparagus. If you're lucky enough to have a home-garden asparagus patch, by all means freeze some for out-of-season enjoyment. At 0°F. or lower, home-frozen asparagus, properly prepared (see special feature: PUTTING FOOD BY), can be kept for 1 year, or it will remain in good condition about 1 month in the frozen-food compartment of a refrigerator.

Other ways, other forms. When the fresh kind is out of season or too budget-bending to be considered, canned and frozen asparagus are the alternatives.

on grocery shelves, in cans or jars: You'll find canned green asparagus cuts (about 1-inch pieces), spears, or tips (just the most tender top of the spear) in cans and jars of various sizes. Luxury white asparagus spears, which are often imported, are available in jars as well. Shop around for a brand you like—some canned asparagus becomes woefully mushy in the processing.

in grocery frozen-food section: Although there's a large rooting section for canned asparagus, the frozen kind is more like fresh, provided you treat it with proper respect; follow package directions, and lean toward under- rather than over-cooking. You'll find 10-ounce packages of cuts and the same size packages of spears, of many brands. There are also, less widely distributed, packages of frozen mammoth spears, which are tender and delectable.

Some perfect partners. Like artichokes, asparagus is often served as a separate course. Dress with plain melted butter or season the butter with lemon juice, capers, or dill. Or serve the asparagus with hollandaise sauce. Or sprinkle with butter-sautéed bread crumbs for Asparagus Polonaise. Cheese-sauced asparagus on toast makes a delightful luncheon dish. For a heartier one, top the toast with thin, lightly sautéed slices of ham or the asparagus with slices of hard-cooked egg; if you're feeling expansive, use both ham and egg. An elegant little sandwich to accompany a salad at lunch, to go on a tea table, or to become part of wedding reception refreshments, goes like this: spread a very thin slice of firm-textured white bread lightly with mustard mayonnaise, top with a thin slice of ham; place an asparagus spear at one end and roll up; secure with a food pick and chill until serving time, at which point remove the pick.

Asparagus has a place in casseroles, too. A combination of asparagus and crabmeat in a very lightly turmeric-flavored sauce makes an exceptional buffet table offering. Chicken or Turkey Divan, with asparagus substituting for the more usual broccoli, will never go begging.

And don't forget that as good as hot asparagus is, cold asparagus is a close contender. Serve the chilled spears on leaves of boston or other pale green lettuce. Dress with vinaigrette sauce, garnish with narrow strips of pimiento or a few very thin slices of brazil nut.

At the height of its glory, the Roman empire originated, among other accomplishments, a large number of what the populace doubtless thought of as snappy sayings. One was the admonition, "Do it in less time than it takes to cook asparagus!" Bear that in mind, and the asparagus on your table will be just as you want it to be—perfectly green and tender-firm, with the promise of spring in every mouthful.

ASPIC

A clear stock stiffened through the good offices of the gelatinous material in the bones of the meat, fish, or poultry from which it was made, or by commercial packaged gelatin, aspic is a cool, beautiful elaboration for a simple dish. You can make the stock yourself at home, or use canned beef or chicken broth (if you choose the condensed variety, dilute with only half as much water as the label calls for) or slightly diluted canned or bottled clam juice if it's a fish aspic you have in mind.

In making aspic, use unflavored gelatin, never the flavored kind, in proportions of 1 tablespoon (1 envelope) of gelatin for each 1½ cups of stock. This produces an aspic with backbone. It will be stiff enough to be turned out of a mold; to be chopped or cut into cubes for garnish; to hold together firmly the diced or chopped food incorporated into it, as in making pressed chicken or jambon persillé (parslied ham); to encapsulate smoothly an entire piece of food, as in making oeufs en gelée (eggs in aspic); or to glaze beautifully a whole ham, chicken, or fish.

Making everything perfectly clear. To be at its best, the stock for aspic should be clarified to produce a cloudless, sparkling coating that allows the food beneath to shine through. This involves heating fat-free stock slowly with beaten egg whites and the shells of the eggs—essential for proper clarifying—until it comes to a boil and a layer of sticky sediment rises to the top. The stock is set aside for 15 minutes, then poured through a strainer lined with several thicknesses of cheesecloth wrung out of cold water. Something of a nuisance, but worth it.

Savor the flavor. Essentially, aspic is flavored by the fish (heads, bones, and trimmings are fine), meat, or poultry from which the stock was made, and the flavor will be all the better if some combination of onion, carrot, celery, parsley, bay leaf, tarragon, or other herbs was simmered along in the pot. Often lemon juice is added for sparkling taste—particularly to fish and chicken aspic—or wine—white for fish or chicken or veal, red for beef—for extra flavor. Sherry and madeira are also often-used flavorings for aspic.

All aspic-glazed food can be—indeed, many must be—prepared up to 24 hours in advance and refrigerated until serving time.

AU GRATIN: see GRATIN

AU JUS: see JUS

AU LAIT: see page 451

AUBERGINE: see page 451

AVGOLEMONO: see LEMONS and SOUPS

AVOCADOS

If this page could be wired for sound, it would be, so that the praises of the glorious avocado could be appropriately set to music. Handsome to behold with its green-to-purple-to-black skin, its green-yellow shading to yellow-green flesh, and a poem to eat with its mild yet unique flavor and its satiny, buttery texture, an avocado at its peak of perfection is a thing of beauty and a joy through the final mouthful.

An American native, the avocado—*ahuacatl*—was served to Hernando Cortez at a banquet given in his honor by Montezuma at Tenochtitlán, now Mexico City, in 1519. Cortez and other visitors to the New World took back to the Old World tales of the exotic fruit of the Aztecs, lamenting that its delicacy would not permit it to make the stormy Atlantic voyage.

Incas, Toltecs, and other Mexican, Central and South American natives cultivated the avocado. In Chile, Peru, and Ecuador, the fruit is still known as *palta,* its Indian name. (In Spain it is *aguacate,* in France, *avocat*—it finally found its way to the Old World.) Probably because of its color and the rough skin of some varieties, "alligator pear" was an early name in the United States, along with even less fitting appellations such as "custard apple," "butter pear," and "laurel peach," until the Department of Agriculture gave its official blessing to "avocado" at the turn of the century.

The first trees in this country were planted in Florida in the early 1830s, but California now leads in production, accounting for about 80 percent of the total crop. Indeed, so highly do Californians regard the fruit that you can find just south of San Francisco a vast avocado replica, in the neighborhood of 20 feet tall, standing at the edge of U.S. highway 1. As art it leaves something to be desired, but as a tribute it is, at the very least, a monumental token of esteem.

Mark of distinction. The growers of avocados have a hallmark of quality, which guarantees that the avocado you buy has met rigid standards concerning color, shape, keeping qualities, and flavor. The name was made up of the first three letters of "California" and the first three of "avocado," and you can be sure that any avocado stamped "Calavo" meets those strict requirements. About two-thirds of the avocado trees in California and nearly three-quarters of those in

Florida are controlled or supervised by the growers' group, and produce fruit worthy of the Calavo hallmark.

AVOCADOS IN YOUR KITCHEN

In color, the skin of an avocado may be one of various shades of green, or brownish-purple, or purplish-black. Thick or thin, the skin may be smooth or slightly pebbled or quite deeply corrugated. Somewhat pear-shaped, the fruit may be long- or short-necked, fairly slim to almost round. It can weigh as little as 3 ounces, as much as 4 pounds. Whatever the color, size, or shape, the meat inside of the avocado is softly green-gold, richly succulent, the Mexican "butter of the poor" that is the delight of good cooks and discriminating eaters everywhere.

how to buy: Avocados are picked and shipped when under-mature because, unlike many fruits, they ripen best off the tree. If you want to use the fruit the day or the day after you buy it, you may be hard put to it to find one ripe enough, unless you search out a gourmet market. Avocado lovers understand that they must wait a while for ripeness, and generally bring home immature fruit to store at room temperature until they have ripened.

Choose unblemished avocados of an allover uniform firmness without any soft or sunken spots. Irregular light-brown markings on the skin do not affect the quality of the fruit, but be sure the skin is unbroken. The fruit should be relatively heavy for its size. From October to May, the California fuerte, green and thin-skinned, is the avocado you're most likely to encounter in the market. Hass, with a dark, thicker, pebbly skin, also comes from California, and is available from May to October. Florida varieties, which are larger, less pear-shaped, and a paler green, are in the market from July to January. So, as you can see, whenever you want avocados they are available—there is really no time when they are out of season.

For immediate use, choose avocados that yield to gentle pressure when cradled between the palms of your hands. Or buy fruit that is uniformly hard to ripen at home. (Don't pinch—avocados bruise more easily than you do and, defenseless, they can't pinch back.)

how to store: Generally, an avocado will ripen to the point where it yields to gentle pressure, and is at its best for eating, in three to five days. Store at room temperature in a bowl with other fruit, if you wish, for an avocado is as good to look at as to eat. If you wish to slow down ripening, store in the refrigerator for up to three days. If you wish to hurry it, snuggle two avocados (or more) together in a paper bag, close the bag loosely, sit back and let nature take its course.

nutritive value: The calorie-counter's lament, "I just love avocados, but they're so fattening!" is a product of fuzzy thinking. In the first place, what is "fattening" and what isn't is all relative. Satiety value—an elegant way of saying that

the food fills you up and keeps you from becoming hungry again until it's time for the next meal—is a very important consideration. Because an avocado is high in fat (mostly unsaturated, if you're about to launch the cholesterol-watcher's lament) and fats are digested slowly, they give the eater a comfortable, lasting feeling of hunger well satisfied.

Half a 10-ounce California fuerte avocado costs the dieter an investment of about 180 calories and contains:

protein	2.4	grams
fat	18.5	grams
carbohydrate	7.1	grams
calcium	11	milligrams
phosphorus	47	milligrams
iron	.7	milligram
sodium	5	milligrams
potassium	680	milligrams
thiamin	.12	milligram
riboflavin	.23	milligram
niacin	1.8	milligrams
ascorbic acid	16	milligrams
vitamin A	330	international units

As you can see, the avocado has protein, seldom found in fruit, and a reasonable supply of vitamins and minerals to make it a useful as well as a delicious part of a normal diet.

Tips on preparing, cooking. To halve an avocado, cut it all around, pit deep, from stem to stern. Holding between your hands, twist the halves gently in opposite directions until they come apart. Spear the pit with the tip of your knife to remove it. To peel, start with a sharp knife, peel off the skin—if the avocado is properly ripe, it will come off readily.

Slice by laying a half, flat side down, on a board and cutting lengthwise. To dice, cut the slices across in pieces of whatever size you wish. To mash, use a fork, to purée, a blender. For neat rounds, use a melon baller. The avocado is an accommodating fruit, easily reduced to any form.

In cooking avocado, be gentle and wary. Brief cooking at low temperature enhances flavor, but long cooking at high heat is ruinous to the avocado's delicate texture. Use a stainless knife to prepare avocado, and brush cut surfaces with lemon juice, a weak (1 tablespoon to 2 cups water) vinegar solution, or an ascorbic acid mixture (follow package directions) to prevent discoloration. Add one of these aids against discoloration to mashed or puréed avocado, too.

Freezing avocados. Don't try it. Freezing causes undesirable changes in color and texture. Well-seasoned avocado dip, protected against discoloration, can be home-frozen with moderate success, but because there are fresh avocados on the market at all seasons, there's no real point to freezing a dip that is reasonably good frozen, spectacularly good when made fresh.

Other ways, other forms. Think of an avocado as a fresh fruit, period. It cannot be successfully canned or otherwise processed or preserved. The only way, other than fresh, that you will find avocado in the market is in the frozen-food section, as a nicely seasoned dip, packaged in cans the size of those used for frozen fruit juice concentrate. This is handy to store in your home freezer—it will keep at least a year at 0°F., or a month or so in a home refrigerator frozen-foods compartment—for it thaws in a very short time, is ready to use as is, or can be quickly dressed up with chopped tomato and/or thinly sliced green onions, or seasoned with a little garlic juice or curry powder.

Some perfect partners. The classic way to serve avocado is on the half shell—simply halved, unpeeled, with lemon juice and salt, or with a light french dressing, or with a dressing of half-and-half honey and lime juice. But that is only the beginning. At any meal, throughout the meal, there are myriad inventive and delectable ways to use avocados.

Guacamole, the classic Mexican sauce-dip, is a delicious appetizer. Puréed avocado is spectacular in a rum-based cocktail. Float thin slices in a clear tomato broth. Serve cream of avocado soup. Crab, lobster, shrimp, and chicken mixtures, hot or cold, can be heaped into avocado halves. Season mashed avocado with lemon juice and salt and use as a spread, in place of butter, on ham or chicken sandwiches. Toss cubes of avocado in green salad, or alternate slices with grapefruit sections on a bed of greens. Add diced avocado to scrambled eggs just before serving. For dessert, marbleize mashed avocado in delicate swirls through vanilla ice cream, or make a beautifully creamy, pale green avocado mousse.

Half an avocado is the usual serving. A medium-size fruit will yield about ⅔ cup of purée, can be cut into eight hearty or twelve thin slices, or about two dozen bite-size cubes.

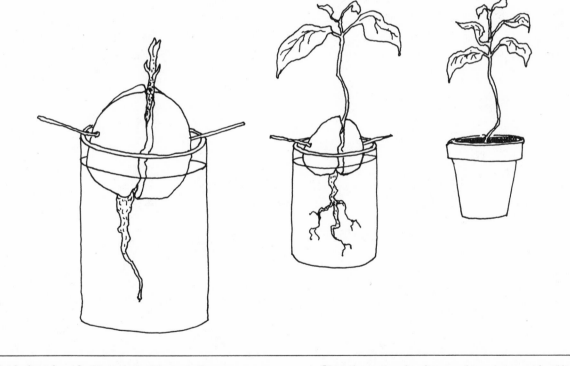

Waste not, want not. There's nothing whatever you can do with an avocado's skin but consign it to the garbage. The pit, however, is another matter. The avocado whose delicious flavor has long become nothing but a pleasant memory can flourish as a handsome semitropical house plant for years to come.

Start the avocado pit one of two ways—plant it in a pot, or suspend it in a glass of water. It will grow equally well either way, but it's more fun—particularly if there are children around to watch nature's goings-on—to use a glass. (Sometimes you'll find that the pit has already split within the fruit, with roots and shoot already starting to grow.) Whichever starting method you choose, wash the pit in lukewarm water and peel off any loose brown skin. Start the pit small end up. If you're using a glass, pour in water to within a half inch of the top, stick the pit with four food picks that will rest on the rim so that only the bottom half inch of the pit is in the water. Add water regularly to maintain the level. Or place the pit in a pot, directly in the soil, with about half the pointed end exposed.

Place the pot or the glass in a warm, dimly lit place until the roots are established and the pit splits and sends up one or more shoots. When the main shoot reaches a height of 6½ inches, cut back to 3 inches. When there are several leaves at the top of the new stem that will appear from the cut-back point, place the plant in soil, bring it out into the light and treat it as you would any other potted plant. Or bring the already potted plant into the light. Cut back judiciously at regular intervals to keep the plant bushy. Uncut, it will grow tall but skinny.

Avocados, oil rich, have another use. They are a favored ingredient in several kinds of skin-improvement preparations.

MEASURING UP TO METRIC

New ways to measure will soon come into your life, particularly into your kitchen—are you ready for the big switchover?

We have, at the present time, what must seem to the rest of the world to be an embarrassment of measurements: avoirdupois ounces, pounds, tons; liquid gallons, quarts, and pints, and fluid ounces; bushels, pecks, dry quarts and pints; inches, feet, yards, rods, miles. And there are fractions of, and multiples of, all these measures. To add to the confusion, we need to be specific when we mention a measure. A quart is not simply a quart—a dry quart is sixteen percent greater in volume than a liquid quart.

To compound the problem, when we cook we measure not only in ounces and pounds and fractions thereof, but also in quarts and pints, in cups and fractions and multiples of cups, in tablespoons and fractions and multiples of tablespoons, and in teaspoons and fractions and multiples of teaspoons. (Some cooks also measure in dashes, pinches, and little-bit-of and quite-a-lot-of quantities, but that way lies culinary madness.)

You didn't realize what a mess we were in, did you?

Because we learned all these measurements by slow progression at home, in school, and out in the world, they don't seem excessively complicated. They are the way everyone else around us measures, the only way used in the world in which we live.

The "mess" works for us but only because we're used to its complications. Out in the wider world, almost everybody has been using the metric system while we plugged along with our own way of doing things. Our British cousins were among the last holdouts, but they've gone metric, too. We are one small star of nonmetric in a firmament of metric.

All the same, we're a big and powerful country, used to doing and getting things our own way. So what if we're out of step with the rest of the world—does it really matter?

METRIC IS SIMPLE, METRIC IS LOGICAL

Yes, it really matters. Just as no man is an island, no country is either. We have to get along with the rest of the world. In the everyday give-and-take of communicating with people and governments and industries in other countries, we can't give inches and take centimeters, give pounds and take kilograms. The first reason for changing over to metric is one of economics, a matter of dollars and cents, a subject we all understand. World business and world trade are based on the metric system. Our economic health derives from buying from and selling to the rest of the world, in which all the measurements—weight, length, volume, and temperature—are metric. It's been estimated that American business loses between 10 and 25 billion dollars a year because it does not measure the way the rest of the world measures.

The second reason is efficiency. We think of ourselves and our ways of doing things as the last word in efficiency. Not true. The last word, as far as measuring is concerned, is being spoken by everybody else, while we're muddling along in a welter of baby talk. Our measurements bear little relation to one another, are not pegged to a common unit. We have 12 inches in a foot, 16 ounces in a pound; water freezes at 32° Fahrenheit and boils at 212°. On the other hand, all metric measurements—whether for weight, length, or volume—are based on the number 10, are expressed in parts or multiples of the number 10. The metric system is a decimal system. But our present systems are based on whole numbers and fractions.

MEETING METRIC HEAD-ON

At first glance, it seems that if you can multiply or divide by 10, you've got metric made. It's not quite that simple—but almost. Here are the basic metric units of measure:

gram – measure of weight (abbreviation: g)
meter – measure of length (abbreviation: m)
liter – measure of volume (abbreviation: l)

Many of the things we measure are too large or too small to be defined in terms of a reasonable number of meters, grams, or liters. For example, if your car's speedometer registers 50 miles per hour, you are rushing along at 80,000 meters per hour—a heady figure. But your speedometer, in the age of metric, will not register meters but kilometers; *kilo* is

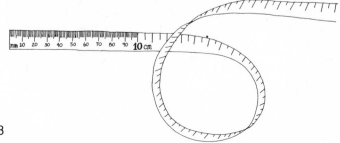

one of the metric prefixes. Combined with the root word, in this case meter, kilo multiplies the root by 1,000. So a kilometer is 1,000 meters. (And a kilowatt is 1,000 watts—but we always knew that, didn't we? We've been operating at least partially on the metric system for a long time—witness 35 millimeter film, medicine that is measured in cc, that is, cubic centimeters.)

Other metric prefixes you'll need to know are:

.001	*milli-*	=	1/1,000 (there are 1,000 millimeters to a meter, 1,000 milligrams to a gram, 1,000 milliliters to a liter)
.01	*centi-*	=	1/100 (there are 100 centimeters to a meter, 100 centigrams to a gram, 100 centiliters to a liter)
.1	*deci-*	=	1/10 (there are 10 decimeters to a meter, 10 decigrams to a gram, 10 deciliters to a liter)

Those are the common "less than" prefixes. There are also three common "more than" prefixes:

10.00	*deka-*	=	(10 times the root; there are 10 meters to a dekameter, etc.)
100.00	*hecto-*	=	(100 times the root; there are 100 meters to a hectometer, etc.)
1000.00	*kilo-*	=	(1,000 times the root; there are 1,000 meters in a kilometer, etc.)

Look at it another way, using the gram (measure of weight) as the root word, and tacking on the prefixes:

1 kilogram	=	1,000 grams
1 hectogram	=	100 grams
1 dekagram	=	10 grams
1 decigram	=	0.1 gram
1 centigram	=	0.01 gram
1 milligram	=	0.001 gram

Or try the liter, the measure of volume, as the root word:

1 kiloliter	=	1,000 liters
1 hectoliter	=	100 liters
1 dekaliter	=	10 liters
1 deciliter	=	0.1 liter
1 centiliter	=	0.01 liter
1 milliliter	=	0.001 liter

All that is nice to know, but how do we convert the everyday measurements we use now to meters, grams, and liters? There are conversion ratios that can be used, but by the time we are well into the conversion to metric (due to be complete by the year 1990), we'll have measuring tools that cope with the problem. Rulers will measure in centimeters and there will be meter sticks instead of yardsticks. Small scales will show grams rather than ounces, large ones, kilograms rather than pounds.

Until these and all the other new measuring tools we'll need are widely available, here are factors you can use for practice, to get the hang of conversion:

if you know:	*multiply by:*	*to get:*
inches	2.54	centimeters
yards	0.91	meters
miles	1.61	kilometers
square inches	6.45	square centimeters
square feet	0.09	square meters
square yards	0.84	square meters
ounces	28.35	grams
pounds	.45	kilograms

If you've always prided yourself on your math, if figuring out how many square yards of carpeting it's going to take to cover a floor 12 feet by 18 feet comes under the heading of a real gas, you're going to have a ball. The rest of us aren't going to be all that overjoyed, but we'll muddle through somehow.

Fortunately, there are some helpful tools that can come to our rescue. One is a device like a slide rule that converts liquid, weight, linear, square, and cubic measures from customary to metric. There are also rulers, tape measures, scales, thermometers, and kitchen measuring devices available to haul us out if we bog down in a morass of metric.

TAKING THE WORLD'S TEMPERATURE

We're used to dealing with degrees Fahrenheit in checking the weather to help us decide how to dress for the day, in taking the children's temperature when they aren't feeling well, in preheating the oven to 350°F. to bake a cake. We've also known—only vaguely, unless science classes in school made a point of it—that there was, somewhere out there, another thermometer that registered temperatures in degrees centigrade.

That other thermometer is still with us, but shortly it will be part of our daily lives. From "somewhere out there" it will come into our homes and we'll learn to live with it. To compound confusion, its name has been changed from centigrade to Celsius—fortunately with the same initial letter—so that we'll still be dealing in degrees F. versus degrees C., instead of having to cope with a third contender.

On the Fahrenheit thermometer, there are some points with which we're particularly familiar. Water boils at 212°, freezes at 32°. Normal body temperature is 98.6°. If the thermometer rises to the neighborhood of 100°, we swelter and suffer; if it drops below zero, we shiver and suffer.

On the Celsius scale we meet these same conditions, but at different points. At rather more logical points, some of them. Water boils at 100°C. and freezes at 0°C., for example. Normal body temperature is 37° on the Celsius scale, certainly no harder—in fact somewhat easier—to remember than 98.6°.

METRIC IN YOUR KITCHEN

You'll soon be "cooking metric." If that throws you into a panic, cool it—help is on the way.

Take a look on your pantry shelves. You may find a can of, say, tomato paste or corn labeled both "12 ounces" and "340 grams" or an 8-ounce package of crackers with its weight also specified as 227 grams. Soon all cans and packages will carry weights in both ounces and grams, so that when a recipe calls for "1 (10½-ounce) can condensed tomato soup," you'll find a 294-gram can ready and waiting.

Moving into metric, you will have one great advantage over many European cooks who've been working under the metric system all their lives. In Europe, recipes specify all liquid ingredients by volume (milliliters, liters) but all dry ingredients by weight (grams, kilograms). But because we are accustomed to measuring both liquid and dry ingredients in cups and spoonfuls, our metric recipes will be tailored so that we can continue to use such tools. Most kitchen measurements will be specified in liters or milliliters, and we'll use familiar cups and spoons, metrically marked. If you've been panicked at the thought of weighing flour, sugar, and the like, take heart. It won't be necessary.

Those ingredients we're accustomed to have specified by weight in a recipe will continue to be—meat, for example. (Who ever heard of a recipe calling for "2 cups lean ground beef"?) But the weights will be specified in grams and kilograms rather than ounces and pounds.

Once you're used to them, you'll appreciate the consistency of metric measurements. In metric, a milliliter is a milliliter, no matter what the ingredient you are measuring. By our present system, an ounce of one ingredient is not necessarily the same as an ounce of another, because we deal in both liquid and solid ounces. If you're measuring milk, there are 8 ounces to a cup, but if you're measuring grated cheese, there are only about 4 ounces to a cup—and confusion reigns.

In changing to kitchen metric—this is true of the tools we'll work with and the recipes we'll be guided by—numbers will generally be rounded off to avoid a rash of decimals, although some few can't be avoided. For example, a quart and a liter are not exactly the same (1 liter equals 1.6 quarts), but for most purposes the equivalent of a 1-quart measurement will be given as 1 liter; 5 milliliters is about the equivalent of 1 teaspoon, 1 cup about the same as 250 milliliters. And, of course, those things measured in numbers (2 onions, 1 bay leaf) will remain the same.

We'll be aware of this only in the transition period, when we're all doing our metric homework. To help us, many new cookbooks being published list ingredients (sometimes pan sizes, oven temperatures, and other kitchen measurements, too) in both the common units we're used to and in metric, using the rounded-off measurements. Here's an example of such a recipe:

Beef Medley, Chinese Style	*6 to 8 servings*
1 kg, cut in 3-cm pieces	2¼ pounds beef for stew, cut in 1¼-inch pieces
30 ml	2 tablespoons vegetable oil
2 ml each	½ teaspoon *each:* salt, ground ginger
1 medium	1 medium onion, chopped
45 ml	3 tablespoons soy sauce
30 ml	2 tablespoons cornstarch
500 ml	2 cups sliced celery
227 g	½ pound mushrooms, sliced
1 small	1 small green pepper, cut in strips
1 (227 g) can	1 (8-ounce) can water chestnuts, drained
1 (454 g) can	1 (16-ounce) can mandarin oranges, drained

In hot oil, brown meat in a deep 12-inch (30 cm) skillet. Drain off excess fat; sprinkle meat with salt and ginger. Add onion, soy sauce, and 1 cup (250 ml) water; heat to boiling. Reduce heat; cover and simmer 1½ hours, or until meat is tender. Combine cornstarch with ½ cup (125 ml) water; stir into meat and cook, stirring constantly, until mixture thickens. Stir in celery, mushrooms, green pepper, and water chestnuts; continue cooking, covered, 6 minutes. Gently stir in orange segments.

Here are some of the rounded-off equivalent measurements you'll soon be dealing with. If you learn them in advance, you'll breeze through the "new" cooking like an old metric hand. The abbreviations: cm=centimeter; ml=milliliter, g=gram, kg=kilogram.

Cup Equivalents (volume)

¼ cup	=	60 ml
⅓ cup	=	85 ml
½ cup	=	125 ml
⅔ cup	=	170 ml
¾ cup	=	180 ml
1 cup	=	250 ml
1¼ cups	=	310 ml
1½ cups	=	375 ml
2 cups	=	500 ml
3 cups	=	750 ml
5 cups	=	1250 ml

Spoonful Equivalents (volume)

⅛ teaspoon	=	.5 ml
¼ teaspoon	=	1.5 ml
½ teaspoon	=	3 ml
¾ teaspoon	=	4 ml
1 teaspoon	=	5 ml
1 tablespoon	=	15 ml
2 tablespoons	=	30 ml
3 tablespoons	=	45 ml

Pan Sizes (linear and volume)

1 inch	=	2.5 cm
8-inch square	=	20-cm square (baking pan)
9- × 13- × 1½-inch	=	23- × 33- × 4-cm
10- × 6- × 2-inch	=	25- × 15- × 5-cm
13- × 9- × 2-inch	=	33- × 23- × 5-cm
7½- × 12- × 1½-inch	=	18- × 30- × 4-cm (baking pans, dishes)
9- × 5- × 3-inch	=	23- × 13- × 8-cm (loaf pan)
10-inch	=	25 cm (skillets)
12-inch	=	30 cm
1-quart	=	1 liter (baking dishes)
2-quart	=	2 liters
5- to 6-cup	=	1.5 liters (ring mold)

Weight (meat and can and package sizes)

1 ounce	=	28 g
½ pound	=	225 g
¾ pound	=	340 g
1 pound	=	450 g
1½ pounds	=	675 g
2 pounds	=	900 g
3 pounds	=	1.4 kg (mostly meats—larger amounts will be weighed in kilograms)
10 ounces	=	280 g (most frozen vegetables)
10½ ounces	=	294 g (most condensed soups)
15 ounces	=	425 g
16 ounces	=	450 g
1 pound, 24 ounces	=	850 g (can sizes)

In baking and broiling, there will be another new element to deal with, temperatures specified in Celsius. Eventually, stoves will come with oven and broiler controls calibrated in Celsius (C) rather than in Fahrenheit (F). Meanwhile, Celsius oven thermometers, the kind that can be set or hung in the oven, on one of the shelves, are appearing on the market. You'll be broiling chops at 260°C. in no time, positioning the pan so that the meat will be 13 cm from the source of heat. You'll be baking in a slow 148°C. oven, or a moderate 175° C. oven, or a hot 230°C. oven, and thinking nothing of it.

Oven Temperatures

275°F	=	135°C
300°F	=	149°C
325°F	=	165°C
350°F	=	175°C
375°F	=	190°C
400°F	=	205°C
425°F	=	218°C
450°F	=	230°C
500°F	=	260°C

Simply by reading the new recipes and by looking more closely at can and package labels, you'll make a start at learning metric. Invest in a measuring cup marked in milliliters as well as the familiar fractions of a cup, and a ruler marked in centimeters as well as inches, and you'll be on your way.

The government is rapidly converting to metric. By the beginning of 1977, more than forty federal offices had made the switch, working first on the double standard of both common and metric measurements, moving eventually to solely metric ones. These offices included such familiar names as the Department of Agriculture, the Central Intelligence Agency, the Justice Department, and the Federal Reserve System. To aid both them and you, the American National Metric Council (referred to, naturally, by its initial letters, ANMC) has been set up. It has published a pamphlet, "A Metric Reference for Consumers," which covers such topics as metric in packaging and pricing and contains a glossary of metric terms and a history of metric. Single copies may be had free from the council's office at 1625 Massachusetts Avenue NW, Washington, D.C. 20036.

SOME THINGS WON'T CHANGE

Certain ramifications of metric will take more getting used to than others—and some will come as agreeable, some as disagreeable, surprises. For instance, if you're accustomed to telling your weight, with a touch of pride, as "oh, somewhere around one hundred ten" (pounds, that is), you'll probably be even more pleased to announce it as "oh, between forty-nine and fifty" (kilograms). If you're 5 feet 2 inches tall,

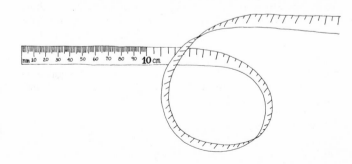

36

you'll stand 1.57 meters—the eyes of blue won't change. If you say, with becoming modesty, that you're a perfect 36, you'll be somewhat upset to learn that under metric you've developed into a perfect 91.44 (centimeters). And there's something chilling about the idea of announcing the measurements of the local beauty pageant winner as 90–60–91. Our 55 miles per hour speed limit will go to nearly 90 per hour measured in kilometers—the same, but giving us a guilty feeling of rocketing along the highway until we get used to the idea. A balmy 75° day will seem suddenly to lose its warmth at only 24° until we can accustom ourselves to the Celsius thermometer.

But in this brave new world, some of our familiar values will remain the same. We'll tell time by the old tried and (if our watches and clocks are accurate) true system, so you won't be able to blame it on metric if you're late for an appointment. An hour will remain 60 minutes, a minute 60 seconds, a comforting fact to rely on. Money, for better or for worse, will remain the same also. Our monetary system is already based on the factor of ten—10 pennies in a dime, 10 dimes in a dollar, 10 ten-dollar units in a hundred, 10 hundred-dollar units in a thousand.

Aside from those two stable items, brace yourself—there's a new world a-coming, and it's metric.

BABA: see page 451

BABY FOOD: see special feature: ON
  FEEDING YOUNGSTERS

BACON

In 1542, when Hernando de Soto landed in what is now Tampa, Florida, thirteen pigs came ashore, too. That was unremarkable, for explorers and conquerors since long before recorded history had carried pigs with them to help in provisioning their men, providing both meat and cooking fat. Because pigs are great scavengers, feed for them did not need to be transported; except during sea voyages, they could fend for themselves.

All America's porkers are descendants of those pigs and the ones brought by waves of explorers and colonists who came later, for we have no native pigs other than the peccary or javelina of Mexico, not a very close relative. There are some wild razorbacks in various parts of the country, but their ancestors were domestic pigs that escaped from sties and took to the woods many generations ago.

The word "bacon" comes from the Old French, and originally meant all pork, fresh or cured. It was also used in England into the sixteenth century for all food pork, and still covers more cuts of cured pork than the term does here. Bacon, in this country, is the cured and smoked meat, striped fat-and-lean, from the side of the hog after the removal of the spareribs. Hogs that yield the best bacon are longer and leaner than the short plump ones that yield the best hams.

BACON IN YOUR KITCHEN

Although it has little to offer from the point of view of nutrition, is high in calories without any great compensating satiety value, and has a high saturated-fat content, Americans love bacon and eat it in great quantities. The kind of person who demands a steady diet of meat and potatoes for dinner is likely to be a bacon-and-eggs eater in the morning at breakfast time, and will fight for his rights. And who but the most dyspeptic can deny that the combined odors of perking coffee and frying bacon are a great eye-opener, especially on a blustery winter morning?

First call for breakfast. In spite of its poor showing as a food, bacon's excellent flavor and crisp texture are relished almost any time, but it is at the breakfast table that bacon truly shines. Some prefer it in very thin slices that reduce themselves to little curls when cooked, others like the thick kind that you can sink your teeth into. Whatever your family's preference, there is a form of bacon to suit it in your market.

thin-sliced: Available in flat 8- and 12-ounce and 1-pound packages. Between 32 and 35 slices to the pound.

regular-sliced: Available in flat ½-, 1-, and 2-pound packages. Averages 22 slices to the pound.

thick-sliced: Available in flat or stacked 1-, 1½-, and 2-pound packages. Up to 18 slices to the pound.

ends and pieces: Available in 1-pound packages and boxes and (not as widely distributed) 3-, 4-, and 5-pound containers. Used largely for flavoring, rather than for eating.

slab bacon: Available by the piece, of almost any weight you wish, to be sliced at home. (Keeps better than presliced bacon.)

bacon squares: From the jowl rather than the sides of the hog; available as whole squares, and generally used for the same purposes as ends and pieces.

fresh bacon: Available only in some markets in some parts of the country. Neither cured nor smoked, it is extremely perishable. Use the same ways as regular bacon. It is much less flavorful than the smoked and cured kind and, to some palates, has a singularly flat flavor—probably because it does not taste like the familiar bacon it so closely resembles.

salt pork: Sometimes called "white bacon," this is salt-cured—either dry salt or brine—but not smoked. Essential ingredient of pork and beans, it is also used to flavor many other foods, for larding and barding and, particularly by those who savor homey, farmstyle cooking, sliced and fried to serve with a milk gravy made of the drippings as an accompaniment for hominy or rice, or on toast or with fried hasty pudding (cornmeal mush).

canadian-style bacon: Meaty, with very little fat, this is the eye of the loin—the muscle that lies along the backbone—sugar-cured and smoked. Available in 2- and 4-pound whole pieces in casings, or canned without casings, or sliced in 4- and 8-ounce packages. In flavor it resembles ham more than conventional bacon, and may be used in many of the same ways.

beef "bacon": Cured like bacon—although by law it cannot be labeled under that name—this is beef rather than pork. It looks rather like bacon and is cooked in the same manner. Many people use it either out of preference or because of dietary restrictions.

In spite of the fact that it is smoked and cured, bacon is quite perishable. And because flavor and texture deteriorate rapidly when it is frozen, freezing bacon is not advisable unless for some reason fresh supplies aren't regularly available to you. Bacon has no season—it is available the year around, in virtually all markets except those that sell only kosher foods.

how to buy: Bacon packages are tightly sealed to preserve quality, but by law the package must have "windows" on both sides through which you can inspect the product. Do so, to make sure the package you buy contains bacon of the proportion of fat to lean that you prefer. Buy no more than your family will use in a week. Bacon becomes moldy quite quickly and the fat turns rancid. Slab bacon is a wise choice both for families that use lots of bacon and those that use little—it is usually somewhat less expensive than the sliced variety, and keeps somewhat longer. Slice with a sharp knife, and don't forget to cut off the rind.

how to store: Keep bacon in the refrigerator, in the unopened package, until you are ready to use it. After opening, return remaining bacon to the refrigerator in the original package if it can be reclosed, or overwrap with foil, or store in a bacon keeper—a flat, tightly covered heavy plastic container designed for the purpose.

nutritive value: Count on bacon for the pleasure of eating it and the flavor it gives to other foods, not for what it will contribute to a balanced diet. Two slices of regular-sliced bacon contain 86 calories, 3.8 grams of protein, 7.8 grams of fat, .5 gram of carbohydrate, no vitamin A or C, small amounts of the B vitamins and of minerals. Because of the salt cure it is high in sodium (153 milligrams in those two slices), making it a forbidden item on salt-restricted diets.

Tips on preparing, cooking. Sliced bacon can be panbroiled, baked, or broiled. Use a rubber spatula for easy separation of the slices. For panbroiling, lay the slices in a cold skillet and cook over low heat, turning several times and draining off fat as it accumulates, until bacon is crisp and well done. (Like all pork, bacon should be well cooked to avoid risk of trichinosis.) Drain cooked bacon on absorbent paper and serve at once, or place—still on the paper—in a very low oven to keep warm. To panbroil canadian-style bacon, grease the pan lightly and cook over low heat, turning frequently, for 5 to 10 minutes, depending on the thickness of the slices.

Broil bacon on a rack 3 to 4 inches below the source of heat for 2 to 3 minutes on each side; turn only once.

Baking is the simplest way to cook bacon, particularly a large quantity, as you don't need to watch it and baby it. It doesn't even need to be turned. Lay slices on a rack in a shallow pan; bake in 400°F. oven (preheated or not as you choose) until crisp, 10 to 15 minutes if oven is preheated, a little longer if not.

An electric bacon baker that cooks slices crisp without curling, and a "bacon ironer"—a flat metal disk to be used in a regular skillet—are available in hardware and housewares stores.

For a heartier dish, with a somewhat different flavor, bacon can be breaded. Dip in flour, then in lightly beaten eggs, then in fine dry bread crumbs or a mixture of crumbs and cornmeal. Panbroil as above.

Canadian-style bacon, in the whole piece, can be roasted in a 350°F. oven. Cook for 25 minutes per pound, or to an internal temperature of 160°F. on a meat thermometer.

Use bacon, cooked crisp and crumbled, to top soups and creamed dishes, to flavor vegetables and salads, to give extra taste and texture to baking powder biscuits, muffins, corn bread, and pancakes. Bacon strips or pieces can be used in dishes such as barbecue-baked lima beans, macaroni and cheese, scalloped potatoes. Or encircle foods that will be broiled or panbroiled, such as filets mignon, with bacon strips, or use in appetizers such as rumaki or angels on horseback. It gives flavor and the "feel" of meat to casseroles or skillets that are largely vegetable in content.

Don't throw out the bacon drippings. Strain them and save—refrigerated—to fry eggs, french toast, potatoes, liver. Combine the drippings with vinegar and seasonings for a hot salad dressing, or use to season vegetables.

Freezing bacon. If for some reason you must freeze bacon, overwrap airtight in freezer paper or heavy-duty foil and store at 0°F. for no longer than a month. Stored for a longer time, the bacon will still be usable, but the flavor, particularly of the fat, will have deteriorated markedly.

Other ways, other forms. Canned bacon is available. Because it is largely imported, butchered from hogs that may have been fed differently from our domestic ones, and cured in a somewhat different manner, it will have a flavor different from American bacon. Some canned bacon is precooked and needs only a 3- to 4-minute heating to ready it for serving.

Bacon bits, in jars, are shelved with spices or near the condiments in food markets. Use in any way that you would use crisp home-cooked and crumbled bacon. (Don't confuse the real thing with protein bacon-flavored bits, which are something else entirely, and may or may not come up to your flavor standards for real bacon taste.)

BAGELS

Someone once described a bagel as a doughnut gone astray. Shaped like a doughnut—round, and with a hole in the center —and made of raised dough as some doughnuts are, bagels are not fried but first simmered in water, then baked. (Some are briefly broiled before simmering.) It's this combination of cooking processes that gives the bagel its hard, glazed brown crust and chewy, "al dente" interior.

One of the many contributions Jewish cooking has made to all-American eating preferences, bagels can be split and toasted, or split and sandwiched with any savory filling. Particularly in New York, bagels are often served for Sunday morning breakfast or brunch with cream cheese and lox—smoked salmon.

Although it was Polish and Austrian Jews who brought bagels to this country, it was a Viennese baker who first made a dough of yeast, eggs, flour, salt, water, and oil and fashioned it into stirrup-shaped rolls. The present doughnut shape evolved later. In Germany they are *buegel* or *bugel*—stirrup—hence "bagel."

The best bagels are shaped by hand. They can be found fresh at bakeries and delicatessens, particularly Jewish ones, and in packages of six or a dozen, plain, or egg- or onion-flavored, in frozen-food cases in supermarkets. For some unfathomably waggish reason, green bagels appear in some places shortly before St. Patrick's Day—perhaps an extension of the Abie's Irish Rose syndrome, of which green-tinted mashed potatoes seem also to be a part? No matter. To each his own.

Bagels may, if you are an indefatigable cook and have a mind to, be made at home. However, since they are not so great a delicacy that the homemade is apt to be infinitely better than the store-bought variety, and considering the broil-boil-bake cooking routine, you might be well advised to skip the whole idea and run down to the deli for your supply.

BAGUETTE: see page 451

BAKE, TO: see page 449

BAKE BLIND

A light, flaky pie shell that must be cooked before filling may puff up, blister, or sag during the baking process. (A heavy, cardboard-type crust isn't as likely to do this, but if you're interested enough in cooking to be reading this book, you aren't going to commit such a culinary faux pas.) To prevent these minor catastrophies, the pie shell is baked blind. Make the pastry according to your favorite recipe, fit into the pie plate with a light hand, form the edge to suit your fancy, and chill until ready to bake. With a fork, prick the crust all over, bottom and sides—again, with a light hand. Very carefully, fit a piece of regular strength foil inside the crust, pressing it gently in place, and weight it with a cupful of dry beans.

Preferably, place the beans in the crust without the foil and run less risk of accidentally tearing the crust with your fingernails. For some reason, however, a great many cooks seem to be horrified by the idea of baking nice, clean beans in their nice, clean pie shells.

Bake the pie shell as the recipe directs, removing the beans (and the foil, if you've used it) about 5 minutes before the baking time is up. The beans, incidentally, may be stored and used for the same purpose over and over again.

BAKER'S CHEESE: see CHEESE

BAKING DISHES, PANS, UTENSILS: see special feature: YOU CAN'T WORK WITHOUT TOOLS

BAKING POWDER

Until the middle of the nineteenth century, leavening a dough or batter—lightening it, that is, causing it to rise—was a somewhat chancy undertaking, and it's no wonder that a good cook was inordinately proud of an airy cake when she managed to produce one.

There was yeast, of course, although it was not nearly as stable, and therefore did not produce as predictable results as today's kind. There were eggs which, when beaten—laboriously, by hand—incorporated air enough to leaven such cakes as angel food, sunshine, sponge. (Martha Washington's favorite cake recipe begins, "Take fifty eggs . . ." We can safely assume that there was company coming.)

The only other leavening agent available was saleratus, a less refined version of what we now know as baking soda. When saleratus was used as the sole leavening agent, it was necessary for the batter to contain an acid ingredient, such as buttermilk or sour milk, molasses, vinegar, or fruit juice. The acid combined with the baking soda, releasing a gas—carbon dioxide—that "raised" the batter. Such mixtures had to be hustled into the oven as soon as mixing was complete, before so much of the gas had escaped that a heavy product resulted.

If what the cook had in mind for that day's baking did not call for an acid ingredient, she had another recourse—to add cream of tartar as well as baking soda to the batter. This wasn't as easy as it sounds. Both the baking soda and the cream of tartar could be purchased only as solid lumps. They had to be pounded to a powder and carefully measured—2 teaspoons of cream of tartar and 1 teaspoon of baking soda for each cup of flour the recipe called for—before they could be used.

There was yet another leavening agent available, carbonate of ammonia, or hartshorn. It too had to be pounded to a powder, and it was very unstable. Purchased at the drug store rather than the grocery, it had to be bought in small quantities, kept perfectly dry and tightly covered, and used soon after purchase.

Considering that leavening a batter was only a tiny facet of living, it's no wonder that woman's work was never done!

Then, in the early 1850s, the first baking powder came on the market—reasonably stable, ready-powdered, ready-combined, ready to use. No word has come down to us as to whether or not it was greeted with shouts of joy, but it should have been, although it isn't hard to imagine some die-hard ladies shaking their heads and clucking their tongues while remarking that this new-fangled idea couldn't last, and surely the old ways were the best ways.

Shortly, baking powder manufacturers produced baking cookbooks loaded with recipes using their product, some of which became kitchen bibles for generations of home bakers. Not to be outdone, flour processors put out cookbooks too, and a whole new era of kitchen expertise was underway.

Up-to-date baking. All present-day baking powders are a mixture of three essential ingredients: 1) baking soda, the source of the still-necessary carbon dioxide, essential for leavening; 2) some kind of acid, to release the carbon dioxide; and 3) a starchy substance, such as flour or cornstarch, to keep the mixture dry and prevent caking. The difference between the various types of baking powder on the market lies in the kind of acid used in each.

tartrate type: Baking powder containing cream of tartar and tartaric acid. Because this kind releases its gases quickly when it is wetted (combined with a liquid), recipes usually call for more of it than of other kinds. Batters leavened with tartrate-type baking powder won't wait. They must be baked as soon as they are mixed or too much carbon dioxide will escape, resulting in a heavy cake, cookie, or quick bread.

phosphate type: Baking powder containing calcium acid phosphate as its acid ingredient; sometimes contains sodium acid pyrophosphate as well. Somewhat slower acting than the tartrate type, this baking powder releases about two-thirds of its gases at room temperature, the remaining third at oven temperature.

combination or double-acting type: Two acid ingredients in this baking powder, sodium aluminum sulphate (s.a.s.—this is sometimes called SAS-type baking powder) and calcium acid phosphate. A small portion of the carbon dioxide is released at room temperature, but this type of baking powder releases the major portion of its leavening gases at oven temperature. It produces a more stable batter, one that can wait a few minutes before being baked without any great loss of leavening, or that can be refrigerated for later (same day) baking.

Emergency measures. If you run out of baking powder, you can use a combination of 1 teaspoon baking soda, 1 teaspoon cream of tartar, and ½ teaspoon salt for each cup of flour the recipe calls for. Use only to save the day, however —don't mix and store your own baking powder, because it will not retain its effectiveness for any length of time.

Even commercial baking powders won't remain effective forever. Home cooks who do very little baking should buy baking powder in the smallest available container, store it tightly covered in a cool place, and make certain that the spoons used to measure it with are entirely free from moisture. If you feel the baking powder in your pantry may need replacing, test it before using it. Stir a teaspoon of the baking powder into ¼ cup of hot water—if the mixture bubbles quickly and cheerfully, the leavening is still useful.

Cautionary note for high-living bakers. Barometric pressure is lower at high altitudes than at sea level. For this reason, carbon dioxide is released more rapidly and thus has a greater leavening action. If you are using a recipe designed for sea-level cooking, the amount of baking powder should be decreased. Better still, follow a recipe designed for your altitude. See also HIGH-ALTITUDE COOKING.

BAKING SODA

Aside from its activity as a leavening agent in baking (see BAKING POWDER), baking soda—bicarbonate of soda and sodium bicarbonate are its other names—has many other household uses. An effective deodorizer (it absorbs odors, rather than masking them), an opened box of baking soda in the refrigerator keeps the interior sweet, helps to prevent the strong odors of such foods as melons and cauliflower from transferring to delicate substances, such as butter. Treat the refrigerator to a fresh box of soda once a month or so, and dump the old box down the sink drain to keep that smelling sweet, too.

Use soda dissolved in water to wipe off the shelves and interior walls of the refrigerator when you clean it. In fact, soda will clean and/or deodorize almost anything, including the family dog.

A box of baking soda was once a standard item in home medicine cabinets, used for, as the television commercials say, "the temporary relief of acid indigestion accompanied by gas." Since so many commercial (not necessarily better) products for that purpose have appeared on the market, the baking soda has retreated to the kitchen in most homes, but it's still a useful emergency measure, provided you know what ails you and why. (Otherwise, a doctor is a lot safer than a teaspoon of bicarbonate.)

A bath with baking soda dissolved in the water will alleviate the itching of a rash until a doctor can determine what caused it. Good to take the heat out of sunburn, too. A paste of soda and water applied to an insect bite will relieve the sting and itching. Washing your hands with soda will get rid of high odors, such as fish or onions. Use it to wash walls and windows, to prevent the streaking soap causes. It cleans and brightens costume jewelry. All in all, a box of old-fashioned sodium bicarbonate is a very useful household staple to have on hand.

BAMBOO SHOOTS

One of the staples of Oriental cooking, bamboo shoots are what their name implies—the young, tender shoots of the bamboo plant (which is, incidentally, a grass, not a tree or shrub). There are many kinds of bamboos, but not all of them produce edible shoots. The shoots are generally cut for culinary purposes as soon as they have poked their heads above ground. Sometimes, to allow the useful part of the plant to grow longer, the shoots are hilled, as asparagus is—that is, earth is heaped around the emerging plant. Winter and spring shoots are delicious, but the ones cut in summer are usually bitter.

Only the white, inner part of the shoot can be used. In preparing it, the tough brown outside sheath, which occurs in overlapping sections rather like tightly wrapped leaves, must be stripped away.

Fresh bamboo shoots are hard to come by in this country, but can sometimes be found in markets in the Chinese or Japanese section of a big city that has a large Oriental population. However, they are available in cans almost everywhere, peeled, cut in pieces, precooked, and ready to use. Imported from Japan and Taiwan, they are packed in water or brine. Store leftover canned bamboo shoots in the refrigerator, covered with water. Change the water every second day.

The crispness of bamboo shoots, which some fanciers say taste rather like artichokes, adds texture to many kinds of dishes. They are particularly suitable for stir-fry mixtures, are often used in soups and salads. There are about 40 calories in a cup. The shoots offer some phosphorus, are high in potassium, and a cupful contains 90 international units of vitamin A—use for texture, not nutrition.

BANANAS

The trading schooner *Telegraph* came to harbor at Kingston, Jamaica, one day in 1870 in search of a cargo to carry back to Boston. Her skipper nosed around for quite a while, got in touch with all his contacts in the port, but couldn't come up with anything he felt was worth loading into the *Telegraph's* holds. Finally, unwilling to make the run home empty, he took on a load of bananas, the only thing available. But he'd lose money on the deal, he told himself dourly.

Those were not the first bananas brought to the United States by any means. In the early 1800s about thirty stems of the fruit had been imported to New York from Cuba. Other captains had carried bananas to various North American ports thereafter, but always as a novelty, almost an afterthought, rather than as a paying proposition.

James Fenimore Cooper, writing of the streets of New York, said that, ". . . bannanas, yams, water-melons &c. are as common as need be in markets." But somehow bananas didn't really catch on until the *Telegraph* brought her cargo to Boston. Her skipper didn't lose money on the deal after all, and other trading ships began picking up such cargoes too, until bananas became an important part of the commerce between the United States and the West Indies and Central America.

Almost any fruit you care to name has had a turn at being the one with which Eve tempted Adam, and the banana is no exception. The Koran claims that the banana, not the apple, was the forbidden fruit of the Garden of Eden. Whatever the truth may be, bananas have been known for thousands of years in Egypt, in the Holy Land, in India. It isn't certain whether they are also native to the countries that now do a thriving business in them—the "banana republics"—or whether only the plantain, a relative, grew there and the banana was brought by Spanish explorers. (Who, by the way, must have been very well organized—as well as loaded down—if they brought with them everything for which they are given credit!)

However, bananas are now grown on vast plantations throughout the West Indies, Central America, and some of the northern countries of South America where the climate is tropical. They are a staple food in those places, as well as a profitable export crop. Widely grown in central Africa, as well, bananas there are more a basic part of the local diet than for export. Hawaii grows a large crop, too.

Although it looks like a tree—it resembles a palm—the banana is an annual plant. It grows rapidly, produces its fruit, and is cut down to make way for the next planting. The fruit grows on long stalks, producing clusters of bananas known as "hands." Each hand has ten to fifteen individual banana "fingers," and there are between seven and twelve hands on each stalk.

Bananas are one of the most popular fruits in the United States, in part because they are available all year around. We import them by the ton, and each of us, from the oldest to the youngest, eats more than eighteen pounds yearly—if you don't consume your quota, someone out there is making up the deficit. The writer of "Yes, We Have No Bananas" must have been living a very sheltered life.

BANANAS IN YOUR KITCHEN

Although there are many species of bananas in several colors, assorted sizes, and various shapes, most of the banana exotica—such as the tiny fig bananas—seldom find their way to our tables. But we have the familiar yellow banana in abundant supply, as well as its cousin, the plantain—which must be cooked before eating—in many markets. There are also red bananas available, with a pulp that tastes richer and sweeter than that of the familiar yellow, but for some reason these have never been popular, and so appear less frequently in stores.

Almost everyone likes to eat bland, gently sweet bananas out of hand. They make an excellent breakfast fruit; they serve as an ingredient in many cooked dishes, as well as—sautéed or broiled—a very good edible garnish for meats, particularly lamb and poultry, and a splendid accompaniment for curries. And what red-blooded American youngster wouldn't fight for his right to fruit gelatin with bananas for dessert?

Yes, we indeed have some. Bananas are generally sold by the pound, as full or part hands. There are three to five medium bananas in a pound, which will yield 2 cups of sliced or 1¾ cups of mashed fruit.

how to buy: If you want fruit to eat at once, choose completely yellow bananas. Fortunately the fruit ripens best off the tree, so that it's perfectly safe to buy bananas when they are green, trusting to nature to have them ready to eat in a few days. Select firm bananas, without soft spots. Choose plump, well-formed fruit; size is not a factor in quality or flavor. If you want only one or two, and find loose ones in the pile, inspect them carefully. Careless fruit-buyers sometimes pull bananas off the hand roughly, stripping away part of the skin near the stem. Exposed to light and air, bananas turn dark and deteriorate rapidly. If you remove some bananas from a hand to leave behind for the next buyer, do it carefully, being sure not to break the skin.

how to store: Ripen bananas at room temperature. Fully green ones will be ripe in about 5 days. Contrary to the advertising jingle, fully ripe bananas may be stored in the refrigerator up to 3 days. However, the skins of refrigerated ripe bananas sometimes turn dark—the banana doesn't suffer at all, but the consumer is often dismayed by this.

nutritive value: Completely ripe bananas are easily digested, and provide an important adjunct to a balanced diet. They are low in sodium, and are a good source of vitamins A and C. Contrary to a popular belief, bananas are not "fattening"—they have excellent satiety value (make you feel full) and because of this have a place in a weight-loss regimen. A medium banana—between 8 and 9 inches in length—contains about 100 calories, and offers:

protein	1.3	grams
fat	.2	gram
carbohydrate	26.4	grams
calcium	10	milligrams
phosphorus	31	milligrams
iron	.8	milligram
sodium	1	milligram
potassium	440	milligrams
thiamin	.06	milligram
riboflavin	.07	milligram
niacin	.8	milligram
ascorbic acid	12	milligrams
vitamin A	230	international units

Tips on preparing, cooking. Peel a banana just before you are going to use it. If it must wait any length of time after peeling, it must be dipped in fruit juice—lemon, orange, lime, pineapple—or given an ascorbic acid treatment to prevent darkening, or immediately incorporated into a mixture that will exclude air, such as fruit gelatin. Any of these measures will halt the darkening process.

Use raw bananas in fruit salads and cups, sliced to serve with cream and sugar, layered—along with whipped cream or a cream filling—between layers of cake or beneath the filling of a cream pie. Try bananas mashed with a little lemon juice as a topping for hot gingerbread, or sliced and folded into almost any flavor pudding of the blancmange or cornstarch variety.

Halved crosswise and sautéed in butter until browned—the process takes only a couple of minutes—bananas are delicious with sausage or bacon as a breakfast or brunch dish. Prepare the same way to accompany baked ham, roast duck, or leg of lamb at dinner time, or as a side dish with lamb or chicken curry. Another wonderful curry accompaniment is a chutney made of bananas and dates with candied ginger. Split one side of the skin of whole bananas, pour in a little orange juice, sprinkle with brown sugar, and bake until heated through for a delectable, unusual dessert. Another time, substitute lime juice and honey. Banana fritters, too, make an excellent dessert.

Candlestick salad is one of the delights of childhood and a way to encourage a youngster to eat fruit; it consists of a crosswise half of a banana upended in the hole in the center of a slice of canned pineapple, topped with a dab of mayonnaise and a maraschino cherry. Or split a banana lengthwise, spread with peanut butter and put back together again. Or sandwich sliced banana and peanut butter on whole wheat bread. Or mash a banana and beat it into milk, with a few drops of vanilla, for a nutritious drink kids love.

Banana-walnut quick bread is great to eat as is, even greater sandwiched with cream cheese. (If you stir a little finely chopped candied ginger into the cheese, so much the better.) Cake-type doughnuts with mashed banana in the batter are a gustatory delight. Banana can go into cake batter, too, or into the frosting. And don't forget that soda-fountain glory, the banana split.

Freezing bananas. Surprisingly enough, they can be frozen very successfully at home, although we don't find commercially frozen bananas in the market. Mashed, treated with ascorbic acid, and properly packaged, they will keep a month in the frozen-food compartment of your refrigerator, or a year at 0°F. or below. It is not necessarily worthwhile, however, as bananas are available the year around, unless you come across a great bargain or for some reason have an excess of the fruit that will spoil unless you preserve it.

Other ways, other forms. Most often, bananas are purchased as fresh fruit. However, there are several other forms available.

on grocery shelves, in jars: Various kinds of puréed or chopped banana or banana-combination baby foods.

on grocery shelves, in packages: Dehydrated banana powder or flakes. Banana chips are also available, to use in cooking or as a snack food—you may have to go to a fruit specialty or health food store for these. At such a source you may also find banana flour, sometimes labeled "bananose." It is designed primarily as a food for invalids and children; it has excellent flavor and can be put to many surprisingly good uses.

in ice cream or dairy stores: As well as the popular banana split, some of these places offer a goodie both children and adults delight in—a whole banana, dipped in chocolate (sometimes, if you're lucky, with a lagniappe of chopped nuts) and frozen.

The botanical name of the banana is *Musa sapientum,* supposedly because Alexander the Great found, when he visited India, that the wise men there relished the fruit. Wisely, we relish it too and use it generously as a delicious and nutritious part of our regular diet.

BARBECUE

All over suburban America, when the weather is balmy and the urge to spend time outdoors comes over everyone, the evening air is filled with the enticing aroma of grilling meat. (And sometimes, when other considerations such as the two-hour cocktail "hour" intervene, with the odor of scorching meat.)

Men who have never so much as boiled water indoors tend to fancy themselves as *cordon bleu* chefs, complete with *toques blanches,* when the cookout season rolls around. To further them in this desire, housewares and hardware stores break out in a rash of fancy barbecue equipment as soon as the weather warms up. There are grills—charcoal briquet- or gas-fired—of all shapes and sizes, rosin cookers, reflector ovens, smoke cookers, turnspits—hand or battery operated, or plug-in electrically turned—special fish grills, chops grills, burger grills, you-name-it grills. There is a formidable array of long-handled tongs, skewers, forks, spatulas, turners, grill thermometers, big-daddy-size salt and pepper shakers, mitts and hotpads, branding irons to separate the rare from the medium from the well-done steaks, basting mops and brushes, all manner of tools and cookware and tableware for outdoor dining. And the aprons! They come in all sizes and colors, made of a variety of materials, many adorned with cutesy art work and cutesier sayings.

More in spite of all this paraphernalia than because of it, some of America's best cooking—and eating—is done on porches and patios or out in backyards.

Getting down to business. In most homes, it all started with a small grill and an occasional hot dog or burger cookout for the kids. From such humble beginnings, there was nowhere to go but up and out—or back into the house, for those people who detest the whole barbecue syndrome, and indeed there are some. The simplest cookout meal is the one in which the main dish is cooked outdoors and everything else is prepared in advance in the kitchen, to be served cold or at most heated up on the grill. But there are many variations. Potatoes, suitably wrapped, can be baked in or on the coals. So can corn on the cob. Many vegetables do very well by themselves seasoned and buttered and pouched in foil to be cooked on the grill. Garlic bread, herb-cheese bread, and the many variations heat up beautifully on the grill, as do plain breads and rolls, and the buns used for hamburgers and frankfurters. There are even some good grill-cooked desserts. Only the salad need come from the kitchen, if you prefer things that way.

Fire without friction. If you own a gas-fired grill, you have no problems. But if you cook over charcoal, you need to know how to build a good fire, one that will cook your food the way you want it cooked, and that will last through the cooking process.

Unless your hobby is scrubbing, line the bottom of the grill pan with foil so that when the party is over you can gather up the whole mess and chuck it in the garbage. Another advantage of the foil ploy is that it reflects heat upward, to the business part of the grill. Because charcoal briquets burn from the bottom up, it's necessary to provide draft from below. If your firebox has a built-in draft, fine. Otherwise, a layer of sand or gravel spread over the foil will serve the purpose. Spread the charcoal briquets over the sand or gravel, and you're ready to light your fire. This can be quite a feat in itself, unless you're an expert.

Everybody has his own favorite way of starting the fire. Duffers use paper and/or kindling, but to coax charcoal to light from kindling usually requires considerable huffing and puffing with the aid of a bellows or a bellows substitute, such as a bicycle pump or the blower of a vacuum cleaner.

starters: A fire starter of one sort or another is a quicker, less traumatic way. Most charcoals respond tractably to an electric fire starter; place the glowing coil on the briquets, wait a few minutes, and you'll see them begin to grow rosy. Or you can use a fire-starting liquid, either by pouring it over some of the briquets, arranged in a pyramid on the firebed, or by presoaking briquets in the liquid, then arranging them in a pyramid. A brick can also be soaked in starter fluid, used to get the fire going, and then removed before the food is placed on the grill.

Cautionary note about starters: Use a liquid manufactured for the purpose, or alcohol. Don't use kerosene or that will be the predominant flavor of the food when it's cooked. And never use gasoline. Gasoline's place is in the tank of your car, as far from the fire as possible. As a fire starter, it's altogether too successful—and exceedingly dangerous.

other ways: If you prefer, you can buy a "kindle can" or, quite feasibly, make one from an empty two-pound coffee can by removing the bottom (as well as the top, of course) and punching vents close to the bottom with a tool such as a beer opener. Set the can on the firebed, put in four or five presoaked briquets or a crushed milk carton (the wax with which the carton is coated burns readily) and light. Be patient for about 15 minutes, at which point you'll see the coals begin to glow. Remove the can—use tongs—and spread the coals out, adding more briquets around the edge, depending on the size fire you need. Before you set the food in place on the grill, be sure that the fire has settled down to an even bed of gray coals. A fire that flames will scorch food on the outside, leave it uncooked within.

Barbecuing calls for patience and forethought. Estimate the time it will take to cook the food, add to that the time it will take the fire to burn down to the proper level for cooking, and get the fire-making process started early enough so that you won't have a mob of starving people staring at you reproachfully when the spareribs won't be ready to eat for another hour.

flavor enhancers. If you want smoke-flavored meat, you can add liquid smoke to the basting sauce, but true smoke-cooking devotees scorn such shortcuts. Or, if you're exceedingly skillful and are prepared for total concentration, including not taking your eyes off your cooking for a moment, you can grill over open flames from burning aromatic wood. But the most satisfactory way to achieve that great smoke taste is to throw a few dampened chips or leaves of aromatic wood on the coals a few moments before the food is removed from the grill. Oak, hickory, bay, alder, and myrtle all work well. So do leaves or chips of the fruitwoods—cherry, orange, apple, lemon. But choose knowledgeably. Eucalyptus will produce meat that tastes like a chest rub and smells like nose drops. Pine will impart the flavor and fragrance of turpentine.

What will you cook? Fire properly built, started, and seasoned down to an even bed of gray coals is ready to do its work. Now what will you put on the grill? Beef steaks seem to be everyone's favorite, closely followed by chicken, with the kids opting for burgers and hot dogs. There are other choices, delectable ones that you should investigate, particularly if cookouts are a summertime way of life with you. Even as gold and diamonds (we're told) become commonplace to those who have an overabundance of them, so will steaks before the season is over—if you can stave off bankruptcy meanwhile. Steak is expensive, and the best steaks are rapidly pricing themselves into a class with gold and diamonds. But as a sometime thing, steak can be a barbecue masterpiece.

beef: Steaks up to about 2½ inches thick can be successfully grilled. The thinnest grillable steak is about ¾ inch—thinner than that and you're likely to have well-done meat even if rare was what you had in mind. All a good steak needs is to have the fat cut at several places around the outside to keep the meat from curling. Otherwise, just throw it on and cook it—don't even salt until the grilling process is complete.

Less tender steaks can be tenderized before grilling. (Tenderized at home, that is. Steaks that have been run through the butcher's tenderizer are usually too thin for outdoor cooking—panbroil them briefly instead.) Use a commercial tenderizer, following label directions, or let the meat luxuriate, before cooking, in a commercial tenderizing marinade or a homemade one containing something acid—vinegar, lemon juice, or wine. A commercially tenderized flank steak is the exception to the rule—even so, it will not be tender unless it is marinated or unless it is to be served rare.

If you can't afford a good steak, don't settle for a lesser one. Have burgers instead. They can be absolutely great with a melting nugget of bleu or jack cheese tucked in the center, or basted with a teriyaki sauce. Any good cookbook will point you to dozens of ways.

If your grill boasts a turnspit, you can spit-roast several cuts of beef—eye of round, a whole fillet (it will need barding), a rolled rump or rib or sirloin roast. Be sure the roast is properly balanced on the spit and held securely by the end forks before you start the cooking, or you're going to be in deep trouble.

Marinated cubes of beef can be cooked on skewers, along with such good things as pepper squares, mushrooms, and onions. Sirloin is a good choice for this, or round if the marinade is also a tenderizer. Or turn the burgers into little meatballs for a change and skewer them to cook on the grill.

lamb: There are barbecuers who will give battle if you deny that butterflied leg of lamb is the greatest of all meats for grill-cooking. It's true that grill-cooking and spit-roasting bring out something in lamb that makes even those who scorn it indoors come ravenously back for seconds. Young lamb is so succulent that almost any cut can be cooked this way—breast and shanks are just as meltingly tender as roasts, chops, and steaks. Lamb kabobs are wonderfully good. So are lamburgers. Season as you will—lamb has a particular affinity for lemon and mint, singly or as a pair; garlic, rosemary, tarragon, and marjoram are fine, too. A side dish of ratatouille is a perfect accompaniment to the outdoor chef's lamb masterpiece.

pork: He who has not savored a barbecued sparerib (or a dozen—who could eat only one?) simply hasn't lived life to its fullest. But other pork cuts make fine barbecue fare too, provided you get them started in plenty of time so that they can be well done, the only way pork should be served. A whole loin of pork or a fresh ham can be spit-roasted with marked success. So can a whole smoked ham. Ham steaks can be grilled, as can fresh pork chops and steaks. Grilled thick-sliced bacon and pork sausage with apple rings can make such a hit at a brunch cookout that wistful strangers may come flocking, holding out their plates like Oliver Twist. As for suckling pig, there's a celebration dish fit for a king. (But ask around if you aren't too certain of your guests' tastes. Some people are appalled at the idea. It's not the flavor, it's the appearance. A woman was once heard to mutter, "I never did like that pekingese of theirs, but I certainly didn't wish him such a fate!")

fowl: Chicken halves cooked on the grill can be delicious indeed, and small whole chickens (or game hens) are elegant when spit-roasted. Ducks and geese—they baste themselves with their own fat—can also be prepared either way for an exceptional cookout treat. A whole turkey can be spit-roasted for, say, an unusual holiday dinner. Just remember to start *far* ahead of the dinner hour. Small game birds, such as quail, pheasant, and wild duck can be grill-cooked or spit-roasted—after all, they have been spitted over an open fire by hunters for generations—but tend to be a bit dry. If you're going to cook these, baste liberally with fat or fasten strips of fat, such as salt pork, to the birds with food picks.

fish and shellfish: A grilled whole bass or salmon is a thing of beauty, its appearance surpassed only by its taste. Steaks of swordfish or tuna do well on the grill. Caught-today trout are unbelievably delicious. Shrimp and oysters can be skewered, well seasoned, and cooked briefly with great success.

Grilled lobster is excellent. And, of course, the lobster-clam-chicken-potato-corn mélange that makes up a clambake is one of the ultimate cookout delights.

and the others: Almost any kind of meat, fish, or fowl can be cookout fare. Try a plump bologna or kielbasa ring. Charcoal broil sweetbreads, beef heart or tongue, pigs' feet, even tripe if you've a mind to. (Some of these will need on-the-stove precooking.) Skewer chicken livers alternately with bacon strips and mushrooms. Spitted kidneys or cubes of calves' liver are delectable. Roast oysters or clams in their shells. Grill or spit-roast venison, antelope, whatever the freezer or the triumphantly returning hunter has to offer. Remember the barbecuer's axiom: If you like it indoors, you'll like it better outdoors.

Keeping the temperature under control. All grills except the most primitive have a device for regulating the amount of space between the source of heat and the cooking food by raising or lowering the firebox or raising or lowering the grill. This is helpful once cooking is underway, but it's also necessary to have the fire at the proper temperature when the food is put on to cook. Some barbecue chefs determine this through a combination of instinct and prayer, but a grill thermometer is likely to be more accurate. Use it to check the temperature at food level—that is, where the meat is going to be placed, whether on the grill or on the spit. Keep these temperatures in mind:

hot fire	=	375°F. or over
medium fire	=	about 325°F.
slow fire	=	200 to 275°F.

In most cases, meat should be at room temperature before it goes on the grill. If frozen, it should be thawed. Fish fillets are the exception—they need so brief a cooking that starting them from the frozen state results in moist, properly cooked fish, not overdone.

Grilled meats can be cooked by timing (see adjacent chart), but the doneness of spit-roasted meats should be determined by checking the internal temperature with a meat thermometer. The "instant" kind is simple to use for outdoor cooking. With it you can check internal temperature simply by inserting the thermometer briefly in the meat, rather than by leaving it in place throughout the roasting.

Finessing the fire. In making a grill fire, most people err on the side of too much rather than too little. It takes about two pounds of charcoal to cook a 5- to 6-pound steak 1½ inches thick. If the fire is too hot for your purpose, spread it out into a more open pattern (using tongs). Keep tools at hand to lift the meat away from the fire for a brief time if flare-ups occur—and they generally will. If you get an extensive flare-up from dripping fat, don't panic. Get the food off the grill if you can. Douse the fire with baking soda or salt or —as a last resort—water.

TIME/TEMPERATURE CHART FOR MEAT COOKED ON THE GRILL

meat cut	thickness, weight, or size	fire temp.	cooking time each side (in minutes)				
			very rare	rare	med. rare	medium	well done
beef:							
beef steak	1 inch	hot	4	5 to 6	7	7½ to 8	10 or more
beef steak	1½ inches	hot	5	6 to 7	8 to 9	10	12 to 15
beef steak	2 inches	med. to hot	7 to 8	8 to 10	10 to 15	16 to 18	20 or more
beef steak	2½ inches	med. to hot	10 to 12	12 to 15	15 to 17	18 to 23	25 or more
flank steak	whole	hot	3 to 4	4 to 5	5 to 6	(must be rare to be tender)	
hamburger	1 inch	med. to hot	3	4	5	6	7 or more
tenderloin	whole	medium	10 to 12	12 to 15	15 to 17	18 to 23	(don't ruin!)
fish:			(all fish: if frozen, do not thaw)				
steak	1 inch	medium	—	—	—	—	3 to 5
steak	1½ inches	medium	—	—	—	—	4 to 6
fillet or split whole	small	medium	—	—	—	—	3 to 6
fillet or split whole	large	medium	—	—	—	—	6 to 9
ham:			(fully cooked ham: reduce time by 5 minutes)				
slice	1 inch	low to med.	—	—	—	—	15
slice	1½ inches	low to med.	—	—	—	—	20
lamb:							
chops, steaks	1 inch	medium	—	4 to 5	6	6 to 7	8 to 9
chops, steaks	1½ inches	medium	—	5 to 6	7	8 to 9	10 to 11
chops, steaks	2 inches	medium	—	6 to 7	8	9 to 10	12 to 14
butterflied leg	whole	low to med.	—	—	—	30, total	40, total (turn several times)
pork:							
chops, steaks	1 inch	low to med.	—	—	—	—	14 to 18
chops, steaks	1½ inches	low to med.	—	—	—	—	16 to 24
spareribs	whole rack	low	—	—	—	—	60 to 90, total (turn often)
poultry:							
chicken half	small	medium	—	—	—	—	15 to 25
chicken half	large	medium	—	—	—	—	18 to 35
cornish hen	half	medium	—	—	—	—	15 to 20
duck	half	med. to low	—	—	6 to 10	9 to 13	15 to 30
turkey half	4 to 6 lbs.	medium	—	—	—	—	23 to 33
lobster:			(if frozen, do not thaw)				
half	1½ to 2 lbs.	med. to low	—	—	—	—	6 to 9

A long-handled, double-sided wire broiler that can be set directly on the grill is a useful gadget. Some foods—burgers, franks, fish, butterflied lamb—are difficult to turn if they're placed directly on the grill. The wire broiler prevents mishaps. Grease the grids, place the meat inside, and lock the broiler securely—usually there's a ring to slip over the handle for this purpose—before placing it over the heat.

Marinades and sauces, bastes and butters. Lily-gilding is one of the sins of cookout chefs. A truly good steak, for example, needs no tampering with to make it tender or improve its flavor. Neither does a thick loin lamb chop, or a lobster.

On the other hand, some foods need all the help they can get. Marinades, sauces, and bastes tenderize, add flavor, and help keep the meat from drying out. Butters add zest when the meat is served.

A marinade—which can usually double later as a sauce or baste during the cooking time—consists of fat (most often oil), seasoning, and an acid (vinegar, wine, lemon or lime or tomato juice) to impart soak-in flavor and/or to aid in tenderizing. A truly tough meat cut can profit from remaining in the marinade two or even three days (why not braise or pot-roast it instead?), but generally a two- or three-hour bath in the flavorful liquid is sufficient. If the meat does not need tenderizing, use a sauce or baste during cooking to add flavor. Apply it with a brush and be generous—not a lot at a time, but often. Sometimes an improvised brush will impart just the necessary extra touch of flavor to sauce and meat—try a bundle of celery, bay, or mint leaves. Leftover sauce or baste can be heated in a small pan on the grill and served with the cooked meat.

Sometimes the chef has his own special, jim-dandy, handed-down-from-daddy barbecue sauce, composed of eighty-four "secret" ingredients. But generally in this, as in almost anything, simpler is better. Lemon juice, corn oil, and tarragon make chicken sing; vermouth, olive oil, and rosemary cause lamb to beam with pleasure; melted currant jelly, orange juice, and brown sugar turn pork into poetry.

Drop a dollop of savory butter on meat hot off the grill to turn a so-so cut into a triumph—and, as a bonus, most such butters are great on roasted potatoes and grilled corn as well. Try creaming butter with lemon juice and minced parsley, or anchovy paste, or red wine vinegar and chili powder, or minced chives, or minced garlic, or crumbled marjoram or oregano.

Grill-roasting. A grill with a hood or dome cover that can be completely closed over the food turns out roasted meats that are tender and succulent beyond a conventional oven's wildest dreams. Food is crisp on the outside, slightly ruddy in color, and delicately char/smoke flavored.

For this kind of cooking, build the fire to one side of the grill rather than in the center. Gauge the size of the fire by the size of the meat you'll be cooking—for instance, less than three pounds of charcoal will cook a 10- to 14-pound turkey. On the side of the grill opposite the fire, place a shallow pan to catch drippings. Put the grill rack in position. If there's a trapdoor for adding more fuel, be sure that's positioned over the fire. Light the fire and, when it is burning well, close the hood and adjust the vents so that the fire will continue to burn properly. Place the food on the grill over the drip pan; close the hood over the food. Check browning time—if the food browns too quickly, close vents somewhat; if too slowly, open them a bit more.

If you have a grill thermometer, use it—it should register whatever a good cookbook tells you is the proper temperature for oven-roasting the food. Also use a roast meat thermometer to keep track of the internal temperature of the meat. If any portion browns more quickly than the rest, protect that portion with a small piece of foil.

Basting isn't necessary with this kind of cooking—the food when done is crisp on the outside, moist within. But baste for extra flavor if you like. A cider-basted turkey, for example, is a not-to-be-missed taste sensation. Because drippings don't fall onto the fire, a minimum amount of smoke results, just enough to give the food a delicate touch of smoke flavor. If you prefer a more pronounced smoke taste, add damp chips or twigs of aromatic wood toward the end of the cooking time.

The all-weather, all-purpose cookout. With the possible exception of a howling blizzard, you can barbecue any time, and enjoy the wonderful flavor of barbecued meats all year around. Set the grill up in a sheltered spot and, if the weather doesn't permit outdoor eating, bring the feast inside. Or, if barbecuing is truly your thing, get a grill to fit your indoor fireplace. For big family gatherings or holiday meals, grill-roasting can free the indoor oven for cooking other components of the celebration dinner. Any time of year, any occasion, it's a great way to cook. See also KABOBS.

BARBECUE SPICE: see SPICES

BARD, TO: see page 444

BAR-LE-DUC: see page 451

BARLEY

Except for those among us who are devoted to tippling beer and/or Scotch whisky, and perhaps those who are very small babies, barley has little place in our scheme of things. Even barley sugar, a brittle, twisted, straw-colored stick candy our grandparents enjoyed as children, and barley water, a cooling, refreshing drink, have all but disappeared from our lives.

But even though we know and use barley so little in this country, it is one of the oldest cultivated foods, and is still an important crop in many parts of the world. Flour made from barley was once widely used in bread, although in many places it has been replaced by wheat flour, which yields a lighter loaf because wheat has a higher gluten content. The two grains, both grasses, are related.

Because it will grow in very cold and in subtropical climates as well as in temperate areas, and because its growing season is short, barley is the grain grown in places where others will not thrive. Scots grow barley in abundance, not only because it is essential for the whisky they drink at home and export to all parts of the world, but because they use it as a breakfast cereal, in Scotch Broth, a delicious mutton-based soup, in baked dishes, and in flat griddle-baked cakes that are split and served with butter, like scones.

It is available as pearl barley (the bran is removed, the grain polished) in fine, medium, and coarse grinds. The grain with the husk removed, coarsely ground, is called Scotch barley, and is not as readily available as pearl barley. Dry "instant" baby cereal made from barley can be found anywhere baby food is sold. Pearl barley can be cooked (until tender, about 1½ hours) as it comes from the package, but Scotch barley must be soaked before cooking.

A pleasant change from other starchy side dishes—potatoes, pasta, rice—a dish of barley cooked in consommé, perhaps with the addition of onion and mushrooms, is a pleasant accompaniment for lamb, duck, or any game.

Barley is high in carbohydrate, contains moderate amounts of protein and small amounts of B vitamins. See also FLOUR and GRAINS.

BASIC FOUR FOODS PLAN: see special
feature: NUTRITION NOTEBOOK

BASIL: see HERBS AND SAVORY
SEASONINGS

BASS: see FISH

BASTE, TO: see page 444

BATTERIE DE CUISINE
The French term for everything—pots, pans, utensils—except the food itself, needed for cooking. For the equivalent in this country, see the special feature: YOU CAN'T WORK WITHOUT TOOLS.

BAVARIAN CREAM
An egg custard with gelatin to stiffen it and whipped cream to enrich it folded in after the basic custard has cooled; it is then molded. A rich yet light and airy dessert, it is one of those handsome yet easily made productions that grace company-coming meals. Almost anything you like, from vanilla through fruit to sweet wines can be used to flavor it; a flavoring of PRALINE is particularly delectable. See also PUDDINGS AND CUSTARDS.

BAY LEAVES: see HERBS AND SAVORY
SEASONINGS

BAY SCALLOPS: see SHELLFISH

BEACH PLUMS
A small fruit, relative of the cultivated plum, that grows wild in sandy soil in the eastern part of the United States, near the seashore. Sour to the point of bitterness when eaten raw, beach plums make delicious jams and jellies.

BEAN FLOUR: see BEANS

BEAN SPROUTS: see SPROUTS

BEANS
Next to the cereals, beans and the other legumes—peas, lentils, and peanuts—are the world's most widely eaten food. Beans are a highly important diet staple, particularly in countries where little meat (from choice or necessity) is eaten, because they are rich in protein, the body-builder, as other vegetables are not. In central Europe, people of the Bronze Age (*circa* 3000 B.C.) ate broad beans. Early Greeks ate broad beans and lentils, Romans, fava beans and garbanzos —chick-peas—and so revered them that two of the great Roman families took their names from the beans. The Chinese cultivated soybeans, the most nutritive member of the entire vegetable family, and mung beans. By the time of the first Elizabeth, the English were eating broad beans—probably reluctantly, because they had no great love for vegetables. (Eat your beans, Cedric, or I won't let you buy oranges from Nell Gwyn at *A Midsummer Night's Dream*.)

Nobody in the Old World, however, had seen or heard of kidney beans, lima beans, navy beans, or snap beans until our industrious friends the Spanish explorers brought them back from their ventures across the Atlantic to North and Central and South America. As fair exchange, they brought garbanzos in the other direction, to the New World.

The few fresh beans. There are many kinds of beans, but only a small number of them are eaten fresh. Fresh as opposed to dried, that is. We eat italian green beans "fresh," but most often they have been cooked from a frozen package; we seldom find them fresh in the market.

green beans: Also called snap beans, because we snap off both ends to prepare them for cooking, or string beans, because although this is no longer true, they once came equipped with a long, tough string down each side of the pod, which had to be removed when the beans were snapped. Green beans are a variety of kidney beans, so tender that— unlike the beans we eat dried—they can be consumed totally, seeds, pods, and all. Today's varieties of green beans are tender in all sizes, as long as they are fresh. It's no longer necessary to root around in the bin of beans, as our grandmothers did, to find small ones tender enough to make an acceptable "mess of beans" for dinner.

wax beans: Like green beans, except that they are yellow

—and except that, for some reason, they don't seem to be as popular as they once were, and are not as abundant in the market as their green relatives. Although it's no longer necessary to string green beans, there are some wax beans that do need stringing.

italian green beans: Broader and flatter of pod than the green beans so readily available, and a brighter green in color, these are not often available in any form but frozen.

lima beans: These made their way north from Peru, and take their name from that country's chief city. Called butter beans in our southern and some western states, there are two kinds, large limas (often referred to as fordhook, although that is only one of several sorts), and baby limas. You can sometimes buy them shelled, in small trays—they're very perishable; rush them home and cook them as soon as possible—but you're more likely to find them in the pod, to be shelled at home. Shelling them isn't the easiest task in the world. Prepare to spend a little time, for the fresh beans are worth it. To help you along, use a vegetable peeler—or even scissors—to cut a strip from the longer, curved side of the pod.

cranberry beans: These, too, must be shelled. The tough pods are big and knobby, beige with splotches of red. The tender, cream-colored beans inside, with their nutlike flavor, are well worth the job of getting them out.

black-eyed peas: In spite of their name, these too are beans. Housed in knobbled, rusty-looking green pods are small, pale green beans with neat black "eyes." These are deep-South favorites—in other parts of the country, unless you buy from the roadside stand of a farmer who thought he'd plant a few to see what came up, you're likely to find them only canned or frozen. If you buy them fresh, shell them and discard the pods.

The many dried beans. The area where dried beans are shelved in a large supermarket offers variety undreamed of unless you are a true bean fancier. There are large and medium and small ones, flat ones and round, black, red, pink, tan, and white beans, neatly lined up in plastic bags or cardboard packages. Each has its particular flavor, its several uses. All offer the basis of nutritious, hearty, economical, delicious main dishes and side dishes, and many have a place in soups and salads, too. Browse among the beans to familiarize yourself with the many kinds, and in a general cookbook to discover the infinite variety of dishes you can make from them.

black beans: Black on the outside, cream-colored within, these are the basis of wonderfully good black bean soup—serve with side dishes of chopped onion and chopped hard-cooked egg for each diner to add to his plate, or float a thin slice of lemon on each dark, steaming-hot serving. Cook in other ways, too. Sometimes you'll find these called turtle beans.

black-eyed peas: The dried version looks like the fresh—small, pale, with one black spot. They are called peas because their flavor is reminiscent of peas to some people, and are often cooked in the South with bacon, salt pork, or fatback, and served with some of the well-flavored "pot likker." Hopping John, a "good luck" dish, is made with black-eyed peas and rice.

yellow-eyed peas: The same bean as the black-eyed pea, except that the single eye-spot is yellow. To further confuse matters, these are also known as yellow-eyed beans. Use wherever you would use black-eyed peas.

cannellini: An Italian favorite, these are white kidney beans, somewhat smaller than the red kidney beans that are so familiar. Use them to make a hearty salad, a nice change from potato or macaroni salad—combine with lots of thinly sliced scallions and about a quarter as much diced celery as beans; season with salt and coarse black pepper and dress with oil and vinegar. They are very good hot, as well. Try them casseroled with tomatoes, onions, and basil.

garbanzos: Most nutlike of the beans in flavor—nutlike in appearance, too, for they are in shape and size quite like a shelled and skinned filbert. They have other names—ceci, Spanish beans, chick-peas. Use in soups, stews, salads. They are popular in our southwestern states, and wherever there is a Spanish-speaking community. Italians like them in minestrone. (See CHICK-PEAS.)

cranberry beans: Dry, these are pale with pinkish splotches. They are used throughout the country in specialty dishes, such as New England's cranberry-bean succotash. In some midwestern states they are known as "shell-outs."

lima beans: Both the big ones and the baby limas are available dried. If there's no particular reason for wanting the big ones, choose the babies. The large beans often lose their skins in the cooking process, making them rather unsightly. They also have a nasty habit of being rock hard one minute and then, as you turn your back, disintegrating into a mush. Baby limas neatly hold their shape and their skins and cook at a reasonable, predictable rate of speed. Big purple-blotched limas are sometimes known as calico beans.

kidney beans: These are old favorites, known and used almost everywhere in this country, from a variation on baked beans in New England to Mexican-style dishes in the Southwest. Purple-red or brown-red, they are big, hold their shape well (kidney-shape, from which their name comes). Smaller, but also kidney beans, are red-brown *red beans*—sometimes called red miners, sometimes chili beans—which are favorites in Mexican and Tex-Mex cooking; and *pinto beans,* particularly pretty with their brown-spotted pink skins. All the kidney beans can be used interchangeably in recipes.

fava beans: Sometimes spelled "faba" and also known as horse beans, perhaps because of their very large size, these are wrinkle-skinned, tan in color, and assertive in flavor.

white beans: This is not one variety, but four. All are white (palest beige, really) and generally can be used interchangeably. Consider them in order of size, from the largest to the smallest. *Marrowfat beans,* or just plain marrow beans, are big and nearly round. *Great Northern beans* are almost as large, but with a distinctive, much more delicate flavor; they are a staple for home-baked beans. *Navy beans,* also known as yankee beans, are what the navy once served for breakfast; canners of pork and beans use them extensively. *Pea beans* are what New Englanders seek out for authentic Boston baked beans. Canners use them interchangeably with navy beans.

soybeans: These are about the size of a pea, and may be any of a number of colors—yellow, green, brown, black, or a mottled combination. High in nutritive value, a rich source of protein, they are a staple in some densely populated areas as food, animal fodder, and as a source of oil. They are strongly, distinctively flavored—so much so that, unfortunately, many people who have other types of beans available pass them by in favor of less dominant flavors.

There are a number of unusual uses for soybeans. They can be made into soy nuts by deep-fat frying or roasting, to be used as a snack food or in any dish in which nuts are called for. The beans are processed into meat extenders in which the protein remains but the flavor is not assertive; mixed with ground meats, such extenders add bulk to stretch the meat by half without seriously decreasing the protein content as other extenders—rice, potatoes, bread crumbs—will do.

A particularly valuable use of soybeans has been the development of spun protein fibers, which are made into simulated meats resembling ham, bacon, pork, beef, chicken, turkey, meat loaf, sausage, frankfurters, and fish. These can be purchased canned, frozen, smoked, diced, sliced, or formed into rolls and sausages. They are particularly a boon to those on low-cholesterol diets, and to vegetarians.

About 90 percent of the soybeans grown in the United States are processed into oil used in margarines, shortenings, cooking oils, salad dressings, and frozen desserts, and for bean meals and flours. There are two kinds of soybeans, the commercial-food type processed for the uses mentioned, and a second variety to be used as a fresh or dried vegetable.

FRESH BEANS IN YOUR KITCHEN

Beans grow on trailing vines or standing bushes, depending on the variety. Because of our widely varying climate and growing seasons, there are virtually always fresh beans in the market, although there may be considerable difference in price from month to month depending on whether the beans are local or shipped from some distant point.

Beans were first grown as a farm crop in the 1830s in New York; cultivation took a leap forward when the army began to buy beans to feed the soldiers in the Civil War and has never looked back.

how to buy: Inspect green or wax beans for fresh-looking pods, pleasingly plump but not too fat—great bulk means the beans are over-mature. These snap beans are available all year, but are at their peak from late spring to early fall. Pods should snap easily, be straight and nicely colored, without scars or rusty-looking spots. Select reasonably uniform beans so they'll all be done at the same time. One pound of green or wax beans will yield about 3 cups cooked.

Lima beans, both the big ones and the babies, are also available all year, with the largest supplies in the market from June to September. The shelled ones should be shiny, a uniformly pale, springy green, and look as if they were bursting their skins with pride. When you buy soy or lima or fava beans to shell yourself, look for clean, unblemished pods—and feel them to make sure there are beans within, for you can sometimes get a nasty surprise. Beans of any kind that feel damp or slimy are well on their way to decay. Two pounds of lima or fava beans in the pod will yield about 2¼ cups shelled and cooked.

how to store: Shelled limas should be cooked the day they are purchased to be certain of best flavor—their keeping qualities leave a good deal to be desired. Limas and favas and soybeans in the pod, and green and wax beans should be stored in the refrigerator in a plastic bag or moistureproof covered container. Plan to use them as soon after buying as possible, for they toughen with each passing day; in any case, three days' storage should be the maximum. Plan to use them up within three days once they're cooked, too.

nutritive value: One cup of cooked cut green beans contains 31 calories; the same amount of cooked lima beans, 191 calories. They offer:

	green	lima	
protein	2	13	grams
fat	.3	.8	gram
carbohydrate	6.8	34.3	grams
calcium	63	81	milligrams
phosphorus	46	220	milligrams
iron	.8	4.3	milligrams
sodium	5	3	milligrams
potassium	189	1,008	milligrams
thiamin	.09	.37	milligram
riboflavin	.11	.19	milligram
niacin	.6	2.2	milligrams
ascorbic acid	15	45	milligrams
vitamin A	680	450	international units

Tips on preparing, cooking. Wash green and wax beans just before you are ready to cook them. Snap or cut off the ends. If the beans are young and tender, leave them whole if you like, or cut them into short lengths. If you prefer, the beans can be frenched—cut into long, thin slivers—with a small, sharp knife or with a frenching tool. Such a tool is often a part of a swivel-bladed vegetable peeler, at the end opposite the blade, or you can buy a rotating bean-slicer machine. Cook covered in a small amount of boiling water (salted if you wish) just until the beans lose their crispness, 20 to 30 minutes for whole beans, 15 to 20 for cuts, 10 to 15 for frenched beans. Season as you like before serving.

Shell lima or fava beans just before cooking. Cook, covered, in a small amount of boiling water until tender, 20 to 25 minutes for limas, a bit longer for favas. Season as you like before serving.

Freezing fresh beans. Green, wax, lima, or fava beans may be home-frozen. Properly prepared (see special feature: PUTTING FOOD BY), they can be stored at 0°F. or below 10 months to a year.

Other ways, other forms. Green, wax, or lima beans can be found in your market in almost any form you might like to use.

on grocery shelves, in cans or jars: Puréed or chopped beans as baby or junior foods. Canned whole or cut snap beans, and shelled limas. Bean combinations to serve hot or cold, such as beans with tomatoes, three-bean salads.

in grocery frozen-food section: Cut or whole or frenched green beans, cut wax beans, large or baby lima beans, italian green beans, black-eyed peas, in 10-ounce packages or larger, family-size plastic bags.

Some perfect partners. When the beans are very young, they really don't need to be gussied up. A little butter, salt, and pepper (white pepper is very good with most vegetables) is sufficient. Or lemon-butter them, as you would asparagus. Try cooking half-and-half green and wax beans together for an attractive dish, or green beans with peas for interesting taste and shape contrast. Beans plus corn add up to succotash, a dish the early settlers learned about from their Indian neighbors. Snap beans or limas go into succotash, depending on what recipe you're consulting. Sometimes the corn and beans stand alone, sometimes they're flavored with bacon or other salt-cured meat to make a whole-meal dish—again, it depends.

Green beans are elegant sauced with butter-toasted almonds for green beans amandine. Hollandaise sauce or one flavored with plenty of sharp cheddar and a little mustard raises them to new heights. Or add a few sautéed mushrooms to the beans, or cook with tomatoes and a little onion.

Serve whole cooked green beans chilled in vinaigrette sauce, or find a recipe for Salade Niçoise and make it for a special treat on a summer's night. Or make a salad of wax beans and thin-sliced sweet onions to serve with french dressing.

Limas take kindly to the addition of chopped bacon or leftover bits of ham. They, too, partner well with tomatoes or onions or a combination of the two. Or sauce them with cheese, or with sour cream and crumbled bacon, or dapple them liberally with chopped parsley or, if your garden has them to offer, tender young nasturtium leaves.

DRIED BEANS IN YOUR KITCHEN

All kinds of dried beans are available all year around, shelved with or near the rice, cereals, and pastas in the market. There is great variety in these beans, and an even greater variety of dishes to be made from them. You owe it to yourself to experiment, to try kinds you haven't used before, to learn new ways to cook and serve these economical, protein-rich adjuncts to the diet.

how to buy: These days, dried beans are almost always packaged, although once in a while you'll find them loose, by the pound—particularly true of pinto or red beans in southwestern markets. Look for 1-pound paperboard packages or plastic bags, or 5-pound bags. Make certain the packages are tightly sealed, that the bags have no breaks or cuts. One pound of raw dried beans measures about 2 cups; cooked, that one pound will measure about 6 cups. Beans expand in cooking, so judge your recipe accordingly.

how to store: On your pantry shelf. Leave sealed until you are ready to use them. If you use less than a full package of beans, transfer the remainder to a closely covered container. Shelf life is approximately 1 year.

nutritive value: Although we've been lauding the protein value of beans, you should bear in mind that this is vegetable protein, inferior to the animal protein found in meat, milk, eggs, and cheese. The addition of a little animal protein to a bean dish improves the nutritional value. Or if the bean dish itself has no animal protein added, make certain each family member has a glass of milk to drink with the meal.

Besides their protein content, dried beans are an excellent source of iron. Although the nutritional value varies somewhat from one kind of bean to the next, an approximation can be had from the listing below. To give you an idea, 1 cup of cooked navy beans contains 224 calories; the same measure of cooked kidney beans, 218 calories; of soybeans, 234 calories. They also offer:

	navy	kidney	soy	
protein	14.8	14.4	19.8	grams
fat	1.1	.9	10.3	grams
carbohydrate	40.3	39.6	19.4	grams
calcium	95	70	131	milligrams
phosphorus	281	259	322	milligrams
iron	5.1	4.4	4.9	milligrams
sodium	13	6	4	milligrams
potassium	790	629	972	milligrams
thiamin	.27	.20	.38	milligram
riboflavin	.13	.11	.16	milligram
niacin	1.3	1.3	1.1	milligrams
vitamin A	0	10	50	international units

Tips on preparing, cooking. Dried beans in packages have generally been picked over and washed before packing, and need only a brief rinsing. If you've bought the beans in bulk, before washing pick over to remove stones, dirt, bits of straw, any foreign matter.

All dried beans must be soaked before they are cooked to replace the water lost in the drying process. There are two ways to go about it, the old-fashioned soak-overnight method, or the more recently devised quick soak. Whichever you choose, don't discard the soaking water, which will have leached out some of the beans' nutrients; instead, use it in cooking the beans. Use the amount of water called for on the package or, if no directions are given, the amount of water called for in the recipe for cooking the beans.

overnight soak: Measure water into a large heavy pan, add washed beans; cover pot, let stand a minimum of 6, a maximum of 8 hours.

quick soak: Measure water into large heavy pan, add washed beans, bring to a boil; cover pot, cook 2 minutes; remove from heat, let stand 1 hour.

In either case, then cook the beans—in the soaking water—as the recipe directs. The quick-soak method is generally preferable, as it results in softer skins on the cooked beans. Unless for some reason you need to start cooking the beans at the crack of dawn, quick-soak them.

Stir dried beans during cooking to make certain they aren't sticking to the pot, but do it carefully to avoid breaking up the beans. Simmer, never boil—simmering keeps the beans whole. Cooking time is generally 1½ to 2 hours. Beans that will be cooked again—in baked dishes or soups for example—should not be fully cooked; the second time around will finish the process. Meat, onions, green pepper, and celery can be added to simmering beans at any time during the cooking period. Acid substances, such as tomatoes, lemon, vinegar, or wine, should not be added until close to the end of cooking time, as they slow down the tenderizing of the beans. Fully cooked, beans should be tender but not mushy; they should remain whole. Cooking in very hard water or at high altitudes will increase the cooking time. Beans tend to foam considerably during cooking—add a tablespoon of fat to help control this.

Freezing dried beans. There's not much point in freezing the plain simmered beans—cook them fresh when you need them. But baked beans, barbecued limas, and all the other good bean dishes, including the many fine bean soups, are great to have stashed in the freezer to get out on busy days or when you invite drop-in guests to stay for a meal. Cooked bean dishes, properly packaged (see special feature: PUTTING FOOD BY), will keep well at 0°F. or below for about 6 months. Remember to allow for ample heat-through time when you serve them.

Other ways, other forms. If you don't want to cook the beans from scratch when you make a bean dish, or if you want to buy the bean dish itself ready-made, browse among the canned vegetables in your market.

on grocery shelves, in cans or jars: All kinds of water-cooked beans—kidney, white, red, chili, pinto, garbanzo, lima, the works—ready to be flavored and seasoned and recooked as you like, or turned into salads. Baked beans—New England style, in tomato sauce, barbecue style, with ham, and lots more—ready to heat and serve, or to doll up a bit to make them your own specialty before heating. Refried beans. Limas with ham. Chill-and-serve bean salads. All these come in cans or jars of several sizes, to feed one or two or a family or a group.

in grocery frozen-food section: Refried beans. Mexican-style TV dinners, which always include beans in some form, most often as chili or refried beans. Black-eyed peas—these were fresh, not dried, when frozen, but can be used in any dried-bean dish calling for black-eyed peas.

bean flour: This reasonably recent addition to grocery shelves can be used in various ways. Follow package directions to use in dips, breads, casseroles, to combine with or substitute for bread crumbs in meat loaves or in breading meats, poultry, or fish, for thickening soups, gravies, and sauces. Because of the protein content of dried beans, from which these flours are made, the use of them contributes to the protein value of any dish to which they are added.

Some perfect partners. Beans and pork—cured or fresh—have an affinity for one another. Cooked with pork of any description, beans are delectable, and the dish provides high-quality protein.

Baked beans are a staple food, not only in New England—where once Saturday night wouldn't have been right without baked beans, Sunday breakfast all wrong without more of the beans plus codfish cakes—but all over the country. Southern-style baked beans add ginger and hot pepper to the beans-pork-molasses combination. Some areas opt for tomato sauce, some for smoke flavoring. The bean soup of the United States Senate commissary is justly famous. Chili has migrated from the southwestern states as far as both oceans and the Canadian border, not only as a great family meal but also as a fine company dish when you have both a crowd to feed and your budget to consider. Cassoulet, with white beans and a multitude of other delights, is a feast for a gourmet. Both black beans and black-eyed peas are delicious paired with rice. Soybeans are super-tasty casseroled with tomatoes, onions, and cheese. Louisiana contributes limas in Creole sauce; Arizona and New Mexico, refried beans; the Midwest, bean loaf. Vegetarians relish a bean-and-peanut "roast," and so will you. Dried beans, one kind alone or in combinations of several, make a delectable, unusual salad. You can serve a dried-bean dish once a week and not repeat yourself for years.

Long before we got here, beans were cultivated in this country by the Indians, then dried and stored against the lean winter months. They generously shared the secrets of growing and storing beans with the settlers when they arrived. Beans played a substantial role in feeding an expanding nation—they provided bulk, satiety, energy; they were easy to store in times when there was no refrigeration, and easy to carry and reconstitute for west-going adventurers, for cowboys on the trail. The navy sailed on them; the army marched on them. Beans arrived early and are here to stay as an important part of a balanced diet.

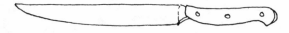

BEAR: see GAME

BEAT, TO: see page 444

BEAVER: see GAME

BEEF

As one facet of the unending search for new things to eat and drink, for new ways to cook and serve familiar foods, or—and this is really reaching—for so-old-they're-new ways to cook and serve familiar foods, the Medieval English Banquet is having its turn in vogue, a new way that's a very old way indeed.

On the surface, it sounds like a fine idea. Picture the Great Hall waveringly lit by candles and flambeaux, serving wenches rushing back and forth with beer and wine, flunkys staggering under the weight of vast spit-roasted haunches of venison and barons of beef, the tables groaning under such exotic dishes as pigeon pie, meat pasties, boiled puddings, and quivering jellies, to say nothing of that new-fangled treat, blank mang. The court fool capering about. Music from the minstrels in the gallery. The nobles seated above the salt, the commoners below. And circulating democratically both above and below the salt, great shaggy dogs to be used in lieu of napkins.

Sound glorious? It wasn't. The Great Hall was cold and drafty, and malodorous with the garbage of previous meals tossed into the corners. The candles and flambeaux were drippy and smelly. The serving wenches got their bottoms pinched during dinner and a lot worse afterwards. The flunkys were beaten regularly. The beer and wine were thin and sour, and so was the music. The court fool, poor wretch, was probably handicapped, mentally or physically or both. Much of the food was overspiced to disguise the fact that it was rotten. If you happened upon a few maggots—well, *c'est la vie!* The pastry was tough; the puddings were abysmally heavy; the jellies resembled mucilage because they were, after all, made of virtually the same ingredients. The blank mang (our present blancmange is a lineal descendant) was a starchy, undercooked disaster. Even the salt was dirty, and there was likely not to be enough of it. The nobles above the salt could barely wait for the meal to be over to settle their differences with the swords they had recently used to hack at the meat. The commoners below the salt fawned and toadied and ate in mortal fear of offending those above. As for the dogs—well, how would your napkins smell if you wiped food all over them and never put them in the laundry? Ah, the good old days!

Wasn't there anything by our standards worth eating or, even, possible to eat on those tables in the Middle Ages? Small, spit-roasted songbirds (and, for heaven's sakes, their tongues) were a delicacy that probably could be called by the same term today, little though we might like the whole idea.

There were often hard-cooked eggs; it's exceedingly difficult to ruin a hard-cooked egg unless, of course, the egg was exceptionally elderly before cooking. Blackbird pie, although it may not appeal to us today, may well have been quite delectable. The venison certainly was edible by our standards, although probably quite dry—venison needs larding or barding, and the English nobles' chefs were unlikely to have employed such niceties.

But oh, those barons of beef! It's very likely that beef, on the other hand, as served at the tables of the high-born (for which read "rich") was at least acceptable. Although the poor slaughtered their cattle—if they had any—in the fall because there was no forage in the cold weather and no fodder to carry them over the winter, the rich used a rough-and-ready version of our present feedlot system to finish their beef. Because there was no refrigeration, the animals were slaughtered as they were used. But not, generally, immediately before being cooked; it simply wasn't handy to slaughter beef and cook it the same day. By sheer lucky accident, some of the meat was hung. (They'd noticed that if they simply tossed it in the corner it rotted, so they strung it from the rafters.)

The beef was spit-roasted, the spit turned by a small boy, called a scullion, or by an ingenious device of a dog that ran on an endless belt that turned massive wooden gears that turned the handle that turned the spit, à la Rube Goldberg. It was then, as it is today, an excellent way of cooking beef. Generally the cut was a baron—both sirloins joined by the backbone—too large to overcook by any other than the most dedicatedly inept chef. Of course, the beef wasn't, to begin with, the beef we know today, lovingly and scientifically bred to insure optimum quality. But it was probably a real joy compared with the rest of what came to the table. No wonder the British have been famous for generations for their roast beef!

Beef goes back a long time. In an Egyptian tomb that experts date from the third millennium B.C., beef ribs were found among the other foods left in the tomb to feed the soul of the dead. In 1750 B.C., Aryan nomads overran India, bringing with them their domesticated cattle and the useful knowledge of *ghee* (or *ghi*), the clarified butter that will keep for months without refrigeration, even in hot climates.

All our modern beef cattle are the result of the crossbreeding of the great ox, or aurochs, and the Celtic Shorthorn. The domestication of the aurochs took place as early as 2500 B.C. in Egypt and Mesopotamia. The Celtic Shorthorn was the cattle breed in Britain up to A.D. 500, at which point the Anglo-Saxons came to England, bringing the aurochs with them, and began the crossbreeding that was to eventuate, over the centuries, in the several kinds of sturdy, meaty beef cattle we know today.

Hoof and horn in the New World. Those indefatigable Spanish explorers (this time Columbus himself) brought cattle to the New World toward the end of the fifteenth century. Small though they were—less than a hundred pounds at full growth—those cattle were a source of surprise to the natives, who hadn't domesticated anything larger than dogs and guinea pigs. But almost all of America's breeding stock—certainly the most important progenitors of present-day breeds—came from England and Scotland when cattle raising got underway as a serious project, although some kinds were brought from Sweden, Holland, France, and Spain, and later from Africa and India.

Products of inbreeding (mating of sister with brother), line breeding (mating of second cousins), and crossbreeding (mating of individuals of one breed with individuals of another) are the beef cattle breeds most important to our vast beef-raising industry of the present time: Hereford, Shorthorn, Aberdeen-Angus, Galloway, Brahman, Africander, Charolais—all originally imported—and Beefmaster, Braford, Brangus, Cattalo, Charbrais, and Santa Gertrudis—all "invented" in the United States.

Much modern breeding—nearly 50 percent in this country—is accomplished by means of artificial insemination, which not only is less chancy than nature's way, but also allows a prize bull to inseminate thousands of cows. Transplantation of ova—sometimes called embryo transfer—is also practiced, making it possible for a nondescript cow to bear a calf with an impressive pedigree; the donor cow can shortly be inseminated again, that fertilized ovum transplanted to another host (hostess?) cow, and so on and on. All of this tampering with nature doesn't seem to upset the four-legged creatures in the least, but certainly it causes the thoughtful reader to pause and reflect upon what we two-legged ones may be coming to in the brave new world ahead.

Who are the champion beefeaters? We are, here in the United States. We do not eat a lot of veal, although people in some parts of the country consume more than those in other parts. The same is true of lamb. Although we do like pork and eat a lot of it, beef still heads our meat shopping list by a wide margin. In the early 1950s we were eating 62 pounds of beef per person per year. By the end of the 1950s that had risen to 89 pounds; by the early 1960s, to 99 pounds; by the early 1970s, to 115 pounds; and the rate is still climbing spectacularly. (All this in spite of the fact that our British cousins at one point thought that eating beef in large quantities caused such problems as depression and mental deterioration.)

Proliferation at the meat counter. Until a short time ago, when we went to buy beef we were dazzled by a vast array of names to choose among. Beef was labeled by all sorts of unlikely, unseemly handles—pike's peak roast, watermelon roast, California roast, spencer steak, filet of bavet, butterball steak, breakfast steak, X-rib roast, market filet, fluff steak, scotch roast, are only a few examples. Even good old soup bones were delicately labeled "bouillon bones" in some places. Worse, if you moved from one part of the country to another and asked for your favorite his-and-hers steak you might be greated by a dull "Huh?" or a put-down, "I assume you mean porterhouse?"

Much of this was our own fault. If you pressed the buzzer in the supermarket and told the answering attendant that you wanted enough beef stroganoff to serve four, he went away and sliced a pound and a quarter of round steak for you. After dozens and dozens had made the same request, he began to cut round and package it, label it "stroganoff," and put it out on the counter—at a price higher than you would have paid if you'd bought the round and cut it yourself. At the same time, there were other customers demanding to know what cut stroganoff came from, and what in the world a watermelon roast was.

The meat industry at last made the move, prompted by the protests of meat dealers themselves, as well as frustrated consumers, organizations of home economists, food authors and editors and many others, that something ought to be—must be—done about meat nomenclature and labeling. The response was the formation of the Industrywide Cooperative Meat Identification Standards Committee (ICMISC for short) in 1972. With the help of the National Live Stock and Meat Board and various federal, state, and local agencies, the ICMISC tackled the morass of meat-cut names and came up with standards that it has urged the industry to adopt at the retail level in order to reduce, and if possible eliminate, consumer confusion. To serve as a guide, the Uniform Retail Meat Identity Standards manual was published.

Just look at the label. The manual of uniform standards lists the single name best suited to each of 314 meat cuts (arrived at after much sifting and discarding), and urges the use of these names, all based on identification of the cut rather than fancy terms of salesmanship. This is the Master List of Recommended Names, designed to make clear to the meat shopper—at last—what it is that she is buying.

Certain standard abbreviations were developed, as well, so that the necessary information could be contained on a label, and so that abbreviations would be consistent and the label brief and specific. The beef abbreviations are:

BAR BQ – Barbecue	BI – Bone In
BNLS – Boneless	DBLE – Double
LGE – Large	N.Y. (NY) – New York
POT-RST – Pot-Roast	RND – Round
SHLDR – Shoulder	SQ – Square
STK – Steak	TRMD – Trimmed

The identification portion of the label—that is, the part that tells you what meat you're buying—should be, the ICMISC recommends, contained in two lines, and combine the name of the species (beef), the primal cut (name of the section of the animal from which the cut comes, as chuck), and the retail name (blade roast). The rest of the label shows the name of the store or the department of the store, the per-pound price, the weight, and the total cost of the piece of meat you've chosen. Like this:

Where did it come from? The key to the relative toughness or tenderness of a cut of meat is the portion of the animal from which it was taken. The key to how to cook that cut is the relative toughness or tenderness. See the adjacent Beef Chart. Approved by the National Live Stock and Meat Board, this chart not only shows you the cuts of beef, and the source of each cut in the beef carcass (primal cut), but also serves as a cooking guide. Tender cuts can be roasted, broiled, panfried, or panbroiled; less tender cuts should be braised or cooked in deep liquid (simmered, that is—no meat, even that served up as "boiled beef" should be boiled).

What do you call it? It wouldn't be possible to list all the fanciful names that various cuts of meat have been called in the hundreds of stores all over the country. But here is a listing of some of the more widely used terms by which cuts were (still are, in some places) commonly called, along with the ICMISC recommended name that you should now find on the label (including abbreviations). These are grouped under the primal cut from which the piece of meat you buy is taken. For how to cook each cut, see the Beef Chart.

Beef Chart

Retail Cuts of Beef—Where They Come from and How to Cook Them

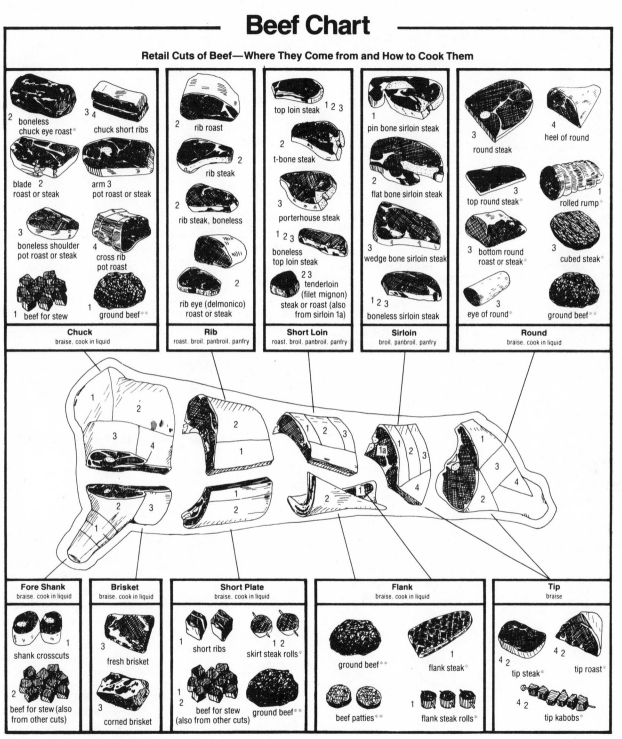

Chuck
braise. cook in liquid

2 boneless chuck eye roast*
3 4 chuck short ribs
blade 2 roast or steak
arm 3 pot roast or steak
3 boneless shoulder pot roast or steak
4 cross rib pot roast
1 beef for stew
ground beef**

Rib
roast. broil. panbroil. panfry

2 rib roast
2 rib steak
2 rib steak, boneless
2 rib eye (delmonico) roast or steak

Short Loin
roast. broil. panbroil. panfry

top loin steak 1 2 3
2 t-bone steak
3 porterhouse steak
1 2 3 boneless top loin steak
2 3 tenderloin (filet mignon) steak or roast (also from sirloin 1a)

Sirloin
broil. panbroil. panfry

1 pin bone sirloin steak
2 flat bone sirloin steak
3 wedge bone sirloin steak
1 2 3 boneless sirloin steak

Round
braise. cook in liquid

3 round steak
4 heel of round
3 top round steak*
1 rolled rump*
3 bottom round roast or steak
3 cubed steak*
3 eye of round*
ground beef**

Fore Shank
braise. cook in liquid

1 shank crosscuts
2 beef for stew (also from other cuts)

Brisket
braise. cook in liquid

3 fresh brisket
3 corned brisket

Short Plate
braise. cook in liquid

1 short ribs
1 2 skirt steak rolls*
1 2 beef for stew (also from other cuts)
ground beef**

Flank
braise. cook in liquid

ground beef**
1 flank steak*
beef patties**
1 flank steak rolls*

Tip
braise

4 2 tip steak*
4 2 tip roast*
4 2 tip kabobs*

* May be roasted. broiled. panbroiled. or panfried from high quality beef.
** May be roasted. baked. broiled. panbroiled. or panfried.

PRIMAL CUT: BEEF CHUCK (ARM HALF)

common name	recommended name
arm chuck roast chuck arm roast chuck round-bone cut round bone pot-roast round bone roast	BEEF CHUCK ARM POT-ROAST
beef chuck arm pot-roast with arm bone removed	BEEF CHUCK ARM POT-RST BNLS
boston cut bread and butter cut cross rib roast english cut roast thick rib roast	BEEF CHUCK CROSS RIB POT-ROAST
boneless boston cut boneless english cut cross rib roast, boneless english roll	BEEF CHUCK CROSS RIB POT-RST BNLS
boneless english roast cross rib roast, boneless honey cut shoulder roast shoulder roast, bnls	BEEF CHUCK SHOULDER POT-RST BNLS
knuckle bone knuckle soup bone soup bone	BEEF SOUP BONE
arm chuck steak arm steak beef chuck arm swiss steak chuck steak for swissing round bone steak round bone swiss steak	BEEF CHUCK ARM STEAK
boneless arm steak boneless round-bone steak boneless swiss steak	BEEF CHUCK ARM STEAK BNLS
barbecue ribs braising ribs english short ribs extra lean fancy ribs short ribs	BEEF CHUCK SHORT RIBS

common name	recommended name
english steak shoulder steak shoulder steak, bnls shoulder steak, half cut chuck for swissing clod steak bnls london broil shoulder clod steak bnls shoulder cutlet bnls	BEEF CHUCK SHOULDER STEAK BNLS
center shoulder roast chuck roast, bnls chuck shoulder roast clod roast	BEEF CHUCK SHOULDER POT-RST BNLS
beef cubed for stew boneless beef for stew boneless beef stew	BEEF FOR STEW
barbecue ribs bottom chuck ribs chuck spareribs	BEEF CHUCK FLAT RIBS
barbecue ribs braising ribs brust flanken flanken short ribs	BEEF CHUCK SHORT RIBS
barbecue ribs braising ribs brust flanken flanken short ribs kosher ribs (usually thinner than Beef Chuck Short Ribs)	BEEF CHUCK FLANKEN STYLE RIB
clear bones marrow bones soup bones	BEEF MARROW BONES

PRIMAL CUT: BEEF CHUCK (BLADE HALF)

common name	recommended name
neck boiling beef neck pot-roast neck soup meat yankee pot-roast	BEEF CHUCK NECK POT-ROAST
beef neck bnls neck pot-roast, bnls yankee pot-roast, bnls	BEEF CHUCK NECK POT-ROAST BNLS
braising bones meaty neck bones neck bone neck soup bone	BEEF CHUCK NECK BONES

common name	recommended name
beef for stew stewing beef boneless beef stew	BEEF FOR STEW

PRIMAL CUT: BEEF CHUCK (BLADE PORTION)

common name	recommended name
boneless chuck roast chuck pot-roast bnls chuck roast boneless	BEEF CHUCK POT-ROAST BNLS
center cut pot-roast chuck roast center cut 7-bone roast	BEEF CHUCK 7-BONE POT-ROAST
center chuck steak chuck steak center cut 7-bone steak	BEEF CHUCK 7-BONE STEAK
blade chuck roast chuck blade roast chuck roast blade cut chuck roast 1st cut	BEEF CHUCK BLADE ROAST
blade steak chuck blade steak chuck steak blade cut chuck steak 1st cut	BEEF CHUCK BLADE STEAK
char broil steak chuck barbecue steak chuck steak 1st cut chuck steak for bar b q	BEEF CHUCK BLADE STEAK CAP OFF
blade roast, bone-in 7-bone roast top chuck roast	BEEF CHUCK TOP BLADE POT-ROAST
blade steak, bone-in top blade steak top chuck steak, bone-in	BEEF CHUCK TOP BLADE STEAK
bottom chuck roast california roast semiboneless roast under cut roast	BEEF CHUCK UNDER BLADE POT-ROAST
bottom chuck steak california steak semiboneless chuck steak under cut steak	BEEF CHUCK UNDER BLADE STEAK
bnls, roast bottom chuck bottom chuck roast, bnls california roast, bnls inside chuck roast	BEEF CHUCK UNDER BLD POT-RST BNLS

common name	recommended name
boneless chuck steak bottom chuck steak, bnls chuck fillet steak under cut steak bnls	BEEF CHUCK UNDER BLADE STEAK BNLS
chuck eye chuck fillet chuck tender fish muscle medallion pot-roast scotch tender	BEEF CHUCK MOCK TENDER
flat iron roast lifter roast puff roast shoulder roast, thin end triangle roast	BEEF CHUCK TOP BLADE ROAST BNLS
book steak butler steak lifter steak petite steak top chuck stk, bnls	BEEF CHUCK TOP BLADE STEAK BNLS
boneless chuck roll boneless chuck filler chuck eye roast inside chuck roll	BEEF CHUCK EYE ROAST BNLS
bnls chuck fillet steak bnls steak bottom chuck chuck boneless slices chuck eye steak chuck fillet steak	BEEF CHUCK EYE STEAK BNLS
boneless chuck pot-roast chuck boneless roast inside chuck roast chuck rib pot-roast	BEEF CHUCK EYE EDGE POT-ROAST

(thin strip from inside chuck, originally attached to rib bones)

PRIMAL CUT: BEEF SHANK

common name	recommended name
center beef shanks cross cut shanks fore shank for soup meat, bone-in	BEEF SHANK CROSS CUTS
boneless beef shanks cross cut shank, bnls fore shank for soup meat, bnls	BEEF SHANK CROSS CUTS, BNLS
center shank soup bone shank soup bone	BEEF SHANK CENTER CUT

beef bones	
clear bones	BEEF SHANK
soup bones	SOUP BONES

PRIMAL CUT: BEEF BRISKET

common name	recommended name
boneless brisket	
brisket boneless	BEEF BRISKET
fresh beef brisket	WHOLE BNLS
whole brisket	
brisket front cut	
brisket point cut	BEEF BRISKET
brisket thick cut	POINT HALF BNLS
brisket first cut	
brisket flat cut	BEEF BRISKET
brisket thin cut	FLAT HALF BNLS

(the two cuts just above are from a brisket that has been cut in half crosswise, those below from a brisket cut in thirds crosswise)

common name	recommended name
brisket front cut	
brisket point cut	BEEF BRISKET
brisket thick cut	POINT CUT BNLS
brisket center cut	BEEF BRISKET
	MIDDLE CUT BNLS
brisket flat cut	BEEF BRISKET
	FLAT CUT BNLS

(the following two cuts are from a brisket in which the pointed two-thirds has been cut in half lengthwise, the remaining third cut off crosswise)

common name	recommended name
brisket edge cut	BEEF BRISKET
brisket side cut	EDGE CUT BNLS
brisket front cut	
brisket point cut	BEEF BRISKET
brisket thick cut	HALF POINT BNLS
corned beef	BEEF BRISKET
	CORNED BNLS

(all cuts of brisket can be corned)

PRIMAL CUT: BEEF PLATE

common name	recommended name
short ribs	BEEF PLATE
	SHORT RIBS
beef spareribs	BEEF PLATE
	SPARERIBS

common name	recommended name
boiling beef	
plate beef	BEEF PLATE
plate boiling beef	RIBS
skirt steak	BEEF PLATE
diaphragm	SKIRT STEAK BNLS
cubed skirt steak	
skirt steak, cubed	BEEF PLATE
diaphragm	SKIRT STK CUBED BNLS
beef london broil	
london broils	
skirt fillets	BEEF PLATE
skirt london broils	SKIRT STEAK ROLLS BNLS
london grill steak	
plate roll	
rolled plate	BEEF PLATE
yankee pot-roast	ROLLED BONELESS

PRIMAL CUT: BEEF FLANK

common name	recommended name
flank steak fillet	
plank steak	
london broil	BEEF FLANK STEAK
jiffy steak	
cubed flank steak	BEEF FLANK STK CUBED
tendered flank steak	
rolled flank steak	
tendered rolled flank steak	BEEF FLANK STEAK
tender roll	CUBED ROLLED
beef london broils	
flank steak rolls	
flank steak fillets	BEEF FLANK STK ROLLS
flank steak london broils	
london broils	

PRIMAL CUT: BEEF RIB

common name	recommended name
beef rib roast, short cut 6–7	
standing rib roast 6–7	BEEF RIB
beef rib roast, short cut 6–7	ROAST LARGE END
rib roast oven ready	ribs 6–7
standing rib roast 8–9	BEEF RIB
rib roast oven ready	ROAST LARGE END
	ribs 8–9

standing rib roast 6–8 rib roast oven ready	BEEF RIB ROAST LARGE END ribs 6–8
newport roast beef rib roast deluxe club rib roast	BEEF RIB EXTRA TRIM RST LGE END
beef rib steak beef rib steak, bone-in	BEEF RIB STEAK LARGE END 7th rib
rib roast oven ready standing rib roast sirloin tip roast	BEEF RIB ROAST SMALL END ribs 11–12
rib roast oven ready standing rib roast	BEEF RIB ROAST SMALL END ribs 9–10
rib roast oven ready standing rib roast	BEEF RIB ROAST SMALL END ribs 10–12
beef rib steak beef rib steak, bone-in	BEEF RIB STEAK SMALL END ribs 11–12
beef rib steak bnls spencer steak bnls	BEEF RIB STEAK SMALL END BNLS ribs 11–12
delmonico steak boneless rib eye steak fillet steak spencer steak beauty steak	BEEF RIB EYE STEAK
delmonico pot-roast delmonico roast beef rib eye pot-roast regular roll roast	BEEF RIB RIB EYE ROAST ribs 6–12
beef short ribs	BEEF RIB SHORT RIBS
beef riblets rib bones finger ribs	BEEF RIB BACK RIBS
cap meat rolled top rib roll bnls	BEEF RIB ROLLED CAP POT-RST

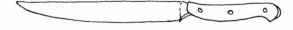

PRIMAL CUT: BEEF LOIN

common name	recommended name
shell steak strip steak club steak chip club steak bone-in club sirloin steak sirloin strip steak, bone-in delmonico steak	BEEF LOIN TOP LOIN STEAK
strip steak Kansas City steak N.Y. strip steak sirloin steak, hotel style beef loin ambassador steak beef loin strip steak hotel cut boneless club sirloin steak	BEEF LOIN TOP LOIN STEAK BNLS
T-bone steak	BEEF LOIN T-BONE STEAK

(diameter of tenderloin must be no less than ½ inch, measured across center)

porterhouse steak	BEEF LOIN PORTERHOUSE STEAK

(diameter of tenderloin must be no less than 1¼ inches, measured across center)

beef sirloin steak, wedge bone beef sirloin steak, short cut sirloin steak	BEEF LOIN SIRLOIN STEAK WEDGE BONE*
sirloin steak	BEEF LOIN SIRLOIN STK ROUND BONE*
beef sirloin steak flat bone sirloin steak flat bone sirloin steak	BEEF LOIN SIRLOIN STK FLAT BONE*
beef sirloin steak pin bone sirloin steak	BEEF LOIN SIRLOIN STK PIN BONE*

(*these four may all be simply labeled BEEF LOIN, SIRLOIN STEAK)

beef sirloin N.Y. steak, bone-in N.Y. sirloin steak shell steak	BEEF LOIN SHELL SIRLOIN STEAK
sirloin steak bnls rump steak	BEEF LOIN SIRLOIN STEAK BNLS

(same as bone-in sirloin steaks, except all bones removed)

boneless sirloin	BEEF LOIN
sirloin steak bnls	
top sirloin steak	TOP SIRLOIN STEAK BNLS

beef tenderloin tip roast	
beef tenderloin, filet mignon roast	BEEF LOIN
beef tenderloin chateaubriand	TENDERLOIN ROAST

filet mignon	
beef fillet steak	
beef tenderloin, filet de boeuf	BEEF LOIN
beef tender steak	TENDERLOIN STEAK
(or may be labeled FILET MIGNON)	

tenderloin tips	BEEF LOIN
	TENDERLOIN TIPS
(from end of tenderloin as it tapers down loin)	

PRIMAL CUT: BEEF ROUND

common name	recommended name
beef round steak	
beef round steak, center cut	BEEF ROUND STEAK
beef round steak, full cut	
(may or may not contain part of the tip)	

beef round steak	
beef round steak, center cut bnls	BEEF ROUND STEAK BNLS
beef round, full cut bnls	

| beef round rump roast, bone-in | BEEF ROUND |
| beef round standing rump | RUMP ROAST |

| beef round boneless rump | BEEF ROUND |
| beef round rump roast, rolled | RUMP RST BNLS |

beef round heel pot-roast	
pike's peak roast	BEEF ROUND
diamond roast	HEEL OF ROUND
denver pot-roast	
horseshoe roast	

| beef stew | BEEF FOR STEW |
| cubed beef for stew | |

first cuts of top steak	BEEF ROUND
short cuts	TOP ROUND STK 1st CUT
top round london broil	
(sometimes cut extra thick—from tenderest portion of top round)	

| beef top round steak | BEEF ROUND |
| beef top round steak, center cut | TOP ROUND STEAK |

braciole round steak	
braciole steak	BEEF ROUND
beef top round braciole steak	TOP RND STK BUTTERFLY
beef butterfly steak	
(cut paper thin and butterflied—for stuffing and rolling)	

| beef top round roast | BEEF ROUND |
| beef top round roast center | TOP ROUND ROAST |

cube steaks	
cubed steaks	BEEF CUBED STEAK
tendered round steak	
(may be from either the top or the bottom round)	

| round tip roast | BEEF ROUND |
| round back of rump roast | BOTTOM ROUND RUMP RST |

beef bottom round pot roast	
beef bottom round oven roast	BEEF ROUND
beef bottom round steak pot-roast	BOTTOM ROUND ROAST

| beef bottom round steak | BEEF ROUND |
| bottom round steak | BOTTOM ROUND STEAK |

beef eye round roast	
beef round eye pot-roast	BEEF ROUND
eye round pot-roast	EYE ROUND ROAST
beef round eye roast	

| eye round steak | BEEF ROUND |
| beef round eye steak | EYE ROUND STEAK |

beef sirloin tip roast	
face round roast	
tip sirloin roast	BEEF ROUND
round tip roast	TIP ROAST
crescent roast	

| beef sirloin tip steak | BEEF ROUND |
| top sirloin steak | TIP STEAK |

| ball tip steak | BEEF ROUND |
| trimmed tip steak | TIP STEAK CAP OFF |

| ball tip roast | BEEF ROUND |
| full trimmed tip roast | TIP ROAST CAP OFF |

| beef sirloin tip kabob cubes | BEEF ROUND |
| beef kabobs | CUBES FOR KABOBS |

Buying the right cut of beef for the purpose you have in mind requires a certain amount of know-how—but it's know-how that can easily be acquired if you're willing to do a little homework, particularly now that the butcher's soaring imagination has been somewhat tempered by common sense.

BEEF IN YOUR KITCHEN

Armed with awareness that beef is bought by cut, not by method of cooking—no part of the critter is a "london broil" or a "sauerbraten" or a "chicken-fry steak"—you can sally forth to the market with a certain amount of sangfroid. However, you do need to know the answers to some other problems you can face while standing at the meat counter—how to judge quality, how many servings to expect from the cut you buy, how to be certain that the cut you choose and the cooking method you intend to use are compatible, and a whole lot more.

Bracing yourself to do battle. If you buy meat in a butcher shop and enjoy the friendship of the butcher to the point where you have confidence in his judgment, you can simply put your problems on his shoulders. Tell him, "I want a tender oven roast to serve six, with enough leftovers for another meal for four," and let him take it from there.

But if you buy beef, as most people do these days, from the meat counter at the supermarket, you're on your own.

rule of thumb to determine servings: A pound of lean boneless beef will yield 3 to 4 servings; a pound of beef with a large amount of fat and/or bone, 1 or 2 servings. That's easy to remember.

tough or tender or in between: The age of the steer before slaughtering in a large degree determines how tender the tenderest cuts will be, how tough the toughest. Almost all beef in the United States—at least, all beef that you buy in a meat department or butcher shop in which you have confidence—will be reasonably young, if only because it does not pay to feed a steer longer than about 18 months. The younger the animal, the more tender the meat.

The color of the meat isn't all that accurate an indication. True, young beef is bright red in color, old beef is dark red, almost purple. But factors other than age, including how long the actual cut you're preparing to buy has been hanging around the butcher shop, influence color, too. Light makes a difference—are you looking at the cut by daylight, incandescent light, fluorescent light? Is the meat unwrapped in the butcher shop's case, or closely wrapped in plastic in the supermarket's?

Aging—that is, how long the beef has been held under certain controlled conditions—also influences tenderness. Meat that has been stored from two to six weeks at a temperature between 34 and 38° F. is called "aged beef." Only the top grades of beef can be aged—Prime and heavy Choice.

Lesser grades don't age, they deteriorate. More than tenderizing, aging develops excellent flavor and texture.

Most important, tenderness depends on the cut. All meat is muscle. The meat of the loin, which lies along the backbone, and of the ribs, is the tenderest simply because it consists of the least-used muscles. The meat of the legs and shoulders—the chuck, shank, and round—the lower belly—brisket, plate, and flank—and the tail (steers twitch their tails a lot) are the tough cuts, because they are the most-used muscles.

inspection and grading: The most reliable guides to good beef are the United States Department of Agriculture's inspection and grading systems. All meat processed in plants that sell their products across state lines must be inspected. Meat grading, on the other hand, is not mandatory.

Inspection service is provided by the USDA's Consumer and Marketing Service. The USDA inspectors not only examine the meat itself for wholesomeness, but also supervise the cleanliness and operating procedures of the meat packing plants to assure that meat is not contaminated or adulterated. Meat that passes the USDA inspection for wholesomeness is stamped with a round mark that bears the legend U.S. INSP'D & P'S'D along with the inspector's number, like this:

The stamp is placed only once on wholesale cuts, so that you are likely to see it only on large cuts of meat (if, for example, you buy beef in quantity for your freezer). Packaged meat foods, however, such as canned meats and frozen dinners, are required to carry the inspection mark on their label if they are to be sold in interstate commerce.

Meat grading is a service provided by the USDA's Consumer and Marketing Service to meat packers and others who request it and who pay a fee for the service. Not all meat is graded, but a large percentage of it is, because packers understand that alert consumers will look for the grade mark.

Highly trained in determining meat quality, the USDA graders grade only whole carcasses or wholesale cuts—quality differences are difficult or impossible to recognize in smaller retail cuts. A purple shield-shaped grade mark containing the letters USDA and the grade name—Prime, Choice, or Good (you are not likely to be able to buy the lesser grades, Standard, Commercial, Utility, and Cutter, at retail)—is applied with a roller stamp all along the length of the carcass and across both shoulders, so that when the carcass is divided into retail cuts, one or more of the grade marks will appear on most cuts. The grade marks look like this:

USDA PRIME is the highest quality, the most tender, juicy, and flavorful. It is available in many butcher shops and some supermarkets. Like all "bests" it is the most expensive grade. USDA CHOICE is the grade most often sold by butcher shops and supermarkets, and by those who supply meat in quantity for freezers. It is tender, juicy, and flavorful. USDA GOOD is lean and fairly tender, though not as juicy and flavorful.

Only meat that has first passed inspection can be graded, so the grade mark assures you of wholesome meat from a healthy animal processed in a sanitary plant, as well as telling you the grade—the quality—of the meat you buy.

how to buy: Fresh beef is available all year around, is most plentiful—and therefore likely to be least expensive—between January and April. Quite often, large cuts cost less per pound than small cuts. If you see a bargain, buy it. Cut it yourself, or have it cut, into sizes useful for your family. For example, the tenderloin—filet mignon—is likely to be cheaper whole than cut, and is easy to slice into pieces of the exact thickness you prefer. A large pot roast can be cut into a smaller pot roast, slices to use for swiss steak, and cubes to make a stew. A large rib roast will yield a roast and rib steaks, as well as short ribs. (In all cases, don't forget to salvage any bones for stock or soup.) Be guided by the USDA grade mark—ask questions about beef that does not carry the mark, and don't buy it if the answers aren't satisfactory.

how to store: If your refrigerator has a meat keeper, store the meat in it, unwrapped. If not, remove or loosen the store wrappings, store loosely wrapped in the coldest part of the refrigerator. Raw ground meat and stew meat can be stored in the refrigerator for 1 to 2 days; steaks and other smaller cuts, 2 to 4 days; roasts, 3 to 6 days. Cooked meat should be cooled slightly and stored tightly covered (meat and gravy separately) in the coldest part of the refrigerator no more than 4 days.

nutritive value: To give the nutritive value of every cut of beef, with all its variables of bone-to-meat and fat-to-lean, would require a book in itself. But there are a number of points concerning nutritional value to bear in mind when choosing and serving meat.

Beef is a fine source of high-quality protein, and also provides good amounts of iron and of niacin (one of the B vitamins). A 3-ounce serving of cooked, boneless, lean beef supplies these percentages of the RDA for an adult: protein, 30 percent; iron, 27 percent; riboflavin, 10 percent; niacin, 22 percent; thiamin, 4 percent. (See special feature: NUTRITION NOTEBOOK.)

As for calorie content, remember that calories from beef are made up largely of high-quality protein, and that 250 calories of good beef are quite different in quality, if not in quantity, from 250 "empty" calories derived from junk food. Calorie counts vary from cut to cut, and actually from serving to serving. Here are some typical calorie counts for various cuts of beef—serving size is 3½ ounces, grade is Choice: chuck, about 250; round, about 195; lean ground beef, about 180; rib roast and porterhouse steak, about 400; sirloin steak, about 320; flank steak (which has little or no fat) about 145. The less fat, the lower the calorie count—but bear in mind that it is flecks of fat distributed throughout the meat (called marbling, as opposed to an outer layer of fat, which can be cut off) that makes meat tender, moist, and juicy.

Tips on preparing, cooking. There are two simple,

easy-to-remember guidelines for cooking beef. If it's a tender cut, use dry heat—roast, broil, panbroil, or panfry; if it's a less-than-tender cut, use moist heat—braise or cook in liquid.

High-quality less-than-tender cuts can be broiled if your family will eat them rare or, at most, medium rare. Or, if you wish, you can use a commercial tenderizer to make cuts such as chuck steak suitable for broiling.

Time and temperature are the two most important factors in cooking meat, and they are both vital to properly cooked tender cuts, using dry heat. You need to take into consideration the size and shape of the cut—weight? thick or thin?—when determining how long a piece of meat will take to cook, and at what temperature it should be cooked.

There are assorted mechanical devices to lend you a hand. Your oven doubtless has a regulator that can be set to any temperature you choose, or (sometimes this is a good idea even if you have faith in your regulator) use an oven thermometer to check temperature. In addition, a meat thermometer, to register the internal temperature of the cut, takes the guesswork out of meat cookery.

You can also rely, but only as a rough guide, on a minutes-per-pound scale. In general, the larger the cut, the fewer minutes per pound it will take to cook. Bear in mind that meat continues to cook after you take it out of the oven. A roast should "rest" for 20 minutes or so between removal from the oven and carving—less juice will be lost, and carving will be easier—but it will also cook a little more during that resting time. Remove from the oven when the meat thermometer registers between 5 and 10 degrees lower than the desired doneness.

For best results in roasting beef, place the roast on a rack, fat side up, in a shallow pan. (The bones of a standing rib roast serve as its rack.) Season if you wish, although salt penetrates the roast only a little more than ¼ inch during cooking. Insert a meat thermometer so that the bulb is in the center of the largest muscle, neither touching bone nor resting in fat. Do not cover. Add no water or other liquid. Roast in a slow oven—300°F. for larger roasts, 350° for smaller ones —until the thermometer indicates the desired degree of doneness: 140° for rare, 160° for medium, 170° for well done. The single exception to this is a whole beef tenderloin. The assumption here is that if you're cooking this cut you like your meat rare. Cook a 4- to 6-pound tenderloin in a 425° oven 45 to 60 minutes total time, to 140° on the meat thermometer. It will cut handsomely into slices, be more steaklike than roastlike, and be totally delicious.

General instructions for broiling beef are more difficult to give than for roasting, not only because broilers differ widely, but also because although most people agree on the perfect roast, everybody has his own ideas about the perfect steak. In general, a boneless steak should take a slightly longer time than a bone-in one, a steak large in area slightly longer than one that is small. A 1-inch steak (don't try broiling thinner steaks—panbroil, instead) should take in the neighborhood of 15 minutes total time for rare, 20 for medium, 25 for well done; a 1½-inch steak, 25, 30, or 35 minutes; a 2-inch steak, 35, 45, or 55 minutes. If you like your steak very rare, you'll want to shorten the shortest time; if you like it very well done, you may want to lengthen the longest time. Even though well-done steak is considered tantamount to heresy by rare-steak buffs, you're entitled to have yours exactly the way you like it.

Less tender cuts should be braised—first browned in a small amount of fat, then cooked, barely simmering, in a small amount of liquid.

Freezing beef. Raw beef, properly prepared for freezing (see special feature: PUTTING FOOD BY), can be stored at 0°F. or lower up to 9 months; beyond that point the meat will not be harmful to eat, but will begin to lose texture and flavor. Store cooked beef under the same condition up to 3 months.

Other ways, other forms. There are beef and beef-combination foods in great variety in supermarkets. Here is a sampling.

on grocery shelves: Sliced beef in gravy, corned beef, roast beef hash, corned beef hash, roast beef sandwich spread, beef jerky.

in grocery frozen-food section: Frozen dinners with various cuts of beef plus vegetables and potatoes; beef-and-gravy combinations in plastic boil pouches; beef potpies; frozen beef sandwiches.

in grocery refrigerated cases: Beef or beef-combination sausages, luncheon meats, corned beef, pastrami.

The shopper's lament, "Why is beef so expensive?" If you've ever seen a beef steer on the hoof at a fair or cattle show, you've probably marveled at all that meat. The trouble is, that's not all meat. Say the steer weighs 1,000 pounds. Dressed, that steer yields only 61.5 percent of that weight, or 615 pounds. The packer sells that 615-pound beef carcass to the retailer, who trims away 183 pounds of bone, fat, and other waste, ending up with 432 pounds—less than half the steer's original weight—to sell to the consumer. More, the best—and the most expensive beef—the rib and loin sections, make up only a portion of that final 432 pounds of beef. The rib section accounts for 47.5 pounds, the loin for

77.7 pounds of salable beef. The chuck accounts for 134.3 pounds; the brisket, 9.4 pounds; the plate, 40.8 pounds; the flank, 15.8 pounds; the shank, 19.1 pounds; the round, 83.8 pounds. (In case you're a swift adder and wonder what became of the rest, our old friend miscellaneous accounts for the remaining amount.)

Raising that beef to the point at which it was a salable 1,000-pound steer took time and money, both of which contribute to the beef's retail price. There's board and room for the cow until the calf is born, followed by six or seven months' time for cow and calf together in pasture, plus 330 pounds of grain, 70 pounds of protein supplement, and 10,000 pounds of hay, silage, and grass before the calf reaches weaning age. After that, 2,200 more pounds of grain, 360 pounds of protein supplement, and 2,300 pounds of hay, silage, and pasture before the steer reaches the 1,000-pound weight at which it is sold to the packer.

Retail beef prices must cover the amount paid to the producer for the steer plus the costs of processing, refrigeration, transportation, rent, taxes, and labor. The retail store manager must price his beef so that all of it is sold—so that he doesn't sell out the steaks and roasts and end up with unsold pot roasts and short ribs.

The law of supply and demand, that bugaboo from Introduction to Economics, plays its part in setting beef prices. When for one reason or another we buy more beef than we were expected to buy, supply is used up and prices rise. When we buy less than expected, there's no way to stop production (you can't ask a cow not to have her calf for another six months, please, or a steer to stop eating for a while), so the supply continues, and the prices go down.

Demand, however, generally continues to rise. We eat 116 pounds of beef per person per year now, and that's expected to go up to 130 pounds by 1980. Beef production will have to be doubled, expert forecasters say, by the end of the century if demand is not to exceed supply by a great deal.

"Why not simply stop producing beef?" That's a question asked by some (obviously not avid meat-eaters) as an answer to those who complain of the high price of beef. We could use the grain with which the beef are fed in other ways, the argument goes, at a far lower cost, to feed more people.

It's a simplistic argument which, like many such, isn't true. To begin with, beef contains about 24 percent protein —the body-builder we need for good health. It is high-quality protein, containing all the essential amino acids, unlike vegetable protein. Of that protein supplied by beef, 80 percent is usable by the human body. Contrast that with corn, for example, which is only 8 percent protein, of which 56 percent is usable by the body. Wheat is 12 percent protein, with 52 percent usable.

Consider also that the beef steer is an efficient machine, capable of converting feed unfit for human consumption into high-quality protein food for humans. Because cattle are ruminants (they have three more stomachs than we were allotted), they can eat and convert to meat roughage and by-products that man cannot eat. More than 80 percent of the feed given to cattle consists of these things not digestible by humans. See also COLD CUTS, CORNED BEEF, GROUND MEAT, MARROW, OXTAILS, PASTRAMI, SAUSAGES, SUET, and VARIETY MEATS.

BEEF STOCK: see HERBS AND SAVORY SEASONINGS

BEER

Beer has been with us a long, long time—longer than we can successfully determine with any certainty. Ancient Sumerians worshipped Ninkasi—called "the lady who fills the mouth"— one of whose areas of expertise was the brewing of beer. Early Egyptians drank beer in sufficient quantity that authorities felt called upon, through a papyrus that has been dated about 1400 B.C., to warn against the hazards of getting drunk in beer taverns "for fear that people repeat words which may have gone out of your mouth without you being aware. . . ." (Similar warnings, in more forthright terms, were posted in English pubs during World War II, proving what we already know, that the more things change, the more they stay the same.)

Although no one seems to be quite certain how brewing originated, an educated guess is that it was a by-product of bread-making. Long before recorded history, women had learned that raw grain could be made digestible by setting it aside until it sprouted. Better still, bread made from sprouted grain that had been dried and pounded to a powder tasted better and had keeping qualities superior to that made from ordinary flour. Some dedicated toper, who up to then had probably been getting his jollies only from the juices of rotting fruit, figured out that sprouted-grain bread, partially baked and then broken up and set to soak, gave the soaking water certain delightfully heady properties. So was beer born.

Until somewhere in the neighborhood of 1500 B.C., however, brewing was a chancy business. Nobody understood why some brews simply spoiled instead of fermenting, why some beers turned out so much better than others made exactly the same way. But bread and beer continued as partners, some people learning that the foam skimmed off the beer could be reintroduced into the bread-making process to produce a lighter, better-leavened loaf. When the workings of yeast were at last understood, things looked up at the brewery. But it was not until the end of the Middle Ages that hops, contributing the bite of their bitterness as well as their preservative quality, were added to beer.

Beer in the Colonies. When the *Mayflower's* Pilgrims landed, their choice of Plymouth Rock certainly was determined in part by the fact that ". . . we could not now take time for further search or consideration: our victuals being spent, especially our beer." The earliest New Englanders learned to their dismay that barley and hops, those essentials of brewing, did not grow well in their new land, and had to make do with a potable made of maple sugar and persimmons. Not beer, but intoxicating, it had to do until transatlantic trade could be gotten underway. Once Pennsylvania—fine barley-and-hops country—was settled and the Pennsylvania Dutch began to brew, everyone breathed a little easier.

Today, beer is brewed in America from malted barley—our old friend, the sprouted barley soaked in water—and hops, sometimes with the addition of other cereals, such as corn and rye. Fermentation has long since progressed from a matter of chance to a consideration of science. Cultured yeast causes carefully controlled fermentation that produces the bitey sparkle characteristic of the beverage. The final important ingredient is distilled water—experts say that beer truly succeeds or fails according to the water used, and reputations have been made for fine beers by the exceptionally clear, sweet water used in their brewing. The proportion of water to malt governs the strength of the beer—the more water, the less alcohol in the finished product.

Most American beers are about 3½ percent alcohol by weight, although some few go as high as 5 percent. In any case, beer's alcoholic content is lower than that of wine and considerably lower than spirits, the "hard" liquors.

The brewmeister's delight. As with the making of anything edible or potable, there is a vocabulary that goes along with the brewing of beer. To make beer, *barley* is dampened, then spread out on a flat surface to *germinate*—that is, to sprout. The germ is heat-dried and becomes *malt*. Ground, the malt becomes *grist*. Mixed in a vat with hot water, grist becomes *mash*. *Hops* (the dried buds of the hop vine) are added, and the mixture becomes *wort*. The wort is drawn into a fermenting vat, *brewers' yeast* is added, and *fermentation* takes place. The result: beer.

The German word *lager* means "to store." Lager beer is beer that has been stored for various periods of time, the exact amount of time depending on the expert in control of that particular beer. The storage period ages the brew, allows it to mellow.

Cooking with beer. As an ingredient in cooking, beer has a long history. It can play an important role in a large number of delicious dishes. Beer and various kinds of cheese are particularly good flavor partners.

Try beer in a recipe for a wine-tomato spaghetti sauce, substituting beer for the wine. Shrimps cooked in beer are delectable. A cheese strata, with beer added to the egg-milk mixture, is a trencherman's delight. Beer makes pancakes puff cloud-light and gives them an elusive flavor resembling sourdough. Beer batter is great for all sorts of deep-fried fish, meat, or vegetables. Sauerkraut, bacon, and apples simmered in beer perfumed with juniper berries makes a mouth-watering accompaniment for a pork roast, or for duck or goose. And there are dozens more ways to go—there are even beer cookbooks to guide you—if you'd like to learn to cook with beer.

BEETS

Beets are a homey, down-on-the-farm-type vegetable. Nobody suggests that they grace a royal banquet, or that the beet, not the apple, was what Adam took and did eat.

The fact that beets are a close relative of chard isn't a big news item, either—if you called this a nation of chard lovers, you'd be stretching the truth beyond the breaking point. Ditto beets. If you announce beets as tonight's vegetable in many families, you're much more likely to elicit "You're kidding!" rather than "Oh, frabjus day!" as a response.

It's hard to say how beets got their unsavory reputation. Perhaps it's because they, like turnips, are one of the root vegetables that will "winter over" in cold cellars and were once one of the very few vegetables available at the end of the long cold season before the early crops came in. But potatoes wintered over, too. So did apples. Nobody complained of those. And beets are not bitter, as turnips often are. So it's not easy to figure out. Nonetheless, when you ask "What's your favorite vegetable?" there are no loud cries of "Beets, beets!"

The trouble, probably, was plain boiled beets, served up over and over again by winter-weary cooks not blessed with much culinary imagination. It still happens today, but it needn't—the beet is a fine (and certainly a handsome) vegetable that can be served in a surprising number of ways hot or cold. It's low in calories, contributes vitamins and minerals to the diet, and has a bonus of edible leaves—beet greens—that are delicious. If you come across (most likely in a farmers' market) fresh beet greens with very tiny, rosy beets attached, you're in for a true table treat.

BEETS IN YOUR KITCHEN

Although they're available all year around, the peak season for beets is June, July, and August. They are shipped to markets all over the country from California, New Jersey, Ohio, Pennsylvania, and Colorado, the main beet-growing states.

how to buy: Choose firm, shapely, unblemished beets that show good color. The smaller they are, the more tender they will be. Count on about 1½ pounds to make 4 servings.

how to store: Keep beets, unwashed until you are ready to use them, in the refrigerator. Loosely packed in the vegetable compartment or in plastic bags, they can be stored up to a month; however, as they are virtually always available, it's wiser to buy beets as you need them, rather than let them occupy valuable refrigerator space.

nutritive value: A cup of diced or sliced beets contains a little less than 55 calories, and offers:

protein	1.9	grams
fat	.2	gram
carbohydrate	12.2	grams
calcium	24	milligrams
phosphorus	39	milligrams
iron	.9	milligram
sodium	73	milligrams
potassium	354	milligrams
thiamin	.05	milligram
riboflavin	.07	milligram
niacin	.5	milligram
ascorbic acid	10	milligrams
vitamin A	30	international units

A cup of cooked beet greens contains 26 calories and:

protein	2.5	grams
fat	.3	gram
carbohydrate	4.8	grams
calcium	144	milligrams
phosphorus	36	milligrams
iron	2.8	milligrams
sodium	110	milligrams
potassium	481	milligrams
thiamin	.1	milligram
riboflavin	.22	milligram
niacin	.4	milligram
ascorbic acid	22	milligrams
vitamin A	7,400	international units

Tips on preparing, cooking. There are two things to remember about cooking beets: don't peel them, and give them time. Beets that are peeled bleed their rich, deep red into the cooking water, and the vegetable turns out an unappetizing brownish color. In preparing beets for cooking, wash them carefully so that you don't break the skin, and leave about 2 inches of both root and stem in place. Obviously, they should be cooked whole, not sliced or diced before they go into the pot. Young beets, half-covered with water, will cook in 25 to 30 minutes; old beets may take an hour and a half, or even longer. When they are tender, let them cool a few moments. The skins will then slip off as easily as if they were zippered.

Freezing beets. Properly prepared for freezing (see special feature: PUTTING FOOD BY), beets can be stored 9 to 12 months at 0°F. or below, or for about one month in a refrigerator frozen-food compartment.

Other ways, other forms. Beets, unlike some vegetables, take very kindly to being canned, so if you don't fancy cooking beets yourself, buy them in a can or jar, to serve however you like.

on grocery shelves, in cans or jars: Whole baby beets, sliced or diced or julienned beets; pickled beets; harvard beets.

in grocery frozen-food section: In packages, beets in orange sauce.

Some perfect partners. Young beets, with or without their greens, are delicious simply served with butter, salt, and pepper. (To tell their age, look at their size—the smaller, the younger. Also, young beets are bright and fresh looking, old ones darker in color.) But that is not by any means the end of the matter.

If the beets you buy come with greens attached, save them to use raw in salads if they are very young, or cook whole or—if very old—cut into slivers, with the beets or as a separate vegetable another day. Hot sliced beets can be prepared with a sweet/sour sauce (listed as Harvard Beets in your cookbook). Or sauce them with sour cream, sprinkle with freshly ground pepper or with grated orange peel or with chopped dill. Or thicken the cooking water slightly with cornstarch, season with salt, white pepper, and ample lemon juice and/or horseradish. Or make the sauce of half cooking water, half orange juice. Heat drained whole baby beets in a little butter, sprinkle with sugar—white or brown—and continue to cook until they are glazed.

Beets and the richly red liquid in which they are cooked are the chief ingredient of borscht of several kinds, made with or without meat, served hot or cold with a boiled potato or a dollop of sour cream. Cooked separately so that they will not stain the whole dish red, beets are an integral part of a proper New England Boiled Dinner. Later, they are chopped and combined with the leftover potatoes and corned beef from that dish to make Red Flannel Hash. Cooked beets with apples and onions make a delicious casserole to serve with pork.

Cold pickled beets—always with onions, vinegar, and sugar, sometimes with oil and cloves or allspice—are delicious summer fare, and a must for smörgåsbord. Dress up pickled beets with sour cream for a salad. Sliced beets alternating with thin slices of orange and, sometimes, onion, make a refreshing salad, too. And don't forget the beet juice, seasoned, that is the medium for pickling red beet eggs, perfect on a picnic or with any outdoor summer meal.

Beets deserve more than the short shrift—or none at all —that they are given in many American homes. A little effort combined with seasoning know-how makes them welcomed by even confirmed beet-haters. They lend versatility to meals as a change from vegetables more usually served.

BEIGNETS: see page 451

BEL PAESE: see CHEESE

BELGIAN ENDIVE

Shaped like large, fat cigars, heads of belgian endive (sometimes called witloof) are small and tightly closed, ivory at the root end shading to a delicate yellow-green at the tips of the blades. With a somewhat bitter flavor that is likely to be an acquired taste, belgian endive can add color and zest to mixed green salads (cut the heads across in thick slices, or separate into individual blades). Or the individual blades can be served as part of a selection of crudités, with an appropriate dip, or they may be stuffed, as celery is, with a savory mixture, often cheese-based. Individual blades spread with such a mixture, reassembled into the original head shape and chilled, then cut into thin slices, make a handsome and tasty garnish for meat, fish, or poultry salads.

As a cooked vegetable—the French are particularly fond of it—whole heads of belgian endive are braised (on the top of the stove or in the oven) in a mixture of butter and beef or chicken broth, and served as is or sauced with hollandaise or a well-seasoned sour cream mixture. Or the endive may be layered with a cream sauce, each layer heavily sprinkled with grated sharp cheese, in a casserole.

Largely imported, belgian endive is in the markets from October through May. It is sold by the pound, but you can determine the amount you need by the head—count on a head for two persons in a mixed salad, two or three heads per person, depending on size, to serve as a hot vegetable.

Choose fresh, crisp-looking, tightly closed heads, without blemishes. Store in the refrigerator, in the vegetable crisper or a plastic bag, for no more than 5 days.

Low in calories, belgian endive is a good source of vitamin A and a moderate source of iron.

BELL PEPPERS: see PEPPERS and HERBS AND
  SAVORY SEASONINGS

BERMUDA ONIONS: see ONIONS

BERRY CURRANTS: see CURRANTS

BEURRE: see page 451

BEVERAGES

If your sole purpose is to quench your thirst, you can't beat water as a beverage. But if you have something a bit more interesting in mind, your choice is virtually limitless.

Beverages may be classified under almost any system that comes to mind—hot versus cold, alcoholic versus nonalcoholic, nourishing versus merely thirst-quenching, and so on. And the paraphernalia used in the making/serving/imbibing is so diverse and (some of it at least) so attractive that an entire kitchen and all its wares could be devoted to drinking, without ever getting around to solid food. Glasses alone —and cups and mugs and other drinking vessels—come in all conceivable shapes and sizes, each one "proper" for a specific drink. But unless you plan on opening a bar or an ice cream parlor, such diversity isn't called for. In fact, in this liberated age, you can offer everything potable that you serve in cheese-spread glasses if you don't mind a few raised eyebrows.

For the show-and-tell set. Here is an area, as with television watching, where firm parental guidance is called for. Stores offer a multitude of drinks and drink mixes for the young, fetchingly named and invitingly packaged. Your job is to read the label. If you are horrified at the idea of your child's drinking coffee or tea, some soft drinks contain enough caffeine so that you can be horrified all over again. With youngsters' teeth in mind, check the sugar content—there's little point in having junior brush with cavity-preventive toothpaste only to allow him to flood his teeth with a sugar bath five minutes later. If the drink or mix touts its vitamin content, determine what vitamins and how much. See what the chief ingredient is (if the drink is a liquid, it's probably water, but don't be too upset by that—a great many of the things we eat or drink are largely water), and the second ingredient— they're listed in descending order of quantity. The day is past when something could be put on the market labeled "pure orangeade" that, in truth, had never so much as been formally introduced to an orange. But label reading is still a very worthwhile live-and-learn practice.

For the kids—adults, too, for that matter—homemade is best: a pitcher of orange juice in the refrigerator to which youngsters are allowed free access—as a privilege rather than a duty; milk-and-fruit mixtures, whirled in the blender; a cup of hot bouillon after school in winter; cocoa topped with a marshmallow for a treat on a cold day; home-squeezed orange- or lemon- or limeade, made with club soda if your children love fizz.

A bit of guile can work wonders. Tomato juice in an on-the-rocks glass, with a celery-stick stirrer, is a very grown-up drink. (Some children don't like the acid taste of tomato juice. Temper it with a few grains of sugar. Sugar, in spite of what you may read here and there, isn't all bad if used as a condiment or flavor-enhancer, not as a way of life.) If you get tearful protests that make you feel like a heel because you won't let your youngsters drink the liquid junk that "all the other kids do," call on a little rough-and-ready psychology to support you. "You mean Esmeralda isn't *allowed* to have orange juice? Poor thing!" Or "Lancelot's mommy can't be

69

bothered fixing him a strawberry shake after school? Invite him over—I don't mind fixing two.''

On the other hand, don't push something to which your child has a real antipathy. There's a forty-two-year-old woman living in Cleveland today who still turns green at the sight of an orange. ''Mother made me drink a glass of orange juice every morning. I am probably the only person in the world who was morning sick from kindergarten through high school.''

The joys of growing up. There's coffee, hot or iced—very little is as tempting as iced coffee with cream slowly finding its way down the inside of the glass—and all its au lait and espresso and viennese and capuccino and other variations. And tea, black or green, hot or iced, plain or lemoned or spiced. There are all the leftovers from childhood that are just as good today—hot cocoa and chocolate, hot and cold coffee/chocolate combinations, milk-and-fruit refreshers, homemade ice cream sodas or shakes, fruit ades. There are tomato and tomato-clam and tomato-vegetable juices, clam juice, carrot and celery and sauerkraut and other off-beat juices, nectars of many kinds, pineapple and grapefruit and apple juices, and many more. There is apple cider, and the delicious but less usual ciders made from other fruits, such as cherries or pears. And there are, of course, the ''soft drinks'' that we deplore our children drinking, yet lap up at a great rate ourselves.

Sterner stuff. Unless you are a teetotaler, you probably remember your first alcoholic beverage. If you were lucky, it was wine or a few sips of something stronger, drunk at home under parental eyes, to ease you into sensible drinking habits. Or, if you go back to the days of prohibition, you may remember with loathing the combination of ''near beer'' spiked with medicinal alcohol, or the lethal qualities of bathtub gin.

Many girls taste their first liquor in the form of sloe gin, relying on the persistent myth that if it tastes like a fruit drink or a soda-fountain drink, it can't do you any harm. Indeed, women's lib notwithstanding, there are still a lot of beverages that are thought of as ''lady drinks'' because the liquor—just as much of it as in other cocktails or highballs or whatever —is well disguised. Alexanders—crème de cacao, cream, and brandy—that taste like a rather sprightly chocolate cream, daiquiris (and the banana, strawberry, peach variations), orange blossoms, and pink ladies are some of them. Other ''sneaky'' drinks, their alcoholic content well disguised, are the bloody mary, the screwdriver (these are often served at brunch, because they don't really seem like ''real'' drinks, do they?) and the fruit-salady mixtures so dear to the hearts of cruise-ship bartenders, such as planter's punch and the libations drunk through straws from pineapple or coconut shells.

Two-fisted—and even many one-fisted—drinkers prefer

their liquor less gussied up. But taken straight, or served over ice with plain water or club soda, liquor needs to be of good quality. Poor quality Scotch, gin, rye, bourbon, and brandy need something to cover, or at least cut, their raw, varnish-remover taste.

The tipples of Polite Society. There was once a very strict pecking order for alcoholic beverages, slavishly followed by anybody who was anybody. Cocktails and aperitifs were served before dinner, dry red wines with beef and game, dry white wines with veal, lamb, pork, and poultry, nothing with the salad, sweet wines with dessert or after dessert, brandy and liqueurs with coffee, highballs (for the men—perhaps a little sherry for the ladies?) during the evening when the spirits or the party began to lag. Punch at balls and receptions. Champagne, anytime. Beer, never—except with curries and at picnics or political rallies.

Such strictures have gone the way of high-button shoes, and today we drink what we choose when and where we choose. But there is something to be said for knowing the rules even in their violation, for the same sensible reason that it is impossible successfully to misuse words as a joke unless you first have a firm grip on an extensive vocabulary. The most delightful cream sherry in the world, for example, is a poor pre-dinner choice, simply because it will spoil the appetite and leave a lingering taste, however pleasant, in the mouth and throat to fight with the first course. A mid-evening martini or two will get the dinner guests hungry all over again or send them off to sleep or reeling around with lampshades on their heads, depending on their previous intake. To each his own, moderated by common sense, is today's drinking rule.

More than anything else today, wine is everyone's anytime drink. Although aperitif wines have been with us a long time—dubonnet, byrrh, and the like—plain, lightly chilled dry white wine as an agreeable pre-dinner drink began to catch on only a few years ago, and preprandial red or rosé still occasions what grandma called "a meaningful look." Kir—white wine with a little crème de cassis—serves the same refreshing, not-too-heady purpose. Wines with dinner—once reserved for those everyone else thought of as snobs—and wines after dinner continue to be acceptable companionable drinks, alcoholic enough to thaw stand-offishness, not alcoholic enough to turn the party into a ringading that some may regret, or at least feel sheepish about, later. Cheese and wine parties (see CHEESE) have become a comfortable, not-too-difficult way to entertain. Pleasant customs, all of these.

The bartender at home. It is possible, without much effort, to spend a small fortune on the gadgetry of drinking before ever getting around to footing the booze bill. There are glasses in vast array, shakers and pitchers in great variety, ice buckets of all shapes and sizes, squeezers and cutters and mixers and stirrers without number, containers—many deplorably cutesy—for such drink accessories as cherries, wedges of lemon or lime, strips of citrus peel, olives, pickled onions, and the rest, to say nothing of peanuts, pretzels, and all the other drink go-alongs. Human nature being what it is, social pressure often causes a modest bar cart to be exchanged for a larger wet bar, which in turn leads to remodeling the game room to include a mahogany bar with brass rail, naked-lady backbar art, and stools upholstered in buffalo hide, all in the name of upward mobility.

What such layouts often do not provide, but should, is a drink-mixing manual. Messed-up drinks make for messed-up evenings. There are a number of good manuals available, and everyone who intends to serve liquor to guests on any but the most modest scale should get one and apply himself to it. To result in a really good drink, ingredients must be measured—neither too much nor too little—must be in proper proportion to one another, must be mixed by the accepted method, must incorporate or be served over the right amount of ice, and should be garnished agreeably if garnish is called for. None of this is difficult and all of it results in the kind of drink that makes people say, "Joe serves the best booze in town"—glorious accolade for one who sets his sights on cut-velvet bar stools when the buffalo hide ones wear out. See also ALE, BEER, CIDER, CLUB SODA, COCKTAILS, COFFEE, COLA, FLOATS, LEMONADE, LIQUEURS, LIQUORS, MILK, NECTAR, ORGEAT, SARSAPARILLA, SOFT DRINKS, TEA, and WINE.

BIBB LETTUCE: see SALAD GREENS
AND PLANTS

BICARBONATE OF SODA: see BAKING
SODA

BIND, TO: see page 444

BISCUIT MIXES

This is one of the earlier of the hundreds of convenience foods that have proliferated in this generation. A great many baked foods can be made with biscuit mix as a base—biscuits, of course, and dumplings, shortcake, simple snack-type cakes, pancakes and waffles, quick breads, coffeecakes, and so on. In fact, the maker of the mix in widest distribution offers a cookbook containing more than two hundred biscuit-mix recipes.

The chief advantage of convenience foods is ease of preparation. Another point in their favor is that they may contain ingredients that the average home cook doesn't store in her kitchen and/or doesn't want to buy in quantity because she may not use them again before they deteriorate from age.

In spite of its wide popularity, neither of these two important points is true of biscuit mix. It is almost as easy—and as quick—to measure and combine the ingredients from scratch as it is to measure and use the biscuit mix. And the ingredients—flour, shortening, leavening, salt, and, in the case of some mixes, dried milk—are available in most kitchens in which any amount of baking is done. (Liquid milk, from the container, can be substituted for the dried milk when baking from scratch, although many kitchens these days use dried milk regularly for both drinking and cooking.) The total cost of those ingredients, when baking from scratch, is less than that of a comparable amount of biscuit mix.

Nevertheless, many households swear by biscuit mix. Part of this is psychological—inexperienced or inept cooks feel that through some magic the foods they bake with a mix will turn out better than if they measured and combined the ingredients themselves—although there is nothing that can be made of biscuit mix alone, without adding, at the very least, water. In the case of even very simple foods—pancakes, for instance—milk, eggs, and often sugar must be added to the mix to make an acceptable product.

If you're addicted to biscuit mix, you might like to try assembling your own. In a large mixing bowl, combine 10 cups of all-purpose flour, 1 tablespoon of salt, ½ cup of baking powder and, if you wish, ¼ cup of sugar. Measure 2 cups of shortening—the type that does not require refrigeration—and cut into the dry ingredients with a pastry blender or two knives until the mixture resembles coarse meal. Store, covered, at room temperature—it will keep about 6 weeks.

Even for the cook who is not intimidated by the thought of whipping up a batch of from-scratch biscuits, this mix or the commercial kind can be useful on occasion—camping trips, visits to summer cottages—when it's expedient to take along as few separate items as possible.

BISCUITS

Biscuits are soda- or baking powder-leavened quick breads, (similar small yeast breads are buns or rolls) generally round but sometimes square, and now and then somewhat lop-sided because the cook has taken a shortcut and made drop biscuits rather than cutting out the dough. Baked in a hot oven they puff up high, have crisp sides if they've been placed on the baking sheet with space between them, soft sides if they've baked huddled together. They are—or should be—flaky within. Serve hot, then split and toast the leftovers, if there are any, for another meal.

Easy to make and quick to bake, biscuits have all sorts of uses. At breakfast or brunch (once breakfast wasn't worthy of the name without a pan of biscuits), hustle them to the table, split and butter while they're still steaming, and serve with honey, jam or jelly or preserves. An old-fashioned dish that deserves greater current popularity is fricasseed chicken and biscuits: the hot biscuits are split and spread on a platter, some of the gravy is dribbled over them, the chicken is placed on top, and extra gravy is brought to the table. Split, buttered, slathered with sweetened strawberries between and on top and drenched with thick cream, biscuits make a most superior shortcake. However and whenever you serve them, you aren't likely to find anyone who says "No, thanks," to fresh, hot biscuits.

Water biscuits and beaten biscuits are two of the South's innumerable culinary claims to fame. The former are hard, with a ring of shiny brown mounds around their top edges and a depression in the center just right for a good dab of jam or peanut butter. Beaten biscuits are small, not browned, and bear neat fork-pricks in their tops. They take their name from one of the preparation steps—they are literally beaten, not in a bowl but on a board. Any handy instrument, such as a mallet, can be used. (One recipe suggests the flat side of an ax.) Twenty minutes to an hour is a proper beating time—reflecting long gone days of gracious living, when not only did the lady of the house have a cook, but the cook had helpers to spell her in her more arduous tasks. Split and sandwiched with a sliver of sharp, salty Virginia-style ham, beaten biscuits were often a feature of buffets and hunt breakfasts.

If you are not in any way a home baker, help is at hand. In the refrigerated case at the supermarket you'll find biscuits of various kinds, packed in tubes. All you need do is put them on a baking sheet and bake them. Bakeries, too, often make biscuits, but they cannot be served hot from the oven as can your homemade ones, or the home-baked ones from the supermarket. Be sure to check the metal top of the tube in which the biscuits are packed. It's dated—don't buy the biscuits if the date has passed, or if you cannot use them by the specified time. See also BREADS and REFRIGERATED DOUGH.

BISQUE: see page 451

BITTERS

Generally a bar item, bitters are a liquid (with, not surprisingly, a bitter taste) usually based on spirits of some sort and flavored with herbs, barks, roots, fruits and/or other aromatics, and distilled. Strong and pungent, a little usually goes a long way, most often as a flavoring agent, although some kinds of bitters are used—usually diluted with water, and sometimes sweetened—as a digestive.

Bitters are a mandatory ingredient in the old fashioned cocktail, and are used in many other kinds of drinks to add flavor and mellowness. Manufactured from "secret" formulas, bitters are made by several companies, one of which issues a small cookbook suggesting many uses other than the usual liquor-oriented ones for their product.

BLACK BEANS: see BEANS

BLACK PEPPER: see HERBS AND
  SAVORY SEASONINGS

BLACK RASPBERRIES: see RASPBERRIES

BLACK TEA: see TEA

BLACK WALNUTS: see WALNUTS

BLACKBERRIES

The blackberry looks as if it were made up of many small, round, purple-black globes—each contains a small seed—clustered into a cone-shaped whole. Once they grew wild, so prolifically that in some places they were considered a nuisance and weeded out. But now, to meet the demand, they are cultivated, although not nearly as many blackberries come to market as the more favored raspberries, strawberries, and blueberries.

BLACKBERRIES IN YOUR KITCHEN

The season begins in May and continues through August, but in few places is there a plentiful supply available throughout the season. Blackberries seem to suffer from the problem expressed by the little boy who, when asked if he liked prunes, answered, "Oh, I love them—but not very much."

how to buy: Select dark, fresh-looking berries of uniform color. Inspect the bottom as well as the top of the container for stains that indicate deterioration.

how to store: Sort the berries, discarding soft ones—like the one bad apple in the barrel, the soft berry will contaminate all the rest. Store, unwashed, lightly covered, in the refrigerator for no more than 2 days.

nutritional value: Not rich in nutrients, blackberries do contain appreciable amounts of vitamins A and C, and traces of some of the B vitamins. A cup of raw blackberries contains about 85 calories, about 18 grams of carbohydrate.

Tips on preparing, cooking. Wash berries just before using. Serve with cream and sugar for dessert or as a breakfast fruit, or add to fruit salads or cups. Use in pie, cobbler, roly-poly—any of the good, down-home-type desserts.

Freezing blackberries. Properly prepared (see special feature: PUTTING FOOD BY), blackberries can be frozen with or without sugar and stored up to a year at 0°F. or below.

Other ways, other forms. Canned blackberries—these are sweetened—and frozen ones, both sweetened and unsweetened, in packages or larger plastic bags, are available in most large markets. So are blackberry preserves, jams, and jellies.

BLACK-EYED PEAS: see BEANS

BLACKSTRAP MOLASSES

Food faddists to the contrary, blackstrap molasses is not the universal panacea many people would like to believe it to be. It is, however, fractionally richer in iron, calcium, and phosphorus than the lighter molasses, fractionally less rich in B vitamins of which, in any case, there are only very small amounts. All molasses is the product of the various boilings of sugarcane which eventually result in cane sugar. Blackstrap is the residue of the final boiling, and contains all the ash, gum, and other (indigestible) leftovers of the sugarcane. Thick and black, it is very bitter—definitely an acquired taste which there seems to be very little valid reason to acquire. See also MOLASSES.

BLANCH, TO: see page 444

BLANQUETTE: see page 451

BLENDERS: see special feature: YOU CAN'T WORK WITHOUT TOOLS

BLEU CHEESE: see CHEESE

BLINTZES

A small oblong or round of batter, griddle-baked, and rolled to enclose a cheese or fruit filling—one of the joys of Jewish cookery. Usually served with sour cream and/or applesauce. Cheese blintzes, with sour cream and strawberry preserve, make a delightful brunch dish.

BLOOD ORANGES: see ORANGES

BLUE CHEESE: see CHEESE

BLUEBERRIES

Picking blueberries is one of those delightful pastimes recalled with sweet sorrow by those nostalgia buffs who prefer the good old days to the good new ones. (They tend to forget the sunburn, the bugs, and sundry other attendant inconveniences.) Pie made from those hand-picked berries grows sweeter, juicier, tastier, in all ways more memorable with each passing year.

Wild blueberries are very small compared to the cultivated variety, and have a somewhat different taste—not surprising, because the commercially grown blueberry is a development of the wild huckleberry, which grows in swampy regions, often closely associated with cranberries.

The terms "blueberry" and "huckleberry" are used interchangeably by many people, and there is a marked resemblance between them, but the blueberry has many tiny seeds, the huckleberry ten larger, harder ones. To further confuse things, our British cousins (and some foreign cookbooks you may encounter) call blueberries "bilberries" or "whortleberries." Although blueberries grow wild in a variety of climates, the cultivated ones you buy in the market are likely to have been grown in New Jersey, North Carolina, or Michigan.

You can, if you wish, cultivate blueberry bushes in a backyard garden almost anywhere in the United States. Cautionary note: You'll have to fight the birds for the fruit every inch of the way—the berry is a favorite food of many species.

BLUEBERRIES IN YOUR KITCHEN

You'll find blueberries in the market at the end of May, and they will continue to be available into early September, but the peak season is June, July, and August.

how to buy: As always in choosing berries, look at the bottom of the container as well as the top, keeping a sharp eye out for damp and/or stained spots that indicate spoilage. Smell them, too—fresh berries smell clean and earthy without any odor of incipient rot. Choose fresh-looking, dark blue, unwrinkled berries that are fairly uniform in size. The silvery powder on the berry's plump cheek is natural bloom, a protective coating.

how to store: In the refrigerator, unwashed, in the original container if you're going to use them soon, or spread out on a flat surface—again, unwashed and covered—if you plan to keep the berries for two or three days, no more.

nutritive value: A cup of raw blueberries contains about 90 calories, about 22 grams of carbohydrate, small amounts of vitamins A and C, even smaller amounts of several of the B vitamins.

Tips on preparing, cooking. Pick over and wash blueberries just before you are going to use them. Serve with sweet or sour cream and a little white or brown sugar—they are sweeter than many other berries—for dessert or as a breakfast fruit (excellent with cereal), or add to fruit salads and cups, or use in any number of delightful cooked dishes.

Blueberry muffins are a Sunday brunch treat; blueberry scones are just as delicious and a bit more unusual. Blueberry pie is beloved of almost everyone, nostalgia buff or not. The berries have a place in a number of wonderful old-fashioned desserts—blueberry slump, blueberry buckle, blueberry fool are among them.

Freezing blueberries. The berries can be satisfactorily frozen with or without sugar, and can be stored at 0°F. or below for about a year, if properly prepared. (See special feature: PUTTING FOOD BY.) Use in any way that you would use fresh berries.

Other ways, other forms. Blueberries are available canned (these are sweetened) and frozen (sweetened or not) in packages and in larger plastic bags. Less widely available is blueberry syrup, great as an ice cream sauce—unless the color puts you off—and on pancakes and waffles. There are also blueberry jams and preserves in the market.

BLUTWURST: see SAUSAGES

BOAR: see GAME

BOCKWURST: see SAUSAGES

BOEUF: see page 451

BOIL, TO: see page 449

BOILED DRESSING: see SALAD DRESSINGS

BOLOGNA: see SAUSAGES

BOMBES

A frozen dessert, bi- or tri-colored and flavored—the sort of culinary triumph that looks and tastes as if you'd labored over it, but actually is quite simple to prepare if you use commercial ice cream and sherbet.

Start, at least eight hours before you will serve the dessert, with high-quality, well-flavored ice cream. One flavor of ice cream and one of sherbet—perhaps chocolate ice cream and orange sherbet—make a simple but handsome bombe. (Be sure the flavors and the colors you choose go well together.) Place a 1½-quart mixing bowl, preferably metal, lined with wax paper or foil, in the freezer to chill. Slightly soften a quart of ice cream. Working quickly, spread the ice cream along the sides (inside, naturally) and bottom of the bowl; return to the freezer until the ice cream is hard again. Fill the center with sherbet. Cover the top of the bowl with wax paper or foil, pressed close to the contents. Freeze until firm. When ready to serve, invert the bowl over a serving dish, and shake out the contents. It may be necessary to place a cloth wrung out of hot water on the bottom of the bowl for a moment or two. Peel off the paper, garnish the bombe appropriately, and bring to the table with pride. Cut in wedges. If you wish to gild your lily, frost all over with whipped cream

before serving and/or pass a sauce—chocolate, butterscotch, a fruit mixture—and let guests help themselves.

BONE, TO: see page 444

BONING: see special feature: CARVING, BONING, AND OTHER KITCHEN TECHNIQUES

BORSCHT: see page 451

BOSTON LETTUCE: see SALAD GREENS AND PLANTS

BOTTOM ROUND: see BEEF

BOUILLABAISSE: see page 451

BOUILLON

Dear to the hearts of weight-loss dieters, bouillon—clear, largely defatted soup based on meat, fish, poultry, or vegetables—is a great deal more than a guilt-free supplement to a sparse meal. Usually a by-product of other cooking (the name comes from the French word for "boil"), bouillon was once, in the days of the back-of-the-stove stockpot, readily available to use as a plain soup, to be suitably added to or garnished, or to employ in cooking to enrich gravies, make sauces, and braise meats. Even though—in this country at least—the stockpot has vanished along with the cook who kept it going, bouillon can still be made at home, or it can be conveniently obtained by opening a can or by dissolving a cube or powder in boiling water.

Homemade bouillon is an excellent way of using up scraps and bones of meat or poultry not sufficient for a meal but too good to throw away. Long and slow cooking is the secret. Put bones and scraps, along with whatever flavoring vegetables you have on hand—onion, carrot, snips of parsley, celery—to cook in water, simmering for at least three hours. The water in which vegetables were cooked is a fine addition, and so are the leftover vegetables accumulated from several dinners. A bay leaf adds good flavor to beef, a pinch of thyme if the scraps are from poultry, rosemary or marjoram if lamb. Season to taste with salt and pepper a half hour before you plan on taking the bouillon off the stove. When done, fish out the bones and put the rest through a strainer, pressing with the back of a wooden spoon so that all the good essence of meat and vegetables goes through. Refrigerate, discard the fat that will rise to the top when the soup is chilled, and it is ready to use as you wish.

Isn't what you have made broth? Or consommé? Yes, it is. The three terms are used interchangeably now, although consommé is usually thought of as being more concentrated—more "cooked down"—than broth, and is clarified.

If you would like to turn your homemade bouillon to consommé, you must clarify it, a process that involves cooking strong defatted bouillon with egg whites and egg shells, then straining it through cheesecloth. (Consult a good general cookbook for step-by-step directions.) To further dress it up, bake an unsweetened egg custard in a thin sheet, cut it into attractive small shapes to float on top of the consommé, and you have produced Consommé Royale, as served in the best restaurants.

On the other hand, if the idea of all this kitchen work makes you a little ill, have recourse to canned, cubed, granulated, or powdered bouillon, which you'll find in quantity under various brand names in your market. Some of these taste, when reconstituted, very much like the good homemade version, while others resemble nothing you'd care to have in your kitchen. Sample various brands, and be choosy.

BOUQUET GARNI

This is a tied-together collection—called a faggot, meaning "bundle"—of flavoring agents for long-cooking dishes such as stews, casseroles, and soups. The point of tying these things together is that they can be neatly and easily taken out and discarded at the end of the cooking process.

The simplest bouquet garni consists of a few sprigs of parsley tied together to be used in a concoction where parsley flavor is wanted but bits of parsley throughout are not desirable. A somewhat more subtle, but still simple bouquet combines parsley, bay leaf, and thyme. All sorts of herbs—tarragon, chervil, basil, savory, rosemary, marjoram, and many others—can be used, alone or in combination with vegetables such as chives, leeks, and celery. In fact, two stalks of celery or a split leek can serve as the outer casing of a faggot, with herbs tied securely within. Use ordinary white kitchen twine to hold the bundle together, tying in several places.

If dried herbs and/or other flavorings, such as garlic, orange or lemon peel, and peppercorns are used, the bouquet is usually placed in a square of cheesecloth, the ends gathered together and tied into a neat little bag so that the small bits of flavoring don't disperse themselves through the liquid. The bag is easy to remove when the dish is ready to be served.

BOURBON: see LIQUORS

BOYSENBERRIES

Would you believe an empire built on a berry? Well, if not exactly an empire, a very large, very profitable family business that provides food, fun, and entertainment for millions of visitors every year as well as an extensive line of food products to be found in quality stores throughout the country?

Knott's Berry Farm is the seat of the "empire," Cordelia and Walter Knott and their second- and third-generation descendants the family that brought the boysenberry to the attention of a world of fruit lovers.

The Knotts planted their first berries on rented land in Buena Park, California, and later bought the land and continued to raise various kinds of berries at a modest profit, augmented by sales of Cordelia's homemade candy and berry pies and jams and, later, her chicken dinners. During the difficult years of the depression, Walter Knott heard of a man named Rudolph Boysen, who had crossed the loganberry, the blackberry, and the red raspberry to produce a new fruit. Apparently berry connoisseurs had not beaten a path to Boysen's door because, Knott discovered, the few boysenberry plants had been left in an orange orchard that Boysen had sold. Knott located them, got permission to cultivate them, and three years later had them ready to present to a welcoming public, and the boysenberry empire was on its way.

BOYSENBERRIES IN YOUR KITCHEN

Today, according to the Knotts, boysenberries are grown in many parts of the United States, and in fifteen foreign countries. They are delicious, combining the flavors of the parent berries with more of the raspberry than of the other two, and are very handsome and reasonably sturdy—not nearly so delicate as raspberries, for example.

how to buy: Look for firm, uniformly colored, fresh-looking berries in unstained boxes. Although boysenberries are widely grown, they do not come into the market in any great supply, even in those areas—such as California—where they are well known and liked.

how to store: In their original container, covered, in the refrigerator, if you are going to use them very soon. Otherwise, sort and discard soft berries; store the remainder, spread out and covered, in the refrigerator.

nutritive value: A cup of raw boysenberries contains 88 calories, about 22 grams of carbohydrate, yields modest amounts of vitamins A and C, and small amounts of B vitamins and minerals.

Tips on preparing, cooking. Wash just before using. Serve raw with cream and sugar for dessert or, alone or with cereal, as a breakfast fruit. Or add to fruit salads and cups. In cooking, any recipe that calls for blackberries can be used with boysenberries instead—jams and jellies, pies, cobblers, and other desserts.

Freezing boysenberries. Properly prepared (see special feature: PUTTING FOOD BY), boysenberries can be frozen with or without sugar, stored at 0°F. or lower up to 1 year.

Other ways, other forms. Canned and frozen boysenberries are available throughout the country, although in a somewhat limited supply. Boysenberry preserves, jams and jellies, and (limited) syrup are for sale in many markets, and can also be mail-ordered from the boysenberry originators.

BRAINS: see VARIETY MEATS

BRAISE, TO: see page 449

BRAN

The coarse, brown outer layer of a kernel of grain, bran is removed during the milling process when a white flour is the desired result. The bran crumbles into particles larger than the flour, and is bolted out—sifted through a fine-meshed cloth. The thin, papery bran is made into breakfast foods of various sorts, alone or in combination with other cereals, or into FLOUR, or is used as fodder for animals.

Whole wheat and graham flour are made with the entire wheat kernel, including the bran. Bran breads and muffins contain relatively large amounts of bran, in combination with white or whole wheat flour and other ingredients. Ready-to-eat cereals may be all bran, or bran combined with parts of other grains.

Various bran products differ in nutritive value, but all are high in carbohydrate and contain some protein and minerals. Most are processed to retain B vitamin content, or the vitamins are restored, and vitamin A, which does not occur naturally in bran, is added.

Miller's bran—that which is left when flour is bolted—began to sell at gold-rush rates (and, in some instances, prices) when, in 1976, the theory that "roughage" was required in the human diet—a fact grandma had known all along—was reiterated by a well-known doctor and supported by many experts in nutrition. The food fiber boom moved miller's bran from the natural-food stores on whose shelves it had languished to supermarkets, where it sold for a while as if going out of style. (See also FIBER.)

Too much bran, as with any good thing, can be a disaster. Mostly cellulose, bran has a laxative effect, and in large quantities can make you sick, because it acts as an irritant to the digestive and excretory systems. Moderation is called for, especially in feeding bran to children.

BRANDY: see LIQUORS

BRANDY EXTRACT: see FLAVORING EXTRACTS

BRATWURST: see SAUSAGES

BRAUNSCHWEIGER: see SAUSAGES

BRAZIL NUTS

If you could visit brazil nuts on the Amazon river in their native country, you'd find that they grow in a large, woody outer shell inside of which a number of individual nuts are neatly fitted together, rather like the segments of an orange, each segment encased in its own triangular hard brown shell. Inside, further protected by a thin but resistant skin, lies the oily white nutmeat with its rich, delicious flavor.

In buying brazil nuts, look for unblemished shells. Shake them—if they rattle, the meat is dry and undesirable. A pound of nuts in the shell will yield roughly a half pound, or 1½ cups, of kernels. Store tightly covered in a cool place, preferably the refrigerator, where they will keep up to 12 months, or the freezer, where they may be stored up to 2 years.

Brazil nuts resist shelling, and they seldom can be found already shelled. To help things along, put the nuts in a saucepan, cover with cold water, bring to a boil, and boil 3 minutes. Cover again with cold water, let stand 1 minute, and drain. After this treatment they should shell easily—or, at least, a great deal more easily than untreated nuts. Or freeze the nuts for several hours and then shell them.

You also need special know-how to slice or sliver the nuts as specified in recipes. Once again, place the shelled nuts in a pan, cover with cold water, and bring to a boil. In this case, reduce the heat and simmer 3 minutes. Now they'll be amenable to being sliced with a sharp knife or to being cut into curls with a swivel vegetable peeler.

One ounce of brazil nuts—3 to 3½ individual nuts—contains 89 calories, nearly 2 grams of protein, a little over 9 grams of fat, and measurable amounts of the B vitamins.

Use brazil nuts in candies, fruit cakes, cookies, to stuff dates or prunes (roll the finished product in granulated sugar and you have produced those sugarplums famous in Christmas song and story), and to add texture and flavor to sauces and main dishes. Ground, brazil nuts substitute for all or part of the flour in some recipes.

BREAD, TO: see page 444

BREAD CRUMBS: see CRUMBS

BREADFRUIT: see EXOTIC FRUIT

BREADS

Once, if Mom sent you to the store for a loaf of bread, you came home with an oblong of spongy, doughy material without substance. It was white or whole wheat, or, if you were lucky, it was rye—not quite so spongy and doughy, but not much to brag about. That was all the grocery store had to offer. If you wanted better bread, you went to a bakery—and you had to search out a good one—or you made bread at home.

Things have improved considerably at the supermarket —at the bakery, too—since those days, and all sorts of staff-of-life firsts have been marked along the way. (Brown-and-serve rolls, frozen bread doughs, to name just two.) Now, if you go to the store for bread, you can come home with a loaf of almost any kind that suits your taste. If you want white, you can buy a dense-crumbed loaf that resembles homemade, or an egg braid, or a long baguette of french, or a crusty italian, or a seed-topped vienna, or a dozen others. (Or you can still buy the doughy white sponge, if you—or your children—happen to like it.) There's also whole wheat, and now it's good —often made with honey—and there's cracked wheat, sprouted wheat, and many other combinations as well. There's rye, dark and light, with and without seeds, or good swedish rye with a touch of orange-peel flavor. There's corn-meal bread, oatmeal bread, dark and hearty pumpernickel, sourdough, fruit breads and cheese breads and herb breads and nut breads, and dozens of others, to say nothing of an assortment of rolls, buns, danish, coffeecakes, and sweet rolls as far as the eye can see.

On the home front.
In spite of the vast variety available to the bread fancier, home cooks all over America have rolled up their sleeves and begun to bake bread. Why, when there's such an incredible bounty available in stores and bakeries? When you can buy whatever bread you could possibly want? Because many people object to the additives incorporated into commercial bread to give it a longer life, keep it from staling and molding. Because nothing tastes quite so wonderful as home-baked bread fresh from the oven. Because nothing can equal, or even approach, the heady aroma of baking bread. But also, most important, because baking bread is an experience for the baker quite different from that attendant on any other cooking—more satisfying, more creative. Making bread at home is a kind of therapy. Yeast, unlike most of the ingredients with which we cook, is a living organism. Like every living thing it must be approached respectfully, handled thoughtfully. In order to grow it needs loving care, and in order to make it grow, the home baker must be lovingly careful.

There's a kind of interpersonal relationship that arises between bread and the baker far superior to that engendered by any other household task, not only because the dough is alive but also because it requires contact—in the kneading and shaping—closer than that called for by any other form of cooking.

The super self.
There's an ego trip in baking bread, and something a little awe-inspiring about your first try. You assemble the ingredients carefully, controlling temperature so that the yeast is neither under- nor over-stimulated. You knead the dough, feeling the elastic life under your hands, feeling the change in texture, feeling the strength in it. You set it to rise, and you must wait until it is ready for you, not you ready for it. Then you punch it down, shape it, put it in its pan and set it to rise again, enjoying the miracle of the yeast's aliveness once more. You bake it, turn it out, thump its backside to be sure it's done (it is if it sounds hollow), and butter its top for a tender crust. And then—well, if you have any pride about you, you call the family to taste this miracle you've wrought while it's still a fresh, new miracle. But proba-

bly you won't have to call. They'll be assembled and waiting, looking wistfully hopeful, drawn to the kitchen by the irresistible aroma. (You may even have drawn a few neighbors, possibly a stranger or two off the street.) Bring out the butter, open a jar of preserves. Be smug. You deserve it. You have mastered a living force.

Backing up a bit.
Baking bread has been a function of the homemaker since we stopped eating our food raw. Certainly, bread was the first "made" food—a mixture of pounded seeds and water, shaped into a cake, baked on a rock. Since that first creative cook thought up the idea, we've been following her example, with flat, unleavened cakes, and then, when the action of yeast was finally understood and so possible to control, fine, high loaves of leavened bread.

As it was in those first days, bread is still the staff of life, a part of each day's—generally, each meal's—provender. Now, once again, whether you bake your own or buy from the store or the bakery, you can have good, substantial loaves of bread in great variety, to satisfy the bread-hunger we all have.

The ingredients and the know-how.
If you want to bake your own bread—and once you've tried it, you'll swear by it—there are a few basics you will need to know, a few rules to understand.

flour: Almost all breads contain at least some white flour. There are special bread flours on the market, extra high in gluten, but recipes in most cookbooks are tailored to the use of all-purpose flour. (A recipe that is not will warn you—a good reason for reading recipes through well in advance of starting to work.) Also available are whole wheat, graham, and rye flours of various kinds. Again, read the recipe to be sure you have on hand what you will need for the loaf you want to bake.

If you buy special flour—whole wheat, for example—in a larger quantity than you will use up in a short time, store it in the freezer.

yeast: There are two kinds, dry granular and compressed. The granular yeast comes in small packages, each holding ¼ ounce, or in jars for those who do a good deal of baking. Compressed yeast comes foil-wrapped in small ⅝-ounce cakes; the cake is the equivalent of the package of dry yeast in that the two may be interchanged in recipes. Store granular yeast on the cupboard shelf, where it will keep for several months, but be sure to use it before the expiration date stamped on the package. Compressed yeast is much more

perishable; it must be stored in the refrigerator, where it will keep 1 to 2 weeks. Preferably, buy it fresh shortly before using.

If you have reason to suspect your yeast is not fresh, test it by adding ½ teaspoon of sugar when you stir it into warm water to dissolve it. After about ten minutes the mixture should be foaming and bubbling, and you'll know that the yeast is alive and ready to do its job. If it just sits there, sulking, don't use it—it won't raise the dough and you'll waste a whole batch of ingredients as well as your time and effort.

Dissolve active dry yeast in warm liquid, 105 to 115°F. Liquid of this temperature will feel comfortably warm on the inside of your wrist, a somewhat chancy way of determining temperature. If you're going to do any amount of baking, invest in a thermometer—it's much more accurate than your wrist, and the temperature is critical. Compressed yeast should be dissolved at 95°F., which is virtually blood temperature, so the liquid should feel neither warm nor cool on the inside of your wrist.

Whichever yeast you use, you must supply warmth so that the living plant will grow. As it grows, it forms a gas that leavens the mixture. This is a continuous action that requires a framework capable of holding the gas over a period of time. The gluten in the flour provides that framework, holding the gas in tiny pockets throughout the dough.

kneading: Kneading is mixing and blending the bread ingredients after the first bowl-and-spoon or electric mixer blending, when the dough becomes too stiff to use anything but those very best of kitchen tools, your hands. If you must, you can use a dough hook (an attachment available for heavy-duty electric mixers) or a dough maker (a tub with a crank fixed in its cover) to do your kneading with virtually no effort on your part. But if you do, you'll be missing a real joy, the high point of bread-making. Kneading is one-on-one contact between you and the living bread. You make friends with it. If you knead it well—and with patience, love, and empathy—the bread will rise magnificently for you, and bake up into handsome, richly scented loaves of excellent flavor and admirable texture.

To knead, turn the dough out on a lightly floured pastry cloth or board. Flour your hands lightly, too. With your fingers, pick up the part of the dough farthest away and fold it toward you. With the heels of your hands, push down and away from you. Give the dough a quarter turn and repeat. Keep kneading and turning until the dough is smooth and elastic, with little blisters on its surface. This will take somewhere in the neighborhood of ten minutes.

rising: Use a buttered bowl large enough to accommodate about three times as much as the quantity of dough. Place the dough in and turn it over so that all sides will be buttered. This keeps the dough from drying out on top as it rises. Cover with a clean dish towel or other cloth.

A room temperature of about 85° is just right for perfect rising. However, most kitchens aren't that hot—and if they are, the cook is pretty uncomfortable and may well be getting a bit crotchety. The solution is to let the bread rise in an unheated oven. Position the bowl on one shelf and on the shelf below place a large pan of very hot water. Close the oven door and let nature take its course. Most bread doughs require about one hour for their first rising. If you prefer, place the dough bowl inside a larger one partially filled with warm water, and place it where no drafts will reach it.

"double in bulk": This means just what it says. Rising should be allowed to continue until the dough is roughly twice the size it was when you set it to rise. This is true of both the first rising and the second, after you have shaped the dough. In both cases, be sure the rising takes place with the dough covered and in a place that is free from drafts. Yeast dough is touchy—if it feels a chill wind it will crouch sulkily in the bowl or pan and refuse to grow.

punching down: How do you know when the dough is sufficiently risen? Stick two fingers firmly into it. If the dough springs back only a little, leaving a definite indentation, it is ready. Still firmly—but not aggressively, unless you have hostilities to work off—push down on the dough with your closed fist, all over, until it gives up and is not much greater in bulk than it was when you set it to rise.

shaping: Follow individual recipe directions. Breads are made in many shapes other than the conventional loaf. For example, three long, thin ropes of dough are literally braided, like old-fashioned girls' pigtails, to form a braid loaf or coffee ring. Cloverleaf rolls are shaped by placing three small balls of dough in each well of a muffin pan. Cinnamon rolls are formed by rolling the dough into a sheet, spreading with butter, and sprinkling with cinnamon and sugar (and nuts and/or raisins, in some cases). The dough is then rolled up jelly-roll fashion, sliced, and the slices placed on a baking sheet for their second rising. There are many, many different shapes into which dough can be formed, none hard to do.

Other days, other ways. One of the bread-making drawbacks, many cooks feel, is that when you make bread you must be on hand to cosset the dough every inch of the way. True, you can do other things while it rises. But when the dough is ready, you must be ready, too, both to prepare and shape it for the second rising, and to bake it when that rising is completed.

To get around these problems, various preparation methods other than the conventional one have been devised, as follows:

the CoolRise way: One of the yeast manufacturers developed this bread-making technique, which incorporates some shortcuts and calls for the second rising to take place in the refrigerator. By this method, the bread or rolls or whatever can be baked when you are ready instead of when they are.

To begin with, the undissolved yeast is combined with sugar, salt, and a portion of the flour. Hot tap water—along with some other ingredients the recipe may call for, such as butter or molasses—is added, and the resulting paste beaten with the electric mixer, and the remaining flour added. The dough is kneaded, "rested" for a short time (this takes the place of the first rising in these breads), shaped, and placed in the pan. It is then refrigerated from 2 to 24 hours, to be baked at the cook's convenience. Don't attempt to adapt your own recipes to this method—you must use recipes especially developed for the CoolRise way of doing things.

batter breads: If you decide that kneading is not your thing —you'll be missing a lot, but that's your problem—you can make batter breads, which are beaten but not kneaded. Specially developed recipes are required for these, too—any good cookbook can provide them. Batter breads are more open, almost lacy, in texture. They do not keep as well as kneaded bread, and should be eaten when freshly baked, at which point they are delicious.

no-yeast breads: If bread in a hurry is your aim—no kneading, no rising—you can make one of the many delicious breads leavened with baking powder or soda or a combination of the two. See QUICK BREADS.

don't-make, do-bake breads: The refrigerated and frozen foods cases at the supermarket are loaded with good breads that ask no more of you than removing them from their containers and baking according to label directions. There are frozen white and whole wheat loaves, and various kinds of sweet or savory buns and rolls available. Refrigerated, in tubes, you'll find a number of good sweet, danish-type breakfast or snack rolls, as well as biscuits, crescent rolls, and several others. The frozen-foods case offers a wide variety of coffeecakes and sweet rolls, many of them fruited or nutted, as well as dinner rolls, parkerhouse, and others. These are already baked and need only heating.

There are also available packaged bread mixes of various kinds, in which the ingredients are all assembled and measured for you. Your task is to add liquid (sometimes eggs, as well), pour into the pan, and bake. These are mostly quick-bread types, and you'll find muffin mixes of various sorts, sweet bread mixes (fruited, and/or with nuts), coffeecakes, corn breads, biscuits, popovers. And they're easy to make— even the most slam-bam-thank-you-ma'm cook can cope with them.

Hot roll mix is also available. This requires a bit more tender loving care, but not a great deal. Follow the package instructions for hot rolls or one of a number of delicious variations. In fact, if you have never made bread and would like to try, but are timid, buy a package of hot roll mix. Follow the directions faithfully, and you'll be delightfully surprised. Who knows where such a step may lead? In a few months, you could be producing your own pumpernickel!

A choice of crusts. To many people, the crust is the best part of the loaf. When you bake bread at home, you can treat the top crust in one of several ways to bring it to what your taste considers perfection.

very crisp crust: Brush the tops of loaves with plain water before baking. If you wish a heavily crisp, resistant crust—as on french or italian bread—brush with water before baking and also several times, after the first 15 minutes, during the baking period.

soft, tender crust: After you take the loaves from the oven, brush with soft butter or shortening, cover the loaves with a towel until they are cool.

highly glazed crust: Brush before baking with dorure—the yolk of an egg beaten with a tablespoon of water. This is the "baker's varnish" that gives a high, glistening shine to much of the baked goods made by professionals.

naturally crisp crust: Don't brush the loaf with anything, before or after baking; simply let it cool, uncovered, at room temperature.

Storing your own or bakers' bread. Homemade bread has a way of disappearing rapidly. But if there's any left, store it—this goes for bakers' bread, too—well wrapped, at room temperature, in a cool, dry area of the kitchen. Storage in the refrigerator defeats freshness. True, refrigerated bread will not mold, but it stales more rapidly than that stored in a cool, dry place.

For longer storage, use the freezer. Home bakers often double or triple their bread recipes, resulting in loaves to stash in the freezer and produce when needed. Wrap tightly in freezer paper or heavy-duty foil and store at 0°F. or below. Bread will retain its moisture and delicacy, and remain mold free, for about two months. If you're a small family, slice bread and package in several-slice quantities. To thaw, place the wrapped bread in a 350°F. oven for 45 minutes for a whole loaf. Thaw individual slices in your toaster if you're in a hurry.

There is no great mystery to baking bread. If you can read, if you have the patience to follow a recipe carefully, you too can know the satisfaction and fulfillment of home baking, the pride of serving your homemade bread while listening, with a modest blush and downcast eyes, to the mighty chorus of huzzahs that will greet its appearance.

Use-it-up ideas for leftover bread. Unless you have a hungry mob of kids to feed, you'll sometimes find yourself with stale bread on your hands. The simplest thing to do with it is make toast to use at breakfast or as a base on which to serve supper-time creamed foods or cheese rarebits. Or serve it up as french toast, or french-toasted sandwiches. Or you can cut it into attractive shapes, and sauté them lightly in butter to provide bases for savory canapés. Or you can crumb it and store it for later use, saving yourself the price of commercially prepared crumbs.

bread crumbs: For breading such foods as croquettes and scallops, for topping casseroles and other baked dishes, for buttering and sprinkling over vegetables, and for a number of other uses your cookbook will lead you to, bread crumbs are a kitchen staple.

Two kinds are called for in recipes, soft and fine dry. There's a difference, one that should be observed for proper results in the finished dish. Fine dry bread crumbs, plain or flavored (herbed, cheesed, spiced), can be made at home from bread that you dry out in a slow oven. Spread bread slices in a single layer on a baking sheet, bake at 300°F. until completely dry and lightly browned. Then process in a blender until you produce fine crumbs—if necessary, sift and reprocess the larger pieces. Six slices of bread will produce about 1 cup of fine dry bread crumbs.

Make soft bread crumbs, crusts removed or not as you choose, by hand. Simply tear slices of slightly stale bread to pieces with your fingers. Or, if you prefer, process these too in the blender, one slice—first torn into several pieces—at a time. Two to 2½ slices will make 1 cup of soft crumbs. For soft buttered bread crumbs, process lightly buttered bread in the blender until the crumbs are the size you want.

cases, croustades, and the like: Looked at from the proper point of view, a loaf of unsliced stale bread is a treasure. With a sharp knife, cut off the crusts on all sides; hollow out the center, leaving a ½-inch case all around. Brush inside and out with melted butter (plain, or seasoned with garlic or onion juice or snipped herbs, depending on the use you'll make of the finished product) and bake at 350°F. until crisped and handsomely browned. You have produced a croustade to fill with a sauced mixture—creamed chicken or oysters, or seafood singly or in any combination, or ham à la king are some examples—a dish handsome and delicious enough to grace almost any company-coming meal.

For individual cases to fill with mixtures of the same sort, or with poached eggs, begin as above by cutting off the crusts of a loaf all around. Then cut into 2-inch slices. Hollow out each slice to leave a ½-inch shell, brush with butter, and bake. Or, if you prefer, omit the butter and deep-fry in oil.

To make a breakfast treat that will seem as if you'd prepared it on purpose rather than to use up the stale bread, start again with a crusts-removed loaf. With a sharp serrated knife, cut it into thin lengthwise slices. Roll each slice firmly with a rolling pin. Spread generously with soft butter and sprinkle thickly with a combination of sugar and cinnamon. Roll up, jelly-roll fashion; cut each roll in half crosswise. Refrigerate an hour or longer. Just before serving, heat rolls in a 350°F. oven until warmed through and beginning to brown.

Turn sliced stale bread into croutons by cutting into cubes and either baking in the oven or sautéeing. Use left-over bread for stuffings, crumb dumplings, bread sauce, bread pudding, brown betty, french toast, cheese strata—a cookbook will show you dozens of ways, all of them great additions to any menu.

Fresh or stale, plain or in any of its guises, bread is a staple part of our diet, a wholesome and delicious part. See also BISCUITS, FRENCH BREAD, LIMPA, MATZOTH, MELBA TOAST, MUFFINS, POCKET BREADS, QUICK BREADS, REFRIGERATED DOUGH, TOAST, UNLEAVENED, and ZWIEBACK.

BREAKFAST

How to break the night's long fast is the subject of considerable—often ascerbic—controversy. Nutritionists are in general agreement that a good, balanced breakfast, particularly one containing some protein, sets you up to face the rigors of the day ahead. Some few, however, flying in the face of their fellows, point out that what you've been doing all night is resting, so why should you need a lot of food, especially if you had a good dinner last night?

People not as concerned with nutrition as with getting the day started somehow, anyhow, present a number of points of view. There are those who want and have a hearty breakfast every day of the week, and would be impossible to live with if they didn't. Others would like that kind of breakfast but a) can't get themselves out of bed in time, or b) have no one to prepare it for them and don't yearn for it sufficiently to fix it themselves.

Some settle for "whole nutrition" drinks from a package, stirred into a glass of milk, or some combination such as orange juice and vanilla ice cream whipped up in a blender. Still others, trying to lose weight, find breakfast the easiest meal of the day to skip. And finally there are those, their eyes barely open, who grope around trying to pull themselves together, drinking cup after cup of coffee to get themselves going, and sometimes, as a concession to good health, use the coffee to wash down a multivitamin/mineral pill.

The bad old days. One thing is sure: None of us eats a breakfast today like the ones our grandfathers and great-grandfathers did. The amount of food those old boys (old girls, too) could put away was downright awe-inspiring. Farm breakfasts were not—and still aren't—hard to understand. After all, before the farmer and his assorted sons and hired hands bellied up to the table they had already been awake

for hours and done an assortment of chores sufficiently formidable to warrant quite an appetite. But how about the ordinary mortals who hadn't done anything more strenuous than (possibly) take a bath? Listen to the president of a railroad, writing to his wife in the 1880s concerning the first breakfast served to him on his new private car:

> There was a nice pair of trout Cook had caught before coming on board this morning, with three rashers of bacon alongside. A couple of good mutton chops, the kind with the kidneys, to follow, with fried potatoes and fried tomatoes, and a batch of hot biscuits with honey, and some muffins with raisins in I didn't care much for, and a platter of fried eggs with ham on the side. Finished off with a stack of griddle cakes and sausage (not as good as your sausages, Annie) with maple syrup. Cook sent out to see if I wanted apple pie. I was near to full, but I had a piece, not to hurt his feelings, with cheese and lemon sauce. Very good.

Stunned, we can only wonder what he had for lunch.

Breakfast up to date. The first meal of the day tends to be a catch-as-catch-can affair now, at least on weekdays, with many families. The kids help themselves to juice from a pitcher in the refrigerator. Then they have dry cereal, perhaps with a sliced banana. If Dad is ambitious, he cooks himself an egg or two, maybe a couple of slices of bacon, and pops bread into the toaster. If not, he settles for a doughnut or a sweet roll from a bakery box. By this time the coffee, set up the night before, has run through. Mom, if she's a working woman, makes do with coffee. If she doesn't go to business, she may stay resolutely in bed until most of the morning's traumas are past, at which point she'll make an appearance, kiss everybody goodbye, and settle down with her first cup of coffee. (Later, she'll have more, and perhaps coffeecake with "the girls.")

That's an unsatisfactory way to start the day for all concerned. Is it universal? No, but it's unfortunately common. Sure, there are still lots of women who get up ahead of the rest of the family, get a good breakfast going, call their husbands and kids (feeling, by the sixth call, pretty put-upon), assemble the group around the family board, alternately order and cajole until everyone's eaten something, find books and boots and lunch money and the papers Dad brought home last night, and shove everyone out the front door with kisses all around and a big sigh of relief.

Neither blessed nor, depending on the point of view, burdened with families, singles tend to breakfast on juice and/or coffee, supplement this mid-morning when the office coffee wagon makes its rounds. Roomies are likely to ignore one another with excessive politeness and, if they're lucky, get the day started without a fight over who ate the last of the strawberry jam and forgot to buy another jar. It may, indeed, be only the recently married who start the morning peacefully, and they can well be so wrapped up in each other that

the idea of breakfast doesn't occur to them at all—until it's too late. Breakfast time is not, generally, an easy, full-of-goodwill occasion. A return to gentler, less hectic ways would be, everyone will agree, a good thing. If you can figure out how to manage it, your fortune is made.

But wait till the weekend. Saturday and Sunday morning, typical American family style, have their own pattern. Dad cuts the lawn or makes forays to the hardware store, to be lost for hours in the beauties of chainsaws and toggle bolts. Kids are packed off for lessons in whatever it's fashionable to take lessons in at the moment, or to Scout meetings or Little League games. Mom shops or gardens or, if she's also a breadwinner, indulges in a frenzy of cleaning and washing. Quite often, everybody gets together for Saturday breakfast out, most likely at whatever fast food emporium is nearby, on anything from bacon and egg on a bun to three eggs, ham, and a stack of pancakes with a choice of six kinds of syrup. Not all that relaxed, but an improvement on weekdays in many cases.

Sunday, in many homes, is Quiet Time. Swingers may entertain or be entertained at brunch, and often families go the brunch party route, too. But many families reserve most Sundays as sit-around-and-pant day, a time to recharge batteries and store up energy to face the coming week. Mom and Dad catch up on sleep while the kids snack on whatever they can find and—quietly, on pain of instant retaliation—watch television. After a while there's breakfast, usually a good one of fruit, eggs, breakfast meat of some kind, perhaps fresh muffins or popovers, or pancakes or waffles. Everyone's relaxed, nobody nags, differences among the kids are half-hearted and quickly settled, Mom and Dad hash over the past week's events. Ah, peace—it's wonderful!

Breakfast around the country. Different parts of the nation favor various kinds of breakfasts—not necessarily every day but on occasion, by tradition. Pancakes are big in the West, accompanied by fresh fruit, bacon or eggs or sausage (or bacon *and* eggs *and* sausage), and a multitude of sweets to slather on the pancakes—syrup, honey, applesauce, sour cream, you name it. Waffles topped with country ham topped with creamed chicken make it big in the South, with country ham and grits and cream-scrambled eggs with beaten biscuits a close second. In New England you might feast on fresh-picked berries, fresh-caught trout with bacon, and float-away popovers. Scrapple and fried apples and fat, raisin-rich cinnamon rolls might greet you in Pennsylvania Dutch country. In the land of the Cajuns, look for Creole sausage (hot enough to wake you up and then some) with hominy grits, and fresh biscuits with wild-grape jelly. Wherever you go in this country, you can seek out a breakfast specialty of some sort—lox with cream cheese and bagels, eggs scrambled with oysters, baby lamb chops, country ham with red-eye gravy, baked eggs with swiss cheese, creamed finnan haddie, sourdough pancakes, steak and eggs, and dozens more.

Breakfast around the world. The English like a hearty breakfast, favoring grilled kidneys, bacon, scrambled eggs, kippered herring. The Danish are so fond of breakfast they have it twice, early and mid-morning. The Dutch are hearty breakfasters, fond of such goodies as pea soup, big wedges of cheese, and good yeast rolls called *broodjes*. The French like continental breakfast—café au lait and croissants or brioche with sweet butter. In the Bavarian section of Germany, they have continental breakfast too, but follow it mid-morning with *veschperlem* made up of black bread and raw bacon washed down with kirschwasser. Russians like smoked fish and cabbage, sauerkraut, or beet soup. Orientals, as in other meals, break the fast with rice and fish.

So, when it comes to breakfast it's not so much *what* you eat as *that* you eat, an idea most of us could adopt and accept with profit.

BREAKFAST CEREALS: see CEREALS

BRICK CHEESE: see CHEESE

BRIE: see CHEESE

BRINE: see special feature: PUTTING FOODS BY

BRISKET: see BEEF

BROAD BEANS: see BEANS

BROCCOLI

Cousin to cabbage—as are brussels sprouts and cauliflower, collards and kale—broccoli was known to the early Greeks and Romans. Prepared in the manner prescribed by the Roman epicure Apicius, broccoli was a favorite dish of the son of the emperor Tiberius, if that sort of trivia intrigues you. In his meticulous accounting of the minutia that made up his world, Pliny mentioned broccoli. We know that the vegetable was eaten in the years when B.C. turned to A.D., but probably not too long before that, as the ancient Eastern languages have no word for the vegetable—nor for any of the cabbage family, for that matter.

However long it has been around in the rest of the world, broccoli did not become widely eaten in America until this century, although Thomas Jefferson, that experimental horticulturalist, grew some in his gardens at Monticello. Emigrating Italians, fond of broccoli, brought seeds with them to the new country and grew them in kitchen gardens, but the vegetable was not produced and distributed commercially until the early 1920s.

BROCCOLI IN YOUR KITCHEN

Grown in California (the major portion of the crop) and in Arizona and Texas, as well as in some of the eastern states, broccoli is in season the year around and at its peak in October and November. Two pounds of broccoli will make four servings.

how to buy: Select fresh-looking, unblemished bunches with compact heads, which may be dark green, dark gray-green, or purplish-green. Stalks and branches should be firm but not hard, and should not feel spongy or woody. If the heads are yellow or opened, the vegetable is old. Look at the ends of the stalks. If they are turning brown or look slimy, the broccoli has been in the market too long. Pick another vegetable for tonight.

how to store: In the vegetable crisper, or in a closed plastic bag, in the refrigerator. Don't plan on keeping broccoli, raw or after it's been cooked, for more than 4 days.

nutritive value: An excellent source of vitamin A, a good source of vitamin C, as well as B vitamins and some minerals, one large whole stalk of broccoli contains about 73 calories, and offers:

protein	8.7 grams
fat	.8 gram
carbohydrate	12.6 grams
calcium	246 milligrams
phosphorus	174 milligrams
iron	2.2 milligrams
sodium	28 milligrams
potassium	748 milligrams
thiamin	.25 milligram
riboflavin	.26 milligram
niacin	2.2 milligrams
ascorbic acid	252 milligrams
vitamin A	7,000 international units

Tips on preparation, cooking. Wash under cold running water. Remove largest leaves, and any others that are blemished. With a sharp knife, cut a deep cross in the bottom of each stalk—heads cook faster than stalks; the cross allows the water to reach into the stalk, assuring that both heads and stalks will be done at the same time. Or, if you prefer, slice the entire stalk lengthwise, with one floweret and a thin piece of stalk in each cut. Cook in a large, flat pan—a skillet is ideal, provided it has a cover—in an inch of water, until barely tender, 10 to 15 minutes. Cover, but remove cover briefly several times during the cooking period. This allows excess steam to escape, and helps keep the broccoli green. Drain well before serving.

An alternative method is to cut off the heads and cut the stalks into 1-inch slices. Cook the stalk slices 5 minutes; add the heads and continue cooking until done.

Broccoli may also be cooked by the stir-fry method. Cut in thin slices and sauté quickly in hot oil, again cooking the stalk sections a bit longer than the heads.

To serve simply, dress with butter, salt, and pepper. Or drizzle with melted butter, sprinkle with cheese, and broil briefly until the cheese melts. Or dress with lemon butter or with hollandaise sauce. Or sprinkle with crumbled crisp bacon. Cooked in advance and refrigerated, cold broccoli is delicious as an appetizer or salad, with vinaigrette or simply with lemon juice, or mayonnaise thinned with lemon juice and sharpened with cayenne, or with sour cream. Use leftover broccoli to make a delicious cream soup. And, of course, broccoli is the base for Chicken or Turkey Divan—broccoli topped with breast slices of poultry, napped with a sherry-flavored cream sauce, sprinkled with parmesan, and baked until bubbling hot and lightly browned.

Freezing broccoli. Properly prepared (see special feature: PUTTING FOODS BY), broccoli may be stored at 0°F. or below for about 6 months, in the refrigerator frozen-food compartment for 1 month.

Other ways, other forms. Baby-food broccoli is available in small jars, puréed or chopped. The vegetable is not otherwise available canned, but can be found frozen, spears or chopped, in the frozen-food case of most markets.

A delicious and versatile vegetable, broccoli is widely liked by both children and adults. Because of its vitamin content and good flavor, serve it often.

BROCHETTE: see page 451

BROIL, TO: see page 449

BROILER/FRYER: see CHICKEN

BROOK TROUT: see FISH

BROTH: see BOUILLON

BROWN RICE: see RICE

BROWN SAUCE: see special feature:
SAUCE SORCERY

BROWN STOCK

Basis of a number of sauces, this is made with beef and beef bones. Meat and bones are baked in a very hot oven until deeply browned, or they may be broiled. Then they and their cooking juices are simmered long and slowly in water (sometimes red wine is added) with flavoring ingredients, such as celery, onion, carrot, bouquet garni. Cool stock, strain, and refrigerate in tightly covered containers up to 4 days; for longer storage return to the kettle after the 4 days, boil 10 minutes, then refrigerate again.

BROWN SUGAR: see SUGAR

BRUNCH

Since the inventive soul who thought up the idea squeezed breakfast and lunch (the words, the food, the times) into one meal, brunch has been a festive occasion, generally a leisurely one. Inviting friends for brunch is an easy and easy-on-the-budget way to entertain. Indoors or out, winter or summer, a brunch party is a good party.

The menu need not be elaborate. Drinks, if they are served, can be confined to one or, at the most, two kinds; most often fruit- or tomato-juice combinations seem right for early-in-the-day imbibing. Make-aheads leave the hostess free to enjoy her own party, or the host may like to do the kind of on-the-spot cooking that allows him to show off his skills with a flourish. Service is simple, usually buffet-style (see BUFFET). The party is over and the subsequent tidying up accomplished early enough so that nobody is short on sleep the following day, especially those for whom dawn tends to come much too soon the morning after they've entertained, particularly if it's Monday, the low point of the week.

What's the occasion? Sundays and holidays are the best brunch days, with an air of relaxed festivity. Brunch on Christmas or Easter morning can be joyous celebrations. New Year's day brunch can take the place of the more usual afternoon-evening open house and leave a bit of breathing time before work the following morning. A cookout brunch is great on the Fourth of July or Labor Day. A birthday brunch, if the big day falls on a weekend, is a fine way to celebrate for young or old. A brunch before a football game—attended in person or by way of the tube—gets the day off to a rousing start. And almost any Sunday the year around is the right day for a pleasant brunch.

What will you drink? If you plan to serve what grandma called "intoxicating beverages"—and if you're the kind of person who entertains at brunch, you're likely also to be the kind who does serve drinks—be certain that there's at least one nonintoxicating beverage available for those who a) don't drink, or b) don't drink before the sun is over the yard-arm, or c) had a bit too much last night. A pitcher of well-seasoned tomato juice (the same mix you'll use for bloody marys if you plan to serve them) or of orange or combination orange-pineapple juice will fill the bill nicely. If there are to be children at the brunch—and this is the kind of party children can and do attend—remember that kids are big guzzlers of juices and soft drinks.

Bloody marys and screwdrivers are the more usual brunch drinks, but there are many others. Bullshots fit in well with brunch menus. So do sours or daiquiris or margaritas or

any other drink in which fruit juice is a part. Beer is the drink for a curry brunch. Champagne or white wine goes well with anything you're likely to serve at such a meal. Whatever you offer your guests, you'll be better off not having an open bar —plan on one, or at the most two kinds of alcoholic drinks, plus one nonalcoholic, and save yourself trouble and mess.

What will you eat? Brunch menus call for drinks to begin with, a sturdy main dish with necessary accompaniments, and something sweet but not too sweet—Rigos Yanci, for example, is wildly out of place at a brunch. Coffeecake or danish or cinnamon snails is the right sort of sweet, along with fruit. Here are typical brunch menus to help you plan:

Bloody Marys   Pineapple Juice
Mushroom-Cream Scrambled Eggs
Toasted French Bread
Cider-Baked Whole Canadian Bacon
Moravian Sugar Cake   Coffee   Papaya with Lemon

Daiquiris on the Rocks   Tomato Juice
Lamb-stuffed Artichokes   Avgolemono Sauce
Tomato Aspic   Rye Toast with Sweet Butter
Orange Baba   Coffee   Strawberries

Cranberry Juice with Vodka   Plain Cranberry Juice
Baked Eggs in Tomato Shells   Grilled Ham
Stuffed Mushrooms   Toasted English Muffins
Cinnamon-Raisin Snails   Coffee   Minted Pineapple

Bullshots   Orange Juice
Onion-Tomato Quiche   Baked Bacon
Dilled Green Beans   Hot Croissants
Cherry-Almond Coffeecake   Coffee   Melon Balls

Champagne   Apricot Nectar
French Omelets with Assorted Fillings
Broiled Sausages   Asparagus Vinaigrette
Brioche with Sweet Butter
Macaroons   Coffee   Raspberry Fool

Brandy Sours   Apple Juice
Chicken Liver-Mushroom Kabobs
Baked Eggs Florentine
Hot Biscuits   Honey   Marmalade
Fresh Pears   Coffee   Brie

Clam-Tomato Cocktail   Clam-Tomato Juice
Hangtown Fry   Toasted French Bread
Barbecued Lima Beans
Mocha Pound Cake   Coffee   Ambrosia

Screwdrivers   Orange Juice
Grilled Fresh Salmon   Broiled Tomatoes
Popovers   Ginger Marmalade
Sour Cream Coffeecake   Coffee
Apples with Camembert

White Wine   Raspberry Shrub
Swiss Cheese Strata   Frizzled Ham
White Bean Salad   Bran Muffins
Lemon Sponge Cake   Coffee   Fresh Figs

Milk Punch   Grapefruit Juice
Country Ham   Corn Pudding   Fried Apples
Buttermilk Biscuits   Peach Conserve
Sticky Buns   Coffee   Honeydew Melon

That ought to get you going—particularly if, as you're reading this, you happen to be hungry. And there are literally hundreds of other combinations suitable for brunch. Be guided by your own tastes, restrained only by your budget.

What will you do? Nothing. That's the beauty of brunch. Shag the children outdoors to play. Set up the stereo or tape player, but keep the music in the background so you can hear yourselves talk. Brunch is a gossippy, yakkity kind of party. No games (except those on television, if that's the point of this brunch). No structured amusements. Just pleasure in good food, in each other's good company.

BRUSH, TO: see page 444

BRUSSELS SPROUTS

The English have the reputation of being terrible cooks, one not totally deserved. Think of noble English roast beef and its Yorkshire Pudding. Think of such goodies as bath buns and sally lunn and sticky, gingery parkin. Think of golden buck, that splendor of rarebits, of glorious English breakfasts (grilled kidneys, kippers), of every-bit-as-glorious English teas (crumpets, scones, cucumber sandwiches). Think of fresh berries with clotted Devonshire cream, the great cheeses, Cornish pasties, Lancashire hotpot.

On the other hand, think also of brussels sprouts and, for that matter, most vegetables. They are cooked, unimaginatively, in the manner the French call (with a sneer) à la Anglaise—plain-boiled. Not only plain-boiled, but boiled to the point where they are fit only to be interred with appropriate prayers for a better life in a future incarnation. Boiled-to-death English brussels sprouts, those cooked by women whose mothers or grandmothers or great-grandmothers learned to cook in the British manner, are the reason many people turn green and avert their eyes at the very mention of the vegetable.

All wrong. Brussels sprouts need not be tasteless or, on the other hand, rankly bitter. They need not be an elderly, spiritless gray. Properly prepared—and it's very easy—brussels sprouts are a delicious (and handsome) vegetable, worthy of a place on any table, at any meal.

BRUSSELS SPROUTS IN YOUR KITCHEN

The vegetable migrated from Brussels, Belgium, where it has been raised since the fourteenth century. A relative of cabbage, brussels sprouts grow in neat miniature cabbage-head rows on the stalk of the plant. They are available—mostly from California and New York—from September through March; peak season is November.

how to buy: Sold loose by the pound, or in small baskets like those in which strawberries come. A pound will make four servings. Look for small, compact, firm heads that are uniformly green. Brussels sprouts with yellow leaves are old; they will have poor flavor. If you pick out your own, choose heads of uniform size—the smaller the better—so all will cook at the same rate.

how to store: Unwashed until just before using, in the refrigerator, in crisper or plastic bag. If possible, buy fresh the day you plan to serve them; in any case, store no more than 4 days.

nutritive value: Low in sodium, brussels sprouts are a good vegetable to keep in mind if you're cooking for someone on a low-salt diet. They're low in calories, too, and high in vitamins A and C. A cup of brussels sprouts—seven or eight individual heads—contains about 55 calories, and offers:

protein	6.5	grams
fat	.6	gram
carbohydrate	9.9	grams
calcium	50	milligrams
phosphorus	112	milligrams
iron	1.7	milligrams
sodium	16	milligrams
potassium	423	milligrams
thiamin	.12	milligram
riboflavin	.22	milligram
niacin	1.2	milligrams
ascorbic acid	135	milligrams
vitamin A	810	international units

Tips on preparing, cooking. Cut off stalk from each sprout, but not so close to the head that you loosen the leaves. Pull off any yellowed or blemished leaves. Wash in deep cold water. Cook, covered, in a small amount of water, 5 to 10 minutes, or until just tender. Overcooked, brussels sprouts lose vitamins and their flavor is intensified to the unpleasant point.

Dress cooked sprouts with butter, lemon-butter, browned butter, cheese sauce, hollandaise, or sour cream. Combine with mushrooms, chestnuts (a traditional holiday vegetable), water chestnuts, almonds, or crisp croutons for texture contrast. Season with black or white pepper, lemon-parsley salt, nutmeg, dill. Serve whole sprouts, cooked tender-crisp and chilled, with a mustard dip or vinaigrette sauce as an appetizer. Bake with potatoes in cheese sauce. Skewer with lamb chunks and tomato wedges for kabobs. Serve on toast, topped with creamed eggs.

Freezing brussels sprouts. Properly prepared (see special feature: PUTTING FOOD BY), brussels sprouts can be stored up to 12 months at 0°F. or below, or 1 month in the refrigerator frozen-food compartment.

Other ways, other forms. Brussels sprouts are not available canned. They are widely available in 10-ounce packages and larger plastic bags, in frozen-food sections, less widely available as frozen combinations (cheese sauce, and such) in boilable bags.

BUCKWHEAT

Buckwheat flours and cereals are prepared from the triangular seeds of an herbaceous plant—not a grass, like wheat—that once grew wild in China and Siberia. It is still used extensively in the latter country and throughout Russia, and in Poland, where the cooked buckwheat is called *kasha.* The name is also used in Jewish cookery.

Early settlers brought the seeds here from Europe. Because buckwheat grows rapidly, flourishes in poor soil, and is easy to mill, it went west to help settle the country. At present, most of our buckwheat is grown in New York and Pennsylvania.

Buckwheat flour. There are two kinds available today, light and dark, both with a portion of wheat flour mixed in to tone down the high flavor of the buckwheat. Used in breads and griddle cakes—buckwheat cakes—the flour should not be sifted. Simply stir, then spoon lightly into a measuring cup. Store in a cool, dry place up to 3 months. See also FLOUR.

Buckwheat groats. These may be brown or white, and are available as whole kernel or coarse-, medium-, or fine-ground. Cooked with egg, salt, and shortening in water, they become *kasha,* to be served as a side dish (often with gravy) or used in soups. Or groats may be cooked in milk, chilled and sliced, sautéed in butter or drippings, and served with maple syrup, à la hasty pudding. Store groats in a cool, dry place up to 1 year; covered, in the refrigerator, store *kasha* up to 1 week.

Buckwheat is high in carbohydrate, and contains small amounts of some vitamins and minerals.

BUFFETS

Since, for the average family, the cook in the kitchen and the servants to wait table have gone the way of the surrey with the fringe on top, sit-down dinners for large numbers of people have been confined to the very rich or heads of state. For the rest of us, when we entertain more than six or eight guests at dinner, the buffet is the way to go.

The buffet meal is an informal one (which doesn't mean slapdash) that is easy on the hostess and pleasant for the guests. It can be as simple as a big platter of spaghetti accompanied by green salad, crusty bread, and red wine, or as elaborate as a collation of several hot main dishes and several cold ones with all the appropriate accompaniments.

Aside from the food—simple or elaborate, it should be *good*—the most important considerations are ease of service and comfort while eating. If you possibly can, provide snack tables or card tables at which guests can be seated after serving themselves. Lacking tables, have individual trays large enough to accommodate several dishes-cups-glasses and silverware. It's virtually impossible to juggle a plate and a glass on your lap without disaster or, at the least, acute discomfort. In any case, don't serve anything that can't be eaten with a fork—knives are verboten at buffets. If you provide tables or trays, these can be set with silverware and napkins in advance, making do-it-yourself service much easier.

Plan of action. Pre-dinner drinks should be dispensed from a bar, barcart, or table reserved for this purpose and set up somewhere apart from the dining room or other area from which food is to be served. The main part of the meal can be set out on the dining room table (if it normally lives in the center of the room, move it toward one wall), from a buffet, from a long hall table, from any convenient surface large enough to hold it. If at all possible, serve beverage and dessert from a separate, smaller table or cart. It saves clutter and keeps things moving.

Arrange dinner plates at one end of the table, where guests will start serving themselves. Main dishes next, then side dishes, salads, vegetables, rolls, relishes. Finally, silverware and napkins, to be picked up last. Everything should be within easy reach. Be sure there are serving spoons and/or forks beside each dish. Cautionary word about main dishes: avoid anything with a great deal of runny sauce or gravy. Cautionary word about salads: nothing drenched in dressing that will spread all over the plate. Cautionary word about bread: pre-buttered, please (parkerhouse rolls are an example of the kind that can be pre-buttered and warmed without being messy), but no bread that needs to be buttered on the spot—this requires tools and holds up traffic on the food line.

Not just for dinner. A buffet can be one of many kinds of meals—a luncheon, a cookout, a buffet tea, an afternoon or evening reception, a dessert-and-coffee buffet, a cocktail party with a substantial buffet spread of canapés, pâtés, dips, and such from which guests can help themselves. Whatever, plan on a bit more food than you would for a sit-down meal.

Portions are not as controllable as at sit-down meals, and neither are the guests as controlled—those who wouldn't think of passing their plates for seconds will trot back to a buffet table twice or thrice and think nothing of it.

BULGUR

Wheat treated to a cleaning-washing-cooking-drying-debranning-cracking-sifting processing, this is a basic food in the Middle East. In recent years (particularly since the upsurge of interest in "natural" foods) it has begun to appear often in homes and restaurants in the United States.

Tender but chewy in texture, bulgur can be used as a side dish, in casseroles, and in soups and stews. It is rich in niacin, riboflavin, and thiamin—B vitamins—and in vegetable protein as well. See also GRAINS.

BUNS: see BREADS

BUTTER

Smooth and yellow and rich, delicately flavored, with a sweet odor that calls up visions of buttercup-dotted pastures filled with bovines amiably grazing, butter is many things to many people—everything from a rare treat to a necessity of life. And part of our nonfood language, too: soft as butter, a big butter-and-egg man, butter wouldn't melt in her mouth, he knows what side his bread is buttered on, she's only trying to butter you up, that chubby little kid is a real butterball, he works hard to earn his family's bread and butter.

And a part, even, of the rhetoric by which the world has been moved to conflict, from the Bible ("The words of his mouth were smoother than butter, but war was in his heart") to the Third Reich's Goebbels ("We can do without butter but, despite all our love of peace, not without arms. One cannot shoot with butter, but with guns").

A.A. Milne wrote a charming poem for children about the King who was without "butter for the Royal slice of bread." A delightful verse Victorian children learned ran like this:

> "Oh, Ma'm," the cook said, all a-flutter,
> "I quote forget to salt the butter!"
> "Don't fret," her mistress calmly said,
> "We'll simply have to salt the bread!"

Then there is the old charm farm wives chanted while churning when the cream refused to clot and the butter was slow in coming:

> Come, butter, come,
> Come, butter come;
> Peter stands at the gate
> Waiting for a butter cake.
> Come, butter, come.

Repeated three times, the charm is supposed to be infallible. It has been in use in England since at least the fifteenth century and was still in use in America in the twentieth.

Through the years, around the world. The elite of ancient Rome had many kinds of bread—with them the word covered not only loaves and rolls, but those things we now call cakes and pastries—but they apparently did not care for butter. This was not because no one had yet gotten around to discovering it. There was butter available, but it was for those associated with cattle, the herding peasantry, and looked down upon as coarse and common by the gentry, who used it only medicinally, for treating burns.

Nomadic tribes not only drank the milk of their mares, but also made butter and cheese from it. In the England of the thirteenth century, farmers used ewes' milk, but by 1500 had discovered that they preferred cows' milk as a beverage, and liked the butter and cheese made from it better as well. The chief problem with butter was that it became rancid so quickly that it was long a staple food of the farmer and herdsman, but a luxury for city dwellers, even the affluent. Then herdsmen discovered that ghee—clarified butter—would keep indefinitely, and farmers, that salt would ward off rancidity, at least for a time. Butter became a more widely used food and, with the development of refrigeration, at last an almost universal one.

Moving to the West. In early America the agrarian way of life was the rule—most people raised their own food, except for such luxuries as tea, coffee, and salt. They grew their own grain and took it to the local mill to be ground, raised and butchered their own meat, made their own butter and cheese from their own cows' milk. Every household had a churn, a wooden tub with a device to agitate milk placed inside it. The most common type was tall and narrow, with a plunger-dasher that the housewife (or a small boy, if he could be cornered into it) moved rapidly up and down, sloshing the milk around until globules of fat separated from the liquid and finally gathered into a cohesive mass. This butter was then washed and pressed to get the remaining milk out of it, salted —if salt was available—and was ready to use.

West-going women had a difficult time keeping their families clean (at least relatively) and fed during the long journeys when the Conestoga wagon was their only home. But they found that the jolting and lurching of the wagon offered two advantages—it churned the butter and it kneaded the bread.

Cattle made the journey on foot, following the wagons. If they dropped calves en route, the calves joined the women and children in the wagon for part of the day until they were old enough to follow along, for the settlers knew that cattle would be a necessity of life—of survival—in their new homes. In the Midwest, dairy farming eventually became a major industry; in the West, raising beef cattle was all-important.

BUTTER IN YOUR KITCHEN

Through the years, farm wives continued to churn their own butter—many still do. In the early part of this century, the town and city housewife got her butter courtesy of the milkman, in his horse and wagon, who used to deliver house to house. (Indeed, he did long after he'd traded Dobbin in on a truck.) This butter came in crocks holding 1, 2, or 3 pounds, with a piece of wax paper, often imprinted with the name of the producing dairy, pressed on the butter's surface. Or the milkman brought butter "prints"—blocks—of the same sizes to the door, roughly wax-paper wrapped. Alternatively, he had a big tub of butter in his wagon (sometimes, happily, imbedded in ice) from which, guided by his practiced eye, he whacked off a hunk of the size the housewife wanted and placed it in the container she had ready for it. She stored it in the coldest part—not all that cold—of her old-fashioned icebox.

Today most of us buy our butter in 1-pound cartons at the supermarket, only vaguely aware, if at all, that the smooth yellow cubes have anything to do with cows. If we want high-quality butter—and why would we not?—we look for the United States Department of Agriculture (USDA) score and/ or grade-mark shield on the carton of the butter we buy.

Knowing the score. Like meat, butter is graded by the USDA on a voluntary fee-for-service basis. That is, inspection and consequent grading of butter are not mandatory by law, and the producer must pay for the services of the government graders.

The grade shield is a reliable guide to butter quality. To earn the right to carry the shield on its butter, the manufacturing plant, as well as the butter itself, must meet exacting requirements. Only butter processed in a plant whose sanitation and good operating practices have been approved by the USDA can carry the shield. The government inspects the plant's premises, facilities, equipment, manufacturing procedures, and packaging operations. As a final step, the butter itself is graded by a USDA inspector trained for the job.

The inspector—in a clean white uniform and cap, with the USDA insignia on his breast—uses a "trier," rather like a large, reverse-action hypodermic, to draw a sample of the butter. He tastes it, because flavor—determined by taste and aroma—is one of the most important factors in determining the butter's grade. Body, texture, and color are also rated, all in accordance with the USDA-established standards. Portions of each sample are packed in sterile jars to be sent for laboratory tests on the butter's keeping quality, another factor in grading.

The grades are AA (93 score), A (92 score), B (90 score), and C (89) score. You'll find the first two grades, AA and A, in most stores, and B in some. Grade C butter is used only by baking and food-processing plants; you will not find it in retail stores. Fat content is not a grading factor. All butter, whatever the grade, must by law have a fat content of 80 percent. The remaining 20 percent is mostly water plus small amounts of milk solids.

Following are the standards that graded butter must meet, according to the USDA.

grade AA butter: Delicate, sweet flavor; fine, highly pleasing aroma; made from high-quality fresh, sweet cream; smooth, creamy texture with good spreadability; (if salted) salt completely dissolved and blended in just the right amount to enhance savory quality.

grade A butter: Pleasing flavor; made from fresh cream, fairly smooth in texture. Grade A rates very close to AA.

grade B butter: May have slightly acid flavor; generally made from selected sour cream. Readily acceptable to many consumers, preferred by some.

You will find the grade shield (less often, nowadays, the score) on the outside of the butter carton, on the front or the side. The label will also show, besides the actual brand name of the butter—Old Bossy's Best Effort, or whatever—the product's net weight and the name of the manufacturer, packer, or distributor.

Knowing the kind. Entirely apart from the grade (quality) of butter is the kind. There are three to choose among, any of which may be any of the three available grades. Which you choose depends on your family's taste preference and/or the use you intend to make of that particular butter purchase.

sweet cream butter: Made from pasteurized cream, with added salt. Sometimes called "salted butter."

sweet butter: Also made from pasteurized cream, but without added salt. Sometimes called "unsalted butter."

whipped butter: Made from pasteurized cream into which air or inert gas has been whipped to improve spreadability and increase volume. To compound confusion, whipped butter may be salted or unsalted but, happily, it is not called by any other name.

Bringing home the butter. Armed with all this information, you doubtless feel ready to sally forth to buy butter as an informed consumer. Wait a minute. You need also to know that both salted and unsalted butter are sold in 1-pound cartons, made of heavily waxed paperboard. Within the carton, the butter is divided into ¼-pound sticks, individually wrapped. Whipped butter, on the other hand, is sold in ½-pound tubs, also heavily waxed, or (less widely available) 1-pound cartons containing 6 sticks.

One more thing—salted butter, regular or whipped, keeps longer than sweet. Now, you can go butter shopping with confidence.

how to buy: Purchase only the amount you can use in a week's time, unless you plan to freeze the butter. It's perishable. Look for the grade shield on the carton, and buy the grade you prefer. If the carton does not carry a grade shield, that's a sign that the manufacturer wasn't interested enough in you, the consumer, to pay for having his butter graded, or perhaps he felt his plant would not pass inspection. There is no way to determine the quality of ungraded butter—caveat emptor.

how to store: Three Cs govern the storage of butter—keep it clean, cool, and covered. Store in the refrigerator, in its original protective wrapping, until you're ready to use it. Once you've opened a stick of butter, store leftovers in the refrigerator tightly covered. Uncovered or carelessly covered butter will pick up the flavors of other refrigerated foods—particularly strong ones, such as melons or fish. So that it will spread well, take butter you intend to use out of the refrigerator about 15 minutes before you sound the chow's-on call. The same is true of butter you intend to use for sandwiches. Those few minutes at room temperature will soften the butter enough to make it readily spreadable.

nutritive value: A serving of butter is considered to be one pat, which the USDA solemnly describes as "1 in. square, ⅓ in. high, 90 per pound." This is, they go on to explain, the common size serving used in institutions and restaurants, although "dimensions may vary from those shown." For our purposes, let's consider the nutritive value of a tablespoon of regular butter (not whipped), which is ⅛ of a stick—¹⁄₃₂ of a pound. That tablespoon contains 102 calories, and offers:

protein	.1 gram
fat	11.5 grams
carbohydrate	.1 gram
calcium	3 milligrams
phosphorus	2 milligrams
sodium	140 milligrams
potassium	3 milligrams
vitamin A	470 international units

Butter contains no iron, and no B or C vitamins. A tablespoon of whipped butter contains 67 calories, and offers about two-thirds of each of the above values—the other third is the nonnutritive air or gas that makes the butter fluffy.

Freezing butter. If for some reason you buy more butter than you can use up in a week, by all means freeze it. Overwrap the original carton with freezer paper or foil, seal it, date it, and store up to 6 months at 0°F. or below. After 2 to 3 months, it will gradually begin to lose its fresh, delicate flavor and aroma.

Measuring butter. When you use butter for cooking, it's far easier to measure it by the stick or portion thereof than to try to cram the waxy, resistant globs into a measuring cup or spoon. Measurements are easy to remember:

1 pound	=	4 sticks	=	2 cups
2 sticks	=	½ pound	=	1 cup
1 stick	=	¼ pound	=	½ cup
½ stick	=	4 tablespoons	=	¼ cup

The thin, inner paper wrappers that enclose the individual sticks of butter of some brands are accommodatingly marked with measurements all the way down to 1 tablespoon. Just cut off the amount that your recipe calls for.

Butter's vagaries. Nothing in the fat/shortening line can come up to the sweet, delicate, almost indescribable flavor of good, fresh butter used on the table or in cooking. In fact, it's so good that we sometimes tend to use too much of it, on the wrong-headed principle that if some is good, more must be better. Not necessarily so. As is true of virtually every good thing in this world other than love, too much butter is too much.

cautionary note: When using butter as a spread for bread or a dressing for vegetables, let your good sense/waistline/ budget be your guide. But when it comes to "made dishes" (particularly baked ones), control yourself. Follow the recipe, measuring the butter as carefully as all the rest of the ingredients. Too much butter in a cake will make it heavy, destroy its texture. Too much butter in a casserole dish will result in a finished product swimming in oily liquid. Take care; measure accurately.

sautéeing and frying in butter: Butter browns—and the next step, burns—much more rapidly, particularly at high temperatures, than oil or shortening. On the plus side, it imparts delicate flavor and a lovely gentle golden-brown color to foods sautéed in it. To have the best of both choices, sauté in half-and-half butter and oil. The oil tames the butter's desire to burn; the butter gives flavor that the oil lacks.

Frying in butter is a chancy business at best. And because fried foods are not by nature delicate, there's little point in trying to fry in all butter or in butter/oil or butter/shortening combinations. (Fried eggs? Good fried eggs are not really fried. They are gently cooked in butter over very low heat.) Particularly, don't attempt to deep fry in butter—both you and the food are likely to be burned, and the whole kitchen may join the holocaust. (To understand the terms "sauté," "fry," and "deep fry" as well as other common cooking language, see the special feature: WHAT DOES IT MEAN WHEN THE RECIPE SAYS . . . ?)

creaming butter: "Cream together the butter and sugar," the directions tell you—but they don't add that if you try to cream ice-cold butter just out of the refrigerator, you've got a problem. Very hard butter chips and flakes. Slightly softened butter will soften more in the creaming process, and mix with the sugar into a desirably light, fluffy mass. On the other hand, butter that is too soft will not cream well, either. Remove it from the refrigerator and let stand about 20 minutes before beginning to cream it, either with sugar for a cake or alone to serve as the basis of a butter-plus spread for sandwiches or canapés. Spread the creamed butter all the way to the edges of the bread or toast—it helps keep the filler or topping from soaking in.

Bettering butter. There are all sorts of shortcuts, dress-ups, and other enhancers for butter available to you. Easy-do, they require only a bit of skill or know-how on your part.

clarified butter: This is also called drawn butter and (but not in this country) ghee. Use it—plain or seasoned—to sauce vegetables and as the dipping sauce served with such foods as artichokes or lobster. To clarify butter, melt it slowly over very low heat. Remove from heat and let stand for a few moments. Carefully skim off the foam of butterfat on the top; gently pour off the clear yellow liquid, leaving behind the milk solids that will have sunk to the bottom of the pan. (You may strain it, as some cookbooks direct, but unless you're the original kitchen klutz, you shouldn't need to.)

browned butter: This is best made with clarified butter—if you make it with unclarified, the milk solids are likely to burn before the butter turns a delightful nut brown (the French call it *beurre noisette*). Melt clarified butter and cook it slowly until it turns a light brown. Use it to dress asparagus, cauliflower, brains, broccoli, and many other foods—wherever a recipe calls for browned butter.

simple butter sauces: Melt clarified butter and flavor to taste with lemon juice, finely chopped parsley, prepared mustard, mixed herbs, onion or garlic juice, wine vinegar, and/or anything else that comes to your mind, depending on the food (vegetables, seafood, steak, whatever) you will sauce with it.

kneaded butter: Used to thicken sauces and cooking liquids, this is the *beurre manié* of French cooking. Add kneaded butter close to the end of the cooking time; do not boil after adding, and allow to cook only long enough to thicken the liquid, and to cook the flour so that it won't taste raw. To make, knead together equal parts of butter and flour —2 tablespoons butter, 2 tablespoons flour, for example— and add to the simmering sauce or liquid in small pieces, stirring gently. The 2-tablespoons-each combination will lightly thicken about 1 cup of liquid.

homemade whipped butter: This is one of those little extras that is not difficult, but gives the impression that you've labored long and lovingly. Whip up a batch when you intend to make homemade bread—the combination will reduce everybody to tears of joy. Or flavor this lovely, airy spread in one of dozens of ways to make perfect little finger sandwiches to serve with salad or soup, or as part of the refreshments at a reception-type party.

To make, let 1 pound of butter—sweet or salted, depending on the use you'll make of the finished product— come to room temperature. Place in the bowl of an electric mixer; add 1 whole egg. Beat at low speed until blended, then at high speed 5 minutes. Add ¼ cup cold heavy (whipping) cream. Blend at low speed; beat at high speed 10 to 15 minutes, or until very light and fluffy. Refrigerate in two 1-pound containers—your butter will have just about doubled in bulk.

Use as is, or flavor to taste with almost anything you like. Here are a few suggestions to get your imagination into gear: grated sharp cheddar cheese plus dry mustard; drained prepared horseradish; lemon juice and grated lemon peel, ditto orange juice and peel, lime juice and peel; mashed strawberries or raspberries plus confectioners sugar; anchovy paste plus a little lemon juice; cinnamon, mace, or nutmeg plus confectioners sugar; garlic juice plus lemon juice plus celery seed; finely chopped nuts of almost any kind; mashed skinless/boneless sardines; grated parmesan or romano; snipped chives or parsley or tarragon; well-drained relish plus onion powder. Get the idea?

Making butter shape up. With kitchen tools you have at hand or can acquire inexpensively at any good housewares store, you can turn butter into delightful shapes to please the eye and tempt the appetite. Some of them take a bit of practice—which is, when you see the result, well worth the trouble.

butter balls: Use the large end of a melon-ball cutter, dipped in hot water; cut balls out of hard butter, then refrigerate. For handsomer, shaplier balls, use butter paddles—a pair of striated wooden paddles some ingenious soul thought up for just this purpose. Cut butter into equal-size chunks and allow to soften slightly. Dip the paddles into scalding water, then into ice water. One at a time, roll the butter chunks between the paddles, moving the paddles in tight circles in opposite directions. Place the finished balls in ice water.

butter curls: For these you need, not surprisingly, a butter curler—it looks like an elongated metal question mark with teeth at the business end. Dip the curler into hot water, then draw smoothly across a slightly softened stick of butter. Drop the finished curls into ice water.

butter molds: These, made of wood, come in various sizes for individual or group servings. Dip the mold into scalding water, then into ice water. Pack softened butter firmly and evenly into the mold; level off with a spatula or the back of a knife. Chill. Depending on the mold's construction, press, tap, or gently force plunger to remove butter. Refrigerate.

fancy pats: Use a stick of cold butter. Dip a knife into cold water, or cover its blade with wax paper; cut pats any thickness you wish. Dip a fork in hot water and draw gently but firmly across the butter pat from one corner to another. Refrigerate. Or decorate a plain butter pat with a tiny sprig of parsley, a couple of small leaves of watercress, or a neat sprinkling of snipped chives or tarragon or other fresh herb.

fancy crocks: Small dishes, generally made of wood or pottery, are available for individual servings of butter. Pack the butter into the crock, decorate as above, refrigerate until serving time.

butter sculpture: Butter is easy to carve. With a little patience and a modicum of talent, you—or one of the adventurous children—can turn a pound of butter into an art form both pretty and functional. By tradition, people in Poland—and many of Polish descent in this country—sculpt butter into the shape of a lamb for Easter breakfast, but almost any shape you have in mind can be readily accomplished. Just be sure that you have a piece of very cold butter of proper size, and go to work. If the butter softens while you work, return it to the refrigerator for a short time. Small, sharp knives, melon ballers, and wire-bladed cheese cutters make good carving tools, as well as your fingers—their warmth helps to shape the butter. For a soft, furlike surface, put small pieces of cold butter through a wire strainer and apply carefully to the main shape. Use bits of nut, fruit, or vegetable to decorate—as the features, if you sculpt an animal, for example.

However you use it, however often, treat butter kindly—

buy only as needed and keep refrigerated—and it will reciprocate. One of the commonest of our kitchen staples, butter is so frequently and so much used we tend not to think about it unless—horrors!—we run out.

BUTTER CAKES: see CAKES

BUTTER FLAVOR: see FLAVORINGS

BUTTER LETTUCE: see SALAD GREENS AND PLANTS

BUTTERCUP SQUASH: see SQUASH

BUTTERFISH: see FISH

BUTTERMILK: see MILK

BUTTERNUT SQUASH: see SQUASH

BUTTERS, FRUIT: see special feature: PUTTING FOOD BY

BUTTERS, NUT: see NUT BUTTERS

YOUR PARTNER IN THE KITCHEN

In staggering (reassuring?) numbers, Uncle Sam's watchdogs test, check, evaluate everything we buy, every regulation we live under

Have you ever had the feeling, while you were out shopping, that someone was looking over your shoulder? Someone was, at least figuratively. Someone was keeping a watchful, avuncular eye on your major and minor purchases, on the prices you were charged, on the clerk who waited on you, on the scales that weighed your choices, on the bank where you cashed a check, on the automobile in which you drove to the store, on the clothes you wore, on—good grief, what *not* on?

If that gives you a creepy sensation, look at it from another point of view. It may not be a matter to which you gave much thought, but wasn't it nice not to find a portion of a deceased rodent in your morning breakfast cereal? Isn't it a pleasure to open a quart of milk that doesn't have assorted multilegged critters taking a bath in it? Isn't it something of a comfort to know that tonight's pot roast didn't come from a steer that died of some mysterious debilitating disease? For all this, and much, much more, thank Uncle.

Would you like to know the safe way to home can green beans? Where to complain about your new slow cooker that keeps blowing a fuse? What to do about those little bugs that are chomping their way through your tomato patch? If microwave ovens are really safe? Whether those alfalfa-and-rose-hips capsules grandpa gulps are good for him? What to pack in a safe and nutritionally sound brown-bag lunch? How to feed your husband on his low-sodium diet? For answers to these and hundreds more questions that plague you daily, ask Uncle.

All of the government's watchdogs and regulating bodies don't, of course, have directly to do with our kitchens. But they have to do with our lives in ways that affect our ability to cope with our kitchens—and our families, our work, our recreation, our living in general, all of our daily concerns.

AN ALPHABET OF AGENCIES

For some reason not totally clear, government agencies and departments tend to be christened with more-than-a-mouthful names, and all their works with jaw-breaking titles. (Perhaps there is an agency whose sole purpose is to name agencies?) As a kind of defensive shorthand, most of the departments and agencies and many of their works are known by acronyms—coined terms made up of the initial letters of the words in their names. Thus our oldest watchdog friend, the United States Department of Agriculture, is known far and wide as the USDA. The Food and Drug Administration is the FDA, and its list of substances Generally Recognized As Safe is the GRAS list. The Federal Trade Commission is the FTC, the Interstate Commerce Commission the ICC, the Internal Revenue Service the IRS, the Federal Communications Commission the FCC—all familiar acronyms that we're so used to seeing in print or hearing on the news that we pay no attention to them.

Consumers take heart. The most important acronym agency concerned with our welfare as consumers (not only with food, but with everything we buy and use) is the OCA—Office of Consumer Affairs—which is a subsidiary of HEW—Health, Education and Welfare, a cabinet-level department. FDA is also an arm of HEW.

OCA monitors the activities and programs of the constantly proliferating government agencies and departments concerned with the consumer, and, in the words of the OCA's director, "has been involved in the creation of many of these new Federal consumer programs, coordinated the Federal response to consumers' rights, and continues to propose and encourage additional recognition of consumer problems by existing Federal Departments and Agencies."

Because the OCA is in existence to see that you have information you need to make a wise selection, a choice available to you, redress if the article you buy does not live up to its claims, and education concerning products and concerning consumerism itself, it publishes a *Guide to Federal Consumer Services*. In this are listed all the government departments and agencies that have in any way to do with the consumer, along with the subsidiaries of each and the functions of each subsidiary, and the name and phone number of the administrator of each of the consumer programs.

This publication, *Guide to Federal Consumer Services*, is DHEW Publication no. (OS) 76-512, available from the Superintendent of Documents, Pueblo, Colorado 81009. Available also, from the same source, is *Consumer Information*, a catalog of approximately 250 selected federal publications of consumer interest, and *Selected U.S. Government Publications*, a monthly catalog of popular government publications. You may have one copy of any of these free for the asking.

The United States Government Printing Office is a busy place, turning out millions of words a year on hundreds of topics. Some of the publications, many of them of consumer and particularly homemaker interest, are free. Some are available at nominal cost. Others—the *Congressional Record,* for example—come high. (It's unlikely you'll want the *Congressional Record* for your home bookshelves, particularly at millions of words and $45.00 a year, but it's worth taking a look at. Ask for it at your public library, and find out what our senators and representatives talk about and consider during congressional sessions. Some of it will please you with its relevancy, some of it stun you with its irrelevancy. Either way, it's a mind boggler.)

Two publications that are totally relevant as far as consumers are concerned are also put out by HEW: *Consumer News* and *FDA Consumer,* both chock full of eye-opening information.

Consumer News. This is a twice-monthly newsletter published by OCA to report on federal government programs for consumers. (Available through Consumer Information Center, Pueblo, Colorado 81009, and is priced at $4.00 for a yearly subscription.)

Information in *Consumer News* is brief, most often summaries of pending conferences, new regulations, and so on, often followed by a source for further information if you wish it. Each issue of the newsletter also contains a supplement, *Consumer Register,* which summarizes federal actions and offers the opportunity for you, the consumer, to comment on these actions before they take effect, through blanks to be filled in and mailed to the agency concerned.

To give you an idea, one issue of *Consumer News* contained the following bits of news, among others. Caution on mounting CB antennas and suggestions on theft alarms for CBs. Nominations to the seventeen-member U.S. Metric Board. Recalls of poultry seasoning (distributors and brand names given) because the products were rodent and insect contaminated. Recalls of various pieces of literature distributed to promote the sale of water stills because the brochures ("Probe U.S. Water for Cancer Threat," for example) were filled with untrue information. Recalls of several makes of tires because of defects, including information as to how to proceed if you owned these tires. A seasonal buying calendar, with best buys—the most for the money—for each month of the year. Recent Supreme Court decisions affecting benefits for dependent children. New ICC regulations concerning household movers. Approval of new bus and plane fares, including amounts and routes covered. Information about state offices to assist consumers in problems concerned with public utility rates. A list of some particularly interesting new federal publications. Investigation of possible unfair or deceptive acts or practices in connection with the

sale of memberships in buying clubs. Recalls of television sets. Notices of hearings on energy-saving household appliances. Recalls of testing strips for diabetics. And much more.

FDA Consumer. This magazine, issued ten times a year, is concerned with recent developments in the regulation of food, drugs, and cosmetics by the Food and Drug Administration. (Also available from the Consumer Information Center, $10.00 a year.) The magazine offers well-written, interesting, illustrated (often in color) information on a variety of topics, each with a considerably greater in-depth coverage than *Consumer News* is able to give. You will find such features as an article on how and why manufacturers of devices must prove they are safe and effective, a discussion of public misunderstandings about FDA functions and policies (entitled, plaintively, "To Serve Well and Not to Please"), information on gearing up to prevent a flu epidemic, how pesticide and bacteriological analyses of food are made, improving food service sanitation, how to read prescriptions. A section, "News Highlights," deals with FDA actions in brief—topics such as withdrawal of approval on use of certain drugs used to promote growth in chickens and turkeys, ingredient labeling on baby food, new regulations governing "hypoallergenic" cosmetics. Another section, "Update," concerns itself with new information on topics previously covered in the magazine—cough-and-cold drugs now available over the counter, breast X-ray examinations, how fats and oil in foods must be designated on labels. Other departments in the magazine report—by state and region—FDA actions such as recalls and seizures of products, closing of plants, including brand names, manufacturers' names—all you might need to know.

OCA also puts out *Directory of Consumer Organizations,* a listing of nongovernmental consumer-service groups at local, state, and national levels, to which you can have recourse if dealing with Uncle directly is not your thing.

Give Uncle a call. In addition to its agencies and departments, the federal government operates a call-for-help hotline—or, rather, a large number of them. If you, as a consumer, have questions about any program or agency or any function or service of any program or agency, you can telephone a Federal Information Center for quick answers, direc-

tions on how to proceed, referral to a proper source for guidance. Here are the hotline locations and phone numbers:

Alabama			**Missouri**	
Birmingham	205/322–8591		Kansas City	816/374–2466
Mobile	205/438–1421		St. Joseph	816/233–8206
Arizona			St. Louis	314/425–4106
Tucson	602/622–1511		**Nebraska**	
Phoenix	602/261–3313		Omaha	402/221–3353
Arkansas			**New Jersey**	
Little Rock	501/378–6177		Newark	201/645–3600
California			Trenton	609/396–4400
Los Angeles	213/688–3800		**New Mexico**	
Sacramento	916/440–3344		Albuquerque	505/766–3091
San Diego	714/293–6030		Santa Fe	505/983–7743
San Francisco	415/556–6600		**New York**	
San Jose	408/275–7422		Albany	518/463–4421
Colorado			Buffalo	716/842–5770
Colorado Springs	303/471–9491		New York	212/264–4464
Denver	303/837–3602		Rochester	716/546–5075
Pueblo	303/544–9523		Syracuse	315/476–8545
Connecticut			**North Carolina**	
Hartford	203/527–2617		Charlotte	704/376–3600
New Haven	203/624–4720		**Ohio**	
District of Columbia			Akron	216/375–5638
Washington	202/755–8660		Cincinnati	513/684–2801
Florida			Cleveland	216/522–4040
Fort Lauderdale	305/522–8531		Columbus	614/221–1014
Miami	305/350–4155		Dayton	513/223–7377
Jacksonville	904/354–4756		Toledo	419/244–8625
St. Petersburg	813/893–3495		**Oklahoma**	
Tampa	813/229–7911		Oklahoma City	405/231–4868
West Palm Beach	305/833–7566		Tulsa	918/584–4193
Georgia			**Oregon**	
Atlanta	404/526–6891		Portland	503/221–2222
Hawaii			**Pennsylvania**	
Honolulu	808/546–8620		Philadelphia	215/597–7042
Illinois			Pittsburgh	412/644–3456
Chicago	312/353–4242		Scranton	717/346–7081
Indiana			**Rhode Island**	
Indianapolis	317/269–7373		Providence	401/331–5565
Iowa			**Tennessee**	
Des Moines	515/282–9091		Chattanooga	615/265–8231
Kansas			Memphis	901/521–3285
Topeka	913/232–7229		Nashville	615/242–5056
Wichita	316/263–6931		**Texas**	
Kentucky			Austin	512/472–5494
Louisville	502/582–6162		Dallas	214/749–2131
Louisiana			Fort Worth	817/334–3624
New Orleans	504/589–6696		Houston	713/226–5711
Maryland			San Antonio	512/224–4471
Baltimore	301/962–4980		**Utah**	
Massachusetts			Ogden	801/399–1347
Boston	617/223–7121		Salt Lake City	801/524–5353
Michigan			**Washington**	
Detroit	313/226–7016		Tacoma	206/383–5230
Minnesota			Seattle	206/442–0570
Minneapolis	612/725–2073		**Wisconsin**	
			Milwaukee	414/271–2273

And here are some further numbers—addresses, too—that may come in handy in your unceasing battle with inanimate objects.

consumer affairs:

Office of Consumer Affairs
Washington, DC 20201
202/755–8830

Consumer Information Center
General Services Administration
Washington, DC 20469
202/566–1794

consumer and homemaking education:

Office of Education
Washington, DC 20202
202/245–3478

food:

Special Assistant to Secretary for Consumer Affairs
Agriculture Department
Washington, DC 20250
202/447–3165

Office of Consumer Inquiries
Food & Drug Administration
5600 Fishers Lane
Rockville, MD 20851
301/443–3170

consumer products:

Bureau of Information & Education
Consumer Product Safety Commission
Bethesda, MD 20207
301/492–6504

Gentlemen's disagreement. Now and then a little agency infighting develops over who does what to whom. Witness this quote from *Consumer News:*

> Consumer Product Safety Commission (CPSC) has reached agreement with Food and Drug Administration (FDA) concerning jurisdiction over such food-related articles as pressure cookers, slow cookers, refrigerators, freezers, and home canning equipment. Agreement was necessary because of the uncertainty concerning which agency had jurisdiction to deal with hazards of food spoilage resulting from home canning lids that fail to seal properly. Under the CPSC and FDA agreement, articles used by consumers for preparation or storage of foods are under the jurisdiction of CPSC. If food becomes contaminated as a result of a substance in the container, FDA has jurisdiction to eliminate the hazard.

Sometimes, as you can see, it's indeed difficult to tell the players without a program. Take pineapple and strawberries as a for-instance. Both are fruit, right? So standards for both should be under the control of the same agency, right? Wrong. Here are two side-by-side quotes from the same issue of *Consumer News,* lumped under the general heading "standards":

PINEAPPLE JUICE—Food and Drug Administration (FDA) has revised its standards of identity and quality for canned pineapple juice. New standards will permit use of concentrated pineapple juice in preparation of canned juice and labeled "pineapple juice from concentrate."

FROZEN STRAWBERRIES—Aug. 31 is deadline for comment on Agriculture Dept.'s proposal to revise standards for grades of frozen strawberries. . . . Proposal revises requirements on color and provides for "halved" berries as a new style that has become popular. Proposal also further restricts the maximum allowance for mushy strawberries in the sliced style.

Besides illustrating a certain overlapping of areas of jurisdiction, those two quotes make another, and more comforting, point: Someone Cares. Federal watchdogs—never mind from which agency—have their eye on every product we lug home from the supermarket, virtually every bite that goes into our mouths. Maybe the idea of Uncle breathing down your neck as you lap up your morning porridge makes you nervous—but it could be a whole lot more nervous-making if you really had no idea whether the porridge would nourish you or knock you off.

YOU AND USDA, HAND IN HAND

According to its own evaluation of its duties and services, these are the functions of USDA vis-à-vis the consumer:

The Department of Agriculture (USDA) is headed by a Secretary, a member of the Cabinet, who is appointed by the President. The Department is directed by law to acquire and disseminate useful information on agricultural subjects in the broadest sense, including areas of research, education, conservation, marketing, regulatory work, and rural development programs.

Agriculture Research Service (ARS) provides the necessary knowledge and technology so that farmers can produce efficiently, conserve the environment, and meet the food and fiber needs of the American people. The agency conducts USDA's basic research in human nutrition and national dietary levels.

Animal and Plant Health Inspection Service (APHIS) conducts regulatory and control programs to protect the wholesomeness of meat and poultry products for human consumption, including meat and poultry inspection, animal and plant quarantine, and disease and pest control programs.

Economic Research Service (ERS) develops and carries out a program of research to provide economic intelligence for agriculture, agriculture-related industries, and the public on all aspects of food production, consumption, and prices.

Extension Service (ES), in cooperation with state and county governments, conducts continuing education programs for youth and adults in agricultural production, home economics, family life, and related subjects.

Farmers Home Administration (FmHA) provides credit for those in rural America who are unable to get credit from other sources at reasonable rates and terms.

Food and Nutrition Service (FNS) administers the USDA's various food assistance programs, such as food stamps and child nutrition.

Forest Service (FS) provides for the conservation and wise use of the nation's forest and land resources, including recreational uses.

Office of Communications provides information on all consumer programs of the USDA. Publications on a variety of subjects of interest to consumers are available free or for a minimal charge. Also available are slides, filmstrips, and exhibits of use to consumer organizations.

Rural Development Service (RDS) coordinates social and economic development programs in rural areas of the nation, including a wide range of assistance measures for communities of 10,000 population or less.

Special Assistant to the Secretary of Agriculture for Consumer Affairs coordinates the USDA actions on problems and issues of major importance to consumers.

One can only conclude that, down there at USDA, they're a busy bunch, most of them involved in one way or another with seeing that what we eat is not only fit to, but good to. Here's a closer look at some of the workings of those services.

A wealth of reading matter. You name it, the USDA has available a pamphlet on it. If you were totally ignorant about food, didn't know a wiener from a waffle or an egg from a chicken, you could find out all you'd need to know to make you an informed shopper and a competent (if not sensational) cook by reading pamphlets published by USDA. There's a pamphlet explaining grading and how to be guided by USDA grades. There are how-to booklets on buying fresh fruits, fresh vegetables, beef, poultry, dry beans and peas, canned and frozen fruits, cheese, lamb, potatoes, dairy products, meat for your freezer, canned and frozen vegetables, eggs, whatever. Each one tells you what to look for, how to choose, differences between grades, and offers tips on care, storage, and cooking. Other leaflets describe basic cooking methods and contain recipes for almost any edible you can think of. Some pamphlets are free, some are available for a very small charge.

USDA is in the bigger-book business, too. Annually it publishes the *Yearbook of Agriculture,* each year's volume dealing in depth with some aspect of homemaking. For example, the 1974 yearbook was a 368-page *Shopper's Guide,* a massive rundown of how to buy wisely everything from steaks to concrete blocks to franklin stoves to apple trees to backpacks to credit. A sampling of some other yearbook titles includes *Food for Us All, Handbook for the Home, Consumers All.*

One of USDA's major triumphs is *Nutritive Value of American Foods in Common Units,* which is just what its title says it is—a listing of the nutritive value of everything edible. To give you an idea of how big Agriculture is in the book business, this monster assemblage of information is labeled "Agriculture Handbook No. 456"—think of all the handbooks that went before, all that follow!

Guides to quality—standards and grading. USDA grades many of the fresh foods in our markets, and formulates and publishes standards—which must be adhered to—for vast numbers of processed foods. It also inspects plants where food is manufactured or processed to make certain the premises are clean, that the food is handled in a sanitary manner.

The USDA shield that marks the grades of meat sold at retail—Prime, Choice, Good, Standard—is a familiar one to most shoppers (see BEEF) and almost as familiar is the grade shield—AA, A, B—on butter (see BUTTER) and eggs (see EGGS). The shield appears on other foods as well. Graded poultry carries the shield on packages of fresh or frozen chickens, turkeys, ducks, geese, guinea hens. (But the USDA shield is not on fish and shellfish. For some obscure reason we won't pursue lest it stir up internecine strife, the DOC—Department of Commerce—through its National Marine Fisheries Service, inspects, grades, and develops standards of quality, conditions, quantity, grade, and packaging for fishery plants, fish, and fishery products.)

Less conspicuous and therefore less familiar to shoppers is the USDA grade shield on fresh fruits and vegetables, cheddar cheese, and processed fruits, vegetables, and related products, such as peanut butter, jelly, and jam. About 35 percent of canned and 65 percent of frozen fruits and vegetables are officially graded. In these areas, Grades A and B are desirable for table use, according to USDA standards; lower grades are suitable for use in stews, casseroles, and puddings because they may consist of less tender, irregularly shaped pieces.

Grading is voluntary, and fees are paid by the food producers or processors for inspection and grading. Thus, there can be much perfectly good food on the market that does not carry the USDA grade shield. But the lack of it causes many shoppers to wonder why a particular plant or processor would not be willing to pay for the service, so that his food can wear the shield in which many consumers have faith.

Establishment of standards is also voluntary. For exam-ple, at the time this is being written the poultry industry has asked the Department of Agriculture to establish standards for cooked sausage—frankfurters, bologna, and knockwurst—made from poultry, to assure uniformity and consistency. A survey indicated that there were, at the time of the request, 344 approved labels for poultry sausage products produced by 66 plants. Products with such labels as "Turkey Franks" and "Chicken Wieners," the industry pointed out, were gaining consumer acceptance.

In response, after a period of investigation, USDA suggested standards. They included such points as a maximum of 25 percent fat to be allowed in the finished product, a minimum of 12 percent protein. A listing of the kinds of binders used—dried skim milk, soy protein concentrate, vegetable starch—would have to be on the label. If giblets were included in the making of the product, that information would be required on the label as well.

The next step in such a procedure is that all details are published in the Federal Register, and a hearing date set. Consumers and other interested parties are invited to send their comments to the USDA's hearing clerk before that date. When the hearing occurs, these written comments are considered, as well as USDA experts' reasons for establishing each detail of the standards, and the industry's objections or questions, or countering points of view. Finally, the standards—perhaps amended, perhaps not—are agreed to by all parties, and go into effect. Once they have, they must be adhered to.

Help is waiting in the wings. Among its multitude of concerns, the USDA administers the federal food stamp program. Food stamps are coupons that can be spent in the same way as money for food at almost any food store. The program was started to help those with low incomes to have an adequate diet. Eligible are people who are unemployed or employed only part time, full-time employed with very low income, those on welfare, and those on Social Security and/or small pensions. The able-bodied between eighteen and sixty-five years of age (with some few exceptions) must register for employment and be willing to accept a job if a suitable one is found, to be eligible for the food stamp program.

Food stamps are purchased. The amount that can be purchased and the cost are determined by the number of members in the household unit and the total amount of household income after certain deductions such as rent, utilities, medical expenses, taxes, and such. The amount a household pays for its food stamps is called the purchase requirement; the total amount of stamps a household receives is the coupon allotment. As an example, a family might be eligible for a monthly purchase requirement of $14, a monthly coupon allotment of $192. That means that the household buys $192 worth of spendable (for food) "money" and pays $14 for it. Or a family with a different number of members, a higher net income, might be eligible to purchase $90 worth of coupons at a cost of $70, and so on.

The coupons can be spent exactly as cash is spent, but only for food items. Such things as cigarettes, alcoholic beverages, soap, paper products, and pet food cannot be bought with food stamps.

AT HOME AND ABROAD WITH THE FDA

"What you don't know can't hurt you," says an old saw. Nothing, the FDA believes, could be farther from the truth. In order to make sure that the food, drugs, and cosmetics we use can't harm us, the FDA is constantly testing and accepting or rejecting all sorts of domestic items in those categories, as well as imported ones that will go on sale here.

To accomplish this requires large laboratories and an enormous number of people who constantly look at products of all sorts and ask questions. Is this just exactly what the label says it is? Does it contain any adulterants? Contaminants? Does it weigh what the label claims? Does the label state all the required information? And, less scientifically and more humanly, does it look good, taste good? If not, why not? What went wrong; why did it happen? By accident or on purpose?

Most interesting of the equipment the FDA uses is that housed in its mobile laboratories—and, indeed, the laboratories themselves, in which Mohammed constantly goes to the mountain.

Here, excerpted from a report in the *FDA Consumer,* is an account of how these laboratories function and the varied work they do.

Watchdogs on wheels. In the old West, circuit-riding federal judges, dressed in black coats, carrying law books, and mounted on horseback or traveling by stagecoach, journeyed throughout their assigned territories to help protect frontier folk by hearing cases against accused law breakers. Today, FDA's version of the frontier circuit rider drives a large, scientifically equipped mobile laboratory, dresses in a white laboratory coat, and carries scientific books and instruments for use in protecting consumers from potentially harmful foods, drugs, and cosmetics.

While the judicial circuit riders of old dealt solely with trying and punishing offenders, FDA's regulatory circuit riders concentrate much of their effort on detecting and preventing offenses by inspecting domestic food processing plants for insanitary conditions, and by examining domestic and imported products for possible health hazards before they reach consumers.

The mobile laboratories, now deployed nationwide by FDA, bear little resemblance to the first of their breed—two heavy-duty World War II army trailers that were towed by

tractor. They were loaned to FDA by the army in the early 1950s for use in inspecting crab-picking houses and strawberry-processing plants. In 1953, FDA purchased two 21-foot trailers, which were towed by car and used primarily for pesticide and bacteriological analyses of foods, and for use in inspecting flour mills and a variety of food-processing plants. In 1964, two 35-foot trailer labs were delivered to FDA and used for similar field work. One is still being used as a permanent lab for pesticide analysis at Nogales, Arizona. The current fleet of self-propelled labs began to take shape in 1972 with the delivery to FDA of three 22-foot mobile vans designed primarily for use in filth-in-food analysis. The fleet now numbers twenty-three, including three remodeled postal vans in use since 1971 in New York for dockside inspections of products offered for import. In addition, four step vans are used for radiological enforcement activities.

The types of inspection and analyses that mobile labs can perform have increased dramatically since the early days of crab and strawberry plant inspections. Today, labs are used by FDA personnel to inspect food warehouses and processing plants for insanitary conditions and to analyze shellfish, fish, low-acid canned vegetables, fruits, and spices for chemical, pesticide, and microbiological contamination as well as for filth. They also have been used to analyze dinnerware for the presence of lead and cadmium that might get into food, to verify economic deception such as mislabeling or short-weighting, and to enforce drug and cosmetic labeling requirements. In all, these labs have been used in twenty-two different types of inspection programs dealing with food, drugs, and cosmetics.

The mobile labs are based in nine of FDA's ten regions, which cover the United States, Guam, and Puerto Rico. Most are based near large metropolitan areas that have port facilities, such as Boston, New York, Miami, Los Angeles, and Seattle.

Because they are mobile, the labs often are assigned to offices other than their home base for use in inspection of food-processing operations of a seasonal nature and for special projects, such as conducting surveys of food-processing facilities known to be chronic violators of FDA regulations.

Versatility is the word that best describes the 22-foot general sanitation labs, which are the backbone of the mobile fleet. They are equipped primarily for use in examining canned and packaged foods for insect and rodent contamination and for use in inspecting food-processing plants and warehouses for similar contamination. For example, FDA's Kansas City District sends its general sanitation lab for a month-long round of inspections of wheat-storage facilities in Kansas and Nebraska. Staffed by an FDA inspector and a chemist, the lab is used for on-the-spot analysis of stored wheat for insect, rodent, and other contaminants, to help reduce shipments of unacceptable grain from the firms.

At one point, the same lab was temporarily assigned to FDA's Minneapolis District, where it was restaffed by a chemist and a physical science technician who spent the next two months—the height of the canning season for corn, peas, and beans—inspecting canneries in Wisconsin. The two-man team checked cans for proper ingredients, weight, and labeling and for compliance with filth-in-food regulations. They also assisted FDA inspectors in checking plants for insanitary conditions.

The mobile labs also have proved to be a valuable and versatile resource in emergencies. In the fall of 1972, the general sanitation mobile lab based at FDA's facility in New York City was sent to Wilkes-Barre, Pennsylvania, to serve as an office for federal employees who were providing help and advice to flood victims in the area. The lab was also used as a station by the Red Cross for inoculation of flood victims.

All the 22-foot labs come equipped with the same basic laboratory equipment, including a ventilation fume hood, refrigerator, freezer, a water bath that can be held at a constant temperature for use in various food analyses, garbage disposal, and balances to weigh and blend samples undergoing analysis. Other equipment, such as centrifuges, microscopes, vacuum pumps, sieves, and calculators are added when needed for a particular investigation. The labs can be modified to meet particular needs. In Boston, for example, the general sanitation lab is equipped to handle microbiological analyses because of the emphasis on seafood inspection at the Port of Boston.

Staffing of the mobile labs depends on the purpose for which they are being used. Usually a specialist—a chemist, an entomologist, or a microbiologist—is teamed with an inspector for inspection of food facilities and collection and analyses of samples.

Bringing a laboratory on wheels to a dock or a food-processing plant, rather than sending samples to a stationary lab, speeds the process of analyzing food for potential health hazards and increases the number of inspections FDA can conduct. In addition, the prominently marked vehicles give increased visibility to FDA. One FDA district official says that several industry people have told him that just the presence of a mobile lab is enough to get industry to "shape up."

MORE GOVERNMENT FINGERS IN THE HOME PIE

USDA is not by any manner or means the only government agency that is largely consumer oriented, nor is FDA the only arm of HEW concerned with the consumer. There are more —many more.

Department of Commerce. As we've seen, DOC inspects and grades fish and fishery products. It also supervises patents and trademarks to protect consumers from confusion—or deception—in brand identification. One of its chief functions, from the consumer point of view, is the National Bureau of Standards. The Bureau develops specifications, rating schemes, and label designs to provide information on the energy efficiency of major household appliances; provides technical assistance in developing safety standards to reduce risk of injury associated with consumer products; and provides product information to guide the consumer in making purchase decisions.

Also an arm of DOC is the National Fire Prevention and Control Administration, which monitors residential fire detectors, assists in the development of fire safety standards for consumer products, and conducts educational programs on methods of fire prevention.

Department of Defense. One of its functions is to check the suitability and condition of perishable food and processed food purchased for military resale through post PXs. The department also inspects all nonfood merchandise sold through the PX system.

Department of Health, Education and Welfare. This is the federal department most concerned with people and with the nation's human needs. It has a number of divisions.

The Office of Consumer Education is responsible for consumer services and provides support to states, local education agencies, institutions of higher education, and a variety of nonprofit organizations—including libraries—for initiation or expansion of consumer education projects. The Consumer and Homemaking Education Program provides funds to states to assist them and through them local education agencies in developing consumer and homemaking education programs. One-third of the program's funds are set aside for projects aiding persons in economically depressed areas and groups with high unemployment rates—migrant workers, Indians, the aged, people in correctional institutions.

HEW's Office for Civil Rights administers and enforces the laws, rules, and regulations that prohibit discrimination with regard to race, color, national origin, religion, mental or physical handicap, and sex.

The Office of Human Development is concerned with "vulnerable" Americans—those with special needs. Among its arms are the Administration on Aging, the Development Disabilities Office, the Office of Child Development, the Office of Native American Programs, the Office of Youth Development (which operates the National Runaway Switchboard —800/621–4000 is its number), and the Rehabilitation Services Administration.

The Public Health Service supervises the Office of Nursing Home Affairs, the Office of International Affairs, and the Office of Population Affairs, and administers six operating agencies: the Alcohol, Drug Abuse, and Mental Health Administration; the Center for Disease Control; the FDA; the Health Resources Administration; the Health Services Administration; and the National Institutes of Health.

The Social and Rehabilitation Service helps the states to provide money, medical care, and social services to people in need through its three arms: Assistance Payments Administration (assistance to blind, aged, disabled persons in Guam, Puerto Rico, and the Virgin Islands; and ill and destitute American citizens returning from foreign countries; and grants to states to assist in providing cash payments to needy families with dependent children); Public Services Administration (programs to serve children, families, aged and handicapped, and others who may not be receiving public welfare); and Medical Services Administration (Medicaid).

HEW also administrates Social Security and Medicare, and a program of cash assistance payments to the needy, aged, blind, and disabled through the Social Security Administration.

We've already taken a look at the Office of Consumer Affairs and Food and Drug Administration, both functions of HEW.

Department of Housing and Urban Development (HUD)
serves the consumer with crime insurance in places where it is difficult to obtain or not affordable, and flood insurance at a subsidized rate. Through Housing Assistance, it insures mortgages to finance the construction, purchase, or improvement of one- to four-family houses for low- and moderate-income families, and to finance rehabilitation or purchase of houses in declining neighborhoods and urban renewal areas. Interstate Land Sales Registration supervises developers of subdivisions.

Minimum Property Standards provides a basis for planning and design, defines minimum level of quality acceptable to HUD, and has developed mobile home construction and safety standards to improve the quality and durability of mobile homes. Mortgage Credit Assistance for Homeownership provides mortgage insurance for low- and moderate-income families whose credit history does not qualify them for insurance through normal channels. Real Estate Settlement Procedures provides consumers with better and more timely information on the nature and cost of closing and settlement of housing purchases than is available from private sources. Structural Defects Repairs provides for federal reimbursement in certain circumstances for the repair of defects affecting safety and habitability of some HUD-insured houses in declining urban neighborhoods.

Department of the Interior.
The function of this department is to appraise, manage, conserve, and develop the nation's public land, park, mineral, water, wildlife, and energy resources, and to protect the environment. It operates the Bureau of Land Management, Bureau of Outdoor Recreation, Fish and Wildlife Service, Geological Survey, Indian Arts and Crafts Board, and the National Park Service.

Department of Justice.
This is the principal law-enforcement arm of the federal government. Among the laws it enforces are those for consumer protection, referred to it through other federal agencies. Also of interest to the consumer is the enforcement of antitrust laws to prevent restraints of trade and mergers or other concentrations of economic power that might lead to monopoly and unfair pricing.

Department of Labor.
Functions are to serve the public through its Bureau of International Labor Affairs, Bureau of Labor Statistics, Employment and Training Administration programs, Employment Standards Administration (workers' compensation, equal opportunity employment), Labor-Management Services Administration, and Occupational Safety and Health Administration.

Department of Transportation.
The concerns of this department are the Coast Guard, Federal Aviation Administration, Federal Highway Administration, Federal Railroad Administration, National Highway Traffic Safety Administration, and Urban Mass Transportation Administration.

Department of the Treasury.
This government arm is concerned with consumers through its Alcohol, Tobacco and Firearms unit; the Internal Revenue Service; and U.S. Customs. Its Comptroller of the Currency oversees national banks with a staff of examiners who audit banks to ensure solvency and protect depositors. The department also controls the U.S. Savings Bonds program.

Consumer Product Safety Commission.
An independent regulatory agency, the commission's purpose is to protect the consumer against unreasonable risks associated with consumer products, to assist consumers in evaluating the comparative safety of those products, to develop uniform safety standards and minimize conflicting state and local regulations, to promote research, and to investigate product-related deaths, illnesses, and injuries. It deals with over ten thousand consumer products, and operates the National Electronic Injury Surveillance System to monitor hospital emergency rooms nationwide for injuries associated with these products. It has authority over the Federal Hazardous Substances Act, the Flammable Fabrics Act, the Poison Prevention Packaging Act, and the Refrigerator Safety Act. Consumers are encouraged to volunteer as Consumer Deputies to assist in surveys to identify unsafe products, and to place their names on the roster from which volunteers are selected to participate in various CPSC activities.

Some of the other government departments and agencies that have various consumer functions include the Civil Aeronautics Board, Commission on Civil Rights, Commodity Futures Trading Commission, Energy Research and Development Administration, Environmental Protection Agency, Equal Employment Opportunity Commission, Federal Communications Commission, Federal Deposit Insurance Corporation (FDIC), Federal Energy Administration, Federal Home Loan Bank Board, Federal Maritime Commission, Federal Power Commission, Federal Reserve System, Federal Trade Commission, General Services Administration, Government Printing Office, Interstate Commerce Commission, Library of Congress, National Credit Union Administration, Pension Benefit Guaranty Corporation, Postal Rate Commission, Postal Service, Securities and Exchange Commission, and Small Business Administration.

Too much, too little, right on the button? We tend to sniff, many of us, at the cradle-to-grave care policies of countries with governments more socialistic than ours. And we tend to complain, many of us, that our own government meddles too much, too often, in our private affairs. We moan about taxes. We chafe under regulations. We deplore bureaucracy, grumble about red tape.

On the other hand, if something goes wrong and the government isn't there to back us up or bail us out, we're resentful. We howl that we pay our taxes and we have a right to help from public servants.

The thing is, we can't have it both ways. This little homily wasn't meant to be either pro or anti government's hand in our daily goings-out and comings-in, but only to point out the multitude of matters in which Uncle tries (sometimes efficiently, sometimes inefficiently, often officiously, always strong-mindedly, once in a while pig-headedly) to help us.

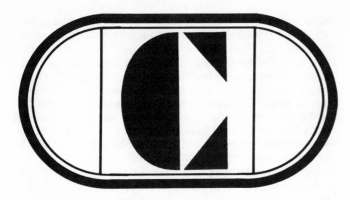

CABBAGE

Caput is Latin for "head" and is probably the root from which —through countless permutations—the word "cabbage" derived. But the early Romans, who were exceedingly fond of cabbage, didn't know the headed-up variety we think of as cabbage today. That sort requires a cooler climate. Roman cabbages were probably loose-leafed—kale, collards, and the like. Cato praised cabbage fulsomely as the best of vegetables, to be eaten either raw or cooked. Raw cabbage, he suggested, should be dipped in vinegar. And, he pointed out, it "promotes digestion marvelously."

Early Greeks appreciated cabbage, too, and not only as a vegetable that could be served in a variety of ways. It was bruted about that a large quantity of cabbage made a good absorber for wine and spirits, and much cabbage was consumed to ward off—or at least stave off—inebriation.

The Celts brought cabbage to northern Europe, where the English, a splendid people in many ways but the world's worst vegetable cooks, boiled it without mercy and served it up looking as if it had barely survived a disaster. That's still the way to deal with cabbage throughout much of the British Isles. Not many years ago an Irish nurse stood up manfully (personfully?) to the doctor who had recommended her and said she could not, despite the patient's precarious condition, remain in that house another moment. "The missus," she explained, "tried to feed me raw cabbage."

Slavs and Germans took to cabbage at once. It has been a part of the daily diet of those peoples ever since, and they have worked out many interesting and delicious ways to serve it. The Scandinavians use a lot of cabbage, too. An explorer, as has so often been the case, was responsible for bringing cabbage here. Jacques Cartier planted the vegetable in Canada during his 1541 venture to the New World. Early colonists raised cabbage to feed both themselves and their livestock.

And, of course, for many years in many countries it has been a close race to see whether the stork brings the new baby or whether it has been fortuitously found in the cabbage patch.

Assorted shapes and sizes. Besides all its collateral relatives—kale, brussels sprouts, cauliflower, collards, and the like—there are several kissing-kin varieties of cabbage to choose among, a kind to suit almost any purpose. As early as 1828, a seed catalog listed eighteen varieties. However, for ordinary kitchen purposes, you need to know only the following kinds.

danish: Matures late, rounding into a solid, slightly flattened head that is smooth on top.

domestic: Not as compact, with somewhat curled leaf edges, these cabbages are an early- to mid-season crop.

"new" cabbage: Smaller, slightly pointy heads of bright, fresh green—matures early, doesn't store as well as other kinds.

savoy: Handsome, crinkled leaves of pale to dark green, overlapping into a rather loose head.

red cabbage: Rather loose-leaved heads of red to purple.

celery or chinese cabbage: Long, slender, and crisp, pale green to almost white—most often used raw, but delicious cooked.

CABBAGE IN YOUR KITCHEN

Sold by the pound, cabbage is one of our less expensive vegetables. Count on a pound for four servings; this will yield about 3½ cups shredded raw cabbage, which will cook down to about 2½ cups.

how to buy: Look for firm heads, solid and heavy for their size (particularly danish and domestic). Pass by any with yellowed or browned leaves. Cabbages with split heads have been left too long before picking—skip them, too.

how to store: In the refrigerator crisper, or in a closed plastic bag, up to 8 days. If there are any wilted leaves, pluck them off before storing the cabbage. Refrigerate cooked cabbage, covered, up to 4 days.

nutritive value: Rich in vitamin C, with some vitamin A, and low in fat and carbohydrates, cabbage is a dieter's delight. One cup of coarsely shredded raw cabbage contains 17 calories; an equal measure of coarsely shredded cooked cabbage, 29 calories. Other values are:

	raw	cooked	
protein	.9	1.6	grams
fat	.1	.3	gram
carbohydrate	3.8	6.2	grams
calcium	34	64	milligrams
phosphorus	20	29	milligrams
iron	.3	.4	milligram
sodium	14	20	milligrams
potassium	163	236	milligrams
thiamin	.04	.06	milligram
riboflavin	.04	.06	milligram
niacin	.2	.4	milligram
ascorbic acid	33	48	milligrams
vitamin A	90	190	international units

The above values are for common cabbage varieties—danish, domestic, new. Red and savoy cabbages vary only slightly from these. Celery (chinese) cabbage is somewhat lower on all counts.

Tips on preparing, cooking. Whatever the kind of cabbage, wash it well and remove any wilted leaves. Quarter, remove most of the core, and cook in wedges or coarsely shredded. Or prepare as the recipe you want to follow directs.

Cook cabbage only a short time, in a small amount of water—an average of 12 to 15 minutes total time for wedges, 5 to 8 minutes for the shredded. Cook, uncovered, over high heat for the first 2 to 3 minutes of cooking time; then lower heat, cover, and finish cooking. Drain well, season to taste. Or do not drain; thicken the cooking water with kneaded butter (see BUTTER) and season to taste.

When you cook red cabbage, add a little vinegar or lemon juice to the water—it helps to keep the color from bleeding.

Instead of boiling, braise cabbage in fat—use butter or, for good farm-style flavor, bacon or sausage drippings. Melt enough fat to cover the bottom of the pan; add shredded cabbage and turn to coat pieces with fat as you cook them for a brief time. Then cover the pan and let the cabbage steam until tender-crisp. If you're cooking red cabbage this way, add a few apple wedges and a little nutmeg for extra-good flavor.

Freezing cabbage. You can freeze cabbage—but why would you want to? Fresh cabbage is available the year around, and fresh in anything is always better than processed. Anyway, freezer space—and the energy it takes to run the freezer—should be conserved for foods that a) would otherwise be wasted, b) have only a brief fresh season, c) are very expensive when bought fresh out of season, or d) are difficult-to-prepare make-aheads for entertaining.

Other ways, other forms. You will not find plain canned or frozen cabbage in the market. However, there are available frozen stuffed cabbage rolls and, less widely distributed, stuffed cabbage in glass jars. Also—particularly in shops that specialize in home-style foods—several kinds of cabbage-based relishes in glass jars.

Some perfect partners. Dress cabbage with lemon butter, cheese sauce or grated cheese, white sauce, mustard-dill sauce, creamed hard-cooked eggs, bacon bits, crunchy croutons, crumbled pretzels, chopped peanuts. Cook celery cabbage very briefly, so that it is still crisp, and dress with hollandaise for a vegetable delicious and elegant enough for any kind of meal. Stuff a whole cabbage or large cabbage leaves with a mixture based on ground beef, pork, or lamb, with or without rice. Simmer a hearty, tasty cabbage soup when the weather turns cold—a leftover ham bone makes a great base for this. Make a sweet/sour sauce with raisins, apples, and caraway seed for red cabbage.

And, of course, make cabbage salad—any kind from the simplest vinegar-dressed coleslaw to down-home slaw with old-fashioned "boiled" dressing to everybody's favorite—jellied perfection salad. Put together a delicate slaw of shredded celery cabbage dressed with a mixture of heavy cream and lemon juice, sparked with white pepper. Add bits of celery, radish, green pepper, and shredded carrot to turn cabbage salad into calico slaw. Make a salad of half green cabbage, half red. Dress up plain coleslaw with chopped peanuts, crushed pineapple, crumbled bacon, pieces of fresh orange or canned mandarin orange segments, chopped chutney, grated apple, shredded carrots, or chopped candied ginger.

It's been a long time since ancient Egyptians raised an altar to cabbage. And it looks as if the versatile, delicious vegetable will be around for many years to come. See also COLESLAW and SAUERKRAUT.

CACIOCAVALLO: see CHEESE

CACTUS PEARS: see EXOTIC FRUIT

CAESAR SALAD: see SALADS

CAKE FLOUR: see FLOUR

CAKE MIXES

A whole cake in a box. And beside it, frosting in a box. What results will you get from these? An edible cake. If you are totally, irremediably a klutz in the kitchen, a result superior to what you'd get if you made a cake from scratch. Or, if you hate to cook and wouldn't be caught dead making a cake from scratch, a treat for the family on the premise that any cake is better than no cake. More economical than from scratch? No, unless your kitchen is as bare as Mother Hubbard's cupboard. A saving in time? Yes, a little, but not all that much.

Then why are the supermarket shelves loaded with cake mixes of all sizes, flavors, and descriptions? Why are women rushing through the stores loading these mixes into their carts? Because home baking, like a great many other things, is rapidly becoming a lost art. Even now, in the midst of a back-to-natural movement in the kitchen, women who are learning to bake bread—and learning to love baking it—blanch and turn aside at the suggestion that they make a cake. To try to reverse that trend would be folly greater than King Canute's, so we might as well offer a few suggestions to guide from-a-mix cake bakers.

Read the directions—and follow them. First light the oven and set it to the temperature called for in the instructions. Despite flack from energy-savers, a cake—from a mix or from scratch—will not bake properly in an oven that has not been preheated. Carefully measure the liquid (usually

water) called for. Break eggs separately into a saucer or cup before adding to the mix—in spite of careful regulation of the egg industry, a bad egg still occurs now and then. Be sure you have a pan or pans of the proper size, and that you prepare them—grease or not, flour or not—as the instructions tell you. Beat the mix for the length of time suggested, scraping the bowl several times (not just the sides, the bottom too) during the beating. If the mixture is to be divided between two pans, divide equally (your eye will tell you—you don't have to measure). Bake for the minimum suggested time, resisting the impulse to open the oven door and peek. At the end of that time, if the cake isn't done, continue to bake until it is. Cool and remove from the pan as directed.

And if you are so cake-shy that making even a from-a-mix cake intimidates you, hear this: No one, repeat no one, who can read and follow simple directions can have a failure with a mix cake. So take heart.

Some easy mix-fixers. The reasons that mix cakes don't taste like the from-scratch variety are several, all involved with two factors: a) mixes must have a long shelf life, and b) they must not price themselves out of the market. Considering that they have both longevity and economy to contend with, mix-makers have done a pretty good job. Shortening must be of a kind that will not turn rancid with passing time. Flour must be moisture reduced. If there is egg in the mix, it must be dried white, not yolk. Flavorings must age gracefully. Leavening must retain its oomph. All in all, it can't be easy.

You can help along the mix you use. If you remember with longing your mother's or grandmother's butter cakes, choose the mix to which butter must be added at home—it shoots the already doubtful economy, but makes a better cake. So does a teaspoonful of good (real, that is) vanilla extract, or some other add-it-yourself flavoring. Cake mixes are relatively sturdy—they can stand some monkeying with and not fail. But don't tamper with the proportions of liquid to dry mix. If you want to add orange juice, for instance, substitute it for all or part of the water, don't use it in addition to the amount of water called for. One extra egg doesn't seem to harm the usual plain mix, but it doesn't seem to do it any good, either, so why bother? The best area for improvement in a plain mix is in flavoring.

By now, everyone has heard about the "pound" cakes made with 2-layer-size cake mix + the usual water + 4 eggs + ½ cup cooking oil + instant pudding mix. This unlikely

sounding combination (baked in a bundt or 10-inch tube pan) produces a very creditable pound-type cake, particularly if you flavor it well—mace for old-time pound cake flavor, or real vanilla or almond extract to upgrade or reinforce the flavoring already in the mix, or lemon or orange juice substituted for part of the water. A very acceptable, darkly rich mocha "pound" cake can be made with a devil's food cake mix, chocolate instant pudding, vanilla, and a rounded teaspoon of dry instant coffee—or substitute strong, cold, brewed coffee for the water.

As part of the frenzied effort proliferating on all sides to save the overburdened housewife time (and ensure that she will never have to think for herself), one company has triumphantly put on the market a mix for these pound-type cakes with the instant pudding already incorporated into the mix. It will, apparently, never end. Perhaps some day cake mix will come with a bottle of pre-measured water, and a hen to lay the eggs attached to the box by a leash.

What's your pleasure? The cake-mix shelves in a large, well-stocked supermarket work on a you-name-it-we've-got-it policy, holding mixes in several sizes and kinds, in a number of flavors.

The most widely distributed foam-type (that is, fatless cake leavened with air rather than with baking powder/soda) mix is angel food, of which several brands (and two somewhat different mixing methods) are available. These are whole mixes, requiring no addition other than water, and make acceptable cakes if you follow the directions, in particular those concerning the amount (time) of beating required. Most have a rather nothing flavor—vanilla or almond extract improves them. There are also available, but not as widely, mixes for sponge cakes (reflavor these, too) and for that neither-fish-nor-fowl, the chiffon cake—neither fatless nor leavenless, but with a high-rise shape and texture reminiscent of angel food and sponge cakes. All of these should be baked in tube pans.

Most of the cake mixes on the shelves are for the type known as butter cakes—except that these contain no butter. Most require the addition of water and eggs, many can (should) have their flavoring improved at home. They can be baked as two layers, in a flat pan as a sheet cake, or as cupcakes. Smaller versions are for small square or round pans, or to be made into cupcakes. Some full-size—they are known as two-layer size—cake mixes, as we mentioned, require the addition of butter; read the label before buying. The label may also offer some acceptable variations—flavor changes, the addition of sour cream, the recipe for the pound-type cakes mentioned above, frosting suggestions and/or recipes, instructions for preparing streusel-type cake from the mix, and so on. There are also full-size bundt cake mixes (although no law says you can't bake them in an ordinary tube pan of comparable size) and "tunnel cake" bundt

mixes, in which a center core of a different flavor/texture appears in the finished product—provided instructions are followed.

Another variety of mix is the quick- or snack-type cake, meant to be mixed faster than even the regular variety, generally right in the pan in which it is to be baked, with the addition only of water. One variation on this provides both the pan in which to bake the cake and the frosting with which to finish it, reducing the fine art of cake baking to nursery-school level. But, as we said before, better any cake than no cake according to most people.

There are also available gingerbread and cakelike sweet bread mixes, honey cake mix, and a number of others in varying degrees of availability.

You pays your money, you takes your choice. What has been said about enhancing flavors might lead that single aborigine in the Australian back country who has never heard of cake mixes to believe that they are available in only a limited choice. Not so. The choice is wide but, in some cases, not all that good. That, however, is subjective judgment. Whether or not you like the flavor of a particular cake mix depends on your taste buds and what you've been used to, and consequently enjoyed, all your cake-eating years. Be that as it may, the plain yellow and white cake mixes are very mildly flavored with (usually imitation) vanilla. These can be reflavored with such extracts as lemon, almond, maple, peppermint, rum or brandy. There are also chocolate and spice cake mixes, and some flavored with lemon, some with orange, and a sprinkling of other flavors, such as mocha, strawberry, butter pecan, banana, and so on. There are mixes that include such extras as nuts, raisins, coconut, or chocolate chips.

If you are a timid baker, by all means make a cake from a mix. Choose a brand you know from experience to be reliable. Follow the directions concerning measuring, beating, pan size, oven temperature, and baking time. If you wish, reinforce the flavor with a teaspoon of good, "real" flavoring extract, added with the liquid. Having faithfully adhered to the simple instructions, you will produce a cake you need have no qualms about serving to anyone. It may not be as good as a baked-from-scratch cake made by a baking-happy cook, but it certainly will be good to eat—and the world is full of people who won't know the difference.

CAKES

Once upon a time there were only two broad, general classifications of cakes: fat-free—called "foam"—cakes leavened with air, and butter cakes, usually leavened with chemicals. (There were, of course, as with everything in this uncertain world, exceptions; butter sponge cake—leavened with air, but not fat free—is one.)

Then, more than thirty years ago, an ingenious experimenter—a man, rumor has it—invented a third type, combining some of the best features of both but mixed in a way quite different from either, and christened it chiffon cake. Now there are three general cake classes, each with its own multitude of variations and permutations, all lovely to look at, delicious to eat, and a source of pride to the baker.

In spite of the proliferation of cake mixes and the trend toward lighter desserts, there are still a great many cake bakers around, dedicated to bringing joy to their families and friends, and taking modest pleasure in that crowning achievement of baking a magnificent, mile-high, truly delectable, homemade cake. A thing of beauty, and a joy as long as it lasts—which generally isn't all that long. If, as the baking is going on, there is a child around to dip a finger into the batter, to lurk on the outskirts until the frosting bowl is ready to be licked, so much the better—he will remember the day sweetly all his life. And so will the cook. Baking is a lovesome thing, God wot.

Some general ground rules. Approach the making of a cake positively. Cowards are poor bakers. You are an intelligent human being, able to reason, to read, to follow directions. So what's to be afraid of?

If you are not a regular, do-it-blindfolded cake baker, choose a recipe from a cookbook you can trust. Read the recipe through well in advance, to make certain you have all the ingredients on hand. When you are ready to go to work, assemble all the ingredients, a pan or pans of proper size, and all the necessary tools. Prepare the pan as the recipe directs. Light the oven so that it can preheat while you're making the cake. Measure carefully and accurately, using standard measuring cups and spoons. Combine the ingredients in the order and manner the recipe calls for. Bake the minimum length of time called for (set a timer, so that you won't get caught up in something else and lose track), test (see below), and continue to bake if the cake isn't done. Cool and remove from the pan according to the recipe directions. Fill and frost as the recipe suggests. Do all these things properly, in proper order, and you'll produce a minor masterpiece. It's really not difficult—scout's honor!

A word or two about ingredients. Leaving aside the skill you bring to the making of a cake, its goodness—or lack of same—depends on the quality of the ingredients you use. Freshness is the most important. The good flavor of fresh ingredients imparts good, fresh flavor to the cake. Unless you are a constant baker, the large, economy size of anything— flour, baking powder, and all the rest—is false economy. Past-their-prime flour, eggs, butter, and some other cake ingredients will impair the flavor of the cake, which is bad enough; leavening that has lost its youthful zest can cause a complete failure.

butter: To cream well, butter should be neither too soft nor too hard. If too hard, it flakes and chips and will not combine smoothly with the remaining ingredients; if too soft, it will not turn into the light, fluffy mass that is the desideratum of the creaming process. Take it from the refrigerator about 20 minutes before you'll be ready to use it. Measure butter by the quarter pound or fractions or increments thereof (see BUTTER) or pack it into a measuring cup and remove it with a rubber spatula.

eggs: Most modern recipes are developed to use large eggs. Eggs separate best when cold, but beat up to their maximum volume at about 70°F. If your recipe calls for separated eggs, separate them immediately after you take them from the refrigerator, then allow both whites and yolks to stand until they reach room temperature before beating. To separate, crack an egg gently but firmly on the edge of a bowl or other hard surface. Using both hands (one-handed egg separators are show-offs and disaster-courters), gently pull the two halves of the shell apart, retaining the yolk in one half and letting the white drip out into a bowl beneath. Carefully slide the yolk into the other half of the shell, letting the remaining white drip down. If you are a kitchen klutz, a gadget called an egg separator was invented just for you; lacking one, pour the whole egg into a small funnel—the white will run through, the yolk remain safe and secure in the top.

Bits of egg yolk in the whites will keep them from beating up to full volume. If you were unlucky enough to break the yolk and much of it runs into the white, use that egg for another purpose. But if only a small bit of yolk drops into the white, fish it out, using a piece of eggshell as a scoop. Fat and some other foreign substances keep whites from doing their best by you, too. Be sure the bowl in which you beat them is scrupulously clean.

sugar: Lumps in the sugar may or may not come out when you beat the batter. Make sure ahead of time by pressing lumps out or sifting the sugar before measuring. Confectioners and brown sugar both tend to be lumpy. Sift the former, remove and discard lumps from the latter. Measure granulated and confectioners sugar by spooning lightly into a measuring cup. Most brown sugar measurements call for packed sugar; spoon into the cup, pack down with the back of the spoon, and repeat until the proper packed amount is achieved.

flour: All-purpose flour labeled presifted does not need to be sifted before measuring unless the recipe specifies that it must. (Those not so labeled must be sifted before measuring.) However, presifted flour should be aerated before measuring; stir the flour with a spoon until it is no longer compacted, then spoon lightly—do not pack—into a measuring cup. Level off with a spatula or the back of a knife. Some flours—as whole wheat, graham—should not be sifted. Be guided by the recipe. At any rate, such flours are seldom used in cakes. However, many recipes do call for cake flour—a lighter, finer type (see FLOUR).

liquids: Measure in a see-through—glass or plastic—measuring cup designed specifically for liquids; do not use a cup designed to measure dry ingredients. Pour the liquid to the specified amount at eye level (set the cup on a flat, level surface, bend down to peer at it—a little mild exercise never hurt anyone). Milk should be whole (homogenized) unless the recipe calls for something else. Evaporated milk, mixed half and half with water, may be used in place of fresh whole milk. Do not use condensed milk unless the recipe specifies it. Dry whole milk, reconstituted as the package directs, may be substituted, but do not use reconstituted nonfat dry milk unless the directions say you can.

Molasses, oil, honey, and corn syrup are a bit easier to get out of the cup if you've first rinsed it in cold water—shake out all the water, but don't dry it. Again, check measurements at eye level. For small amounts of these ingredients, measure by the tablespoonful rather than fractions of a cup, bearing in mind that ¼ cup equals 4 tablespoons. Gooey substances come more easily out of a spoon than a cup. In either case, remove the last drops with a rubber spatula.

flavorings, spices: Use the amount the recipe directs unless you know, from previous experience with this same recipe, that the called-for amount wasn't quite enough for your taste. Measure flavorings and spices with standard measuring spoons. Pour extracts into a proper-size spoon until it is full; measure rounded spoonfuls of spices, then level off with a spatula or the dull side of a knife.

leavening: Measure as for spices, above. If you are not certain of freshness, test chemical leavenings (see BAKING POWDER) or yeast (see BREADS) before using. Yeast is seldom used in cakes, but there are a few (a notably good devil's food is one) that call for it.

A word or two about ovens. Unless you are following a recipe that specifically tells you not to do so, preheat the oven before you put the cake into it. Most ovens come up to the required temperature in about 10 minutes. Be sure your oven thermostat is properly calibrated—if you're not certain, check it against an oven thermometer. Set the regulator carefully for the temperature that the recipe calls for. (If you need glasses, put them on. Proper temperature is critical to a well-baked cake, and a by-guess-by-gee setting won't do.)

A word or two about pans and placement. In some culinary efforts, substitutions can be made in a fairly offhand manner, but baking is not one of those areas. You need, among other things, a pan or pans of the proper size for the

volume of batter the recipe you are using will produce, or an acceptable substitute. Your recipe will tell you the proper size. If you don't have it, or if you want a cake of a different shape, don't choose a substitute at random. These alternates will work:

a recipe that yields:	*can also be baked as:*
two round 8-inch layers	two thin 8-inch squares *or* 18 to 24 2½-inch cupcakes
three round 8-inch layers	two round 9-inch layers
two round 9-inch layers	two 8-inch squares *or* three thin 8-inch layers *or* one 15- × 10- × 1-inch rectangle *or* 30 2½-inch cupcakes
one 8- × 8- × 2-inch square	one round 9-inch layer
two 8- × 8- × 2-inch squares	two round 9-inch layers *or* one 13- × 9- × 2-inch rectangle
one 9- × 9- × 2-inch square	two thin round 8-inch layers
two 9- × 9- × 2-inch squares	three round 8-inch layers
one 13- × 9- × 2-inch rectangle	two round 9-inch layers *or* two 8- × 8- × 2-inch squares
one 9- × 5- × 3-inch loaf cake	one 9- × 9- × 2-inch square *or* 24 to 30 2½-inch cupcakes
one 8- × 4- × 3-inch loaf cake	one 8- × 8- × 2-inch square
one 9- × 3½-inch tube cake	two round 9-inch layers *or* 24 to 30 2½-inch cupcakes
one 10- × 4-inch tube cake	two 9- × 5- × 3-inch loaves *or* one 13- × 9- × 2-inch rectangle

cautionary note on pans: Even though the capacity of the pans may be the same, don't bake a recipe calling for a flat pan (layer, square, or sheet) in a high pan (loaf or tube); the proportions in the recipe may not be right for the high-type cake. However, high-type cakes generally may be baked in same-capacity flat pans, or as cupcakes.

preparing pans: Follow the recipe's directions on greasing the pan or not, on flouring it, on lining it with paper. Grease, if the recipe directs, with shortening—the white, needs-no-refrigeration kind—spreading it evenly over bottom and sides, unless the recipe tells you to grease the bottom only. If the directions call for both grease and flour, sprinkle flour lightly and evenly over the greased surface, then tap the pans, face down, to shake out the excess flour. If you're told to grease and line the pans, cut a piece of wax paper to fit the bottom of the pan, place it, then grease the paper.

When you bake a sponge, angel food, or chiffon cake, the tube pan should not be greased. In fact, make certain the pan is totally fat-free—cakes of this kind "climb" up the side of the dry, ungreased pan during baking to attain their desirable lofty height.

Sometimes, the recipe for a very small sponge cake will direct you to grease the pan. There's always an exception—follow the directions. Another such exception is the pans in which jelly rolls and similar cakes—usually a type of foam cake—are baked; they are always greased, and lined with paper as well.

Even if you bake your cakes in pans lined with no-stick coatings, you'll get better results—browner, tastier crust and easier removal—if you prepare (grease, line, flour) the pans as the recipe directs you.

placing pans: Once your cake is in its pan(s), it must be put in the oven, and there are right and wrong ways for that, too.

If there is only one shallow pan of batter, round or square or rectangular, place the rack in the center of the oven and the pan in the center of the rack. If you are baking two layers, place them on opposite corners of the centered rack, making sure they touch neither each other nor the walls of the oven.

Three or four layers or squares call for two oven racks, placed in the center third of the oven. Position two pans in opposite corners of the top rack, two on the different opposite corners of the bottom rack, so that no pan is directly above or below another pan. This allows for optimum heat circulation.

Tube and loaf pans should be centered (or, if two, side by side but not touching) on a rack placed in the lower third of the oven.

Is it done? Bake to the minimum time the recipe suggests, then touch the center of the cake lightly with your finger. If it is done, it will spring back, leaving no indentation. If a depression remains, bake 5 minutes longer, test again; if necessary, repeat. A cake that is ready to be taken from the oven will have shrunk a little away from the sides of the pan—a backup for the finger test.

If you prefer, use a cake tester, which looks like a thin wire skewer, or a wooden food pick. Insert in the center of the cake; if it comes out dry, with no batter or soft crumbs clinging to it, the cake is done.

Patiently waiting. A cake must be properly cooled before it is frosted and/or cut. If there are young predators about, two-footed or four-footed, cool it out of their reach or your efforts will have been in vain—fresh cake is notoriously tempting.

butter cakes: Cool on a wire rack. This allows air to circulate on all sides. Leave in the pan, on the rack, for 10 minutes. Then loosen the sides of the cake gently with a thin-bladed knife or spatula. Invert on the rack or a plate, and shake gently. If the pan was lined, carefully peel off the paper. Turn right side up on the rack—again, easy does it—to finish cooling. The cake should be entirely cool before you frost it.

foam cakes: Tube-pan cakes—angel food, sponge, chiffon —must cool completely before you take them from the pan. As soon as they come out of the oven, invert and hang them to cool. Some tube pans have little attached feet, some have elongated tubes—if yours has either, balance the cake upside down on them. If not, insert the neck of a bottle into the tube and let the cake hang, upside down (don't worry, it won't fall out), until entirely cool. Alternatively, balance the rim of the pan on inverted cups or other small dishes—but the bottle ploy is easier.

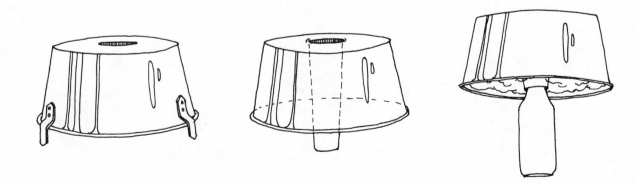

When the cake (any kind) is completely cooled, it can be frosted. (See FROSTINGS, ICINGS, AND FILLINGS and DECORATING FOOD.) Or serve it plain, sprinkled with sifted confectioners sugar, or topped with whipped cream or custard or fruit sauce.

Keeping cakes. If you're lucky, there may be cake leftovers for tomorrow or the day after. A covered cake keeper is the place for frosted cakes, either butter or foam; if you don't have one, invert a big bowl, large enough so that it doesn't touch the frosting, over the cake. If the cake has a cooked cream filling or a whipped cream filling or frosting, store it in the refrigerator. If it has an ice cream filling, store it in the freezer. Otherwise, store at room temperature.

Wrap up unfrosted cake in plastic wrap or foil, store at room temperature.

How many will it serve? That's more or less up to you and how generous/miserly you are in cutting it. However, there are some rules of thumb to guide you.

Cut butter cakes with a thin, sharp knife, using a sawing motion. Cut foam cakes with a long knife that has a serrated blade or, better, with a cake breaker (a gadget that somewhat resembles a rat-tail comb grown long in the tooth), or gently pull apart, using two forks. Cut a jelly or similar roll cake with a long piece of heavy thread; loop it around the cake, crossing the ends, then pull the ends gently in opposite directions.

Divide a round cake into wedges; an 8-inch layer cake should yield 12 servings, a 9-inch one, 16. If you have larger (12- or 14-inch) layer pans, cut a center rectangle through the cake first and divide into slices; cut the remaining side pieces into wedges. Such cakes yield 30 to 40 servings. A 10-inch tube cake yields 12 to 16 servings—the smaller number for a foam cake, the larger for a butter cake.

An 8- × 4- × 3-inch loaf cake will yield 8 servings; a 9- × 5- × 3-inch loaf will serve 10. Cut an 8-inch square cake into 9 square servings or 10 rectangular ones. A 9-inch square cake yields 12 generous square servings, 16 smaller ones. Cut a 13- × 9- × 2-inch cake twice lengthwise, nine times crosswise, to yield 30 servings.

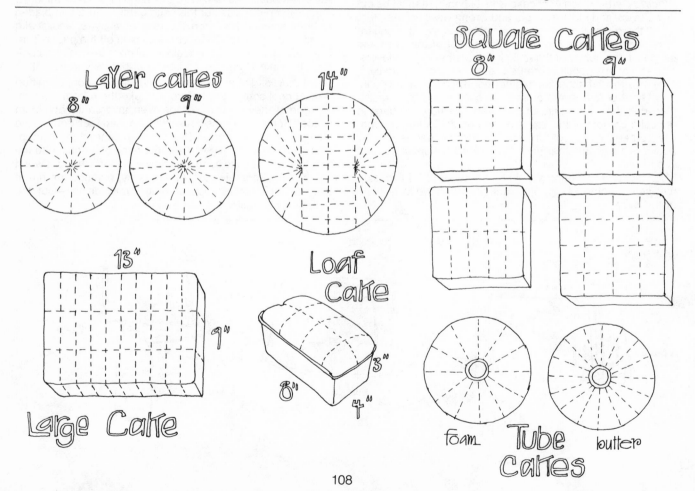

Layer cakes — 8" 9" 14"

Large Cake — 13" 9"

Loaf Cake — 8" 3" 4"

Square Cakes — 8" 9"

Tube Cakes — foam, butter

Any good cookbook will offer you a wide variety of cakes to try, from simple to complex—none too difficult, even for the novice baker, provided you follow directions to the letter. Browse among such delights as Jam Cake, Lady Baltimore, Maple-Nut Chiffon, Wellesley Fudge, Burnt Sugar, Banana Cake, Mahogany Cake, Fudge-Frosted Lemon Layers, Hot Milk Sponge, Old-Fashioned Marble Cake, Strawberry Angel Food, Carioca Mocha, Applesauce Spice, Red Devil's Food, and literally hundreds more. (Even Tomato Soup Cake, for heaven's sake—a lot better than it sounds.) Choose one that takes your fancy, and go to it—you can make it happen!

Understanding butter cakes. When grandma made a butter cake, it was a longer process than is called for today. In the first place, it was truly a *butter* cake—there was no other shortening available. Now we have margarines of various kinds (but use only regular, not whipped or "diet" margarines) and hydrogenated white shortenings that we use in these cakes sometimes in place of butter, although we still call them "butter" cakes. Lacking an electric mixer, grandma creamed and folded and beat by grandma-power. We have helper tools, although some cooks still prefer the old-time hand mixing.

hand-mixed butter cakes: Sift together dry ingredients. In a large bowl, cream butter until light and fluffy; gradually add sugar, creaming until fluffy. Add eggs—or yolks, if eggs are separated—one at a time, beating well after each addition. Add flavoring. Add dry ingredients alternately with liquid, beginning and ending with dry ingredients. Beat until well blended. If whites are to be added, beat them in a separate bowl until stiff but not dry; fold into butter mixture. (This is known as the "cake method of mixing" as opposed to the "muffin method," in which everything is swooshed together and beaten as little as possible, and the "biscuit method," in which shortening is cut into dry ingredients with a pastry blender or two knives.)

mixer-made butter cakes: In large bowl of an electric mixer, combine shortening (butter or other) with sugar, eggs, and flavoring extract; beat at high speed 3 minutes. Add liquid and sifted dry ingredients alternately, beginning and ending with dry ingredients, with mixer at low speed; scrape bowl often. Beat only enough so that ingredients are blended.

all-in-one butter cakes: These are made, not with butter but with vegetable shortening. In large mixer bowl, place sifted dry ingredients, shortening, and a portion of the liquid; beat 2 minutes at medium speed. Add remaining liquid along with the eggs and flavoring extract; beat 2 minutes at medium speed, scraping the bowl frequently.

cautionary note: Don't try to juggle these methods of cake mixing—one method won't necessarily work with a recipe that calls for a different approach. Be guided by the recipe instructions.

Understanding foam cakes. When grandma made an angel food cake, she placed the egg whites on a large platter and beat the dickens out of them with a flat wire whip, a time-consuming, to say nothing of grandma-consuming, task. With all those yolks on hand and chancy refrigeration to cope with, she made a baked custard or a sunshine cake from the leftovers, wasting not in order to want not.

Foam cakes—angel food, sponge (including sunshine cake, ladyfingers, and jelly roll), and chiffon—are leavened with air that is beaten into the egg whites in angel food, into both whites and yolks in the others. Sometimes the recipe will call for a little cream of tartar to be beaten with the whites to help things along in angel food and sponge; chiffon cake recipes call for baking powder.

angel food cakes: Only the whites of the eggs, beaten to their greatest volume, go into these cakes. Egg-white measurements in angel food recipes are given by the cup, not by the number of eggs—the amount of white is critical and we can't count on hens to care enough about our baking to lay eggs with identical amounts of white. Usually, 10 to 12 whites are required to make the 1½ cups most recipes call for. Some angel food recipes specify confectioners or superfine sugar rather than the regular granulated, or part confectioners, part regular. Egg whites, cream of tartar, and salt are combined in a large mixer bowl and beaten until foamy; sugar is added gradually until the mixture stands in stiff, glossy peaks. Flavoring extract is folded in by hand, using a rubber spatula or flat wire whisk, then flour is folded in, a quarter at a time, in the same way. The batter is pushed out of the bowl into the (ungreased) pan and a thin-bladed spatula drawn through to break up large air pockets.

sponge cakes: Sponge cakes begin the same way as angel food, with an egg-white-plus-sugar meringue. Yolks are beaten separately with more sugar and the flavoring, and the yolk mixture is folded into the egg-white meringue. Flour and salt are folded in, a quarter at a time.

There are variations on this true sponge cake, some made with hot milk, some with boiling water, some leavened with baking powder, some calling for melted butter (the French génoise is one of these), some with cocoa substituting for part of the flour.

chiffon cakes: These are not truly foam cakes, because they contain shortening and baking powder; not truly butter cakes, because the shortening is liquid and the cakes rely on stiffly beaten egg whites for a measure of their leavening. They are baked in ungreased tube pans, but some variations can be baked in greased and floured layer pans. Neither fish nor fowl nor good red herring, these.

Cake flour, sugar, baking powder, and salt are sifted together into a large bowl. A well is made in the center of these ingredients, into which are poured vegetable oil, egg yolks, liquid (sometimes milk, sometimes fruit juice, sometimes another liquid, such as coffee), and flavoring, and the mixture is beaten until smooth. Egg whites and more sugar (and sometimes cream of tartar) are beaten separately until stiff and glossy; then the yolk mixture is folded into the whites. Many flavors of chiffon cake can be made—mocha, chocolate, orange, lemon, maple, and so on.

A word or two about pound cakes. In the beginning, pound cakes were literally made pound for pound: 1 pound of sugar (2¼ cups), 1 pound of butter (2 cups), 1 pound of eggs (about 8 large ones), 1 pound of flour (4 cups). After that, the pound theory broke down—you couldn't add a pound of flavoring, which was most often mace, sometimes vanilla. Nowadays, the pound theory is totally shot. We make "pound" cakes with varying amounts of ingredients and even, sometimes, with baking powder. However made, they are close-grained, rich cakes, usually baked as loaves and served thinly sliced, unembellished or sprinkled with confectioners sugar.

Most cakes freeze well, baked but not frosted, and thaw rapidly. (See special feature: PUTTING FOOD BY.) A cake in the freezer is like money in the bank when unexpected guests drop in. Or, if your family is small, serve half and freeze half for another day. See also CHEESECAKES, FRUIT-CAKES, GENOISE, ICEBOX CAKES, RUM CAKES, SHORT-CAKES, and WEDDING CAKES.

CALAVOS: see AVOCADOS

CALCIUM: see MILK and the special feature: NUTRITION NOTEBOOK

CALF

This is meat from a steer neither as young as the animal used for veal nor as old as the one called beef. Its flavor is neither as delicate as veal nor as assertive as beef. Calf is not as tender as veal, and in cooking, instructions for beef should be followed—that is, cook with dry heat those cuts that in beef are cooked in that manner, and braise or simmer all other cuts.

Calf appeared on the market a number of years ago at the time of a consumers' rebellion against soaring beef prices, resulting in a partial beef boycott. Because the very young beef was not feed-lot "finished," it could be put on the market at prices lower than similar beef cuts. Unfortunately —from the producers' point of view—calf was not greeted with appreciable cheers from the public. Neither a substitute for beef nor a substitute for veal, home cooks didn't really know what to do with calf, and what they did do often produced unacceptable results. Calf does not have a great deal of flavor; about all it has going for it is that it is cheaper than either veal or beef—except when wily butchers try to pass it off as veal and charge veal prices for it. Don't be taken in. Veal—true, milk-fed, delicate veal—is gray when raw. Beef is red. Calf is a deep rose-pink.

You may or may not find calf in your market, depending on the part of the country you live in and whether or not calf has been generally accepted there. It has certainly not been the rousing success producers hoped it would be. Buy it, by all means, if your family likes it, but don't pay veal or beef prices for it.

CALORIES: see special feature: NUTRITION NOTEBOOK

CAMEMBERT: see CHEESE

CAN, JAR, AND PACKAGE SIZES

In New England, they often categorize things by saying that they "weigh heavy" or "weigh light," which is really a consideration of bulk rather than weight—a pound of feathers, for example, weighs light, and so is considerably bulkier than a weighs-heavy pound of iron.

The same, although generally within a narrower range, is true of foods. A pound of chow mein noodles weighs light, is much bulkier—greater in volume—than a pound of canned tuna. In fact, a large can of chow mein noodles has a net contents of 3 ounces, a small flat can of tuna, 6½ or 7 ounces.

The weight of the food within a can or package is the net weight (the weight of the edible contents) meaning that two cans or two packages identical in *size* may have contents that differ in *weight*. Condensed soups all come in the same size can, but their net weight ranges from 10½ to 11½ ounces.

Serving size and number of servings per container also differ with bulk. An ounce or two of dry cereal is considered a serving, but an ounce or even two of canned tuna is a rather measly offering unless mixed with a lot of other ingredients in a salad or casserole. What we're saying is this: You can't always count on the size of the container to guide you to the number of servings it contains. The same size can, 303, to cite one more example, contains 1 pound of baked beans, but only 14 ounces of blueberries.

The great can revolution. At one point, when canning foods had become a big industry, can sizes proliferated to an amazing degree. Whatever the food, a can size was developed for it, to the point where neither the consumer nor the canning industry had any real guidelines.

About a decade ago, the industry decided that this nonsense had gone far enough. In cooperation with the Bureau of Standards of the United States Department of Commerce, the industry made an in-depth study of can sizes and, flum-

moxed by what they found, promptly set up standards to guide commercial canners.

It was recommended that canners confine themselves to only thirty-two can sizes. (If "only" seems to you to be the wrong word, remember that this number includes institution-size cans, as well as containers for products that never appear on your supermarket shelves.) Of the thirty-two sizes, nineteen are used for the majority of foods. The other thirteen sizes are designed for specific foods that require odd-size cans, such as pimientos, mushrooms, one-serving main dishes, olives, and so on.

The ten can sizes below are the ones you'll most commonly encounter. The term "specialties" in the *products* column covers such things as macaroni and spaghetti in cheese or tomato sauce, Spanish rice, various Mexican-style and Chinese-style foods, tomato aspic, and others.

container name	approximate weight	approximate net contents in cups	principal products	number of servings
8-ounce	8 ounces	1	fruits, vegetables, specialties	2
picnic	10½ to 12 ounces	1¼	condensed soups, some fruits, meat, vegetables, fish, specialties	3
12-ounce	12 ounces	1½	principally vacuum-pack corn	3 to 4
no. 300	14 to 16 ounces	1¾	pork and beans, baked beans, meat products, cranberry sauce, blueberries, specialties	3 to 4
no. 303	16 to 17 ounces	2	most usual size for fruits and vegetables, some meat products, ready-to-serve soups, specialties	4
no. 2	1 pound, 4 ounces *or* 20 ounces	2½	juices, ready-to-serve soups, some specialties; apple, pineapple slices	5
no. 2½	1 pound, 13 ounces *or* 29 ounces	3½	fruits, vegetables such as pumpkin, sauerkraut, tomatoes, greens	7
no. 3 special *or* 46-ounce	2 pounds, 14 ounces *or* 1 quart, 14 fluid ounces	5¾	family economy size for fruit and vegetable juices, pork and beans	10 to 12

In some markets that make a specialty of catering to large families, you may also find condensed soups and some vegetables in the no. 3 size; you may also find a no. 10 size, with a weight of 6½ pounds to 7 pounds, 5 ounces, a contents of 12 to 13 cups, offering 25 servings. These are generally for fruits and vegetables, and a few other foods. Both of these are really institutional sizes, useful only to the extra-large family or to someone doing quantity cookery for a party or for such an occasion as a church supper or a group picnic.

The contents of the cans in the above list are averages; there can be certain differences in the cup yield between one food and another in the same or similar-size containers. To give you an idea of this spread, here are some typical canned vegetable container net weights and their yields:

vegetable	net weight	yield in cups
asparagus, cut	14 ounces	1⅓
beans, green or wax, cut	15½ ounces	1¾
beans, lima	16 ounces	1¾
carrots, diced or sliced	16 ounces	1¾
corn, whole kernel	16 ounces	1⅔
kale	15 ounces	1⅓
okra	15½ ounces	1¾
peas	16 ounces	1¾
spinach	15 ounces	1⅓
tomatoes	16 ounces	1⅞

The serving size commonly used—and calculated in recipes —for most canned vegetables is ½ cup for adults, scaled down for children and light eaters, up for teenage boys and other notable trenchermen. The same amount, ½ cup, is considered an average serving of canned fruit, too—or two halves, if you're measuring large pieces. Weight listed on

cans of fruit includes both the fruit itself and the syrup, because the syrup is usually served along with the fruit.

Packaged goods. Let the net weight, printed on the outside of the package, be your guide. Dry packaged foods are much more influenced by the weigh-heavy/weigh-light principle than canned foods are, and the size of the package can fool you. Bear in mind, as well, that food in the large economy package is not economical at all if a good part of the contents becomes stale before your small family can eat it up. Feeding stale dry cereal to the wild birds is humanitarian, but it's no bolster to the food budget.

Whether or not leftovers in a package can be stored usefully and without going stale should guide the size you buy and the kind of pack. Loose pie crust mix in the 2-crust size is difficult to measure for a 1-crust pie. But pie crust mix that comes packed as two separate sticks can be easily divided, one stick used for a 1-crust pie and the second stored for another such pie another day. If you buy the loose mix and need only a single crust, you're better off (and that much ahead on a future occasion) if you prepare the entire package as two 1-crust pie shells—use one and freeze the second. The same is true of a 2-layer cake mix—it's difficult to divide and store, but you can make and bake the whole mix as two layers, use only one layer (cut in half, fill and frost) and freeze the second.

On the other hand, biscuit and pancake mixes are measured by the cup, and leftovers can readily be stored in the original package or transferred to a glass or plastic or metal container with a tight closure. The same is true of such foods as rice, dried beans, and many others. Pudding mixes and flavored gelatin come in packages small enough to be used up at one meal, at two at the most. Refrigerated biscuits come in 5- and 10-biscuit sizes. Many packages have smaller 1- or 2-serving packages within (dry soup mixes, for example), so that you can conveniently use one, store the remainder. Most packaged foods come in several sizes, one of which should be the right size for your purpose.

It all boils down to this: Buy the can or package size that's useful for you and your family. Economize on large sizes only when the contents will either be used up in a short time or will store easily and without growing stale. See also FROZEN FOODS, COMMERCIAL.

CANAPES: see APPETIZERS

CANDIED FLOWERS, FRUIT

Makers of holiday fruit cake, candied-fruit pound cake, and such specialty breads as panettone are probably those most familiar with commercial candied fruits; dedicated consumers of petits fours from elegant bakeries, those most familiar with candied flowers. Cut-up candied orange and lemon and (less widely available) grapefruit peel, candied pineapple slices and whole cherries, candied pieces of citron and angelica are widely available in supermarkets throughout the year or, at least, during the extraordinary baking season that precedes the winter holidays. These come in several sizes of plastic tubs—often with some of the syrup in which they were candied—or in small cans or jars.

Candied ginger root is available the year around in small glass jars shelved with the spices in your market. Guava "shells"—large pieces of candied guava rind—a dessert staple (with cream cheese) of some Latin American people, can be found in specialty food shops or in gourmet-food sections of some supermarkets.

Candied flowers are less easy to come by. Most usual are candied violets, to be found most readily in elegant confectionary shops, in bulk or (imported from France) small metal containers. These violets, as well as similar confections such as candied rose petals and mint leaves, may be made at home by a simple method that uses egg white and superfine granulated sugar, or a more elaborate one using a cooked sugar-water syrup. Candied fruits and fruit peels may also be made at home. Fruit peels can also be candied in chocolate, resulting in a delicious sweet-tart confection. Complete instructions for making all of these can be found in a good general cookbook, or in a specialty cookbook devoted to confectionary.

CANDY

The ancient Persians developed a confection made from a sweet reed combined with honey and spices, and called it *kand.* Nearby, certain Arabs worked out a rough-and-ready sugar-refining process, combined the product with gum arabic to make a confection called *quand,* the Arabian word for sugar. From those two terms came our word, "candy."

For many years, in both Europe and America, commercial candy-making was the province of the apothecary—the druggist—who devised sugar-coated pills to make medication more palatable and manufactured simple candy lozenges (often mint or horehound flavored) to soothe sore throats and quiet coughs. When people bought these in quantity, not for medicinal purposes but because they were so good, many druggists experimented with new flavors and kinds and sold them simply for the pleasure they brought to customers. Homemakers learned to prepare confections, too —hard and stick candies, taffies, caramels, maple-sugar treats.

About the middle of the nineteenth century, commercial candy-making on a large scale was begun in the United States, thanks to the invention of specialized machinery and equipment. Early in the twentieth century, that joy of the hearts of young and old, the candy bar, came on the market; it was first mass-produced during World War I, as a quick pick-me-up for the troops.

What does candy have to offer? Nutritionally, candy is

almost a total loss. Sugar, its chief component, contains no protein, vitamins, or minerals. It does produce quick energy, but more often because we want it to—because we offer ourselves that need for an energy boost as an excuse for eating the candy that we know has no nutritional value to speak of and is bad for our teeth besides. The best that can be said for candy is that it's good because it's good—we consume it in vast quantities because we love it, in all its infinite sweet variety. True, some candy ingredients, such as milk, nuts, fruit, do have nutritional value to offer, but the quantities are generally small. We eat candy because we like it, not because it's good for us.

Candy-making at home. Homemade or commercial candy is based on sugar crystals or the lack of them, dividing the confection into two general classifications, sugar-crystal candy and dense-syrup candy. The ingredients used, the proportion of each to the others, the care taken in measuring and combining them, plus cooking temperature and cooking time, determine the kind of candy—and whether or not it's successful.

the ingredients: The chief component of most candy is granulated sugar. Sugar-and-water syrup, concentrated by boiling down, then turned out and cooled, results in a hard, grainy, crystallized candy hardly worthy of the name. But when other ingredients are added, both to flavor the finished product and to influence the texture of it by controlling or preventing the crystallization, candy as we know it today results.

One of the control ingredients is corn syrup. Combined in proper proportion to sugar, corn syrup makes candy creamy or soft and chewy. Acids—vinegar, cream of tartar, lemon juice—used judiciously, will slow down crystallization, but an excess makes a too-thin, never-congeals candy. Fat —butter, as well as the fat content of milk and/or chocolate —also slows down crystallization, as well as adding flavor and mellowness.

Those ingredients, and water, are the chief components of most candy, other than flavoring extracts, nuts, and fruit such as raisins that are added after the cooking process is complete.

the equipment: Candy is boiled and, because it is a sugar mixture, rises high and boils over readily if the pan is too small. So you need a large pan—one with a cover—for candy-making. It should be heavy-duty; candy has a nasty habit of sticking and scorching that a heavy pan helps to prevent.

You will also need spoons for stirring and beating. Wooden spoons are the best choice; they never get too hot to handle, and they cut down on clatter when you're beating candy in a metal pan. A large pastry brush is useful for washing down sugar crystals that cling to the side of the pan.

Most useful of all is a candy thermometer. This gadget, with an easy-read dial and a clip to fasten it to the side of the pan, eliminates all the guesswork of cold-water testing. Removing candy from the heat at the moment it reaches the proper temperature is critical to good results, so such a thermometer is a good investment for the home candy-maker— and it can also be used to test the sugar syrup for seafoam and allied frostings, and is useful in jelly-making.

the techniques: Sugar must be completely dissolved for proper texture, so the sugar mixture should be stirred until it comes to a boil. Thereafter, most candies are not stirred— follow the recipe directions. As the candy cooks, crystals of sugar, sometimes in clusters, tend to form on the sides of the pan. Covering the pan during the early part of the boiling period allows steam to accumulate, which washes these crystals back into the candy mixture. Some recipes will tell you to wash these crystals away with a brush; others suggest buttering the sides of the pan to prevent crystal formation. Trust the recipe to guide you to the right technique for the kind of candy you're making.

Candies in which the liquid is water can be cooked over a medium-high heat (always keep a sharp eye out, to make certain that the mixture doesn't stick to the pan and scorch). When milk is the liquid, cook over moderate heat, as milk compounds the tendency to scorching.

testing, testing: Cook the mixture to the correct temperature, remove it immediately from the heat once that temperature is reached—those two points are all-important to success. Before the candy thermometer was available, cooks tested the hot syrup by dropping a small amount from a spoon into cold water to determine whether or not it had reached the proper consistency, and a great many cooks still rely on this method. It is, however, not nearly as accurate as a thermometer. Most candy recipes specify a thermometer reading, followed by the alternative cold-water test, such as soft ball or hard ball. If you use a thermometer, keep a sharp eye on it during the last few minutes of cooking. That's when the temperature rises rapidly. If you water-test, be sure that the water is very cold, but don't use ice water. Take a clean cup and spoon, and fresh water, for each test.

To make the cold-water test, remove the pan from the heat and drop a little of the mixture into the water. Use your fingers to gather the drops into a ball and feel it for firmness. If the candy isn't yet ready, return it at once to the heat.

Here are the stages, tests, and equivalent temperatures:

stage	cold-water test	temperature
thread	syrup runs off in a 2-inch thread as it is dropped from metal spoon	230–234°F.
soft ball	syrup can be shaped into ball in water, flattens when removed from water	234–240°F.
firm ball	syrup can be shaped into firm ball in water, does not flatten when removed	244–248°F.
hard ball	syrup forms hard, but still pliable, ball	250–266°F.
soft crack	syrup separates into firm, but not brittle, threads in water	270–290°F.
hard crack	syrup separates into hard, brittle threads	300–310°F.

cautionary notes: Humidity is the candy cook's enemy. On damp or rainy days, cook candy to a degree or so higher on the thermometer than the recipe calls for. Or, if there's no howling mob clamoring for the product, put off the candy-making session till the weather clears up. Be aware that altitude also affects candy (see HIGH-ALTITUDE COOKING). Temperatures given in recipes are for sea level.

If you are not of a placid disposition, leave candy-making to others. It's a phase of cookery that requires a large helping of unflappable patience. Leaving aside the beating, pulling, kneading, or whatever is required, the cooking alone sometimes seems to take just short of forever. And there's no way to hurry it without disaster.

Sugar-crystal or creamy candy.
Fondant, made of sugar, corn syrup, cream of tartar, and water, and flavored and colored to suit the cook's taste, is the simplest of these candies. Mints are made of fondant; so are the centers for many kinds of chocolate creams. Fudge—chocolate, mocha, penuche, peanut butter, walnut, are some of the varieties—is made with milk rather than water, sometimes has butter added after the syrup is taken from the heat, and is beaten to gain the proper consistency and texture. Divinity is made by slowly adding hot cooked syrup to beaten egg whites, resulting in a delicate, pale, porous confection to which nuts or candied fruits are often added.

Dense-syrup or noncrystalline candy.
These candies are smooth rather than creamy, and include both hard and chewy kinds. Some of the hard ones are brittles, toffees, fruit-flavored drops, lollypops. These are poured out and allowed to cool after cooking. Some chewy ones are caramels, marshmallows, and taffy of assorted kinds. Caramels cool to proper consistency. Taffy is pulled. Marshmallows add a new ingredient, gelatin, combined with sugar, syrup and egg whites.

Chocolate-dipped candies.
Coating various kinds of candy with chocolate is a most felicitous form of lily-gilding. Nuts and fruits (candied fruits, too), caramels and nougats and toffees all take kindly to a chocolate bath and, of course, various kinds and flavors of fondant, chocolate-dipped, result in chocolate creams, the home candy-maker's crowning achievement.

There is an assortment of equipment available to aid in the making of chocolate-coated candies, such as little wire dippers to hold the candy, special racks, tiny paper bonbon cups, and, indeed, special kinds of chocolate, with a waxy consistency, for the dipping. Some of these are useful, particularly if you are going to make chocolate-dipped candy on a fairly regular basis. But you can get along, at least until you see whether or not you enjoy making such candies, with two forks, a candy thermometer, and a double boiler.

Temperature is of first importance—the temperature of the chocolate and of the centers you are dipping in it, and of the room in which you work. Heat and humidity defeat the most skillful chocolate dipper, so choose a cool, dry day and work in a kitchen where the temperature is about 65°F.

Making chocolate-dipped candies requires considerable patience and skill—and a lot of experience and experimenting—before you will be able to produce results like those on display in a good candy store. If you want to try, consult a reliable cookbook that has an extensive section on candy-making. Consolation: If you use fresh, high-quality ingredients, your candies will taste as good as those from the best candy shops, even though at first they may not equal them in appearance.

Now that you've got it made.
Most homemade candies store well, can be kept for several weeks if hidden from marauding snackers. All candies should be stored airtight, in a cool, dry place. Sticky and chewy kinds—taffies, caramels, and the like—and hard candies should be individually wrapped. The exception to the storage rule is divinity; it stales rapidly, and should be eaten within a day or two of making.

Homemade candies—the commercial kind too for that matter—freeze well. Place in a box or other container, individually wrapped or not according to the kind; overwrap with freezer paper or foil.

Confections, but not really candy.
Many kinds of sweets that don't meet the "candy" definition are nevertheless eaten and enjoyed for the same purpose. There are glacéed fruits and peels, fondant-dipped strawberries and other berries, crystallized flowers or flower petals, stuffed dried fruits such as dates and prunes, fruit pastes often called leather—peach leather, apricot leather, and so on—and a number of popcorn-based confections. There are also some quick/easy candies for the undermotivated or too-timid candy-maker to try—melted chocolate drops with nuts or dry cereal or coconut or, even, chow mein noodles, stirred in, or

melted commercial caramels or marshmallows given the same treatment, for example. They are simple to make. Some commercial boxed frosting mixes can be made into acceptable candy, too. Follow instructions on the label.

Candy calorie counting. As we remarked before, we eat candy because it's good, not because it's good for us. Now and again you'll find a bit of nutritional value—a little protein here, a trace of vitamin A there. But nothing to brag about. What candy does have to offer is calories (call it food energy, if that's any comfort to you). Almost all candy is high in carbohydrate. Confections can be a disaster on a weight-loss diet, whether it's calories or carbograms that you're counting.

It's impossible to give accurate counts for various kinds of candy. Each recipe is different from others for the same confection. But here are some approximations:

candy (1 ounce)	calories	carbohydrates
butterscotch	113	27 grams
milk chocolate	147	16 grams
chocolate cream, vanilla	123	20 grams
chocolate fudge	113	22 grams
gum drops	98	25 grams
jellybeans	104	26 grams
marshmallows	90	22 grams
chocolate-coated almonds	161	12 grams
peanut brittle	119	23 grams

You get the idea, don't you? And one ounce, unfortunately, is a shockingly small measure in the eyes of a true candy lover.

Worth it? To a great many of us, it most certainly is. Please pass the chocolates—there may be a destiny that shapes our ends, but their girth remains our own business. See also FUDGE, KISSES, and PRALINE.

CANNED AND PACKAGED FOODS

Most present-day commercially canned foods are packed and processed to keep for a long time on your pantry shelf. But not forever. If you have on hand a large amount of food in cans (or jars), it's wise to place the new cans at the back of the shelves when you bring them home, pulling the older ones forward so that they will be used first. As a double precaution to protect a heavy canned-goods investment, date cans as you bring them into the kitchen. That way, you can be certain of using up older foods before new ones.

Stop, look, and read. The label on a can can tell you a lot. Canned fruits and vegetables may carry the USDA inspection shield (if the producer wishes and pays for inspection and grading) and the grade name. For vegetables, these are:

U.S. Grade A or *Fancy:* Carefully selected for color, tenderness, and freedom from blemishes; the most tender, succulent, and flavorful vegetables produced.

U.S. Grade B or *Extra Standard:* Excellent quality, but not quite so well selected for color and tenderness as the top grade; slightly more mature, and therefore have a slightly different flavor from those of top grade.

U.S. Grade C or *Standard:* Not as uniform in either color or flavor as the higher grades, and generally more mature; use when appearance is not important.

Grades and standards for canned fruits are:

U.S. Grade A or *Fancy:* The very best; excellent color, uniform size, weight, and shape, and properly ripe, having few or no blemishes.

U.S. Grade B or *Choice:* Very good quality, only slightly less perfect than the top grade in color, uniformity, and texture; suitable for most uses.

U.S. Grade C or *Standard:* Can may contain some broken and/or uneven pieces and flavor may not be quite as good (sweet) as in higher grades; use where color and texture are not of great importance.

labels have a lot to say: Federal regulations require that the labels carry the common or usual name of the product, and the form—style—of the product (such as slices, halves, or diced). The form may be illustrated, rather than stated. In fruit, the pack must also be listed—that is, whether in heavy syrup, light syrup, or water. Also mandatory is the net contents in total ounces for containers of a pound or less, in pounds and ounces for those holding over a pound but less than 4 pounds. (At the time this is written, consideration is being given to requiring drained weight—that is, solids without liquid—to be given as well.) Many labels now carry weight in grams too and many more will soon do so, as we move closer to metrication.

Other information on the label may include spices or seasonings if used in the packing, and number of servings—if servings are stated at all, they must be given in common measures (cups or ounces). Mandatory on the label is the packer's or distributor's name and place of business. Not mandatory, but nice to find there, may be cooking directions and even recipes using the product in various ways.

Snoop a little to protect yourself. Inspect the cans or jars of foods you choose in the store before you put them into your shopping cart. Make certain can seams are not leaking, that the labels are clean, that there are no serious dents (small dents won't affect the contents). Swollen or bulging cans are dangerous; don't buy them and, if you have a sense of obligation toward your fellow mortals, call them to the manager's attention. (At home, dispose of swollen or bulging cans unopened; if you accidentally open such a can, do not taste the contents—throw it away where children and animals can't get at it.)

Glass jars in which food is packed are especially sealed to keep the contents safe. If tops are not tightly in place, or there is any other evidence that the jar has been tampered with, don't buy it; call it to the manager's attention.

The choice is yours. Many foods are packed in various styles—be aware that you have a choice, and be guided accordingly. Peaches, for example, come packed in heavy syrup (extra sweetness, extra calories as well), in light syrup, and in water (diet pack). Pineapple comes packed in syrup or in its own juice. Tomatoes are packed whole peeled, sliced, in chunks, "stewed"—with celery, onion, and peppers—and as purée, plain or variously flavored sauces, or as paste. Green beans come whole or cut, as well as pickled. It pays to read the label for grade and style to choose the pack that's right for the purpose you have in mind. Buying expensive whole tomatoes, for example, is wasteful if you're going to cook them down into spaghetti sauce or cut them up into a casserole.

The variety of canned goods available in today's markets is almost infinite. Choose a day when you're not rushed, and the store is not too busy—a Monday morning, say—to browse a little. You may find some treasures you weren't even aware existed, to lend variety to meals and to lend you a hand in the kitchen.

Store canned-goods leftovers, covered, in the original container in the refrigerator, or transfer to another covered container. Don't plan on keeping them more than 4 days.

Anything, everything comes in a package. Packaged foods do not, in general, have as long a shelf life as canned ones. However, packaging has been so much improved in the past generation (waxed interiors, plastic inner wraps, and so on) that you are exceedingly unlikely to bring home a stale packaged product from a busy market. Always inspect packages before you buy them. Some

market shelf boys are very cavalier with their box knives, cutting not only the big carton but some of the packages as well, often all the way through the inner wrap. The contents of such slit packages are exposed to air and will rapidly go stale. Be sure every package you buy is securely sealed on all sides. And, again, read the labels—they will tell you what you need to know about the contents of the package.

Contrary to ads and commercials, the big economy size is not always economical. A large box of dry cereal, for example, even though it may cost less per ounce than a smaller package, is not a good buy if half of it goes stale before you can use it up. Check the price per ounce for another reason: the big economy size is sometimes not economical; if the 32-ounce size sells for $3.10 and the 12-ounce size for 96 cents, you'll be ripped off if you don't stop and think a moment. That's what unit pricing is all about.

At home, rotate packaged goods in the same manner as canned ones, using the oldest first. If a package has a closure that can be securely refastened, be sure to open it and close it again as directed. If the package cannot be securely closed, transfer the contents to a tightly covered jar or canister for longer life. If you have a problem with pantry pests —ants or weevils—always transfer the contents to a tightly closable glass or metal container as soon as you open a package. And be certain that the place you choose for package storage is cool and dry—moisture is the enemy of packaged foods of all kinds.

CANNELLINI: see BEANS

CANNELONI: see PASTA

CANNING AT HOME: see special feature: PUTTING FOOD BY

CANTALOUPES: see MELONS

CAPERS

The unopened flower buds of a shrub native to the Mediterranean, capers are preserved in vinegar with a touch of salt. They add piquant flavor to hot and cold sauces, particularly those that garnish fish or shellfish, and to salads of several kinds. A superb salad combines cold poached chicken breast masked with homemade lemon mayonnaise and sprinkled with capers—simple, but perfect as so many simple things often are.

Along with onion and egg yolk, capers are an accompaniment for Steak Tartare. Use capers as a garnish for appetizers, as a condiment with meat dishes, as an enlivener in salad fillings for sandwiches.

Buy capers in small glass jars, refrigerate after opening. They can be stored for at least 6 months. The smaller the bud, the better the flavor—and the more expensive.

CAPONS: see CHICKEN

CAPPICOLA: see SAUSAGES

CARAMELIZE, TO: see page 449

CARAWAY: see SEEDS

CARBOHYDRATE: see special feature:
 NUTRITION NOTEBOOK

CARDAMOM: see SEEDS and SPICES

CARDOONS: see UNUSUAL VEGETABLES

CARIBOU: see GAME

CAROB

This enjoys (or suffers from) a number of different names—caroub, algarroba, locust bean, St. John's bread. Whatever you choose to call it, it is the long, brown pod of the carob tree, which grows in Palestine and in various other places along the Mediterranean. Sweet and quite chocolatelike in flavor, except for a few small, hard seeds, the entire pod is edible. It is sold fresh—sometimes by street peddlers, to be eaten out of hand—in the places where it grows, and is available dried elsewhere. Look for carob in natural-food stores if you have difficulty finding it.

The dried fruit is powdered, resulting in a meal that resembles a pale cocoa powder. This powder, as well as a carob syrup, is used to flavor such foods as puddings and candies, delicious in their own right and particularly useful to those who are allergic to chocolate. Carob is a favorite of natural-food nuts (as opposed to those who approach the subject sensibly) as a chocolate substitute; actually it is in no way more "natural" than chocolate—both are derived from plants, both are cultivated, both are processed. As a substitute for chocolate or cocoa, carob must be used in recipes tailored for its use.

Rich in sugar and fairly high in protein, carob is also used extensively as a food for cattle, as well as a flavoring for chewing tobacco and dog biscuits. Carob bean gum is used as an additive—a thickener/stabilizer—in many foods.

CAROB FLOUR: see FLOUR

CAROLINA RICE: see RICE

CARP: see FISH

CARROTS

Inexpensive, enjoyed by almost everyone, available everywhere all year around—you can't ask more of a vegetable.

As is true of many vegetables, carrots once grew wild in Europe, free for the gathering. Very early, they were more likely to be used for medicinal purposes than as part of the menu. Pliny recommended carrots to his fellow Romans as an excellent tonic for the stomach, and they were also thought to have remarkable curative effects on those suffering from bronchitis. The Greeks made a love potion, called *philtron,* from the vegetable. Elizabethan ladies liked the tops of domestic carrots, mingled with the carrot's wild relative, Queen Anne's Lace, woven into wreaths to wear on their heads.

Oddly, carrots were among the first canned foods—turned out with (one assumes) pride by a factory in England, along with boiled beef, corned beef, mutton and vegetable stew, and several soups. These were greeted with particularly joyous gratitude by ships' provisioners, we are told, for fresh meat could not be served other than for the first few days after leaving port on long voyages, and dried and salted meats could become very monotonous. But why carrots? Carrots keep—they are one of the root vegetables that "winter over" well. Ships could carry them raw, serve them fresh. Perhaps that early canner also had a truck farm and a crop excess, and tried canning carrots just to see if the process would work.

Carrots came to Virginia in 1609, shortly after the Jamestown settlers, and to the New England colonists less than ten years after the first of them had arrived.

CARROTS IN YOUR KITCHEN

You will find carrots available all year long, but the treat of the carrot world is the small, fresh "baby" carrots that come to market in the spring. These tender young roots need be neither peeled nor scraped, only washed and cooked—preferably whole.

Bringing home the carrots. "New" carrots—you can tell them because they have their green tops still in place—are widely available much of the year, thanks to modern shipping, which whisks them easily and rapidly from warm climates to cold ones. "Old" carrots—they may have been out of the ground and in storage for a time—are always available. Local carrots (tops on) are available in season; out of season (topless) they are shipped from California, Texas, Arizona, and Florida.

how to buy: Purchase carrots loose, by the pound—a pound will yield 2½ cups when cooked, make 3 to 4 servings —or in plastic bags. Either way, look for shapely firmness, a fresh, clean look, and a good golden-orange color. Pass by any with blemishes or soft spots. Carrots that have split or those that have forked into two ends may be woody, so may carrots with a dry, too-pale, flaky appearance. Carrots begin to rot at both the root and the stem ends—make certain that those you buy are solid and not starting to turn brown in those places. If the tops are still on the carrots, they should be fresh and green.

how to store: If the tops are still in place, remove them. Refrigerate, in plastic bags or wrapped in foil, preferably in the refrigerator's vegetable crisper, up to 4 weeks. Cooked carrots—covered and refrigerated—keep up to 5 days.

nutritive value: Low in calories, rich in vitamin A (one of the major sources), carrots should be a part of the diet of young and old. Fortunately, they are widely liked. One cup of sliced cooked carrots contains 48 calories and offers:

protein	1.4 grams
fat	.3 gram
carbohydrate	11 grams
calcium	51 milligrams
phosphorus	48 milligrams
iron	.9 milligram
sodium	51 milligrams
potassium	344 milligrams
thiamin	.08 milligram
riboflavin	.08 milligram
niacin	.8 milligram
ascorbic acid	9 milligrams
vitamin A	16,280 international units

Tips on preparing, cooking. Very young, small fresh carrots need only be washed, then cooked whole until just tender in a small amount of water (salted if you wish). Larger, older ones should be scraped or peeled—a very thin peeling—with a vegetable parer. Quarter, dice, cut in crosswise slices or lengthwise strips, depending on the use you will make of the vegetable after it is cooked.

Serve carrots plain, with a little butter, salt, and pepper. Or cook until almost tender, drain, return to pan, add butter and a sprinkling of sugar—white or brown—or a tablespoon or two of honey, and glaze over low heat; if you prefer a sweet/sour glaze, add lemon juice. Or try a glazed combination of carrots and apples. Cream carrots and sprinkle the dish very lightly with ground nutmeg or cloves. Or sprinkle plain or creamed carrots with chopped parsley, dill, or mint, or with parmesan or cheddar. Or lightly season the liquid in which the carrots were cooked with grated orange peel, ginger, celery seed, thyme, or rosemary, or with garlic or onion juice, and thicken slightly with cornstarch; reheat carrots in this sauce. Or grate carrots coarsely and steam briefly in butter and a little water until liquid evaporates; season and serve.

All sorts of stews and casseroles are the better for having carrots added; the vegetable teams well with almost any meat or poultry. And it partners well with other vegetables, too, as a side dish or in a main dish; pair carrots with peas, celery, zucchini, small whole onions, green beans. For a change, serve mashed carrots, alone or cooked and mashed half-and-half with potatoes. Or roast whole carrots in the pan with beef or lamb.

And don't forget that carrots are just as good—maybe better—raw. "An apple a day keeps the doctor away" may be an old wives' tale, but one carrot—medium size, raw—gives you your entire day's requirement of vitamin A. Coarsely grated, combine carrots with cabbage for better-than-ever slaw, with nuts and raisins for a salad kids (adults, too) love, with pineapple in lemon-flavored gelatin for old-fashioned sunshine salad. Or heap on sandwiches as a change from lettuce. Or toss with greens for added color and flavor. Cut carrot sticks or curls to add to a platter of crudités or for a deliciously edible garnish for cold meats or poultry.

If you don't have carrots in the main part of the meal, bring them on at the end, for they add sweet color and flavor to all sorts of desserts. Try carrot cake with cream cheese icing, crunchy carrot cookies, baked or steamed carrot pudding (with lemon sauce). Or substitute for pumpkin in a wonderful pie. Or combine carrots with figs, raisins, lemon, grapefruit, and orange for a delectable Creole carrot conserve.

Freezing Carrots. Properly prepared (see special feature: PUTTING FOOD BY), carrots may be stored at 0°F. or below up to a year. However, unless you have exceptionally ample freezer space (or carrots from your own garden that you can't otherwise preserve), carrots should be low on the freezing list, as they are available fresh all year around. Save freezer space for seasonal foods.

Other ways, other forms. You'll find carrots, in one form or another, in many departments of your market.

fresh produce: Besides the loose, bunched, or packaged carrots, look for shredded carrots in coleslaw-mix plastic bags, as well as bags of whole baby carrots (but buy these only in a market you trust—sometimes, rather than being tiny young carrots, these are very old ones trimmed to shape, and may be packaged this way to disguise the fact).

on grocery shelves, in cans or jars: Whole baby carrots, sliced or julienned carrots, dilled or otherwise pickled carrots. Baby food puréed or "junior" carrots.

in grocery frozen-food section: Whole baby or sliced or julienned carrots; carrots and peas in combination; in packages of mixed vegetables; as the vegetable in some kinds of TV dinners.

However you serve carrots—and there are so many ways you need never grow tired of them—serve them often. The yellow-orange carotene that colors them is obligingly converted by our bodies to vitamin A, essential for normal growth, good eyesight. A raw carrot makes a great munch-on snack for a child—and his enthusiasm for it is shared by horses, donkeys, rabbits, and some discriminating dogs. Great for waistline-watchers, too. Great, in fact, for everyone.

CARVING, BONING, AND OTHER KITCHEN TECHNIQUES: see page 298

CASABAS: see MELONS

CASERTAS: see SQUASH

CASHEWS

A nut that, considerately, has no shell. A nut that is the seed of an applelike, but pear-shaped, fruit of a tropical evergreen tree. A nut that grows outside, not inside, the fruit, hanging neatly at the bottom to invite the picker. In short, the crisp, buttery, kidney-shaped cashew nut.

Cashews are native to tropical America, but have spread to many hot, moist parts of the world. Most of the cashews we eat in the United States are imported from Brazil and from India. Most of them are roasted and salted, although diligent effort will search out unsalted nuts, if you prefer them. Usually, because the nuts themselves are high in fat, cashews are dry-roasted, without oil.

CASHEWS IN YOUR KITCHEN

how to buy: Cashews are available in 3-ounce or larger plastic bags, or ½- or 1-pound jars or vacuum-pack cans or, in specialty shops, in bulk. And, of course, as part of the combination in mixed nuts. Choose whole cashews for eating out of hand, less expensive pieces for cooking.

how to store: Keep cashews in the refrigerator, where they will remain fresh up to 6 months, or in the freezer up to 1 year.

nutritive value: One ounce of cashew nuts—about 18 of medium size—contains 159 calories, 4.9 grams of protein, 13 grams of fat, 8.3 grams of carbohydrate, and small amounts of some of the vitamins and minerals.

Some perfect partners. For a simple dessert, team cashews with fruit and cream cheese. Add to curry dishes for an authentic Indian flavor. Chop and include in stuffing for all kinds of poultry, and for breast of veal. Enhance fruit or meat or poultry salads with cashews, or add them to casserole dishes based on the same foods. Make cashew cookies and candies. Or—using the meat grinder or the blender—whip up a batch of cashew butter, an exotic and delectable change from peanut butter.

However you use cashew nuts, in cooking or for snacking, they will reward you with their excellent flavor, their unusual buttery-yet-crisp texture. Substitute cashews in recipes that call for peanuts or almonds, for a change of pace.

CASSEROLES

Here in the United States, we use the same word, "casserole," for the food and for the pan in which it's cooked. And we make casseroles of virtually anything edible you can think of, because the casserole spans a wide range of culinary virtues.

To begin with, it's a make-ahead dish, put together—sometimes partially, sometimes fully cooked—at your leisure, in the morning or even the day before. It needs only to be popped into the oven in advance of dinner, requiring no tiresome, inconvenient standing over at a time when you're busy with other things, would like to sit down for a preprandial drink-and-nibble session with family or guests, or simply yearn to drop into a chair and pant for a little while.

Casserole constituents. Main-dish casseroles usually have meat or fish or poultry as a chief ingredient, a starch (often inelegantly referred to as a "filler"), and a sauce. Sometimes a vegetable joins in, once in a while a fruit. More often than not there's a crisp topping to add texture, or a finishing touch of cheese for extra flavor.

Although casseroles are a dandy way to use up leftovers, it's the sweep-the-kitchen idea that has given casseroles a bad name, particularly with men. Throwing in a tired leftover, whether or not it has any affinity with the dish, leads to dialogue like this:

Wife: Do you like the casserole?

Husband (warily): What's it called?

Wife: Fruits de Mer chez McGillicuddy. I added some pea soup from Tabitha's lunch and what was left of the strawberry Jello we had Tuesday. Oh, and those crackers you said were getting stale.

Husband: Um.

Wife (anxiously): Don't you like it? Really? Tell the truth.

Husband (with patience and fortitude): I love it. It's very good. Please don't ever make it again.

Moral: a good casserole should be made on purpose, not because it's your day to clean out the refrigerator.

the meat/fish/poultry: These are the stick-to-your-ribs ingredients. Ground beef, that American dietary staple, is the backbone of many a delicious casserole, from tamale pie to quick/easy lasagna. Ground lamb, often available as lamb patties, is a change of flavor, and more authentic, in casseroles with a Mediterranean flavor. (Ground turkey, which has begun to appear in markets all over the country, substitutes well for beef or lamb, is lower in fat and calories than either.) Ground pork has great flavor; best to brown it first and pour off the excess fat. Or, instead of buying raw ground meat, grind your own leftovers, or dice them.

But ground meat is only the beginning. Casserole chops, too, particularly the less delicate kinds, such as lamb shoulder (perfect with eggplant, garlicky tomato sauce, mozzarella cheese). Pork chops in a casserole are much more tender and juicy than when they're broiled or fried. Bony cuts of meat, such as beef shortribs, lamb neck, veal breast, profit by long oven braising in a casserole with vegetables or a bread stuffing. And don't overlook sausages of various kinds, gently or assertively spiced according to the use you intend to put them to.

Chicken, as bone-in parts or precooked and boned, is a casserole favorite. So is turkey. So, more surprisingly, is duck —think of a casserole of quartered duck with sweet potatoes and orange segments, and salivate.

Fish does well in delicate, quick-to-cook casseroles. Shellfish is equally good—crab, rice, and asparagus, for example, in an egg-enriched, sherry-flavored cream sauce. As for canned fish, this country would go straight to the dogs if a law against the ubiquitous tuna-noodle casserole were passed. Tuna—salmon, too—has many other roles to play in all-in-one oven dishes.

the "fillers": Pasta of all shapes and sizes shines here, with egg noodles leading the pack, and seashells, lasagna noodles, linguine, fettucine (plain or spinach), regular spaghetti, elbow macaroni, and all the others following close behind.

But don't forget potatoes. A great way to use up leftover roast is to dice it, cook onion, and celery (carrot, too, if you like), and combine with the meat in its gravy; layer with mashed potatoes into which grated cheese has been folded. A casserole of leftover ham with scalloped potatoes, perked up with onion, is so good you'll be tempted to buy ham especially if there's none in the refrigerator. Cooked dried beans of various kinds make excellent casserole extenders. Experiment with cornmeal mush or polenta layered with spicy, savory meat mixtures. And rice, white or brown, is second only to pasta as a universally used casserole extender.

the vegetables: Add them by all means—but not just because they're hanging around, growing elderly. Make certain the vegetable flavor is compatible with the other casserole components. Cabbage stands up to ham or other pork, and to spicy beef mixtures, but kills veal. Spinach is a welcome addition to the cheese layer in lasagna. Peas and green beans can make a place for themselves in many casserole dishes. Lima beans and corn, separately or together, partner well with bacon or salt pork. Eggplant is wonderfully good in Italian- or Greek-type combinations. Remember that carrots and turnips are strong flavored, as well as tending to sweeten any dish in which they are cooked, and be guided accordingly. Water chestnuts, bamboo shoots, and nuts add crunch.

the sauces: Tomato sauce is often what binds a casserole together, particularly if pasta is the starch ingredient. Use your own, made from scratch from fresh tomatoes (the Italian plums are perfect for tomato sauce; add a small can of tomato paste for body and reinforced flavor), or sauce from a can, gussied up a bit with garlic, basil, oregano, a speck of sugar, whatever it needs to give it oomph. Sometimes the binder is a simple white sauce. Sometimes it's a cheese sauce. Sometimes it's a special make-at-home sauce tailored just for the recipe you're following.

More often than not, the sauce is one of the canned condensed soups. These soups serve exceptionally well in casseroles—they're time- and work-saving, and they have good flavor and body. Cream of chicken, cream of celery, cream of mushroom, and cheddar cheese make some of the best casserole sauces, but there are many others. Be sure, though, unless your recipe directs you otherwise, not to dilute the soup one-for-one when you're using it as a sauce. And go easy on the salt—taste the casserole mixture first, season after tasting.

the toppers: Some go on early in the game, some are added the last few minutes of cooking—either way, toppings for casseroles are many and various, all add the finishing touch, the final fillip that makes a good dish better. Bread crumbs are good, are better for having been sautéed lightly in butter. Crushed chips—corn or potato—are very tasty. Crushed crackers ditto—plain, buttery, cheese- or otherwise flavored. Just a sprinkling of paprika shows you cared, and helps the top of the dish to brown. Crunchy dry cereal is fine. So are broken-up pretzels. Cheese, grated or cut in neat squares or triangles, makes a deliciously chewy topping. Biscuits—homemade or from a dairy-case package—bake up high and handsome, and can take the place of a filler ingredient in the dish itself. Mashed potatoes, plain or cheese-flavored or -sprinkled, make a fine topping and serve the same purpose. Or prepare a batch of pie crust or crust mix and cut into pretty shapes with a cookie cutter to top the dish. Or sprinkle the top of the dish with toasted slivered almonds. Whatever, do something—don't let a casserole come naked to the table.

Treasures waiting in the wings. One of the great advantages of casseroles is that most of them freeze well. A good casserole or two tucked away in the freezer makes it easy for you to invite drop-in friends to stay for dinner. When you're planning a big party, prepare your main-dish casserole a few days—or weeks, or up to 3 months—in advance and stash it in the freezer, ready and waiting. When you make a casserole for a family dinner, double the recipe, serve one and freeze the second to serve you well on some busy day in the future.

It's not practical, of course, to tie up all those casserole pans in the freezer. For a casserole that you plan to freeze, line the pan with heavy-duty foil, fitting and shaping it well to conform with the dish. Fill, bake (if the recipe requires), cool, and freeze. Then remove the frozen food, still foil-wrapped, from the casserole dish. Overwrap, label, date, and return to the freezer. When you're ready to use it, peel off the wrappings, put the frozen food into the dish in which you originally prepared it, and pop it into the oven. Remember that you'll need to add at least half an hour for a small frozen casserole, an hour or more for a large one, to the normal baking time.

An eye on the purse strings. In France, the casserole is looked upon as a specialty, the gratifying achievement of a good cook. Here, we tend to view it as that which we serve a) when the food budget is at a low ebb, b) when we can't think of anything else to have for dinner, or c) both. We tend to be grim about it. Learn to think "I guess I'll make a casserole" with an exclamation point at the end of the sentence, and eating will start to look up around your house.

Although casseroles—good ones and bad—generally are relatively low-budget dishes (low as compared to a standing rib roast, say), this isn't necessarily the case. Consider Cassoulet, for example, that great, long-cooking based-on-beans dish from the Toulouse region of France, that harbors a multitude of delights, such as pork, lamb, and sausages. One of them, if you're following an authentic recipe, is *confit d'oie*—preserved goose—an item which, provided you can lay hands on it, will deliver a blow to your food budget that will send it reeling. *Chacun à son goût.*

CASSOULET: see STEWS

CAST IRON KITCHEN UTENSILS: see
    special feature: YOU CAN'T WORK
    WITHOUT TOOLS

CATFISH: see FISH

CATSUP

A thick, usually tomato-based sauce that probably got its name from *kecap,* the Malay word for "taste." Catsup is a condiment used by children on virtually anything that isn't breathing and running around—burgers, hot dogs, eggs, sandwiches, french fries (and mashed and baked potatoes, too), vegetables, meat, salads, whatever. There is doubtless a benighted kid somewhere who relishes catsup on his chocolate ice cream. This unfortunate habit often carries over into adulthood. Good cooks are annoyed when a diner reaches for the salt and pepper before tasting his food—how much more infuriating to have him reach for the catsup and slather it on!

This is not to say that catsup doesn't have a place in the comestible scheme of things, but only that it should be kept in its place. On cookout burgers and frankfurters, for example —well, all right, on eaten-indoors burgers, too, if that's your pleasure. On, in fact, any sort of informal food, such as fast-food fries. And if Junior wolfs down peanut butter-and-catsup sandwiches, that's his problem. But please, not on the lobster thermidor, not on the breast of duckling Montmorency, not on the fettucine Alfredo.

Catsup can be a useful cooking adjunct, used judiciously. A tablespoon or so lends body and color to beef gravy, makes stews a bit gutsier, improves some nothing salad dressings.

"Catsup" is, by the way, the generic spelling— "KETCHUP," a processor's spelling of the word. However spelled, it's the same, except that each manufacturer's brand tastes slightly different from his competitor's, depending on his "secret" formula.

There are catsups other than tomato—cranberry, cucumber, grape, walnut, mushroom, and more; these are most usually homemade, and often very good indeed. Excellent tomato catsup too can be made at home—consult a good general cookbook.

CAULIFLOWER

Part of the family that includes broccoli and brussels sprouts, as well as the various kinds of cabbage, cauliflower was once characterized by Mark Twain as "cabbage with a college education."

Known and loved in Italy since the days of the Roman Empire, cauliflower, like broccoli, was developed for its flower rather than its leaves. It was brought to the United States by Italian immigrants and grown almost exclusively in backyards and small truck gardens until the 1920s, when quantity commercial growing and distribution began.

The tight cluster of creamy-white flower buds that makes up the head of cauliflower is called the curd—not surprisingly, because it does resemble the curds formed by milk as it sours.

The vegetable is grown throughout the United States, with New York, Washington, and Oregon producing large amounts. Because cauliflower likes a moist climate, warm in the daytime but cooling off at night, California is the chief supplier of the vegetable to the nation.

CAULIFLOWER IN YOUR KITCHEN

To decide how much cauliflower to buy, you need only to look at it. The vegetable shrinks little in cooking; only the white flower portion is eaten. You can choose a small head to serve 3 or 4, or a larger one for 5 or 6 servings.

You will find cauliflower in the market throughout the year, but the peak season starts in September, ends in November. Fresh cauliflower is sold only as whole heads, either "as is" or in a protective wrapping of clear plastic.

how to buy: Choose a head that is heavy for its size, firm and compact. The size of the head bears no relation to its quality or age. The condition of the leaves—green and fresh-looking, or yellow, withering, and limp—is a guide. Avoid bruises and more than a minimum of brown spots, as well as a head that is darkening and seems to be shrinking in upon itself. This condition is called "riciness" and is a sign of old age.

how to store: Refrigerate, closely covered—with foil, plastic wrap, or in a plastic bag—up to 5 days. Cooked cauliflower, in a covered container in the refrigerator, may be kept up to 4 days.

nutritive value: As many vegetables are, cauliflower—raw or cooked—is a weight-loss dieter's delight. It's also a good source of vitamin C, especially when eaten raw. Cooked and drained, one cup of cauliflower contains 28 calories, and offers:

protein	2.9 grams
fat	.3 gram
carbohydrate	5.1 grams
calcium	26 milligrams
phosphorus	53 milligrams
iron	.9 milligram
sodium	11 milligrams
potassium	258 milligrams
thiamin	.11 milligram
riboflavin	.1 milligram
niacin	.8 milligram
ascorbic acid	69 milligrams
vitamin A	80 international units

Tips on preparing, cooking. Wash the cauliflower; remove the leaves and the lower part of the stem. If you are going to serve it raw, or if you plan to cook it whole, soak the head in cold water for a few minutes to entice out any lurking insects. Cook, whole or broken (or cut) into flowerets, in a small amount of boiling water, salted if you like, until just tender. This should take 20 to 30 minutes for a whole head, 7 to 12 minutes for the flowerets. A small amount of lemon juice added to the water will help keep the cauliflower white if you suspect yours of being a bit on the elderly side.

Freezing cauliflower. Properly prepared (see special feature: PUTTING FOOD BY), cauliflower may be kept at 0°F. or below up to a year. Again, though, cauliflower is available fresh most of the year; freezer space, unless you have a great deal of it, is better devoted to truly seasonal foods.

Other ways, other forms. There are not a great many choices other than the fresh form.

in grocery frozen-food section: Frozen plain cauliflower in 10-ounce packages (be careful not to overcook), and, with cheese sauce, in boil-in bags.

Some perfect partners. Serve raw cauliflowerets or slices as a deliciously tasty, crunchy addition to a platter of crudités, or to add texture and variety to a tossed green salad or a main-dish ham salad, or simply—in the manner of carrot or celery sticks—as a snack food. Or offer a salad of the vegetable, cooked just until tender-crisp and chilled, with a vinaigrette sauce.

A whole cooked head of cauliflower can be a handsome separate course when masked with a light curry sauce, one made with cheddar cheese, or a cream sauce blushed with tomato. Or sprinkle with butter-browned bread crumbs, then with chopped pimiento, for cauliflower Polonaise. Sauced with creamed shrimps, eggs, or ham, a whole cooked cauliflower becomes a most acceptable main dish, especially if given the added fillip of the butter-browned bread crumb treatment. Or serve more simply, whole or in flowerets, with browned butter, or with plain butter lightly sprinkled with nutmeg or chopped dill.

Cooked tender-crisp, drained, and batter-dipped, cauliflower can be turned into delectable fritters. Make a great cream soup with cauliflower leftovers.

For a change, seek out a greengrocer in an Italian neighborhood, where you may find exotic green- or purple-curded cauliflowers. But exotic or old standby, serve cauliflower regularly, as one of the variety of vegetables available in such profusion that we never hear the complaint that our families are tired of "the same old thing."

CAVIAR

The glorious—or absolutely appalling, depending on your taste buds, upbringing, and outlook on life—fish roe (eggs) of several finny critters. Those of the sturgeon, which yield the finest quality, are used generally, but also used are those of cod, carp, whitefish, and others. Salmon yields red caviar, with eggs much larger than most others.

Years ago, kids used to (perhaps they still do) sing a song they considered pretty daring:

> Caviar comes from a virgin sturgeon;
> A virgin sturgeon's a very rare fish,
> Very few sturgeons ever need urgin'—
> That's why caviar's such a rare dish.

Whether or not that sums up the truth of the matter, caviar is indeed a very rare dish, at least in the sense that it is in short supply and, therefore, breathtakingly expensive.

One of the ladies of the group known as the Beautiful People claims that her favorite low-calorie lunch consists of a baked potato split and heaped high with caviar (the finest beluga, it goes without saying), accompanied by a glass of champagne. Not exactly a Weight Watchers' special, although indeed it does add up to about 500 calories.

For kinds, sources, how to serve, and other information about caviar, see APPETIZERS.

CAYENNE: see CHILIES and HERBS AND SAVORY SEASONINGS

CELERIAC or CELERI-RAVE: see UNUSUAL VEGETABLES

CELERY

Once a wild herb that grew free for the picking across Europe and Asia (it still grows wild in some parts of England), celery was chiefly used medicinally. But it has been cultivated for centuries and now has a part in our cooking/eating scheme of things almost daily, although many of us don't use it in as many ways as its versatility deserves.

Dutch farmers around Kalamazoo, Michigan, first grew

celery commercially in the United States in the 1870s. Here we eat celery most often raw, but Europeans prefer it cooked.

Celery nomenclature tends to get a bit confusing. The whole bunch of celery is technically a stalk. The single branch or piece, which we often call a stalk, is technically a rib. Celery isn't going to care a bit what you call it, but watch out in the recipes of certain cookbook writers who pride themselves on their culinary vocabularies, or you may end up with too much or too little.

CELERY IN YOUR KITCHEN

Two varieties of celery are available, the golden or yellow, which is often referred to as "white," and the larger, green pascal celery. "Be sure to get the *white* kind," grandma admonished the child she sent to the store for celery, but by now we have come to appreciate—and buy more of—the pascal, which—although large—is tender and not as stringy as the paler variety. Yellow celery would also be green, if allowed, but it is grown under little paper tents that prevent chlorophyl from developing. Nowadays, most of the celery in our markets is pascal, and we find yellow celery rarely except when packaged and labeled "celery hearts."

how to buy: Celery should be so crisp it snaps at you. Choose such stalks, making certain the leaves are fresh-looking and have not begun to wilt. When you get the celery home, don't make the mistake of whacking off the tops and throwing them away—in them lies a bouquet of delicious flavor for soups and other cooked foods, and a bonus of pretty leaves for garnishing.

how to store: Keep celery cool and dry, in a covered container, in a closed-up plastic bag or closely wrapped in foil; store leaves and stalk separately, but do not cut off the root end—celery keeps better with it in place. Well stored, it will keep 8 days, often as long as 2 weeks. Freshen in ice water celery that has begun to grow limp. Cooked celery, covered and refrigerated, will keep up to 5 days.

nutritive value: As we all have heard until we're tired of hearing it, celery is the weight-loss dieter's security blanket. One cup of diced raw celery "costs" only 17 calories. One large rib of pascal celery, about 8 inches long and 1½ inches wide at the root end, contains 7 calories, and offers:

protein	.4	grams
fat	trace	gram
carbohydrate	1.6	grams
calcium	16	milligrams
phosphorus	11	milligrams
iron	.1	milligram
sodium	50	milligrams
potassium	136	milligrams
thiamin	.01	milligram
riboflavin	.01	milligram
niacin	.1	milligram
ascorbic acid	4	milligrams
vitamin A	110	international units

Tips on preparing, cooking. Separate ribs from root end just before using; wash in cold water, pat dry with absorbent paper if the celery is to be served raw. Rule of thumb: Save the tender, inner ribs for serving raw, use the outer ones for cooking.

Raw celery, just in ribs, has been so much a part of our eating habits for generations that once there were handsome, long and slender cut-glass dishes reserved for that vegetable alone (often grandma cheated and tucked in some radishes, or perhaps olives, on festive occasions such as Thanksgiving). Those celery dishes, incidentally, fetch a pretty penny nowadays in antique shops.

Stuffing celery brings up the calories, but adds flavor. Bleu cheese or sharp cheddar cheese mixtures partner beautifully with the crispness of celery hearts or sections of larger ribs. For a change, try minced raw mushrooms bound with a little mustard-spiked mayonnaise. Or cream cheese liberally laced with chopped toasted almonds or minced chives. Or chopped hard-cooked eggs bound with curry-flavored sour cream. Or peanut butter with lots of crumbled crisp bacon—kids love this one.

Add sliced celery to tossed green salads; dice it into meat, fish, or poultry main-dish salads, and to add crunch to potato or macaroni salad mixtures. Or slice celery very thinly across the rib, mix with grated carrot, finely diced green pepper, and grated onion for a fine "health slaw"; dress with sour cream plus salad oil, salt, pepper, a little wine vinegar, and a bit of sugar to taste.

To cook celery as a side-dish vegetable, slice ribs or quarter hearts lengthwise and cook, covered, in a small amount of boiling (salted) water until just tender, 10 minutes or a little longer. Or braise, in the French manner, in beef or chicken bouillon. Serve as is (a sprinkling of white pepper lends zest), buttered, combined with mushrooms, with a cheese sauce, or creamed and sprinkled with crisp bacon crumbles or toasted nuts or buttered bread crumbs.

Celery belongs by right in stir-fry mixtures, in soups and stews, and in stuffings for poultry or fish or pork.

Freezing celery. Don't—it loses all its zing. Besides, it's available all year around. However, you can bag celery leaves and freeze them to use in flavoring soups and stews when you're caught without fresh celery on hand.

Other ways, other forms. You may find canned cooked (usually braised in bouillon) celery hearts, imported from France or Belgium, in specialty food shops or the gourmet-food sections of large supermarkets. Otherwise, use fresh celery—there are no other forms generally available.

Because it is an everyday kind of food, so often used that we add it almost without thinking as we cook, we tend to forget about the less ordinary ways to enrich our diet with celery. For a change, serve it as a vegetable rather than as a relish or part of a tray of crudités. Or make a good cream of celery soup. Next time you entertain, offer your guests celery remoulade—julienne strips of celery blanched briefly in boiling water, drained and chilled, and served with a sauce of mayonnaise made lively with chopped pickles, capers, parsley, and herbs and spiked with mustard and anchovy paste. Strictly speaking, this should be made with celeriac—but it is every bit as good using regular celery.

CELERY CABBAGE: see CABBAGE

CELERY SALT, POWDER: see HERBS
AND SAVORY SEASONINGS

CELERY SEED: see SEEDS

CELLOPHANE NOODLES

These are thin, round noodles made, most usually, from powdered mung beans. Used in a number of kinds of Oriental dishes, cellophane noodles should be cooked very briefly; they are translucent when cooked. Find them (sometimes called bean threads) in Oriental markets, specialty food shops, or Oriental-food or gourmet-food sections of large supermarkets. They have very little flavor, but absorb the taste of the liquid—meat, fish, or poultry broth—in which they are cooked.

CELSIUS TEMPERATURE SYSTEM: see
special feature: MEASURING
UP TO METRIC

CERAMIC KITCHEN UTENSILS: see
special feature: YOU CAN'T WORK
WITHOUT TOOLS

CEREALS

In every gathering-together of people, there are some who are more alert, more aware, than the general run. Sometime, long before recorded history, some alert someone noticed that the food plants his tribe gathered produced seeds, and that when those seeds fell on the ground some of them grew into new plants. Ah-ha! If the seeds were gathered and put into the ground in a cleared spot, when they had (by magic, probably) sprouted and grown tall, it would no longer be necessary for the tribe to scrounge all over hell's half acre to find the makings of a meal.

Having implemented this excellent idea, he worked on another one. There were good times, when the food plants grew and animals to hunt were plentiful; bellies were full, the people were contented. But there were also bad times, when the earth offered nothing edible and the animals hid from the hunters; then hunger plagued them all, and the weak died. If, he reasoned, they put into the ground seeds of more plants than they would need in the good times, the plants could be harvested and stored against the bad times.

In time, refinements were developed. A hooked piece of wood was used to scratch the soil where the seeds were planted, and so the plow was invented. Then someone realized that if one man pulled the wood and another guided it from behind, the ground could be scratched deeper. Someone else took a good look at the jaw of that excellent ruminant, the sheep, found a like-shaped curve of wood, studded it with teeth made of flint chips, and invented the sickle. (From then on, all sickles were made in that manner—until man finally learned how to temper metal.) Later, man hitched his ox to the plow in place of one of his brothers. Primitive gleaning and winnowing tools were developed.

On the sum of those principles, arrived at and improved upon by trial and error, civilization as we know it was born. The magnificent cultures of the early Egyptians and Sumerians were based on improved growing techniques and the use of granaries—on the ability to raise and store food in such quantity that parts of the populace need not be agriculturists, but were freed to develop and follow other pursuits.

Feeding the few, feeding the millions. Somewhere along the way, someone figured out that land planted to cereal grains would feed more people than land of like size used to support livestock. (Now we have learned that some land will raise food which, while unfit for human consumption, can be efficiently turned into milk or meat by livestock, and we have arrived at what all but the vegetarians among us consider a nice balance.) Some clever early agronomist started the use of animal droppings as fertilizer—indeed, human wastes have been used for that purpose too by various cultures. Where no livestock was raised and so animal droppings were not available, other methods were arrived at. The local Indians, for example, showed the Plymouth colony pilgrims their method of burying a small fish in each hill of corn to rot there and fertilize the grain.

At first, most of the people worked the land, while some few—fed with food raised by the many—developed other skills. But as agricultural methods increased in efficiency, more and more people were released from the land, until finally—as it remains today—the few could feed the many.

Gifts of a goddess. "Cereal" is a word that covers three terms we use regularly in talking about the plant foods: 1) the edible seeds of certain food grasses, 2) the grasses (grains) themselves, and 3) the various food products that are manufactured from grains. The word comes from the ancient roman festival, *cerealia,* which honored the goddess of grain, Ceres, and sought her favor in assuring a fruitful harvest.

The chief cereal grains are wheat, corn, rice, oats, rye, and barley, all plants of the grass family. Not grasses, although they are used in cereal products, are buckwheat and millet. These grains are used in the form in which they grow, or are processed to make various kinds of flours (and further processed into breads, pastas, and other grain foods) or breakfast foods, which are also commonly called cereals.

Cereals of one kind or another grow in most climates, under all sorts of conditions. Barley and rye are raised in the cold North, wheat, corn, and rice where the climate is more kindly. Rice has been cultivated in the Orient for thousands of years. In the western hemisphere, the Aztecs were growing maize (corn) when those ubiquitous Spanish explorers arrived, and had been doing so for a long time. More than any other crops, the cereal grasses provide man with the most food for the least effort. They supply more carbohydrate than other plants used for food and contain, in amounts depending on the particular grain, appreciable protein, as well as some fat and vitamins.

Taking grain apart. Each individual grain of cereal—each seed, that is—of whatever kind, can be broken down into three elements.

the bran: This is the grain's protective outer covering; the thin papery layers are often removed when the grain is milled.

the endosperm: This is the main part, the "meat" of the grain; it is the food supply for the growing plant when the seed is cultivated.

the germ: This is the embryo, the part that contains all the elements of the new plant, the part that awaits bringing to life in earth and moisture if the seed is planted.

In the milling, one or more of these parts of the original cereal grain may be removed, but cereals that are labeled

"whole grain" retain bran, endosperm, and germ. Processing grain results in various types of flours and meals from which, in turn, a wide variety of food products are made that find their way to market and from there to your home. See also FLOUR, and additional information under each grain name: BARLEY, BUCKWHEAT, CORN, OATS, RICE, RYE, WHEAT.

BREAKFAST CEREALS

There was a time when breakfast simply was not breakfast without several cereal-based foods. Breads, for example—at the very least there was toast, most likely supplemented by a plate of fresh-from-the-oven biscuits, and/or (most likely and) a few waffles or a stack of pancakes. But the heart of that meal, the part that stuck to your ribs and carried you through until noontime, was the cereal itself, the porridge. A bowl of oatmeal, say, or of whole wheat cereal or the more effete cream of wheat, or good old cornmeal mush, all served with sugar (brown or white) or syrup, and butter or cream, or both. That's really what "cereal" meant, once upon a time.

Some of those cereals had to be cooked for hours to render them edible—or, at least, digestible. They were put on early in the morning by some hapless slavey (the lady of the house, more often than not) who had risen before the crack of dawn. Or, in "modern" homes, they were set to cook the night before in an ingenious device known as a fireless cooker. This wooden box had a metal-lined, insulated well into which fitted a heavy round of soapstone and, on top of it, an especially designed metal pot with a clamp-on lid. Over all, a wooden cover could be dropped snugly into place. The soapstone was set on the stove to heat; meanwhile, the cereal was started over another burner on the stove. When the stone was hot and the cereal boiling, the pot's lid was clamped in place. The stone was transferred to the cooker, the pot placed on it, and the cooker cover set over all. Through the night the cereal cooked, to be ready for breakfast in the morning. Sure, this wasn't the jolliest of tasks for the housewife, but after all, in the evening she had only the dishes to wash, the bread sponge to set for tomorrow's baking, and the family mending to get through, and it certainly beat standing over that pot of cereal in the dismal pre-dawn hours.

Times they are a-changing. Nowadays, we have a number of cereal processes to choose among, none of them as formidable as what grandma was faced with. You can find cereals of various kinds, made from individual grains or a combination of several, labeled "cooked," "quick," "instant," "ready-to-eat," and (recently) "natural."

cooked cereal: A misnomer, because the cereal is not cooked when you buy it, but must be, at home. Cereals of this kind may also be labeled "hot"—not because they are, but because that is how they are to be served. In other words, these must be cooked—but not for endless hours, fortunately, unless you buy them at a store that specializes in old-type cereals, such as Irish oatmeal.

quick cereal: These cereals are made of finer, thinner particles so that they will cook in a much shorter time than their "cooked" counterparts.

instant cereal: These cereals are precooked; they are served by placing the cereal in a dish, stirring in boiling water —presto! a bowl of porridge.

ready-to-eat cereal: These are the dry cereals so many kids swear by—because of their flavor or because of the surprises contained in the box, or because Cap'n Camelhumpher, their favorite TV hero, told them to go out and buy some or else. There are puffed, flaked, shredded, biscuited, and assorted other kinds; single-grain or in multiple-grain combinations; with or without fruit; sweetened or not; plain or variously flavored.

natural cereal: There is nothing more "natural" about many of these cereals than about any others—all the cereal grains are, of course, natural (as opposed to synthetic), no matter what kind of food they appear in. What these are, generally, is at least in part whole grain, which is one of the several possible kinds of processing, and has nothing to do with natural or unnatural. They are not, as many cereals are, enriched with vitamins and minerals not found in the plain product—that this "natural" lack of enrichment exists is a dubious, certainly an arguable, advantage. But they are, some of them, extremely delicious, being savory combinations of one or more cereal grains with nuts and/or fruit, mixed with brown sugar or molasses or some other sweetening agent. Granola was the first of these to be rediscovered; there are many variations on granola available, as well as many other kinds of "natural" cereals, both ready-to-eat and "hot."

Processing cereals. Since the first Stone-Age cavewife ground a few seeds between two rocks and produced a mishmash that was more palatable than the untreated seeds, processing of cereal has come a long way.

Consult the label to find out what type of treatment the cereal you intend to buy has undergone. Whole-grain cereal is the nutritional standard to which the others are compared.

whole-grain: This cereal retains all the nutrients of the three elements of the grain seed—bran, endosperm, and germ.

enriched: These cereals add vitamins and minerals to bring the food above the level of the whole-grain product. Some breakfast cereals provide the entire adult RDA of these nutrients in the recommended serving.

restored: These cereals have had nutrients removed in the processing, which have been returned to the product to bring the level up to the equivalent of whole-grain cereal.

Breaking the fast at your house. If you never served anything for breakfast other than cereal, you still would not need to repeat yourself often. The variety of breakfast cereals available is staggering—stroll past the supermarket shelves and see for yourself. There are a number of kinds of must-be-cooked products, but it is in the field of ready-to-eat cereals that the manufacturers really outdo themselves. Besides the more pedestrian flaked, puffed, nutlike, and biscuit types, there is an awesome array of shapes, sizes, colors, and flavorings designed to titillate the eye and appetite of the young. These are marketed under a variety of names that, unless you house some of the show-and-tell set, you simply would not believe, in intriguingly decorated boxes, many harboring a cheap toy within or a cutout of some sort on the back. What it comes down to is that there is a cult of cereal eaters with its own involved, inviolable mystique.

buying cereal: Since it is impossible to inspect the contents of the package, buy cereal put out by a manufacturer you know and trust. Choose an amount that will be eaten within a reasonable time. Check to make certain that the package is intact—between box boys' knives and hungry little vandals who have escaped their mothers, cereal packages sometimes get opened long before their day has come.

storing cereal: A cool, dry place in your cupboard is right for unopened cereal packages of all kinds. Opened and tightly reclosed, all types except whole-grain can remain on kitchen shelves. Whole-grain cereals (and jars of wheat germ) should be refrigerated after opening.

Open packages carefully, following label instructions, so that they can be reclosed. Fold and close the inner wrapping as well as the box in which ready-to-eat cereal is sold. Either the to-be-cooked or ready-to-eat kind of cereal will store longer, keep fresher, if you transfer it to a jar or cannister with an airtight closure that helps defeat humidity.

Don't plan to keep opened cereal, uncooked or ready-to-eat, longer than 3 months in the kitchen cupboard. Uncooked whole-grain cereals can be stored in the refrigerator up to 6 months after opening. Cooked cereal, refrigerated and covered, will keep up to 4 days.

nutritive value: It's impossible to give, in limited space, specific nutritive values for each of the enormous number of cereals on the market. As a rule of thumb, whole-grain cereals offer better nutrition, are high in vitamin E. All cereals are low in vitamins A, D, and C, except for yellow corn cereal, which does have some A. Enriched cereals may supply these lacks. Consult the labels of restored and enriched cereals for nutrient values—if a cereal makes any nutritional claims, all nutrients must be listed.

As a rule of thumb, a whole-grain, enriched, or restored cereal, plus milk, provides a suitably nutritious breakfast. If you add fruit to the bowl, you improve the value. A 1-ounce serving of dry cereal will contain somewhere in the neighborhood of 100 to 150 calories, depending on the kind; a serving of cooked cereal, from 40 to 80 calories. Remember that anything you add—milk, sugar, fruit—brings up the calorie count in proportion.

Tips on preparing, serving. Follow label instructions when cooking cereal for the proper proportion of water to cereal for a smooth, palatable product. Have the water boiling briskly; add cereal slowly, stirring constantly to avoid lumps. Continue to stir until the mixture thickens, then reduce heat and cook as the label directs.

To add interest to hot cereal, cook it in milk or part milk—or even, for chocoholics, chocolate milk—instead of water. Or add a little spice, such as nutmeg or mace. Or stir in chopped nuts or whole or cut-up fruit or chocolate bits. In place of the usual milk, top the serving of hot cereal with a pat of butter and sprinkle with cinnamon sugar. Or top cereal with a poached or coddled egg and sprinkle with crumbled bacon or grated cheese.

To add interest to dry cereal, add miniature marshmallows or semisweet chocolate bits or fruit—dried or fresh—of almost any kind. Instead of plain milk, serve with chocolate milk or eggnog. Or omit the milk and mix with small cheese cubes and/or crisp slivers of bacon.

Vary the sweetening for cereal, cooked or dry, with brown sugar, maple-flavored syrup, honey, or preserves.

Although some of us tend to disparage cereals, particularly the ready-to-eat ones, as "empty calories," this need not be true if you buy whole-grain or restored, or—particularly—enriched varieties. Be more influenced by what the label tells you than by what Junior says all the other kids are eating. See also FARINA and OATMEAL.

CERVELAT: see SAUSAGES

CHAMPAGNE: see WINE

CHANTILLY: see page 451

CHAPON: see page 451

CHARD: see UNUSUAL VEGETABLES

CHARLOTTE: see page 451

CHAUD-FROID: see page 451

CHAYOTE: see SQUASH and UNUSUAL VEGETABLES

CHEDDAR: see CHEESE

CHEESE

Long ago, ages before it occurred to man that those who followed after him might like to know about his doings if he would only write an account of them, the happy—probably accidental—discovery of cheese was made. That discovery is lost in the mists of time, but there are legends about it that persist to this day. Two such stories are interesting enough, and credible enough, to bear repeating.

Tribesman's ride, shepherd's lunch. The first legend concerns a long-ago desert tribesman who set out on a journey with a container of milk—probably mares' or camels'—in that day's ordinary milk container, the dried stomach of a sheep. In the broiling desert sun, he mounted his camel and took off on a ride as bumpy and lurchy in those days as a camel ride remains to this day.

When he stopped to refresh himself, he found the milk separated into a thin, watery substance (whey) and a thickened mass (curds)—a result of the warmth of the day and the churning motion of the ride he had taken, helped along by the action of the rennet, an enzyme in the sheep's stomach. He tasted the mass of curds and was delighted—probably could hardly wait to get home to share his discovery with family and friends.

The second story is about a long-ago herdsman who took along a lunch of fresh ewes' or goats' milk cheese and a chunk of bread when he went out to tend his sheep. He laid his lunch aside—perhaps in the shade of a tree, perhaps in a cave to keep the food cool—and went about his business. Something kept him from his lunch that day and for several days thereafter. When he finally did get back to it, he found the cheese in a condition that he doubtless thought of as spoiled. It was veined with blue mold. Gingerly he tasted the cheese and, to his surprise, found that it was delicious.

History takes cheese into account. However cheese came to be discovered, it has been a staple—and nutritious and tasty—food of many peoples for many years. The Sumerians of 4000 B.C. ate cheese, as tablets dating back to that time testify. Archaeologists have established that long-ago Egyptians and Chaldeans knew what a wonderful food could be made from clabbered milk. The ancient Greeks thought it a fit offering to their gods. David, on his way to deliver cheese to Saul's camp, interrupted his journey to fight Goliath.

Among the many things of which Homer sang, cheese was one. The Greeks trained their athletes on cheese and made their wedding cakes of it. The Romans knew a number of kinds of cheese. Returning from his journeys, Marco Polo told of, among other wonders, the many varieties of cheese, and the secrets of making it, that he had encountered.

Armies, so the old saying goes, travel on their stomachs, and the men of many an ancient army, including those of Julius Caesar and Genghis Khan, carried cheese to sustain them. Visitors to ancient Sicily brought home tales of incredibly delicious cheesecakes. Charlemagne, it is said, had a great fondness for roquefort.

Indeed, a history of cheese might be said to be a capsule history of the world.

What's in a name? How did we come by the word "cheese"? The ancient Greeks drained their cheese in wicker baskets called *formos.* The word became *forma* in Latin, and from that root came today's Italian *formaggio* and French *fromage.* The Latin word for cheese was *caseus,* from which sprang the German *käse,* Dutch *kaas,* Gaelic *cáis,* Welsh *caws,* Portuguese *queijo,* and Spanish *queso.* The same root produced the Old English word *cese* and a variation, *cyse,* which evolved into "cheese."

Everywhere, any time. Whatever it is called in whatever country, whatever milk it is made from and however it is made, cheese now exists in a great many varieties—estimates range from 700 to 2,000, depending on who's counting. France alone claims 500 kinds, the United States, 200.

Cheese is a hearty, nourishing fare. Bread and cheese —sometimes with a handful of olives or a fresh fig or two or some apricots from a nearby tree, along with a beaker of the sour local wine—has fed many a peasant in many a land. But cheese has snob appeal, too. Gourmets speak of fine cheeses in hushed tones: Crottin de Chavignol, for example, a small, medium-firm salted goats' milk cheese from the Berry district of France that sells in Paris markets during its short season at the kind of price one ought to pay only for something that would last forever.

Many cheeses are named after the places in which they are made, or were first made. Cheddar is the name of a village near Bristol, England, where its namesake cheese first saw light; today the town is still the center of a thriving cheese industry. Limburger is named after Limburg, Belgium.

Eating your curds and whey. Cheesemaking may have begun as a happy accident, but it has grown into a huge industry based on scientific principles, surrounded by strict regulations. Nevertheless, it all begins now, as then, with the separation of milk into curds and whey.

The kind of milk—sheep, buffalo, reindeer, cow, or goat —begins the determination of the taste and texture of the finished cheese. The differences among the many kinds of cheese are caused by variations in preparation of the curds, by the addition of friendly bacteria and mold, and by the conditions of the curing or ripening.

Reduced to its simplest definition, natural cheese is the solid or casein portion of milk (curds) separated from the whey and coagulated by the action of rennet or lactic acid or both.

preparing the milk: Fresh milk, received at the cheese factory from farms, is scientifically tested and heat treated. Fat content is adjusted; the milk is pumped into vats.

adding coloring, starter, and rennet: Coloring is not used in all cheeses, but for a golden-colored cheese, for example, a vegetable coloring is added to the milk. Then the starter, a pure culture of microorganisms, is added to help firm up the curd particles and develop the individual characteristics of the cheese. Rennet extract, containing the enzyme, coagulates the milk into a custardlike mass called "curd."

cutting and cooking: After the curd reaches custard firmness, it is cut into small cubes; the watery whey begins to separate. Curds and whey are heated to the required cooking temperature for the kind of cheese being made. This firms the curd and hastens the separation of whey from curd.

draining the whey: The whey is removed from the curd by simple drainage or by one of several mechanical methods.

salting: The time that salt is added, and the amount, has a definite effect on the type of cheese produced. Sometimes salt is added now, sometimes after pressing.

pressing and curing: The salted curd is weighed and pressed into forms to produce a solid block of cheese, which is kept in temperature-controlled storage rooms to cure until the desired texture and flavor develop.

Tracing the cheese family tree. Each cured cheese (cured, as opposed to the fresh varieties, such as cottage and cream) has its own range of time and temperature, its own conditions of curing which, taken together, result in the development of that particular cheese, which is different from any other. Sharpness depends on age—some cheeses are aged up to 12 months, some few as long as 24 months.

There are nine basic families—related groups—of cheeses. Most of these originated in various countries of the Old World, but when we buy them today they may have been imported from one of those countries, or they may have been manufactured right here in the United States.

the cheddar cheeses: These are the most popular cheeses in the United States. Like all other varieties of natural cheese, cheddar is made according to the six basic steps. The variation that sets cheddar apart occurs in the whey-draining step. At this point the curd is allowed to knit together and is turned and piled to expel the whey. This procedure— known as cheddaring—develops the characteristic body and texture. The flattened slab is then milled—cut into smaller pieces—and placed in a hoop or mold.

Colby is another member of the cheddar family. In making it, the curd particles are stirred instead of being allowed to knit together, resulting in a more open-textured cheese. The drained curd is washed with cool water, which gives higher moisture content and milder flavor.

Monterey or monterey jack cheese was developed by monks in southern California in the early days of that area's history. This creamy white cheese is similar to colby, although it has a higher moisture content, a softer consistency, and a more open texture.

the dutch cheeses: The most popular varieties of cheese from Holland are edam and gouda. Both are semisoft to hard sweet-curd cheeses made from cows' milk. Both have a characteristic milky, nutlike flavor that varies in intensity with the age of the cheese.

In the United States, edam is the familiar red cannonball-shaped cheese, usually weighing from ¾ pound to 4½ pounds. In Holland, edam is often found in the natural gold color, without the waxy red covering.

Gouda comes in one of two shapes, a flattened sphere or a rectangular loaf. A gouda may weigh from 6 to 50 pounds, but probably the most familiar is the "baby gouda," weighing a pound or less. Gouda, too, may or may not have a red wax coating.

Special metal or hardwood molds lined with cheesecloth are used in the pressing step of the manufacture of edam and gouda. These molds, which give the cheeses their characteristic shape, consist of a round lower section perforated for draining, and a round cover.

Cheeses made by this same method may include mixtures of cumin, caraway, and other spices. Some examples are noekkelost, leyden, and cuminost.

the provolone cheeses: The provolone family is technically known as *pasta filata* (spun) cheese. The curd is placed in either hot water or hot whey, which changes it into a stringy, plasticlike mass that is stretched, much the way taffy candy is, and molded into the desired size and shape. It is salted by being soaked in brine and, following that, may or may not be smoked.

The most commonly used member of this cheese family is provolone, which is slightly cured and usually smoked. It has a very important place in Italian cooking.

Mozzarella, another member of this cheese family, has become very well known in the United States because of the increased popularity of pizza. A fresh cheese, originally made of buffalos' milk, it originated in Italy just south of Rome. Buffalo-milk mozzarella is still sold in that area of Italy, but it is always made from cows' milk in the United States.

Originally, mozzarella was sold and consumed the day of manufacture, but national distribution and commercial sale no longer permit that kind of treatment. However, mozzarella is still a fresh, uncured cheese. It is particularly adaptable to cooking, for it melts into a smooth, stringy mass desirable for such dishes as pizza and lasagna.

Scamorze cheese is a close relative of mozzarella. Both are fresh—uncured—and mild in flavor.

the swiss cheeses: Swiss is the second most popular variety of cheese in the United States. In Switzerland, it is called emmentaler, a name also used to some extent in the United States. The distinguishing feature of swiss cheese is its "eyes"—holes that develop throughout the cheese during ripening. These are the result of propionic acid bacteria that

produce carbon dioxide bubbles throughout the body of the cheese. The size of the holes is controlled to some extent by regulating the temperature and time of ripening. The bacteria also produce the characteristic sweet, nutlike flavor.

Gruyère is related to swiss cheese, although the characteristic eyes are not as fully developed. A certain amount of surface growth is allowed to take place, resulting in a somewhat sharper flavor.

To avoid confusion, cheese buyers should understand that much of the gruyère sold in the United States is a pasteurized process cheese containing emmentaler and gruyère. This is usually sold in small individually wrapped wedges, in round or half-round packages. It is not the same as the gruyère found in Europe.

the blue-veined cheeses: These are characterized by the distribution of blue-green mold throughout the cheese, which results in a characteristic flavor. This is the result of inoculation with a strain of penicillium mold that grows throughout the body of the cheese.

Almost every cheese-consuming country of the world has developed a blue-veined cheese very similar to the bleu cheese produced in the United States. The best known are Italy's gorgonzola, England's stilton, France's roquefort, and Denmark's danablu. All these bleu cheeses with the exception of roquefort are made of cows' milk. Roquefort is produced from sheeps' milk in a region of southeastern France, and is cured in caves in the same area.

During the manufacture of bleu cheeses, the penicillium mold is mixed with the curd either while it is in the vat or while it is being placed in molds or hoops, where it is held for twenty-four hours. After removal from the hoops, the cheese is salted over a period of approximately one week under conditions that simulate the temperature and humidity of the Roquefort caves. Approximately one week after salting, the cheese is pierced to produce holes that allow the air penetration that is essential for mold growth. The cheese then cures for a period of about five months.

the parmesan cheeses: Members of this "hard-grating" cheese family, primarily associated with Italian cooking, were originally developed in Italy in the vicinity of Parma. They are grated and sprinkled on spaghetti, pizza, minestrone, and tossed salads, and are used in baked dishes, such as veal parmigiana and lasagna.

These cheeses are characterized by the hard granular texture that makes them ideal for grating. In fact, much of the parmesan and romano cheese produced in the United States is sold grated or shredded, in jars or cardboard containers.

Parmesan is the most familiar cheese in this group and one of the best-known Italian cheeses in the United States. Made from a mixture of whole and skim milk, it is usually cured from fourteen to twenty-four months to develop the characteristic texture and flavor. Romano, the other member of the family well known in the United States, originated near

Rome. Very similar to parmesan, it is used in the same manner, but it has a sharper, more piquant flavor. Both parmesan and romano are excellent seasoning cheeses.

the fresh, uncured cheeses: The fresh cheeses do not follow exactly the six major steps of cheese manufacture. Coagulation of the curd is started by the addition of lactic acid, with or without a small amount of rennet. Also, as their name implies, these cheeses are not cured, but are sold fresh. They have a mild flavor.

Cream cheese is an American original. It starts as a mixture of milk and cream, which is pasteurized and coagulated by a starter. Originally the curd was poured into cloth bags and pressed to expel the whey, but in 1945 a method of removing the curd by centrifugal force was perfected. It produces a fine, smooth-bodied cheese that has greater keeping qualities than cheese produced by the bag method.

Neufchâtel (spelled without the *f* when the product is made in Switzerland) is a lower-fat product similar to cream cheese. Because of their mild flavor and smooth, creamy texture, both cream cheese and neufchâtel blend readily with other ingredients and are called for in a wide variety of recipes.

Cottage cheese is a third member of the family of fresh, uncured cheeses. In making cottage cheese, skim milk is coagulated by adding lactic acid starter and sometimes a small amount of rennet. When the curd is sufficiently firm, it is cut into cubes and heated in the whey. After the whey has been removed, the curd is washed and salted. The cheese is usually improved in flavor and texture by adding a mixture of cream and milk. Cottage cheese can be purchased in small or large-curd form.

the surface-ripened cheeses: Members of this family include camembert, brie, brick, muenster, bel paese, port du salut, and limburger. In all surface-ripened cheeses, a bacterial or mold culture is grown on the surface of the cheese. The enzymes produced by the growth of these organisms penetrate the cheese and bring about the development of the characteristic flavor and texture of each variety.

Two basic subfamilies within this large group of cheeses are differentiated by the type of organism used for ripening—mold or bacteria. Characteristic of the mold-ripened varieties are camembert and brie, both of which originated in France. The best-known variety of bacterial-ripened cheese is limburger, which originated in Belgium. Other popular cheeses of this type are bel paese of Italy and port du salut of France.

Brick and muenster, which were originally included in this family of cheeses, can no longer be considered true members, for today they have little or no surface ripening. This is because of changes in consumer preferences for milder and milder versions of these cheeses.

the whey cheeses: These are produced from whey rather than curd, and so are not true cheeses, as whey is a by-product of cheese manufacture. Perhaps the best-known whey cheese is ricotta, used frequently in Italian cooking. Ricotta was originally produced by the coagulation of the albumen portion of the whey, which resulted in a soft, fresh cheese similar to cottage cheese. Today ricotta is made by the coagulation of a mixture of whey and whole or skim milk. It is a soft, grainy cheese, and can be purchased either dry or moist.

Two other cheeses of this family, gjetost and primost, are Scandinavian. They are prepared by condensing whey and adding small amounts of fat. Gjetost is rather hard; primost is a semisoft product. Another member of the family is sapsago, a Swiss type of whey cheese. It is the result of the acid coagulation of the protein in a mixture of skim milk, buttermilk, and whey. The addition of the leaves of a clover-like plant leads to the characteristic flavor and light green color. A hard cheese, it is primarily used grated.

"The wife takes the cheese." To a very large segment of the population, there is only one kind of cheese, which is in reality several varieties. The consumers of this cheese call it loosely, "American," but its straight name is pasteurized process cheese.

To cheese snobs, this mild-flavored, somewhat waxy-textured substance doesn't deserve to be called cheese at all. But how can you knock a food that millions of women buy and use each week, millions of husbands and kids take to work or school every day between two slices of bread? A food that, literally, has had a major influence on the eating habits of the nation? So, if you're a head-held-high connoisseur of fine cheeses, skip the next few paragraphs.

The whole pasteurized process cheese business started with a young man named Kraft, a cheese door-to-door merchant who, back in the early 1900s, began to toy with the idea of somehow treating cheese so that it would keep longer. His many experiments eventuated in a product that, when it went on the market in 1920 as a 5-pound loaf in a little wooden crate, was an instant, spectacular success.

process cheese products: Process cheese starts with natural cheeses—several kinds, in a blend—that are heated with an emulsifier. Pasteurization halts the aging of the natural cheese that is used. The result is a homogenous product that is consistent in flavor, body, and texture, and has excellent keeping qualities. It melts smoothly, so it is often used in cooking.

Pasteurized process American cheese is further treated—with the addition of milk or whey solids—to form pasteurized process cheese *food,* and—with the addition of moisture—to form pasteurized process cheese *spread.* To both of these variations, ingredients other than cheese (meats, vegetables, fruits, such flavorings as pimiento, chopped olives or pickles, spices) may be added.

CHEESE IN YOUR KITCHEN

In 1624, only four years after they had landed at Plymouth Rock, the Pilgrims welcomed their first cows to the new land, and promptly set about making cheese, an item of diet they had sorely missed since the Dutch cheeses they had brought with them had been used up. We've been making cheese here ever since.

Admirers presented Thomas Jefferson, when he was the nation's third president, with a whopping 1,235-pound cheese. From that unusual gift the catch-phrase "big cheese" came into our language.

Cheesemaking was a cottage industry—most families made their own cheese at home—until the mid-1800s, when it became a business enterprise, manufacturers sending their cheeses to the large indoor or outdoor markets that every city of any size boasted in those days, or delivering the product to customers' doors. One of the country's first cheese manufacturers was Jesse Williams, who opened a cheddar factory at Oneida, New York, in 1851.

A practically perfect food. One of the most nutritious and palatable of foods, delicious to eat and readily digestible, cheese provides a great many of the elements our bodies need to keep us in working trim. Milk, from which cheese is made, is considered by nutritionists to be a nearly perfect food, containing proteins, minerals, vitamins, and fat. Casein, the protein found only in milk, is a complete protein, for it contains all the amino acids—the building blocks—that the body requires to maintain life and support growth and tissue repair.

Cheese is made in virtually every state of the union, with Wisconsin leading the way. There is also a practically unlimited supply of imported cheese of countless varieties. Sold in many outlets, from small grocery stores through delicatessens and supermarkets to specialty cheese-only shops in many cities, cheese is available whenever and wherever you want it.

how to buy: Soft and fresh cheeses are very perishable. Buy only as much as you'll use within a few days. On the other hand, hard cheeses keep well. It may be more economical to buy a large cut of hard or very hard cheese of which your family is fond; you can count on its storing well until used up, if you take good care of it. Process cheese and cheese spreads also have excellent keeping qualities.

You'll find natural cheeses in the dairy case at your market in wheels, wedges, balls, loaves, sticks, and packages of slices. Processed cheese comes in loaves, slices, "links" (like sausage links), and in variously flavored dips and spreads.

how to store: Soft and fresh cheeses should be kept closely covered, in their original container if it can be reclosed or transferred to another container that has an airtight cover.

Store in the coldest part of the refrigerator. Molding and drying out are the two unfortunate conditions cheese is heir to. Tightly wrap hard cheeses in foil or plastic wrap and refrigerate; if you plan to store hard cheeses for more than a few days after cutting, butter the cut edge or seal it with melted paraffin. If the cheese seems to be getting dry, wrap it in a clean cloth wrung out in vinegar; keep the cloth damp. Mold that may develop on hard cheese will do no harm—scrape or cut it off. Storing basics: keep moisture in, air out.

Strong cheese offers another problem—its smell, which will transfer itself (if you're not careful) to other refrigerated items with more delicate flavor, such as butter. Wrap the cheese well, as suggested above, and then put the whole package in a container with a tight cover.

Process cheeses and spreads can be kept on a cupboard shelf at room temperature before they are opened; after opening, store in the refrigerator in their original container or wrapping, or enclose tightly in foil or plastic.

Plan on storing soft and fresh cheeses in the refrigerator for no more than 2 weeks (although you may find some cream cheese especially processed so that it will keep well, as long as it is unopened, for considerably longer). Hard cheeses can be refrigerated, properly cared for, up to 9 months. Spreads and cheese in jars can be shelved unopened at room temperature up to 1 year; opened, covered and refrigerated, they may be kept up to 3 weeks.

nutritive value: Cheeses vary in nutritive value from kind to kind, although you can be safe in assuming that the cheese you like, of whatever sort, will have appreciable amounts of protein, calcium, and riboflavin. Most natural cheeses average between 300 and 400 calories for 3½ ounces; the exception is cottage cheese, which has about 85 calories for the uncreamed variety and 105 for the creamed for a 3½-ounce portion.

To give you an idea of nutritive value, here are listings for 1 cubic inch of three favorite natural cheeses:

	camembert	cheddar	swiss	
calories	51	68	39	
protein	3	4.3	4.1	grams
fat	4.2	5.5	4.2	grams
carbohydrate	.3	.4	.3	gram
calcium	18	129	139	milligrams
phosphorus	31	82	84	milligrams
iron	.1	.2	.1	milligram
sodium	115	120	107	milligrams
potassium	19	14	16	milligrams
thiamin	1	1	trace	milligram
riboflavin	.13	.08	.06	milligram
niacin	.1	trace	trace	milligram
ascorbic acid	0	0	0	
vitamin A	170	230	170	international units

You might also like to compare the nutritive values of two of the fresh cheeses:

	creamed cottage cheese (1 ounce)	regular cream cheese (1 cubic inch)	
calories	30	60	
protein	3.9	1.3	grams
fat	1.2	6.1	grams
carbohydrate	.8	.3	gram
calcium	27	10	milligrams
phosphorus	43	15	milligrams
iron	.1	trace	milligram
sodium	65	40	milligrams
potassium	24	12	milligrams
thiamin	.01	trace	milligram
riboflavin	.07	.04	milligram
niacin	trace	trace	milligram
ascorbic acid	0	0	
vitamin A	50	250	international units

Tips on serving cheese. Most cheeses, other than the fresh ones, offer their optimum character and flavor when served at room temperature. To enjoy them at their best, remove them from the refrigerator 30 minutes to an hour before serving. Camembert is most appreciated by those who love the cheese when it is so soft it is almost runny, so take it from the refrigerator at least 2 hours in advance of serving. But bring cottage, neufchâtel, and cream cheese to the table straight from the refrigerator. They are at their best chilled.

Freezing cheese. Freezing extends the (already quite long) storage life of cheese, but often adversely affects body and texture. Frozen cheese may be crumbly or mealy after it is thawed. The flavor remains, but the cheese is best suited for cooking.

Cheese for freezing must be tightly sealed in moisture- and vaporproof material. Such cheeses as cheddar, swiss, edam, or gouda can be successfully frozen, if the freezing process is completed rapidly, in small packages of about a half pound each. If the cheese is cubed, plan on storing in the freezer no more than 3 weeks; slices and loaves of natural cheese and pasteurized process cheese may be kept frozen up to 3 months. Always thaw cheese slowly, still wrapped, in the refrigerator.

Some perfect partners. Cheese and crackers are as much a taken-for-granted pair as ham and eggs. Preferably, choose plain crackers whose neutral taste won't interfere with enjoyment of the cheese. If you want to serve flavored crackers, choose a flavor, such as bacon, that complements the taste of the cheese. Serve crackers and cheese as an appetizer, with drinks before the meal, after the meal in place of dessert, or almost any time as a very good snack.

Fruit and cheese are good friends, too; served together —with or without plain crackers—they make a perfect dessert. Add a few (unsalted) nuts, and your cup runneth over. Cheese pairs beautifully with fresh, crisp apples or winter pears, equally well with the softer summer fruits, such as peaches, apricots, and nectarines. Bleu cheese and big, fresh bing or other dark-fleshed cherries have a particular affinity for one another. Fresh figs with brie make a spectacular treat. Top a block of cream cheese with fresh strawberries or raspberries. In winter, when choice of fruit is not wide, try oranges or grapefruit with sharp cheddar. Or serve almost any cheese with dried figs, apricots, or raisins—nuts are virtually a must with this combination.

As for wine and cheese, those two are not only delicious together, they add up to an occasion. Wine-and-cheese parties are a great informal way to entertain, easy on the hostess and not too budget-bending. See WINE.

Cooking with cheese. Cheese is best cooked briefly, at a low to medium temperature—high heat and prolonged cooking make the food tough and stringy. Here are some good-to-know ideas about cheese cookery.

adding to hot foods: Add only shredded natural cheese or cubed process cheese; larger pieces will not melt properly.

making sauces: Add cheese at the end of the cooking period; heat the sauce just until cheese is melted.

broiling: Place the pan so that the cheese is several inches below the heat source; broil just until cheese melts.

in baked dishes: Bake at a temperature range between 325 and 375°F.—in other words, at a moderate temperature.

topping casseroles: Place cheese on top of casserole just before the end of the baking period; continue to cook only until melted.

Recipes often call for cubed, shredded, or grated cheese. *Cubed* is easy—cut the cheese into blocks; about half an inch all around is a convenient measurement. *Shredded* means cheese that has been prepared on the coarse openings of a grater, so that it comes out in long, thin strips. *Grated* means cheese that has been prepared on the fine openings of a grater. To put it another way, shredded is softer and larger than grated—indeed, generally only very hard cheeses, such as parmesan or romano, are grated. If you want to skip the trouble, buy ready-shredded or -grated cheese in jars or plastic bags. However, freshly shredded or grated cheese has better flavor and texture than the pre-prepared kind.

Measuring cheese. How much cheese do you need to produce the measurement that the recipe calls for? Easy. Four ounces—¼ pound, that is—of cheese will yield a full cup of shredded cheese. This rule works whether you are applying it to any of the natural cheeses or to any of the forms of pasteurized process cheese.

When using cream cheese in any of the many excellent recipes that call for it (ever made cream cheese pastry?), let the cheese come to room temperature before using it. In that softened state it will blend readily and easily with other ingredients. The same rule applies to neufchâtel.

The imaginative cook. Cheese can be used in dozens of inventive ways. Crumble any of the bleu family of cheeses into almost any favorite salad dressing. Stir small cubes of cheese or shredded cheese into scrambled eggs. Add julienne strips of cheese to salads—mixed greens, fruit salads, or let cheese add authority (and protein) to hearty macaroni salads. Vary the cheese in a cheeseburger—bleu is great, so is swiss, so is a heavy sprinkling of grated romano. Don't reserve parmesan only for pasta—stir it into soups and sauces, sprinkle it on cooked vegetables. Top desserts— especially hot ones—such as fruit cobblers, deep-dish pies, gingerbread, with whipped cream cheese. And never forget that what grandpa maintained is true: pie without cheese is like a kiss without a squeeze. Well, true at the very least of apple pie—there ought to be a law against serving apple pie without a wedge of cheddar or colby or, for sturdier souls, stilton.

CHEESE FROM A TO Z

Here are some of the better-known (and greatly enjoyed) cheeses from all over the world. You should be able to find them all in a well-stocked cheese store, many of them in a large supermarket cheese department. Browse here for varieties with which you are not familiar, then buy some of kinds that sound good to you and broaden your cheese horizons.

asiago: Made from whole or part-skim milk; dark surface, cream inside; texture hard, granular; piquant flavor; use for eating (fresh type) or cooking (aged type).

baker's cheese: Made from skim milk; white, resembles cottage cheese, but is softer, fine grained; slightly sour flavor; use for eating, cooking.

bel paese: Made from whole milk; gray-brown surface, light yellow inside; soft texture; delicate flavor; use for eating.

blue or bleu: Made from whole milk; white interior with blue veins; semisoft, crumbly; piquant flavor that gets stronger with age; use for eating, cooking.

brick: Made from whole milk; yellow-brown surface, creamy yellow inside; semisoft; mild but pungent flavor; use primarily for eating.

brie: Made from whole milk; brown, edible crust; creamy yellow inside; soft; mild to pungent flavor; use for eating.

caciocavallo: Made from whole milk; light-brown, glossy surface, yellowish-white color; smooth, firm body; slightly salty, smoky flavor; spindle-shape, cord bound; use for eating, grating when dry.

camembert: Made from whole milk; gray-white, edible crust; soft, creamy interior; full flavor; use for eating.

cheddar: Made from whole milk; yellow-brown surface, cream to deep-orange color; firm texture; mild flavor when fresh; sharper the more aged; use for eating, cooking.

cheshire: Made from whole milk; yellow surface, cream to deep-yellow color; firm, more crumbly than cheddar; sharp flavor the more aged; use for eating, cooking.

colby: Made from whole milk; deep yellow; softer body and more open texture than cheddar; use for eating, cooking.

coon: Made from whole milk; cheddar-type cheese with dark surface; crumbly texture; sharp tangy flavor; use for eating, cooking.

cottage cheese: Made from skim milk with cream and salt added; white; soft; pleasant mildly sour taste; use for eating, cooking. *Skim milk cottage cheese:* a form with no cream added. *Pot cheese:* skim milk cottage cheese with a larger, dry curd; neither cream nor salt added.

cream cheese: Made from cream and milk; white; smooth, soft texture; delicate, very slight acid taste; use for eating, cooking.

edam: Originally made of whole milk, now fat content is reduced; red waxed surface, yellowish inside; semisoft to hard; mild flavor; use for eating, cooking.

farmer (or pressed): Made from whole or partly skimmed milk; white, dry form of cottage cheese; pressed into parchment paper packages; use for eating, cooking.

feta: Made from ewes' milk, sometimes goats' milk; white, soft; salty; use for eating, cooking.

fontina: Made from whole milk, sometimes from ewes' milk; slightly yellow with oiled surface; semisoft to hard; delicate, nutty flavor; use for eating, cooking.

gjetost: Made from cows' and/or goats' milk whey; golden brown; hard, buttery; rather sweet caramel flavor; use for eating.

gorgonzola: Made from whole milk; clay-colored exterior, white with blue veins inside; semisoft, crumbly texture; piquant flavor; use for eating.

gouda: Made from whole or partly skimmed milk; usually red surface, yellow interior; semisoft to hard; mellow flavor; use for eating.

gruyère: Made from whole milk; light yellow, firm with small holes; flavor like swiss but somewhat sharper; use for eating, cooking.

liederkranz: Made from whole milk; russet surface, creamy inside; soft; robust taste and aroma; use for eating.

limburger: Made from whole milk; grayish-brown surface,

creamy white inside; semisoft; full, aromatic taste; use for eating.

monterey jack: Made from whole, partly skimmed, or skim milk; mild, cheddar-type cheese; whole-milk jack is semisoft, jack made from partly skimmed or skim milk is grating type; use for eating, cooking, grating.

mozzarella: Made from whole or partly skimmed milk; white; semisoft; mild flavor; use for eating, cooking.

muenster: Made from whole milk; yellow-tan surface, white to light yellow interior; semisoft; tastes like milder brick; use for eating, cooking.

mysost: Made from cows' milk whey; light brown; sweetish taste; use for eating.

neufchâtel: Made from whole or skim milk, or mixture of milk and cream; white; soft; mild flavor; use for eating.

parmesan: Made from partly skimmed milk; dark-green or black surface, whitish inside; hard, granular texture; flavor gets stronger with age; use for eating (fresh), grating (aged).

petit suisse: Made from fresh, whole milk with added cream; soft, rich, unripened; use for eating.

pineapple: Made from whole milk; cheddar type, shaped like a pineapple; usually hard; use for eating, cooking.

pont l'évêque: Made from whole or partly skimmed milk; yellow; soft; sharp flavored; use for eating.

poona: Made from whole milk; pale; soft; aroma like mild limburger; use for eating.

port du salut: Made from whole or partly skimmed milk; russet surface, creamy inside; elastic curd, semisoft; mild flavor like gouda; strong aroma; use for eating.

primost: Made from whey; light brown; soft; mild sweetish flavor; use for eating.

provolone: Made from whole milk; yellowish; hard; smoky flavor; link-shape or round; use for eating, cooking.

ricotta: Made from whey; white; soft, granular; use for eating, cooking.

romadur: Made from whole or partly skimmed milk; soft; similar to liederkranz; aroma like limburger but milder; use for eating.

romano: Made from partly skimmed cows', goats', or ewes' milk; greenish-black surface, creamy white inside; granular, hard texture; sharp flavor; use for grating.

roquefort: Made from ewes' milk; white, blue-green veins; crumbly, semisoft to hard; strong, sharp flavor; use for eating, cooking.

sage: Made from whole or partly skimmed milk; green, mottled appearance throughout; sage flavor; use for cooking, grating.

samsoe: Made from whole milk; semihard; mild, sweet, nutty flavor; use for eating, cooking.

sapsago: Made from slightly sour skim milk; light green color; very hard; pungent, flavored with powdered clover leaves; use for eating, grating.

sardo: Made from whole milk; cream to grayish color; firm and smooth; use for eating, cooking.

sbrinz: Made from whole or partly skimmed milk; gray-green surface, white inside; hard, granular texture; medium-sharp flavor; use for grating.

stilton: Made from whole milk; cream-colored with blue-green veins; wrinkled surface; crumbly; sharp flavor; use for eating.

swiss: Made from whole milk; deep cream-colored interior with holes that develop as the cheese ripens; springy texture; mild, nutlike flavor; use for eating, cooking.

tilsit: Made from whole or skim milk; light yellow; medium firm; moderately sharp flavor; use for eating, cooking.

trappist: Made from whole cows' milk, sometimes with ewes' or goats' milk added; pale yellow; semisoft; mild flavor; use for eating.

vacherin: Made from whole milk; firm, hard rind, very soft interior; aromatic; use for eating.

wensleydale: Made from whole milk; white; soft; delicately flavored; when aged, a medium-hard, blue-veined cheese with a strong flavor; use for eating, cooking.

ziegel: Made from whole milk, sometimes with added cream; creamy white; medium-soft texture; mild, somewhat salty flavor; use for eating.

A whole wide world of cheese. The cheeses listed above are only a sampling of the many kinds available. In fact, the USDA listing of cheese varieties fills a 150-page book printed in small type! It includes such exotica as glumse, the cottage cheese of western Prussia; dotter, a German egg-and-skim-milk variety; commission, an 8-pound Dutch cheese rather like edam; cornhusker, "invented" by an agricultural experiment station in Nebraska nearly 80 years ago; hopfen, cured between layers of hops, which lend it flavor; isigny, originated in America but named for a French town, with a very assertive flavor and aroma; majocchino, made of ewes' milk and olive oil. And there are literally dozens upon dozens more. Whatever your taste, from very pedestrian to highly esoteric, there is a cheese—or two or three, or many —to fill your needs and keep you cheese-happy. See also CHEESECAKES, CLUB CHEESE, FETA, FONDUE, GOUDA, GRUYERE, JACK CHEESE, MOZZARELLA, RACLETTE, and RAREBIT.

CHEESECAKES

These are desserts whose chief ingredient is a mild cheese —most often cream cheese, but sometimes cottage or farmer or ricotta. Eggs give the sweet a custardy texture. Cheesecakes are usually baked in a springform pan that has been lined with a cookie- or cracker-crumb crust; some of the crumbs are reserved to sprinkle over the top of the cake. The dessert may be simply flavored with lemon or vanilla or may be topped with fruit in a glaze—cherry, pineapple, and strawberry are favorites. There are caramel and chocolate cheesecakes as well. Because the dessert is dense and rich, it should be offered in small servings.

CHEF'S SALAD: see SALADS

CHERIMOYAS: see EXOTIC FRUIT

CHERRIES

The Cree Indian word for fat is *pemmican*. The term was extended by white men to mean the food, made in the Cree manner, that sustained explorers and fur traders who opened up the American West. Pemmican was made by drying thinly sliced lean elk, deer, or buffalo meat over a slow fire; the dried meat was shredded, mixed with melted fat, bone marrow, and wild cherries, and packed in rawhide sacks that were sealed with tallow. Properly prepared, its keeping qualities were great, its nutritive values high, and its flavor very acceptable (particularly, one supposes, when the food comprised the entire menu, so that the Hobson's choice was between pemmican and starvation).

North America was not the only place where cherries grew wild, providing a delicious food for whoever would go to the trouble of picking them. The fruit has been known since biblical times, and began to be cultivated at least as early as 300 B.C. Cherries have been a favorite fruit in Europe for many hundreds of years; the seeds were brought there from their Asian origins, many authorities believe, by homing birds who had wintered near the Caspian Sea. In this country, cherries grew wild before the first settlers arrived, bringing with them cultivated varieties.

Thanks to Parson Weems's *Life of George Washington,* we know that the father of our country confessed to having cut down the family cherry tree: "I did it with my little hatchet." (The parson may, however, have made the story up out of whole cloth, as a handy illustration of Washington's honesty. The book is loaded with other dubious "facts.")

Cherries ripe, cherries red. There are two major kinds of cherries: sweet—usually eaten raw, out of hand, or in salads or fresh-fruit desserts—and sour—used in cooked foods, such as cherry pies and cobblers. Each of these two divisions is broken down into several varieties.

sweet cherries: These are red, ranging from a light shade to a deep almost-black purple, and white, ranging from palest yellow to golden. The best-known kinds are:

bing—very large, shaped like a heart; thin, smooth, glossy skin; flesh that ranges from deep blood-red to virtually black; firm, meaty but juicy; rich, full flavor.

chapman—very large, early-maturing variety; ball-shaped, with tender skin and purple-black flesh; sweet, full-bodied flavor.

lambert—extra large, round; firm, meaty flesh; deep, dark red; good flavor, but not very juicy.

republican—small to medium in size, heart-shaped; flesh and juice are purple-black; very mild but sweet flavor (also called lewelling).

royal ann—both skin and flesh pale golden in color, usually with a light red blush on one or both sides; firm, meaty but juicy, with excellent flavor; thin-skinned and easily bruised; most often used for canning, but delicious eaten out of hand when available (also called napoleon).

black tartarian—mid-season variety; large, heart-shaped; flesh deep purple, almost black; thin-skinned; tender, sweet, fine distinctive flavor.

sour cherries: These occur in colors that range from red to almost black, are usually smaller and less firm than the sweet varieties. Most sour cherries are cooked in various ways, seldom eaten raw—except by the birds, as you know if you have a cherry tree. Kinds are:

early richmond—round and full; medium red; flesh tender and juicy, but skin inclined to be tough; first sour cherry to appear on the market each spring.

english morello—smallish, round; deep red to almost black; tender, tart, juicy.

montmorency—most popular sour cherry; round; medium red; the fruit that turns up most often in cherry pies—also makes fine jelly.

maraschino cherries: These are not a variety—although they are most often made from royal anns—but a process. To make them, the cherries are bleached (sometimes stemmed, sometimes not), pitted, steeped in a syrup made of sugar, water, oil of bitter almond, and red food coloring. The name comes from the Italian liqueur, maraschino, which is made of a cherry variety called mascara. Originally, maraschino cherries were soaked in the liqueur; it was the French who worked out the sugar-syrup method, retaining the name. They are sold only in jars or cans, in their syrup, and are used in cookies, cakes, and candies, as well as for garnishing drinks, salads, and desserts. A soda fountain sundae looks undressed without a fluff of whipped cream topped by a shiny red maraschino cherry. There are also green, mint-flavored maraschino cherries available.

CHERRIES IN YOUR KITCHEN

Most of our sweet cherry crop is now grown west of the Rockies, although there is some cultivation in New York state and in the area around the Great Lakes. You will find sweet cherries in the market from May through August. Sour cherries have a shorter season, beginning sometime in June, ending near the middle of August. Seasons for both kinds may vary a bit, depending on where you live. The major sour-cherry crop is grown east of the Mississippi, with New York, Michigan, and Wisconsin the biggest producers.

Two pounds of stemmed and pitted cherries will measure about 4 cups and will yield about 2 cups of juice.

how to buy: Look for fresh appearance, plump fruit without blemishes or soft spots; sweet cherries, when ripe, are firmer than sour cherries, but neither kind should be soft. If the skin has a dull look and/or the cherries are leaking juice, they are too old to be a good buy. Cherries with their stems still in place will keep longer, but if you're buying by the pound you'll be paying for the weight of the inedible stems.

Cherries are sold loose, by the pound—in which case you can take time to choose the best from the batch available —or in ventilated plastic bags—in which case you should inspect carefully for leakage, and smell the bag to make sure there's no odor of rotting fruit.

how to store: Look through the batch to make certain you haven't come home with any decaying fruit—one bad cherry, like one bad apple, can quickly contaminate its neighbors. Don't wash the cherries until you are ready to use them— water also encourages decay. Refrigerate them in a plastic bag. Plan on keeping fresh cherries no more than 3 to 5 days, although they may last—if you have a very restrained, disciplined family—as long as 2 weeks. Cooked cherries, closely covered, will keep up to 5 days in the refrigerator.

nutritive value: There are about 90 calories in 1 cup of stemmed and pitted sour cherries, slightly over 100 calories in the same measure of sweet cherries prepared in the same manner. Other values, for 1 cup stemmed and pitted, are:

	sour	sweet	
protein	1.9	1.9	grams
fat	.5	.4	gram
carbohydrate	22.2	25.2	grams
calcium	34	32	milligrams
phosphorus	29	28	milligrams
iron	.6	.6	milligram
sodium	3	3	milligrams
potassium	296	277	milligrams
thiamin	.08	.07	milligram
riboflavin	.09	.09	milligram
niacin	.6	.6	milligram
ascorbic acid	16	15	milligrams
vitamin A	1,550	160	international units

Tips on preparing, cooking. Before eating them raw or using them in a cooked dish, sort over cherries once again, and wash them. Recipes often direct, in a cavalier manner, "wash and pit cherries." Washing is no problem, but pitting isn't all that offhand a job. For the effete, there are cherry-pitters available—metal gadgets, looking rather like a reverse hypodermic with a pair of grabby little tongs on the business end. Or use a thin, pointed knife or the tip of a swivel vegetable peeler. Or press a paper clip into service to hook the stone and pry it out. In any case, don't squeeze—you'll lose juice, flavor, and nutrients. And bear in mind that cherry juice, especially that of dark, sweet cherries, stains everything it touches, including clothes, fingers (particularly under fingernails), counters, and utensils. Wash up right away.

Freezing cherries. Properly prepared (see special feature: PUTTING FOOD BY), both sweet and sour cherries may be frozen; they can be stored at 0°F. or below up to 1 year.

Other ways, other forms. When fresh cherries aren't in season, or you don't want to bother preparing them, have recourse to the many kinds of processed cherries you'll find at your market.

on grocery shelves, in cans, jars, or bottles: Canned sweet cherries, both dark and light varieties, in light, heavy, or extra-heavy syrup, or diet-packed in water, pitted or not; canned sour cherries, always pitted; cherry sauce; cherry juice; cherry syrup; cherry jelly and preserves; maraschino cherries, red or green, with stems or stemless.

on grocery shelves, in packages: Candied and glacéed cherries, red and green; dried cherries (not widely available).

in grocery frozen-food section: Frozen whole cherries, both sweet and sour; cherry pies, ready to bake.

Some perfect partners. Cherries make delicious desserts in great variety. But don't neglect cherries in main dishes. Pork with a sweet/sour cherry sauce is wonderful. Duck Montmorency, the rich meat bathed in a wine-based cherry sauce, is a glorious experience. Ham with a cherry glaze is almost—but not quite—too pretty to eat. Try ringing a change on Sole Veronique by using cherries instead of green grapes. A busty capon reaches new heights when its stuffing is thick with chopped cherries. Cherries and slivered orange peel turn pedestrian shoulder lamb chops into poems.

Back in the Victorian era, young ladies of the upper classes were sent to finishing school where they learned to speak (a little) French, play (a little) piano, embroider passably, flirt in a genteel manner, and make Cherries Jubilee at the table in a chafing dish, amid oohs and aahs from the assembled guests of both genders. If they could do it, so can you—and a chafing dish of cherries in sauce, set aflame before being ladled slowly and lovingly over vanilla ice cream, is still an easy but big-production dessert today.

Don't stop there. Make puddings, pies, tarts, cakes, sweet breads, dumplings, roly-polys, preserves—a whole repertoire of cherry sweets. To say nothing of a gorgeous mishmash known as Cherry Bounce, which is absolutely delicious, wildly intoxicating, and guaranteed to turn the dullest party into an occasion long remembered.

Americans consume about 150,000 tons of cherries, fresh and processed, a year. Are you taking care of your quota?

CHERRY TOMATOES: see TOMATOES

CHERVIL: see HERBS AND SAVORY
  SEASONINGS

CHESHIRE: see CHEESE

CHESTNUTS

According to John Evelyn—diarist and government official who lived for eighty-six years in the seventeenth and eighteenth centuries, and spent many of those years writing about a mixed bag of topics—chestnuts provide "delicacies for princes and a lusty and masculine food for rustics." Until the present era of general plenty supported by rapid, refrigerated transportation that moves edibles quickly and safely from their place of origination to the world at large, there was usually a class of food for the poor, and another —almost totally different—for the rich and high-born. But chestnuts, as few other foods did, bridged the wide gaps of cost and quality between the two.

The edible chestnut (there is also its relative, the horse chestnut, which cannot be eaten) grows on a large and handsome tree with big, shiny deep green leaves, producing clusters of creamy flowers that turn into rough burrs, each of which encloses two or three of the hard-shelled, dark brown nuts. (The exception is the queen of chestnuts, the French marron, whose burrs hold only one nut each. See MARRONS.) The tree was so much admired that the early Greeks envisioned Mount Olympus, where their gods lived, as planted with groves of beautiful chestnut trees.

The everywhere, all-purpose nut. Chestnuts grow all over the world. They were being enjoyed by native Americans at the time Columbus came, probably had been long before that, and continued to be grown and used extensively in this country until 1904, when a blight destroyed all edible chestnuts in America. Chestnuts of Chinese stock (although the destructive blight originated in Asia) have since been planted in this country with moderate success in an effort to produce a homegrown crop for us. But nowadays most of the chestnuts we eat are imported from Italy, from Sicily in particular.

The smell of hot roasted chestnuts is familiar and welcome in many of the world's great cities, New York among them, a concomitant of autumn along with football fever, threatening skies, underfoot slush, and pre-holiday sales.

Fresh-roasted chestnuts are a treat, but that is only one of myriad uses to be made of the versatile nuts, which can serve as a vegetable, the basis for delicious soups, a chief ingredient in savory stuffings for poultry, duck, and goose, as well as chicken and turkey, and the heart of some very elegant desserts, as well as a wonderfully edible garnish for many kinds of dishes.

The considerable differences. Unlike other nuts, chestnuts are never served without being cooked: roasted, as many nuts are, or boiled, as most are not. Getting them shelled and skinned is something of an effort—they don't give up without a struggle—but if you go about it properly it's not too bad a job. Or you can bypass that task by buying dried chestnuts or several kinds of canned ones, all of them ready to use however you wish.

Chestnuts differ from other nuts in a second way: they are considerably lower in both fat and carbohydrate, and so are lower in calories, than most nuts—which are, admittedly, as calorie-high as they are delicious. To understand, compare these examples:

nut	amount	calories
almond	1 pound	2,896
brazil	1 pound	3,120
chestnut	1 pound	1,140
macadamia	1 pound	3,400
peanut	1 pound	2,610
pecan	1 pound	3,300
walnut	1 pound	3,075

The counts above are for the edible portion of the nuts, so don't be too frightened. Shelled nuts are light, so a pound is made up of a large number. Only a pig would eat his way through a pound, isn't that true? Now that you give the matter mature consideration, do a number of your friends and family appear to have developed snouts and curly little tails?

CHESTNUTS IN YOUR KITCHEN

At large greengrocers and in the produce departments of well-run supermarkets, you can buy almost every kind of nut two ways, both in and out of the shell. But not chestnuts. They are available only with their shells still in place, unless you choose the dried or canned kind. One reason, a good one, is that unlike other nuts chestnuts must be cooked to a degree before the shell can be removed. And because— again unlike other nuts—chestnuts aren't eaten without some preliminary cooking anyway, the cooking-shelling-skinning process is best left until just before they are to be used.

how to buy: Look for clean, shiny, richly brown shells, free of soft spots and of such blemishes as worm holes. Nuts should fill their shells snugly; those that rattle are shriveled and inedible. Chestnuts are available to a limited extent the year around, in quantity from the middle of September through March.

There are between 30 and 40 chestnuts to a pound; the pound, when shelled, will yield about 2½ cups of nutmeats. If you are using the chestnuts as a vegetable, count on 3 rather meager servings per pound, or 2 very generous ones. If chestnut purée is your aim, buy 1¼ pounds of nuts to yield 2 cups of purée.

how to store: In their shells, chestnuts will keep up to 6 months if stored in a cool, dry place. In the refrigerator, count on their remaining fresh a year, or even longer.

nutritive value: One cup of shelled chestnuts contains 310 calories; the same measure offers:

protein	4.6	grams
fat	2.4	grams
carbohydrate	67.4	grams
calcium	43	milligrams
phosphorus	141	milligrams
iron	2.7	milligrams
sodium	10	milligrams
potassium	726	milligrams
thiamin	.35	milligram
riboflavin	.35	milligram
niacin	1	milligram

The nuts have no vitamins A or C.

Shelling chestnuts. Into each life, they say, some rain must fall. If you wish to savor the joys of chestnuts, you must first remove the shells and the bitter thin brown inner skins that encase the nutmeats. This is not particularly easy—not as easy, say, as shelling and blanching almonds. But on the other hand, neither is it particularly difficult unless you prefer to make a big production of it so that you can later complain about how much time you've spent in the kitchen, working your fingers to the bone for the sake of the Mont Blanc that everyone is eating with little moans of delight.

You will need a sharp knife. With it, cut gashes in the shape of a cross on the flat side of the shell. Put the nuts in a deep pan, pour on boiling water so that it covers the nuts with at least an inch to spare; let stand 10 minutes. Or cover with cold water, bring to a boil, and boil 1 minute. Remove nuts one at a time and peel off both shell and inner skin. If the use to which you are going to put them requires whole nuts, work carefully—they break easily.

Roasting chestnuts. Again, do the crisscross cutting with a sharp knife. Place the nuts in a skillet with an ovenproof handle; add 1 tablespoon vegetable oil for each pound of chestnuts. Shake the skillet over moderate heat until all the nuts are oil-coated and beginning to sizzle. Place the skillet in a 350°F. oven and bake about 30 minutes, at which point the shells and skins will come off easily, and the nuts will

have a delicately roasted flavor—for a stronger roasted flavor, add 10 minutes to the baking time.

Tips on preparing, cooking. The roasted chestnuts are for eating as is—or with a light sprinkling of salt—but not for use in cooking. For that you want the plain, unroasted flavor of the nuts shelled by the boiling-water method. Such nuts may be added to any recipe that requires further cooking. If the recipe calls for chestnut purée, boil the shelled nuts in plain water until tender, drain and force through a food mill or purée in a blender. If the purée is for a dessert, you might like to flavor the cooking water with a little vanilla, or boil the chestnuts in milk or in a lightly vanilla-flavored sugar syrup. If you are going to serve the nuts as a vegetable, cook in plain water, in water with a little onion and celery (discard before serving), or in chicken or beef broth. Drain, serve with butter, season as you like. Or cook the shelled chestnuts in water for 10 minutes, drain the nuts and pat them dry, then sauté in butter over moderate heat until the nuts are tender, lightly browned, and beginning to crisp.

Other ways, other forms. If you are a chestnut nut, there's no reason to deny yourself even at times when chestnuts in the shell may be hard to come by. There are always chestnuts available in one form or another.

on grocery shelves, in cans or jars: Whole (most expensive) or pieces, canned in water; whole (most expensive) or pieces in syrup (vanilla- or rum- or brandy-flavored), most often in jars; canned chestnut purée, sweetened or unsweetened. All are most likely to be found in a supermarket's gourmet-food department.

on grocery shelves, in packages: Chestnut confections, preserved in sugar; dried chestnuts (to be reconstituted by soaking overnight in water); chestnut flour. You may have to seek out an Italian grocer for these.

Some perfect partners. Look for recipes that combine chestnuts with poultry, that use them in stuffings and in curries, that team them with vegetables such as red cabbage or brussels sprouts. Or cook the chestnuts in a vanilla-sugar syrup and serve the confection over ice cream or plain cake. Or make Mont Blanc, a heavenly dessert that combines chestnut purée with a hot syrup, the chilled result served with sweetened, vanilla-flavored whipped cream. Seek out ways to make other wonderful chestnut desserts, too—tortes, mousses, sauces, preserves, and a glorious is-it-cake-or-pudding? concoction, rich with chestnuts and chocolate, called Turinois.

Although we use chestnuts as a sometime thing, in many countries—particularly those around the Mediterranean—they are a household staple and have often meant the difference between preservation of life and starvation in times of crop failure. A versatile food, the chestnut, deserving of more attention than most of us in this country give it.

CHICKEN

The pièce de résistance of countless meals in all the far and near corners of the world, chicken has been a favorite food for a number of years that defies imagination, and shows no signs of going out of style.

Long before recorded time, chickens were pecking and cackling around in the jungle—as much as 150 million years ago, fossils discovered in Bavaria attest. People of India and the East Indies coaxed the fowl out of the wilds and into the barnyard well before 1000 B.C., and chickens have been domesticated ever since.

In ancient Rome, a proper flock comprised two hundred hens, because someone had figured out that this was the maximum number that could be cared for by one adult with the aid of one child. Romans were so fond of chicken, and ate so much of it, that a law was passed restricting its use. So much enjoyment, the lawgivers thought, couldn't possibly be good for the common people.

That well-known potful of chicken. The Republican party leaders who fixed on "a chicken in every pot" as a slogan for the 1932 campaign, in the depths of the Great Depression, may have thought they'd come up with a breath-takingly new idea. Wrong—as politicians often are. Henry IV of France, at the beginning of the seventeenth century, be-nignly wished for his peasants a chicken in every pot every Sunday—perhaps while, with the other hand, lightening the burdens of the Hugenots by signing the Edict of Nantes.

Writing more than 150 years later, Scottish poet Alexander Smith echoed him with, "Just consider what a world this would be if ruled by the best thoughts of men of letters! Ignorance would die at once, war would cease, taxation would be lightened, not only every Frenchman, but every man in the world, would have his hen in the pot." (He also wrote: "To be occasionally quoted is the only fame I care for." Alexander, wherever you may be, we have obviously just made your day.)

Sunday dinner, company dinner. Once upon a time in this country, chicken appeared on tables only at feast-day meals. The affluent (or affluent chicken farmers) ate chicken every Sunday, the less fortunate had to wait for a special occasion, such as a birthday or the preacher coming to dinner. First, as in the old joke, you had to catch your chicken, either literally in the backyard, or at the market where you inspected the fowl on, so to speak, the hoof, and chose one that looked good to you. After you got it home and wrung its neck—woman's work is never done—there were still the matters of drawing and plucking, often delegated to some hapless child who had ventured into the kitchen to steal a cookie. (The feathers went into pillows and bed ticks.) Chicken dinner, as with many things in what people tend, misty-eyed, to think of as the good old days, wasn't easy to come by.

Sometimes a hen past her laying years or a rooster too elderly to crow, much less perform other roosterish functions, was retired to the cooking pot, where she/he had to be boiled for hours on end before the meat became tender enough to eat. Dumplings—plain or herbed or made with cornmeal—were the usual accompaniment, and some good, thick cream went into the gravy. A fitting end to a long and useful life.

The price flip-flop. In those times, chicken was a costly delicacy. Beef and pork and lamb were for everyday eating. Nowadays, chicken is relatively inexpensive—compared, at least, to the red meats—and turns up on the menu at least once a week in many homes. Fortunately, almost everyone likes its mild, delicate flavor, and it lends itself to so many kinds of dishes that no one need ever tire of chicken, no matter how often it is served.

CHICKEN IN YOUR KITCHEN

Ready-to-cook chicken can be found in the market both fresh and frozen. More, you may choose it whole, halved, quartered, or in parts—a selection of breasts (boned or bone-in), wings, thighs, drumsticks, or necks and backs, packaged separately, or a whole chicken cut up. And you'll also find hearts and gizzards, usually packaged together, and livers, separately packaged.

Assorted shapes and sizes. A chicken is not just a chicken. There is a kind suitable to whatever ultimate end you have in mind for it, from a plain broiled half to the makings of a hearty, tasty Marengo or Cacciatore.

broiler/fryer: Ranges in weight from ¾ pound to 3½ pounds. Use it, not surprisingly, for broiling or frying, although you may roast it if you have a mind to.

capon: A male, desexed in its infancy, the better to grow tenderly meaty. Ranges in weight from 4 to 8 pounds. For roasting.

roaster: Larger than a broiler/fryer, it ranges in weight from 2½ to 5 pounds. For roasting.

rock cornish hen: Miniature chicken; ranges in weight up to 2 pounds. For roasting (whole) or broiling (halved).

stewing chicken: May be hen or fowl; ranges in weight from under 3 pounds to over 5. More mature than other chickens, it should be stewed or braised.

Inspection, grading. As with many other foods we shop for, poultry is inspected and graded by the USDA. Bear in mind though that the grade mark indicates quality, but not tenderness—that is determined by the age classification of the bird, above.

The familiar grade shield can be found on the outside of the package, if the chicken you buy is packaged; if not, you'll find the shield on a tag attached to the bird's wing. In order to be graded for quality, poultry must first be inspected for wholesomeness; the inspection stamp assures you that the chicken was butchered and processed under completely sanitary conditions.

U.S. Grade A: The highest quality; bird is fully fleshed and meaty, well finished, and attractive in appearance.

U.S. Grade B: Lesser quality; less attractive in finish and appearance; slightly lacking in meatiness.

You are most likely to find chickens proudly wearing the U.S. Grade A shield, or no grade at all. Producers of Grade B chickens would prefer their birds to wear no shield rather than one that proclaims them less than the very best. As with other foods, grading of poultry is voluntary, provided on a fee basis by the USDA to processors who request it. But inspection, at least of chickens shipped from state to state, is mandatory, and all graded chickens must first be inspected.

Sometimes the inspection stamp and the grade shield are combined on a wing tag, along with the class of chicken —roaster, capon, or whatever. When grading is done in cooperation with the state, the official grade shield may carry the phrase "federal-state graded."

Chicken for dinner. Because it is relatively inexpensive, because there are so many savory ways to prepare it, and because almost everyone likes it, chicken is always a good choice.

how to buy: Choose by class—as broiler/fryer, roaster— depending on how you are going to cook the bird. Look for plump, meaty, short-legged birds; skin color should be creamy-white to creamy-yellow, but not blue. If the chicken is packaged, look for a last-day-of-sale date on the package, and do not buy beyond that date; chicken is very perishable. If it is not packaged, don't be shy about smelling the cavity. A fresh chicken has a very faint, clean odor; the smell of one not so fresh is unmistakably unpleasant. Use your eyes, too; look for bruises or cuts in the skin. A good covering of fat is an indication of tenderness. If you're paying for a top-quality bird, you want to get one.

how to store: If the chicken is in a transparent-wrap package, loosen the wrapping; if not, wrap the chicken lightly, not airtight. Remove package of giblets (the neck is often in that package, too), rewrap, and store separately. Keep the chicken in the coldest part of the refrigerator, and plan to use it within 2 days. Cooked chicken, tightly covered and refrigerated, should also be used within 2 days. Store stuffing, broth, or gravy separately.

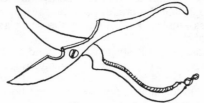

nutritive value: Chicken provides high-quality protein; the white meat is lower in fat, lower in iron, higher in niacin than the dark. One cup of diced white meat of roasted chicken, skin excluded, contains 255 calories; a similar portion of dark meat, 258 calories. These are the nutrients in one cup diced roasted chicken:

	light	dark	
protein	45.2	41	grams
carbohydrate	0	0	
fat	6.9	9.1	grams
calcium	15	20	milligrams
phosphorus	381	329	milligrams
iron	1.8	2.5	milligrams
sodium	92	123	milligrams
potassium	591	462	milligrams
thiamin	.11	.17	milligram
riboflavin	.14	.27	milligram
niacin	16.5	7.4	milligrams
ascorbic acid	trace	trace	milligram
vitamin A	150	220	international units

Tips on preparing, cooking. Broiler/fryers may be, to belabor the obvious, broiled or fried; they may also be roasted. Roasters and capons are generally too large for either broiling or frying, and are best roasted, stuffed or not as you choose. All three kinds are also delectable baked in one of several kinds of savory sauces. Cornish game hens are too small and delicate for frying, and, many think, for broiling, too. They are best roasted or baked. Or they may be halved, lightly browned, and braised—a treatment that is excellent for broiler/fryers as well. An older chicken, hen or fowl, must be cooked in liquid until tender, by which process you gain a bonus of chicken broth. There is no law, certainly, against cooking any of the tenderer varieties of chicken in the same manner if you wish.

Choose the right bird for the cooking treatment you intend to give it, and proceed like this:

to panfry: Have broiler/fryer quartered or cut into serving pieces; pat dry—it will not brown as well if it is damp. In a large skillet, heat a combination of ⅔ butter or margarine and ⅓ vegetable oil, or if you prefer, use all vegetable shortening. Use sufficient fat so that it is ¼ to ½ inch deep, and heat to a high-moderate temperature, 360°F. if you are using an electric skillet. Dredge chicken pieces in seasoned flour. Place chicken in skillet, skin side down, the large meatier pieces first. Cook from 15 to 25 minutes on each side, turning once, for a crisp, brown skin. Or you may brown for 15 minutes total, then cover skillet tightly and cook 20 to 30 minutes longer (the skin will not be as crisp). Either way, cook until chicken is fork-tender and the juices, when the meat is pricked, are yellow, with no tinge of pink. If you prefer, chicken may be deep-fat fried.

The flour in which the chicken pieces are dredged may be seasoned simply with salt and pepper, or you may add onion powder, celery salt, sage, thyme, or any combination. Or chicken may be dipped in a fritter-type thin batter before frying—any good general cookbook will tell you how. Or pieces may be breaded by dredging with flour, then dipping in beaten egg or heavy cream, then in cornmeal, dry bread crumbs, or crushed cereal flakes.

to roast: Sprinkle neck and body cavities of broiler/fryer, capon, roaster, or cornish hen with salt. Stuff if you wish. Hook wing tips onto back to hold neck skin down, or tie snugly to the body; tie legs together and to the tail, or press legs through the loop of skin some butchers provide for the purpose. Spread the bird all over with softened butter. Place breast side down on a rack in a shallow roasting pan; cook at 325°F. about 15 minutes per pound, more or less, or until drumstick moves easily in its socket and drumstick meat feels soft when gently pinched with your (protected) fingers. Turn breast side up and raise heat to 425°F. for the last 15 minutes of cooking time if you wish the chicken well browned and the skin crisp.

If you stuff the bird, you may prepare the stuffing in advance and refrigerate it, but don't spoon it into the bird until just before you are ready to put it in the oven. A stuffed chicken will require 15 to 20 minutes extra roasting time. If you do not stuff the chicken, you can place several large pieces of onion and several chunks of celery into the cavity for extra flavor. Or place a quartered orange along with a few onion slices in the cavity for a delicious change.

For optimum juiciness, cook the bird under a tent of foil. Fold foil of generous size down the middle and tent it, with the crease up, over the breast-side-up bird, securing the foil at the four corners to the edge of the roasting pan. Remove tent the last 20 minutes for browning. Be sure that the foil does not touch the bird at any point, or enclose the bird airtight. Do not wrap a chicken—or turkey or any other bird—tightly in foil for roasting; the bird is then steamed rather than roasted, and does not have the good roasted flavor.

to broil: Preheat the broiler, if your range use-and-care booklet tells you to preheat. Season chicken, brush with melted butter or margarine. Place halves or quarters of broiler/fryer skin side down on lightly greased broiler pan rack; place pan about 7 inches from source of heat. Broil 20 to 30 minutes on each side (be guided by the size of the bird). Brush again with melted butter after turning. Prick the thickest part of the meat with a skewer or cake tester. If the juices run yellow, the chicken is done; if pink, it requires further cooking.

to braise: Pat chicken parts dry. Brown in a butter/oil mixture or vegetable shortening, as for frying, 10 to 15 minutes. Drain excess fat; add liquid—water, bouillon, tomato juice—to a depth of ¾ inch. Lower heat, cover pan, and cook until chicken is fork-tender, adding more liquid as necessary. Turn chicken pieces twice during braising period.

If you like, vegetables may be added to braise with the chicken.

to stew: Place stewing chicken in a deep kettle with seasonings—pieces of onion, celery, carrot, bay leaf, parsley sprigs, or branches of fresh tarragon or basil or thyme—and water to cover. (If your aim is a rich, strong chicken stock at the end of cooking, make the liquid part water and part chicken broth, or all broth.) Cover kettle and simmer until chicken is tender, anywhere from 1 to 3 hours, depending on the bird's size and age. If not to be used immediately, refrigerate the chicken and stock separately.

to spit-roast: Use an oven or barbecue-grill rotisserie, or a specially designed spit-roaster. You can roast whole chickens—stuffed or not—or halves, but bear in mind that you are limited by the length of the spit. Salt, stuff if you wish, and tie or skewer wing tips over breast. Push spit through bird from tail toward front so that the point emerges between the branches of the wishbone. Cross drumsticks and tie them and the tail together. The bird must be evenly balanced or the spit won't turn properly. Push the pronged anchors into place securely. For halves, push spit evenly through thigh meat, then breast meat, and anchor.

Brush all over with melted fat or oil. No further basting is necessary, but if you wish you may baste with a savory sauce several times during the final 30 minutes of cooking time. Over glowing coals, roast 1 hour or more for a 2-pound chicken, about 2 hours for a 3-pound bird. In oven or electric rotisserie, follow manufacturer's directions. When the bird is done, the breast meat near the wing will be fork-tender and the drumstick meat soft when pinched between your fingers.

to barbecue: Place broiler/fryer halves or quarters, skin side up, on grate set 3 to 6 inches from hot coals—make it 5 inches if you're using a barbecue sauce with a high sugar content. Brush with cooking oil, or a combination of 2 parts oil to 1 part vinegar, or your favorite barbecue sauce. Cook until tender, turning and brushing several times during cooking. Total time will be 45 minutes to 1¼ hours, depending on the weight of the chicken pieces and the distance from the coals. Test for doneness as for broiled chicken.

to bake: Brown the chicken first, if you prefer, but in most cases this is not necessary—baked chicken is an easy-do dish for family or company, one that can be as simple or as dressed-up as you please. Use a shallow casserole dish for halves or pieces, a deeper one for a whole chicken. There should be room for the chicken to fit snugly, but not be crowded, in one layer. From here on, you are on your own—there are more savory ways to bake chicken than you can shake a stick at. Dip pieces in melted butter, then in fine bread crumbs. Or dip into sour cream mixed with lots of snipped chives. Or place in a greased casserole and pour in a well-seasoned tomato sauce, or a combination of red or white wine and chicken broth. Or tuck in quarters of fresh tomato and pieces of onion, eggplant, and mushrooms; sprinkle lightly with thyme or oregano and, close to the end of baking time, a good drift of grated parmesan or romano or shredded mozzarella. Or bake in a sauce made of canned condensed soup, diluted with half as much water or milk—cream of tomato or celery or mushroom or cheddar cheese soups make good sauces. Add vegetables or not, as you like.

One of the great farm-style dishes, fit for a king, is chicken baked in cream. Place a whole chicken in a buttered deep casserole. Around it pack a mixed bag of matchstick-size pieces of celery and carrot, tiny parsley sprigs, very thin slices of onion, sliced or whole button mushrooms, thin strips of lean cooked ham, seasoning lightly with salt and white pepper as you go. Then pour in heavy cream, enough so that the whole deal is covered. Add fresh or thawed frozen peas 20 minutes before the end of the baking time—the other vegetables will have cooked down enough by then so that there will be room. Long, slow cooking is the ticket—300°F., until the chicken is meltingly tender. Bring to the table as is, or remove the chicken and thicken the vegetable-laden gravy lightly if you prefer. If you have a sense of the fitness of things, you'll serve this with spoon bread.

For this or any other baked chicken, cover the casserole —use foil if the dish doesn't have a cover of its own—until about 20 minutes before cooking is complete; remove the cover for the remaining cooking time. These baked chicken dishes cry out for something over which to ladle the good sauce they've manufactured during cooking. Spoon bread is one idea. Mashed potatoes, fluffy biscuits, rice, noodles, or corn pudding are others. (Corn and chicken are very close friends.)

Consult a good cookbook for dozens of ways to cook chicken. You'll find Pennsylvania Dutch Bot Boi, Country Captain, Corn Soup with Rivels, Chicken Marengo, Chicken Cacciatore, Southern Fried Chicken with Cream Gravy, Florentine Chicken, Suprêmes Cordon Bleu, Sherried Chicken with Artichokes, Circassian Walnut Chicken, Orange-Cream Chicken Salad in Avocados, Coconut Cream Chicken, Country Scallop, Broiled Chicken and Yams with Marmalade Sauce, Chicken with Snow Peas and Almonds. Doesn't even so short a list set your imagination soaring, to say nothing of sending your salivary glands into high gear?

As for chicken leftovers, they are like an unexpected legacy. Think about Monte Cristo sandwiches. Or old-fashioned pressed chicken. Or Chicken Divan. Or crepes stuffed with a savory chicken mixture. Or crisp chicken croquettes. Or chickenburgers with bleu cheese. Or a chicken-ham-macaroni loaf. Or Chicken à la King. Or creamy chicken hash. Or chicken fried rice. Or farm-style creamed chicken on fried bread. The list could go on for pages.

Freezing chicken. If you buy chicken already frozen, hustle it home from the market and into the freezer before it begins to thaw, unless you are going to cook it that day or the next. When unfrozen chickens are on sale, buy extras to freeze at home—whole or cut up. Properly prepared and wrapped (see special feature: PUTTING FOOD BY), raw chicken can be stored at 0°F. or lower up to 7 months, giblets up to 3 months. Cooked chicken may also be frozen. Plan on storing properly prepared fried chicken at 0° or below up to 3 months, chicken main dishes made with sauce or gravy up to 6 months.

Other ways, other forms. You'll find cooked chicken of various kinds throughout your market, to serve as is or to use in the preparation of other dishes.

on grocery shelves, in cans or jars: Whole canned chickens—not economical for general use (it's cheaper to buy the chicken fresh, cook it yourself), but useful when refrigeration is nonexistent or at a premium, as on camping trips. Small cans of boneless cooked chicken, generally light meat, are useful when only a small amount is wanted, as for a small salad or a sandwich filling. Jars of chicken-and-noodle main dish, ready to heat and serve—not economical for family eating, but useful as a change for a single person, particularly one who doesn't like to (or know how to) cook. Canned chicken-based soups of several kinds. Canned chicken gravy. Canned chicken broth.

in grocery frozen-food section: Boxes of fried chicken, ready to heat and serve. Whole-meal tray dinners, with fried chicken or roast chicken (usually with stuffing and gravy) as the chief component. Frozen main-dish items, such as chicken and noodle casserole, chicken-stuffed pasta shells, creamed chicken, chicken à la king. Frozen chicken livers. Frozen potpies—chicken and vegetables in gravy, with a crust.

in grocery refrigerator cases: Chicken breast roll, in slices or ready-to-slice pieces, for sandwiches. Chicken wieners.

Getting your chicken money's worth. Chicken, in whatever form you purchase it, is a good buy. Scientific breeding and feeding and modern methods of processing now bring to the market in weeks chickens that it used to take months to raise, making the bird that was once comparatively expensive now comparatively cheap.

If you're willing to devote a little time and effort, you can cut the price even more. Bone chicken breasts yourself, for example, instead of buying the elegant suprêmes ready-boned. Bone-in breasts cost less per pound, and if you bone them yourself you get a bonus of bones and skin to use for chicken stock or soup. See the special feature: CUTTING, BONING, AND OTHER KITCHEN TECHNIQUES for boning how-to.

Although this is not universally true, whole chickens are

generally lower in price than either parts or cut-up chickens. When chickens are on sale, buy the whole ones and cut them up into packages of parts to freeze. Once again, there's a bonus attached—you'll get necks and giblets to stockpile for chicken soup or a meal of chicken livers.

There are times, however, when chicken parts are a bargain—and this is particularly true for families in which most of the members prefer light meat or dark meat. Use this chart to determine when whole chickens and parts are an equally good buy.

when per-pound price of broiler/ fryers is:	parts are equal buy at per-pound price of:			
	breasts	drumsticks	thighs	wings
59¢	83¢	72¢	78¢	47¢
65¢	91¢	79¢	86¢	52¢
69¢	97¢	84¢	92¢	55¢
75¢	$1.05	92¢	$1.00	60¢
79¢	$1.11	96¢	$1.05	63¢
85¢	$1.19	$1.04	$1.13	68¢
89¢	$1.25	$1.09	$1.18	71¢

Thrifty chicken know-how. Look for "three-legged" chickens—packaged with an extra drumstick—if you have kids who like drumsticks best. When choosing a broiler/fryer in the 2- to 3-pound range, the larger bird is the better buy —ratio of meat to bone is greater. Count on 3 to 4 servings from a 2-pound bird, 4 to 6 from a 3-pounder. Or put it another way—for frying or roasting, count on ¾ to 1 pound of chicken per serving; for broiling or barbecuing, 1 pound or ½ of a whole chicken; for stewing, ½ to 1 pound per serving. None of these quantities allows for second helpings, remember. Always stuff a roasting chicken—stuffing is delicious and a great portion-stretcher. Always buy stewing hen or fowl (lower priced) for stews and fricassees, and when the meat is to be used for sandwiches, salads, or casserole dishes. Substitute boned chicken breasts, pounded thin, in recipes calling for veal cutlets or scallops—they have fine flavor and are much less expensive.

Since long before Chicken Little rushed around announcing that the sky was falling, we've eaten—and enjoyed eating—chicken prepared in dozens of ways, and doubtless will continue to do so for generations to come. Not only good but good for us, the birds offer high-quality protein (and, if you're counting, they're low in cholesterol), at a reasonable price.

Here's an illuminating comparison. Suppose you wanted to get your total daily protein requirement from meat, and chose bacon as the meat. You'd need well over a pound to get the edible 6 ounces necessary (nearly 70 percent of the weight of bacon is lost in cooking) at a cost of at least $2.00 and a "cost" of a staggering 1,010 cholesterol-loaded calories. On the other hand, suppose you chose chicken. You'd

need less than a pound that, cooked, skinned, and boned would be reduced to 7 ounces. It would cost about 55 cents, add up to about 260 calories, and be far lower in cholesterol. Worth thinking about.

CHICKEN STOCK: see HERBS AND
SAVORY SEASONINGS

CHICK-PEAS

Not peas, really, but beans, these are the most nutlike of the legumes in flavor, shape, and color. Most often available canned, they're also called garbanzos and ceci. See also BEANS.

CHICORY: see SALAD GREENS AND PLANTS

CHIFFON CAKES: see CAKES

CHILDREN, FEEDING: see special feature:
ON FEEDING YOUNGSTERS

CHILI

A wonderfully spicy, long-cooked thick stew of meat (chili con carne) and sometimes beans (con frijoles) in a richly flavored sauce. There are as many "real thing" recipes for chili as there are chili lovers, and that's a lot. Chili purists opt for varying degrees of hotness, varying amounts of tomato, varying types of beans or no beans at all. The ground beef versus diced beef controversy heats up whenever chili is served or even mentioned. The Southwest is chili country, where you'll find the dish served in homes and restaurants, at cookouts, even at chili festivals and cook-offs.

CHILI POWDER: see CHILIES, SPICES, and
HERBS AND SAVORY SEASONINGS

CHILI SAUCE

A condiment sauce, made at home or purchased. It is based on tomatoes and contains sweet and hot peppers, onions, celery and mustard seeds, bay leaves, cloves, ginger, nutmeg, cinnamon, brown sugar, vinegar, and salt—it contains most of these, dropping some out, adding others, depending on the home recipe you use or the formula followed by your favorite commercial maker of the sauce.

Chili sauce is most often served with meats, on sandwiches, or with clams, oysters or, often combined with

mayonnaise, as a sauce for lobster or crabmeat cocktail. A tablespoon or so folded, along with a liberal squirt of lemon juice, into the mayonnaise to be used to bind a seafood salad of any kind lends flavor and character to the mixture.

CHILIES

These are the fruit of a plant of the Capiscum family, to which all PEPPERS, including the familiar green (bell) variety, belong. The flavor of chilies—or call them chili peppers—is pungent, hot to fiery, dominating any food to which they are added without caution. They are the smallest and most bitingly hot of the pepper family. As with all peppers, the seeds are even hotter than the vegetable itself, so watch out. A broken chili pepper can be added to soup or stew, fished out a bit later before its taste becomes too dominant in the food.

Cayenne, the hot red pepper seasoning, is made from chilies. So is the dried pepper-flake seasoning that, used with discretion, adds heat to Mexican, Italian, and some Indian foods. Ground chilies make chili powder. This seasoning, in a reasonably mild form, can be found in small tins or jars on the spice shelves of markets nationwide. But in the Southwest it comes in varying strengths, ranging from hot to blow-your-head-wide-open. Approach with caution.

CHILL, TO: see page 444

CHINESE CABBAGE: see CABBAGE

CHINESE GOOSEBERRIES: see EXOTIC FRUITS and KIWIS

CHINESE NOODLES

These are familiar to most people as the crisp-fried brown noodles that come as part of a take-out or eat-in Chinese meal that includes chow mein. But there's more to the noodle story than that. Chinese cooking also embraces several kinds of soft noodles, including translucent bean threads (see CELLOPHANE NOODLES) and a kind made of yams or sweet potatoes—the latter most often found in cans in supermarkets; you are likely to be able to buy them freshly made only if there is a Chinese section, with active markets, near you.

CHIPPED BEEF: see DRIED FOODS

CHIPS

Mutt and Jeff, ham and eggs, boys and girls, chips and dips —all these are partnerships so rooted in convention no one would dream of breaking them up. Think of the hundreds of thousands of parties that could never have been held had chips and dips been outlawed!

First were potato chips, "invented" in Victorian times by an imaginative chef at one of the old hotels in Saratoga Springs, New York, a fashionable spa. In fact, for a long while potato chips were known as "saratoga chips," and were very stylish indeed. Cooks vied with one another to make the thinnest, airiest, daintiest saratogas. Now we've come full circle—the most trendy potato chips today are labeled "old-fashioned," are somewhat thickish, and cut from potatoes with the skins left on. There are variations on the potato chip available, too: "manufactured" chips made of ground and re-formed potatoes, and chips with various added flavorings such as bacon and barbecue.

Corn chips next appeared on the scene—that is, they appeared bagged in the supermarket, although broken pieces of tortilla had been used in various ways by Mexicans and Central Americans for generations, notably in casserole dishes and as scoops for guacamole. Besides the plain corn chips, there are available barbecue-flavored and nacho (cheese) flavored chips.

Shrimp chips are feather-light pale pink goodies that originated in the Far East. (Some, now, are made as far east as Brooklyn.) They make fine, exotic nibbles to serve with cocktail-hour drinks. So do toasted coconut chips. Both of these kinds are available in cans, most likely in the gourmet-food section of your market.

The chips that are half the partnership of authentic British fish 'n' chips resemble much more closely what we call french fries than what we think of as potato chips. In Britain, our chips are their "crisps."

Two delicious do-it-yourself chips can be deep-fried at home, made of yams or of bananas. Slice thinly (the bananas should be underripe) and fry a few at a time in deep fat. Salt lightly and serve soon—their goodness is short-lived.

CHIVES: see ONIONS and HERBS
AND SAVORY SEASONINGS

CHLORIDE: see special feature:
NUTRITION NOTEBOOK

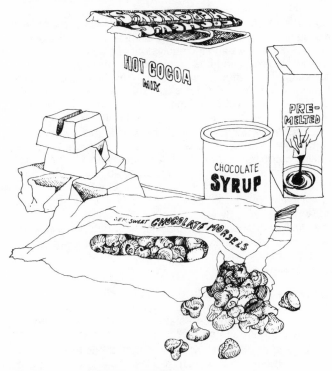

CHOCOLATE AND COCOA

A whole cookbook, bulging at the seams with seductive recipes, could be written on the subject of chocolate alone. As a matter of fact, there are several such books in existence, which gives the dedicated chocolate freak a feeling of no more worlds to conquer, nothing left but to indulge the craving until he/she also bulges at the seams in a state of chocoholic bliss.

Fantasy aside, chocolate is America's favorite, and "give me any flavor as long as it's chocolate" is a mild joke that carries more truth than comedy.

Gift of the gods, fit for a king. Returning from one of his later voyages, Columbus brought back to King Ferdinand of Spain a collection of the treasures to be found in the New World. Among them were a few dark brown beans, to which not much attention was paid, because no one had any idea of what use to make of them. It wasn't until Hernando Cortez drank a magic brown brew from a golden goblet in the court of Montezuma, emperor of the Aztecs, that any European knew what chocolate was.

The Aztecs believed that *cacahuatl*—their word for "chocolate"—was a gift from their gods. When, later, a botanical name was given the cacao tree, *Theobroma cacao,* food of the gods, was chosen, reflecting the same feeling. Cortez (those enterprising Spanish explorers again!) brought more cocoa beans—and this time the method of preparing them—back to Spain. The king and his court were so enchanted that the secret of the dark, rich, frothy drink was kept from the rest of Europe for more than a century, until Spanish monks shared it with their Italian brothers.

Meanwhile, the Spaniards improved on what was already a good thing, adding sugar to the chocolate, serving the beverage both hot and cold, flavoring it with vanilla and cinnamon. When word leaked out, the chocolate craze spread rapidly across Europe. By the middle of the seventeenth century, chocolate houses sprang up in England, where those who had the price could go to kill time in learned discussions while drinking cup after cup of the exotic beverage. Chocolate had slipped out of the control of the aristocrats and, inevitably, means of mass production were set in motion to produce an ever finer, more flavorful drink at reduced cost. In this country the first chocolate factory opened in 1765, in Massachusetts.

The great Swiss idea. Two centuries after the beginning of the chocolate house fad in England, an inventive Swiss gentleman asked himself a question (probably while sipping a cup of his favorite beverage). Could chocolate be somehow congealed and dried, turned into a solid instead of a liquid, so that it could be eaten rather than drunk? From that cogitation arose the method of producing milk chocolate. When it appeared on the market the revolution began, until today chocolate for eating outstrips chocolate for drinking by many millions of pounds.

From tree to kitchen. The cacao grows only in tropical areas not far north and south of the equator. At maturity the trees are twenty to twenty-five feet tall, bearing long, shiny leaves and clusters of pink and white scentless flowers that turn, in their season, into pods six to eight inches long, each bearing from twenty to fifty cacao beans. Each tree produces between twenty and forty pods a year, and the growth cycle is continuous—leaves, blossoms, and pods appear at one time on the tree.

The mature pods are harvested and the beans removed. Fermentation separates the beans from the pulp; then the beans are dried in the sun. They are shipped from their tropical home to processing plants, where they are cleaned, roasted, and husked. Milled, the beans release a large amount of their "butter," the natural fat of the cocoa bean, so that a liquor is formed. From this liquor all the various forms of chocolate are processed.

In making baking chocolate, the cocoa butter content is maintained; in making cocoa—chocolate in a powdered, less rich form—more than half the butter is removed. That cocoa butter is added, along with milk and sugar, to chocolate liquor to produce milk chocolate. Omission of the milk results in the semisweet chocolate used for some kinds of baking—chocolate bits, for example—and for eating as candy.

Shopping for chocolate products. Whatever chocolate delicacy—and their name is legion—you have in mind to make, there's a chocolate product to serve your purpose.

unsweetened chocolate: This is often called baking chocolate. It's pure chocolate liquor, with nothing added, that has been poured into molds, where it hardens into cakes. When a recipe calls for "2 squares chocolate," this is what is required; a square weighs 1 ounce, in case the recipe calls for measurement in ounces. Buy it in packages of 8 individually wrapped squares, shelved near other products for baking, such as flour, baking powder, and so on.

cocoa: Part of the cocoa butter is removed from chocolate liquor, the liquor is pressed into cakes, and the cakes are pulverized to result in the fine chocolate powder that is cocoa. Use this plain cocoa in recipes calling for the product, and to make—with milk and sugar—the cups of cocoa in which children delight (particularly with a marshmallow afloat). Usually shelved in the markets with other products for baking, or with beverages, most often in cardboard cartons with pry-off metal lids.

breakfast cocoa: This has somewhat more cocoa butter left in. Use interchangeably with regular cocoa.

dutch cocoa: Treated with an alkali, this cocoa is darker and has a slightly different taste and aroma. It, too, can be used interchangeably with regular cocoa.

instant cocoa: Sugar is added to cocoa for convenience in making a hot beverage at home; don't use in cooking unless the recipe specifically calls for it. Shelved with beverages.

hot cocoa mix: Cocoa plus sugar plus dry milk—again for making beverages, but not for cooking. It is also shelved with beverages.

semisweet chocolate: A blend of unsweetened chocolate plus sugar and extra cocoa butter. Comes in 8-ounce bars, marked into segments for easy measuring. Can be eaten out of hand or used in recipes that specifically call for it. Do not substitute for regular baking chocolate in cooking. Shelved with baking products.

chocolate chips: Also called, depending on the manufacturer, pieces or bits. For eating out of hand, or use in cooking. Packed in 6- and 12-ounce bags, the chips are generally made of semisweet chocolate, although at least one manufacturer also makes milk chocolate chips. These milk chocolate chips can be used interchangeably with the semisweet ones in cookies and for toppings, but where the recipe calls for melting the chips, stick to the semisweet kind for best results. One manufacturer also makes miniature semisweet chocolate chips, each about half the size of the usual kind.

sweet cooking chocolate: Also a blend of unsweetened chocolate, sugar, and cocoa butter, this is lighter and milder than semisweet. Comes in individually wrapped squares, in packages. Shelved with baking products. Do not substitute for regular baking chocolate in cooking unless recipe specifically calls for it.

liquid chocolate: Unsweetened, for cooking; made with cocoa and vegetable shortening. Comes in packages of individual envelopes, each the equivalent of a 1-ounce square of regular unsweetened baking chocolate, for which it may be substituted. In effect, this is premelted baking chocolate. However, the flavor is not exactly the same—you may be delighted to skip the melting, or prefer to melt chocolate yourself for the familiar flavor. Shelved with baking products.

chocolate syrup: Ready-to-use, made of cocoa sweetened with sugar. Comes in cans or jars or bottles, shelved near baking products or sometimes near ice cream. Add it to milk for a chocolate beverage, or use as a sauce over ice cream or cake. Can be used in cooking, but not unless recipe specifically calls for it.

milk chocolate: Sweetened chocolate with milk added—the familiar chocolate bar, plain or with nuts; also used to coat chocolate creams and various kinds of candy bars. Find it at the candy counter. Do not cook with it unless recipe specifies.

Cooking with chocolate. Although chocolate products keep well, you're better off buying no more than you'll use up within a couple of months—stale chocolate is still usable, but the flavor's not quite so richly, deep-down good.

melting chocolate: Bear in mind that chocolate scorches easily, and burned chocolate has a terrible taste. Melt over hot but not boiling water, in a double boiler (first choice) or a cup or small bowl set in a saucepan. Make sure the water doesn't boil for two reasons—if even a tiny amount of water sloshes into the chocolate, the mixture will thicken and become somewhat granular (this is called "seizing") and will be difficult to incorporate evenly into whatever you're making; even steam may cause chocolate to seize, the second reason for not allowing the water to boil.

More than a drop or two of water will change the chocolate too much for use, but the effects of a little steam can be rectified. Soften the chocolate again by adding 1 to 2 tablespoons of vegetable shortening (butter won't do) and stir the mixture fiercely until it becomes tractable.

In some recipes, chocolate can be melted in the liquid called for—milk, water, brandy, whatever—in a heavy saucepan placed directly over low heat. Be sure the recipe calls for at least ¼ cup liquid for each 6 ounces of chocolate.

If the recipe calls for melted fat, melt the fat and chocolate together, again in a heavy pan over low heat. In both cases, keep your eye on the mixture.

storing chocolate: A temperature between 60 and 70 degrees is best for storing chocolate. In too warm a place, or in hot summer weather, chocolate may develop a gray-white film over the outside. This is called "bloom," and is caused by part of the cocoa butter content rising to the surface. It's not particularly pretty, but it does not affect the usefulness of the chocolate. The same thing sometimes happens to chocolate candy in warm weather.

In storing cocoa, the thing to remember is to replace the top of the carton firmly. Humidity makes cocoa lumpy and hard. The 60 to 70 degree range is best for cocoa, too.

We generally bake cakes containing chocolate at a somewhat lower temperature than white cakes—usually about 25 degrees lower—because too high a temperature can change the flavor of the chocolate. Also, the crust of a chocolate cake scorches more easily than that of its white counterpart.

Cooking with cocoa.
If you want to make a chocolate dessert and have no chocolate on hand, you can substitute cocoa. Use 3 level tablespoons of cocoa plus 2 teaspoons of shortening for each ounce of baking chocolate the recipe calls for. The shortening is required to make up the fat that chocolate contains but cocoa has in lesser quantity.

In any recipe that calls for cocoa, or in which you're substituting cocoa, mix the cocoa thoroughly with the flour or the sugar called for before adding the eggs or liquids.

The goodness of chocolate.
We eat chocolate, those of us who do, because we love it, and we pity those poor souls allergic to it. But it's certainly the pleasure we derive from it, not the nutritive value, that puts chocolate high on our goodies list.

Milk chocolate contains 147 calories per ounce, a little protein, an appreciable amount of fat, more carbohydrate than carbogram-counting dieters can afford, and minor amounts of some vitamins and minerals. Not, you'll have to admit, an exceedingly worthwhile addition to a balanced diet. Nor is baking chocolate, which has virtually the same number of calories and the same nutrients—or lack of them—to offer.

When we cook with chocolate, though, things look up a bit. A chocolate pudding, for example, has the goodness of eggs and milk to mitigate the nutritional curse of the chocolate. A milk drink flavored with chocolate has all of milk's nutrients.

But that's not really the point. It's safe to say that no one who loves chocolate rejects it for its lack of contribution to nutrition—and that "no one," without a doubt, embraces some very dedicated nutritionists. Chocolate candy, pies of various sorts, many kinds of cakes and cookies, puddings, bavarians, frozen desserts, sodas and sundaes—just listing them starts the taste buds dancing. What are we having for dessert tonight?

CHOICE (one of the USDA meat grades):
see BEEF

CHOLESTEROL: see special feature: NUTRITION NOTEBOOK

CHOP, TO: see page 445

CHOPPED MEAT: see GROUND MEAT

CHOPS: see under kind, as: LAMB, PORK, VEAL

CHORIZOS: see SAUSAGES

CHOU(X) PASTE
You may find it in your cookbooks under its full French name, pâte à chou. Whatever you call it, it's the pastry from which the shells for cream puffs and eclairs are made, as well as some other elegant concoctions, such as paris brest. The familiar pastry we use for pies is made by cutting fat into flour, adding ice water. The totally different method for chou paste consists of melting butter in water, vigorously stirring in the flour, then beating in eggs one by one.

Cookbooks often call for shaping chou paste with a pastry tube, but you can manage very creditable cream puff and eclair shells by shaping them with two spoons. Tiny puffs of chou paste, filled with a savory mixture after baking, serve as handsome and delectable appetizers, not at all difficult to achieve, but looking and tasting as if you'd labored long and lovingly.

Baked chou paste freezes well. Keep a stock of appetizers on hand. Eclair or cream puff shells filled with ice cream and stashed in the freezer equal instant—and impressive—dessert. Serve with hot fudge or butterscotch sauce for total bliss.

CHOWDER: see page 451

CHRISTMAS MELONS: see MELONS

CHROMIUM: see special feature: NUTRITION NOTEBOOK

CHUCK: see BEEF

CIDER
Made of the juices of apples (sometimes, but much less widely, of cherries or pears), the mere mention of cider con-

jures up visions of country living—hoedowns, barn raisings, harvest home festivals. With a deliciously distinctive, sweet-with-a-bite flavor, sweet cider is a refreshing, thirst-quenching beverage. Hard cider, which has been allowed to ferment, has all of those qualities and because of its 4- to 8-percent alcohol content, packs a mild wallop as well.

In the United States, cider-making is a farm-based business, a by-product of apple growing. Some local sweet cider appears in supermarkets in the fall and some domestic hard cider in liquor stores, but most cider purchases are made at farmers' produce stands along country roads. In England and France, however, cider-making is a big business; the beverage is produced by highly developed processes in factories, and is government regulated. Imported cider is "hard" and can be found in liquor stores.

Cider makes an excellent baste for baked country ham. A cider gelatin salad, brimful of chopped apples, celery, and walnuts, is an autumn treat, as is a spice loaf cake that uses unfermented apple cider as its liquid ingredient. And in many places, such occasions as after-football gatherings and Halloween parties would not be complete without mulled cider —the beverage heated with orange and lemon juice, brown sugar and spices, and served steaming in a mug, with a cinnamon-stick stirrer.

CIDER VINEGAR: see VINEGARS

CILANTRO: see SPICES

CINNAMON, CINNAMON-SUGAR: see SPICES and SUGAR

CIOPPINO: see page 451

CITRONS: see EXOTIC FRUIT

CITRUS FRUIT: see individual fruit, as: ORANGE, LEMON

CLAMS: see SHELLFISH

CLARIFIED BUTTER: see BUTTER

CLARIFY, TO: see page 449

CLOVES: see SPICES

CLUB CHEESE

A combination of two or more natural cheeses, often cheddars, flavored with a variety of spices and herbs, often mixed with wine. Club cheese is spreadable, usually served with crackers as an appetizer. It comes packed in crocks or jars.

CLUB SODA

Water highly charged with carbonic acid gas. Sold bottled, used plain as a beverage or, more often, as the base to which fruit syrup is added for a nonalcoholic drink, or some kind of liquor for an alcoholic one. Liquor plus club soda plus ice equals a highball. Flavoring syrup plus club soda plus ice cream equals an ice cream soda. The club soda has virtually no flavor of its own, but adds fizz and sparkle.

COAT, TO see page 445

COBALT: see special feature: NUTRITION NOTEBOOK

COBBLER: see page 451

COCKLE: see SHELLFISH

COCKTAIL MIXES, READY-MIXED COCKTAILS

Useful for those whose bartending skills are minimal, cocktail mixes are available for any type of drink you might want to serve and a number that may never have swum into your ken. They are made up of all the necessities for the particular kind of cocktail, and require only the addition of liquor and ice— specific directions are on the labels.

For those whose bartending skills are nonexistent, or who wish to serve a wide variety of drinks but only a few of each, ready-mixed cocktails, containing the liquor as well as all the other ingredients, are available bottled and (what isn't nowadays?) canned—the latter just the ticket for bibulous picnics and beach parties.

All this instantizing may be well and good, but there are those among us who wouldn't be caught dead with a canned cocktail, or even one made with a ready mix, believing that in this, as in most things, prepared-on-the-spot is better, and therefore preferable.

COCKTAILS

"The curse of the upper classes," according to one strident prohibitionist, the cocktail is an American invention. Mixed drinks, based on one or another kind of liquor, cocktails are drunk before (sometimes instead of) lunch or dinner. Like the drink itself, the cocktail hour is an American institution, a period of relaxed enjoyment between the day's work and the evening meal. So is the cocktail party, a favorite way of paying social obligations, at which guests stand around (there are never enough chairs) guzzling and nibbling and making remarks such as "My, hasn't she put on weight!" and "She looks great—what a marvelous plastic surgeon she must have!"

Some cocktails are stirred, some shaken with ice to chill them before they are served "up"—without ice—or "on the rocks"—over ice cubes. They are usually garnished in some manner—the martini chastely with an olive, onion, or twist of lemon peel, the old fashioned more gaudily with a slice of orange and a maraschino cherry, as examples.

There are also nonalcoholic cocktails of two classes: 1) preprandial drinks, such as tomato or orange juice, served to those who don't, or don't want to, indulge, and 2) sit-down-type APPETIZERS that start the meal—fruit cup, shrimp cocktail, oysters on the half shell, and the like. See also BEVERAGES.

COCOA: see CHOCOLATE AND COCOA

COCONUTS

You can, if you have a mind to, bring home a coconut from the market, rend it asunder, chip off the brown inner skin, and grate the meat. But not too many of us have such a mind. Or you can sit beneath a coconut palm and bribe a small boy to shinny up, bring back a nut, whack at it with his machete and offer it. You can drink the sweet liquid, cool because the shell and husk insulate it. You can eat the meat, soft and succulent, because the nut is fresh, not dried. But few of us have such an opportunity.

That coconut palm under which not many of us, alas, will ever get to sit, is a native of Malaya, but it now is grown in many tropical and subtropical countries—where, in most cases, it is vital to the economy. It is, indeed, an all-purpose tree, yielding food—the nut and the tender buds, which are eaten as a vegetable—and drink—the milk of the nut, and the tree sap, which is made into wine and vinegar—as well as fiber for rope and nets, and leaves for thatching, mats, and baskets. The wood of the tree is used for building, the roots for fuel, and the nut shells, when the meat has been scooped out, go into service as bowls. The dried nutmeat is called copra, an important commercial crop from which coconut oil, an ingredient of soap, cosmetics, candles, and margarines, to name only a few of its uses, is obtained. All things to all men, the coconut palm.

COCONUTS IN YOUR KITCHEN

If, indeed, you do have a mind to tackle a whole coconut or two in your kitchen, you need some basic guidance.

how to buy: Peak season for coconuts runs from October through December, but they are available in some quantity all year around. There are three indentations, called eyes, at one end of the nut. Look at those to be sure they are dry, hard, and free of mold. Choose a coconut heavy for its size; shake it to see that it is full of liquid, not dried out. One coconut of medium size will yield 3 to 4 cups of grated meat.

how to store: The whole nut, unopened, should be stored at room temperature. After the nut is broken apart, store the meat, grated or in pieces, tightly covered in the refrigerator.

nutritive value: One cup of fresh coconut meat, grated, but not tightly packed, contains 277 calories; a cup of dried coconut meat (from can or package) contains slightly less than double that number. Coconut water—that is, the liquid within a fresh coconut—has 53 calories per cup. Other values for fresh coconut in 1-cup measure are:

	meat	liquid	
protein	2.8	.7	grams
fat	28.2	.5	grams
carbohydrate	7.5	11.3	grams
calcium	10	48	milligrams
phosphorus	76	31	milligrams
iron	1.4	.7	milligrams
sodium	18	60	milligrams
potassium	205	353	milligrams
thiamin	.04	trace	milligram
riboflavin	.02	trace	milligram
niacin	.4	.2	milligram
ascorbic acid	2	5	milligrams

Coconut contains no vitamin A.

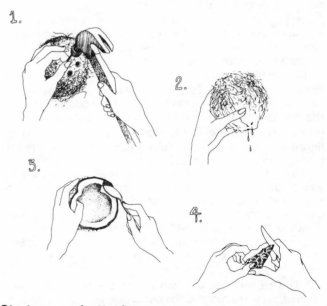

Strategy and attack. To separate the edible from the inedible part of your coconut, start by piercing each of the three "eyes" with something sharp, such as an ice pick. Pour out and reserve the liquid. Bake the coconut in a 350°F. oven for 20 to 25 minutes. Tap all over the outside with a hammer, and break the nut open. Take out the meat—you'll need a tool, such as a heavy metal spoon, to pry with. Using a sharp knife, pare off the thin brown skin.

grating coconut: Grate by hand on a grater—not one of the foremost joys of kitchen work—or let the blender do it for you.

toasting coconut: Spread in a thin layer in a shallow pan and bake at 350°F. 10 to 20 minutes, or until lightly browned; stir several times during baking. Keep a sharp eye open—when it starts to brown, it browns very rapidly.

tinting coconut: Combine a few drops of food coloring and a few drops of water, bearing in mind that the finished product will be a paler tint. Toss coconut and food-coloring mixture lightly until the color is even and of a shade that suits you.

making coconut milk: Recipes for such dishes as curries and puddings sometimes call for coconut milk or coconut cream, or your family may enjoy the milk as a beverage. If a small amount of liquid is called for, use the water drained from the coconut, or enrich it by squeezing coconut meat through several layers of cheesecloth into the water; stir well. Or place in a saucepan equal amounts of milk (cows', not coconut) and broken or coarsely grated coconut meat. Simmer over low heat until the mixture foams. Strain; use as recipe directs. Or chill to use as a beverage, alone or combined with fruit juice—pineapple juice is just right, but experiment with others, too.

Freezing coconut. Place grated fresh coconut into a freezer container, leaving 1 inch of head space. Fill container with coconut milk (above) or a mixture of half coconut milk and half white corn syrup; store in freezer, at 0°F. or below, up to 9 months.

Other ways, other forms. If you have no desire to do battle with a coconut, it's still feasible to use coconut in your kitchen, for you'll find several kinds of it in the market.

on grocery shelves, in cans or packages: Shredded or flaked coconut in cans is shelved near other products for baking. The canned coconut is moist, very like fresh, and may or may not be sweetened (check the label). It comes dried, as well, both shredded and flaked, in plastic or treated-paper bags, shelved in the same section. Not as widely available is canned coconut-milk beverage, intended for use in mixed drinks, but fine as is, or diluted with milk or fruit juice.

in grocery frozen-food section: For nonbakers or victims of sudden droppers-in, baked coconut custard pies are available, ready to thaw and serve.

The canned coconut can be pantry-shelf stored, unopened, up to 18 months, the packages, unopened, up to 6 months. After opening, store either kind in the refrigerator up to 1 month.

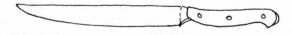

If you need coconut milk or cream for a recipe, you may make it from the canned or packaged product by the same milk-plus-coconut formula as for fresh coconut, above. For a discussion of coconut oil, see OILS, SALAD AND COOKING.

Cooking with coconut. Use flaked or grated coconut, fresh or from a can or package, in home-baked coconut custard or cream pies, piled high on the boiled frosting of a layer cake (if there's lemon filling between the layers, so much the better), drifted over fresh fruit salads or cups or compotes, in ambrosia (layered orange slices and coconut), in chewy coconut macaroons and other cookies, in candies and confections. Use coconut milk in the making of an authentic lamb or chicken curry, and offer toasted coconut as one of the sambals—curry accompaniments. Use the milk in puddings and custards, too. It lends distinctive flavor to any dish.

COCOZELLE: see SQUASH

COD: see FISH

CODDLE, TO: see page 449

COFFEE

In a quiet way, coffee has influenced if not the history, then at least the lifestyle, of many people in many lands. Coffee in any quantity was confined to the Middle East until Muhammadan priests realized that their people were spending their daily hour of prayer gossiping over little cups of thick, dark brew, and banned the drinking of coffee. Pope Clement VII, on hearing of this—doubtless working on the principle that what was wrong for Infidels must be right for Christians—gave coffee the blessing of the church, opening the way for a wide brown river to flood Europe.

Viennese coffee houses became the office-away-from-office for Austrian businessmen, who conducted their affairs over steaming cups of the beverage, topped with glistening mounds of *schlagobers* (whipped cream)—and a few pastries on the side couldn't hurt, could they, to keep body and soul together between breakfast and lunch, between lunch and dinner?

London's coffee houses were known as "penny universities"—anyone with the price of a cup of coffee (generally a penny, two at most) could sit and listen to the wits and sages, poets and philosophers of the time practicing their version of oneupmanship. Samuel Pepys' diary entry for February 3, 1663, reads: "I just looked in, on my way home from Covent Garden, at the great coffeehouse there where I never was before; where Dryden, the poet I knew at Cambridge, and all the wits of the town were assembled."

German coffeehouses kept men away from home so much that their women retaliated by organizing kaffeeklatsches for their own socializing, where coffee, coffeecake, and gossip were consumed in equal quantities.

Music was composed immortalizing the beverage—witness Bach's *Coffee Cantata*. Poetry was written lauding it—witness Talleyrand's ode:

> *Noir comme le diable,*
> *Chaud comme l'infer,*
> *Pur comme un ange,*
> *Doux comme l'amour.*

Black as the devil and hot as hell we can buy—but pure as an angel, sweet as love? Come now. Considering the haphazard methods of brewing that once prevailed, our old friend Anonymous probably came closer to the truth when he wrote:

> A loathsome potion, not yet understood,
> Syrup of soot, or essence of old shoes.

English women, socially conscious then as now, got up a petition in the late 1600s pointing out the dreadful consequences that would befall those who persisted in the drinking of coffee, including the threat that "the offspring of our mighty ancestors would dwindle into a succession of apes" if this pernicious habit continued—a sort of *Origin of the Species* in reverse.

On the other hand, Englishmen welcomed the drinking of coffee by the lower classes, pointing out, as one writer put it, that coffee had caused an unprecedented wave of sobriety among apprentices and clerks, who "used to take their morning draughts of ale, beer, or wine, which often made them unfit for business." The switch to coffee, he went on, turned them into "good-fellows in this wakeful and civil drink."

The ingenious French, however, figured out a way to drink coffee and still avoid the unhappy fate of remaining sober. They devised an after-dinner ritual in which ten cups of coffee were drunk. The first was plain coffee, the second had a small amount of brandy added, and the third through ninth (by which time, probably, nobody was counting) decreased the coffee and increased the brandy until, by the tenth, coffee was omitted entirely and the cup was filled with brandy. That tenth was called the stirrup-cup, but it is unlikely that the inbiber could see his horse by then, much less the stirrup.

Evolution of a happy habit. Legend credits a young Ethiopian goatherd with the discovery of coffee somewhere in the neighborhood of A.D. 500. He observed the *joie de vivre* displayed by his goats after eating the berries of a certain bush, the story goes, tried them himself and so enjoyed the result that he shared the discovery with family and friends. Coffee remained the Ethiopians' secret for many hundreds of years, but eventually they gave—or were forced to give—the plants to outsiders. By the fourteenth century, coffee plants were being grown in Arabia, where the people concocted a strong, black, very stimulating beverage they called *qahwah*—"that which gives strength." The Turkish version of the word was *kahvah*. From those two terms come the words for coffee in many languages: the French and Spanish *café*, the Italian *caffè*, the German *Kaffee*, the Finnish *kahvi*, the Dutch *koffie*, the Greek *kafeo*, and all the rest. The word in English did not remain constant. In 1590 it was spelled *chaoua;* by 1610 it had become *cahoa;* five years later the spelling was *cahue;* by 1640 it had been simplified to *coho.* Ten more years, two more spellings: *coffey* and, finally, *coffee,* and so it has remained.

Spreading the word. Almost a thousand years ago on the streets of Damascus and Cairo, vendors sold tiny cups of black coffee from copper vessels heated by spirit lamps. As the taste for the beverage spread, coffee peddlers like those early ones spread with it, to make the brew available to everyone. By the sixteenth century, peddlers had given way to coffeehouses—in one case at least to coffee "speakeasies," where Egyptians went to drink their favorite beverage, although authorities had banned it in 1531 in a kind of early-days "noble experiment."

In Paris in 1689, a street peddler named François Procope opened an elegant, gracious coffeehouse, Café de Procope. About the same time another former vendor opened the rival Café de la Regence. Today, both those coffeehouses are still serving regular customers and visitors to Paris.

In America, the first coffee peddler on record was licensed in Boston in 1670—a woman, one Dorothy Jones. About twenty years later there were coffeehouses in several cities here, but the beverage did not really become popular until after the Boston Tea Party in 1773. By the time of the Civil War, coffee was a part of daily living. When the war began, each Union soldier's haversack contained these staples: hardtack (a dry, crackerlike bread that resisted mold, humidity, and, quite often, human teeth), salt pork, coffee, and sugar. John D. Billings, who served in the war and later wrote about his experiences in a book called *Hardtack and Coffee,* described the scene at the end of a day's march. Each soldier, he said, made a campfire, got out his tin dipper, filled it with coffee and water, and brewed himself a comforting cup. "The little campfires," he went on, "rapidly increasing to hundreds in number, would shoot up along the hills and plains, and as if by magic, acres of territory would be luminous with them."

Like soldiers, explorers too sought relaxation in a cup of coffee at the end of the day. Everyone knows what Sir Henry Morton Stanley said on the occasion of his famous encounter: "Dr. Livingstone, I presume?" But Livingstone's answer is not so widely known. He is said—and there is documentary evidence to support it—to have replied, "Just in time for coffee, Stanley." That dialogue is so typical of British reserve and understatement, one wonders how the two of them were able to drink anything, hampered as they were by their stiff upper lips.

Coffee from plant to pot. As demand for coffee grew and spread, ways had to be devised for supply to keep pace. Cultivation of the plant was tried in many places. The soil and climate of Latin America were found to be favorable, and the altitude of the mountain areas of Brazil, Venezuela, Colombia, the Central American countries, and Mexico proved to be ideal. The rich, volcanic-ash soil, combined with abundant rainfall, provided a perfect medium for the growing of the coffee plant, an evergreen shrub. Started in a nursery, the plants are set out in rows about ten feet apart, like an apple orchard. The coffee trees begin to bear in their sixth year.

Much coffee is grown on small farms, but the bulk of it comes from large plantations—*fincas* in Spanish, *fazendas* in Portuguese. These plantations are virtually self-sufficient communities; the owner provides houses, a church, a meeting place, and a school for the large number of workers the plantation requires. When the crop is ready, everyone—men, women, and children—participates in the harvest.

The coffee bean is the seed or pit of the cherry that grows on the coffee tree. Separated from the meat and skin of the cherry, the beans are known as "green coffee," which must be prepared for market by one of several methods of drying and milling, then shipped by truck, riverboat, railroad, or sometimes—still—by mule pack to the nearest seaport. In the neighborhood of 34 million bags of coffee are produced annually for export, 28.5 million of them grown in Latin America—of those, all but half a million bags are used in the United States.

Lower Manhattan, near the Wall Street area in New York City, is the heart of the world's largest coffee market. Here are clustered shippers' agents, coffee importers, green-coffee jobbers, and the green-coffee buying offices of the country's large coffee processors. Here the imported coffee is inspected by FDA agents.

Green coffee is prepared for the consumer in plants equipped to blend, roast, and grind the coffee beans to suit the varying tastes of coffee drinkers. A small part of the imported coffee goes to small specialty coffee merchants who blend, roast, and grind coffee to the individual preferences of devoted coffee lovers who buy from them, or who make up their own special blends that their customers return for time and again.

Coffee-roasting equipment, both that of the large coffee processors who supply the many brands available in supermarkets, and of the small, individual coffee merchants, is geared to roast the green beans the shortest possible time at the lowest possible temperature to achieve the wanted result. The many kinds of coffees have varying characteristics that require differing approaches in the roasting and blending, which are very specialized skills.

COFFEE IN YOUR KITCHEN

One coffee tree's entire annual production comes down, in the final roasted and ground form in which you buy it, to one pound of coffee. If your family uses a pound a week, there are fifty-two trees, somewhere on Latin America's fincas and fazendas, that are dedicated to you and yours.

Buying your share. Supermarket shelves are stocked with many brands of ground coffee; among them there should be one that seems just right for your taste. There are a great many "standard" brands, a number of "extra quality" coffees, and, if your market is a large one or part of a large chain, one or perhaps two house brands. The house brands will be lowest in price, the standard brands next—all priced about the same amount per pound—with the extra quality coffees—again, all priced alike—costing the most. Or, if you are a true coffee fancier, you may patronize a small coffee merchant who grinds and blends coffees to his own formula —or to yours. For that, you will pay more than for the supermarket brands. If you have never ventured into the blend-your-own area of the coffee world, you might like to try. See the adjacent charts as a guide to what kinds of experiments you can make to find what is, for you, the perfect coffee.

the alternatives: Americans—in fact, many people in many parts of the world—use large quantities of instant and freeze-dried coffee. The early experiments with these make-in-a-minute beverages resulted in something pretty dreadful (and pretty uncoffeelike), but improvements have been made along the way.

Instant coffee is a powder; freeze-dried occurs as tiny nuggets. Both are, contrary to some widely held opinions, real coffee, not imitations. Both start in the producer's plant with freshly brewed ground coffee. The difference lies in the method of production from that point: oversimplified, instant coffee is dried by heat, freeze-dried is frozen into a slush and the water evaporated away. There is a certain amount of price difference, too. Generally, instant is cheaper than—and inferior to, many claim—freeze-dried.

Both are for your average, everyday coffee drinker, a category into which a great many of us fall. Speed and convenience are the keys here in producing an acceptable, but in no way a magnificent, cup of coffee.

For those allergic to, or adversely affected by, caffeine, there is the alternative of decaffeinated coffee, available ground or freeze-dried or as an instant powder. Some feel the removal of most of the caffeine also takes away part of the flavor; others feel that this isn't true or, at least, that coffee without the drug they can't tolerate is far preferable to giving up the beverage entirely.

Keeping coffee. Store vacuum-packed cans of coffee on your kitchen shelf until opened. But, unless you live far from

WELL-KNOWN VARIETIES OF COFFEE AND THEIR CHARACTERISTICS

Here are some of the universally enjoyed varieties of coffee and the attributes that have endeared them to American coffee lovers. For dedicated aficionados of the brew, flavor is not the sole criterion. Aroma (as with wine) is also important. So is acidity —high-acid varieties are often combined with lower-acid types for distinctive flavor but softened "bite." Body is the fourth consideration in choosing a coffee. Connoisseurs buy their favorite beverage in the bean and have it roasted to order, as type of roast affects both flavor and aroma. Often they grind it themselves, or have it ground to their specifications by the coffee vendor. If you like the idea of getting into coffee seriously, you may want to experiment with some of the nearly hundred varieties (only the more widely known ones are listed here) or with combinations of varieties, as well as with various roasts, until you find the flavor, aroma, acidity, body, and roast just right for you.

variety name	where grown	aroma	flavor	acidity	body
antigua	Guatemala	moderate	full, rich	high	full to medium
armenian	Colombia	strong, distinctive	full, rich	high	medium to full
blue mountain	Jamaica	strong	full, rich	high	full
bourban santos	Brazil	strong	full	low	light
celebes	Indonesia	strong	light	low	full
coatepec	Mexico	strong, distinctive	full, rich	high	medium to light
coban	Guatemala	light, spicy	full, distinctive	high	full to medium
harar	Ethiopia	moderately strong	full, slightly sour	high	full to medium
java	Indonesia	strong	full	low	full
kona	U.S.–Hawaii	moderately strong	delicate, distinctive	low	light
malabar	India	delicate	strong, distinctive	low	full
mandheling	Indonesia	light	delicate	low	full
manizales	Colombia	strong	full, rich	fairly high	medium
maracaibo	Venezuela	light	delicate, distinctive	high	light
medellin	Brazil	strong, distinctive	full	fairly high	medium to full
mocha	Yemen	strong	full, chocolatelike	high	full
orizaba	Mexico	strong, distinctive	full	fairly high	light
sumatra	Indonesia	delicate	full	low	heavy, syruplike

COFFEE ROAST CHARACTERISTICS

The roast you choose, from the lightest to the darkest, enhances—sometimes almost changes—the characteristics of the coffee or blend of coffees; specify roast choice to the coffee vendor.

American roast

lightest in color, imparts mildest flavor to the coffee; widely favored in this country for breakfast coffee, general use

New Orleans roast

(also called Continental or European roast) renders coffee somewhat darker, heavier than American; New Orleans used to roast chicory with coffee to produce distinctive flavor

French roast

produces coffee still darker and heavier than previous two; excellent roast for after-dinner coffee to be served in demitasse

Italian roast

strongest, darkest of the roasts; imparts an almost-burned flavor resulting in a rich, slightly bitter beverage with espressolike flavor

civilization, don't buy more than you'll use up in a couple of weeks. Although it will remain usable for much longer, coffee deteriorates even in the unopened can, and the devoted coffee-lover will notice the difference. If possible, buy at a busy market where turnover is rapid.

After the can is opened, keep it in the refrigerator. Treat jars of instant and freeze-dried coffee the same way. If you buy freshly roasted coffee in the bag, transfer it to a container that can be tightly closed, and store in the refrigerator. If you grind your own, store unground beans at room temperature in a cool, dry place, and grind only as much at one time as you need to make one pot of coffee. In all cases, plan to use up opened, refrigerated coffee within one week.

The quest for that perfect cup. Until about 1700, there was only one way to make coffee. Boil it. The result was a muddy, bitter brew that was enjoyed only because no one knew that there was a better way. Shortly after the turn of the eighteenth century, the French began to steep the beverage instead of boiling it. Things were looking up. But not until 1800, when the French-designed drip pot made its appearance, did coffee as we know it become available. Shortly after that, in quick succession, the first pump percolator and the first vacuum pot came on the market. Although there have been changes and improvements, these three basic types of coffee makers are the ones in general use today.

making good coffee: Start with the best coffee—that is, the best for you, the brand or private blend that best suits your taste.

Next in importance is the proper grind for the kind of coffee maker you use: regular for percolators, drip grind for drip pots, fine (or drip) grind for vacuum coffee makers. Some brands also categorize grinds for electric percolators and electric coffee makers, but the three usual grinds will serve any purpose. Choosing the proper grind is necessary for optimum efficiency of your coffee maker—fine enough to allow the water to circulate freely and extract all the good, rich flavor, but not so fine that the brewed coffee is cloudy and leaves a muddy sediment in the cup.

clean counts: Even if you use the best of coffees, blended to your taste and ground to suit your maker, you can't get a good cup of coffee unless the coffee maker is scrupulously clean. Wash all parts after each use in hot water and detergent. Be sure to rinse well. Then, just before brewing another batch, rinse the pot again with hot water. Because it is impossible to wash the innards of the drip mechanism of an electric drip machine, it's important never to put anything other than water through the mechanism. Don't use it to heat soup, for example.

meticulous measuring: Use your coffee maker to at least three-quarters of its capacity—there is no way that you can brew 2 cups of really good, rich, satisfying coffee in an 8-cup maker. If you want an occasional cup during the day, buy a small 1-cup drip filter and reserve the larger maker for those times when you want a number of cups.

Start with fresh coffee—that means coffee that you use up within a week of opening. Or, if you're a coffee purist, grind it fresh each time. The second ingredient is water—fresh from the cold-water tap; sometimes hot-water pipes deposit minerals in the water that give coffee an off flavor.

For each cup, measure 2 level tablespoons of coffee and ¾ cup (6 fluid ounces) of water. Don't skimp on the coffee or be over-generous with the water—coffee can't be stretched. Two tablespoons to ¾ cup is the standard ratio of

coffee to water, one that produces a beverage to most people's liking. However, if you prefer a stronger or a weaker brew, adjust the amount of coffee until you get just the strength you like, and then always measure accordingly, so that each pot you make will be the way you want it.

Coffee measures that hold exactly 2 level tablespoons are handy to use. Use a standard measuring cup for water, unless your maker is conveniently marked off in cups.

pleasure in the cup: For the very best coffee, serve it as soon as it is made. Despite all the promises made by the manufacturers of coffee makers, coffee that has stood for a time is not as good as the freshly made beverage. If you must hold coffee for a while, follow manufacturer's directions if you use an electric maker; for a nonelectric type, immerse the pot in a pan of very hot water, or set it over a low flame. But make sure that it doesn't boil—even a moment of boiling will spoil the flavor. In all cases, remove the container that holds the coffee grounds as soon as the coffee is brewed, and cover the pot to keep the coffee warm and ensure that evaporation doesn't make the brew strong and bitter.

The right coffee maker. Obviously, the right maker is the one that makes coffee as you like it. There are three main kinds of coffee makers, and the principle that governs each is the same whether the pot is electric or not.

the percolator: Water boils in the bottom of the pot, bubbles up through a central tube to spray gently over the ground coffee, which is held in a basket at the top of the pot. The water seeps slowly down through the coffee and trickles back to the bottom of the pot, carrying with it the full essence of the coffee.

To use a percolator, measure fresh cold water into the bottom of the pot, and regular grind coffee—in proper proportion—into the basket. (Some percolators require flat paper filters for the bottom of the basket, others do not.) The water level must be below the bottom of the basket—don't try to make more cups of coffee than the pot is designed for. Put the basket in place in the pot, cover, and heat until the water begins to bubble up to the top. Reduce heat. When the water becomes amber colored, begin timing; let the brew percolate gently 6 to 8 minutes. Remove the basket. If your percolator is electric, it probably will do the timing for you.

the drip pot: In this method, freshly boiled water trickles slowly through the ground coffee. Preheat the pot by rinsing with boiling water. Measure drip grind coffee into the center filter section; put it in place and top with the upper section. Measure fresh boiling water into the upper section (which, in some pots, is marked off in cup measurements) and cover. When all the water has dripped through, remove the upper and the filter sections, stir the coffee, recover the pot, and serve.

Most of the newest kinds of electric coffee makers brew the beverage by the drip method. Cold, rather than boiling water, is measured into the maker's reservoir; the maker heats the water, which then drips through the coffee into a carafe.

the vacuum pot: By this method, steam from boiling water creates pressure that forces most of the water from the bottom bowl into the top one, where it bubbles gently through the ground coffee. When the pot is removed from the heat, the bottom bowl cools, creating a vacuum that draws the brewed coffee through the filter down to the lower bowl. To brew by this method, measure fresh cold water into the lower bowl; set over heat. Position the filter in the upper bowl, measure in fine or drip grind coffee. When the water boils, insert the upper bowl, twisting slightly to ensure a tight seal. Most of the water will rise into the upper bowl. When it has, reduce heat, stir well, and allow the brew to bubble for a minute or two. Remove the whole contraption from the heat —in three minutes or less the brewed coffee will flow down into the lower bowl. Remove the upper bowl and serve the coffee.

the hurry-up way: A fourth coffee-making method uses a carafe, of which there are two kinds—one, with a plunger, that uses ground coffee, and a second, plungerless type, in which to brew instant or freeze-dried coffee (which, incidentally, tastes much better brewed in bulk than a serving at a time, in a cup).

Follow carefully the manufacturer's directions for using the plunger-type carafe. This gadget was invented to brew ground coffee "instantly"—a coffee-lover's answer to the ease of instant coffee. The result is better than instant coffee, if you are the kind of coffee aficionado who faints dead away at the very mention of instant or freeze-dried, but not as good as coffee made by one of the three standard methods. These plunger carafes had a flurry of popularity when they were introduced. They are still on the market, but it's easy to suppose that many of them are gathering dust on kitchen shelves, their owners having gone back to one of the good old ways, or surrendered to instant.

To make instant (or freeze-dried) coffee in a plain carafe, measure into the vessel a rounded teaspoon of coffee powder for each cup you wish to brew. Gradually add, stirring as you go, 5 ounces of cold water for each spoonful of coffee. Set over heat and bring just to the boiling point, but do not allow the beverage to boil. Or—not as good as the cold-water method, but still superior to the by-the-cup variety—stir boiling water into the coffee, and let it steep (stand) 4 minutes. In either case, keep the coffee hot, but never allow it to boil.

the distillation way: There is available (from specialty cookware shops, at a rather steep price) a gadget that uses cold water to distill, over a period of time—generally 24 hours —the essence of ground coffee. The result is a kind of liquid instant coffee. It is stored in the refrigerator, a small amount spooned into a cup, and the cup filled with boiling water to produce a beverage many coffee lovers feel is the equal of freshly brewed.

When there's a crowd coming. There will come a time in your life when you're faced with producing what seems like an ocean of coffee—for a big party, a church supper, a monster family reunion, a fund-raising get-together. Don't despair. Quantity coffee-making is simple. You can use a large coffee maker, if one is available, or a big kettle if one is not.

with a coffee maker: Follow the manufacturer's directions, if previous users were thoughtful enough to leave them behind. If not, work from these formulas:

servings	ground coffee	cold water
50	1 pound	2½ gallons
100	2 pounds	5 gallons
150	3 pounds	7½ gallons

Follow previous instructions for percolated or drip coffee— whichever kind your maker produces.

without a coffee maker: Into a cheesecloth or muslin bag that will hold at least twice that amount, put 1 pound of ground coffee. Tie the neck of the bag tightly. In a large kettle, bring 2 gallons of water to a boil. Drop in the bag of coffee, cover the kettle, reduce the heat and simmer gently 10 to 12 minutes, plunging the bag up and down in the water several times during the process. Don't let the mixture boil. Remove the bag, cover the kettle, and keep the coffee hot —but, once again, don't allow it to boil. This makes 45 to 50 cups, 5 to 6 ounces each. If you need more than this amount, make it in two kettles. Use a dipper with a spout for pouring into individual cups or into carafes for table service.

Facts and figures. Coffee, particularly for those who drink many cups a day, can take a big bite out of the food budget. But no matter whether the price is relatively high or relatively low, we still buy coffee. In 1975, when beef prices rose alarmingly, many women boycotted beef. But at the end of 1976, the early months of 1977, when the price of coffee spiraled upward and upward until it came close to four dollars a pound for supermarket brands, very few people boycotted coffee. Some people drank less (and some drank weaker coffee than they preferred), but very few gave it up entirely. We Americans like coffee—we'll give up other things, but not that.

In its several grinds, coffee is available in 1-, 2-, and 3-pound vacuum-pack cans, and in 1-pound or larger bags in those places that grind coffee to the customer's order. A pound of coffee yields about 42 (6-ounce) cups when brewed to the average strength—2 level tablespoons per cup. Instant and freeze-dried coffee comes in 2-, 6-, and 10-ounce jars. It is somewhat cheaper to use than ground coffee, but does not take the place of their favorite beverage for those who truly enjoy well-brewed ground coffee.

Also available are various kinds of flavored instant coffee—with coconut, with orange, with chocolate, with spice—in small cans or jars. Some of these, besides the flavoring, contain dry milk. They can be made in the cup or by the carafe method. Some take on added flavor and richness if they are made with hot milk rather than the hot water the directions call for, or if they are made with less than the called-for amount of water, and cream is added to the finished product.

We are so fond of coffee, it's logical for us to learn to judge a really good cup of the beverage: it has clear color, is not cloudy, has a fresh and pleasant aroma, has full flavor—neither watery nor overstrong—and is never bitter. If your coffee comes up to these standards, you're doing things right. See also DEMITASSE.

COLA

Of all the many soft drinks available to us, those that are cola flavored are right at the top of most people's lists, although cola is a love-it-or-leave-it taste that nobody seems to feel neutral about. From can or bottle, or made fresh from cola syrup at a soda fountain, a cola drink is the daily (often many times a day) pick-me-up large numbers of people prefer.

There are many brands, all depending on the tropical cola nut for flavor and each on its manufacturer's "secret" formula for flavor differences. Caffeine, a drug present also in coffee, tea, and cocoa, accounts for the lift a cola drink gives. Many call such drinks "cokes," although the technical truth is that the term is a trademark of the largest bottler of cola beverage, and should not be used to describe any other.

Occasional scare rumors circulate about the pernicious effects of the consumption of cola—that an engine block immersed in cola beverage will rust (so will one immersed in plain water) or be eaten away (so will one immersed in hydrochloric acid, which the human stomach generates in quantity to aid digestion). The truth is that—as with anything—cola in moderate amounts seems to do no harm, unless you are particularly sensitive to caffeine.

COLBY: see CHEESE

COLD CUTS

Also called luncheon meats and sandwich meats, these are available in wide and tempting variety in supermarket refrigerated cases in packages—cooked, sliced, and ready to serve. They can be had at meat markets, too, and at delicatessens or delicatessen departments, sometimes packaged in the same manner, sometimes sliced to order.

Considering that we are gobblers of sandwiches in huge numbers, it's no wonder that tasty and convenient cold cuts are so popular. But their usefulness and goodness doesn't end there. A platter of cold cuts makes a welcome change as a main dish, particularly on a warm summer night, accompanied by potato salad (hot or cold) or macaroni salad, with a platter of raw vegetables and a savory dressing to dip them in, or a bowl of zippy coleslaw. Or if you have a family turned off by liver, try them on lightly sautéed slices of liver sausage accompanied by creamed new potatoes and peas and a salad of pickled beets.

One of the easiest and most welcome meals for a large crowd is a spread of build-your-own sandwich makings, with several kinds of cold cuts, several cheeses, and several breads, plus mustard, pickles and relishes, and a bowl of crisp lettuce leaves for the finishing touch. If you want to be a bit more elaborate, add a dish of three-bean or white-bean salad, or a salad made of several cooked vegetables mixed with minced celery and onion, dressed with garlicky mayonnaise. This is the blame-it-on-someone else mixture called French Salad by the English, Italian Salad by the French, and Russian Salad by the Italians—heaven only knows what the Russians call it—probably because in its early versions it was a sort of sweep-the-kitchen mélange. Made on purpose, rather than to use up leftovers, it's truly delicious, and a nice change from potato salad. With all this, beer is the beverage of choice, coffee is always acceptable, and big glasses of (don't turn up your nose) icy cold milk taste just right. On a hot day, iced tea and/or cold fruit punch.

Back to business. We've strayed somewhat from cold cuts—thinking up party refreshments, even the simplest, can do that to you.

Cold-cut fanciers, whose name is legion, probably have a list of availabilities at their fingertips. But for those of you who haven't ventured far into the field, tending to think of cold cuts as bounded on the north by bologna and on the south by liver sausage, with no man's land between, there's a wide world a-waiting. Here's a sampling to get your thinking aimed in the right direction. All of these are ready to eat straight from the package, but some may be warmed if you prefer. Heat them, foil-wrapped, in regular or microwave oven, or frizzle briefly in fat in a skillet, or steam gently in the top of a double boiler.

sliced meats: corned beef, smoked beef, tongue, pastrami, baked or boiled ham, pork loin, breast of chicken or turkey, smoked turkey.

sausages: bologna in various sizes, several kinds of cervelat, summer sausage, mortadella, hard or genoa salami, pepperoni, thuringer, lebanon bologna, new england-style sausage.

liver luncheon meats: braunschweiger (sometimes with flecks of green pistachio nuts), liver sausage (often flavored, as with bacon), and white-rimmed liver cheese loaf.

luncheon loaves: peppered loaf, pickle and pimiento, chopped ham, honey loaf, headcheese (and souse, its close kin), olive loaf, jellied tongue, blood-and-tongue pudding, jellied corned beef, jellied veal loaf, ham-and-cheese loaf, dutch loaf.

A recent development is turkey cold cuts. In plentiful supply and low in fat and in calories, turkey is being used as a substitute for the more usual meats (beef or pork or a beef-pork combination) in many kinds of luncheon meats. Look for turkey bologna, salami, pastrami, ham, summer sausage, and old-fashioned meat loaf, as well as sliced cooked turkey breast, smoked turkey, and smoked turkey breast. Your favorite flavor a new way—isn't modern technology wonderful?

Luncheon meats are high in protein. Store them, unopened, in the refrigerator—be guided by the "last day of sale" date stamped on them. After the package is opened, keep the meats refrigerated and closely covered; store up to 1 week.

COLESLAW

Primarily, to Americans, this is shredded cabbage salad, combined or not with other ingredients—carrots, onions, green peppers, celery, whatever—and dressed with mayonnaise, bottled salad dressing, seasoned sweet or sour cream, homemade boiled dressing, or simply vinegar and a little sugar.

Ready-shredded coleslaw is available in bags in many produce markets and is usually higher in price than cabbage. This could be useful to a person living alone, who doesn't want to buy a whole cabbage. But the bagged amount is too much for one serving of coleslaw anyway, and a person who can't manage to use up a small head of cabbage is fairly unimaginative. More, unless you're lucky enough to arrive at the market at the right moment to snatch a freshly bagged batch, packaged coleslaw tends to be limp and elderly. However, if you're a convenience-food addict, admittedly some coleslaw is better than no coleslaw.

COLLARDS

Referred to in the South, where the warm climate helps them to flourish, simply as "greens," collards are a part of the cabbage family, kissing cousin to kale.

The Southern way is to cook the greens with a piece of bacon or salt pork. The resulting "pot likker" is served over corn bread, with the collards on the side. But collards can be cooked in any way suitable for spinach, chard, or kale. The big point to remember is not to boil the greens to death— usually, 15 minutes does the job. (But if you're cooking with salt pork or bacon, the meat—pork must be well done—will not be sufficiently cooked in that time. Start the meat first, add the greens later.)

Collards are available all year around; the height of the season is early winter through early spring. Look for fresh green leaves that are neither wilted nor beginning to turn yellow. Remove any discolored leaves before storing collards in the refrigerator, up to a week, in a moistureproof container or plastic bag. After cooking, store in the refrigerator, closely covered, up to 5 days. Properly prepared (see special feature: PUTTING FOOD BY), collards may be stored in the freezer up to 1 year—however, once again, because the greens are almost always available, freezer space and energy are better devoted to seasonal foods.

High in vitamins A and C, as well as iron and calcium, collards also offer limited amounts of some of the B vitamins.

COLORING AGENTS: see ADDITIVES AND PRESERVATIVES

COLORINGS, FOOD: see FOOD COLORINGS

COMMERCIAL (one of the USDA meat grades): see BEEF

COMPOTE: see page 452

COMPUTERIZED SUPERMARKET CHECKOUT

You can hardly have missed the UPC—Universal Products Code—on the labels of all sorts of supermarket items, from food through paper and cleaning products to magazines to nonprescription drugs. It consists of many closely spaced lines, bars, and numbers, printed in black on white, occupying a space roughly ¾ inch by 1¾ inches. The symbols may all look alike to you, but the computer can tell one from another as easily as mother can tell her children (even twins) apart, for each symbol is unique.

The UPC symbol heralds a whole new system of supermarket checkout, in use now in some experimental stores, soon to be used universally—its sponsors hope.

To aid us in understanding the new system, the Department of Health, Education and Welfare's *FDA Consumer* gathered all the facts, pro and con, on UPC. Here is an abridged version of its findings.

How UPC works. When the customer finishes shopping and reaches the checkout stand, the clerk slides the product, UPC side down, over a scanning device that uses a laser beam. As the product is passed over the scanner, a message is sent to the store's computer, which identifies the item, "rings" it up on the computer terminal at the checkout counter, and prints a description of the item and the price on the customer's receipt. In addition to identifying the product, the UPC, when used in conjunction with a computer, also can function as an automated inventory system, informing management how much of a specific item is on hand, how fast it is being sold, when and how much to order, and community buying patterns.

The UPC symbol itself does not contain the price, only information about the name, manufacturer, and size of the product. The computer is programmed to reflect the current price. For chain stores, price information can be stored in a central computer serving an entire city or similar geographic area. The central computer will feed data to smaller computers located in each of the chain's stores.

The quick-thinking computer. Under the UPC system, each item is rung up separately. The computer can be programmed, however, to permit volume discounts, such as an item that is priced at "3 for 29 cents." In this instance, the computer would charge 10 cents for the first and second items, but 9 cents for the third. The computer also can be programmed to permit the use of food stamps and special promotional campaigns, such as cents-off coupons that are acceptable as partial payment for certain products.

Cash register receipts that customers get at the checkout counter will vary somewhat, depending on the type of computer-assisted system used. In one system, the customer sees the brand name and price of each item flashed on an electronic screen as it is rung up at the checkout counter, and the brand name and price are both printed on the receipt. Not all systems show the name of the product on the receipt, however.

All this new technology and equipment does not come cheap. The supermarket industry estimates that it costs about $100,000 per store to set up the computerized UPC checkout system, but maintains that the equipment ultimately will more than pay for itself through increased operating efficiency, and that the savings could be passed on to the consumer in the form of lower food prices.

The major supermarkets and the food manufacturers, processors, and distributers have agreed on the design of the UPC symbol and on the technology needed to make it work. But the system is not being implemented without controversy. Consumer and labor groups have raised a number of questions and issues.

checkout speed: Industry contends that the checkout process will be much faster and that each checker will be able to handle more customers. Consumer and labor groups see a potential for increased checkout speed, but say the supermarket may use the faster-moving lines as a justification for reducing the number of checkout stands. If this happens, the result would be faster-moving but longer lines, with little or no time saved by the customer.

checkout errors: Industry says that because most of the

prices will be "rung up" on the register automatically by the computer, there will be fewer errors caused by the checkout clerk ringing up the wrong price. Those opposed to the system agree that fewer errors of this type will occur, but point out that the information fed into the computer could be wrong, or the computer could malfunction. They also argue that price increases may be coded into the computer before the price posted on the shelf or stamped on the product is changed. Customers would pay more than the posted price —and might not be aware of the difference.

sales receipts: Some computer-assisted checkout systems produce receipts that show the price, size, type, and brand name of each product purchased. Under this system, the consumer can save receipts to check back on past prices, and also comparison-shop prices from store to store. Under a system that does not have this feature, the customer is no better off than with the familiar cash register tapes that show prices, and sometimes the type of product, but not the brand or size.

check cashing: Because the computer can store information on regular customers, a check can be approved immediately. Consumer advocates agree that this would save much time, but are concerned that this information might be sold to credit bureaus or to direct mail organizations.

item pricing: This is the most controversial part of the system. Industry maintains that to make the most efficient use of the UPC computer checkout system, and to achieve maximum savings from it, prices should no longer be stamped or otherwise marked on individual items. The industry wants to continue the practice of placing the prices on the shelf under the product to which it applies but eliminate the price on each item. Industry points out that in addition to being posted on the shelf, the price of each item appears on the cash register receipt and, in some UPC systems, is flashed on the electric monitor at the checkout counter.

The Consumer Federation of America—CFA—calls the proposed elimination of item pricing "a new supermarket ripoff" and charges that package price information is second only to supermarket cleanliness as a consumer desire. If prices are not placed on individual items, the Federation says, shoppers will have difficulty comparing the price of various products—such as canned versus frozen versus fresh—since these are in separate parts of the store and the customer would have to remember a shelf-tag price instead of being able to look at the package. Also, the rapid checkout and bagging could make it difficult for the purchaser to keep up with the price information being flashed on the monitor at the checkout counter.

Other consumer objections are that prices placed on very high or very low shelves will be hard to read, and that unless the shelves are kept neat, the customer may not know which posted price refers to which product.

Some consumers also complain that if the price is not stamped on each item, they will not be able to compare the current price of a product with what it cost the last time they purchased it. Even regular receipts will not make price comparisons possible unless they include information on the brand and size of the products purchased.

The result, CFA feels, will be reduced price consciousness by consumers, a tendency that can lead to wasteful buying practices.

Supermarket firms estimate that use of the UPC system would result in monthly savings to the company of $10,000 per store or $120,000 per year. The supermarkets say that if they eliminate marking prices on individual items, food prices may not go up as quickly and, in some cases, may be stabilized. CFA estimates savings to the industry at considerably less than $10,000 per store, per month. It says that if item pricing is eliminated, a supermarket with annual sales of $3 million would save $34,700 per year by using the UPC system. The same store would save $23,000 if it continued to mark the price on each item, CFA contends. The weekly difference in savings—$225—is worth it to the store to satisfy consumer desire for price information, CFA believes.

California, Connecticut, Massachusetts, Rhode Island, and the city of Chicago have at the time this is being written, prices on each item. Several other states and cities are considering such laws. The supermarket industry says it should be given a chance to try out a system without prices on packages. Consumer advocates fear that if item pricing is once eliminated, it will never be brought back.

FDA concerns. As the agency with primary authority over food labeling, FDA has no objection to use the UPC on the labels of regulated products so long as its location does not interfere with the placement or clarity of certain required information. Information required by FDA on the label of a food product includes a list of ingredients (except on some standardized foods), the name and address of the manufacturer, the name of the product, net contents, and nutrition information if nutrients are added or a nutritional claim is made for the product.

Although it is most often associated with food and related products, the UPC system also can be used on drugs. Under its National Drug Code (NDC), FDA is assigning an identification number to every drug—prescription as well as over-the-counter. This will help FDA to identify all drugs commercially marketed in this country, and to track more effectively drug products that are recalled from the market. A company may voluntarily list this NDC number on the label of the drug. Since the NDC number can be read by the scanners used in the UPC system, the NDC number on a nonprescription drug sold in a computerized supermarket will also be used as the UPC for that product.

Prescription drugs bearing the NDC/UPC number on the label and packaged in the most commonly prescribed sizes could be processed through the computer checkout systems of supermarkets that offer pharmacy services or at drugstores that might adopt computer checkout.

Many medical products, such as crutches, bandages, and similar items, also are sold in supermarkets. Since the National Health Related Items Code established by FDA for these products is compatible with the UPC, they too can be incorporated into computerized checkout systems.

One other use of the compatible NDC/UPC number is in health insurance reimbursement for drug expenses. The pharmacist, instead of filling out the name, quantity, and description of a drug, would only need to put down the NDC/UPC number on insurance forms to provide the insurance company with a complete identification of the drug.

Will the UPC system be adopted nationwide? Time will tell. Will we, the consumers, like it—or, even, hold still for it? Time will tell that, too. We'll have to wait and see.

CONCH: see SHELLFISH

CONCHIGLIE: see PASTA

CONDENSED MILK: see MILK

CONFECTIONERS SUGAR: see SUGAR

CONSERVES: see special feature: PUTTING FOOD BY

CONSOMME: see BOUILLON

CONVENIENCE FOODS

Every supermarket is a treasure house for the dedicated short-cut lover. Women pour through the stores stuffing their shopping carts with convenience foods like kids let loose in a candy store. A new one comes out, claiming convenience superior to last week's offering, and it is gobbled up by shoppers as if the manufacturer had threatened to snatch it back tomorrow.

Hold it! Some convenience foods aren't really all that convenient. Some are hideously expensive when compared to the same food made from scratch. And some, though convenient and/or less expensive, are so inferior to the from-scratch variety they aren't worth buying at any price. In the jungle of convenience foods, the discriminating shopper needs not only to tread softly and carry a big stick, but also to ask herself some pointed questions.

Is it really convenient? It is if a) it saves a good deal of time and effort, or b) it is made from ingredients not stocked in your kitchen; c) it is less expensive than the same food in another form, or d) it is something you would not attempt to make yourself, but would like to give your family as an occasional treat or serve when you're entertaining.

What is a convenience food, anyway? The list would surprise you. Certainly a frozen, ready-to-bake apple pie is one—more convenient than making crust from shortening, flour, and ice water, rolling out half of it, fitting it in a pan, peeling and slicing apples, seasoning with sugar and spices, rolling out and fitting in place a top crust. Biscuit mix is another—somewhat more convenient than measuring flour, baking powder, and salt, measuring shortening and cutting it into the dry ingredients. From there on, mix and from-scratch are the same—measuring liquid and mixing it in, rolling or patting out the dough, cutting out the biscuits, baking them. Actually, a tube of ready-made refrigerated-dough biscuits from the grocer's dairy case is more convenient still.

Or take a whole dinner in a tray—say salisbury steak, mashed potatoes with gravy, buttered carrots and peas, a muffin, and blueberry cobbler. Leaving aside considerations of flavor and acceptability, that heat-and-eat dinner is infinitely more convenient than cooking the whole thing from scratch.

But how about a can of peaches? A can of frozen orange juice concentrate? A package of frozen peas? A bag of ready-to-dress shredded cabbage for coleslaw? Are these, too, convenience foods? Indeed they are—by a sort of rough-and-ready definition, a convenience item is any food to which something has been done that you would otherwise have to do at home.

The USDA takes a long, hard look. The United States Department of Agriculture's Economic Research Service, intrigued by the proliferation of convenience foods, decided to survey the field. Although, of course, prices have fluctuated since the study was made, the price spread—the difference in price—between convenience and nonconvenience foods, or between one kind of convenience and another in dealing with the same food, remains reasonably constant.

Price was the only consideration in the ERS survey, as it is a major consideration with most home cooks. Comparisons of flavor, texture, general goodness—all of which are subjective, and differ from one person's tastes to another's —were not made.

convenience, as defined by ERS: For purposes of the survey, ERS defined convenience foods as "any fully or partially prepared food in which significant preparation time, culinary skills, or energy inputs have been transferred from the homemaker's kitchen to the food processor and distributor." Convenience foods in this context correspond to our broader definition, and include everything from canned and frozen single-ingredient fruits and vegetables, to meat entrées with built-in "chef service"—as sauces, special seasonings.

ERS ground rules: Price information was collected from leading retail chain stores in cities in different areas of the country, reduced to cost per ounce, then converted to cost per serving. Recipes for home-prepared foods were adjusted, wherever possible, to fit ingredients in corresponding convenience foods—thus, if a convenience food was prepared with nonfat dry milk, that was also used, rather than whole fluid milk, in the home-prepared version.

The cost of each ingredient used in the home-prepared food was based on the original amount of food required to yield the final amount needed—for example, the cost of chicken in a recipe calling for 2 cups of cooked, diced chicken was based on the cost of raw chicken needed to produce that much meat. Costs for vegetables that had to be trimmed or peeled, or canned ingredients that had to be drained, were also figured on the whole item.

In the year-long study, no comparisons or allowances were made for nutritive value or culinary skills, or for equipment and time involved in food preparation—all of which are considerations important to home cooks in varying degrees.

You learn something every day. More than 160 convenience foods were studied versus their home-prepared counterparts. Of those, about one-third of the convenience foods cost less (some significantly) than the same dish made from scratch. Many, however, cost far more in the convenience form than when prepared at home. Here are some examples.

vegetables: Prices of some vegetables, particularly those that have a short peak season (lowest prices) when fresh, offer a good argument for buying the convenience kinds. Peas are a case in point. Canned and frozen peas were priced virtually alike—and 16 cents cheaper than fresh peas. Fresh lima beans cost 15 cents more a serving than canned limas, and 18 cents more a serving than frozen. Fresh spinach was 12 cents more a serving than canned, 14 cents more than frozen.

The prices above hold true the year around, because those vegetables are more expensive fresh, even in their peak season. But asparagus spears, brussels sprouts, and corn are cheaper fresh during their peak season, and become a somewhat better buy frozen or canned (the two forms cost virtually the same) out of season.

Some vegetables virtually never appear in the fresh form in general distribution, and can be found fresh only in certain areas or from certain outlets, such as farmers' produce stands. Then it becomes a matter of choosing between two or more processed forms. Butter beans are an example—dried butter beans cooked at home cost 7 cents less per serving than canned cooked butter beans.

When it comes to vegetables with built-in chef service

(such dress-ups as hollandaise, butter sauce, and so on), it's a whole new ball game. Invariably, these vegetables are more expensive frozen than home-prepared. So are scalloped, stuffed, or au gratin potatoes, whether frozen or packaged. But if it's any comfort to you (and it is, flavor aside, to those to whom deep-fat frying is a traumatic experience), frozen french fries and potato puffs cost less than the fixed-from-scratch ones.

fruits: Do you home-squeeze orange juice? If you do, it's costing you money. A 4-ounce glass of freshly squeezed orange juice costs about 8 cents more per glass (three times as much) as the same amount made from frozen concentrate, and a little less than 6 cents a glass more than canned orange juice. Lemon juice, too, is cheaper in the ready-squeezed bottles than squeezing fresh lemons at home.

Consider tart red cherries—the kind used for pies, cobblers, and the like. There is virtually no price difference between fresh and canned (and, because cherries of this kind are used only in cooked foods, not eaten fresh, there is virtually no taste difference, either). Considering that the canned ones are pitted for you, and pitting is a time-consuming, finger-staining job, canned cherries are a better buy even when fresh ones are in season.

Strained cranberry sauce—often called cranberry jelly—is cheaper canned than made fresh; but whole-berry sauce is cheaper if you make it yourself. Here, though, you have to take into consideration the price of sugar, which fluctuates considerably. If you're making the sauce when sugar prices are relatively low, you'll save; if when relatively high, it could be cheaper to buy the canned variety, which may well have been processed at a time when sugar was cheaper.

There is no argument when it comes to strawberries—they are cheapest when bought fresh. When fresh berries are not in season, frozen berries in the bulk bag (you take out as many as you need, return the remainder to the freezer) are cheaper than the smaller frozen packages or the canned berries. The same is true of peaches—fresh ones are cheapest. But out of season, canned peaches are less expensive than frozen ones.

"made" dishes: Homemade baking powder biscuits cost less than those made from a mix which, in turn, cost less than the ready-to-bake kind. But pancakes and waffles made from a complete mix (one to which only water must be added) cost only about two-thirds as much as homemade ones; however, frozen pancakes and waffles cost about 3 times as much as the homemade kind.

Frosting mixes can save you money. Pudding mixes can, too. Chocolate pudding made from scratch costs 2 cents more a serving than pudding made from a mix. Small snack-type cans of pudding, on the other hand, cost considerably more than homemade.

Apple pie, the all-American dessert, is least expensive when you make it at home from scratch. Homemade, but using piecrust mix and canned apple pie filling, costs nearly 6 cents more per serving; frozen pie costs about 8 cents more per serving than homemade; ready-to-serve (from a bakery) almost twice as much as homemade. Other pies follow the same pattern: they are least expensive when made at home from scratch.

main dishes and whole meals: Here is the area in which, by and large, you save the most by preparing at home. The difference between a frozen beef dinner and the same dinner made at home was 28 cents per person in favor of homemade; a frozen turkey dinner cost nearly 42 cents more than if made at home.

Frozen chicken chow mein costs more than when you make it at home, but the canned kind costs less than homemade. And some main-dish mixes offer bargains—lasagna mix, for example, cost 9 cents a serving less than homemade, and tuna casserole mix was 3 cents cheaper. But packaged stroganoff mix was more expensive—though only about 1½ cents a serving—than the homemade variety; chili-macaroni mix ran 2½ cents per serving more than homemade. Canned spaghetti and packaged spaghetti mix were both cheaper than homemade—probably, the ERS postulated, because the convenience versions use less expensive cheeses than are generally used at home in these dishes.

If you're a pizza fan, make it from scratch or use a mix —they cost virtually the same. But frozen pizza is something else again, coming in at a big 24 cents a serving more than the homemade or mix-made kinds.

Perhaps you like to use soy protein (see TEXTURED PLANT PROTEIN) to extend ground meat. If you do, buy the ready-combined ground meat and soy protein, rather than mixing in the extender at home—it's considerably cheaper. Again, the ERS has an explanation: markets buy soy protein in bulk, getting a price break.

fishing for bargains: Frozen crab cakes, if they are a family favorite, will save you money—about 8 cents a serving—over homemade. Both frozen and canned shrimp are cheaper than fresh by 11 cents a serving. But a frozen haddock dinner costs almost 45 cents more per person than the same dinner prepared at home, and frozen shrimp newburg was 44 cents more per serving than homemade.

in the dairy: Comparatively few Americans—more's the pity, if you're a back-to-earther—milk their own cows, pasteurize the milk at home, skim their own cream, and churn their own butter these days. So, when shopping for dairy products, it does most of us no good to draw comparisons between what's offered and the home-fashioned version. However, here are a few pointers to bear in mind. Reconstituted nonfat or part-skim dry milk is less costly than fresh milk, whole or skim. Even if your family refuses to drink it, use it in cooking. Or try combining one quart reconstituted dry milk with an equal amount of fresh whole milk—you'll still save, and most milk drinkers can't tell the difference. Reconstituted evaporated milk, whole or skim, is less expensive to use in cooking than fresh milk, and there is no detectable flavor difference.

American cheese prices are about the same for the loaf or the slices, but individually wrapped slices cost more, and cheese food in a squeeze can is triple the price of the same product in loaf form. Margarine is less expensive than butter, and stick margarine less expensive than the same product in a tub or a squeeze bottle.

Summing it up. Considerations other than price do count, of course. There are some who won't eat anything except fresh spinach, some who consider frozen just as good as fresh but canned spinach an abomination. Most people prefer fresh peaches when they're in season, but will make do with canned when they're not; others would rather have no peaches than canned ones. Some wouldn't be caught dead eating a whole-meal frozen dinner if it were free. In homes where there's a good baker, homemade cake is the only way to go; in other homes, frozen cake is far superior to no cake. Some people prefer frozen peas even when fresh ones are widely available. It takes all kinds.

Convenience foods offer an important benefit in getting home cooks to try a project they might otherwise not attempt. Many a good home baker was lured into bread-baking by experimenting with a package of hot roll mix; enjoying the results (and her family's enchanted reaction), she ventured into from-scratch baking and discovered what a satisfaction it can be.

And there are, of course, many families whose home cook's interests lie far afield from the kitchen, where his/her skills are only minimal. Such families, if they eat reasonably well, do so thanks to convenience foods.

But when price is the primary consideration, it pays to keep a sharp eye out, to compare prices between one store and another, between one buying period and another, between fresh and frozen, between frozen and canned. The canny shopper (excuse it, please) often saves a pretty penny.

CONVERSIONS: see special features:
MEASURING UP TO METRIC and
THE HOME COOK'S NEW MATH

CONVERTED RICE: see RICE

COOKIES

There are a number of laws governing cookies. 1) A cookie snitched behind mother's back is somehow sweeter than one offered for dessert. 2) A grandmother whose cookie jar is empty is subject to being drummed out of the regiment. 3) Those who do not request a snack of cookies and milk on coming home from school are ill, and should have their temperatures taken at once. 4) People who do not like cookies should be looked upon with suspicion and given a wide berth —they probably have other bad habits, such as tying cans to cats' tails or going to bed with their shoes on.

A map of the world, dotted with cookies. This very moment, there are cookie munchers in every corner of the globe enjoying their favorite snack. The French are eating langue-de-chat—cats' tongues—slim cookies that manage to be crisp and spongy at the same time. Dutch youngsters are enjoying speculaas, crisp and spicy form cookies with a bonus of slivered almonds. In Italy, twice-baked anise rusks, also with almonds, are being downed at a great rate. English nannies are offering jumbles and rocks, cinnamon sweet and crammed full of raisins and walnuts, for nursery tea. In Germany, lebkuchen—glazed honey bars with candied citron and orange peel—are big favorites. In Russia, crisp fried cookies are a treat, along with a glass of tea. In Mexico, the cookies are fried, too—buñuelos, honey-dribbled, so richly fragile they fall apart at the first bite. In Scandinavia, there are spritz, buttery cookie-press mouthfuls with a hint of orange peel or cardamom. But if you think that in China youngsters are snacking on fortune cookies, you're much mistaken— they're probably nibbling rice cakes or tea eggs, not being much for sweets; fortune cookies were invented (some say in Brooklyn) to intrigue Westerners who enjoy dining in Chinese restaurants.

Here at home? Depends on where you are. In New England, you might find fat ginger cookies, with a lemon glaze if you're lucky. On a farm in Iowa, big round sugar cookies or chunky drops redolent of nutmeg. Down South, thin brown-edge wafers or pecan lace. Wherever you are, you might feast on chocolate sour-cream drops with a top hat of pistachio-sprinkled fudge frosting. Or everybody's favorite, butter-rich toll house cookies, chock full of chocolate bits and chopped walnuts. (Grandmothers earn extra brownie points by doubling the amount of chocolate bits the recipe calls for.) Or coconut bars. Or butterscotch oatmeal cookies. Or almond crescents. Or brownies. Elmer, stop drooling at once, or go to your room!

Making, baking, storing (if they last that long). The home cook who has an attack of the vapors at the suggestion that she bake a cake or make a pie can tackle cookies—at least the ordinary run of them—with confidence and a clear conscience. Cookies are not, repeat not, hard to make. It has been said that anyone who can read and follow directions can learn to cook, but if the directions are as long as your arm and consist of forty-nine separate and distinct steps, they can be more than a little daunting. Cookie recipes are not like that. Cookie recipes are comparatively brief and simple. In fact, cookies are a perfect jumping-off point for the home cook who wants to learn to bake. And cookie-making can be learned in easy steps, starting with simple bars, progressing to easy drop cookies, and then exploring bit by bit the world of roll-outs, refrigerator cookies, forms, meringues, press cookies, and fried cookies, as well as frostings, decorations, and such esoteric matters.

making cookies: The ingredients are few, the mixing easy. Most cookies contain fat. Butter, or at least part butter, gives a taste no other fat can duplicate, but in cookies with high flavor, such as spice or chocolate, butter isn't critical; indeed, some other fat may be called for, as lard in a particular type of thin, gingery German Christmas cookie. Most cookies contain all-purpose flour, although some few substitute ground nuts or cracker meals or rolled oats or some other bulky dry ingredient for all or a portion of the flour. Some cookies are leavened, some not. Some contain eggs—generally added whole and beaten in, rather than separated and beaten separately; some do not call for eggs. Virtually all cookies call for sugar—by nature cookies are sweet—but some specify part or all light or dark brown sugar, or molasses or honey. Most cookies, other than crisp little wafers that rely on the taste of butter alone, are flavored—with extracts of various kinds, an array of spices, chocolate. Some have additions—chocolate bits, nuts, candied fruits, raisins, dates.

The simplest cookies call for simply stirring the ingredients together. Cakelike cookies cream the butter and sugar first. Some are made in the manner of pastry, combining fat and dry ingredients by cutting together.

Unlike most baked goods, cookies may be chilled before baking—in fact, most kinds profit by a time in the refrigerator, rendering the dough easier to handle. In this, as in all cookie matters, do as the recipe recommends. Follow the simple directions in a reliable cookbook—and have fun, because that's what cookie-making is, for the cook and for the mob that will gather as the glorious aroma of baking fills the house and wafts down the block.

baking cookies: You need special pans, called cookie sheets or baking sheets, for most cookies other than squares or bars. Cake pans or other deep pans won't do; their too-high sides deflect the heat and keep cookies from baking properly, and also make them difficult to remove. Cookie sheets are metal—aluminum, usually—with low rims, sometimes no rims on at least one side. In a pinch, you can turn a metal baking pan of another kind upside down and use the bottom of it as a temporary baking sheet, but over the long cookie haul, you'll need proper pans.

Sometimes cookie sheets are not greased—when you're baking very high-fat cookies—but most often they are. Use unsalted fat for greasing. Unsalted butter is fine, so is white solid vegetable shortening. Oil doesn't work well—it tends to turn brown and sticky in the spaces between the cookies. Some recipes call for the sheet to be lined with foil or parchment paper—follow directions.

Sheets should be cold when you drop or place cookies on them; if they are warm, they will start the baking process before the cookies get into the oven, making them unshapely. Sheets should be filled with cookies, spaced as the particular recipe directs. If you haven't enough cookies at the end of the batch to fill a sheet, resort to a small upside-down baking pan for the last few, because a partially filled sheet draws heat to the few cookies on it, and they may burn on the bottom or be overcooked.

Bake in a preheated oven at the temperature the recipe requires. Preheating—energy-savers to the contrary—is critical for the baking of cookies, cakes, and pies. (In any case, even where preheating isn't critical, baking time must generally be lengthened, so energy watchers—most of whom don't seem to understand cooking well—are stealing time from one end and adding it to the other.) Most cookies bake in a relatively short time. Keep an eye on them.

Remove cookies—with a broad spatula—from the baking sheet as soon as it is removed from the oven, unless the recipe directs you otherwise. If you don't you'll have a stick-to-the-pan problem. Besides, cookies continue to bake from the heat of the pan. If a ringing telephone or some emergency calls you away and the cookies do stick, return the sheet to the oven briefly, then remove the cookies from it at once. Cool them, not touching each other, on wire racks.

storing cookies: Two problems beset cookies that are not carefully stored—soft ones dry out, crisp ones get limp. Tightly covered metal containers are the answer in both cases. Squares or bars can be stored in the pan in which they were baked, tightly topped with aluminum foil, if they're going to be eaten today or, at most, tomorrow; otherwise, take them out of the pan and wrap them individually in foil.

Unless you live alone, or unless you have tried to break the record for the number of dozens made in one day, cookies usually don't last long enough to get stale if properly stored. However, it's good to know that you can restore crispness to limp cookies by placing them on a baking sheet in a 300°F. oven for about 5 minutes. To restore moisture to dried-out soft cookies, dampen a paper napkin, tear off a piece of foil large enough to accommodate the napkin, and puncture it in several places with a skewer or the tines of a fork. Wrap the napkin in the foil and store it with the cookies. You can, alternatively, store the cookies with a piece of bread or apple, but they tend to mold—the foil-wrapped napkin is safer and surer.

freezing cookies: Most cookies freeze well. Because they also thaw quickly, they are a great emergency-dessert item for the freezer. Freeze flat, on a baking sheet or stiff cardboard covered with foil; when they are frozen, bundle them into plastic freezer bags in suitable numbers. Be sure all the air is pressed out. Seal, label with kind and date—voilà, money in the bank! Baking a batch—or several—of cookies for freezer storage is a great way to work off your aggressions/frustrations and do the whole family a favor.

Thaw cookies unwrapped; if necessary, warm them in a 300°F. oven 5 minutes or so to crisp them.

packing cookies: Cookies make fine gifts, at Christmas or any other occasion, for faraway friends; all year around, cookies are a great homesickness remedy for youngsters away at school or camp. To ensure that they will travel well, wrap individually or pack lightly into a plastic bag, and surround them with popcorn, filling all the spaces above, below, and on the sides.

Cookie primer. To give you an idea of the length, breadth, and scope of the cookie field in all its ramifications, here are the basic kinds, starting with the easiest.

squares, bars, and fingers: These are the most cakelike of cookies, many of them with a wonderful characteristic chewiness. The genre covers such delights as brownies—chocolate and blond—nut bars of several kinds, and various two-layer goodies with crusts below, fillings on top.

drop cookies: Made from a dough that can be dropped from a spoon—if it's on the stiff side, give a nudge with a second spoon. Toll house belong in this category, as well as a wide range of flavors: butterscotch, lemon, spice, old-fashioned molasses chews, gingersnaps and chocolatesnaps, the elegant Florentines, fruit-rich hermits, kids' favorite peanut butter cookies, meringue kisses, almond macaroons, and a host of others.

formed cookies: These are rolled into balls or otherwise shaped with the hands before baking, from a dough somewhat stiffer than for drop cookies. They include such treats as thumbprint cookies, tiny jam tarts, almond pretzels, Christmas pfeffernüsse, nut balls, and cookies of various flavors shaped and then pressed (gently) with old-fashioned—now back in style with craftpersons—stamps that imprint a pattern on the cookies. A cookie press forms butter-rich cookies into pretty shapes.

rolled cookies: The trick here is to chill the dough after mixing, so that it will require little extra flour when the cookies are rolled. Rolled cookies come in many flavors, and can be cut out with a variety of cutters—alphabet letters, animals, leaves, flowers, gingerbread people, hearts, card pips, you name it. As an alternative to cookie cutters, special gadgets can be used, such as the springerle rolling pin that imprints a pattern on the dough as it is rolled.

refrigerator cookies: These have been around so long they started life as icebox cookies before the electric refrigerator was a twinkle in GE's eye. The dough is made into a roll that, foil wrapped, is refrigerated 12 hours or more, at which point it is of a consistency to slice and bake. Make these any flavor you like—but if you include such extras as nuts, raisins, or candied fruit, chop them very fine or the dough won't slice neatly.

filled cookies: These are generally rolled cookies, cut in two rounds—or squares or whatever—for each cookie, with a sweet filling stashed between before baking. Or they can be one big round, with the filling placed at one side, and the other side of the cookie folded over to cover it. Or the cookie dough can be pressed into tiny muffin tins or tart shells, and the filling spooned into the hollows. The filling? Mincemeat, date-nut, marmalade-nut, prune, what you will. Alternatively, the cookies may be baked first, sandwiched later—thin chocolate with a marshmallow filling, for example, or butter wafers with jam. A third way is to form (with fingers) a stiffish dough around a central nugget of goodness, such as a chocolate kiss or a mint wafer, before baking. Still another variety is made by baking a special, very thin wafer, curling it around a handy object—such as the handle of a wooden spoon—the moment it comes from the oven, then filling the resulting tube with crème pâtissière or buttercream or whipped cream, with the aid of a pastry tube.

Other days, other ways. Not all cookies are baked, at least not baked in the oven. There are several kinds of irons —cousins of waffle irons—to be used over a burner on the top of the stove to produce entrancingly thin, crisp cookies that may be served flat or rolled to hold a filling or to make small, superior ice cream cones. The Scandinavian version is called a krumcake iron, the French one a gaufrette iron. Directions and recipes come with the utensils and should be carefully followed.

Or you might like to experiment with fried cookies. One kind is Mexican buñuelos—consult a south-of-the-border cookbook for these delights. A second kind is rosettes, for which a gadget called, not surprisingly, a rosette iron, is required; this consists of a wooden handle from which juts a metal bar to which several kinds of interchangeable metal shapes can be attached. The procedure is to dip the shape into the thin, fritterlike dough, then quickly into deep hot fat, holding it there very briefly until the rosette turns a lovely golden, at which point the cookie will slip off the iron easily onto absorbent paper to drain. These rosettes, as well as kiflis, a fried cookie that does not require an iron, are usually served with a drift of confectioners sugar, as the dough itself is not very sweet. All these are melt-in-your-mouth crisp.

The Pennsylvania Dutch, those wonderfully inventive cooks, make funnel cakes, in which the dough is put through a funnel directly into hot fat, round and round in a plump circle that curls in on itself. These are served with confectioners sugar too, or with honey or cinnamon-sugar.

Whatever kind you make, however often, cookies are their own reward—an easy, not overrich dessert or snack. Did you ever hear anyone say, "No thanks, I really don't like cookies"? See also DECORATING FOOD, HERMITS, ICEBOX COOKIES, JUMBLES, KISSES, LACE COOKIES, LADYFINGERS, MACAROONS, MADELEINES, and MERINGUES.

COOKING OILS: see OILS, SALAD AND COOKING

COOKING PANS, POTS, UTENSILS: see
special feature: YOU CAN'T WORK
WITHOUT TOOLS

COOKOUT: see BARBECUE

COOL, TO: see page 445

COON CHEESE: see CHEESE

COOT: see GAME

COPPER: see special feature: NUTRITION
NOTEBOOK

CORAL: see TOMALLEY

CORIANDER: see SEEDS, SPICES, and HERBS
AND SAVORY SEASONINGS

CORN

As was the custom when manhood was near, the Indian boy went along into the woods to fast and pray. He was used to fasting, for this was a year of famine; there was very little food for any of the tribe. And his prayers arose from that."Great Spirit, send me a gift to take back to my people, who are sorely in need."

For days, nothing happened. The boy grew so weak he had difficulty moving about. At last a spirit, a youth like himself, appeared, dressed in a robe of green. "My name is Mahiz," the spirit told him. "You must wrestle with me if you wish your prayers to be answered." So the boy summoned his strength, and they wrestled until the boy fell exhausted to the ground and could not rise again. This happened on each of the following three days, at the end of which the spirit told the boy, "Tomorrow when we wrestle you will triumph. Then strip off my green robe and bury it. Tend the plot, water it, weed it, and your prayers will be answered."

The boy did as he was told, tending the plot where the robe was buried with great care. After some days, a green shoot came through the ground. The plant grew miraculously, producing ears of a grain that was sweet and good to the taste, that stayed the pangs of hunger gnawing at the boy's belly. The boy carried the new food back to his tribe. They called the grain "mahiz," after the kindly spirit who had sacrificed himself for them. And ever after, even in the years when the animals hid from the hunters and there was no meat in the kettle, there was mahiz to hold hunger at bay.

A matter of definition. In Europe, before white settlers came to the New World, there was no corn as we know it (although Icelandic sagas tell of the grain grown in the land to the west, which Norsemen had explored in the eleventh century and named Vineland). But the British and other Europeans called all the grasses that produced edible seeds—the grains—"corn." So it was natural that when the colonists learned of maiz (the "h" disappeared in the pronunciation), they called it Indian corn, and finally, just corn. In Europe today, corn is still the generic name for the cereal grains, and what we call corn is known as maize.

The early Indian corn was many-hued—red ears and blue ones, some black, some a mixture of variously colored kernels. Horticulturists bred for white or yellow ears; we still use the brightly colored Indian corn for decoration at harvest time, but to eat we opt for white or yellow kernels.

Two kinds are grown, field corn to feed livestock and sweet corn for human consumption. The grain is one of our major crops, with a variety of uses. Besides fresh corn as a vegetable and dried ground corn as cornmeal, the grain gives us cornstarch, a thickening agent; corn syrup, used in cooking and—usually maple flavored—on pancakes and waffles; corn oil, for cooking, for making some kinds of margarines, and for salad dressings; and laundry starch to give clothing a perky finish. Heat-puffed corn gives us everyone's favorite treat, popcorn; puffed by another method, corn is turned into big, sweet grains of hominy. The whole plant is used as animal fodder.

CORN IN YOUR KITCHEN

With fresh corn, time is of the essence—the briefer the span between picking and eating, the sweeter and tenderer the vegetable will be. After picking, the sugar in the kernels gradually changes to starch, losing sweetness in the process.

how to buy: If you're a resident of the suburbs, not too far from a farmer who grows his own sweet corn, you're in. Learn his schedule of picking times and be waiting—it's not polite to shove—to rush the corn home, strip it, and cook it. That way, you'll discover how wonderful corn at its best can be.

Lacking such a blissful circumstance, you can still enjoy the gustatory delight of fresh sweet corn if you shop wisely for it. The season lasts from May—in most places, this is corn shipped in from Florida—to the beginning of September, when the last local corn is picked in the East and Midwest; again, there may be shipped-in corn available until December. For the best choice, get to the supermarket in the morning. Choose ears with fresh-looking, clean green husks and golden-brown silk that is not wet and matted but has a look of life to it. Pull back the husk and look at the kernels—they should be plump and evenly full, never dry looking. Kernels can be white or yellow, but the old-fashioned white types such as country gentleman and shoepeg, once most popular, are no longer considered as desirable as the yellow kinds, the new and improved relatives of golden bantam.

how to store: In a word, don't. If at all possible, cook and serve fresh corn immediately. At any rate, don't keep it overnight if you truly enjoy the vegetable at its best. Store briefly in the refrigerator; do not strip off husks and silk until just before cooking.

Cooked corn (off the cob) can be stored in the refrigerator, closely covered, up to 3 days.

nutritive value: One average ear of corn, about 5 inches long, has 70 calories; 1 cup of kernels cut off the cob, 137 calories. Other nutrients that corn offers:

	ear	kernels	
protein	2.5	5.3	grams
fat	.8	1.7	grams
carbohydrate	16.2	31	grams
calcium	2	5	milligrams
phosphorus	69	147	milligrams
iron	.5	1	milligram
sodium	trace	trace	milligram
potassium	151	272	milligrams
thiamin	.09	.18	milligram
riboflavin	.08	.17	milligram
niacin	1.1	2.1	milligrams
ascorbic acid	7	12	milligrams
vitamin A	310	660	international units

Tips on preparing, cooking. Hurry, hurry! Strip away husks and silk (a dry vegetable brush gets obstinate silk from between rows of kernels) just before cooking. Have ready a large kettle of boiling water. Do not salt it (salt makes the corn tough); for fresh-tasting sweetness, you may add a tablespoon or so of sugar if you like. If you suspect the corn of being close to retirement age, make the cooking liquid half water, half milk. Rinse the corn briefly in cold water. Add to the pot, bring again to a boil, and boil gently no more than 5 minutes for young corn, 6 or 7 for older.

If it becomes absolutely necessary to cook corn that must be held for a time, pack the prepared ears into a pan that has a tight-fitting lid. Do not salt, but add ½ teaspoon sugar and 1 inch of water. Cover and place over the lowest possible heat for 15 minutes or longer—as long as dinner will be delayed up to ¾ hour. This method cooks corn by steaming. If you are cooking as many as a dozen ears or more, you may even extend the holding time up to an hour. The corn will not be quite as toothsome as when briefly cooked, but this way serves far better than endlessly boiling it until it hollars "Uncle!"

To remove kernels from the cob before cooking, cut off with a sharp knife. Or, if you wish only the sweet, tender interior of the kernel, cut down the middle of each row of kernels with the tip of a sharp knife, slitting the kernels but not reaching the cob; then scrape off the milky contents with the blunt side of the knife. A stripper, a gadget that looks like giant tweezers with a central toothed circle, is available to strip kernels readily from the cob.

If you prefer, you can roast young, tender whole ears of corn in the oven, on the barbecue grill, or even in the coals of a campfire. Pull back the husks, but don't pull them off. Remove the silk, then bring the husks back around the ear of corn and tie them in place. Soak in salted water for 5 minutes. Drain. Roast on the grill, over a hot fire, 10 to 12 minutes, turning often. Or, after draining, bury the corn in hot coals for 10 to 12 minutes. Or roast in a 350°F. oven for 20 minutes.

Alternatively, strip husks and silk from the corn. Spread ears liberally with softened butter or margarine. Wrap each ear in aluminum foil. Roast over hot coals for 10 to 15 minutes on each side; in a 350°F. oven for 15 to 20 minutes, depending on how young the corn is.

Other ways, other forms. Corn is all over the market, in many delicious and widely useful guises.

on grocery shelves, in cans, jars, or bottles: Yellow corn, whole kernel or cream-style; white whole-kernel corn; Mexican-style whole-kernel corn with red and green pepper bits; corn relish; golden or white hominy (see below); corn syrup, dark or light or maple flavored (see SYRUPS); corn oil (see OILS, SALAD AND COOKING).

on grocery shelves, in packages: Cornmeal (see below); cornstarch (see below); hominy and hominy grits; masa harina (see below); corn muffin and corn bread mixes; tortillas and taco shells; popcorn (see below); parched (dried) corn (limited availability).

in grocery frozen-food section: Cream-style and whole-kernel corn, and corn on the cob, in packages and plastic bags; frozen tortillas; frozen ready-to-finish-baking corn muffins in boxes of 6.

in grocery refrigerated cases: Fresh corn tortillas.

Some perfect partners. Corn is a versatile vegetable, agreeable to being cooked and served in many guises. Corn chowder—made with salt pork or bacon, plus milk, onions, and potatoes—is a hearty soup for sturdy appetites. So is chicken corn soup with rivels. Delicate corn custard and the slightly more substantial corn pudding and spoon bread are perfect to serve with ham or chicken. Corn soufflé is a high-rise delight, as beautiful to look at as to eat. Pancakes with corn kernels stirred into the batter provide a breakfast for trenchermen. Corn fritters, whether the deep- or shallow-fat-fried variety, or lighter-textured corn oysters, make a perfect all-American supper with country ham. Corn leftovers add extra substance to scrambled eggs. Scalloped corn is a great way to use the vegetable when it gets a bit elderly, at the end of the season. And never forget succotash, made with lima or shell beans, sometimes green beans, sometimes with bits of salt pork—one of the mahiz dishes that the Indians taught early settlers to make.

A cook's tour of corn country. If you remember, in *Yankee Doodle* they saw the men and boys "as thick as hasty pudding." Cornmeal mush, called (more agreeably) hasty pudding, was a mealtime staple in colonial days and was often served for both breakfast and supper, with other foods reserved for the midday main meal.

cornmeal: The meal may be either yellow or white, and is processed in one of two ways—old-style water ground (because the mill wheels were turned by water power) or stone ground, and modern-day electric milled. The old-style cornmeal is ground between two enormous millstones. The skin and the germ of the kernel are not removed before grinding, and although some of both are lost in the milling, old-style cornmeal contains some of the skin and most of the germ in the finished product. Because of this, the meal does not keep as well as the new-process variety; it should be stored in the refrigerator. It feels soft to the touch.

New process cornmeal is ground between huge metal rollers. The latter break and remove the husk and germ almost entirely. This kind feels dry and granular to the touch. It can be stored, both before and after opening, on the kitchen shelf. It must, however, be kept dry—transfer it to a can or jar with a tight closure.

Use hasty pudding today as a breakfast cereal or refrigerate, slice, and sauté to serve with butter and syrup. Make various breads, muffins, pancakes, waffles, and spoon bread with white or yellow cornmeal.

cornstarch: This is the dry "flour" of corn, the starch from the endosperm portion of the kernel. It is used as a thickener in sauces, puddings, and the like. Stir-fry mixtures are often tossed in cornstarch before cooking. In puddings, cornstarch and sugar are combined before liquid is added. For thickening hot mixtures, cornstarch is combined with cold liquid before adding. In many European recipes—particularly those of Scandinavian countries—cornstarch substitutes for part of the wheat flour, giving a finer, more compact (and often drier) texture to cakes, and conferring longer keeping qualities.

In cooking with cornstarch, do not stir too vigorously and do not cook too long—bring to the boiling point, cook 1 minute longer, and that's enough. Cool without stirring. In substituting cornstarch for flour in thickening sauces and gravies, use 1 tablespoon of cornstarch in place of 2 tablespoons of flour. Such sauces and gravies will have a translucent appearance, rather than the opaque look of flour-thickened substances.

masa: Parched corn is made by drying corn kernels slowly over fire, and is used (reconstituted by soaking, and long-cooked) as a vegetable, particularly in the West, and by the Pennsylvania Dutch. This same parched corn, limed, cooked, washed and husked, and ground into a flour produces masa, the basic ingredient of corn tortillas. It is available in supermarkets, particularly in the West and Southwest, shelved near other flours.

hominy: Corn kernels are hulled and dried to make hominy, a truly American dish known nowhere else in the world. Also called "samp," hominy was another of the Indians' food gifts to the early settlers. The corn kernels can be hulled mechanically or chemically—with lye—but the result is virtually the same. It is available dry by the pound (it must be soaked, then cooked in water or milk first, before using in various dishes) or ready-cooked, in cans. Ground, it becomes hominy grits, available in fine, medium, and coarse grinds. Hominy grits are served at breakfast—with butter or gravy—in the South as hash-browned or cottage-fried potatoes are served in the North. Cooked hominy can be used as a vegetable, and both hominy and grits are used as the basis of various kinds of casserole dishes.

popcorn: This is a special variety of corn with small, hard kernels. Dry heat causes the moisture and air in the kernel to explode into a white, wrongside-out ball many times its original size. Dress with salt and butter, or with a syrup for caramel corn or popcorn balls. What would movies be without popcorn, Halloween without popcorn balls? Where, indeed, would we all be without corn in its multitude of forms to use every day in so many ways? See POPCORN.

CORN BREAD: see CORN and JOHNNY CAKES

CORN FLOUR: see FLOUR

CORN OIL: see OILS, SALAD AND COOKING

CORN SYRUP: see SYRUPS

CORNED BEEF

Boneless beef, most often brisket, that has been cured in a 20-percent-salt brine containing sugar, nitrate, nitrite, and sometimes flavorings such as allspice and cloves. The beef remains in the pickle about a month at a temperature a few degrees above freezing. Most corned beef in markets is packed in heavy plastic. Wash before cooking, then simmer until fork tender, a matter of 3 hours or more. If you like, glaze in the oven—in the manner of a ham—after simmering. Corned beef on rye is a favorite sandwich; so is the reuben, which adds sauerkraut and swiss cheese. Corned beef and cabbage is a hearty cold weather standby, and the meat is the heart of New England boiled dinner. Corned beef hash or red flannel hash (beets added) makes a hearty breakfast or supper dish, topped with a poached egg or two. See also BEEF.

CORNISH GAME HEN

Small, generally individual-serving-size chicken—young, tender, toothsome. Most often available frozen, to be roasted—stuffed or not, sometimes with wild rice—or baked. Also available ready-stuffed. A platter of these little birds makes a very handsome entrée when you're entertaining. See also CHICKEN.

CORNMEAL: see CORN, SCRAPPLE, and SPOON BREAD

CORNSTARCH: see CORN

CORRECT, TO: see page 445

COTTAGE CHEESE: see CHEESE

COTTONSEED FLOUR: see FLOUR

COTTONSEED OIL: see OILS, SALAD AND COOKING

COUNTRY HAM: see HAM

COUPONS

Cents-off coupons—7 cents off on a package of cake mix, 25 cents off on a bag of dry dog food, and so on—are a fact of life with American shoppers. Some of us ignore them, on the theory that, because they are a form of advertising, they raise prices. Be that as it may, the price as set is what you pay, and if it's possible to knock 7 or however many cents off that price, then ignoring coupons becomes one of the many methods available for cutting off your nose to spite your face. Think of it this way: with inflation nibbling away at our food budgets, a cents-off coupon is a way of reducing the price of an item to what it was a year ago, or two, or three.

Rather than wishing coupons would go away and stop bothering you, think of shopping as a business (it is, you know) and yourself as an on-your-toes executive. Have a place to keep coupons until you're ready to use them. When you prepare to shop, make a list, then go through your cache of coupons and take out the ones that correspond to items on the list.

Coupons are printed on the backs of packages or enclosed within them; they are printed or bound into magazines; they arrive through the mail. Weed them out as you come upon them, ignoring or throwing away the ones that have to do with items you will never buy, saving the rest.

But—and this is a big enough BUT to print in capital letters—don't fall into the coupon trap. Don't let the lure of cents off charm you into buying something you don't need, don't want, will never use. Twenty cents off a frozen pie your family won't eat is a bad bargain, which is no bargain at all. Don't be wooed into buying soap the family hates the smell of, paper towels that are more expensive than the kind you regularly buy, stuffing mix when you always make your own, or anything else you can't or don't want to use. That's the con-game aspect of coupons.

On the other hand, a cents-off coupon can introduce you to a new product (that's what the manufacturer has in mind) that may be superior in some way—better, cheaper, or both—to the brand you've been using. That's a plus. But if you don't like the new product, then avoid it no matter if you've accumulated a pile of coupons for it.

COURT BOUILLON: see page 452

COUSCOUS: see page 452

CRAB: see SHELLFISH

CRAB APPLES

A crab apple tree in full bloom and, later, in full fruit, is one of the sensational sights nature has to offer us. But the pretty little rosy-cheeked crab apple isn't all that sensational as a fruit. Kids like to snitch them off trees and then nibble their hard, sour meat while wearing expressions of martyrdom, but otherwise their use is confined to jelly-making and preserving. There they shine. Golden, tart-sweet crab apple jelly is great on hot toast or biscuits or muffins, or as a condiment with meats—lamb chops and chicken livers come to mind. Whole spiced crab apples make a look-pretty/taste-good accompaniment for poultry and pork, particularly ham.

There is one excellent use for raw crab apples. Piled in a bowl—with some of their leaves, if you can come by them—they make a handsome wears-well centerpiece.

CRACKER CRUMBS, MEAL

Unsweetened crackers are crushed and sifted to produce cracker meal, sold in packages to be used for thickening chowders, coating croquettes, breading meats and fish before cooking, and for topping casseroles. Graham cracker crumbs are available—also in packages—for use in making graham cracker crusts for cream-filled pies, in tortes, and as a dessert topping.

CRACKERS

There was a time when a cracker was a small, crisp, white square of unleavened bread, suitable for serving with soup or coupled with a square of rat cheese as a snack. Things have indeed changed—today crackers come in all sizes and shapes; include such uncrackerlike flavors as chicken, cheese, garlic, bacon, celery, and beef; and are made of such varied grains as corn, rye, and rice, as well as white wheat flour, whole wheat and graham flour. In the cracker family are flat breads, rusks, and crisp square crackers like tiny, thin-shredded wheat biscuits.

Besides serving as a base for snacks and canapés, crushed crackers go into scalloped dishes. Rolled ones are used for breading, are made into "crusts" for pies, and are used to replace some or all of the flour in certain tortes. See also GRAHAM CRACKERS.

CRACKLINGS: see page 452

CRANBERRIES

There were cranberries in the bogs not far from the Pilgrims' landfall at Plymouth Rock. There had been cranberries in Europe, too—smaller than these, and even more acid—growing wild as these did in turfy bogs. No matter that the two berries were different species of the same family. They were there for the picking, and they were edible, and they made the wanderers feel a little less "strangers in a strange land," all important considerations.

Gifts of cranberries were among the many kindnesses—often life-sustaining in those first long, hard winters—which the Indians showed the early settlers. The native Americans had been using the berries for generations, not only as a food —cooked with honey or maple syrup, and dried for wintering over—but also employing the bright red juices as a dye, the crushed berries as a poultice.

The fruits are sometimes called craneberries, for the pale pink blossoms of the shrub resemble the head of a crane, and cranes often wade in the bogs where the berries grow, enjoying the fruit as a nice change of diet.

Today cranberries are cultivated—plump, juicy berries that bear little resemblance to their wild ancestors. However, more than two hundred years passed after the Pilgrims landed before a bright idea occurred to a canny New Englander. He observed that the best wild cranberries grew in places where sand blown in from the seashore covered the plants. On this principle the first commercial cranberry bog was laid out. It produced exceptional berries, and is still doing so today.

Now commercial cranberry production has spread from Massachusetts (where about 70 percent of the crop comes from) to New Jersey, Wisconsin, Washington, and Oregon and, to a lesser degree, Maine, Michigan, and Rhode Island. The plants grow in peaty soil topped with a layer of sand, which is replenished as needed. The berries are ready for marketing in the fall, when gathering them becomes an iffy business—which will come first, the proper ripeness of the berries for harvesting, or the killing frost? If frost is forecast, the plants are protected by flooding the bog. Flooding is also a method of harvesting in some cases; the berries are knocked off the plants into the flood waters and floated out. Whether by flooding or not, cranberries are no longer harvested as they once were, hand-picked berry by berry. When the wooden cranberry scoop with "fingers" to pull off the berries was devised, harvesting was accelerated, but holding the scoop was still a by-hand process. Finally, various kinds of mechanical pickers were invented that make the harvesting quicker and easier.

CRANBERRIES IN YOUR KITCHEN

Cranberries were one of the first American exports. Their keeping qualities are excellent, and tons of them were shipped to the Old World in the early days of the colonies. They also were later carried on ships as a scurvy preventative, for the berries are rich in vitamin C.

Those excellent keeping qualities make them available fresh in markets nowadays throughout the fall and winter, and they can be had frozen and in various preserves all year around. Sold by the pound, 1 pound of the berries will result in 4 cups of jellied or unstrained cranberry sauce, in 4 cups of whole, or 4½ cups of chopped raw berries.

how to buy: Look for firm, plump berries with a shiny brightness. They may vary in color according to the variety—light to bright to dark red—but should never be dull-looking. Avoid, of course, shriveled or soft berries, or those with brown spots.

how to store: Sort through them before storing, discarding any berries with soft or brown spots. Do not wash. Store, covered, in the refrigerator up to 4 weeks. Cooked cranberries may be refrigerated, in a closed container, for the same amount of time.

nutritive value: Calorie content of raw cranberries is low.

However, unsugared cranberries, raw or cooked, are disastrously sour, and the sugar necessary to make them palatable brings up the calorie count considerably. A whole pound of raw cranberries has only about 200 calories. However, a 1-pound can of strained, sweetened cranberry sauce has more than 660 calories, proving once again that you probably can win, but it isn't easy. For 1 cup of whole raw cranberries, other values are:

protein	44 grams
fat	.4 gram
carbohydrate	10.3 grams
calcium	13 milligrams
phosphorus	10 milligrams
iron	.5 milligram
sodium	2 milligrams
potassium	78 milligrams
thiamin	.03 milligram
riboflavin	.02 milligram
niacin	.1 milligram
ascorbic acid	10 milligrams
vitamin A	78 international units

Tips on preparing, cooking. Wash cranberries just before cooking, for moisture—as with all berries—hastens spoilage. Cranberries combine well with other fruits, notably with oranges and apples. Go through a good general cookbook for recipes to try, such as cranberry-nut quick bread, cranberry muffins, cranberry-raisin pie, many kinds of jellied salads—side- and main-dish—old-fashioned roly-poly made with the berries, and various cranberry jellies, chutneys, and relishes.

Freezing cranberries. Properly prepared (see special feature: PUTTING FOOD BY), cranberries can be stored at 0°F. or below up to 1 year.

Other ways, other forms. It's a shame to confine cranberries to the holiday season, when they're delicious—and available in several forms—all year around.

on grocery shelves, in cans, jars, or bottles: Canned cranberry sauce, either strained (cranberry jelly) or whole-berry; cranberry-apple sauce; cranberry-orange relish; cranberry juice cocktail, both (nutritive sweetener) regular and diet-pack (artificial sweetener); cranberry-apple juice cocktail, sometimes labeled "cranapple."

in grocery frozen-food section: Frozen whole cranberries in 1-pound boxes; at the holiday season, cranberry ice or sherbet.

Here in the United States we consume cranberries in large amounts, particularly from Thanksgiving through New Year's day. Only the Scandinavian countries rival us in enjoyment of the fruit, using lingonberries—a smaller, spicier variety of cranberry than our native ones—in many ways as a relish or a sauce. Tiny, thin Swedish pancakes *(plättar)* come

to the table with lingonberry sauce, for example. The tart goodness of cranberries complements many flavors throughout the meal, at home and abroad.

CRANBERRY BEANS: see BEANS

CRANSHAWS: see MELONS

CRAYFISH: see SHELLFISH

CREAM

Years ago, the milkman delivered whole milk in bottles to our door, white in the bottom three-quarters of the bottle, richly yellow in the top quarter where the cream had risen. If we were thrifty, we poured off the "top milk" to cream our coffee or to use over cereals and puddings, and drank the milk or used it in cooking. Nowadays, milk is homogenized (the cream permanently incorporated into it), and it is seldom delivered to our doorsteps. Instead we buy milk and cream separately at the market or dairy store. Sweet cream can be had in several degrees of richness, depending on the butterfat content (regulated), so that it does not vary from brand to brand. Dairy sour cream—a far cry from sweet cream that has soured naturally in the refrigerator—is also available.

Fat and other nutrients. Thick and rich and ineluctably smooth, cream both sweet and sour plays a stellar role in our kitchens, as an ingredient in cooked foods and as a topping for a wide variety of dishes.

As the butterfat content varies with the type of cream, so does the calorie content. Here are figures, in 1-tablespoon amounts:

cream type	butterfat	calories
half-and-half	11.7%	20
light ("coffee cream")	20.6%	32
light whipping	31.3%	45
heavy whipping	37.6%	53
dairy sour cream	18.0%	30

In the way of nutrients other than the butterfat, cream offers protein—the higher the fat content, the lower the protein—calcium, and vitamin A, as well as small amounts of other minerals and of the B vitamins and vitamin C.

Dried cream, consisting of milk solids and light cream solids plus stabilizers, is also available. The butterfat and calorie content of these varies from brand to brand—read the label. And there are nondairy "creamers" on the market as well, both dried and frozen liquid, which do not contain any cream at all. Don't be misled into believing that these are necessarily lower in calories than the real thing—again, read the label.

Topping and cooking with cream. Highly perishable, cream must be stored in the coldest part of the refrigerator.

When you buy it, check the date on the carton, and do not buy more than you will use in up to 4 days. Half-and-half (half milk, half light cream) and light cream are the choices for pouring over cereals and pudding and for creaming beverages. They are also used in cooking, to enrich custards and sauces. Half-and-half is sold in pint (2-cup) containers, and in quarts (4 cups); light cream is most often sold in half-pint (1-cup) containers.

heavy cream: This used to be the most perishable of the lot, but a few years ago a heavy cream appeared on the market that was processed by a new method that, to put it untechnically, postponed souring. Heavy cream of this kind can be refrigerator-stored for a matter of weeks rather than days, allowing us to have it on hand as we need it.

Although some markets stock both kinds, the heavy (37.6 percent butterfat) whipping cream is the more widely available. When whipped, heavy cream doubles in volume— 1 cup fluid cream produces 2 cups of whipped cream. For best results, the cream should be beaten in a chilled bowl with a chilled beater—electric or dover beater, or a wire whisk. If you use the electric mixer, set it at medium speed until the cream begins to thicken, then at low speed until the cream retains a soft shape. For decoration—to be piped through a pastry tube, for example—cream must be whipped until stiff. But be careful, because at that stage, you have stiffly whipped cream one moment and butter the next.

Fold sugar (superfine or confectioners dissolves better than regular granulated) and flavorings into the cream after it has been whipped. Properly prepared, whipped cream should hold in the refrigerator for about 2 hours. If for some reason you wish it to retain its shape and consistency for a longer time, it can be stabilized with gelatin. Soften 1 teaspoon (about ⅓ of an envelope) gelatin in 2 tablespoons cold water. From 1 cup heavy cream, remove 3 tablespoons and scald it; add to gelatin and stir until dissolved. Refrigerate until thickened but not set, and beat until frothy. Whip remaining cream; add a few grains salt, 2 tablespoons confectioners sugar, ½ teaspoon vanilla. Fold in the gelatin mixture. This stabilized cream—tinted a delicate pastel with food coloring if you like—pipes beautifully through a pastry tube, holds its shape overnight. (Refrigerate the cake or whatever you've used the cream to decorate.) If you wish chocolate cream, melt one 6-ounce package of semisweet chocolate pieces, cool slightly, and fold into the stabilized whipped cream.

Whipping cream is sold in half-pint (1-cup) and quart (4-cup) containers. Whipped cream in a squirt-top can is available in dairy cases. It is not as thick or rich as cream whipped at home. Similar cans of nondairy whipped topping are shelved close by.

sour cream: "Dairy sour cream" is its proper name, to distinguish it from cream that has soured by accident, of old age, or in your refrigerator. (Don't throw out such accidents, though—they enrich pancakes and waffles and biscuits, making them delicately tender.) Dairy sour cream is made of sweet cream to which a culture has been added; it is timed and temperature-controlled until it develops just the right degree of that wonderful tart/nutty flavor. Chilling at that point halts the action of the culture, and dairy sour cream results.

Available in pint and half-pint cartons, commercial sour cream has innumerable kitchen uses. It is a superlative topping for fruit desserts—try it on an old-fashioned blueberry roly-poly, or with light brown sugar on fresh strawberries. Dabbed on a slice of toast already spread with strawberry jam, sour cream is the ultimate in lily-gilding.

Added to sauces—beef stroganoff comes to mind—sour cream smooths and enriches and imparts a wonderful flavor. When you add sour cream to such sauces, let it heat through but do not allow the sauce to boil. If sour cream is to be added to a sauce that must boil, stir flour into the cream before adding it to keep it from curdling.

Polish mushrooms are a simple but heavenly sour-cream concoction. Sauté mushrooms lightly in butter with a little onion, stir in sour cream and heat through. Season to taste with salt and white pepper, and serve on toast triangles— which, if you wish to make a more substantial dish, may first be topped with thin slices of ham or frizzled dried beef (watch the salt in both cases) or soft-scrambled eggs. Baked potatoes feel undressed without a topping of sour cream. But enough, enough—this is a kitchen book, not a cookbook.

Freezing cream. Don't—not liquid cream, that is. It separates and is barely usable, if at all, when thawed. However, whipped cream can be successfully frozen in small amounts. Drop spoonfuls, or pipe small mounds through a pastry tube, onto aluminum foil. Freeze flat, uncovered; when frozen, overwrap and return to freezer.

CREAM, TO: see page 445

CREAM CHEESE: see CHEESE

CREAM OF TARTAR

A leavening agent, most often beaten into egg whites, as a recipe directs. It stabilizes the egg whites and (as in meringues) increases their tolerance of heat. A natural fruit acid made from grapes, cream of tartar is an ingredient of commercial baking powders. Alone, it is used in candies and frostings for creamier consistency. See BAKING POWDER.

CREME BRULEE: see PUDDINGS AND CUSTARDS

CREME PATISSIERE: see page 452

CREPES

About the middle of the 1970s, these thin, delicate pancakes began to sweep the country. Before that they were chiefly found—most often in good restaurants—as Crêpes Suzette (orange-and-brandy-sauced dessert crepes) or as the wrapping of quality canneloni or, less frequently, in a dish of seafood crepes with a mousseline sauce.

The batter, which may be sweetened or not, is rather thin, made of milk, eggs, butter, and flour. Unsweetened crepes—for appetizers or main dishes—may be filled with any meat or fish or poultry or vegetable mixture thick enough to stay within the rolled crepe, and are most often served with a sauce. (Filling for crepes is an elegant way to use up leftovers.) Sweet crepes take a cream or fruit filling or, unfilled and folded rather than rolled, rely on their sauce (often flambéed) for flavor.

Crepes are cooked one at a time in a 6- or 7-inch skillet or in one of the top-of-stove or electrical crepe-making pans that have proliferated since the crepe craze came into being. They usually are browned on one side only, and that becomes the outside when the crepes are rolled or folded.

Easy to make, once you get the hang of it, crepes can be manufactured in large batches and stashed in the freezer (separate with pieces of wax paper, overwrap in convenient numbers) for later serving. Great for expected or unexpected company.

CRIMP, TO: see page 445

CRISP, TO: see page 450

CROOKNECK: see SQUASH

CROQUETTE: see page 452

CROUSTADES: see BREADS

CROUTONS

Small bread cubes, oven-toasted or butter-browned in a skillet, croutons are used for garnishing soups, salads, and vegetables, and as casserole toppings. They may be made at home or purchased packaged, plain or perked up with cheese, onions or garlic, or herbs in various combinations. See BREADS.

CRUDITES: see APPETIZERS

CRUMBS

Used as a (major) ingredient in stuffings and a (minor) one in several kinds of ground-meat mixtures, notably meat loaves, and as a coating when breading meats, fish, or poultry, crumbs may be soft or dry. The soft crumbs are made at home by the simple expedient of crumbling day-old bread between the fingers, crusts removed or not as you choose. Dry bread crumbs may be made at home by first drying the bread in the oven, then crumbing it in a blender, or they (and various kinds of cracker crumbs) may be purchased, plain or seasoned, in pour- and/or shaker-topped packages. See also BREADS and CRACKERS.

CRUSH, TO: see page 445

CRUSTS: see PASTRY

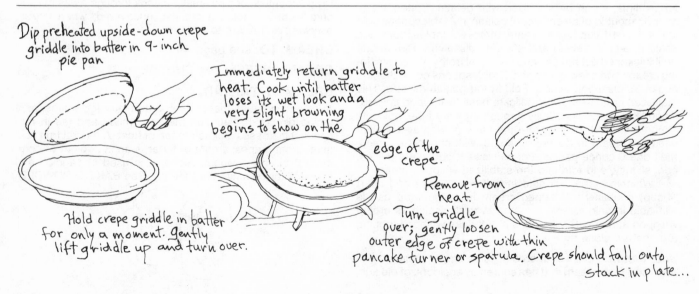

Dip preheated upside-down crepe griddle into batter in 9-inch pie pan

Hold crepe griddle in batter for only a moment. Gently lift griddle up and turn over.

Immediately return griddle to heat. Cook until batter loses its wet look and a very slight browning begins to show on the edge of the crepe.

Remove from heat. Turn griddle over; gently loosen outer edge of crepe with thin pancake turner or spatula. Crepe should fall onto stack in plate...

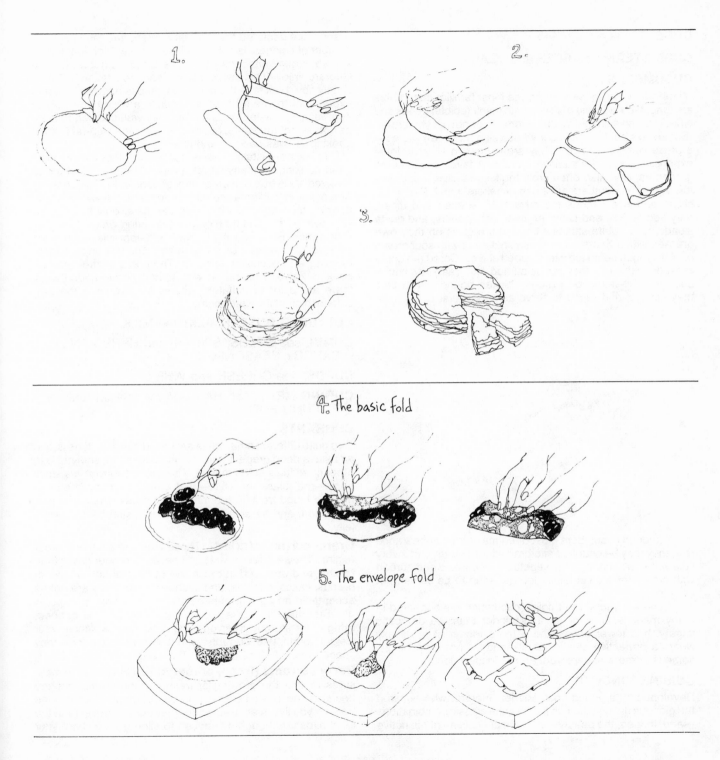

1.

2.

3.

4. The basic fold

5. The envelope fold

CUBE, TO: see page 445

CUBE STEAK: see BEEF and VEAL

CUCUMBERS

Members of the squash family, the most familiar cucumbers are long, tapered, mild of flavor, with many (edible) seeds and a deep-green skin that you may remove or not, as you prefer. (But always peel a cucumber whose skin has been waxed—a preservative measure.) They are in season all year, least expensive during the summer months. A favorite with home gardeners, who also often grow the less-familiar round, yellow variety, cucumbers are a salad-makers' must. Cartwheel slices enhance various tossed salads; seeded and diced, they add texture and flavor to meat, fish, poultry, and pasta salads, give potato salads a lift, and are great on their own dressed with a vinegar-sugar combination or with sour cream or plain yogurt sprinkled with snipped chives. Cored (an apple corer does the job), they can be stuffed with a savory mixture, such as well-seasoned minced chicken bound with a little mayonnaise, and sliced to serve as appetizers.

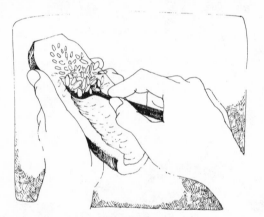

Although cucumbers most often make their appearance raw, they may be chunked and braised with butter and a very little water to serve as a hot vegetable, or cooked and puréed with cream for a delectable, delicate soup to be served hot or cold.

In recent years, the English cucumber has appeared in many markets. It is longer and thinner than the domestic variety, has fewer seeds and a more tender skin, usually wears a protective plastic jacket—and is, not surprisingly, somewhat more expensive than the local product.

CUISINE MINCEUR

Developed by a young chef, Michel Guérard, who admired the glorious flavors, the rich sauces, the classic combinations—and, indeed, the beauty—of the haute cuisine of his native France, but deplored the high-fat content and the incredible number of calories, la cuisine minceur is diet food that tastes superb, looks handsome. The idea arose from the fact that Guérard enjoyed his own cooking—and grew fat on it. But he simply could not face the usual weight-loss diet. He began to experiment to see if he could produce a whole new way of approaching low-fat foods so that they would look and taste as good—not the same, but as good—as the high-fat French cooking he was used to and loved.

Make no mistake, this is not throw-it-together-and-forget-it cooking. In many cases, preparation time is long and involved, as is true of a great deal of nondiet French cooking. And some ingredients are difficult to come by—fresh thyme flowers, for example, which you can have only if you grow your own herbs, and then only in the spring when the thyme is flowering. But if you like to cook and appreciate subtleties of flavor and beauty of presentation, you will enjoy experimenting with la cuisine minceur. There is a Michel Guérard cookbook available and, as with so many other good things, there are a lot of imitators who've latched onto the low-calorie/high-style gastronomy.

CULTURED BUTTERMILK: see MILK

CUMIN: see SEEDS, SPICES, and HERBS AND SAVORY SEASONINGS

CURDS: see CHEESE and WHEY

CURING MEAT: see HAM and the special feature: PUTTING FOOD BY

CURRANTS

Two quite different small fruits are called currants. One is, like a raisin, a dried grape; these we find packaged, shelved with other dried fruits in the market. The second currant is a small berry—red, black, or white—that grows in cool climates; it may be found fresh in the markets of areas where it grows, in season, and as preserves, the most usual being currant jelly.

Grape currants (dried). These look like smaller, harder raisins. They are less sweet and have a stronger flavor than raisins, and are used in much the same manner—in sweet breads, cakes, cookies, and such. However, they are not as acceptable an eat-out-of-hand sweet as raisins.

Buy them in packages for shelf storage until opened, refrigerator storage after opening. If you are watching your weight, don't use currants with too lavish a hand—they "cost" nearly 210 calories per half cup.

Berry currants (fresh, preserved). Conservation measures restrict the growing of fresh currants in this country because the bush carries a fungus harmful to white pine trees. If you live in an area where they can be grown (and the local birds are thoughtful enough to allow you to share your crop), or if you find the fresh berries in the market in their brief season, serve them fresh with sugar and cream, or make currant jelly. Tart and richly red, the jelly is good on toast or biscuits, comes into its own as an accompaniment for meats —a sparkly glaze for ham, the chief ingredient in Cumberland Sauce, and a fine game or poultry condiment.

Bar-le-duc, that elegant French preserve, is made of red or white currants by a time-consuming process that requires pricking each individual berry with a needlelike instrument before cooking. Black currants are used to make crème de cassis, a liqueur. Kir, a refreshing aperitif, is made by adding a little crème de cassis to chilled white wine.

Store fresh currants, unwashed, in the refrigerator for no more than 2 days. Count on less than 35 calories per half cup of fresh currants, of whatever color.

CURRY

Devised to hide—before the days of refrigeration—the flavor of too-old meat, curry seasonings are an assertive blend of spice flavors that add piquancy to many dishes. Curry powder (see SPICES and HERBS AND SAVORY SEASONINGS) is available commercially, but if you're adventurous, you can blend your own curry seasoning mixture as cooks in India do. If you can't find all the ingredients, there are substitutes available. Besides, no two curry seasonings are exactly alike— blend yours to suit your own taste.

Curry seasoning ingredients. Some of these you'll find in the produce section of your market, some in the spice section. And some you may have to go far afield for, or omit, or use a substitute. Here are basics to pick and choose among.

peppers: Green chilies (fresh or canned), dried red chilies, or use chili powder for a mild, red curry, adding a bit of cayenne for bite; if you use fresh or canned chilies, remember that the seeds are the hottest part—remove them all, or leave some for extra heat.

spices: Coriander seeds and cumin seeds for pungency; cinnamon, cloves, cardamom for sweet spicy flavor; turmeric for both flavor and golden color.

vegetables, herbs: Cilantro (or find it labeled fresh coriander or chinese parsley)—if you can't find fresh, use the dried leaves from the spice shelf; onions and garlic are old friends; fresh ginger is often available—if not, add a bit of dried ginger, or wash the sugar from candied ginger and chop it; lemon grass—most often available in health food stores, where it is sold (dried) as a tea; tamarind pods are for flavor and tartness—available in Mexican or Oriental food stores, or substitute lemon juice.

seasonings: Shrimp paste is a smelly concoction of fermented shrimp—if you can't find it, use anchovy paste; fish soy is equally smelly, a thick sauce used for salty flavor— substitute soy sauce or plain salt.

Curry seasonings should be mixed before adding to the dish they are to flavor. Experiment until you get a taste you like, then mix with a little liquid or heat in a little fat before adding to the dish. And gently is the watchword—you can always add more, but you can't remove too much.

Curry on the menu. Almost all meats and poultry are delicious in a curry dish. Brown, then braise, beef, lamb, veal, chicken—whatever meat you want as the basis for your curry —using little water. If you wish, cook with celery, onions, and add peeled and sliced apples near the end of the cooking period. For mellowness, add coconut milk (see COCONUT) or plain yogurt or sour cream to the sauce. Season to taste with commercial curry powder, or your own curry mixture.

Serve the curry with fluffy rice, white or brown, chutney —homemade or one of the many bottled varieties—a salad of cucumbers dressed with plain yogurt and chopped mint, another of cooked lentils in oil and vinegar, and bananas briefly sautéed in butter or oil and very lightly sprinkled with mace. Provide a selection of sambals. A curry meal is built on a foundation of rice, the curry is spooned over, sambals are sprinkled on top.

sambals: Serve each of these in its own small bowl or dish, and let guests help themselves. Choose six or seven from the list below—they add flavor and texture to the curry.

chopped peanuts	julienne green pepper
toasted coconut	chopped (fresh or canned) mango
pickled lemons (buy	sieved hard-cooked egg yolk
them in specialty	chopped hard-cooked egg white
shops, in jars)	grated raw turnip
thinly sliced scallions	slivered preserved ginger
thinly sliced radishes	or grated fresh ginger
tiny whole shrimp	french fried onions (from a can)
diced fresh melon	white raisins
pomegranate seeds	chopped tomato
chopped apple (if you	snipped dried apricots
have not used	
it in the curry)	

A curry meal is fine for a crowd. Make the curry in advance—it's one of those blessed dishes that improves on standing. Serve buffet style, with lots of cold beer to soothe the fire. (Don't offer wine with curry—it's an insult to the wine to expect it to compete, and besides, the flavors hate one another. For nondrinkers of beer, offer iced tea.) Fresh fruit for dessert, or guava shells—find them in the gourmet-food section—with cream cheese.

CUSTARD APPLES: see EXOTIC FRUIT

CUSTARDS: see PUDDINGS AND CUSTARDS

CUT IN, TO: see page 445

CUTLERY: see special feature: YOU CAN'T WORK WITHOUT TOOLS

CUTLET: see page 452

CYCLAMATE: see SACCHARIN

CYMLING: see SQUASH

NUTRITION NOTEBOOK

The Compleat Kitchen Executive must be (as well as chief cook and bottle washer) something of a juggler—keeping the family diet properly balanced is no mean feat

If we indeed were what we eat, as the old saying tells us, we'd be a pretty sorry lot. We all have met the woman who bears a striking resemblance to a cream puff, the man who is best described as a string bean, the cute, baby-fat little girl who looks like a bonbon—these are unfortunate coincidences.

Aside from the obesity of those who will eat anything and everything that isn't nailed down, the damage we do ourselves through improper diet is insidious. There is no scarlet letter blazoned on the bosoms of careless eaters like Hester Prynne's "A" to make them stand out in a crowd.

The teenager who subsists largely on colas and potato chips doesn't look all that different from his proper-diet peers. But he *feels* different. He's listless, lacking in energy. He's not the bright-eyed, bushy-tailed fellow he'd (perhaps secretly) like to be, popular with everyone, participating in sports, very big with the girls. Schoolwork, as does everything else, comes hard. And it's not, as parents sometimes like to comfort themselves, because "he's growing so fast—he's putting all his energy into growing, and hasn't any left over for anything else." The blunt truth is that he's not getting enough to eat. Not enough of the right foods. Even the teenager who seems to eat enough to keep an army on the move may well be, in a sense, starving. And so are thousands of adults—tall ones and short, fat ones and thin, successful ones and failures—suffering from poor nutrition.

The simple fact is this: If you eat a nourishing, well-balanced diet you will be, all other things being equal, a healthy, sturdy, energetic human being. Probably a contented one, too, because feeling well physically has a lot to do with being able to face each day with a positive, optimistic attitude.

THE BASIC FOUR

Before we go any farther, let's get one thing straight. Feeding your family a properly balanced diet is not a matter of constant weighing and measuring, of relentless adding-to and subtracting-from. Nor is it a matter of serving dull, regimented meals. Nor of constantly prohibiting the things that are each family member's favorite foods. Once you master the basics —and even that is no overwhelming learning experience— you'll find that you can serve nutritionally balanced meals that are also delicious, welcomed meals, as automatically as you accomplish dozens of other daily chores.

Each of the foods we eat falls into one of the Basic Four food categories: meat, fish, and poultry; fruits and vegetables; breads, cereals, and pastas; milk and dairy products. There is a certain amount of crossover among these categories. Meat—and that includes poultry and fish—is the prime source of protein, but cheese, a dairy product, is also protein-rich. Dried peas and beans, certain nuts, and some cereal products also contribute protein to the diet.

From these four groups come all the nutrients that sustain our lives. Proper quantities of each of those nutrients ensure us of the feeling of well-being that comes from good health.

The chart on the next page shows *minimum* daily portions for adults in good health on a regular (not a weight-loss) diet. Most adults eat more than this daily minimum from some or all of the groups, supplemented with nonrequired food, such as butter and sugar.

A CLOSER LOOK AT THE NUTRIENTS

From the foods of the Basic Four in proper balance we derive the nutrients we need to stoke our engines and keep them in good repair. What's a nutrient? The dictionary says "that which furnishes nourishment," which is encouraging but not all that helpful. Why do we need to be nourished? Let's take a one-by-one look at the nutrients to find out.

Protein, the builder. The enzymes controlling the processes that keep the body in working order are made of protein, which is also part of the hemoglobin molecule in red blood cells that carries oxygen through the system. Also protein are the antibodies, carried in the blood stream, that fight off disease and infection. The body uses protein to build muscle tissue that holds our skeletal structure together and gives us the ability to move, to work and play and carry on our daily lives.

Made up of substances called amino acids, protein from the food we eat is broken down by the body into the separate amino acids, which are then rearranged by means of our unbelievably intricate body chemistry into the particular combinations needed to build the various types of tissue. Some of the needed amino acids can be produced by the body. Others, which the body cannot manufacture, must come from the foods we eat. The latter are termed "essential" amino

Food Group	Serving Size	Nutrients Supplied
meat and protein-rich foods	*one serving is:*	
2 servings of meat, fish, poultry, eggs, or cheese; occasionally dried beans, peas, nuts, etc., may be substituted for the meats	3 ounces lean cooked meat, fish, or poultry 3 eggs 3 slices (ounces) cheese 1 to 1½ cups cooked beans or peas ⅓ cup peanut butter	protein, iron, niacin, and the other B vitamins
fruits and vegetables	*one serving is:*	
4 servings of fruits and vegetables; be sure to include 1 serving of citrus fruit or tomatoes and one of dark green or leafy vegetables daily	½ cup canned or cooked fruit 1 fresh peach, pear, etc. 1 cup fresh berries or cherries 1 cup uncooked leafy vegetables ½ cup cooked vegetables	vitamins A and C, plus the other vitamins and minerals, as well as food fiber
breads, cereals, pastas	*one serving is:*	
4 servings of enriched or whole-grain cereals and breads	1 slice bread 1 small biscuit, muffin, or roll ½ cup potatoes, pasta, or rice ¾ to 1 cup flaked or puffed dry cereal ½ cup cooked cereal	important sources of B-complex vitamins; supplemental amounts of protein and iron; some food fiber
milk and milk products	*one serving is:*	
2 servings of milk and other dairy foods for adults; 3 or more servings for children; 4 or more servings for teenagers	8-ounce glass whole or skimmed milk 1 ounce (1 slice) cheese ½ cup cottage cheese	significant amounts of calcium, protein, and riboflavin, as well as vitamins A and D and the B-complex vitamins

acids, although all of them are necessary to the body's well-being. Proteins containing all the essential amino acids in the proportions needed by the body are of superior nutritional quality. These come from animal sources—meat, fish, poultry, eggs, cheese, and milk.

The animal foods provide what is called the "high-quality protein." Bread and cereals supply some protein, too, as do such vegetables as soybeans, chick-peas, dry beans, and peanuts. Combining cereals or vegetables (imperfect protein) with a small amount of animal (high-quality) protein provides the kind of protein the body needs and is able to utilize. Examples of such combinations are cereal with milk, rice with fish, spaghetti with meat sauce. When you serve a meal low in protein, either vegetable or animal, making sure everybody drinks a glass of milk with the meal will take care of the deficiency.

Fat, for energy—and for flavor. The stick-to-the-ribs quality that makes meals satisfying is a result of the fat content. Fat gives you the feeling of having eaten well, of being comfortably and contentedly full and prepared, according to your preferences, to take a cosy nap or round up a few friends for a game of touch football. (You're better off if you choose football. Or even a brisk walk. Or even a not-so-brisk one.)

But the feeling of satiety they produce is far less important than the fact that fats are an essential part of the structure of the cells that make up the body's tissues. Fats also carry vitamins—the fat-soluble ones—throughout the body. And fats provide the cushioning that protects vital organs. Women, no matter how fashionably thin or pleasingly plump, all have a subcutaneous—just under the skin—layer of fat that is lacking in men. It's believed to have been provided by nature long ago, when the world was a very chancy place in which to live, to help protect a woman's unborn child.

Butter, margarine, shortening, oils, cream, most cheeses, mayonnaise, salad dressings, nuts, and such high-fat meats as bacon provide plentiful fat. Some people delight in the fat that edges a good steak, while others carefully cut it away. Whichever is your preference, you'll get sufficient fat from other sources without the crisp steak edging. Most meats have considerable fat throughout, not as apparent—and not as easily removed—as that on a steak. Fats are one of the leading cut-downs in most weight-loss diets.

Carbohydrates, the fuel we burn. Starches and sugars—the carbohydrates—are found in cereal grains, in fruits and vegetables (and, of course, in the foods we make from them), and in the sugar we add to food for sweetening. These are the major sources of energy in our diet. Wheat, oats, corn, and rice and their products—bread, pasta, grits, cakes, pastries, and so on—provide starch in the diet along with other nutrients. So do potatoes, both white and sweet, as well as such other vegetables as peas, dry beans, peanuts, and soybeans.

Other vegetables also supply carbohydrates, although in lesser amounts, and so do fruits. The carbohydrates in vegetables generally occur as starch, in fruits as sugar. And, of course, the sweet things so many of us crave (and craving, indulge in, to the detriment of our waistlines) are primarily sugar: candies, jams and jellies, molasses and honey and syrup, as well as the sugar itself—white or brown, it makes no difference—with which we sweeten our coffee and liberally "improve" our cereals, desserts, and fruits.

Water—is that a nutrient, too? It is indeed—the most essential one. Only air is more vital to life than water. You can live—perhaps not pleasantly, but at least surviving—for many days without food. But you will last only a very few without water.

Our bodies' digestive and elimination processes depend on water. Dissolved in water, other nutrients can pass through the intestinal wall and into the blood stream, to be carried throughout the system to the bodily structures that require them. Water carries waste out of the body. And it helps to regulate body temperature.

The primary source of this essential fluid is the water we drink—eight glasses every day, grandma used to advise, and it's as sound an idea today as it was then. Other fluids—coffee, tea, fruit juices, even milk—are mostly water. Even meat, so solid-seeming, can be up to 80 percent water. In fact, we ourselves are largely water. Only nature's magnificent structural arrangements keep us from flowing out to sea with the tide.

VITAMINS: WHAT THEY DO AND DON'T

Our affluent society has fostered a lot of silly notions that can be grouped under the general idea that "if some is good, more must be better." True of some things (such as education—a little learning is indeed a dangerous thing), but untrue of many more. Among the foolish, and sometimes dangerous, untruths is the belief that the more vitamins you ingest the better off you'll be. So, being inclined anyway to the unfortunate—and also dangerous—habit of pill-popping, we solemnly swallow our morning multivitamin pill and imagine that we feel strength and energy flowing through our bodies at a great up-and-at-'em rate. If one is good, two must be better, some of us reason. Or three? Or four? A whole lot of people, the two or three or four proponents, are this very minute wondering where that strange rash came from, or why they have chronic diarrhea, or what they should take (more pills of another kind, perhaps?) to make that nagging, persistent headache go away.

Here is a fact worth digesting: The food you eat, unless you are a small child, or on a stringent and unsupervised weight-loss regimen, or are suffering from a diet-related disease, will supply all the vitamins you need.

Babies, subsisting mostly on milk—their mother's or that of the benevolent cow—need supplemental vitamins until they are of an age to eat a more varied diet. Many weight-loss dieters, particularly those who swear by the odd crash diets that are made up mainly of one food (bananas, grapefruit, steak, rice, whatever), do themselves a favor by taking one, repeat *one,* broad-spectrum multivitamin tablet daily (it should contain the essential minerals as well as vitamins). As for those with a health problem, they are—or should be—under a doctor's care; he is the one to decide whether or not supplemental vitamins are necessary. The rest of us, if we eat a nutritionally balanced diet, can swear off pill-popping. It's a useless, sometimes harmful habit. And also an expensive one.

There is one shortcut to getting all the vitamins we need from the food we eat. The well-known (and well-understood) ones are vitamin A, the B-vitamin complex, vitamin C, and vitamin D. However, there are others—vitamin K is an example—which are known to exist, but about which very little other than their existence is known. What effect they have on body functions, what the optimum amount should be, in what foods they occur—all these are still mysteries. However, because a person in good health who gets the proper quantities of the known vitamins daily remains in good health, scientists infer that the foods in which the known vitamins occur also harbor the unknown ones. Eat a balanced diet and your vitamin intake will be adequate, they assure us. But some are what might be called sketchy eaters, to whom a balanced diet is a desirable goal seldom achieved. For them, as for weight-loss dieters and any others whose daily food intake doesn't adequately supply vitamins and minerals, *one* multivitamin mineral tablet, geared to the U.S. RDA for adults, is a sensible precaution.

Cautionary note: There are several substances that health-food promoters and certain pseudoscientific pontificators like to call vitamins—and like to attempt to sell us through scare-tactic advertising. Among these substances are inositol, para-aminobenzoic acid (called PABA for short, and no wonder), citrus bioflavonoid complex, hesperidin, and rutin—and there are others. These are not vitamins and, more to the point, they have no importance in the diet for human nutrition. Their absence from the human diet does not cause any disease or any form of illness, nor does it constitute a vitamin inadequacy.

From the negative back to the positive, the chart on the next page shows vitamins we do need, the way each affects our bodies, and the foods in which each one is found most plentifully.

Vitamin	Functions	Best Sources
vitamin A	helps keep eyes healthy, able to see in dim light * helps keep skin smooth * helps keep mucous linings of mouth, nose, throat, and digestive tract healthy, resistant to infection * aids normal bone growth and tooth formation	deep yellow and dark green leafy vegetables * cantaloupe, apricots, and other deep-yellow fruits * butter, fortified margarine * egg yolk * whole milk and vitamin A-fortified nonfat and lowfat milk
vitamin C (ascorbic acid)	helps bind body cells together * strengthens walls of blood vessels * aids normal tooth and bone formation * aids in healing wounds and broken bones * helps body to utilize iron * helps body resist infection	citrus fruits and juices * strawberries, cantaloupe, watermelon * tomatoes, broccoli, brussels sprouts, kale, green peppers * smaller but useful amounts also in cauliflower, sweet potatoes, white potatoes, raw cabbage
thiamine (vitamin B$_1$)	promotes normal appetite and digestion * helps body convert carbohydrate to energy * helps maintain healthy nervous system	lean pork * liver, heart, kidney * dry beans and peas * whole-grain and enriched breads and cereals * some nuts
riboflavin (vitamin B$_2$)	helps body cells use oxygen to obtain energy from food * helps keep eyes healthy, skin around mouth and eyes healthy and smooth	milk and milk products * liver, heart, kidney, lean meats * eggs * dark green leafy vegetables * dried beans * almonds * enriched breads and cereals (also in small amounts in many other foods)
niacin	helps body cells use oxygen to obtain energy from food * helps maintain healthy skin, digestion, and nervous system * helps maintain life of all body tissue	tuna, liver, lean meat, fish, poultry * peanuts * whole-grain enriched or fortified breads and cereals * peas
vitamin B$_6$	helps body use protein to build tissue * helps body use carbohydrate and fat for energy * helps keep skin, digestion, and nervous system healthy	pork, liver, heart, kidney * milk * whole-grain and enriched cereals * wheat germ * beef * yellow corn * bananas
vitamin B$_{12}$	aids in normal function of all body cells * helps body form red blood cells	liver, kidney * milk * eggs * fish * cheese * lean meats
vitamin D	helps body use calcium and phosphorus to build and maintain strong bones and teeth * promotes normal growth	fish liver oils * milk fortified with vitamin D * irradiated evaporated milk * liver * egg yolk * salmon, tuna, sardines (direct sunlight on skin produces vitamin D from a form of cholesterol in the skin)

Multivitamyths. We've already taken a look at the "more is better" theory and found it wanting, but there are some other old wives' (and, particularly in the case of vitamin E, old husbands') tales that need to be examined.

Vitamins give you energy, some say—particularly vitamin B. Not true. Energy comes from food. Vitamins do not supply calories. True, some of the B-complex vitamins aid in *converting* food to energy, but dosing yourself with more than the body can use is fruitless.

There are so many claims made for vitamin E that it begins to sound like the universal panacea. Vitamin E, its proponents (particularly those whose business is selling it) claim, can promote physical endurance, enhance sexual potency, prevent heart attacks, reverse baldness, protect against air pollution, and slow the aging process. For most of these claims, there is not an iota of back-it-up evidence. Previous claims for vitamin E, that it is both a preventative and a cure for cancer, a treatment for muscular dystrophy, ulcers, burns, and various skin conditions, have long since been disproved.

The point is that it is virtually impossible to have a vitamin E deficiency unless you are starving to death, in the face of which a little extra vitamin E isn't going to save the situation. The vitamin is present to some extent in most foods and in large amounts in vegetable fats and oils. Almost any daily diet supplies more vitamin E than the body can use, which is why many lists of recommended daily vitamin intake do not include E—just by the act of eating, you supply yourself with more than you need.

Vitamin E supplements have been found useful in two conditions: in premature babies who, because of poor placental transfer, have received too little of the vitamin before birth; and in persons with intestinal disorders in which fats are poorly absorbed—E is a fat-soluble vitamin. There is no E deficiency in those suffering from muscular dystrophy. Large doses of E have no effect on human impotence or sterility, on cancer, or on any of the other conditions for which it is touted.

C is for colds? We know, and have known since 1747, that vitamin C prevents scurvy, once the scourge of sailors on long sea voyages, where fresh foods were not available. (Citrus fruit, rich in vitamin C, was discovered to be the preventative, not the vitamin itself, which was not isolated and named until 1933.)

A number of years ago, a very well-known doctor wrote a book which claimed that vitamin C was both a preventative of and a cure for the common cold. If he said so, it had to be true, didn't it? Not necessarily. What people lost track of was that he was a doctor of physics, not of medicine. The book, however, gave rise to a number of tests of the theory, properly administered and controlled by doctors of medicine. Definite conclusion: Vitamin C does not cure colds. Iffy conclusion: Vitamin C may or again may not lessen the number and severity of colds a given person may have. In several clinical studies, persons who believed they were being given C but were actually given inert tablets reported fewer colds than usual. And some who were actually given C reported no difference, believing that they were the ones who were taking the inert tablets.

"It's all in your mind." Experts have by and large concluded that any benefits reported from megadosage with any of the vitamins is purely psychological. And, indeed, in rare cases where deficiencies do occur, it is because of poor absorption of the vitamin. Therefore, additional quantities of the vitamin taken by mouth—the only way vitamins can be purchased without prescription—are useless. Such rare deficiencies must be remedied by vitamin shots administered by a physician, not by self-administered pills.

Trouble in the vitamin-gulper's paradise. Those who can't convince themselves that nature knows what she's doing and decide to give her a little help by taking additional vitamins may be laying up troubles for themselves. Some of the vitamins can, in excessive doses, cause a wide range of complaints. And some are definitely toxic. A child who recently ate a whole bottle (forty tablets) of children's multivitamins "to make me strong" spent several days in the local hospital's intensive care unit with vitamin A and iron poisoning. Another reminder to us to keep all medicines out of the reach of children. Vitamins aren't "medicine"? Tell that to the little boy and to all the other children who have made themselves sick on vitamins.

toxicity of A and D: Excessive amounts of vitamin A taken over long periods can increase pressure within the human skull and may mimic a brain tumor. In fact, one teenager actually was hospitalized and prepared for brain surgery only to have it discovered that the real trouble was an overdose of vitamin A. Large doses of A taken over extended periods have been known to retard growth in children and to cause dry and cracked skin, headaches, bone pain, and other symptoms—in fact, almost the same symptoms as for a severe deficiency of the vitamin.

Excessive doses of vitamin D have been known to retard

mental as well as physical growth in children. Such doses can also cause nausea, weakness, stiffness, constipation, hypertension, and even, in the persistently foolish, death.

problems with C: Associated with large doses of vitamin C are such conditions as kidney stones and severe diarrhea. Because the body passes off excessive doses of C, its presence in the urine makes accurate testing for diabetes impossible, since it gives a false indication of sugar levels.

There is also increasing evidence of an antagonistic effect of a high intake of vitamin C on the nutritional status of vitamin A. That's another good example of the foolishness, sometimes the danger, of tampering with the body's tried-and-true way of doing things.

Getting back to nature. A few years ago, when the big push for what were termed "natural" and "health" foods was at its peak, a corollary demand for so-called "natural" vitamins arose. People eagerly paid five times as much, for example, for vitamin C extracted from rose hips or acerola cherries as for the synthesized vitamin. Two beliefs supported this craze: 1) natural vitamins are superior to those synthesized by man, and 2) vitamin products labeled "natural" do not contain synthetic ingredients. Both of those suppositions are fallacious.

Each vitamin has a molecular structure peculiar to it alone, and that structure is the same whether the vitamin is synthesized in a laboratory or extracted from an animal or plant—or consumed as part of an animal or plant in the daily diet. To be called "vitamin A," for example, the substance must have a specific molecular arrangement that is identical no matter where it is found or how it is derived. The body cannot distinguish in any way between a vitamin from a plant or animal and the same vitamin from a laboratory. Even more revealing is the fact that some synthetic ingredients are present in "natural" products—synthetics that are what the "natural" vitamin purchaser is trying to avoid and believes he is avoiding. The manufacturer of "natural" vitamins uses excipients and binders to hold his product together—such things as ethyl cellulose and Polysorbate 80 (a synthetic emulsifier).

So it comes back down to simple terms: neither you nor your body can differentiate between a "natural" and a synthesized vitamin. Only your pocketbook knows the difference.

MACROMINERALS AND TRACE ELEMENTS

While everybody seems to be vitamin-conscious, minerals seldom come up as a subject of conversation. But minerals, too, are essential for growth and good health. Just-right amounts of the minerals in our diet are necessary. Tamper with the supply, and we find ourselves with varying types of deficiency diseases.

Some minerals are required by our bodies in relatively large amounts—more than a hundred milligrams a day; these are called the macrominerals. Others, called trace elements, are important to bodily function as well, but are needed in smaller amounts. The macrominerals are calcium, phosphorus, sodium, chloride, potassium, magnesium, and sulphur. The trace elements are iron, manganese, copper, iodine, zinc, cobalt, fluorine, selenium—and there may be others whose relationship to the body are as yet not identified. And there is a third group of minerals—including lead, mercury, and cadmium—that is regarded as harmful.

The why and what. Minerals have two important functions in the body: building and regulating. The building functions affect the skeleton and all the soft tissues. The regulating functions include a wide variety of body systems, such as heartbeat, blood clotting, maintenance of the internal pressure of body fluids, nerve responses, and transport of oxygen from the lungs to the tissues. Lacking minerals, our bodies would be in a sorry state.

The macrominerals. These are the minerals needed in large amounts—"large" being relative—up to a gram a day.

calcium: This mineral is present in the body in greater amounts than any other. Almost all of the two to three pounds present in the body is concentrated in the bones and teeth. Calcium helps to regulate certain body processes, such as the normal behavior of nerves, muscle tone and irritability, and blood clotting. Although growing children and pregnant and lactating women have the highest calcium needs, all people require calcium in their diets throughout life. *Sources:* milk and milk products are best sources; other good sources are leafy green vegetables (except spinach and chard), citrus fruits, dried peas and beans.

phosphorus: This is present with calcium in almost equal amounts in the bones and teeth, and is an important part of every tissue in the body. It is widely distributed in foods, so a sufficient supply is easily obtained in the normal everyday diet. *Sources:* meat, poultry, fish, eggs, and whole-grain foods.

sodium and chloride: These two combine to form sodium chloride (table salt), but each has separate functions in the body.

Sodium is found mainly in blood plasma and in the fluids outside the body cells, helping to maintain normal water balance inside and outside the cells. The daily American diet provides a high intake of sodium and of the sodium/chloride combination added to food in the form of salt. Many authorities believe this intake is higher than desirable. A reduction of salt is often prescribed by physicians to lower the sodium intake of those with high blood pressure, kidney disease, cirrhosis of the liver, and congestive heart disease. A decrease in sodium intake can reduce the retention of water in the system, typically associated with these health problems. Under conditions of heavy sweating or vomiting, salt

intake may need to be increased, but the usual diet provides more than enough of the mineral to cover sodium losses from normal activities.

Chloride is a component of hydrochloric acid, which is found in quite high concentration in the gastric juices and is very important to proper digestion of food in the stomach. *Sources:* animal foods—meat, fish, poultry, eggs, milk—are sodium-rich, and many processed foods—ham, bacon, bread, crackers—have a high sodium content because salt is added in the processing; chloride sufficient for the body's needs is obtained from the table salt in the normal diet.

potassium: This mineral is found mainly in the fluid inside the individual body cells. Along with sodium, it helps to regulate balance and volume of body fluids. A potassium deficiency is very uncommon in healthy people, but may result from prolonged diarrhea or from the use of diuretics, which cause high urine volume. Deficiency has also been associated, in children, with diets extremely inadequate in protein. *Sources:* the mineral is abundant in almost all foods, both plant and animal.

magnesium: This mineral is found in all body tissues, but principally in the bones. It is an essential part of many enzyme systems responsible for energy conversions in the body. A deficiency of magnesium in healthy persons is uncommon, but it has been observed in some postsurgical patients, in alcoholics, and in certain other disease conditions. *Sources:* a nutritionally balanced diet supplies the body with adequate amounts.

sulphur: This is also present in all body tissues, and is essential to life. It is related to protein nutrition because it is a component of several important amino acids. It is also a component of two vitamins, thiamin and biotin. The complete function of sulphur in the human body has not yet been established. *Sources:* as far as is presently known, a nutritionally balanced diet supplies the body with adequate amounts.

The trace elements. The essential trace elements are present in extremely small amounts in the body but, as with the other necessary nutrients, we could not live without them. Most of them do not occur in the body in their free form, but are bound to organic compounds on which they depend for transport, storage, and function. Our understanding of the importance of some trace elements comes primarily from studies of animals.

iron: This is an important part of compounds necessary for transporting oxygen to the cells and making use of the oxygen after it arrives. Iron is widely distributed in the body, mostly in the blood, but with relatively large amounts in the liver, spleen, and bone marrow. The only way that the body can lose a significant amount of iron is through a loss of blood. This is why those who have periodic blood losses or who are forming more blood have the greatest need for dietary iron. Women of childbearing age, pregnant women, and growing children are the ones most likely to suffer from iron-deficiency anemia because of their higher needs for the mineral. *Sources:* only a few foods provide iron in useful amounts; liver is an excellent source; other sources are meat products, egg yolk, fish, green leafy vegetables, peas, beans, dried fruits, whole-grain cereals, and foods prepared from iron-enriched cereal products.

manganese: Normal tendon and bone structure requires manganese, and it is part of some enzymes. A deficiency in humans is unknown. *Sources:* abundant in many foods, especially bran, coffee, tea, nuts, peas, and beans.

copper: This mineral is involved in the storage and release from storage of iron to form hemoglobin for red blood cells; the need for it is particularly important in the early months of life. If the intake of the mother is sufficient, an infant is born with a store of copper to use in the early months. *Sources:* occurs in most unprocessed foods; particularly abundant in organ meats, shellfish, nuts, and dried legumes.

iodine: Although iodine is required in extremely small amounts, the normal functioning of the thyroid gland depends on an adequate supply. Goiter, caused by iodine deficiency, was common in some inland areas of the United States where the soil contains little iodine until iodized salt was introduced in 1924. Iodization of salt is not mandatory, but FDA regulation requires that noniodized salt must be labeled with the statement, "This salt does not supply iodide, a necessary nutrient." *Sources:* iodized salt; seafood is the richest natural source of the mineral.

zinc: This mineral is an important part of the enzymes that, among other functions, move carbon dioxide—by way of the red blood cells—from the tissues to the lungs, where it can be exhaled. It had been thought that a zinc deficiency did not exist in the United States until studies in the early 1970s, concerned with the loss of the sense of taste and with delayed wound healing, indicated that a deficiency may exist in some persons. *Sources:* meat, fish, egg yolks, milk; although whole-grain cereals are zinc-rich, the presence of certain other substances keeps the zinc from being completely available for absorption.

cobalt: By itself, the mineral is not essential in the body, but it is part of vitamin B_{12}, which is an essential nutrient. Vegetarians who eliminate meat, eggs, and dairy products from their diets can become vitamin B_{12} deficient. *Sources:* animal foods and products made from animal foods.

chromium: It is known that chromium, acting with insulin, is required for the body's utilization of glucose—a deficiency can produce a diabeteslike condition. However, much remains to be learned about the functions of the mineral. *Sources:* dried brewer's yeast, whole-grain cereals, liver.

selenium: This mineral appears to have a "sparing action" on vitamin E. A variety of problems occur in animals that have a deficiency of vitamin E and selenium—most of these are cured by providing the animal with vitamin E and/or selenium. From the information concerning the importance of selenium to animals, it becomes reasonably certain that the mineral is equally important for man, and studies concerning the mineral in the human body are being made to determine its function. *Sources:* the amount of this mineral in foods depends on the amount of selenium available to the growing plant or animal.

fluorine: Like iodine, this is found in small and varying amounts in water, soil, plants, and animals. Research has proven one benefit to be derived from the mineral and provides strong evidence for a second. Proven: that fluoride contributes to solid tooth formation and results in a decrease of dental caries (cavities), especially in children. Strong evidence: that fluoride helps retain calcium in the bones of older people. *Source:* in drinking water; acceptable level is one part per million.

Other minerals. Studies are constantly being carried out on the functions of various other minerals in the human body. Some are known to be important to the health of certain plants and animals, but as yet none of these has been demonstrated as being beneficial to man. Research continues to seek answers to these questions.

the harmful ones: Cadmium, lead, and mercury have no demonstrated essential function in the human body and have, indeed, been proven harmful. Cadmium interferes with the functions of the essential minerals iron, copper, and calcium. People exposed to large amounts of cadmium may develop anemia, kidney damage and, finally, marked bone mineral loss. These effects are lessened with adequate intake of zinc, iron, copper, calcium, manganese, and ascorbic acid—in other words, a normal diet. Lead and mercury accumulated in the system are toxic.

A final cautionary note, applicable to both vitamins and minerals: inunction doesn't work. You can slather yourself with vitamin creams unremittingly from now till doomsday and nothing will happen. Nutrients are not absorbed through the skin. If you are determined to madly grease yourself, try crankcase oil—it will be just as effective, and a whole lot cheaper. You may as well come to terms with the fact that eternal youth does not reside in jars or tubes of vitamin or mineral skin creams. Give up and grow old gracefully.

A FEW THOUGHTS ON CALORIES

First, a calorie is not a nutrient. It is a unit of measure—a measurement of the energy we derive from the food we eat. If you consume the exact amount of food—the exact number of calories—you need for proper body functioning, your body will acknowledge this by neither putting on nor losing weight. Consume too little, and your body will "burn up" some of its own substance (first fat, and then, in dire circumstances, tissue) and you will lose weight. Consume too much, and the body will store it as excess fat, and you will gain weight.

Almost all foods provide energy, some considerably more than others. The energy, large amount or small, is measured in calories. Except as a convenient way of expressing how much energy is supplied by one food or another, calories make no contribution to a discussion of nutrition.

AND ON FIBER

Food fiber is not a nutrient, either—at least, it is not in the sense that protein, carbohydrate, fat, vitamins, and minerals are. But discussions of, and speculations on, and research into food fiber in the diet have, since the mid-1970s, occupied a number of nutritionists. There is a considerable body of medical evidence, growing all the time, supporting the contention that a diet containing adequate amounts of high-fiber foods can reduce impressively the risk of cancer of the colon, and can also help protect against cardiovascular problems—ailments of the heart and circulatory system. And a case for fiber as protection against diverticular disease of the colon, appendicitis, phlebitis and resulting blood clots to the lungs, obesity, hemorrhoids, and varicose veins can be convincingly made, if not yet proven.

The consensus seems to be that the average American now consumes between two and three grams of crude fiber a day, and should be taking in closer to six or seven.

Food fiber is what grandma used to call "roughage." Plant foods provide it, animal foods do not. Grains, vegetables, fruits, nuts, and seeds all contain varying amounts of food fiber, while meat, fish, poultry, and dairy products provide none. For optimum amounts of fiber, whenever possible eat vegetables and fruits raw rather than cooked, unpeeled rather than peeled. If there's a choice between whole-grain and refined foods, choose whole-grain.

AND ON CHOLESTEROL

To begin with, a lot of us are still confused about the whole subject. We know vaguely that egg yolks are cholesterol-loaded, that some kinds of fats (saturated) are more dangerous than other kinds of fats, and that a high level of cholesterol is somehow related to heart disease.

Cholesterol does not only occur in the foods we eat or avoid eating. Our bodies manufacture cholesterol, a fatlike material essential to life. It is often referred to as "blood cholesterol" because its measurable presence is in the blood of the human body. "Dietary cholesterol" is found in some of the foods we eat—foods of animal origin, such as meat, egg yolks, and dairy products.

A medical theory subscribed to by many experts holds that high blood cholesterol is associated with the increased incidence of heart disease. Corollary to that is the belief that the amount of dietary cholesterol a person consumes raises the level of his blood cholesterol. The latter has been proved to be true in some cases, but not in all. It should follow, then, that a diet low in dietary cholesterol should prevent heart disease—however, this has not been clearly demonstrated. (Indeed, there is a second body of medical belief which holds that dietary cholesterol has nothing to do with the incidence of heart disease.)

What causes a heart attack? Fatty deposits build up on the inner walls of the arteries; gradually, the passageway for blood through the arteries is narrowed by these deposits. When the coronary artery becomes clogged, heart attack occurs.

Blood cholesterol is a major ingredient in the fatty deposits that build up in the arterial walls. In fact, certain studies indicate that of all the factors thought to increase the probability of heart attack—including hypertension, cigarette smoking, and diabetes—high blood cholesterol is the chief culprit.

A major breakthrough. In 1977, the Framingham Heart Study, a Massachusetts research center funded by the National Heart, Lung, and Blood Institute, announced the confirmation of an ongoing study of cholesterol in relation to heart attack.

It has been known for some time that cholesterol is carried through the blood in a series of "packets," which contain other fats and protein as well as cholesterol. The Framingham research demonstrates that not all of these packets are important in the prediction of heart disease. Only two of them are: the packets called low-density lipoproteins (LDLs) and the ones called high-density lipoproteins (HDLs). The LDLs have proved to be an excellent indicator of heart disease—the higher a person's LDL level, the greater his chances of having a heart attack.

The big breakthrough, however, concerns HDLs. Researchers in this study found that the cholesterol in the HDL packets had an inverse relationship to the incidence of heart disease. That is, the higher the HDL cholesterol level in the blood, the lower the risk of heart disease. Thus, a test for overall blood cholesterol level is no longer a reliable indicator of whether or not a person runs a risk of heart disease. Tests must differentiate between levels of LDLs and HDLs in the blood.

HDL cholesterol appears to have the ability to attract excess cholesterol from the tissues and carry it to the liver to be excreted; it is also believed to prevent the cells' intake of LDL cholesterol and thus help prevent buildup of fatty deposits in arteries—the buildup that causes blockage and the consequent heart attacks. For some reason as yet un-

RECOMMENDED DAILY (DIETARY) ALLOWANCES
Designed for the maintenance of good nutrition of healthy people in the U.S.A.

	Age (years)	Weight (pounds)	Height (inches)	Energy (calories)	Protein (grams)	Fat-Soluble Vitamins (international units)				Water-Soluble Vitamins (milligrams)							Minerals (milligrams)					
						vitamin A	vitamin D	vitamin E	ascorbic acid (C)	folacin	niacin	riboflavin	thiamin	vitamin B_6	vitamin B_{12}	calcium	phosphorus	iodine	iron	magnesium	zinc
children 1–3	28	34	1300	23	2000	400	7	40	100	9	0.8	0.7	0.6	1.0	800	800	60	15	150	10
4–6	44	44	1800	30	2500	400	9	40	200	12	1.1	0.9	0.9	1.5	800	800	80	10	200	10
7–10	66	54	2400	36	3300	400	10	40	300	16	1.2	1.2	1.2	2.0	800	800	110	10	250	10
males 11–14	97	63	2800	44	5000	400	12	45	400	18	1.5	1.4	1.6	3.0	1200	1200	130	18	350	15
15–18	134	69	3000	54	5000	400	15	45	400	20	1.8	1.5	2.0	3.0	1200	1200	150	18	400	15
19–22	147	69	3000	54	5000	400	15	45	400	20	1.8	1.5	2.0	3.0	800	800	140	10	350	15
23–50	154	69	2700	56	5000	—	15	45	400	18	1.6	1.4	2.0	3.0	800	800	130	10	350	15
51+	154	69	2400	56	5000	—	15	45	400	16	1.5	1.2	2.0	3.0	800	800	110	10	350	15
females 11–14	97	62	2400	44	4000	400	12	45	400	16	1.3	1.2	1.6	3.0	1200	1200	115	18	300	15
15–18	119	65	2100	48	4000	400	12	45	400	14	1.4	1.1	2.0	3.0	1200	1200	115	18	300	15
19–22	128	65	2100	46	4000	400	12	45	400	14	1.4	1.1	2.0	3.0	800	800	100	18	300	15
23–50	128	65	2000	46	4000	—	12	45	400	13	1.2	1.0	2.0	3.0	800	800	100	18	300	15
51+	128	65	1800	46	4000	—	12	45	400	12	1.1	1.0	2.0	3.0	800	800	80	10	300	15
pregnant			+300	+30	5000	400	15	60	800	+2	+.3	+.3	2.5	4.0	1200	1200	125	18+	450	20
lactating			+500	+20	6000	400	15	80	600	+4	+.5	+.3	2.5	4.0	1200	1200	150	18	450	25

known, women appear to have higher HDL levels than men of the same age, which may well explain why fewer women than men have heart attacks.

What can we do, nutritionally, to lower LDL and raise HDL levels? Research on this is underway, and seems to indicate, from the early studies, that a low-cholesterol diet—a diet low in saturated fats—may raise the HDL level. Exercise, particularly running, may have the desired effect. And some drugs seem to raise HDL levels. But more investigation must be carried out before any of these moves from the class of a possibility to that of a certainty.

THE WHAT AND WHY OF U.S. RDA

Labels on many foods you buy show the percentage of the U.S.RDA of proteins, vitamins, and minerals in one serving of the food. RDA stands for Recommended Daily Allowance—amounts of each of the nutrients established by the Food and Nutrition Board of the National Academy of Sciences, National Research Council (NAS-NRC, if you're an acronym fancier) as optimum for an individual in good health. From the research of this body, our old friend the FDA has established the U.S. RDAs.

RDAs were first published in 1943, and have been revised a number of times since then, keeping pace with the advance of knowledge and research in the field of nutrition.

For example, RDA for zinc was added to the list in 1973, as it became clear that zinc was required by and used by the human body; in the same year, RDA of vitamin A for adult females was reduced, but no change was made for adult males, reflecting the latest findings concerning the amount of that vitamin the body requires.

The chart above shows in detail RDAs for healthy children, male adults, female adults, and pregnant and lactating women. As you will see, there are RDAs for protein, vitamins, and minerals, but none for carbohydrates and fats —the theory being that the daily diet supplies virtually everyone sufficient, or more than sufficient, amounts of these nutrients. The chart also lists an amount of calories (energy) proper for various age/sex groups. Note that the iron requirement for pregnant women is 18+ milligrams—an amount that cannot be met by ordinary diets. Pregnant women need iron supplements over and above diet-furnished iron.

THE BALANCING ACT

To help you acquire the knack of using U.S.RDAs in planning meals for your family, here are a few of the sources of some of the nutrients—not by any means a complete list, but a sampling of a wide variety of foods, to give you an idea of how you can use a knowledge of RDAs to your advantage. In the following lists, it is assumed that the food is ready to serve

—that is, cooked if it is a food that requires cooking, peeled if it is a food that requires peeling, and so on.

SOME SOURCES OF PROTEIN

food	quantity	percent of U.S.RDA
beef, lean	3 ounces	52%
cheddar cheese	2 ounces	30%
chicken (excluding skin, bone)	3 ounces	44%
dried peas, beans	1 cup	23%
egg	1 large	13%
fish	4 ounces	45%
liverwurst	2 ounces	18%
milk	1 cup (8 ounces)	20%
oatmeal	1 cup	8%
peanut butter	2 tablespoons	12%
tuna (canned)	3 ounces	53%
turkey (excluding skin)	3 ounces	56%

SOME SOURCES OF VITAMIN A

food	quantity	percent of U.S.RDA
beef liver	3 ounces	995%
broccoli, cut up	1 cup	78%
calves' liver	3 ounces	510%
cantaloupe	¼ of 5-inch-diameter melon	65%
carrots, diced	⅓ cup	101%
cheddar cheese	2 ounces	14%
chicken livers	3 ounces	274%
eggs, large	2	24%
greens: mustard, collard	⅔ cup	120%
milk, whole or vitamin A-fortified nonfat	1 cup (8 ounces)	7%
orange juice (from concentrate)	1 cup	11%
papaya, diced	1 cup	64%
pepper, sweet red, diced	1 cup	44%
pumpkin, mashed	½ cup	146%
squash, acorn	1 cup	56%
squash, butternut	1 cup	256%
sweet potato	1 medium	178%
tomatoes (canned)	½ cup	21%
tomato juice	1 cup	39%
watermelon	4- × 8-inch wedge	50%

SOME SOURCES OF VITAMIN C

food	quantity	percent of U.S.RDA
broccoli, cut up	1 cup	233%
brussels sprouts	1 cup	225%
cabbage, shredded raw	1 cup	55%
cabbage, shredded cooked	1 cup	35%
cantaloupe	¼ medium	105%
cauliflower	½ cup	55%
grapefruit juice, unsweetened	½ cup	160%
orange juice (from concentrate)	½ cup	103%
peas, green	½ cup	18%
pepper, green, raw	½ large	107%
pepper, sweet red, raw	½ large	170%
potato, white, baked	1 medium	33%
radishes	4 small	16%
sauerkraut	½ cup	27%
spinach, cooked	1 cup	83%
squash, winter, mashed	1 cup	172%
sweet potato, baked	1 medium	178%
tomato, raw	1 medium	70%
tomatoes (canned)	½ cup	33%

SOME SOURCES OF IRON

food	quantity	percent of U.S.RDA
beans (canned) with pork, molasses, and tomato sauce	1 cup	33%
beans, dried	1 cup	30%
beef, lean	3 ounces	18%
beef liver	3 ounces	31%
bran flakes, with added thiamin and iron	1 cup	68%
bread: enriched white, whole wheat	2 slices	9%
chicken livers	3 ounces	37%
eggs, large	2	12%
oatmeal	1 cup	8%
oysters, raw	1 cup	73%
pasta, enriched	1 cup (cooked)	7%
pork, fresh or cured (ham)	3 ounces	14%
pork liver	3 ounces	91%
rice, enriched	1 cup	10%
sweet potato, baked	1 medium	5%
turnip greens	1 cup	8%

SOME SOURCES OF THIAMIN

food	quantity	percent of U.S. RDA
beef heart	3 ounces	61%
beef liver	3 ounces	15%
bread, enriched	2 slices	8%
ham	3 ounces	27%
peas, green	½ cup	14%
pork liver	3 ounces	17%
pork roast	3 ounces	52%
rice, enriched	1 cup	15%
split peas	1 cup	26%
wheat germ	3 tablespoons	31%

SOME SOURCES OF RIBOFLAVIN

food	quantity	percent of U.S.RDA
beef, lean	3 ounces	11%
beef heart	3 ounces	61%
beef liver	3 ounces	164%
broccoli, cut up	1 cup	18%
brussels sprouts	1 cup	12%
cheddar cheese	2 ounces	15%
cottage cheese, creamed	½ cup	18%
eggs, large	2	16%
milk, whole	1 cup (8 ounces)	24%
milk, skim (nonfat) or buttermilk	1 cup	25%
pork liver	3 ounces	153%
split peas	½ cup	6%
squash, winter, mashed	1 cup	16%

SOME SOURCES OF NIACIN

food	quantity	percent of U.S.RDA
beef hamburger, lean, broiled	3 ounces	26%
beef liver	3 ounces	58%
beef roast, lean	3 ounces	23%
chicken (excluding skin, bone)	3 ounces	37%
cod, fillets	4 ounces	13%
ham	3 ounces	16%
lima beans	⅔ cup	8%
liver sausage	2 slices	8%
mackerel, fresh	4 ounces	47%
peanut butter	2 tablespoons	24%
peas, green	½ cup	10%
pork roast	3 ounces	24%
tuna (canned)	3 ounces	51%

SOME SOURCES OF CALCIUM

food	quantity	percent of U.S.RDA
american cheese	2 ounces	40%
broccoli, cut up	1 cup	16%
cheddar cheese	2 ounces	43%
cottage cheese, creamed	½ cup	12%
greens: collard, mustard, turnip	⅔ cup	15%
kale	⅔ cup	9%
macaroni (enriched) and cheese	1 cup	36%
milk, whole, skim (nonfat), or buttermilk	1 cup	29%
milk, evaporated, undiluted	½ cup	63%
milk, instant nonfat dry	1 cup	88%
parmesan cheese	1 ounce	36%
sardines (with skin and bone)	3 ounces	37%
swiss cheese	2 ounces	50%
yogurt, lowfat, plain	1 cup	29%

Again, these are not by any means all the foods you eat, nor all the nutrients you need. But the listings above will give you an idea of the RDAs supplied by a variety of foods. Make it a habit to read the nutrition labels of all the foods you buy for percentages of U.S.RDAs per serving.

STUFF AND NONSENSE

There are all sorts of food supplements on the market, and all sorts of ideas and rumors circulating that concern nutrition. Some are useless, some at best harmless, but some— both supplements and ideas—are dangerous. Here are a few of them.

rumor: For optimum good health, everyone ought to take a protein supplement to augment the food protein.

fact: This is one of the dangerous ones. If you or any of your family are taking protein supplements—stop! For infants and children, too much concentrated protein can cause kidney damage or kidney failure, coma, even death. The Federal Trade Commission, which made an in-depth study of protein supplements on the market, warns that feeding babies concentrated protein (as in a protein supplement) could take a baby from good health to "desperate dehydration" in a matter of a few hours. Infants in the United States, the FTC continues, presently ingest two to four times as much protein as they need. Added protein from supplements is exceedingly dangerous to their health.

Although risk of dehydration in young children—one to three years old—is less than for infants, it is still a possibility. At any rate, children, too, do not need more protein than they get from their daily diet. Excess protein, particularly in the concentrated form of protein supplements, can damage the liver and/or kidneys of a child.

In adults, the danger of protein supplements is acute for those with liver or kidney diseases—these organs may be unable to handle the by-products produced by the metabolism of high levels of protein, causing even further damage.

At the very least, protein supplements are a waste of money for the average healthy American. The total protein intake of an average adult male is about 115 grams. But the U.S.RDA is 54 to 56 grams. Healthy people get more than enough protein from their daily diet, without protein supplements, even if such supplements did not carry any risk.

rumor: All food additives are bad and should be banned.

fact: Some additives serve a useful purpose. Those that preserve food, prevent spoilage, are very useful, provided they have been tested and found safe. In fact, the shelves of the present-day supermarket would be virtually as bare as Mother Hubbard's cupboard if all foods containing additives were removed from them. However, there are a number of so-called "cosmetic" additives that serve no purpose other than making the food look more appealing—for instance, yellow coloring in a pudding to give it an egg-yolk color. These are without any real benefit.

rumor: Sugar is harmful. There is no place for sugar in a normal diet.

fact: True, sugar is without much to offer in the way of nutrition. But that doesn't mean it should be done away with. Good nutrition does not by any means demand that everything you eat must be nutrition-loaded. There is room in the diet for balanced nutrition and for the things that make the nutrients taste good, make them acceptable to us, as well. Used as a condiment—a flavoring agent—sugar does no harm. Nor does occasional indulgence in the sugar-loaded sweets so many of us enjoy, as long as we take them in addition to a well-balanced diet, not as a substitute for good nutrition. Moderation is the key. Sugar, in moderation, is a nutritional "luxury" we can allow ourselves. But an excess of sugar is nutritionally unsound and should be avoided.

rumor: Our soil has lost its vitamins and minerals—because of this, our food crops have little nutritional value. To add to the problem, chemical fertilizers are poisoning the soil. Natural, organic fertilizers are not only safer, but produce crops that are nutritionally sounder.

fact: Plant nutrients are added to the soil through fertilizers—food crops, today as yesterday, contain the expected nutrients. Modern chemical fertilizers are needed to produce enough food to support the population. There is no evidence to support the contention that the soil is being poisoned. Organic and chemical fertilizers produce crops that are of equal quality and equally safe for human consumption. Chemical fertilizers supply nutrients—potassium, phosphorus, nitrogen—to the growing plants directly and more quickly, therefore more efficiently. Organic ones must first be broken down by bacteria in the soil before those nutrients can be released.

rumor: Processing removes most vitamins and minerals from foods.

fact: Cooking a food at home is, in reality, a form of processing. Like commercial processing, cooking at home does reduce to some extent the nutrient quality or content of foods—the reason that some commercial foods are enriched after processing. In any event, modern processing methods are designed to keep such losses as low as possible. Home cooking should be accomplished with this same goal in mind.

rumor: Aluminum cooking utensils are dangerous to health. So are Teflon-coated ones.

fact: Aluminum is the second most abundant element in the soil—by reason of this, aluminum occurs naturally in many foods. Cooking in aluminum utensils is harmless. Careful testing of Teflon-coated utensils has proved that there is no danger from them to the foods cooked in them and, therefore, to those who eat the foods.

rumor: If you feel tired, you are suffering from a vitamin deficiency.

fact: You might be. But most people feel tired—or suffer from assorted aches and pains—now and then. Overwork, emotional stress, disease, lack of sleep—all these can cause that tired feeling. Whatever the cause, don't make your own diagnosis. If the weariness persists, see your doctor. He can find the cause and prescribe the treatment, neither of which any layman is equipped to do.

These are just a few of the ideas that people latch onto and, without thinking about it, without any attempt to check the source, accept as gospel. A grain of salt—even if you're on a low-sodium diet—is what you need in dealing with these rumors. If you hear something that sounds reasonable, that sounds as if it might apply to you, check it out. Ask your doctor or consult a nutritionist, and get your facts straight before you take up any food fads or believe any food fancies.

PUTTING IT ALL TOGETHER

Your body can pick and choose whatever it needs from the nutrients in your diet—provided, of course, that what you eat includes everything the body needs, and in quantities sufficient for the body's use. In other words, a nutritionally balanced diet. If the diet lacks some needed nutrients, the body has no way to get them. If it can, it steals the needed nutrient from body structures.

Like a factory on a twenty-four-hour schedule, the body works around the clock—building itself up, repairing itself, discarding waste products. Supplied with proper amounts of raw materials to use and energy to keep it running, the factory goes chugging along day after day, giving you no trouble. But cut off some of the needed supplies and you have problems.

The sad thing is, some of the problems can go on for a long time before you are aware of them.

Take calcium as an example. The body needs calcium to clot blood, to make the nerves function properly, to develop bones. If the body does not get enough calcium from the food you eat, it will take what it needs from your bones. If what it takes is not promptly replaced, your body is in trouble, although you may not realize this for some years. As much as one-third of the normal amount of calcium can be lost from an adult's bones before it shows up in an X ray.

It is not only the use for which a nutrient is needed by the body or the use to which it is put that is important, but also the interaction of the various nutrients with one another, because no single nutrient can function properly by itself. Without vitamin D, calcium is not absorbed from the intestines. Protein is needed for the framework of the bones, and to form part of every cell and all the fluids that circulate in and around the cells. Vitamin C is needed to help produce the materials between the cells. All the nutrients are necessary, because they all must work together.

The foods you eat today must sustain your body today and help build it for your lifetime. The more varied your diet, the closer it comes to nutritional balance, the better off you will be—tomorrow as well as today.

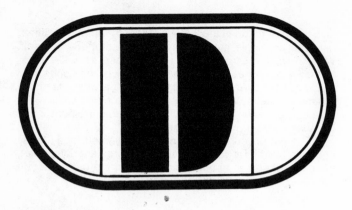

DACQUOISE: see page 452

DAIRY PRODUCTS: see individual product:
BUTTER, CHEESE, CREAM, ICE
CREAM, MILK, YOGURT

DAIRY SOUR CREAM: see CREAM

DANDELION GREENS: see SALAD
GREENS AND PLANTS

DANISH BLUE CHEESE: see CHEESE

DANISH PASTRY: see PASTRY

DASHEENS: see UNUSUAL VEGETABLES

DATES: see EXOTIC FRUIT

DECORATING FOOD

By kitchen tradition, garnishes are savory, decorations are sweet. That is, we garnish everything until we get to dessert, and then we decorate. And, as a general rule, we tend to garnish modestly—a little parsley here, a few chopped olives there—but when we get to decorating we go overboard. We slather on whipped cream, pile up garlands and pyramids of decorator-frosting flowers that make Mother Nature blush and hang her head, pour sauces with reckless abandon, and then toss on chopped nuts as if trying to mend the dike.

Moderation should be the decorator's foremost attribute. Beautifully—and restrainedly—decorated desserts are a joy to the eye and a source of pride to their producer. Just try to remember that it's something to eat that you're preparing, not a funeral set-piece or a floral blanket to toss over the horse that just won the derby, and everything will work out fine.

Basic goodness counts most. The most untrammeled extravaganza of decoration will not serve to lift the food it covers out of mediocrity if the food wasn't very good to begin with. If you're going to stint somewhere along the line, stint on the decoration itself, not on what it decorates. There's something basically dishonest about flinging roses riotously on an eggless, milkless economy cake that might have been better gone with the wind in the first place.

Not that there's anything wrong with the eggless-milkless wonder in its place. Make and serve it by all means on a suitable occasion. But don't try to turn it into a symphony when the best it can hope for is a harmonica solo. Simple cookies, wholesome and delicious, cry out for drifts of sugar on their tops, not a ring-a-ding of royal icing, candied violets, and silver dragées. A cup of weak instant coffee cringes under the café brûlot treatment. A down-home apple pie is embarrassed if you smother it in caramel sauce, whipped cream, chopped pecans, and maraschino cherries. That prissy old saying about a place for everything and everything in its place goes double for food.

Concentrating on cakes and cookies. Some of us, alas, were born with ten thumbs and cannot, to save our lives, learn to sashay around the kitchen with a lineup of pastry tubes, manufacturing floral tributes and frosting basketry with a hand that is quicker than the eye. If you are one of the only-God-can-make-a-tree set, come to terms with the problem. There are plenty of other ways to go.

Cakes can be decorated with good, rich frosting, lavishly swirled on or smoothed and patterned with the tines of a fork or with an edging of nutmeats. Or drizzle a white frosting with melted chocolate. Or top a hot-from-the-oven unfrosted cake with peppermint patties and swirl with a knife when the heat softens them. Make a tasty spice cake or gingerbread better with whipped cream cheese and a sprinkle of grated lemon peel. Drift confectioners sugar over a bundt or pound cake. Or serve any cake plain and pass a good fruit or fudge or caramel sauce, or a bowl of sweetened, flavored whipped cream.

If you yearn to be an accomplished cake decorator (and know in your heart that you can restrain yourself once you've got the hang of it), take a course in cake decorating—some bakeries offer them, so do YWCAs, adult education departments—there are even entire schools devoted to teaching the art. Unless you are exceedingly skillful with your hands and adept at reading and following directions, the more elaborate kinds of cake decorating aren't a do-it-yourself learning experience. Find a school where techniques are demonstrated, where you can learn by watching a pro and following her/his example.

There are dozens of available cake decorations that can ornament a simply frosted cake without benefit of pastry tube: candies of many kinds, coconut—toasted or colored or plain—store-bought or homemade marzipan fruit or flower shapes, tiny cookies, fresh flowers. You don't need to know or to be a pro.

Cookies, lightly frosted or glazed, can take almost any decoration suitable for a cake—provided it's also suitable for the particular cookie. And cookies shaped with decorative cutters—letters of the alphabet, flower shapes, a whole zoo of animals and birds and fish, and dozens more—are decorative in and of themselves. There are molds and forms and presses available too in which to shape cookies, and patterned pins with which to roll them. Cookies are fun to make, fun to decorate—easy, too.

Personality pies. A good general cookbook or, even better, an all-purpose decorating and garnishing book, will show-and-tell you how to make delightfully ornamental pie-crust edges and decorative top crusts in amazing variety. A mile-high, beautifully browned meringue is an intrinsic decoration. Some pies like cheese. Others take to a sauce of some sort. A pie should not be too plain, but don't overdo.

Decorated desserts of other sorts. There are many decorations you can try your hand at for gussying-up puddings, bavarians, frozen desserts, and the like. Find a food-decorating book that will tell you how to make glacéed strawberries, crystallized violets and rose petals, candied citrus peel, spiced and glazed nuts, chocolate curls and cones and other fancy shapes—they're all fun to do, not difficult provided you are blessed with a certain amount of patience.

If you are interested in decorating desserts—and in garnishing the savory part of the meal—browse the library or a bookstore for a good, down-to-earth book on the how-to, what-to, and when-to. Food decorating and garnishing is a craft, very satisfying and well worth investigating. See also CANDIED FLOWERS, FRUIT, SPUN SUGAR, and TOPPINGS, DESSERT.

DEEP-FAT FRYING

Deep-fried foods tend to fall into two categories, exceedingly good or exceedingly bad, with no in-between. That is because the temperature of the fat is all-important. Foods fried in too-hot fat brown too fast, look done on the outside before they are cooked on the inside. Foods cooked in too-cool fat are boiled rather than fried, are soggy with soaked-in fat and, all in all, unappetizing, indigestible, and totally undesirable.

So it is important to follow recipe directions concerning fat temperatures. Precooked foods, such as croquettes, need only to brown and to be heated through, but uncooked deep-fried foods—doughnuts, for example—must be cooked as well as browned. Generally, the precooked foods are fried at slightly higher temperatures than the uncooked ones.

If you have an electric deep-fat fryer, set the dial to the required temperature and don't start to cook until the indicator shows you that the fat has reached that temperature. If you deep fry in a kettle on your stovetop, you will be well served by a deep-fat thermometer to gauge the readiness of the fat—not only before you put the first food in, but between batches, for fat cools somewhat each time more cool food is put into it.

Never fill the container or kettle more than half full of fat —there must be room for the food that will be cooked in it,

and also room for a certain amount of bubbling-up, as when somewhat damp foods, such as potatoes, are put into the fat. (Very damp foods should be patted dry with absorbent paper before they are lowered into the fat.)

Fats with low smoking points—and low burning points—such as butter and margarine are never used for deep-fat frying. Instead, use solid shortening—of the kind that need not be refrigerated—or cooking oil. Lard may also be used, but it has a characteristic odor and flavor that it may impart to delicate food. The others are bland, odorless, and flavorless. Fat may be reused for frying several times, particularly if you add a little more fresh fat of the same kind each time. After frying, wait until the fat has cooled somewhat, strain it through cheesecloth, place in a tightly covered container, and refrigerate.

DEER: see GAME

DEGLAZE, TO: see page 445

DEMITASSE

In French, "half cup"—the small cup in which we serve after-dinner coffee when we're feeling elegant and, by extension, the coffee served in these small (and usually very handsome) cups.

After-dinner coffee should be stronger than the usual brew. Make it by using only ½ cup of water for each standard coffee measure—that is, for each 2 level tablespoons of coffee.

An elegant—and-easy-on-the-hostess—way of finishing the meal, in place of dessert, is by serving demitasse with appropriate accompaniments in the living room. Bring in the coffee in a pretty pot. Have a warmer at hand, because most people will want a second or even a third cup. You'll also need demitasse cups and saucers, small liqueur glasses, small—also called demitasse—spoons, some attractive serving dishes, and small napkins. Put out several kinds of liqueurs—an orange-flavored one, such as curaçao or grand marnier; a plain brandy; crème de cacao for those who love the mocha flavor of coffee-plus-chocolate; and one exotic, such as framboise or crème de noyeaux—are all good choices. Have cream and sugar available—such additions to after-dinner coffee were once frowned on, but in our freer/easier days are perfectly respectable. A bowl of whipped cream. A small dish of grated orange peel. Another of lemon peel twists. Something sweet, anything from a plate of plain but rich cookies to fancy petits fours (a bakery can supply these, if you quail at making your own).

Indeed, if you invite guests just for after-dinner coffee, skipping the dinner invitation, you'll find this a pleasant, unusual, and welcomed way to entertain.

DESSERTS

A meal without dessert is like a telephone that stops ringing before you reach it, leaving you with a frustrating sense of incompleteness. It doesn't have to be elaborate—a piece of fruit will do fine, thanks—but the meal needs something to round it out, to bring it to a satisfactory conclusion.

The day of the dessert table. Long ago in Europe—and in this country too at the time when our forefathers were trying to get the democracy going—a dessert buffet was the accepted form of refreshment to be served at a ball, a concert, a wedding, almost any sort of entertainment or celebration. Indeed, in many elegant homes, dessert was considered a separate meal, not a separate course, on an everyday basis. The main meal would be served at anywhere between noon and three in the afternoon, followed as the night followed day by dessert a couple of hours later.

They were something to see (and, for the dedicated lover of sweets, to wallow in), those dessert tables, especially the ones fabricated to mark some special occasion. One such, described by John Adams in a letter to his wife Abigail in 1776, listed curds and creams, jellies, sweetmeats of various kinds, twenty sorts of tarts, fools, trifles, floating islands, whipped syllabubs, pastries, parmesan cheese, punch, wine, and beer. Martha Washington's famous cake recipe begins offhandedly, "Take fifty eggs. . . ." Obviously, she had more dessert-eaters than herself and George in mind.

Even much earlier, not long after they had arrived in this country, the sweets-loving English settlers managed to have desserts for themselves and to offer their guests—quince and pear and pumpkin tarts, and those preserved fruits they called sugarplums. John Josselyn, a traveler from England inspecting the colonies, recorded in his 1638 *Two Voyages to New England* that "Marmalad and Preserved Damsons is to be met with in every house," and added the information that "the Women are pitifully Tooth-shaken, whether through the coldness of the climate, or by sweet-meats of which they have store, I am not able to affirm."

About a century later, *The Art of Cookery, or Accomplished Gentlewoman's Companion* was published, with one chapter each on soups and sauces, flesh and fish, bread, garden stuff and salads, preserves and pickles, and four chapters on sweets—pastries and cheesecakes, confectionery, cakes, and desserts. Even the chapter devoted to preserves and pickles lists heavily to the sweet side, with recipes for apricots in brandy, cherries in brandy, pickled figs, preserved greengages, conserve of lemons, orange marmalade, candied orange and lemon peel, peaches preserved in sugar, sugar-preserved quinces, quince marmalade, and sweet watermelon pickle.

The sweetmeats ground rules. There was a mystique surrounding the setting up and decorating of a sweetmeat table, a large number of do and don't-do regulations that were, apparently, inviolable. The large table, covered with a "fair damask" cloth, was arranged buffet style, and guests were expected to serve themselves. The dishes that held the sweetmeats were silver or, less elegantly, pewter, and the edibles were arranged according to an elaborate pattern—sugared nuts and seeds (comfits) here, custards and flummaries there, cheesecakes and pastries, cakes, preserved and sugared fruits—all occupying their appointed positions, surrounding, more often than not, an elaborate carved-from-ice centerpiece.

So—we shake our heads in disbelief over the dear dead days, and say, "We don't do that sort of thing any more, and (sigh!) it's probably just as well." We don't? Well, true, we don't put out quite such a tooth-eroding array of sweets. But we do end our meals with dessert. And how about our very pleasant custom of inviting friends to "come for dessert and coffee" as a way to start an enjoyable evening? And how about the dessert buffet that has become so "in" a thing—joyously welcomed by guests—among good cooks who love to show off their prowess?

What's for dessert tonight? For the family, custards and puddings supply nutritious milk and eggs. Children love gelatin, fruited or plain, and so do their elders. If you're worried about a nondrinker of milk, make a light custard sauce for the gelatin. Fruit is always welcome, eaten out of hand, served with cheese, in a mixed-fruit cup or compote, or dressed up a bit. Try fresh strawberries with brown sugar and sour cream, fresh peaches dribbled with honey and sprinkled lightly with mace, honeydew or casaba melon with salt and lime juice, blueberries with sour cream and cinnamon, apricots with crumbled almond macaroons, figs with cream cheese and walnut halves, pears with chocolate sauce, cantaloupe made into an old-fashioned ice cream parlor treat with vanilla ice cream and a crushed pineapple sauce.

We all, the old song says, scream for ice cream. And ices and ice milk and sherbets, too. For a company-coming change of pace, sauce ice creams and ices with liqueurs or fruit brandies for a dessert that combines elegance with ease. What goes with what? Almost anything. Here are some ideas to get you started:

caramel ice cream, crème de noyaux
chocolate ice cream, cherry heering
banana ice cream, coffee liqueur
vanilla ice cream, crème de cassis
lime ice, crème d'ananas
chocolate-almond ice cream, curaçao
orange ice, green crème de menthe
peach ice cream, amaretto
pineapple ice, crème de cacao

For further dressing-up, add chopped nuts if you like. Even maple syrup, a staple in most pantries, will turn a dish of plain vanilla into a handsome dessert, especially with plenty of chopped pecans. Or dress chocolate ice cream with softened marshmallow creme and a substantial sprinkling of chopped salted peanuts or crushed peppermint candies. If you have a jar of homemade praline on hand and ice cream in the freezer, you have the makings of a superb sweet to serve drop-in or invited guests.

There's nothing mysterious about praline, in spite of the fact that it turns up most often in elegant French cookbooks. Go about it this way: in a heavy skillet, cook 2 cups of sugar over low heat until it begins to melt; stir in, all at once, ¾ cup each of shelled filberts and almonds; continue to cook, without further stirring, until the mixture turns a rich golden amber. Pour onto a lightly buttered baking sheet; allow to cool and harden completely, then crush between wax paper with a rolling pin or a mallet, or pulverize in the blender. Store in an airtight jar—and hide it, or there will be nothing there but a few crumbs when you go to use it. Praline is addictive.

Dessert in a crust. When the fruits of summer are abundant but the family wants a change from eating them fresh, turn them into big pies or little tarts. Blueberries, cherries, blackberries, boysenberries, peaches, apricots, nectarines— all make sumptuous double-crust pies, juicy and sweet. Or put a custard or cream cheese filling into a baked or a crumb crust, top it with whole or halved fruit—strawberries, peaches, apricots, sweet cherries, raspberries, and such— and glaze the fruit with a little melted jelly.

When autumn comes, it brings all-American apple pie, and pumpkin and mince, too. And custard or cream pies— chocolate, banana, lemon, butterscotch. Through the wonders of preserving, we have fruits to use in pies all year around—cherries, cranberries, blueberries, and all the other favorites, canned or frozen. When we're feeling fancy, we can whip up very special pies for family or company meals— angel pies with meringue instead of crust, green grasshopper pies rich with crème de menthe in chocolate crumb crusts, rum custard pies with marrons glacés, chocolate-topped crème pâtissière in pâte à chou crusts, and dozens more.

If not pie, cake. A beautiful made-from-scratch cake used to be an ordinary thing, but no more. These days, if you offer guests such a cake—lemon filled and boiled-icing topped with coconut frosted, or darkly rich fudge with seafoam frosting, or Lady Baltimore, or strawberry angel food, or burnt sugar cake with walnuts, or chocolate cream roll, just for openers—you can expect to be mobbed. Baking is not by any means a lost art, but neither is it one practiced as routinely as once it was. Our grandmothers had only their own arms to power the beating, and chancy ovens for baking, but they managed. We can—when we want to—do better. Try it. A truly perfect cake is a good cook's poem, her play, her sculpture, her symphony. It's creative, and creativity is eminently satisfying.

Those are special cakes. How about everyday ones? How about gingerbread, or lemon sponge cake, or a plain cake with a broiled topping, or some spice cupcakes with maple frosting, or a pound-type or bundt cake with a drift of

confectioners sugar or a light glaze? If you're by no means a baker, how about cakes from a mix, even those made-in-the-pan snack cakes? Some cake is better than no cake, any cake will be welcomed by a sweet-hungry family.

If not cake, cookies. A cookie jar is a lovesome thing, full or almost empty, warning that it's time to bake another batch. A great snack, cookies—and if you feel they are "empty calories" (they really aren't) concentrate on things like apple-cinnamon-bran jumbles, oatmeal-raisin cookies, ground-nut-and-apricot bars, peanut butter cookies, and the like. Wheat germ makes a nutty-flavored, fiber-rich addition to cookies. Any kind of fruit or nuts up their nutritive value.

Alone or partnered with fresh fruit, cookies make a fine family dessert, too. And there are some company-coming kinds, such as almond macaroons, florentines, pecan lace, gaufrettes, that are elegant enough for any occasion, yet far easier to make for the timid baker than almost any other dessert.

The all-out efforts. If you're a true dessert fancier, and like to show off a bit besides, you probably enjoy making a smashing dessert for a special occasion. A towering croquembouche, perhaps, or melting chocolate velvet, or almond-meringue dacquoise. Or perhaps crème brulée, with its soft and gently sweet custard topped with the brittleness of burnt sugar. Or you may choose a cold strawberry soufflé or a hot chocolate one. Whatever, you know what you like and you know what you're doing, so any advice from us is bound to be superfluous.

On the other hand, if you yearn to venture into the realms of the fanciful but are timid about your capabilities, don't be. Start with a bavarian cream—find a recipe in a reliable cookbook (bavarians can be made in a multitude of flavors) and follow instructions to the letter. You'll produce a mini-masterpiece that will surprise everyone—you included. Or cheat a little. Buy an angel food cake from a good bakery, cut a slice off the smaller end, hollow out the center and pile it high with sweetened, grand-marnier-flavored whipped cream into which you've folded fresh raspberries. Or rely on surprise— peel and halve kiwis (chinese gooseberries) and sandwich them with softened whipped cream cheese flavored with grated orange peel. Or make chocolate stabilized whipped cream (see CREAM) and layer it alternately with store-bought ladyfingers in a loaf pan, frosting the turned-out loaf just before serving with more of the cream heavily sprinkled with toasted almonds. Or make packaged butterscotch pudding (the cooked kind) with 1¼ instead of 2 cups milk; when it's cold, fold it into 1 cup heavy cream, whipped, and then fold into it ½ cup each crushed butterscotch hard candy and chopped walnuts. Serve it in individual dishes with small packaged vanilla wafers lining the sides. All of these are easy —and sensational, either intrinsically or because they are out of the ordinary or both.

So, don't let a meal, family or company, end before it is

really over. Give it an upbeat finish by serving something, anything appropriate, for dessert. Make it, buy it, improvise it. Have it just plain good, or both good and good for you. But don't skip it. See also BAVARIAN CREAM, BOMBES, CAKES, COOKIES, CREPES, FLOATING ISLAND, GELATIN, ICE CREAM, JELLY ROLL, JUNKET, MERINGUES, NESSELRODE, OMELETS, PASTRY, PIES, PUDDINGS AND CUSTARDS, SHERBET, TOPPINGS, WAFER PAPER, WAFFLES, and ZABAGLIONE.

DEVIL, TO: see page 445

DEWBERRIES

These are a type of blackberry—the difference is that dewberries grow on trailing vines, blackberries on climbing ones. Wild dewberries were another of those native food plants to which the Indians introduced the settlers. Ripening earlier than regular blackberries, they will appear a few weeks before their cousins. However, few dewberries reach market— they are, these days, almost entirely a backyard or wild fruit, not raised commercially. See also BLACKBERRIES.

DEXTROSE: see GLUCOSE

DICE, TO: see page 445

DIET-PACK FOODS

If a food makes a nutritional claim—that it is low-calorie, low-cholesterol, or low-sodium, for example—the ingredients must be listed, with their nutritional value per serving, on the label. (See special feature: A SHORT COURSE IN LABEL READING.)

"Diet" is a catchall word—what diet, whose diet, for what purpose? Most of us, unless we have a medical problem that requires a special, prescribed diet, or cook for someone with such a problem, think of the word as synonymous with "low-calorie." But that's not necessarily so. A bland diet— sometimes prescribed for those with ailments of the stomach or intestines—can be quite high-calorie, deriving much of its blandness from carbohydrates. A low-sodium diet limits salt but, unless the patient is also overweight, does not restrict calories. A low-cholesterol diet limits saturated fats, but other components of such a diet are not necessarily aimed at weight loss.

If you're looking for low-calorie foods for a weight-loss diet, make certain that's what you're getting. There are many low-calorie or reduced-calorie "diet-pack" foods on the market. Fruits canned in water, rather than the heavy syrup of the usual pack, are an example. But if you're searching for foods for, say, a low-sodium diet, don't assume that because the food is labeled "diet pack" or some other phrase that means the same thing, that it is safe for your diet. Know what you want, what you need, and get it by taking the time to read labels. That's smart shopping—and a good habit to get into.

DIETS

We have corrupted the use of the word "diet" to mean a special food regimen of some sort—weight-loss, low-cholesterol, low-salt, and other specialized food-intake patterns. But to use the word in its strictest meaning, our diet is the sum of what we eat, whether good for us or bad for us or in between. If a benighted individual fed himself on nothing but cream puffs, cream puffs would constitute his diet.

However, the looser usage is the one we use more frequently, saying, "I must go on a diet," if we are overweight, or that "My doctor has prescribed a low-salt diet" for hypertension, or "I'll be on a bland diet for a few days," when we have an upset stomach. In this sense, we tend to speak of "free" diets—salt-free, fat-free, and so on—although actually no diet can be totally free of any of the nutrients.

A salt-free diet, for example, is impossible, because sodium is a component of almost all foods—so, instead, it is on a low-salt (not no-salt) diet on which we avoid those foods high in sodium, and refrain from adding salt in cooking or at the table. A low-carbohydrate diet cuts carbohydrate intake to between 50 and 60 grams a day, but does not eliminate carbohydrates totally—not only because that is virtually impossible to do, but also because it is dangerous.

There is, of course, one legitimate "free" diet—the starvation weight-loss diet, and what it is free of is food. It supports the body with predigested protein, must be resorted to only under constant medical supervision, and is, even so, the subject of considerable controversy in the medical world, being called everything from "the greatest breakthrough of the era" to "irresponsible and dangerous," depending on what physician you talk to.

Indeed, any diet should be undertaken only under the supervision of, or at least the permission of, your doctor. Except for weight-loss diets for the somewhat overweight (not the obese), these diets should be prescribed by the physician, who takes into account the idosyncrasies of your personal body chemistry as well as the problem for which the diet is indicated. However, with your doctor's permission, rather than his constant supervision, you may strip away a little excess avoirdupois on a weight-loss diet. (Or put on a few pounds, lucky you, if that's your problem.)

DIJON MUSTARD

This savory seasoning, which originated in France—in Dijon, quite reasonably—is an excellent accompaniment for many foods, including meats, fish, and eggs, and is used to add zesty good flavor to sauces and soups. A combination of dry mustard with herbs, spices, and white wine, dijon mustard can be found in most markets—if not with the other condiments, try the gourmet-food section—in jars or crocks.

DILL: see HERBS AND SAVORY SEASONINGS and SEEDS

DILUTE, TO: see page 445

DINNER

Always the main meal—no matter at what hour it was served —dinner was once the only meal. On the Niña and the Pinta and the Santa Maria, the sailors seeking a new route to the Indies were fed one meal a day (if they were lucky) from a huge kettle suspended over a charcoal pit in the hold, and made do with a snack of ship's biscuit—kissing kin to cement blocks—the rest of the time. In Elizabethan England, dinner was eaten by daylight; before bedtime everyone had a snack of comfits and sugarplums, sweetmeats so relished by the Virgin Queen that her teeth were black with decay before she reached her middle years.

Long after the day's food intake had been broken up into three meals, dinner was customarily served at noon with a lighter supper (or, in England, high tea) in the evening; on many farms and ranches, noon dinner is still the big meal. In the days before the expense-account lunch had been thought of, businessmen went home to dinner at noon, and although some laborers carried their midday meal, many more had it brought to the job by their wives, steaming hot in metal dinner pails. As a matter of fact, a number of nutritionists urge the return to eating the main meal in the middle of the day, so that the afternoon's active work (or play) will burn up this fuel. Under such a system, they say, not nearly so many people would be overweight. Of course, many business people, particularly men, eat what amounts to dinner twice a day, at lunch time and again in the evening—a sad state of affairs from the nutritionists' point of view.

Family patterns. Little by little, whether we purposefully seek out the information or simply absorb it from the bombardment that occurs in the press and on radio and television, we are learning the essentials of healthful eating patterns, learning to plan and serve balanced meals. We have become weight-conscious, calorie-conscious, vitamin-conscious, cholesterol-conscious, and all this has led to better family eating, from the nutritional point of view. (For an in-depth discussion of optimum daily eating patterns, see special feature: NUTRITION NOTEBOOK.)

Although improved knowledge of nutrition has helped us to plan and serve better meals on the one hand, our changing habits of living have eroded the custom of enjoying meals as a family group. Both husbands and wives often work late, and both, in these consciousness-raised times, also tend to take evenings off from the family. Or there are events that lure at least part of the family away at the normal dinner hour—such things as Little League games, special classes, peer-group activities that trespass on time normally spent at home.

So, even though dinner may be better nutritionally than once it was, it also may be kept warm in the oven or sitting in the freezer prior to being microwaved, waiting to be dealt with by each individual as his time or his social engagements or his stomach prompts him. Togetherness, touted so widely in the late sixties, was a concept whose time came and went with embarrassing rapidity. Not that we no longer all sit down together as a group, but that family-group dining is no longer the always-thing it once was.

Company coming. We entertain a lot and, although brunch is popular and cocktail parties continue to proliferate, we entertain most often at dinner. But most of us have learned, happily, that dinner consists of something good to eat rather than a lavish and budget-busting spread calculated to one-up the guests and send them home to the bicarbonate of soda. We've learned, too, both by preference and through force of circumstance, that a company-coming dinner need not be—cannot any longer be—a sit-down affair of at least six courses, complete with grandma's double-damask banquet cloth and yard-square napkins, an array of silver that dazzles the eye (which bent the mind and back of the unfortunate soul who had to keep it polished), and selected wine for each course served in its glass of proper shape. Now, unless it's a very small party, we offer dinner buffet style and the serving table may be set up in the living room, on the patio, out in the backyard, or even in the kitchen, where hosts and guests combine their talents to cook the meal. Perhaps company dinners were more elegant in those gone-and-all-but-forgotten days, but is elegance so important? Isn't having enough energy left to enjoy your own party even better?

Dining on the go. On the fabulous trains of the past, such as the Twentieth Century Limited and the Super Chief, the highlight of the trip, anticipated for hours in advance, came when the dining car steward made his way through the train banging a small gong and singing out, "First call for dinner!" As you entered the dining car, if you were lucky you might get a glimpse of one of the cooks, dressed all in white and with a toque blanche set jauntily on his head, working with incredible speed and efficiency in the miniscule kitchen. You were seated with a flourish, handed a menu of considerable complexity considering the size of the kitchen, and invited to write your own order. When you had, a dinner of incomparable food was served you with both grace and speed. However did they manage it! A child of those times remembers that there were always fresh strawberries, even in the dead of winter, and that the black waiters were always friendly and smiling —probably as southern plantation owners tended to remember that their "darkies" were always singing joyously as they toiled in the cotton fields. Things just couldn't have been that wonderful, but in memory they certainly seem to have been.

Food in transit is a far cry from that too-good-to-be-true picture these days. For those who still ride trains, there are sandwiches and drinks—sometimes not even those—or, on long journeys, "snack cars" serving microwave-heated foods, or a few remaining dining cars serving food that will, indeed, stave off starvation, but that's about the best to be said for it. Long-distance buses have added rest rooms but not kitchens. Understandably, first-rate restaurants aren't happy about busloads of people coming in at odd times, so buses generally stop at second-rate ones. Airlines serve full meals to passengers on journeys that extend through mealtimes, and make quite a to-do in their advertisements about the gourmet dining they offer. However, the big to-do is often confined to the ads and doesn't extend to the kitchens that prepare the food.

When we're on the go on our own, we generally fare a little better if we're discriminating. Buying food on which to picnic is one good way of beating the greasy-hamburger routine—milk in cartons, coffee in a carry-along thermos, the makings of really good sandwiches, little cups of salad from a good delicatessen, even a whole spit-roasted chicken to tear blissfully limb from limb and wash down with a bottle of wine. Roadside restaurants generally do better with breakfast than with other meals, and often serve breakfast all day. A good ploy is to have the thermos filled with coffee in the morning, carry small cans of fruit juice, buy sweet rolls fresh from the oven at a bakery, and enjoy a light breakfast en route. Then stop for the full-breakfast treatment at what ought to be lunch time. Of course, if it's a recreation vehicle in which you're traveling, you can have things your own way at any meal.

Backpackers carry high-energy mixtures of fruit, nuts, popcorn, cereals, chocolate or carob, and the like, christened gunk, goop, and glop but tasting much better than they sound. Dehydrated foods are available in amazing variety to be reconstituted over campfires; they may not be the epitome of elegant dining, but after a day of exercise outdoors, you can count on their being fallen on with shouts of joy and consumed to the last morsel.

Let's eat out. Once, some of the best eat-out food in the world could be found at countryside farmhouses where home-style meals were served. For instance, there was a big white farmhouse in Minnesota, in a town that rejoiced in the name of Young America, at which mammoth dinners were served every Sunday. Outside, there were animals for city children to get acquainted with—to learn that eggs were not produced in cartons, that milk came from a cow before it was put into a bottle, that a brand new woolly lamb might be the softest, sweetest-smelling thing on the face of the earth.

Indoors there were long tables, with white tablecloths and big napkins, on which everything was served from help-yourself bowls and platters. Smiling women, all looking as if they ate substantially of their own cooking, cheered the diners on with, "Come on, you haven't eaten enough to keep a bird alive!" and "I'm going to get my feelings hurt if you don't try some of my piccalili."

What was on the menu? On a typical Sunday, platters piled high with crispy fried chicken, roast turkey with sage dressing, slabs of rare roast beef, pork chops with fried apples, cider-basted home-cured ham. To accompany them, big bowls of mashed potatoes with melted butter dribbling down, casseroles of scalloped potatoes, home-fried potatoes, dishes of green beans with bits of bacon, wax beans and peas, glazed carrots, creamed onions, jerusalem artichokes, salsify, corn on the cob. Homemade bread and rolls and biscuits. Bowls of coleslaw dressed with cream and vinegar, homemade cottage cheese, wilted cucumbers, platters of sliced tomatoes sprinkled with fresh basil and black pepper. Apple butter, applesauce, pickled watermelon rind, crispy cucumber pickles, mixed mustard pickles. Fresh celery and radishes and little green onions. And for dessert? Well, always a big three-layer cake—sometimes chocolate with white mountain icing, sometimes lemon with fudge frosting. Pies in abundance—peach, cherry, apple, coconut custard, butterscotch cream, raisin, mince, pumpkin. Piles of cookies. Squares of gingerbread with lemon "soft sauce." Bowls of nuts to crack. No place for a picky appetite.

For all we know, that same farmhouse in Young America may be serving such Sunday dinners today. Certainly its counterparts still exist in many places, notably the Amish and Mennonite and Gay Dutch country of Pennsylvania. In any case, there are many choices today when the family decides to eat out—everything from fast-food places (there are good ones as well as bad) to a restaurant in an apartment building in New York City where the check for a dinner for two may well run as high as $300.00, and many, many good eating places in between those two extremes. You can have a juicy hamburger, a light meal at one of the newer soup-salad-sandwich places, a hearty full dinner—whatever you want, at whatever price, is available to American diners-out.

Back home again. The good cook is a good planner, a good shopper. She makes optimum use of what's in season—and therefore both freshest and cheapest—when deciding what to serve the family. She learns delicious ways to prepare the less usual—and generally less expensive—cuts of meat, and to give her family protein from foods other than meat. She isn't afraid to experiment with foods that were not part of her mother's kitchen repertoire, to cook familiar foods in new ways and combinations.

DIPPING CHOCOLATE: see CANDY

DIPS

The day someone thought of mixing dry onion soup mix and sour cream and serving the mixture with chips to dunk in it, the whole appetizer/snack world turned upside down. There had been few-and-far-between dips before, notably one made of cream cheese softened with sour cream and liberally laced with snipped chives, but dip on a scale that swept the country, dip you met everywhere you turned? Never before—and, if heaven smiles on us, never again. Good as it is, that onion soup mix got pretty tiresome before it began to occur to people that there must be other combinations that would make great dunks. And so there are, so there are.

Dips are thinner than the canapé spreads from which they sprang, but should be thick enough not to be a threat to clothes and carpets when used by speeding, starving dunkers, especially the stand-up ones of the cocktail party circuit. Sour cream makes a fine base. So does softened cream cheese. So does mayonnaise—in some cases. So do, less calorifically, plain yogurt and lowfat cottage cheese whirled smooth in the blender. As for flavoring, the dip-maker has wide scope. Make any dip as above, add a zipper-upper from the list below, season to taste, and you're ready to let the party get underway.

snipped fresh dill
drained minced clams
snipped chives
chopped parsley + onion juice
basil + tomato paste
snipped dried beef + garlic juice
mashed avocado + lemon juice + onion juice
thinly sliced small scallions
chopped hard-cooked egg + relish
finely chopped raw mushrooms
chopped chutney + curry powder
crumbled bleu cheese
sharp cheddar + bacon bits
grated orange peel + chopped mint (for fruit)
chopped shrimp + dill
mashed kidney beans + chili peppers
chopped lobster + grated onion + sherry
chopped chicken livers + sautéed onion
deviled ham + chopped onion + chopped sweet pickle
mashed liver sausage + chopped pistachios

And those are only to get you started on ideas of your own.

As for dippers and dunkers, there are dozens available —corn or potato chips, toasted bread strips, sautéed bread shapes, pretzel sticks, commercial (flavored or not) small bread sticks, shredded-wheat wafers, crackers by the dozens of all shapes and flavors. Vegetables of many sorts are fine, too—thin strips or sticks or slices of carrot, celery, zucchini, jicama, turnip, cucumber; cauliflower and young broccoli flowerets; whole radishes and scallions. Fruit, too—apple wedges, pineapple fingers, whole strawberries, melon balls, halved fresh apricots, quartered fresh peaches, halved fresh figs. Dip in! See also APPETIZERS and GUACAMOLE.

DISHWASHERS: see special feature: YOU CAN'T WORK WITHOUT TOOLS

DISSOLVE, TO: see page 445

DISTILLED VINEGAR: see VINEGARS

DITALI: see PASTA

DONENESS

"How do I know when it's done?" That's a niggling question for all cooks, an exceedingly important one to beginning cooks who are trying to learn that piece of high-ranking kitchen legerdemain: how to have all the components of a meal done and ready to serve at the same time.

There are ways. Expert cooks can tell by looking. And by smelling. Try this simple trick—put a piece of bread in the toaster and stand beside it, sniffing. You can tell by the difference in smell the point at which it's warming up, the point at which it's a lovely, golden brown, and the point at which it's beginning to burn. A more aware sense of smell, highly developed by those who spend their lives and earn their livings in kitchens, gives those same clues for all kinds of food. And their eyes also tell such cooks, at a quick glance, that the cauliflower needs another three minutes, the pie another six, the lamb chops two minutes more before turning.

Those of us not blessed with such skills use other methods—timing, various gadgets, common sense. When we're first learning to cook, we need to add it all up: put the potatoes on ten minutes before the roast is done; take the roast out and let it "rest" twenty minutes; ten minutes after the roast comes out, drain and mash the potatoes, and put on the frozen green beans; make the gravy, let it simmer; send in the roast for carving, put the rolls in to warm; drain and dish the beans, dish the potatoes, dress the previously prepared salad, take out the rolls. Then, if the table has been set in advance, the whole dinner will be ready simultaneously. Later, such planning comes automatically to the cook, without having to be thought through, as she masters the techniques of doneness-scheduling.

"Cook until done." Some recipes say cavalierly, "cook until done," assuming you'll have the good sense to know when that happy moment arrives. But suppose you've never cooked that particular food before—will it be done in ten minutes? Two hours? Other recipes helpfully add to the phrase: "cook until done, about 20 minutes," giving you a pretty good clue as to when the food will be cooked in relation to the other parts of the meal. Still others state categorically: "bake 30 minutes"—a chancy business because all ovens are not the same. And there are other variables: food that is icy cold will take longer to cook than that at room temperature, for example, a bit longer when the oven is not preheated than when it is, a somewhat shorter time if the food is particularly young and tender of its kind or longer if it is older and/or tougher than the average food in that category.

Gadgets and helpers. An oven whose thermostat is properly regulated is a must. Your local gas or electric company will test the controls and regulate the thermostat if it requires an adjustment.

Meat can be roasted by timing, but it's a lot less certain a method than using a meat thermometer. Candy and cooked frostings and syrups and the like can be tested by the cold-water method, but a candy thermometer is much more precise. If your family enjoys deep-fat-fried foods, you can use the browned-cube-of-bread method to see if the fat has reached the right temperature, but a thermometer—or the gauge on an electric fryer—is much more accurate.

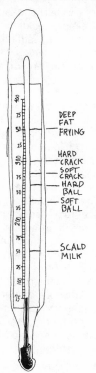

DEEP
FAT
FRYING

HARD
CRACK
SOFT
CRACK
HARD
BALL
SOFT
BALL

SCALD
MILK

Every cook needs a timer to ring or buzz a reminder when cooking time is up. Many stoves have one; if yours doesn't, invest in a mechanical timer. They come in all shapes and colors, most of them timing by the minute up to one hour, but some with timing periods up to five or even seven hours. Microwave ovens have built-in timers; so do some other kitchen appliances, such as some brands of electric mixers. Electric appliances often have timers that flash a light when they have reached cooking temperature or when the food—such as waffles—has reached the required shade of brown. Toasters obligingly pop the toast up when it's done. Automatic ovens turn themselves off, or down to a keep-warm temperature, when the pre-selected cooking period is up. We live in an era of automation.

Indeed, in a world where we have dozens of gadgets, comparable to extra pairs of hands in the kitchen, a world in which we no longer scrub our clothes on a washboard, get down on our hands and knees to tackle the kitchen floor, flatiron weekly mountains of clothing and linens, make all our own clothes and our children's, and wrestle with the dozens of other tasks that once made up the daily lot of the housewife, some of us—the unliberated ones—feel stirrings of primordial guilt on occasion. Sure, we're busy, we're pushed. But really, taking care of a house is pretty easy compared to what it once was. Somehow, it ought to be harder—and being harder, nobler, loftier as well. So we spend our days in a sort of wild chase through our daily chores, pursued by a panting protestant work ethic. But that's another story. Back to doneness—a state which the guilty ones believe never occurs.

Knowing fingers, all-seeing eyes. Even with gadgets to aid us, we need to have in our minds—or in some other place where we can refer to it when we need it—a kind of overall cooking timetable. Cooks develop it over the years, but beginners do a good deal of floundering around until they get the hang of kitchen scheduling. "Cook until done" or "cook until tender" are all very well—but how long will it take? How can you be sure it's ready? Here are some of the rough rules of thumb for doneness.

Timing meats. Relatively speaking, tougher cuts of meat, cooked with moist heat, require longer cooking times than tenderer cuts, cooked by dry heat. But the reverse is true of poultry—it cooks somewhat faster by moist heat than by dry. Fish cooks in quite brief a time by either method.

beef: There was a home cook, some years ago, who timed her large Sunday roast of beef not by clock, but by dog. She put the roast on late in the morning and went off to church. Home again, she continued to cook it until a neighbor's dog, a family friend, appeared at the back door, sniffing and drooling. At that point she took the roast out of the oven, cut Rex off a juicy, rare slice—and then shoved the roast back into the oven for three more hours, bringing it to the table shrunken, dry, cooked within an inch of disaster.

Beef connoisseurs like their meat, both roasts and steaks, bloody rare. To serve a roast in that delicious condition—barely heated through, dissenters claim—count on roughly 20 minutes per pound in a 325°F. oven. Add 4 minutes per pound for medium rare, 4 or 5 more for medium, 5 more for (fie!) well done. Use a meat thermometer for on-the-nose doneness—internal temperature of 140° for rare, 160° for medium, and 170° for well done—but these increments of time will help you know at about what point the meat will be ready. Count on 15 to 20 minutes standing time after you take the roast out of the oven—it will carve better.

Steaks less than an inch thick do not broil satisfactorily for any but medium and well-done eaters; steaks of 1- to 1½-inch thickness will broil very rare in a hot broiler when cooked 5 minutes per side. Add 2 minutes per side more for each increased degree of doneness. Steaks 2 inches thick will be rare after 7 minutes per side; add 2 minutes more per side for each increased degree of doneness.

Braised beef in one piece—pot roasts and the like—should be cooked until tender, a matter of 2 to 4 hours, depending on size. Whole smoked or otherwise cured beef—corned beef and tongue are examples—requires longer cooking, in larger amounts of liquid. Count on 3½ to 4 hours, or even a little longer if the piece of meat is very large. The beef in stews will be ready in 2½ to 3 hours. Be aware that these meats will be edible before those times, but they will not be tender, and tenderness is the criterion of doneness in tougher cuts of meat. Poke the meat with a long-tined fork to test for tenderness.

pork: Well-done is the only way pork of any kind can be safely served. For a roast, count on about 35 minutes per pound, in a 350°F. oven, and time with a meat thermometer to an internal temperature of 185°. If you broil pork chops, they must be cooked through, which tends to make them dry—better to pan brown them, then cover the pan, lower the heat and cook, with or without the addition of a small amount of liquid, until they are done, from 30 minutes for thin chops to an hour for thick ones. Or brown in a skillet, finish the cooking in a 325°F. oven, adding 10 to 15 minutes to the cooking time.

Spareribs can be cooked in water on top of the stove for an hour, finished for another hour in the oven, sauced or glazed if you like; or cook them covered in the oven for the first hour, drain the fat and cook uncovered for the second hour.

Ham should be cooked to an internal temperature of 170° unless it is labeled "fully cooked," in which case an internal temperature of 150° will send it to the table hot and ready to carve.

veal: This tender meat is also served well done. Roast in a 325°F. oven, counting on 35 minutes per pound; use a meat thermometer to bring the internal temperature to 180°. Veal scallops—pounded thin—will cook briefly in a skillet in about 7 minutes for each side; give veal cutlet, which is thicker, 10 minutes for each side; give chops, even thicker, a total cooking time of 45 minutes to an hour, depending on their thickness—they are best treated like pork chops because veal dries out all too easily. Veal breast is best braised, most acceptably in the oven, and requires long, slow cooking—count on 2½ to 3 hours, depending on size.

Calf's liver (this is veal, too) should be very briefly sautéed, no more than 3 minutes a side for thin slices, and served pink—but not bloody rare.

lamb: Some like lamb well done, some contend that it must be pink—medium rare to medium—to be at its best. Count on 30 minutes per pound in a 325°F. oven, to an internal temper-

ature of 180° for well-done roasted lamb—leg or shoulder—25 minutes per pound to an internal temperature of 165° for a lovely pink. Rib or loin lamb chops, too, may be broiled well done or pink; count on 7 to 10 minutes per side, depending on thickness, for pink; add 2 minutes per side for well done. Lamb shoulder chops, lamb shanks and riblets (lamb spareribs) should be braised—stovetop or oven—until well done. All lamb is relatively tender and cooks in a shorter time than beef. (What's "relative"? Einstein, explaining relativity, remarked that when a man spends two hours with a pretty girl it seems a very brief time, but two minutes spent in pain can seem very long indeed.)

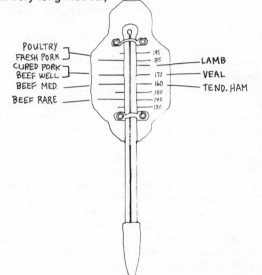

Timing poultry. To paraphrase a TV commercial, nobody doesn't like chicken. This is generally true of chicken's small relatives, the cornish hens, and big cousins, the turkeys. Duck doesn't meet with such wide acceptance. Neither does goose—perhaps not only because of its flavor but also because of its limited availability. Chicken and turkey can be purchased in several forms—whole, halved, in parts, and either fresh or frozen. Cornish hens are generally available only frozen, although they are widely distributed. Duck and goose are also available frozen, and less widely distributed—this is particularly true of goose.

chicken and turkey: Count on about 15 to 20 minutes per pound for a tender roasting chicken; 35 to 40 for a small turkey, about 20 for a large. Both should be well done, cooked to an internal temperature of 185° in a 325°F. oven. Using a meat thermometer is less easy—and more chancy—with poultry than with meat. The thermometer, in all cases, must be inserted into the meat so that the bulb is not resting in fat or against bone, as either of those conditions lead to unrealistic readings. In a good-sized roast of meat, this poses no problem—but how do you insert a meat thermometer in poultry without encountering bone? Put it into the heaviest part of the thigh, avoiding both the hip socket and the thigh bone. It's difficult with a small chicken, not so troublesome if you're dealing with a large turkey. But there are other ways to judge doneness in poultry. Insert the tip of a thin-bladed knife between the body and the thigh of the bird—juices should run clear or somewhat yellow, but never even slightly tinged with red or even pink. The breast meat near where the wing joins the body should feel softly tender when pricked with a fork; so should the meat of the drumstick when pinched between your fingers—protect yourself from burns with absorbent paper.

Roast a duck or goose 35 minutes per pound at 350°F. to an internal temperature of 185°. (If you wish crispy skin and less rich meat, prick with a fork—but don't overdo it, for even a pleasingly plump duck or goose can lose too much fat during cooking, turn out dry and tasteless.) Goose is virtually always served well done, but some duck lovers want their birds rare—for them, cook to an internal temperature of 165°.

Fried chicken should cook in about 40 minutes or—less crisp, but also more certain of being cooked completely—can be browned on all sides, then cooked over lower heat, covered, until the juices show no sign of pinkness, about 35 to 40 minutes after the browning period. Delicate suprême de volaille—boned breast of chicken—or "scallops" (thin slices) of turkey breast cook in a brief time, about 6 minutes per side sautéed, or 15 minutes total time gently braised in butter. Count on about 70 minutes for chicken parts baked in a casserole or in sauce, longer for turkey parts, depending on size—again, test for pinkness in the juices.

Timing fish and shellfish. Brevity may or may not be the soul of wit, but it is indubitably the essence of cooking fish of all kinds, no matter by what method.

fillets: Of whatever fish, poached or broiled (broiling is wrong for all but thick fillets of fat fish), or breaded and pan- or deep-fried, fillets generally take between 9 and 12 minutes to cook. They are done when the flesh loses its translucency and flakes readily when gently poked with a fork. In the oven, cooked in liquid or butter-braised, the time may be as long as 17 or 18 minutes; test for doneness in the same way.

whole fish: Baked on a rack in the oven, stuffed or not as you like, whole fish will bake in 30 to 50 minutes, unless you are cooking a monster—a whole salmon, say. Small whole "panfish"—sunnies and the like—should be done in about 10 minutes per side, sautéed in a skillet. Again, test all fish, however cooked, for doneness by flaking with a fork.

big cuts of fish: One of the world's great treats is a large center cut of salmon, poached in COURT BOUILLON and served hot with lemon butter or hollandaise, or cold with a cucumber-sour cream sauce. You'll need a deep kettle and an unusual kitchen tool, a ruler, as well as a piece of cheesecloth large enough to enclose the whole piece of fish with enough left over for a handle. Measure the fish at its thickest point; count on poaching the fish exactly 10 minutes for each inch. Bring the court bouillon to the boiling point. Tie the fish in the cheesecloth and lower it into the liquid, which should be deep enough to cover it completely. Turn down the heat and barely simmer until done. Take out and drain in the cheesecloth, remove carefully to a serving platter.

fish steaks: These—swordfish, tuna, salmon, and the like— are most often broiled. A 1-inch-thick steak should be done in 10 to 12 minutes—do not turn. Test by flaking.

shellfish: Again, be brief. Oysters need only be cooked until their edges curl, a matter of 3 to 4 minutes in their own liquor or in an oyster stew, or baked on a (filled) half shell. Clams take a little longer—their muscles are tougher. Shrimp can be simmered until they turn pink, 3 or 4 minutes, perhaps 5 if they are very large. A chicken lobster (1 pound) will cook whole in boiling water in 10 minutes, will broil—split—in about the same amount of time; for larger lobsters, add 4 minutes a pound. Abalone, sliced and pounded into submissive tenderness as abalone steaks, must be very briefly sautéed, or it will get tough all over again—3 or 4 minutes should do it. Bay scallops are at their best dipped in melted butter, rolled in dry bread crumbs, and sautéed no longer than 4 minutes; larger scallops will take proportionately longer. (As for those fake "scallops" stamped out of a piece of flat fish, forget it —caveat emptor.) Mussels in their shell can steam in court bouillon 6 to 8 minutes.

Casseroles and other mixed-food main dishes. If the ingredients of such a dish are uncooked (chicken baked with vegetables, for example), plan on timing by the normal cooking time of the longest-cooking ingredient—in this case, the chicken; if that is done, everything else will be, too. This is the rule for all casseroles in which uncooked meat or poultry is used. You need to be guided, as well, by the size of the pieces of meat—chicken parts will cook in a shorter time than a whole chicken, cubed lamb in a shorter time than whole lamb shanks, and so on.

If all the ingredients in a casserole are precooked, oven time required is only long enough to meld flavors and get the mixture piping hot—20 minutes or so in a 350°F. oven for a 4-serving casserole, 30 minutes for 6 servings, 35 for 8. If the casserole has been prepared earlier and refrigerated, add an extra 5 minutes for a small casserole, 10 for a larger one. If the casserole has been frozen, baking time doubles and may even triple for a very large casserole.

If the casserole ingredients are bubbling, you can safely assume that it is ready to serve. If you still aren't sure, plunge the blade of a table knife into the center of the casserole and let it remain there a full minute. Take it out and immediately feel it—gingerly—with your fingers. If it is very hot, so is the center of the casserole, and the dish is ready to serve. A frozen casserole of uncooked ingredients takes an unconscionably long time to thaw-then-cook. Better let it stand in the refrigerator in advance of cooking, in plenty of time so that it will be completely thawed—the center gives up last—when it goes into the oven. Then time it as you would a refrigerated raw-ingredient dish.

Vegetables and fruits. Vegetables are iffy. "Cook until tender," older recipes recommend; "cook until tender-crisp" many newer ones advise. There are a few general rules to guide you. Root vegetables take longer to cook than those that grow above the ground. Cut-up vegetables cook in less time than whole ones, and the smaller the pieces the shorter the cooking time. "Tender" means that a two-tined fork or a small, thin knife blade meets no resistance when you stick the vegetable with it. "Tender-crisp" means that you will meet some resistance. Some vegetables—potatoes are a sterling example—should never be cooked tender-crisp, and if your family's reaction to any vegetable cooked to that state is, "Hey, this stuff isn't done!" you may as well go back to cooking everything until tender. There's no point—and no nutrition—in cooking foods nobody will eat.

How long? Potatoes and other root vegetables will be tender in roughly 20 minutes if cut into medium pieces. New potatoes take a bit longer to cook than old ones, and whole new potatoes, unless they are tiny, will be tender in about 30 to 35 minutes. Beets, unless they are very small and garden-fresh, require 40 to 50 minutes, because beets are always cooked whole to avoid "bleeding"; if they are very old, they may need an hour or more.

Celery and onions, sliced, will be tender-crisp in 8 to 10 minutes, tender in 15 to 20, depending on age. Ditto green and wax beans, and peas. Cauliflower, broken into flowerets, is tender in about 12 minutes, unless it's very old; this is another vegetable that doesn't take too kindly to the tender-crisp treatment—if you like it crisp, serve it raw. Broccoli, if you split the stems, takes about the same time or a little less. Coarsely shredded cabbage can be "panned" in butter and a very little water in 6 to 8 minutes; quartered, it will take 15 to 20. Spinach, cooked in only the water that clings to the leaves, is ready in 3 to 5 minutes (frozen spinach should be thawed before cooking, or cooked long enough to thaw it). Corn on the cob, if it's young and fresh, cooks in 5 minutes after the water returns to a boil; pan corn off the cob in butter and a little cream in 3 minutes.

Fruit tends to take a little longer to cook than you'd think. For sauce, pies, and other desserts, choose the right variety of apple (see APPLES); some cook in a very brief time, some resist lengthily. Peaches and pears poach in syrup in about 40 minutes if whole, 30 if halved. Rhubarb cooks into sauce in about 10 minutes if it's young, proportionately longer the older (larger) it is. Berries generally cook quickly—about 10 minutes of brisk cooking for sauce.

Wednesday and Saturday are baking days. Perhaps not now, though they used to be—Monday was washday; Tuesday, ironing; Wednesday, baking; Thursday, upstairs cleaning; Friday, downstairs cleaning; Saturday, baking again; Sunday (thank goodness!), a day of rest. How pleasant that we've managed, between consciousness-raising and the acquisition of a flock of gadgets and appliances, plus easy-care furniture and floor and window coverings and table and bed linens and clothing, to pry ourselves out of that destructive rut.

Still, we bake, some of us at least. Not because our families will starve, there being no alternative, but because we like to.

cakes: As an overall rule, flat cakes (in layer or square or sheet pans) bake in a shorter time than those in deep and/or tube pans. Layer cakes bake in 25 to 30 minutes, squares and rectangles in 30 to 45, deep cakes (depending on their kind) in 45 to 75 minutes, except for fruit cakes and real pound cakes, which take even longer.

How do you tell when they're done? First, let the cake bake at the oven temperature called for in the minimum amount of time the recipe suggests. If at that point it is nicely, evenly browned, and has shrunk a bit from the sides of the pan, it is probably done. Press it lightly in the center with the tip of your finger—if the indentation springs back, you're in. Or stick a food pick or cake tester (grandma tore a straw out of the kitchen broom, but sanitation has overtaken us) in the center; if it comes out clean, the cake is done. The cake tester doesn't work for sponge or angel cakes, but the finger-tip test does. Cupcakes, depending on the size of the cups in which they are baked, should be done in 12 to 18 minutes.

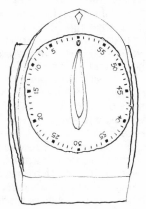

quick breads, yeast breads: Biscuits bake in about 12 minutes in a hot oven, muffins in 15 to 20 minutes; small, square-pan coffeecakes and corn bread in 30 to 35 minutes, larger rectangular ones in 10 minutes more. Let your eyes tell you when they are well risen and nicely browned, and if you're uncertain, use a cake tester. The "quick" in quick breads means that they are quicker to prepare, not necessarily to bake. Yeast breads bake in relatively short times, too. Small yeast breads—rolls and buns—bake in 15 to 20 minutes; so do various kinds of sweet rolls. Loaves of bread and raised coffeecakes take longer, 40 to 50 minutes. If you are uncertain about the doneness of a loaf of bread, at the end of the recommended baking time, turn it out of the pan—it will drop out easily—and thump its bottom with your knuckles. If it sounds hollow, the bread is done; if not, back to the oven for another 5 to 10 minutes.

pies: The top should be pleasantly, richly brown, whether the top is a crust or the surface of an open-face pie's filling. Fruit pies should bubble to thicken their juices; they bake in about an hour, the first 10 to 15 minutes at a high temperature, the remaining time at a somewhat lowered one. Custard-type pies—including pumpkin—are slow cookers and may take 40 to 80 minutes, depending on the ingredients. Check for doneness by inserting the blade of a table knife into the filling halfway between the center and the rim—if the knife comes out clean, with no filling clinging to it, the pie is done. Don't count on the pie being done in the time the recipe says; it may be, so check it, but this is an area in which many cookbooks err on the side of brevity. Pie shells, which are baked before a precooked filling is added, should be nicely browned, ready to cool and fill, in 10 to 15 minutes in a hot 475°F. oven.

custards and egg-based puddings: These require take-it-easy treatment. "Cook," recipes say of stovetop custards made in a double boiler, "until mixture coats the spoon." A metal spoon that is, and the "coating" is a very thin, translucent film, not a heavy covering. Stir with the metal spoon, take it out of the mixture, and—if a thin film clings to the spoon and does not run off—remove the custard from the heat—and from the bottom of the double boiler, or it will continue to cook. Incidentally, the water in the bottom of the double boiler, over which the mixture cooks, must be hot, but never boiling. Desserts of this ilk thicken as they cool. Baked custards and similar desserts are cooked in a water bath—*bain marie,* if you encounter the term in a French cookbook. That is, the custard is poured into its baking dish or dishes, then placed in a larger pan into which water is poured to half the depth of the custard dish. Test such desserts by inserting the blade of a table knife halfway between the center and the rim; if it comes out clean, with no bits of the food clinging to it, the dessert is done. Remove at once from the water bath—if you let the food cool in the bath, it will be overcooked.

DOT, TO: see page 445

DOUGHNUTS

These wonderful sweets, reminiscent of country kitchens—hear the fire crackling in the wood stove?—barn-raisings, cider-pressings, square dances, and Halloween, fall into two well-known classes. One kind is leavened with yeast, one with baking powder. The yeast-leavened ones are called raised doughnuts; their dough, like bread dough, is not very sweet; they derive their sweetness from a sugar dipping or a topper of glaze or frosting. The baking powder-leavened kind are called cake doughnuts—their dough is sweet, but that doesn't prevent us from shaking them in a bag full of confectioners sugar or cinnamon-sugar, or giving them the glaze or frosting treatment too. A third kind, the french doughnut, is seldom seen these days—not often enough at any rate. It is made of choux paste—the dough from which cream puffs are made—and pressed into a ridged ring through a pastry tube. Often glazed, they are the most delicate of doughnuts.

In each of the two main categories there are several subclasses. Raised doughnuts may be the familiar doughnut shape—round, with a hole in the middle—or they may be a long, éclair shape, or twisted; or square (New Orleans type, for dunking) or round, but without a hole, so that they may be filled after frying with tart-sweet jam or jelly or smooth cream. Cake doughnuts are most often round, but inside the crispy brown crust can lurk any number of flavors—nutmeg, orange, chocolate, lemon, and more. They can be sugar-shaken, frosted, or sprinkled after frosting with chocolate shot, coconut, chopped nuts, crushed hard candy.

Raised doughnuts must rise before they are fried. Cake doughnuts can be fried at once, but they profit from an hour or so in the refrigerator to firm up the dough—that way, very little flour is needed to roll them out, and added flour makes the finished product less tender.

Be certain that the fat you use for frying is at the proper temperature—for most doughnuts, 365°F. For techniques, see DEEP-FAT FRYING.

Cautionary note: When you make cake doughnuts, don't neglect to fry the "holes"—some people claim they're the best part. The world is filled with disappointed children whose grandmothers forgot to fry the holes.

DOVE: see GAME

DRAIN, TO: see page 445

DRAWN BUTTER

This, served as a sauce with vegetables or seafood, is melted butter; most elegantly, it is clarified. See BUTTER.

DREDGE, TO: see page 445

DRESSINGS: see MAYONNAISE, SALAD DRESSINGS, and STUFFINGS

DRIED FOODS

Once, drying—in a current of air or spread out in the sunshine —or packing in salt or sugar were the only ways to preserve food when there was plenty against the lean and hungry times. All over the world, for centuries, people have dried beans and peas and lentils to store for the season when there would be no fresh vegetables. The "pease" of the old English nursery rhyme, "Pease Porridge Hot," were dried— and whether hot or cold or nine days old, were far more nourishing than their alternative, nothing, for long-ago British peasants in times of famine. American Indians dried (sometimes smoked) all sorts of foods—meat, fish, cranberries and other berries, cherries, corn, and beans among them—and shared this method of preserving, and the foods themselves, with settlers, many of whom would have starved without such acts of charitable neighborliness.

Today we still eat and enjoy many kinds of dried foods. Those same beans, peas, and lentils are with us in abundance, for savory wintertime soups and casseroles. Raisins (dried grapes) are the most common dried fruit, but there are also prunes (dried plums), apples, peaches, pears, apricots, figs, and cherries. In the seasonings section of a large supermarket you will find dried herbs and spices of many kinds, dried orange and lemon peel, dried mushrooms in both the Chinese and American style, dried onion and parsley and green pepper and celery "flakes," and dried hot red peppers.

Dried fish is available in several varieties, particularly in various ethnic delicatessens and those corners of paradise for dedicated eaters, the "appetizing stores." Dried meat is not as widely available as it once was, when various kinds of jerky were laid away for winter or as provisions for long journeys. But in the last several years jerky has begun to appear in supermarkets for general consumption, instead of only as the province of hunters and campers. Jerky makes a fine snack for youngsters and oldsters alike, infinitely more nutritious and less calories-making than, say, cookies or candies, and it has found its place among the many other nibbles and munchies we serve with cocktails. One meat, dried (sometimes known as chipped) beef has been with us all along, and is still a favorite. (Actually, it is pickled, smoked, then dried, then thin-sliced and packaged or packed in glass jars.) It can be frizzled to serve with eggs for breakfast, creamed on toast for lunch or supper (it sometimes appears that way at breakfast, too), or incorporated into any number of casserole dishes. Spread with softened cream cheese, plain or mixed with snipped chives, then rolled, dried beef makes a zippy snack with drinks, or a splendid accompaniment to a luncheon salad, making the meal both tastier and considerably more substantial.

Other such foods available to us are dry soup mixes, dried eggs, and dried milk. The advantages of all of these dried foods are that the unopened package requires no refrigeration (often the opened package need not be refrigerated, either) and the concentration of moisture removal makes for smaller, easier to store packages. Year-around availability is also a factor.

Since the trend back toward the natural way of living began, many people have begun to experiment—many very successfully—with drying foods at home as an alternative to canning and freezing as a way of storing home-raised (and sometimes store-bought) foods.

DRIP GRIND: see COFFEE

DRIZZLE, TO: see page 445

DRY MILK: see MILK

DRYING FOOD AT HOME: see special
    feature: PUTTING FOOD BY

DUCHESSE: see page 452

DUCK, DUCKLING

Web-footed and aquatic of habit, the duck has been hunted for its dark, succulent flesh since before recorded history.

Egyptians were so fond of it that they salted and dried ducks to ensure a constant supply. The Chinese—first in so many things—brought the ducks out of the wild, raising them for food rather than depending on the uncertainties of the hunt. The Japanese kept ducks in a semiwild state, in large enclosures netted at the top to prevent them from flying away. To domesticate ducks, the Romans took eggs from the wild birds' nests and put them under their setting hens. The ducks were fed on figs and dates to sweeten their flesh; they were cooked with wine and truffles.

In colonial times in this country, wild ducks—mallards— were an important part of the food supply. In the United States today, more than half of the five million domestic ducks that will eventually come to our tables are raised on Long Island, in an area about seventy-five miles from New York City, all descended from three ducks and a drake brought from China in the 1870s.

DUCK IN YOUR KITCHEN

Actually, "duckling" is a more accurate term, for most of the ducks we eat are young birds. Fresh duck is available from May to January, but only near places where the birds are raised. Broiler/fryer ducklings are very young birds, under 8 weeks old; roasters are larger, ranging in age up to 16 weeks and in weight from 3 to 5½ pounds. Frozen ducks—the ones most of us encounter—are usually roasters. We buy them from meat departments' frozen-food sections, securely dressed in sturdy, shape-fitting plastic wraps.

how to buy: Choose a fresh duck that is broad-breasted, well padded with fat; the skin should be elastic rather than flabby. The bird should be clean, almost free of pinfeathers. When you buy a frozen duck, make certain the plastic wrap is unbroken, that the bird looks clean, white, unbruised.

how to store: Cover fresh duck loosely, store in the coldest part of the refrigerator up to 3 days; store giblets separately. If frozen, duck may be stored in the freezer at 0°F. or below up to 3 months; thaw just before cooking. Refrigerate cooked duck, closely covered, up to 2 days; remove stuffing and store separately.

nutritive value: Higher in fat than chicken or turkey, duck— it follows—is also higher in calories, about 315 for 3 slices of roasted breast meat. The same amount offers nearly 23 grams of high-quality protein, about the same amount of fat. Duck is a good source of the B vitamins thiamin and riboflavin, and a fair source of iron.

Freezing duck. Since frozen duck is available the year around, there is no point in doing something that the processors can do better and more quickly. If frozen duck is on sale, by all means buy a supply to be used within 3 months, and store in your freezer.

Duck on the table. In Europe, duck is considered one of the greatest delicacies. Here, it is not served as often—nor, in many cases, is it greeted as joyously. For the sake of variety, and for very good eating indeed, learn to prepare duck. It's easy.

thawing: Thaw frozen duck, still in its plastic wrap, in the refrigerator. The process will take from 24 to 36 hours, depending on the size of the bird. Plan on cooking the bird as soon as it is thawed. If you're in a hurry, thaw—again, still in its plastic overcoat—in a pan of cold water; it should be ready to cook in 1½ to 3 hours.

preparation: Remove giblets and neck from the cavity of the bird. Rinse the fresh or thawed duck in cold water, and pat dry. Leave the duck whole, or split it and remove the backbone; a sharp knife and a pair of poultry shears are the tools you will need. Leave halved, or cut into quarters. Bear in mind that the edible meat is on the breast and thighs and drumsticks—the back and wings have virtually nothing to offer.

stuffing: About 4 cups of stuffing will fill an average duck, both body and neck cavities. Stuffing can be one of many varieties, based on bread (try corn bread, rye, or pumpernickel, rather than white, for a change), brown or white or wild rice, or mashed potatoes. It should be highly seasoned with onion and celery, with sage and/or thyme, or rosemary, and can incorporate such delightful surprises as sliced almonds, dried fruit such as prunes or apricots or raisins, or fresh fruit such as apples or oranges. Stuffing should be moist, but does not require as much fat as that for chicken or turkey, as it will acquire fat from the duck during cooking. If you prefer not to stuff the bird, put a quartered onion, a couple of pieces of celery, and a quartered apple or orange into the cavity for extra flavor.

roasting: Stuffed or not, truss the duck by fastening the neck skin to the back with a skewer and tying the ends of the legs together. Prick the skin—but not deeply into the meat— to allow some of the fat to drain away, so that the meat will not be too rich and the skin crisply browned. Rub the outside of the duck with salt—this, too, helps to crisp the skin as well as flavor it. Place on a rack in a shallow roasting pan; ideally, the rack should raise the bird to the level of the rim of the pan or slightly above it. Roast in a preheated 325°F. oven. A 4-pound duck will be done in about 2½ hours, a 5-pound bird in 3 hours. If you like your duck somewhat rare, as many people do, shorten the roasting time by 30 minutes or so. To test for doneness, gently pinch the drumstick meat; it should be soft. If you like a very brown, crisp skin, turn the heat up to 450°F. for the final 10 minutes of roasting time.

cooking giblets: Simmer neck, heart, and gizzard for 1¾ hours in salted water to which a little onion and celery have been added; add liver and cook 15 minutes longer. Add chopped giblets to gravy, or cook in advance and add to stuffing. Use the broth in which the giblets were cooked to make gravy, or for cooking rice to serve with the duck.

finishing: If you would like the skin to have a sweet glaze, brush with honey or with melted apple jelly several times during the last half hour of cooking time, raising the oven temperature during that period to 400°F.

other ways: Duck may be broiled—halves or quarters—if you prefer. Broil slowly, 7 or 8 inches from the heat source. Or braise duck by browning first, on top of the stove, pouring off all the fat, adding liquid (water alone, or in combination with cider, apple juice, orange juice, or white or red wine) and seasonings; cover and simmer until tender.

Some perfect partners. Duck and mushrooms go well together. So do duck and turnips, sweet potatoes, corn, panned cabbage, broccoli or cauliflower, or sauerkraut— with, if you like them, caraway seeds. Duck takes kindly to all sorts of fruit accompaniments, such as dried fruit compote, poached oranges, nut-stuffed prunes, fried apple slices, applesauce, watermelon pickles, sautéed canned pineapple slices or halved bananas.

For a wonderful, unusual duck dish, a day in advance of serving, cook giblets as above and roast unstuffed duck as above, glazing the skin with honey. Remove meat from bones in large pieces. Cut skin in strips. Make gravy from drippings in the usual way, using orange juice in place of water. Cut orange peel into thin strips and simmer 2 hours in light sugar syrup. Refrigerate all. On the day of serving, cook wild rice in the giblet broth and combine half-and-half with sautéed mushrooms on an ovenproof platter. Cover with duck meat; spoon orange gravy over. Sprinkle with strips of duck skin; garnish with orange peel. Bake at 325°F. until heated through.

Besides being delicious, this dish is a duck stretcher— a 5-pound duck which, roasted, will serve two generously or four rather stingily, will serve 6 to 8 when prepared this way. Serve with sautéed bananas, crisp corn sticks, green beans amandine, and sauerkraut salad for a perfect and unusual company-coming dinner.

Wild duck is a gourmet delight. It is sometimes available in elegant butcher shops in large cities, but most often is the result of a hunting trip, yours or a friend's. See GAME.

DUMPLINGS

There are two kinds of dumplings, those—usually steamed—that are a light and delicious accompaniment to soups and stews and main dishes, and those—steamed or baked, most often enclosing fruit or cooked in a fruit sauce—that are served as dessert.

We get our love of dumplings from English or Scandinavian ancestors, or those from middle Europe—Germany, Austria, Czechoslovakia, Poland—where wonderful dumplings of infinite variety are a culinary way of life.

Base of dumplings is a starch of some sort—flour, cornmeal, bread crumbs, farina, matzo meal—with liquid and/or eggs, butter or other fat, and leavening. Savory dumplings are simmered, covered, in soup or stock or even plain water (the latter are then drained and served with butter or gravy as a meat side dish) or on top of a thicker mixture, such as a stew. Some dumplings hide a surprise, such as a browned bread cube or a slice of sausage, in their centers; others are made more substantial with ground or chopped liver, or flavored with herbs or spices, or incorporate cheese or tomato paste into their dough.

Chicken soup with matzo balls—knaidlach—is a Jewish dish that all the rest of us have taken to our hearts. Pennsyl-vania Dutch chicken-corn soup with rivels—dumpling dough crumbled or put through a strainer into the soup—is a hearty delight on a cold day. New England chicken fricassee with cornmeal dumplings is a homestyle treat. Italian mashed-potato dumplings—GNOCCHI—with parmesan in the dough, and served with tomato sauce, are a delicious change from the more usual pasta.

For dessert, dumplings are perfect as a hearty finish to a light meal. Baked apple dumplings are most familiar, but just as delicious are nutmeg-flavored dumplings steamed in a sauce made of fresh peaches, or yeast-raised dumplings in plum sauce, or dumplings cooked in butterscotch or orange sauce, or berry—blackberry, blueberry, whatever—dumplings—all of these served with light cream.

DUNGENESS CRAB: see SHELLFISH

DURIANS: see EXOTIC FRUIT

DUST, TO: see page 445

DUXELLES

One of the graces of French cooking, made by simmering finely chopped mushrooms and shallots (or scallions, if shallots are not available) in a stock or broth until the liquid has evaporated. Used where the flavor of mushrooms is wanted, but large pieces of mushroom are undesirable. Beef Wellington blankets the fillet of beef in pâté, then in duxelles, before the crust encloses it. Veal Prince Orloff flavors sliced roasted veal with duxelles and soubise (onion purée) between the slices. The cook who is deeply into this sort of thing can make duxelles in quantity, store in the refrigerator up to 2 weeks, or freeze the mixture up to 6 months.

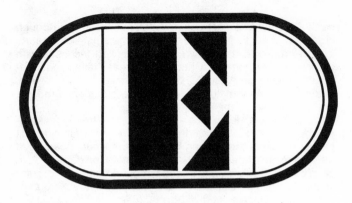

ECLAIR: see page 452

EDAM: see CHEESE

EELS

Like a snake in shape and in movement, and apparently without scales, the eel is nevertheless a fish, not a reptile. Indeed, it does have scales, but they are very tiny and buried in the skin. Eel is one of the fat fish—its flesh is rich, with excellent flavor. It is not the taste, but the shape, that makes fishermen shudder and throw them back, that makes some people exclaim, with little whinnies of disgust, "I wouldn't eat that thing for a million dollars!" (Get up the million, though, and eel would doubtless be on the menu at breakfast, lunch, and dinner.) It does no good to point out that some people eat snakes, and that rattlesnake meat, for example, is very like chicken. Snakes are snakes and so, in many minds, are eels—and let's talk about something else, please!

On the other hand, all sorts of splendid people eat eels, and all sorts of splendid cooks prepare them. The French are very fond of eel. So are the Spanish. So are the Scandinavians, and there are many others who consider eel a delicacy. Aside from their edibility, they are an interesting fish, driven by some atavistic memory and guided by some natural homing device to make incredible journeys through fresh water and salt to seek the place that to them is home.

Eels reverse the spawning habits of salmon. Salmon return from the ocean to their freshwater spawning ground; eels spawn at sea, swim to fresh water to live. From both Europe and America, eels migrate to the sea around Bermuda to spawn; afterwards they die, but when the young eels —called elvers—are born, they take off for the fresh waters where their parents lived, somehow (unless they are caught or become dinner for some larger fish) managing to find their way home.

Eel at the market, at home. You can find eel fresh— particularly in the fall—smoked, or canned (in jelly). Like all fish, fresh eel is very perishable. Refrigerate, and plan on using it the day you buy it, or certainly the next day. Refrigerate up to 3 days after cooking, if you wish. Smoked eel should also be refrigerated—up to 3 months—and so should canned eel after opening, at which point keep it no longer than you would fresh cooked fish.

A serving (in the neighborhood of 3 ounces) of cooked fresh eel—remember, it is one of the fat fish—has about 300 calories; it is rich in high-quality protein and contains vitamin A and the B vitamins. Smoked, a serving has 160 to 170 calories and the same protein, but the vitamins have been lost in the smoking process.

Skin fresh eel before cooking: cut the skin all the way around just back of the head, grasp the skin and strip it off in one piece. Cut off the head, eviscerate the fish, wash it and divide it into pieces of the size you wish. You may broil eel, bake it, poach it, or fry it. For eel recipes, consult a fish cookbook or one that specializes in European recipes. Serve smoked or canned eel as an appetizer, with lemon juice and black pepper. Offer mayonnaise on the side with canned eel for those who wish it.

EGG NOODLES: see PASTA

EGGPLANT

Considerably more handsome than its relative the potato, the eggplant always appears to have just finished polishing its fashionably wet-look skin. The kind familiar to most of us is pear-shaped and a deep plum-purple, but eggplants grow in many shapes and colors—round, long and narrow, egg-shaped, oblong, white, violet, red, light yellow, and even striped—and in a variety of sizes scaled to feed one person or many.

Turkish and Arabian cuisines would be far poorer without the eggplant, a favorite vegetable (actually it's a fruit used as a vegetable) in those countries. One Turkish dish of eggplant cooked in olive oil with garlic, onions, and tomatoes, is called Imam Bayeldi. This translates roughly as "the priest fainted" —from sheer, unadulterated joy at such a treat, one must assume.

The Balkan countries and France and Spain have many inventive ways to use eggplant, but in Britain (where it's known as aubergine) and in the United States, the vegetable never really caught on. Or, at least, it's neither served as regularly nor greeted with as much enthusiasm as it is in other parts of the world. In fact, in the United States in the 1800s, the eggplant was used, if at all, as a table decoration. It was thought (as the tomato once was) to be poisonous, and was known as "the mad apple."

EGGPLANT IN YOUR KITCHEN

Although no one seems to be quite sure, the eggplant is believed to have originated in the East Indies, whence it migrated to China, India, Turkey, and in the Middle Ages, to

Spain, courtesy of the conquering Moors, and finally to the rest of Europe and to South America.

Because it requires a lengthy growing season, eggplant is raised where the summers are long, chiefly in Texas and Florida, although New Jersey grows some. The vegetable is at the height of its season in August, but is available all year around.

how to buy: Choose eggplants heavy for their size, with smooth, unblemished skin. Rough, spongy places are a sign of poor quality; brown spots indicate incipient decay.

how to store: Refrigerate—eggplants like high humidity— up to 6 weeks in the raw state. Cooked, refrigerate, tightly covered, up to 5 days.

nutritive value: Eggplant contributes good flavor and considerable variety to the menu, but not a great deal in the way of nutrition. One cup of diced cooked eggplant has about 38 calories—a good dieters' item—and supplies:

protein	2 grams
fat	.4 gram
carbohydrate	8.2 grams
calcium	22 milligrams
phosphorus	42 milligrams
iron	1.2 milligrams
sodium	2 milligrams
potassium	200 milligrams
thiamin	.10 milligram
riboflavin	.08 milligram
niacin	1 milligram
ascorbic acid	6 milligrams
vitamin A	20 international units

Tips on preparing, cooking. Eggplant can be peeled or not as you choose. Unless the skin is unusually tough, leave it in place—it has excellent flavor, and helps hold the eggplant together in the finished dish.

However you prepare it, eggplant cooks in a short time. Boiling (cubes, 6 to 7 minutes) is the least desirable method; it leaches out most of the flavor. It may be sliced and pan-fried in oil—preferably olive oil, as the two flavors have an affinity for one another—either plain or breaded (5 to 8 minutes, depending on thickness of slices), but it absorbs a lot of oil in the process. If you want plain sliced eggplant as a vegetable, brush the slices on both sides with oil or soft butter and broil (5 to 10 minutes per side) until brown. It may also be deep-fried—again, plain or breaded. Or it may be baked whole (20 to 30 minutes) until tender, halved, the meat scooped out and combined with other ingredients, returned to the half shells and reheated in the oven.

Lamb and eggplant are the best of friends, and the flavors of that excellent combination are enhanced with onion, tomato, garlic, and mushrooms. Eggplant parmigiana—with not only parmesan but also mozzarella, and a richly sea-soned tomato sauce—is a classic Italian dish. Eggplant caviar—caponata—is another. Stuffed eggplant, particularly if the stuffing combines the eggplant pulp with rice and either ground lamb or pork sausage—particularly the anise-flavored Italian sweet sausage—is a gustatory triumph. Ratatouille, a superb hodgepodge of eggplant, onion, tomatoes, and zucchini or little yellow summer squash cooked in a garlicky olive oil, is delicious hot or cold.

Some eggplants are bitter. To avoid carrying this taste into the finished dish, slice the eggplant and place the slices on a flat surface in a single layer. Sprinkle liberally with salt; turn over and repeat. Cover with wax paper or foil and weight with a cookie sheet on which you have placed several heavy food cans. Let stand about an hour. Rinse the eggplant very well under cold running water, and pat dry with absorbent paper.

Freezing eggplant. Although eggplant can be frozen, it is another of the vegetables that, because it is available all year, needlessly takes up freezer space and energy. As a general rule, freeze it only if you grow it. Dishes with eggplant as an ingredient—as parmigiana, eggplant lasagna—can be frozen, properly prepared (see special feature: PUTTING FOOD BY), up to 6 months.

Other ways, other forms. Except for caponata, usually found in a flat glass container, eggplant is not available canned. Nor can it be purchased frozen in the plain, uncooked state. However, breaded and deep-fried fingers or slices of eggplant are available frozen, and so is parmigiana.

Eggplant is, of course, to eat. But it can also be for show. An attractive centerpiece—for, say, an autumn buffet—can be composed of sleek purple eggplants, green peppers, small yellow crookneck squash, and ears of colorful Indian corn, liberally heaped on a flat wooden tray or directly on a brightly colored tablecloth.

EGGS

The creation legends of many ancient peoples center around the egg. American Indians believed that in the beginning the primeval waters produced a golden egg from which the Great Spirit burst forth to create the world. The Chinese told the story of how the Supreme Being dropped from heaven an egg that floated on the waters until, after a long time, man hatched from it. One Egyptian legend has it that a sky goddess produced a huge egg from which the earth and the sky were hatched; a second says that an ancient god gave to the universe the three vital elements from which all else emerged: the egg, the sun, and the moon. Early Phoenicians believed that an egg mysteriously appeared in the primeval slime, split in half to form heaven and earth. Finns once believed that a teal—a wild duck—laid an egg that broke to form the earth. So it seems, from these and countless other such legends, that the age-old question of which came first, the chicken or the egg, is answered. The egg did.

The hen's production schedule. A fertile egg needs approximately 20 days of incubation at 100°F. About 5 months elapse from the time the chicken is hatched to the time it becomes a hen and begins to lay eggs of salable size. A hen will lay at the rate of about 1 egg every 25 hours for 10 to 12 weeks, then go into a 6- to 8-week period of rest (molt), before the laying cycle begins again. What other small factory, with so low an overhead, can boast such a production record?

Eggs in the market. The important thing to know, to begin with, is that eggs are graded for both size and quality, and that one has nothing to do with the other. For example, extra-large eggs (size) may range from AA to C (quality).

egg size: There are 6 egg-weight classes, sized by the minimum weight per dozen. These standards of size/weight are set by the USDA—as are the quality standards.

size	minimum weight per dozen
jumbo	30 ounces
extra large	27 ounces
large	24 ounces
medium	21 ounces
small	18 ounces
peewee (sometimes called bantam)	15 ounces

Large eggs are usually the right size for most household uses. A rule of thumb in purchasing, as far as price is concerned: if there is a more than 7-cent difference between two sizes, the smaller size is the better buy.

Most recipes in standard cookbooks are based on the use of large eggs. Where the amount is critical, as in the volume of egg whites in an angel food cake, a cup measurement will often be given as well as the number of egg whites to be used.

egg quality: A process called candling determines quality. Eggs are passed over a light and rotated; the light reveals the condition of the shell; size of the air cell; condition of the white; and size, color, and mobility of the yolk.

Eggs are graded AA, A, B and, in some parts of the country, C. In a Grade AA egg, the broken egg covers a small area, the white is thick and stands high, the yolk is firm and high. A Grade A egg covers a moderate area, the white is reasonably thick, and both white and yolk stand fairly high. A Grade B egg covers a wide area, has a small amount of thick white with the remainder quite thin, the yolk is somewhat flattened and enlarged. Grade C is even thinner and flatter. Yolks of B and C eggs break easily, will probably be off center if the egg is hard cooked.

Grade AA and A eggs are both excellent for any use, but are particularly desirable for poaching, frying, and soft- or hard-cooking in the shell. Grade B eggs can be used for scrambling and in baking, and in other cooked foods such as custards. Supermarkets in some states do not sell Grade B eggs, and Grade C are not available in many areas.

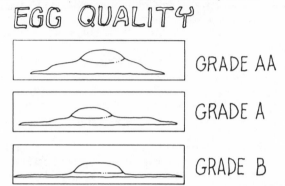

EGG QUALITY

GRADE AA

GRADE A

GRADE B

The savvy shopper. Before you buy eggs, arm yourself with a little more knowledge of what is inside that epitome of handsome and practical packaging, the egg shell.

shell color: There are eggs with white shells and eggs with brown ones. The color you choose is entirely a matter of preference, because—contrary to a widely held belief—the quality, the nutritive value, and the taste do not differ between the two colors.

The color of the shell of an egg is determined by the breed of the hen that laid it. Larger birds, such as the Rhode Island Red and the Plymouth Rock, lay brown eggs. These larger birds are, understandably, more expensive to feed—explaining why there are usually fewer brown eggs than white in a given market, and why the brown eggs will probably be higher in price. The White Leghorn, lighter and therefore less expensive to feed, lays white eggs and is the breed that produces most of the eggs that come to market at the present time.

blood spots: Most eggs with such spots are culled during the grading and sorting process and never find their way to market, but once in a while one will slip by. These naturally occurring blemishes are caused by the rupture of a blood vessel on the yolk surface during the formation of the egg, or by some similar accident of nature. These spots in no way affect the taste or the food value of the eggs, although they may mar its appearance.

Are such eggs fertile? No—the chances of buying a fertile egg at your market are virtually nonexistent, because commercial egg-production hens never even see a rooster. If you want fertile eggs, you must go directly to the producer (the farmer, not the hen), or to a specialty store, such as a health food shop.

chalaza: This is the thick white, ropy material that appears on either side of the egg yolk. Its purpose is to hold the yolk in place in the center of the egg. Chalaza does not affect the taste or nutritional value—indeed, a prominent amount indicates a high-quality egg. Removal is very difficult and besides, you'll lose a lot of the egg's goodness, so trying to get rid of the chalaza is an exercise in futility.

light yolks, dark yolks: There's no difference in flavor or in nutritional value. What the hen had for dinner determines the color of the yolk in her eggs—hens that eat grass, yellow corn, and alfalfa lay eggs with darker yolks than those fed mainly on wheat.

storage eggs: These are eggs that have been held under refrigeration for more than thirty days, rather than being taken immediately to market. In that time they lose some carbon dioxide, which results in a larger air cell than in a fresh-laid egg and, in turn, a flatter egg when broken. They are best used for scrambling, or in baking or other cooking. Varying state laws govern the classifying of storage eggs— for example, in many cases they must be classified Grade B, and are not widely distributed.

Composition of the Egg

Air cell · Shell · Yolk · Shell membranes · Chalaza · Chalaza · Germinal Disk · Vitelline (Yolk) Membrane · Thick Albumen · Thin or fluid Albumen

Why are hard-cooked eggs difficult to peel? Not all of them are, but a freshly laid egg will not peel easily. Buy eggs for hard-cooking four to six days before you plan to use them. Stored in your refrigerator, they will lose a little carbon dioxide and moisture and take in air through the shell, which will form a barrier between the shell membranes and make the egg easier to peel. Plunge hard-cooked eggs immediately into cold water—preferably ice water—which will not only make them easier to shell but also prevent a dark area (unsightly, but in no way harmful) from forming around the yolk. But don't let them sit in the water. One minute is about right. Then gently crack the shell all over, roll the egg between your hands—easy does it—to loosen the shell. Begin peeling at the large end, holding the egg under cold running water or submerged in a bowl of cold water to help ease off the shell.

EGGS IN YOUR KITCHEN

Fresh, in-the-shell eggs are available the year around. They are most plentiful—and therefore least expensive—in the spring and summer, when hens are at their peak of production. However, modern egg ranching has just about convinced the hen that there are no longer any seasons, assuring an ample egg supply at all times.

how to buy: Nowadays, most eggs are packed in resilient foam cartons that cushion them well against the vicissitudes of packing and shipping. However, don't just pick up a closed carton and put it in your shopping cart. Open the carton (never mind that the dairy department manager may glower at you; the price you are paying is for a dozen whole, usable eggs) and check to make certain that none of the eggs is cracked or broken. Be sure too that the whole dozen is there —in some areas where there is a high incidence of shoplifting, taking one or two eggs from a carton is a common practice. It pays to check.

A word about price: By USDA standards, a dozen large eggs must weigh at least 24 ounces—a pound and a half. If the eggs are selling at 80 cents a dozen, you are paying 53 cents a pound. Stop to consider the price per pound of other high-protein foods—particularly meat—and you'll see that eggs are a good buy on a pound-for-pound basis.

Buy eggs only from a refrigerated case. Quality deteriorates rapidly when eggs are stored at room temperature. Many stores stamp egg cartons with an expiration date— check it to assure yourself that the eggs are fresh when you buy them. If the carton wears the USDA shield, this assures you that the eggs were packed under federal/state inspection and have met the Department of Agriculture's requirements for quality and size.

how to store: Place eggs in the refrigerator immediately after you get them home. They lose more quality in one day at room temperature than in one week under refrigeration. Leave eggs in the carton in which they came—store in the egg-holder section of your refrigerator only if you are going to use the entire dozen (or twenty, as eggs are also packed in some areas) within a day or two. Always store eggs large end up, to keep the yolk centered.

Never wash eggs before storing them. Eggshells are hard, but they are also porous, and so most eggs we buy nowadays have been treated with a light odorless, tasteless mineral oil to seal the pores and thus slow the loss of carbon dioxide.

In their carton, large end up, fresh eggs will keep in your refrigerator (at a 45 to 55° temperature) up to five weeks without significant loss of quality. In any event, loss with age is only of moisture and carbon dioxide, not nutrient value. Practically, don't buy more eggs than you'll use in a two-week period. They must be stored with care, and take up valuable refrigerator space.

Raw eggs, separated, may be kept on the refrigerator shelf one or two days. Cover whites tightly; cover yolks with cold water, then cover tightly, and drain before using. Leftover whites or yolks may be frozen (see below) and stockpiled until a sufficient amount is accumulated for, say, a sponge cake (about six yolks) or an angel food cake (eleven to twelve whites) or for use in custards, soufflés, sauces, puddings, and in baking.

nutritive value: A large egg contains 80 calories, 60 in the yolk, 20 in the white. The normal serving, 2 eggs, offers 26.6 percent of the adult RDA protein requirement, at only 160 calories—an excellent protein source for those on weight-loss diets. Nutrient content of 1 large egg is:

protein	6.5	grams
fat	5.8	grams
carbohydrate	.5	gram
calcium	27	milligrams
phosphorus	103	milligrams
iron	1.2	milligrams
sodium	61	milligrams
potassium	65	milligrams
thiamin	.05	milligram
riboflavin	.15	milligram
niacin	trace	milligram
vitamin A	590	international units

A word about cholesterol: About two-thirds of the fats in eggs are unsaturated. However, if you are on a low-cholesterol diet, the physician who prescribed the diet has probably limited your intake of egg yolk, the portion of the egg which contains cholesterol—275 milligrams per large egg.

There is, of course, no such thing as a cholesterol-free diet—cholesterol is a fatty substance vital to the development of the human body, particularly of the brain and of sex hormones, and is present in every body cell. Our bodies manufacture up to 2,000 milligrams of cholesterol each day. A person in good health, with a normal rate of metabolism, handles excess cholesterol through normal bodily elimination processes.

Be guided by your physician. Don't decide for yourself that you should go on a low-cholesterol diet, or any other kind of diet that limits a normal, average daily intake of a balance of nutrients, or of any one kind of nutrient.

Tips on preparing, cooking, serving. Our love affair with the egg has been going on so long it's as familiar, and often provokes as little thought, as a marriage sneaking up on its golden anniversary. But in dealing with eggs, as with everything else (including marriage), there are easy approaches and difficult ones. Knowing the easy and/or best ways cuts loss of time and temper to a minimum.

separating eggs: If a recipe calls for yolks only, whites only, or yolks and whites used separately, separate the eggs when you take them from the refrigerator. They separate more easily, and the yolks are less likely to break, when they are cold. Crack the shell with a sharp tap at the center and gently pull apart. Retain the yolk in one half of the shell while you let the white pour out into a bowl; gently drop the yolk into the other half of the shell, and repeat until all the white has drained away. Gently is the watchword. If you're heavy-handed, there's a gadget called an egg separator that will do the job for you. Or break the egg into a small funnel—the yolk will remain in the top while the white drains out the bottom.

beating eggs: Whole or separated, eggs will produce the greatest possible volume if allowed to come to room temperature before beating.

If the recipe says "slightly beaten," use a fork to beat whole eggs just until yolks are broken and somewhat mixed with whites. If "lightly beaten," beat with a fork or whisk just until whites and yolks are well combined.

The recipe that directs you to beat yolks until they are "thick and lemon colored" is leading you astray. Thick, yes; lemon colored, no. They will get pale, a lovely pale golden yellow, but they will never take on the color of a lemon. So when your yolks are very thick and pale, quit while you're ahead—you can beat until doomsday waiting for that lemon color to put in a miraculous appearance.

There is considerable mystique surrounding the beating of whites. Certain things are true: For best results, they should be brought to room temperature before beating; the bowl and beaters must be completely clean, free of the least speck of grease, or the whites will not beat up to full volume; neither will they achieve full volume if there is the tiniest bit of yolk in them—if a little falls in, remove it with a corner of absorbent paper or a piece of eggshell. Whites will achieve their greatest volume if beaten with a balloon whisk in an unlined copper bowl, but such equipment isn't necessary unless you are a fanatic (and fantastic) cook. Grandma always beat the whites for her angel food with a flat whisk on the enormous platter that otherwise came into service only to hold the festive bird on holidays. But a bowl with a rounded bottom plus a whisk, rotary or electric beater will do.

"Slightly beaten" whites are frothy and foamy, with discernible large air bubbles, but are still liquid and flow easily. "Soft peaks" describes whites that, when the beater is removed, stand in points whose tops turn over as the beater comes out; they will slide if you tip the bowl. "Stiff but not dry" describes whites that stand in stiff peaks behind the beater as it is drawn out; the peaks will not turn over, and the mass will slip only slightly or not at all if the bowl is tipped. Do not beat until the whites lose their moisture, however—they should not be dry.

In beating whites to which sugar is to be added, as for meringues and similar mixtures, beat until very foamy and beginning to turn white, then add sugar 1 tablespoon at a time, continuing to beat until all sugar is added and dissolved and the whites are very stiff and glossy.

adding eggs to hot mixtures: Slightly beat the whole eggs or yolks (whites are never added to hot mixtures). Add a small amount of the hot mixture to the eggs and mix well. Gradually add the eggs to the remaining hot mixture, stirring constantly. This method assures a smooth result. If you simply dump the eggs into the hot mixture without adding a little of the heated mixture to them first, you'll end up with strings of cooked egg no matter how vigorously you stir.

boiling eggs: In a word, don't. When cooking eggs, in the shell or out of it, you'll get a finer, tenderer result if you cook gently, at a low temperature. This is true of baking, poaching, shirring, scrambling, and frying as well as of "boiling"—the only exception is french-style omelets, which are cooked briskly. To cook eggs in the shell, gently prick the large end of each egg with a needle (there's an egg-pricking gadget for the effete, but that's not necessary). Place in a pan that will accommodate all the eggs you're cooking in one layer. Cover with cold water. Place over medium heat; bring to a boil.

The moment the water boils, turn off the heat, cover the pan, and start timing. One minute will produce a very soft, coddled egg; two minutes, what is thought of as a "soft-boiled" egg, and so on. A little experimenting will determine the optimum degree of cooking for your taste. If you want hard-cooked eggs, leave them covered sixteen minutes. When cooking time is up, plunge the eggs—hard- or soft-cooked—immediately into cold water to prevent further cooking. Unless you do, the first egg you remove will be perfectly cooked, but the others will overcook.

Freezing eggs. Broken eggs, whole or separated, should be frozen in moisture- and vaporproof containers. Add 1 teaspoon salt or 1½ teaspoons sugar per cup to whole eggs or yolks to be frozen; label as to content. Whites may be frozen without any addition. Both whites and yolks, prepared as directed, may be held in the freezer up to one year.

Other ways, other forms. Fresh eggs in the shell are, of course, the form in which we usually buy them. But there are others.

on grocery shelves, in cans, jars, or bottles: Dried eggs, whole or the whites and yolks separately processed, are available—as everyone who has ever served abroad in the armed forces remembers. For babies, yolks only, whole eggs, and eggs in combination with other foods are available.

in grocery frozen-food section: Frozen eggs are available, although not widely distributed, as whole eggs or as whites and yolks frozen separately. Whole-egg substitutes, made with only the egg white plus other ingredients, are available (for scrambling, omelets, and for use in cooking) for those on low-cholesterol diets. Thaw before using; follow label directions.

Dozens of eggs, dozens of uses. If you have eggs in the kitchen, you need never be at a loss for something very good to serve for a family or a company meal. All the breakfast ways—soft-cooked, scrambled, fried, poached, baked, shirred—are delicious, and can double at later-in-the-day meals with aplomb. Soufflés—handsome, top-hatted, and golden—make great main dishes at luncheon or dinner, and are a fine way to use up leftovers—a bit of chicken, too little to use alone; one or several kinds of leftover vegetables; a dab of ham, a drib of veal, those two slices of bacon left from breakfast—to add flavor and substance. Or make a dessert soufflé, baked while the main part of the meal is being consumed, then rushed to the table amid squeals of delight from the admiring audience.

For an elegant luncheon dish or as the first course for a very special dinner, serve make-ahead eggs in aspic—the superb French oeufs en gelée. Top veal cutlet with a fried egg and capers for Austria's incomparable schnitzel à la holstein. And don't forget the coddled egg that made Caesar salad what it is today.

Kids dote on eggs goldenrod—creamed hard-cooked egg whites on toast, the yolks sieved in a golden mound to top off the dish. If you put a little something between the toast and the creamed eggs (such as frizzled ham or dried beef, well-seasoned spinach or broccoli, sautéed and chopped chicken livers, sautéed mushrooms, a slice or two of cheese), you'll have a dish that is substantial, tasty, and very good to look at.

When you'd like to invite drop-in company to stay for supper and there's nothing in the house, potluck deliciously with baked eggs. Trim crusts from very thin bread slices and halve them. Heat butter and half-and-half together until butter is melted; dip the bread quickly in and out of the butter-cream mixture and use to line individual casseroles. Put a dab of something savory in the bottom of each dish—crumbled crisp bacon, slivered ham, mushrooms, any vegetable, any chopped leftover meat or poultry or fish or, if you have nothing, put in nothing and the dish will still be good. Into each dish, break two eggs. Season lightly with salt and white pepper, and spoon about two tablespoons of the butter-cream mixture over them. Top with grated cheese if you like, or sprinkle lightly with paprika for color. Bake at 350°F. for 10 to 15 minutes, depending on how firm you like your eggs, and serve with pride.

In desserts, eggs truly come into their own. Angel food and sponge and chiffon cakes. Custards, baked or stovetop-cooked. Puddings of many kinds. Cloud-light floating island. Fruity trifle. Cream pies and cream fillings for cakes and éclairs and cream puffs.

And who would be so presumptuous as to pack a picnic lunch, especially when there are children about, without deviled eggs? For perfect deviled eggs, ranging from simple to elegant, properly hard-cook the eggs; shell, halve the long way, and separate yolks from whites. Mash the yolks well, moisten with a little melted butter or salad dressing or sour cream or mayonnaise, season with a bit of cayenne and salt to taste, and add one—or a combination—of savory ingredients for zesty flavor. To get your thinking started, here are some ideas:

chopped olives, stuffed green or ripe
crumbled crisp bacon
chopped dill or sweet or mustard pickle
slivered smoked salmon + dillweed
finely flaked tuna or crabmeat or lobster
chopped shrimp + chopped capers
thinly sliced scallions + finely chopped celery
minced raw mushrooms
grated romano or parmesan cheese
minced clams + finely chopped celery
snipped chives
mashed avocado + lemon juice
salmon or black caviar + finely chopped onion
minced anchovies or anchovy paste
finely chopped sautéed chicken livers
minced smoked tongue or ham
drained and minced marinated herring with onion
mashed liver sausage + minced onion
mashed sardines + lemon juice

Well, you get the idea. And should heaven rain on your picnic, serve the deviled eggs heated in the oven with a blanket of good, sharp cheddar cheese sauce, on toasted english muffins or on a bed of hot parslied rice.

One fad, one foolishness. An egg dish that is excellent for a company-coming brunch, luncheon, or light supper began to catch on a while back and is growing in popularity. Because it's so good, so handsome, and has so many possibilities for variation, it's likely to be with us a long time. Soufflé Roll is its name, a seven-egg soufflé baked in a jelly roll pan, rolled around a savory filling, served in slices as is or with a sauce. Cheese is often a part of the plan, either in the soufflé mixture or as a sauce to serve over it. Mushrooms ditto. Often the filling is a spinach-sour cream mixture, but other vegetables, such as broccoli or asparagus, do beautifully. So do creamed mixtures, such as chicken or ham. However you vary the dish, it's a winner. Any good general cookbook will give you how-to details.

Now the fad. If you have ever fruitlessly tried to pound a square peg into a round hole, this gadget may ease your frustrations. It's an egg squarer, a plastic doohickey into which you drop a hot hard-cooked egg. Press down the top, and voilà—a square egg. Why should you want a square egg? Who knows? Square egg canapés, maybe? Whatever, we can only surmise that, nationwide, hens are going to be very upset.

However you serve it, the egg is one of nature's master-pieces, a neatly prepackaged container of high-quality protein and other essential nutrients, with flavor almost everyone enjoys, with kitchen versatility unmatched by any food other than milk. Bless you, Henny-Penny. We trust the sky never falls on you and yours. See also OMELETS and SCOTCH EGGS.

ELBOW MACARONI: see PASTA

ELDERBERRIES

The plant on which these berries grow is a kind of all-weather, all-purpose wonder. The berries, of course, are eaten—in a darkly rich jelly, in homemade elderberry wine (with quite a kick to it—no wonder the abstemious among our forebears touted its high medicinal value), in a glowing purple-red syrup for pancakes and waffles, and in farm-style pies. The flowers—white, growing in flat clusters—make delicious fritters when young and tender. The flower buds can be pickled before they open, resulting in a product resembling capers. Dried flowers are made into a tea or steeped for elderflower water, an ingredient in a number of perfumes and lotions. Old-wives' country medicine employs the bark of the shrub as a laxative, the dried-flower tea as a cure for colic, the boiled leaves as a poultice. Hollowed out, young stems of the plant can be fashioned into a variety of toys—whistles, pea shooters, waterguns—and the older wood provides raw material for small wooden household utensils.

But here, we're concerned with food. If you have never lived where elderberries grow wild (they are not cultivated) you have not partaken of their joys, unless Aunt Maud thoughtfully sent you a bottle of her Elderberry Elixir at the holidays. But if elderberries grow—which they do with reckless abandon—near where you live, plan on gathering some when they come ripe in August and September. Raw, the flavor and the odor are exceedingly off-putting, but cooked, they're great. Try an old-time cookbook for jelly, syrup, and wine recipes.

And be sure to bring back a few branches of the shrub to hang around your windows and doors on Halloween. They ward off evil spirits, we are told.

ELECTRIC APPLIANCES: see special
feature: YOU CAN'T WORK WITHOUT TOOLS

ELK: see GAME

EMMENTHALER: see CHEESE

EMULSIFIERS: see ADDITIVES AND
PRESERVATIVES

ENCHILADAS: see page 452

ENDIVE: see BELGIAN ENDIVE and
SALAD GREENS AND PLANTS

ENGLISH MUFFINS

Flat, round, yeast-raised breads, english muffins are baked on a griddle rather than in the oven, on a surface sprinkled with cornmeal in lieu of fat. They are not difficult to make, but they are one of the few breads of which the store-bought variety is just as good as, sometimes superior to, the home-made kind. Once made only of plain white bread dough, there are now whole wheat, sourdough, cornmeal, and raisin-studded varieties to be found in the bakery department of supermarkets.

The muffins are doughy if not toasted, but when they are —and buttered at once—they are delightfully crisp, full of neat little hills and vales that trap the butter. Toast in a toaster, if yours is made to take thick slices, or under the broiler. Serve with orange marmalade or, even better, cream cheese and strawberry preserve.

Attacking english muffins with a knife amounts to heresy. Instead, pull them apart gently with your fingers or, more refinedly, with two forks. Cut, they develop an unpleasantly gummy texture; pulled apart, they are great.

ENRICHED

Generally said of white flour, and of the white bread made from the flour—enriching restores the nutritional elements removed when the flour is milled. See also BREADS and FLOUR.

ENRICHERS: see ADDITIVES AND
PRESERVATIVES

ENTERTAINING

"Every time the world goes around," an old Finnish proverb has it, "something falls off." If this sounds rather gloomy (the Finns tend in that direction), think about it for a minute. We are inclined to nail down, one way or another, those things we care about—so what can fall off but the useless, extraneous things?

The world has made a great many turns since the days of formal entertaining, and each time we've lost something that we are better off without. Vast amounts of heavy silver that required constant polishing. A number of courses from the menu for almost any occasion. The ladies retiring to the parlor for coffee, leaving the gentlemen to their port. Afternoon "at homes." Place cards. Jack Horner pies. (You don't know what a Jack Horner pie is? You're lucky.) Salt spoons, fish forks, jelly servers, and other related table tools once laid out in so ostentatious an array that half the guests pretended to be engaged in enthralling conversation until the other half began to eat, in order to see which tool was proper for the course being served. And more, dozens more, that have now gone the way of the antimacassar, lace curtains, and high-button shoes. It's nice to think of them in some Great Beyond populated by the cooks, butlers, footmen, parlor maids, up-stairs maids, scullery girls, and ladies who "came in to oblige," all of whom fell off the turning world too.

We're speaking, of course, of ordinary you-and-me type people, entertaining their friends at home. Not the beautiful people, not the jet set. When we have guests for dinner, we are more likely to telephone them than to send them an engraved invitation. Dinner may still be consumed in the dining room, but it is just as likely to be the patio, the backyard, the living room, or even the kitchen—in which latter case, the company may well be invited not only to eat dinner but to help cook it. If there are more than two or four or at most six guests, the service will probably be buffet style. Many of us still have elegant silver and china, but it's likely to be squirreled away, brought out on only the most elegant of occasions or not at all. We eat from handsome and colorful dinnerware with attractive stainless steel flatware. The handmade lace tablecloth (it had to be hand-washed, too) and the double damask have given way to place mats and permanent-press, soil-release napkins.

What we eat has changed as much as how we eat. Grandma *might*—just *might,* mind you—have served spaghetti with clam sauce, a big tossed green salad, grissini, and red jug wine to the family, but she would have dropped over in her tracks if anyone had suggested such a meal for guests. These days, dropping over in one's tracks is as out of style as suet pudding—anything goes, as long as it's very good of its kind and there's plenty of it. There's not a truffle in sight.

We still entertain at dinner, even if differently. But we also give brunch parties, tailgate picnics, cookouts. We invite friends for dessert and coffee, or for drinks and an appetizer spread. Afternoon tea has given way to the cocktail hour, but morning coffee as a way to entertain has taken its place. The musicale is among the missing, replaced by an evening of cards and games or just talk, followed by a dessert buffet or a selection of good things for make-your-own sandwiches. Any time is as good as any other for entertaining today, any kind of party a good party. See also BRUNCH, LUNCH, and DINNER.

ENTREE: see page 452

ENTREMETS: see page 452

EQUIVALENTS: see special feature: THE HOME COOK'S NEW MATH

ESCARGOT: see SNAILS

ESCAROLE: see SALAD GREENS AND PLANTS

ESPRESSO: see page 452

EVAPORATED MILK

This is fresh milk—whole or skimmed—from which about 60 percent of the water has been removed; the milk is then canned. Reconstituted with the same amount of water, the milk can be used in cooking just as fresh milk is; that is, if the recipe calls for 1 cup milk, measure ½ cup of evaporated milk and add cold water to fill to the 1-cup measurement.

Undiluted evaporated milk, just as it comes from the can, may be used to "cream" coffee. It makes a rich mixture, like coffee that has been lightened with heavy cream. However, the "canned" flavor remains—many like it, an equal number do not. The flavor, which some people find objectionable, is lost in cooking. Undiluted evaporated milk can be used in place of cream in cooking—it makes a fine, rich custard, for instance, or a superlative pumpkin pie.

The concentrated canned milk is generally cheaper than fresh milk—whole or skimmed—which is why many people use it in cooked foods. Also, it is useful where milk or cream is hard to come by—on camping trips, for example—or where refrigeration is not available. Evaporated milk can be stored at room temperature until the can is opened. However, after it is opened, it must be treated like fresh milk; it must be refrigerated, and should be used within a few days. Cover tightly in the refrigerator to prevent the milk from picking up tastes and odors of other foods.

Evaporated milk production. Whole or skim milk is heated in a vacuum evaporator, which draws off more than half of the water content. The milk is homogenized, cooled, placed in cans (6-ounce and 14½-ounce sizes for home use, 6¾-pound size for institutions), and sealed. The cans are then sterilized at high temperatures. This kills bacteria that might cause spoilage, and makes it possible for the unopened cans to be stored at room temperature.

Federal standards require evaporated milk to contain not less than 7.9 percent milk fat and not less than 25.9 percent total milk solids. Vitamin D is added to all brands of the milk to increase nutritional value.

Whipping the milk. Whipped evaporated milk can be used in many recipes in place of whipped cream—it is considerably less expensive. Pour undiluted milk into a freezer tray and freeze until soft ice crystals form around the edge of the tray. Turn into a bowl and whip, using a dover beater or electric mixer, until the milk triples in volume and forms stiff peaks. Like whipped cream, the whipped milk may be sweetened and flavored if you wish. See also MILK.

EVISERATE, TO: see page 446

EXOTIC FRUIT

Some of us are adventurous eaters, willing to sample almost anything edible as long as it isn't walking around. Others, although they may not phrase it that way, are locked into the "what was good enough for grandma" theory—if everybody else isn't eating a certain food, they won't eat it either. They won't even try it. Even those who regularly ask their children with an air of sweet reasonableness, "How do you know you

don't like green beans if you don't try them?" are guilty of turning up their noses at the very mention of a persimmon or a kumquat, a plaintain or a kiwi.

Too bad, because hidebound eaters forget that some of the foods they enjoy were once considered unusual and exotic. Bananas were, when first brought here from the tropics. So were pineapples. So were avocados. The grapefruit was once new-fangled and thought to be the result of "tampering with nature." And it is still a suspect curiosity in many European countries.

At various times during the year, a well-stocked market (with an aggressively curious-minded produce buyer) will have many of the out-of-the-ordinary exotic fruits on display. If you aren't willing to experiment, you'll never know what you're missing—and you're missing a great deal. Some few of the fruits listed below you may encounter only on a trip to some far (or nearby—the world is getting smaller and smaller!) place. Try them when you have the opportunity, remembering that even in places where you need to be careful about what you eat, fruit—secure inside its skin, which can be stripped away—is always one of the "safe" foods.

Here is a sampling of the pleasures that await the adventurous. Seek them out at home or abroad.

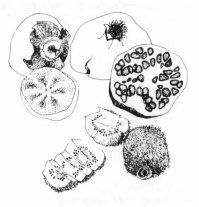

Akee. Are you fond of scrambled eggs? You'll enjoy the akee, which, although it is a fruit, is served cooked as a vegetable. You don't have to wonder whether an akee is ripe. It signals its readiness by bursting open its thick, rosy skin to reveal creamy yellow flesh (the edible portion) and three shiny black seeds.

Banana (see main entry). There are many varieties of bananas other than the yellow ones with which we are familiar. Try red bananas—sweeter, richer in flavor—if you come across them in the market, or tiny finger bananas, or fig bananas. Many of the unusual kinds have distinctive, unusual flavors, too. There are more than a hundred kinds of bananas in all.

Breadfruit. This is the starchy mainstay, literally the staff of life, of many native populations in the tropics, particularly in the South Pacific. Round, with a netted green rind, breadfruit resembles a melon in size and shape. Inside, the flesh is white, like that of a potato. It is roasted or baked before it is ripe, and tastes like bread. Or it may be sliced and fried in oil at this stage. Riper, the flavor more resembles that of a sweet potato. Fully ripe—now the rind has turned yellow—it is sweet, and can be made into a dessert. Even the seeds, which resemble chestnuts, are edible.

Cactus Pear. Fruit of the prickly pear cactus, this is really more egg- than pear-shaped. Ripe, it is rusty rose-pink or brownish-yellow, depending on the variety, and covered with a formidable array of spikes, with which nature has provided it to protect the ripening seeds. A desert plant that is high in water content—about 85 percent—the prickly pear has given many a parched animal a lifesaving drink. Indeed, it has also done the same favor for people lost in the American desert. Mild-flavored and sweet, the fruit is usually eaten raw. It's in season from October through January, when you'll find it in limited supply in many markets in the West, mostly in gourmet markets in the East. Choose fruit reasonably bright in color, firm but not hard. Store at room temperature. Slit the fruit lengthwise and the skin, with its prickles, will come off easily. Serve with lemon juice, or with sugar and cream, or in fruit salads.

Cherimoya. A subtropical green fruit, grown now in California and Florida as well as in Hawaii, Central America, and the Caribbean islands. The flesh is soft, white, juicy, and exquisitely flavored, so delicious that once tasted it is never forgotten. The texture is almost that of ice cream, the flavor a cross between banana and pineapple, with overtones of something else indescribably good. Cherimoyas turn up in many fancy fruit stores throughout the United States.

Citron. Highly aromatic, with a thick, somewhat warty skin and a very sour pulp, citron is not eaten raw, but is often made into jams and jellies, alone or in combination with other fruits. "Citron" or a close approximation of it is the word for lemon in French and many other languages. The use with which we are most familiar is the candied peel—the citron called for in many cakes and breads, particularly those we enjoy at the holiday season.

Coconut (see main entry). You're surely familiar with the dried coconut, whether as a whole hairy brown sphere or shredded or flaked in cans or packages. But if ever you get a chance, on a trip to a place where coconuts grow in green clusters on tall palm trees, try a fresh coconut for a treat you'll remember forever. The water is cool and refreshing, the soft, translucent flesh superb. There are always boys about who will, for a small fee, shinny up a tree to obtain a coconut for you, whack it open with a formidable knife, and present it with a smile worth many times the price.

Custard Apple. Also called imaginatively if not very appetizingly, "bullock's heart." Large tropical fruit whose skin has neatly arranged markings somewhat like those of a pineapple. The flesh is sweet and creamy, its flavor and texture resembling custard closely enough to have given the fruit its common name—it's true one is "sweetsop." Grown in Florida and the Caribbean, custard apples can sometimes be found in markets throughout the United States. A relative of the cherimoya, the two bear a kissing cousin resemblance in flavor.

Date. The small golden to dark brown to almost black fruit occurs in clusters under the leaves of a tall, stately palm tree. Dates are grown extensively in California for shipment all over the country, although only some of the many varieties take kindly to traveling. The type most often found in the states other than California is the deglet noor, which is dried for shipment. Dates are very sweet, sometimes almost cloyingly so. The flesh between the stiff, papery skin and the long, slim pit is brown and sticky. They are eaten out of hand, as a confection, and used in puddings, quick breads, cookies, and other sweets. For those who find dates too sweet, a stuffing of nuts or cream cheese or both makes them more palatable, so that the flavor can be better appreciated.

Durian. This takes some getting used to. Not to put too fine a point on it, it stinks. Large and pear-shaped, with a prickly skin, the fruit has cream-colored, rich, somewhat gelatinous flesh that is delightfully sweet. Chilling helps to tame its put-offish odor somewhat. The durian can be eaten as is, or made into candy or various desserts, including ice cream.

Fig. Although fresh figs appear in season at greengrocers and supermarkets, most Americans, if they give thought to figs at all, have in mind the dried or the canned variety or the filling in a long-popular commercial cookie. (One little boy liked them so much that when he was presented with a puppy he promptly christened it Fig Newton.) Fresh figs are a taste sensation that should be sampled when the opportunity offers. There are many kinds, but the ones most likely to be encountered fresh are California's black mission figs (brought from Spain to grow in the missions established by Father Serra and other doughty priests to spread Christianity, cleanliness, and better eating habits to the Indians), and the kadota and calimyrna, both white figs. Actually, the black figs are a deep purple, the white ones a creamy greenish-yellow. Fresh figs are very soft when ripe, and should be eaten only when they are. The fruit has many tiny—edible—seeds and is, unfortunately, very perishable. Serve as an appetizer with proscuitto or as a dessert with a mild cheese or sliced, with cream. (It is said that the wisdom of Buddha came to him while he was seated under a fig tree. Remembering what occurred to Newton under the apple tree, there seems to be a message here for thinkers: Go sit under a fruit tree, and something nice will happen.)

Jackfruit. A huge fruit—some of them weigh more than 60 pounds—this, like the durian, fortunately tastes considerably better than it smells. The skin is dark green and bumpy. Both the seeds and the pulp are edible. The flesh, the color of rich cream, may be treated as a fruit and eaten raw, or as a vegetable and boiled or fried.

Jujube. This is the name of not one but two exotic fruits. The jujube is a datelike Oriental fruit, often dried as a date is, and used for flavoring. It has a place in several Oriental cuisines, notably Chinese. The jujube plum, the second fruit, is berrylike, a native of China as well as north Africa and several Mediterranean countries. It is most often used to make jellies and paste-type confections.

Kiwi. There is something endearing about this fuzzy little brown fruit—and something spectacular when it is cut to reveal sweet, juicy flesh of a glorious light green with a neat pattern of (edible) tiny black seeds, rather like poppy seeds, around a firmer, paler core. Sometimes called, for obscure reasons, the chinese gooseberry, the kiwi was almost unknown here until the 1960s, then suddenly began appearing in markets and finding acceptance—such as few "new" foods do—all over the country. Although its flesh is so beautiful and its taste so delightfully delicate, the kiwi is a sturdy fruit. Bought to eat when the fruit yields to gentle pressure, it is singularly hardy. Refrigerated, it may be kept several weeks. Cut in half and eat out of hand (but only the flesh, not the skin) or peel and slice as a splendidly edible garnish or a welcome addition to fruit salads and fresh compotes.

Kumquat. In season in the winter, kumquats are the color of an orange but much smaller and more oval-shaped. They are most often sold in baskets, like strawberries, on stems with some of the shiny green leaves still in place. The flesh and juice are tart, but in combination with the skin—which is entirely edible—they take on an agreeable tart-sweetness. Cut them in half, pop out the few rather large seeds, and eat as a snack. Or slice very thin for a delightful addition to fruit salads or cups. Or preserve them whole for an unusual accompaniment to meat—pork and poultry, particularly—or to serve as dessert, perhaps with cream cheese. Commercial kumquat preserves are widely available. Kumquats are or are not a citrus fruit, depending on what authority you consult, but whatever, they're refreshing and exceedingly pretty.

Loquat. Golden yellow, with an enjoyable sweet/sour flavor, this plumlike fruit is from the medlar tree, which was cultivated for centuries in Japan, and is now grown in California and Florida. Loquats can be eaten out of hand when ripe, but are more often used in the making of jams, jellies, and preserves.

Lychee. Often spelled "litchi" or "lichee" or in various other ways, you may have encountered this dried (lychee nuts) or canned, offered as a dessert on the menu of a Chinese restaurant. But the fresh lychee, sometimes made available here by Oriental markets and specialty greengrocers, is something else entirely. Small—about the size of a large strawberry—the lychee when ripe has a skin that is red and brittle and easily stripped away. The luscious flesh is white, translucent, and juicy, with a flavor entirely its own—though somewhat reminiscent of a very good tokay grape. There is only one seed, good-sized and a polished brown.

Mango. More familiar than some of the other tropical fruits, the mango appears regularly in markets all over the country in the fall. Generally oval or kidney-shaped, its skin is most likely to be yellowish-green, sometimes with a blush on one side like the blush on an apple. But it can be wholly green, or shade from green to red, or have an entirely gold-colored skin, or even be so dark it appears black, depending on the variety. Cradle the mango between the palms of your hands and press lightly. If there is a little "give," the mango is ripe. If not, take it home anyway and in a few days it will be. Under the (inedible) skin, the flesh of the ripe fruit is a bright light orange and very juicy, clinging stubbornly to the large central pit. Eat from the half shell with a spoon, plain or with a squirt of lime or lemon juice. The flavor is distinctive—you're likely either to fall under its spell or vow never to buy another. Not only for eating raw, mangoes can be made into ice cream, preserves, jellies, and that relish that is the curry lover's favorite, mango chutney.

Mangosteen. In size and structure, this fruit is much like an orange—the flesh is segmented, and the fruit is about the size of a large navel orange. But there the resemblance ends. In color, the mangosteen is a red/brown/purple combination, rather like the skin of an eggplant. The flesh is white, soft, and juicy, with a delicious is-it-sweet-or-is-it-sour flavor, combining hints of peach and pineapple with its own individual taste. Its home is southeast Asia.

Papaya. Like the mango, this has become more familiar in American markets—and homes—than most of the exotic fruits. Shaped like an oversized pear, the immature papaya is green and hard; ripe, it turns yellow and softens. If you can't find a ripe papaya, buy a green one and let it ripen at room temperature, which it does most obligingly. The flesh is orange, and the center of the fruit is occupied by many small, shiny black seeds—which may be eaten, if you're a seed fancier. Sweet and tender, the papaya (sometimes called the pawpaw) is excellent as a breakfast fruit eaten as we eat melons—plain, with salt or sugar, or with a little lemon or lime juice—or it may be incorporated into any raw fruit mixture, or serve as a "half shell" to fill with chicken or shrimp or crabmeat salad. Papaya nectar is available canned or in bottles in many areas. The leaves of the plant, as well as the green fruit, contain papain, sometimes called vegetable pepsin, a digestive enzyme from which commercial meat tenderizers are made. You'll find papayas in the market through the winter months and into the spring.

Passion Fruit. Its straight name is granadilla, but "passion fruit," certainly more romantic, comes from the flower of the plant, which supposedly, in all its parts, represents the passion of Christ. Sweet to smell and sweet to eat, the fruit is pulpy, with small black seeds, a tough purple-brown skin, and a hauntingly delicate flavor. It is so juicy that it is generally eaten with a spoon. Delicate, refreshing passion fruit ice is a tropical treat.

Persimmon. These grow on a shapely, pretty tree in several of our southern states, and are such a favorite of possums that if you have a persimmon tree, you're hard put to it to get any of the fruit for your own use. Persimmons appear in our markets in the autumn, along with a Japanese variety called kaki. The fruit is yellow-orange or red-orange, the flesh about the same color as the skin; there is a thin, central paler-colored core in the fruit, but seldom do you find seeds. To buy and enjoy a persimmon, you must be aware of one thing—if it is so soft that it appears to be well on its way to rotting, it's just nicely ripe and ready to eat. Until it reaches that stage, the flesh is so astringent that it is totally unpleasant, but there are few things as sweet, as interestingly textured (jellylike), as delightfully flavored as a fully ripe persimmon. Eat out of hand, in a salad—perhaps with a garnish of nut-rolled cream cheese balls—or in a persimmon pudding, a favorite throughout the South. The skin is edible, if you're a roughage buff.

Plantain. This larger, sturdier, less-sweet cousin of the banana is most often cooked, although there are a few kinds that can be eaten raw. The fruit can be roasted in its skin, or peeled and then baked or boiled. Thin, deep-fried plantain chips, in the manner of potato chips, are a delicious, crisp snack food. Plantains—also called "adam's fig"—are a starchy fruit usually treated as a vegetable, and are a staple food in the tropics. They're available the year around in North American markets. Even though ripe, they are fairly hard—they never get as soft as a banana.

Pomegranate. About the size of a large apple, round with a slightly worn-looking skin of either yellow-to-orange or rusty-red-to-deep-purple, the pomegranate saves the surprising beauty of its appearance until it is cut open. Then the richly wine-red, translucent flesh is revealed, encapsulating a multitude of seeds. Eat the fruit by sucking the juicy flesh away and discarding the seeds, or by consuming seeds and all. The flavor is tart-sweet, as cranberries are. Use the flesh-covered seeds in fruit cups and salads, or ream the halved fruit in a juicer for a refreshing drink or to use in making a fruit ice. Grenadine syrup is prepared from pomegranates.

Prickly Pear. Fruit of a cactus called the tuna that grows in various tropical countries and in the semitropical parts of our southwestern states, the prickly pear is shaped like a small pear, shades in color from green to rosy, and is covered with sharp spines of several colors. The "prickles" can be burned off, as the Indians did (a lot of trouble, and hardly worth it because the skin isn't edible), or the fruit can be halved for eating. Take the trouble of avoiding the spines, because the fruit is juicy, with a delightful, unique flavor.

Quince. Inedible raw—the flesh is exceedingly bitter—quinces are quite another matter when cooked for pies, puddings, or jellies. The fruit is hard, yellowish-green, and has the contours of a rather chubby, rather misshapen pear. Inside it is somewhat applelike—another name for the fruit is "emu apple"—with the seeds held in stiff, papery capsules. When quinces come on the market, experiment to expand your cooking and eating experiences. Any good cookbook concerned with preserving will offer you recipes for quince jelly, preserves, and paste, the latter an interesting confection.

Rambutan. A close relative of the lychee in size, shape, flavor, and consistency. Like the prickly pear, it is off-putting in appearance, for the beige-yellow skin is covered with sharp red spikes. Get past the armory, and you'll find delectable, juicy flesh well worth the trouble.

Sapodilla. When it is fully ripe, the beige flesh of this fruit is richly sweet and juicy, and slightly grainy in texture as pears sometimes are. It can be eaten raw or used in cooking, principally in desserts and ice creams. The evergreen tree on which this brown, rough-skinned fruit grows is the same one from which chicle, used in chewing gum, is harvested.

Soursop. This big, dark green fruit, which is covered with fleshy spines, often weighs five pounds or more. Its flesh is like that of the custard apple, to which it is related, but not as sweet. It is often used in making sherbets and refreshing drinks. Picture yourself on the veranda of a slightly tacky hotel in a backcountry tropical town, eating soursop ice—romance is where you find it.

Sweetsop. See Custard Apple.

Tangelo. If you appreciate the good flavor and zip-off skin of the tangerine, you'll like this child of the marriage between tangerine and grapefruit. Larger than a tangerine and with a somewhat thicker skin, more tangerine- than grapefruit-colored, it's in season in our markets from late fall to early spring.

Ugli Fruit. True to its name, this fruit is so homely you'll want to buy one and take it home to comfort it. Instead, it will comfort you—it's a citrus, as large as a big, misshapen grapefruit, with a dusky yellow-orange-green-brown warty skin, but ah, inside! The flesh is segmented, and tastes like a particularly good, juicy tangerine. Ugly, like beauty, is only skin deep. It comes into our markets in the winter and spring, shipped here from the Caribbean.

For information on the more common fruits, see each listed under its individual name, as APPLE, PEAR.

EXTRACTS: see FLAVORING EXTRACTS

EYE OF ROUND: see BEEF

217

THE HOME COOK'S NEW MATH

Here's a mixed bag of equivalents, substitutions, conversions, and other useful measurement information for the aid and comfort of the home cook

Suppose you want to make a batch of chocolate cookies, but you have run out of chocolate. Can you substitute cocoa? Suppose a recipe calls for buttermilk. Is there a substitute? Suppose you'd like to use brown sugar rather than granulated in a pudding. Are they measured equally, or should you use more brown sugar than you would white? If you'd like to thicken your gravy with cornstarch instead of flour, how much should you use? Your grandmother's recipe for pound cake calls for a pinch of mace. How much is a pinch? A sauce you've found in a British cookbook calls for a gill of burgundy. How much is a gill? How much juice can you expect a whole lemon to yield? How much cheese should you buy to end up with 1 cup, grated? How many pecans in the shell to yield 1 cup of nutmeats? How many apples to yield 3 cups of slices? How many oranges to yield 2 tablespoons of grated peel?

If you have ever been plagued by these questions or dozens of others like them, you've needed a place to go for answers. This is the place.

CONVERSIONS: MULTIPLYING AND DIVIDING

Many recipes can be doubled or halved if you have it in mind to serve twice as many or half as many as the recipe yield specifies. This is not, however, universally true. Many cakes resent this sort of treatment. If you want to make 12 cupcakes from a recipe that yields 24, you can divide each ingredient by 2 and probably come out with a dozen good little cakes—provided you do your division accurately. However, if you wish to serve each of 24 to 32 people a slice of angel food cake from a recipe that yields 12 to 16 slices (a 10-inch tube pan), make the cake twice from scratch. Angel foods are finicky. They don't like being tampered with. Anyway, most kitchens don't have the equipment to handle such mass— have you a bowl and a beater that can cope with beating 16 to 20 egg whites (with sugar) to full volume and still leave room for folding in the dry ingredients? On the other hand, if it's a fruit cake—especially the almost-all-fruit sort—that you plan to double, go right ahead. You'll develop your biceps mixing it (who would think that cooking could be better exercise than tennis?), but it will yield the expected result if, once again, your math is accurate.

The sturdier sauces double well—white sauce, béchamel, fruit concoctions are examples. But watch the seasonings. Salt, in almost all cases, should not be doubled.

Neither should herbs and spices. Neither should flavoring extracts. Here's where the familiar phrases "season to taste" and "taste and correct seasoning" come into their own. Adding a little is easy, removing a little is impossible, so take it slowly and taste as you go. Casseroles also double—or halve —well, but again, watch the seasonings.

Dividing each ingredient by two to halve a recipe or multiplying by two to double it generally isn't difficult. But if you want to make a third of a recipe or one-and-one-half times the original amount, you're going to run into difficulties. In such cases you may be well advised to reduce amounts of ingredients to lower denominations—fractions of a cup to tablespoons, for example, tablespoons to teaspoons, using some of the equivalents from this table:

3 teaspoons	=	1 tablespoon
1½ teaspoons	=	½ tablespoon
2 tablespoons	=	1 (fluid) ounce
4 tablespoons	=	¼ cup = 2 ounces
5 tablespoons + 1 teaspoon	=	⅓ cup = 2 ⅔ ounces
8 tablespoons	=	½ cup = 4 ounces = 1 gill
10 tablespoons + 2 teaspoons	=	⅔ cup = 5⅓ ounces
12 tablespoons	=	¾ cup = 6 ounces
16 tablespoons	=	1 cup = 8 ounces = 2 gills
2 cups	=	1 pint = 16 ounces
4 cups	=	2 pints = 1 (liquid) quart = 32 ounces
4 (liquid) quarts	=	1 gallon

There are also some less usual measurements that you may on some occasion (if you're using an old-fashioned recipe, or if you're called upon to do a bit of bartending) need to know:

dash (liquid)	=	6 or 7 drops
dash (dry)	=	less than ⅛ teaspoon
60 drops	=	1 teaspoon
pinch	=	amount that can be picked up between thumb and first finger
jigger	=	1½ fluid ounces = 3 tablespoons
⅜ cup	=	¼ cup + 2 tablespoons
⅝ cup	=	½ cup + 2 tablespoons
⅞ cup	=	¾ cup + 2 tablespoons
fifth (of a gallon)	=	25 fluid ounces = 3 cups + 2 tablespoons

Speaking of bartending, punches and eggnogs and such beverages for a crowd can generally be doubled, tripled, or quadrupled with reasonably reckless abandon, unless the recipe calls for spices or bitters, in which case taste as you go. But don't make a punch bowl full of mixed drinks, particularly cocktails, that depend on a delicate balance of ingredients. Somehow, something always gets lost in the translation. Besides, large quantities of such drinks often get warm from not enough ice or diluted from too much of it.

Back to food and cutting or increasing recipes for same. Pastry for pie shells increases well—providing, as always, that you measure carefully—allowing you a use-some/freeze-some bonus. Most cookie recipes can be doubled or tripled, with the same benefit. Many appetizers ditto, particularly cheese pastries (allumettes, cheese dollars, and so on) and savory mouthfuls made of pâte à choux.

Ground rules for dividing or increasing recipes: Most can be doubled (except for foam-type or delicate butter-type cakes) or halved unless the original recipe yields less than four servings. Tread with exceeding caution when tripling and quadrupling. In any case, do your math accurately, and write down the changed amounts of ingredients, lest you double the butter but forget to double the flour. Measure carefully. Let your taste govern the amount of seasoning.

If you are increasing or decreasing a recipe with one or more ingredients in difficult-to-work-with amounts, use ratios. For example, suppose you want to triple a recipe calling for ¾ cup flour. The recipe serves four—tripled, it will serve twelve. Your ratio goes ¾ (cup flour) is to 4 (servings) as X (the quantity you're searching for) is to 12 (servings). Stated as a ratio, it will look like this:

$$¾ : 4 :: X : 12$$

Recalling your junior-high math, you will multiply the outside factors by one another ($¾ \times 12$) and the inside factors by one another ($4 \times X$); the result:

$$9 = 4X$$

Divide 9 by 4, and your answer is $2¼X$—or 2¼ cups of flour.

Simple? No. But it will get you there, especially in recipes where you are dealing with multiples of fractions.

CONVERSIONS: METRIC

Along with other inevitables, metric is coming our way, slowly but surely. In our kitchens, signs point to the new direction—cookbooks with metric conversion tables or with ingredients stated in both metric and the familiar measurements; cans and packages with metric weight as well as avoirdupois printed on their labels.

This should not give rise to panic. You will not have to learn how to cook all over again. Neither will you be required to burn your cherished cookbooks, or to chuck out all the measuring devices that have been your friends for years. Nor will you have to weigh every ingredient you use. Rumormongers would have it that the advent of metric will give rise to a kitchen upheaval such as hasn't been seen since Cro-Magnon woman left her campfire and brought her culinary activities indoors. T'ain't so. (It may cause something of a hoo-haw in heavy industry, but we aren't going to worry about that, are we?)

In the first place, metric is easy to learn. It progresses neatly and reasonably by increments of ten, rather than being all over the place with pounds and ounces, bushels and pecks, fluid versus dry measure, here a pint, there a quart. Second, familiar cups and spoons will still serve you, because American cookbook writers aren't about to make you weigh everything, knowing that if they did you'd figure out a way to make them sorry for it.

So brew yourself a cup of tea, sit back and take it easy. Metric is out to help, not harm you. For some simple, comforting words about metrication plus easy-to-understand metric conversion tables, see the special feature: MEASURING UP TO METRIC.

SENSIBLE SUBSTITUTIONS

Some Ms. Hubbards, finding a particular corner of their cupboards bare, fall victim to instant hysteria. This is sheer self-indulgence. No chocolate? Use cocoa. No honey? Try corn syrup. No sour milk? Sour some yourself in five minutes. No sour cream? If you have a can of evaporated milk and a lemon, you're in.

But you can't win this game of kitchen put-and-take unless you play by the rules, unless you fiddle with the measurements somewhat. In many cases, one-for-one substitutions won't give you the results you're looking for. But these will:

if the recipe calls for	use instead
2 tablespoons all-purpose or whole wheat or graham flour (for thickening)	1 tablespoon cornstarch *or* arrowroot *or* potato starch *or* quick-cooking tapioca
1 cup beef or chicken broth	1 bouillon cube, *or* 1 envelope *or* 1 rounded teaspoon bouillon powder, + 1 cup boiling water
2 egg yolks	1 whole egg
1 cup grated coconut	1⅓ cups flaked coconut
1 pound fresh mushrooms	12 ounces canned mushrooms, drained, *or* 3 ounces dried mushrooms, rehydrated
1 teaspoon lemon juice	½ teaspoon white vinegar

if the recipe calls for	use instead
1 teaspoon grated lemon peel	½ teaspoon lemon extract
1 cup homogenized milk	1 cup skim milk + 2 tablespoons butter or margarine *or* ½ cup evaporated milk + ½ cup water *or* ¼ cup powdered whole milk + 1 cup water
1 square (1 ounce) unsweetened chocolate	3 tablespoons cocoa + 1 tablespoon butter or margarine
½ cup (1 stick) butter or margarine	7 tablespoons vegetable shortening
1 cup sifted cake flour	⅞ cup sifted all-purpose flour
1 teaspoon baking powder	½ teaspoon cream of tartar + ¼ teaspoon baking soda
1 cup sour cream	1 tablespoon lemon juice + evaporated milk (undiluted) to make 1 cup *or* ⅓ cup butter + ¾ cup yogurt or buttermilk (for use in cooking)
1 cup buttermilk (or sour milk)	1 tablespoon lemon juice or white vinegar + homogenized milk to make 1 cup (let stand 5 minutes)
1 cup honey or 1 cup corn syrup	1¼ cups sugar + ¼ cup liquid
1 tablespoon chopped fresh herb (any kind)	1 teaspoon dried leaf herb of same kind
1 medium onion	1 tablespoon instant minced onion, rehydrated
1 cup light cream (20% butterfat)	3 tablespoons butter + ⅞ cup milk (for use in cooking)
1 cup heavy (whipping) cream (36% or more butterfat)	⅓ cup butter + ¾ cup milk (for use in cooking)
2 cups tomato sauce	¾ cup tomato paste + 1 cup water
1 cup tomato juice	½ cup tomato sauce + ½ cup water

if the recipe calls for	use instead
1 small clove garlic	⅛ teaspoon garlic powder *or* ¼ teaspoon commercial garlic juice *or* 1 teaspoon garlic salt (cut salt in recipe)
1 tablespoon gelatin	1 envelope
1 cake compressed yeast	1 envelope active dry yeast
1 cup yogurt	1 cup buttermilk

HOW MUCH, HOW MANY?

The recipe calls for 3 cups cooked rice—how much raw rice should you start with? You need ½ cup of blanched almonds—how many almonds in the shell should you buy? You're going to have green beans for dinner—how many will a pound serve? There's a special on breast of veal—how many pounds will serve six?

Questions like these face us every day, creating small math problems one after another. Labels on packages are generally helpful, but many of us prudently transfer the contents of packages, once opened, to canisters or screw-top jars and are left without guidance. (Exceedingly prudent, we cut out the useful label information and tape it to the top or bottom of the canister, but that forethoughtful few of us are.)

Calculating servings. You, of course, know better than anyone else the eating habits of your family. A 6-foot-3, 210-pound man quite naturally eats more than one who weighs 140 pounds. Aunt Emma may merely pick at her food, but if she picks relentlessly day and night, she's a factor to contend with. A teenage daughter may eat like a horse today, a bird tomorrow, depending on whether or not she's dieting. A teenage son can consume as much as two or three grown men and still look as if not a morsel has passed his lips in weeks; several teenage sons can blow your calculations (and your food budget) sky high—just prepare enough for an army, and hope for the best.

On the other hand, there are normal, average eaters. It is those—bless 'em—on whom our calculations are based.

meats: If the cut has a large amount of bone (spareribs, veal breast, oxtails, and the like), count on ¾ to 1 pound, in the raw state, per serving. A medium amount of bone (as chuck steak or roast, chicken), count on ½ pound per serving. Boneless meat (round steak, boneless roasts, boned chicken breasts, and so on), count on ¼ pound per serving.

casseroles, skillets, thick stews: Total the ingredients into cups; count on ¾ cup per serving if the food is a main dish, ½ cup if a side dish.

soups: Again, total the ingredients into cupfuls; ¾ cup is 1 serving of a meal-starter soup, 1¼ cups of a main-dish soup.

salads: Tossed or mixed greens, 1 cup per serving before dressing; gelatin, a recipe calling for 2 cups liquid will serve 3 or 4, depending on how many other ingredients are added —tomato aspic, 3 servings, jellied gazpacho, 4, for example.

vegetables: As a general rule, a 10-ounce or thereabouts package of frozen vegetables yields 3 servings (never mind that the package may say 4); fresh vegetables with little waste, such as green beans, usually yield 4 servings per pound. (See individual vegetables by name for more accurate calculations.)

bread: By the piece, it's easy—1 roll or bun or muffin or biscuit is 1 serving. A commercial loaf of bread averages 16 to 20 slices. Homemade hot breads give 6 servings if baked in an 8-inch square pan, 9 in a 9-inch pan, 11 or 12 in a 10-inch tube pan—but bear in mind that the demand for seconds runs high on these.

sauces and gravies: Count on 2 to 4 tablespoons as 1 serving.

desserts: A pudding or custard based on 2 cups of milk will serve 3 generously, 4 adequately. An 8-inch layer cake yields 8 to 10 servings; a 12-inch layer cake, 10 to 12 servings; a 9-inch square cake yields 9 servings; an 8-inch square, 6 servings; a 12- × 9- × 2-inch rectangle, 20 servings. An 8-inch pie cuts into 6 servings; a 9-inch into 6 if you're lavish, 8 if you're restrained; a 10-inch pie, 10 to 12 servings.

fruit: Again, by the piece it's easy. Canned fruit—2 halves of peaches or pears, 3 of apricots make a serving; of canned berries or sliced fruits, count on ¾ cup including juice.

BIG OAKS FROM LITTLE ACORNS

In order to end up with what the recipe calls for, you often need to calculate what quantity you must have on hand—how many bananas to mash for that new dessert you want to try, how much elbow macaroni for the picnic salad, how many slices of bread to make the soft crumbs for the meat loaf, how many pounds of cabbage to yield the amount required for your mother-in-law's coleslaw recipe.

Niggling questions like these, and dozens more, arise to confront us regularly. Some of us, wedded to our kitchens, may carry a wealth of such information around in our heads. Others, more diversified in interests, need a look-it-up list.

start with	to finish with
almonds in shell, 1 pound	1¾ cups shelled
whole, shelled, 6 ounces	1 cup
whole, blanched, 5⅓ ounces	1 cup
apples, 1 pound	3 cups, pared and sliced
apricots, dried, 1 pound	3 cups

start with	to finish with
bananas, 3 to 4 medium	1¾ cups mashed
beans, green, fresh, 1 pound	2½ cups cooked
beans, dry kidney, 1 pound	6 cups cooked
dry navy, 1 pound	5 cups cooked
brazil nuts in shell, 1 pound	1½ cups shelled
bread crumbs, packaged, 10 ounces	2¾ cups
butter, 1 pound	2 cups
1 stick	½ cup or 8 tablespoons
whipped, 1 pound	3 cups
cabbage, 1 pound	4½ cups shredded
celery, 4 medium ribs	1 cup chopped
chocolate, unsweetened, 1 square	1 ounce
semisweet bits, 6 ounces	1 cup
cocoa, dry powder, ½ pound	2 cups
coffee, ground, 1 pound	about 46 6-ounce cups of prepared beverage
instant, 2 ounces	about 25 6-ounce cups
freeze-dried, 4 ounces	about 60 6-ounce cups
cornmeal, white, 1 pound	3½ cups
yellow, 1 pound	3 cups
cranberries, fresh, 1 pound	4 cups sauce
cream, whipping, 1 cup	2 to 2¼ cups whipped
sweet or sour, ½ pint	1 cup
dates, 1 pound	about 2½ cups pitted and chopped
eggs, extra large, 4	about 1 cup
large, 5	about 1 cup
medium, 6	about 1 cup
extra large whites, 6	about 1 cup
large whites, 8	about 1 cup
medium whites, 11	about 1 cup
extra large yolks, 11	about 1 cup
large yolks, 12	about 1 cup
medium yolks, 16	about 1 cup
frozen whites, thawed, 2 tablespoons	1 fresh egg white
frozen yolks, thawed, 3½ teaspoons	1 fresh egg yolk
filberts in shell, 1 pound	1⅓ cups shelled
flour, all-purpose, 1 pound	4 cups
cake, 1 pound	4¾ cups
graham cracker crumbs, 1 pound	4⅓ cups

start with	to finish with
honey, 1 pound	1⅓ cups
lard, 1 pound	2 cups
lemon, 1 medium	2 tablespoons juice *and* about 1¼ teaspoons grated peel
lentils, 1 pound	5 cups cooked
lime, 1 medium	about 1½ teaspoons juice *and* about ¾ teaspoons grated peel
macaroni, elbow or shell, 1 cup uncooked	about 2 cups cooked
meat, no bone, uncooked, 1 pound	2 cups ground
milk, 1 quart	4 cups
whole dry, 1 pound	14 cups reconstituted
nonfat dry, 1 pound	5 quarts reconstituted
molasses, 12 ounces	1½ cups
mushrooms, fresh, ½ pound	1 cup sliced, cooked
canned, 4 ounces	⅔ cup
noodles, wide, uncooked, 8 ounces	about 3½ cups cooked
fine, uncooked, 8 ounces	about 5½ cups cooked
nuts, ¼ pound meats	1 cup, chopped
onions, 2 medium	1 cup, chopped
frozen, chopped, 12 ounces	3 cups
orange, 1 medium	about 7 tablespoons juice *or* ¾ cup peeled, diced, *and* about 1½ tablespoons grated peel
peaches, 4 medium	about 2 cups peeled, sliced
peanut butter, 9 ounces	1 cup
peanuts in shell, 1 pound	2 cups shelled
pears, 4 medium	2 cups peeled, sliced
peas, dried split, 1 pound	5 cups cooked
fresh, in pod, 1 pound	1 cup, shelled and cooked
pecans in shell, 1 pound	2¼ cups shelled
pepper, green, 1 large	1 cup seeded, diced
potatoes, 1 pound	about 3¾ cups peeled and sliced or diced = 2¼ cups cooked *or* 1¾ cups mashed
prunes, dried, 1 pound	2½ cups pitted *or* 2 cups cooked, drained

start with	to finish with
pumpkin, canned, 16 ounces	2 cups
raisins, seedless, 1 pound	2¾ cups
seeded, 1 pound	3¼ cups
rhubarb, 1 pound	2 cups cooked
rice, regular, 1 pound	2 cups uncooked, about 5½ cups cooked
precooked, 2 cups	about 2⅔ cups cooked
shortening, hydrogenated, 1 pound	2⅓ cups
spaghetti, 12-inch length, 1 pound	about 6½ cups cooked
strawberries, 1 quart	about 4 cups, hulled, sliced
sugar, granulated, 1 pound	2 cups
brown, 1 pound	2½ packed cups
superfine, 1 pound	2 cups
confectioners, 1 pound	3½ cups
tea, 1 pound	about 125 cups
walnuts in shell, 1 pound	2 cups shelled
wheat germ, 1 pound	4 cups
yeast, 1 cake compressed	⅗ ounce
active dry, 1 envelope	1 tablespoon

NEED-TO-KNOW MISCELLANY

Recipes have a nasty habit of calling for things you don't know how to measure, or for measurements other than ones you're familiar with. It's difficult to look at a baking dish or pan and determine whether or not it will hold 4 cups. A nice piece of cheese, but how much will it yield when you grate it? A crumb crust for a pie—how many crackers or cookies, crushed, will make the amount called for? Marshmallows for Cousin Susie's heavenly hash salad—how many in a cup? Once again, you've come to the right place.

Crumbs from crackers, cookies, bread. Make these crumbs yourself to save a pretty penny over the packaged kind. Place cookies or crackers in a plastic bag and crumb with a rolling pin—the bag keeps the crumbs from shooting all over the kitchen, and provides a handy way to pour them into a measuring cup. Or make cracker, cookie, or dry bread crumbs in your blender. Make soft bread crumbs by crumbing the bread—any kind—with your fingers into a measuring vessel. Use the crusts or not, depending on the dish you're making—if you don't, remember that the wild birds will thank you kindly for small favors.

desired result	use to achieve it
1 cup soft bread crumbs	2 slices 2-day-old bread
1 cup zwieback crumbs	9 slices zwieback

desired result	use to achieve it
1 cup graham cracker crumbs	12 graham crackers
1 cup white cracker crumbs	20 soda crackers
1 cup vanilla wafer crumbs	22 vanilla wafers
1 cup cornflake crumbs	2½ cups cornflakes
1 cup chocolate wafer crumbs	26 chocolate wafers

In measuring all of these, pile into the cup—don't pack. To substitute dry bread crumbs for cracker crumbs (as in coating food) remember this: 1 cup fine dry bread crumbs = ¾ cup fine cracker crumbs.

Cheese, grated, shredded, crumbled. These, too, you can buy in packages, some kinds in heavy plastic bags, some in little flat boxes, some in tube-shaped containers with sifter tops. But you can also prepare them at home—indeed, it's a great way to use up tag ends of cheese. Crumble with your fingers, shred with the big-opening side of your grater, grate with the small-opening side. Sometimes recipes call for cream and cottage cheese in cup measures—we give you these, too.

desired result	use to achieve it
⅓ cup cream cheese, softened	3-ounce package, brought to room temperature
1 cup cream cheese, softened	8-ounce package, brought to room temperature
1 cup cottage cheese	½-pound carton
2 cups shredded or cubed cheddar or swiss	8-ounce cut or piece
1 cup crumbled bleu cheese	¼- to ⅓-pound piece
1 cup grated parmesan	½-pound piece *or* 3-ounce container of ready-grated

Marshmallows. You can make even these at home, but that may be pushing back-to-the-good-old-days a bit too far. So measure the commercial kind this way:

desired result	use to achieve it
1 cup large marshmallows	11 pieces
1 cup miniature marshmallows	60 pieces
1 cup cut-up marshmallows	16 large whole ones

To cut up marshmallows, use the kitchen scissors, and constantly dip the blades in water.

POTS AND PANS AND SUCH

You've found a recipe for a bundt-type cake you want to try, but you don't own a bundt pan—will your angel cake pan do? If they are the same capacity—that is, if they hold equal amounts—go ahead, because they are the same general shape, both being deep, round pans with a center tube. But substitution of cake pans is chancy. For more about this, see CAKES.

The big gelatin salad you're making for a party is supposed to jell in a 12-cup mold. By filling them with measured water, you discover that your 3-inch springform pan and your 13½- × 8½- × 1-inch glass baking pan each hold 12 cups. Which should you choose? The glass pan is safer, even if the shape is not as appealing. Springform pans, by their design, can leak—and gelatin is liquid when it goes into the mold. A denser substance, such as cheesecake, is what a springform is all about. Or use it to mold a gelatin salad that is whipped, that incorporates mayonnaise and/or cream cheese—that is, one that is already past the liquid stage when it goes into the mold.

Suppose the new casserole or other baked food recipe you're trying calls offhandedly for a 6-cup or 1½-quart baking dish. Use too small a dish, the food will cook over onto the oven floor; too large a dish, the food will be spread out, may get too crusty, may be overcooked. You can use the measured-water trick to find a dish of the right size. (Sometimes, mercifully, the capacity is marked on the bottom.) Or you can consult this list for cup capacity. When a size may be called for in quarts, that capacity is listed, too.

pan size	capacity
9-inch pie plate	4 cups (1 quart)
7⅜- × 3⅝- × 2¼-inch loaf pan	4 cups (1 quart)
8½- × 2¼-inch ring mold	4½ cups
10-inch pie plate	6 cups (1½ quarts)
8- × 1½-inch layer cake pan	6 cups (1½ quarts)
8½- × 3⅝- × 2⅝-inch loaf pan	6 cups (1½ quarts)
7½- × 3-inch bundt pan	6 cups (1½ quarts)
9¼- × 2¾-inch ring mold	8 cups (2 quarts)
8- × 8- × 2-inch square pan	8 cups (2 quarts)
11- × 7- × 1½-inch baking pan	8 cups (2 quarts)
9- × 5- × 3-inch loaf pan	8 cups (2 quarts)
9¼- × 2¾-inch ring mold	8 cups (2 quarts)
9- × 3½-inch bundt pan	9 cups
9- × 9- × 2-inch square pan	10 cups (2½ quarts)
11¾- × 7½- × 1¾-inch baking pan	10 cups (2½ quarts)
13½- × 8½- × 2-inch baking pan	12 cups (3 quarts)
9- × 3½-inch tube pan	12 cups (3 quarts)
10- × 3¾-inch bundt pan	12 cups (3 quarts)
8- × 3-inch springform pan	12 cups (3 quarts)
13- × 9- × 2-inch baking pan	15 cups
9- × 3-inch springform pan	16 cups (4 quarts)
10- × 4-inch tube pan	18 cups (4½ quarts)
14- × 10½- × 2½-inch baking pan or roaster	19 cups

A STEADY HAND, A SHARP EYE

There are superior cooks who can throw in a pinch of this, a little of that, a trifle of something other, and turn out a masterpiece. And then there are the rest of us.

If it's a masterpiece you contemplate, begin by measuring carefully and accurately, bearing in mind that a kitchen masterpiece can be anything from an easy-mix quick bread to a Soufflé à l'Orange Grand Marnier Flambé provided it's the best of its kind that you can turn out.

Some matters of measurement—and semantics. In cooking, you need to keep your wits about you. Daydream about a Duckling Montmorency in advance if that pleasures you, but while you're producing it don't let your mind go wool-gathering. Be aware that if a recipe calls for 1 cup of whipping cream, it means 1 cup of heavy cream in the state in which it comes from the container; but if it calls for 1 cup of whipped cream, it means you must whip the cream before you measure and add it. If the recipe directs you to add 1 cup almonds, chopped, you chop after measuring; if it's 1 cup chopped almonds, you chop before measuring—and there can be quite a difference. If the method tells you to add 3 eggs one at a time, beating well after each addition, that instruction wasn't put there just to tire your beating arm; it can make a big difference in the finished product. If the ingredient is ½ cup butter, melted, measure first and then melt; if it is ½ cup melted butter, melt first, then measure—the difference is slight, but in a génoise it counts, even if it wouldn't in waffles. If you're told to sift before measuring (confectioners sugar, for example), don't skip it—the volume will be different, and besides, you'll get out all the lumps that the ingredient is heir to.

Measuring isn't all that's required of you—*how* you measure matters too. You need tools, the proper tools, for the best results.

dry measure: A set of cup-shaped containers, usually metal, holding ¼, ½, ¾, and 1 cup—some well-thought-out sets also have ⅓- and ⅔-cup measures, and are worth shopping around for. If the recipe calls for a sifted ingredient, sift first. Spoon the ingredient into the measure until it heaps above the brim, then level off the top with a rigid spatula or the dull side of a knife. Some ingredients—brown sugar is the chief example—call for packing. Do this with the back of the spoon, making sure there are no air pockets and that the ingredient is so firmly packed it will turn out of the container in one solid mass.

liquid measure: Cup-shaped see-through containers, usually glass but sometimes plastic, in 1-, 2-, and 4-cup sizes, with fractions of those sizes (¼, ⅓, ½, ⅔, ¾, and 1 cup) clearly marked. Set the container on an even, flat surface—don't trust the steadiness of your hand—and pour in the ingredient to be measured to exactly the right marked level. If the ingredient is sticky—molasses and corn syrup are—you can grease the inside of the measuring cup very lightly if you like, but a rubber scraper will usually get every drop out of the cup and into the mixture you're working on. Rinsing the cup in cold water—shake out all the water—before measuring oil or sour cream will help, but again, the rubber scraper will do the job. In measuring sour cream, be sure there are no air pockets, that the cream fills the container on all sides to the required level.

small measures, dry and liquid: A set of graduated measuring spoons, usually metal or plastic, that measure ¼-, ½-, and 1-teaspoon amounts, and 1 tablespoon. (Some come with extras, such as ⅛ teaspoon, 2 teaspoons, ½ tablespoon, but the 4-spoon set plus a little rudimentary ingenuity will see you through.) Measure dry ingredients to heap the spoon, then level off with a rigid spatula or the dull side of a knife. Liquid ingredients are easy—your eye will tell you if the spoon is not full enough; if it is too full, it will run over. (Remember what you learned in Physics I—water seeks its own level.)

Old math, new math in the kitchen. If you sometimes feel as if you should have gone to circus school and learned how to juggle before you ever set foot in the kitchen, you are not alone. We hope we've offered some aid with the numbers side of kitchening. We haven't included every problem you'll face. We couldn't. That would take a book in itself. (A book could be written about any subject in the world—and somewhere out there, someone is writing it.) But we trust these lists and ideas will help you, because cooking is—ought to be —a pleasure, not a pain.

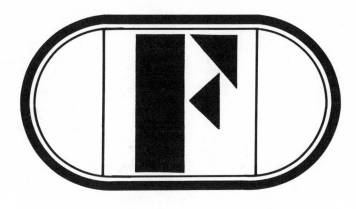

FARINA

Cream colored, relatively high in protein, and easily digested, farina is a cereal made from hard wheat from which the bran and most of the germ have been removed. A standard baby cereal, farina is the first solid food that millions of European infants taste. It is used in the United States as a breakfast cereal—cooked in milk or water, eaten with milk or cream and sugar—and as an ingredient in puddings and such dishes as spoon bread, muffins, and dumplings. Most farina on the market today is enriched with iron and the B vitamins. Water-cooked, 3½ ounces of farina furnishes about 43 calories.

FARM OR FARMER CHEESE: see CHEESE

FASHIONS IN FOOD: see page 585

FAST FOODS

Millions of Americans eat out at inexpensive, fast-food restaurants on an average of once a week; millions more, on a once-a-week basis, buy fast foods from a take-out restaurant to serve at home. And a whole lot of us do both. Fast-food outlets have proliferated to a tremendous degree during the past decades. Most of them are attractive, brightly decorated places with (usually young) help wearing cheery uniforms—a far cry from the drab "hamburger joints" that once were virtually the only kind of fast-food restaurant available.

Why has this happened? Because eating out is one—a very popular one—of our forms of entertainment, and fast-food restaurants offer that entertainment at a price which, if not as cheap as the same dishes could be made and served at home, is at least affordable by a large segment of the population. By far the most popular of the fast-food places are those offering hamburgers and french fries as the chief items on the menu. Pizza "palaces" are next on the list of favorites. Places offering fish and chips, late-comers in the fast-food hierarchy, are very popular. Fried chicken, as an eat-in or take-out item (more often taken home than eaten on the spot), wins a lot of votes from fast-food devotees. New in the field but climbing rapidly are soup-salad-sandwich restaurants, most of them with a down-home flavor (in decor, if not in food). Tex-Mex food, gaining popularity at a great rate, has spread its charms, in ersatz-Mexican drive-throughs, from the southwest to the entire country.

Some places specialize in roast beef sandwiches. Some are light-snack places, offering only cookies or doughnuts along with coffee, tea, or milk. Many fast-food restaurants have added a make-your-own salad bar in recent years, in an attempt to avoid being classified as places where only high-calorie foods are available.

Since eating breakfast out—on Saturdays or Sundays as a family treat, on weekdays for singles or when home proves too hectic—has become popular, many fast-food places have begun to serve the morning meals. Indeed, the kinds of foods we think of as breakfast items, such as ham and eggs, waffles or pancakes, are so much in demand that some places serve breakfast all day. (The day for many fast-food outlets starts at 6 a.m. and ends at midnight or 2 a.m.; many are open 24 hours.)

Time was when all fast-food—from the hamburger joint, the lunch counter, the highway diner—was uniformly terrible, with absolutely nothing to recommend it except that it filled the aching void (and, quite often, made the void ache even worse shortly after eating in such a place). They smelled of rancid oil. The coffee was watery. The hamburgers were more filler than meat. The french fries were limp and leaked dreary puddles of grease on the plate. However you ordered your eggs, you got them some other way. The pancakes were heavy enough to go to sea as ship's ballast. The toast was either undertoasted or burned, and smeared with something that tasted like mucilage.

But things have undergone a radical change. Fast-food outlets have smartened up both their food and the environment in which it is served. No one is claiming that this is gourmet food, of a quality sufficient to stand Escoffier on his ear. But it's edible, much of it has good flavor, and some of it is superior, all things considered. And one is no longer required to perch on a backless stool designed for the derriere of a midget in order to get a bite to eat.

The meal that is the overwhelming favorite of customers of the quick-service/low-price eateries consists of a "deluxe" hamburger, french fries, and a chocolate shake. Such a meal, at the time this is written, ranges from $1.65 to just under $2, depending on the restaurant. Additions, such as a double order of fries, onion rings, a cola drink instead of a shake plus a sundae for dessert, bring up the tab.

The interesting thing is that while all the fast-food places of today are far superior to those of yesterday, quality varies considerably from one to another—but the low-quality places seem to be as heavily patronized as the high-quality ones. That says something dismal, we fear, about the average American's gustatory discernment.

Most fast-food establishments are franchise operations. Some franchisers keep close watch on the outlets bearing their names, inspecting them regularly for cleanliness as well as adherence to the formula-recipes for the various foods served. Others seem to feel that, having let the franchise, they have done all that is required of them.

Virtually all the fast-fooders employ gimmicks of one sort or another to bring in eaters—particularly adamant kids with docile parents in tow. Such premiums as free drinking glasses abound. Two-for-one coupons appear regularly in advertisements. Some chains have a live "image"—a clown, a king, whatever—who appears (in his many numbers, if the chain is nationwide) at fairs, carnivals, ball games, and does charity performances, such as at childrens' hospitals. TV advertising—for the chains, rather than a single outlet—is all over the tube, accompanied by relentlessly cheery jingles.

All in all, it's a big business. And because it filled a need (or created one?), it's a very profitable business.

FATS

Fats are edible oils or greases used in cooking and at the table. They may be animal fats: butter, lard, bacon fat, suet, chicken fat; or derived from vegetables: corn, cottonseed, olive, peanut, safflower, sesame, and soy oils. Margarine can be wholly vegetable or made of a combination of animal and vegetable fats. Shortenings of the solid-mass variety—the ones that come in cans—are generally made up of vegetable oils with incorporated hydrogen, which gives them solidity. Some lard is also hydrogenated in this manner.

In the kitchen, fats have three principal uses:

a) To add flavor and richness—butter or margarine used to dress vegetables and as spreads for breads, oils used in the making of mayonnaise and other sauces and dressings.

b) As a cooking medium—oil, shortening, lard, and sometimes chicken or bacon fat, less often butter or margarine, in which foods are sautéed, panfried, or deep-fried; best for these purposes are fats with a high smoking point, which do not burn easily.

c) In baking, to shorten (make tender and/or flaky) batters, doughs, and pastries—butter, margarine and, less often, hydrogenated shortening for cakes and cookies; shortening or lard for pastries; any of the fats, depending on the recipe, for various other baking purposes.

Margarine and butter are interchangeable in recipes. Beyond that, follow the suggestion of the recipe you use for the type of fat. For example, there is an excellent oil pastry and certain cakes can be made with oil, but these require special recipes—you cannot simply substitute oil for butter, shortening, or other fat called for and expect satisfactory results.

Measuring fats. Most butter or margarine that is packed in quarter-pound sticks has by-tablespoonful measurements printed on the paper that wraps each stick; use this handy arrangement for measuring, bearing in mind that ¼ pound of butter or regular margarine—1 stick—is ½ cup. (Do not attempt to substitute whipped butter or margarine or imitation margarine in baking unless the recipe specifies this kind.) Other solid fats can be measured in a measuring cup; spoon the fat into the cup in small quantities, pressing lightly as you go so that there will be no air pockets. Oils, of course, can be measured like any other liquid, in a measuring cup.

Storing fats. Butter, margarine, suet, bacon fat, chicken fat, and regular lard will retain their freshness for about 2 weeks when stored, tightly covered, in the refrigerator. Hydrogenated products—lard and shortenings—can be kitchen-shelf stored, tightly covered, kept cool and dry, up to 3 months. Oil can be shelf-stored up to 2 months; keep oils in a dark place, as light fades them, and tightly covered, as air —particularly in the presence of moisture—turns them rancid, shortening their useful life.

Oil or shortening used for deep-fat frying can be reused. Cool, then strain into a storage can through a strainer lined with a double thickness of cheesecloth. Cover tightly and store in a cool, dry place.

Cholesterol-watchers special. All foods containing fat contain more than one kind, but generally one is dominant. If you are on a low-cholesterol intake, you know that the saturated fats are the cholesterol-heavy ones. Here are some guidelines.

predominately saturated, high in total fat: Beef, lamb, pork, and ham, hard yellow cheeses and cream cheese, cream (both sweet and sour), luncheon meats, cold cuts, sausages, frankfurters.

predominately saturated, low in total fat: Veal, organ meats (liver, kidney, etc.), whole milk, part-skim milk, yogurt, cottage cheese, farmer cheese, neufchâtel.

predominately monounsaturated, high in total fat: Duck, goose, eggs.

predominately monounsaturated, low in total fat: Chicken, turkey.

predominately polyunsaturated, low in total fat: Fish, shellfish.

saturated fats and oils: Butter, lard, coconut oil, palm oil, hydrogenated vegetable oils in margarines and other similar products.

monounsaturated fats and oils: Olive oil, peanut oil.

polyunsaturated fats and oils: Safflower, corn, cottonseed, sesame, and soybean oils.

For a discussion of fat as a nutrient in a balanced diet, see the special feature: NUTRITION NOTEBOOK; see also BACON; BUTTER; LARD; MARGARINE; OILS, SALAD AND COOKING; and SUET.

FAUFAL

Tiny pellets of semolina (wheat). The basis of couscous, a classic Algerian dish. Used throughout North Africa.

FAVA BEANS: see BEANS

FELL: see page 452

FENNEL

A vegetable, this somewhat resembles celery, but the stalk is more bulbous. It can be used as celery is, on a relish tray or sliced into salads, or it may be braised in the Italian manner and served with a liberal sprinkling of parmesan. The flavor is reminiscent of licorice or anise. See SEEDS.

FERNS

Handsome plants of many varieties that grow in what romantics like to term "bosky dells," ferns are edible when they are young and tender. They must be in the "fiddlehead" stage—when the new-growth fronds are tightly furled. Ostrich fern and pasture brake are two edible ferns. The flavor is rather like asparagus with a hint of mushroom. It is sometimes possible to find canned fiddlehead ferns in gourmet food shops.

FETA

A white Greek cheese, crumbly of texture, made of goats' or ewes' milk. Its salty, somewhat astringent flavor is particularly good in salads. Make a simple Greek salad with greens, tomato wedges, chunks of feta, and ripe olives—dress with a combination of garlic, olive oil, lemon juice, and anchovy paste. See CHEESE.

FETTUCINE: see PASTA

FIBER

This is what grandma called roughage, as in "Eat your celery —the roughage is good for you." The premise that food fiber is beneficial to the human system is not a new one, but rather an old idea whose time came once again in the mid-1970s. As always happens when something new is talked about or something old-new has a renascence, everybody has hopped on the bandwagon. There was, for example, the baking company that solemnly announced, in 1977, a brand new bread—with wood fiber added, for heaven's sake!

Fiber is found in plant—never in animal—foods. One of the most concentrated sources is miller's bran, the part of the wheat milled away in making flour. For more on fiber, see the special feature: NUTRITION NOTEBOOK.

FIGS: see EXOTIC FRUIT

FILBERTS

Filberts and hazelnuts are the same thing, although the cultivated variety is generally called filbert, the kind that grows wild, and that some of us remember gathering as children, is usually referred to as hazelnut. To further confuse matters, in England they are called cobnuts. Whatever called, they are (in several varieties) the fruit of shrublike trees of the Corylus family, differing somewhat in size and shape, depending on the parent tree. All grow in most parts of the northern hemisphere, in clusters on the tree, each nut in its separate husk, which opens as the nut ripens. In Turkey, where the best filberts came from before we began to cultivate them in this country, the nuts are picked green, then dried before shipping. In Washington and Oregon, where they have been an important crop since the turn of the century, they are allowed to mature on the trees, and are gathered after they fall to the ground.

As filberts, there is some dispute over the origin of the name. Some feel that the nuts were named after St. Philibert, whose name day falls in August, when the nuts ripen. As hazelnuts, however, there is no dispute: in Anglo-Saxon, the word *haesel* means "helmet," which perfectly describes the nut's shape.

However named, the nuts have been of gastronomic and commercial importance since at least 1000 B.C. In the time of Christ, the nuts were being shipped from the Black Sea to ports on the Mediterranean. At one time, the tree was thought to have certain supernatural powers—the divining rod, used to search for both water and precious metals, had to be a hazel branch.

Filberts in cooking. The nut has a slightly sweet flavor, and is less oily than either the walnut or the pecan. Ground, it is a major ingredient in all sorts of glorious tortes and confections of Austria, Hungary, and other middle-European countries. Chocolate and filberts have a special affinity for one another.

But the use of filberts is not confined to sweets. The nuts make a splendid addition to poultry stuffings—cornish hens, for example, with a wild rice stuffing that incorporates a generous amount of coarsely chopped filberts is a very special dish. (Serve with a sauce made of melted tart currant jelly liberally seasoned with orange peel and you will have produced a minor masterpiece.) Sliced filberts are flavorful in fruit salads. Substitute the nuts for walnuts or pecans in nut bread, cake, and cookie recipes. Toast and lightly butter them to serve as an appetizer—they are the perfect accompaniment for a good sherry. Add the nuts to melted, lightly browned butter to use as a sauce for asparagus. Add to maple syrup as a wonderful waffle topping or ice cream sauce. Fold into softened vanilla or coffee ice cream, refreeze, then serve with chocolate sauce as a sundae.

Buying and using filberts. The nuts are generally sold in the shell, although it's sometimes possible to find shelled filberts in small plastic bags. When buying them in the shell, choose nuts with shiny, unblemished shells. Shake them—if they rattle, the nuts are old and dried. Store at home in a cool place, where they will keep for at least 5 months. Store shelled filberts in the refrigerator, closely covered.

yields: 2½ pounds of filberts in the shell will yield about 1 pound shelled—that will be about 3½ cups of nutmeats.

One cup of whole filberts will yield slightly more than 1 cup when coarsely chopped, about 1¼ cups finely chopped.

skinning filberts: The nuts have a thin, papery pinkish-brown skin between shell and meat. In many cases, this skin is left on, as it adds flavor. However, for some purposes the skin must be removed. To do so, spread the nuts in a single layer on an ungreased baking sheet; roast in a 350°F. oven about 15 minutes. Remove and immediately rub the nuts vigorously with a towel. Or roast as above, then cover with boiling water; let stand 2 minutes, drain, rub with a towel. The first method will remove most of the skin, the second will remove the entire skin.

toasting filberts: Spread filberts (with skins) in a single layer in a shallow pan. Bake at 400°F. for 12 minutes, stirring the nuts occasionally for even browning.

butter-roasting filberts: Spread in a shallow pan; pour melted butter over the nuts in proportions of ½ cup butter for each cup of filberts. Bake at 300°F. until crisp and light brown, 15 to 20 minutes, stirring frequently.

salting filberts: Butter-roast as above. Cool slightly, then sprinkle with salt—about ½ teaspoon for 1 cup of nuts.

Because they are not grown in as large quantities as, say, almonds or pecans, filberts are generally more expensive than those and other nuts.

FILE

A powder made from young leaves of the sassafras tree, filé is a component of Creole cooking—Gumbo Filé, for example.

The powder becomes stringy when cooked. It should be added to the dish immediately after it is taken off the stove, or sprinkled over just before serving. Choctaw Indians used the black-green filé powder, and taught its use—as a flavoring and thickening agent—to Creole cooks.

Gumbos, the dishes in which filé is most oftened used, are pungent mixtures that came to Louisiana from Africa by way of the West Indies. Seasoned with onions, garlic, and hot pepper sauce, gumbo is a kind of stew, made of almost any meat, fish, shellfish, or poultry or a combination, always served with rice, and always flavored with filé. Gumbo Zhebes, based on seven greens—mustard, spinach, turnip, beet, collard, lettuce, cabbage—boiled for three hours with ham hock or bacon for added flavor, is served on Holy Thursday for good luck. Hunters make a gumbo of duck gizzards and livers in hunting camps, to use up those very perishable parts of their bag. Hot french bread and red wine are customary gumbo accompaniments.

FILET MIGNON: see BEEF

FILLED MILK

This is fresh milk from which the milk fat has been removed and replaced with another kind of fat, most often coconut oil. The oil is often added to skim or reconstituted nonfat dry milk to make what passes for whole milk, but may or may not be nutritionally equal to fresh whole milk, depending on the maker. Filled milk is generally cheaper than whole milk. It is sometimes used by those allergic to the butterfat content of milk—however, the substitution of coconut oil does not reduce the cholesterol content, and it should not be used by those on low-cholesterol diets.

Filled milk is not available in many places; its sale is subject to many state regulations. See also MILK.

FILLETS

Boneless, most often flat, slices of meat, fish, or poultry. A fillet is a delicacy and, generally, one fillet is an individual serving. Although fillets may seem high-priced, considering that there is no bone or waste, they are often a good buy. Fillets of fish are made of the sides of the fish; poultry fillets are halves or slices of breast meat; beef or pork fillets are slices of the tenderloin.

FILLINGS

In the Midwest, and particularly in Pennsylvania Dutch country, "filling" is the word for stuffing, and a stuffinglike dish of bread crumbs (waste-not/want-not use of stale bread), well-seasoned and moistened with broth or water, is often served in lieu of potatoes or as an additional dish on the laden tables of those splendidly hearty eaters. Filling, in those parts of the country, is also that mixture which stuffs a bird to be roasted.

Elsewhere, filling is savory or sweet—savory sandwich fillings, for example, or sweet custard or fruit or similar fillings for cakes, cookies, and pies. Although almost anything that goes between two slices of bread is the "filling" of a sandwich, actually those substances generally thought of as fillings are "made" mixtures, a combination of several ingredients with a binder of mayonnaise, salad dressing, sour cream, or the like.

Sandwich fillings may be made with chopped, ground, or diced meat, fish, or poultry; with hard-cooked eggs; with various types of sausage; with cold cuts and luncheon meats, canned or from a delicatessen or supermarket; with many kinds of cheese. Peanut butter is a big sandwich-filling item. And don't think for a minute that it's only kids who dote on peanut butter sandwiches. One thirty-eight-year-old kid of our acquaintance often sneaks downstairs after the house is quiet at night and makes himself his favorite: a peanut butter and mustard sandwich on rye, accompanied by a glass of milk and a large dill pickle. He goes back to bed and sleeps the sleep of the just—or, at least, the sleep of one blessed with a remarkable digestive system.

Added to the basic sandwich filling can be a wide selection of secondary ingredients: chopped celery or onion or cucumber, nuts of various kinds, chopped ripe or stuffed green olives, sliced or chopped pickles or pickle relish, crumbled crisp bacon.

Sweet sandwich fillings get a big play, too. More often than not based on peanut butter or cream cheese, they add honey, jelly, preserves, marmalade, dates, raisins, nuts, candied ginger, coconut, what have you.

Cake, pie, and cookie fillings range broadly over the whole sweet field. Jelly fills an old-fashioned jelly cake or jelly roll. Whatever frosts a cake may also fill it, or a separate filling —custard, lemon, chocolate, caramel, orange, coconut, almond, maple, pineapple, date-nut, fig, raisin—may be used. (See FROSTINGS, ICINGS, AND FILLINGS.) Mixtures such as dates with nuts, marmalade with nuts, mincemeat, lemon curd, and others may fill cookies or coffee-time sweet rolls. As for pies—well, almost anything fills a pie deliciously, whether it be the kind of filling that is cooked and goes into an already-baked pie shell, or the kind that is placed in the pastry and cooked with it.

Omelets, a third use for fillings, employ both savory and sweet foods and combinations to enhance their beautiful simplicity. Fanciers often prefer only a drift of cheese—cheddar, fontina, parmesan—to fill their omelets, but there are many who relish a thick cheese sauce, a ratatouillelike vegetable mixture, a spicy spanish sauce, crumbled crisp bacon or sautéed chicken livers or slivers of country ham or sausage of one kind or another. One of the better omelets is filled with long, thin slices of avocado and topped with sour cream—a symphony of gold and green and white, and a delicate triumph of flavor blending. Diced cooked chicken breast in mornay sauce is another. Jelly or jam (don't use grape—it turns gray), or either in combination with cream cheese, is a favorite sweet filling for an omelet. Fresh or stewed dried fruit also ranks high, as does lightly spiced applesauce. Grated semisweet chocolate and finely chopped almonds folded into whipped cream produce a superb dessert omelet.

This is only a minor sampling of the myriad fillings available for whatever you have it in mind to fill. And this is an area where even the timid can safely let their imaginations run riot.

FINES HERBES

A mixture of several chopped fresh herbs, this is the BOUQUET GARNI of uncooked or briefly cooked dishes. Fines herbes should consist of a combination of some or all of these: chervil, parsley, tarragon, watercress, chives, and sweet marjoram. At one time, salad burnet and mushrooms were also a part of the mixture.

In the days when most people had a patch of herbs as a part of their garden, fresh herbs were not difficult to come by. Indeed, most of them are easily grown, and the flavor of fresh herbs, incomparably superior to the dried variety, is worth the small effort needed to cultivate them. Many will grow in a box on a kitchen windowsill, or in a series of small pots—a delightful addition to kitchen decor and a treasure to use in cooking. Most herbs, chopped, freeze well in small, one-use packets; the flavor of frozen herbs is much closer to fresh than that of the dried ones.

Today, fines herbes may be reduced to a combination of parsley and chives, those two standards virtually always available at the supermarket or greengrocer, and sometimes even the chives are lacking. If you don't grow your own, the components of a proper fines herbes are worth seeking out. An Omelette Fines Herbes is one of the simple but simply perfect dishes not to be missed. A veal cutlet laved with lemon juice and sprinkled with fines herbes just before it is brought to the table is another such culinary triumph.

Italian gremolata, a chopped mixture of parsley, lemon peel, garlic, and anchovies, is a relative of fines herbes, used to garnish such dishes as Osso Buco.

Lacking fresh herbs or frozen ones, look on the spices and seasoning shelves at your supermarket for dried fines herbes. The little jar will give you a hint of the pleasures of this combination of flavors—perhaps next year you'll decide to plant an herb garden of your own.

FINNAN HADDIE

Named after Findon, a village near Aberdeen in Scotland famous for preparing the fish, finnan haddie is smoked haddock. The fish is split, partially boned, lightly salted, and then smoked. Once the smoking was done over peat fires, which lent the fish a superb flavor. Although commercial smoking on a broader scale has robbed the fish of that delicate nuance of flavor, finnan haddie is still a delightful dish.

Available whole or in fillets, finnan haddie may be broiled

with butter, baked in milk, or poached and served with a cream sauce plentifully decorated with hard-cooked eggs, or

with a not-too-spicy tomato sauce, or a mushroom sauce well laced with dill.

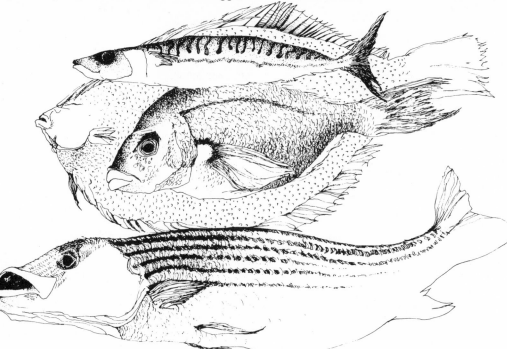

FISH

At the opening of the second act of Shakespeare's *Pericles,* there is a relevant bit of dialogue between two fishermen.

Third fisherman: Master, I marvel how the fishes live in the sea.

First fisherman: Why, as men do a'land; the great ones eat up the little ones; I can compare our rich misers to nothing so fitly as to a whale; a' plays and tumbles, driving the poor fry before him, and at last devours them all at a mouthful. Such whales have I heard on o' the land, who never leave gaping till they've swallowed the whole parish, church, steeple, bells, and all.

We tend to think of the bounty of ocean, lake, river, and stream as having been put there for our use, a source of pleasure for the sports fisherman, a living for the commercial fisherman and, most important, a food supply for all of us. But in larger numbers and greater predation, the fish are themselves fishers and are the food supply for one another. When we catch and eat fish, we interrupt one small link in a vast chain, begun when the action of the sun produces phytoplankton in the sea, which nourish zooplankton, which nourish small fish, which nourish the larger fish that eat them, which nourish the still larger fish . . . "as men do a' land; the great ones eat up the little ones."

"The seas, and all that in them is." We can only suppose that the first fisherman caught a lazy fish in some quiet pond or stream with his bare hands. Having discovered so tasty a food (and, although they didn't know it, so valuable a source of protein), men quickly thought up ways less chancy than hands to catch their dinner—nets, weirs, traps, hooks. And then, because fish spoil so quickly, and because the catch could not always be counted on, they developed ways to preserve part of a bountiful catch to fill their stomachs in leaner times—salting, smoking, pickling, and finally, commercial canning and freezing.

Wherever there is water, salt or fresh, there are fish of one or many kinds. Early on, people ate the kinds that inhabited the waters near their homes, but with the development of rapid transportation and dependable refrigeration, fresh fish from far away became available everywhere.

A fish by any other name . . . . Some saltwater fish— tuna and bonito among them—range throughout the world and can be found in seas everywhere. Others are peculiar to smaller areas, but these generally have close-relative counterparts in other fishing grounds. Sometimes these relationships are obscured by language differences or by lack of knowledge. For example, a fish of South African waters was called salmon by English settlers; Dutch settlers called the same fish *kabeljou*—cod. Neither salmon nor cod, the fish is the same one known in Australia as the mulloway and in North America as the croaker. The rouget, delight of gourmet Romans in the empire's heyday, is not, as they thought, peculiar to the Mediterranean—it is the same fish as the red mullet of the Atlantic, and the goatfish of the Indo-Pacific area. Sometimes it is size that is the determining factor in the naming of fish—a sardine, if it escapes catching and canning, is called a pilchard when it attains greater age and larger size.

Some of the fish that occur in many areas are highly regarded by some people, considered not worth eating by others. (Carp is an example.) In general, people who live near colder water—inhabitants of North America and of Great Britain, for example—eat fewer varieties of fish (because fewer are available) than those near warmer water—the Mediterranean, the Caribbean—where fish are plentiful not only in numbers but in variety.

Saltwater and freshwater varieties. Of the tens of thousands of species of fish in the sea, hundreds are counted on by man for his food supply. Some of the saltwater fish that appear regularly at fishmongers' shops in many places (and, some of them, canned or frozen at the supermarket) include cod, mackerel, swordfish, bonito, bluefin tuna, halibut, gray mullet, haddock, croaker, red bream, sea bass, red snapper, sole, whiting, herring, turbot—and there are many, many more. Freshwater fish exist in considerable variety as well, some of them fished commercially, many of them brought home by dedicated fishermen whose idea of the greatest relaxation in the world is to sit on a sunny bank or wade a stream or putter around in a boat, waiting for a fish to accept their invitation. Freshwater fish are most appreciated—probably because they are at their best—in the northern hemisphere. Among the freshwater varieties most sought after are the carp (prized in Europe and Asia, not thought of as highly here), lake and brook trout, Atlantic and sockeye salmon, bream, grayling, pike (the oldest surviving species of fish), chub, perch, large-mouth and small-mouth bass, whitefish, char; and there are many more, including some peculiar only to relatively small areas. One of these is the huge, fierce-fighting muskelunge; many a fisherman has devoted the entire recreation side of his life to landing just one muskelunge . . . and failed. Fish of moving waters—rivers and streams—are generally better flavored than those of still waters—lakes and ponds; fish from waters where the bottom is sand and/or stone are generally better flavored than those from mud-bottom waters.

Watery pride and prejudice. All sorts of stories surround fish and fishing, some of them true, some simply matters of legend. North American anglers regularly throw back carp because "they feed on garbage," although their flesh is delicious and greatly prized elsewhere in the world. Many people will not eat eel because "they look like snakes," and

pickerel, although the resemblance is not as great, suffer from the same comparison.

Some fish are wisely given a wide berth because their flesh is poisonous. Blowfish—puffers—produce the most virulent of the fish poisons, and eating their flesh can be fatal. Yet the Japanese regard the toro fugu, the tiger blowfish, as the height of finny delicacy. Properly prepared, making certain that the liver and the ovaries are removed, the tiger is not only safe but loved by Oriental fish connoisseurs.

The legends of the salmon's vast endurance and tenacity are true. A salmon will travel as much as 3,000 miles, enduring incredible hardships, to return from the sea to the stream in which it was spawned. Freshly hatched, the salmon remains in the stream that was its hatching ground until it becomes about six inches long, when it begins to make its way downstream. It grows in the course of the journey, lingers for a while at the mouth of the stream or river, and finally moves out into the ocean. While it matures to a full-grown salmon, a matter of something like four years, the fish remains in the ocean; at the end of that time, it begins to retrace its journey—navigating by the sun, experts say—finally reaching the estuary of the home stream, which it recognizes—again, in experts' opinion—by the smell. Then begins the upstream journey, full of hazards, during which the salmon does not eat until, exhausted, it reaches the spawning grounds. Few live after spawning to return to the sea and make the entire incredible journey a second time.

FISH IN YOUR KITCHEN

Although it has been considered a fine and plentiful food by most peoples from the Stone Age to the present, fish has played other roles, among them as a kind of money and a medium of barter, as a religious symbol (early Christians), and as a proper sacrifice to the gods (early pagan Aegean islanders). But the food aspect of fish has been the most important, both yesterday and today. Many colonists and settlers of various lands carefully chose homesites near the sea or a lake or river to assure a supply of fish. And at one time the Roman Catholic church, to bolster the fishing industry of Catholic countries, banned the eating of meat on Fridays and saints' days to encourage the people of that faith to eat more fish.

Shopping for fish. We buy most of the fish we eat, but we still catch a good deal of it. Caught or purchased, the key word in handling fish is speed. Anglers know they must keep the fish they have caught alive if they are going to continue fishing for some time, and that when the day's sport is done, the fish must be cleaned and iced as rapidly as possible. Speed counts with purchased fish, too. If you are shopping for any length of time, buy fish last, hurry them home and into the refrigerator, and plan on cooking and eating them that day or, at most, the next.

There are certain fish-shopping terms you should know to make choosing fish at the market easier.

round: Fish as it comes from the water. If you buy round fish, it must be eviscerated (internal organs removed) and scaled preparatory to cooking—either by the fish merchant or, at home, by you.

drawn: Whole fish, eviscerated, but with head, tail, fins, and scales still in place.

dressed: Eviscerated and scaled, with the head, tail, and fins cut off.

fillet: Boneless (usually) slice cut lengthwise from the side of the fish.

steak: Crosscut slice from a large dressed fish, such as salmon or swordfish. If you buy at a fish store, you can have the steaks cut to the exact thickness you prefer. Steaks are bone-in.

piece: Section of a large fish, such as a salmon, for baking or poaching; it will be eviscerated but bone-in.

Both your eyes and nose are useful in buying fish. Here are some indications of quality to keep in mind.

whole fresh fish: The gills (if they are still in place) should be red, and the flesh light red or pink, and translucent. Fresh fish does not have a strong, fishy odor—if it does, it's getting old and should be avoided. Skin should be shiny, and never look or feel slimy. Flesh should spring back when pressed with the fingertip.

fillets and steaks: The flesh should look fresh and firm and moist, at the edges as well as in the center. Again, smell it —if the fish has a strong, fishy odor, pass it by. Flesh should spring back when you touch it with a fingertip. The skin, if it is still in place, should be shiny, but never slimy.

how to buy: Choose your fresh fish or portion thereof by the above criteria. It's helpful to know that you will be able to cook and eat about 60 percent of a round fish, 80 percent of a dressed fish, 90 percent of fish steaks, and 100 percent of fish fillets. If you plan on flaked fish for a salad or a casserole dish, 1 pound of fillets will yield 2 cups of flakes.

amounts to buy: Amounts below will make one average serving of fish as a main dish; if served as an appetizer, less will be needed; for hearty appetites, you may need more.

round fish	12 ounces
dressed fish	8 ounces
fillets or steaks	5 ounces
piece	5 ounces
fish sticks	4 ounces
canned fish	3 ounces

how to store: From the time you buy it until the time you use it, keep fresh fish tightly enclosed in moisture- and vapor-proof material, constantly refrigerated. Plan to use the fish within 2 days. Store cooked fish in a tightly closed container in the refrigerator; plan to use within 2 days.

nutritive value: Fish varies somewhat in nutrients and considerably in calories, depending on the kind. However, all fish is high in protein; it's also low in calories compared to other main-dish foods.

It's helpful to know that some fish are classified as fat, others as lean. This makes a certain amount of difference in the nutritive value, and a considerable difference in the best cooking methods for each type—lean fish if broiled must be basted with butter or other fat, if baked, should be cooked in milk or a sauce; fat fish are sufficiently moistened by their own fat so that basting or sauce is not necessary to keep them from drying out during the cooking process. Lean fish include catfish, yellow perch, cod, flounder, sole, halibut, red snapper, sea and striped bass (rockfish). Among the fat fish are lake and rainbow trout, whitefish, eel, herring, mackerel, pompano, salmon, and tuna.

To give you an idea of the nutrients in fish in general, and a comparison of a lean fish and a fat one in nutrients, below is a table of nutrient values for one serving of cod and one of salmon. The cod furnishes 111 calories, the salmon 232, and the nutrient yields are:

	cod	salmon	
protein	18.5	35.4	grams
fat	3.4	9.4	grams
carbohydrate	0	0	
calcium	20	18	milligrams
phosphorus	178	528	milligrams
iron	.7	1.5	milligrams
sodium	72	148	milligrams
potassium	265	565	milligrams
thiamin	.05	.20	milligram
riboflavin	.07	.08	milligram
niacin	2	12.5	milligrams
ascorbic acid	trace	trace	milligram
vitamin A	120	200	international units

Tips on preparing, cooking. With fish, the simple ways are best. Fish flavor is delicate—it's a shame to mask it with spicy or otherwise strong-flavored sauces and seasonings. (Except, of course, if you hate fish. During rationing in World War II, when few meats or poultry were available and some fish unobtainable, scrod—young cod—was plentiful and un-rationed. One good and imaginative cook boasted that she had invented twenty-two ways to serve scrod, "and you can't guess what any of them is!") But in general, fish is at its best briefly cooked and delicately seasoned. That doesn't mean, however, that there aren't dozens of delightful ways to prepare and serve it.

Fish may be poached, broiled, baked, or fried (usually breaded when fried). Whatever method you use, the big thing is not to overdo it. The method of timing fish cookery worked out by the Canadian Department of Fisheries is an excellent one. You time, not by minutes but by inches, and it works amazingly well for almost any type of fish. Measure the fish at its thickest point—depth, not width—and cook it exactly 10 minutes for every inch. For rolled fish fillets, measure after rolling. When poaching, lower the fish into the boiling poaching liquid, let the water return to the simmer point, and then start timing. For example, suppose you are poaching a thick piece of salmon. Bring the poaching liquid to a boil. Measure the salmon and find that it is, say, 8 inches deep at its thickest. For easy handling, encase the whole piece of salmon in cheesecloth; lower it into the liquid. Bring the liquid back to the simmering point, lower the heat so that a bare simmer is maintained, and poach the fish 80 minutes—an hour and 20 minutes. (Now that it's done, you'll serve it hot with lemon butter or hollandaise, or chilled with cucumber-dill sauce, won't you?)

If you want to double-check, test with a fork—always choosing the thickest part—twisting the tines a little. If the fish does not flake easily and is still even slightly translucent, it isn't done. In other words, fish ready to serve is opaque and flakes easily when tested.

Freezing fish. Fresh-caught fish, properly prepared (see special feature: PUTTING FOOD BY), may be frozen and held at 0°F. or below up to 6 months for lean fish, 3 months for fat fish. Never refreeze thawed fish, your own or commercially frozen.

Some perfect partners. As we hinted above, fish and lemon are great friends, and there's been a long love affair between fish and dill that started in Scandinavia and spread worldwide.

When you poach fish, thicken some of the poaching fluid with egg yolk, season with salt and white pepper and a liberal splash of lemon juice, and serve it over the fish with a bit of chopped parsley for color and extra flavor. Or bake fish in milk, then use the milk to make a white sauce; add chopped hard-cooked egg whites and spoon the sauce over the fish; sieve the hard-cooked yolks over the top of the dish in a golden drift.

Cucumber goes well with almost any fish. Peel, seed, and grate cucumber, bind with just enough sour cream to hold it together, season with the faintest touch of onion powder and cayenne, and serve with cold fish. Or poach peeled and seeded quartered cucumbers with the fish and serve them, with a drizzle of melted butter, beside it (they will be tender-crisp, not soft, and delicious).

As for dill, that feathery herb gives the just-perfect flavor touch. Melt butter, pour it over fish, then sprinkle very liberally with snipped dill fronds. Or add dill to the poaching liquid or baking sauce, or make a well-dilled cream sauce.

Capers are a nice change with fish, especially when the dish is a cold one. Make a salad of leftover or poached-on-purpose fresh salmon with plenty of chopped cucumber and a liberal lacing of capers; mayonnaise with lemon juice is the dressing.

And there's tartar sauce, best when it accompanies breaded and fried fish.

Other ways, other forms. Many supermarkets, particularly those near large bodies of water, have fresh-fish departments. And all of them sell fish processed in various ways.

on grocery shelves, in cans: Canned tuna, salmon, sardines, and mackerel; fish cakes and fish balls; kippered herring; in jars, gefilte fish—airy quenelles of pike and other fish in jellied fish stock that you definitely don't have to be Jewish to enjoy; anchovies, anchovy paste; soups, stews, and chowders of several kinds.

in grocery frozen-food section: Frozen raw fish fillets of many kinds; fish sticks, ready to heat and eat; whole trout; breaded raw or cooked fillets; fish dinners.

in delicatessens or supermarket deli counters: Fillets of herring in wine, in sour cream with onions, other ways; many kinds of delicately cured and/or smoked fish; if the deli is Scandinavian, sample gravlax, a marinated/pickled salmon that is one of the ultimate delicacies—expensive, but then so are diamonds and mink.

Canned fish, frozen fish. There is no federal inspection program for fresh fish—as there is for meat and poultry—but canned and frozen fish may be, at the option of the processor, inspected by the Department of Commerce National Marine Fisheries Service. Such products will carry one or both of two inspection marks. The first is round, and carries the words "U.S. Dept. of Commerce, Packed Under Federal Inspection." The mark is given only to inspected fish, and means that the product has been sampled and found to be of good quality, wholesome and safe. The second mark is a shield, similar to the USDA's meat and poultry quality inspection shields, bearing the words "U.S. Grade A." This mark is given only to top-quality products that are uniform in size, free of blemishes and defects, and possess fresh flavor and odor.

handling canned fish: Store on pantry shelf, at room temperature but away from a source of heat. After opening, store in glass or plastic containers, tightly covered, in the refrigerator up to 3 days.

Before you buy, check the condition of the can. If it is bulging, something has broken the seal—the fish may be spoiled. If the can is dented or rusty, there is no way to tell if the seal has been broken—don't buy.

At home, when you open the can check to make sure the flesh is firm. If the meat is overcooked, the flesh next to the can will be darker than that in the middle—if so, return the can to the store. If the fish is packed in oil, the oil should be clear, not milky. The can should be properly filled to the top.

Most tuna is packed in vegetable oil; some is packed in water, and there is a diet pack in distilled water, without salt. Read the tuna label; albacore is the only tuna that can be labled "white meat"—tuna labeled "light meat" comes from the yellow fin, skipjack, and blue fin varieties. If the can contains bonito, a fish very like tuna, it must be so labeled. Contents of tuna can may be 6½ or 7 ounces or 12 ounces —in some stores, smaller and larger sizes may be available. And there is one more thing the label will tell you: the piece-size—solid pack, chunk-style, grated, or flaked. (See TUNA.)

Canned salmon labels will also tell you a good deal. The color of the salmon is an indication of the oil content of the fish, and also determines the price. The deeper red the color, the higher the oil content will be. Sockeye salmon, a deep red color, has the highest oil content. Pink varieties are paler in color, lower in oil. Salmon is packed in 7- and 16-ounce cans. Years ago, before food processing was regulated, an enterprising canner put out a pale pink salmon the label of which carried the legend: "Guaranteed not to turn red in the can" and charged a fancy price for this "special" product. (See SALMON.)

Sardines come in a variety of packs, but virtually always in flat cans, most of which have to be opened with a key. They can be whole—heads, tails, skin, and bones—or skinless and boneless (also, although the label doesn't say so, headless and tailless), packed in oil, in tomato sauce, in mustard sauce, sometimes in wine sauce. (See SARDINES.)

handling frozen fish: Hustle it home to your freezer as fast as you can. But before you buy, make sure that the fish is solidly frozen, and has no objectionable odor. Avoid damaged packages. Fish is packed in moisture- and vaporproof material to prevent dehydration and contamination. A damaged package can mean loss of quality. Don't buy packages stacked above the freezing line in the store freezer—they may be thawed or in the process of thawing. If the frozen fish you buy is breaded, the label will tell you the amount of breading: if marked "regular breading" the contents is 50 percent fish, 50 percent breading; if marked "lightly breaded" the contents must be at least 65 percent fish.

In your freezer, at 0°F. or below, you can store commercially frozen fish up to 6 months. To thaw, place the wrapped package in the refrigerator; a 1-pound package of fish should thaw in about 24 hours. Whole fish should be completely thawed, fillets only sufficiently so that they can be separated; do not thaw breaded fish portions—heat or cook from the frozen state, as the label directs. You can thaw fish more rapidly by setting the wrapped package under cold running water; the fish will thaw in between 1 and 2 hours per pound. Do not thaw at room temperature or in warm water. Once thawed, fish should never be refrozen.

Ways with fish. A good fish cookbook will lead you to dozens and dozens of ways to prepare fish: mousses, salads, casseroles, puddings, fishcakes and fishballs, and many more. Look for recipes for specialty dishes such as coulibiac, a Russian hot fish pie that makes an excellent, unusual brunch-party dish.

The sociable side. At one time, the fish fry was an agreeable get-together, especially in the South. Often such gatherings were sponsored by politicians who furnished the food and drink to get constituents (or prospective ones) into a receptive mood for having the political facts of life hammered home. Probably too replete to flee, the crowd listened to the speakers, and no doubt some of them were convinced— either by the free food or the free-flowing rhetoric. Catfish were the fish of choice for such an occasion, and crisp hush puppies (cornmeal cakes, sometimes with onion in the batter) were fried along with the fish, ostensibly to quiet the hungry dogs that had joined the party, but often eaten by the people as well.

Today, the fish fry—minus the politicians—is regaining popularity as a way to entertain outdoors, another variation on the cookout that Americans are so fond of. Breaded fish, hush puppies, big bowls of potato salad and coleslaw, perhaps hot dishes of baked beans or barbecued limas, with beer to wash it all down and slabs of watermelon for dessert, add up to a perfect old-timey menu for such an occasion.

Fish, grandma used to say, is brain food. It isn't, any more than other protein foods are. But it's good and good for you. If you've never fried trout fresh from the stream or little sunfish from the lake over an open fire, you don't—as the Pennsylvania Dutch say—know what good is. See also ANCHOVIES, CAVIAR, EELS, FINNAN HADDIE, GEFILTE FISH, GROUPER, HERRING, KIPPERS, MACKEREL, ROE, AND SHELLFISH.

FLAKE, TO: see page 446

FLAMBE

Flambéed dishes are foods—generally main dishes or desserts—set aflame; the flames are allowed to die down (or are doused, if the cook has been too liberal with the brandy) before the food is served. Crepes Suzette and Cherries Jubilee are two of the commonly flambéed dishes, but restaurants with delusions of grandeur tend to set fire to everything in sight.

To flambé, you must use liquor with a high alcoholic content, such as brandy—wines and liqueurs often stubbornly refuse to go up in flames. Heat the liquor until it is well warmed, pour over the food to be flambéed, and set afire. Let the flames die away, and serve the food at once.

FLANK, FLANK STEAK: see BEEF

FLAPJACKS

Pancakes by another name, one that is used most often in the West, the Northwest, and Canada. There are many other names for this familiar breakfast favorite as well. In New England and parts of the South they're flannel cakes, a large pancake with a rather dense consistency—served with butter and maple syrup, with sausage cakes on the side, for a great New England breakfast; often with fruit as dessert in the South. Other names to which pancakes will answer include griddle cakes, batter cakes, wheat cakes, hotcakes. And there are special kinds of pancakes, such as corn cakes in the Midwest, blueberry pancakes, sourdough flapjacks, buckwheat cakes, and those big, popoverlike cakes called, oddly enough, Dutch Babies. Also dollar-sized Swedish plättar—with lingonberries and sour cream, ambrosial! And big German apple pancakes, cinnamon-sugar sprinkled, laved with melted butter. And latkes—potato pancakes—best with applesauce. And many others, surely. How splendidly varied our melting-pot food heritage is! See also PANCAKES.

FLAVOR

Food must be pleasing to the eye and to the nose, but it is food's good flavor that draws us to it, that impels us to eat it with pleasure.

Flavor can be an iffy thing—what one of us relishes, another rejects, for this is a highly individual, very subjective matter. Supposedly, human taste buds can detect four flavors: sweet, sour, salty, and bitter. Of those all the flavors we enjoy are made, enhanced by aroma. The smell of perking coffee, of frying bacon, of baking bread—we find in our mouths the flavor of those and many others simply by smelling them.

The shape and size and color of the food affect our perception of its flavor, and so does the texture when we take a bite—smooth or lumpy, crisp or soggy, tough or tender, whatever. Whether the food is pleasantly hot if it should be, or well chilled if that is how it ought to be served, is another flavor-perception factor. All of these influence our judgment of flavor, sending "it's good" or "it's terrible" or "it's only so-so" messages to our brains.

FLAVOR ENHANCERS: see ADDITIVES AND PRESERVATIVES and BARBECUE

FLAVORING AGENTS: see ADDITIVES AND PRESERVATIVES

FLAVORING EXTRACTS

Produced by dissolving the essential oils of various edibles —nuts, barks, seeds, seed pods, flowers, and others—in alcohol, these extracts impart to food the flavor of the edible from which they are derived. Some of the common extracts:

almond	coffee	pistachio
anise	ginger	raspberry
banana	lemon	rum
brandy	maple	sherry
celery	mocha	spearmint
cherry	orange	strawberry
cinnamon	peach	vanilla
clove	peppermint	walnut
coconut	pineapple	wintergreen

Most of these are the pure extracts—the real thing, taken from the fruit or nut or bark. But there are several, pineapple and black walnut among them, which in no way resemble the flavor they are supposed to impart, and so are made of chemical compounds which do give the expected flavor although they contain none of the original food they resemble. (Pineapple flavoring is among the better known ones, but black walnut is a love-it-or-hate it flavor that inspires more hate than love.)

In general, however, natural flavorings are more desirable—and much closer, understandably, to the real thing. Imitation vanilla, for example, is a very poor substitute for the flavoring made from the vanilla bean.

Flavoring extracts find their widest acceptance in desserts of many kinds, although some are useful in nonsweet foods. The ones made from spices are most often used in dishes where the tiny specks of the spice would not be desirable—custards are an example. This is also true of extracts made from nuts, used in dishes where the nuts themselves would not be acceptable or in dishes where the flavor is wanted, but too many nuts (to a balance of other ingredients) would be required to give a flavor strong enough.

The strength of extracts varies considerably, a good reason for approaching their use cautiously. Almond is the strongest—a quarter teaspoon of almond is sufficient to flavor a dish for which a whole teaspoon or more of vanilla would be required. A few drops of almond make a particularly good flavor-enhancer for dishes made with cherries or peaches—pies, cobblers, and such. A quarter to a half teaspoon of almond extract gives an angel food cake a delightful difference.

VANILLA is the flavoring most commonly used by both commercial bakers and home cooks. It blends with and enhances many other flavors exceptionally well, and is an especially good companion for chocolate and coffee. A mocha

235

(coffee/chocolate) cake, enlivened with a teaspoon of vanilla, is a subtle flavor experience.

Pure vanilla extract is made from a tropical plant of the orchid family. Imitation vanilla—which bears some, but not a great deal of resemblance to the real thing—is made with artificial flavorings, colored with caramel, and may contain a small amount of the pure extract. A few drops of vanilla in a glass of milk can turn some balky milk drinkers into lovers of the beverage; in hot cocoa, it smooths and reinforces the chocolate taste; the addition of vanilla, with a little sugar, to whipped cream produces a delightfully airy dessert sauce.

Rum and brandy flavorings are for those who like the taste but not the alcoholic content of those liquors, and are also used in some cases where an amount of the actual liquor sufficient to give good flavor would alter the consistency of the food. Use either of the extracts in holiday pies and cakes and cookies, and to flavor hard sauce.

All flavoring extracts are volatile. They should be added to stovetop-cooked foods—candies, frostings, and so on—at the end of the cooking period. Because the flavors "fade" after a time, foods to be frozen should be flavored more heavily with extracts than those to be eaten within a couple of days.

Some brands of flavoring extracts are put up in dark-glass bottles to protect them from the effects of light. Store extracts in a cool, dark place, making certain that caps are screwed on tightly after each use. Buy the smallest available size of an extract not often used. See also CHOCOLATE, MAPLE, MOCHA, and LICORICE.

FLAVORINGS

Other than extracts, there are many kinds of flavorings accessible to the home cook. Herbs and spices are kitchen standbys. Grated orange and lemon peel are available in small jars, and orange-flower water and rosewater in bottles—if not at the grocer's, try the pharmacist. Mushroom, garlic, and onion powders are useful; so are bottled onion and garlic juices. Combination flavorings appeared toward the end of the 1960s, small packets of a mixture of proper seasonings for various kinds of salad dressings, for stews and pasta sauces and chili con carne and a dozen more, conveniently measured in proper proportions, valuable for inexperienced cooks who want foods to taste "the way they ought to." Supermarket spice shelves yield various seasoned salts and peppers and spice-herb combinations such as italian seasoning, salad mixtures, and others.

There are sauces for flavoring on the market as well—soy sauces, steak sauces, liquid smoke flavoring (also smoke salt), tomato sauces—plain and with such added flavorings as onion, garlic, and mushroom—bottled gravy enhancers that add both flavor and color, bouillon cubes and powders

that produce "instant" beef or chicken broth to use as a flavor-improving cooking medium, barbecue sauces with flavors ranging from very mild to extremely assertive, worcestershire sauce, hot pepper sauce to add zip by the drop, flavored vinegars—dill, garlic, tarragon, and more—prepared mustards of several kinds and strengths, and fruit-based sweet glazes for ham and poultry. And there is MSG—monosodium glutamate—which is without flavor of its own but which, when added to a variety of foods (never to sweet ones), brings out and enriches the natural flavor.

Also available are butter-flavored extract and butter-flavored salt (artificial flavors, both) to add the familiar taste without the calories and cholesterol of the real thing.

There are other flavor-improvers in most kitchens. Sugar has its place as a condiment; in small quantities it smooths and mellows too-acid tastes without imparting sweetness. Try a half teaspoon of sugar in spaghetti sauce or in any other tomato dish for a vast flavor improvement. A tablespoon or two of catsup added to beef gravy leaves no catsup flavor but makes the gravy taste more richly and fully of the beef itself. A quarter cup of the liquid from a jar of sweet pickles improves the braising liquid for pot roast immeasurably. Wine, both white and red, are flavorful cooking mediums. Brandy and rum, as well as many of the liqueurs, are great flavor-enhancers when used judiciously. See also SPICES and HERBS AND SAVORY SEASONINGS.

FLOATING ISLAND

An old-fashioned dessert made of a custard with "islands" of meringue on top. The meringues are poached in milk, set aside to drain, and the same milk is used as the base of the custard. Fresh fruit is sometimes added—strawberries, raspberries, peaches, or nectarines are good choices.

FLOATS

Beverages made of a flavoring syrup (chocolate, coffee, any fruit) with carbonated water added, and a scoop of ice cream floated on top—a substantial, refreshing snack for droppers-in, or a good dessert to climax a family meal. Flavored carbonated beverages can stand in for the flavoring syrups and charged water. A root beer float, commonly known as a black cow, is a favorite with youngsters. Cream soda with chocolate ice cream is an excellent combination. For a lighter version, use water ice or sherbet in place of the ice cream; for a more substantial one, stir one ball of ice cream into the beverage until it melts, float a second on top. Floats can be decorated with slices or wedges of fresh fruit, sprigs of mint, or maraschino cherries.

FLORENTINE: see page 452

FLOUNDER: see FISH

FLOUR

A finely ground meal, made chiefly from grain, flour is as old as the beginnings of civilization. As soon as man added agriculture to his hunting and foraging for food, he worked out ways to turn the grain he grew into flour.

At first the grain was ground between two stones—any two of reasonable size that came to hand. But it soon became clear that if the bottom stone were concave (having a hollowed center) and the top stone fit the hand easily, the process went faster. This method, actually a mortar and pestle, is still in use in Mexico—the hollow stone is the *metate,* the hand-fitting one is called the *mano,* which means "hand" in Spanish.

For thousands of years, a slight refinement of this method was used. A sloping stone—called a saddle stone—was placed on a pedestal so that it slanted away from the hand-held grinding stone; as the flour was ground, it was pushed into a bowl or basket positioned under the lower edge of the saddle stone.

Then along came the Romans—always inventive when it came to anything that made food better—to revolutionize the whole process with the quern. It was round and stationary, with a flat or slightly convex surface into which grooves were cut. Another grooved stone was rotated over it, this one with a central hole through which the grain was poured. The two stones were positioned so that the space between them was narrower at the outside edge than near the center where the grain was fed in, so that the grain was first crushed, then ground finer and finer as it was pushed out toward the edge. The larger the stones, the Romans realized quite reasonably, the more flour could be milled.

In time, the state took over the task—and a new craft, milling, and a new kind of craftsman, the miller, came into being. From professional millers, it was a short step to professional bakers and community ovens. Woman's work, still never done, was eased a trifle.

After querns came millstones, great slabs of stone engineered to fit together two by two to grind between them flour finer than had previously been thought possible. No single miller could run this device, so a long wooden arm, something like a singletree, was attached in such a way that when men (slaves, usually) or draft animals pushed the wooden arm, the stones revolved.

About 100 B.C., ingenious Greeks worked out a device, the waterwheel, to power the big stones. Later, wind power was harnessed, when the windmill was invented by some unknown genius long lost to history. Finally steam power took over, in the early part of the nineteenth century.

By the 1870s, millstones had given way to the roller process, the one still in use, in which the grain is ground by a series of steel rollers, both smooth and corrugated.

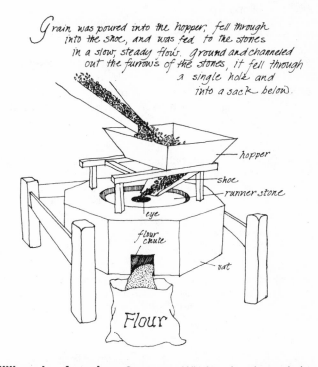

Grain was poured into the hopper, fell through into the shoe, and was fed to the stones in a slow, steady flow. Ground and channeled out the furrows of the stones, it fell through a single hole and into a sack below.

hopper
shoe
runner stone
eye
flour chute
vat

Flour

Milling in America. Governor Winthrop's *Journal,* in which that assiduous collector and recorder of facts made note of almost everything that went on in the Massachusetts colony, mentions a windmill used to power the grinding of flour that was moved from Newton—now Cambridge—to Boston in 1632 because the prevailing winds at Newton came from the wrong direction. The first recorded water mill was built in 1634 in Dorchester. The raising and milling of wheat quickly became an important business in New England, from where flour was exported to the other colonies and to the West Indies. Wheat flour was expensive, however, and most of the ordinary run of colonials made do with corn bread.

Near the end of the next century, in 1787, Oliver Evans began operation of a water-driven flour mill that ground wheat by a process that included bolting (sifting) through fine-meshed cloth, and produced a superior product—so superior that he was able to patent the process. His automated mill was almost certainly the first real "factory" in the country, and soon many other mills were using the process—some legally, some not—to produce the fine bolted flour. By 1837 there were some 1,200 such mills producing about two million barrels of flour a year, most of them in the western (west of the Alleghenies) states.

White flour made by the bolting process produces a fine, light bread. In the 1870s, a Hungarian count perfected a bolting method that produced so fine a white flour that the governor of Minnesota sent for Hungarian engineers to build a similar rolling mill in Minneapolis. Operated by two gentlemen named Washburn and Crosby, whose flour brand name was Gold Medal, that mill developed into a business familiar to all home cooks today—General Mills.

Milling and flour today. One of the major industries in the United States, flour milling is carried on in huge mills under conditions carefully regulated by the government, which specifies the type of wheat or other grains that must go into the making of a particular kind of flour, the way the flour is processed and packaged, and the nature of enrichment if the flour is enriched.

To begin the process of flour-making, the wheat seed or kernel must be separated into its component parts:

a) bran, the papery outside covering
b) the endosperm, the "meat" of the grain
c) the germ, the embryo (from which new wheat would grow if the seed were planted rather than milled)

When the kernel is broken, the bran and the germ readily split away, leaving the protein-carbohydrate endosperm. There are four major steps in the process of flour milling:

1) cleaning the wheat
2) tempering or conditioning
3) separating, by means of grinding and sifting
4) post-treating

cleaning: This step is exactly what it sounds like—removing any foreign matter and extraneous material, so that nothing but the wheat itself remains.

tempering: This step determines the moisture content of the wheat, then adds or removes moisture until the proper level for separation is attained.

separating: This is actually a combination of two steps, grinding and sifting; the two are alternated, and repeated many times. The grain goes first through corrugated metal rollers and a series of pegs very like hammers to break up the kernels. The size of the particles is reduced by each new set of rollers, which are placed closer and closer together. After each rolling, the ground particles are sifted through sieves of increasingly fine mesh; this system of alternate grinding and sieving is continued until the endosperm is separated from the bran and the germ insofar as possible.

post-treating: The grain, by the time it reaches this stage, has become flour. There are various post-treatments, including blending, maturing, and bleaching, each designed to improve the baking characteristics of the flour. Depending on the use for which a particular batch of flour is intended, it may be given additional treatment, such as instantizing, enriching, and enzyme replacement (enzymes are lost in the milling process).

For whole wheat flour, blending recombines the milled white flour with the bran and germ removed in the milling. All-purpose flour blends hard and soft wheats according to a specific formula. Blending also produces the various grades of flour.

Matured flour—that is, flour that has been aged—has better baking qualities than flour freshly milled. Long-time storage will produce this desirable quality, but so will harmless chemicals, which reproduce natural aging in a shorter time and at a lower cost.

Wheat, hard and soft, for various wheat flours. There are several kinds of wheat, all of which fall into one of two groups—hard and soft. Hard wheats, grown principally in the Midwest, are higher in gluten—structure-building protein —than soft ones. Flours incorporating a large quantity of hard wheats are good for making yeast-raised breads and rolls and all the other good things that are yeast-leavened. Some of these wheats are planted in the fall, harvested the following spring, and are called hard winter wheats; others, planted in the spring and harvested the following summer, are called hard spring wheats.

Grown principally in the eastern states, soft wheats, lower in gluten, produce flours just right for baked goods leavened with baking powder—cakes, quick breads, and the like.

Grading wheat flours. Flour comes off the mill's rollers in several streams, according to the fineness of the grind. Blending specified amounts of some or each of the streams produces the flour grades—straight, patent, and clear—as well as the several types of flours. "Straight" is the term for all the milled flour that has been separated from the embryo and the bran. "Patent," the highest grade of white flour, contains only select flour streams with a low percentage of residual germ and bran; "short patent"—the most select patent grade—contains the least amount of germ, bran, and ash. Clear flour is less refined, and is not available for home use.

FLOUR IN YOUR KITCHEN

Available to you are many varieties of wheat flours as well as flours made from other kinds of seeds, grains and, sometimes, nuts. You'll find many at your supermarket, but some you'll have to seek out at specialty food shops.

The wheat flours. When first milled, flour has a yellowish color. Aging and/or chemicals not only mature the flour so that it will "bake well" but also bleach it. Chlorine dioxide is a typical aging-bleaching agent; flours treated with it produce cakes that, because the flour will tolerate a higher percentage of shortening and sugar, are tenderer and sweeter—and a cake, as a kind of bonus, less likely to fall. There are also other chemicals used for maturing and/or bleaching. If these optional chemicals are used, the flour must be labeled "bleached." (See WHEAT.)

whole wheat flour: Also called wheat flour or graham—made from any cleaned, unrefined, unbleached wheat other than durum or red durum, the proportions of natural constituents of the flour (bran, embryo, endosperm) remain unchanged. Brown in color.

all-purpose flour: Also called white, plain, general-purpose, or just plain "flour"—refined wheat flour that may be bleached or unbleached, and can be used in any recipe that calls simply for "flour," without any qualifying adjective. Various blends of all-purpose flour are prepared to conform to the baking habits of different sections of the country. A blend from soft wheat is marketed in the South, where quick breads are a specialty; harder-wheat blends are sold in the North, where considerable yeast-leavened baking is done. All-purpose flour is white if bleached, yellowish if unbleached.

bran flour: All-purpose flour into which bran has been mixed.

cracked wheat flour: All-purpose flour into which cracked wheat—the entire wheat kernel, somewhat crushed—has been mixed.

wheat germ flour: All-purpose flour into which wheat germ—the embryo—has been mixed.

cake flour: Highly refined, bleached flour—uniformly and finely ground, it feels soft and very silky to the touch. Available for home baking, and also used in commercial cake mixes.

self-rising flour: Bleached flour into which leavening and salt have been incorporated in proper proportions for home baking. This flour should not be used in any yeast-raised baking. Available as self-rising all-purpose and self-rising cake flour.

enriched flour: Certain nutrients are lost in the refining and bleaching of white flour; enriching restores these to a level approximately equal to whole wheat flour. The amounts added to each pound of flour are government regulated; minimums and maximums are specified, so that there is a certain amount of leeway. Iron, niacin, riboflavin, and thiamine must be added, within the prescribed amounts, for a flour to qualify as "enriched," and calcium and vitamin D may also be added.

instant-type flour: Granular texture makes this flour easy to measure, easy to pour. It need not be sifted, and it blends readily with cold liquid without producing lumps. It cannot be used interchangeably in baking with regular all-purpose flour, but should be used only in recipes specially developed for its use. Particularly useful in making white sauce and as a thickener, it also has many other uses.

Flours other than wheat. Although when we think "flour" we generally are also, at least subconsciously, thinking "wheat," there are a number of other kinds of flours. These are usually sold mixed with a certain proportion of wheat flour because they lack the gluten necessary for baking—of them, only rye provides sufficient gluten for successful baking without the addition of wheat flour. Many of them, however, are available without added wheat in various specialty food stores.

arrowroot flour: From the roots of the tropical maranta plant; used by home cooks as a thickening agent, by commercial bakers—because of its easy digestibility—in biscuits and cookies for children and for adults on certain restricted diets. (See ARROWROOT.)

barley flour: Lower in protein than wheat, barley is rich in minerals; more popular in Europe than in the United States, it is difficult to use in making yeast breads. (See BARLEY.)

buckwheat flour: Finely ground flour made by sifting buckwheat meal. It has the sweet/sour flavor peculiar to buckwheat. (See BUCKWHEAT.)

carob flour: Made from the pods of the carob tree—also called St. John's bread or locust pods—the flour is high in protein, has a sweetish, faintly chocolatelike flavor. (See CAROB.)

corn flour: Finer than the cornmeal of which it is a by-product, it may be made of white or yellow corn. (May be labeled "masa harina.") (See CORN.)

cottonseed flour: Made from the residue that remains after the extraction of oil from specially treated cotton seeds.

lima bean flour: Made from ripe, dried lima beans.

oat flour: Made from refined and ground oats; requires the addition of wheat flour to produce acceptable yeast-raised breads. (See OATMEAL.)

peanut flour: What remains after the oil has been extracted from peanuts.

potato flour: Made from cooked potatoes, dried and ground. Used more in Europe than here, an important ingredient in several kinds of Jewish cooking.

rice flour: Starchy flour made from white rice. A second kind, *waxy rice flour* is made from a variety of rice with waxy, adhesive qualities; it is used as a stabilizer in sauces and gravies, and prevents separation of these foods when frozen. (See RICE FLOUR.)

rye flour: Made from finely ground and sifted rye meal. (See RYE.)

soy flour: There are two kinds: full-fat and low-fat. The former is made from soybeans with only the hull removed, the latter from the residue after the oil is expressed from treated soybeans.

tapioca flour: Made from the roots of tropical manioc or cassava plants—both high in carbohydrate nutrients. (See TAPIOCA.)

Although you may never buy many (or any) of these flours to use at home, a study of labels on many of the processed foods you purchase will reveal the commercial uses for them. And many of the nonwheat flours find their chief use in foods for those allergic to wheat.

Buying, keeping, and using flour. Unless you do a good deal of baking, the larger sizes of flour, even though they may cost less per pound, are not necessarily a good buy. This is particularly true in warm weather. You're better off buying the smaller sizes, and bringing home a fresh batch more often. Even if you use enough all-purpose flour to warrant buying the large size, the other household-use flours, such as whole wheat and rye, should be purchased only in quantities that will be used up within a month or so.

how to store: Remove the flour from the bag (or box) in which you buy it to a container—metal, glass, plastic—with an airtight cover as soon as you bring it home. This helps to keep the flour fresh, and it also discourages weevils, those pantry pests to whom flour is especially appealing. White all-purpose and cake flour can be stored at room temperature, in a cool, dry place. Those that incorporate the embryo —whole wheat and wheat germ flours—should be refrigerated, also in a container with an airtight cover, as the germ deteriorates rapidly at room temperature and the oil it contains becomes rancid. Flours from grains other than wheat should also be refrigerated, and if your kitchen shelves do not offer a sufficiently cool storage place, refrigerate flours of all kinds. Tightly covered containers prevent flour from losing its own moisture content and from absorbing moisture from outside sources.

nutritive values: Starch is proportionately greater in white than in whole wheat flour—the white flour, then, is also higher in calories (and is also more easily digested) than the whole wheat. Calories furnished by flour, however, are fairly similar in amount throughout the range of the kinds, although there is some variation. Below are listed nutrients in whole wheat and in white enriched flour in 1-cup amounts. One cup of whole wheat flour furnishes 400 calories, a like amount of white enriched, 499.

	whole wheat	enriched white	
protein	16	14.4	grams
fat	2.4	1.4	grams
carbohydrate	85.2	104.3	grams
calcium	49	22	milligrams
phosphorus	446	119	milligrams
iron	4	4	milligrams
sodium	4	3	milligrams
potassium	444	130	milligrams
thiamin	66	60	milligrams
riboflavin	.14	.36	milligram
niacin	5.2	4.8	milligrams

Neither whole wheat nor white flour furnishes vitamin A or ascorbic acid (vitamin C).

Measuring flour. Stir the flour first, as it often becomes compacted on standing. Then spoon lightly into the measuring cup; do not pack. Or, if the flour container is large, dip the measuring cup into the stirred flour, spoon out any excess. In either case, use a cup made for dry measuring and level off the top gently with a dull knife or a spatula.

Sifting flour. Many brands of white all-purpose flour are now presifted and need not be sifted again before using; however, they should be stirred before measuring. Let the recipe you are using be your guide as to whether or not to sift. If it calls for sifted flour, sift—in a flour sifter or through a fairly fine-mesh sieve—before measuring, then spoon the sifted flour lightly into the measuring cup. Cake flour should always be sifted. Whole wheat and wheat germ flour should not be sifted—it removes the bran and wheat embryo, the reasons you bought that kind of flour in the first place. These, too, should be stirred before measuring.

Sifting flour onto a piece of wax paper or foil makes it easy to return unused flour to the container; just pick up the paper or foil and pour. Use the same trick when sifting flour with other dry ingredients; foil or paper makes it simple to add the dry ingredients to the dough or batter.

Using flour. Most of us are aware of the many good foods, particularly the baked ones, of which flour is a chief ingredient. There are many kinds of cakes and cookies, pies (flour in the pastry and sometimes in the filling as well), quick breads and yeast-raised ones, and more. Flour gives these mixtures structure and elasticity because of its gluten protein content.

We also use flour in the kitchen for dredging, coating, and thickening. Dredging, we sprinkle food with flour or shake it in a bag containing flour—and sometimes seasonings of various sorts—to give the food a light dusting so that it will brown better. Pieces of meat and poultry to be fried or browned are often dredged. We also speak of dredging in connection with sticky fruits—raisins, dates—fruit peels, and sometimes nuts, which are to be incorporated in a batter. The flour coating helps to distribute them throughout the batter and hold them there during baking (undredged, they may sink to the bottom). Use part of the flour from the cake or cookies you are making for this kind of dredging—otherwise you will incorporate too much flour into the batter, resulting in a dry product.

In coating foods to be sautéed or deep-fat fried—generally these are pieces of meat, such as veal scallops or cutlets, or such things as croquettes or patties—dip first in flour, making sure the food is well coated with it, then in beaten egg, then in flour again or in fine dry bread or cracker crumbs.

The presence of flour as an ingredient in many kinds of foods thickens them. In such foods as puddings and pie fillings, the flour is mixed with other ingredients before cooking or heating takes place. Flour is used at the end of cooking time to thicken gravies or during cooking to thicken sauces. There are four ways to approach this kind of thickening. Sometimes a roux is made by melting fat, then stirring in flour before liquid is added. Or a smooth flour-cold water mixture can be made and poured slowly into bubbling liquid—soup or sauce, for example—while the mixture is stirred constantly until it thickens. Or instantized—granular—flour may be mixed with cold fat and cold liquid and then cooked, stirring, until the mixture thickens. Or some soups and stews may be thickened with beurre manié, a mixture of flour and butter kneaded together; small bits are broken off and dropped into the bubbling soup or stew, and the mixture is stirred until it reaches the required thickness. See BUTTER.

Freezing flour. Flour in itself cannot be frozen, but many of the foods made from flour, particularly breads, cakes, and cookies, freeze very well (see special feature: PUTTING FOOD BY).

When you use flour today, give a kind thought to yesterday's cooks. Before modern methods of flour processing were perfected, flour for every use had to be dried—in the sun, over a fire, or in the oven—before the cooking could begin. In many ways, things are constantly improving for the home cook! See also INSTANTIZED FLOUR, SAGO, and TRITICALE.

FLOUR, TO: see page 446

FLOWERS

In cooking? Yes, indeed—well, yes in some limited uses. Early Persian cooking, in particular, made excellent use of flowers, adding fresh or dried ones to soups and meat dishes as well as to confections. Oriental cultures added dried flowers, notably jasmine but other kinds as well, to tea to improve flavor and fragrance; they also added flower petals to wines to increase bouquet, and used them to flavor sweets. Nero, notable for his violin virtuosity while Rome went up in flames around him, is also remembered for his love of rose petals as a seasoning for all sorts of foods.

But that was long ago and far away. How about today? Look around your kitchen—it's very likely that you regularly use flowers without even thinking about it. If you're addicted to capers, remember that they are pickled flower buds. Fond of broccoli? Cauliflower? The best, most delicate parts of both vegetables are unopened flower buds. Saffron is the golden stamen of a certain kind of crocus.

In fancy baking we use rosewater and orange-flower water to flavor cookies and sometimes custards. We decorate cakes and other special desserts with candied violets and rose petals. Nasturtium flowers and leaves add a lovely touch to salads, and the pickled buds much resemble capers. Rose petals and hips—the large fruitlike pod that forms when a rose is allowed to die on the bush—make a wonderful jam. If you raise squash in your home garden, pick off some of the flowers (not all, or you'll have no squash crop), dip them in light fritter batter and deep fry for a taste sensation. Pass the flowers, please. See also CANDIED FLOWERS and NASTURTIUMS.

FLUORINE: see special feature: NUTRITION NOTEBOOK

FLUTE, TO: see page 446

FOAM CAKES: see CAKES

FOIE GRAS

Incredibly rich, ineluctably smooth, sinfully good—and horribly expensive—foie gras is the fat liver (that's the English translation of the French) of a goose who gave her all for the gustatory delight of such as we. Our laws against cruelty to animals prevent the production of foie gras here; our supply is imported, generally in tins or earthenware terrines, from France, Austria, and Czechoslovakia. The delicacy is produced by force-feeding geese kept in small enclosures; their rich diet and lack of exercise cause their livers to grow to enormous size.

Pâté de foie gras (perhaps it would not sound so elegant if we called it paste of fat liver?), a smooth concoction made of the liver, is sometimes lily-gilded with truffles. But it is not considered the ultimate—foie gras *au naturel* is, for that is the whole liver, cooked, with nothing added or taken away.

If you are truly into foie gras, or would like to be, you'll want to know the various grades and kinds we import:

grades—in descending order, Extra, Sur-Choix, and Choix.

foie gras au naturel—the finest; one whole liver

pâté de foie gras—at least 75 percent whole foie gras, the remainder minced foie gras

crème de foie gras—at least 75 percent minced foie gras, plus other liver, such as pork

crème de foie d'oie—at least 55 percent foie gras

crème au foie—30 percent foie gras

This is the sort of information that food snobs love to bandy about, in the hope of intimidating other food snobs. Have fun.

FOLD, TO: see page 446

FONDANT: see page 452

FONDUES

Gruyère—sometimes other cheeses—melted with white wine, a sprinkle of pepper, and a little kirsch compose the true Swiss fondue. Served in a chafing dish or a casserole placed over an alcohol burner or canned heat or some other mechanism to keep it warm, fondue is not only delicious but makes one of the warmest, friendliest possible ways to entertain. It's virtually impossible to remain standoffish when you're part of a group gathered around a fondue pot, dipping in chunks of crusty bread and dribbling cheese down your chin.

Fondue Bourguignonne is another cook-it-yourself dish —in this case, pieces of meat (often fillet of beef) cooked in a community container of hot oil, dipped into one of several sauces, and popped into your mouth. Fondue Oriental operates on the same principle, except that the cooking medium is hot broth rather than oil; chicken, fish, and vegetables are often a part of the spread of good things to be cooked in the broth. Finally, there's dessert fondue—chocolate melted in milk or cream or liquor or liqueur, with pieces of doughnut, squares of sponge or angel food cake, marshmallows, and pieces of fruit to be dunked in it, then into dishes of chopped nuts or coconut.

FONTINA: see CHEESE

FOO YONG

Chinese in origin, foo yong combines bits of almost any meat, fish, poultry, or vegetable with eggs into a cake rather like a thick omelet. Great way to use up leftovers at lunch time.

FOOD ADDITIVES: see ADDITIVES AND PRESERVATIVES

FOOD ADULTERANTS

Anything that gets into food that doesn't belong there, whether added on purpose or accidentally, constitutes adulteration. It's been a problem for a long time, and for as long a time those in authority have been trying to do something about it. As early as 300 B.C., a Sanskrit law forbade the adding of foreign matter to foods and medicines, and the wine-bibing ancient Romans passed laws against the dilution of their favorite tipple.

The earliest law prohibiting the adulteration of food in the United States was passed in 1890, but it was the Pure Food and Drug Act of 1906 that first made a wide, general attempt to control the problem. Correcting the lacks of that law was the 1938 Federal Food, Drug and Cosmetic Act, which— along with subsequent amendments—forbids adulteration of any sort and lays down penalties for those who flout it.

The FDA is the watchdog. FDA teams inspect and spot-check all sorts of foods in all stages of processing; the agency has the ability—and the clout—to force recall and/or destruction of foods that are harmful, or that do not meet standards set for them.

FOOD ALLERGIES: see ALLERGIES, FOOD

FOOD COLORINGS

The more familiar form of this is liquid, packed in small bottles of four colors—red, green, blue, and yellow—to a set, or in individual somewhat larger bottles similar to those used for flavoring extracts. Its purpose is to lend color to foods, partic-

ularly frostings and confections. Sometimes nonsweet foods are colored too, as when yellow coloring is added to sauces to make them look egg-yolk rich—a mild form of culinary cheating. Be cautious in using food coloring. A little goes a long way. Add a drop or two, stir in, add more if necessary.

Paste food coloring, less widely available, comes in a wider range of colors and is easier to control. It is used principally to color the frostings from which cake decorators fashion flowers, leaves, swags, and other doodads.

FOOD FADS

Foods come, foods go, and most of the time it's difficult to figure out why they do either. Some of the fads begin when a piece of information concerning the food in question finally becomes widely disseminated—such as the fact that fish is high in protein and low in fat. Weight-loss and low-fat dieters take the food to their bosoms—actually, their mouths—and a new fad has started; not wanting to be left out, nondieters hop on the bandwagon. Natural cereals are another example —they are "natural" and have excellent flavor and texture, so what could be bad about them? Many dedicated natural cereal eaters have an extra ten or fifteen pounds to show for what's bad: such cereals are high in fats and carbohydrates.

Or perhaps a respected food columnist or one of the women's magazines prints a recipe, and the informational copy surrounding the recipe is particularly winning. A large number of home cooks try it, and they all tell their friends, and pretty soon we're all up to our armpits in gnocchi or chicken kiev or pavlova or whatever. Then, when we've reached the point where we turn pale at the very mention of the food, the fad mercifully disappears and we coast a little until another one comes along. (What's pavlova? Besides a ballerina, a dessert from Australia, made of meringue, fruit, and whipped cream. Very good, too—wonder whatever happened to it?)

Sylvester Graham, a health-food faddist of many years ago, gave us graham flour. Thereafter for a time, everything that could be, and a whole lot that couldn't, was made with graham flour; today we retain a legacy from the gentleman —graham crackers.

Then there was Horace Fletcher, a turn-of-the-century nutritionist who held that what you ate didn't matter so much as how you ate it. Fletcherizing—chewing each bite at least thirty times—was all the rage for a while, until most people's jaws rebelled and the fad died away. We're told that a large family seated around the dinner table all rhythmically masticating was a sight to see.

As this is written, we're having a sesame-seed fit. Sesame seeds are very good (toasted, they're even better)—but not, for the love of Escoffier, in everything! It has become virtually impossible, for example, to buy a hamburger on a plain bun. If you plaintively ask for one, you are given what grandma used to call "a certain kind of look"—the kind that curdles your blood. Sesame seeds turn up in crackers, in cookies, in candies, in cakes, in pie crust, in breads and rolls, sprinkled over puddings and sundaes, in the breading for veal cutlet, incorporated into meat loaves, in assorted appetizer dips, drifting over various vegetables (green beans sesame instead of amandine), and a dozen more places, some acceptable, some totally inappropriate. Enough, already.

FOOD GARDENS: see special feature: THE GROW-IT-YOURSELF BOOM

FOOD PICKS

"Secure with a food pick," the recipe says blandly. But if you ask for food picks in the supermarket, you're going to get a blank stare and a shake of the head. Some time ago, the recipe would have directed you to "secure with a toothpick," but somewhere along the line someone decided that toothpick was a vulgar word—to say nothing of a vulgar concept—and that such vulgarity must cease. So now we are burdened with the excessive gentility of food picks.

Toothpicks! So useful that no kitchen can afford to be without them for pinning foods together to hold them in shape, for plunging into foods to test them for doneness, for spearing appetizer goodies, for a dozen other uses. Cautionary note: If someone has made you a present of deluxe colored plastic picks, put them aside. If you use them in food to be cooked, they'll melt, spoiling your dish with a mishmash of glop that, if not poisonous, looks as if it ought to be. And another: Make sure you remove picks from food before you serve it, lest you have an accident on your hands. Wooden picks, eminently useful, are nevertheless not edible.

So—let's hear it for toothpicks. Plain wooden toothpicks.

FOOD PROCESSING

There's a lot of flack to be heard about processed foods—all bad. Before you join the sounding off, remember that anything—anything at all—that is done to a food is a form of processing. Peel a potato, you've begun to process it. Cook it, and you've processed it some more. Mash it, and you've processed it again. Dish it up, decorate with a pat of butter and a sprinkling of parsley—oops, further processing. So watch those derogatory remarks about food processors and processed foods. You might be talking to yourself.

FOOD PROCESSORS: see special feature: YOU CAN'T WORK WITHOUT TOOLS

FOOD SHOPPING

As with virtually everything else in the world, there's a right way and a wrong way to go about food shopping. Haphazard is wrong; organized is right.

To begin with, you need a blackboard or a comparable device in the kitchen on which to jot down those things you are about to run out of. Indoctrinate the whole family—tell them that they are required to list any item of which they have eaten or used the next-to-the-last, on pain of being drummed out of the regiment.

Have a work place, in the kitchen or elsewhere in the house, that is yours. A place where you can make menus and lists. Menus come first. From flyers left at the door or picked up at the market, or from food ads in the local newspapers, determine good buys this week (on foods your family likes, of course) at your favorite market. Let those be the basis on which to build your menus. Choose the main dish of each menu first, then the vegetables and side dishes that go well with it (many of these will be in the ads, too), then any extras —hot breads, pickles, relishes, and so on—that you want to add to round the menu out; finally, the dessert, bearing in mind that a heavy meal calls for a light dessert, and vice versa. But don't feel that the menus constitute an inviolable contract—be flexible enough to make changes if you come on an unadvertised special that's a good buy.

Armed with your week's menus plus the kitchen list of items that need replenishing, make your shopping list. (Never shop without a list, even if you're going after only three items —which you should never have to do, if you've planned efficiently. You're sure to meet the woman from down the street who wants to tell you all about her son's hernia operation, and the gory details will drive those three items right out of your head.)

Make your list with the layout of the supermarket in mind. Start with nonfood items—paper and cleaning supplies, soap and detergents, polishes and the like. Next, the canned and packaged staples—flour, sugar, crackers, cereals, tomato sauce, whatever. Now the bakery area for bread, rolls, buns. Then the meat department where, guided by your menus and how the advertised specials will look when you meet them face to face, you'll make the final main-dish selections that will determine other menu items to go with them. Next the fresh produce, the fruits and vegetables. Then the dairy department—milk, cream, butter, eggs, cheese. Finally, frozen foods, juices, ice cream. Organize your cents-off coupons and fasten them to your list. Then it's off to the market to shop in the same order as the list was made out.

Then checkout—and home. Don't plan to do anything after food shopping. If you have other errands, do them before food shopping. In warm weather, bring along an insulated food bag or cooler to get the frozen things and milk, cream, and butter home in mint condition.

Do anything, short of giving them away, to avoid taking the children with you on the big weekly shopping trip. Husband and kids both? That way lies madness. You'll come home with frazzled nerves, an out-of-shape food budget, three cans of smoked oysters, two pounds of imported bleu cheese, and grounds for divorce.

Final cautionary notes: Don't shop when you're hungry, or appetite will overcome discretion. And be aware of the fallacy, no matter how economy-minded you are, of driving all over town from market to market to save two cents on kitchen cleanser at one, four cents on ground beef at another, while you burn up thirty cents' worth of gas in the process.

FOOD STAMPS: see special feature:
YOUR PARTNER IN THE KITCHEN

FOOD STORAGE

There are three main food storage areas in the home cook's kitchen: cupboards, refrigerator, and freezer. Using each to optimum advantage—a combination of know-how and organization—results in the best possible food for your family with the least possible waste. Storing foods properly takes no more time and energy than storing them improperly. And there's a bonus attached to proper storage: you know what you have and where to lay hands on it.

Storing in the cupboard. Keep the coolest, darkest, driest cupboard areas in your kitchen for food storage. Other cupboards—over the stove, for example, or near the refrigerator exhaust, or above the washer and dryer if they are in the kitchen—should store dishes, glassware, and pots and pans.

Dry foods store best if transferred to airtight containers after opening; such containers help prevent the absorption of moisture, and keep out insects. Canned goods should be arranged by kind, and rotated—put the new ones of each kind at the back of the shelf when you get them home from the market, bringing the older ones forward to assure that they will be used first. Or if that system doesn't work for you, date the cans and packages before putting them away. Even if a food is on sale at an inviting price, don't buy more than you can use up before its optimum storage time is over. Although many foods are perfectly edible longer than the storage times shown in the charts below, flavors will begin to fade and nutrients be lost.

Storing in the refrigerator. Refrigerator temperature should be between 34 and 40°F. Below that range, delicate foods will freeze; above it, they will spoil. Keep all refrigerator-stored foods in containers with tight covers, in closed plastic bags, or well wrapped in foil. This keeps the contents from drying out, and prevents flavors and odors from transferring from one food to another. Fruits and vegetables should not be washed before storing—moisture encourages spoilage. Wash just before using. Again, foods may well be usable if 'stored longer than the recommended times, but quality will have deteriorated.

Storing in the freezer. Freezer temperature must be maintained at 0°F. or below. If your freezer is a part of your refrigerator but has a separate door, or if your freezer is a separate appliance, you should be able to maintain the proper temperature. However, if the freezer section is a compartment within your refrigerator and the refrigerator itself has only one main door, you will not be able to keep the compartment at 0°F. or below. Foods stored in such compartments must be used within two weeks. In any case, you should have a freezer thermometer (from a housewares or hardware store) to keep a check on the freezer temperature. If a freezer is well stocked, it will maintain proper temperature better than one with only a few items stored in it.

If the electricity goes off, keep the freezer door closed—don't open it, even once, for any reason. A full freezer should keep food solidly frozen for at least two days without electricity; a freezer with relatively few items in it will begin to warm up more rapidly. It is safe to refreeze foods that have begun to thaw provided they still contain ice crystals. And foods that have been frozen raw, thawed, and cooked, may be frozen again in the cooked state—that is, if you make stew from frozen stewing beef, you may freeze the finished stew.

Store commercial frozen foods in their original packages in your freezer; if the package is not entirely secure, overwrap with moisture/vaporproof freezer paper or heavy-duty foil. Freeze prepared foods from your kitchen only in plastic or other containers made especially for freezer storage.

STORING IN THE CUPBOARD

food item	storage time	bear in mind
baking powder, baking soda	18 months	keep dry
bouillon cubes and powders	1 year	
bread and cracker crumbs	6 months	
breads and rolls	3 days	in original wrapping
cake mixes	1 year	
cakes, baked	2–3 days	refrigerate if with cream or custard fillings
canned foods (all kinds)	1 year	use oldest first
coffee, vacuum can	1 year	refrigerate 1 week after opening
coffee, instant	6 months	only 2 weeks after opening
coffee lighteners, nondairy dry	6 months	keep dry
cookies, packaged	4 months	1 week after opening

food item	storage time	bear in mind
crackers	3 months	keep dry, tightly closed
flour, all-purpose and cake	6 months	keep dry, tightly closed
frosting mixes and canned frostings	6–8 months	
fruit, dried	6 months	keep dry
gelatin, plain and fruit	18 months	keep dry
herbs, spices		
whole	1 year	keep tightly closed
ground	6 months	
honey	1 year	do not refrigerate
hot-roll and quick-bread mixes	1 year	keep dry
jam, jelly	1 year	refrigerate after opening
molasses	2 years	
nonfat dry milk	6 months	keep dry, refrigerate after reconstituting
oil, salad and cooking	3 months	close tightly after use
pancake and waffle mixes	6 months	keep dry
pasta (all kinds)	1 year	2 months after opening
peanut butter	6 months	2 months after opening
piecrust mixes	6 months	
pies and pastries	3 days	refrigerate custard, cream
potatoes, dry mixes	18 months	keep dry
pudding mixes (all kinds)	1 year	
rice, brown and wild	1 year	
white	2 years	
flavored mixes	6 months	
salad dressings	3 months	refrigerate after opening
sauce, soup, gravy mixes	6 months	keep dry
sauces: barbecue, chili, catsup	2 months	keep tightly closed
shortening, hydrogenated	8 months	keep tightly covered
soft drinks	3 months	
sugar, granulated	2 years	keep dry
brown and confectioners	4 years	
syrups	1 year	close tightly after use
tea, loose and bags	6 months	
instant	1 year	
vegetables: onions, potatoes, rutabagas, sweet potatoes, winter squash	1 week (room temperature)	keep dry, out of sun; provide for air circulation (will keep 2–3 months at 55° F. but not refrigerated)
whipped-topping mixes	1 year	

STORING IN THE REFRIGERATOR

FRUITS AND VEGETABLES
(in crisper or closed plastic bags)

food item	storage time	bear in mind
apples	1 month	or at cool room temperature
apricots, avocados, bananas, grapes, melons, nectarines, pears, peaches, plums	5 days	if necessary, ripen at room temperature before refrigerating
berries, cherries	3 days	
citrus fruit (all kinds)	2 weeks	or at cool room temperature
pineapples	2 days	

food item	storage time	bear in mind
asparagus	3 days	
beets, carrots, parsnips, radishes, turnips	2 weeks	remove leafy tops before storing
broccoli, brussels sprouts, green onions, summer squash	5 days	
cabbage, cauliflower, celery, cucumbers, green beans, eggplant, peppers, tomatoes	1 week	if necessary, ripen tomatoes at room temperature (not in light) before refrigerating
corn on cob	1 day	refrigerate in husks
lettuce, spinach, all green leafy vegetables	5 days	remove damaged leaves before refrigerating
lima beans, peas	5 days	leave in pods

DAIRY PRODUCTS
(keep tightly covered or wrapped)

food item	storage time	bear in mind
butter	2 weeks	in butter keeper (spreading consistency) 2–3 days only
buttermilk	2 weeks	
cheese, spreads	2 weeks	if mold forms on surface of hard or semisoft
cottage and ricotta	5 days	cheeses, remove before serving—no harm done
cream and neufchatel	2 weeks	
sliced cheeses	2 weeks	
whole cuts	2 months	
cream, sweet and sour	1 week	
eggs, whole in shell	1 month	store in original carton—if in egg keeper,
whites, separated	4 days	1 week only; cover yolks with water
yolks, separated	4 days	
margarine	1 month	
milk, whole and skim (also reconstituted nonfat dry, condensed, and evaporated—after opening)	1 week	never return unused milk to original container—will spread bacteria

MEAT, FISH, AND POULTRY
(before cooking)

food item	storage time	bear in mind
fresh beef, lamb, pork and veal: steaks, chops, roasts	5 days	leave in store plastic wrap, or wrap loosely to allow for air circulation
ground and stew meat	2 days	
fresh sausage	2 days	
variety meats	2 days	
bacon, frankfurters	1 week	after opening
ham, canned	6 months	unopened
slices	3 days	
whole	1 week	
luncheon meats, cold cuts	5 days	after opening
sausage, dry and semidry	3 weeks	
fish, shellfish (all kinds)	1 day	keep closely wrapped
poultry, fresh or thawed	2 days	

PREPARED FOODS, LEFTOVERS, AND PACKAGED FOODS
(after opening)

food item	storage time	bear in mind
broth, gravy, soup	2 days	keep all tightly covered
cakes, pies (cream or custard fillings)	2 days	
casserole dishes, stews	3 days	
coffee	1 week	after opening
coffee lighteners, frozen	3 weeks	after thawing
flour: rye, whole wheat, wheat germ	1 year	tightly covered container, not original package
fruits	3 days	
juices, beverages	6 days	
meat, fish, poultry	2 days	remove stuffing from poultry, refrigerate separately
nutmeats	6 months	keep tightly covered
pickles and olives	1 month	original container
refrigerated doughs:		check final-use date on package;
biscuits, cookies, rolls		do not open until ready to use
salad dressings	3 months	original container
salads: potato, chicken, coleslaw	2 days	tightly covered container
wine, table white	3 days	after opening

Food to be refrigerated should be dealt with promptly. Do not allow food to cool to room temperature before refrigerating, but place in a container, cover tightly, and refrigerate at once— hot foods will not raise the temperature of the refrigerator excessively, and the extra expenditure of energy by the refrigerator to cool the food is worth it to avoid food poisoning.

STORING IN THE FREEZER

COMMERCIAL FROZEN FOODS

food item	storage time	bear in mind
breads, rolls (baked); unbaked loaves	3 months	overwrap commercial wrappings
cakes, butter, unfrosted, and pound-type	6 months	overwrap all except boxed cakes
angel food	2 months	
frosted layer cake	4 months	
coffee lighteners	1 year	
doughnuts, danish pastry	3 months	
fish (fat types): trout, mackerel, salmon	3 months	overwrap all if package is damaged
fish (lean types): cod, flounder, sole	6 months	if fish is thawed in transit,
		do not refreeze—use at once
shellfish, breaded, cooked	3 months	
lobster, scallops	3 months	
king crab	10 months	
shrimp, uncooked, not breaded	1 year	
fruit	1 year	
ice cream, sherbet	1 month	overwrap leftovers after opening
main dishes, pies:		
fish or meat	3 months	
poultry	6 months	
meats, beef: roasts, steaks	1 year	overwrap all if package is damaged or flimsy
ground beef	4 months	
lamb, veal: roasts, steaks	9 months	
pork chops	4 months	
roasts	8 months	

food item	storage time
pancake, waffle batter	3 months
pies, unbaked	8 months
ready to thaw and eat	4 months
poultry: chicken, turkey parts	6 months
whole chicken, turkey	1 year
duck, goose	6 months
turkey rolls, roasts	6 months
vegetables	8 months

These times apply to commercially frozen foods only—foods bought already frozen, not thawed before they are placed in your home freezer. For storage times for home-frozen foods, see the special feature: PUTTING FOOD BY.

FOOD STORAGE CONTAINERS: see special feature: YOU CAN'T WORK WITHOUT TOOLS

FOOD VALUES: see individual food by name and the special feature: NUTRITION NOTEBOOK

FOODS, COMPOSITION OF: see individual food by name and the special feature: NUTRITION NOTEBOOK

FORCEMEAT

Composed of fine-ground or minced or chopped meat—and in some cases other foods as well—along with such ingredients as eggs and cream to bind and smooth the mixture, forcemeat is essentially an elegant sort of stuffing. Unlike the bread or rice or potato stuffings we use for poultry, forcemeat is a dense, smooth, compact mixture, usually highly seasoned. It is used for garnishing, and in pâtés and galantines and terrines, and for stuffing boned poultry. The chief ingredient of a forcemeat is finely ground—often put through the grinder's fine blade several times—to achieve fine texture. The finished product is velvety smooth. Egg-sized portions of forcemeat are poached to make quenelles; these are generally served with a sauce.

FORTIFIERS: see ADDITIVES AND PRESERVATIVES

FOWL

An elderly hen, fowl is also called a stewing chicken—the basis of soups, stews, fricassees, or any other dish using a moist-heat method of cooking. On the farm, a hen past her prime as an egg factory, no matter what her age, was used for these purposes, but fowl that come to market today are generally hens over ten months old, weighing up to six pounds. See also CHICKEN.

FRANGIPANE

A term with two meanings. The first frangipane is a mixture of flour, egg yolks, butter, and milk, resembling—and cooked in the same way as—pâte à choux. The resulting puffs are often filled with chicken or fish forcemeat. The second, frangipane cream, is a rich, thick sweet custard, flavored with almond and often incorporating ground almonds or finely crushed almond macaroon crumbs.

FRANKFURTERS: see HOT DOGS and SAUSAGES

FRAPPE: see page 452

FREEZE-DRIED FOODS

This is a commercial method of preserving food that combines aspects of both freezing and drying. It is based on the principle of sublimation: although water generally evaporates from its liquid state, under certain conditions it will go directly from a solid to a gas—from ice to vapor—bypassing the liquid stage.

Dehydration—drying—has been a method of preserving food for thousands of years, long before canning was thought of, even longer before freezing. And in spite of these later methods of preserving, drying is still used for some foods because dried food is light in weight, compact in volume, and does not require refrigeration. Freeze-drying, an extension of this method, offers further advantages: freeze-dried foods retain their original color, shape, and structure much better than foods that are simply dehydrated.

As with plain dried foods, those that are freeze-dried must be rehydrated (have their water content restored) before they are used. Foods to be eaten raw must first be soaked in water; cooking in liquid rehydrates freeze-dried foods (mushrooms are an example) used in cooked dishes.

The armed forces are the leading users, and were the pioneer developers, of freeze-dried foods in a continuing search for high-quality foods not requiring refrigeration. Freeze-dried orange juice was an armed forces specialty in World War II. Today, the services remain the largest users of freeze-dried foods, although a number of single items and combinations have been developed for use by campers and backpackers.

Only a few freeze-dried foods have gained wide public acceptance, freeze-dried coffee leading the list. The method is costly (freeze drying is a large-scale commercial effort and cannot be accomplished at home). Packaging, because of the tendency of these foods to break or crumble, is also expensive. And Americans, with a prejudice against dried foods, have not offered a wide market. Consequently, the freeze-drying of most foods, although it works well and results in an acceptable rehydrated product, is not profitable.

FREEZING FOODS: see individual food by name and the special feature: PUTTING FOOD BY

FRENCH BREAD

A long cylinder of heavily crusted bread; it is made with water rather than milk, and brushing with water during baking creates the characteristic munchy crust. The very long, very thin loaf that is more crust than bread, seen peeking out of French shoppers' bags or baskets, is called a flûte. See BREAD.

FRENCH DRESSING: see SALAD DRESSINGS

FRENCH FRY

Another term for DEEP-FAT FRYING.

FRESH HAM: see PORK

FRICASSEE, TO: see page 450

FRITTATA: see OMELETS

FRITTERS

Deep-fried delicacies, either sweet or savory, fritters may be made either by dipping solid pieces of food into a special batter before frying, or incorporating chopped or ground food into such a batter. The French are fond of fritters—*beignets*—and make them also of pâte à choux, often with cheese stirred into the pâte before it is dropped by small spoonfuls into deep, hot fat.

Corn fritters, made when the vegetable is in season from fresh sweet corn cut off the cob, are an American specialty. They are especially delicious served with honey butter, and make a very welcome brunch dish, especially when fried "to order" for hungry guests. Apple fritters are American, too. They can be served as a main-dish accompaniment—with poultry or pork in particular—or as a dessert, dusted with confectioners sugar.

FRIZZLE, TO: see page 450

FROMAGE: see page 452

FROSTINGS, ICINGS, AND FILLINGS

Sometimes, to frost a cake is a redundancy. If it is already richly sweet, almost stickily so—fruitcake, jam cake, and the like—or pristinely plain—pound cake, bundt cake—anything more than a little confectioners sugar or a modest decoration of fruit and/or nuts or, at most, a thin glaze, is almost an embarrassment.

But then there are other days, other ways, occasions when the frosting makes or breaks the cake. A grandchild summed it up by glaring at a pan of cupcakes and demanding, "They've got no frosting—what good are they?"

Frosting versus icing. Asked to differentiate between the two, that grandchild might well say, "Icing is a little bit, frosting is lots." And, although by now the terms have become interchangeable, that definition works for most people. Frosting is generous in amount, lavishly piled on, swirled and peaked; icing is flatter, sparser, more restrained. Frosting is for lady-of-the-evening cakes, ample of proportion, cushiony of structure, outgoing of disposition. Iced cakes are spinsterish, introverted, and always wear their hats and gloves to church.

By another kind of differentiation, icings are uncooked and frostings are cooked, a definition that works very well to keep the two separated in your mind. But actually, no separation is required—that delightful lily-gilding that resides on top of a cake (or cookies) is frosting or icing, whichever you prefer.

How much will you need? On the principle that anything worth doing is worth doing well, a cake that is frosted at all should be frosted generously.

Here are some frosting amounts to guide you. In all cases, we presuppose that you wish to frost both the top and the sides of the cake, and to use the frosting for filling as well if it is a layer cake that you are working with.

cake size	frosting amount
8- or 9-inch square	¾ to 1¼ cups
8- or 9-inch 2-layer	1¾ to 2⅔ cups
8- or 9-inch 3-layer	2¼ to 3 cups
9½- × 5½- × 3-inch loaf	1 to 1½ cups
13- × 9- × 2-inch sheet	1½ to 2 cups
11- × 7- × 1½-inch sheet	1 to 1¾ cups
9- or 10-inch tube	3 cups
16 large or 24 small cupcakes	1½ to 2¼ cups

further guidance: When you use a fluffy frosting, such as one made by beating hot syrup into egg whites, use the larger amount in the range given above; when you use a dense frosting, such as fudge, use the smaller amount. But be guided by your own and your family's preferences—a complaint that there is too much frosting on the cake is seldom heard.

A few words about uncooked icings. These are easy to make and to work with, and it is equally easy to gauge their readiness to be spread on the cake. Those made with heated liquid—melted butter and/or milk or cream—will thicken somewhat as they cool. If too thick, add cold liquid in ¼-teaspoon increments, beating after each addition until you achieve the consistency you want; if too thin, beat in more confectioners sugar, a tablespoon at a time.

Uncooked icings made with cool or room-temperature ingredients should be of a proper consistency when all ingredients are combined. They will not thicken on standing unless refrigerated, nor thin on standing unless made with a large amount of butter on an exceedingly hot day.

Uncooked icings made with cream cheese have good body and consistency. Good flavor, too.

Rather more words about cooked frostings. Success with these depends not only on your relative skill, but also on the weather—it should not be unconscionably hot, nor should the humidity be high. Put off the project or choose another type of frosting if the weather is against you.

white cooked frostings: These are made by cooking beaten egg whites by pouring into them a hot syrup—the italian meringue principle. The egg whites must be absolutely without a speck of yolk (separate the eggs when you take them from the refrigerator, then allow the whites to stand until they come to room temperature), and must be beaten in a clean, grease-free bowl with clean, grease-free beaters. The syrup is cooked to 238 to 240°F. on a candy thermometer and added gradually to the beaten whites, as you continue to beat all the while. By the time the syrup is used up, the volume will have increased enormously, and the frosting should be nearly ready to spread—if not, continue to beat.

Sometimes a stabilizer is used in this type of frosting to keep the mixture from "sugaring"—becoming gritty with sugar crystals. Cream of tartar, lemon juice, white vinegar, or light corn syrup all serve well as stabilizers, added after the syrup is completely incorporated into the egg whites, and just before flavoring extract is added in the final moments of beating.

White Mountain frosting varies this method by beating a portion of partially cooked syrup into the egg whites, continuing to cook the remaining syrup to the proper temperature, then gradually adding it, while beating constantly.

Seven-minute frosting, another variation, combines all ingredients in the top of a double boiler, where they are constantly beaten over hot water until the frosting reaches spreading consistency.

fudge frostings: Chocolate or vanilla or penuche or caramel, the making of these is very like making their candy counterparts. Ingredients are cooked to the proper stage, then taken off the stove and beaten until they reach spreading consistency.

A variation on the fudge-type frostings is one that is half-cooked, half-uncooked. Butter and brown sugar are cooked together to a very thick syrup, then taken off the heat. Confectioners sugar is then beaten in until the mixture reaches the right consistency. This is failureproof (which cannot be said of the "boiled" or fudge types—we all have our bad days) but makes a very dense and heavy, though flavorful, frosting.

And a few about not-really-frosting toppers. If you are a frosting klutz, these are for you. There is a baked frosting that you spread in place before the cake goes into the oven. There is a broiled topping that looks and tastes delightful after a few well-watched minutes under the broiler. Look in a good general or dessert cookbook for the simple how-to of these. Or resort to cream-filled peppermint patties (great on chocolate cake), which are placed on top of the cake the moment it leaves the oven and then, after a few minutes to soften the candies, are swirled over the top of the cake. Or combine grated semisweet chocolate with finely chopped nuts and sprinkle liberally over a hot cake—the chocolate will soften to an icinglike consistency (don't try to spread this one) and anchor the nuts in place. Or top a cake with miniature marshmallows and broil briefly until they are softened and lightly browned. Or, if the top of your cake is flat, position a paper doily on top, sprinkle with confectioners sugar, and then—exercising considerable care—remove the doily, leaving a sugarlace pattern behind. Or roll out commercial almond paste to a thin layer for a topping sure to win compliments.

Some nuggets of frosting know-how. Cakes to be iced with cooked frosting must be thoroughly cooled before the frosting is applied; those using uncooked frosting may be cold or very slightly warm.

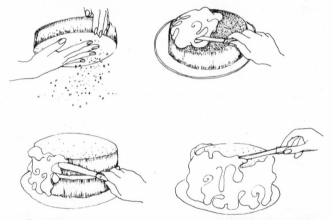

Brush cake gently to remove loose crumbs. If it is a layer cake, place the bottom layer topside down on the serving plate; the second layer, after frosting or filling is spread over the first, should go in place with its topside down as well.

If possible, frost the cake on its serving plate; protect the plate from dribbles of frosting by placing strips of foil or wax paper on the plate and positioning the cake on them. Later, they can be tugged out gently, leaving the plate clean. If you must frost the cake on a different plate or on a revolving stand, place several strips of heavy paper under it, long enough to protrude on each side and be used as handles.

Even with this precaution, moving a large frosted cake from one plate to another is a chancy business.

Use between one-fourth and one-third of the frosting between the layers; put the second layer (and the third, if there is one) in place on the frosting or filling, and then let the cake stand for about 15 minutes before proceeding; this gives the frosting time to set. Then cover the entire outside of the cake, top and sides, with a very thin layer of frosting. Again, give this time to set—it captures the crumbs and gives you an excellent working surface. Add the remaining frosting, swirling it on as fancy dictates. Let it set somewhat before you cover the cake. A cake keeper with a high domed cover is ideal. If you don't have one, invert a large mixing bowl over the cake, making sure it doesn't touch the frosting.

If the frosting is to have a decoration—coconut, say, or chopped nuts or candied fruit—put that in place before the frosting sets, pressing it down lightly. See also GLAZES, MARZIPAN, ROYAL ICING, STREUSEL, and TOPPINGS, DESSERT.

Coping with fillings. Jelly cake—and, of course, jelly roll —use jelly as a filling; it should be of a reasonably firm consistency and a full flavor. Neither the cake nor the roll needs frosting. Sprinkle with confectioners sugar or, if you must frost, make it a light glaze on the top only.

Lady Baltimore Cake uses some of its white cooked frosting for the filling, adding chopped figs, raisins, and nuts. German Sweet Chocolate Cake uses some of its caramel-pecan-coconut frosting to fill the layers.

But in some cases you'll want to make a special filling, having nothing to do with the frosting other than compatibility of flavors. Lemon filling goes well with a white cake whose frosting you plan to snow under with coconut. Orange filling is a delicious surprise in a chocolate cake. A custard filling into which finely chopped candied ginger is stirred is just right for spice cake. Whipped cream into which sliced strawberries have been folded fills a hollowed-out angel food deliciously —use plain whipped cream, without the berries, to frost the cake. Another time, fill the cake with a chocolate or caramel bavarian cream. Or add to 1 cup heavy cream ⅓ cup confectioners sugar, 3 tablespoons cocoa, a dash of salt, and ½ teaspoon vanilla; chill 3 hours, whip until it holds its shape, and use to fill the hollowed angel food.

Vanilla custard with ground almonds is perfect for a white cake to be chocolate frosted; without the almonds, but with slices of banana arranged over it, it's superb with a nut cake. Split a square gingerbread and fill it with milk-softened whipped cream cheese; serve it with lemon sauce instead of frosting. Make a Boston Cream Pie by liberally spreading crème pâtissière between two white cake layers; give the top, but not the sides, a thin chocolate frosting. Fill a chocolate roll with a custard made with coconut cream in place of part of the milk, or with frangipane cream. Douse two white-cake

layers with rum, fill them with a ricotta cheese filling rich with shaved chocolate and candied fruit. Or use a fruit-pie filling, your own or from a can, between the layers of lemon-flavored cake. Or layer it with almond paste softened with a little unbeaten egg white. Or split vanilla layers, spread with different flavors of slightly softened ice cream, then place in the freezer until ready to serve.

Remember that cakes filled with custard or whipped cream must be refrigerated. And this: If you have cake layers in the freezer (they freeze very well) you always have dessert on hand to fill and frost at the drop of a dropper-in.

In filling a cake—in frosting it, too—there are many ways to go, with only the outer limits of your imagination setting the boundaries. See also FILLINGS.

FROZEN FOODS, COMMERCIAL

If you are old enough to have lived in the days before frozen foods were a twinkle in Mr. Birdseye's eye, you'll remember the first time you tasted this new wonder. For many of us, our first frozen food was strawberries. Imagine that, strawberries right in the dead of winter—not exactly like fresh strawberries, but certainly tasting more fresh than canned.

Nowadays, the freezer shelves of large supermarkets hold as much promise to home cooks as the Big Rock Candy Mountain to kids. There they are, row on row on row of smartly designed packages, all crying, "Eat me—I'm delicious!" Foods that don't have to be washed or peeled or cut up. Foods that don't have to be fixed or mixed. Foods, some of them, that don't have to be cooked, or that can be cooked by thrusting them, untouched, into the oven or plumping their plastic boil-in bags into hot water. Hallelujah—it's Beulah Land!

Well, yes. Yes, certainly, for the well-heeled person who hates to, or can't, cook. And for all of us, even the most dedicated cooks, a blessing some of the time. Truly an unmixed blessing when it comes to fruit and vegetables. Winter used to back the home cook into a corner with a rutabaga in one hand and a head of cabbage in the other. Now we can serve green or wax beans, broccoli, asparagus, brussels sprouts, peas, all the rest, as readily out of season as in. Suddenly inspired to make a gumbo, frozen okra is there to help us. Succotash? There are frozen limas and corn to hand. The same with fruit, although some of us feel that frozen fruits are not quite as widely varied, and often not quite as uniformly good, as frozen vegetables.

Good cooks generally agree: nothing beats fresh—but frozen beats canned nine times out of ten. Frozen foods are there, all year around, so that you can serve asparagus in November, cherries in February, whatever you want whenever you want. And there are times when frozen beats fresh even in the fresh season. Tender young frozen peas are better than leathery, wizened fresh ones, if that's all the market has to offer. And frozen raspberries may not be superior in taste, but neither are they such terrific budget benders as fresh ones at $1.25 for a tiny box, particularly if a number of the fresh ones (raspberries are exceedingly perishable) have to be discarded when you pick them over.

Shopping guidelines for vegetables. Most frozen vegetables are packed and priced according to the grade (quality); this is true even when the grade is not indicated on the package.

Frozen Vegetable Grades

U.S. Grade A or Fancy: Top quality, tender, succulent vegetables with excellent flavor and color.

U.S. Grade B or Extra Standard: Slightly more mature vegetables with good flavor and color.

U.S. Grade C or Standard: Mature vegetables, not as tasty or as attractive in appearance as A or B.

Whole vegetables or specially sized vegetables usually cost more than cut styles; diced, short cuts, and vegetable pieces are least expensive. Take green beans as an example. Whole beans are more expensive than cut ones, because the whole beans must be selected for uniform size and color, and must be unblemished. French-cut green beans are also more expensive, in this case because of the cutting process. There could be a considerable price differential between a package of Grade A whole green beans and one of Grade C cut beans. Be guided by your needs and your pocketbook, secure in the knowledge that all frozen vegetables are wholesome and nutritious.

Frozen vegetables are generally packed in 9- or 10-ounce boxes, and the more common vegetables (as well as certain combinations) are also packed in larger plastic bags. Often the bags are a better buy than the boxes, especially for large families. They are also useful for singles and families of two, because the bag can be opened to remove enough for one meal, then closed again and returned to the freezer.

The USDA grade shield with the legend "Packed under continuous inspection of the U.S. Department of Agriculture" may appear on the label of the frozen vegetables you buy, or it may not—inspection here, as with all other foods, is voluntary and paid for by the processor. Sometimes you will find the grade designated on the label without the letters "U.S." preceeding it—Fancy or Grade A, for example. A frozen vegetable labeled in this way must measure up to the quality stated even though it has not been officially graded.

more label information: The label on a frozen vegetable should enable you to tell, in a quick glance, what you're buying—and make it simple for you to compare prices among the various packs as well as the many brands.

Government regulations require that the following information must appear on the label of the package as it faces the customer:

- the common or usual name of the product, and its form and style (style—whole, sliced, diced—may be illustrated rather than spelled out)
- the net contents in total ounces, and in pounds and ounces if the package contains 1 pound or more

Labels may also give the grade, variety, size, and maturity of the vegetable, as well as seasonings and number of servings. If the number of servings is given, the law requires that the size of a serving must be stated also, in common measures—cups or ounces. The serving size commonly used for adults is ½ cup for most cooked vegetables, but small children and light eaters may want less, large adults and heavy eaters more, so be guided by your knowledge of your family's eating habits as well as by the label. Because frozen vegetables are packed by net weight rather than volume, and because the number of cups obtained from a container of a particular size varies somewhat from vegetable to vegetable, here are yields of some common vegetables to give you an idea of servings to be expected.

vegetable	package size	yield
asparagus, cut	10 ounces	1¼ cups
beans, green or wax, cut	9 ounces	1⅔ cups
beans, lima	10 ounces	1⅔ cups
broccoli, cut	10 ounces	1½ cups
carrots, diced or sliced	10 ounces	1⅔ cups
cauliflower	10 ounces	1½ cups
corn, whole kernel	10 ounces	1½ cups
kale	10 ounces	1⅛ cups
okra	10 ounces	1¼ cups
peas	10 ounces	1⅔ cups
potatoes, french-fried	9 ounces	1⅔ cups
spinach, leaf or chopped	10 ounces	1¼ cups
summer squash, yellow, or zucchini, sliced	10 ounces	1⅓ cups

Vegetables for freezing are grown especially for that purpose, are harvested at their peak, and processed to preserve nutritional values. Freezing plants are usually located at the growing areas so that vegetables can be picked and quickly brought to the plant for processing while they are at their fresh best. Most of the processing is done by automated equipment working at high speed to bring us sanitary, wholesome products preserved at the peak of their goodness and flavor.

forms and styles: Plain frozen vegetables, unseasoned (other than with salt), make up the bulk of the frozen vegetable line. In this plain state they can be found whole, sliced, diced, cut, french cut, or in julienne strips, depending on the particular vegetable. And there are plain vegetable combinations, such as carrots and peas, mixed vegetables, corn with red and green peppers. But there are other packs, too, with various kinds of sauces and seasonings added. Beets are not available frozen plain, but can be had in a thickened, orange-flavored sauce. Carrots are packed plain, but also in butter sauce and in a brown-sugar glaze. Many vegetables are available in butter or cream sauces, or with mushrooms or other garnishings and flavorings. There are combinations here, too—potatoes with onion-flavored cheese sauce, creamed peas and baby onions, and many more. These gussied-up vegetables are more expensive than the plain ones, but allow you to serve something different without extra work.

Shopping guidelines for fruit. Much of the above information holds true for frozen fruit as well as for vegetables. Preserved at the peak of goodness, frozen fruit is ready to serve as it comes from the package, or can be used in cooked dishes—main-dish garnishes and desserts—and in salads.

Grade standards have been established by the USDA for frozen fruit; most fruit is packed and priced according to these quality standards even if the grade is not shown on the label.

Frozen Fruit Grades

U.S. Grade A or Fancy: Top-quality, delicious, full-flavored fruits with excellent color; uniform in shape and size.

U.S. Grade B or Choice: Very good flavor and color, not quite as attractive in appearance as Grade A.

U.S. Grade C or Standard: Not as sweet or uniform in appearance as A or B; pieces may be broken, uneven in size.

The USDA grade shield may appear on the package with the "continuous inspection" legend; or the fruit may be labeled Fancy or Grade A without the letters "U.S."—if so, the fruit should meet the standards for that grade, even though the product has not been officially inspected.

more label information: Federal regulations require certain information to appear on the front panel of a frozen fruit package:

- the common or usual name of the fruit
- form (or style) of the fruit, such as whole, slices or halves; if the form is visible on or through the package, it need not be stated
- for some fruits, the variety or color
- syrups, sugar, or liquid in which the fruit is packed must be listed near the name of the product
- total contents (net weight) must be stated for containers holding 1 pound or less; from 1 to 4 pounds, weight must be given in both total ounces and in ounces and pounds or pounds and fractions of a pound (net weight includes the syrup or liquid)

Also required on the label, although not necessarily on the front panel, are a listing of ingredients such as spices, flavoring, coloring, and special sweeteners if used; any special type of treatment; the packer's or distributor's name and business address. At the option of the processor, the label may also include the quality or grade, size and maturity of the fruit, cooking directions and/or serving ideas. If the label lists number of servings, it must also give the size of a serving in common measures.

processing and packing: Fruits for freezing are harvested at the proper stage of ripeness so that optimum texture and flavor are preserved. Much of the processing is done by automated equipment—the fruits are handled very little by plant workers. All and all, processing methods assure us of wholesome, sanitary frozen fruits of good flavor and quality.

At the plant, fruits are sorted by size—machinery does it—and washed in continuously circulating water or under sprays. Some fruits—apples, pears, and pineapples among them—are mechanically peeled and cored, while others require hand treatment for these steps. The fruits are moved along on conveyor belts to workers who do any other necessary hand work to be certain that all skins and stems are removed. Pits and seeds are taken out by automatic equipment and machines also prepare the various styles—halves, slices, pieces. Inspectors remove any undesirable pieces.

Frozen fruits are most often packed with dry sugar. Packages are filled with fruit by automatic equipment, sugar or syrup is added, and the packages are automatically sealed. The packaged fruit is immediately frozen in special low-temperature chambers, then stored at 0°F. or below.

fruit serving sizes: Serving sizes vary because of the different styles in which fruits are packed and the varied ways of using fruit in the home. For mixtures or small fruits, ½ cup is the serving size commonly used for adults. Two pieces make up the usual serving of halved fruit.

A wide, cold world. Fruits and vegetables—vegetables

in particular—are the frozen foods most often purchased. But there is a multitude of other kinds of food in those big supermarket freezer cases, some of it very good indeed, some so-so. Such judgments are subjective, governed by personal prejudices and preferences developed over the years. To a very good cook, many frozen foods, particularly "made" dishes and desserts, are acceptable but not approaching within a million miles their made-at-home counterparts. But a poor cook, and the family of a poor cook, may find the same dishes wonderful beyond their stomach's imagining. It takes all kinds.

From soup to nuts. You could, if required, eat frozen foods exclusively; every menu item is there in those cases. It would be a rather expensive diet, but not necessarily a dull one.

beginnings: For family meals and for company-coming ones, freezer cases offer all sorts of appetizers and a number of soups. There are puff-paste goodies with savory fillings, ready to be baked. There are frozen mixtures, such as guacamole and chopped chicken livers, that need only thawing. And there are soups in considerable variety, depending on the size of the market, from Chinese to Midwest homestyle, ready to thaw and heat.

main dishes: Variety is enormous here, everything from whole chickens, turkeys, ducks, and geese through prime grade filet mignon and ready-to-cook hamburgers to macaroni and cheese, with dozens in between. You can have gourmet chicken kiev or homey tuna casserole with noodles. All kinds of heat-and-eat pasta dishes. Pizzas galore. Stuffed cabbage and stuffed peppers. Creamed chicken, lobster newburg, scampi, goulash, gumbo, blanquette de veau—you name it. And, of course, the bases for make-it-yourself meals—frozen fish and shellfish, meats and poultry to cook and serve as you will.

side dishes: Besides the vegetables we've already considered, there are potatoes in many guises—french fried, cottage fried, nuggets, home-fried, whole small peeled potatoes, and more. There are bags of mixed vegetables especially for soups and stews. And there are heat-and-eat side dishes such as scalloped apples, several flavored rice combinations, breaded and deep-fried eggplant sticks or slices, and dozens of others.

breads: For breakfast or brunch, for lunch or dinner, frozen bread is available in many kinds, from raise-and-bake loaves of uncooked dough, to heat-and-eat garlic and cheese and herb breads, rolls in abundance, corn and bran and blueberry muffins, sweet rolls and danish pastries and coffeecakes in wide variety.

desserts: Ice cream, of course, and all its cousins—ices and sherbets, ice pops and ice cream bars and sandwiches for the kids, chocolate-cake ice cream rolls, and more. Layer cakes, large and small, nicely filled and frosted; pound cakes, crumb cakes, cheesecakes, ready-to-bake cookies. Elegant specialties, such as bavarians. Bake-and-serve fruit pies in wide variety, plus thaw-and-serve cream and chiffon pies. Whipped topping to dress up any one of them.

don't overlook breakfast: The frozen-food cases hold all sorts of breakfast goodies. There are frozen waffles and french toast to be heated in the toaster. There are waffle and pancake (and crepe, too) batters if you prefer to bake your own. Frozen sausages, both brown-and-serve and cook-from-scratch. Many kinds of fruit juices as well as drink mixes—fruit punch, lemonade, limeade. Nondairy coffee "creamers." All those breakfast sweet breads. And a collection of foods for cholesterol watchers—low-fat egg substitutes, and simulated bacon, sausage, and ham to go with them.

That list hardly begins to tap the variety to be found in the freezer cases of a large supermarket, including a number of specialties of dieters. And we haven't yet touched on one broad frozen-food category.

"The blue-plate special." In other words, the frozen dinner that offers main dish and side dishes, sometimes bread, sometimes dessert, in one neat package. To some, the very idea of these TV dinners, as they used to be called, is anathema; to others, those dinners are virtually a way of life. Without attempting to pass judgment, let's take a look at them.

Most of them are routine meat-and-potatoes meals—nothing fancy, nothing out of the ordinary. A few processors put up "ethnic" frozen dinners, particularly Italian and Mexican specialties, but three companies produce nearly 90 percent of the frozen dinners purchased by American consumers, and all of those dinners consist of very down-to-earth foods. All three of the producers put out "regular" dinners and extra-portion meals tagged with such phrases as "man-pleaser" and "country table" to imply heartiness.

what's on the menu?: The combinations put out by all three producers are very much alike. So are the prices, although there is a wider price variation among the extra-portion dinners. It becomes a matter of choosing for appetite-appeal rather than price.

All three producers put out a fried chicken, a turkey, and a salisbury steak (ground beef) dinner in both the regular and the extra-portion sizes. In all cases, the fried chicken is accompanied by mashed potatoes, except one extra-portion dinner, which has crinkle-cut potatoes; all offer carrots and peas or mixed vegetables, except that same extra-portion dinner, which offers corn. One brand's regular dinner includes a bonus apple cobbler; all the extra-portion dinners include such a dessert, or an apple-cranberry compote plus corn bread. All the turkey dinners offer gravy, dressing, mashed potatoes, carrots and peas. Other dinners have beef with gravy, chopped sirloin beef with gravy, fish fillets, and meat loaf with tomato sauce as the main dish, with side dishes ranging through carrots and peas, green beans (one innovator), mixed vegetables, mashed potatoes, potato nuggets, corn, and apples and cranberries. One beef with gravy dinner unfortunately includes both mashed potatoes and macaroni and cheese in its extra-portion menu. Desserts are apple or apple-raisin or apple-cranberry cobblers, chocolate cake, chocolate brownie.

With all these, it is assumed that the diner adds a beverage to the meal—hopefully, if the diner is a child, milk.

nutritional considerations: How do these dinners stack up nutritionally? Not too badly. Assuming that the person who eats such a dinner has had two other meals that day, the frozen dinners offer a reasonable number of calories for one-third of the day's food intake; a few are on the high side, more are on the low. In fact, most of the regular dinners contain too few calories to provide complete meals for men and children. (Add milk, fruit, and cheese to make a nutritionally acceptable meal.) The amount of protein is reasonable; indeed, some of the extra-portion dinners provide sufficient protein for two-thirds of the day's supply. Carbohydrate content of most of the dinners is just about right, also. But fat content is generally too high.

Conclusion? That frozen dinners are acceptable from a nutrition point of view, particularly if augmented a bit. Whether or not they are acceptable from the points of view of flavor, texture, and appearance—well, that's another story, one that differs considerably from one individual to another.

Buying frozen foods. Dealing responsibly with these foods that are such a boon to busy home cooks is worth a little time and effort. If it is possible, shop at a large, busy supermarket where the volume is great and the turnover rapid. Upright freezer cases with doors keep foods in better condition than open cases.

Choose only packages that are in good condition—they should show no discoloration or signs of leakage, no breaks in the packaging material. And, of course, the food should be solidly frozen. Heavy frost on the outside of the package indicates improper storage at some point along the way.

Do your grocery shopping the last thing before you go home, and make frozen foods your last pickup when you shop. At the checkout counter, ask for insulated bags for your frozen foods. If your market doesn't supply them, bag all your frozen foods together—they help keep each other cold. In hot weather, carry a cooler in the car and put the frozen foods into it.

At home, put frozen foods away first; date each package (a grease pencil works fine) before you store it. Don't plan on storing frozen foods in the ice-cube compartment of a conventional one-door refrigerator for more than a few days; temperature in these compartments is generally 15 to 20 degrees above zero, and foods begin to thaw slowly at these temperatures, even though the package may feel hard. In the freezer compartment of a two-door refrigerator, you can usu-

ally count on a temperature range of from 0 to 8°F., at which foods will keep well for 4 to 6 months. In a separate freezer, the temperature should be zero or below, at which many foods will remain in good condition up to a year. If your freezer does not have a thermometer, one is a worthwhile investment. The inventory in the average home freezer represents quite an outlay of money. After spending that much, it's poor planning to keep the food in anything less than tip-top condition.

"Wholesale" meat for your freezer. If yours is a big meat-eating family, at some point or another you'll consider buying large cuts of meat for your freezer. It's possible to save money this way. It's also possible to lose money. You need to tread warily.

Remember that a large cut of meat, a side of beef for example, has a tremendous amount of waste. Also remember that the ratio of cuts such as steak and roasts to items like ground meat and stew meat is very heavy in the direction of the lesser cuts. Although the price per pound for the side of beef may sound enticingly low, it's the price per pound after the waste has been eliminated that really counts. If that price per pound is about the same as for the lesser cuts in your supermarket, you'll be saving; if it is about the same as for supermarket best cuts—the roasts and steaks—it means that you'll be paying far too much per pound for ground beef, stew meat, and all the (preponderant) lesser cuts. It pays to do the math.

If you do buy "wholesale" freezer meat, be certain you make your purchase from a reliable dealer. Final cautionary note: that "free" freezer sometimes offered is *not* free. One way or another, you'll pay for it.

Special circumstances, special benefits. As a rule of thumb, the frozen foods most economically feasible for a large family are the vegetables, the fruit juices and, sometimes, the fruits. Main dishes can be duplicated less expensively from scratch. So can the specialty vegetables—the soufflés, those in sauces, and the like. So can desserts. So —if there's a baker in the house—can the breads.

But for a person living alone, and sometimes for a family of two—particularly if both have full-time jobs—those frozen main dishes, desserts, and other dressed-up dishes can be a boon and a blessing at the end of a long, hard day.

Many of the best cooks among us simply won't bother to cook for themselves if they live alone. It's a combination of inertia and the need for applause. They'll put together a gourmet feast when they've invited guests, but when no company is coming, they open a can of soup or soft-cook a couple of eggs at best, throw together a sandwich at worst. The monotony—and the nutritional imbalance—of such a day-in-day-out diet can be devastating. And, of course, there are the live-alones who couldn't manage anything more complicated than a soft-cooked egg or a peanut butter sandwich if their lives depended on it. For them, frozen main dishes, vegetables, breads, and desserts spell salvation—variety, good flavor, improved nutrition.

Even in big families, these frozen foods have their place. On mom's night out, for instance, when dad and the kids fix their own dinner. Or when mom's alone for a change, and can have a treat of something she likes very much that the rest of the family won't eat. (We know a woman who, on a night when her husband and teenagers are away, cooks a package of french-style green beans, wolfs the whole thing, and calls it dinner—her family hates green beans.)

Big families and small, alone at the table or in a crowd, we owe a lot to those ingenious souls who worked out the intricacies of freezing food.

FRUIT

We used to be able to mark the arrival and the passing of summer by the succession of fruits that came in season. In these days of rapid and refrigerated transportation, the seasons of fruit are neither as brief nor as circumscribed as once they were. But those of us who live in cold climates still feel our hearts lift when the first shipped-in strawberries appear in February—can spring be far behind? With warmer weather, cherries appear, and apricots, and green grapes. Then peaches, pears, nectarines, plums, melons, and the rest of summer's bounty.

When fresh fruits are in season and (relatively, at least) low-priced, home cooks can and freeze or, at the least, serve the fruits often. When there's a surfeit, and everyone grows tired of fresh fruit eaten out of hand or with cereal or with sugar and cream, we make some of the old-fashioned fresh-fruit desserts—cobblers and flummeries and slumps and fools, juicy pies and shortcakes. Or we serve the raw fruit with brown sugar or honey, with sour cream instead of sweet for a change, or make up a handsome and delicious fruit and cheese platter.

France provides one of the great dress-ups for fresh fruit, crème fraîche. This heavy, thick, slightly soured sweet cream is available here only in a few very elegant markets in the largest cities, and at breathtaking prices. Although we can't make the real thing at home, we can produce an acceptable substitute. Here are two ways to go about it, each resulting in a delightful approximation of the true crème fraîche:

Combine 1 cup heavy cream and 1 teaspoon buttermilk. Heat until the mixture is lukewarm. Cover loosely and let stand at room temperature 6 to 8 hours. Stir, cover, and refrigerate—it will become considerably thicker. Store up to 1 month. Makes about 1 cup.

The second way uses sour cream:

In a small saucepan, place 1 cup dairy sour cream; very gradually add 2 cups heavy cream. Over lowest heat, warm slightly—just enough to take the chill off (85 to 90°F.). Pour into a large jar; cover loosely and let stand at a temperature of 75 to 80° for 8 to 12 hours, until thickened to the consistency of very heavy cream. Stir, cover tightly, and refrigerate. Will keep well up to 3 weeks. Makes about 3 cups.

Serve either of these versions with almost any fresh fruit or berries for a simple yet exotic dessert.

Another make-an-impression dessert with fresh fruit, which is easy to prepare, uses seedless green grapes:

Wash 1 pound seedless green grapes and remove stems. Drain thoroughly; chill. Place in individual serving dishes. In separate bowls, place 1 pint dairy sour cream and ½ cup light brown sugar combined with 3 tablespoons cinnamon. Pour 1½ cups kirsch or cointreau into a pitcher or small decanter. Each diner prepares his own dessert, adding to his portion of grapes the amount of cream, sugar-cinnamon, and liqueur he prefers, as they are passed.

How much for how many? Sometimes a recipe will call for a pound, or some other weight, of fruit. How many pieces is that? Or if the requirement is 2 cups of fruit slices, how much fruit should you buy to make that amount? Here are useful-to-know yields of some of the more common fruits.

fruit	weight/amount	yield
apples	1 pound	3 medium size
	1 medium size	1 cup peeled, cored, and chopped
apricots	1 pound fresh	8 to 12
	1 pound dried	about 50 large halves 3 cups, 4 cups cooked
bananas	1 pound	3 medium size
	1 medium size	¾ to ⅞ cup, peeled and sliced
berries	1 pint fresh	1½ to 2 cups, hulled
cherries	1 pound fresh	2 cups, pitted
cranberries	1 pound, fresh or frozen	4 cups
dates	1 (8-ounce) package	1¼ cups, pitted and finely diced
lemons	1 medium	2 tablespoons juice, 1 teaspoon grated peel
limes	1 medium	1½ to 2 tablespoons juice, ¾ to 1 teaspoon grated peel
oranges	1 medium	⅓ to ½ cup juice, 1 tablespoon grated peel
peaches	1 pound fresh	4 medium 1½ to 2 cups peeled and sliced
pears	1 pound fresh	4 to 5 medium 1½ to 2 cups peeled, cored, and sliced
pineapple	1 medium	5 cups, peeled and diced
plums	1 pound fresh	12 to 14 medium
prunes	1 pound	55 to 65 medium 3 cups, 4 cups cooked
raisins	1 (15-ounce) package, seedless	3 cups, loosely packed

Summer—held over for another season. When summer fruits are at their best, you may can them or freeze them (see special feature: PUTTING FOOD BY). But you can also preserve them other ways—in TUTTI-FRUTTI (with brandy) or RUMTOPF (with rum). Either way, these are "crocked" fruits in both senses of the word. Either is headily delicious to serve as a relish with meats or a sauce for plain cakes, puddings, or ice cream, and also makes a splendid gift from your kitchen, if you can bring yourself to part with some of the fruity delight.

You will need a large stoneware crock, sugar, and brandy or rum, plus fruit as it comes into season. Start by placing 1 quart of brandy or rum in the crock. Add 4 cups of whole hulled strawberries and 4 cups of sugar. Stir, cover, and let stand at room temperature. As they come into season, add (in 4-cup increments—it's easier to keep track that way) pitted cherries, raspberries, currants, gooseberries, peeled and sliced apricots, peaches and nectarines, peeled and cut-up pineapple—in any amount or combination you like. Each time you add fruit, add the same amount of sugar; but you will need no more liquor, as the fruit is busily manufacturing its own. Stir every day until after the last fruit of the season has been added, putting the cover back on the crock each time.

Once you've made this heady concoction the first time, you can perpetuate it by adding 1 cup of fruit plus ¼ cup each of sugar and brandy for every cup of the crocked fruit you remove to use.

See also each fruit listed under its individual name, as APPLES, CHERRIES, GUAVAS, PEACHES. See also EXOTIC FRUIT.

FRUIT, CANDIED: see CANDIED FLOWERS, FRUIT

FRUIT, HOME-GROWN: see special feature:
THE GROW-IT-YOURSELF BOOM

FRUIT COCKTAILS, COMPOTES, CUPS, SALADS

These mixtures of several fruits are all close relatives, the compote—often served hot, often made of dried fruit—being a cousin once removed. Cups, cocktails, and salads are always served chilled, and may be a mixture of whatever compatible fruits are in season, often with canned fruits added when there are few fresh ones available.

Obligingly, these fruit mixtures can begin a meal, accompany one, or serve as its sweet ending. Cocktails and cups are actually two names for the same thing, a sit-down fruit appetizer to get a meal off to a good start. Try a combination of honeydew, cantaloupe, and watermelon balls for a handsome color combination as well as a delightful assortment of close-but-different flavors. Or mix fresh pitted bing and royal ann cherries. Or fresh pineapple chunks and halved strawberries. Kiwis, grown now in the United States, make a beautiful (incredibly green, with tiny coal-black edible seeds) addition to any combination of fruits.

In the winter, grapefruit segments and slices of avocado taste as lovely as they look, or cheer up orange segments and banana slices with frozen raspberries, not quite thawed. Almost any fruit mixture looks good and tastes good. Generally not dressed with anything but the fruits' own juices, cups and cocktails profit by wearing a sprig of mint for flavor and color, or by being served with a wedge of lime or lemon. For a change, serve the fruit in ginger ale or quinine water instead of fruit juice.

The pieces of fruit in salads are generally somewhat larger than the small dice of cups and cocktails. Again, almost any combination of fruits will be welcome, and sometimes a vegetable-fruit alliance makes a nice change, as when you compose a salad of alternating slices of peeled oranges and paper-thin red sweet onions, or mix artichoke hearts with grapefruit segments.

Salads need dressing. A half-and-half combination of mayonnaise and dairy sour cream or whipped cream is very good. So is honey and lime juice in equal parts. Or make a fresh pineapple salad and sprinkle it liberally with grated cheddar cheese in lieu of dressing. Or find a recipe for old-fashioned boiled salad dressing and substitute orange juice for the vinegar it calls for. Fold a drop or two of almond extract and a liberal sprinkling of nutmeg or slivered mint leaves and grated orange peel into sour cream to dress peaches, nectarines, or apricots. Thin whipped cream cheese with orange juice. Nuts of almost any kind are an excellent addition to any fruit salad. So are slivered dates. For children, combine bananas, white raisins, and pineapple, and dress with a mixture of three-fourths mayonnaise and one-fourth chunky peanut butter well blended.

Compotes, baked or simmered on top of the stove, may be made of fresh fruits, but more often are an excellent way to take advantage of the many wonderful dried fruits available—peaches, pears, apricots, prunes, raisins, figs. Bake a mixed dried fruit compote, well seasoned with curry powder, to serve hot with duck, goose, or pork. Or serve the same mixture minus the curry, but with slivers of lemon peel and a generous measure of blanched almonds, for dessert along with crisp butter cookies or madeleines.

Fruit is versatile, and it's difficult to find someone who doesn't like it. Make use of it often in your menus, in many good and different ways, to please yourself and your family.

FRUITCAKES

Made of a molasses-and-spice-flavored batter, thick with fruit and nuts, laced with rum or brandy, this is our traditional holiday-season cake. Wrapped in cheesecloth dipped in brandy or rum, overwrapped in foil or stored in a metal container, the cake mellows and enriches in flavor as time goes by, so it can be—and generally is—made well in advance of the holidays, usually before Thanksgiving. Loaves of the cake, or individual fruitcakes in gold- or silver-colored foil cups are perfect for holiday entertaining, or make a welcome gift, especially for friends who don't bake.

A white-batter fruitcake, made with almonds and the paler candied fruit—orange and lemon peel, pineapple, citron, sometimes with red and/or green candied cherries for contrast—and often flavored with sherry, is another version of this popular cake. And there is an unbaked cake, almost entirely fruit with melted butter and graham cracker crumbs replacing batter.

FRY: see DEEP-FAT FRYING

FRYER: see CHICKEN

FUDGE

When grandma was a girl (or great grandma, depending on your age), a young lady was considered suitably "finished" if she knew a few French phrases, could embroider well, and could play a few "selections" on the piano. Oh, and one more thing. Grandma did not go riding with a boy in order to make out. Grandma went to the kitchen, in order to make fudge.

Fudge, in later days, threatened to become a lost art. It was something of a nuisance, had a way of sugaring just when you'd cornered a boy you really wanted to impress with your culinary skills, needed to be beaten within an inch of its life (and yours), and took an unconscionable time to set—if indeed, it didn't balk and refuse to set at all.

But some years back a genius thought up a new way to make fudge. You boil together sugar, evaporated milk, and marshmallow creme (never mind how it sounds—concentrate on how it tastes) for a matter of five minutes or so, stirring industriously. You take it off the stove, stir in semi-sweet chocolate bits, vanilla, and—if you wish—nuts. Turn into a pan, and wait a very short while until it sets. That's all. It's easy, creamy, and good. Better still, it's failureproof. A cookbook, the back of the chocolate bits bag, or the label of the marshmallow creme jar will tell you exactly how.

If you yearn for a return to the good old days, any cookbook will also give you the recipe for the old-fashioned kind of fudge. And for the other fudges: divinity (tricky, this one), penuche, and peanut butter. Make candy for the kids or with the kids. It won't hurt a bit.

FUMET: see WHITE STOCK

FUSILLI: see PASTA

WHAT'S IN A FOOD'S NAME?

A meat or poultry product that carries the mark of federal inspection is formulated to meet USDA standards—your assurance that the name on the label truly represents what's inside the package

A food package labeled "Aunt Lizzie's Delight" gives no clue to the contents—a piece of misguided foolishness on the part of the producer, because no one wants to buy a pig in a poke.

But a food package labeled "Mrs. Partridge's Game Bird Ragout" gives, if the ragout is made of one sliver of partridge and a whole lot of chicken, a deliberately misleading clue—a piece of cupidity on the producer's part. And a package labeled "Meatballs in Sauce" that turns out to contain an ocean of sauce and two tiny nubbins of meatballs is a piece of deliberate fraud on the producer's part. Either case may cause a richly deserved backfire of consumer indignation, and bring the wrath of the USDA down on the producer's head.

The dilemma's familiar horns. Ethical producers of food have no problems with the USDA. Agriculture and the processor have an identical interest in that case: to provide consumers with good, wholesome food, an honest value that conceals no nasty surprises. But those with larceny in their souls are caught in a "damned if you do, damned if you don't" situation. On the one hand, they know consumers look for and rely on the USDA's little round "inspected and passed" stamp. On the other hand, they lust after the dishonest buck, and know that the way to make it is to cheat the consumer.

If they could have both, they'd chortle all the way to the bank with their ill-gotten gains. But it doesn't work out that way—or, if it does, it is only for a brief time. Uncle Sam's watchdogs are soon yapping at their heels. Comeuppance is swift and gets them in the most pain-prone portion of the larcenous anatomy, the wallet.

USDA standards—guidelines for producer and consumer. Meat and poultry products are the chief concerns of the standards-setting and -maintaining experts at the USDA, because it is one of the Department of Agriculture's functions to inspect meat and the plants in which it is processed. And it is in these areas that consumer confusion can easily arise and that producer skulduggery can readily be perpetrated.

Specialists at the Department of Agriculture check each food product name against the recipe to be used—before the name ever goes on the label—to see that it tells what's really inside the package. For example, products labeled "beef with gravy" must contain at least 50 percent cooked beef; "gravy with beef" must contain at least 35 percent cooked beef. Spot checking of the keep-'em-honest variety after the product is on the market assures consumers that the contents continue to meet the standards.

How can you use a knowledge of these standard formulations in your job as home cook? One area is in planning nutritionally balanced meals. Another is in informed purchasing. A third, know-how to enable you to make useful price/value comparisons between two products that seem on the surface to be identical.

Following are listings of some of the most popular products in the meat and poultry areas, along with the major USDA formula requirements for each of them.

STANDARDS FOR MEAT PRODUCTS

All percentages of meat in the following list are on the basis of fresh uncooked weight, unless an individual entry indicates otherwise.

baby food:
    high meat dinners: Must contain at least 30 percent meat.
    meat and broth: Must contain at least 65 percent meat.
    vegetable and meat: Must contain at least 8 percent meat.

bacon (cooked): Weight of cooked bacon cannot exceed 40 percent of cured, smoked (but uncooked) bacon.

bacon and tomato spread: Must contain at least 20 percent cooked bacon.

bacon dressing: Must contain at least 8 percent cured, smoked bacon.

barbecue sauce with meat: Must contain at least 35 percent meat, measured on cooked basis.

barbecued meats: Weight of the meat when barbecued cannot exceed 70 percent of the fresh, uncooked meat; must have barbecued (crusted) appearance and be prepared over burning or smoldering hardwood or its sawdust. If cooked by other dry heat means, the product name must mention the type of cookery.

beans and meat in sauce: Must contain at least 20 percent meat.

beans in sauce with meat: Must contain at least 20 percent cooked, or smoked and cooked, meat.

beans with bacon in sauce: Must contain at least 20 percent bacon.

beans with frankfurters in sauce: Must contain at least 20 percent frankfurters.

beans with meatballs in sauce: Must contain at least 20 percent meatballs.

beef and dumplings with gravy or *beef and gravy with dumplings:* Either way, must contain at least 25 percent beef.

beef and pasta in tomato sauce: No matter what the type of pasta, contents must be at least 17.5 percent beef.

beef carbonade: Must contain at least 50 percent beef tenderloin.

beef burger sandwich: Must contain at least 35 percent hamburger, measured on cooked basis.

beef burgundy: Must contain at least 50 percent beef; must also contain sufficient wine to characterize the sauce.

beef sauce with beef and mushrooms: Must contain at least 25 percent beef and at least 7 percent mushrooms.

beef sausage (raw): Must contain no more than 30 percent fat; must not contain any by-products or any extenders.

beef stroganoff: Must contain at least 45 percent fresh, uncooked beef or 30 percent cooked beef; must also contain at least 10 percent dairy sour cream, or a "gourmet" combination sauce that contains at least 7.5 percent sour cream plus 5 percent wine.

beef with barbecue sauce: Must contain at least 50 percent beef, measured on cooked basis.

beef with gravy: Must contain at least 50 percent beef, measured on cooked basis; on the other hand, *gravy with beef* is required only to have a minimum of 35 percent beef, again on cooked basis.

breaded steaks, chops, etc.: Breading must not exceed 30 percent of the finished weight.

breakfast product (frozen, containing meat): Must contain at least 15 percent meat, measured on cooked basis.

breakfast sausage: Must not contain more than 50 percent fat.

brown and serve sausage: Must not contain more than 35 percent fat, nor more than 10 percent added water.

brunswick stew: Must contain a minimum of 25 percent of at least two kinds of meat and/or poultry; also, must contain corn as one of the vegetables in the mixture.

burgundy sauce with beef and noodles: Must contain at least 25 percent beef, measured on cooked basis, as well as enough wine to characterize the sauce.

burritos: Must contain at least 25 percent meat.

cabbage rolls with meat: Filling of the rolls must contain at least 12 percent meat.

canneloni with meat and sauce: Sauce and/or filling of the pasta must contain at least 10 percent meat.

cappelletti with meat and sauce: Must contain at least 12 percent meat.

cheesefurter: Must contain at least 15 percent cheese.

chili con carne: Must contain at least 40 percent meat.

chili con carne with beans: Must contain at least 25 percent meat.

chili hot dog with meat: There must be at least 40 percent meat in the chili—in other words, it must comply with the regular chili con carne (without beans) standard.

chili macaroni (also known as chilimac): Must contain at least 16 percent meat.

chili pie: Must contain at least 20 percent meat; also, the filling must make up at least 50 percent of the product.

chili sauce with meat or *chili hot dog sauce with meat:* Both must contain at least 6 percent meat.

chop suey (American style) with macaroni and meat: Must contain at least 25 percent meat.

chop suey vegetables with meat: Must contain at least 12 percent meat.

chopped ham: Must be prepared from fresh, cured, or smoked ham, plus certain kinds of curing agents and seasonings; may contain dehydrated onions and/or garlic, corn syrup, and not more than 3 percent water to dissolve the curing agents.

chorizos empanadillos: Must contain at least 25 percent fresh chorizos or 17 percent dry chorizos.

chow mein vegetables with meat: Must contain at least 12 percent meat; *chow mein vegetables with meat and noodles* must contain at least 8 percent meat, and the chow mein must make up two-thirds of the total product.

condensed, cream dried, or *chipped beef:* Must contain at least 18 percent dried or chipped beef, figured on reconstituted total product.

corn dog: Must meet standards for frankfurters; batter cannot exceed the weight of the frankfurter.

corned beef and cabbage: Must contain at least 25 percent corned beef, measured on cooked basis.

corned beef hash: Must contain at least 35 percent corned beef, measured on cooked basis; must contain potatoes, curing agents, and seasonings. May contain onions, garlic, beef broth, beef fat, and other ingredients, but no more than 15 percent fat; moisture must not exceed 72 percent.

country ham: Must meet the definition, "a dry-cured product frequently coated with spices."

crackling corn bread: Must contain at least 15 percent cracklings, measured on cooked basis.

cream cheese with chipped beef (sandwich spread): Must contain at least 12 percent chipped beef.

crepes: Filling/sauce must contain at least 20 percent meat, measured on cooked basis, or at least 10 percent meat (cooked basis) if the filling has another major characterizing ingredient, such as cheese.

croquettes: Must contain at least 35 percent meat.

curried sauce with meat and rice (casserole dish): Must contain at least 35 percent meat (cooked basis) in the sauce and meat portion; total dish must contain no more than 50 percent rice.

deviled ham: Must contain no more than 35 percent fat.

dinners (frozen, containing meat): Must contain at least 25 percent meat or meat food product (cooked basis), figured on total main portion of meal—that is, minus appetizer, bread, and dessert. Minimum weight of a consumer package in this category, 10 ounces.

dumplings and meat in sauce: Must contain at least 18 percent meat.

egg foo yong with meat: Must contain at least 12 percent meat.

egg rolls with meat: Must contain at least 10 percent meat.

enchilada with meat: Must contain at least 15 percent meat.

entrées (main course, consisting of meat or meat food product, plus one vegetable): Must contain at least 50 percent meat or meat food product, measured on cooked basis. But entrées labeled *meat or meat food product, gravy or sauce, and one vegetable* are required to have only a minimum of 30 percent meat or meat food product (cooked basis).

frankfurter, bologna, and similar cooked sausage: May contain only skeletal meat; no more than 30 percent fat, 10 percent added water (exclusive of water in formula), 2 percent corn syrup, and 15 percent poultry meat.

frankfurter, bologna, and similar cooked sausage with by-products or variety meats: Same limitations as above on fat, added water, and corn syrup; must contain at least 15 percent skeletal meat. Each by-product or variety meat (these include heart, tongue, spleen, tripe, stomach) must be specifically named in the list of ingredients.

frankfurter, bologna, and similar cooked sausage with by-products or variety meats, and which also contain nonmeat binders: Products are made with the above formulas and also contain up to 3.5 percent nonmeat binders or 2 percent isolated soy protein. These products must be distinctively labeled, in a manner such as, "frankfurters with by-products, nonfat milk added." The binders must be named in their proper order in the list of ingredients.

fried rice with meat: Must contain at least 10 percent meat.

fritters (breaded): Must contain at least 35 percent meat.

german-style potato salad with bacon: Must contain at least 14 percent bacon, measured on cooked basis.

goulash: Must contain at least 25 percent meat.

gravies: Must contain at least 25 percent meat stock or broth, or at least 6 percent meat.

ham (canned): Limited to 8 percent total weight gain after processing.

ham, cooked or cooked and smoked (not canned): Must not weigh more after processing than the fresh ham weighed before curing and smoking; if it has up to 10 percent added weight, it must be labeled "Ham, Water Added"; if more than 10 percent, it must be labeled "Imitation Ham."

ham à la king: Must contain at least 25 percent ham, measured on cooked basis.

ham and cheese spread: Must contain at least 25 percent ham, measured on cooked basis.

ham chowder: Must contain at least 10 percent ham, measured on cooked basis.

ham croquettes: Must contain at least 35 percent ham, measured on cooked basis.

ham salad: Must contain at least 35 percent ham (cooked basis), but *ham spread* must contain at least 50 percent ham, measured on cooked basis.

hamburger, hamburg, burger, ground beef, or chopped beef: Must contain no more than 30 percent fat; must contain no extenders.

hash: Must contain at least 35 percent meat (of whatever kind the label specifies, as beef, corned beef), measured on cooked basis.

hors d'oeuvres: Must contain at least 15 percent meat (cooked basis) or at least 10 percent bacon, measured on cooked basis.

jambalaya with meat: Must contain at least 25 percent meat, measured on cooked basis.

knishes: Must contain at least 15 percent meat (cooked basis) or 10 percent bacon (cooked basis).

kreplach: Must contain at least 20 percent meat.

lasagna with meat and sauce: Must contain at least 12 percent meat.

lasagna with sauce, cheese, and dry sausage: Must contain at least 8 percent dry sausage.

lima beans with ham or bacon in sauce: Must contain at least 12 percent ham or bacon.

liver products such as liver loaf, liver paste, liver pâté, liver cheese, liver spread, and liver sausage: Must contain at least 30 percent liver.

macaroni and beef in tomato sauce: Must contain at least 12 percent beef.

macaroni and meat: Must contain at least 25 percent meat.

macaroni salad with ham or beef: Must contain at least 12 percent ham or beef, measured on cooked basis.

manicotti (with meat filling): Must contain at least 10 percent meat.

meat and dumplings in sauce: Must contain at least 25 percent meat.

meat and seafood egg roll: Must contain at least 5 percent meat.

meat and vegetables: Must contain at least 50 percent meat.

meat casseroles: Must contain at least 25 percent fresh uncooked meat, or at least 18 percent cooked meat.

meat curry: Must contain at least 50 percent meat.

meat loaf (baked or oven-ready): Must contain at least 65 percent meat, can contain no more than 12 percent extenders, including textured vegetable protein.

meat pastry: Must contain at least 25 percent meat.

meat pies: Must contain at least 25 percent meat.

meat ravioli and *meat ravioli in sauce:* Both must contain at least 10 percent meat in the ravioli.

meat salads: Must contain at least 35 percent meat, measured on cooked basis.

meat shortcake: Must contain at least 25 percent meat, measured on cooked basis.

meat soups:
    ready-to-eat: Must contain at least 5 percent meat.
    condensed: Must contain at least 10 percent meat.

meat spreads: Must contain at least 50 percent meat.

meat taco filling: Must contain at least 40 percent meat. On the other hand, *meat tacos* must contain at least 15 percent meat.

meat turnovers: Must contain at least 25 percent meat.

meat wellington: Must consist of at least 50 percent cooked tenderloin, spread with a liver pâté or similar coating, and covered with not more than 30 percent pastry.

meatballs: Must contain at least 65 percent meat; can contain no more than 12 percent extenders (cereals and such), including textured vegetable protein.

meatballs in sauce: Must contain at least 50 percent meatballs, measured on cooked basis.

mincemeat: Must contain at least 12 percent meat.

oleomargarine or margarine: If the fat in the product is entirely animal fat, or contains some animal fat, it is processed under federal inspection and must contain—individually or in combination—pasteurized cream, cows' milk, skim milk, a combination of nonfat dry milk and water or finely ground soybeans and water. It may contain butter, salt, artificial coloring, vitamins A and D. The finished product must contain at least 80 percent fat, and labels must clearly state which types of fat are used.

omelet with bacon: Must contain at least 9 percent bacon, measured on cooked basis; *omelet with dry sausage* must contain at least 12 percent dry sausage (cooked basis); *omelet with liver* must contain at least 12 percent liver (cooked basis); *omelet with ham* must contain at least 18 percent ham (cooked basis).

pan haus (panhas): Must contain at least 10 percent meat.

pâté de foie: Must contain at least 30 percent liver.

pepper steaks: Must contain at least 30 percent beef, measured on cooked basis.

peppers and italian brand sausage in sauce: Must contain at least 20 percent sausage, measured on cooked basis.

petcha (pcha): Must contain at least 50 percent calves' feet.

pizza sauce with sausage: Must contain at least 6 percent sausage.

pizza with meat: Must contain at least 15 percent meat.

pizza with sausage: Must contain at least 12 percent sausage, measured on cooked basis, or 10 percent dry sausage (such as pepperoni).

pork and dressing: Must contain at least 50 percent pork, measured on cooked basis; *pork with dressing and gravy* must contain at least 30 percent pork (cooked basis).

pork sausage: Can contain no more than 50 percent fat; can contain no by-products or extenders.

pork with barbecue sauce: Must contain at least 50 percent pork, measured on cooked basis.

proscuitto: Must conform to definition, "a flat, dry-cured ham coated with spices."

salisbury steak: Must contain at least 65 percent meat and no more than 12 percent extenders, including textured vegetable protein.

sandwiches (containing meat): Total sandwich must contain at least 35 percent meat; filling must be at least 50 percent of the sandwich.

sauce with chipped beef: Must contain at least 18 percent chipped beef.

sauce with meat or *meat sauce:* Must contain at least 6 percent meat.

sauerbraten: Must contain at least 50 percent meat, measured on cooked basis.

sauerkraut balls with meat: Must contain at least 30 percent meat.

sauerkraut with wieners and juice: Must contain at least 20 percent wieners.

scalloped potatoes and ham: Must contain at least 20 percent ham, measured on cooked basis.

scallopine: Must contain at least 35 percent meat, measured on cooked basis.

scrambled eggs with ham in a pancake: Must contain at least 9 percent cooked ham.

scrapple: Must contain at least 40 percent meat and/or meat by-products.

shepherd's pie: Must contain at least 25 percent meat; can contain no more than 50 percent mashed potatoes.

sloppy joe (sauce with meat): Must contain at least 35 percent meat, measured on cooked basis.

snacks: Must contain either 15 percent meat, measured on cooked basis, or 10 percent bacon (cooked basis).

spaghetti with sliced franks and sauce: Must contain at least 12 percent frankfurters.

spanish rice with beef or with ham: Must contain at least 20 percent beef or ham, measured on cooked basis.

stews (beef, lamb, etc.): Must contain at least 25 percent of whichever meat the label specifies.

stuffed cabbage with meat in sauce and *stuffed peppers with meat in sauce:* Each must contain at least 12 percent meat.

sukiyaki: Must contain at least 30 percent meat.

sweet-and-sour pork or *beef:* Must contain at least 25 percent meat and at least 16 percent fruit.

sweet-and-sour spareribs: Must contain at least 50 percent bone-in spareribs, measured on cooked basis.

swiss steak with gravy: Must contain at least 50 percent meat, measured on cooked basis, but *gravy and swiss steak* must contain at least 35 percent meat (cooked basis).

tamale pie: Must contain at least 20 percent meat, and filling must make up at least 40 percent of the total product.

tamales: Must contain at least 25 percent meat.

tamales with sauce (or with gravy): Must contain at least 20 percent meat.

taquitos: Must contain at least 15 percent meat.

tongue spread: Must contain at least 50 percent tongue.

tortellini with meat: Must contain at least 10 percent meat.

veal birds: Must contain at least 60 percent veal and no more than 40 percent stuffing.

veal cordon bleu: Must contain at least 60 percent veal and 5 percent ham; must contain swiss, gruyère, or mozzarella cheese.

veal fricassee: Must contain at least 40 percent veal.

veal parmigiana: Must consist of at least 40 percent breaded meat product in sauce.

veal steaks: Can be chopped, shaped, cubed, frozen. Beef may be added with product name shown as "Veal Steaks, Beef Added, Chopped, Shaped, and Cubed" if beef amounts to no more than 20 percent; if more than 20 percent beef, must be labeled "Veal and Beef Steak, Chopped, Shaped, and Cubed." In all cases, the product can contain no more than 30 percent fat.

vegetable and meat casserole or *vegetable and meat pie:* Each must contain at least 25 percent meat.

vegetable stew and meatballs: Total product must contain at least 12 percent meat.

won ton soup: Must contain at least 5 percent meat.

POULTRY PRODUCTS

All percentages of poultry in the following list—chicken, turkey, or other kinds—are on cooked, deboned basis, unless otherwise indicated in individual entries. When standard indicates poultry meat, skin, and fat, the requirement is for skin and fat to be in proportions normal to the type of poultry.

baby food
   high poultry dinner: Must contain at least 18.75 percent poultry meat, skin, fat, and giblets.
   poultry with broth: Must contain at least 43 percent poultry meat, skin, fat, and giblets.

beans and rice with poultry: Must contain at least 6 percent poultry meat.

breaded poultry: Can contain no more than 30 percent breading.

cabbage stuffed with poultry: Stuffing must contain at least 8 percent poultry meat.

canelloni with poultry: Must contain at least 7 percent poultry meat.

canned boned poultry:
   boned (kind), solid pack: At least 95 percent poultry meat, skin, and fat.
   boned (kind): At least 90 percent poultry meat, skin, and fat.
   boned (kind) with broth: At least 80 percent poultry meat, skin, and fat.
   boned (kind) with specified percentage of broth: At least 50 percent poultry meat, skin, and fat.

chicken cordon bleu: Must contain at least 60 percent boneless chicken breast, measured on raw basis, 6 percent ham, and swiss, gruyère, or mozzarella cheese.

creamed poultry: Must contain at least 20 percent poultry meat; product must also contain some cream.

entrées (main course):
poultry or poultry food product and one vegetable: At least 37.5 percent poultry meat or poultry food product.
poultry or poultry food product with gravy or sauce and one vegetable: At least 22 percent poultry meat or poultry food product.

poultry à la kiev: Must be breast meat (with or without attached skin) stuffed with butter and chives.

poultry à la king: Must contain at least 20 percent poultry meat.

poultry amandine: Must contain at least 50 percent poultry meat.

poultry barbecue: Must contain at least 40 percent poultry meat; must have barbecued appearance, and be prepared over burning or smoldering hardwood or its sawdust.

poultry blintz filling: Must contain at least 40 percent poultry meat.

poultry brunswick stew: Must contain at least 12 percent poultry meat; one of the vegetables must be corn.

poultry burgers: Must be 100 percent poultry meat, with skin and fat.

poultry burgundy: Must contain at least 50 percent poultry meat, with sufficient wine to characterize the sauce.

poultry cacciatore: Must contain at least 20 percent boneless poultry meat or 40 percent bone-in.

poultry casserole: Must contain at least 19 percent poultry meat.

poultry chili: Must contain at least 28 percent poultry meat.

poultry chili with beans: Must contain at least 17 percent poultry meat.

poultry chop suey: Must contain at least 4 percent poultry meat; but *chop suey with poultry* must contain at least 2 percent.

poultry chow mein without noodles: Must contain at least 4 percent poultry meat.

poultry croquettes: Must contain at least 25 percent poultry meat; *poultry croquettes with macaroni and cheese* must have at least 29 percent croquettes in the dish.

poultry dinners (frozen product): Must contain at least 18 percent poultry meat, figured on the total meal minus appetizer, bread, and dessert.

poultry empanadillo: Must contain at least 25 percent poultry meat, measured on raw basis, including skin and fat.

poultry fricassee: Must contain at least 20 percent poultry meat.

poultry fricassee of wings: Must contain at least 40 percent poultry wings, measured on cooked basis, with bone.

poultry hash: Must contain at least 30 percent poultry meat.

poultry lasagna: Must contain at least 8 percent poultry meat, measured on raw basis.

poultry livers with rice and gravy: Must contain at least 30 percent poultry livers in poultry and gravy portion of dish, or 17.5 percent in total product.

poultry paella: Must contain at least 35 percent poultry meat or 35 percent poultry and other meat, measured on cooked basis; can contain no more than 35 percent cooked rice; the dish must also contain seafood.

poultry pies: Must contain at least 14 percent poultry meat.

poultry ravioli: Must contain at least 2 percent poultry meat.

poultry roll: Can contain no more than 3 percent binding agents, such as gelatin, in the cooked product; no more than 2 percent natural cooked-out juices; *poultry roll with natural juices* may contain more than 2 percent natural cooked-out juices; *poultry roll with broth* may contain more than 2 percent poultry broth in addition to natural cooked-out juices. In *poultry roll with gelatin,* the gelatin may exceed 3 percent of cooked product.

poultry salad: Must contain at least 25 percent poultry meat, including normal amounts of skin and fat.

poultry scallopini: Must contain at least 35 percent poultry meat.

poultry soup:
ready-to-eat: At least 2 percent poultry meat.
condensed: At least 4 percent poultry meat.

poultry stew: Must contain at least 12 percent poultry meat.

poultry stroganoff: Must contain at least 30 percent poultry meat, as well as at least 10 percent sour cream and 5 percent wine.

poultry tamales: Must contain at least 6 percent poultry meat.

poultry tetrazzini: Must contain at least 15 percent poultry meat.

poultry wellington: Must consist of at least 50 percent poultry breast spread with a liver or similar pâté coating, covered in not more than 30 percent pastry.

poultry with gravy: Must contain at least 35 percent poultry meat; but *gravy with poultry* must contain at least 15 percent, while *poultry with gravy and dressing* must contain at least 25 percent boneless poultry meat or 30 percent bone-in; *noodles* or *dumplings with poultry* must contain at least 6 percent poultry meat.

poultry with noodles au gratin: Must contain at least 18 percent poultry meat.

poultry with sauce or sauce with poultry: Either one must contain at least 6 percent poultry meat.

poultry with vegetables: Must contain at least 15 percent poultry meat.

AND SOME ANCILLARY CONSIDERATIONS

It should be borne in mind that foods will not necessarily be labeled quite so flat-footedly as in the lists above. A food processor who put out cans or jars or frozen packages labeled "Beans with Bacon" might get the leather medal for honesty, but wouldn't necessarily attract a rush of customers. However, if he (just as honestly) calls his product

RED BEANS WITH BACON
in Zesty Mexican Sauce

he has a fighting chance. And, no matter how cross you may be with them on occasion, food processors need a fighting chance and should be expected to grab it when opportunity offers.

On the other hand, if they grab the opportunity to substitute salt pork or hog jowl for the bacon, or to trim the amount of bacon to under 12 percent, Uncle's watchdogs will shortly be at their door.

There is no reason why consumers, the victims of this and other kinds of food shortchanging, should be tolerant. The pass-it-on system of protest should be put into motion every time you buy a product that does not live up to the promises made on the label. Tell your friends and neighbors, who in turn will tell theirs. Besides being vocal, be verbal. Write to the food processor, stating your objections fully. (If he gets a lot of protests it will become clear to him that ultimately he will cheat himself in lost customers if he doesn't mend his ways—or, at least, his products.) And write to the USDA and the FDA, too. Those mills may grind slowly, but sooner or later your protest—and those of others who have been motivated to sound off—will be acted upon.

Ongoing governmental concerns. For some time, the Department of Agriculture has been working—along with its many other concerns—on the problem of ice cream. That frozen dessert dear to all our hearts is one of the foods that need not list ingredients on the label (mayonnaise is another example, and there are more) because, presumably, the makers conform to a sort of "universal recipe" for the product. If a manufacturer strays from the standard, he must list ingredients on the label for the consumer to use as a yardstick in comparing his product with the standard.

But since the time the standards were set, all sorts of nontraditional ingredients have been making their appearance in ice cream to the point where the question of what is

ice cream and what is not has become a very iffy one. So once again the Agriculture Department took a hand, to solve the problem or, at least, to make it easily possible for the consumer to find his way through the ice cream maze. The Food and Agriculture Act of 1977 enables consumers to distinguish between ice cream as it has been traditionally made and ice cream containing, for example, unlimited amounts of whey and caseinates. (Whey is the thin, watery substance separated out of milk in cheesemaking; caseinates are milk proteins that are separated from milk by special processing methods. Both are by-products of types of food manufacturing other than ice cream-making.)

USDA's new formula for ice cream—"traditional recipe" —requires, among other things, that minimum-standard ice cream must:

- contain at least 1.6 pounds of total solids per gallon
- weigh at least 4.5 pounds per gallon
- contain at least 20 percent total milk solids, constituted of 10 percent milk fat and at least 6 percent nonfat milk solids; whey cannot, by weight, constitute more than 25 percent of the nonfat milk solids

Under the new law, manufacturers whose ice cream meets the Agriculture Department's standard may label their products with an identifying Department of Agriculture symbol. Use of the symbol is voluntary; however, manufacturers who wish to use it must:

- operate a USDA-approved plant
- use dairy ingredients from a USDA-approved plant
- produce ice cream according to the Department's standard of composition and (for the usual fee) operate under continuous USDA inspection

The Department is also considering (still in the feeling-the-way stage at the time this is written) the establishment of an ice cream grading system that would allow consumers to make an at-a-glance quality determination, based on milkfat and milk solids content, on flavor, body, texture, color, and appearance.

Meanwhile, down the road a piece, the FDA is also reconsidering amended standards of identity for ice cream, frozen custard, ice milk, and sherbet, particularly in regard to establishing minimum milk protein requirements. They are also taking into consideration comparison and relative importance of physical characteristics and nutritional value of ice cream manufactured under present and pending standards.

What does all this mean? That the government is busily looking after your welfare. Here we've discussed ice cream. It boggles the mind to imagine all the dozens, hundreds, thousands of foods also under examination at the same time, being analyzed for nutritional content, inspected for cleanliness, considered for eye- and appetite-appeal, scrutinized for conformance to standards.

For example, as this is being written, one of the USDA's other concerns—one of dozens—is the problem of MDM (mechanically deboned meat), over which the Department is feeling its way through considerations of definition, permitted uses, and labeling requirements for meat food products prepared in this manner.

"This manner" is a process in which hand-trimmed bones, primarily soft bones that have considerable muscle tissue (meat) on them, are ground and then forced through sieves that separate the meat from most of the bone. The Department feels it should permit 0.75 percent calcium (from bones) in the MDM product.

An earlier regulation covering the subject was withdrawn as the result of a suit by a coalition of consumer groups in which the court ruled in favor of the consumer groups, holding that the USDA had not adequately assessed MDM's potential health hazards. The new proposed regulation is based on scientific data evaluated by a select panel of government scientists who are considered experts on the health and safety aspects of foods. It provides that what had previously been referred to as MDM could be called "Tissue from Ground Bones"—TGB. It classifies TGB as a "meat food product" rather than as "meat," as the previous regulation had classified the substance. By the new regulation—which, remember, may or may not go into effect—TGB could constitute no more than 20 percent of the meat portion of any meat food product, and would have to be of the same species as the formulated product—that is, only pork TGB in pork sausage, as an example.

More, the new regulation prohibits the use of TGB in baby, junior, or toddler foods, as well as in ground beef, fabricated steaks, barbecued meats, roast beef, corned cuts, lima beans with ham, and similar products, such as beef with gravy and meat pies.

A lot of concern, a lot of people concerned in the concern. And it all may mean, as well as concern, that Uncle's minions are rushing around in all directions, getting in each other's way, duplicating each other's efforts, tangling themselves and each other in red tape, churning out memos in sextuplicate. But surely it is better to be over rather than under cared for?

And private concerns, as well. In spite of what some consumers think, most food processors and manufacturers are not out to bilk them in assorted devious ways. On the contrary, processors know that to build and maintain consumer acceptance, they have to offer good value, good appearance, good flavor, and—insofar as possible within the limits of the food in question—good nutrition. To help acceptance along, they package food as attractively as they can and spread the word endlessly through advertising. But in the long run it's what's inside the package that really counts. That's the bottom line for getting—or losing—consumer acceptance of the products.

Many food manufacturer/processor/packer groups maintain industrywide agencies that help in such divergent areas as promoting the food, determining policies, originating and testing recipes using the product, and setting standards. One of the concerns of some such agencies is consumer relations. Other companies have their own consumer advocates or departments—full-time, on-staff people who are there to help you vis-à-vis the manufacturer and his product.

What we're trying to say is this: You are not alone. Speak, and you will be heard—and listened to.

GALANTINE

This is not one of your simple, easy indoor sports. It requires a sharp eye and a sure hand, considerable skill and even more patience. And, just for openers, large quantities of courage and supreme self-confidence. Unless you can truthfully say to yourself, "There is nothing concerned with the kitchen that I cannot accomplish," you should never decide, "Today I will make a galantine."

But ah, the ineluctable joys of the finished product—the beauty, the flavor, the aroma! (To say nothing of the cook's button-bursting pride.) Having produced so superb a culinary effort, you have every right to make up your mind that tomorrow you will try walking on water.

What is it? Well, to be brutally frank, it's a sort of sausage. But, we hasten to add, the perfect sausage, the epitome of sausages, a sausage to put all others to shame.

Let's consider a galantine of turkey as an example, following it (not the recipe, just the steps of preparing) from lowly beginning to triumphant conclusion.

Gathering your forces. You will need, obviously, a turkey. One 12 to 15 pounds in weight will make a galantine sufficient for 16 to 20 servings as a part of a buffet dinner (this is not the sort of thing one whips up for the family on PTA night), or 28 to 32 servings if you offer it as an appetizer. Better to count on the low side rather than the high—Joe, the one who always ends the evening with a lampshade on his head, will gobble it up as if it were hamburger.

Besides the ordinary staples—eggs, seasonings, and so on—you will also need fine, lean, milk-fed veal; lean pork; cooked tongue and ham; brandy; truffles (whole, not the cheap pieces and trimmings that cost only an arm and a leg); and shelled whole pistachio nuts.

The early stages. To begin with, you must bone the raw turkey. You must do it with neatness and aplomb, never—except for the initial cut—breaking the skin anywhere. (The special feature: CARVING, BONING, AND OTHER KITCHEN TECHNIQUES will tell you how.)

If, having accomplished this, you feel like an early Christian martyr with a lion nibbling at your vitals, make yourself a cup of tea or pour yourself a drink, according to your lights, sit down and pull yourself together. The worst is over.

When you have recovered sufficiently, put the turkey bones on to cook, to make the stock you will need later. Now tackle the do-aheads. Cut the cooked tongue and ham into neat finger-shaped strips. Shell and skin the pistachios. Prepare a mirepoix (diced carrot, onion, and celery, simmered in butter with bay leaf and thyme, with a little madeira wine added at the end). Make a Sauce Chaud-Froid (well-seasoned béchamel stiffened with gelatin) and set it to cool.

Onward and upward. Your next move is to cut half of the turkey breast meat into strips like those of the tongue and ham. Then assemble the remaining turkey meat, the raw veal and pork, and grind it all together three times. To the ground mixture you'll add brandy, various seasonings, eggs, and minced parsley, making a fine, smooth paste—a forcemeat, as a matter of fact.

Now you'll need a large piece of clean linen or, lacking that, cheesecloth. Spread it on a flat surface and on top of it, in the center, gently spread out the turkey skin, outside down. Over it spread the ground mixture, gently pushing and pulling and tucking until you have achieved a shape roughly rectangular.

Over the center of the ground mixture, arrange the ham and tongue and turkey breast strips in a pleasing pattern. In the very center, arrange a neat row of small black truffles. Sprinkle the whole deal with pistachios and minced parsley.

At this point, it's possible you'll need to ask for assistance—preferably of someone who won't think the whole deal is a joke. Together, starting at the long side farther from you, the two of you will gently roll the filled turkey skin into a sausage shape, using the cloth under it to help you, and ending with the cloth covering the entire outside of the roll. With white kitchen string, tie cloth and all securely at both ends, then several times in the middle, then lengthwise.

The garrison finish. Put the mirepoix in the bottom of a large, deep kettle; place a rack over it and position the galantine on the rack. Add turkey stock to cover. Put the lid on the kettle and simmer the contents gently until the galantine is firm to the touch, up to 2 hours. (Rest now, having another cup of tea or whatever.) Remove the galantine, when it is done, to a large platter and cool it. When it is only barely warm, carefully cut the string and remove the cloth wrapping. Refrigerate until very cold, decorate with the Sauce Chaud-Froid, and bring it triumphantly to the table, to be served with buttered toast.

Our wish for you is this: that you've invited to share the galantine someone who will appreciate your efforts, someone who wouldn't rather have had a nice fried pork chop.

Now that you're in the swing of it, you'll be happy to know

that you can also make galantines of duck, chicken, capon, veal—the latter beginning with a boned breast of veal—and eel—in which the eel skin is removed whole, then stuffed and cooked. And there are others. But poultry is by far the most common base for a galantine.

Any galantine may be served hot, with or without a sauce, if you prefer.

GALLINULE: see GAME

GAME

Those who live in cities and lead cosmopolitan lives tend to think of hunting as something people did a long time ago—for food, because food was needed, or for sport, because there wasn't much of anything else to do.

Not true. There are still a great many men—and women, too—who hunt. The only real change is that almost everyone today frowns on killing for killing's sake. People who hunt intend to eat what they bag, perhaps sharing it with friends and neighbors.

Properly cared for in the field and, later, properly cooked, virtually any game is a feast for the connoisseur. Game is not just food, but excellent, gourmet food. But both care and cooking do require know-how.

Preparation begins in the field. Delicious meat on the table starts with the hunter, with how he handles the game he takes. With all game, large or small, and game birds and waterfowl as well, it is absolutely mandatory that the animal be gutted on the spot. Speed is essential, both in removing the entrails and getting the body cooled as soon as possible. Keep open the incision through which the animal is gutted, so that air can circulate. In big-game animals, prop the abdominal cavity open with a stick to let as much air in as possible; if you are staying out overnight, hang the animal in a tree, off the ground, for better air circulation.

If there's snow on the ground, the body cavities of small game can be packed with it for a few minutes after gutting to cool and clean the animal. Birds, both waterfowl and upland game, also require immediate dressing. Carry birds on a game hanger for optimum air circulation.

In cold weather, it's not difficult to keep game cool; in warm weather, it's essential to get your game home, or to a locker or refrigerator plant, as rapidly as possible. In any weather, don't carry game home on the hood of the car. The heat of the engine may start spoilage in the meat.

The four divisions. Although the in-the-field-rule of gutting and keeping cool applies to all game, somewhat different subsequent approaches can be taken to the bag in each of the four game categories: upland game birds, waterfowl, small game, and big game. Both hunter and home cook (in many cases they are the same person) need to know what to expect and how to cope.

UPLAND GAME BIRDS

Game birds offer the most varied—and perhaps the most delicious—wild meat. From the miniature woodcock to the magnificent wild turkey, they provide a range of flavor as wide as the variation of sport in hunting them. The quality and flavor of game birds depend to a great extent, however, on the care they receive after the hunter has bagged them.

The rules are simple: The birds should be drawn very soon after they are shot, body heat should be encouraged to dissipate as quickly as possible, and the birds should be kept at a cool—better still, cold—temperature until they are cooked.

In testing game birds to identify those that are young and tender, the condition of the bill is a useful guide. If pheasant and grouse, for example, can be lifted by the lower jaw without breaking it, they are mature birds whose jaws are set. They will not be as tender as the younger, less developed birds, and will require longer cooking, preferably by a moist-heat method such as braising.

Young pheasants' spurs will be pliable. The breast bone of a young partridge will break easily, and the leg will be plump close to the foot. The claws of a young—and, it follows, tender—bird of any kind are sharp; in an older bird, the claws are blunter at the tip. If the bird is old, a commercial tenderizer will be a help before cooking. Follow the package directions, but use the tenderizer in the cavity rather than on the outside flesh of the bird.

Game birds in the field should not be packed together in a mass if there is any warmth left in them or if the weather is mild. In camp, at a distance from any settlement where cooling facilities are to be had, the birds should be allowed to air thoroughly each night, or should remain hung in a cool, airy place until the trip is over. If a freezing locker is available, the birds should be cleaned and packaged separately in heavy-duty foil or other moisture/vaporproof material.

How many will your bag serve? That depends partly on the recipe you will use—is the bird to be stuffed, braised with accompanying vegetables, cooked in a potpie? If so, a single bird will go farther than one simply roasted. In general, however, a pheasant will serve three or four, a partridge one—or two if it is very large. With quail and woodcock, count on one bird per serving.

When you stuff a game bird, deal with it the same way you would with domestic fowl: do not stuff until a short time before the bird is to be cooked. If you wish, prepare the stuffing ahead of time, and refrigerate the stuffing and bird separately. If there are leftovers, once again refrigerate them separately rather than leaving the stuffing in the cavity.

Grouse, partridge, and prairie chicken. A debate has gone on among hunters for years as to whether upland birds should be plucked or skinned. Some wild-game cooks insist that the skin be left on to preserve the layer of fat that lies just beneath it. However, that fat is not as plentiful as in domestic birds, and in many cases isn't enough to be taken into account. Some birds—ruffed grouse is one—have very tender skins, and plucking them can be quite difficult. Skinning, on the other hand, is simple and easy. (Incidentally, there's an unwritten law among fishermen and fishermen's wives that goes: "Them as catches 'em cleans 'em." There is no reason it shouldn't hold true for game as well.)

So, skin or pluck the bird as you prefer. Remove the head and cut the legs off at the middle joint. Wipe the cavity with a cloth wrung out of cold water, and you're ready to cook the bird in any manner you prefer—and there are many ways to go about it. A large general cookbook or, preferably, a game cookbook, can introduce you to a wide variety of game-bird recipes. To tempt you into pursuing the matter, look for:

partridge: Casseroled with vegetables and mushrooms; cooked hunter's style with bacon, cabbage, and herbs; breasts stroganoff; fricasseed in cream; grill-baked in foil; braised with onions; breasts with dumplings; braised in wine sauce; barbecued, with sweet/sour sauce; partridge pie; roasted with fruit stuffing.

grouse: Breast with tomato sauce; pressure-cooked with peppery béchamel; with poppy-seed dumplings; stuffed with oysters; broiled with olive oil; smothered with mushrooms in cream; with lemon-butter sauce and almonds; roasted with oranges; pot-roasted with black currant jelly.

prairie chicken: Sautéed suprêmes; fruit-stuffed; scalloped in cream with mushrooms; roasted with celery and apple; chicken-fried, with old-fashioned milk gravy; braised with rice creole; creamed on toast.

Wild turkey. Those who have had the pleasure of tasting them consider wild turkeys the most delicious of all game birds, making the domestic turkey seem bland and flavorless in comparison. They should be plucked (not skinned) and the down singed off in a flame—just as we used to treat domestic poultry before the processors began to do all the work for us. Remove the head; cut off the lower part of the legs at the middle joint. Wipe clean, inside and out, with a hot cloth.

Here are some of the many ways to prepare wild turkey:

Roasted, with chestnut stuffing flavored with juniper berries; in spanish sauce, with ham, rice, grated cheese (for leftovers); braised in white wine; roasted, with pork sausage stuffing or celery-sage stuffing.

Count on an 8- to 10-pound wild turkey to serve 4 to 6 people amply, with some leftovers—in other words, about 2 pounds per person (wild turkey is not as meaty as its pampered domestic cousin; it's had to forage for itself). Some people like certain wild birds served rare, but turkey should not be one of them. As with domestic turkey, the bird is done when the juices run pale yellow, with no tinge of pink or red.

Woodcock. These are small, migratory game birds of delicious, delicate flavor. Count on one bird for each serving. Even more important than with other game birds, woodcock should be cleaned as soon as possible after being shot.

Look for woodcock recipes such as these:

Broiled, served with parsley butter on toast; roasted, with lingonberry stuffing; glazed with orange jelly, served on toast with poached orange slices; marinated and braised in wine; baked in sour cream.

Quail. These little birds—one to a serving, or even two for quail-loving trenchermen—may be either plucked or skinned. Most dyed-in-the-wool quail hunters maintain that it's worth the trouble of plucking and singeing them to conserve the extra bit of flavor and moisture the skin affords.

Remove heads, cut off legs at the first joint above the foot. Wipe the cavity clean with a cloth wrung out of hot water.

Here are some of the many ways to serve the succulent birds:

Breaded with cornmeal, browned and braised; sautéed with grapes and hazelnuts; baked in wine; roasted in grape leaves; roasted with sausage stuffing; casseroled with vegetables and mushrooms in white wine; sautéed, served on sautéed hominy slices; barbecued in peppery lemon sauce; quail pie; broiled, with lemon-butter sauce; foil-roasted with blueberries; southern-fried with mushroom gravy.

Pigeons and doves. Both of these are all-dark-meat birds. They should be handled as you would any other game bird. Although the pigeon has an excellent flavor, the meat is not always tender and is best cooked by braising or some other slow, moist-cooking method. Doves, smaller in size, are also flavorful but more tender. One pigeon makes one serving. So does one dove, unless they are very small—then count on two per person.

Here are some of the delectable ways with these birds:

Dove breasts stroganoff; braised doves with pan gravy; doves in wine sauce; country-style doves with bacon; foil-roasted doves with vegetables; sherry-roasted doves; oven-braised doves in white wine; pigeon potpie with biscuit topping; pigeons in beer-tomato sauce; English cold pigeon pie; potted pigeon; pigeon hunter's style, with lemon and sage.

Pheasant. These birds can be either dry-plucked or skinned. Skinning is quicker and easier, and doesn't seriously affect the flavor. If the birds are to be roasted, however, they should be plucked, as the meat will dry seriously without the skin's protection. Plucking should take place as soon as possible after the birds are shot because the feathers tend to stiffen into the skin as the bird cools, making the plucking more difficult.

Pheasant meat is all white, and almost any recipe good for chicken is good for pheasant as well. Here are some special ways with this bird, many hunters' favorite game:

Potpie with peas and onions; roasted, with sour-cream gravy; baked in wine; baked, with horseradish-cream sauce and wild rice; barbecued in tomato sauce; braised with cabbage; foil-roasted with apricot nectar; casseroled breasts with onions and rice; fricasseed with wine-olive sauce; casseroled with raisins and muscatel, served with nutted rice; Spanish style, with spices and almonds; curried with rhubarb; paprikash; roasted, with rice-pecan stuffing; oven-fried with eggplant parmesan; stewed, with parsley dumplings; roasted, with purple plum sauce; sherried, with wild rice and figs.

Upland birds in general. These delicious birds can be very dry if not carefully cooked. Stuffing for a bird to be roasted should contain plenty of butter or other fat. Bacon or salt pork—preferably blanched before using—can be tied over the breast of the bird to keep the meat moist; if these are not used, the roasting bird must be basted frequently. Or use the old-fashioned way with domestic chickens and turkeys: melt fat in a pan on top of the stove with just a little liquid—broth, white wine, or water; dip a clean cloth (an old towel or napkin, or several layers of cheesecloth) in the fat and place over the bird, covering it completely. Redip several times during the roasting period. Or you can smear the bird liberally with butter and cover it with a foil tent; do not close the bird airtight in the foil.

WATERFOWL

When brought well-prepared to the table, waterfowl offer the hunter pleasure at least equal to that he enjoyed in bagging them. Duck hunting, in particular, has always been so popular that at one time ducks were threatened with extinction. Conservation measures now protect them to make sure that these, and the other water birds, can be enjoyed by all.

In dealing with waterfowl, follow the rules for all game birds. Draw as soon as possible after the birds are shot. Body heat should be encouraged to dissipate rapidly by keeping bagged birds separate from one another and allowing for free air circulation. As with all birds, waterfowl must be kept cool until it is time to cook them.

There has been for a long time considerable controversy over the cooking and serving of wild duck. Some connoisseurs maintain that the birds should be cooked only briefly, at high heat, and served very rare. Others believe that such a method barely warms the duck, and that it is not edible unless it is well done. However, the longer roasting that a well-done bird will require produces a drier, less palatable dish. A compromise suits most people—for a duck of medium size, roughly three-quarters of an hour results in a flavorful, juicy bird that is by no means rare, but neither is it overcooked.

Older ducks should be cooked by moist-heat methods. Early in the season it is possible to determine whether or not

a bird is young by examining the tail feathers. If the stem of the feather extends about an eighth of an inch beyond the fibers, the bird is a young one, and will take well to roasting.

Count on a wild duck yielding two servings. Like its domestic brother, most of a wild duck's meat is on the breast and thighs. Wings, drumsticks, and back have very little to offer that is edible. Usually, a wild duck has less meat, even in the meaty spots, than the domestic, raised-for-the-table bird.

Coot and mud hen. Properly handled and prepared, these birds make excellent eating. Those who turn up their noses at the mention of a coot are missing a very tasty wildfowl meal. These birds are easier to prepare than duck. There is no choice between plucking and skinning—the birds must be skinned, as the skin has a strong, disagreeable flavor. After skinning, all fat must be removed, because it too has an unpleasant flavor which it imparts to the meat if left in place. After skinning and removing the fat, soak the bird —in a salt solution to which 2 tablespoons of vinegar have been added—for 4 to 6 hours before cooking.

Count on one coot or mud hen to serve one person, or even a bit less—three birds for two people makes a good, hearty dish. To prepare, after skinning and defatting, cut off head, wings, feet, and tail.

Here are some of the ways to cook these birds—look for recipes for these and other coot and mud hen dishes in a game cookbook:

Coot braised in bacon drippings, with onions; coot marinated in lime juice, casseroled in cream with green beans and mushrooms; coot stewed with carrots, tomatoes, and bay; mud hens in cream gravy, with onion and apple; mud hens braised with celery in sherry sauce.

Wild duck. Ducks should be drawn at the earliest opportunity, particularly in warm weather, and the empty cavity wiped out with a cloth dipped in cold water and well wrung out.

As mentioned before, ducks should be plucked rather than skinned, so that the skin can help retain moisture in the bird during cooking. Remove wings at the joint nearest the body and cut off legs at the first joint above the feet. Pull out all the larger feathers near the wings and tail, and pick the bird roughly. Paraffin and water will finish the job for you, neatly and with dispatch.

For 6 ducks, place three 12-ounce cakes of paraffin in a pot (use an old one, kept for this and other rough uses) with 6 quarts of water. Heat to about 160°F.—if you get it much hotter, little paraffin will cling to the birds and you'll have defeated your purpose. Immerse the birds one by one in the paraffin solution, dipping each one three times and allowing the paraffin that will adhere to the feathers to harden after each dipping. When the final dipping has hardened, small feathers and down can be easily removed by scraping with a knife, removing paraffin and feathers together. Paraffin may be reused several times if you remove the feathers caught in it each time it is heated. If paraffin is not available, the birds should be plucked clean, then singed to remove remaining down.

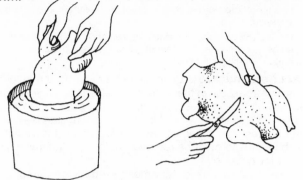

When you clean a duck, be sure to keep the heart, liver, and gizzard to cook, chop, and use in stuffing or gravy. They should be wiped thoroughly before cooking. Do not use liver or gizzard that has been penetrated by shot.

If there is not time to do a complete and thorough job of drawing ducks soon after they are shot, it is wise to remove, at least, the craw and intestines. This will go a long way toward ensuring good keeping quality.

After ducks have been plucked and drawn, a thorough washing in cold water, inside and out, followed by a soaking in very cold water overnight, then wiping dry with clean cloth or absorbent paper, will ready the birds for shipping or freezing if they are not to be cooked immediately. Ducks to be hung immediately or shipped in ordinary ice (not dry ice) should not be plucked; the body cavity should be stuffed with grass or clean crumpled paper for this type of shipment. However, ducks to be frozen must be plucked before freezing —it is exceedingly difficult to pluck a bird that has been frozen and allowed to thaw.

There are great numbers of delightful ways to cook duck. Consult a game cookbook for ways such as these:

Lemon-roasted; pecan-stuffed, basted with savory sauce; smothered in onions and beer; raisin-orange stuffing, orange sauce; in grand marnier sauce; braised with red cabbage; spit-roasted, flamed with cognac; roasted with juniper-seasoned sauerkraut; Chinese style, with apricot preserves; Mexican style, in red wine; roasted, sausage-stuffed; Cantonese style, with ginger, orange peel, and aniseed; broiled breast with lemon butter; cassoulet; sweet/sour braised; duck-leg pie; roasted, with apple-sage stuffing.

Wild geese. A sure sign that winter is approaching is skeins of wild geese high in the sky, flying south in disciplined formation, honking goodbye until next year. And a sure sign that the geese will soon be migrating is the large numbers of hunters out to bag a goose or two before they take off.

Knowledgeable hunters say that cutting the throat of a downed goose as soon as you get to where it has fallen, and allowing the bird to bleed out completely, will ensure a fine bird for the table.

As with other birds to be roasted, a goose is better plucked than skinned. Follow the method of drawing and plucking given for duck. A larger kettle and a larger amount of paraffin solution will be needed, of course. Because of the size of the bird, instead of dipping, pour the melted paraffin over it. Count on a pound of goose per serving.

Wild goose is not as fat as its domestic relatives, but it is, as an old hunter describes it, "a mighty fine-eatin' bird." Here are some of the many possible ways to prepare it:

Roasted, with apple-apricot stuffing; wild pot au feu; oven-braised with parsnips and garlic; cider-basted, with cinnamon apples; fruit-stuffed, with red cabbage and corn fritters; grape-stuffed, with orange sauce; fruit-stuffed, oven-braised in red wine; stuffed with mushrooms and wild rice; herb-seasoned, baked in sour cream.

Gallinule and rail. Although gallinule does not rank among the most delectable of game birds, it can be delicious when skinned and braised. Rail, which inhabits tidal marshlands, has many devoted advocates; the bird is excellent either roasted or braised. Unlike gallinule, rail should be plucked.

Here are some ways to serve the birds:

Bacon-roasted rail with wild rice; chicken-fried rail with lemon and marjoram; curried rail; butter-browned gallinule with sour-cream sauce; Italian-style gallinule in spicy tomato sauce with peppers.

SMALL GAME

The handling of small game animals differs from that of birds in several ways. To start with, there is no question of whether to pluck or skin—small game is invariably skinned (except for that proverbial, eat-it-or-starve porcupine, baked in an open fire in a coating of mud).

In skinning small game, you need to take care in order to keep loose fur from getting into the meat. A cloth dipped in scalding water will wipe away stray bits of fur from the carcasses. Small game should be dressed as soon as possible, and allowed to cool thoroughly; it should then be hung in a cool place. Musk glands are present in most small game; they must be removed very carefully to avoid spillage, or the meat will be spoiled by the strong flavor.

Generally speaking, small game animals are hunted near home and the problem of shipping them does not arise, as it often does with big game and with some of the birds. But although hunting them is a "backyard" sport, small game animals form a large share of our wild meat and deserve equal consideration with any other game in both dressing and cooking. It is estimated that one wild rabbit is bagged for every other item of game of all kinds taken by American hunters, and that the total weight of bagged rabbits is equal to or greater than the weight of all other game combined.

Squirrels, like rabbits, are nationwide in distribution and, in spite of their small size, form an important part of our wild meat supply. Other small game, neither hunted as avidly nor eaten as generally as squirrel and rabbit, includes beaver, opossum, woodchuck, raccoon, and muskrat.

Beaver. There's lots of good meat on a beaver—and although it's not true that the tail is the best part, as some claim (that tail gets a lot of exercise, and overexercised muscles tend to be tough), the tail, as well as the rest of the animal, is very edible indeed when properly prepared and cooked. A mature beaver may weigh as much as 60 pounds, but younger, smaller animals are better eating, as they are more tender. The first step in preparing to cook beaver is to remove all surface fat—the fat has a strong unpleasant flavor.

Beaver meat is dark, rich, and delicious. Here are some of the ways to serve it—consult a game cookbook for details:

Roasted, with onions and bacon; pot-roasted, seasoned with bay and cloves; barbecued, with a spice-and-herb sauce; roasted, larded with salt pork; cooked with onions, carrots, and celery; beaver-tail soup with noodles; tail roast, marinated in red wine and vinegar.

Rabbit. Most hunters prefer to dress rabbits immediately after they are shot, removing entrails and letting blood drain. This practice offers a twofold advantage: immediate draining of blood gives the meat better quality, and discarding the entrails removes the chief cause of spoilage. The body cavity should be wiped out with a cloth, dry grass, or absorbent paper immediately after cleaning. The skin is left on the rabbit until just before cooking or freezing. (See RABBIT.)

Rabbit meat is light in color and delicious in flavor. Some feel that a rabbit should be soaked in vinegar or wine or salted water before cooking; this is a matter of taste.

Cooked in any number of ways, rabbit is delicious. Here are a few of the possibilities:

Baked, with mashed potato-sage stuffing; deviled with wine and dijon mustard; Italian style, with mushrooms and oregano; ham-rabbit pie; batter-fried; fricasseed, with dumplings; old-fashioned jugged hare; stewed, with fruited gravy; sherry-baked; roasted in cream; baked, with prosciutto-liver sauce; rabbit-potato salad; smothered in onions; curried, with vegetables; Mennonite style, with bot boi; fricasseed in beer; stewed, with lima beans and carrots; honey-glazed; paprikash; Creole style; goulash, with potato dumplings—and, of course, hasenpfeffer.

Opossum, woodchuck. Both animals should be hung for 48 hours after they are dressed. Opossum meat is light-colored and tender; surface fat may be removed if you wish, but it does not have a strong odor or flavor.

It is the usual practice to parboil all opossum and wood-chuck, other than the youngest animals, before frying or roasting. Here are some of the ways to cook:

opossum: Roasted, with bread-and-egg stuffing; baked, with sweet potatoes and apples; roasted, with cinnamon-sugared apples; batter-fried.

woodchuck: Baked, with winter squash and raisins; barbecue burgers; braised in basil-tomato sauce; baked, butter-basted and brown-sugar glazed.

Raccoon, muskrat. Every bit of fat must be scrupulously removed from both of these animals before cooking—any left behind will impart undesirable flavor and odor to the meat. There are also small, round "kernels"—scent glands—under the front legs, on either side of the spine, and in the small of the back; these must be removed before the animal is prepared for cooking.

Both animals have dark meat; properly prepared, they make tender and flavorful main dishes such as these:

raccoon: In sweet/sour sauce; baked, with bread dressing; sloppy joes in buns; deep-dish pie with biscuit topping; barbecued in chili-tomato sauce; baked, with onions and bay leaves; bacon-roasted; roasted, with chicken-liver stuffing; raccoonburgers; corn-fried, with milk gravy; with sour cream sauce; roasted, with sauerkraut stuffing.

muskrat: Southern-fried, with cream gravy; oven-barbecued, in tomato sauce; bacon-roasted; curried, with chutney; marinated and batter-fried, with fruit sauce.

Squirrel. Mild flavored, rarely "gamey," squirrel is one of the finest—and one of the most tender—of all wild meats. In the field, the animals are handled the same way as rabbits. At home, the animal should be skinned just before cooking. There is never any need for soaking, and it takes a mighty old squirrel to require parboiling.

There are dozens of wonderful ways to prepare squirrel for the table. Make a search for recipes such as these:

Broiled, butter-basted; baked, sausage-stuffed; Southern-style stew with vegetables; braised, with fruit; brunswick stew; jambalaya; baked in onion-cream sauce; roasted, with sherry-grape sauce; baked, with apples and rutabagas; batter-fried, with milk gravy; squirrel chowder; sautéed, with white wine and rosemary.

Whatever small game the family hunter bags can serve as meat on the table for many a hearty, delicious meal.

BIG GAME

When the hunter approaches the big-game animal that he has dropped, the main object of his trip into the wilds has been attained: before him are enough steaks, chops, roasts, stew meat, ground meat, and other cuts to provide the average family with its main dishes for a great many meals. Getting the meat out of the woods in perfect shape and into a freezing locker or refrigerator is the next consideration, and it's important that the hunter's solution to the problem allows none of that good meat to go to waste.

Accurate shooting means that the animal the hunter has brought down can be reached immediately; this is important to both the tenderness and the flavor of the meat. Deer, moose, caribou, elk, antelope, bear, mountain sheep and goat, and boar are the big-game animals taken in this country —some prevalent enough so that a good hunter may bag many in his hunting lifetime, some so few in numbers or situated in areas so remote that a hunter may never so much as lay eyes on the animal.

Deer. A deer should be bled and gutted as soon as possible after it is taken to ensure optimum tenderness and flavor. Wipe out the abdominal cavity with moss or leaves—don't use water—and prop it open with a stick to allow for circulation of air. As soon as they are cleaned and cooled, the heart and liver are ready for cooking and are usually welcome meat to be prepared and eaten in camp.

The dressed deer must somehow be transported to the highway or to the camp. The best method is dragging (all hunters should be supplied with rope), particularly if the terrain is snow-covered. When the deer reaches the destination, it should again be hung immediately, propped open, so that the cooling process can continue.

Much meat spoilage occurs while the carcass is en route home from the hunting area. No one in his right mind would walk into a meat market, buy a large and expensive roast, strap it unwrapped to a fender of his car, drive a hundred miles or more, subjecting it to heat and dirt, and then expect to eat the meat.

A hunter should carry a certain amount of equipment with him. Besides a knife and a rope, he should have a saw, a hatchet or ax, and a quantity of clean cheesecloth to wrap the meat in after it has been skinned and quartered. Cheesecloth not only protects the meat from dust and grime, but also from insects if the weather is warm enough so that they are still about.

Once the meat is wrapped, it should be packed securely in the hunter's car in such a way that air can circulate around it but it will not be subjected to dust from the open road. In warm weather, the meat should not be placed in a car trunk with the lid closed—prop the lid ajar and secure it, so that air can get in. Cautionary note: Be aware of state laws where you hunt—some require that evidence of the sex of the animal must not be destroyed, and/or that carcasses must be kept whole.

When you have the deer home, take it to a professional for butchering, or butcher it yourself if you have the skill and the proper tools. The loin yields roasts and steaks. Chuck and rump are good for pot-roasting, or can be cut up for stew meat, or ground. The round yields good steaks if the animal is young and tender enough, or can be used for swiss or spanish steaks (braised) or, again, ground. If the leg is small, it can be roasted in one piece, like a leg of lamb; larger legs can be divided into two roasts, the leg and the haunch. The neck, with tendons removed, makes an excellent roast. Meat from the shank, flank, and spareribs can be cubed for soups and stews, or ground.

By convention, the animal is deer until it is butchered into edible cuts; at that point it is called venison. Some people complain of the strong flavor and/or odor of venison before or after it is cooked, an excessively gamey taste or smell that they find objectionable. These conditions are under the control of the hunter who takes the game and brings it home. If the animal is properly treated in the field and during transportation, strong flavors and odors will not develop.

Venison is a rather dry meat, and is usually improved by the addition of suet, butter, or other fat during the cooking process. Roasts should be larded or barded. The characteristic flavor of venison, which some rejoice in and some are put off by, lies largely in the animal's fat. Cutting away most of the fat will remove the wild-game flavor.

Here are some ways to prepare venison:

Ragout, with bourbon and beer; roasted, buttermilk-basted; rump roast with onions; venison mincemeat; roasted, with red wine and juniper berries; port-marinated steaks; chicken-fried round steak; baked in sweet/sour sauce; stroganoff; venison sauerbraten; foil-roasted in burgundy, with polish sausage stuffing; braised chops; meat loaf; venison-stuffed cabbage; venison-potato sausage; broiled steaks; stewed, with vegetables; barbecued short ribs; Bohemian-style pickled, with cream gravy; steaks with Hawaiian sauce; hunter's pie with vegetables, flaky pastry.

And that barely scratches the surface of the methods of cooking venison so that the whole family will not only eat it, but enjoy it. A freezer filled with cuts of venison is a treasure house of great meals.

Moose, caribou, elk. Methods used for dressing and butchering deer also apply for moose, caribou, and elk, although these three larger animals may present more problems. Immediate and thorough bleeding, and gutting as rapidly as possible, are essential for meat of good flavor, texture, and tenderness. (A saw, useful in cutting up a deer, is essential with these larger animals.) The animal must be completely cooled without delay, handled so that air circulation is provided, and protected from dirt, water, and insects.

Meat from any of these three animals may be cooked in the same ways as venison. If the "wild" flavor and odor are objectionable, try marinating the meat in cultured buttermilk, which will both tenderize it and also remove a large part of the gamey taste and smell. Cover the meat completely with the buttermilk and refrigerate; steaks and chops should be marinated 4 to 5 hours, roasts 12 hours. Wipe off the excess buttermilk with absorbent paper or a damp cloth, and cook

273

as you wish. The meat will be tender, and have delicious, mild flavor.

Here are some of the ways with these game animals:

moose: Stuffed steak; braised steak with mushroom cream gravy; moose meat loaf; stuffed and rolled steak in red wine; moose chili con carne; swissed steak with bay and basil; stroganoff pie with biscuit topping; roasted, with apricots and prunes.

caribou: Collops in port wine and currant jelly sauce; braised chops with mushroom gravy; stew with winter vegetables; chops braised with parsnips; round steak with panned cabbage; pot roast with sauerkraut.

elk: Chops, braised in sherry gravy; strip steaks with beaujolais; elk sauerbraten; casseroled steak with scalloped potatoes; steak, broiled with mushrooms; roasted, with peppers and onions; stewed, with dried fruit.

Bear. This game appears on fewer tables than venison or any of the hoofed animals. A full-grown bear is an awesomely ponderous creature, but the effort of butchering it and bringing home the meat is well worth it. Mature bear is often too tough to be palatable, and should be served in a highly seasoned ragout or stew, or tenderized before cooking. The haunch or saddle of a young bear, however, takes very well to roasting.

The old hunter's precept, "How they taste depends on what they've been eating," applies in some degree to all wild game, but is particularly true of bear. Bear grease, however —unlike the fat of many game animals—is highly prized. Many hunters consider their winter store of supplies incomplete until they have bagged a bear and rendered the clear, sweet lard for cooking. (Folk medicine swears by bear grease smeared on the chest for a bronchial cough, but you needn't go that far.)

Ways to approach the cooking of bear include:

Broiled loin steaks au jus; stewed, with mushrooms, carrots, and onions; braised roast in mustard-tomato sauce; pot-roasted, in red wine; marinated rump chops; bear mincemeat; deviled steak; mulligan stew, with tomatoes; barbecued, with mustard-brown sugar baste; steak in orange/tomato juice; breaded chops with sherry.

Mountain sheep, mountain goat. Usually found only at high altitudes, a long way from civilization, these animals can pose a considerable problem. Packing the meat out is difficult, for the going is steep and the country rough. But the effort is worthwhile, for the meat is both delicious and unusual. The sheep is tender and has fine flavor; however, the goat meat is dark—virtually black—and strong, tougher than most game meats. It is an acquired taste.

Treatment in the field is the same as for deer.

At home, use any venison recipe for cooking either mountain sheep or mountain goat; the goat meat, however, will require both soaking overnight (vinegar fortified with cloves, cinnamon, mustard, salt, and pepper will do the trick) and parboiling. Pressure-cooking is a fine way to deal with mountain goat. Sheep, on the other hand, may be roasted as beef is, and served with its own thickened gravy.

Antelope. Relatively small animals—averaging about 80 pounds dressed weight—antelope are found in rolling country or wide open plains. Packing them back to camp is not as difficult as with some of the larger animals—a mountain sheep, for example, can weigh 300 pounds, and is taken in country where transporting the meat can be very wearing and time-consuming.

Bleeding and drawing antelope should be done in the same way as for deer, and butchering follows the same methods, too.

Antelope meat is slightly gamier than venison, but any venison recipe can be used. Or look for recipes such as these:

Braised steak with celery and onions; potted steak; roasted saddle au jus; charcoal-broiled steak; wine-marinated grilled chops; honey-baked, with sour cream gravy; hunter's stew with tomatoes and parmesan; pot-roasted, with vegetables; steak smothered in mushrooms.

Boar. This is wild pig, and the flavor is deliciously porklike. However, unless the boar is a young one, the meat will not be as tender as pork from the local butcher shop. For best results, use slow, moist-heat methods of cooking.

Properly prepared, boar is a great delicacy. A good game cookbook should supply you with recipes for dishes such as these:

Roasted saddle with yams and applesauce; spareribs with caraway-seed sauerkraut; pot-roasted shoulder, in cider; chops braised in milk, with onions; wild boar chow mein (leftovers); stuffed chops, with candied apples; curried, with pineapple chunks.

WHAT DO YOU SERVE WITH A BEAR?

What do you serve with any kind of game, for that matter? The answer lies in thinking back to those times when our ancestors' main source of meat was what they acquired by hunting. With your game dinner, serve country-style, down-home foods and you can't go wrong. What you can do is serve a hearty, satisfying meal that will delight the family and the guests you've invited to share the hunter's bounty.

Here are some ideas to help you plan game menus:

Vegetables. Green beans and peas, cooked together; sautéed mushrooms; succotash, made with fresh corn and shelly beans; corn in other ways—fresh corn custard, corn with peppers, sautéed corn, or oven- or campfire-roasted corn on the cob; brussels sprouts—even better with chestnuts; fried green tomatoes; fried parsnips; sweet/sour red cabbage with plump apple wedges; pan-glazed baby onions;

baked stuffed white onions; beet greens with a few tiny beets still attached to them; rutabagas and potatoes, mashed half-and-half; jerusalem artichokes. Those are only a few of the ways with vegetables that have a just-right flavor with game.

Breads. Buttermilk biscuits; anadama bread; beaten biscuits; any of the many varieties of corn bread, made with white or yellow meal; sally lunn; blueberry or cranberry or spice-nut muffins; orange bread, with nuts or plain; sweet-potato rolls; spicy pumpkin bread; sourdough bread or rolls —sourdough and game were made for one another. Bring on fresh comb honey or honey butter with these.

Side dishes. Cottage fried potatoes; scalloped potatoes— a topping of grated cheddar won't hurt a bit; potato pancakes or old-time mashed potato cakes; twice-baked potatoes with thin-sliced scallions in the stuffing; spoon bread made with stone-ground cornmeal; fried hasty pudding (cornmeal mush, refrigerated and sliced); rice cooked in broth, with mushrooms; brown rice cakes; wild rice, which has a special affinity for game of all sorts; hominy, white or golden, and hominy grits; homemade egg noodles; sweet potatoes or yams, mashed or sliced and glazed with brown sugar. With game, any of these will hit the spot.

Desserts. These, too, should be what kids call "old-timey" in kind and flavor. Try gingerbread—perhaps with a dollop of softened cream cheese on top; pound cake, butternut or hickory nut cake; those colonial standbys, Gooseberry Fool and Blueberry Slump; cranberry and pumpkin and sweet potato pies; deep-dish blueberry and blackberry and apple pies; mince pie with brandy hard sauce; Indian pudding, topped with a scoop of vanilla ice cream; persimmon pudding with foamy sauce; sponge cake with soft custard; floating island; syllabub. Any of these will give a good game dinner the right finishing touch.

The go-alongs and serve-withs. Exceedingly important to a successful game dinner is the just-right stuffing and/or sauce and/or relish to go with the meat or bird. Accompaniments that complement the main dish are needed in such cases, perhaps more than with any other sort of meal.

Fruit and game are excellent partners; spiced fruit, in particular, seems to round out the game dish perfectly. Vegetable relishes, too, are fine with game, and take the place of the salad that we are used to, but that our forefathers seldom ate. Almost any good general cookbook should afford recipes for game accompaniments such as these: poached cinnamon apples; candied cranberries; cranberry-orange-walnut relish; spiced prunes (at another meal, stuff these with cream cheese and almonds, serve as a salad); orange-glazed apples; savory jellies—port wine, parsley, marjoram, thyme, white wine with mint; pickled walnuts; gingered pears; fresh peach chutney; apple chutney, with walnuts and golden raisins; concord grape conserve; fresh corn relish; sweet red-and-green pepper relish; wilted cucumbers; fresh pickled cabbage; tomato-onion relish; jellied apricot relish; spiced crab apples; minted pears; pickled lemons; spicy cranberry conserve.

Good game sauces include the English favorite, bread sauce; orange sauce—there are both hot and cold varieties; madeira wine sauce; chestnut sauce, made with cream; wild grape sauce; the French sauces, robert and poivrade; mint sauce, made with wine vinegar; tart, light lemon sauce for light-meat game birds; hunter's sauce, made with mushrooms and game stock; brown game gravy with port wine and grated orange peel; cherry sauce with brandy, perfect with wild duck; mint-currant sauce; cumberland sauce, the classic accompaniment for venison; fluffy horseradish sauce for meats with an assertive flavor; celery sauce—particularly for partridge; sweet/sour mustard sauce; cider sauce; cream gravy with tart jelly and minced onion.

For game that can be stuffed—and all that can be, should be—there are stuffings in wide variety, most of them a bit higher in flavor than those we use for blander foods, such as chicken and turkey. All these are good: old-fashioned bread stuffing, well-seasoned with sage and thyme, or with celery and summer savory; mashed-potato stuffing, just right with goose; oyster stuffing; Southern-style corn bread stuffing with pecans; goose stuffing borrowed from Alsace, with chestnuts, dates, prunes, and almonds, and moistened with grand marnier; chestnut-apple stuffing; nut-rice stuffing with mushrooms; pumpernickel-apple stuffing for wild duck.

Smoking and smoke-cooking game. If you have never tasted smoked venison, wild turkey, wild duck, pheasant, or quail, you have a pleasant surprise in store. Smoking and smoke-cooking develop delicate and tantalizing flavors in the game you have taken.

There is nothing new about smoking game—the native Americans were doing it long before we came here. It is not difficult to do, and although it requires a certain amount of equipment, none of it is complicated or expensive.

If you would like to try your hand at smoking game, see the special feature, PUTTING FOOD BY, for instructions.

Freezing game. If you bag big game, or if you hunt often for small game and game birds, you will obviously have a surplus that cannot be consumed immediately. The answer is to freeze what you won't eat, putting by the basis for wonderful meals in the months to come—or for holiday gifts, if you feel like sharing.

Your aim should be to get the game, of whatever kind, from the field to the freezer in the shortest possible time. Birds to be frozen should be scrupulously clean—drawn and plucked or skinned—and wrapped individually, no matter how small, in heavy-duty foil or other moisture/vaporproof material. Package them separately so that they can be handled as single units, and as few or as many removed for use at one time as you wish.

Meat to be frozen should be cut into pieces of convenient size for a meal or two. Stew meat should be cut up before you freeze it, and meat for grinding should be ground; if it is to be used as patties or burgers, they should be shaped before freezing and separated from one another by sheets of plastic film. If several pieces—chops, for example—are to be packaged together, sheets of plastic film should be placed between the cut surfaces—otherwise the pieces will freeze into a solid block difficult to separate unless completely thawed. Wrap the package in moisture/vaporproof wrap.

In all cases, make certain to use wrapping materials designed for freezer use. Regular foil is not heavy enough, nor is butcher paper; the wrapping must form a barrier for moisture and vapor or the frozen food will not hold up well.

Label and date each package. If you cache more than one bag in the freezer, plan on abiding by the old "first in, first out" rule, using the oldest packages first. Besides labeling and dating individual packages, keep a freezer inventory. It's difficult to remember exactly what's still in the freezer and what has been used, and it wastes freezer energy to fumble through a bunch of look-alike packages searching for something no longer there. Enter each item on the inventory as you put it in the freezer, cross it off as you take it out.

Meat frozen and maintained at 0°F. or colder will lose none of its fine qualities over a period of 6 to 12 months. Plan on using stew meat within 9 months, ground meat and the variety meats—heart, liver—within 6 months.

Frozen game can be cooked from the solidly frozen state, but for uniform cooking, meat should be at least two-thirds thawed. You can't, of course, stuff a frozen bird. In thawing, the rule is the slower the better. In the refrigerator, thawing will take about 5 hours per pound. Do not thaw at room temperature. Stew meat can be put on to cook solidly frozen, unless you intend to brown it. Burgers and patties can always be cooked from the frozen state. To hasten thawing of large cuts of meat, put the package, still wrapped, under running cold—never warm—water.

Game, large or small, and game birds can provide many enjoyable meals if properly cared for. And if it was worth going after, it's worth handling correctly and sensibly.

Preparing game for shipment. Game taken far from home must be shipped—a perfectly safe procedure if done properly.

There is rarely any certainty, even in the coldest season, that game being shipped for any distance will not encounter a period during which it will be subject to temperatures high enough to cause spoilage. For that reason, game should be shipped frozen whenever possible, and every precaution should be taken to protect the meat against its worse enemy, heat.

Birds should always be cleaned before shipment. When they are to be shipped in dry ice, they should also be plucked or skinned before freezing. If shipped with ordinary ice, the feathers should be left on, or each bird individually enclosed in moistureproof wrapping. Birds should never be frozen with the feathers on.

When the game is frozen and separately wrapped, it can be packed in a carton with dry ice, then wrapped with a moistureproof outer covering and sealed completely. The carton containing the game and the dry ice should be surrounded by a layer of crumpled newspaper or other insulating material and placed in a slightly larger carton to protect it from the heat.

The average loss of dry ice through evaporation during shipment is about 20 percent in each 24 hours, and allowance for such loss should be made when ordering it for shipping. If possible, game should be frozen before packing in dry ice—unfrozen game will freeze quickly, but will use up a good deal of the dry ice, leaving less for the job of keeping the meat frozen on its journey. It is safer to be generous than skimpy—a little left over at the end of the trip is far better than having the ice give out en route and subject the meat to heat damage. A 50-pound block of dry ice in a 100-pound carton will provide package allowance for more than 40 pounds of meat. To ship frozen game safely, allow 25 pounds of dry ice for each 75 pounds of meat to maintain the frozen state for 5 days or longer.

Check state laws well in advance of a hunting trip to be sure you fulfill all necessary conditions when you ship your game. All game should be plainly labeled. When you ship migratory birds, the number and species must be marked plainly on the outside of the package, together with the shipper's name and his hunting license number.

Large and small game, game birds, and waterfowl can provide many enjoyable meals if properly cared for and handled every step of the way from field to home. Half the fun is in the hunting, but the other half is in the eating—don't rob yourself of that great second half.

GARBAGE DISPOSALS: see special feature: YOU CAN'T WORK WITHOUT TOOLS

GARBANZOS: see BEANS

GARDENS: see special feature: THE GROW-IT-YOURSELF BOOM

GARLIC

There are those who, while wolfing their way through your well-garlicked salad, will congratulate you on not using garlic in it. Their stomachs, they maintain, simply can't take garlic. Never could. Pass the salad, please.

Among a number of people, the myth has grown that garlic is somehow indelicate, rather vulgar, not the sort of thing that nice people would indulge in or their nice digestive systems can tolerate. Garlic and garlic eaters have been the butt of a great many jokes of the "deflect the blast" variety, the cause of many head-shakings, sighs, and casting of eyes heavenward.

Mistaken, misled, these poor souls. In the first place, they have been eating garlic all this time without knowing it. Well used, by a cook who has sense enough to know when to stop, garlic is the subtle what-is-it seasoning in dozens of dishes that would be bland to the point of blah without it.

Garlic down the ages. Like other members of the onion family—indeed, like almost all foods not "invented" by selective breeding and hybridizing—garlic once grew wild. But it was soon cultivated. Herodotus, the Greek historian, says that the builders of the great pyramid at Giza—about 2900 B.C.—lived mainly on garlic and onions, which were grown in the lush Egyptian bottomlands seasonally flooded by the Nile. But the pungent bulb had its detractors even in those days. The peoples of ancient India so disliked garlic that it was forbidden in many communities. Those who wished to eat it were required to go outside the town when they did so. But the Chinese, who have been great cooks and cooking innovators for thousands of years, were using garlic as their chief seasoning at least as early as 250 B.C.

On the other hand, ancient Greeks used some garlic, but not much, and Greek cooks today emulate them. Early Roman nobles fed garlic to their workmen to make them strong and their soldiers to make them courageous, but did not eat it themselves. In fact, one of the first sumptuary laws (designed to regulate personal habits on moral or religious grounds) passed by the Roman Senate forbade citizens who had recently eaten garlic to enter the temple of Cybele, the goddess of nature. Later Romans took more kindly to the flavorful bulb, but even today most of Italy, except Sicily and Calabria, uses garlic sparingly.

Cooking with garlic. That is exactly how garlic should be used—sparingly—unless the food it seasons is to be cooked for a lengthy period. Long, slow cooking tames and softens and smooths garlic's assertive flavor and its odor as well. Discretion and moderation produce the foods that guests consume with relish while pausing between mouthfuls to congratulate you on not spoiling your dishes with so vulgar a seasoning.

salads: We all know the trick of rubbing the salad bowl with the cut side of a clove of garlic, leaving behind only the subtle essence. If you wish a somewhat stronger flavor, add a peeled and split clove (or two) to a bottle of red wine vinegar. Let it stay there for 24 hours and then remove, leaving behind a vinegar delightfully but not too strongly flavored. Or you can give oil (preferably olive oil, with which garlic long ago struck up a lasting friendship) the same 24-hour treatment.

If you wish a rather stronger garlic flavor, add a few drops of garlic juice to your oil-and-vinegar dressing when you make it. But never add the garlic itself, no matter how finely minced, to a salad of any kind. It's raw garlic that has given the seasoning its bad reputation.

sauces: In a sauce that is going to simmer for a long time, you can use garlic freely, minced or slivered or crushed, for fine flavor. In a sauce less lengthily cooked, crush the garlic (in a garlic press, or with the back of a spoon), or use garlic juice. Or spear a—peeled, of course—bulb or two with a food pick, let it cook in the sauce, then scoop it out before serving. (The food pick helps you locate it.) Or stick a garlic clove on the tines of a fork and use the fork to stir the sauce as it cooks.

But there are some sauces that depend on garlic as their reason for being. How about the exceedingly garlicky butter we use on snails? How about aioli, that splendid mayonnaise-like sauce, redolent of garlic, served with hot or cold fish, or with vegetables or eggs, or as a dip for raw vegetables?

main dishes, too: Leg of lamb is very good roasted plain, but it is infinitely superior if, before you put it in the oven, you cut a number of little slits in the leg and into each stuff a sliver of garlic. Vary this by putting a very tiny piece of lemon peel in each slit as well. Try the same thing with a roast or a pot roast of beef.

If you have never enjoyed Forty-Garlic Chicken, promise yourself—and guests, it's a fine conversation piece—this exceptional dish very soon. You need a large, shallow casserole dish with a well-fitting cover. To serve 8, pour 1 cup of melted butter into the casserole. Add 1 cup thinly sliced celery, ¼ cup snipped parsley, ½ teaspoon dried tarragon. Add 2 quartered broiler-fryers, and turn them in the seasoned butter until they are well coated with it. Sprinkle with salt and white pepper. Add 40 peeled cloves of garlic, distributing them about the dish. Cover securely and bake at 375°F. for 1½ hours without removing the cover. Have ready cooked green noodles. Toss the noodles with the soft, cooked garlic and the butter and chicken juices remaining in the casserole, and serve with the chicken.

When next you make a baked chicken liver pâté, butter the baking pan well, then rub the buttered surfaces with a cut clove of garlic for heavenly flavor.

To provide your guests with a sensational appetizer, place 25 peeled cloves of garlic in a heavy skillet just large enough to accommodate them nicely. Sprinkle with salt and crush lightly with the back of a spoon. (Salt softens garlic almost at once, making it easy to crush—a good trick to remember when making other dishes, too.) Add olive oil to a depth of about ⅛ inch. Cook over the lowest possible heat until the garlic is very soft, adding more oil if necessary and making certain that the garlic does not brown. Spread on small squares of pumpernickel.

Garlic bread, particularly when served with cookout steaks, has become such a tradition that the steaks feel undressed without it. But there is another sort of garlic bread, focaccia, that is truly superb, and worth the very small effort it takes to make it, particularly when you use a biscuit-mix shortcut. Into a small pan, put ⅓ cup finely chopped garlic and 6 tablespoons olive oil; cook over low heat until the garlic is soft—do not brown. Strain, reserving the garlic and the oil separately. Combine 3 cups buttermilk biscuit mix, the cooked reserved garlic, and 1 cup milk; mix to make a soft dough. Pour about ⅓ of the reserved garlic oil into a 9- × 13-inch baking pan, spreading it over the bottom. Place biscuit dough in the pan and pat it out into an even layer. Poke holes in the dough with your finger at about 1½-inch intervals. Pour remaining garlic oil over the dough and spread evenly to cover the entire surface. Sprinkle with ¼ cup grated parmesan. Bake at 400°F. until nicely browned, about 25 minutes. Cut into finger shapes; serve hot.

The several forms. Fresh garlic (it is dried, not actually fresh) is available all year around, and will keep well in your kitchen. In fact, you can buy a string of bulbs, the dried stems braided together, to hang up as a useful decoration. Store garlic where air circulates, where it won't become damp.

Garlic salt, powder, and juice are also available, these in the spices and seasonings section of any market. Of the three, garlic salt is not recommended—much better to use garlic powder, if you wish the seasoning in a dry form, and control the quantity of salt in any dish yourself. Garlic juice, in small bottles, is handy for anything in which you wish the flavor but not the garlic itself. Like any other herb, spice, or seasoning, don't expect either garlic powder or juice to keep fresh-flavored for a long period of time. See HERBS AND SAVORY SEASONINGS.

A garlic press is a gadget that reduces a clove or two of garlic to a pulp. You can use either the juice expressed by the press, or the pulped garlic. Wash the little press immediately after each use; it is very difficult to get clean if the remains of the garlic are allowed to dry in it.

Outside the kitchen. If it happens that you are bothered by vampires, plagued by werewolves, or reduced to a bundle of nerves by a witch giving you the evil eye, wear a little bag of garlic cloves around your neck. Specialists in the black arts insist that this will do the trick, successfully warding off any or all of these creatures. (And, probably, your family and friends as well, in case you don't like them, either.)

The medicinal and antiseptic qualities of garlic have long had their place in folk medicine, and they seem to be—in some cases, at least—more than myth. Applied externally, garlic will keep biting and stinging insects away, or heal the bites if you haven't resorted to garlic soon enough. Taken internally, so its proponents claim, garlic will relieve bronchial congestion, lower blood pressure, rid the intestines of parasites, and reduce cholesterol levels in the blood. (The latter claim, at least, seems to be true. A study was carried out at Michigan State University, in which patients with high blood cholesterol were fed the equivalent of two ounces of garlic after each meal; their cholesterol levels were lowered in each case.)

Some farmers and gardeners swear by garlic as a natural pesticide. Organic gardeners claim that planting alternate rows of garlic and other vegetables keeps the insect population under control. Peach orchardists say that garlic planted under their trees will protect them from peach borers. Garlic supposedly increases the flow of milk in lactating animals—but it must be administered immediately after milking, or the milk will taste of garlic.

The taste and the smell. Garlic on the breath, after indulging in a heavily garlicked dish, can be removed (or covered) by chewing a sprig of parsley. It takes away the lingering taste, too, if you prefer the taste of parsley to the one you were already burdened with.

Garlic on the hands can be persistent if not tended to promptly and effectively. Rinse your hands in cold water. Rub with a piece of cut lemon; sprinkle with salt, then wash again in cold water. Now wash with soap and warm water.

Pungent and flavorful, enough garlic can make a dish; too much, even for the most dedicated garlic lovers, can ruin it. Use it well and wisely.

GARNISHING

By convention, one garnishes savory foods—appetizers, soups, main dishes, and so on—and decorates sweet ones —desserts of many kinds. In practice, many of us seldom extend ourselves further in the garnishing department than tucking a few sprigs of parsley or watercress here and there, accompanying a serving of fish or a cut of melon with a lemon wedge, or shoving a sprig of mint into the iced tea glass.

Those tokens are certainly not the end, hardly the beginning, of garnishing. There are many directions to go in to make the good food we serve just a little better, a little prettier, when we bring it to the table.

Garnishes are meant chiefly to be pleasing to the eyes, but they should be pleasing to the palate as well, because this is the cardinal rule of successful garnishing: never use anything that can't be eaten—'tain't cricket. Inedible garnishes have no more right on a plate of food than plastic flowers have as a centerpiece. Less, perhaps. An unwary diner might nibble an inedible garnish, but is very unlikely to browse on the bouquet that occupies the center of the table.

More, not only should garnishes be edible, they should be temptingly delicious, add something to the dish rather than just sit there as part of the scenery, to be pushed aside as the diner works his way around the plate. However, appealing as it may be, a garnish should never overpower the flavor of the food. Nor should it be relied upon to make a poor dish seem better than it is. It won't. What it will do is call attention, by contrast, to the food's deficiencies.

Garnishing—decorating, too—is a craft, one that gives pleasure and satisfaction to the doer and the beholder alike.

Marching through the meal. Almost everything we eat is the better—in looks, at least, and most often in flavor, too—for a bit of garnishing. But that's not to say that it should be overdone. Discretion and moderation, as in all things, are virtues in this area as well. Sauce in quantity that requires a dam to hold it in check, an avalanche of chives, a landslide of chopped pickles, a jungle of dill—all these are excesses to be avoided.

But a little something pretty here, a little something tasty there—that is what garnishing is all about. A morsel to titillate the appetite and ravish the eye, judiciously applied throughout the meal, moves garnishing into the field of an art and ups the knowing garnisher to the status of artist.

appetizers: Here, more than anywhere else, the garnish can well be an intrinsic part of the dish itself, added not only for its appeal but also because it complements and reinforces the flavors.

The field is wide open. For simple canapés, such as good cheese on a good cracker, there are all sorts of possibilities that will not only look attractive but measurably improve the savory mouthful. A rolled anchovy with a caper at its heart, a tiny pickle sliced into a fan shape, a neatly arranged heap of tiny red onion rings, a smoked oyster or clam, even something so simple as three overlapping slices of stuffed olive—any of these makes a cheese-topped cracker much more delicious and, incidentally, much better to look at.

Something stuffed makes a pretty and savory appetizer. There are dozens of things waiting to be stuffed, from ribs of celery and blades of endive through cherry tomatoes and cooked baby beets and mushroom caps to dill pickles and cucumbers. Make the filling flavorful—half-and-half bleu and cream cheese, for instance—and tuck a little pickled onion on the top for the final fillip. Refrigerate big items like pickles and cucumbers, then slice just before serving.

A cold pâté is much dressier if you have set small, decorative vegetable shapes in aspic on the bottom of the mold. A baked pâté with a crust is handsomer if you cut leaf shapes of leftover pastry, set them on the top, and glaze the whole thing with an egg wash before baking.

If your dip is delicious but pale, sprinkle it with something colorful—minced chives or parsley or watercress, chopped nuts, thinly sliced scallions, even, in a pinch, paprika. If you make a cheese ball or cheese log, roll in any one of those garnishes.

By now, you must get the idea. Dress up whatever you choose to serve as an appetizer, and it will be the better for the moment's thought and time you devote to it.

soups: Almost anything that won't sink to the bottom is fine as a garnish to break up the plain, flat surface of soup. Drift chives on cold soups, or perk them up with avocado slices or a dollop of cream—whipped sweet or sour—and a sprinkle of snipped parsley or a few chopped nuts. Croutons decorate hot or cold soup as well as adding crunchy texture.

On black bean soup or on consommé, float a thin lemon slice. Or sprinkle on cheese or sieved hard-cooked egg or snipped fresh dill or basil or thyme. Or shape thin raw vegetable slices with miniature cookie or canapé cutters to float on soup. Popcorn sits up perkily on a soup's surface. So does a whole pretzel. So do chinese noodles. So do canned french-fried onions.

main dishes: Instead of serving the potatoes plain, serve them fancily and fancifully; then they are not only part of the meal, but a garnish for the meat or fish or poultry as well. Shredded potato baskets, deep-fried, serve that purpose. So do golden potatoes duchesse, piped into a border through a pastry tube, and lightly browned under the broiler.

When you're preparing vegetables, cut them into uniform shapes and sizes, using a ball cutter or a french-fry cutter with a wavy blade, or trim by hand with a small, sharp knife into neat cubes or rectangles or large olive shapes. (It's not wasteful; make soups of the trimmings.) Flute the tops of mushrooms to make a handsome garnish. Buy artichoke bottoms in cans or jars and fill them with something cold—whole shrimp or crab salad—to garnish a cold dish, or heat and fill with something hot—baby peas, onion purée—to serve with a hot entrée. Hollow out lemon halves to hold mayonnaise or hollandaise, orange halves to hold mashed sweet potatoes or cranberry-orange relish, small cooked beets to hold horseradish sauce, green peppers to hold coleslaw.

Instead of on a slice of toast, serve creamed or sauced mixtures in patty shells or in croustades (see BREADS), or in a ring of parslied or saffron rice. Briefly sautéed fruit—halved bananas, rings of apple or pineapple—or spiced or pickled or brandied fruit—such as crab apples, peaches, or pears—make delightful and flavorful garnishes for many kinds of main dishes. Vegetables such as beets, carrots, onions, and tomatoes can be cut into a variety of handsome shapes—a good cookbook or a specialty garnishing/decorating book will tell you (and show you) how. And it will lead you to dozens of other appealing ways to add pretty, edible garnishes to your main dishes.

sandwiches, salads: Almost anything will cheer up an individual serving of salad or a sandwich—a handful of potato or corn chips or shoestring potatoes, a couple of olives, a pickle or two. But you can do better. Small vegetable shapes or small stuffed vegetables add appeal and good taste. A deviled egg is pretty, and adds substance to the meal. Marinated vegetables, such as asparagus or artichokes vinaigrette, mushrooms à la grecque, or wilted cucumbers make a fine addition to a salad or sandwich plate. Or sandwich halves of pitted cherries or walnuts with a half-and-half mixture of bleu and cream cheese for a delectable garnish. Jel-

279

lied relishes and herb-and-wine jellies make unusual and tasty garnishes, too.

As for a tossed green salad, there are literally dozens of additions that not only garnish it but improve it immeasurably. Among them are cubes or slivers of cheese, broken pretzel sticks, sliced raw mushrooms, sliced or shredded red or white radishes, coarsely crumbled corn or potato chips, crumbled crisp bacon, chinese noodles, rings of sweet onion, nuts—plain, salted, or toasted—sliced water chestnuts, canned french-fried onions, hard-cooked egg slices, anchovies, bamboo shoots, and many more.

Whatever you serve, for the simplest of meals or the most elegant, garnish it attractively—and deliciously—to delight the eyes and the taste buds of family and guests. For dessert ideas, see DECORATING.

GAZPACHO

A tomato-based soup of Spanish origin, gazpacho has been with us for a long time—and with the Spaniards even longer—but it is only within the past ten years that it has become well known and widely appreciated in this country.

Made with tomato juice or, better, puréed fresh tomatoes, gazpacho is flavored with onions, celery, and garlic, and often smoothed and mellowed with the addition of a little olive oil, and/or sharpened with wine or wine vinegar. The soup can be served hot, but it is almost always offered well chilled—a very refreshing part of the meal in hot weather. The usual method of making is to combine rather finely chopped vegetables with tomato juice, seasonings, and olive oil, and to allow the mixture to chill for several hours, during which the flavors will meld. This is often served over an ice cube or two in the soup dish.

A somewhat more attractive service, as well as a better-flavored soup, is achieved by puréeing peeled tomatoes, olive oil, red wine vinegar, celery, garlic, onion, and green pepper with salt and freshly ground pepper in the blender; this results in a liquid with more·flavor and more body. Serve it in bowls or flat soup plates, accompanied by dishes of snipped parsley, thinly sliced green onions, crisp croutons, chopped celery, slivers of green pepper, and chopped cucumber, which each diner adds to his plate of soup in any combination and quantity he desires. Not strictly authentic, but good, are additions such as thin slices of raw cauliflower, mushrooms, and zucchini, and grated cheddar or parmesan cheese. You can also offer wedges of lemon to sharpen the soup flavor for those who wish it, and hot pepper sauce to "heat" it.

GEFILTE FISH

These round or egg-shaped fish balls—they are really quenelles—are one of the many delightful contributions of Jewish cuisine to our American melting pot of good foods. Made with boned pike, carp, or whitefish, sometimes a combina-

tion, they are bound with egg and matzo meal, nicely seasoned, and poached in fish stock. Served cold on lettuce with some of the fish stock, which jellies as it chills, gefilte fish makes a delightful summer luncheon dish, or an appetizer at any season. Horseradish is the usual accompaniment, along with vegetable relishes such as sweet/sour carrots and pickled beets.

GELATIN

Powdered gelatin, the kind we use in our kitchens today, is one of many American success stories.

Until virtually the end of the nineteenth century, when the home cook wanted to make an aspic, a jellied soup or salad or dessert, she was faced with two choices, either one a task of considerable difficulty. She could boil calf's feet and veal knuckles at length to extract the gelatinous material in them, then clarify the mixture before it was ready for use. Or she could resort to a sheet of isinglass—made from the air bladders of fish—or collagee, a foul-smelling derivative of seaweed, soak it until it softened, and go on from there. It is no wonder that gelatin dishes had no great popularity in those days.

In the 1840s, Peter Cooper—an inventor of considerable stature, to whom we owe a great debt for dozens of things that make our lives easier—put together a mixture of gelatin, sugar, and artificial fruit flavors. Apparently the world wasn't ready. This kind of flavored gelatin was not embraced by the American housewife until half a century later. In the 1890s, Charles Knox, a New York salesman, watching his wife struggle to make calf's-foot jelly, remembered hearing about powdered gelatin. He packaged it, sold it door-to-door with a demonstration of its easy use thrown in with each sale, and revolutionized the use of gelatin in our kitchens.

280

Those two types of gelatin are the ones familiar to us today: unflavored, in envelopes that hold ¼ ounce (about 1 tablespoon) and will gel two cups of liquid; sweetened and flavored, in 3- and 6-ounce packages, to gel 2 or 4 cups of liquid.

Commercial edible gelatin in today's granular form is made from animal bones and connective tissue. The unflavored variety, pure protein, is easily digestible. It contains seven essential amino acids, but is not a complete protein. (See special feature: NUTRITION NOTEBOOK.) Useful as a diet supplement (it strengthens brittle fingernails), it may be mixed into a drink with orange juice. Each envelope furnishes only 25 calories.

GELATIN COOKERY KNOW-HOW

One of the pleasant things about dishes made with gelatin is that they can be prepared in advance. Indeed, they must be, because it is refrigeration for a period of hours that sets the gelatin and readies the dish for serving.

Ahead-of-time variety. All sorts of dishes, for any course of the meal, can be gelatin-based—unusual appetizers, soft-gelled soups, hearty whole-meal salads and various other main dishes, side-dish salads of fruits or vegetables, inventive relishes, and a wide world of delightful desserts.

Although the sweetened and flavored fruit gelatins produce many delicious dishes, an inventive home cook can find a much wider variety of uses for the unflavored kind. It can be flavored as you like, sweetened or not as you choose, made into creative dishes using fresh, canned, or frozen fruits and vegetables; meats, poultry, and fish (gelled dishes are great for the undetectable use of leftovers); fresh eggs and milk and cream—whatever you like, to make a large assortment of dishes.

Unflavored gelatin basics. There are several ways, all of them simple and easy to learn, to work with unflavored gelatin. First, there are two basic gels, one sweetened to use as a base for desserts, the other unsweetened to use as a base for main dishes, salads, soups—all the rest of the menu.

basic unsweetened gel: In a bowl, soften 1 envelope unflavored gelatin in ½ cup cold liquid (water, broth, or juice). Heat to boiling 1½ cups liquid; pour over softened gelatin and stir until dissolved. Refrigerate.

If you are adding another liquid—vinegar or lemon juice, say, for a salad—about 2 tablespoons should be stirred in after the gelatin is dissolved; if the dish is to be molded, reduce the cold liquid in which the gelatin is softened to ¼ cup.

basic sweetened gel: In a bowl, combine 1 envelope unflavored gelatin with 2 to 4 tablespoons sugar. Heat to boiling 2 cups liquid (fruit juice or fruit drink or water); pour over softened gelatin and stir until dissolved. Refrigerate.

If the mixture is to be molded, reduce liquid to 1¾ cups.

cautionary note: There is an enzyme in fresh pineapple that prevents gelatin mixtures from gelling. Do not use fresh or frozen pineapple juice, or pieces of the fruit, in a gelatin mixture without first cooking (boil for 4 minutes). Canned pineapple and juice may be used as they come from the can—their processing has tamed the enzyme.

basic add-to ideas: To either of the basic gels above, you can add about 1½ cups of cut-up food—cooked meat, poultry, or fish, raw or cooked vegetables or fruits, or combinations such as nuts and fruit, marshmallows and fruit, and so on. Refrigerate the basic gel until it is the consistency of unbeaten egg white; fold in the cut-up food; return mixture to the refrigerator until it is firm.

What goes with what? As a starting point for inventing your own gelatin dishes, here are some of the good-flavor combinations. But these are only a jumping-off point—you'll think of others, prompted by the preferences of your family and, often, by the leftovers in your refrigerator, begging to be used up in some way that won't bring cries of "That *again?*"

liquids: Fresh, frozen, or canned fruit juices, alone or in combinations. Tomato and other vegetable juices, alone or in combinations. Beef, chicken, veal, or vegetable broths, or vegetable cooking liquids, or packing liquids from canned vegetables. Fruit punches, nectars, and ades.

fruit: Fresh, frozen, or canned peaches, plums, pears, apricots, grapes, cherries. All varieties of berries and melons. Canned pineapple and fruit cocktail. (When you use canned fruits, drain them well—use the juices in the basic gelatin mixture, then fold in the solids later.)

raw vegetables: Finely shredded cabbage (green or red), spinach, carrots. Chopped celery, green pepper, cucumber, cauliflower. Sliced green onions or radishes.

cooked vegetables: Canned, frozen, or fresh cooked cut green or wax beans, corn, asparagus, lima beans, sliced carrots, peas, kidney beans, chick-peas (garbanzos).

meat, poultry, fish, shellfish: Diced cooked chicken, ham, tongue, pork, veal, beef. Flaked cooked fish of any kind. Flaked canned tuna or salmon. Flaked crabmeat. Diced shrimp or lobster, or whole tiny shrimp.

And that's not the end—only the beginning.

Some simple salad ideas. Combine clear gel (made with water or vegetable cooking liquid and lemon juice or vinegar) with cabbage, carrots, green onions, radishes. Combine tomato juice gel with tuna or shrimp, adding cucumber, green onions, sliced stuffed or ripe olives. Combine beef broth gel with ham or beef, adding lima beans, cauliflower (raw or cooked), radishes, green pepper. Combine chicken broth gel with veal or chicken, adding celery, pimiento, onion. Combine vegetable broth gel, spiked with lemon juice, with shrimp, lobster, or crab, adding celery, sliced green onions, and chopped, peeled, and seeded cucumber.

Some simple dessert ideas. Combine orange juice gel with peaches and strawberries. Combine lemon gel (drained fruit juices, plus lemon) with fruit cocktail. Combine cranberry juice gel with oranges and walnuts. Combine fruit punch gel with pears and grapes. Combine apricot nectar gel with melon balls and blueberries. Combine raspberry gel (drained frozen raspberry juice plus orange juice) with the raspberries and miniature marshmallows. Serve any of these with whipped cream or topping, or custard sauce.

Gelatin know-how. Recipes based on gelatin sometimes give directions that are puzzling to home cooks, especially beginners. Here's what the gelatin recipe terms mean.

"stir until gelatin is completely dissolved": Use a rubber spatula, stirring constantly and scraping the sides and bottom of the bowl or pan as you stir. Make sure all gelatin granules have dissolved before you go on to the next step. If the gelatin is not completely dissolved, the dish will not gel properly. Stir well, but not so vigorously that you splash.

"chill until mixture is the consistency of unbeaten egg whites": This is rather vague, but it describes the proper consistency perfectly. "Until the mixture is the consistency of honey" also does it pretty well. Chilling times vary with the temperature of individual refrigerators, so it's impossible to set a time when this condition will occur—however, it's usually between 20 and 25 minutes. Why not just skip this step, add the remaining ingredients, and chill the whole smagula until it's firm? Because then the added ingredients would not be distributed throughout the mixture, but would sink to the bottom. Chilling to the consistency of unbeaten egg whites ensures the even distribution of the solid ingredients—vegetables, fruit, meat, or whatever you add.

"chill until mixture mounds slightly when dropped from a spoon": This direction is most often given when beaten egg whites or whipped cream are to be incorporated into the gelatin mixture, in such dishes as chiffons or bavarians. To test, follow the directions—spoon up a little of the mixture and slide it off the spoon, back into the bowl. It should make a little, very soft mound, rather than just streaming off the spoon.

"fold in": Gently is the word. Using a rubber spatula, cut down into the mixture in the center of the bowl; turn the spatula flat, sweep gently across the bottom, and bring the spatula up to the surface of the mixture near the edge of the bowl closest to you. Give the bowl a quarter turn and repeat; continue to repeat until the gelatin mixture and the other ingredient are well—but lightly—blended. Whipped cream and beaten egg white need particularly gentle treatment, or you will lose some of the air trapped in the beaten mixture and the volume of the finished dish will not be as great, the texture not as fluffy as you'd like them to be.

"chill until firm": You know what firm is—but how long does it take? As with everything else in life, this varies—it depends on the quantity of the mixture, the ingredients, and the temperature of your refrigerator. Individual molds and shallow dishes such as pies will be firm in less than 3 hours. A big soufflé or other large gel may take 4 to 6 hours, or overnight. To be on the safe side, make a dish that will serve a large number the day before the party. Not only does this ensure a perfectly firmed product, but it also makes life easier for the cook on party day.

"turn into a mold or individual serving dishes": Molds lend flair to party tables, and make the dish more attractively inviting even for family meals. A fish-shaped mold of salmon mousse can be the hit of the buffet, both in looks and flavor. Tall molds of gelled salad or dessert are very handsome. Or use individual molds, or press cups or custard cups into service. Any kitchen bowl of pleasant shape will do very well. Try unusual containers, too—demitasse cups, brandy snifters, parfait glasses, shells of fruits or vegetables—oranges, tomatoes, grapefruit, green peppers—for mixtures that are not to be unmolded before serving.

"unmold to serve": This is, indeed, one more river to cross, but not nearly as iffy as it sounds. Dip the mold into warm—not hot—water to the depth of the gelatin mixture for about 5 seconds (keep an eye on the clock, or count as the kids do—one raccoon, two raccoons, and so on). Remove the mold from the water. Carefully loosen the mixture from the sides of the mold with the tip of a thin, sharp knife. Invert a serving dish on top of the mold. Hold mold and serving dish firmly together and turn both over. Shake gently until the gelatin slips from container to serving dish. What if it doesn't? You've probably been too cautious. Repeat the process as required.

"garnish, if desired": For desserts: whipped cream or topping, fresh cooked or candied fruit, custard sauce, mint or grape leaves, cookie crumbs, crushed hard candies, grated chocolate or chocolate curls, whole or chopped nuts. For salads and main dishes: salad greens, parsley or watercress sprigs, nasturtium or grape leaves, cucumber slices or fingers, tomato wedges or cherry tomatoes, carrot curls, lemon wedges, strips of pimiento, sliced olives. These are only suggestions—almost anything pretty and edible can be used as a garnish.

Gelatin, incorporated. As you've probably gathered, all sorts of foods or mixtures can be folded into partially stiffened gelatin that will change the texture or flavor or both. These include beaten egg whites, whipped cream, sour cream, softened cream cheese, softened flavored cheese spreads, mayonnaise, mayonnaise-type and other salad dressings. The results are chiffons, mousses, bavarians, soufflés, and dozens of other handsome and delicious dishes to add to your kitchen repertoire.

Flavored gelatins. Packaged fruit-flavored gelatin mixes are only about 15 percent gelatin. The remainder of the granulated mixture in the package is made up of sugar, flavorings, colorings, and acids. Basic preparation for these is to dissolve the mixture (3-ounce size) in 1 cup of boiling water, then stir in 1 cup of cold water. When the mixture is partially set, up to 2 cups of drained cut-up or chopped fruits or vegetables may be added—indeed, many of the suggestions for additions to unflavored gelatin mixtures hold good here, too. Sometimes fruit juice or a carbonated beverage are added in place of the cup of cold water. Fruit-flavored low-calorie gelatin mixes are also available; these substitute artificial sweeteners for sugar.

Any good cookbook will offer you many recipes using both unflavored and fruit-flavored gelatins, and the makers of both kinds have leaflets and cookbooks to introduce you to the many and varied uses of their products.

Some specials. One of the makers of unflavored gelatin has introduced two unusual uses for the product. The first is a snack food that, in some cases, combines both unflavored and fruit-flavored gelatins with other ingredients, and in other cases, the unflavored gelatin with sweet ingredients, such as juices and beverages, or savory ones, such as salad dressings or broths. In all cases, a considerable amount of gelatin is required, and the finished product—which may have many kinds of added ingredients—is very firm, and is served cut in squares or blocks. Although they are chilled in the making, these snacks remain firm at room temperature after they are finished. A low-calorie version, made with sugar-free carbonated beverages, makes a good snacking sweet for weight-loss dieters.

The second innovation is jams, jellies, and preserves made with unflavored gelatin. The advantage here is that not nearly as much sugar is required as with such products made the conventional way. Usual-method jams, jellies, and preserves have about 60 calories per tablespoon. The range for these new-method ones is 10 to 30 calories per tablespoon, and they may be made with a sugar substitute for a further calorie reduction. Most fruits are naturally sweet to a certain extent; the large amounts of sugar added to them to produce conventional jams, jellies, and preserves is to make them jell, not to sweeten them. Unflavored gelatin takes care of this, and so excess sugar is not required. These new-fangled spreads store well—short-term (up to 4 weeks) in the refrigerator, or long-term (up to 1 year) in the freezer. They must be stored in small jars with tight-fitting lids, but sealing with paraffin is not necessary. A wide variety of fruits—fresh or canned—and fruit juices can be used in these recipes.

GELLED FOODS: see GELATIN and JELLIED FOODS

GELS: see ADDITIVES AND PRESERVATIVES

GENOISE

This is a French adaptation of a cake originally Italian, made like a sponge cake—that is, by the foam method, leavened with air beaten into eggs—but with clarified butter folded into the batter for added richness.

Genoise is simple and easy to make, provided you follow directions, and provided you don't try to shortcut the time required for beating the eggs. Heating the eggs prior to beating encourages them to attain greater volume; they (and the sugar) are beaten up to 15 minutes, until the mixture triples in volume and has the appearance of whipped cream.

The basis of many handsome French cakes (gâteaux), genoise may be flavored with vanilla, or cocoa may substitute for a part of the flour to create a feathery chocolate version.

GHERKINS

A small and prickly variety of cucumber that is usually pickled—and, by extension, any small cucumber pickle. Most gherkins are grown in the southern United States, or in their native West Indies. The name for both pickles and cucumbers comes from an old Dutch word, *augurk.*

GIBLETS

Portions of the viscera of poultry—the heart, gizzard, and liver; the neck and wing tips are also counted in with the giblets by some butchers (and some cooks) but really are not.

Considered without prejudice, giblets are delicious. They are welcomed with pleasure when cooked, chopped, and included in the stuffing of the holiday bird. And how can you have the traditional giblet gravy without giblets? But try to serve some people a main dish of giblets, and you'll be told that they don't eat innards, thank you. Even many of those who enjoy chicken livers balk when the heart and gizzard are included. (If you added coxcombs, which are really a delicacy too, you'd have a rebellion or mass nausea on your hands.)

But a dish of braised giblets, cooked with celery and onion and a little thyme, served on toast points or over fluffy rice, is truly delicious. You can make an excellent sandwich spread of giblets, too. Chopped, they are flavorful in soups. And the southern dish that unfortunately suffers under the name "Dirty Rice" is a classic use of giblets.

Giblet gravy. To cook, put the gizzard, heart, neck, and wing tips in a pan; cover with water. Add a little salt, a few slices of onion, a few pieces of celery or celery leaves. Bring to a boil; turn down the heat and simmer 1 to 2 hours, until the gizzard is tender. Add the liver and simmer 5 to 10 minutes longer. Use the stock as the liquid in gravy. Chop the giblets and add to the gravy just before serving.

Waste-not/want-not item. If your family is discerning enough to enjoy a meal of giblets, you'll sometimes find them packaged at the chicken section of the supermarket meat department—happily low in price. An even less expensive dish comes from giblets that are a by-product of a number of chicken dinners, stockpiled in the freezer until you have sufficient for a meal. Or accumulate them to make an elegant, flavorful pâté, almost certain to be appreciated by one and all, including snobs who don't eat innards, provided you do not share your secret with them.

GIN

A colorless alcoholic beverage, made from rectified (twice distilled) spirits, flavored in many ways but most usually with juniper berries. Cereal grains are the base. See LIQUORS.

GINGER

Queen Elizabeth I of England had in her employ an artistic baker whose sole occupation was fashioning portraits of members of the court in gingerbread. Russian royalty, equally fond of the sweet, celebrated the birth of Peter the Great in 1672 by presenting the infant prince with a gingerbread modeled after the Kremlin, weighing in the neighborhood of 150 pounds.

But those were not gingerbread's beginnings. The Egyptians created it, centuries before. Whether Confucius enjoyed gingerbread is not recorded, but he loved ginger. Chinese traders carried the spice to the Greeks and Romans, brought back gold and silver, handsome glassware, and fine wine in return. Trading carried the spice north in Europe; it had reached England before William did in 1066. In Switzerland in the Middle Ages, one of the spice markets was called "Ginger Alley." The first Oriental spice to reach North America, it was brought by the Spanish envoy to Mexico in 1535.

Ginger is the rhizome of an orchidlike plant that today grows in many tropical countries. It is available to home cooks in six forms, the most familiar of which is the dry, ground spice. But you can also buy the whole fresh rhizome in season, dried pieces of it (most often called ginger root), canned slices, sweet preserved ginger in syrup, and dry candied ginger.

Like many other spices, ginger was once used as a medicine—for toothache and digestive problems by the Greeks, as an antidote for poisoning in a number of Middle-European countries, to ward off the plague by the English. It was also taken, in Great Britain, to assuage the pangs of unrequited love. ("Ethelbert has scorned me. Please pass the cyanide. No, on second thought, pass the ginger.")

Gingerbread is certainly not the only ginger-flavored food we eat, although it may be the one in which we most clearly discern the flavor of the spice. But ginger is part of the flavoring—along with cinnamon and nutmeg—of pumpkin pies, and some use it in apple pies as well. There are ginger cookies, too—fat, soft ones, made even better with a thin lemon-flavored icing, and crackly gingersnaps topped with sugar. Many pickles and preserves owe part of their goodness to the spice. And a little of it on carrots, squash, and sweet potatoes gives them a wonderful what's-that? taste.

We drink beverages flavored with the spice as well, notably ginger ale and ginger beer. It holds a high place in both Chinese and Indian cuisines, and is one of the components of curry powder.

Ginger oil, distilled from the root, is used in some cosmetics, in particular a delightfully pungent cologne for men. See also SPICES.

GJETOST: see CHEESE

GLASSWARE KITCHEN UTENSILS: see special feature: YOU CAN'T WORK WITHOUT TOOLS

GLAZES

A light coating, usually sweet, with which we improve the flavor of many foods is called a glaze. Here are some of them, to give you a sampling of the wide variety of glazes and the kinds of foods we can glaze:

ham: In the last half hour of baking, glaze with pineapple juice and light molasses, stud with cloves; or with cider and brown sugar; or beer and brown sugar; or melted cherry jelly, stud with halves of glacéed cherries.

spareribs: Glaze with melted apple jelly; or with combination of tomato sauce and molasses; or with honey and lime juice.

potatoes: Shake small peeled new potatoes, cooked and drained, in a skillet with melted butter until they begin to brown; sprinkle lightly with sugar; shake pan over flame until potatoes are well browned (this is a Danish way).

sweet potatoes or yams: Glaze cooked and sliced potatoes in the oven with a combination of orange juice, orange peel, and brown sugar; or cover with miniature marshmallows, brown briefly under broiler.

cold meats, fish, poultry, eggs: Glaze elegantly with aspic; glaze and decorate with Sauce Chaud-Froid.

carrots: Glaze lightly with butter and sugar, sprinkle with snipped mint leaves; glaze with maple or maple-flavored syrup.

fruit, nuts: Glaze with a crystal-clear sugar syrup.

bananas: Bake halves brushed with a combination of melted butter, lemon juice, ginger, and honey.

sweet rolls, coffeecakes: Dribble with a glaze of confectioners sugar and water, vanilla flavored; or combine confectioners sugar and lemon juice; or confectioners sugar and coffee; or confectioners sugar, light cream, and maple or almond flavoring.

babka or sally lunn: Glaze with orange juice, grated orange peel, and honey, stud with blanched almonds.

custard: Glaze under broiler with heavily sprinkled brown sugar (result is Crème Brûlée).

cream pie: Cover top with whole strawberries, glaze with melted strawberry jelly.

venison steaks: Glaze with melted tart currant jelly.

lamb chops: Brush lightly with melted mint jelly.

chocolate pound cake: Pour over a glaze of melted chocolate, butter, confectioners sugar, vanilla extract.

tortes: Some of the best are given a hard, shiny caramel glaze made with melted sugar.

pies, top crust: Before baking, brush with slightly beaten egg white or with undiluted evaporated milk, sprinkle lightly with sugar.

breads, rolls: Some are glazed before baking with an egg-milk wash (dorure) that causes them to brown handsomely.

And that's only the beginning of glazes, the sweet and glossy coatings we give many foods to enhance both flavor and appearance.

GLOBE ARTICHOKES: see ARTICHOKES, GLOBE

GLUCOSE

Also called dextrose, this is the natural sugar found in fruits, vegetables, and honey. Less sweet than table sugar (sucrose), it does not crystallize as readily; thus it is often used in commercially made candies and confections, sometimes also in baked goods and in wines. The corn syrup we use in home cooking is glucose, prepared from cornstarch.

GLUTEN

This is a protein that is found in flour; various kinds of flours have differing amounts and kinds of gluten. In cake flour there is a small amount of soft gluten, which gives cakes their light and delicate texture. On the other hand, bread flour has more gluten and it is stickier—"elastic" is the commercial cook's term for it. This elasticity allows the cells of yeast dough to enlarge and expand without rupturing.

Gluten is developed in yeast doughs by kneading. Quick breads, made with the same flour, are mixed lightly—only until the dry ingredients are moistened—to avoid developing gluten that would coarsen and toughen the texture of the finished product.

GNOCCHI

The Italian word for dumpling—gnocco is one (and who would eat only one?), gnocchi more than one. They may be made of farina, of potatoes, or—like pasta—of flour; often there are eggs in the dough, sometimes there is cheese, sometimes there is finely chopped, well-drained spinach. Sometimes they are boiled in salted water, sometimes the dough is chilled, cut into shapes, and then baked. A good, well-seasoned sauce usually accompanies gnocchi—at the very least, melted butter and a hefty sprinkling of parmesan, or it may be a flavorful tomato sauce or, for the cheeseless gnocchi, a cheese sauce seasoned with onion and pepper.

Worth trying as a change from the omnipresent potato, gnocchi are an excellent accompaniment for meat or poultry.

GOLDEN SYRUP

A translucent syrup—golden in color, not surprisingly—that is very popular in Great Britain, where it is used to top many kinds of desserts. It is made of corn syrup, molasses, and sugar and, it follows, is very sweet. Not widely available here, it can sometimes be found in specialty food shops.

GOOSE

If ever, as a small child, you had an encounter with a goose, you almost undoubtedly came off second best. Geese are known for irascibility and have a short fuse.

But they have many good qualities—indeed some very admirable ones. They mate for life, and are exceedingly loving and fiercely loyal to one another. A goose who loses her mate, or a gander who loses his, may pine away and die, showing every sign of heartbreak. They're good parents, too, and share the burdens of nest-guarding and gosling-rearing equally, willing to defend each other and their young with their lives. They even share the same plumage, unusual in the bird world, where the male is generally much more showily, sometimes gaudily, attired.

Strong, brave, and intelligent, geese have many uses on a farm other than as meat for the table. A watchgoose can be every bit as effective as a watchdog in keeping away intruders or fending them off. And the big birds are expert gardeners. Turned loose in a field of grain or vegetables, a goose will waddle down the rows, pulling and eating weeds but never touching the planted crops. If you are lucky enough to gain his confidence, a goose can be a loyal friend. He'll even go on walks with you, making grouchy-sounding comments along the way.

The long goose story. The goose has been known since the beginnings of history, and raised as a barnyard fowl almost that long. Folktales of many countries, in many languages, include the one about the goose who laid the golden egg and the greedy, stupid owner who killed it. In Hindu mythology, the god Brahma is depicted riding a huge and handsome gander. The Chinese, who have raised geese for 3,000 years, once considered a pair of geese an excellent wedding present, because the birds symbolized faithfulness.

The succulent goose. Having praised the goose so fulsomely, it seems an embarrassment, if not a sin, to discuss the bird's virtues as a pièce de résistance. However, as food is our chief concern here, we'll muddle ahead.

In England and throughout Europe, a farm wife would not consider her little domain complete without a few geese to fatten for holiday meals—and, incidental to those good meals, to supply feathers and down for the featherbeds and pillows, goose quills to use as pens, and goose grease to use as a liniment, a leather polish, and—rendered and strained—as a cooking fat and a spread for bread.

As a bird for the table, the goose has never been as popular here as in Europe, where it is the center of the traditional Christmas dinner in England and the Scandinavian countries, and in Austria and Germany as well. Properly cooked, it is indeed a succulent bird—if more people would bring themselves to try it, the goose would undoubtedly make many new friends.

Young geese, raised for the table, appear in our markets in the fall, weighing from a bit more than 4 up to 13 or 14 pounds. Frozen geese, in the 5- to 8-pound range, are available all year. In buying, look for unbruised skin, a fresh and clean appearance—and, if frozen, unbroken packaging material. Store fresh goose in the refrigerator up to 3 days, frozen goose in the freezer, at 0°F. or below, up to 6 months; once thawed, plan on cooking that day or the next. Cooked goose, bird and stuffing separated, can be refrigerated, closely covered, up to 5 days.

Higher in fat than duck, considerably higher than chicken or turkey, goose has more calories than those birds; a 3½-ounce serving of roast goose yields about 425 calories.

Stuff goose with a bread or mashed-potato dressing made with onions and celery and seasoned with plenty of sage and thyme. Or make a dried-fruit stuffing, with prunes and apricots. Or an apple-walnut-raisin stuffing. Serve with pickled crab apples, brandied peaches, or spiced applesauce. Sauerkraut is one of the traditional goose accompaniments; turnips or rutabagas are another. Wild rice is not traditional, but be an innovator—throw tradition to the winds and serve it anyway.

A goose of 4 pounds should be done at the end of 2¾ hours or a bit longer; one of 8 pounds, 3½ hours; one of 14 pounds, about 5 hours.

For a discussion of wild goose, see GAME.

GOOSEBERRIES

More often grown and used in Europe—especially in England, where they are much enjoyed—than here in the United States, gooseberries are a relative of the sassafras, and grow on a prickly bush. Picking the berries is more chore than pleasure, but once past that point there is a delicious, juicy pie, or an old-fashioned Gooseberry Fool in store for you, or simply the fresh berries with cream and sugar.

As they are available only in June and July, and not widely distributed even in those months, most of us who use gooseberries at all are more familiar with the canned kind, which are very good. The berries can be green to red-blushed amber to dark purple when ripe, depending on the variety, but virtually all the canned ones are green. Unsweetened, they are low in calories—about 40 for a generous ⅔ cup—but they tend to be tart, and must be sugared to be palatable. As with most berries, don't plan on keeping them long; refrigerate, loosely covered, up to 2 days.

A Gooseberry Fool, if you would like to experiment, is made with sweetened stewed berries folded into whipped cream, which may be deliciously flavored with a little mace.

GORGONZOLA: see CHEESE

GOUDA

A plump yellow cheese that wears a red-wax overcoat, gouda originated in the Netherlands but is now made in many places, including the United States. It is semisoft to hard, and has a mild, slightly nutty flavor. See also CHEESE.

GOULASH

Gulyas in its native tongue, Hungarian, goulash is a stew made of veal (preferably) or beef, with vegetables, and seasoned with Hungary's wonderful paprika. Sometimes sour cream, another Hungarian specialty, is stirred into the flavorful gravy of the goulash just before it is served.

GOURMAND, GOURMET

Both are appreciators of fine food. The gourmand's sin is gluttony, the gourmet's vanity. The former falls on his food heartily, often greedily, while the connoisseur gourmet needs only a little, but that little must be the very best. Often, although not always, the gourmand is fat, the gourmet thin.

GRADES, UNITED STATES DEPARTMENT OF AGRICULTURE

The USDA inspects and grades meat, poultry, eggs, butter, cheddar cheese, fruits, and vegetables both fresh and processed. Food processors, packers, and distributors pay for the grading service in return for the right to have their products carry the USDA's quality grade shield, which canny consumers look for. See also individual foods by name, and the special features: YOUR PARTNER IN THE KITCHEN and A SHORT COURSE IN LABEL READING.

GRAHAM CRACKERS

Thin, crisp wafers made with whole wheat flour, graham crackers are always sweetened, sometimes with honey.

Although almost everyone enjoys them, graham crackers are a great favorite with children. Peanut butter has a special affinity for the crackers, which long-ago generations of kids discovered. They also learned to make S'mores: place a whole marshmallow on a graham cracker, top with several squares of plain milk chocolate candy bar; warm (in the oven or, more chancily, over a fire) until the chocolate softens to coat the marshmallow, the marshmallow softens to spread onto the cracker, and the whole becomes a sublimely sweet, gooey mass of delight. A second school of thought on S'mores places the chocolate on the cracker, then the marshmallow. A second cracker is added after chocolate and marshmallow are melted, to create what is certainly the messiest sandwich in the world, but the sweetest, and most widely loved by children.

Graham cracker crumbs are used to make crusts for unbaked pies, and the crumbs also replace part or all of the flour in several kinds of delectable tortes. The crackers plus a glass of milk make an excellent after-school snack for youngsters. See also FOOD FADS.

GRAINS

These are the seeds of cereal grasses or other plants, which we use in various (processed) ways in our kitchens. The most familiar, most-used ones—wheat, rice, rye, oats—are dealt with individually, under their own names. So is corn, which is not a grain in the sense that the others are, but some products of which we use in the same manner as the grains.

But there are others, little known (by some home cooks, even knowledgeable ones, virtually unknown), although they, or foods made from them, are delicious and nutritious. You may have seen packages of these grains in the market, and wondered in passing what they were and how they could be used. And there are also some products of the familiar grains that are unfamiliar in themselves, the uses of which you might like to explore.

Grains on the menu. The grains listed below make tasty and interesting alternatives to the starch side dishes that most of our main meals include—substitutes for potatoes, pasta, rice, and stuffings. Nutritionally they are low in fat, high in carbohydrate. None, except the corn products, supplies vitamins A or C; most are a good source of vitamin B and of iron, one of the nutrients less easy to come by in a normal diet. Kasha and millet, in particular, supply more than 20 percent of the adult RDA of iron. The grains also provide food fiber, of which the amount needed by the average person remains to be determined.

Here are some of the unusual grains and their uses.

barley: We may be most familiar with this as malted barley, an ingredient of beer and ale. A malted barley breakfast cereal, ready to cook, is available in some areas. But it is as pearl barley that we should learn to use it, as a delicious natural thickener for soups and stews, an ingredient in casseroles. It is available in regular and quick-cooking forms, and should be added to the dish 30 to 45 minutes before the end of cooking time. Mushroom and Barley Soup is a wonderful old-world dish.

bulgur: This is hard red winter wheat that has been cooked, dried, and cracked. It has been used in the Middle East for centuries as a staple food. Three grinds—fine, medium, and coarse—are available, each with its particular uses, although one can be substituted for another in almost all recipes. In general, the fine and medium grinds are used in casseroles and other main dishes, the coarse in salads or as a side dish.

Because it is already cooked, bulgur can be prepared in two ways—simmered in liquid, or simply soaked in boiling water, which rehydrates the grain.

grits: This, at least to cooks in the northern and western parts of the country, is the least-familiar processing of corn. But in the South it's a different story—grits are virtually a way of life. They are served at breakfast with ham and eggs, as home-fried or hash-brown potatoes are in some other places. Or they may accompany fried country ham with red-eye gravy, or be cooked with eggs and milk into spoon bread or corn custard. Topped with a pat of butter or served with gravy, grits are an out-of-the-ordinary side dish at any meal.

kasha: This is toasted and hulled buckwheat—familiar to some of us as an ingredient of a variety of pancake and to others as an ingredient of a widely enjoyed dry breakfast cereal—but to few in this form. You may also find kasha labeled "buckwheat groats." The word "groats" is used to designate grain that is hulled and broken up—"grits" is a synonym.

masa harina: Again, a processing of corn that is not well known; the exceptions this time are the West and Southwest. It is corn flour (not cornstarch) and, among other uses, is the chief ingredient in corn tortillas. At the rate Americans in all parts of the country are becoming enamored of Mexican and Tex-Mex foods, masa harina should soon be well known everywhere.

millet: A spoonful of millet looks like a spoonful of tiny yellow decorettes, the sort used to gussy-up cake or cookie frosting. You can buy the grain this way, or ground as flour. Toast the yellow grains lightly in a skillet before cooking—this reduces considerably the unconscionably long time it otherwise takes.

Buying, cooking the off-beat grains. Some you will find in your supermarket, among the cereals or flours, or in the health-food sections that some supermarkets have these days. If not there, try a specialty food shop or health food store.

To cook the grains as a starch-type side dish, you'll need a heavy pot with a well-fitting cover. Cook in liquid—water, broth, fruit or vegetable juices. Whatever the liquid, long and slow cooking is the rule. To serve as a side dish, top with butter or gravy or grated cheese or plain yogurt. Or you may add vegetables—mushrooms and/or onions and/or eggplant are particularly good with kasha and bulgur—or nuts or fruits, particularly dried ones. Stir often during cooking, because these foods have a nasty habit of sticking and scorching. Adequate liquid helps prevent this, too. Lamb has an affinity for these grains. So do chicken and chicken livers. So do clams and shrimp, and good, spicy sausages. See also BARLEY, OATMEAL, RYE, TRITICALE, and WHEAT.

GRANITE: see page 452

GRANULATED SUGAR: see SUGAR

GRAPE CURRANTS: see CURRANTS

GRAPE LEAVES

Handsome of shape, tender of texture, pleasantly neutral of flavor, the large green leaves of the grapevine are a traditional part of the cuisines of many countries, particularly those of the Near East. Rolled around a savory mixture of well-seasoned meat and rice, they make a tasty and attractive appetizer—these are "dolmas" in several languages. If you wish to make them and don't have the requisite vine in your backyard, grape leaves are available in jars. So are the dolmas themselves, if you prefer someone else to do the making. In this country, we are likely to use grape leaves, if at all, as a garnish or decoration—a large leaf on the plate under a sherbet dish, for example, or a number lining a salad bowl.

GRAPEFRUIT

By 1300, a tree called the pomelo—handsome and fruit-laden—had been brought to many parts of Europe from its native Malaya. The trees were planted as ornamentals, but the fruit—called by some "Adam's apple"—was not eaten. The tree was later taken to the West Indies by one Captain Shaddock, where, in Barbados, a happy accident of nature crossed the pomelo with the sweet orange, to produce the ancestor of today's grapefruit. They were given their name because the fruit grows in clusters, like grapes.

Even then, nobody got very excited. The West Indies are a fruit-lover's paradise, and one more fruit hardly made an impression. Seeds brought to the United States in the mid-1800s were planted in some suitable areas, but still no one ate many grapefruit until an advertising campaign just after the turn of the century promoted the fruit. Little by little it caught on. Today, grapefruit are enjoyed throughout the United States, and there are many who feel the day gets off on the wrong foot if it doesn't start with half a grapefruit for breakfast.

GRAPEFRUIT IN YOUR KITCHEN

There are two classes of grapefruit, seeded and seedless (those categorized as seedless may actually have up to five seeds), and two kinds, white and pink—the pulp, that is; the rind of the grapefruit is greenish yellow. The pink grapefruit is a mutation of the white, another happy accident that delighted growers encouraged and exploited because, although it is not true, consumers tend to think of pink grapefruit as sweeter than white.

Citrus the year around. Florida and Texas send fresh grapefruit to market in October, and continue through June. In January, fruit from California and Arizona appears in the stores, continuing through the summer.

how to buy: Grapefruit are available singly, by the dozen, or by the pound. Weight is a good indication of juiciness—the heavier a grapefruit is for its size, the juicier it will be. Look for fine-textured skin of bright color. Small blemishes do not affect the quality of the fruit, but bad bruises or breaks in the rind do. Don't judge quality by the color of the rind—top-quality, fully ripe fruit may be yellow, somewhat russet, or tinged with green. Because the tree's growth cycles overlap, producing new blossoms while some of the last cycle's fruit remains on the tree, extra chlorophyll manufactured to support the new blossoms may tint the older fruit with green. This is true of other citrus as well as of the grapefruit.

how to store: Do not keep at room temperature for more than a day or so. Store in the refrigerator, preferably unwrapped in the crisper, up to 1 month. Remove fruit to be juiced so that it can reach room temperature—you'll get a better volume of juice.

nutritive value: Grapefruit's big contribution to nutrition is vitamin C. Half a 4-inch fruit supplies the entire day's requirement of the vitamin. As that same half furnishes only 40 calories, it is clear why grapefruit is consumed in quantity by weight-loss dieters.

Tips on preparing. The grapefruit knife is a useful gadget with which to loosen grapefruit segments and remove the pulpy core, so that the fruit may be easily eaten. This process generally occurs in the kitchen, but in these days of equal opportunity, a grapefruit spoon, serrated on one edge, is available so that each diner can prepare his own fruit as he goes. (As with many other things designed to free women from their kitchen "slavery," this doesn't work too well. Unless the fruit is to be eaten unsweetened, it should be prepared and sweetened about 30 minutes in advance for much better flavor and optimum juiciness.)

Grapefruit can be juiced, using a hand or electric fruit juicer. Segments can be removed—the grapefruit knife again—for use in fruit cups or in salads.

Some Spartan souls eat their grapefruit as is, holding forth on the fruit's natural sweetness between mouth-puckering bites. Others sugar theirs, with white sugar or brown, or sweeten with honey or (these are likely not to be the greatest admirers of the fruit) with maple or maple-flavored syrup.

Freezing grapefruit. Although the peeled and sectioned fruit freezes well, it is another of those foods that, because it is so readily available in a number of forms the year around, should not be allotted home freezer space in other than exceptional circumstances.

Other ways, other forms. Fresh grapefruit is virtually always available in the produce section of the market, but it can also be found in other forms. Indeed, some who really don't like fresh grapefruit will happily eat the canned or frozen kind.

on grocery shelves, in cans or jars: Grapefruit segments, grapefruit juice (both sweetened and unsweetened), and combination orange-grapefruit juice; candied grapefruit peel.

Grapefruit marmalade, not widely distributed, is worth seeking out, particularly the kind that incorporates bits of candied ginger.

in grocery frozen-food section: Grapefruit juice, sweetened or not, plain and in combination with orange juice; grapefruit segments in sweetened juice or in syrup.

Some perfect partners. The tangy flavor of grapefruit perfectly complements the buttery blandness of avocado—indeed, some of us had our first taste of avocado combined with grapefruit in a salad, long ago when avocados seldom traveled far from where they were grown. Alternating wheel-pattern segments of the two fruits are very good to look at, too. Dress such a salad with simple oil and vinegar, or with a bleu cheese dressing to add a third fine flavor.

Grapefruit is excellent in molded salads, using grapefruit juice as part of the liquid to reinforce the flavor. Crisp apple (don't peel it) and smooth banana are good texture-flavor contrasts in such a mold. Or mold a salad that combines grapefruit, cranberries, and pecans.

Shellfish and grapefruit can be combined in an interesting appetizer. Crab, lobster, and shrimp, separately or in combination, can be layered with the fruit in lettuce-lined cups or on small plates, or in grapefruit "half shells." This is a particularly good dressing for such a mixture: blend 1 cup mayonnaise, 1 tablespoon tomato paste, 2 tablespoons lemon juice, a dash of hot pepper sauce. Or dress with mayonnaise sharpened with curry powder.

Broiled grapefruit can serve as either appetizer or dessert. Section and core grapefruit halves, leaving the segments in the shell, and dot with butter. Sprinkle liberally with combined sugar and cinnamon; broil until heated and bubbling. Or sprinkle with brown sugar, pour over a tablespoon of dry sherry for each half, and broil.

Grapefruit is an American specialty. In other countries, even those in which other citrus fruits are grown in abundance, grapefruit is virtually unknown.

GRAPES

Grapes grow wild in temperate climates over most of the world, and are cultivated in many lands for the fruit of the vine and for the wine that is made from that fruit.

Ranging in color from pale green (white grapes) through rosy russet to deep blue-purple (red grapes), grapes are one of the oldest of fruits, mentioned in both the Old and New Testaments of the Bible. Wine is spoken of, too, and has a part in the sacraments of several faiths. Early writings of Greeks and Romans include mentions of grapes and wine; grape seeds have been found in Swiss archaeological digs and in ancient Egyptian tombs. And during the same time, different kinds of grapes were growing wild or being cultivated in other lands—growing so abundantly in North America that when the Vikings explored here they named the country Vineland.

Grapes used for the table and those employed in wine-making are of different varieties. Some kinds are cultivated primarily for the production of grape juice, others to be dried and sold as raisins. Although some grapes grow well in the eastern parts of the United States—the native fox grapes, from which have been bred the concord and the muscadine and the scuppernong—California is America's great grape-growing country. Huge vineyards of wine grapes flourish there on hillside terraces, and large amounts of table grapes and raisin grapes are grown as well.

GRAPES IN YOUR KITCHEN

Though grapes come chiefly from California, some come from New York and other eastern states. There are thirteen major varieties of table grapes available in the United States, most of them nationally, but some—that do not ship well—obtainable only locally. See the chart on the following page.

how to buy: Look for proper color for the variety. Dark-colored grapes should show no tinge of green; pale grapes are sweetest when just beginning to show a touch of amber color. Ripe grapes yield to the touch, but should not be very soft. Bunches should not look dull or feel sticky; grapes should not be falling from their stems—these are overripe.

how to store: Sort and remove any shriveled or rotting grapes. Store in a ventilated plastic bag or covered container, in the refrigerator, up to 3 days.

nutritive value: Although grapes contain some vitamins and minerals, in quantities that vary with the kind, we cherish them more for their beauty and the pleasure of eating them than for what they contribute to the diet. Slip-skin varieties are lower in calories (about 18 calories furnished by 10 grapes) than the adherent-skin kinds (about 35 to 45 calories, depending on variety).

Tips on preparing. To eat out of hand, grapes need only be washed and have their stems removed. For fruit cups and salads, halve the grapes and seed them, using the point of a sharp, thin-bladed knife. Grapes are not often used in cooking, other than in jams, jellies, and preserves. Two exceptions to that are Concord Grape Pie (the skins are slipped off, the pulp heated to boiling and sieved to remove the obstinate seeds, and the reserved skins returned to the pulp for the pie filling), and Fillet of Sole Veronique, which incorporates seedless green grapes into a delicate sauce for the fish. Grapes are used, however, in many cold dishes; besides all-fruit cups and salads, grapes combine well with chicken or turkey in a salad, and add attractive texture and flavor to fish and shellfish salads as well.

Sugared grapes are delicious as a dessert with cream cheese, or as a garnish for other desserts. Slightly beat egg

variety	characteristics	season
almeria (California)	medium size; greenish-white; heavy, tough skin; not very juicy; mild flavor	September to November
catawba (East)	medium size, oval shape; red-purple; slip-off skins; very sweet, strong flavor	September to November
cardinal (California)	large, dark red; rather tough skin; few seeds; sweet flavor, pungent odor	June to August
concord (East)	medium size; deep blue with a silvery, powdery blush; slip-off skins; mild, sweet flavor	September and October
delaware (East)	small, pale red; tender skin; very juicy, sweet flavor	August and September
emperor (California)	large, oval "finger" shape; pale red-purple; thin skins; mild flavor	November to May
niagara (East)	large, somewhat egg-shaped; white or pale amber; slip-off skins; juicy, sweet flavor	September and October
olivette blanche (California)	long finger-shaped; pale green; tender skin; few seeds; very sweet; distinctive odor	June to August
red malaga (California)	large and round; pale to deep red-purple; rather tough skin; mild flavor	July to October
ribier (California)	large and round; coal black; tough skin; not highly juicy; mild but sweet flavor	July to February
thompson seedless (California)	medium size; slightly elongated; pale green; tender, thin skin; without seeds; mild flavor	June to November
tokay (California)	large, elongated shape; red; tough, thick skin; mild flavor	August to January
white malaga (California)	large; green-white to pale yellow; tough, thick skin; mild flavor	September to November

white with a teaspoon of water; with a brush, apply this to small clusters of grapes. Sprinkle liberally with sugar, set to dry on a rack. Give a holiday fruit cake a festive air by surrounding it with clusters of sugared grapes.

Freezing grapes. In a word, don't. They do not take kindly to freezing. The juice, yes, but the grapes themselves, no.

Other ways, other forms. Wine, of course—many, many kinds. But we're dealing with the unfermented grape here.

on grocery shelves: Canned seedless green grapes, alone or with other fruits in canned fruit salads; bottled grape juice —red, purple, and white—as well as sparkling catawba, a sort of alcohol-free champagne; in jars or glasses: grape jam, jelly, and preserves—most of these made with concords— and, less widely, spiced grape conserve; in packages: raisins —dark seedless or seeded, and white (golden) varieties.

in grocery frozen-food section: Frozen concentrated juice.

If there is room on your property, and you live in a proper climate, a grape arbor can be a very attractive addition to the landscaping, offering shade and grape leaves for use in cooking and for garnishing, to say nothing of the fruit itself. See also RAISINS and WINE.

GRAPE-SEED OIL: see OILS, SALAD AND COOKING

GRATE, TO: see page 446

GRATIN

A baked dish with a crisp, golden-brown crust on its top is said to be gratinéed. This pleasant attribute is achieved by covering the surface of the food with buttered crumbs and/or grated cheese, and baking at high heat for the last few minutes of cooking. Potatoes au gratin are liberally mixed and topped with cheese, then baked to assure that good brown crust.

GRAVAD LAX

A triumph of the Swedes, those splendid kitchen innovators, this is raw pickled salmon. As an appetizer delicacy, it puts lox (smoked salmon), even the elegant Nova Scotia variety, to shame.

Scout around for a Scandinavian delicatessen to find

gravad lax. Serve on small squares of dense, dark bread with a squirt of lemon and a bit of dill or a few capers. Or soften cream cheese, add fresh snipped chives, and spread on slices of the salmon; roll, chill, cut into ¼-inch slices and impale on a food pick. Or make a sandwich (again, dark bread) of cream cheese or sliced hard-cooked egg and gravad lax. Or fold slivers into soft scrambled eggs just before you serve them. Sometimes you will find the name shortened to gravlax.

GRAVIES

Made of fat, meat drippings, and juices, plus a liquid and a thickening agent, gravy is a sauce served with meat or poultry. It differs from other sauces in that its flavor and a part of its ingredients derive from the dish with which it is served.

The fat comes from the cooked meat, but sometimes must be augmented with another fat. The meat juices also come from the cooked meat. The liquid may be water, milk, broth or stock, liquid saved from the cooking of vegetables, tomato juice, or commercial bouillon or consommé. The thickener may be flour, cornstarch, potato starch, or something out of the ordinary, such as the gingersnaps used to thicken the gravy of sauerbraten. It may be made by stirring the thickener into melted fat, then adding liquid; this is the pan gravy made to accompany roasted meats and poultry. Or it may be made with a smooth paste of thickener and cold liquid stirred into hot braising liquids; this is the pot gravy made with stews and pot roasts.

However made, gravy should be flavorful, totally free from lumps, and about the consistency of heavy cream.

The broad gravy spectrum. Gravy has an honored place in many cuisines, for it stretches the good flavor of meat when it sauces any of the traditional meat accompaniments—potatoes, rice, pasta, grits, dumplings, stuffings. Here is the how-to for many kinds.

pan gravy: Make in the pan in which the meat or poultry was cooked—roasted, baked, or fried. Remove the meat to a serving dish and keep warm. Pour or skim off excess fat, leaving behind only enough for making the gravy; leave drippings and meat juices in the pan. You will need 1 tablespoon of fat for thin gravy, 2 for medium consistency, 3 for medium-thick. Place the pan over low heat. Stir in flour briskly—the same measurement of flour as of fat—combining it with the fat and drippings until you have a smooth, bubbling paste. Very slowly, continuing to stir, add 1 cup liquid; cook, stirring constantly, until thickened and smooth, and the mixture bubbles—3 to 4 minutes. Season to taste.

braising-liquid gravy: If the meat is in one piece, such as a pot roast, remove it. Turn up heat so that the mixture bubbles. In a small bowl or shaker, combine 1 part flour to 2 parts liquid (2 tablespoons flour to ¼ cup liquid, for example) and stir or shake until smooth and well combined. Slowly add

to braising liquid, stirring constantly; cook until smooth and thickened, 3 to 5 minutes. Season to taste.

vegetable-thickened gravy: When you cook vegetables in a stew or with a pot roast, cook half again as many vegetables as you will need. Remove the excess vegetables to a blender container, with a little of the braising liquid. Purée, then return to the cooking pan. Season to taste. The puréed vegetables will thicken the cooking liquid slightly, making a very flavorful gravy.

cream gravy for fried chicken: Remove chicken to a serving dish; keep warm. Measure fat in cooking pan, return 3 tablespoons to pan. Stir in 3 tablespoons flour; cook over low heat until the mixture is smooth and bubbling. Add ½ cup water; cook, stirring, until all browned particles in pan are incorporated into the mixture. Slowly add 1 cup light cream, stirring constantly; cook, stirring, until thickened and smooth. Season to taste with salt, white pepper, and thyme.

fricassee gravy: Remove chicken; keep warm. To cooking liquid in pan, add chicken stock or broth to make 1½ cups. Cook, stirring, until all brown bits and pan juices are incorporated into mixture. Combine ½ cup heavy cream with 2 tablespoons flour; stir or shake until smooth. Add slowly, stirring constantly, until the mixture bubbles and thickens. Season to taste with salt and white pepper and, if you wish, with thyme or sage.

sour-cream gravy for veal: Remove roasted veal to serving dish; keep warm. Place roasting pan over low heat. Add ½ cup water; cook, stirring, until meat juices and browned particles are loosened and combined in mixture. Into 1 cup sour cream, stir 2 tablespoons instantized flour until smooth and well combined. Add gradually to pan, stirring vigorously; cook until mixture bubbles and thickens. Season to taste with salt and paprika. (When flour is mixed into sour cream, the cream will neither separate nor curdle, even if boiled.)

mushroom gravy for broiled steak: In a skillet, place ¾ pound fresh mushrooms, sliced; 2 tablespoons butter; 2 tablespoons water. Cover skillet; cook over medium heat 3 minutes, or until mushrooms have released their liquid. Uncover, and cook until all liquid has evaporated and mushrooms have browned lightly. In blender container, place 1 cup cold beef stock or broth, 1 tablespoon instantized flour, ¼ teaspoon garlic juice; blend briefly. Add one-third of the mushrooms from the pan; purée. Return mixture to pan and cook, stirring, until bubbling and thickened. Add 2 tablespoons heavy cream, 2 tablespoons minced parsley. Cook, stirring, until heated through. Season to taste.

red-eye gravy for country ham: Remove fried ham from skillet to serving platter. To skillet drippings add 1 cup strong black coffee. Cook, stirring, until well combined and the liquid has come to a boil. Pour over ham. (Serve grits with this, if you want an authentic—and fantastically good—dish.)

tomato gravy: Cook 6 thick bacon slices slowly until done. Keep bacon warm; pour off drippings and reserve. Combine ½ cup flour, 1 teaspoon salt, ¼ teaspoon pepper, and ½ teaspoon sugar. Dip 6 thick-sliced underripe tomatoes in flour mixture; sauté in same skillet in bacon drippings, a tablespoon at a time, until well browned and beginning to soften. Remove to a warm platter. Return remaining drippings to skillet; heat to bubbling. Add remaining flour mixture; stir rapidly until combined with drippings and browned pieces in skillet. Add cold milk slowly, stirring until smooth, and mixture bubbles and thickens. Taste, and correct seasoning if necessary. Pour over tomatoes; place bacon on top.

vegetable gravy: Remove vegetables—carrots, green or wax beans, broccoli, peas, little boiled onions, whatever—from their cooking liquid, and keep warm. To the cooking liquid, add a good-sized lump of butter (or you may omit this if there are weight-loss dieters at the table). Let butter melt and blend with cooking liquid over low heat. Combine 1 tablespoon cornstarch with 2 tablespoons cold water until smooth. Add slowly to liquid, stirring constantly until mixture bubbles and thickens. Pour over vegetables, stir gently to combine.

poached-fish gravy: Remove 1½ cups poaching liquid to a small pan. Add 2 tablespoons butter; melt over low heat. Combine 1½ tablespoons cornstarch with 3 tablespoons water; add slowly to liquid, stirring constantly, until mixture bubbles and thickens. Stir in 2 tablespoons lemon juice, ¾ teaspoon dillweed. Pour over fish or serve separately. (Substitute 2 tablespoons fresh dill for dillweed, if you like.)

Gravy fix-ups. You may vary these—and any other gravy you make—as you see fit by substituting a different liquid, and/or by the addition of herbs and seasonings of any kind compatible with the basis of the gravy. Here are some gravy additions that may be added during the cooking for excellent, sometimes unusual, flavor.

> garlic juice or pressed whole garlic cloves
> onion or garlic powder
> minced celery or onion or parsley
> basil or oregano (tomato-flavored gravies)
> tarragon (chicken)
> marjoram or summer savory (lamb)
> chopped fresh or canned mushrooms
> sage and/or thyme (chicken, turkey)
> chopped giblets (any poultry)
> dry or prepared mustard
> ginger and turmeric (lamb or veal stews)
> curry powder (braised lamb or chicken)
> juice from pickles (beef stews, pot roasts)
> chopped parsley or watercress, snipped chives
> worcestershire sauce, other meat sauces
> hot pepper sauce
> canned soups, clear or cream (to stretch gravy)

And in a pinch. There are canned gravies and packaged gravy mixes available if you need gravy and don't have the makings. You'll find them in various kinds and flavors—brown gravy, chicken, mushroom, onion, and beef, and a canned chicken gravy complete with giblets. You can add to these any of the gravy fix-ups listed or season as you like to give these substitutes a made-at-home flavor.

Natural gravy. This is made simply from the pan juices—with most of the fat removed—diluted with a little water or bouillon and brought to a boil while being stirred, so that the browned particles will be loosened and incorporated. No thickening is added, but the mixture may be seasoned to taste. On many menus, this is called "jus"—French for juice, referring to the natural juices of the meat that drip out during cooking. "Prime ribs of beef au jus" means a cut of prime rib, served with this natural gravy.

Gravy gadgetry. Gravy is served, if not over the meat, in a gravy boat—a somewhat boat-shaped dish with a matching plate beneath it. (Sometimes the plate is attached to the gravy boat, making serving easier and accidents less likely.) A small ladle is used to serve the gravy. However, no law says that gravy cannot be served in a bowl of appropriate size, with a plate beneath it to catch the drips, or even in a small pitcher.

There is on the market a two-sided gravy boat designed for the Spratt family—Jack could eat no fat, you'll recall, and his wife could eat no lean. In natural (unthickened) gravy, the fat tends to rise to the top. This gravy boat has a spout at the top for Jack's wife, a spout lower down on the other side for Jack. Lacking this, the Jack Spratts of the world can dip the gravy ladle deep into the boat and bring up the leaner *jus* at the bottom. There is also available a large-bowled ladle that works on the same principle—and that invites catastrophe for all but the most agile-handed.

GRAVY BROWNING AGENTS

These are bottled liquids used to add color (sometimes flavor) to gravies, or to the braising liquid of such dishes as stews and pot roasts. They are deep in color, and a little goes a long way. Browning agents are composed of caramel (carmelized sugar), various dried vegetables, salt, and various other seasonings.

One excellent use for these products is in broiling tougher-cut steaks, such as chuck, which must be tenderized. In a cup, combine ¼ teaspoon garlic juice, 2 tablespoons water, 1 tablespoon gravy browning agent. Use to moisten the surface of the meat. Sprinkle with unseasoned meat tenderizer; pierce the meat deeply all over with a sharp kitchen fork. Turn the meat over and repeat. Broil immediately or let stand up to 30 minutes. This method gives excellent flavor and the meat browns well, as often it will not when plain water is used to moisten it for the tenderizer.

GRAY MULLET, SOLE: see FISH

GREASE, TO: see page 446

GREAT NORTHERN BEANS: see BEANS

GREEN BEANS: see BEANS

GREEN ONIONS

Tender young onions, also called spring onions and scallions. To be eaten raw with salt or a dip, or sliced thinly (including some of the green tops) to add to salads, cottage or cream cheese. Or they may be braised in butter, with a little water, seasoned, and served as a hot vegetable. See also ONIONS.

GREEN PEPPERS: see PEPPERS

GRENADINE: see page 452

GRIDDLES: see special feature: YOU CAN'T WORK WITHOUT TOOLS

GRILL, TO: see page 450

GRIND, TO: see page 446

GRITS

The South's answer to hashed-brown potatoes as a breakfast side dish, this is corn processed as for hominy, then finely ground. See GRAIN.

GRITS, HOMINY: see CORN

GROATS: see GRAIN

GROUND MEATS

All over America last night, as families gathered at the dinner table, the plaintive cry rose from a million throats: "Hamburger? *Again?"*

This form of torture is totally unnecessary. There are so many ways to go with ground beef—and lamb and veal and pork—that ground meat could appear on the table 365 days of the year without once repeating itself. And ground meat has so many things going for it—adaptability, versatility, acceptability, and (relatively) low cost—it's no wonder that home cooks depend on it as a mainstay, often the backbone, of their menu planning.

Tender, boneless ground meat has been depended on in that same manner by generations of home cooks all over the world. Russians relish raw ground beef, nicely seasoned. Swedish meatballs, those tasty little one-bite nuggets with a whif of nutmeg or allspice, are popular far beyond Sweden's borders. Frikadeller are the larger Danish version. Mexicans stuff their tasty tacos and tamales with ground meat; Germans stuff their savory cabbage rolls with it. Italians make richly tomatoey meat sauce for pasta and meatballs for lasagna. Everywhere, everyone makes one kind of sausage or another—hot or mild, delicately or assertively seasoned, composed of one ground meat or a combination of two or several.

A hamburger by any other name. Not too long ago, when you bought a package labeled "hamburger" or "ground beef," you had no way of knowing what you were getting. You paid your money and you took your chances, or you picked out a nice piece of chuck or round steak and had it ground to order, paying the marked price for the meat and, sometimes, a little extra for the grinding. Then the USDA took a hand, setting standards for ground beef according to fat content and the beef cut from which the meat came. Here are those standards.

hamburger: A package labeled hamburger contains ground beef from an unspecified cut, and can be up to 30 percent fat. Extra fat may be added, since beef usually does not carry this much fat. (See HAMBURGER.)

ground beef: This may also contain up to 30 percent fat, but no extra fat may be added; only the fat attached to the beef may be ground with it. In practice, this generally means that meat labeled ground beef contains only 20 to 25 percent fat. No extenders may be added—no nonfat dry milk, soy protein, cereals, or water.

ground chuck: This must be meat from the chuck primal cut; it contains 15 to 25 percent fat and will be more expensive per pound than either hamburger or ground beef.

ground round: Meat must come from the round, generally contains only about 11 percent fat, and is accordingly more expensive per pound than ground chuck.

ground sirloin: It is not the lower fat content, but the cut, that makes this the most expensive ground beef. Sirloin steaks and roasts are tender and have excellent flavor; most people prefer to eat sirloin in those forms, using ground beef from lesser cuts.

Getting a second opinion. The National Live Stock and Meat Board feels that there should be a better way to label ground meats, ground beef in particular. The Industrywide Cooperative Meat Identification Standards Committee (IC-MISC) considered ground meats as well as the primal cuts when recommending standards for meat labeling (see BEEF for an in-depth discussion of this).

The committee realized that the obvious reason for such a wide variety of names in the labeling of ground beef was that the various grounds came from various specific sections of the beef carcass. But, they further determined, customers over the years have attached certain properties to these names—round, chuck, and sirloin—believing that there are differences in flavor, nutritive values, or some mysterious unidentified properties inherent in the meat, depending on what cut from the beef carcass was used in the ground beef.

To further complicate accurate by-cut identification, retailers have made it a practice to "balance" the content of their specifically labeled ground beef with trimmings from other parts of the carcass—for example, "ground round" might contain trimmings from the chuck or loin in some cases. To meat cutters there is nothing unusual or deceptive in this practice, especially since they try to maintain the lean-to-fat ratio for the kind of ground beef that the package label specifies. The purpose of this practice, the ICMISC points out, has been purely and honestly economic—to utilize (not waste) perfectly good meat trimmings, and thus keep costs and prices down.

Unfortunately, this practice of selling "ground round" with chuck trimmings added, or any other label that contains meat other than the kind specified, has the appearance of deception. In the minds of meat-industry critics, it is cheating. The ICMISC feels that suspicion and criticism in this area of meat merchandising will be allayed forever through the use of the singular, all-inclusive label "ground beef," qualified by the lean-to-fat ratio on the label. This lean-to-fat ratio is, many experts in the field agree, the most important factor, not the point of origin on the carcass of the meat in the package.

Lean-to-fat ratio is important in relation to the use of the ground beef in recipes, and it also affects the retail price. The less lean (therefore the more fat), the lower the price per pound.

ICMISC guidelines for retailers. In deference to the industry and in fairness to consumers, the ICMISC has recommended that nomenclature and specifications for retail ground beef be based on the following provisions:

1. That all ground beef be identified as GROUND BEEF on the label.
2. That standards or categories for all ground beef be decided by lean-to-fat content, and that this quality be shown on the label as NOT LESS THAN X% LEAN. So, the label on a package of ground beef might read:

GROUND BEEF
NOT LESS THAN 70% LEAN

or

GROUND BEEF
NOT LESS THAN 83% LEAN

Percentage, of course, would depend on the lean-to-fat ratio. Conceivably, the number of ground beef categories handled by any retailer would depend on the individual and the trim he could generate from his own merchandising methods. *But in no case should the lean content of ground beef ever be less than 70 percent.*

3. All ground beef should contain *only* beef, with *no* trimmings from veal, pork, lamb, or cuts of other meat added to the product.

4. Only skeletal meat should be used in ground beef unless labeled otherwise. (This means no visceral or "variety" meats—liver, kidney, and such.)
5. An added descriptive name can be used where the ground beef is ground from a specific beef cut such as the chuck, round, and sirloin. In cases like these, the top line of the label could read:

GROUND BEEF CHUCK

or

GROUND BEEF ROUND

or

GROUND BEEF SIRLOIN

But in all cases the second line on the label would give the lean-to-fat information. Thus, the full label for a specifically ground cut might read:

GROUND BEEF CHUCK
NOT LESS THAN 75% LEAN

or

GROUND BEEF ROUND
NOT LESS THAN 85% LEAN

To play safe, the retailer should aim for at least 2 to 3 percent above his "not less than" guarantee, *especially since the statement will almost always pertain to batches rather than individual packages.*

Consumers, the ICMISC, points out, are always willing to buy ground beef with 1 to 2 percent greater leanness than listed on the label, but they're sure to object to ground beef with more fat—or less lean, the other end of the ratio—than stated. There is no doubt, the committee continues, that if there is to be allowable error in labeling, the error should be in favor of the consumer. When it's the other way around, the retailer is wide open for criticism and even prosecution.

Labeling ground pork, lamb, and veal. For economic reasons, as well as service to customers, meat retailers often grind trimmings from species other than beef. These are sold as fresh (unseasoned) ground pork, lamb, or veal; sometimes they are sold as combinations—of pork-beef-veal, for example, to be used in meat loaves. Some retailers season such packaged combinations—in which case, they must be clearly marked as such.

Because, the National Live Stock and Meat Board says, there have been very few consumer complaints on lean-to-fat ratios in ground meats other than beef, no present attempt is made to define these ratios on the labels, although this may be a future step.

Recommendations for the labeling of nonbeef ground meats:

Ground Pork *or* Ground Pork Sausage
Ground Lamb *or* Ground Lamb Patties
Ground Veal *or* Ground Veal Patties
Ground for Meat Loaf—Ground Beef, Pork, and Veal

GROUND MEAT IN YOUR KITCHEN

All the ground meats are highly perishable. Unless you intend to freeze the meat (which you should do immediately after you get it home, shaping it before freezing with an eye to its future use), plan on using it the day you buy it or, at the outside, the following day. Dating, mandatory in some states and optional in others, will help you determine how freshly ground the meat is at the time you buy it.

As certain as death and taxes. Ground meat appears on American menus on an average of once a week, in—if the home cook is on her toes—one guise or another. Most often, it's ground beef. But the other ground meats (lamb, pork, veal) are delicious and can be used in many ways to help vary the menu. Watch for them in your market. Ground beef is always available, but the others may not be at the meat counter every day or, if they are, may be there in smaller numbers of packages. They're very much worth your seeking out, to use in many ways.

how to buy: In selecting a package of ground beef, the color of the meat may be a factor, but not necessarily for the reason you may think. The time that has elapsed since grinding, rather than the age of the meat, determines the color of ground beef. Immediately after grinding it is a bluish-red. After exposure to air for a brief time it may vary from pale to bright red. After prolonged exposure to air, the meat becomes brownish-red. Take these color cues into consideration when you choose a package of ground beef.

Ground veal is pinkish-gray; the nearer to red that pink is, the older the calf when it was slaughtered. Very young veal is gray in color. Because almost all veal is tender, there are not many trimmings to make into ground veal; that makes it scarce at the meat counter. Ground pork is also pinkish-gray, but deeper in color than veal. Ground lamb is gray-brown to red-brown.

When choosing any ground meat, make certain that the package is well sealed. Avoid any meat that looks dried out.

At the market, keep in mind the use you intend to make of the meat, and let that help guide your purchase. Some home cooks believe that the leanest ground beef is the best

buy, for example, but that is not necessarily so. Some fat is necessary to give beef flavor and juiciness—between 15 and 30 percent, the USDA's Consumer Marketing Service suggests as reasonable ratios.

how to store: Leave prepackaged ground meat in the original wrapper, and store in the coldest part of the refrigerator. Ground meat that is not prepackaged should be removed from the butcher's wrapping paper, wrapped loosely in wax paper, and stored in the coldest part of the refrigerator.

nutritive value: Although values vary with the cut from which the ground meat was taken, the lean-to-fat ratio, and (beef in particular) the grade of the meat, here are some rough guides. All are in 1-cup measurements (two medium-size patties); ground beef furnishes 470 calories in this amount, lamb 287 calories, pork 388 calories, and veal 296 calories.

	beef	lamb	pork	veal	
protein	24.6	37.5	24.8	29.9	grams
fat	40.4	14	31.4	18.6	grams
carbohydrate	0	0	0	0	
calcium	11	17	11	13	milligrams
phosphorus	121	307	252	273	milligrams
iron	3.2	2.7	3.2	3.7	milligrams
sodium	43	92	61	73	milligrams
potassium	197	420	278	335	milligrams
thiamin	.05	.21	.55	.14	milligram
riboflavin	.19	.39	.25	3.4	milligrams
niacin	3.9	8	4.8	8.6	milligrams
ascorbic acid	0	0	0	0	
vitamin A	80	trace	trace	trace	international units

Freezing ground meat. If you come upon a sale of ground meat at a good price, you can avail yourself of the bargain if you have a freezer in which to store it. Ground meats do not have as long a freezer life as other meat cuts, but you can safely freezer-store them for 2 to 3 months.

Portion the meat into meal-size packages for freezing. If the meat is to be cooked as patties, shape it that way before freezing, stacking patties in meal-size numbers, separating them with pieces of plastic wrap. Portion meat not to be used as patties in··recipe quantities—enough for a meat loaf, enough for spaghetti sauce, enough for your favorite casserole dish, and so on. Patties can be conveniently frozen in round plastic freezer containers or freezer-weight plastic bags. Other portions of ground meat should be tightly enclosed in moisture/vaporproof wrappings—heavy-duty foil, or other freezer-wrap material. Be sure to date packages and observe the first-in/first-out rule.

In recipe-size portions, ground meat will thaw readily in the refrigerator or, if the package is waterproof, under cold running water. Do not thaw at room temperature. Do not season ground meats or add other recipe ingredients—bread or cracker crumbs, eggs or milk—before freezing. However, the dish may be completely prepared, cooked (preferably somewhat undercooked), and then frozen, needing only re-heating (about one and one-half times as long as the original cooking time) for serving.

Some ideas on shaping ground meats. If you have a practiced eye, you can probably attack a mountain of ground meat and whack it up into patties that vary only a hair's breadth from one another in size and weight. But we are not all thus blessed. Use a ⅓- or ½-cup measure; gently pack meat into it, turn out, and shape into patties between damp hands. (Gently is the operative word—the more you handle ground meat, the drier and more compact the finished product will be.) Or shape the meat into a long roll of the proper diameter and divide into slices. Or pat the meat into a layer of even depth on wax paper; with a dull knife, divide into equal squares, gently round the corners with your fingers. You can cut the layer with a large cookie cutter, but then you have the scraps to contend with, and no guarantee that they will make a patty to conform with the rest.

For the effete there is a gadget called a meat-baller—two hollow half-balls at the ends of a scissorslike doohickey; dip into the meat mixture, close the handles, and hey, presto! But just as fingers were made before forks, hands were made before meat-ballers. Rinse your hands in cold water and go to it. But do use a measuring tool—tablespoon, scoop, whatever—to make sure the balls are all approximately the same size. Again, gently does it.

No law requires that a meat loaf be baked in a loaf pan, or even that it be loaf shaped. Try a 9-inch square pan for 6 neat rectangular servings. If you have individual bread-loaf pans, they can be used for meat loaf, too. Or bake the meat loaf mixture in large muffin pans or custard cups for individual servings. Or bake the mixture in a deep ring mold.

Borrow grandma's trick of burying hard-cooked eggs in a line down the center of the loaf—that way, each serving has a neatly centered slice of egg. Or hide a cube of cheddar or a ball of bleu cheese in the center of each meatball. To extend a meat loaf, pat out the prepared mixture into a rectangle on a sheet of wax paper. Spread with a well-seasoned bread stuffing or with not-too-soft mashed potatoes (with grated cheese folded in, if you like), roll up jelly-roll fashion, and—using the wax paper to help you—transfer to a baking pan. Or frost a meat loaf after baking with hot mashed potatoes, sprinkle lightly with paprika or with grated parmesan, and broil for a moment or two to brown; or skip the browning and sprinkle lightly with snipped parsley.

A meat loaf of plain beef is neither as tasty nor as juicy as one made with pork and veal as well. Good proportions are 1½ pounds of beef to ½ pound each of veal and pork. A lamb loaf is a nice change of pace; make it all lamb, or a quarter as much veal as lamb. Tomato and lamb are good partners—make a lamb loaf, using half of an 8-ounce can of tomato sauce as all or part of the liquid in the loaf. Season the remaining half can of sauce with a little salt, a speck of sugar, a few drops of garlic juice, and ½ teaspoon of basil or oregano, and pour over the lamb loaf before you put it in to bake.

There are literally hundreds of dishes to be made with ground meat—pies and pasta sauces; casseroles and skillets; stuffings (with rice) for such vegetables as peppers, eggplant, squash; loaves and patties; soups and stews; and that's not half of it. Consult a good general cookbook—or two or three—for new approaches to serving the home cook's best friend.

Last word on the subject. Here's a hamburger trick worth knowing. Season the meat as you like, then mix it with a little crushed ice, ice water, or cold club soda. Use enough to make the mixture soft, but not so much that the patties won't hold together. Cook as usual, and you'll find that you are serving the tenderest, juiciest hamburgers that you've ever produced. It's one of those sounds-terrible ideas that turns out to be worth a mint.

GROUPER

A lean, saltwater fish, relative of the sea bass. Buy whole, filleted, or steaked. See also FISH.

GROUSE: see GAME

GROW-IT-YOURSELF BOOM, THE: see page 383

GRUYERE

A Swiss cheese made of whole cows' milk—a close relative in color, flavor, and shape to emmenthaler, the cheese we know as swiss cheese. Gruyère "eyes"—the holes in the cheese—are somewhat smaller than those in emmenthaler. See also CHEESE.

GUACAMOLE

Savory and very handsome mixture, Mexican in origin, used as an appetizer dip or spread, sometimes as a sauce, sometimes as a salad dressing. Made of mashed or puréed avocados, guacamole is usually flavored with onion and lemon juice, sometimes with cumin.

Avocado with plenty of lemon juice and thinly sliced scallions, seasoned with salt and a dash of hot pepper sauce, makes the basic guacamole. To this can be added—and often is—almost anything, such as chili powder, diced tomato, chopped green chilies, chopped stuffed green or ripe olives, bits of crisp bacon, diced cheese, and even deviled ham or mashed liverwurst. Seems a shame, when the simplest version is so lovely to look at and so delightful to taste.

GUAVAS

Tropical or subtropical fruit which may be eaten raw—the flavor is somewhat acid—but is more often encountered in jam or jelly. Guava paste, which you may find offered among the desserts on the menu of a Mexican restaurant, is made by boiling the fruit until it forms a mass so dense it can be sliced. It is delectable served in the company of fresh cream cheese.

GUM

A thick, sticky substance used as an adhesive or thickener in food processing. It is an additive, but a natural one, obtained from various plants. On a label listing of ingredients you may find Gum Acacia, Gum Arabic, and Gum Tragacanth; all are natural plant materials.

GUMBO

A thick soup-stew, native of New Orleans, which almost always contains okra and which is thickened at the last minute, off the heat, with FILE (a powder made from young leaves of the sassafras tree).

CARVING, BONING, AND OTHER KITCHEN TECHNIQUES

Far better than rending the food limb from limb is to master the niceties of cutting, boning, and carving—easy to learn and satisfying in the accomplishment

There was a time (the Middle Ages) when the common folks ate with newfangled tools—forks, they were called—that some upstart had invented. Well-bred people would have no part of such a vulgar notion. They continued to eat, as their ancestors had, with their fingers. This conservative approach to table manners obviated the necessity for much in the way of carving other than for large fowls (swans were considered very tasty, so were peacocks, and both came to the table in their plumage) and for big cuts of meat, such as barons of beef. Dividing these up was accomplished by a system that made up in efficiency what it lacked in grace: the carver got a firm handhold on a part of the meat and with his knife in his other hand hacked off suitable portions, presenting them to the diner on the flat of his knife. The dogs who ranged around the dining halls—they worked as efficient garbage disposals, and also doubled as napkins for the greasy-handed—were thrown the parts that the carvers' hand had touched, which further demonstrates the delicate sensibilities of the elite of those times.

Don't think for a moment that the carver was an ordinary kitchen menial, pressed into service in the Great Hall. The carver was always a gentleman, sometimes a member of the nobility, never lower in rank than the guests. In the great houses of England, there was a Carver in Chief with a number of assistants called Carvers in Ordinary, along with various Servers in Chief and in Ordinary, Cupbearers, and assorted Knights—accompanied by their Squires, serving as the genteel equivalents of the modern bouncer. And, finally, there was that poor fellow, the Taster, whose duty it was to eat and drink, in advance of his master, everything that was served just in case the household poisoner (he had no official status, but there seemed always to be one or two lurking behind the arras) had managed to do his dirty work.

There was even a book on carving to guide the Carver in Chief, in case his previous duty had been Lord of the Bath or some other service unrelated to food. Grasp a fowl by one leg, the book directed, and cut off suitable portions; balance them on the knife blade and pass along. As for meat, cut it in one long, continuous piece (the way, apparently, that young girls peel apples to ascertain the initials of their future husbands), cutting off the piece when it reached a length of

serving size and, again, passing it along on the flat of the knife.

CARVING BECOMES AN ART

As all things must, the Middle Ages came to an end, and its customs gave way to a whole new mode of living. Now there was glass in the windows instead of arrases hanging over the openings. There were carpets on the floors instead of rushes. Fuzzy dogs were replaced by napkins. Each person at the table had his own plate, knife, fork, and spoon, and the table was covered with a "fair cloth of fine linen." Wine replaced such potables as small beer and mead with meals. Things were indeed looking up.

But the carver was still a man, still a gentleman. Now he was the head of the house, the father of the family—and, in his own opinion and that of those gathered at the table, the center of the universe. He had two roles concerned with the food served in his home. One was to criticize it if it did not meet his standards. (He didn't know beans about cooking, but he knew what he liked.) The other was as the carver; stern yet kindly dispenser of the food that was the heart of the meal, master of a new and delicate art form that caused the beholders—when he was good at it—to ooh and aah at his skill, to shower him with compliments that he accepted as no more than his just due.

Carving, then, was a ceremony; the carver was a devoted craftsman. And he was always a man. Women were not equipped, mentally or emotionally or physically, for so elegant a duty. The best they were fitted for was to clean up afterwards.

As with all such ceremonies, a certain mystique surrounded carving, as well as a rigid set of standards and rules that only the vulgar would violate. To begin with, at least among the upper classes, carving was always done in the dining room. The master stood at his rightful place, the head of the table, a stack of hot-from-the-warming-oven plates at one side, his tools laid out in splendid array. These included two carving knives, a large one with a long, flexible blade and a smaller one with a shorter, inflexible blade and a pointed end; plus a third knife, long, thin, sometimes with a serrated blade, always with a rounded tip, called a slicer. Two forks, of a size to match the carving knife, were supplied, double-tined and each with a turn-down guard to protect the carver in the event the knife—oh, the shame of it!—should slip. There was also a long sharpening steel, with a handle, to which the master would give a couple of preparatory licks with a knife already at the ultimate stage of sharpness.

A small gadget, dumbbell-shaped and fashioned of silver or of cut crystal, was a knife rest. A plate or small platter or tray was provided on which bones could be discarded, as was a large extra napkin to keep the artist's hands tidy in the event of splashes. A long-handled dressing spoon, when it would be required, completed the array. Presently, when poultry shears were invented, they were added to the armory.

In from the kitchen would come the roast or bird, on a hot platter large enough to accommodate, also, the servings that the master would carve. A hush would fall over the table. With a dignified inclination of his head, the master would pick up his tools. The ceremony was underway. Neatly, deftly, the carver separated the meat or fowl into servings, following the rules given for each separate cut of meat. Neatly, deftly, he portioned the servings onto the plates. They were passed; vegetables, gravy, condiments were also passed. His work done, the carver laid aside his tools, delicately mopped his hands on the napkin, and sat down. With a heartfelt sigh of relief, the diners fell on their food. It was all over—until tomorrow, when it would be solemnly repeated.

CARVING UP TO DATE

Today, carving is not so formal. It's no longer a ceremony, but merely one of the assorted concomitants of cooking a meal and getting it on the table. Sometimes, still, it's done at the table by dad, sometimes by mother in the kitchen.

But in spite of informality, there are still rules to be followed—not because the right way is the only way genteel people attack a problem, but because the right way is the best way to carve a given piece of meat, fish, or poultry for optimum flavor, juiciness, and ease of eating.

Some tools are still necessary. On the theory that a job worth doing is worth doing well, they should be the right ones and they should be good ones. Below are the choices.

standard carving knife: Most often used for roasts. Blade is 7 to 9 inches long, of medium width, and tapers to a point.

short carving knife: For steaks, poultry. It has a shorter (7-

or 8-inch), narrower, curved blade, easier to maneuver where there are many bones, or for simple slicing.

electric carving knife: There are both plug-in and battery models. Gives excellent control over slices—they can be as thick as you wish, or see-through thin. Easy to use. (Don't carve meat on a platter with an electric knife; meat must be placed on a carving board to avoid damage to the knife blade.)

slicing knife: Also known as a ham slicer. Has a long (up to 10-inch), narrow, blunt-tipped blade. Just right for thin slicing of cold meats, which tend to stick to a wider, less flexible knife.

carving fork: Has two long tines, a long stem, and a turn-down guard to protect the carver against knife slippage. Use to anchor the meat—keep it from slipping on the platter—as it is carved. An alternative is a wicked-looking meat holder called a carving aid; it has two very long, very sharp tines, a very short stem, and a sturdy, fist-grip handle. It does the job,

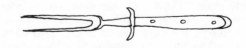

but don't leave it (or knives, or anything else sharp) where the kids can get at it.

poultry shears: They look somewhat like grass trimmers, with short, sharp, pointed blades and a handle that works them scissors-fashion. With these you can carve poultry easily. Use the shears to separate bones at the joints or cut off a whole portion—wing, thigh, drumstick; go back to a knife for slicing.

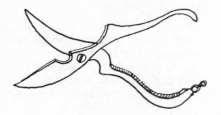

Tools must be sharp to do a good job. Use a steel or a whetstone or an electric knife sharpener (provided you know how to use it properly—improperly used it can hack up the blades) to keep the carving tools sharp. And use them only for the purpose for which they were designed. Carving knives are not for prying caps off jars, hammering nails, or use as substitutes for a cleaver. Wash knives in warm, soapy water, rinse well, and dry by hand, paying particular attention to the point where the handle joins the blade. Don't put them into the dishwasher.

DEALING WITH MEAT

Meat should stand for a time between coming out of the oven and being carved ("rest a spell," was grandma's term for it). This sets the juices and firms the meat, making it easier to carve. In general—although there are some exceptions—carve all meats across the grain, all fowl with the grain. Move with reasonable speed, with broad—not short, choppy—strokes of the knife, to ensure attractive, even portions.

Carving beef. Properly handled in the cooking, beef is tender and succulent. Properly handled in the carving, it is juicy and delectable. Here are the ways with the usual cuts.

standing rib roast (A): Place the roast with the meaty, flat side down on a platter large enough to hold the juices that carving will release. It should be positioned so that the ends of the bones are to the carver's left. Trim off excess fat, but bear in mind that some people think that the fat is the best part of the meat. Anchor the meat firmly by piercing it between ribs with a carving fork. With the carving knife, slice the meat toward you, from the outside of the roast toward the bones, parallel to the platter, making the slices of whatever thickness you like. (Very thin slices are called "English-cut," very thick ones "pub-cut.") When you have carved as many slices as you wish, cut down, from top to bottom, along and

as close as possible to the rib bones—this frees the slices from the bones.

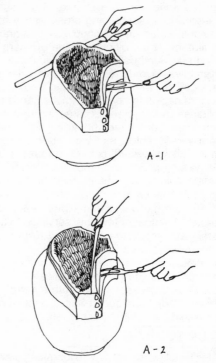

rolled roast (B): Stand the roast up on the platter, with the meat side up, the tying strings parallel to the platter. Anchor firmly with the carving fork. Slice, toward you, as thickly or thinly as desired, starting at the top. Although it may seem as if it would be simpler to place the roast on its side and slice as you'd slice a loaf of bread, the position described keeps juices in the roast, instead of allowing them to run out on the platter.

steaks, sirloin, and porterhouse (C): It's not necessary, of course, to carve a single-portion steak—that's the individual diner's problem. But when a steak is large and thick, it will serve a number of people and must be carved. Place steak flat on a platter, anchor firmly with carving fork. With the tip of the carving knife (the shorter one is better here), cut closely around the bone. Lift out bone and lay aside. Carve across the steak, including in each slice meat from either side of the bone. Cut the slices slightly on the diagonal, across the grain. Cut the tail of the steak in slightly diagonal slices across the width.

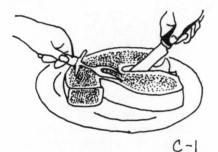

C-1

C-2

C-3

blade pot roast (D): Place meat flat on a platter. Anchor with the carving fork. With (short) carving knife, cut between muscles and around bones to remove meat one solid piece at a time. Turn the cut-out piece of meat so that its fibers (grain) are parallel to the platter. Holding the piece with the fork, slice down, across the grain. Repeat with remaining pieces.

D-1

D-2

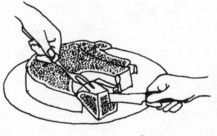

D-3

tongue: The tongue should be skinned in the kitchen, and the root end—the schlung—trimmed away. (If the tongue is smoked, save the schlung for soup—bean, pea, or lentil—which it flavors gloriously.) Carving is then very simple; cut the tongue in thin, crosswise slices. The tip, which would make very small slices, can be put aside to chop for a delicious sandwich spread, or to scramble with eggs.

corned beef: The usual cut of corned beef is boneless brisket. Simply cut in thin slices, across the grain. If you have a piece of bone-in corned beef, remove the bones before bringing it to the table.

Carving lamb. Young lamb (and most all available to us is young) is tender and juicy. Only roasts need carving; steaks

—cross-cut slices of the leg—and chops are single-serving items.

crown roast (E): The butcher who prepared the roast will have done all the hard work, making this the easiest of roasts to carve. It should be placed on the platter with the bone-ends up. All you need to do is steady it with the carving fork and use the knife to slice down through the ribs, cutting it into servings that are, in effect, chops. If the roast has been stuffed, add a spoonful of stuffing to each serving.

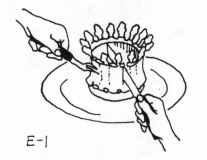

E-1

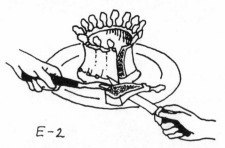

E-2

leg of lamb, American style (F): Place the lamb on the platter with the leg bone to the carver's right. From the thin side of the leg, facing you, cut three thin, lengthwise slices. Turn the roast so that it stands on this flat, cut surface. Starting at the point where the shank joins the thigh portion, cut ¼-inch slices perpendicular to the leg bone. Then loosen the slices by cutting under them, along the top of the leg bone.

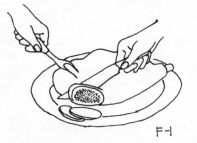

F-1

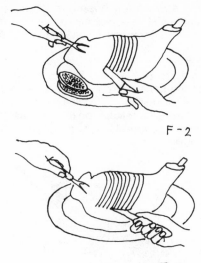

F-2

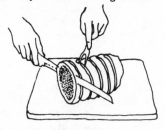

F-3

leg of lamb, French style (G): This is very simple, and more or less harks back to the Middle Ages carver. Hold the end of the leg bone with your hand, lifting it a little off the platter. Cut thin slices parallel to the leg bone.

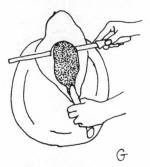

G

boned-and-rolled shoulder (H): Place the roast flat on the platter. Anchor with the carving fork, and cut neat, even, round slices, as if you were slicing bread.

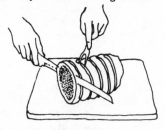

H

302

Carving pork. Ever since Charles Lamb's "Dissertation on Roast Pig," people have been enjoying pork. (In it, people had been eating their meat raw. However, when the house burned down and the family's pig was caught in the conflagration, it smelled so good in its roasted state they were tempted to try it, and we've been eating our meat cooked ever since.) Properly cooked—it is not necessary to burn the house down—pork is tender and juicy. Onion seasons pork excellently, and apples, sauerkraut or cabbage, and sweet potatoes go particularly well with it.

crown roast: Carve in the manner of crown roast of lamb (E).

loin roast (J): First, remove the backbone, taking with it as little meat as possible. This can be done in the kitchen, before the roast is brought in, or by the carver. Then set the roast with the bone ends up and the concave side of the ribs facing you. You need only cut down between the ribs, separating the roast into chops for serving.

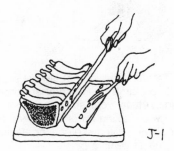

J-1

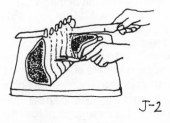

J-2

rolled roast: Carve in the manner of a boned-and-rolled shoulder of lamb (H).

whole ham (K): Position the ham on the platter with the fat side up and the shank bone to the carver's right. Anchoring the ham with the carving fork, cut two or three thin slices off the thin side of the ham, to make a flat resting place. This will be the side nearest you if the ham is from a left leg, away from you if a right leg. Turn ham so that it rests on this cut, flat portion; slice straight down, from the top to the leg bone,

making narrow, even cuts. Cut parallel and close to the leg bone beneath the slices to free them for serving.

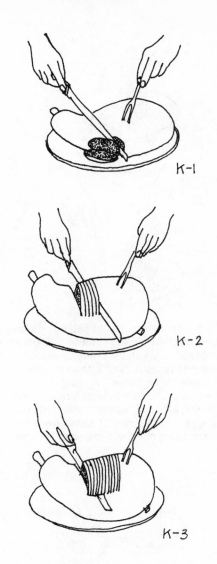

K-1

K-2

K-3

shank-half ham (L): Position the meat on the platter so that the shank end is at the carver's left. This puts the thick "cushion" meat on top. Anchor ham with a carving fork; cut along and close to the leg bone. Lift off this all-meat top portion, and carve by cutting straight down through it in thin, even slices. Cut around the bone of the remaining piece; turn so that it rests on its flat side. Cut straight down into thin, even slices.

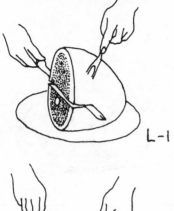

L-1

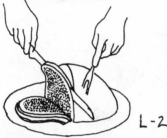

L-2

butt-half ham (M): Position meat flat-side down on the platter. Cut along the h-bone and remove the boneless piece; place this cut-side down on the platter and slice in thin, even pieces from top to bottom. (You'll have to explore a bit—this meaty piece may be on either the right or the left side, depending on whether the ham is from a right or left leg.) Holding the remaining piece of ham with your fork, cut across the meat, toward you, in a series of slices from outside to the bone. Cut down along bone with the tip of the knife to release the slices.

m-1

m-2

m-3

Carving veal. Tender—though not always juicy—veal can be carved exactly as lamb is. Remember, always, to slice against the grain. Letting veal stand or "rest" for twenty minutes or so between taking it from the oven and bringing it to the table for serving will make carving easier, true of all meats but most true of veal.

DEALING WITH POULTRY

There was a time when a chicken dinner was an event, in the days when (unless you raised the fowl yourself) chicken was expensive compared to meat. Some lucky folks had chicken every Sunday, others only on special occasions, such as when the minister was invited to dinner. But today, meat has long since elbowed its way past chicken—and turkey, too—in price, and we can enjoy poultry meals as often as we like.

Carving chicken, turkey, and capon. Meat, you'll remember, is carved for the most part across the grain. The opposite is true for fowl, which is carved for the most part with the grain. You'll need a carving knife and fork, of course, and a long-handled stuffing spoon as well, if the bird is stuffed. Before beginning to carve, remove all the trussing paraphernalia—wooden or metal trussing picks, cord, sewing thread, whatever. An extra plate or smaller platter is useful to hold drumsticks and wings as they are removed.

chicken, turkey, capon (N): Position fowl on the platter breast-side up, with legs toward the carver's right. Hold the end of the leg nearest you with your fingers, pulling gently away from the body as you cut through the skin between leg and body. With the flat side of the knife, press the leg away from the body; anchor with carving fork. Cut through the joint holding the leg to the body. Separate drumstick from thigh, cutting through at the joint; set the two portions aside.

Anchor fowl with fork near the breastbone; cut off the wing close to the body, slanting the knife slightly inward to locate the joint; set wing aside. Repeat these two steps on the other side of the fowl. Slice breast meat, beginning at the tip of the breastbone and cutting down toward wing joint; repeat on the other side. If you are dealing with a small chicken, the wings, drumsticks, and thighs will each make a single serving. These portions of a large bird, however, require carving.

Anchoring with the fork, separate the wing at the first joint, making two servings. Slice drumstick meat by holding drumstick firmly at the end with your fingers; cut down, away from you, turning the leg to get uniform slices. Anchor thigh firmly on the platter with the fork; cut slices of meat through thickest portion, parallel to the bone. Transfer meat to serving plates, giving each diner some light, some dark meat, and a spoonful of stuffing.

N-3

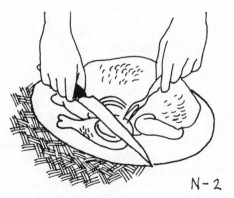

N-1

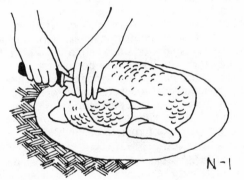

N-2

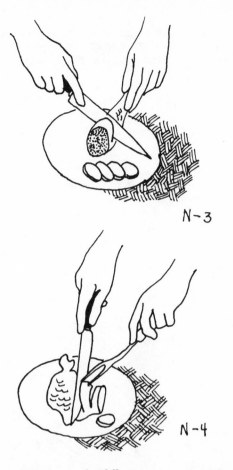

N-4

Carving duck or duckling, goose, game birds.

Though slightly more complicated than chicken or turkey, the secret of carving these birds is not to allow yourself to be seized by stage fright. As with other fowl, start by removing all the trussing and/or sewing materials. Have a long-handled spoon ready if the bird is stuffed.

duck, duckling (O): Anchor the duck firmly with the carving fork. Cut the skin at the inside hip joint; run the point of the knife all the way around the thigh where it joins the body, to cut the skin. Pull the leg away from the body and cut through the joint to remove the leg. Set leg aside; repeat with the other leg. Remove the wishbone by cutting around it on both sides; using the fork, pull out the bone and lay it aside. Cut from the top of the breast down to the wing joint; sever the joint with the point of the knife and lay the wing aside. Repeat with the other wing.

Again anchoring the bird firmly with your fork, cut down the length of the bird on each side of and very close to the breastbone. Slide the knife gently down along the ribs on each side, loosening the breastbone. If the bird is large, the breast meat may be sliced; if small, each half of the breast meat is one serving, each leg one serving. (The wings are

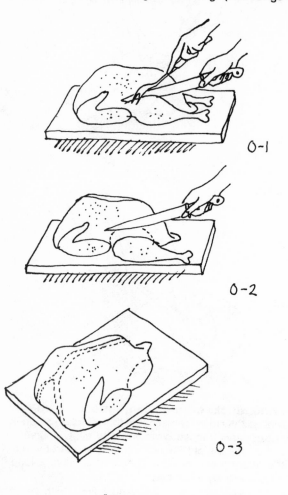

O-1

O-2

O-3

O-4

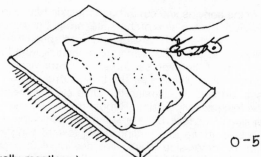

O-5

virtually meatless.)

goose: Wild or domestic, carve this in the same manner as a duck. The goose, being somewhat larger, is easier to carve. Slice the breast meat, from the top of the breastbone downward, before removing from the carcass.

pheasant, other wild birds: Pheasant is carved exactly as a chicken is. Small game birds are simply split in half, each half making a serving; start at the breastbone and work gently downward. Very small birds are served whole.

DEALING WITH FISH

Cutting a fish into servings is more a matter of boning than of carving. Here a carving knife is excess baggage, although in some cases you may need a fork—but use it very carefully, or you will tear the tender fish. A small, blunt knife—such as a butter knife—is fine for small fish, a table knife for larger ones. In a large fish, the choice portions are in the center. When you serve a portion of a large fish, or of a piece of such a fish—a poached center cut of salmon, for example—lift the meat away from the bones, preserving it in sizable sections, and using the natural flakes as your guide. A large server or, in a pinch, a pancake turner, is useful here.

Boning whole fish, fish steaks. At first sight, boning a whole cooked fish looks like a job for a professional chef, but it's really quite easy. Word of advice: tackle a small fish, such as a trout, rather than a monster of the deep for your first try. Fish steaks (a slice cut through the entire fish, including the bones) are sometimes boned—before cooking—to form elegant servings called medallions. Steaks from large fish, such as salmon, are the only ones suitable for this process.

boning a whole cooked fish (P): Anchor the fish by holding it with a fork placed—not too deeply—in the gill section. Use a butter knife or some other short, blunt-tipped knife; slip it through the skin and—gently—along the entire length of the backbone. Lift the entire top piece (this is a fillet), including the backbone and tail, away from the bottom fillet; place it, skin-side down, on the platter. By sliding the knife closely underneath them, lift away and discard the tail, the backbone with its attached lateral bones, and the head. If this is a small fish—one serving—replace the top fillet over the bottom one,

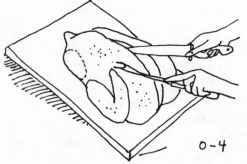

306

and serve. If a large fish, cut each fillet into serving pieces gently, using the natural lines of the flakes as a guide. The skin is left on a small fish, such as a trout; it can be removed or left in place on a large fish, as you wish.

P-1

P-2

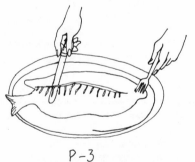

P-3

boning fish steaks for medallions (Q): Lay a raw steak, ¾ to 1 inch thick, flat on a cutting board with the open end toward you. With the point of a small, sharp knife, remove the skin and discard (or save skin and bones to make court bouillon, if the medallions are to be poached). Working with the knife tip, cut and gently pry away the central bone and the sets of long, thin bones that are attached to it, making certain not to break off and leave behind any of these bones. You now have two boneless, skinless halves. Turn one of these upside down, and place it very close to the second. Press the large ends together and wrap the small ends around them, until you have a solid, circular piece. Secure with food picks,

which will stay in place during cooking but be removed before the medallions are served.

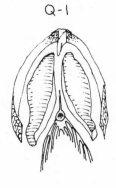

Q-1

Q-2

THE HOME COOK AS BUTCHER

Armed with sharp knives of several sizes, a certain amount of skill with your hands, and the determination to forge ahead, you can save a considerable amount on your food budget by doing simple butchering procedures at home.

Think of it this way: every time the market butcher takes knife to meat, it costs you money. So if you buy meat in large pieces and take knife to them yourself, you'll be way ahead. Don't tackle anything that requires great skill as well as a knowledge of the anatomy of the animal, such as cutting up a side of beef for your freezer. But smaller, simpler jobs are easy to handle in the home kitchen with a minimum of know-how.

First, do your math. It's almost always true that a large piece of meat will cost less per pound than a collection of small pieces—a whole pork loin less than pork loin chops, a whole chicken less than chicken parts, bone-in chicken breasts less than the boned ones. If the per-pound price differential between the whole and the cut-up versions is very small, a matter of two or three cents, the work involved isn't worth it unless you really enjoy this kind of thing and have nothing better to do with your time. If the price differential is larger, the work involved will be worth it.

307

working on pork loin: If you see a whole pork loin in the market at a good price, by all means take it home. You can easily cut it up—into chops, or into a small roast plus chops. If there is an excess amount of fat, start by trimming it off. Then cut off the backbone as in carving a loin of pork. (Use this piece as the basis of a good, hearty soup.) Turn the meat—on a cutting board—so that the bone ends of the ribs are up, the concave side of the loin toward you; this is the best position for locating the ribs. If you wish very thick chops (perhaps to stuff and bake, like small, individual roasts), cut each one two ribs thick. For chops of normal thickness, cut between each two ribs, making the cut in the middle of the meat between the ribs. For thin chops, make a cut down each side of each rib, very close to the bone. If you do this thriftily, there will be small collops of pork left over, one between each two ribs. (Braise these with onions and mushrooms, seasoned with paprika; stir sour cream in just before dishing up, and serve over parslied rice.)

If a whole fresh ham (leg of pork) is on sale, bring it home even if it is too large for a first meal plus a leftovers meal for your family. Cut the ham in half crosswise, to make two roasts—cook one, freeze one. Or cut off two even slices, ½ inch thick, from the large end. These pork steaks can be browned and then, with liquid added (water, chicken broth, tomato juice), cooked, tightly covered, until done and tender. Or the second step of cooking can be accomplished in the oven if you prefer. Serve with baked yams and sautéed apple rings.

working on lamb: Lamb breast is sometimes on sale. Bring it home, cut it into lamb riblets (in this form, they are usually considerably more expensive in the market). Treat these riblets as you would pork spareribs, with a barbecue sauce or a sweet glaze, or braise with a ratatouillelike vegetable mixture. The cutting up is no work at all—just place the breast on a cutting board and, with a large, sharp knife, slice between the ribs.

If you see a bargain leg of lamb too big for your family, buy it and slice off steaks from the large end—depending on the size of the leg, these steaks will serve one or two persons. A small saw is useful here, as well as in some other home butchering. A hacksaw (with a clean blade, naturally) will do fine, or the family tool chest may turn up another useful saw.

A rack of lamb may be very easily sliced into french-style rib chops, if the whole rack is less expensive than the chops packaged individually. However, the rack will be juicier and more delicious if you cook it whole.

working on beef: Sometimes a large standing rib roast is less expensive per pound than a smaller one. If your meat-counter prowling turns up one too large to be consumed by the family in two meals, buy it anyway and cut off rib steaks. Attack this as if you were going to carve a roasted standing rib, but instead of disengaging slices from the bone, cut off ribs and all. If the roast is not oven-ready (has not been trimmed), cut off the ends of the ribs of the entire roast, almost down to the big eye of meat, and put them away to braise or devil for another meal. (The saw will come in handy here, too.)

A too-large pot roast of the chuck-eye, eye-of-round, rump, or cross-rib variety can yield slices (about ½ to ¾ inch thick) from which to make swiss or spanish steak. A rib-eye roast will yield delmonico steaks, but broil or panfry these—they are too tender (and expensive) to braise. In any case, the cutting-up is easy. Simply cut off even slices, as if you were carving the cooked roast.

working on chicken: There are two sides to the home butchering of chicken, cutting up and boning, and both are money-savers of considerable merit. Broiler-fryers are virtually always less expensive per pound whole than when they appear in the market as chicken parts. And bone-in chicken breasts cost a good deal less than the boned suprêmes. Since both the cutting and the boning are easy to do at home—why not? You'll save even more if you keep a sharp eye out for specials. Have a big-project home butchering, stash the proceeds in the freezer, and save yourself a bundle. Tools? A sturdy cutting board and a small, pointed knife, very sharp.

CUTTING UP A WHOLE CHICKEN

1) Start with the legs. First, with the chicken on its back, sever the skin all the way around between the thighs and body. Lift the chicken firmly by both legs; bend the legs back until hip joints are loose. With a sharp knife, remove the legs from the body—cut from back to front, keeping as close to the backbone as possible.

2) Separate thigh from drumstick of both legs. Locate the joint by pressing the area with your fingers. When you have the proper place, cut neatly through the joint with your sharp knife.

3) Next, remove the wings. Begin on the inside of the wing, just over the joint that connects it to the body, and cut all the way around the joint. Then cut through the joint.

4) Now separate breast and back sections. Stand the carcass up on the neck end. From the tail, cut along each side of the backbone through the rib joints to the neck. Cut through the skin that joins the breast to the back. Place the back skin-side up on the board. Cut into two pieces, making your cut just above the two spoon-shaped bones in the back.

5) Finally the breast. Place it skin-side down on the board. Cut through the white cartilage that shows in the V-shape at the neck end of the breast. Hold the breast firmly with both hands, one on each side, and bend back. Push up with fingers to snap out the breastbone. Cut the breast in half lengthwise.

And there you are—chicken parts. Plus a bonus of giblets, neck, bones, skin, and fat, which add up to chicken stock to use in cooking or as the basis of a good soup.

BONING CHICKEN BREASTS

Use whole breasts that weigh about 1 pound each—of which about 2 ounces will be skin, 6 ounces bone. You need a thin, sharp knife about 6 inches long—the thinner and sharper the blade, the easier and neater your task.

1) Place breast skin-side down on the cutting board. Cut just through the white cartilage at the neck end of the keel bone—the dark bone at the center of the breast. Bend the breast back with both hands and press flat to expose the keel bone.

2) Loosen the keel bone by running the tip of your index finger around both sides. Remove keel bone—it may come out in one piece or in two.

3) Working on one side of the breast, insert the tip of the knife under the long rib bone. Gently work the knife underneath the bone to cut it free from the meat. Lifting the rib bones as you go, cut the meat away from the rib cage, cutting around the outer edge of the breast up to the shoulder joint; then cut through the shoulder joint. This removes the entire rib cage on one side. Turn breast and repeat on the second side.

4) Working from the ends of the wishbone, gently scrape flesh away from each side of the bone. Cut out the wishbone, now free of meat. Slip your knife under the white tendons on either side of the breast to loosen them; pull them out. If you wish, pull off the skin. (Use skin and bones for stock.)

BONING A WHOLE FOWL

This can be tricky. But take comfort: it looks trickier than it turns out to be. Why would you want to bone a whole fowl—chicken, turkey, duck? For a GALANTINE or similar dish, such as a boneless stuffed chicken. Boning a whole bird is not something the average home cook does often—indeed, it's something that vast numbers of home cooks go through life without doing, without wanting to do, without the idea even occurring to them.

Boning a whole fowl—that is, taking out the bones, but leaving the meat and the skin intact—is something of a learn-by-doing process. We can give you directions, which are relatively short and simple, but you'll have to practice. Try a chicken of which you intend to make not a galantine but a stew or soup. Your first attempt may be botched a bit, but the stew/soup won't suffer. And you'll be surprised how well the second one will go if you're at all skillful, and if you enjoy nit-picky jobs. If you aren't and don't, this type of boning is not for you. Make some other kind of elegant dish when you want to impress guests.

1) Place the fowl breast-side down on a cutting board. With a boning knife (or a very sharp knife with a thin, short, pointed blade), slit the skin down the back from the neck to the tail.

2) Moving slowly, exploring gently with both knife and fingers, work the blade of the knife down both sides of the incision, keeping as close as possible to the bone. Scrape the meat from the bone little by little, separating the flesh from the rib cage by running your fingers between the two. Continue to scrape the meat from the bones, and sever the joints, until the backbone, rib cage, and breastbone are removed.

3) Scrape the meat away from the top of the leg joints and down the bones. Grasp the top of the leg joint with a towel (fingers will slip), and pull the flesh free from the bone, turning it inside out as you would strip off a glove. Scrape and remove the tendons from the leg meat. Repeat with second leg.

4) Scrape the meat from the bones at the neck end. Cut off and discard (save for stock) the last two joints of each wing. Scrape and remove the remaining wing bones in the same manner as you used for the legs.

If you are intrigued with boning chicken or any other meat, you may want to acquire a boning knife. These knives have short, narrow blades and heavy handles that are easy to grip. Some come with finger guards. But whether you use a boner or simply a small kitchen (paring) knife, make certain it is very sharp. Otherwise you'll hack away and make a mess of the job.

Man's place is in the kitchen. You'll remember that for a long while woman, that inferior soul, was not considered capable of so intricate a job as carving. That day is gone, but it's true that today many men—even those who would starve if left to fend for themselves culinarily speaking—enjoy the intricacy of cutting up and boning. (This is particularly true of those who like to carve.) So if you have two left hands but your husband is skillful with both of his, here's a kitchen job he can do and will probably enjoy doing. Perhaps he'll have Mitty-type dreams of being a famous surgeon. If he does, indulge him—it'll get a job done for you that you can't, or would rather not, do yourself.

HADDOCK: see FISH

HALF-AND-HALF: see CREAM

HAM

Meat from the hind leg of a hog, ham may be fresh, cured, canned, or cured and smoked. Tender, delectable of flavor, delicately rosy-pink in color, it is one of our favorite meats—in steaks or small cuts for family meals, as whole ham for festive occasions, as leftovers that supply dozens of delicious dishes.

An old wives' tale maintains that the hog's left leg makes a ham superior to the right leg, based on the fact that human right sides (of those of us who are righthanded) get more exercise, and should therefore be tougher than the left ones. Inasmuch as very few pigs write letters, open doors, play quarterback or center field, or do any of the myriad other things we do with our right arms (not to mention that hams come from *hind* legs) it's safe to discount the tale and go on about our business.

Turning pork into ham. A fresh ham is like any other fresh pork, neither cured nor smoked (see PORK). But the pink-fleshed leg that is truly ham has been treated in one of several ways before it comes to the market.

Like many of the other things we do to food, curing ham started as a necessity—a way to preserve meat long past the time it would remain edible when freshly butchered. Some such cures were successful only in that they preserved the food, even though the finished product was pretty unpalatable. But curing ham was, and is, such a success that we continued the process long after it was necessary.

the curing process: Hams may be dry-salt cured or cured in a salt/water brine. But by far the most common curing process these days involves pumping into the meat, before it is smoked, a liquid made up of salt, sodium or potassium nitrite, and sugar, dissolved in water. During the smoking that follows, hams lose some of the moisture from the curing liquid. Those that return to their original weight are labeled

simply "ham," but those that retain up to 10 percent of the moisture, adding that much to their weight, must be labeled "ham, water added." (Retention of more than 10 percent is not allowed; if more than 10 percent is retained, the product must be labeled "imitation ham.")

The label on the ham you buy should also give you other information—the weight, the price per pound, and the total price, of course, but also whether or not the ham is smoked (some are simply cured, not smoked afterwards) and whether or not it is fully cooked.

fully cooked: This ham has been smoked and cooked to an internal temperature of at least 150°F. It does not require further cooking. You may serve it cold or, if you prefer, you may heat it (in the oven) to serve hot.

cook before eating: This ham will have been heated to an internal temperature of at least 140°F. during the smoking process. It should be cooked to an internal temperature of 160°F. for optimum flavor and tenderness.

If the ham you buy does not have a label, you should assume that it is the cook-before-eating type, and cook it.

Styles, types, and kinds of ham. Whatever you have in mind as a ham main dish, you can buy a kind to suit your purpose. Here are the choices.

bone-in: These are sold as whole ham, half ham, shank portion, butt (rump) portion, and as center slices. Shank portion is the shank half with center slices removed. Rump portion is the butt half with center slices cut off.

semi-boneless: These hams are partially boned, have at least one bone—usually the round leg bone—remaining.

boneless: These hams, or parts of hams, have all the bones removed. Most of the external and internal fat has been trimmed away as well. The lean meat is shaped and enclosed in a casing, or it may be placed in a can for processing.

canned: These are boneless, cured sections of ham, placed in cans, vacuum-sealed, and then fully cooked. A small amount of neutral, unflavored dry gelatin (about ¼ ounce in a 5-pound canned ham) is added before sealing to absorb the natural juices that the ham releases during the cooking process.

All canned hams may be served without further cooking, although they can be oven-baked if you wish to serve them hot. Most canned hams must be stored in the refrigerator—both at the store where you buy them and after you get them home. Check the label for storage instructions. Those that require refrigeration (a few small sizes do not) will be marked "Perishable—Keep Refrigerated."

cooked ham: This is available at delicatessens, supermarket deli counters, and—sliced and packaged—in supermarket refrigerated cases. It will have been either boiled or baked, the latter often referred to as Virginia ham, although the hog may never have seen Virginia.

prosciutto: This is Italian-style ham, dry-cured and ready to eat. Highly seasoned, it is best sliced very thin. Available at specialty food shops or Italian grocery stores or delicatessens. (See PROSCIUTTO.)

westphalian: Also ready to eat, this is a very firm ham from Germany. It gets its characteristic flavor from the juniper wood used in smoking it. Get it at specialty stores and delicatessens, or, sometimes, sliced and packaged in supermarket refrigerated cases. Best sliced thin. (See WESTPHALIAN HAM.)

scotch-style ham: This is boneless and uncooked cured ham, packed in a casing or a stockinette bag.

country ham: This is bone-in ham, uncooked, dry-cured—after which it may or may not be smoked. Scrub with a stiff brush to remove excess salt and pepper and, sometimes, harmless mold on the outside; soak overnight to get out some of the heavy salt, then simmer at length (after which it may be glazed and baked if you like). A long process and worth every moment of it. Country hams come from many states, and are likely to be labeled with the state of origin—Georgia, Kentucky, Missouri, North Carolina, Tennessee, or Virginia.

country-style ham: Bears a taste-and-appearance resemblance to country ham, but is not produced in rural areas. May or may not need soaking; either way, it must be cooked before eating.

smithfield ham: This, the producers would have you believe, is the only "real thing" country ham, and once you've tasted it you will be inclined to agree. So long and lean you'll really believe this hog did play center field, the ham must be scrubbed and soaked, and it requires long cooking. Smithfield, Virginia—named after the London livestock center—was founded in 1752, but citizens of the area had been exporting ham to England since 1640.

As with anything very, very good, all sorts of imitators began labeling their hams "Smithfield." Patience is certainly a virtue in Virginia, because it wasn't until 1926 that the state's General Assembly passed a law stating that "genuine Smithfield hams are . . . cut from the carcasses of peanut-fed hogs, raised in the peanut-belt of the State of Virginia and the State of North Carolina . . . cured, treated, smoked, and processed in the town of Smithfield, in the State of Virginia."

Testament to the superb quality of Smithfield hams is the fact that Queen Victoria placed a standing order for six hams a week.

Other products, hamlike but not ham. Hams, we pointed out, are from the hog's hind legs. Other parts of the porker are often cured, smoked, and treated in the manner of ham to produce hamlike flavor, color, and texture in the meat. Smoked shoulder rolls and smoked picnics (sometimes incorrectly called "picnic ham") are from the shoulder of the hog. They are flavorful, less tender than ham, and have a higher fat content. These may be either fully cooked or cook-before-eating types. The fully cooked kind may be served cold, or heated if you wish. Cook-before-eating rolls and picnics (sometimes called butts) may be baked or cooked in liquid. In either case, follow the instructions on the package.

Also kissing kin to ham are canadian bacon—the cured and smoked "eye" of the loin, a long, boneless roll of lean meat—and smoked loin pork chops. Both have the good, tangy flavor of smoked ham. Chops are sold four or six to the package; cook them following label directions. Canadian bacon may be whole or packaged in slices; sometimes the whole kind is canned.

HAM IN YOUR KITCHEN

When you decide to have ham for a meal—or several—you need to have in mind before you buy it the number (and appetites) of the people you are going to serve. Ham as one facet of a buffet spread will yield more servings than if it is the main dish of a sit-down meal, for example. You also need to bear in mind your time and facilities for cooking and storage of the meat.

how to buy: Don't make a snap judgment of "it's too expensive," and pass ham by. Instead, compute servings per pound—it's the cost of edible meat per serving that really counts. Here are some serving sizes to guide you: allow ¼ to ⅓ pound per serving for boneless meat, ⅓ to ½ pound for semi-boneless, up to ¾ pound per serving for bone-in meat. Remember, too, that there is virtually no shrinkage to fully cooked ham, and not much to the cook-before-eating variety.

Perhaps guided by a memory—real or atavistic—of hams hanging for months, sometimes for years, from the rafters of the kitchen or smokehouse, some of us tend to buy ham and to store it as if it were as imperishable as honor. Not so—not present-day. Today, hams are cured (and smoked, if they are) much more lightly. Unless canned or packaged in special ways to preserve them, they are as perishable as any fresh meat, perhaps rather more so. Accordingly, it behooves us to buy ham only if it is to be brought to the table within a short time, and to use up leftovers promptly. Make sure, if you buy a canned ham, that it is stored in a refrigerated case at the market. If packages of ham or other smoked products are dated, observe the dates as sensibly as you would those on any other dated, perishable food.

how to store: All types and styles of ham and other cured or cured and smoked pork cuts should be stored in their original wrappings in the coldest part of the refrigerator, at a temperature as low as possible without freezing the meat. Except for dated packages, store up to 1 week, no longer; store center ham slices up to 3 days. Follow the instructions on dated packages; date indicates approved storage time of the *unopened* package. After opening, treat as you would any fresh meat.

Check individual canned ham labels for storage instructions. Unless labels state otherwise, canned hams and picnics may be stored, *refrigerated and unopened,* up to 1 year. After opening, treat as you would any fresh meat.

Ham leftovers should be tightly enclosed in plastic wrap or in a container with a tight-fitting cover, and stored in the coldest part of the refrigerator up to 5 days. (Ham is one of the few foods that should not be stored in foil—the salt of the cure eats little holes in foil.)

nutritive value: Values depend on many variables, particularly proportion of fat to lean, but also somewhat on the kind of ham or hamlike cured pork. To give you an idea, compare 3½-ounce servings of cooked lean meat from four types.

	smoked ham	canned ham	smoked picnic	smoked shoulder roll	
calories	211	193	211	243	
protein	25.2	18.3	28.4	27.8	grams
fat	11.5	12.3	9.9	13.8	grams
calcium	8	11	13	12	milligrams
phosphorus	201	156	220	218	milligrams
iron	3.2	2.7	3.7	3.6	milligrams
potassium	398	340	326	326	milligrams
thiamin	.78	.53	.65	.64	milligram
riboflavin	.24	.19	.26	.25	milligram
niacin	4.1	3.8	5	5	milligrams

Ham contains no carbohydrate, vitamin A or C (ascorbic acid). The sodium content varies with the cure; although the range is broad, you can count on a high sodium content in any ham.

Tips on preparing. Most cook-before-eating hams have some rind (skin), which should be removed before cooking. Otherwise, there is little to do to prepare it for cooking, and virtually nothing to do to a ready-to-eat ham to prepare it for heating, if you wish to serve it hot. Ham steaks (center slices) probably will have no rind; however, if there is any, remove it. Slash the edges of steaks in several places to prevent curling during cooking.

Country and other specialty hams ask more of you. First, read the label—almost all of these hams are uncooked, but a few sources cook them (often in wine), glaze them, and send them to you ready to slice and eat. Uncooked hams of this kind should be unwrapped and soaked in cold water to cover for 24 hours. Drain off the soaking water and place the ham in a large kettle. This may be easier to tell you than for you to accomplish—these hams are big. A covered roaster may have to be pressed into service; if you can, position it over two burners of the stove. Cover the ham with water. Bring to a boil; lower heat and simmer, covered, until tender, or until the large bone in the heavy end of the ham becomes loose and protrudes. Count on 25 to 30 minutes per pound

for this step. Remove the ham from the water and cut off the rind. Slice (very thin slices for this kind of ham) and serve, or glaze and oven-bake.

Freezing ham. Long-term freezing is not practical because flavor deteriorates seriously. The Pork Industry Group of the National Live Stock and Meat Board suggests that hams, arm picnic shoulders, loins, and shoulder rolls—butts—may be frozen and stored for not more than 1 month. Ham will not be inedible if frozen for a longer period, but flavor goes rapidly downhill after 1 month. (Incidentally, acronym fanciers, take a look at the initials of the Pork Industry Group.)

Other ways, other forms. In a manner of speaking, ham is ham. It is to be found in the meat, delicatessen, or refrigerator cases at the supermarket in the many forms listed at the beginning of this section. Other than those forms, look on the canned-meat shelves for small cans of deviled ham and ham-peanut butter spread. Flaked chunky ham in tunafish-size cans (6¾ ounces net weight) is a relatively new product. It is mild in flavor, packed in juices that can be stirred into whatever you're making of this ham—which can be sandwich spreads, salads, casseroles, or wherever you might use tuna. There are also ham or part-ham canned luncheon meats available.

Cooking ham. A handsome ham, well glazed, is a sight to behold, and will be fallen on with joy. You can achieve this desirable effect with either fully cooked or cook-before-eating hams. A meaty center slice, broiled or panbroiled, is certainly not to be sneezed at, plain for breakfast or brunch, gussied-up with a tasty sweet or savory or sweet/savory glaze at dinner.

If cooking instructions come with the ham you buy, follow them. If not, be guided by these.

baking: Place meat on a rack in a shallow roasting pan. Insert meat thermometer so that the bulb is centered in the thickest part of the meat, but does not rest in fat or on bone. Do not add water to the pan; do not cover the pan. Bake in a 325°F. oven until internal temperature reaches

140°F.—fully cooked or canned hams, picnic shoulders
160°F.—cook-before-eating hams, loins, canadian-style bacon
170°F.—cook-before-eating arm picnic shoulders, shoulder rolls (butts)

If the ham is to be glazed, apply the glaze 15 to 30 minutes before the end of the cooking time.

broiling, panbroiling: Broil slices that are 1 inch or more thick; panbroil thinner slices. Slash edges of fat in several places to prevent curling. Broil 3 inches from source of heat, or panbroil in a hot, ungreased skillet; in either case, turn and brown second side when first side is browned. Thin slices may also be fried, using a little oil or shortening, in a skillet over medium heat.

cooking in liquid: Cook-before-eating arm picnic shoulders and shoulder rolls can be cooked in simmering water, covered. You'll need to allow about 1½ hours for the shoulder and 3½ to 4 hours for the picnic. Make an old-fashioned meal of these by serving with boiled potatoes in their jackets, coleslaw with shredded carrots and onions and snippets of green pepper, sautéed apple rings sprinkled with cinnamon-sugar, and a relish for the meat of half-and-half prepared horseradish and yellow prepared mustard. Rhubarb sauce and plump, homemade ginger cookies with a thin lemon glaze would make a perfect ending to such a meal.

Here, to get down to specifics, are cooking timetables.

BAKED HAM
(in a 325°F. oven)

cut	weight in pounds	approximate oven time in hours
boneless ham, fully cooked (to an internal temperature of 140°F.)	3 to 4 (portion)	1½ to 1¾
	5 to 7 (half)	2 to 2¼
	7 to 10	2½ to 3
	10 to 12	3 to 3½
	12 to 14	3½ to 4
bone-in ham, fully cooked (to an internal temperature of 140°F.)	10 to 13	3 to 3½
	13 to 16	3½ to 4
semiboneless ham, fully cooked (to an internal temperature of 140°F.)	4 to 6 (half)	1¾ to 2½
	10 to 12	3 to 3½
canned ham (to an internal temperature of 140°F.)	1½ to 3	1 to 1½
	3 to 7	1½ to 2
	7 to 10	2 to 2½
	10 to 13	2½ to 3
arm picnic shoulder, fully cooked (to an internal temperature of 140°F.)	4 to 8	1¾ to 2¾
boneless ham, cook-before-eating (to an internal temperature of 160°F.)	8 to 11	2½ to 3¼
	11 to 14	3¼ to 4
bone-in ham, cook-before-eating (to an internal temperature of 160°F.)	3 to 4 (portion)	2½ to 2¾
	5 to 7 (half)	3 to 3¼
	10 to 12	3½ to 4
	12 to 15	4 to 4½
	15 to 18	4½ to 5
	18 to 22	5 to 6
loin, cook-before-eating (to an internal temperature of 160°F.)	3 to 5	1 to 2
canadian-style bacon (to an internal temperature of 160°F.)	2 to 4	1¼ to 2¼
arm picnic shoulder, cook-before-eating (to an internal temperature of 170°F.)	4 to 8	2½ to 4
shoulder roll (butt), cook-before-eating (to an internal temperature of 170°F.)	2 to 3	1½ to 2

BROILED HAM
(cook 2 to 3 inches from source of heat)

cut	approximate thickness	approximate total cooking time
ham slice	½ inch	10 to 12 minutes
	1 inch	16 to 20 minutes
smoked loin chops	½ to ¼ inch	15 to 20 minutes
canadian-style bacon slice	¼ inch	6 to 8 minutes
	½ inch	8 to 10 minutes
ham kabobs	1 to 1½ inches	16 to 20 minutes
ham patties	1 inch	16 to 20 minutes

Carving ham. How-to for whole, half, and portions of ham is covered in depth in the special feature, CARVING, BONING, AND OTHER KITCHEN TECHNIQUES.

The sweet and pretty shine. Without a glaze, a whole or half or portion of baked ham looks forlorn. And though the good ham flavor will be there without a glaze, it will be enhanced and reinforced by one, particularly a substantial and colorful topping with a tasty bonus, such as pieces of fruit. Sometimes a sauce, used to baste the ham throughout its cooking time, stands in for a glaze.

Here are some tried-and-true sauces and glazes to turn a great ham into a symphony, gustatorially speaking. Unless otherwise directed, spread glaze over ham 20 to 30 minutes before the end of baking time, return to the oven.

orange sauce: Baste ham with 1 can condensed frozen orange juice, thawed and combined with 1 cup brown sugar, ½ cup A1 Sauce.

cider baste: Combine 1 cup apple cider, 1 cup brown sugar. Decorate ham with spiced crab apples.

apricot sauce: Combine 1 cup apricot nectar, ½ cup honey; use to baste ham last hour of cooking.

sherry sauce: Pour 1 cup sherry over ham just before placing in oven. Half an hour before ham is done, sprinkle with brown sugar, baste with an additional 1 cup sherry.

french-style ham: Pour over whole ham 1 cup madeira wine; sprinkle on ½ cup each sliced onions and carrots, 1 sliced rib celery, several parsley sprigs, 1 bay leaf, ½ teaspoon thyme. Bake. Make madeira sauce when ham is almost done—combine pan juices, 1 cup beef broth, 1 cup madeira; thicken with 1½ tablespoons cornstarch dissolved in a little more madeira; simmer 5 minutes. Score ham fat, sprinkle with brown sugar; return to oven for 10 minutes. Baste with 2 tablespoons of the madeira sauce, bake 5 minutes longer. Serve with remaining madeira sauce.

honeyed country ham: Soak and simmer ham according to directions. When done, transfer to a baking sheet. Spread liberally with honey, sprinkle lightly with grated orange peel; bake until glazed.

applesauce glaze: Combine ½ cup corn syrup, 1 cup applesauce, 2 tablespoons prepared mustard.

mustard-sugar: Combine ¾ cup dark brown sugar, 2 teaspoons dry mustard, enough ham drippings to moisten.

british-pub glaze: Combine ½ cup dark brown sugar, ¼ cup dark beer, ½ teaspoon summer savory, ¼ teaspoon basil. Garnish the ham at serving time with thick sautéed tomato slices; serve with brussels sprouts.

sugaring-off glaze: Cut ham fat crisscross style; stud with cloves where cuts meet. Pat maple sugar thickly over surface. Garnish with sautéed pineapple rings.

midwest glaze: Combine 1 cup orange marmalade, ¼ cup cider vinegar, ¼ teaspoon nutmeg; spread over ham.

deep-south style: Combine 1 cup peach nectar, ½ cup honey; spoon over ham. Garnish serving platter with brandied peaches.

cumberland glaze: Melt 1 glass tart currant jelly; add 1 teaspoon dry mustard, 2 tablespoons sherry, 1 teaspoon grated orange peel.

grandma's way: Glaze ham with a combination of 1 cup molasses, ½ cup cider vinegar. Garnish platter with whole baked apples stuffed with mincemeat.

ham in cream: Bake a 1½-inch slice of ham in 2 cups heavy cream at 300°F., turning over once during cooking. Fifteen minutes before it is done, spread top very lightly with apple butter.

Sometimes a ham—particularly a boneless or canned one—tastes fine, but doesn't look all that much like ham. Then dress it up by baking it in a jacket of pastry—ham en croute. Use pie crust mix, thawed and rolled-out frozen patty shells, or refrigerated crescent rolls, the edges of their "seams" pinched together. Make decorations of scraps of pastry, place on top, and brush the whole thing with 1 egg yolk beaten with 1 tablespoon cream. Garnish with lemon cups filled with currant jelly.

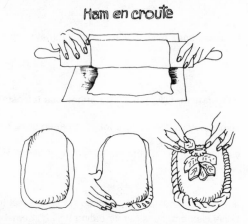

Ham en croute

The wide, wide world of ham leftovers. Nothing, not even a turkey, produces such bountiful and versatile leftovers as a ham. And when most of the meat is gone, use the bone and scraps for pea or bean or lentil soup, or chicken-ham chowder, or ham-corn soup.

Here is a random sampling of ham-leftovers ideas. Chicken breasts or thighs, boned, stuffed with ham. Ham and lima bean bake. Grilled ham and muenster sandwiches. French-fried ham and turkey (or chicken) sandwiches. Salad of fresh peach halves filled with ham-pickle relish-mayonnaise mixture. Old-fashioned ham and scalloped potatoes. For breakfast, split and buttered biscuits sandwiched with country ham, or ham and grits with red-eye gravy (see GRAVIES). Baked ham slices with sage-celery stuffing. Upside-down ham loaf with pineapple. Ham balls in sweet/sour sauce with dried apricots. Ham à la king in a corn bread ring. Ham croquettes with creamed peas and little onions. Ham shortcake made with buttermilk biscuits. Individual orange-glazed ham loaves. Corn fritters with slivers of ham. Molded ham-and-egg salad. Creamy scrambled eggs with frizzled ham. Ham soufflé. Ham-rice salad with pineapple chunks. Ham mousse. Ham creole over fluffy rice. Spaghetti with olive oil, grated cheese, ham chunks. Ham pie with cheddar crust. Ham succotash. Baked eggs with ham. Ham-stuffed cabbage. Ham-pecan waffles. Ham and eggs mollet in aspic. Well, you get the idea.

Happy ham match-ups. What does ham go well with? What doesn't it! Eggs, of course. With fruit—serve a baked or broiled ham steak with cherry sauce, peach sauce, raisin sauce. With vegetables—sweet potatoes or yams, cabbage or sauerkraut, brussels sprouts or broccoli, corn fritters or corn custard or spoon bread. With relishes—cranberry-orange-walnut, watermelon pickle, any kind of chutney.

In fact, think of ham not as a main dish for a meal or two, but as an investment in half a dozen great meals.

HAMBURGER

Americans young and old, male and female, have been conducting an aboveboard but nonetheless passionate love affair with the hamburger for generations. Hamburger in buns —plain or sesame seed or onion—as is or with a sauce or filling of cheese or chili, or in dozens of other ways, is a food everyone takes to. It's an American institution, right up there beside Home and Mother. The hamburger-on-a-bun tradition began at the St. Louis Exposition of 1904, and has never looked back. For more on hamburgers and all hamburger's relatives, see GROUND MEATS.

HARD SAUCE: see special feature: SAUCE
  SORCERY

HARD-SHELL CLAMS: see SHELLFISH

HASTY PUDDING

This is the diet staple of people everywhere who grow corn. It answers to many names—cornmeal mush, loblolly, stir-about pudding, and samp are some of them—but it was hasty pudding to our colonial ancestors, who learned from their Indian neighbors how to grow corn, how to grind it, and how to make the thick, hot, stick-to-the-ribs mush that the settlers ate morning and evening.

Although many disparaged hasty pudding as poor fare indeed, American poet-diplomat Joel Barlow wrote a paean of praise to the dish in the flowery terms of the time:

E'en Hasty-Pudding, purest of all food,
May still be bad, indifferent, or good,
As sage experience the short process guides,
Or want of skill, or want of care presides.

Unmindful that his third line doesn't scan, and warming to his work, the poet at unbelievable length describes the growing, husking, grinding of corn, and finally gets down to:

In *haste* the boiling cauldron, o'er the blaze,
Receives and cooks the ready-powder'd maize;
In *haste* 'tis served, and then in equal *haste,*
With cooling milk, we make the sweet repast.
No carving to be done, no knife to grate
The tender ear, and wound the stony plate;
But the smooth spoon, just fitted to the lip,

And taught with art the yielding mass to dip,
By frequent journeys to the bowl well stor'd,
Performs the hasty honors of the board.

Well, you get the idea. Barlow loved hasty pudding.

And well he might, because it's very good indeed. At least it is to many of us now, in a time when we are not required to eat it twice a day the year around.

The mush itself, prepared from water and cornmeal with a little salt, long cooked until it is thick and smooth, makes a deliciously unusual breakfast. Serve with milk, as the settlers did (when the cow wasn't dry), and sweeten as they did, too—with maple sugar or honey or molasses—or with white or brown sugar. Or pour the hot mush into a buttered loaf pan and refrigerate overnight. In the morning, cut into slices about ¾ inch thick. Dredge with flour and brown in bacon drippings or shortening. Serve with bacon, ham, or sausage, and with heated maple syrup or butter and brown sugar. A trencherman's breakfast, an unusual supper dish, or great for an old-fashioned brunch.

HAZELNUTS: see FILBERTS

HEAD LETTUCE: see SALAD GREENS
  AND PLANTS

HEADCHEESE: see COLD CUTS and SAUSAGES

HEALTH FOODS

Cyclamates are banned, and controversy rages over whether or not to ban saccharin. Carrots, those golden vegetables grandma said would make your hair curly and mother said would help you see better at night, are suspected of harboring more residual pesticides than any other vegetable. TV and newspapers tell us of soups put out under a respected brand name that harbor the killer botulism, beef "poisoned" by growth hormones, fish contaminated by mercury. How has all this happened? Why have we let it happen? Where will it all end?

The thing to bear in mind, before we get panicky and start running around in circles, is that these things are accidents. Isolated incidents. They are governed by two principles that weren't in existence in our forefathers' days:

1) We know a lot more now than we used to.
2) Based on ever-increasing new knowledge, we increasingly attempt to improve our way of living and, as part and parcel of our way of living, our way of eating.

We know a lot more now than we used to. Once upon a time we simply bumbled around, doing our best—a best that was none too good. Crowds of people who went to the Sunday school picnic and ate potato salad came down with something called "stomach complaint." It was simply one of those things that happened to people, and no one identified it as food poisoning or pointed a finger at the potato salad as the culprit.

After a meal that included grandma's home-canned green beans, everyone in the family fell ill; some of them died, some lived because they were stronger or because, not liking green beans, they'd taken only a taste to avoid hurting grandma's feelings. The consensus was that a flu epidemic took them off. Nobody had ever heard of botulism.

An entire farm family contracted typhoid fever. Exceedingly unfortunate, but no one suspected that it was because the family well was too shallow and situated too close to the barn.

Many of these catastrophes, and others like them, no longer occur because we know better. If they do occur, we know why. We are able to pinpoint the source of the problem rather than simply shaking our heads and saying "God's will be done." Sometimes when we identify a problem, find a name to call it, the solution is inherent in the identification. But sometimes—this is what everyone finds so hard to understand, to believe, to live with—when the solution becomes apparent, it turns out to be a good deal worse than the problem itself.

We increasingly attempt to improve our ways.

We are a people enchanted with knowledge and, because we are an impulsive people as well, demand that any new nugget of knowledge our scientists and researchers come up with be put to work at once. We find out the functions and sources of vitamins, for example, and immediately can't understand why it might not be wise to fortify every food with a load of vitamins. We learn that egg yolks are high in cholesterol, and the hotheads among us immediately want to organize a purge of hens.

But we are also, unfortunately, a gullible people, many of us totally unable to differentiate between the discoveries made by qualified people working under scientific conditions and "discoveries" made by con men over a beer in the local bar. We tend to take them all to our bosoms—the information supplied by qualified nutritionists and medical authorities, the hoaxes supplied by con men, the fads supplied by quacks. Perhaps not totally understanding any of them, we nevertheless embrace them all.

One of the results of all the fears—legitimate or not—and the pressures, the fads and fancies and pseudoscientific gibberish, as well as established scientific findings, has been the proliferation of health food movements and their concomitant health food stores, where "health" and "organic" and "natural" foods are sold. There are no official standards for the foods that fall under any of these terms, but the Office of Consumer Affairs has suggested definitions.

natural foods: Products marketed without preservatives, emulsifiers, or artificial ingredients.

organic foods: Essentially the same as "natural" foods, but with the added implication of the exclusion of pesticides and chemical fertilizers during the growing.

health foods: An all-inclusive term, embracing not only "natural" and "organic" foods, but dietetic, vegetarian, and other products, some of which contain artificial chemicals.

Many of these products are nutritious foods, but no more so than the equivalent product as sold in a grocery store or supermarket at a price far lower than the health food store asks. And many are exactly the same product as the supermarket variety, packaged differently, labeled "organic," and sold at a huge markup. For example, Connecticut's State Consumer Protection Department tested seven foods labeled as organically grown and sold in health food stores; six of them had pesticide spray residues.

Exploitation of our anxieties about our food supply is rampant. Buyers should beware, tread cautiously, investigate. But they seldom do—to the detriment of their food budget and, much more important, sometimes to the detriment of their health.

How did it all begin? The health food movement started in the sixties, in the days of the flower children—the hippies. Seeking lifestyles alternative to the home-mother-apple pie image of American living against which they rebelled (more realistically, in some cases, the cocktail party-swinger-french fry image), they dressed themselves in a ragbag couture, tried out mantras to focus their meditation, muttered "Om mani padme hum" as they put the arm on the straighter citizenry for "a little change for something to eat." Change in hand, did they head for the golden arches? No way. They sought out granola, brown rice, goats' milk, and fertile eggs, prompted by the gurus who had replaced football players as the all-American heroes.

Frantic mothers, who had been brought up to believe that the future of the world was in their hands, saw civilization slipping through their fingers daily. Fathers brought up to equate long hair with sissies and dirty fingernails with the "lower classes" laid down the law. Mothers wept, fathers raged, and the kids ran away from home in droves to form the counterculture. Some of them took to drugs. Appalled parents poured themselves another drink or two to see them through the crisis. O tempora! O mores!

Times change, so do customs. That generation has grown up now. The strong have sorted themselves out from the weak, and everyone has discovered what everyone ought to have remembered in the first place: Come what may, life goes on. Even the health food movement has shaken itself down. But it is nevertheless still with us, evolved into a pursuit of "natural" foods. As a concomitant, health food stores have proliferated. They were a $100-million a year business in 1970; only two years later, they had grown to $400-million a year, with 3,500 health food stores in the country. The growth rate has leveled off, and some of the more extreme stores have gone out of business, but the health food movement remains healthy.

What do they sell? Mainly foods without additives or preservatives, which makes the rate of spoilage great, the turnover rapid, and the prices outrageously high. A look at the shelves of a typical store reveals a large number of "natural" vitamins made from such foods as alfalfa, rose hips, garlic. (Synthesized vitamins are absolutely no different from the "natural" ones, except that they may be cleaner and purer.) Raw milk—pasteurization is not "natural" but the bacilli against which pasteurization protects us presumably are. Brown eggs in parts of the country where most home cooks prefer white ones, and vice versa. Fertile eggs. Yogurt. Wheat germ. Brewers' yeast. An abundance of "natural" cereals. Some 26 different kinds of nut butters, 79 different herb teas, 52 different "natural" cheeses (presumably made from the milk of "straight" cows?), 102 different kinds and blends of honey. In the world of health food "freaks"—as opposed to those who take a more cautious view of the matter—natural bees are always preternaturally busy, and honey is a cure for a wide spectrum of diseases from warts to tuberculosis.

Along comes the flim-flam artist. As with everything else in this imperfect world, exploiters found a fertile field in the counterculture. Extravagant claims were made for all sorts of foods. Milk—raw milk, that is—was touted as a cure for cancer. So was the diet regimen of one rabid health food advocate, who insisted that those who adhered to her diet would never die of cancer right up to the day she died . . . of cancer. Honey was both the preventative and the cure for arthritis, the faddists claimed. As for vitamin E, that was the long-sought universal panacea.

If you abided by the strictest of the macrobiotic diets, one of its leading exponents (now dead) declared, you would be spared Armageddon. "A macrobiotic person," he maintained, "cannot be killed by an atomic bomb." Probably quite true—those who adhered to the third-stage macrobiotic diet (brown rice only) would die of malnutrition long before the bomb fell.

Where does it hurt? Right here, in the pocketbook. Perhaps it is just as well that few of the young people who advocate organic and "natural" foods as offering more nutrition and more "meaning"—as well as defiance of the status quo—can afford to live by their principles. A comparison made in the early 1970s between two dozen foods purchased in health food stores and the identical two dozen foods bought in a supermarket showed that the health food store items cost an average of 70 percent more than those from the supermarket.

So most health food advocates—all but the most rabid —content themselves with fresh produce in abundance, dried beans, cheese, yogurt (without preservatives), granola, and other "natural" foods to be found these days in supermarkets, with only occasional desiccated liver pills or wild honey shampoo (just shy of $16.00 a bottle) as a sop to their counterculture leanings.

That's all to the good. Nobody is going to quarrel with fresh fruits and vegetables. Many "natural" cereals are higher in calories than in nutrients, but do no harm if your waistline can take it. Dried beans are protein-rich, especially if eaten at a meal that includes the high-quality protein of milk. Cheese is a splendid food. So is yogurt. And if they want to grow their own bean or alfalfa sprouts, though these appear in many markets today, why not? Only the rabid faddists are likely to do themselves harm—and they tend to be the kind of people to whom harm gravitates anyway, if not in one form, then in another.

The chief trouble with health food and natural food and organic food freaks is that they diagnose their own ills and then exacerbate the problems by prescribing for them. None of us without a medical education can make a viable diagnosis of any ailment beyond the point at which, if we injure a leg and see a piece of broken bone sticking up, we can say with confidence that we have a compound fracture. Like the man in the old Jerome K. Jerome story who read a medical book and immediately decided he had a bad case of housemaid's knee, we label our complaints unrealistically. But the more interesting-sounding the label, the more righteous we feel as we decide upon a remedy or at least an amelioration.

And therein lies the real danger. Listen to this list of available products, which people all over the country are busily shoving into their mouths. Megadosage of "natural" rose-hip vitamin C. Instant protein powder, "sugar free, with natural vanilla flavor," consumed in appalling amounts. Superpotent vitamin and mineral supplements—never mind what vitamins and what minerals; just be sure to take plenty, because if some is good, more must be better. Full-range amino acid chelated multi-minerals. Acidophilus powder, an aid in restoring favorable intestinal flora, containing five strains of lactobacilli. Red zinger sleepytime herb tea. D-alpha tocopherol vitamin E. All of these are from a recent "health food" company catalog, and all are nutrition supplements. Don't they sound impressive? Don't they sound good for what ails you, even if you haven't the vaguest idea what ails you or even if anything does?

The choosing of food and vitamin nostrums, instead of seeking—and following—medical advice, is the great folly of

the health food faddists. The danger is that some who have undiagnosed and untreated diseases "medicate" themselves with such things as honey, blackstrap molasses, or brewers' yeast, none of which (in reasonable amounts) will do any harm, but it will do no good either if a medical problem exists.

Exaggerated claims are made for health food products and, unfortunately, are believed. Most are untrue. Blackstrap molasses will not restore natural color to gray hair. Honey does contain calcium and iron, but is not "rich" in either mineral as claimed—there is a great deal more iron, measure for measure, in semisweet chocolate, cocoa, brown sugar, dates, prune juice, sweet potatoes, cucumbers; there is a great deal more calcium in raisins, dates, carob flour (if you want a calcium-rich health food, there's one), cocoa, sesame seeds and, of course, milk and milk products. Wheat germ is indeed high in protein compared to some of the other grain products, but not nearly as high (or as high-quality protein) as cheese, meat, poultry, and fish.

The list could go on forever. But who's listening? Probably only the people who knew all this before. Only the people who know that optimum nutrition, the well-known balanced diet, can be obtained by a proper selection and preparation of a wide variety of foods, all to be found in the ordinary stores at ordinary prices, rather than in health food stores at exorbitant prices. The health food "freaks" aren't listening—they're too busy scratching around to get enough money to buy blackstrap molasses, lecithin, avocado oil, and all the other requirements of their habit, which may not be as costly as a monkey on your back, but comes very, and very uselessly, high. For the opposite side of the coin, see the special feature: NUTRITION NOTEBOOK.

HEART: see VARIETY MEATS

HEARTS OF PALM

The terminal bud and the interior of the thick stem of one variety of cabbage palm. Fresh hearts of palm are available only in Florida and in some tropical countries, but the canned kind may be found in specialty food shops and in the gourmet-food sections of some large supermarkets. The taste is mild and delicate—and it grows on you. Which can be unfortunate, because they are expensive.

They may be served chilled, on lettuce, with a simple dressing. Or as a component of a tossed green salad. Or heat hearts of palm and serve with lemon butter, as a vegetable.

HEAVY CREAM: see CREAM

HEAVY SYRUP

The thick, sugar-rich syrup in which some kinds of canned fruits are packed; the label will tell you whether or not the fruit is packed in heavy syrup, which is high in calories and contributes little or nothing to the real flavor of the fruit.

Also, a sugar-and-water syrup made at home and used for sweetening, particularly in beverages in which dry sugar does not dissolve well. See also SYRUP.

HEN: see CHICKEN and CORNISH GAME HEN

HERBS AND SAVORY SEASONINGS

In colonial times, and for a considerable period afterward, nearly everyone had a vegetable garden. And nearly everyone who had a garden set aside a patch in which to grow herbs. Today, some of us still grow herbs—in gardens, or in boxes or pots on the kitchen windowsill—but most of us use dried herbs bought at the supermarket in little glass jars or metal or plastic boxes. How could we cook without them?

To make sure we all know what we're talking about, we need to understand the difference between the two broad categories, *herbs* and *spices,* as well as the origins of some of the other plant foods that we use in the same manner as those two.

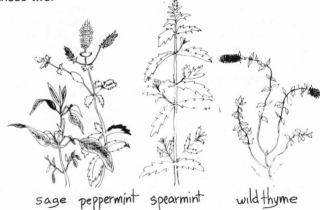

sage   peppermint   spearmint   wild thyme

herbs are the leaves of low-growing plants, some annual, some perennial. Examples are basil, marjoram, thyme, and rosemary.

spices come from the bark, roots, fruit, or berries of perennial shrubs and trees. Examples are cinnamon (bark), ginger (root), nutmeg (fruit—the interior; mace comes from the exterior of the same small, aromatic fruit). See SPICES.

seasoning blends are usually combinations of several herbs and/or spices and/or seeds, generally prepared for a specific purpose. Examples are poultry seasoning, chili powder, apple-pie spice.

savory seasonings are our old friends garlic, onion, bell peppers, horseradish, mushrooms, and others, put up in easy-use powdered or flaked form.

seeds are, quite reasonably, the flavorful seeds of various annual plants. Examples are anise, celery, caraway, mustard, dill, coriander, fennel. See SEEDS.

"Parsley, sage, rosemary, and thyme . . . ." As in the old song, these and the other herbs and savory seasonings are our concern here. They are important enough to our good cooking to consider them one by one.

Basil first grew in tropical Asia and Africa. Between thirty and forty different species of basil grow at present in many of the warmer parts of the world; although only one is generally used by spice processors, several kinds can be grown in home gardens.

Long before the time of Christ, foods were being seasoned with basil. In this country it was raised in Virginia well before 1800, and is now commercially grown here, chiefly in California. Fields of basil are beautiful, the plants growing to about eighteen inches high and giving off an enticing scent. The large leaves are harvested for commercial use just before the flower buds open, when their flavor is at its best. Fresh basil tastes mildly like licorice; the dried leaves have a lemon/anise flavor.

Use basil in many dishes, but particularly those made with tomatoes, for which the herb has a special affinity—tomato juices, soups, sauces, main dishes, salads. It is also very pleasant with fish, eggs, and cheese, and with such vegetables as eggplant, squash, peas, onions, and new potatoes.

Bay Leaves are the leaves of the sweet bay or laurel, an evergreen tree native to the Mediterranean area but grown now extensively in mild parts of North America. Crowns of laurel played their part in early Greek and Roman ceremonials, and bay still has a role in both religious and social festivals in parts of Europe.

There are several kinds of bay, each slightly different in taste from the others. But all are pungent and should be used with discretion, so that the bay flavor does not overpower all others in the dish. Greek and Turkish bay leaves are greenish-brown in color, with a slightly toothed edge, and are not as assertive in flavor as the California bay laurel's long, bright green leaves, which are up to three times more pungent than the European varieties.

Use bay leaves sparingly in soups and stews based on beef or lamb. If your bay leaves are the California variety, simmer the whole leaf in the soup or stew for half an hour, then remove. Use also in the poaching liquid for fish—again, with discretion—and in pot roast cooking liquids and marinades. Potatoes and carrots are two vegetables cheered up by bay flavor.

Beef and Chicken Stock Bases are invaluable savory seasonings to have on hand. They'll make you a quick, flavorful (and low-calorie) cup of beef or chicken broth as a pick-me-up, but they have dozens of other uses. Added to the cooking liquid, they turn plain rice into a delicious side dish. Pasta profits from cooking in such a liquid, too, in some cases. If you wish to make béchamel or brown sauce without

stock on hand, turn to these powders. Add to vegetable cooking liquid, too, for excellent flavor-reinforcement.

Celery Salt or Powder imparts familiar celery flavor in cases where the bulk of pieces of celery would not be desirable (and in cases, too, where the home cook finds herself without celery, but needing the flavor). Although the flavors of the two are very similar, celery salt comes from our familiar friend, the domestic stalk of celery—the leaves are dried, powdered, and combined with salt. Celery powder, on the other hand, is the ground seed of the wild celery plant, a relative of parsley.

Use celery salt or powder in any dish that would welcome the flavor of celery. The salt is not as strong as the powder; use the latter sparingly. However, because it is not salty, the powder is the more useful of the two, allowing you to add salt as you wish. The flavor of either is compatible with a wide spectrum of foods: eggs, cheese, vegetable-juice cocktails, salads and salad dressings, sandwich spreads, sauces, such vegetables as eggplant, tomatoes, peppers, and potatoes.

Chervil is a low-growing annual plant, a handsome sea-green color, and a relative of parsley. Believed to be native to what is now the southern part of Russia, the herb has been used throughout Europe for centuries. It is commercially grown today in Belgium and other central-European countries. But in America it is not widely known, is even less widely used—a pity, because it imparts a delightful flavor to certain foods. Fine-quality chervil is now grown in California, and is available almost everywhere.

Use chervil in egg dishes—soufflés, omelets, scrambled eggs—and with lamb, veal, and pork, as well as all fish and shellfish. It is a proper component of several elegant French sauces.

Chili Powder is used chiefly in chili con carne, but there is a variety of other uses to which it can be put. The powder is a nicely balanced blend of cumin, garlic, coriander, oregano, and several kinds of chili peppers; it is dark red-brown in color. Pungent when fresh, it loses flavor rapidly in storage—don't buy more than you can use up in a short time.

Use chili powder in chili con carne, of course. (In chili country—Texas and the Southwest in general—packets of "our own special blend" of chili powders are available, ranging in heat/strength from mild to blow-your-head-off. Shop around, sampling with restraint and discretion, until you find one to suit you.) Chili powder, used sparingly so that its flavor is not overpowering, adds piquancy to cheese sauces, dips, rarebits and soufflés, marinades and basting sauces for pork chops and ribs, lamb or beef ribs, and chicken. Corn, rice, and kidney beans also profit from the addition of chili powder for unusual flavor appeal.

Cumin comes from the seed of a rather tacky-looking plant native to the Mediterranean regions, particularly Egypt. It has been used as a flavoring since the early Christian era, and is still used extensively, particularly in Chinese, Spanish, and Mexican cuisines. In earlier times, the Dutch and Swiss used cumin to flavor cheese, the Germans to enliven sauerkraut, but did not add its seasoning to any other food. Early Hebrews flavored unleavened bread with cumin.

Use cumin in baked or scrambled eggs, omelets, deviled eggs, egg salads. Flavor french dressing or mayonnaise with cumin to dress macaroni or potato salad or chicken salad. Just a touch improves chicken, lobster, and shrimp, and barley, lentil, and pea soups. Enhance the flavor of tomato sauce and meat marinades with cumin. It is a component of a number of relishes and of sausages or dishes made with sausage.

Curry Powder is not a single flavor, but a compound of many. The seasoning is familiar in India, where meat, poultry, fish, and vegetable curries are made, but where none is seasoned with the curry powder we find on spice shelves in our supermarkets. Indian cooks make their own curry seasonings, a different one for chicken than the one used for lamb, different again for fish, for beef, for vegetable mixtures. But here, where a curry dish is a sometime rather than everyday thing, we use curry powder. It varies from blend to blend, from manufacturer to manufacturer, but will generally be composed of six or more (or all) of these: cumin, coriander, fenugreek, turmeric, ginger, pepper, dill, mace, cardamom, and cloves. To whatever dish it is added, curry powder imparts unique flavor as well as a deep saffron- or mustard-yellow color. Some like only a touch of curry powder, some like a lot. When you use it, add a teaspoon or so, stir in and taste; continue to add, stir, and taste until you've achieved the flavor you want.

Use curry powder in meat, poultry, fish, and vegetable Indian-style curry dishes, of course. But add its bright flavor to marinades, to mayonnaise-dressed salads such as potato and chicken, to deviled eggs and egg salads, to butter used to season broiled lamb or fish, and to hot dried-fruit compotes to use as a relish with meats and poultry.

Dillweed is the dried leaf of the dill plant, which is feathery, lively green in color, with many yellow blossoms. Unlike other herbs, dill is at its fullest flavor when flowering. An annual related to parsley, it is native to Europe and Asia Minor, but can be grown in any temperate zone. Most of the dried dillweed we use comes from India, although fresh dill can be had at specialty food shops and elegant greengrocers, as well as at some large supermarkets. The flavor is delicate; so is the aroma.

Use dillweed in poaching liquid and sauces for fish, particularly salmon and shrimp, and in pickles and relishes (who has never tasted a dill pickle?), with lamb and pork, in salads—particularly cucumber—to perk up tomato juice, and with vegetables such as green beans, squash, beets, turnips, and potatoes. A salad of cold beets and paper-thin onion slices, dressed with dill-laden sour cream, is a taste sensation.

Dried Hot Peppers are small flakes (and sometimes the seeds) of little fiery-red, fiery-hot peppers, generally of the Capiscum family. The seasoning is orange-red in color, with the seeds tending more toward yellow. You will often find a shaker of these on the table in an Italian or Mexican restaurant. The peppers are native to tropical America; the major supply comes from Mexico. Use with restraint—dried peppers are hot, *hot,* HOT!

Use dried hot peppers in sauces for spaghetti, enchiladas, tacos, and tostados, in meat sauces and gravies, and in stews. But be careful. Until you get used to this seasoning, what you think ought to be just the right amount will be four or five times too much. The peppers are also used in pickles and relishes, and in a pepper sauce you can buy or make simply at home by combining 1 tablespoon dried peppers with 4 ounces dry sherry, 1 teaspoon garlic powder, 1 teaspoon red wine vinegar; let stand for a week, shaking or stirring every day. It will then be ready to use—sparingly!—on meats and fish, in gravies and sauces.

Garlic is available in whole heads in produce departments, of course, but also on the spice shelves as garlic salt, powder, dried minced, and juice, giving you a wide choice of ways to add the pungent, robust flavor to a variety of foods. Garlic in dried forms needs liquid to work with—garlic salt and powder may not smell pungent, but the liquids in the foods to which you add them will quickly release the high flavor and odor. The powder is preferable to the salt for kitchen use, as it imparts the garlic flavor only and allows you to salt your dishes as you wish. Dried minced garlic, rehydrated, is ideal for dishes in which the texture as well as the flavor is wanted, wherever you would use whole or chopped cloves of garlic. The juice is excellent for flavoring as well, and does not require liquid to release its pungent flavor and aroma. (See GARLIC.)

Use garlic salt, powder, dried minced garlic, or juice wherever and whenever you'd use garlic in cooking—and, with many home cooks, that's often. Sprinkle the salt on raw vegetables or green salads. In cooked dishes, use the juice or the powder; in adding garlic powder to acid foods (as relishes, pickles, salad dressings), blend with a small amount of water before adding, as acid slows down the release of the garlic flavor; in adding it to soups, stews, sauces, gravies, and meat dishes, blend the powder with a small amount of the liquid from the dish, then return to the dish—this makes for quick and thorough blending. Garlic in whatever form has a place in appetizers, soups, meat dishes of many kinds, sauces and gravies and dressings, salads and vegetables—in anything, in fact, except desserts.

Horseradish can be purchased fresh, to be grated and

prepared at home; it can also be purchased, ready-prepared, in small jars to be found in refrigerated cases at supermarkets and delicatessens. It can also be bought in a dehydrated, granular form that has certain considerable advantages: it is always on hand, it never dries out or spoils, it needs only one of several moisture-making ingredients to rehydrate it for on-the-spot use, and you can prepare as much or as little as you need at one time, then rehydrate a fresh batch when you wish to use horseradish again.

Horseradish belongs to the mustard family, a perennial root that, pale in color, somewhat resembles a parsnip. In the Middle Ages, it was widely used as a medicine; about 1600 it began its career as a seasoning and condiment. Like the parsnip, horseradish is harvested after the first frost, which enhances the flavor, color, and texture of the root.

Use horseradish in sauces for oyster and other shellfish and seafood cocktails; to add zing to barbecue sauces for beef, lamb, and pork; in various pickles and relishes; in a simple creamy sauce for beef (boiled beef isn't quite right without horseradish sauce); and with some of the high-flavor vegetables, such as beets and rutabagas. In all cases, rehydrate granular horseradish in a small amount of water before adding to any dish, cooked or uncooked. To make a simple horseradish cream sauce, rehydrate 1 tablespoon dried horseradish in 2 tablespoons water; add 1 teaspoon white vinegar, ½ teaspoon onion powder. Whip ½ cup heavy cream and fold the horseradish mixture into it, or omit vinegar and use 1 cup sour cream in place of the heavy cream.

Juniper Berries are the fruit of an evergreen shrub native to southern Europe, but now grown all over Europe, Asia, and North Africa. The berry is a hazy blue when it is ripe, a matter of as much as 2½ years. Picked then, it is dried and becomes bluish-black in color, looking something like a considerably larger peppercorn. Most juniper berries imported by the United States come from Italy and Hungary. The berry has been known for a long time, but its use in the kitchen is relatively recent. Previously it was used medicinally, and as a flavoring agent in the distilling of gin.

Use juniper berries to season pork or lamb and almost all wild game, including upland game birds and waterfowl. Be parsimonious—the flavor is strong and pervasive. Crush the berries and rub into meat before cooking, or add to the dressing for a duck, turkey, or chicken salad.

Lemon Peel and Orange Peel can be acquired, to use as a seasoning, by grating the rind of a lemon or orange. But such rinds are not always on hand, and if you grate the rind of a fruit you propose to use later for another purpose, you will shorten its life considerably. So both lemon peel and orange peel, ready-grated, dried, ground, sold in small jars to be found on the spices-and-herbs shelves, can be a good investment. (See LEMON PEEL.)

Use lemon peel and orange peel in the dough for quick and yeast breads and sweet rolls; add to all kinds of desserts; to marinades and bastes for veal, chicken, and lamb; and as a seasoning for vegetables and for fish. For a pleasant change, stir a little into a fresh, hot cup of tea or coffee, or use in iced tea.

Marjoram, a compact, low-to-the-ground shrub, often called "sweet marjoram," first grew in Portugal. It is a relative newcomer in the kitchen, having been associated with food for only the past two hundred years or so. Now it grows in southern France and other European countries with a Mediterranean seacoast, as well as in parts of the Orient; in the United States, it flourishes in California. Its uses in medicine and pagan religious celebrations almost forgotten, it's now a spice-shelf staple.

Use marjoram with a light hand for delicate, distinctive flavor in cream and sour cream and brown sauces, with broiled or baked fish, in egg dishes, in soups (it makes clam broth sing), and with such vegetables as carrots, peas, mushrooms, spinach, and zucchini. Marjoram and lamb have a particular affinity for one another—use the herb in the braising liquid for lamb shanks and riblets, in lamb stew, in the stuffing for a boned and rolled leg of lamb, or rubbed all over a bone-in leg before roasting. Pork and veal take kindly to marjoram, too.

Mint is a large family, growing in many places, in many kinds. But only two—peppermint and spearmint—go to work in the kitchen. Peppermint is bright green, so pungent it is almost peppery; the stems wear a light purple haze. The fragrance of spearmint is milder; the plant is a pale gray-green. Native to the Mediterranean area, mint is now cultivated throughout Europe, in the Orient, and on our own west coast and in some of the central states. It will grow almost anywhere, and many people who raise nothing else plant a patch of mint for use in beverages and sauces. Hardy, it multiplies rapidly and will drive you out unless regularly cut back. Fortunately for those of us living in climates where the winter is cold, dried mint leaves (as well as mint extracts) are available for kitchen—and bartending—use.

Use peppermint in fruit cocktails, fruit juices, fruit and gelatin salads, in hot and iced tea or chocolate, and in mint juleps. Also, it is the proper mint for the sauce without which lamb doesn't taste quite right to many people.

Use spearmint—the crushed dried leaves or the shredded fresh ones—on vegetables such as carrots, zucchini, cabbage, potatoes, and peas, in fruit drinks and punches—including wine punch—and in salads and sauces.

Mushrooms are a vegetable (actually fungus, but thought of and used as a vegetable) when we use them whole or sliced or chopped in sauces and gravies, meat and other main dishes. But when they are dried and powdered, they become an exceedingly useful and delicious savory seasoning. The flavor accentuates others but does not—unless you're too liberal-handed—overpower them.

Use powdered mushrooms in soups, stews, and gravies for added flavor and richness, add to hamburgers, meat loaves, hash, croquettes, and casseroles. In a pinch, make a double-quick mushroom soup of powdered mushrooms, chicken stock base, onion powder or juice—rehydrate all in water, heat to boiling, add heavy cream and heat again, but do not boil. (See MUSHROOMS.)

Mustard was first used—at least its use was first recorded—in A.D. 75; since then it has been widely employed both as a medicine and as an herb. The plant grows prolifically, a hardy annual that reseeds itself. When doughty Fr. Junipero Serra came up from Mexico and made his way through what is now California, establishing missions and mission schools and spreading the Word, he and the other missioners planted mustard seed along their route. When they returned, their trail was marked by large numbers of yellow-flowered mustard plants. In fact, the plant grows so readily that in many places it is considered a weed. Dry mustard is made of a number of varieties of mustard seeds, the kinds and amounts determining the relative hotness of the product. (See MUSTARD.)

Use dry mustard in casseroles—particularly those with cheese—and in soufflés and sauces; add it to glazes for ham or corned beef, to dressings for potato, macaroni, tuna, and shellfish salads. Combine with melted butter and lemon juice to dress vegetables. Add to coating or dredging mixtures for such foods as fried chicken and swiss steak. Combine mustard with vinegar for a pungently hot dipping sauce, with sour cream for a milder one.

Onion is a kitchen standby we couldn't do without, and the bulbs in several varieties are available in produce markets all year around. Although most of us have whole onions in the house at all times, we still make room on our spice shelf for a number of onion seasoning products: onion salt, juice, and powder; minced and diced dried onions; toasted dried onions. Related products are dried shredded green onions, from the tender young tops of spring onions, and dried snipped chives. All are easy to use, requiring no peeling, slicing, chopping, or other preparation. (See ONIONS.)

Use onion products of all kinds in the same foods and in the same manner as you would use fresh onions, scallions, and chives. Again, onion powder is often a wiser choice than onion salt, because it leaves you free to salt the dish as you choose. In dishes that have liquid ingredients, you can add

dried minced or diced onions just as they come from the container; to add them to dry foods, rehydrate first in a little water. The toasted dried onions have a mild sautéed-onion flavor; they should not be rehydrated. Use them in dishes where their flavor and crunchy texture will be an asset—in dips and spreads, as a casserole topping, mixed into hamburger before cooking, in tossed salads, or as a crisp garnish for vegetables.

Oregano is a member of the mint family, and a close relative of marjoram—in fact, it is often called "wild marjoram." Known and used since the days of ancient Rome, oregano did not find its way into American kitchens until less than fifty years ago. Once it had made its appearance, however, it was warmly welcomed and now is widely used. There are two strains, the Mediterranean, which is delicate in both flavor and fragrance, and the Mexican, which is pungent.

Use oregano in meat mixtures—hamburgers, meat loaves, stews—in stuffings, in salad dressings, and particularly in tomato-based sauces for pasta and barbecue. The flavor of oregano teams well with vegetables, too, particularly eggplant, zucchini and, above all, fresh tomatoes.

Parsley belongs to the celery family, and was cultivated long before celery was brought in from the wilds to the garden. Although it's impossible to pinpoint its origin, parsley was known as early as the third century B.C. Ancient Greeks and Romans used parsley for its flavor and—as we do—to garnish various dishes with a frill of green. It was known throughout Europe by the 1400s, had moved to England by the mid-1500s, and came to America with colonists in the seventeenth century. Although we use fresh parsley for garnishing, the dehydrated herb (sometimes labeled "parsley flakes") is exceedingly useful in the kitchen. In order to pack it for us to use, parsley is first stemmed—the stems make up at least half the weight—and the stems are discarded. The parsley is dried, and more stems are removed. In all, it requires twelve pounds of destemmed fresh parsley to make one pound of the dried herb. (See PARSLEY.)

Use dried parsley in salads and dressings, in sauces, in bastes and marinades, in stuffings for meat, poultry, and fish. Add to soups and stews and chowders for color and flavor. Make parsley butter; place on fish or steak to melt into a simple, delicious sauce, or spread on very thin bread to make finger sandwiches, perfect with a salad meal. However you use parsley, you're doing yourself a favor—it is rich in vitamins A and C, and contains appreciable quantities of iron, iodine, manganese, and copper.

Pepper is so familiar a savory seasoning that it's impossible to imagine a kitchen without at least one kind. Native to the East Indies, pepper is the berry of a perennial vine, which produces both black and white pepper. For the black variety, the berries are picked when slightly underripe; for white pepper, the fully ripe berries are gathered. Both kinds are dried in the sun or over charcoal fires, both become wrinkled and black in the process. When the outer hull of the ripe berries is removed, leaving the creamy core, the result is white pepper, less pungent than the black.

The properties of pepper were first recognized in India and influenced, more than any other single thing, the wide exploration of parts of the world previously uncharted. Later, the pepper trade supported the building of America's early merchant fleet, bringing more than five million dollars into the young nation's treasury.

Other kinds of pepper are also available for our spice shelves. Fiery *cayenne*—a relative of paprika and the bell peppers—is orange to bright red in color, and a little goes a very long way. Dried *sweet green* and *red peppers* are available in jars, and are exceedingly useful when only a little of their seasoning is needed. (The fresh peppers, although widely available, do not keep well and are a poor bargain if only a small part is to be used.) *Paprika,* also originally from Central America, is now widely grown in Europe, and used extensively there, especially in Hungary. The bulk of the paprika we use in the United States is imported from Spain, but some is produced in California.

Use black pepper in all kinds of meat dishes, in soups and stews, in salads—and, of course, at the table so that each diner can pepper his food to his individual taste. Available as *whole black peppercorns* for seasoning in the kitchen and, in a pepper grinder, at the table; *cracked black pepper,* peppercorns that are crushed but not ground; and *medium grind* and *fine grind black pepper.* From so wide a selection, you can choose a variety to suit any kitchen or table need.

Use white pepper where a flavor more delicate than that of black pepper is wanted, and in pale dishes—poultry, fish, light-colored sauces, gelatin salads, pale vegetables—where specks of black pepper offend the eye. Available as *whole white peppercorns* and *ground white pepper*—a shaker of the latter, along with the shaker of black pepper, is a nice addition to the table.

Use paprika as a savory seasoning as well as a garnish—its mild flavor goes well with many dishes. Include it liberally in the coating for breaded foods, such as chicken, veal scallops, and fish, where it will not only add delightful flavor but also aid in browning the food. This aid-to-browning feature of paprika can be a help in other cases, too—on the surface of pale-colored casseroles, for example. Use the color and flavor of paprika to pep up french and thousand island dressings, to add eye-appeal color to creamed dishes and soups.

Use cayenne with restraint—indeed, caution—in dips, spreads, and sauces. Let it be the savory seasoning for all kinds of egg dishes, and the devil of deviled eggs. Cayenne also has a particular affinity for fish and shellfish, used sparingly, and "heats up" barbecue and pasta sauces. Hollandaise sauce isn't quite right without a little cayenne.

Use dried sweet green and red peppers, rehydrated in a small amount of water, in any dish where you would use the fresh ones.

Rosemary is a native of the Mediterranean area, and another member of the mint family. Today, it is cultivated commercially in Spain, Portugal, and France, and in California. As a seasoning—particularly in combination with wine—its use dates back before recorded history. By A.D. 500, a simple sauce of three parts wine to one part crushed rosemary leaves was widely used on meats, perhaps because the good and strong flavor of such a sauce effectively disguised the fact that the meat was beginning to spoil. It was also recommended, in an early herbal, as a wine preservative. Today, wine and rosemary still form a splendid partnership, particularly in bastes and marinades for lamb, chicken, and veal.

Use rosemary (as well as for remembrance) in quick breads, such as muffins and dumplings, and in poultry and fish stuffings. Make little slits in a leg of lamb or veal for roasting and into each put a tiny sliver of lemon peel and a few bits of rosemary. Add rosemary to the cooking liquid for potatoes, green beans, and summer squash.

Saffron has always been and still is the world's most expensive spice, which is not difficult to understand when you know that it takes about 225,000 stigmas from a certain fall-flowering Spanish crocus to produce one pound of saffron. The stigmas, even after drying, are a rich red-gold color, and impart that color—as well as subtle, indescribable flavor—to the dishes in which the seasoning is used. When a recipe specifies a certain amount of saffron, be guided by it. This is not a case where more is better. Too much saffron gives the dish an unpleasant medicinal taste.

Use saffron in buns, rolls, and sweet breads, in rice and chicken-with-rice and fish-with-rice dishes, in fish soups and stews, and in butter sauces for fish. Veal fricassee is improved in both flavor and color by the addition of saffron, and it is a proper ingredient in France's bouillabaise and Spain's arroz con pollo.

Sage is perhaps the best known of all the herbs. Native to south-central Europe, where most of the herb comes from today, sage is also raised commercially on the west coast of the United States. Although it grows wild everywhere in one form or another—the sagebrush of America's plains is a collateral relative—only one kind of the herb is used in cooking. A wide array of dishes profit from the judicious use of sage, but pork and chicken partner particularly well with it. And where would we be without old-fashioned sage dressing for our holiday turkeys?

Use sage in stuffings for almost any meat or bird, in cream of mushroom soup, in fish chowders. Flavor the basting butter for broiled fish with sage, and use it to flavor sausage, meat loaves, and chicken and veal stews. Rub sage over

HERBS IN YOUR KITCHEN

	basil	bay leaves	chervil	dillweed	marjoram	oregano

APPETIZERS	cheese spreads
	seafood
	   cocktails
	tomato juice
		poaching medium
		  for shellfish
		pickles
			avocado dip
			cheese dips
			  and spreads
			canapés
			butters
				cheese dips
				  and spreads
				seafood
				  cocktails
				  and spreads
				deviled eggs
					savory butters
					cheese dips
					  and spreads
					liver pâtés
					stuffed
					  mushrooms
						avocado dip
						cheese spreads
						stuffed mushrooms
						mushroom spread
						tomato juice
						pizza-type
						  canapés

SOUPS and CHOWDERS	fish chowders
	minestrone
	pea
	spinach
	tomato
	vegetable
		bean
		beef stock
		bouillabaise
		chicken-corn
		oxtail-vegetable
			chicken *or*
			  beef stock
			vegetable
				bean
				borscht
				chicken
				fish, shellfish
				  chowders
				pea
				tomato
					chicken noodle
					clam chowder
					onion
					oyster bisque
					spinach
					tomato
						bean
						minestrone
						mushroom
						onion
						tomato
						vegetable

SALADS	chicken cucumber fruit tossed green seafood tomato	aspics beef	beet coleslaw cucumber fruit tossed green tomato	beet coleslaw cucumber potato seafood mixed vegetable	asparagus chicken fruit tossed green seafood	avocado white bean three-bean tossed green potato seafood tomato

FISH and SHELLFISH	crab
	halibut
	mackerel
	salmon
	shrimp
	tuna
		poaching medium
		  for shellfish
		halibut
		salmon
			poaching
			  medium for
			  fillets
				halibut
				salmon
				shrimp
				sole
					clams
					crab sauté
					creamed tuna
					halibut
					salmon
						clams
						creamed lobster
						  or crab
						shrimp

POULTRY and GAME	chicken
	duck
	rabbit
	turkey (wild
	  and domestic)
	venison
		fricasseed or
		  creamed
		  chicken *or*
		  rabbit
			stuffing for
			  all game
				creamed chicken
				chicken pie
					chicken
					duck
					goose
					rabbit
					turkey
					venison
						chicken
						guinea hen
						stuffing for
						  pheasant

MEATS	beef
	lamb
	liver
	pork
	sausage
	veal
		pot roasts
		kabobs: lamb
		  or beef
		stews
		tongue
		tripe
			stews
			seasoning
			  for all
			  kinds of
			  ground
			  meats
				beef
				corned beef
				lamb
				pork
				sweetbreads
				veal
					beef
					pork
					pot roast
					sausage
					stews
					veal
						ground beef
						lamb
						liver
						sausage
						stews
						veal

SAUCES	butter
	orange sauce
	  for game
	spaghetti
	spanish
	any tomato
		barbecue
		curry
		spaghetti
		spanish
		sour cream
		tomato
			barbecue
			butter
			cream
			spaghetti
			sour cream
			tartar
				cream sauce
				  for fish
				tartar
					brown
					cream
					spanish
					sour cream
					tomato
						barbecue
						brown
						mushroom
						spaghetti
						spanish
						tomato

EGGS and CHEESE	cheese soufflés
	cream cheese
	  spreads
	omelets
	rarebits
	scrambled eggs
			cream cheese
			  spreads
			deviled eggs
			omelets
			rarebits
			soufflés
				cottage cheese
				omelets
				scrambled eggs
					omelets
					rarebits
					scrambled eggs
					soufflés
						soft-cooked
						  eggs
						cheese soufflés
						omelets
						rarebits
						scrambled eggs

VEGETABLES	beans
	eggplant
	onions
	peas
	squash
	tomatoes
		beets
		carrots
		potatoes
		stewed
		  tomatoes
			beets
			eggplant
			peas
			potatoes
			spinach
			tomatoes
				beans
				beets
				cabbage
				celery
				parsnips
				potatoes
					brussels
					  sprouts
					carrots
					onions
					peas
					spinach
					zucchini
						broccoli
						cabbage
						lentils
						mushrooms
						onions
						tomatoes

HERBS IN YOUR KITCHEN

parsley	peppermint	rosemary	saffron	sage	savory	tarragon	thyme

avocado dip
savory butter
canapés
cheese dips
   and spreads
	cranberry juice
	garnish for
	   fruit salads,
	   cups
		fruit cups
		pickles
			savory
			  butters
				sharp
				  cheese
				  spreads
					cheese spreads
					liver pâtés
					deviled eggs
					tomato juice
					vegetable
					  juices
						cheese spreads
						liver pâtés
						seafood
						  cocktails
						  and spreads
						deviled eggs
						tomato juice
							liver pâtés
							sauerkraut juice
							seafood spreads
							  and cocktails

chicken *or* beef stock vegetable	bean pea	chicken fish chowders pea potato spinach turtle	bouillabaise chicken-rice turkey	chicken pea potato tomato turkey vegetable	bean chicken chowders lentil pea vegetable	bean chicken mushroom pea tomato	borscht clam chowder consommé gumbo pea vegetable

fruit
tossed green
potato
seafood
vegetable
	fruit
	  gelatins
	celery
	coleslaw
	tossed green
	waldorf
		fruit	chicken
			fish and
			  shellfish
					white bean
					tossed green
					potato
					tomato
					vegetable
						chicken
						coleslaw
						egg
						fruit
						fish and
						  shellfish
							aspics
							beet
							chicken
							coleslaw
							tomato

poaching
  liquids
	shrimp
	prawns
		poaching
		  liquid for
		  salmon,
		  halibut
		broiled salmon
			baked
			  halibut and
			  sole
				baked
				  halibut
				  and sole
				poached
				  salmon
					halibut
					shrimp
					sole
					crab
					salmon
						salmon
						crab
						halibut
						lobster
						shrimp
						sole
							cod
							crab
							creamed tuna
							halibut
							scallops
							sole

stuffings
  for all
  poultry
  and game
		capon
		duck
		chicken
		quail
		rabbit
			lamb
			veal
			all kinds
			  of curries
				chicken
				duck
				goose
				rabbit
				turkey
				stuffings
					chicken
					duck
					squab
					turkey
					venison
					stuffings
						chicken
						duck
						goose
						squab
						turkey
							chicken
							duck
							pheasant
							quail
							turkey
							stuffings

stews
ground meats
garnish for
  steaks,
  chops
	ground beef,
	  lamb
	lamb stew
	roast lamb
	veal
		beef
		ham loaf
		lamb
		pork
		stews
		veal
			lamb *or*
			  veal curry
			veal stew
				beef
				lamb
				pork
				sausage
				stews
					kidneys
					lamb shanks
					meat loaf
					pot roast
					spareribs
					veal cutlets
						lamb
						pork chops
						pot roast
						stews
						sweetbreads
						veal
							beef
							lamb
							pork
							veal
							all variety
							  meats

barbecue
butter
cream
spaghetti
sour cream
tartar
	cranberry
	currant
	mint
		barbecue
		brown
		butter
		cream
		spanish
		tomato
			cream sauce
			  for fish
			curry sauces
				brown
				  butter
				cheese
				  sauce
				  for eggs
					butter for
					  steak
					butter for
					  fish
					horseradish
						béarnaise
						mustard
						sour cream
						tartar
						vinaigrette
							creole
							curry
							mustard
							spaghetti
							spanish
							tomato

cream cheese
  spreads
deviled eggs
omelets
rarebits
soufflés
	cream cheese
	  spreads
		deviled eggs
		scrambled eggs
		soufflés
			cream cheese
			  spreads
			scrambled
			  eggs
				cottage
				  cheese
				creamed
				  eggs
					deviled eggs
					omelets
					scrambled
					  eggs
					soufflés
						cottage cheese
						deviled eggs
						omelets
						scrambled eggs
						baked eggs
							cottage cheese
							deviled eggs
							omelets
							shirred eggs
							soufflés

carrots
potatoes
tomatoes
	carrots
	peas
	potatoes
	spinach
	zucchini
		cauliflower
		cucumbers
		mushrooms
		peas
		potatoes
		spinach
			vegetable
			  combinations
			  with rice
			squash
			zucchini
				carrots
				eggplant
				lima
				  beans
				onions
				peas
				tomatoes
					artichokes
					asparagus
					beans
					lentils
					rice
					sauerkraut
						cauliflower
						celeri-rave
						mushrooms
						potatoes
						spinach
						tomatoes
							asparagus
							beans
							beets
							carrots
							onions
							zucchini

325

lamb or pork to be roasted, and add it to the breading for pork chops.

Savory comes in two varieties distinct from one another—summer savory and winter savory, names which have nothing to do with the times when the herbs are planted or harvested. Because summer savory is more delicate of both flavor and aroma, it is used more widely than its winter relative, which has a somewhat resinous taste. Native to southern Europe, savory is now cultivated commercially in France and Spain, and also in California. Early American colonists used the herb as both medicine and seasoning.

Use savory in lentil and bean soups, in the poaching liquid for fish, in stuffing for chicken or turkey, in hamburgers and meatballs, and—in butter—to season such vegetables as cabbage, spinach, and carrots. Toss hot noodles with butter, cheese, and savory; add the herb to the cooking liquid for rice.

Tarragon migrated centuries ago from Siberia to central and eastern Europe, where the warmer climate fostered a more pungent strain. Now it is grown commercially in Russia, France, and in California, and it can be raised successfully in home gardens everywhere.

Use tarragon to season tongue or chicken in aspic; in all sorts of salads from chicken and seafood to mixed green and fruit; to lend delicate flavor to sweetbreads or veal; in sauces for meat, fish, and poultry; in egg dishes of many kinds.

Thyme is a favorite of poets, bees, and cooks, beloved for its delicate fragrance. Although there are many kinds of thyme, only two are commercially important, the gray-green, small-leafed French thyme, whose odor is reminiscent of balsam, and lemon thyme, with its clear, clean citrus fragrance and incisive flavor. Greek bees have been producing honey from thyme blossoms for centuries, and some feel it is the finest honey in the world. Scandinavians flavor certain cheeses with thyme, and have for generations, but the use of the herb in other foods has not been widespread until the present century.

Use thyme in stuffings for poultry and rabbit, in the breading for chicken and veal, to season sweetbreads and all sorts of egg dishes, in sauces, in fish and shellfish dishes.

Turmeric is a relative of ginger. Like saffron, it imparts not only flavor but deep golden color as well. Used with discretion, the taste is at once both hot and delicate, but too much turmeric will give an unpleasant, medicinal flavor. Although it has been in use since biblical times—as a perfume and dye, as well as a seasoning—turmeric has never gained wide favor. It is a component of commercial curry powder, and is employed in pickle-making.

Use turmeric in old-fashioned boiled dressing for a most superior potato salad, and add to mayonnaise to dress seafood salads. A small amount gives warm color and flavor to cream soups and fish chowders, to the yolk mixture for stuffed eggs, and to bland sauces. Added to curries, it reinforces flavor.

How, and how much, to use. With herbs and savory seasonings, it pays to be delicate-handed. The right amount can be heavenly, but too much can be horrid. The point is to complement the other flavors in the dish, not overpower them. As a general rule, count on ¼ teaspoon of dried herbs to be about right for a dish that yields four servings, and a tablespoon of the chopped fresh herb to season a dish of the same size. Give the herb a few moments to spread its goodness; then taste, add more if necessary. Before adding dried herbs to a dish, crumble them to release the flavor.

Some herbs and savory seasonings live well together—sage and thyme, for example. But in general one herb per dish is the best policy, for often their flavors cancel each other out or combine into a third, sometimes unpleasant, taste. Dill with caraway is an example of an unfortunate combination. Be guided by the recipe you are following, or experiment judiciously. If you're uncertain about combining seasonings, you might like to try some of the ready-made combinations your supermarket's spice shelf has to offer—herbs for salad, for example, or Chinese five spices, or one of the seasoned salts or peppers.

Be restrained, also, about the number of herbed dishes you serve at one time. If the main dish is herbed, let the side dishes be dressed with butter or an herbless sauce, or plain—sometimes plain is better than any embellishment.

Opposite are some conversions and equivalents to guide you in using and substituting herbs and savory seasonings in your cooking.

Buying, storing herbs/savory seasonings. Buy in small quantities that you will be able to use up in a matter of weeks, three or four months at most. Herbs (spices, too) "fade" in a relatively short time, and you want peak flavor and aroma when you use them. It's a good policy to buy these good seasonings at a large market, where the turnover is rapid—herbs and seasonings get old on supermarket shelves just as readily as they do in your kitchen.

If you buy herbs in cardboard containers, transfer them to jars with airtight lids as soon as you get them home. Each time you use an herb, make certain that the lid is tightly screwed on when you are through with it.

Store herbs in a cool, dry place, not above or near the stove, dishwasher, or clothes washer and dryer. A sunny window is a poor choice, too—a dark corner is better.

Freezing herb-seasoned foods. This can be a bit tricky. Some herbs and seasonings lose strength in the freezing process, notably chili powder and the various onion seasonings, as well as table salt. When you thaw and heat these foods for serving, be sure to taste and adjust the seasoning if necessary. On the other hand, some of the herbs and seasonings gain strength in the freezing process, notably

herb/seasoning	amount	equals
beef or chicken stock base	4 teaspoons, dissolved in 1¼ cups water	1 (10½-ounce) can undiluted bouillon or consommé
	2 teaspoons	1 bouillon cube
bell pepper, green or red	1 tablespoon, rehydrated	3 tablespoons chopped fresh pepper
bell pepper, red	1 tablespoon, rehydrated	2 tablespoons chopped pimiento
garlic, minced	⅛ teaspoon	1 medium clove garlic
garlic powder	⅛ teaspoon	1 medium clove garlic
horseradish	1 tablespoon, rehydrated	2 tablespoons prepared horseradish
lemon peel	1 teaspoon	1 teaspoon fresh lemon peel *or* grated peel of 1 medium lemon *or* ½ teaspoon lemon extract
mint (peppermint or spearmint)	1 tablespoon	¼ cup chopped fresh mint
mushrooms, powdered	1 tablespoon	3 tablespoons whole dried mushrooms *or* 4 ounces fresh *or* 2 ounces canned
onion powder	1 tablespoon	1 medium onion, chopped, *or* 4 tablespoons
onions, minced	1 tablespoon	1 small onion, chopped, *or* 2 tablespoons
parsley	1 teaspoon	3 teaspoons chopped fresh parsley

black pepper, green pepper, garlic, and celery. Use these very lightly in foods you are going to freeze; if you're making a serve-some/save-some double batch, season lightly and then add more of these seasonings if necessary to the portion that's to be served right away.

Feel free. Experiment with herbs and savory seasonings. Once you are certain of the ones you and your family like best, try them in new dishes. And try something different every now and then, giving special, unusual flavor to old family favorites. For get-you-started ideas along these lines, see the herb chart on preceding pages. See also BOQUET GARNI, FINES HERBES, LICORICE, SEEDS, SORREL, SPICES, and WOODRUFF.

HERMITS

Spicy drop cookies, chock-full of nuts and raisins. See COOKIES.

HERRING

An impressive fish, this, not only for its place on the table, but also for its effect on world trade, on the fate of nations, and on the livelihoods of thousands of people.

You doubtless consider yourself—as all well-adjusted people do—a creature of some importance. But have you ever had a battle named after you? The herring has. Have you ever played a part in the overthrow of a monarch? The herring has. Has a city ever been built because you were at that spot?

The battle: During the Hundred Years' War, the British were laying siege to Orleans, held by the French. Anxious to give their troops a proper Lenten diet, the British sent rations of herring to the scene. The French intercepted the fish, the indignant and deprived British fought all the harder, and the French lost what is known to this day as the Battle of the Herrings.

The monarch: Charles I of England was deposed because of his interference with the fishing rights of his subjects and the imposition of high taxes on them, in order to finance a navy to destroy the great Dutch herring trade of the time. (It is said that "the foundations of Amsterdam were laid on herring bones.")

The city: Not only Amsterdam, but many others, located at the sites of herring spawning and feeding grounds, because of the ability of those little fish to support a huge fishing industry, and so large a number of people.

And those are only a few of the facets of the herring's position in the world scheme of things.

"Flesh, fowl, or good red herring." The herring family numbers some two hundred kinds, most residing in cool northern waters. Great Britain alone takes hundreds of thousands of tons of herring each year. Off the coast of Norway, herring fishing has been a way of earning a living since the beginning of the eleventh century; the art of salting the fish dates back to the fourteenth century, the smoking of it to the fifteenth. In the north Atlantic, herring is fished from north of Cape Cod to Greenland and Iceland, and is found as far south as the Carolinas, to latitude 35 degrees but never beyond that.

Exceedingly prolific, the herring has prompted science into one of those useless but fascinating calculations it often comes up with. Like this: If a male and a female herring, just one pair, reproduced unmolested and with no accident to eggs or offspring, in seven years' time their issue would choke up all the oceans, seas, and rivers of the world. Mother Herring lays an average of 50 million eggs annually. It has been estimated that the yearly billions of herring man takes from the sea is only about 5 percent of the total number, which shows no signs of extinction or exhaustion.

That concludes biology class. For more about herring as food, see FISH. See also KIPPERS.

HICKORY NUTS

The wood of the hickory tree is of iron hardness and boundless durability—the attributes that gave Andrew Jackson his nickname, "Old Hickory." They are tall and handsome trees, with rich, dark green summer foliage that turns to a brilliant yellow in the fall.

Don't look for hickory nuts in the market. You might find a few in a small country store, but not elsewhere. The resistance of the shell—as hard as the wood itself—plus the imbalanced proportion of shell to nut, makes commercial production unfeasible. If you do come upon some of the nuts, and are blessed with the patience of Job and the strength of Hercules, you will be rewarded by splendid flavor. A hot water bath will assist in the shelling, but not much. Recipes calling for hickory nuts are to be found only in old cookbooks, harking back to the days when everyone sat around the fire, Pa read aloud or told stories, and Ma found work for idle hands by setting the children to shelling nuts.

HIGH-ALTITUDE COOKING

It must have been very unsettling indeed to good cooks who migrated west and found themselves suddenly bad cooks when they tried to prepare meals in the mountains. Biscuits burned. Dried beans, the old standby of those on the trail, were hard as pebbles when cooked the back-home way. Vegetables had to be boiled to death before they were edible. Even boiled coffee, cooked over a campfire, acted most peculiarly. And when the travel-weary pioneer woman got around to making a cake—perhaps to celebrate the arrival at a mile-high destination—it promptly fell.

Most of the recipes she knew had been developed by trial-and-error methods in European lowlands or American eastern seacoast altitudes. Now the trial and error had to be gone through all over again, often under conditions to try the patience of a saint. Blizzards, hostile Indians, sandstorms, alkali-poisoned waterholes—and now this! No wonder the pioneer woman's litany, even as she rolled up her sleeves and learned how to make do, was "Why did we come, why did we ever come?"

The why and how of altitude. To begin with, air—like everything else around us, that we deal with in our daily lives—has weight. The higher we climb, the nearer to the top of the air mass we get and the less the air weighs.

The weight of air is termed "air pressure." At any given altitude, the air pressure is the same on everything—on a person, on a cake in an oven, on a dog and the cat he is chasing, on water boiling in the teakettle—on everything. At sea level, the air exerts a pressure of roughly 15 pounds per square inch. As the altitude increases the air pressure decreases, until at 13,000 feet it is only 7½ pounds per square inch, half that of sea level. Although pressures at altitudes up to 2,000 feet make virtually no difference in cooking, above that point pressure must be taken into account and allowances made. Cooking can still be just as good, and no more or less trouble than at sea level. But the approach has to be somewhat different. Temperatures must be adjusted, and amounts of ingredients—particularly liquids and leavening agents—must be modified.

To illustrate the changes air pressure makes at various levels, consider these temperatures at which water boils:

altitude	Fahrenheit	Celsius
sea level	212°	100°
2,000 feet	208°	98°
5,000 feet	203°	95°
7,500 feet	198°	92°
10,000 feet	194°	90°
15,000 feet	185°	85°

Climbing the mountain. If you move from an area close to sea level, or at least below 2,000 feet in altitude, to a high-altitude area, you will need to make certain basic changes in cooking procedures, and you'll need some new recipes. You will find the home economics department of your state university or the office of your county agent willing—and well prepared—to help you.

Some areas of cooking remain unchanged. Roasting, for example, doesn't differ appreciably whatever the altitude. But foods cooked in liquids—boiled, braised—require adjustment because of the different boiling points of liquid. However, it is leavened foods—cakes, breads—and those with a heavy sugar content—candies, frostings—that require the most high-altitude know-how. And if you use a pressure cooker, you will also have to make adjustments.

HIGH-ALTITUDE BAKING

Breads and cakes depend upon the leavening effect of yeast or baking powder to make them rise. This is achieved by the release of carbon dioxide by the leavening agent within the dough or batter; the gas forms bubbles within the mixture, causing it to rise. Because the air pressure grows less as the elevation increases, the leavening expands more, and more readily; the bubbles become larger and more numerous, the walls of the bubbles thinner and weaker. When the bubble walls collapse, the cake falls.

Low humidity in high altitudes (such places as the high deserts of the west) also affects baking. Baked goods prepared from a sea-level recipe will be overly dry and crumbly, because moisture vaporizes at lower temperatures as air pressure is lessened.

A third condition that affects baked goods is reduced

internal temperature at higher altitudes—this can produce a soggy, underdone cake. At higher altitudes, oven temperatures are increased to counteract this effect.

To avoid all these hazards, use recipes tailored for the altitude in which you live. If you attempt to adjust sea-level recipes, you give yourself many chances for error. And you may waste a great deal of time and a great many ingredients in the process.

Using high-altitude recipes. In these, others have gone through the trial-and-error procedures for you. Ingredients are balanced and proportioned to strengthen the walls of air bubbles so the product won't fall. Amounts of leavening have been adjusted. And increased temperatures are called for.

Here, to help you understand such recipes, are adjustments that must be made in some familiar types of cakes.

ALTITUDE VARIATIONS FOR ANGEL FOOD CAKE

altitude	amount of sugar	oven temperature
sea level	1¾ cups	350°F.
2,500 feet	1½ cups + 2 tablespoons	350°F.
5,000 feet	1½ cups	350°F.
7,500 feet	1¼ cups + 2 tablespoons	350°F.
10,000 feet	1¼ cups	360°F.

The second is a butter cake which calls for both baking powder and baking soda as leavening agents.

ALTITUDE VARIATIONS FOR BUTTER LAYER CAKE

altitude	soda	baking powder	oven temperature
sea level	1⅛ teaspoons	¾ teaspoon	350°F.
2,500 feet	1 teaspoon	¾ teaspoon	350°F.
5,000 feet	¾ teaspoon	½ teaspoon	350°F.
7,500 feet	½ teaspoon	¼ teaspoon	350°F.
10,000 feet	¼ teaspoon	⅛ teaspoon	360°F.

The third is a sponge cake, made from a recipe tailored to high altitudes, calling for variations in amounts of baking powder and milk, plus some temperature adjustment.

ALTITUDE VARIATIONS FOR SPECIAL SPONGE CAKE

altitude	baking powder	milk	oven temperature
sea level	¾ teaspoon	2 tablespoons	375°F.
2,500 feet	⅝ teaspoon	2 tablespoons	375°F.
5,000 feet	½ teaspoon	2 tablespoons	375°F.
7,500 feet	¼ teaspoon	2 tablespoons	375°F.
10,000 feet	⅛ teaspoon	¼ cup	395°F.

More sky-high baking. The listings shown above pertain to specially tailored recipes, each differing from the others. There are certain baking generalizations that can be made,

however, that will help you understand the basic differences between sea-level and high-altitude baking, and the areas in which adjustments are made.

Butter cakes need the most careful—and the most extensive—adjustments. A butter cake in which the ratio is

1 part shortening : 2 parts sugar : 4 parts flour

needs less adjusting for altitude variables, and is more successful, than recipes calling for ingredient amounts that vary from this ratio. Generally a cake that conforms to this ratio will require only a substitution of all-purpose for cake flour, a reduction in amount of baking powder, and a hotter oven.

To adjust a sea-level butter cake recipe to high-altitude level, the experimenter follows these steps:

a) temperature is increased 25 degrees

b) baking powder is decreased to ¾ teaspoon at 5,000 feet for each 1 teaspoon at sea level; to ½ teaspoon at 7,000 feet

c) all-purpose flour is substituted for cake flour to provide a stronger wall-structure for carbon-dioxide leavening bubbles

d) large-size eggs are always used; if the recipe calls for eggs in a varying measure, the larger amount is used

If the cake produced by these adjustments is not satisfactory, further adjustments are made, dealing with only one variable at a time in the experimenting.

Here are the basics that govern adjustments for high-altitude cake-making.

liquid: If the cake is dry or the batter very thick, 1 to 4 tablespoons of liquid may be added, starting with the smaller amount and increasing the amount until a satisfactory result is obtained.

flour: All-purpose flour is preferred for high-altitude baking. If cake flour is used, the amount is increased by 1 tablespoon for each cup the recipe calls for, and the liquid is increased by 1 tablespoon for each tablespoon of flour added. In some cases, adjustments in both shortening and sugar will be required before a satisfactory product using cake flour is arrived at.

Self-rising flour is not used, except in recipes tested and offered by manufacturers of such flour especially for high altitudes.

shortening: If a recipe requires more shortening than called for in the optimum 1:2:4 ratio, shortening is reduced 1 tablespoon plus 1 teaspoon (4 teaspoons in all) at 5,000 feet for each cup called for; at 7,000 feet, it is reduced by 2 tablespoons plus 1 teaspoon (7 teaspoons in all) for each cup of shortening the sea-level recipe calls for.

sugar: This is a critical ingredient in high-altitude baking. Too much sugar will result in a coarse-textured, crumbly cake that may well fall. On the other hand, if the sugar is too much reduced, the cake will be neither sweet enough nor tender enough. Maximum safe reduction at 5,000 feet is 1 tablespoon for each cup called for; at 7,000 feet, the maximum reduction should be 2 tablespoons per cup.

leavening: All types of baking powder require adjustment for altitudes above 3,000 feet. At 5,000 feet, ¾ teaspoon of baking powder is used for each teaspoon called for at sea level; at 7,000 feet, the amount is ½ teaspoon for each teaspoon. Baking soda requires less adjustment; in any case, it should not be reduced to less than ½ teaspoon for each cup of sour liquid—sour milk or fruit juice. In a recipe that calls for both baking powder and soda, it is best to reduce the baking powder rather than the soda.

eggs: The function of eggs in a cake is as emulsifiers, to distribute the fat and the liquid evenly throughout the batter. If a recipe calls for a range of amount, the larger amount is used. In by-cup measurements, if there is a choice between adding a yolk or a white to complete the measurement, the white is the right choice. Often the addition of an extra egg, plus a temperature increase of 25 degrees will convert a very rich sea-level cake recipe to an acceptable high-altitude one.

Adjustments for other high-altitude baking. Breads, pies, and cookies also call for certain changes to convert sea-level recipes to high-altitude baking. None of these, however, is as chancy as cake baking, and none requires nearly as much fiddling with the recipe in order to produce acceptable results.

yeast breads: Here, the only adjustment needed is to shorten the rising time. Test by poking a finger into the dough. Be firm. You won't hurt it. (However, if it giggles, hide the cooking sherry and leave the room at once to summon assistance.) If your finger goes easily into the dough and leaves a hole when you pull it out, the bread is sufficiently risen. If the hole closes up behind your retreating finger, allow more rising time.

quick breads: Oven temperature should be increased by 25 degrees. Baking powder must be decreased—¾ teaspoon at 5,000 feet for each teaspoon required at sea level; ½ teaspoon at 7,000 feet.

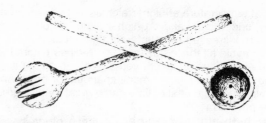

pies: Always bake at the bottom shelf position. Other than that, no adjustment is required. Oven temperature remains the same as that called for at sea level.

cookies: Rolled or dropped, if the cookie is thin, no recipe adjustment is needed, nor should any oven temperature change be made. Very rich cookies require the addition of 1 tablespoon flour for each cup called for in the sea-level recipe, plus 1 tablespoon additional liquid for each tablespoon of added flour. Bake at the called-for temperature. Bar cookies, however, require a temperature 25 degrees hotter than that called for at sea level.

CONFECTIONS AND FROSTINGS

If you are a confectioner of homemade candy, you'll have some adjustments to make. They all concern cooking, however. No changes in ingredient amounts are needed. Candies are cooked to a lower temperature at high altitudes than at sea level to compensate for more rapid evaporation of liquid. (Water boils at a lower temperature, remember?) The general rule is to lower the temperature 1 degree for each 500 feet of altitude. These changes apply also to the boiled-type frostings. If you are unsure of yourself, be guided by both the candy thermometer and the old-fashioned cold water test until your confidence returns. In everything else, abide by the sea-level rules—always remove the candy from the heat while you test, use very cold but not ice water, and don't expect optimum results on rainy days or any day when the humidity is very high.

CANDY AT 5,000 FEET

cold-water test		thermometer reading
soft ball	when dropped into the water, syrup forms a soft ball that flattens on removal from the water	224 to 230°F.
firm ball	when dropped into the water, syrup forms a firm ball that does not flatten on removal from the water	232 to 238°F.
hard ball	when dropped into the water, syrup forms a ball hard enough to hold its shape yet still be plastic	240 to 258°F.
soft crack	when dropped into the water, syrup separates into threads that are hard but not brittle	260 to 280°F.
hard crack	when dropped into the water, syrup separates into threads that are both hard and brittle	290 to 300°F.

Farther up the mountain, there are more adjustments to make.

CANDY AT 7,000 FEET

cold-water test		thermometer reading
soft ball	as above	219 to 225°F.
firm ball	as above	227 to 233°F.
hard ball	as above	235 to 253°F.
soft crack	as above	255 to 275°F.
hard crack	as above	285 to 295°F.

OTHER HIGH-ALTITUDE COOKING

Concerning everything you cook at high altitude versus sea-level methods, you need to know what adjustments must be made. And if no adjustments are necessary that, too, is a fact you must know before you can attempt increased-elevation cooking with any degree of comfort and self-assurance.

stovetop cooking: Foods cooked in liquid will need a longer time allowed, to compensate for the lower boiling point of the liquid.

pressure cooking: In this method of cooking, the temperature within the unit must be considered as well as the pressure. In a pressure cooker, identical pressure will produce a lower temperature at high altitudes than at sea level. So it is necessary to increase the pressure of the cooker beyond that required at sea level to produce a satisfactory high-altitude result. As an example, a food cooked at a pressure of 10 pounds at sea level will have a temperature of 240°F.; at an altitude of 6,000 feet, the identical food must be cooked at 13 pounds pressure to reach the same temperature. The pressure, in all cases, will require adjustment, but not the cooking period.

boiling vegetables: Here, experience will have to be your teacher. In all cases, the vegetables will take longer to cook at high altitudes than at sea level, but the additional time is not a constant factor—it is not possible to offer you a chart to follow. The moisture within the vegetable (an indicator of its age) will also affect cooking time at high altitudes, and so will the humidity of the air. Start by giving the vegetable half again as much time as required at sea level; test for doneness. If not done, continue cooking. To keep the cooking time within a manageable period, be certain the water is boiling briskly when you put the vegetables in to cook, and that it returns to boiling as rapidly as possible.

oven-baking of fruits, vegetables: No adjustments need be made.

deep-fat frying: Temperature must be lowered 2 to 3 degrees for each 1,000 feet of altitude above sea level—that is, 10 to 15 degrees for 5,000 feet, 16 to 21 degrees for 7,000 feet.

canning: Processing time for water-bath method should be increased 1 minute for each 1,000 feet of elevation if the sea-level processing time is 20 minutes or less. If the called-for time is more than 20 minutes, increase processing 2 minutes for each 1,000 feet of elevation above sea level.

For pressure canning, the gauge pressure ordinarily used should be increased 1 pound for each 2,000 feet above sea level.

In making jams, jellies, and preserves, follow the sea-level directions with this exception: the mixtures are done when they reach 7 degrees above boiling. Or use the old-fashioned sheet test—jelly slides off a metal spoon in one large sheetlike drop when done. Jellies should be cooked to 209°F. at 5,000 feet and to 205°F. at 7,000 feet.

broiling: To broil meats successfully in a high/dry climate, food should be placed 1 inch farther from the source of heat than the broiler's use-and-care manual states. If a use-and-care manual is not available, and all your broiling experience has been in the neighborhood of sea level, try the following suggestions, adjusting them to suit your own tastes.

RARE—broil 4 inches from source of heat
MEDIUM—5 to 6 inches
WELL-DONE—7 to 8 inches

As it is with almost everything else, facing the fact that you must learn to cook in a way different from the one with which you are familiar can be considerably more frightening and nervous-making than the cooking itself turns out to be. Some good general cookbooks have sections on high-altitude cookery, but your best bet is a cookbook tailored to your altitude. Consult your public library and browse until you find a book to suit you. Take it home and use it as a guide; if it proves satisfactory, buy a copy and cook from it until you get the hang of it.

HIGHBALL

The most simple of alcoholic beverages—and the one that allows the flavor of the liquor to shine through most clearly—is the highball. To make it, place ice cubes in a tall glass. Add a jigger of liquor—rye, bourbon, or scotch are the usual ones, but a highball may also be made of brandy or rum—and fill the glass with either club soda or plain water. That's it. No fruit, no doodads. See also BEVERAGES.

HOLLANDAISE SAUCE

A smooth, rich, butter-egg yolk-lemon sauce used on such fresh vegetables as asparagus and broccoli, and on fish. Made in a double boiler or (if you're both careful and self-assured) in a heavy saucepan over direct heat, or—this is the easiest—in the electric blender. With orange instead of lemon juice, it becomes Sauce Maltaise; with whipped cream folded in, it becomes a mousseline. See LEMONS and the special feature: SAUCE SORCERY.

HOME CANNING: see special feature:
  PUTTING FOOD BY

HOME COOK'S NEW MATH,
  THE: see page 218

HOMEMADE

The text of our sermon for today: store-bought is (sometimes) good; homemade is (sometimes) better.

Nothing in heaven above, the earth beneath, or the waters under the earth is going to make you a good cook if you don't like cooking. You can be a competent one, and you owe it to your family and your own self-respect to achieve that much. But you'll never waltz around the kitchen to the sound of your own whistling. You'll never pat loaves of bread when they come from the oven as you would pat the head of a child. You'll never wear a slightly foolish-looking smile of sheer pleasure as you attack some time-consuming, non-creative task such as shelling peas. For you, the embroidery needle or the hypodermic needle, the tennis court or the court of law, but not the kitchen. And for you, store-bought may well be best, conserving your minimal kitchen energies for what cooking absolutely must be done, channeling your remaining energies to those things that are important to you.

And then there are the rest of us, the other face of the kitchen coin. We enter the kitchen in the mood in which Cinderella went to the ball. We sing (even the tone-deaf) as we work, producing at one and the same time a croquembouche and all three voices of the final trio from Faust, without turning a hair. We may be unable to jog more than ten feet or climb a flight of stairs without sitting down to pant, but in the kitchen our stamina knows no bounds. We beat with zest, knead with reckless abandon, fold with fairytale delicacy, stir up a storm.

For us, homemade is better. Homemade is the only way to go. If we are told, "You are beautiful," we acknowledge the compliment gracefully and forget it. But if we are told, "Your aioli is a poem, your dobosch torte a dream," we swoon with unalloyed joy. The tears we shed over each peeled onion are tears of sensual pleasure.

That's how it is. *Chacun à son goût*—as long as the homemades don't scorn the store-boughts, or vice versa.

HOMINY: see CORN

HOMOGENIZED MILK: see MILK

HONEY

How doth the little busy bee improve each shining hour? Gathering nectar and returning it to the hive to be converted into honey. And no wonder he's busy, poor creature—to make one pound of honey requires 40,000 bee-loads of nectar brought by more than 550 bees flying 36,000 miles (that's 1⅓ times the distance around the world). Meanwhile, back at the hive, thousands of other bees are at work, beating their wings over the combs to circulate air and evaporate water from the nectar, converting it to honey. Over 5 million colonies of honey bees (a colony consists of about 30,000 individuals) annually produce over 50 million dollars' worth of honey and beeswax. Busy is no word for it.

Honey down the years. Certainly the first sweet that man tasted was honey—and having sampled its goodness, he must have replenished his supply whenever he found a bee tree, doubtless at the expense of considerable effort and many stings, but worth all the trouble.

Almost every civilization has valued honey as a food, a medicine, a trading commodity, and a spiritual gift. Egyptians offered it to their gods, buried it with their dead, and used it in virtually all their medicines. In many lands, taxes were paid in honey, or it was offered as tribute to rulers and leaders.

Early Celts made mead from fermented honey and water, flavoring it with spices; a seat at a ceremonial where mead was the drink of the day was called the Mead Bench, and the festival gathering place was Mead Hall.

The Promised Land, if you know your Bible, was a place flowing with milk and honey, and there are many other biblical references to the natural sweet, which must have seemed a gift from a kindly deity.

For many centuries the major source of sweetening in the diet, honey is still important in the sweet scheme of things. To children, honey, besides being a delicious spread for bread, is a commodity valued by Winnie-the-Pooh (all bears have a weakness for honey), and the Owl and the Pussycat who, when they set sail, took honey along in their beautiful pea-green boat.

Today—although we turn elsewhere for most of our sweets—honey bees are still important for the major agricultural role they play. As the bees go about their nectar-gathering business, they incidentally (to the bees, but indispensably to the farmers) pollinate a billion dollars' worth of valuable crops. Those who raise food rent in the neighborhood of a million colonies of bees each season to pollinate more than fifty different crops, including melons, squash, pumpkins, and fruits and berries, as well as alfalfa, clover, flax, and buckwheat.

"A taste of honey." Natural and unrefined, honey is uniquely the only unmanufactured sweet available in commercial quantities. It varies greatly in flavor, color, and consistency—all three factors dependent on the kind of blossoms from which the bees gathered the nectar.

Generally, the honey lightest in color is mildest in flavor. There is a flavor of honey to suit almost any taste, nearly a hundred of them, from the familiar clover and buckwheat to exotics such as tupelo, raspberry, sage, orange, cotton, coffee, heather, pine, acacia, dogwood, and eucalyptus. Why are the flavors not mixed? Because the honey bee is selective. It may make more than a dozen trips from the hive each day, visiting thousands of flowers, but on each trip it gathers nectar from only one type of blossom. Not only busy, the bee, but also smart.

HONEY IN YOUR KITCHEN

Honey is composed of two simple sugars, levulose and dextrose, both of which require very little digestive change before they can be absorbed by the human body. Levulose is almost twice as sweet as cane sugar, dextrose about half as sweet. Athletes are partial to honey because, they say, it provides an almost instant energy "lift" with no strain on the digestive system.

Cooking with honey. For cooking purposes, liquid honey is what a recipe means when it calls for honey as an ingredient. Measure it easily by measuring the shortening first, then the honey in the same cup—because of the grease lingering in the cup, the honey will slide out easily.

To replace sugar with honey in a cake or cookie recipe, reduce the liquid called for by ¼ cup for each cup of honey used. Beyond that, substitute honey for sugar measure for measure—1 cup of honey for 1 cup of sugar. Reduce baking temperature 25 degrees to avoid overbrowning. You'll find that cakes and cookies and cereals made with honey keep fresh longer than those with sugar because of the ability of honey to absorb and retain moisture, which retards drying out and staling in baked goods. For safest results in baking, however, use recipes developed especially for the use of honey.

how to buy: There are five types generally available, each with its best uses and its own charms.

 liquid: Also called extracted honey, this is obtained by uncapping the combs and removing the honey by centrifugal force; generally sold in jars, sometimes in small crocks.

 comb: This is honey as it was made and stored by the bees; to serve, cut in 1-inch squares.

 cut comb: This is comb honey cut in bars about 4 inches long by 1½ inches wide, each separately wrapped.

 chunk: This is liquid honey in which are suspended small pieces of the comb.

 granulated: Also called solid, candied, honey spread, or creamed, this is honey from which some of the moisture has been removed—just as delicious and much less messy a spread than the liquid.

Choose a honey type and flavor that suits your taste and purpose. For cooking, liquid mild-flavored clover honey is a good choice. Some honey is graded and labeled according to standards set by the USDA or by the various state departments of agriculture.

how to store: Room temperature is best. Be sure that the container is tightly covered—honey will absorb other odors, which impairs its flavor, and moisture, which can dilute the honey sufficiently so that fermentation will set in—or it will mold.

Honey may crystallize as it gets older, or if it is stored in the refrigerator. Restore it to liquid form by setting the jar in a container of water no warmer than 200°F.

nutritive value: Despite the all-embracing claims made by the health food culture, honey does not have a great deal to contribute to nutrition. However, it is a cut above sugar from a nutritional point of view—it contains trace amounts (very small, but measurable) of iron, copper, sodium, potassium, manganese, calcium, magnesium, and phosphorus, seven of the vitamins in the B complex, vitamin C, and certain amino acids and enzymes, although it would require a considerable honey intake to obtain much benefit from these elements. One tablespoon of honey furnishes 65 calories; sugar furnishes 40 in the same measure. Both are composed largely of carbohydrate—sugar almost totally so.

Freezing honey. It can be done, and the honey will remain liquid and undamaged. However, considering that honey is available virtually everywhere at all times, knowing no season, to devote freezer space to it seems wasteful unless you are a beekeeper burdened with an excess.

333

Honey on the table. There are literally hundreds of ways to use honey, all of them delightful, many of them so different from our ordinary fare that they come as a happy flavor/texture surprise to cook and diners alike.

There are honey cookbooks available to show you the way to such delights as pork chops with a honey-tomato sauce, pot roast with a honey-onion-wine braising liquid, chicken with a soy-honey basting sauce, honey-sweetened whole wheat bread, honey-and-spice green apple pie, honey-drenched baklava, honey-flavored ice cream, dozens of honey-based salad dressings, and a great many more, all delicious.

Here are some quick/easy honey treats:

- sweeten tea with honey rather than sugar
- glaze ham with honey and chopped dried apricots
- substitute honey for sugar on hot cereal
- sweeten whipped cream with honey to top desserts
- use honey to replace sugar in lemonade, orangeade, eggnog
- top fresh fruit for dessert with ¼ cup honey stirred into ¾ cup dairy sour cream
- for breakfast, dip orange segments in honey, then in coconut
- sauce chocolate ice cream with honey, sprinkle with nuts
- combine half-and-half honey and butter to use on waffles, pancakes, and french toast, or to serve with hot biscuits or muffins
- blend honey and peanut butter to sauce a ham steak
- top sautéed apple rings with honey, cinnamon and grated orange peel; cook a few moments longer to glaze
- honey and peanut butter make a sandwich loved by children; for a change, try honey with cream cheese, with chopped nuts, with chopped dried fruit
- pep up baked beans with honey, mustard, and ginger
- make a nut cake in a square pan; prick it deeply all over with a skewer or kitchen fork and pour slowly over it a hot syrup made of 3 parts honey to 1 part lemon juice

These and many other quick tricks with honey persuade the home cook to keep it on hand as a pantry staple.

A word about royal jelly. A milky white substance that is the sole food of the queen bee, royal jelly—rich in protein and containing appreciable amounts of other nutrients—has given rise to considerable speculation about its possible effects on human beings. Although the life span of a worker bee is brief—a few weeks to a few months—queens live up to seven years. If we too ate royal jelly, might it not lengthen our lives?

Armed with that galvanizing question, and basing their activities on a knowledge of the human tendency to embrace new (and peculiar) ideas, some venturers have put royal jelly on the market, both as a food supplement and as an ingredient in cosmetics. But the worth of royal jelly has never been proved, and those who have spent a great deal of money on preparations containing it seem to be no better off (true, no worse either, except for the unstemmed advancing of the years) than their peers who have never tried the stuff. If royal jelly has special powers, a way to release and employ them has not yet been found. Science is investigating, but the returns are not in.

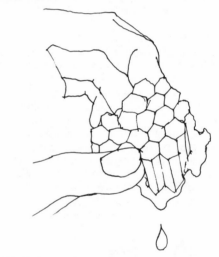

Love rhymes with honey. Somehow, the mellifluous pale-gold liquid has overflowed from pantry to poetry, in a sweet richness of words as in the honey itself. Yeats lived "in the bee-loud glade" at Innisfree. And young Rupert Brooke, sitting in a café in Berlin just before World War I, lonely and homesick for England, wrote:

> Say, is there beauty yet to find?
> And Certainty? and Quiet kind?
> Deep meadows yet, for to forget
> The lies, and truths, and pain? . . . oh, yet
> Stands the Church clock at ten to three?
> And is there honey still for tea?

Killed in the war, he is buried far from England on the Greek island of Scyros. Around his grave the wild thyme grows. Bees feast on its blossoms, gathering nectar for their honey.

HONEYDEWS and HONEYBALLS: see MELONS

HORS D'OEUVRES: see APPETIZERS

HORSEMEAT

Although it is nutritious and has a good—if somewhat sweetish—flavor, horsemeat has never gained favor at the table in the United States. Most people have qualms (of conscience or stomach, who can say) about eating it, although on quiet, nonhysterical consideration, it is difficult to see why. Perhaps because some of us love and ride horses? But it is just as easy to make friends with a steer, or a lamb, or even a chicken, and just as easy to become attached to it.

The 4-H club youngsters raise steers as projects, grow to love them, but sell them for beef. So why not horses? And why should city dwellers who have never encountered a living creature on the hoof still shy away? For that matter, why should country folk, to whom living and dying among their animals is a fact of their occupation?

During World War II there were efforts to popularize the eating of horsemeat both here and in England, but they met with total lack of success. One doughty Britisher went on record as preferring to eat his neighbor (a singularly cantankerous old boy) to eating a horse.

Yet in France, horsemeat is consumed in considerable quantity, particularly by the poor. It is eaten in Austria, Denmark, Germany, and Sweden to some extent. Some horseflesh is sold in the United States, by strictly regulated dealers, and is used for the feeding of dogs.

HORSERADISH: see HERBS AND
SAVORY SEASONINGS and
PREPARED HORSERADISH

HOT DOGS

The succulent wiener—or weenie, or Coney Island Red Hot, or frank, if you prefer—is an American custom if not a shibboleth, without which no fair, circus, or ball game would be complete. It is served on a bun, eaten out of hand, and mustard is a necessity—although some prefer catsup, some pickle relish, some chopped onion, some a messy but fragrantly delicious helping of sauerkraut, and some are not content unless they pile on all of these. Hot dogs are cookout and campfire fare, too. See SAUSAGES.

HOT PEPPER SAUCE

A thin, pale orange-red bottled sauce used for seasoning. It must be approached with caution, for it is hot almost beyond belief. Remembering that a little goes a long way, use it to season sauces, seafood (particularly raw oysters), chili—for those to whom chili powder just never seems to have enough bite—and to add a little fire to a bloody mary. Also called tabasco.

HOT PEPPERS: see PEPPERS and HERBS AND
SAVORY SEASONINGS

HOT-WEATHER COOKERY

In summertime, Porgy tells us, the livin' is easy. And so it should be, for everyone including the cook.

High on the list of hot-weather treats is the cookout, a term that embraces everything from a few frankfurters sizzled on the grill to the whole-ox barbecue put on as a fund-raiser by church or other groups. If there's a nearby beach, there are beach parties, perhaps climaxed by a glorious clambake with lobsters and chicken and potatoes and corn roasted along with the clams, a niagara of butter on everything including people's chins, and big slabs of watermelon to top things off. If not the beach, there are always pools and where there's a pool there's also a pool party, with steaks on the grill or perhaps a plump smoke-cooked turkey or a whole salmon.

Think cool, cook cool. For everyday meals, the smart cook goes to work in the coolest part of the day, early in the morning or after sundown. There are so many dewy vegetables, so much juicy fresh fruit, that no one need ever be at a loss for what to serve.

The trick is to plan so that the oven need not be lighted during the heat of the day, and so that the cook doesn't have to stand at length over a hot stove to get dinner on the table. Salads are fine—the hearty, meal-in-one kind. So are soups, to serve cold or to reheat briefly at mealtime. So are sandwiches, cold cuts, cheese.

But that sort of food, welcomed as a change when hot weather sets in, grows tiresome as summer wears on. Vary it with quick-cook hot food, such as skillet or stir-fry dishes. Try an eat-on-the-patio fondue, or bake-at-table waffles to top with creamed dried beef or chicken or fish. Something hot, such as a mug of hearty soup, takes the chilly curse off otherwise cold meals. Or accompany cold meat with a hot stovetop noodle dish—buttered, with poppy seeds, or sauced with sour cream and parmesan. If it must be sandwiches, make hearty ready-to-grill ones in advance, let everybody cook his own at mealtime.

Desserts can always be make-aheads, hearty if the meal is to be light, simple if the meal has more substance. Serve cheese with some of that good fresh fruit. Ices—lemon, lime, orange, pineapple—are easy to make, even easier to buy, and fit well into the summer season. If you want to zip them up a bit, top each serving with a spoonful of liqueur. Or make a cake or pie in the morning when it's cool, serve after a light

meal and nobody will remember that dinner was soup and salad again.

Hot-weather cookery doesn't call for a great deal of work, but it does need some beforehand planning to serve meals that everyone will enjoy, including the cool cook.

HUBBARD SQUASH: see SQUASH

HUCKLEBERRIES: see BLUEBERRIES

HULL, TO: see page 446

HUNG MEAT

There was a time when meat—particularly beef, often game —was aged after slaughter by hanging it for a period of time at a cool room temperature. This helped to tenderize the meat and to develop good flavor. Now this process is called aging. Beef is held at a temperature of 34 to 38° F. for three weeks or more. This allows enzymatic activity to break down complex proteins, improving flavor and tenderness.

The same end can be reached by quick-aging the beef at 62 to 65° F. for two to three days—a variation of the old hanging process, except that today a relatively high humidity is maintained to prevent dehydration of the carcass, and growth of unwanted bacteria and microbes is controlled with ultraviolet lamps. Either way, the meat we buy today is superior to newly slaughtered, unaged beef because of this aging process.

HUSK, TO: see page 446

PUTTING FOOD BY

Bounty of earth and sea and sky, gathered and preserved against the lean time—our forefathers took pride and comfort in food laid by and today, happily, so can we

There are many ways to lay seasonal foods away for the days when they will not be available fresh, or surplus foods in time of plenty against periods of scarcity. Once the home preserving of supplies for the winter was a necessity. Today, everything we could ask for is available to us all year around in one form or another, in one sort of market or another. Yet we still preserve, some of us, and take enormous pleasure in it. Indeed, even for some of us to whom it is no pleasure, but a backbreaking chore, there is an inner urging that drives us.

Perhaps it is pride: it is far more satisfactory to open a jar of home-canned peaches than one from the market. It is far more satisfactory to say, "Won't you try my apple chutney?" than to pass a dish of it brought home yesterday from a store. And atavistic memory prompts us to take immense comfort from a cellar filled with preserves, a freezer well stocked with food. We are prepared. All will be well.

Certainly it is not economics: unless we have raised the food ourselves, home laying-by can cost as much as, or more than, the same preserved food purchased from the market. Indeed, unless we are farmers and geared for this sort of thing (raising food efficiently on a grand scale, doing our own butchering and slaughtering), even the produce we grow may be more costly, all things considered, than if we had gone to market and bought it.

Not long ago, a cynical guest asked his hostess how much she thought the home-frozen peas and white onions she had served for dinner had cost. When she said she had no idea, he persisted, leading her through all the steps—preparing the soil, fertilizing, buying and planting the seeds and sets, cultivating, weeding, finally picking the vegetables, shelling the peas, peeling the onions, preparing them for freezing, the cost of the necessary equipment, the energy used by the freezer and, finally, her reasonable hourly wage for the work. Warming to his point, he led her through the same process with a jar of homemade strawberry jelly—again, all those steps, plus the sugar and pectin, plus the energy used in cooking, the jars and the sterilizing, the sealing material and, again, the worth of her own time. They reached a figure of $3.20 for the peas and onions (to serve 6 people) and $2.95 for the 10-ounce jar of jelly.

Oddly, the home cook was unperturbed. Instead of saying she'd had no idea of what had been spent, she turned the conversation to her plans for next year's expanded bout of home preserving. So it must be the pride, the satisfaction.

Ways and means. There are a number of available approaches to the laying away of provender for future use.

- *canning:* fruits, vegetables, meats, poultry, fish; soups; meat combinations
- *curing and smoking:* meats, poultry, fish, game
- *drying:* fruits, vegetables (and a few specialties, such as jerky)
- *freezing:* fruits, vegetables, meats, poultry, fish; a wide range of ready-to-eat or ready-to-cook dishes ranging from soups through desserts
- *pickling:* several vegetables, some fruits, assorted relishes
- *preserving:* fruit jams, jellies, preserves, conserves, butters
- *wintering:* certain garden vegetables, unprocessed

Those are the usual ways. There are more: you can make wine at home; you can preserve fruit in alcohol; you can make cheese at home. But few of us venture that far afield. Indeed, canning and freezing—with perhaps some pickling and preserving—are about as far as most home cooks, other than farm wives, care or are able to go.

CANNING AT HOME

Before the invention of the steam-pressure canner, housewives either packed cooked foods into sterilized jars, sealed them, and let it go at that, or packed raw or partially cooked food into jars and processed them in a water bath. Those methods are still employed for many fruits, but we know now that pressure canning is the only safe way to process foods that are low in acid—corn, beans, carrots, beets, greens and, indeed, most garden vegetables, as well as meats, poultry, and fish.

Before you begin. Indeed, even before you make up your mind whether or not to try your hand at home canning, take an up-front, overall look at what is involved in the way of know-how and equipment, as well as time and labor on your part.

raw materials: What you get out of a can depends on what you put into it. Choose only fresh, young, tender, ripe produce, and plan on canning it as soon as possible after it's picked.

preparation: Soil contains bacteria. The produce may have a residue of insect spray. So wash everything well—several times, changing the water often.

containers: Use only jars made for home canning; they are tempered in the manufacturing to withstand the necessary heat and pressure. Empty mayonnaise, peanut butter, and other jars won't do—they may crack or break in the processing or, if they survive that, may fail to seal properly. You make a big investment of time, effort, and money in home canning, so it's foolish to use jars that can make all that expenditure fruitless.

Check the rims of the canning jars—run a finger lightly around—for nicks, cracks, or chips. Discard any jars that are in any way damaged. The rims must be smoothly intact in order to effect a proper seal.

methods: There are three ways to process home-canned foods:

- water bath
- steam pressure
- open kettle

The third, open kettle, is used only for making jellies. Preserves in which a large amount of sugar, which retards spoilage, is used are also kettle-cooked, but they are then processed in a water bath.

For the *water-bath method* you will need a large pot made especially for this purpose; it has a rack in the bottom to hold jars off the bottom and apart from one another, and a cover to keep steam within the pot.

Briefly, this is how it works: The canner, with 4 to 5 inches of water in it, is set on the stove to heat; at the same time, more water is set to heat in another vessel, such as a teakettle. Liquid—juice or syrup—is prepared and kept warm. The jars are packed with food and liquid and their lids put in place, following directions on the package that contains the lids. As each is filled it is placed on the rack in the canner. Don't try to crowd—no jar must touch another. More water is added to the canner to bring the level to 1 to 2 inches above the tops of the jars. The canner is covered (more water may be added as necessary during processing) and the water is maintained at a gentle boil for the amount of time required for the food you are processing. When the time is up, the jars are removed and cooled at room temperature.

The *steam-pressure method* generally follows these same steps, except that the vessel used is a pressure canner —like a home pressure cooker, only much larger. The spoilage-causing organisms that may be present in low-acid foods are killed at the high temperature of the pressure canner. A use-and-care booklet, including recipes, comes with each of the various makes of pressure canners, and its instructions should be followed carefully.

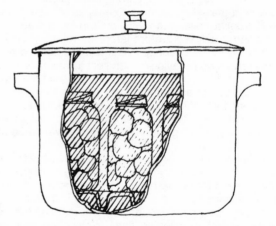

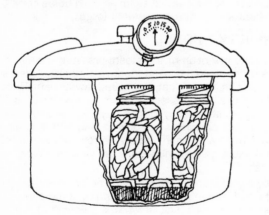

raw-packing: This means that uncooked food is placed in the canning jar and is covered with a boiling liquid—syrup, water, or fruit juice—before processing.

hot-packing: This means that hot, partially cooked food is placed in the canning jar, then covered with boiling liquid before processing.

cautionary notes: When you are canning, keep your work area clean and dry. Do not fill jars too full—headspace must be left for expansion during processing, usually ½ to 1 inch between the top of the food and the jar lid. When a jar is filled, run a rubber spatula or a knife carefully around inside it to release air bubbles that may have formed. After filling, wipe off the rim of the jar before putting the lid in place, to assure a tight seal. Above all, follow the instructions of a good, reliable cookbook. Don't ever try to can "by ear."

storage: Store your home-canned foods in a cool, dark, dry place. Label each jar with the contents and the date it was processed.

Equipment is all-important. Glass jars for home canning are of two kinds, and each has its own type of lid and seal. Lids and seals are not interchangeable between the two kinds of jars.

metal-screwband jars: The closures for these jars are in two parts—a metal screwband in the form of an open-topped ring, threaded to match the threading of the jar, plus a flat metal lid that is coated on the side that goes next to the food and has an edge of sealing compound. This type of closure makes its seal at the rim of the jar. Jars and screwbands (provided they are not damaged) may be reused, but the metal lids with the sealing compound can be used only once.

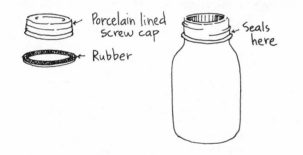

zinc-cap jars with rings: Again, the closure is in two parts —a porcelain-lined screw cap, plus a rubber ring. This type of closure makes its seal on a lip that is part of the jar; it is just below the threading, and it is on this "shoulder" that the wet rubber ring is placed. Jars and caps may be reused if in good condition, the rubber rings can be used only once.

Another type of container used in home canning is the metal can, similar to those in which store-bought canned food is packed. These are generally used only in farm homes, where a great deal of food is processed. A special machine, a can sealer, is required for closing the cans.

Canning safety. A few years ago, the USDA surveyed home canners. About 25 percent of the homes surveyed reported some type of food spoilage in home-canned products—most of it due, the home cooks believed, to improperly sealed jars.

Less than half of the home canners, the survey discovered, carefully followed reliable canning instructions—in cookbooks, in USDA pamphlets on the subject, in information accompanying jars and closures or their water-bath or pressure canners. In other words, carelessness. Almost a third of the households had used jars not meant for canning. About one-tenth had reused metal lids with sealers, contrary to recommendations of the maker. A like number had reused rubber rings, also contrary to the makers' recommendations. Some had used the open-kettle method for fruits and vegetables, although this method should be used *only* in making jelly and as an initial step in making jam.

"How can you tell when food is spoiled?" the home cooks were asked. Most recognized spoilage when they saw it—bulging lids, unpleasant odor, spurting of liquid when the jar was opened, leaking jars, mold on the food. But virtually none was aware that spoilage can be present without exhibiting any signs, and that this sort of spoilage—the invisible botulism toxin, which can be fatal—is the most dangerous of all. (See following chart for various kinds of food spoilage, the "food-poisoning" illnesses they can cause, and how to control such spoilage.)

If food is processed according to reliable instructions for that particular kind of food, and if reliable instructions are followed for packing and sealing it—using proper jars and new closures—there is no reason why spoilage should occur.

Reasons for spoilage. Here are the common causes of canned food spoilage, all of them due to errors in the canning process:

- pressure in the pressure canner was not held at 10 pounds during processing—usually caused by an inaccurate pressure gauge, or by uneven heat maintained under the canner, allowing pressure to drop; also caused by failure to make necessary pressure corrections at altitudes over 2,000 feet
- all the air in the canner was not exhausted before pressure was built up
- water in water-bath canner was not kept at a boil during the entire processing time, or water level was allowed to fall below the tops of the jars at some point during processing

BACTERIAL ILLNESSES CAUSED BY FOOD SPOILAGE

illness	caused by	symptoms	characteristics	control
botulism	*Clostridium botulinum,* spore-forming organisms that grow and produce toxins in absence of oxygen, as in sealed containers; bacteria can also produce toxin in low-acid food refrigerated for 2 weeks or longer; spores, extremely heat-resistant, are harmless, but toxin is a deadly poison.	double vision, inability to swallow, difficulty with speech, progressive respiratory paralysis; fatality rate is high—about 50% in U.S.	transmitted by eating food containing the toxin; onset usually 12 to 36 hours or longer, duration is 3 to 6 days.	spores in food destroyed by high temperature obtained only in pressure canner; more than 6 hours needed to kill spores by boiling; toxin destroyed by boiling 10 to 20 minutes, depending on type of food.
salmonellosis	*Salmonellae,* widespread in nature, live and grow in intestinal tracts of humans, animals; grow and multiply at 44° to 115°F. temperatures.	severe headache is followed by vomiting, diarrhea, cramps, and fever; infants, elderly, and those with low resistance most susceptible; severe infections may cause high fever, even death.	transmitted by eating contaminated food, by contact with infected persons or carriers, and by insects, pets, rodents; onset, 12 to 36 hours; duration, 2 to 7 days.	bacteria in food destroyed by heating to 140°F. and holding 10 minutes, or to higher temperature for less time; refrigeration inhibits growth but they remain alive in refrigerator or freezer, and in dried foods.
perfringens poisoning	*Clostridium perfringens,* spore-forming bacteria grow in absence of oxygen; spores withstand temperatures reached by usual cooking methods; surviving bacteria continue to grow in cooked meats, meat dishes, gravies held without proper refrigeration.	nausea without vomiting, diarrhea, acute inflammation of stomach and intestines.	transmitted by eating food contaminated by abnormally large numbers of the bacteria; onset usually 8 to 20 hours; may persist for 24 hours.	control growth of surviving bacteria on cooked meats to be eaten later by cooling rapidly and refrigerating promptly at 40°F. or lower.
staphylococcal poisoning (sometimes called "staph")	*Staphylococcus aureus,* fairly resistant to heat, grow in food and produce a toxin extremely resistant to heat; profuse growth and production of toxin at temperatures between 44° and 115°F.	vomiting, diarrhea, prostration, cramps; generally mild, and often attributed to other causes.	transmitted by food handlers who carry the bacteria and by eating food containing the toxin; onset within 3 to 8 hours; duration, 1 or 2 days.	growth of bacteria that produce toxin inhibited by keeping hot food above 140°F. and cold foods at or below 40°F.; toxin destroyed by boiling for several hours or heating in pressure cooker at 240°F. for 30 minutes.

other errors: Sometimes food changes color or floats after the canning process is complete and the jars have cooled. Most likely reasons for food color change are:

- too much time elapsed while preparing the food for canning
- food was not processed sufficiently to kill the enzymes that destroy color
- food in the jars wasn't completely covered with liquid
- all air bubbles were not removed before processing was begun
- ascorbic acid was not used where needed with fruit, to prevent darkening
- high color of foods (cherries, beets) was dissolved in liquid or syrup
- area where food jars were stored was too warm or too sunny

Most likely reasons for food floating (food at top of jar, liquid without food in it at bottom) are:

- food was too loosely packed in jar
- food was packed raw, contrary to the best recommendations for that peticular type of food (directions must be followed)
- food was processed too long
- if fruit, the syrup was too heavy
- if fruit, the fruit was too ripe

Once again—it can't be said too many times—reliable home canning instructions (good cookbook, USDA bulletins, manufacturer of home canning supplies) must be followed to the letter. And it must be remembered that even the most reliable instructions for one type of food can be inadequate or totally wrong for another type. Otherwise you are wasting your time and the cost of the food and equipment, as well as exposing your family to health hazards.

Proper equipment is a big help. Besides a water-bath canner and/or a pressure canner, and undamaged jars of the right kind plus their proper lids and new closures, other kitchen equipment—which you most probably have at hand —is useful in home canning.

spoon, ladle: A slotted spoon and a large ladle will assist you in getting and packing food into jars.

funnel: A funnel with a wide mouth and a wide neck is necessary for efficient jar filling.

tongs: Long-handled, sturdy tongs or, better yet, a gadget called a jar-lifter are essential for safely transferring jars to and from the canner. Cloth—pot holders or folded towels— that may work well in protecting you from heat when they are dry are no protection when they are wet, and it's virtually impossible to keep from getting them wet in canning.

sieve: A sturdy sieve or colander is necessary for draining foods.

teakettle: This—easiest to use because it has a spout—or another kettle, preferably with a pouring lip, keeps water boiling to add to the water-bath canner to maintain the proper level (2 inches above jar tops) during processing.

rack: A rack or a wooden board or, lacking either, a folded towel should be used to set hot jars on for cooling. Keep in mind that an abrupt change in temperature can break a jar; so can water in the area where you set the jars down to cool.

measuring containers: Heatproof glass measuring cups, in both the 2-cup and the 4-cup sizes, are useful in pouring hot liquid.

Another important tool is time. Canning cannot be hurried, time cannot be shortcut in the canning process, no step can be skipped. If you have neither the time nor the patience for a job that can be very rewarding but sometimes tedious, don't start.

High-altitude canning. As with other cooking, the altitude must be taken into consideration when you plan to do home canning, particularly when you use a steam-pressure canner. Up to 2,000 feet, the 10-pound pressure required in most recipes (which are tailored to sea level) will give the desired results. Above that point, follow this table:

at this altitude:	process at a pressure of:
2,000 to 2,999 feet	11½ pounds
3,000 to 3,999 feet	12 pounds
4,000 to 4,999 feet	12½ pounds
5,000 to 5,999 feet	13 pounds
6,000 to 6,999 feet	13½ pounds
7,000 to 7,999 feet	14 pounds
8,000 to 8,999 feet	14½ pounds
9,000 to 10,000 feet	15 pounds

Canning low-acid vegetables. In this, as in any other type of canning, follow to the letter instructions given you for that particular vegetable in a reliable cookbook or a government canning bulletin, or by the maker of the canning equipment you are using. Following, to show you the amount of time involved, are processing times for the various low-acid vegetables (any not listed are not suitable for canning). Low-acid vegetables are canned only by steam pressure.

STEAM-PRESSURE CANNING
(240°F., 10 pounds pressure)

vegetable	type of pack	½ pints and pints	1½ pints and quart
asparagus	raw or hot	25 minutes	30 minutes
beans: green, snap, or wax	raw or hot	20 minutes	25 minutes
beans: lima, butter	raw or hot	40 minutes	50 minutes
beets	hot	30 minutes	35 minutes
broccoli	hot	30 minutes	35 minutes
brussels sprouts	hot	30 minutes	35 minutes
cabbage	hot	30 minutes	35 minutes
carrots	raw or hot	25 minutes	30 minutes
cauliflower	hot	30 minutes	35 minutes
celery	hot	30 minutes	35 minutes
corn, whole kernel	raw or hot	55 minutes	85 minutes
corn, cream-style	hot	85 minutes	not recommended
eggplant	hot	30 minutes	40 minutes
greens (all)	hot	70 minutes	90 minutes
hominy	hot	60 minutes	70 minutes
mixed vegetables	hot	time required for vegetable with longest processing time	
mushrooms	hot	30 minutes	not recommended
okra	hot	25 minutes	40 minutes
parsnips	hot	30 minutes	35 minutes
peas: blackeyed and field	raw or hot	35 minutes	40 minutes
peas, green	raw or hot	40 minutes	not recommended
peppers, green	hot	35 minutes	not recommended
peppers, sweet red	hot	15 minutes	not recommended
potatoes, white	hot	30 minutes	40 minutes
potatoes, sweet	hot and wet	55 minutes	90 minutes
pumpkin	hot	65 minutes	80 minutes
rutabagas	hot	30 minutes	35 minutes
salsify (oyster plant)	hot	25 minutes	35 minutes
spinach (see *greens*, above)			
squash, summer	hot	30 minutes	40 minutes
squash, winter	hot	65 minutes	80 minutes
tomatoes, stewed	hot	15 minutes	20 minutes
turnips	hot	30 minutes	35 minutes

Canning meats, fish, and poultry. These, like the low-acid vegetables, are canned by steam pressure. Fresh, wholesome food, properly prepared and processed, results in a safe product and in one that is appetite-appealing as well.

Usual meats for canning include beef, veal, mutton, lamb, and pork, as well as portions of both small-game and big-game animals. Poultry includes chicken, duck, goose, guinea hen, squab, turkey, and game birds. Fish includes clams, oysters, and shrimp among the shellfish, and mackerel, trout, salmon, and shad.

Meat, fish, and poultry for canning must be refrigerated until time to prepare them. Follow canning instructions to the letter—there is considerable risk of botulism in these foods if they are not properly prepared and processed. Make certain that all your equipment is scrupulously clean, scrubbed in hot soapy water, then rinsed in boiling water. Wooden utensils—cutting boards, wooden work surfaces, and wooden spoons require special attention when you are working with meat in order to keep spoilage bacteria under control. If the surfaces are soiled (with blood, scraps) scrape them first. Scrub with hot soapy water, rinse with boiling water. Then disinfect with liquid chlorine—household laundry bleach—diluted according to the directions on the label

Cover the wooden surfaces with the solution, leave it in place 15 minutes, then wash it off well with boiling water.

preparation: As much fat as possible should be removed from meat and poultry; indeed, excessively fat meat or poultry should not be canned. Salt may be added for flavor, but it does not act as a preservative—add it or not as you choose.

Meat can be *hot packed*—precooked before packing in jars, and broth added before processing—or it may be *raw packed*—packed uncooked, then heated to 170°F. before processing to exhaust (remove) air from the cans or jars, so that a vacuum will be formed in the jars after processing and cooling. Meat and poultry can be packed either boneless or bone-in.

Follow recipes and instructions faithfully. Here, as a guide, are processing times for some of the commonly canned meats, fish, and poultry. Remember that time and temperature remain constant at high altitudes, but pressure must be adjusted.

STEAM-PRESSURE CANNING
(240°F., 10 pounds pressure)

| | | processing time for: | |
| | | ½ pints and pints | 1½ pints and quarts |
food	type of pack		
chili	hot	75 minutes	90 minutes
chopped beef, veal, lamb, mutton, pork, venison	hot	75 minutes	90 minutes
corned beef	hot	75 minutes	90 minutes
meat sauce, stew	hot	60 minutes	75 minutes
headcheese, sausage	hot	75 minutes	90 minutes
pork tenderloin	hot or raw	75 minutes	90 minutes
roasts (all meats)	hot	75 minutes	90 minutes
spareribs	hot	75 minutes	90 minutes
steaks and chops (all meats)	hot or raw	75 minutes	90 minutes
poultry, rabbit, and squirrel (boned)	hot	75 minutes	90 minutes
poultry and rabbit (bone-in)	hot or raw	95 minutes	90 minutes
chicken à la king	hot	65 minutes	75 minutes
roasted poultry	hot	65 minutes	75 minutes
clams	these shellfish are usually	70 minutes	not recommended
crabmeat	brine-soaked or otherwise	100 minutes at 5 pounds	not recommended
shrimp	treated before packing—	45 minutes	not recommended
mackerel, trout, salmon, etc.	follow individual recipes	100 minutes	not recommended
fish in sauce (tomato, etc.)	hot	50 minutes	60 minutes

Canning fruits and acid vegetables.

All the various admonitions, suggestions, and cautions given before apply in this instance, too. But these foods are processed in a water-bath instead of a steam-pressure canner.

Choose sound, fresh, firm-ripe fruits and vegetables. Wash and drain before any other preparation steps required, such as peeling, seeding, hulling, coring, and so on. Prepare only enough produce for one canner load at a time.

Sugar is not required for fruits processed in this manner; that is, it is not needed to act as a preservative. However, for best flavor, color and shape-holding, sugar—in the form of syrup—can be added. Three types of syrup can be used; individual recipes will suggest the right type for each fruit. To make syrups:

syrup type:	for 1 quart water add:	yield:
light	2 cups of sugar	5 cups
medium	3 cups of sugar	5½ cups
heavy	4¾ cups of sugar	6½ cups

Syrups may also be made with part corn syrup or part honey. For medium syrup, use 3 cups of water with 1½ cups of sugar and 1 cup of corn syrup, or use 4 cups of water, 1 cup of sugar, and 1 cup of honey. Bear in mind that corn syrup does not change the flavor of the fruit, but honey does. Fruit juices may be used in place of water in these syrups. Sometimes very juicy fruits are packed with dry sugar rather than syrup.

To prevent darkening. There are several commercial preparations available that keep fruit from darkening; they are made of ascorbic/citric acid. Follow label instructions. Or, if you prefer, as you prepare them, drop the fruits that darken —apples, apricots, peaches, nectarines, pears—into a solution of 2 tablespoons each of salt and vinegar to a gallon of water. Don't leave them in the mixture longer than 20 minutes, and rinse them well before packing.

To prevent darkening in the jar, use ascorbic and citric acid mixtures, again following label instructions.

Higher altitudes. Most canning recipes are tailored for altitudes of less than 1,000 feet; above that point, processing times must be increased. The longer the processing time called for at sea level, the greater the high-altitude increase. Here are the adjustments:

	if time called for is	
at an	*20 minutes*	*more than*
altitude of:	*or less*	*20 minutes*
	increase processing time by:	
1,000 feet	1 minute	2 minutes
2,000 feet	2 minutes	4 minutes
3,000 feet	3 minutes	6 minutes
4,000 feet	4 minutes	8 minutes
5,000 feet	5 minutes	10 minutes
6,000 feet	6 minutes	12 minutes
7,000 feet	7 minutes	14 minutes
8,000 feet	8 minutes	16 minutes
9,000 feet	9 minutes	18 minutes
10,000 feet	10 minutes	20 minutes

For exact sea-level processing time for each kind of fruit, follow instructions given in individual recipes.

Processing times. To give you a general idea of how long a processing time individual fruits will require, here is a chart of typical times for fruit "put up," as grandma called it, in syrup. Fruit butter, jams, conserves, and so on will require different times, and some will call for lower temperature. In

all cases, consult a reliable recipe for step-by-step processing instructions.

WATER-BATH CANNING AT 212°F.

fruit	pack	½ pints	pints	processing time in minutes for 1½ pints and quarts
apples	hot	15	20	20
applesauce	hot	15	20	20
apricots	raw	20	25	30
apricots	hot	15	20	25
berries	raw	10	15	20
berries	hot	10	10	15
cherries	raw	15	20	25
cherries	hot	10	10	15
currants	raw	10	15	20
dried fruits	raw	10	15	20
figs	hot	80	85	90
grapefruit	raw	10	10	10
grapes, ripe	raw	10	15	20
grapes, unripe	raw	15	20	25
guavas	hot	10	15	20
loquats	hot	10	15	20
mixed fruits	hot	15	20	25
nectarines	raw	20	25	30
nectarines	hot	15	20	25
peaches	raw	20	25	30
peaches	hot	15	20	25
pears	hot	15	20	25
persimmons	hot	10	15	20
pineapple	hot	10	15	20
plums	hot	15	20	25

Certain acid vegetables—rhubarb, sauerkraut, tomatoes, and tomato juice—are also water bath-canned, as are fruit juices and various pickled vegetables. Consult individual recipes. It is worth knowing that strains of low-acid tomatoes have been developed within the last few years; for safety, these should be pressure-canned.

The finishing touches. After processing—whether water bath or steam pressure—is complete, the jars are set on a rack, board, or folded towel to cool. When they are completely cool (at least 12 hours, and up to 24—this is a next-day job), the seal on each jar must be individually tested.

one-piece seals: These are the lids sealed with rubber rings. Turn each jar partly over. If there is any sign of leakage, the seal is not tight. Some of these lids are made with a dome top; in this case, if the top of the cap is low in the center, the jar is sealed.

two-piece seals: Press the center of the lid—if the lid is down and will not move, the jar is sealed. Or tilt the jar slightly —if there is no leakage, the jar is sealed. Or tap the center of the lid with the back of a spoon—a clear, ringing sound indicates that the jar is sealed. When you have determined that the jar is tightly sealed, remove the screw-on band. (Jars sealed in this manner are stored without the band.)

Wipe jars clean with a damp cloth; label, date, and store.

CURING MEAT AT HOME

This is not, believe us, the sort of thing a swinging single in a one-room apartment might take up as a hobby. Home-curing of meat is virtually always done on or near the spot where the animal was raised and slaughtered. Instructions offered by one of the manufacturers of curing ingredients begin: "To produce the highest quality cured meat, it is important that every step—the selection of the live animal, the butchering, and the curing—be handled with the utmost care and attention." Obviously, it is not a task one does between getting home from the office and going out on a date, while rinsing out pantyhose in the bathroom sink. Those who do cure meat at home, almost always on farms, know how and need no instructions from us. Just the same, it's useful for all of us to take a brief look at how meat is cured, if only to understand what goes into the production of the sausage, ham, corned beef, and other cured meats that we feed our families.

Two kinds of cure. Our forefathers cured meat by salting it—rubbing it all over with salt, or submerging it in a salt/water brine. Today, the methods are the same, but certain refinements that give the meat both better flavor and more secure keeping quality have been added.

Salt is still the basic in meat cures, but today other ingredients such as sugar, saltpeter, pepper, and combinations of spices are added. Wood-smoke flavor is often a part of the cure. These cures can be concocted at home or bought ready-mixed in proper proportions, and can be used for either of the two cure types: dry or sweet pickle (also called brine cure). When a piece of meat to be cured is large—a ham, for example—bacterial action in the center, around the bones, can be stopped by pumping the cure into the center of the meat along the bone area. The meat is then treated in the regular way to cure it from the outside toward the center. The pumping is a precaution to assure safety and to hurry the curing. It is accomplished with a gadget that resembles an oversized hypodermic needle.

Accomplishing the cure. After the meat animal is slaughtered, the meat is chilled, divided into cooking-size cuts (butchered), and chilled again. It is lightly salted, and set to drain for 6 to 12 hours. Large pieces with bone are pumped with pickle, then thoroughly rubbed with a dry-cure mixture or immersed in a cure brine and weighted down. If dry-cured, something like 6 pounds of curing mixture is used to each 100 pounds of meat; it is rubbed into the meat by hand, taking care to cover the entire area and to work it in well around joints. Four or five days later the process is repeated, and the meat is repacked in a position different from the first time.

The amount of cure used depends on several factors. Meat cured in high, dry altitudes does not require as much curing compound as in more humid areas. If the meat is to be used shortly after it is cured, the amount of curing compound can be reduced, but if it is to be held for long periods, more must be used.

Meat remains in the cure about 2 days per pound for large pieces, 1½ days per pound for smaller pieces—that is, a 20-pound ham should cure 40 days, a 10-pound side of bacon 15 days. The meat is inspected during the cure to make sure all is well, and to rub curing compound into any bare spots.

After the meat is removed from the cure, it is washed in lukewarm water and thoroughly dried. It is then wrapped—first in cloth, then in paper—placed in strong paper bags with the tops securely tied, and hung in a dark, cool, well-ventilated place. For best flavor, meat should be held—"seasoning out," it is called—for a period before using, the length of time depending on the size of the piece of meat.

The peripheral benefits. When a hog, for example, is butchered, nothing goes to waste. Perhaps a couple of pieces, part of a ham or a loin, may be used fresh as a roast. The other large parts are cured—hams, shoulders, loins, as well as bacon and fat back. Lard is rendered from the fat. From the trimmings and small pieces, sausage is made—and the small intestine is used for the sausage casings. The liquor in which meat was cooked for sausage or headcheese is used, too. Cornmeal is added to it to make panhas; cooked, formed into a loaf, it is chilled, then sliced and fried. If bits of meat are added to the cooking mixture along with sage or thyme, the loaf is no longer panhas, but scrapple. Even the blood is used, to make blood sausage. Scraps are ground for patties.

Beef, lamb, and veal are also cured in mild variations of the process used for pork, but generally not as many cuts are cured. When lamb and calf—relatively small animals—are butchered, heavy cuts (leg, shank, breast) may be cured, other portions used fresh or canned. Large and small game, game birds, and domestic birds may be cured as well.

The "kitchen cure." Individual cuts of fresh or thawed frozen meat can be lightly cured, then refrigerated after the cure is complete, to be cooked within 5 days. The meat (if frozen, it must be entirely thawed) is rubbed with commercial curing compound, then placed in a plastic bag; the neck of the bag is tightly twister-tie closed, and the meat refrigerated to cure—slices and thin pieces in 1 to 3 days, large pieces in 7 to 10 days. This quick-cure/quick-eat method is something to experiment with—if not exactly while rinsing out pantyhose, at least while feeding a family in an ordinary home.

Smoking meat, game, poultry, fish. Any meat—or fish or game or poultry—that you can cure may also be smoked, giving a finish of flavor and color to the meat. Hardwood is used for the smoking; hickory is preferred by many, but almost any hardwood will do. If you're in doubt, burn a couple of chips of the wood and smell the smoke—if it smells pleasant, it will impart a pleasant flavor to the meat. Don't use any kind of resinous wood, or the food you have worked on so hard will taste like furniture polish.

All food to be smoked must first be cured by one of the methods already outlined; the single exception is very small fish.

There are many kinds of smokers available at a wide range of prices, starting at about twenty-five dollars for a very small, simple one. If you or someone else in the family is handy, smokers that work very well can be made at home. Once you decide this is for you, you can build or have built a small smokehouse on your property.

It is impossible to give accurate instructions for the use of a smoker or how long various meats should be smoked—both of these are variables that differ from one device to another and from one meat to another depending on what kind of smoker you use. If you buy a smoker, explicit instructions will come with it, and they should be followed to the letter. If you make one, instructions for use will be included with the instructions for construction.

Remember that smoking does not cook the meat; all meat smoked at home—again with the possible exception of very small fish—must be cooked before eating.

DRYING FOOD AT HOME

Of all the ways to put food by, drying is the oldest. Preserving some seasonal foods by drying is still useful and convenient, in spite of the fact that we are now able to can or freeze them.

Why does drying preserve food? Because sufficient moisture is removed from the food to prevent its decay—moisture is the culprit in spoilage. Properly dried food, depending on the kind, will have a water content of from 5 to 25 percent.

A hot, dry climate will reduce many foods in a very few days to a moisture level that will preserve them. But in any climate you can create satisfactory drying conditions, using artificial heat and circulating air.

Ways and means. If you want to dry fruits and vegetables, there are three courses open to you.

- Use your kitchen oven

  (you will need drying trays, an oven thermometer, and a small fan)
- Use a portable dehydrator

  (there are natural-draft and electric models—either may be purchased or made at home by a reasonably handy person in a reasonably short time)
- Use the sun

  (you will need drying trays, low relative humidity, and a temperature of 98°F. or higher)

If you are not blessed—or cursed?—with a very hot, dry climate (even then, it's a rather chancy business), you'll probably want to do your first drying in the oven, reserving the construction or purchase of a portable dehydrator until you decide whether or not you enjoy drying food and like the food itself.

Drying trays to fit your oven can be made at home. Turn the handiest person in the family loose on the project. Trays consist of simple rectangular frames, 1½ inches narrower than the inside of your oven to allow for air circulation. The floor of each frame may consist of thin wooden slats, positioned so that there is air space between them, or of stainless steel hardware cloth. (Do not use aluminum or galvanized screening. A floor of slats is best, as such trays can be used for all sorts of drying, as the metal-floored trays cannot.) Finally, on each corner of each tray, fasten a small wooden block 2½ to 3 inches high, or an empty thread spool. This allows for air circulation when loaded trays are stacked.

Drying vegetables. Ideally, vegetables should be washed and prepared, ready to dry, on the same day they are harvested. This isn't always possible, but at least select fresh vegetables, in prime condition. If they are not suitable to cook, neither are they suitable to dry.

Before the drying can begin, preparation includes picking over, washing, draining, peeling, and pitting where required; cutting into slices, strips, or segments; and blanching.

blanching: This is a process in which the vegetables are heated sufficiently to inactivate enzymes that would otherwise cause color and flavor to deteriorate during drying and storage. It is possible to dry vegetables without blanching, but the blanched ones will be superior in both flavor and color.

blanching with steam: You need a kettle with a tight-fitting cover, and a colander, wire basket, or sieve that will fit in the kettle. Place 1½ to 2 inches of water in the kettle; heat to boiling. Fill colander with vegetables, loosely packed, and place in the kettle. Leave until vegetables are heated through and wilted. Test by cutting through a piece of the vegetable—it should appear cooked (translucent) nearly to the center.

blanching with water: Place in the kettle just enough water to cover the amount of vegetable you are going to blanch. Bring to a boil. Gradually add vegetables, stirring gently. Cover and cook until heated through and wilted, as for steam blanching.

oven-drying: If food pieces are very small, cover the surface of the tray with cheesecloth spread under the food. Load two to four trays with no more than 4 to 6 pounds of the prepared vegetable, spread in a single layer on each tray. More than one kind of vegetable may be dried at one time, but dry strong-smelling vegetables separately. Place an accurate, easy-to-read thermometer toward the back of the top tray.

Preheat the oven to 160°F. Place the loaded trays inside. Prop the oven door open at least 4 inches. Position a fan outside the oven so that it will direct air through the opening and across the oven; change the position of the fan frequently during drying to vary the air circulation.

The temperature will lower when the food goes in to dry. Bring it up to 140°F. and maintain that during drying. As the food dries it will take less heat to maintain the temperature, so watch carefully toward the end of drying time. Check the progress of the vegetables frequently, turning the trays each time. There is little danger of scorching at first, but as the vegetables dry they may scorch quite easily; be sure the temperature never rises above 140°F., particularly toward the end of drying time.

See the following chart for drying time for the vegetable you are using. These times are only a guide, however. You will have to judge for yourself when the vegetables are ready to come out of the oven. They should contain 2 to 6 percent moisture when drying is completed. Drying time varies with the type of vegetable, size of the pieces, and tray load. Cool a piece of vegetable before testing it for dryness.

dehydrator-drying: The principle and method are the same as for oven-drying. Time, in most cases, will be shorter than for oven-drying. If you are pleased with oven-drying and wish to buy or make a dehydrator, the library or your state agriculture extension service will doubtless have plans for you to follow or a book on drying to guide you. If you buy the dehydrator, follow instructions that come with it.

sun-drying: Both high temperature and low humidity are essential. If temperature is too low or humidity too high—or both—spoilage will occur before drying is completed. Vegetables should be spread in a single layer. In the sun, trays are not stacked. Cover food with cheesecloth to protect from insects. Turn the vegetables once a day to facilitate drying. If night temperature is more than 20°F. lower than daytime, trays must be placed under shelter at night. Depending on piece size, air temperature, and kind of vegetable, drying will probably take 3 to 4 days.

packaging dried vegetables: When they come out of the dehydrator or oven, vegetables are insect free. To keep them that way, package as soon as they are cool in dry, scalded containers with tight-fitting lids, such as home-canning jars. Coffee cans may be used, but in that case package the vegetables in plastic bags before putting them into the cans.

Either way, pack as tightly as possible without crushing.

Sun-dried vegetables, no matter what precautions you take, may be insect-contaminated. Package the dried vegetables and place the packages in the home freezer for 48 hours to kill any possible insects or their eggs.

storing dried vegetables: A dry, cool, dark place is best. Low storage temperatures extend the life of the vegetables. All dried vegetables deteriorate somewhat as they age. Carrots, onions, and cabbage deteriorate more rapidly than other vegetables; they will generally have a shelf life of about 6 months. Some vegetables will be good after a year's storage.

cooking dried vegetables: Water removed during drying must be replaced through soaking, cooking, or both. Root, stem, and seed vegetables should be soaked from ½ hour to 2 hours in cold water to cover. After soaking, simmer (in the same water and uncovered so that excess water will evaporate) until tender. Greens, cabbage, and tomatoes do not need soaking—place in a pan, add water to cover, and simmer until tender.

Dried vegetables are at their best in soups, stews, casseroles, stuffings, and skillet dishes, rather than served plain as a side dish. They may be cooked singly or in combinations. Cautionary note: Dried onions and garlic are very strong—use them with discretion.

Drying fruit. As with vegetables, drying does not improve the quality of the fruit. Dry only fully ripened fruit of the quality you would be willing to serve fresh—if it's not good enough to serve fresh, it's not good enough to dry, either.

pre-drying steps: Fruit should be sorted and defective pieces discarded. Wash, peel, pit, halve, or cut in pieces as needed, depending on the kind of fruit.

To maintain an appetizing appearance, prevent darkening and loss of flavor and vitamin C, most fruit must be pretreated immediately before drying. Steam- or water-blanching may be used, as for vegetables, but sulfuring—exposing the fruit to sulfur fumes—is the preferred treatment for fruit. Sulfuring is not difficult, and it effectively maintains the quality and the nutrients of the fruit through both drying and storage.

For sulfuring fruit, you will need these materials:

- trays—slatted wooden ones, as previously described; do not use aluminum or galvanized screening, as sulfur fumes corrode most metals

- thread spools or small wooden blocks, placed at the corners of the trays to stack them 1½ inches apart

- a heavy cardboard or wooden box, with no cracks or openings, large enough to place over the stacked trays with 1 to 1½ inches to spare between the trays and the inside of the box

- fire bricks to raise the stack of trays high enough off the ground to accommodate a container of burning sulfur underneath

HOME DRYING OF VEGETABLES

vegetable	preparation	blanching method	time (minutes)	drying method	time (hours)
artichoke, globe	cut hearts into ⅛-inch strips	heat in boiling solution of ¾ cup water and 1 tablespoon lemon juice	6 to 8	dehydrator oven sun	2 to 3 4 to 6 10 to 12
asparagus	wash thoroughly, halve large tips	steam water	4 to 5 3½ to 4½	dehydrator oven sun	1 to 3 3 to 4 8 to 10
beans, green	wash thoroughly, cut in pieces or lengthwise	steam water	2 to 2½ 2	dehydrator oven sun	2½ to 4 3 to 6 8 to 10
beets	cook as usual; cool and peel; cut in strips ⅛ inch thick	already cooked—no further blanching required		dehydrator oven sun	2 to 3 3 to 4½ 8
broccoli	trim, cut as for serving; wash; quarter stalks lengthwise	steam water	3 to 3½ 2	dehydrator oven sun	2½ to 4 3 to 4½ 8 to 10
brussels sprouts	cut in half lengthwise through stem	steam water	3 to 3½ 4½ to 5½	dehydrator oven sun	2 to 3 4 to 5 9 to 11
cabbage	remove outer leaves; quarter and core; cut in ⅛-inch strips	steam (until wilted) water	2½ to 3 1½ to 2	dehydrator oven sun	1 to 2 1 to 3 6 to 7
carrots	use only young, tender ones; wash; cut off roots, tops; peel; cut in slices or ⅛-inch strips	steam water	3 to 3½ 3½	dehydrator oven sun	2½ to 4 3½ to 5 8
cauliflower	prepare as for serving	steam water	4 to 5 3 to 4	dehydrator oven sun	2 to 4 4 to 6 8 to 11
celery	trim, wash stalks and leaves; slice stalks	steam water	2 2	dehydrator oven sun	2 to 3 4 to 6 8
corn on the cob	husk, trim	steam (until milk does not exude from cut kernel) water	2 to 2½ 1½	dehydrator oven sun	1 to 2 2 to 3 6
corn, cut	as above; cut kernels off cob after blanching	as above		dehydrator oven sun	1 to 2 2 to 3 6

HOME DRYING OF VEGETABLES

vegetable	preparation	blanching method	time (minutes)	drying method	time (hours)
eggplant	wash, trim, cut into ¼-inch slices	steam water	3½ 3	dehydrator oven sun	2½ 3½ to 5 6 to 8
mushrooms	scrub, discard tough woody stalks, slice; do not peel small mushrooms, do peel large ones	no blanching		dehydrator oven sun	3½ 3 to 5 6 to 8
okra	wash, trim, cut into ⅛- to ¼-inch slices	no blanching		dehydrator oven sun	2 to 3 4 to 6 8 to 11
onions	wash, skin; cut off tops, root ends; cut ⅛- to ¼-inch slices	no blanching		dehydrator oven sun	1 to 3 4 to 6 8 to 11
parsley	wash; separate clusters, discard tough stems	no blanching		dehydrator oven sun	1 to 2 2 to 4 6 to 8
peas	shell	steam water	3 2	dehydrator oven sun	3 3 6 to 8
peppers, green and sweet red	wash, stem, core, seed; remove pithy strips; cut into squares about ⅜ × ⅜ inch	no blanching		dehydrator oven sun	3½ 2½ to 5 8 to 11
potatoes	wash, peel; cut into shoestring strips or ⅛-inch slices	steam water	6 to 8 5 to 6	dehydrator oven sun	2 to 4 2½ to 3½ 8 to 11
spinach and other greens	trim; wash thoroughly	steam (until completely wilted) water	2 to 2½ 1½	dehydrator oven sun	2½ 2½ to 3½ 6 to 8
squash, summer	wash, trim; cut in ¼-inch slices	steam water	2½ to 3 1½	dehydrator oven sun	2 to 4 4 to 5 6 to 8
squash, winter	cut in pieces, peel, seed; cut in pieces ⅛ to ¼ inch thick	steam water	2½ to 3 1	dehydrator oven sun	2 to 4 4 to 5 6 to 8
tomatoes (for stewing)	peel, cut into ¾-inch sections or slice; halve pear or plum tomatoes	steam water	3 1	dehydrator oven sun	3½ to 4½ 6 to 8 8 to 10

HOME DRYING OF FRUITS

fruit	preparation	before drying, treat by one of following methods:			drying time		test for dryness (cool before testing)
		sulfur	steam	water	sun	dehydrator	
apples	peel, core; cut in ⅛-inch slices or rings	45 minutes	5 minutes, depending on texture	—	3–4 days	4–7 hours	soft, pliable, no moist areas in center
apricots	pit; halve for steam or sulfur; leave whole for water, pit and halve after blanching	2 hours	3–4 minutes	4–5 minutes	2–3 days	4–7 hours	same as apples
figs	in dry, sunny areas, leave on tree—fruit will drop when ⅔ dry; elsewhere, pick when ripe	no treatment necessary			4–5 days	4–7 hours	flesh pliable, slightly sticky but not wet
grapes (muscat, tokay, any seedless)	remove stems, leave grapes whole	no treatment necessary			3–5 days	3–5 hours	raisinlike texture, no moisture in center
nectarines and peaches	for sulfuring, pit and halve, peel if desired; for blanching, leave whole, pit and halve afterward	2–3 hours	8 minutes	8 minutes	3–5 days	4–7 hours	same as apples
pears	halve and core, peel if desired	5 hours	6 minutes	—	5 days	4–7 hours	same as apples
persimmons	peel and slice with stainless knife	no treatment necessary			5–6 days	4–7 hours	light to medium brown, tender but not sticky
plums	use only prune plums; for oven, rinse in hot tap water, leave whole; for sulfuring, halve and pit	no treatment necessary, but sulfuring 1 hour will produce good flavor			4–5 days	4–7 hours	leathery; pit should not slip when squeezed if plum not cut

- the sulfur itself—use elemental sulfur, also called sulfur flowers or flowers of sulfur; it is free of impurities, burns readily, and may be purchased at most drugstores
- a clean metal container to hold the sulfur; for small amounts of fruit, a 1-pound coffee can or an aluminum pie plate will be large enough

how to sulfur: Always sulfur outdoors, away from close contact with plants, shrubs, and trees. The adjacent table gives correct sulfuring time periods for various kinds of fruit. Here are the step-by-step instructions:

1. Spread fruit in a single layer on trays, cut side up; pieces must not touch one another.
2. Stack trays, separated by spools or blocks at the corners, so that they are 1½ inches apart.
3. Cover trays with the box. Cut a small flap near bottom of box on one side, a second near top of box on the opposite side—these can be opened when required to encourage circulation of the sulfur fumes.
4. Measure the sulfur and place it in the container. The amount varies with the length of time the fruit is to be sulfured, the weight of the fruit, and the dimensions

of the box. With a cardboard box, you will need 1 tablespoon of sulfur per pound of fruit (weighed before drying). A stack of four trays holds about 40 pounds of fruit.

5. Place the can of sulfur under the box near the lower flap. Light the sulfur. Do not leave burned matches in the container.

6. Immediately lower the box over the stack and seal the bottom edges with dirt. Start timing. When the sulfur is burning well, close the flaps.

Sulfuring Box

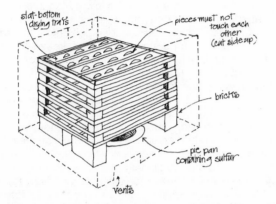

slat-bottom drying trays
pieces must not touch each other (cut side up)
bricks
pie pan containing sulfur
vents

The burning time of the sulfur will vary with the ventilation, the shape of the box, and weather conditions, but it is the fumes that do the work, not the burning. Sulfuring is complete when the fruit looks bright and glistening, and a small amount of juice appears on the surface or in the pit cavities.

blanching: Blanching, as an alternative to sulfuring, results in a darker, less flavorful and less nutritious product. It also produces a slightly cooked flavor in the fruit, and it may loosen the fruit skins and/or make the fruit soft and difficult to handle. Fruits that lose their skins may stick to the drying trays.

blanching with steam: Blanch in a colander or strainer, as for vegetables.

blanching with water: Do not cut fruit; place whole in enough boiling water to cover, with ¼ cup lemon juice or 1 tablespoon lemon juice plus 1 tablespoon ascorbic acid to each quart of water. Cut and pit fruit after blanching is complete.

drying methods: Fruits may be dried, as vegetables are, in the oven, in a dehydrator, or in the sun, following the directions given for vegetables. However—and this is a point that may well influence your choice of method of preparing the fruit if you are a beginner—*oven drying is not recommended for sulfured fruits because of the objectionable odor of the sulfur fumes.*

packing and storing: Follow directions given for packing and storing dried vegetables. Do not use metal lids with sulfured fruit unless a sheet of plastic wrap is placed under the lid to prevent the sulfur fumes from reacting with the metal. Storing dried fruit in plastic bags, tightly sealed, will help retain the original fruit color.

The pleasures of drying foods. If you try drying vegetables and fruits and find that this method of preserving appeals to you, there are many ways to go to expand your food drying activities. There are old-fashioned fruit leathers, for example, delicious totally natural confections that can be eaten out of hand or used to make beverages or in pie fillings, in cookies, and as a dessert topping. You can also make beef jerky, smoke-flavored or not, given extra taste-appeal with garlic, onion, teriyaki sauce, hot chili sauce, or a sweet/sour sauce. Venison strips can be dried in the same manner, and so can salmon fillets.

FREEZING AT HOME

Since the freezer came to live in our homes, the whole world of preserving food has made a gigantic leap ahead. Not only is freezing the easiest kind of home food preserving, but in almost all cases it's the best. Frozen vegetables are by all odds the nearest thing to fresh. Frozen fruits are great. Frozen meats, fish, and poultry are not only very good indeed, but they're on hand when you need them. (Yes, so are the home-canned variety, but in a flavor/texture comparison between the two, the frozen ones win going away. There is a dull, boiled-taste sameness to most of the canned meats, fish, and poultry.)

But perhaps the greatest breakthrough is in freezing prepared foods—foods that there was no way to preserve before the freezer came along. You can't can a pie—the filling perhaps, but not the finished product, ready to pop into the oven. Nor can you can (or dry, or pickle, or smoke, or cure) casserole dishes, ready-prepared main and side dishes, sandwiches for at-home or eat-away lunches, all kinds of breads and sweet breads, and a multitude of desserts. Soups and stews are good when canned, but better when frozen.

As for entertaining, with a freezer to help you it's a whole new ball game. With a bit of planning, you can make and freeze-ahead a sit-down or buffet meal as simple or as glamourous as you like, for ten people or a hundred. About the only nonfrozen food at such a meal is a salad, and anyone who can't get a salad made when the rest of the meal is prepared in advance would be well advised to take guests out to a restaurant.

Ready meals are a boon for the family, too—on busy

days, on days when the cook won't be home at dinner time, on days when you draw a blank trying to decide what to feed the hungry mob.

Kinds of freezers. There are actually four kinds of freezers, but only three can be used for long-term storage; of the three, only two are sizable enough to store large amounts of food.

refrigerator-freezer, 1-door model: If your refrigerator has a freezer compartment, but only one door for the entire appliance, the freezer will not maintain a temperature cold enough for long-term storage of frozen foods, nor will it freeze foods properly. Some such freezer sections have separate inner doors; even so, the section is not cold enough.

refrigerator-freezer, 2-door model: When the freezer compartment has a separate door (top, bottom, or side) of its own, it may—or it may not—maintain a temperature low enough to freeze foods and to hold them for long-term storage. To make certain, you need a freezer thermometer. Leave it in the freezer for several days, checking at intervals. If the freezer maintains 0°F. or lower, it can be used both for freezing food and for long-term storage of frozen foods.

upright freezers: These are separate appliances. They are shaped like a refrigerator—that is, they stand upright, with a "front door" like a refrigerator and a number of (often adjustable) shelves. They come in a range of sizes and, being separate from the refrigerator, can be stored elsewhere if kitchen space is at a premium. The garage, if attached to the house, is a good place. So is a back entryway. So is the basement, provided you plan your puttings-in and takings-out so that you aren't always galloping up and down stairs.

chest freezers: These, too, are separate appliances, shaped like large, rectangular boxes; they have lift-up doors on top. They do the job equally as well as the uprights, but it is easier to lose track of food in them if you don't keep an absolutely accurate inventory—and, sometimes, even if you do. Also, they're more difficult to use, particularly for a short woman. Lower parts are hard to reach, baskets in which food is stored are heavy, and all in all they are harder to organize efficiently than their upright brothers. These also come in several sizes.

Some secrets of success. Good results in freezing are easier to come by than when you can or use other preserving methods. And freezing is easier than other methods, as well. All the same, you cannot simply dump any old leftover into the freezer and expect to find a masterpiece next time you open the door. In order to take good food out, you have to put good food in.

When fruits and vegetables are at their very best for table use, they are also just right for freezing. Once you have brought fruits and vegetables home (or picked them), don't let them hang around the kitchen. If they are in their prime, as they should be for freezing, they can lose a lot of goodness in a day's time.

Keep your preparation area scrupulously clean, to avoid contamination of the food. Freezing does not kill bacteria, it only holds them in abeyance until the food is thawed.

When you freeze cooked foods, chill them rapidly so that they can be wrapped and frozen as soon as possible. Cool in the refrigerator or, if they are packed in tightly closed containers, in an ice-water bath: run cold water into the sink, add ice, and set the containers in the water until cooled. Do not put hot foods into the freezer—it will take too long for them to freeze, and they will raise the freezer temperature unduly. On the other hand, don't allow perishable foods to stand at room temperature until they are cool enough to freeze—that way, you're courting food poisoning. Nor should you refrigerate food for several days, then freeze it, and expect it to be top quality when thawed. What comes out of a freezer is exactly what went into it, good, bad, or indifferent.

Where you place foods when you put them in to freeze can make a big quality difference. Place packages near the outside walls of the freezer, whether it is an upright or a chest model. If your freezer has a quick-freeze shelf, place the unfrozen food on that, again close to an outside wall. Move already frozen packages a little away from the new, unfrozen ones to allow cold air to circulate, and leave in this position for 24 hours. Never freeze more than 3 pounds of food per cubic foot of storage space in any 24-hour period. More than this taxes the freezer too much, and means that the food will freeze slowly and quality will be impaired.

Don't skimp on packaging. Use only materials designed for freezer use. Refrigerator containers and plastic bags won't do—you'll only be cheating yourself. It's false economy to spend a lot of time and money on food for the freezer, then impair its quality or even make it unfit to use through improper packaging. This is no place to cut corners.

wrappings: Heavy-duty foil, heavy-duty plastic wrap, and paper especially made for freezer storage are available. All are moisture/vaporproof, and that's the name of the game in preparing foods for freezer storage. Foil and plastic wrap can be used either side out; when wrapping food in freezer paper, make sure the shiny (treated) side is next to the food.

containers: Rigid plastic containers with tight-fitting lids are available for freezer storage, and are reusable. Glass jars designed for canning may also be used in the freezer. Do not use waxed cartons in which ice cream, cottage cheese, or other foods were purchased. When you fill a container for the freezer, be sure to leave headspace—room at the top for the food to expand as it freezes. Round freezer containers do their job well, but take up more storage space than cube- or box-shaped ones. Heavy-duty foil pans come in almost any shape and size you can imagine. When you bake for freezer storage, use those pans; overwrap for freezer storage, then unwrap and heat the food in the same pan.

bags: Again, any old bag won't do; freezer-weight plastic bags must be used. Bags are fine for odd-shaped foods that won't fit well into a container. Make certain that all possible air is pressed out of the bags before you seal them. (There's an inexpensive gadget on the market, a freezer vacuum pump designed to remove air from freezer bags to create an airtight seal. Easy to use, it's worth having if you do a lot of freezing.) Close the necks of freezer bags this way: Squeeze out all the air; twist the neck several times, as close as possible to the food; turn the top down; seal both thicknesses with a tightly closed twister tie or a pipe cleaner. (Pipe cleaners are great; they can be reused many times, and the exterior will not strip down to wire—which can cut you or a plastic bag with equal ease—as twister ties often do.) Or you may tie the bag tightly with cord. But don't use rubber bands—they deteriorate in freezer temperature.

Freeze/cook bags, sometimes called boil-in bags, are great for freezing—then heating—such foods as stews, chili, sauces, and gravies—virtually anything that you would ordinarily cook in boiling water. The bags suffer intense heat and intense cold—from below zero to above 235°F.—with equal nonchalance. To use them, a special sealer machine is needed; it is electric and operates from the kitchen counter, or it can be wall-hung. A worthwhile investment—under fifteen dollars—if you do, or plan to do, considerable freezing.

No-wrap freezing. A certain small number of foods should be frozen before they are wrapped. Examples are frosted cakes (but it is much better to freeze the cake unfrosted, frost after thawing), other delicate cakes, fragile cookies, chiffon pies, whipped cream for topping. Freeze such items until solid, then wrap quickly and return to the freezer. Cookies frozen this way can be spread out—don't stack—on a baking sheet, packaged after freezing in bags or rigid freezer containers. Dabs of whipped cream—never throw-away leftovers—dropped from a spoon or fed through a pastry tube, can be frozen the same way, then packaged. Set delicate pies and frosted cakes on the freezer shelf until they are frozen, then wrap the usual way and return to the freezer. Use this method for anything that may be damaged or crushed by packaging before it is frozen.

Some foods freeze poorly. Although most foods can be frozen and come through with flying colors, some don't take kindly to the cold. Salad greens are an example; frozen and thawed, they are limp. However, they can be used in soups. Other salad-type vegetables, such as scallions, radishes, and tomatoes, turn disagreeably soft when frozen, although some tomato products—juice, stewed tomatoes, tomato soup base—freeze beautifully.

Most cheese that has been frozen is crumbly—it won't do for eating out of hand, but can be used in casseroles and sauces, in salad dressings and dips. Cream cheese in mixtures such as sandwich spreads freezes very well.

Canned hams get watery, and the texture changes for the worse. Bacon, luncheon meats, and other processed meats can be frozen for short periods, but the high salt content encourages rancidity in the fat.

Gelatin dishes become watery, and so do custards, creamy puddings, and pies made with such fillings. (Why do commercial cream and custard pies hold up? They incorporate additive stabilizers in their fillings.) Meringues toughen. Potatoes darken and become mealy; if you wish them in soups and stews, add when you heat the frozen food. Mayonnaise and salad dressings separate, and many white sauces curdle on reheating.

Stockpiling in the freezer. Cats and dogs are big losers when there's a freezer in the home. When there's chicken for dinner, the cat no longer gets a tasty tidbit of liver—it's added to the others, stockpiling in the freezer until enough accumulate for a meal. Instead of being tossed to Fido, bones and meat scraps go into the freezer until there are enough to use as the basis of a hearty soup. Leftover vegetables get the same treatment. Extra egg whites are frozen to stockpile for an angel food cake or a blitz torte or a batch of meringues; yolks for a custard, for hollandaise. The home cook's watchword should be, "If it'll freeze, freeze it!"

Organization is the key. On the other hand, it's wasteful and foolish to fill your freezer with dribs of this and drabs of that which you promptly lose track of and don't find again until they're past their usefulness.

The way to avoid this sort of thing is to be efficient, even if it goes against the grain. Like this:

- label everything, always, stating clearly what the package contains and the date it was frozen; often it's convenient to include number of servings on the label; adhere religiously to the first-in/first-out rule in using your freezer foods

- instead of tossing packages helter-skelter, organize freezer space into separate areas: fruit, vegetables, main dishes, breads, desserts; assign a separate area to unfinished dishes, such as pie shells, soup or stew ingredients, stacked crepes waiting to be filled, and so on; make a place for breakfast/brunch specialties, such as frozen waffles, pancakes, french toast, sweet rolls, coffeecakes; make another for company-coming specialties—frozen appetizers, casseroles, or other dishes that will feed more than the family, a special dessert or two

• keep an inventory and keep it faithfully; add to it each item you put into the freezer, remove from it each item you take out—it's the only way to know at a glance what you have on hand; don't trust your memory, or you'll be in for a series of surprises

If you plan well, know at all times what you have on hand, use foods before they have passed their maximum best-condition storage time, store a mixed bag of foods to meet a mixed bag of emergencies as well as for day-to-day family meals, you'll find that your freezer is a couldn't-be-better kitchen helper.

Emergency! If the freezer breaks down or if there is a power failure, you need to know how to cope. A well-stocked freezer represents a big outlay of time, effort, and money; the contents must be preserved in good condition if that is at all possible.

A full or nearly full freezer will preserve food with very little thawing for 12 to 20 hours after the power goes off, provided the door is not opened. If you are certain that the power will go back on or the freezer will be repaired within that time span, leave the freezer door closed and sit tight. If you have no such assurance, play it safe with dry ice, or move the food to someone else's freezer or to a locker plant. Even if you are certain that the freezer will be operating again within 24 hours, bear in mind that it might not be able to bring a full load of food back down to zero or below before spoilage starts. Fifty pounds of dry ice, placed in the freezer soon after it ceases operation, will prevent thawing for 2 to 3 days. Handle the dry ice with gloves to prevent burns. Put pieces of the ice on cardboard or some other nonfood material, rather than placing it directly on food packages.

Freezing cooked foods and prepared dishes. Wrap and store—that's all there is to it. Double-batching is common since the invention of the home freezer, and serve-one/save-one is an unbeatable system for keeping a supply of heat-and-eat meals on hand. For instance, if you cook a turkey too big for the family to finish before tiring of it, chunk or slice some of the meat and freeze it in chicken or turkey broth. Thawed, you have the makings of a delicious main dish —turn the broth into sauce, season well, add the meat until it is heated through, serve on toast or frozen-in-advance rice or waffles. When you make a stew, it's no trouble to make twice as much and freeze half; store the frozen half slightly undercooked, so that it will be just right when thawed and heated. You can thus double-batch all sorts of main dishes.

When you make two casseroles, one to serve and one to freeze, bake the freezer-bound one in a casserole dish lined with foil; freeze it, too, slightly underdone. When it is frozen, slip it out of the casserole in its foil covering, overwrap and return to the freezer, freeing the casserole dish for kitchen use in the meantime.

Breads, muffins, cakes, cupcakes, pies, and dozens of other good things freeze beautifully (freeze all but the pies after cooking, the pies before). Freeze crepes, pancakes, and waffles for hurry-up breakfasts or to act as the foundation for served-in-sauce main dishes. Indeed, whenever you make anything good, ask yourself "Will it freeze?" before you begin. If it will, double-batch it and put away a ready-made meal.

sandwiches: Make them production-line style, particularly if there are brown-baggers in your family. Spread the bread to the edges with butter to keep fillings from soaking in. Don't use fillings made with hard-cooked eggs or bound with mayonnaise. Package the sandwiches individually, label and date each, and plan on using within a month. Frozen sandwiches lunch-packed in the morning will be nicely thawed and in prime condition by lunch time.

Freezing fruit. Fruit may be packed one of three ways for freezing—in syrup, in sugar (sometimes called dry pack), or plain.

Choose ripe, ready-for-eating fruit. Sort, wash it in cold water, and prepare it (peel, pit) as you would for table use, working rapidly. Have syrup or sugar ready and, if it will be needed, ascorbic acid or commercial color-protector.

syrup pack: Of the three, fruit packed in syrup retains the most vitamins; it will have good flavor, color, and texture. Make syrup a day or so ahead and refrigerate; when added to the fruit, it must be cold. Individual recipes in a good cookbook or canning-and-freezing book will guide you concerning the kind of syrup to use for each fruit. Add the sugar to the water and let it dissolve by itself, stirring occasionally. Or heat the syrup, stirring, until the sugar dissolves, then cool and refrigerate.

syrup:	sugar:	water:	amount:
30%	2 cups	4 cups	5 cups
35%	2½ cups	4 cups	5⅓ cups
40%	3 cups	4 cups	5½ cups
50%	4¾ cups	4 cups	6½ cups
60%	7 cups	4 cups	7¾ cups

Fill containers one-third full of cold syrup. (If color protector is needed, stir it into the syrup before pouring it into the container.) Add fruit, cover with more cold syrup if necessary, remembering to leave headspace for expansion during freezing. To keep fruit submerged in syrup, crumple a large piece of wax paper on top of the fruit before putting the cover on the container. Don't forget to label and date each one.

sugar pack: Place the fruit in a bowl. If color protector is needed, add it to the sugar, mixing well. Sprinkle sugar over fruit (recipe will give you the proportions). Mix gently with a rubber spatula until the sugar releases some of the fruit's juice and each piece is coated. Gently fill containers, leaving headspace; cover, label, and date.

plain pack: There are two ways to go here, dry pack or with water. If the fruit needs a color protector, it's best to use water, stirring the protector into the water before adding it to the fruit. Put fruit into container, pour water over (leaving headspace), and cover. To pack the fruit dry, carefully place in container, leaving as little space between pieces as possible. Cover, label, and date.

In all cases, place containers one by one on freezer shelf, allowing airspace between them. Do not stack or place close together until the fruit is solidly frozen.

Follow the guidance of a good cookbook or food-preserving book as to which fruits may be packed by which method.

Not true of vegetables, some fruits—especially if you plan to use them as dessert—are better canned than frozen. Among these are applesauce, unpeeled apricots, pears, and plums. Fruits that do freeze well, keeping summer on the table all year around, are apple slices, peeled apricots, avocado purée, all kinds of berries, both sweet and tart (pie) cherries, citrus fruits (although they are a waste of freezer space in most cases, as they are available in all seasons), cranberries, currants, dates, figs, grapes (seedless or tokay or muscadine), melons (balled or cut in chunks), nectarines, peaches, persimmons, pineapple, and rhubarb. Spiced apples, cranberry and cranberry-combination sauces and relishes, mixed fruits for salads and cups, fruit chutneys, and many (special recipe) fruit jams and preserves also freeze beautifully. So do nutmeats, including coconut.

How much makes how much? When you plan to freeze fruit, it's helpful to know how much to buy for the number of containers you'd like to have. Here are the answers:

fresh fruit:	amount:	pint containers:
apples	1 bushel	32 to 40
	1 box (44 pounds)	29 to 35
	1¼ to 1½ pounds	1 pint
apricots	1 bushel	60 to 72
	1 crate (22 pounds)	28 to 33
	⅔ to 1 pound	1 pint
berries	1 crate (24 quarts)	32 to 36
	1½ pint boxes	1 pint
cherries	1 bushel (56 pounds)	36 to 44
	1¼ to 1½ pounds	1 pint
cranberries	1 peck (8 pounds)	16
	½ pound	1 pint
currants	2 quarts	4
	¾ pound	1 pint

fresh fruit:	amount:	pint containers:
peaches	1 bushel (48 pounds)	32 to 46
	1 lug (20 pounds)	14 to 20
	1 to 1½ pounds	1 pint
pineapple	5 pounds	4
rhubarb	15 pounds	15 to 21
	⅔ to 1 pound	1 pint

Freezing vegetables. Unlike fruit, vegetables—most of them—must be blanched before freezing. Blanching prevents toughening and loss of flavor, retains vitamins, and increases the possible freezer storage time. Blanching consists of plunging the vegetables into rapidly boiling water for a short period (chart below tells you how long for individual vegetables), then into cold water—preferably ice water—to reverse the cooking process.

how to blanch: Place water in a large kettle (aluminum, stainless steel, or enamelware), using 1 gallon of water for each pint of vegetables, except for leafy greens, which require 2 gallons per pint. Bring the water to a full, rolling boil. Prepare the vegetables as you would for cooking and serving —peel, cut up, or such as required. Place in a wire basket or loosely in a cheesecloth bag and submerge in the boiling water. Start timing at once. Proper timing is vital—use a timer. Keep heat high, water boiling, kettle covered. Avoid overblanching, which not only destroys vitamins and other nutrients, but will result in a too-soft vegetable when it is cooked for table use.

If you live at a high altitude, you will need to increase blanching time:

at:	add:
2,000 to 4,000 feet	½ minute
4,000 to 6,000 feet	1 minute
over 6,000 feet	2½ minutes

how to chill: Speed is important here. Plunge the basket or bag of vegetables immediately into ice water, using about 1 pound of ice for each pound of vegetables. Test by biting into a piece of vegetable. If it is cold all the way through, the vegetables are ready to drain and pack.

processing: Follow a good cookbook or food-preserving book for preparation and blanching time for individual vegetables, or the listings given in the following chart. Chill, pack (rigid plastic containers with tight-fitting covers are best), and place immediately in the freezer, spreading containers in a single layer with airspace between them. Later, when the contents are solidly frozen, containers may be stacked for more compact storage.

vegetable	preparation	blanching time
asparagus	choose young, tender stalks; place in freezer container with heads in alternate directions	3 to 4 minutes
beans, green	choose young, tender beans; wash, tip; cut into desired lengths after blanching and chilling	2½ to 3 minutes
beans, lima	wash in pods, shell	2½ to 3 minutes
beets	cut off tops, root tips; cook until tender-crisp; chill; peel; slice, dice, or pack whole	until tender-crisp
broccoli	wash, discard woody stems; separate into ½-inch-thick sections	3 minutes
brussels sprouts	wash well, trim	4 to 5½ minutes
carrots	wash; peel; slice or dice	3 to 4 minutes
cauliflower	choose compact white heads; wash, trim off leaves and tough stem ends; divide into flowerets	3 minutes
corn, whole kernel	if possible, use corn just picked; husk, cut kernels from cob	6 to 8 minutes
corn, cream-style	husk, score each row of kernels with a knife, then scrape from cob into pan, bring to boil, chill by placing pan in ice water	no blanching
corn on the cob	husk, remove silks; after blanching and chilling, wrap cobs individually in heavy-duty foil or plastic	6 to 8 minutes, depending on size
greens: collard, kale, mustard, spinach, turnip	choose young, tender leaves; remove coarse stems; wash thoroughly; chop or leave whole after blanching	2 minutes
mixed vegetables	prepare, blanch, quick-chill each vegetable separately; mix before packaging	follow times for individual vegetables
peas, green	choose tender, young pods; wash, shell	2 minutes
pepper, sweet green or red	wash, halve, core, seed; slice if desired or leave as halves	2 minutes
pumpkin and winter squash	steam or bake until soft; quick-chill; peel, seed; mash before packaging	cooked; no blanching
summer squash and zucchini	choose tender, young squash; wash, cut in ½-inch slices	3 minutes

How much makes how much? As with fruit, it's useful to know how many containers to expect from a given amount of vegetable. Let this table guide your purchases (or garden-fresh pickings):

vegetable	amount	pint containers
asparagus	1 crate (12 2-pound bunches)	15 to 22
	1 to 1½ pounds	1 pint
beans, lima (in pods)	1 bushel (32 pounds)	12 to 16
	2 to 2½ pounds	1 pint
beans, green and wax	1 bushel (30 pounds)	30 to 44
	⅔ to 1 pound	1 pint
beets (topped)	1 bushel (52 pounds)	34 to 43
	1¼ to 1½ pounds	1 pint
broccoli	1 crate (25 pounds)	23 to 25
	1 pound	1 pint
brussels sprouts	4 (quart) boxes	6
	1 pound	1 pint
carrots (topped)	1 bushel (50 pounds)	33 to 39
	1¼ to 1½ pounds	1 pint
cauliflower	4 medium heads	6
	1⅓ pounds	1 pint

vegetable	amount	pint containers
corn (in husks)	1 bushel (35 pounds)	14 to 17
	2 to 2½ pounds	1 pint
eggplant	10 pounds	9 to 11 pints
	1 pound	1 pint
greens, beet	15 pounds	10 to 14
	1 to 1½ pounds	1 pint
greens, chard, collard, mustard	1 bushel (12 pounds)	8 to 12
	1 to 1½ pounds	1 pint
kale	1 bushel (18 pounds)	12 to 17
	1 to 1½ pounds	1 pint
peas (in pod)	1 bushel (30 pounds)	12 to 15
	2 to 2½ pounds	1 pint
peppers	10 to 11 pounds	15 to 17 pints
	3 peppers	1 pint
pumpkin and winter squash	12 pounds	8
spinach	1 bushel (18 pounds)	12 to 17
	1 to 1½ pounds	1 pint
squash, summer and zucchini	1 bushel (40 pounds)	32 to 40
	1 to 1¼ pounds	1 pint
sweet potatoes	10⅔ pounds	15 to 17
	⅔ pounds	1 pint

Freezing homemade and store-bought food. Many of us fill our freezers only with food processed at home. Many more process very little, and stock their freezers with a selection of store-bought foods, purchased on sale or simply for the sake of convenience. And many pursue a middle course, never freezing such foods as fruits and vegetables at home, but stocking their freezers with such homemades as appetizers, main dishes, breads, and desserts, produced in intermit-tent flurries of cook-and-freeze activity and augmenting those with commercially frozen fruits, vegetables, and other items to maintain a well-balanced stock in the freezer.

One of the chief items we use to stock our freezers is meat—and poultry and, to a lesser degree unless there is an avid fisherman in the family, fish and shellfish. For information on how to prepare, wrap, freeze, and ultimately use these, consult the following chart.

HOME FREEZING

THAW/HEAT/EAT FOODS

food	preparation	wrap/freeze	store/use
breads (loaves, biscuits, muffins, rolls, sweet rolls, coffeecakes)	make and bake as usual; cool to room temperature; bread may be presliced if desired; do not glaze sweet rolls, coffeecakes	package loaves in plastic freezer bags; bake others on foil pans and freeze in pans in bags or overwrapped	thaw in package or warm in oven; storage time, 3 months
cakes, pies	bake cakes as usual, cool, do not frost; freeze double-crust fruit pies unbaked; fill baked crust with chiffon fillings, set before freezing	wrap layers separately; freeze large cakes before wrapping; bag or wrap unbaked pies, freeze chiffon pies before wrapping	bake fruit pies frozen, thaw chiffon pies; thaw cakes at room temperature, then frost if desired; storage time: cakes 3 months, pies 8 months
casseroles and combination dishes, meat loaves	cook as usual, but rice and pasta for casseroles should be slightly undercooked; slightly underseason; omit potatoes in stews; cool all rapidly; drain fat from meat loaf before wrapping	line casserole dishes with heavy-duty foil, freeze, remove from dish and overwrap; or bake in foil dishes, overwrap; freeze stews, curries, chili, etc. in meal-size plastic containers	thaw in refrigerator, bake or heat as usual (foil-baked casseroles in original dish); storage time, 3 months
cooked meat, poultry	slice, cube, or chop; freeze in gravy or broth to retain moisture; freeze stuffing separately	sliced meats in portion sizes, cubed or chopped in recipe sizes, in containers or boil-in bags	thaw in refrigerator, heat or use in casserole, etc., recipes; storage time, 3 months
soups, stocks	prepare as usual, but omit milk or cream until heating to serve; cool rapidly; defat stock before freezing	pack in plastic containers	thaw, heat; storage time, up to 3 months

RAW MEAT, POULTRY, FISH

food	preparation	wrap/freeze	store/use
chicken, turkey (whole or parts)	whole: rinse and dry, freeze without stuffing; parts: sort for use in recipes, or as portions	freeze giblets separately; wrap parts individually for faster thawing; wrap all airtight	thaw until can be handled or separated; storage time: giblets 2 months, poultry 6 months
beef, lamb, pork, and veal roasts	trim off excess fat; pad all bone ends and edges with foil to avoid puncturing outer wrappings	wrap closely, pressing wrap to meat; seal airtight	thaw and cook as usual; storage time: beef up to 12 months, lamb and veal to 9 months, pork 6 months
steaks and chops	trim off excess fat, pad bone ends with foil	wrap airtight in meal-size amounts; separate layers with double fold of wrap or plastic	thaw thick pieces, cook thin pieces unthawed; storage times same as for roasts

357

food	preparation	wrap/freeze	store/use
ground meats, stew meats	trim excess fat on stew meat, form ground into patties if desired; package in recipe or 1-meal amounts	separate patties with double fold of wrap or plastic; wrap airtight	thaw until meat pieces or patties can be separated without damage; storage time, 3 months
ham, bacon, sausage	trim excess fat from ham, slice or halve if desired; form bulk sausage into patties if desired	leave bacon in package and overwrap; wrap ham closely, airtight; package sausage (bulk or link) in 1-meal amounts	these are iffy freezer items because of high fat content; storage time, 1 month only
fish (whole, fillets, steaks)	prepare, cut up as for cooking; wash, leave wet	package individual pieces, then overwrap 1-meal amounts; whole fish can be frozen in water in tightly closed container	cook frozen or partially thawed; do not thaw completely; storage time, up to 6 months
shellfish (clams, shrimp, oysters, lobster)	rinse all; shrimp may be shelled or not as you prefer; shuck clams, oysters; cook lobster, remove meat from shell	freeze shrimp before wrapping, then pack in bags or containers; pack clams, oysters with their liquor, adding mixture of 1 teaspoon salt to 1 cup water to cover; pack lobster meat in airtight containers	thaw only enough to separate, prepare; storage time, 3 months

Large-quantity meats for the freezer. "Wholesale sides of beef—20 pounds of pork chops free!" the ad reads —and it sounds tempting, particularly to the home cook with a budget-busting family of meat eaters. But it pays to pause and consider. In fact, the answer to "Should I buy a side of beef for my freezer?" is, unfortunately, "It depends."

In buying meat for your freezer, there are three ways to go: buy a whole carcass or a side or a quarter; buy wholesale cuts (that's *cuts*, understand, not necessarily wholesale *prices*); or buy cuts at retail, keeping a sharp eye out for specials and sales. Which way you choose depends on a lot of variables.

points to ponder: Good value for your money heads the list. That means getting quality meat—the grade you want, the cuts you want—at a reasonable price.

Bear in mind that when you buy a whole carcass or a side (half a carcass, including both fore- and hindquarters), you will get a wide variety of cuts, both those that are high-priced at your retail market and those that are low-priced, including some that you may never have bought and don't know how to cook. (You can learn.)

Bear in mind, too, that the carcass or side is sold at "hanging weight"—the gross weight, including all the inedible fat, bone, and connective tissue. Cutting loss on a beef carcass can range from 25 to 30 percent, meaning that a 300-pound side of beef would yield about 225 pounds of edible meat cuts, both desirable and undesirable ones, depending on your point of view. A rule of thumb for carcass beef yield is 25 percent waste, 25 percent ground and stew meat, 25 percent steaks, 25 percent roasts—and, of course, not all the steaks and roasts are from the loin and rib, the tender portions; there will be steaks that must be braised and roasts that must be pot-roasted.

When you buy a quarter, you must be aware of the different kinds of cuts that come from the hind- and the forequarter. Hindquarters yield more steaks and roasts, but will also cost more per pound, and there is more waste; forequarters are less tender, cost less, and yield more usable meat.

more variables: Grade affects price, both quality grade and yield grade. (For a discussion of quality grades, see BEEF.) Yield grades run from 1 to 5, 1 being the best—that is, the most usable meat from the carcass; you are not aware of yield grades when you buy single cuts from a supermarket or butcher shop, but when you are dealing with sides or wholesale cuts, they do matter. You will also want to make sure the large-quantity meat you buy is stamped with the USDA grade mark you are paying for, and that it bears the circular U.S. INSP'D & P'S'D mark, assuring wholesomeness. Ask to see the grade and inspection marks before the meat is cut and trimmed—you have that right, and it's foolish not to exercise it, to make certain that you are getting what you pay for.

buy only from a reliable dealer: A dealer who knows that he sells quality meat and gives good service should be willing to supply you with the names of previous customers with whom you can check. On the other hand, so will a fly-by-night dealer—they'll be the names of his dear mother and great-aunt Bessie, who will praise him fulsomely. So check with friends who have bought meat in quantity and go to a dealer with whom they are satisfied. Your local Chamber of Commerce and Better Business Bureau are other good check points.

The "bait and switch" sham is rampant among unreliable meat dealers. They advertise a side of beef for a ridiculous price (that ought to clue you in right off). When you go to buy, they show you a carcass that will make you weep with compassion for the sufferings of the poor animal before it died of starvation, or one so obese it's virtually impossible to find the meat in that welter of fat. That's the meat at the advertised price, the dealer says. But he can tell, he continues, that you want better than that for your family. Now here is a handsome side of beef, prime quality, yield grade 1. Well, of course it costs more, but . . .

So, when you go to buy meat in quantity, be armed with all the knowledge of meat quality and meat cuts you can get, plus a rigid backbone and a stiff upper lip. Before you make up your mind, determine what the price per pound covers. Does it include cutting, wrapping, and quick-freezing? If not, you'll pay fifteen cents a pound or more for those services. Does it include delivery? If not, and if you can't transport the meat yourself (which is somewhat chancy unless you live very close to the meat dealer), you'll have to pay for that, too.

beef-buying homework: Here are some approximate yields from wholesale cuts and from a side of beef, to guide you:

WHOLESALE CUTS OF BEEF
(grade: choice; yield grade: 3)

wholesale cut: round table cut:	percent of wholesale cut	weight in pounds
round steak	39.7	27.0
boneless rump roast	14.6	9.9
lean trim (stew, ground)	17.9	12.2
waste (fat, bone, shrinkage)	27.8	18.9
	100.0	68.0
wholesale cut: trimmed loin table cut:		
porterhouse, T-bone, club steaks	30.6	15.3
sirloin steak	49.8	24.9
lean trim	6.4	3.2
waste	13.2	6.6
	100.0	50.0
wholesale cut: rib table cut:		
rib roast (7-inch cut)	67.8	18.3
lean trim	12.6	3.4
waste	19.6	5.3
	100.0	27.0

wholesale cut: square-cut chuck table cut:		
blade chuck roast	33.0	26.7
arm chuck roast (boneless)	21.5	17.4
lean trim	25.9	21.0
waste	19.6	15.9
	100.0	81.0

SIDE OF BEEF (300 pounds)
(grade: choice; yield grade: 3)

hindquarter	percent of quarter	weight in pounds
round steak	18.8	27.0
rump roast (boneless)	6.9	9.9
porterhouse, T-bone, club steaks	10.6	15.3
sirloin steak	17.3	24.9
flank steak	1.0	1.5
kidney	.6	.9
lean trim (stew, ground)	14.6	21.0
waste (fat, bone, shrinkage)	30.2	43.5
	100.0	144.0
forequarter		
rib roast (7-inch cut)	11.7	18.3
blade chuck roast	17.1	26.7
arm chuck roast (boneless)	11.2	17.4
brisket (boneless)	4.0	6.3
lean trim	31.6	49.2
waste	24.4	38.1
	100.0	156.0

Still uncertain? Consult the chart on the next page to figure the price and value of retail cuts versus a side of beef. It's simple math, and will really show you the way.

Whatever became of those twenty free pork chops we mentioned? Well, they certainly weren't free—no businessman can afford to give his product away in quantity. The price of them was hidden somewhere in the price of the meat and, as always, it's up to the buyer to beware.

other quantity-buy freezer meats: Although a great deal more beef is bought in quantity than other meats, lamb and pork are also available as sides for freezer storage. Let what you have learned about beef guide you in making these other meat purchases.

Lamb is quality- and yield-graded in the same manner as beef. Pork and lamb are generally from young animals, and therefore less variable in quality than beef. USDA grades for pork reflect only two levels of quality: acceptable and unacceptable. Unacceptable (meat that is soft and watery) is graded U.S. Utility; acceptable pork is graded U.S. No. 1 through No. 4—these are yield grades of the four major lean pork cuts: the ham, loin, boston butt, and picnic shoulder. Buy

FIGURING THE VALUE OF BEEF IN CARCASS FORM VERSUS PURCHASE AT RETAIL

EXAMPLE: Say that you buy a 300-pound beef side (USDA choice, yield grade 3) for $1.00 per pound hanging weight, and the price includes cutting, wrapping, and quick-freezing.

cost of carcass purchase: Hanging weight × quoted price = amount required to buy side of beef

300 pounds × $1.00 = $300.00

but total usable beef (see below) is only 72.8 percent of the hanging weight. So, 72.8 × 300 pounds = 218.4 pounds of usable beef. Therefore, actual cost per pound is $300 ÷ 218.4 pounds = $1.37 per pound for usable beef from carcass.

cost of equivalent meat at retail: Determine the prices, at the retail store where you usually buy meat, for each of the retail cuts listed below, making sure grade and yield grade are the same, and that the trim is comparable to that of the carcass beef. Then multiply each price by the number of pounds shown in the second column of the table below. Now total the "retail value" column, which will give you your total cost at retail for the equivalent of a 300-pound side of beef. To get the average cost per pound, divide this total by 218.4 pounds (of usable beef from the 300-pound side). Now you have retail price per pound to compare with the $1.37 per pound you would pay for usable beef from the side.

retail cut	% of side	pounds		local price per pound		retail value
round steak	9.0	27.0	×	_____	=	_____
rump roast (boneless)	3.3	9.9	×	_____	=	_____
porterhouse, T-bone, and club steaks	5.1	15.3	×	_____	=	_____
sirloin steak	8.3	24.9	×	_____	=	_____
rib roast (7-inch cut)	6.1	18.3	×	_____	=	_____
blade chuck roast	8.9	26.7	×	_____	=	_____
arm chuck roast (boneless)	5.8	17.4	×	_____	=	_____
ground beef	11.1	33.3	×	_____	=	_____
stew meat	12.3	36.9	×	_____	=	_____
brisket (boneless)	2.1	6.3	×	_____	=	_____
flank steak	.5	1.5	×	_____	=	_____
kidney	.3	.9	×	_____	=	_____
total retail cuts	72.8	218.4	×	_____	=	_____
waste (fat, bone, shrinkage)	27.2	81.6				
TOTAL	100.0	300.00	×	TOTAL RETAIL VALUE		_____

total retail value ÷ 218.4 (usable beef from side) = retail price per pound

compare retail price per pound with usable beef side price per pound to determine whether or not the side of beef is a good buy

lamb or pork for the freezer as you would buy beef, but bear in mind that if you are buying a pork carcass or side, the dealer from whom you buy it should be equipped to render the lard and to cure the parts you may not wish to use as fresh meat.

Before you buy. When you plan on quantity-buying of meat for your freezer, you must be aware of the amount of freezer space it will occupy. On the average, 1 cubic foot of freezer space will accommodate 35 to 40 pounds of cut and wrapped meat.

Be sure to buy from a dealer equipped to quick-freeze the meat, because a side of meat is too much to ask a home freezer to cope with properly. Meat should be quick-frozen at −10°F. or lower for best quality; it can then be stored at home-freezer temperature of zero or below. And, of course, for best quality the meat must be properly wrapped in moisture/vaporproof freezer paper or heavy-duty aluminum foil; it must also be labeled and dated.

Last word. If you organize it efficiently, stock it with quality food, and abide by the first-in/first-out rule, your freezer will be like money in the bank, there to draw on whenever you need it, a backstop in emergencies.

PICKLING, PRESERVING, JAM- AND JELLY-MAKING

All of these good things—including conserves, butters, marmalades, and various relishes—can be produced at home with relative ease at times when fruit and vegetables are at their peak season (highest quality, lowest price), and laid away for the bleaker months. All are water-bath processed except jelly, which goes from cooking kettle to container without processing. Some pickles are cured in brine (fermented) before being processed.

Pickle pointers. Follow up-to-date recipes in making pickles for most satisfactory results. Read the recipe carefully before you shop for ingredients, to make certain that you will have everything you need on hand. Alum and lime are not used in modern pickling—if top-quality ingredients are used and a reliable recipe followed, there is no need for them.

salt: If it is available, use pure granulated salt. Table salt may be used, but ingredients added to table salt to prevent caking may make pickle brine cloudy. Under no circumstances use iodized salt—it turns pickles dark.

vinegar: Use high-grade cider or distilled white vinegar. The flavor of cider vinegar is preferable, but white may be called for in recipes for pale-colored pickles, such as cauliflower or pears. Never dilute the vinegar unless the recipe directs you to do so; if you prefer a less sour pickle, add sugar rather than decreasing vinegar.

water: Soft water must be used for pickle brine. If your water is hard, boil it for 15 minutes; let it stand 24 hours, then skim it carefully and ladle out the water rather than pouring it, so that the sediment on the bottom is not disturbed. Before using, add 1 tablespoon vinegar to each gallon of boiled water.

cucumbers: Make certain the ones you buy (which should be pickling, not salad varieties) have not been waxed. The brine cannot penetrate the wax coating, and the pickles will be spoiled.

Heat pickle liquids in kettles of unchipped enamelware, stainless steel, aluminum, or glass. Copper, brass, galvanized, or iron vessels may react with the acids and cause undesirable changes in the pickles. For fermenting or brining, use crocks or stone or glass jars, or large stoneware or glass bowls.

For successful pickle-making, you will need a kitchen scale, as many ingredients are measured by weight rather than by volume. You will need, as well, a large water-bath kettle, canning jars and their closures, large wooden or stainless steel spoons for stirring, measuring cups, sharp knives, a large-mouth funnel, a large ladle with pouring lip, tongs or jar lifter, a footed colander, a food grinder, and a cutting board.

But most of all you need the desire to make pickles and good, modern recipes that you will follow to the last dotting of i and crossing of t. Armed with those, you can produce such homemade good things as sauerkraut, dilled beans, icicle pickles, pickled zucchini, artichoke relish, chow-chow, picalilli, corn relish, chili sauce, pickled pears, spiced peaches, tomato catsup, pickled figs, sweet crab apple pickles, peach chutney, watermelon rind pickles, and dozens more.

Butters, conserves, jams, and preserves.
These sweet spreads and main-dish go-alongs are all kettle cooked, then water-bath processed for a short period.

butters: These are made by cooking fruit pulp with sugar—and, often, spices—long and slowly. The fruit is cooked first, then pressed through a food mill; sugar is added and the mixture stirred over heat until the sugar dissolves. Cooking continues until the mixture is very thick. Frequent stirring is necessary to prevent scorching. Apple butter—particularly the old-fashioned kind in which the apples are first cooked in cider—is the most familiar, but there are peach, pear, and apricot butters as well as several others.

conserves: These are two-fruit or three-fruit combinations, sometimes spiced, sometimes with nuts added, often with lemon juice included to perk up the flavor. They are kettle-cooked until thick. If nuts are required, they are stirred in during the final few minutes of cooking. Apples are a favorite conserve fruit, as in apple-blueberry, apple-cherry, and apple-pineapple conserves. Other good combinations are cherry-pineapple, apple-pineapple-coconut, apricot-orange, peach-orange, blueberry-orange, cherry-raspberry, cranberry-orange-raisin-walnut, grape-walnut, and strawberry-rhubarb, and there are many more.

jams: Like conserves, these are fruit/sugar mixtures, cooked until thick, but jams are generally made of only one fruit. Berry jams, particularly strawberry and raspberry, are great favorites. Carrot jam, deliciously spiced, is unusual and unusually good. Grape, plum, fig, peach, pineapple, and currant are other popular kinds. Because the fruit is not sieved, the jam is a thick mixture with small fruit pieces suspended in it. Jam requires frequent stirring during the long cooking period to prevent it from sticking to the pan.

marmalades: Soft, transparent fruit jelly with small pieces of fruit or fruit peel, marmalades may be made of one or two or three or even more fruits, one of which is virtually always citrus; part of the white inner peel of the citrus fruit is included, because it contains large amounts of pectin—to make the jelly gel. Orange marmalade is perhaps the favorite, but lemon and lime are also delicious. Lemon marmalade with chopped candied ginger is sensational. Other marmalade combinations include cherry-orange, carrot-orange, grapefruit-orange-lemon, cranberry-concord grape, peach-orange, and such out-of-the-ordinary ones as marmalades made from quinces or from prickly pears.

preserves: These consist of a syrup—as thin as honey or as thick as jelly—in which whole or large pieces of fruit, retaining their shape, are suspended. Often lemon juice or thin, quartered lemon slices are added to point up the flavor. Like conserves and jams and marmalades and butters, preserves are kettle-cooked, then water-bath processed. Preserving is a bit more tricky, however. Sometimes the syrup becomes too thick before the fruit is tender, and must be very carefully thinned with boiling water. In other cases, the fruit is ready but the syrup is too thin, in which case they must be separated and the syrup boiled down until it is of the right consistency, then the two recombined.

Berries, other than strawberries, behave more satisfactorily in jam than in preserves. Cherries, figs, peaches, pears, plums, apricots and, oddly, tomatoes—particularly the small, pear-shaped red or yellow ones—are all good candidates for preserving. Perhaps the most elegant preserve is bar-le-duc, made of red currants. In France, the preserving is a laborious —and therefore an expensive—process, in which each currant is individually pricked with a needle. The American kind asks less of the cook, and is still very good indeed.

jelly: No pieces of fruit, but only the richly delicious strained juices appear in jelly which, when it is as it should be, is clear and jewellike. Kettle-cooked, jelly is not processed, but is put immediately into jars.

In order to gel properly, jellies require pectin, either that of the fruit itself or, more usually, commercial powdered or bottled pectin. Acid, generally supplied by lemon juice but sometimes by citric acid, is also required for gelling. A proper jelly is firm enough to hold its shape when it is turned out of its jar, yet soft enough to spread with a knife.

A jelly bag is necessary, made of several thicknesses of cheesecloth or of cotton flannel with the nap side in. Through this the fruit juice drips at its own pace; the bag must not be squeezed or the jelly will be cloudy, a condition that made grandma hang her head in shame. A large kettle is required, too; one with a flat bottom allows the jelly to come to the necessary full, rolling boil without boiling over—an accident that makes a mess of unbelievable magnitude. A jelmeter, a gadget to determine the pectin content of the fruit juice, and a cooking thermometer—jelly, candy, or deep-fat all work well—are not essential, but very helpful.

Determining when jelly is done can be tricky when commercial pectin is not used. You can try the sheet test, dropping some of the jelly from a metal spoon until the point is reached at which no single drops fall but the jelly comes off the spoon in a sheet. Or do it by temperature; the jelly is ready when it has reached 8 degrees above the boiling point of water—which may be 212°F. or may not. Boiling point varies with a change in altitude and also with a change in barometric pressure. So boil some water and use the thermometer to determine the boiling point for water in your kitchen on that particular day, then proceed from there. Let a reliable recipe guide you.

Jelly is stored in sterilized jars that have a two-piece sealer lid like that of canning jars, or in jelly glasses, which are sealed with melted paraffin and then protected with lids.

The rewards. Preserving fruits and vegetables in one or several of these ways results in a store of sweet goodness that keeps summer on the table the whole year around and is exceedingly satisfying to the home cook and all who know her/him.

WINTERING FRESH PRODUCE

Long after the garden is bare and the produce markets are spreading out citrus fruits and apples to fill the empty spaces, you can still enjoy the fresh taste of some of summer's vegetables. Not all kinds, and generally not all winter, but if you have a proper place to store them they will keep for many weeks. What's a proper place? An area cool enough to hold off enzyme action within the vegetables, and sufficiently well-ventilated to prevent decay.

The best solution is the old-fashioned root cellar, with its stone walls and tramped-earth floor, but these days few of us are blessed with such a place. Many of us do have basements, however, and many of us have attics. Most of us— excepting only big-city apartment dwellers—have garages. All of these, provided the climate in which we live is not extreme, can be adapted for winter storage of certain fresh vegetables.

Readying the produce. Don't try to store anything that is not in prime condition, unbruised and unblemished. The adage about one rotten apple spoiling the whole barrel is literally true. No matter if you're Mrs. Clean herself, restrain yourself from washing anything you intend to store. That can come later, before cooking. Anything damp on its surface when you lay it away is doomed to rot.

The latest, most mature crops are the best for wintering, but that does not mean that they should be overripe. Some wintering experts swear by the trick of burying produce in sand or sawdust for storage, but others say that it impairs the flavor of some foods. Pears and apples, though, can be individually wrapped in one layer of tissue paper when stored loose in a box or barrel. This prevents contact of sound fruit with one or two that may have unnoticed bruises.

In the basement. Root vegetables—beets, carrots, parsnips, radishes, turnips, and rutabagas are examples—as well as certain green and leafy kinds—cauliflower, cucumbers, peppers, cabbage, broccoli—can be basement-stored if the temperature there is in the 50- to 55-degree range. These need high humidity, and should be packaged in perforated plastic bags to prevent shriveling. Place on wooden shelves or in wooden boxes near an outside wall, which is the coolest spot. However, if the walls and floor are concrete, don't put them directly on the floor or against the walls, or you'll have trouble with mildew.

Potatoes, squash, and pumpkins must be "hardened" in a room where the temperature is between 75 and 80 degrees for about 10 days to dry up excess moisture. After that period, they can be moved to the basement. Store these loose, not in plastic bags.

In the attic. Vegetables that need colder temperatures, in the 32- to 40-degree range, are candidates for storage in an unheated attic. Garlic, dried peppers, and onions are among these. Onions in particular must be kept moisture-free on trays with slatted wooden or wire-mesh bottoms. Or braid onion tops and hang them from the rafters, along with bunches of dried herbs.

The vegetables suggested for basement storage can also be wintered in an unheated attic, in slatted crates or open-weave bags set on wooden shelves, or in wooden boxes. In all cases, don't pack vegetables too tightly—give them air.

In the garage. This is something of a last resort, but an unheated garage can be used for wintering if basement or attic aren't suitable or available. Pack vegetables in covered, sand-filled boxes, and retain humidity by insulating the outsides of the boxes with straw or bags of leaves. If temperatures in your area drop below the freezing point, store the vegetables in plastic-foam chests of the kind used for picnics.

Leaving them where they grew. Easiest storage of all for the root vegetables is to leave them in the ground. (Parsnips, in fact, need to be left in the ground until after the first frost—it's the nip of frost that gives them their best flavor.) Before the first frost, cover the ground where the vegetables have grown with straw 15 to 18 inches deep (mulch parsnips after the frost). The straw mulch prevents hard freezing. When you want a vegetable, simply go and dig it. However, be certain you keep a garden plan. Bare, straw-covered ground looks quite different from a growing garden, and you may lose track of where your underground treasure is waiting.

Last words. If you've never preserved food before, whatever you choose to try, move slowly. Old hands at the game can zip around keeping track of several things at once, but until you get the hang of it, take one step at a time. If you like to cook, you're almost sure to like any of the various kinds of food preserving. Bonne chance!

ICE

Dim caves, so far underground that the sun never warmed them, and springhouses, with cold water chuckling through them, were the first refrigerators. As early as 1000 B.C., the inventive and practical Chinese were cutting and storing ice, having discovered that perishables were not nearly as much so when kept cold. Rome's caesars had ice brought down from the mountains—indeed, Nero had a large number of slaves whose sole task was to run back and forth between Rome and the Apennines, carrying snow to cool the royal food and drink and to make the fruit ices of which the emperor was inordinately fond. French kings had storage chambers constructed in the bowels of the earth beneath their castles, and imported ice from Norway to cool them.

How it works. If you remember the second law of thermodynamics (heat cannot pass from a colder body to a warmer one, but passes readily from a warmer body to a colder one), you understand why ice cools those things stored with or near it: because it absorbs heat as it melts. This principle of heat transference lies behind all refrigeration, of whatever kind.

Keeping the family's cool. Early Americans (as did people elsewhere at the time, and as some still do today) stored perishables in basements, cold cellars, and springhouses, sometimes in a nearby cave if there was one and it was sufficiently deep to maintain a constant low temperature.

Then, in the early 1800s, the icebox moved into the family kitchen (or back entryway) and revolutionized the American menu. No longer did fish caught today have to be cooked and eaten today or thrown away; it could safely lie—usually wrapped in newspaper—on the block of ice in the family icebox. Cream- and custard-type puddings could be made in double quantity, half served tonight, half reserved for tomorrow. As a matter of fact, the icebox gave rise to the leftover, which a great many people consider something of a mixed blessing.

More utilitarian than beautiful, the outside of the icebox was wood, usually varnished. Between it and the galvanized (ice compartment) and white-enameled (food compartment) interior, there were layers of insulation. Each compartment had a door of its own or, in some models, a door was provided for the food compartment and a lift-up top for access to the ice chamber. Later improvements produced three- and even four-door models, the very last word in kitchen equipment sophistication.

The food compartment had several shelves, made of metal grids to allow for air circulation. Up top, the ice sat on a metal hill-and-valley floor, slightly tilted backward to channel the water to the drain pipe. This led down, through the food compartment, to a pan placed on the floor, sometimes concealed by a flap-on-hinges arrangement.

This pan, which required emptying at least twice a day and sometimes more often, depending on its capacity, was from the start a bone of contention in most families. Whose duty was it to empty the pan? If there was a young son or a sufficiently sturdy daughter, the task fell in that direction. Otherwise, the housewife added it to her long-as-your-arm list of other kitchen chores. The master of the house could not, of course, be expected to do it—that sort of thing, in those days, was women's work.

Whoever was supposed to empty the pan usually forgot to do so several times a week, resulting in a flood on the floor and recriminations heaped on his or her head. If there were still icebox pans to be emptied, families would still be yelling at one another about them. The pans are gone, but the icebox lingers on—or, rather, has made a comeback. Old-fashioned iceboxes, refurbished, are very chic these days, usually as holders of bar supplies.

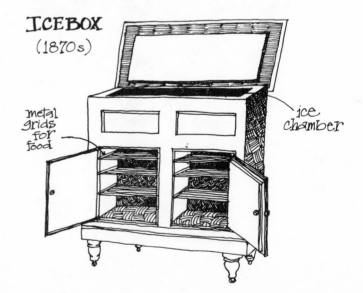

ICEBOX (1870s)

metal grids for food

ice chamber

"Here comes the iceman!" As we need air for our existence, the icebox was useless without ice—a fact that gave rise to a new trade, iceman, and a new business, ice harvesting and storage.

Winter, of course, was harvest time for this crop. An acre of water froze, in cold weather, into a thousand tons of ice, and that amount was considered a good day's haul. A young Boston man, Frederic Tudor, became known as the Ice King. He parlayed blocks of ice from northern lakes and rivers into a big business, supplying ice domestically and exporting it as well. Sawdust, a by-product of the lumber industry and previously considered waste, was brought into service to help insulate the ice and prevent the big blocks from freezing together. By the mid-1800s, Tudor was exporting ice from Boston to storage houses all over the United States and to many foreign countries, some of them tropical. A decade later, cookbooks assumed that their readers all had iceboxes in their kitchen and planned recipes accordingly.

Hauling ice from icehouses to kitchens, the burly iceman, with his two-horse wagon, became a familiar sight on the streets. The horses (like those that pulled the milk wagon, the bakery cart, and rigs of other door-to-door deliveries) learned their route, sauntering down the street and making regular stops. The ice company provided each housewife with a card printed with the numbers 25, 50, 75, and 100. She stuck the card in the window each delivery day, positioning the number corresponding to the amount of ice she wanted so that the iceman could see it from the street. Panic, topped only by that ensuing from forgetting to empty the pan, came each time the lady of the house forgot to put up the ice card.

He was usually a big fellow, the iceman—to a child he seemed enormous—and somehow invested with an air of excitement that the milkman and the bakeryman didn't have. Like the Pied Piper, he generally had a queue of youngsters trailing out behind him, begging for a piece of ice, waiting to pounce on scraps that were dropped, or (the bolder ones) lurking until the iceman made a delivery to hop up into the back of the cold wagon to experience a momentary preview of air conditioning on a hot day.

With a pick, the iceman chipped around a block of the proper size until it came away from the larger piece. Hooking it with huge pincerslike tongs, he slung the ice up to his shoulder—it was protected by a rubber poncho—and carried it indoors. There he passed the time of day with the housewife, provided her with tidbits of gossip he had picked up along his route, and sometimes accepted a cup of coffee or a glass of lemonade (or other favors, coarse men's-club-type jokes of the time used to suggest).

And then, suddenly, it was all over. In 1918 the first practical mechanical refrigerator went on sale, and the iceman's days were numbered.

Ice up to date. Today's automatic refrigerators manufacture ice in compartmented trays, present it to us in neat cubes or slices. Some are even obliging enough to empty the ice into a bin and refill the trays. For those of us affluent enough to require them, separate kitchen ice makers, which put out huge supplies, are available. Lacking such a gadget and needing extra ice, we can buy bags of cubes at the supermarket or liquor store, or from corner vending machines. Insulated buckets keep ice from melting when we serve beverages. Electric crushers reduce ice to slivers. My, my, how times do change!

Dressing ice for a party. Sometimes we need large pieces of ice when we are going to entertain—perhaps to hollow out and fill with shrimp for a spectacular buffet presentation, or to chill the punch in a large bowl. Big chunks of ice can be bought from an ice dispenser, but if you have a freezer, you can fabricate much more interesting shapes at home.

To make an ice bowl to hold shrimp or cut-up fruit or any other food you want to keep cold and serve handsomely, fill a large metal bowl with water. Place it in the freezer until the water is frozen solid. Take it out, and work rapidly. Carefully position a smaller bowl, also metal, in the center of the ice. Holding it in place, fill it with hot water. The smaller bowl will gradually sink into the larger, melting the ice as it goes. Make sure to keep it in the center, and change the water as needed to speed up the melting process. When the center is hollowed to your liking, remove the small bowl and turn the big one upside down. If the big bowl will not come off, wring out a towel in hot water and place it on the bottom and sides until it relents. Lift off the metal bowl and there's your ice bowl. Return it to the freezer until serving time.

Punch needs a large piece of ice to cool it, for cubes melt rapidly and dilute the punch too much too soon. As long as you must provide it, it might as well be attractive and have a secondary usefulness corollary to its chilling properties. Start with a metal ring mold, mixing bowl, or large loaf pan. Fill half full with water, or with fruit juice or whatever base you are using for the punch. (No alcohol, though—it doesn't freeze. Add it to the punch later if you wish. And bear in mind that carbonated beverages lose their fizz if frozen.) Put the container into the freezer until the liquid is partially frozen.

On the surface of the ice, arrange pieces of fruit—any kind that will complement the flavor of the punch, or a mixture of several kinds. Around the fruit arrange mint or nasturtium or small grape leaves in a decorative pattern. Return the container to the freezer until the decoration is solidly frozen in place. Gently fill the container with refrigerated water or fruit juice, and freeze solid.

Approach decorative ice cubes for drinks the same way, using pieces of fruit and small leaves, or a twist or curl of citrus peel or, for nonsweet drinks, a small vegetable shape or a twist of cucumber peel. For iced tea, make cubes of water-diluted lemon juice garnished with pieces of orange, lemon, or lime, or with mint leaves, or slivers of candied ginger. For iced coffee, freeze brewed coffee in cubes for a full-bodied beverage, as strong at the end of the drink as in the beginning. Freeze fruit or vegetable juice, full strength or diluted, to use for making crushed ice that will not water down, but only improve, the beverage in which you use it.

Same song, second verse. The word "ice," aside from meaning frozen water, has other definitions in the domestic scheme of things.

An ice is a frozen dessert made of water, sugar, and fruit juice or purée; sometimes it harbors small chunks of fruit as well. "Water ice," it is often called to distinguish it from sherbet: ice does not contain milk or cream, sherbet does.

Ices can be made at home, in refrigerator or freezer, or they are widely available in markets and ice cream shops. Common flavors are orange, lemon, lime, pineapple, and raspberry. Cranberry appears at the holiday season. Some ice cream stores feature other flavors—tangerine, coffee, grape, and many more. Rainbow ice, a favorite with children, is three or more flavors frozen together. Also for the younger set are ice pops of several kinds.

Third verse. To "ice" a cake—or cookies—means to coat the top or top and sides with frosting. Icing and frosting are synonymous, but in many people's minds icing is thin and spread on lightly; frosting is thick and piled high.

ICE CREAM

You can, if you've a mind to, define ice cream as a frozen dessert made with dairy products. But, as in a saying popular in the day when ice cream freezers were cranked by hand, "Lady, that ain't the 'alf of it!" It says nothing of the wide range of flavors, the vast numbers of toppings, the many ice cream-based goodies, the deliciously dripping cones, the sheer, unspeakable joy of a dish of ice cream on a hot summer's day—or even the sharp ache/pain between the eyes when, as a youngster, you gobbled too much too fast. It says nothing of the dressed-up pleasures of ice cream socials, the cool marble-topped elegance of old-fashioned ice cream parlors. It says nothing of the special Saturday mornings when mom made the custard, dad cracked the ice and packed the freezer, the kids took turns working the crank, and the one who had complained the least was accorded the honor of licking the dasher. Oh, bliss!

Backing up a bit. George and Martha Washington counted two ice cream "machines" among the amenities of Mount Vernon. Thomas Jefferson brought home from France "receipts" for preparing the delicacy. At the 1812 inaugural festivities, Dolley Madison served strawberry ice cream among the other refreshments.

But that was by no means the beginning. Returned from his travels, Marco Polo reported that the Chinese made ice made with milk, an improvement over the early Roman fruit-flavored ices. The idea spread, as good ideas will. Charles I of England pensioned off his chef handsomely with the proviso that he keep secret his way of making ice cream (he didn't, despite the bribe). At a French banquet, Louis XIV's guests were served egg-shaped confections in silver cups, the first ice cream any of them had ever tasted.

Before the nineteenth century, making ice cream was a long and wearying process. The freezers of that time consisted of a metal container within a wooden tub; the container was filled with the ice cream mixture, the tub with ice, and the mixture was frozen by shaking the freezer. Then someone discovered that salt added to the ice speeded the freezing, and things began to look up. They looked up even more when, in 1846, an American woman named Nancy Johnson took a long, hard look at the ice cream freezer and decided she could do better. She came up with one that featured two innovations, the dasher and the hand crank. The dasher, constantly stirring the mixture, resulted in a smoother product. The crank speeded up freezing. Her principles, somewhat refined, are still the ones by which ice cream is made today.

EARLY ICE CREAM FREEZER (1910)

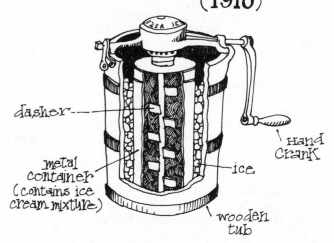

dasher---

metal container (contains ice cream mixture)

ice

hand crank

wooden tub

Five years after her discovery, the first commercial ice cream factory opened in Washington D.C., and the industry has never looked back. More factories were built, all over the country. Today, the frozen dessert is manufactured. Daring druggists added soda fountains to their stores. Ice cream parlors (parlours, it was spelled then) sprang up everywhere. In 1904, at the St. Louis Exposition, the ice cream cone was first offered to a waiting public—delicious and certainly more convenient than ice cream served in an inedible dish. Meanwhile, Nancy Johnson's invention had found favor in American homes, and ice cream—still a great treat, because it was still a great nuisance to make—became a dessert at company meals and the big draw at such occasions as church-sponsored socials. Later, an inventive genius topped the freezer with a small electric motor and the days of hand cranking were over.

Little by little, the ice cream craze died away. At home, freezers gathered dust in the pantry. Ice cream parlors went out of business; you bought ice cream at the drug store, and later at the supermarket. Then, for some unknown reason, the familiar frozen dessert experienced a revival. Ice cream parlors made a comeback—chains of them now, advertising 21 or 39 or 44 or whatever delicious flavors, to be eaten on the spot or hand packed to carry home. Connoisseurs began to talk as knowledgeably about ice cream as wine snobs about their favorite tipple, pointing out that so-and-so's product was made with (fie!) evaporated milk instead of cream, whatchmacallit's cinnamon apple was flavored with real Saigon cinnamon (the very best), and while whoopanhollar's chocolate and mocha fudge were superb, their strawberry left something to be desired, and their pistachio—well, my dear, you wouldn't be caught dead with it! Just absolutely awful!

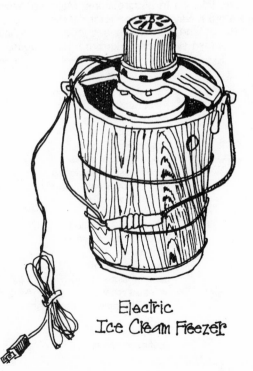

Electric
Ice Cream Freezer

"Make mine vanilla." Vanilla still is, as it always has been, America's favorite ice cream flavor. (It was once the only one.) Chocolate and strawberry follow right along, but after that opinion diverges. Makers vie with one another to produce more and more exotic flavors. Some achieve public acceptance, others die a-borning. Coffee is one that has lasted—although in some ice cream stores you're hard put to it to identify it under such names as kona-mona or sidewalk café. Variations on chocolate—fudge ripple, chocolate almond, and so on—do quite well, too. So do butter pecan, english toffee, and—but only in season—peach. But the makers continue to out-outrageous one another with such offerings as chitty-chatty cheesecake, bubble gum, confetti betty, sticky-gooey, raisin pie, mummy's rummy, nutty old caramel, and so on. (It occurs that the same people who invent names for shades of nail polish must moonlight in the ice cream business.)

Vanilla goes two ways: Philadelphia vanilla, made of cream, sugar, and flavoring, frozen uncooked; French vanilla, based on a rich egg custard, cooked and cooled before freezing. Either way, it's everybody's flavor favorite. Nobody, as they say, doesn't like vanilla. Indeed, nobody doesn't like ice cream. You may acquire a taste for caviar and champagne, but your taste for ice cream, born in your youth, will never fade.

Homemade is heavenly. Making ice cream at home as a family project or an everybody-pitch-in party can be fun. And it's no longer the hard work it once was. The ingredients for the mix are easy to come by, and so is the small amount of personpower required. But you do need a freezer of one sort or another.

churn freezers: These are the old-fashioned jobs—a cannister to hold the mixture (the dasher to stir it goes inside), plus an outer tub to hold ice and salt jacketed around the cannister, plus power—electric or elbow-grease variety. If the latter, the buddy system is best; a lone cranker is inclined to get cranky over the long haul.

First, fill the freezer cannister two-thirds full (ice cream expands as it freezes). Fit the cannister into the freezer. Set the dasher in place, and put on the cover securely. Pack crushed ice and rock salt around the cannister to the top of the freezer, 6 parts ice to 1 part salt. Turn the handle, adding more ice and salt as necessary, until it becomes very difficult to turn. Then stop—all the cranking in the world won't improve things past this point. Take out ice to below the cannister cover; uncover and take out the dasher. Cover the cannister with several thicknesses of foil or wax paper and replace the cover, corking or otherwise plugging the hole in it. Again pack the freezer with ice and salt, 4 parts to 1 this time, and let the whole business stand, covered with a heavy cloth or newspapers, for about four hours to ripen. Or, if there's room, place the covered cannister in your home freezer for the ripening period. And, of course, if your machine is electric, all that cranking isn't necessary—just follow the maker's instructions. Churn freezers usually produce 6 to 8 quarts of ice cream, making the game well worth the candle.

little electric freezers: There are two kinds of these, one that goes inside your home freezer, substituting the freezer's cold air for salt and ice; and a tabletop model that uses ice cubes and regular table salt. Both may be battery operated or be plugged into a receptacle (the in-freezer kind has a flat cord that does not interfere with closing the freezer door). Both these freezers make 1 quart, a few models up to 2 quarts of ice cream at a time.

These little jobs are not particularly expensive, but they have a rich relation, product of a San Francisco gourmet food/utensil specialty store, that would knock your eye out in more ways than one. This is a white countertop dingus with a removable stainless steel tub in its center. Fill the tub with whatever ice cream, ice, or sherbet mixture you wish, plug the thing in, turn it on—and that's it. No salt. No ice. The freezer has its own self-contained, sealed, refrigeration unit. It makes only a quart at a time, but can turn out a quart every fifteen minutes.

There is, unfortunately, one catch. The freezer costs, at the time this is written, $650.00.

ice-tray freezing: Here you pour the ice cream mixture into an ice cube tray or trays, minus the divider. Cover with foil, stick the tray back where it came from, and go about your business. When the top and sides are frozen but the center is still soft, remove from the freezer, turn the ice cream into a bowl, and beat it. Return to the tray and the tray to the freezer, and let it freeze firm. Beating breaks up frozen lumps as well as ice crystals, making for a smoother product.

Which makes the best ice cream? In the same order—churn freezer, small freezer, ice cube tray.

Other ways to go. Freezer cases at the stores offer an array of ice cream treats that is dazzling, especially to youngsters. There are ice cream pops in several flavors, their chocolate or caramel jackets plain or nut-dipped. There are frozen bananas, ice cream bars, chocolate-cake ice cream rolls, bonbons (chocolate-cream-size vanilla ice cream with a chocolate coating), ice pops and bars, fancy decorated ice cream pies and cakes in many sizes and flavors, and more.

Now that ice cream parlors are back—some of them are very elegant indeed—you can drop in and order a sundae or soda whenever you feel the urge. Or you can do the same at home, with homemade or store-bought ice cream, tailoring each serving to taste. There are many kinds of bottled sauces available—or make your own. Set out nuts, candies, cherries, whipped cream, fresh fruit—you name it, it has a place in a soda or sundae. Serve sundaes the way the ice cream parlors did, and some still do, with a sugar wafer or some other thin, crisp cookie.

Sodas follow a pattern—fruit or other sauce for flavoring, cream for richness in the liquid, ice cream, charged water—but sundaes take off in all directions. Make-your-own sundaes are a great way to end an informal meal, especially in summer. Put out the ingredients, and let each drooling diner compose his own symphony. Here are some ideas.

ice cream:	*topping:*	*add if you like:*
chocolate	marshmallow cream	sprinkle of instant coffee powder
lemon	boysenberry syrup	fresh berries
coffee	chocolate fudge	chopped almonds
vanilla	crushed pineapple	melon balls
vanilla	raspberry syrup	fresh peach slices
butter pecan	butterscotch syrup	broken pretzel sticks
strawberry	almost-melted vanilla ice cream	sliced fresh strawberries
chocolate	whipped cream	crushed peppermint candy
vanilla	maple syrup	chopped walnuts
butterscotch	shaved semisweet chocolate	chopped peanuts
vanilla	applesauce	sprinkle of cinnamon
peach	raspberry syrup	crushed vanilla wafers
mint	orange liqueur	mint leaves
toffee	caramel liqueur	shaved chocolate
butter pecan	butterscotch syrup	banana slices
chocolate-cherry	kirsch	whipped cream
vanilla	chocolate and marshmallow syrups	crushed peanut brittle
lemon	orange sections	coconut
vanilla	brandied peaches	grapenuts cereal
fudge ripple	soft custard sauce	sunflower seeds

Well, you do get the idea, don't you? So go and do likewise, allowing your imagination and all your suppressed cravings to run wild. It's good for everyone to let go and wallow once in a while.

Good—but is it good for you? A chubby lady of our acquaintance, addicted to ice cream, answered her husband's protests with, "Would you rather I got drunk every day? Or shot H? Or sniffed coke? Or molested children?" As she was pointing out, everything is relative. So, yes, ice cream is relatively good for you—even the worst of it is a lot better for you than alcohol or drugs. And the best of it is very good indeed, composed largely of eggs and cream, with sweetening and flavoring and, in some cases, fruit and/or nuts.

Like other dairy products, ice cream is a source of protein, calcium, phosphorus and other minerals, and some vitamins. But it is also loaded with carbohydrate (sugar) and fat (butterfat), so it costs the weight-loss dieter a load of calories. In store-bought plain vanilla ice cream, of the kind purchased at the supermarket—not by any means the richest sort—there are about 260 calories in a half pint, an amount any ice cream lover can toss off without blinking an eye and pass his plate for seconds. And, unfortunately, it is generally true that the better the ice cream the higher the calories.

What's it made of? It would be quite natural to assume that ice cream contains cream, and the assumption is true of the very good, high-quality, hand-packed brands. But run-of-the-mill commercial ice cream contains no cream, and has not for a long time. Neither does it contain any eggs.

The problem is, you can't tell by reading the label. Ice cream is one of those few foods that fall under the FDA's "standards of identity" rule, which says that as long as ingredients used are ones that have previously been permitted, no label disclosure is necessary. Under the standards of identity, commercial ice cream must contain at least 8 percent butterfat, a total of 16 percent milk solids, and must weigh no less than 4½ pounds per gallon. For comparison purposes, a gallon of homemade-type ice cream, made from a milk-cream-eggs-sugar-flavoring formula, weighs about 8 pounds. What the other product lacks in weight it makes up in air, which, on the one hand, has no nutritive value but, on the other, isn't in the least fattening.

The "standards of identity" condition is about to change. In fact, as this is written, California has just passed the first law requiring ice cream labels to list ingredients. Other states will doubtless follow, but in any case, the FDA proposes to require listing of ingredients in ice cream nationwide within a short time.

What are some of those ingredients? Whey, a by-product of cheesemaking, is one. Carrageenan, a seaweed derivative. Dry milk solids. Casein, a milk-derived chemical. And a multitude of artificial colorings, flavors, emulsifiers, and stabilizers from the FDA's GRAS (Generally Recognized As Safe) list. Many of these will still be allowed under new labeling laws and will, unfortunately, be lumped in ingredients lists as "artificial flavors and colorings," with no further clue as to what they are.

It's possible to do a bit of detective work in relation to at least some of these. Consider flavoring. If a vanilla ice cream is flavored with pure vanilla, it may be called:

VANILLA ICE CREAM

However, if it is flavored with both pure vanilla and artificial flavoring, but the pure flavoring predominates, it must be called:

VANILLA FLAVORED ICE CREAM

When the artificial flavor predominates, or when the ice cream contains only artificial flavoring, it must be called:

ARTIFICIALLY FLAVORED VANILLA ICE CREAM

This is in line with the FDA's rules concerning the names that products can be called—for instance, a package labeled "beef with gravy" must be more beef than gravy, but one called "gravy with beef" can reverse those proportions.

Assembly-line dessert. In many places, with the exception of some independent stores and small chains that make their own ice cream from scratch, the ice cream you buy comes from a ready-prepared mix bought in bulk. For example, in California, 90 percent of the ice cream purchased is based on ready-mixes made by fifteen large manufacturers. They put together a combination of dry milk solids, sugar, butterfat, and emulsifiers and stabilizers and sell it in bulk to ice cream stores and chains, which add their own combination of colorings and flavorings, as well as, in some cases, air and water. This same assembly-line basic-ice-cream-mix technique occurs all over the country, for outlets and chains that sell "our own ice cream." The odd thing is that some of these "our own" ice creams are very good indeed, at least as far as flavor and texture are concerned.

What to do? Go on as you have been—counting on ice cream more for the pleasure it gives than for anything else. Enjoy it, because enjoyment is what ice cream is all about, whether you will eat only homemade, whether your family is content with an air-filled prepackaged brand from the market, or whether you choose the product of one of the ice cream specialty chains. See also FLOATS, PARFAITS, SHERBET.

ICE MILK

Made in the same manner as ice cream, ice milk contains smaller amounts of milk fats and milk solids. Many weight-loss dieters who turn away from ice cream with tears in their eyes fall on ice milk with reckless abandon, deluded into thinking that the calorie content is very low. It is lower than ice cream, but not all that much. In an effort to put out a taste-tempting product, makers of ice milk often beef it up with extra sugar and nonfat milk solids, and whip less air into it than they do into ice cream. The result is an improvement in taste and texture, and an increase in calories. Plain vanilla ice cream furnishes about 260 calories a half pint; the same amount of plain vanilla ice milk yields about 200 calories.

ICEBERG LETTUCE: see SALAD GREENS AND PLANTS

ICEBOX CAKES, COOKIES

These are names left over from earlier days. Icebox cookies are still with us—stiff cookie dough, formed into a roll and further stiffened by a period of storage in the icebox, then sliced and baked—but are now known as refrigerator cookies. Icebox cake seems to have disappeared. A pity, because it was good, particularly so in days when such a dessert, icebox chilled, was an innovation. It consisted of split ladyfingers or thin slices of sponge cake layered with sweetened and flavored (sometimes chocolate) whipped cream. Overnight in the icebox it stiffened sufficiently so that it could be turned out of its mold and sliced. On second thought, mindful of today's gelatin desserts and cold soufflés and bavarians and such, icebox cake would seem to be a poor relation. Perhaps it's just as well it's retired to icebox heaven, where doubtless it consorts with those other long-gones, the iceman and the little boy who constantly forgot to empty the icebox pan.

ICINGS: see FROSTINGS, ICINGS, AND FILLINGS

IMITATION

This is a word we shy away from. An imitation diamond is only a poor copy of a real one, imitation leather isn't as good as the real thing, imitation fur bears no resemblance to animal pelts, imitation chocolate isn't in the same league with the genuine article, imitation bacon can't compare with that from a good old corn-fed porker.

Right? Yes, in one sense. But in another, wrong.

Most of us were brought up to believe that imitation is a dirty word, and we've lived by this precept for years. Now, all of a sudden, some imitations are sounding better, looking better, *being* better. It all depends on the point of view.

Imitation diamonds aren't the hedge against inflation that the real ones are thought by many to be. But if a girl's heart yearns for a handsome piece of jewelry, and all she (or a gift's donor) can afford is imitation, where's the harm? Imitation furs are far better than the hides of endangered creatures slaughtered to feed female vanity, and there's a third choice—no furs at all for those to whom "imitation" is anathema. A print of a piece of fine art can lift the spirit and nourish the soul of its owner far better than an original executed by a color-blind painter with two left hands. It's all in the point of view.

Where food is concerned, we've begun to take a second, more informed look at imitations. And we've found to our hidebound notions' surprise that "imitation" is not necessarily synonymous with "bad." Sometimes it is. Sometimes it isn't.

Much of our second-looking is because of more stringent product labeling laws that have been introduced in the past few years. Now some products must be labeled "imitation" that we never before considered in that light. Imitation mayonnaise must be so labeled because it does not meet the FDA's standards of identity for mayonnaise. But it has good flavor and texture and, because the fat content is considerably lower than that of mayonnaise, it is a boon to those who watch their weight. Also, it's less expensive. All those points hold true with imitation cream cheese, as well. Imitation ice cream is too low in butterfat to meet ice cream's standards of identity, and may be artificially sweetened as well, but it's a boon to those who because of weight or medical problems can't enjoy the real thing. Many candies were once made with imitations for those allergic to chocolate. More recently, though, these have begun to call themselves carob-flavored and be proud of it. The trend is now very much in that call-a-spade-a-spade direction.

Some manufacturers of imitation foods find new names for their products. Better than "imitation eggs," makers of egg substitutes have called their products by names that connote eggs and are clearly identifiable, but avoid the word "imitation." The same is true of soy-protein and other products that imitate meats—bacon, ham, sausage. All these products have a place in some kitchens, providing menu variety for vegetarians and for those who must abide by a cholesterol-reduced diet.

Emptor need not totally resign the right to *caveat,* but can afford to be more lenient—and more imaginative—where the word "imitation" is concerned these days. See also the special feature: A SHORT COURSE IN LABEL READING.

INDIAN PUDDING

A traditional colonial dessert, still a favorite in New England, Indian pudding was not one of the many gifts from the settlers' aboriginal neighbors, but was named for its chief ingredient, cornmeal, which the settlers called "Indian meal."

A hearty dessert, just right for topping off a not-too-heavy meal in cold weather, Indian pudding combines cornmeal with molasses and spices and other ingredients. It is started on top of the stove, then transferred to the oven for long baking, and is served warm with heavy cream or ice cream.

INDIAN TEA: see TEA

INFANT FEEDING: see special feature: ON FEEDING YOUNGSTERS

INFUSION

Water or other liquid, flavored with an ingredient that has steeped in it, is an infusion. Tea is one—rather than boil tea leaves and water together, which would produce a black and bitter brew, boiling water is poured over the leaves and the mixture set aside to steep; when the tea is strong enough to suit the drinker's taste, it is strained and is ready to drink. Dunking a tea bag in boiling water also produces tea by infusion. Herbs are also sometimes steeped in hot water to produce an infusion, which is strained and used to flavor a food in which the pieces of the herb might not be desirable.

INMEATS

This is one of those over-delicate terms that have crept into our language in great numbers. Inmeats are the visceral meats—liver, kidneys, heart, gizzards, lungs—whatever from inside the animal is eaten. Those who say "passed away" rather than "died" are likely to call these inmeats. The other term for them, variety meats, also tends toward the over-delicate side, but has been so generally used for so long a time that we're stuck with it. See VARIETY MEATS.

INSTANT

This, like "imitation," is a word to which a certain amount of stigma is attached, not always justifiably. We have in our markets today many instant foods that are time-, energy- and, in some cases, cognition-savers—they are prepared in little time, require little energy in their preparation, and little thought on the part of the preparer.

Instant foods range from good to awful, not as absolutes but depending entirely on the point of view of the person who eats or drinks them. Instant coffee is undrinkable to some, delicious to others. The same is true of the many other instant foods—tea, hot cereals, rice, puddings, and a dozen more. It all depends on what you're used to and the degree of education your palate has acquired.

INSTANTIZED FLOUR

Wheat flour, creamy in color and granular in texture, instantized flour has many kitchen uses, notably in producing smooth gravies and easy-make white sauces. Available in shake-or-pour cylindrical packages or heavy paper bags, it may be used in many foods, but should not be substituted for all-purpose flour in baking unless you use a recipe especially developed for it. The label supplies some such recipes. See also FLOUR.

INVERT SUGAR

The process used in making jams, jellies, candies, and frostings results in invert sugar. The action of heat and acid on granulated white sugar turns it from sucrose to a mixture of fructose and glucose, and results in a smooth product because invert sugar keeps the sugar crystals small. Heat alone can cause the inversion of sugar, but the change takes place more readily and more rapidly in the presence of an acid such as vinegar, lemon juice, or cream of tartar. Acid in fruit juices keeps the sugar in jams and jellies from recrystallizing, so that they remain smooth and clear.

IODINE: see special feature: NUTRITION NOTEBOOK

IRON: see special feature: NUTRITION NOTEBOOK

IRONWARE

Kitchen pots and pans made of iron, a metal that heats evenly and retains heat well. Utensils most often made of iron are skillets and dutch ovens, which are sometimes coated with a durable, handsome, brightly colored finish that improves both the appearance and the usefulness of the ironware. See the special feature: YOU CAN'T WORK WITHOUT TOOLS.

IRRADIATED MILK

Evaporated milk is the most common irradiated food. It is exposed to ultraviolet rays to fortify it with vitamin D. See MILK.

ITALIAN GREEN BEANS: see BEANS

ITALIAN HAM

When, in this country at least, we speak of Italian ham, we mean prosciutto, the delectable, highly flavored ham often served with fruit—melon or figs, for example—as an appetizer. Slices should be very thin. See also HAM.

ITALIAN MERINGUE: see MERINGUE

ITALIAN ONIONS: see ONIONS

ITALIAN SAUSAGE

Most often marketed as plump links, Italian sausage is flavored with finocchio or anise. It comes in two varieties, hot—highly seasoned with pepper—and sweet, which is much milder. As it is largely pork, it should be well cooked. See also SAUSAGES.

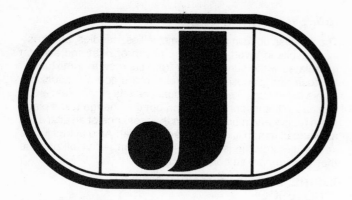

JACK CHEESE

An American cheddar-type cheese, pale cream in color, used both for cooking and for eating out of hand. Mild in flavor when young, it becomes sharper as it ages. Its full name is Monterey Jack. See also CHEESE.

JACKFRUIT: see EXOTIC FRUIT

JAFFA ORANGES

A thick-skinned, rather bitter orange, originally grown in Jaffa, in what is now Israel. See also ORANGES.

JALAPENO PEPPERS

A small, smooth-skinned green pepper, the jalapeño is most often encountered in Mexican and Tex-Mex dishes. Since those foods have become increasingly popular throughout the United States, rather than solely in the Southwest, jalapeños are to be found in many markets. By our standards they are fairly hot—by Mexican standards, only pleasingly so. Use with discretion.

JAMBALAYA

This is a Creole dish, a wonderfully flavorful medley of ham, sausage, chicken, and shrimp combined with rice in a well-seasoned tomato sauce. Jambalaya is obviously a relative of Spanish paella, although the flavors are somewhat different, and a more distant relative of that other famous Creole dish, gumbo, although jambalaya is without gumbo's distinctive filé powder seasoner-thickener.

Paella came to Louisiana with the Spanish. French cooks there added ham; Creole cooks added shrimp, so abundant in local waters. The dish is seasoned with garlic, onions, bay leaf, thyme, and chili powder. Some versions incorporate sliced pitted ripe olives, some add green pepper.

Speculation says that the name of the dish is derived from *jambon,* the French word for ham. When the French added ham to paella they called the dish Provençal jambalaia, which later was corrupted to jambalaya.

JAMS

A thick, sweet fruit-and-sugar mixture, used as a spread for all sorts of breads and in many ways in cooking, jam is distinguished from preserves by being thicker and by the fact that no attempt is made to retain whole pieces of fruit in jam.

A wide variety of single-fruit and fruit-combination jams is available in markets everywhere. Perhaps the most familiar is strawberry jam, very good on hot toast, even better if the toast is first spread with cream cheese, which cuts the jam's sweetness somewhat.

There are two sorts of jams, cooked and uncooked. The cooked variety keeps well, can be stored for long periods at cool room temperature. Uncooked jam, which must be long-term stored in the freezer or short-term in the refrigerator, retains both the flavor and color of the fresh fruit better than the cooked variety. See also the special feature: PUTTING FOOD BY.

JAPANESE TEA: see TEA

JAR SIZES: see CAN, JAR, AND PACKAGE SIZES

JASMINE TEA

Tea that has been blended with the flower petals of the jasmine. It is very fragrant, has a flavor that many people—including most Orientals—are very fond of; others say that the addition of jasmine spoils an otherwise good beverage. See TEA.

JAVA

An area where coffee is grown, and also slang for coffee, as in "Gimme a cuppa java."

JELLIED FOODS

Particularly in summer, and at all seasons as a contrast for hot dishes, often on occasions when the meal is a buffet, jellied foods are both delicious and handsome. Their range is wide, from the beginning of the meal to the end, and they may be gelled because they consist in part of meat, fish, or poultry stock that, when chilled, gels on its own, or through the good offices of commercial gelatin.

Oeufs en gelée—eggs in aspic—provide a beautiful and delectable sit-down appetizer or, in a double portion, an excellent luncheon entrée, particularly in summer. Poached eggs or oeufs mollet (medium soft-cooked eggs, carefully shelled and left whole) are gelled in a well-seasoned aspic in individual molds, and are unmolded for serving.

A familiar jellied appetizer is consommé madrilène, beef-tomato soup softly gelled, spooned into cups for service, and accompanied by a wedge of lemon. But madrilène is not the only jellied soup. Strong, well-seasoned chicken or beef broth may be gelled and served in the same manner. Tiny flecks of snipped parsley or watercress, stirred into the soup before it is completely congealed, add to both the flavor and appearance of the chicken version. Fresh tomato that has been peeled, seeded, and chopped does the same for jellied beef broth. Any of these may be served in an avocado half for added flavor and eye-appeal.

GEFILTE FISH—cold fish quenelles, served in the fish stock in which they were poached, which gels when chilled —is also a jellied appetizer. Horseradish sauce and pickled beets are traditional accompaniments.

There are large numbers of gelled main dishes and main-dish salads, suitable for luncheon or dinner. A good cookbook will tell you how to prepare such dishes as:

mousse of sole with lemon and capers
sliced tongue in aspic with fresh tarragon
old-fashioned pressed chicken
ring-molded avocado mousse with shrimp
chicken-liver pâté in port aspic
cold beef in aspic with horseradish-mustard sauce
molded crabmeat salad with lemon mayonnaise
pork-and-veal headcheese with wilted cucumbers
clam-tomato aspic with white-bean salad
parslied ham (the glorious Jambon Persillé of France)
gingered pear-cheese mold with sliced cold duck
aspic-glazed open-face turkey and scallion sandwiches
gazpacho ring with chived sour cream, deviled eggs
chicken breasts in aspic with orange chutney
curried lamb tongues in aspic
jellied beef borscht with cucumbers, dilled sour cream
jellied veal loaf with green mayonnaise
crabmeat and asparagus in white-wine aspic
salmon mousse with red caviar
lobster and grapefruit in sherry aspic
creamy seafood mousse with stuffed cherry tomatoes
mousseline of shellfish with fresh apricots

Surely by now you have the idea well in hand—or in head. The variety of main-dish gels is wide, and their appeal lies not only in their fine flavor, but also in the fact that they are very good indeed to look at—and, certainly not least, that they are all make-aheads, always an added attraction when you entertain.

Gelled side-dish salads range all the way from old-favorite sunshine salad through all sorts of molded fruit or vegetable or fruit-and-vegetable combinations. Tomato aspic is another specialty from way back; mold it in a ring and fill the center with cottage cheese into which you have folded generous amounts of seeded chopped cucumber and thinly sliced green onions. Indeed, you can mold virtually any sort of salad, using unflavored or fruit-flavored gelatin as the base.

As for gelled desserts, there's a whole wide wonderful world of them, from simple fruit-juice gels with fresh or canned fruit through impressive cold soufflés and bavarians to chiffon pies of many kinds. Once again, their appeal lies

not only in exquisite flavor and impressive appearance, but in the fact that they can be—indeed, they must be—prepared in advance.

Although gelled foods may be molded in almost any container—a mixing bowl, loaf pan, square or round cake pan, or individual servings in coffee or custard cups—handsome molds made especially for the purpose are available in many shapes and sizes. There are single-serving round or square or ring molds, designed to imprint an attractive pattern on the food, as well as a wide variety of larger ones, to hold a main dish or salad or dessert to serve anywhere from four to twenty-four people. As an example, a fish-shaped mold is just right for, say, a salmon mousse; if you wish, you can set an "eye" of a stuffed-olive slice and "scales" of whisper-thin unpeeled cucumber in clear gelatin in the bottom of the container (it will be the top when unmolded) before adding the fish mixture. Such a dish, prepared in such a mold, makes a handsome luncheon entrée, a center of attention at a buffet meal.

There are special occasion molds for almost any celebration you might have in mind. A ring with fruit shapes in its pattern can turn out a Della Robbia fruit salad or cranberry-orange-nut relish wreath at the holidays. A heart shape celebrates Valentine's day and comes into service again when you give a shower. Little individual pumpkin shapes can make an appearance on Halloween and Thanksgiving tables. And there are dozens more.

But don't go overboard. One jellied dish at a meal can be a pleasant experience, but a whole meal of gels, marching by course by course, is a disaster no matter how perfect of its kind each individual dish may be. See also GELATIN.

JELLIES

Fruit juice and sugar cooked together, then strained, then cooked again, jelly attains its quivering, sparkling finished state because of pectin—in the fruit itself, or added to it in the form of commercial liquid or powder. There are also savory jellies, based on wines and/or herbs, to serve with meat.

Like jams, there are some jellies that can be made without cooking. They must be kept in the refrigerator for short-term or the freezer for long-term storage.

Fruits with definite flavors are best for jelly-making because so large a proportion of sugar to fruit is used that fruits of delicate flavor lose their identity. The large amount of sugar is necessary to help make the jelly gel and to assure good keeping quality.

Jellies should be see-through clear when you hold them up to the light, bright-colored (consonant with the fruit used), stiff enough to be turned out of their containers and retain their shape, but never so stiff that they have a rubbery quality nor so lacking in stiffness that they are syrupy. (See also the special feature: PUTTING FOOD BY.)

Commercial jellies are available in a wide range of single

fruit flavors and combinations at most markets. See also WINE JELLY.

JELLY ROLL

A dessert favorite for generations, jelly roll is made of sponge cake baked as a flat sheet, then spread with jelly and rolled. Traditionally it is not frosted, but instead sprinkled liberally with confectioners sugar. Although jelly is the usual filling, no law says that a custard—vanilla, chocolate, or butterscotch flavored—cannot be used instead, or a sweetened and flavored whipped cream, if that is your pleasure.

The cake is simple to make. The only trick lies in turning it out of the pan immediately after it is done, onto a towel sprinkled with confectioners sugar. Roll up at once, using the

be sure to roll cake from narrow end

towel to help you—easy does it—and allow it to cool. Then unroll and spread with jelly of any flavor, and reroll.

So familiar is this good old-fashioned dessert, that many cookbooks use it as an example for other rolled foods. "Roll up, jelly-roll fashion," they direct.

Sometimes slices of jelly roll, rather than plain sponge cake, are used to line the bowl in which English trifle is served.

JERKED MEAT, JERKY

Beef or other meat—in previous eras, often venison—cut in long strips and dried in the sun. Explorers, hunters, and trappers who opened the West counted on jerky (the word is a corruption of a South American Indian word, *charqui*) to sustain them, for it keeps almost indefinitely, is light and compact so that it is easy to carry, and retains a good deal of the food values of the meat from which it is made. It is also, unfortunately, almost unbelievably tough and hard. Even after long soaking and stewing, it obstinately resists any but the strongest teeth and most determined jaws.

There is a present-day snack food called jerky, prepared in a different manner. It, too, is dry, but it is flavorful and much easier to cope with.

JERUSALEM ARTICHOKES

Neither an artichoke nor a native of the Holy Land, this is a vegetable cultivated by the Indians long before we intruded.

It is the root (tuber, really) of a variety of sunflower—in the market, it may be labeled "sunchoke." It is not widely available, but very good if you come upon it. See ARTICHOKES, JERUSALEM.

JICAMAS: see UNUSUAL VEGETABLES

JIGGER

In bartending, at home or commercially, a jigger is a unit of measurement for liquor, and also the container in which the measurement is made. The problem here is that there seems to be no universal agreement on the amount of liquid that goes to make up a jigger. Generally, however, a jigger is considered to be 1½ fluid ounces. To complicate things somewhat, a large jigger is 2 ounces, a small jigger 1 ounce.

As for the container (made of metal, glass, or plastic), it resembles a small whiskey glass—the kind that is often called a shot glass. It is marked in ½-ounce increments to facilitate measuring.

JOHNNY (or JONNY) CAKES

A native of Rhode Island, johnny cake is a type of corn bread. The authentic johnny cake of Roger Williams' colony was made of white stone-ground cornmeal, scalded in boiling water, then drained, mixed with milk and salt, and baked on a griddle.

Nowadays, additions have been made—eggs, melted butter, leavening—and the bread is more often oven-baked than griddle-cooked. One version calls for pouring milk over the top of the bread, after it is in the pan but before it is baked, to form a double-deck johnny cake with a crisp, crusty bottom and a delicate, custardy top. This version makes a perfect base on which to serve chicken à la king or creamed dried beef.

Some say the true name is "journey cake," because pieces of the older griddle-baked variety were often part of the provisions for a journey. Nobody, however, seems to be quite certain of this, even those who declare it authoritatively.

JORDAN ALMONDS

Imported almonds with long, plump kernels of excellent flavor. Also a confection—shelled almonds encased in variously flavored pastel-colored hard candy.

JUG

A container for liquid, usually made of earthenware, with a stout body tapering to a narrow, corked neck.

Also a kind of stew, generally made of game, cooked in an earthenware or stoneware container. Jugged hare is the most common, but all sorts of game and game birds can be jugged.

JUICER

A device for extracting juice from fruit or vegetables, but most commonly from citrus fruit—oranges, lemons, limes, grapefruit. It may be hand operated or electric powered. An older word for the same object is "reamer." See the special feature: YOU CAN'T WORK WITHOUT TOOLS.

JUJUBES: see EXOTIC FRUIT

JULEP

A drink based on wine or liquor—most notably in this country the mint julep, around which considerable mystique has arisen. Bourbon is the liquor of choice—in fact, any Kentucky colonel who was served a julep made of another liquor would doubtless go into shock. It must be served in glasses or, preferably, handleless silver cups that have been chilled until they are frosted. And the garnish, in this case a very liberal one, is fresh-cut mint.

JULIENNE, TO: see page 446

JUMBLES

Pudgy, down-home-type cookies, jumbles are made from a spice-fragrant dough, and are often rich with fruit—raisins, figs, dates—or nuts, or both. See also COOKIES.

JUNIPER

An evergreen tree or shrub, the juniper produces aromatic berries that, when dried, are used as a seasoning in stuffings or basting sauces for wild game and for duck, lamb, or goose. The berries are also the principal flavoring used in the distilling of gin. See HERBS AND SAVORY SEASONINGS.

JUNKET

Besides being a trip on which congressmen go to inspect that which requires inspection or ascertain that which needs ascertaining, a junket is a simple milk-based dessert. The milk is mixed with rennet—which contains rennin, a gastric enzyme that curdles milk—to thicken it, and is sweetened and flavored. Junket tablets are available, and also junket powder, which is both sweetened and flavored (vanilla, chocolate, lemon, orange, and others), so that only lukewarm milk is required to produce the dessert.

JUS

French word for the natural, unthickened juices of meat or fowl. Meat served *au jus* is accompanied by these juices. *Jus lié* is, in French, thickened gravy. See GRAVIES.

KABOBS

A kabob is a small piece of meat. Add "shish," a skewer, and you have shish kabob (or kebab or cabob), a Near Eastern dish that we have made our own, particularly since the cookout became a warm-weather way of life in this country.

Arabians, Armenians, Persians, Syrians, and Turks all cook kabob style, and so do the French (en brochette), but it was probably primitive man who got the idea going. Once he learned that he preferred his meat cooked, it must have been a relatively short step from throwing a chunk of meat into the fire where it was burned on the outside and raw within, to impaling the meat on a stick to cook it over rather than in the flames.

As time went by, refinements were added. Meat was cut into uniform pieces so that it would cook evenly. Presently vegetables (found growing wild, later from cultivated patches) were strung on the skewer to add variety to the meal. When the people were on the move—hunting, fighting, taking their flocks to new pastures—their spears and presently their swords did double duty as weapons and as al fresco cooking equipment.

Bettering a good idea. Before anyone understood that cold would help preserve meat, or had any way to harness the necessary cold, meats were often cooked with spices and herbs and other savory seasonings to disguise the fact that they were—in the genteel term for it of a later day—"turned." From this arose the use of marinating mixtures to tenderize the meat, and sauces and bastes to add succulence as it cooked.

The skewers themselves were refined, too. From swords and spears and fresh-cut green sticks they evolved to kitchen utensils designed for this particular use: pointed pieces of wood or bamboo or metal, sometimes with handsome handles of elaborately carved or chased wood or metal. Presently the spit was devised, turned by hand- (often a small boy) or sometimes by dog-power. Then came the idea of stewing meat in liquid. Stoves were invented, and their ovens in which meat could be roasted. For a time, except for nomadic peoples, the kabob was out of favor. But now here we are again, kabobing all sorts of food and enjoying these tender, deliciously flavored morsels cooked on a skewer.

String it on a stick. Lamb was the earliest domestic meat to be skewer cooked—the Near Eastern peoples did not raise beef, but they had flocks of sheep. Kid (tender and juicy) and goat (strong and tough) were also used. Beef and pork and fowl joined the list when skewer-cooking spread to other parts of the world. Lamb was—and is—still one of the choice kabob meats; it (and mutton) are liked throughout Europe, and particularly in the British Isles.

Meat for skewer-cooking may be from tender cuts, or can be tenderized by marinating or by the use of a commercial meat tenderizer. For those who like beef rare, cubes should be strung very close together; for those who like their beef well done, cubes are allowed air space all around. Pork, although delicious when cooked in this manner, is the hardest meat to control—it must be served well done, and that is sometimes difficult without drying the meat or burning it. Spareribs, cut in narrow strips, and threaded back and forth on a skewer with vegetables between the folds, are probably the best pork choice. Shrimp kabobs are very good, and cook in a brief time. The same is true of oysters and scallops and chunks of lobster tail. Sausages of several sorts and slices of bacon (fold slices accordian-style) add variety. So do lamb or veal kidneys, and chicken livers. Often today, several kinds of meat join on one skewer for a mixed-grill meal.

There's room for more. What goes well on a skewer along with the meat? All sorts of good things. Here are some ideas:

whole, medium-size mushroom caps
pitted ripe or stuffed green olives
squares of seeded green or sweet red peppers
mild chili peppers
chunks of zucchini or yellow crookneck squash
small whole potatoes, or pieces of larger ones (parboiled)
small whole white onions (partially cooked)
fresh or preserved kumquats
whole cherry tomatoes or halved or quartered larger ones
spiced crab apples
chunks of yam or sweet potato (partially cooked)
cubes of tofu (bean curd)
wedges of lemon, lime, or orange (unpeeled)
strips of pimiento
1½-inch cuts of carrot or parsnip (partially cooked)
cubes of eggplant
cubes of turnip or rutabaga (partially cooked)
fresh or canned pineapple chunks
halved fresh peaches or apricots, unpeeled
small whole or chunks of large dill pickles

water chestnuts, bamboo shoots
halved artichoke hearts or whole bottoms
fresh or dried dates or figs
chunks of banana (lemon-dipped)
whole small sweet pickles, watermelon pickle
2-inch chunks of corn on the cob
chunks of jerusalem artichoke (partially cooked)

The only thing you need to bear in mind, when you are deciding what goes with what on a skewer, is the length of time the meat will require to cook. That should guide you in choosing appropriate go-alongs that will cook in about the same length of time.

Marinades and bastes. Generally, a marinade is used to soak the meat to tenderize it and/or give it added flavor. Quite often, such a marinade can double as a sauce with which to baste the kabobs as they cook, or a different basting sauce may be used. (Bear in mind that highly sweet things—syrups, molasses, sugars—tend to burn easily.)

Marinades usually consist of a fat (salad or olive oil), an acid (vinegar, wine, lemon juice), and seasonings such as soy sauce, worcestershire sauce, prepared mustard, puréed fruit, crushed garlic or garlic juice, grated onion or onion juice, smoke flavoring, and a variety of herbs and spices. Tender meats, such as shellfish, chunks of lamb leg or sirloin steak, sausages, and so on, need not be marinated to tenderize them, but can be to flavor them if you wish. Marinated or not, all kabobs profit from being brushed with a savory sauce as they cook.

Ways and means. Over coals on a grill is the most popular way to cook kabobs, but they can as readily be broiled in the oven, the skewers placed on the broiler pan. Or cook kebabs in an electric broiler oven. Or, if you wish, roast kabobs made of tender or tenderized meat in the oven of your stove, although they will not be as well-browned as those from the grill or broiler.

What goes with a kabob? Rice is the usual choice, brown or white or wild. Or a well-seasoned pilaf, the rice cooked in chicken or beef broth with parsley, diced onions, and chopped mushrooms. But rice is not the end. There's no law against pasta or potatoes. Roasted-in-the-coals potatoes are good with almost anything. Riced potatoes make a nice change. Noodles, well buttered and liberally sprinkled with parmesan, are delicious. Or serve kabobs (pushed off the skewer, naturally) in warm buttered buns or rolls, or in long loaves of french or italian bread.

A mixed green salad seems just right as an accompaniment. Vary the shades of green. Depending on what you've used with the meat on the kabobs, add croutons, cheese cubes, cucumber, thin slices of zucchini. A well-dressed coleslaw, bright with flecks of carrot and green pepper, is also good. And/or a platter of thick slices of beefsteak tomatoes, dressed simply with oil and vinegar, sprinkled with lots of cracked black pepper and snipped fresh basil.

Other days, other ways. Miniature kabobs, smaller than the dinner-size ones, make excellent appetizers. They can be small versions of the main-dish kind, or you can go in different directions. Tiny meatballs alternating with small mushrooms are excellent. So are chunks of chicken liver and water chestnuts, threaded on a small skewer with bits of bacon separating them. A slice of bacon, threaded accordian-style around three plump oysters, makes a triple-barreled angel on horseback. Or substitute little bay scallops for the oysters. These and many other combinations can be cooked in advance and kept warm in a chafing dish, or grilled to order on a small hibachi.

There are, also, dessert kabobs—items such as chunks of cake, pieces of fruit, marshmallows, and the like, laved with melted jelly or fruit syrup. One simple sentence describes these adequately: "Good grief, what a mess!" In short, make kabobs the appetizer or main dish, and serve something—anything—else to top off the meal.

KAFFEEKLATSCH

This was originally, in Germany, the women's answer to the coffeehouse, where men congregated and spent, from their wives' point of view, too much time and money. Literally "coffee gossip," the kaffeeklatsch afforded the women an opportunity to rest their feet, grow daily chubbier from quantities of good pastries and coffeecakes, exchange recipes, discuss ideas their menfolk considered to be beyond the grasp of mere females.

Today, the kaffeeklatsch is still alive and well and living in countries all around the world, wherever there are women —particularly women who, because their chief role in life is as wife and mother, tend to be thought of (and, sadly, think of themselves) as second-class citizens, or at least somehow set apart from the world where worthwhile things happen and are made to happen. They draw together for coffee, cake, and comfort.

KALE

This is another of the many members of the cabbage family, a variety that does not form a head. Its leaves, which are cooked in the manner of spinach, are gray- or bluish-green, fine-toothed and curly. Kale was known to the early Greeks and Romans, who lived in climates too warm for the familiar headed cabbage to flourish. It is, horticulturists believe, the earliest cultivated form of cabbage.

KALE IN YOUR KITCHEN

Gray-green kale is prickly-leafed and very curly. The blue-green kind is less tightly curled. The leaves form into a rosette, and the plant is so handsome that it is sometimes grown as an ornamental plant in flower gardens, particularly a variety that shades from white in the leaf's center through soft green, to purple at the edges.

Kale is most widely available—and therefore at its budget best—in the winter months.

Shopping for kale. When buying kale, take into consideration that only the leaves will be cooked; they must be stripped away from the white midrib, which is strong and tough.

how to buy: Look for bright, fresh color. Wilted leaves or those turned or turning yellow tell you that the kale is old. The midrib should break sharply and cleanly, and not be limp.

how to store: Keep in a plastic bag or other covered, moistureproof container in the refrigerator, up to a week. True of all leafy vegetables, but especially of kale, it should be promptly refrigerated when you bring it home. Cooked kale may be refrigerated, covered, up to 5 days.

nutritive value: Kale is rich in vitamins A and C, as is true of many dark green leafy vegetables. It is low in calories, and so is another of the weight-loss dieter's allies; 1 cup of cooked kale furnishes 43 calories, and these nutrients:

protein	5 grams
fat	.8 gram
carbohydrate	6.7 grams
calcium	206 milligrams
phosphorus	64 milligrams
iron	1.8 milligrams
sodium	47 milligrams
potassium	243 milligrams
thiamin	.11 milligram
riboflavin	20 milligrams
niacin	1.8 milligrams
ascorbic acid	102 milligrams
vitamin A	9,130 international units

Tips on preparing, cooking. To ready the vegetable for cooking, cut off and discard any roots that are still in place. Strip the leaves from their center midrib, and discard the rib —or if you wish, it may be cut into small pieces and cooked with the leaves. Wash in cool water, lifting the leaves in and out of it until they are clean and free of sand and grit; then shake to remove excess water. Cook, covered, in a small amount of boiling salted water until tender, 10 to 15 minutes. That is ample time. Some cook kale for a long time in large amounts of water, during which water-soluble and heat-sensitive nutrients are destroyed.

Serve the cooked greens as they are, or chop them coarsely. Dress with butter, salt, and white pepper. Or kale may be creamed, or the cooking water reduced and slightly thickened with cornstarch, flavored with lemon juice, and served over the kale. Or dress the kale with ham drippings,

or with crumbled crisp-cooked bacon or slivers of leftover ham, or chopped hard-cooked eggs.

Freezing kale. Properly prepared for freezing (see the special feature: PUTTING FOOD BY), kale may be freezer-stored up to 1 year at 0° or below, or up to 3 months in a separate-door refrigerator freezing compartment.

Other ways, other forms. Kale must wonder sometimes if it is invisible, because so many people pass it by at the produce counters. The same is, unfortunately, true of kale in the other forms in which it can be found at the market.

on grocery shelves, in cans: Cooked kale (which, like canned spinach, is generally overcooked).

in grocery frozen-food section: Frozen, ready to cook.

Kale is worth investigating, if you've never tried it. Remember to cook it briefly, and it will be a delightful change from the more usual vegetables—and think of all those good-for-you vitamins!

KASHA: see BUCKWHEAT and GRAINS

KEDGEREE

This dish originated in India. Based on rice, it generally contains fresh, dried, or smoked fish, and may also incorporate one or several such ingredients as lentils, onions, hard-cooked eggs, parsley, chives, and peppery seasonings such as cayenne or paprika, and often curry powder.

British army people stationed in India years ago learned to like kedgeree, and when they returned home continued to enjoy it. It is often served as a breakfast or brunch dish, and is sometimes accompanied by an egg-rich cream sauce.

KETCHUP

Spelled also "CATSUP" and "catchup," this is a thick, well-seasoned condiment sauce, named for the Malay ketjap, a spicy fish sauce with many uses in that cuisine.

Originally, ketchup's chief ingredient was salted and spiced mushrooms, but now—although mushroom ketchup is still made—the most familiar kind is based on a thick tomato purée, from which it gets its cheerful red color.

Many commercial ketchups are available, ranging in seasoning from mild to hot. And tomato ketchup may be made at home, as well as mushroom, walnut, apple, concord grape, and a number of other varieties.

KETTLES: see special feature: YOU CAN'T WORK WITHOUT TOOLS

KID

Latin Americans, as well as citizens of Latin countries elsewhere in the world, enjoy the meat of kid, which is sometimes served as an Easter dinner main dish in place of the more usual lamb. Any lamb recipe can be used in preparing kid, which is a young goat, slaughtered before it is time for it to be weaned. The meat is mild flavored and delicate and requires care in the cooking so that it will not dry out.

KIDNEY BEANS: see BEANS

KIDNEYS

One of the edible visceral or organ meats. The size and flavor of kidneys depend on the animal and its age. Beef, pork, lamb, and veal kidneys all make delicious dishes; veal and lamb are the most tender and delicate. Large and stronger beef kidneys may need soaking before cooking. It is best to braise beef kidneys because they are not tender, and pork because they must be well cooked. Sautéing or broiling works well for lamb or veal.

The English are fond of kidneys, often serving them at breakfast, or in steak and kidney pie, or as part of a mixed grill of kidneys, bacon, lamb (or mutton) chops, and sausages, often accompanied by broiled tomatoes. The French also enjoy them, sautéed or served in a rich brown wine sauce, often with mushrooms. Rognons in French, rognoni in Italian, and riñones in Spanish, kidneys often appear on menus in foreign restaurants. See also VARIETY MEATS.

KIELBASA: see SAUSAGES

KILO: see special feature: MEASURING UP TO METRIC

KING CRABS: see SHELLFISH

KIPPERS

Many fish—salmon, halibut, bloater, mullet, shad, sturgeon, and trout are some of them—are kippered, but when kippers are spoken of it is generally herring that the speaker has in mind. The kippering process includes splitting, cleaning, salting, drying, and smoking the fish, resulting in a golden brown color that comes from the smoke of the wood used in curing. Grilled kippers are a favorite breakfast dish in England, where curing and preparing the herring is closely supervised and regulated to ensure that the fish are colored only by smoking, rather than artificially.

Fishmongers sell kippered herring and other kippered fish, and so do specialty food stores and delicatessens. Kippered herring is also available canned.

Heavily smoked kippers should be soaked in boiling water for a few minutes before they are cooked. They can be broiled—brush with melted butter during the process—or sautéed in butter. See also FISH and HERRING.

KISSES

Leaving aside considerations of osculation, kisses may be either a) small, bite-size candies, usually individually wrapped, or b) small, mound-shaped cookies made of meringue with various sweet inclusions. The candy kisses may be drop-shaped milk chocolate wrapped in foil, or lozenge-

shaped and taffylike, flavored with vanilla, peanut butter, chocolate, lemon and other fruits, and wrapped in a twist of wax paper. The cookie kisses, usually vanilla flavored, may include, among other things, chopped nuts, coconut, candied cherries or other candied fruit or fruit peel, dates, grated chocolate. The cookies are easy to make, and a great way to use leftover egg whites.

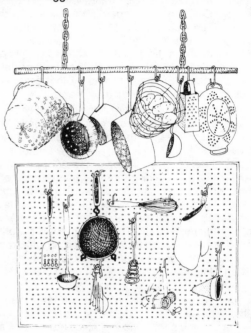

KITCHEN

Like it or not, you spend a lot of hours in the kitchen—a great deal of time if you love to cook, perhaps more than you care to if you don't. One way or another, families have to be fed, even by "I-hate-cooking" cooks. If the kitchen is a sorry place, badly arranged, cramped, poorly organized, lacking adequate storage space, a loving cook will make do while dreaming of kitchen heaven, a sort of Promised Land of pots and pans, stoves and sinks, freezers and refrigerators, cupboards and drawers. But a hating cook will be constantly looking for a place to throw in the towel and never being able to find one.

There is no way to turn a hating cook into a loving one, but an attractive, roomy, well-designed kitchen can go a long way toward easing the pain. And for a loving cook, such a room is unadulterated bliss.

Let there be light. A small kitchen, of dimensions such that when two people work in it they constantly bump bottoms, is bad enough. But if it is gloomy as well as small, it bears all too great a resemblance to a prison cell. Even if there is no way to stretch the room, you can at least light it up. A new ceiling fixture—fluorescent, not incandescent—with a diffuser will cheer up the whole place. Add under-cabinet strips to illuminate counters, stove, and sink, so that there is no area in which you must work in your own shadow.

One of the great ways to bring both light and cheer to a kitchen is to replace a plain window with a bowed, greenhouse one. Even though it does not actually add to the dimensions of the room, it will make the place seem bigger, airier, infinitely more inviting. Such a window juts out from the wall, is shaped like a three-fold screen made of glass, and is topped with glass as well. Glass shelves hold potted plants. The combination of more light and all that greenery transforms the meanest kitchen as if by magic.

Elbow room. Old houses are often blessed with big kitchens that, if not well organized are at least roomy. But some old ones were built on the theory that nobody but hired help would ever use the room anyway, so why bother to make it workable? Such skimpy kitchens, however, generally have breakout space surrounding them—a pantry, a big entryway, an enclosed back porch. Several undersized, underused areas such as these can be pooled into one fabulous kitchen, with plenty of working space, an area in which to serve family meals, a spacious central table or island, a laundry area if that is needed, perhaps even room for a comfortable rocker into which a footsore cook can drop and pant between chores. More than a kitchen, it can become a great place to entertain cookery-minded friends.

Newer houses seldom have such a bonanza of space available. You may defeatedly tell yourself there's nowhere to go—but are you sure? One ingenious home cook acquired the necessary extra space by redesignating rooms: with a minimum of remodeling (and the addition of a fireplace that the family had always yearned for), the garage became the living room, the old living room the dining room, and the old dining room a part of the kitchen, to more than double its size. A house built on a sloping lot, so that the basement was underground at one end of the house but ground level at the other, solved two problems at once—the kitchen was dropped to the ground-level end of the basement, leaving the old kitchen to be remodeled into the den that the man of the house sorely needed. In another case, washer, dryer, and tubs were moved to the basement, and the vacated laundry room incorporated into the kitchen. In still another smart move, a deck beyond the kitchen was enclosed, to add a 5-by 8-foot area to the kitchen and a tiny greenhouse at one end as a bonus. Another moved the dining room furniture to one end of an oversize living room and tacked the small dining room onto the kitchen. There are probably ways to go, if you stop to think about it.

What if there's absolutely no way? Then you must really call on your ingenuity to improvise and organize, to make a small kitchen so workably efficient that it seems, if not spacious, at least adequate.

Start by ventilating. A tiny room seems smaller when it's hot and stuffy with the smells of a dozen different foods. If your stove doesn't have a hood, buy one. Or install a fan above the window to pull out heat and odors.

Make certain the place is adequately lighted, that there are no dark corners. If there is a cupboard so deep you can't really see what's at the back of the shelves, put a light in it.

Color helps, too. Light colors move the walls out, away from you; dark colors pull the walls in around you. Decide on a cheerful color scheme, invest in a couple of gallons of paint, and go to it. If the ceiling is too high, giving you the feeling of working in an airshaft, paint it a darker color to bring it closer. And don't forget the insides of dim cupboards—enamel them white or a pale color for better visibility.

If cupboard and drawer space are inadequate, hang everything you possibly can. Suspend a hanger with hooks from the ceiling to hold pots and pans—low enough to reach, but not so low you bang your head into them. Hang wire mesh baskets to hold fruits and vegetables that don't require refrigeration. Put up pegboard on any empty wallspace to hang smaller objects such as spice jars, spoons, measuring tools. Knives should have a home of their own, not only because they are dangerous stored loose in a drawer but because they become nicked and dull that way—a knife rack is the answer. Magnetized hooks and bars of pegs give you hanging room on the sides of the refrigerator.

If the kitchen has two doors, is it feasible to close one permanently, gaining room for a 3-foot counter with new cupboards above and below it? Is there room to install a large, deep cupboard over the refrigerator? If the washer and dryer must be in the kitchen, can a let-down panel be hinged on the wall behind them to turn their tops into counter space when they are not in use? Is there room anywhere to place a small let-down or pull-up table that can be closed when you don't need it, put into service when you do? Is there a long wall area where very narrow shelves could be put up, 4 or 5 inches deep, to store canned goods without impeding passage? Is there a broom closet whose contents could be stored elsewhere, leaving you room to install shelves in it?

However inadequate the cupboard space, it probably can be improved. There are available small shelves to be hung under cupboard shelves to hold short items, such as spices. There are file-type racks to hold pan lids, trays, and baking sheets. There are, finally, the outsides of cupboard doors, blank spaces much better used for hanging attractive kitchen paraphernalia such as bread baskets, crepe and omelet pans, gelatin molds. There is no law that says everything must be stored out of sight. This is, after all, a kitchen, a work place. Let the tools hang out.

The organized cook. If at all possible, keep the kitchen appliances such as toaster, mixer, processor, blender, and the like out on a counter. Such items as waffle irons and deep-fat fryers, not used everyday, can be stored away, but you'll find that you resent having to haul out the mixer or the blender every time you want to use it, or you'll skip using those tools and find your culinary repertoire growing smaller and smaller.

Organize your kitchen so that like is stored with like—all the baking supplies in one place, for example, with mixer and pastry board on the counter below; rolling pin, spoons, and rubber spatula hanging close by; baking pans under the counter. Store pots in which you cook vegetables near the sink where you prepare them. Make it a rule to store least-used items in least-accessible places—and if you are hoarding never-used items, perhaps as a legacy from your mother's kitchen, isn't it time to chuck them out?

Get your kitchen into the most efficient and attractive condition possible within its limitations, and love-it or hate-it cook, you'll be happier—and you'll set a better table.

KITCHEN EQUIPMENT: see special feature: YOU CAN'T WORK WITHOUT TOOLS

KIWIS

Also called Chinese Gooseberry, this small fruit resembles a fur-coated egg that might have been laid by the flightless down-under kiwi bird from which it takes its name. But once you get past its fuzzy brown exterior, there's a beautiful surprise waiting—brilliantly green flesh, patterned with tiny black edible seeds. And the flavor! Rather like that of pineapple? Somewhat resembling strawberries? Not really. The kiwi's incredibly good subtle taste is all its own.

Until a few years ago, kiwis were imported from Australia and New Zealand. But now we grow them here, in California. Besides good flavor and beauty, the fruit has something else going in its favor: longevity. Refrigerated, kiwis can be stored up to 6 weeks. See also EXOTIC FRUIT.

KNEAD, TO: see page 446

KNOCKWURST: see SAUSAGES

KOHLRABI

Still another member of the far-flung cabbage family, it is neither the leaves nor the root of kohlrabi that is eaten, but rather a bulbous, pale green thickened portion of the stem that occurs just above the ground. When young and tender, the leaves may also be eaten, cooked like any leafy green vegetable such as mustard greens, turnip tops, and spinach.

The bulb is sliced or cut into julienne strips and steamed or boiled, served hot with butter or a cream or sour-cream sauce, or chilled with vinaigrette sauce. Kohlrabi may be served raw in salads or with a dip, when very young. See also UNUSUAL VEGETABLES.

KOLACHKY

This is one of the delights that emigrating Bohemians and Czechoslovakians brought here with them. Yeast-raised, finished kolachky look rather like nicely browned, puffy square envelopes, with one of several delicious fillings peeking through the seams, and topped with a sprinkling of confectioners sugar. The dough is rich with butter, sugar, and eggs. Some appropriate kolachky fillings include poppy-seed, cinnamon-apple, date-and-nut, prune, fig-and-nut, and cinnamon-nut. They fill the house with a heavenly aroma as they bake.

KOSHER FOODS

The Jewish cuisine has evolved in accordance with a set of regulations laid down centuries ago in the Old Testament books of Leviticus and Deuteronomy for the protection of the health and welfare of the people. They deal with sanitary conditions and humanitarian considerations, and spell out in detail how food must be acquired, prepared, and cooked.

Under these regulations, certain foods are acceptable, others are not; moreover, some foods that are acceptable under certain conditions are not under others. Cattle, sheep, goats, and deer—those that chew the cud and have the cloven hoof—are suitable animal foods, but swine and hares are not. Shellfish are forbidden, but fish that have both fins and scales are acceptable. Other than birds of prey, various fowls are acceptable. So are some creatures seldom taken into consideration today as food: locusts and a single category of insects.

No diseased animal or fowl may be used as food, nor may be one mangled in the killing—slaughtering must be done as rapidly and humanely as possible, by a highly skilled person, a "shochet," whose business it is. Meat and poultry, after slaughtering, are "koshered"—they are soaked in water, salted, and drained thoroughly to remove as much blood as possible. Only the forequarters of meat animals are acceptable as food. (Thus there are no tenderloin or sirloin steaks on orthodox Jewish menus.)

Foods are classified by kind: mammals and poultry are "fleishig," milk, cheese, and other milk-derived foods are "milchig," while fish, eggs, vegetables, and fruits are neutral, or "pareve." Fleishig and milchig foods are never served at the same meal, but pareve foods may be served with either. It is required that four to six hours elapse between a fleishig and a milchig meal.

In the kosher kitchen, two sets of cooking utensils, dishes, flatware, and dishcloths and dish towels are required for the preparation and serving of fleishig and milchig meals, and the equipment for each is stored completely apart from the other.

Cooking mediums must be separate too—shortening, for example. Butter is right for milchig meals only, while vegetable oil is chosen for fleishig ones. Kosher margarine, which is pareve, may be used in either case.

Today's supermarkets carry many foods prepared according to Jewish dietary laws. These wear an identifying symbol. It may be the letter U enclosed by the letter O, or K (for kosher) alone or in a circle. Foods kosher for Passover, one of the chief Jewish holidays, are specifically marked by adding a P to the U and O symbol, or by adding the words "Kosher for Passover" to the label. Neutral foods carry the word "pareve" on their labels.

Many wonderful foods are enjoyed today by Jews and non-Jews alike, some so much taken for granted—particularly in areas where there are large Jewish populations—that their origins have been forgotten, or were never known, by many of us who feast on them. There is chopped chicken liver, for instance. Rich chicken soup with matzo balls (feather-light when made by a good cook, lethally heavy by a bad one). High, airy sponge cakes, honey cakes, nut cakes. Potato pancakes and potato knishes. Cheese or fruit-filled blintzes, with accompanying sour cream. Hamantaschen with prune or poppy-seed filling. And there are dozens more.

KUMQUATS

A small, egg-shaped citrus fruit with a yellow-to-orange rind that, as is not true of other citrus, is eaten along with the flesh. See also EXOTIC FRUIT.

THE GROW-IT-YOURSELF BOOM

Being midwife to the mystical burgeoning of seed into plant is an experience like no other; a garden is indeed a lovesome thing—but it is also backbreakingly hard work

Here is a riddle for you: What do zucchini and kittens have in common? Answer: When you have an excess of either, it is virtually impossible to give them away.

Some people irresponsibly let their cats have litter after litter of kittens, in the full knowledge that we already have an overpopulation of cats, reaching the saturation point. And some novice gardeners plant zucchini with reckless abandon—even those who aren't all that fond of the squash, even those who know that neighbors all around them are also relentlessly planting them—because they have heard that zucchini is easy to raise and they are anxious to "get into gardening."

Actually, this is not a perfect parallel. Although it is almost impossible to give away zucchini because everyone else is trying to give away his excess as well, zucchini can be canned or frozen or, as a last resort, added to the compost heap. None of these avenues is open in the matter of excess kittens. Further, a zucchini never fixes you with large yellow eyes and asks to sit on your lap. But the point is this: For manageable results in almost any endeavor, advance planning is essential.

The nervous novice. Those of us old enough to remember World War II also remember Victory Gardens. They were everywhere—in backyards, vacant lots, wherever there was a piece of unused land. We worked them with care and enthusiasm, proud of our produce and of our contribution to the war effort. But when the war was over, we went inside the house and slammed the door thankfully, or returned to our roses and sweetpeas and dahlias. Some few of us raised a patch of herbs and called it a garden, but that was the sum of it.

Now again, in the past few years, we have begun to plant vegetable gardens—both, unfortunately, those of us fitted for the task and those abysmally unfitted. A garden can indeed be a great pleasure. Those who claim that no food can compare with your own produce, freshly picked in your own garden, speak no more than the truth. But before the produce can be picked, a great deal of time, hard work, and money must be expended. And a good deal of know-how must be acquired. Too many people who talk almost religiously of getting back to the land have lost sight of the fact that you cannot return to a place you have never been.

Before you are seduced by seed catalogs and/or friends' glowing accounts of their gardening endeavors, give thought to these considerations:

- a garden requires a certain amount of room; make sure that you have space to devote to it—space that is not now being used for some other purpose your family enjoys, such as horseshoes, badminton, shuffleboard, or such
- make certain that those who will be required to do at least a part of the work—wife, husband, children, teenagers—are agreeable to taking it on; ask yourself if you are prepared to devote a couple of hours several nights a week to the garden after a hard day at business, to give up golf or tennis or whatever is your weekend pleasure in favor of the garden
- be aware that a small family garden will repay you in delicious fresh food, but not in a great deal of money saved
- make sure that whoever will be required to preserve the garden produce not eaten fresh is willing and able to can and freeze it, that you have proper storage space for the canned and frozen foods, and have or are willing to buy the equipment essential to proper—and safe—preserving (see special feature: PUTTING FOOD BY)

Summing it up, a garden should be a joint decision, not a pleasure to one family member but a cause for frustration and resentment to the others.

A preliminary overview. If everyone professes to be ready, willing, and able to cope with the pangs as well as the pleasures of gardening, understand that the project is not merely a matter of sticking seeds into the ground and then, after a suitable interval, reaping the rewards. Take a long, hard look at what making a garden will entail:

- the garden must be located in a suitable spot—one that is well drained, gets plenty of sun, is protected from high winds, can be protected from prowling dogs, foraging rabbits, and kids on tricycles
- the soil must be prepared—by hand with a spade or fork for a very small plot, with a rented or borrowed

383

plow/harrow for a plot large enough to supply most of the family's vegetables for the season and the winter; the soil must be fertilized, limed, and otherwise treated, depending on its original condition and the area in which you live

- seeds must be sown or sets (young plants) put out; seeds are purchased, sets can be purchased or raised from seed in hotbeds or coldframes—which is another whole new ball game; you must know how to plant each individual vegetable—how deep, how far apart, singly or in hills, and more; planting is not a do-it-and-forget-it-task—early crops should be followed by plantings of later ones
- many plants must be thinned when young—an on-the-knees, by-hand job, ruthlessly done
- support must be provided for plants that need something to grow on—such as beans, peas, tomatoes
- war must be waged against weeds and pests and plant diseases
- the garden must be watered; irrigation equipment is necessary in some areas, desirable in virtually all; nowhere can rainfall be counted on to supply adequate water
- the soil must be cultivated—hoed, to the uninitiated—so that it will not form a resistant crust; mulching helps to keep the soil workable and also assists in keeping weeds in check, but it won't do either job totally
- you will need tools—not a great many, but some; gardening is not bare-hands work

As you can see, "Come into the garden, Maude," is an invitation that should be critically examined before it is accepted.

PART-TIME, FULL-TIME, VERY LITTLE TIME AT ALL

Some people are born gardeners. They enjoy every moment of their hours in the sun—even their hours in the rain. Others can take it or leave it, but nevertheless garden because they think it is a good thing to do; they enjoy the fresh produce and/or they feel the outdoor exercise is good for them and/or they believe home gardening is a money-saving proposition—or they garden for some indefinable but compelling reason, possibly for the good of their souls.

If you truly love to garden, but are realistically aware that the time you can devote to it is limited, perhaps the "unbuyable" garden is the right choice for you. In it, you raise those of summer's delights that you and your family particularly enjoy but that do not usually come to market in your area. Small pear-shaped yellow tomatoes, perhaps. Golden globes of lemon cucumbers. Or regular green cucumbers to be picked immature for salads, delicately delicious as those

from the greengrocer can never be. Leeks, because the market variety is always out-of-proportion expensive. Okra, because it is virtually impossible to buy fresh in the area where you live. Tiny potatoes, to be brought in and eaten when they are much smaller than any the market has to offer. Small white eggplants, because no one you know grows them. Salsify, which you often had and loved at your grandmother's house, but have never been able to find in any market since. Herbs, because your good-cook family knows how to use them fresh in season, freeze them for out-of-season to produce a taste of summer when it's snowing. These and other unusual produce are fine for the gardener who is long on love but short on time, who feels somehow incomplete without a garden but can't cope with a full-size one.

But if you have large supplies of time, patience, planting space, and enjoyment of gardening, you can go all out. Equipped with all of these but lacking experience, you will need more detailed how-to information than there is room to give you here. If you're lucky, you have a father or grandfather, neighbor or friend willing to lead you through the many-faceted mysteries.

Or you can easily get a book and read it. Not simply a seed catalog, but a spell-it-out book that will lead you step by step from selecting a site through harvesting your crops. (Not the least of these is knowing when to pick what you've grown; for example, squash picked too soon is rock-hard, resistant to all the blandishments of the kitchen; broccoli picked too late will have formed flowers and seeds, will be tough, strong, and unpalatable). There are many such books available, to be purchased or borrowed from the library. Or send to the Superintendent of Documents, U.S. Government Printing Office, Washington D.C. 20402, for the USDA's Home and Garden Bulletin Number 202, "Growing Vegetables in the Home Garden." It will hold your hand all the way.

Meanwhile, here are some bits and pieces of information to help you decide whether or not to put in a garden and, if the decision is yes, what you might like to plant, how much space it will take, how much of any vegetable you'll need to feed your family fresh, and to can or freeze.

HOW DOES YOUR GARDEN GROW?

You may, if the amount of land available to you will permit, want to make it garden"s"—two plots rather than one. Two plots allow for optimum use of space: vegetables such as lettuce, radishes, beets, spinach, and others requiring only a small amount of growing space can occupy a small kitchen-garden plot. Those needing more room—potatoes, sweet corn, pumpkins, melons—can be planted separately—between rows of trees in a small orchard is ideal for some of them. Permanent crops such as rhubarb and asparagus should be placed where they will not interfere with the plowing and cultivation for annual crops.

Where the growing season is sufficiently long, plan to plant early-maturing vegetables so that as soon as one crop is harvested another can take its place. Follow early peas or beans with late celery cabbage or carrots, early corn or potatoes with late turnips or spinach. Often a late crop, to give it a head start, can be planted between the rows of the early one—sweet corn between rows of early potatoes, for example. Second, even third plantings of crops adapted to late-season growth can supply vegetables for the end of the season and for canning, freezing, or wintering-over.

Before you order seeds, plan the garden on paper so that you will know how much of what you will need. (Your state's agricultural experiment station, your county agricultural agent, or an experienced gardener in your area can advise you about the varieties of vegetables that are successfully grown where you live.) The following table will guide you in early planning subject to modification when you have consulted an expert if you need to. Buy seeds from a reputable seedsman.

A comprehensive plan. Here is a plan for a garden plot 15 feet wide by 25 feet long, utilizing space wisely and counting on second plantings. Many of the first plantings are from seed, the second from sets—either started by you from seed or purchased. You may, of course, wish to grow more of some vegetable, to eliminate some entirely, to add some not mentioned here. Tailor your scheme to suit your own needs. But here is how such a plan can be made.

Plan for garden plot

early peas followed by cucumbers
garden cress followed by brussels sprouts
lettuce
bush green beans
radishes
peas followed by green peppers

first row: Sow early peas as soon as the frost is out of the ground; meanwhile, start early cucumber seeds indoors. Between 72 and 77 days after planting, the peas will be exhausted; set out cucumbers, plan on picking them 56 to 60 days later.

second row: Sow garden cress in early spring, start harvesting in 9 to 11 days, finish 19 to 22 days after planting; meanwhile, start brussels sprouts to set out when cress is exhausted.

third row: Sow lettuce in early spring, begin harvesting in 78 to 82 days, and continue throughout the season.

fourth row: Sow bush green beans, start picking in 48 to 52 days; when exhausted, sow more of the same beans for late season.

fifth row: Sow early radishes to pick in 22 to 24 days; meanwhile, start early tomatoes indoors some 6 weeks before the season's final frost is expected so that seedlings will be ready to set out when radishes are exhausted.

sixth row: Allow 2 to 3 weeks to elapse after sowing the early peas in the first row, then sow peas in this row. Meanwhile, start green pepper seeds indoors; set out when peas are exhausted, harvest in 68 to 74 days.

seventh row: Sow more radishes in this row 14 to 16 days after sowing early radish seeds in the fifth row. Meanwhile, start zucchini indoors, plant when radishes are exhausted; they will be ready in 55 to 60 days.

eighth row: Sow oakleaf (lettuce), pick steadily as plants mature; they will be exhausted in 48 to 52 days, at which point plant green bean seeds to be harvested in another 48 to 52 days.

ninth row: Sow carrots in half the row, sow remaining half in 13 to 18 days; between carrots, plant radishes; they will serve to mark the row, as they germinate much more rapidly than carrots. You can begin to pull fully mature carrots 68 to 74 days after the first sowing, baby carrots sooner.

tenth row: Sow early beets, which you can begin to harvest in 78 to 83 days; when plants must be thinned, use the culls for a dish of tender beet greens. When beets are exhausted, sow any hardy, quick-germinating lettuce for a late crop.

eleventh row: Sow early turnips, which you can harvest in 43 to 46 days; turn the soil and leave until heat of summer is nearly over, then plant a second batch of turnips for a late crop.

twelfth row: Put out broccoli sets (raised from seed or purchased) in early spring, begin to pick in 43 to 47 days; again plant seedlings, for a late crop, when summer heat has passed.

thirteenth row: Sow spinach in mid-spring; begin to pick in 68 to 72 days, continue picking until frost.

PLANNING A GARDEN

The USDA's estimates of quantity of seed/number of plants required for 100 feet of row, plus depths of planting, and distances apart for rows and plants

crop	requirement for 100 feet of row		depth to plant seeds (in inches)	distance apart	
	seeds	plants		rows (hand cultivated)	plants in the row
asparagus	1 ounce	75	1–1½	1½ to 2 feet	18 inches
beans:					
lima, bush	½ pound		1–1½	2 feet	3 to 4 inches
lima, pole	½ pound		1–1½	3 feet	3 to 4 feet
snap, bush	½ pound		1–1½	2 feet	3 to 4 inches
snap, pole	4 ounces		1–1½	2 feet	3 feet
beets	2 ounces		1	14 to 16 inches	2 to 3 inches
broccoli:					
heading	1 packet	50–75	½	2 to 2½ feet	14 to 24 inches
sprouting	1 packet	50–75	½	2 to 2½ feet	14 to 24 inches
brussels sprouts	1 packet	50–75	½	2 to 2½ feet	14 to 24 inches
cabbage	1 packet	50–75	½	2 to 2½ feet	14 to 24 inches
cabbage, chinese	1 packet		½	18 to 24 inches	8 to 12 inches
carrots	1 packet		½	14 to 16 inches	2 to 3 inches
cauliflower	1 packet	50–75	½	2 to 2½ feet	14 to 24 inches
celeriac	1 packet	200–250	⅛	18 to 24 inches	4 to 6 inches
celery	1 packet	200–250	⅛	18 to 24 inches	4 to 6 inches
chard	2 ounces		1	18 to 24 inches	6 inches
chicory, witloof	1 packet		½	18 to 24 inches	6 to 8 inches
collards	1 packet		½	18 to 24 inches	18 to 24 inches
corn, sweet	2 ounces		2	2 to 3 feet	drills, 14 to 16 inches; hills, 2½ to 3 feet
cress, upland	1 packet		⅛–¼	14 to 16 inches	2 to 3 inches
cucumbers	1 packet		½	6 to 7 feet	drills, 3 feet; hills, 6 feet
dasheen	5 to 6 pounds	50	2–3	3½ to 4 feet	2 feet
eggplant	1 packet	50	½	2 to 2½ feet	3 feet
endive	1 packet		½	18 to 24 inches	12 inches
fennel, florence	1 packet		½	18 to 24 inches	4 to 6 inches
garlic	1 pound		1–2	14 to 16 inches	2 to 3 inches
horseradish	(cuttings)	50–75	2	2 to 2½ feet	18 to 24 inches
kale	1 packet		½	18 to 24 inches	12 to 15 inches
kohlrabi	1 packet		½	14 to 16 inches	5 to 6 inches
leeks	1 packet		½–1	14 to 16 inches	2 to 3 inches
lettuce, head	1 packet	100	½	14 to 16 inches	12 to 15 inches
lettuce, leaf	1 packet		½	14 to 16 inches	6 inches
muskmelon	1 packet		1	6 to 7 feet	hills, 6 feet
okra	2 ounces		1–1½	3 to 3½ feet	2 feet
onions:					
plants		400	1–2	14 to 16 inches	2 to 3 inches
seeds	1 packet		½–1	14 to 16 inches	2 to 3 inches
sets	1 pound		1–2	14 to 16 inches	2 to 3 inches
parsnips	1 packet		½	18 to 24 inches	2 to 3 inches
peas	½ pound		2–3	1½ to 3 feet	1 inch
peppers	1 packet	50–70	½	2 to 3 feet	18 to 24 inches
potatoes	5 to 6 pounds (tubers)		4	2 to 2½ feet	10 to 18 inches
pumpkin	1 ounce		1–2	5 to 8 feet	3 to 4 feet
radishes	1 ounce		½	14 to 16 inches	1 inch
rhubarb		25–35		3 to 4 feet	3 to 4 feet
salsify	1 ounce		½	18 to 26 inches	2 to 3 inches
shallots	1 pound (cloves)		1–2	12 to 18 inches	2 to 3 inches

crop	requirement for 100 feet of row		depth to plant seeds (in inches)	distance apart	
	seeds	plants		rows (hand cultivated)	plants in the row
sorrel	1 packet		½	18 to 24 inches	5 to 8 inches
soybeans	½ to 1 pound		1–1½	24 to 30 inches	3 inches
spinach	1 ounce		½	14 to 16 inches	3 to 4 inches
spinach, new zealand	1 ounce		1–1½	3 feet	18 inches
squash:					
bush	½ ounce		1–2	4 to 5 feet	drills, 15 to 18 inches; hills, 4 feet
vine	1 ounce		1–2	8 to 12 feet	drills, 2 to 3 feet; hills, 4 feet
sweet potatoes	5 pounds (bedroots)	75	2–3	3 to 3½ feet	12 to 14 inches
tomatoes	1 packet	35–50	½	2 to 3 feet	1½ to 3 feet
turnip greens	1 packet		¼–½	14 to 16 inches	2 to 3 inches
turnips and rutabagas	½ ounce		¼ to ½	14 to 16 inches	2 to 3 inches
watermelon	1 ounce		1–2	8 to 10 feet	drills, 2 to 3 feet; hills, 8 feet

fourteenth row: Sow butternut squash in mid-spring, to be picked beginning in 108 to 112 days; leave on vine until heavy frost is imminent. Winter-over the last of the crop in a cool place (see special feature: PUTTING FOOD BY).

fifteenth row: Sow green onions in early spring; in 58 to 64 days, thin as necessary (use the thinned-out plants, they are tender and delicate); start pulling full-size onions 118 to 122 days from planting, continue until frost.

This is the sort of plan you need to make, enlarging or cutting down on the size, adapting plantings to your family's tastes. If you need to visualize, plot the garden on ¼-inch crosshatch graph paper, counting each ¼ inch as 1 foot.

A PATCH OF HERBS

Fresh, fragrant herbs are a delight to the palate. If you have never grown them, try planting a small patch. You'll be able to enjoy a wide variety of almost-new flavors, the fresh herbs are so much more flavorful than the dried variety.

Buy plants (most nurseries carry them) rather than starting herbs from seed. Most need very good soil, at least half a day's sunshine, and must be fertilized. Mint is the exception. It needs very little fertilizer, can stand more shade than most herbs, and once it gets a foothold can overrun the whole patch if you aren't firm with it; fortunately, most households require more mint than other herbs—whole sprigs to add fragrance and flavor to glasses of iced tea and lemonade, for instance.

A well-rounded herb garden might consist of two plants each (four, if you wish to freeze some) of basil, dill, mint, marjoram, oregano, rosemary, sage, tarragon, and thyme, plus three or four of chives and the same number of parsley if you're a lavish user of them. To convert your favorite recipes calling for dried herbs to the use of fresh ones, start with twice as much of the fresh as the recipe calls for, taste

and add a little more—up to three times as much—if you wish.

Fresh herbs are delightful in butters to spread on bread or sandwiches or to melt on hot-off-the-grill steaks. They improve salads immeasurably, both mixed green and such hearty ones as potato and macaroni. They add elegance to scrambled eggs and omelets. Try fresh sage in ham loaf, fresh thyme in the stuffing for roast chicken or turkey, basil sprinkled thickly over sun-warmed beefsteak tomatoes, tarragon over lamb chops before broiling, dill in sour cream to dress cucumbers or sauce fish, oregano in salmon salad, marjoram in lemon butter for green beans or asparagus. Those are only a few of the dozens of ways that fresh herbs can enhance your reputation as a cook.

Even if you have no garden space, you can grow herbs in pots or a planter box on the kitchen windowsill for all-year-around harvesting, even in winter.

TLC IN THE GARDEN

Mulching is a good idea for a number of reasons. It helps keep weeds down, it encourages the soil to conserve moisture, and it modifies soil temperature, keeping it warmer or cooler than the air, so that the growing plants are not subjected to extremes. When the soil is mulched, the vegetables are less likely to be mud spattered during a rain—and you'll have a less muddy place to walk between the rows as you work or pick.

Organic mulches will decompose and can be turned over into the ground at the end of the growing season to improve the structure of the soil. Some good organic mulches are clean straw, ground corncobs, sawdust, and spoiled hay; use whatever is most widely available—and therefore cheapest—in your area. Best of the organic mulches is well-rotted compost; if you're going to get into gardening you'll probably also get into composting. Whichever organic mulch you choose, don't be chintzy—it should be spread 4 to 6 inches deep. Put it on when the soil is moist, but not soggy wet.

The inorganic compost most widely used in recent years is black plastic. You can buy it in sheets or rolls and, while it's generally more expensive than the organic mulches, it does a great job and can be saved and reused year after year. Cover the ground with the plastic, cutting circles out of the material for plants to come through and making X-shaped slits at intervals to allow water to reach the soil and the plants.

Doing something about the weather. Depending on temperatures—and their fluctuations—in your area, you may at some point need to modify the weather in temporary ways. Sometimes sets you put out react to their first experience with strong sunshine by wilting. During their first few days, the critical ones in their new environment, tent them loosely with newspapers held in place by bricks or stones during the hottest part of the day. Remove the tents when the sun fades, and be sure that you don't cut off the circulation of air.

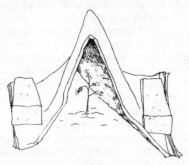

If the weather turns unseasonably cold after you've put sets out or seedlings have pushed their way through the ground, you may have to give them "hothouse" protection for a few nights. For individual plants, cut the bottom off a half-gallon plastic milk carton; place the top part over a plant at

sundown, but make sure to remove it during the day. If you need to protect whole rows of plants, nail 1- by 1-inch stakes into V-shapes and stick into the ground at the ends of rows; connect with a strip of lath. At night, tent plastic over this framework, removing it during the day.

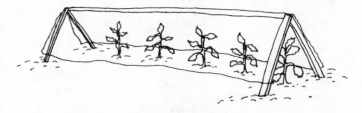

In areas where high winds are a problem, a large shingle pushed into the ground on the windward side of a plant will help to shield it. Use two or even three shingles per plant if necessary, to give two- or three-sided protection.

Cold and wind are not likely to be your only problems. Wherever there's a garden, two- and four-footed predators gather in response to some silent dinner bell within them. Rabbits adore lettuce, but they'll willingly eat anything young and tender that you're thoughtful enough to plant for them. So will woodchucks. Raccoons are a little choosier, but not much. Birds are always on the lookout for seeds, and they'll fight you to the last ditch for berries. Bluejays are mad for fallen berries that have fermented, and an inebriated bluejay can be pretty rowdy. (Look on the bright side, though: in Africa, elephants often get drunk on fallen fruit. Given your druthers, wouldn't you prefer a tipsy bluejay to a drunken elephant rampaging around your garden?) Cotton netting thrown over the bushes or vines will often allow you to get your share of berries. Wire netting of 2- to 4-inch mesh, bent into a three-sided cage, will protect lettuce and other tender young plants. Consult an experienced gardener or a nursery in your area to learn what predators to guard against and how to protect your crop from them.

There are smaller crop devastators, too—slugs, bugs, worms, beetles, and sufficient diseases and blights to keep a medical school in business. Start by buying disease-resistant strains of seeds. Water well and regularly; well-watered plants are healthier, better able to fend off diseases and pests. Using a soaker hose gets the water to the roots, where it is needed, helps keep the leaves dry and mildew down. Stiff paper collars at the bases of tomato plants will repel cutworms. Hand pick and destroy any creepers and crawlers you spot. Again, consult experienced gardeners and/or local nurserymen concerning the pests and diseases your area is heir to and the best ways to cope with them. But be sure the advice you take is sensible—it would be a safe bet that there isn't an old-hand gardener in the country who doesn't have his own pet nostrum, some of them so foul and noisome you'll be tempted to abandon the garden to the beasties and find another hobby.

The compleat composter. Entirely organic, compost improves soil as a plant-growing medium. As it continues to decay, it releases nitrogen, minerals, and other nutrients the plants need. Virtually any plant material—even some things that up to now you've called garbage—can be composted for use in your garden. Lawn clippings, discarded sod, straw, all the leaves you never before knew what to do with after you'd raked them, kitchen refuse (as long as it is organic)—all these can go into the compost heap. Rabid composters have been known to relieve their neighbors of leaves and lawn clippings, even to chase the street sweepers down the block, begging for a handout.

There is method to what at first blush seems like the madness of composting. Why bother? Why not just shovel all those miscellaneous discards onto the garden and let it go at that? In the first place, you'd turn your lovesome thing into an unsightly mess. Neighbors who have cheerfully donated leaves to you can become somewhat miffed if their largesse blows back to their yards in the first high wind. But the important reason is that the compost materials must decay before they can be optimumly useful and easily worked into the garden soil.

So in the autumn, when fallen leaves are plentiful, choose an out-of-the-way corner of your yard and enclose it. Make a bin out of cinder blocks, old boards, wire fencing, what have you, as long as the sides are not air- and watertight. Spread out a layer of plant refuse about 6 inches deep. Over it sprinkle ½ pound of 10–10–10 or 10–20–10 or 10–6–4 commercial fertilizer for each 10 square feet of surface. Next, add a 1-inch layer of soil. Water sufficiently to moisten the materials, but not to make them soggy. Keep repeating layers in this manner, whenever new material comes to hand, until the pile is 4 or 5 feet high; make a basin in the top to catch rainwater. If an alkaline compost is required, spread ground limestone on the pile in the same proportions as fertilizer.

Now you wait, because except in the most ideal of climates the compost pile will not decay well until the weather warms up the following spring. In the heat of summer, turn the pile with a fork to make certain that moisture reaches all parts of it. At the end of the first summer, the compost should be ready to use. And it will be time to start a new heap, for next year.

The necessities. You will almost certainly need to use commercial fertilizer, and you may well need to use lime as well, to make a proper environment in which your seeds or sets will thrive. Requirements of these differ widely, depending on the area—once more, follow the advice of an experienced gardener or your local nursery or seed house. Good drainage, plenty of organic matter in the soil, moderate amounts of commercial fertilizer, and lime if needed, will prepare your garden to meet the growth requirements of virtually any vegetable you plant.

SING THE SONG OF HARVEST HOME

After you have prepared and planted and fertilized and bugsprayed and cultivated and watered until you're blue in the face, cricked in the back, and fungused in the feet, all at once the big venture begins to pay off. The first of the crop is ready for picking, a heady moment indeed.

Here are some guidelines. For many of the vegetables you grow, the younger you pick them the tenderer and better they'll be. Young onions, lettuce, and radishes will make a salad your taste buds won't believe. Pull a mess of beets when the tops are gently green and the beets themselves the size of marbles; cook just until tender, and enjoy a dish that no bought-at-the-market vegetable can provide. Dig baby new potatoes, cook them in their jackets and serve with sour cream and coarsely ground pepper. Bring in little 2-inch carrots, wash—they don't need peeling or scraping—cook and serve them whole, either buttered or honey-glazed.

Pick summer squash—zucchini, yellow crookneck, little pattypans—when they are small and their skins are soft; a monster crookneck might get you somewhere at the state fair, but in the kitchen it's a disaster. On the other hand, winter squash—acorn, butternut, hubbard, and the like—need maturing time; don't pick until the rinds are hard and the side next to the ground turns creamy yellow.

Gather peas and beans by feel—beans before the inner beans start getting fat, peas not until there is something inside the pods, unless you yearn to try grandma's way of cooking pods and all. Wait for broccoli to head up, then catch it before it flowers and seeds; cut off 6 to 7 inches below the top, and new heads will form. Vine-ripened tomatoes have superb flavor; pick them when they are ripe but still firm. Gather brussels sprouts—picking from the base of the plants first—when the little heads have just turned firm. Gather eggplants as soon as they firm up, while the skin is glossy and bright in color. Parsnips aren't choosy; bring them in when they are well developed, or leave them in the ground, harvesting as you need them until early spring. Muskmelons signal their ripeness by developing a crack around the base of the fruit stem.

All leafy vegetables should be picked in the early morning, while the dew is still on them. Gather others as close to mealtime as possible, hurrying them from garden to cooking pot for the very best flavor. More than of any others, this is true of corn; if you have never eaten sweet corn picked only a few minutes before a very brief cooking, you really don't know what this vegetable is all about.

Whatever quantity you plant in your first garden may be regrettably too little, but it is more likely to be too much. So share. And calculate how much to plant in next year's garden by keeping a record of the amounts you harvest from this year's.

PROBLEM SOLVERS

In the garden, as elsewhere in this perverse world, that which can go wrong will do so. If you raise more lima beans than any normal family can eat, freeze, can, or give away during one season, that is your poor planning. So is a crop of weeds so lush it chokes out the vegetables. But there are some not-your-fault problems, and when you run into one of those, it's good to know to whom you can turn for help. Or you may have questions that local friends can't answer. Help is at hand for those, too.

A for-instance: You buy beet seeds from a reputable seedsman, and start them indoors. When you put out the sets you have a feeling that something is amiss, but this is your first gardening venture so you tell yourself to hang in and see what happens. What happens is carrots. Enter your state department of agriculture to the rescue. When you plant seeds, any seeds at all, save the package in which they came and a few of the seeds. The Federal Seed Act says that when in good faith you plant a beet and get a carrot, the seed company has to make good. Get in touch with your state D of A, and an agent will take over from there.

Indeed, your state agricultural experiment station can be a sturdy, dependable shoulder to lean on. Here is a list of all fifty states, along with the cities in which the stations are located. Your library or local telephone company will have a directory of each city in which you can look up the station's address and phone number. Those stations are there for you, the taxpayer. Don't hesitate to call on them for answers to your problems.

Alabama	Auburn	Mississippi	State College
Alaska	College	Missouri	Columbia
Arizona	Tucson	Montana	Bozeman
Arkansas	Fayetteville	Nebraska	Lincoln

California	Berkeley, Davis,	Nevada	Reno
	Los Angeles,	New Hampshire	Durham
	Riverside, Parlier	New Jersey	New Brunswick
Colorado	Fort Collins	New Mexico	Las Cruces
Connecticut	New Haven,	New York	Geneva, Ithaca
	Storrs	North Carolina	Raleigh
Delaware	Newark	North Dakota	Fargo
Florida	Gainesville	Ohio	Columbus,
Georgia	Athens, Tifton,		Wooster
	Experiment	Oklahoma	Stillwater
Hawaii	Honolulu	Oregon	Corvallis
Idaho	Moscow	Pennsylvania	University Park
Illinois	Urbana	Rhode Island	Kingston
Indiana	La Fayette	South Carolina	Clemson
Iowa	Ames	South Dakota	Brookings
Kansas	Manhattan	Tennessee	Knoxville
Kentucky	Lexington	Texas	College Station
Louisiana	Baton Rouge	Utah	Logan
Maine	Orono	Vermont	Burlington
Maryland	College Park	Virginia	Blacksburg
Massachusetts	Amherst	Washington	Pullman
Michigan	East Lansing	West Virginia	Morgantown
Minnesota	St. Paul	Wisconsin	Madison
	Wyoming	Laramie	

WAIT TILL NEXT YEAR

When you have made your first garden and have experienced the tremendous amount of work it can be, you will agree with Charles Dudley Warner that "what a man needs in gardening is a cast-iron back, with a hinge in it." But by the end of the season when you also know how much joy a garden can give, you'll agree too with Bronson Alcott that "who loves a garden still his Eden keeps."

Some autumn night, when there is a huge, bright moon with tatters of clouds skipping across its orange face, you'll walk out to take a last look at the frost-blackened garden. You'll remember the toad—no garden is complete without one—who lived down among the turnips, wonder where toads go in the winter, and promise yourself to look it up. You'll see rime on the bird bath and remember how pleased the birds were when you set it up for them in the heat of summer, especially the rose-breasted grosbeak who used to sit on the lowest branch of the apple tree and talk about the most important things in the world, such as a drink of cool water when you are thirsty. You'll remember the brazen rabbit who nightly shopped the rows, choosing just the right lettuce for his supper. And that will remind you of a hundred suppers with your family, all of them superior to those of past years, because some part of each came from this garden.

You'll shiver a little and go inside to sit by the fire. Will they come again, the toads, the birds, the rabbits? Will they take it for granted that you will be there, too? So you get a pencil and paper and begin planning next year's garden.

390

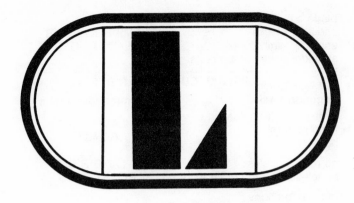

LABELS

Portion of the outside of a commercial food package that identifies the kind of food, the manufacturer or processor and his address, and offers information concerning the contents. See the special feature: A SHORT COURSE IN LABEL READING.

LACE COOKIES

Very thin cookies, so delicate that they have a lacy appearance. They may be very small, or baked as a circle 3 inches or so in diameter. In the latter case, they are usually shaped into cups (to hold ice cream or a mousselike mixture) over the bottom of a buttered tea cup, or into rolls (to serve plain or with a pastry-tube squirt of flavored and sweetened whipped cream) over the handle of a wooden spoon.

LACTOSE: see MILK

LADYFINGERS

Small, airy sponge cakes, roughly finger shaped (the lady in question must have been an amazon, however), plain vanilla-flavored ladyfingers are a perfect accompaniment for ice creams and ices, or for fruit desserts. For a less mild sweet, they can be sandwiched with buttercream of any flavor or with other fillings, such as lemon curd. They play a role in various refrigerator desserts that layer the little cakes alternately with a cream or custard filling and/or fruit, such as sliced strawberries or whole raspberries. Finally, they serve as the outer, stand-up rim that surrounds a charlotte russe and holds it together.

Ladyfingers may be made at home, a simple process. Batter can be baked in a special ladyfinger pan, or shaped with a pastry tube or even with two spoons on a cookie sheet. Or the little cakes may be purchased. Most bakeries and many supermarkets carry ladyfingers, the latter in packages of a dozen that, when split (as they often are in desserts), yield twenty-four pieces.

LAMB

Tender in all its cuts, delicately distinctive of flavor, versatile in its many uses, lamb deserves a place in the forefront of American meat dishes. A leg of lamb for Sunday dinner (serve it with tart mint or cumberland sauce, pan-browned potatoes, frenched green beans or new peas) leaves a bonus of leftovers for more good meals: perhaps a handsome Shepherd's Pie on Tuesday, stuffed eggplant on Thursday, and a hearty lamb-mushroom-barley soup with vegetables, made from the bone and scraps, to be frozen for a later meal.

Sound good? Unfortunately, if you're the average American, it probably doesn't. Or perhaps it does, but you have no idea how to approach such a selection of delights, and feel you can't learn. We don't, relatively speaking, eat much lamb in this country. And that's a pity. In a way, however, it's a comfort to those of us who do love lamb, because even the best cuts are seldom as expensive as beef, and the lesser cuts—large numbers of people don't know what to do with them—are often the best bargain in the meat department.

Mrs. Beeton, First Lady of household management (what a formidable woman she must have been, the sort who makes grown women weep and grown men feel like four-year-olds caught with their hands in the cookie jar), said of lamb that it is of all "wild or domesticated animals," without exception, the "most useful to man as food." That's the British point of view. There they extravagantly admire lamb and its older relative, mutton. So do the Irish—how can you make Irish stew without lamb? So do those excellent cooks, the French and the Italians. As for people of the Mediterranean and Middle East, lamb is their first meat choice, served in dozens of ways so savory that it makes one's mouth water just to think of them.

Back home, at the meat counter. If you're a lamb lover in the midst of a family of them, more power to you. If you're not, here's a challenge: before you go shopping next time, browse a good cookbook until you find a lamb dish that sounds good to you. Buy the lamb, prepare and serve the dish, and see if it doesn't meet with pleased acceptance, if not with loud huzzahs.

All cuts of lamb are easily cooked so that the meat is tender, juicy, and attractive. Lamb's tenderness comes about in part because the animal is young; it must be under a year old to be sold as lamb. After that it's mutton, a meat for which there is virtually no acceptance whatever in this country; consequently, most of those who raise lamb don't allow their animals to reach the mutton stage, although there is some small demand for the meat by gourmet restaurants. Lambs come to market about 60 pounds dressed weight. Generally the heaviest supply occurs in the autumn, but good lamb is available all year around. Some lamb is imported (frozen) from Australia and New Zealand.

Selection of lamb. Many Americans who do eat lamb

never venture beyond a leg to roast or loin or rib chops to broil, but there are many other possibilities.

shanks: Meaty and tender, these can be roasted, but are at their juicy, flavorful best when oven-braised with vegetables in a small amount of liquid.

chops: There are sirloin, loin, rib and blade and arm shoulder chops to choose among; all can be broiled, but like the shank, meaty shoulder chops are best braised. There are also boneless chops, from the inside shoulder muscle.

roasts: Leg of lamb can be purchased whole or, for smaller families, as the shank or butt half. There are also loin roasts, rib roasts (the elegant rack of lamb that many excellent restaurants feature), shoulder roasts, and boned shoulder (rolled, or with a pocket to accommodate a savory stuffing).

steaks: The sirloin steak—because lamb is so small an animal—is usually considered a chop. Leg steaks are cut from the center of the leg when it is divided into two roasts.

breast: The breast can be boned and rolled, or the breast bone removed to form a pocket for stuffing. Or the section may be cut into tasty lamb riblets.

and more: Ground lamb is available to serve as relief-from-beef patties, or to use in casseroles and for stuffing vegetables such as eggplant and peppers. Lamb stew meat, bone-in or boneless, is often cut from the neck and shoulders, but can come from any part of the carcass. And, of course, lamb supplies all the variety meats—brains, heart, kidneys, liver, sweetbreads, and tongue—for many kinds of good main dishes.

Calling it by its right name. As with beef, the meat industry's ICMISC—Industrywide Cooperative Meat Identification Standards Committee—has arrived at a master list of recommended names for lamb, in the hope that retailers will follow these guides and make purchasing of lamb easier for the consumer through universally precise and consistent labeling of the various cuts. (See BEEF for a more detailed discussion.)

PRIMAL CUT: LAMB SHOULDER

common name	recommended name
shoulder block shoulder roast square cut shoulder	LAMB SHOULDER SQUARE CUT WHOLE
boneless shoulder netted rolled shoulder roast	LAMB SHOULDER ROAST BNLS
boneless lamb shoulder lamb shoulder roast (ingredient listing required if stuffing other than ground lamb is included)	LAMB SHOULDER CUSHION ROAST BNLS
shoulder blocks shoulder roast	LAMB SHOULDER BLADE ROAST
blade cut chop shoulder blocks shoulder lamb chops shoulder blade lamb chops	LAMB SHOULDER BLADE CHOPS

PRIMAL CUT: LAMB RIB

common name	recommended name
lamb rib rack for roasting lamb rack roast hotel rack	LAMB RIB ROAST
rib roast boneless boneless rib lamb roast	LAMB RIB ROAST BNLS
rack lamb chops lamb rib chops fresh lamb rib chops rib lamb chops	LAMB RIB CHOPS
lamb crown roast	LAMB RIB CROWN ROAST
rib kabobs french chops french lamb chops	LAMB RIB FRENCHED CHOPS

PRIMAL CUT: LAMB LOIN (trimmed)

common name	recommended name
saddle roast full-trimmed loin roast lamb loin roast loin lamb roast	LAMB LOIN ROAST
lamb loin chops loin lamb chops	LAMB LOIN CHOPS
double chops english chops	LAMB LOIN DOUBLE CHOPS
english chops boneless double loin chops	LAMB LOIN DOUBLE CHOPS BNLS
rolled double loin roast double loin roast boneless	LAMB LOIN DOUBLE ROAST BNLS

PRIMAL CUT: LAMB LEG

common name	recommended name
leg, sirloin on leg-o-lamb leg of lamb—oven ready full-trimmed leg roast	LAMB LEG WHOLE
leg of lamb—boneless boneless lamb leg	LAMB LEG ROAST BONELESS
leg, sirloin off (tibia bone and sirloin section removed by cutting 3 or 4 chops)	LAMB LEG SHORT CUT SIRLOIN OFF

Lamb Chart

Retail Cuts of Lamb—Where They Come from and How to Cook Them

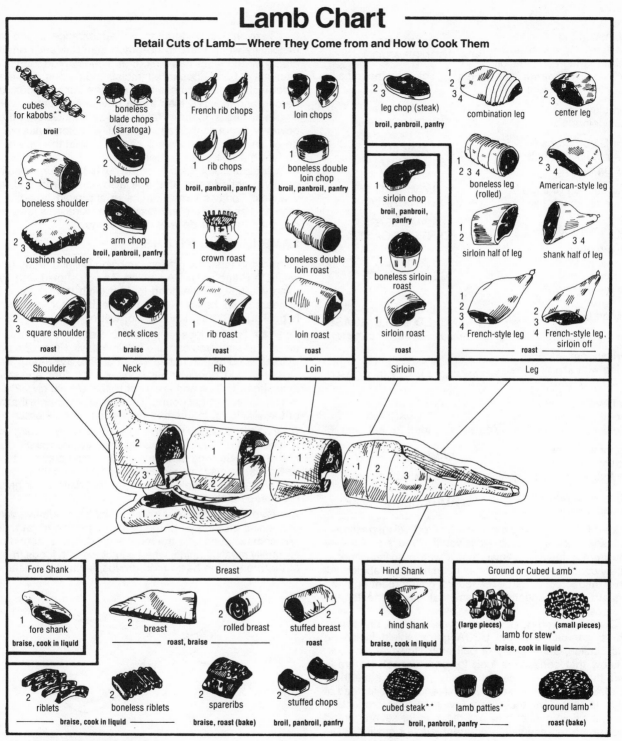

Shoulder

cubes for kabobs **
broil

2 boneless blade chops (saratoga)

2 3 boneless shoulder

blade chop

2 3 cushion shoulder

arm chop
broil, panbroil, panfry

2 3 square shoulder
roast

Neck

1 neck slices
braise

Rib

1 French rib chops

1 rib chops
broil, panbroil, panfry

1 crown roast

1 rib roast
roast

Loin

1 loin chops

1 boneless double loin chop
broil, panbroil, panfry

1 boneless double loin roast

1 loin roast
roast

Sirloin

2 3 leg chop (steak)
broil, panbroil, panfry

1 sirloin chop
broil, panbroil, panfry

1 boneless sirloin roast

1 sirloin roast
roast

Leg

1 2 3 4 combination leg

2 3 center leg

1 2 3 4 boneless leg (rolled)

2 3 4 American-style leg

1 2 sirloin half of leg

3 4 shank half of leg

1 2 3 4 French-style leg

2 3 4 French-style leg, sirloin off
roast

Fore Shank

1 fore shank
braise, cook in liquid

2 riblets

Breast

2 breast
roast, braise

2 rolled breast

2 stuffed breast
roast

2 boneless riblets

spareribs
braise, roast (bake)

2 stuffed chops
broil, panbroil, panfry

braise, cook in liquid

Hind Shank

4 hind shank
braise, cook in liquid

Ground or Cubed Lamb*

(large pieces)   (small pieces)
lamb for stew *
braise, cook in liquid

cubed steak **   lamb patties *
broil, panbroil, panfry

ground lamb *
roast (bake)

* Lamb for stew or grinding may be made from any cut.
** Kabobs or cube steaks may be made from any thick solid piece of boneless lamb.

combination leg 3-in-1 lamb leg combination 2-in-1 lamb leg combination	LAMB LEG COMBINATION
(2 to 3 sirloin chops cut from the full leg, sold with the remaining portion of the leg)	
sirloin lamb chops lamb sirloin steak	LAMB LEG SIRLOIN CHOPS
leg of lamb butt half leg-o-lamb sirloin half lamb leg butt half	LAMB LEG SIRLOIN HALF
shank half leg of lamb leg-o-lamb shank half	LAMB LEG SHANK HALF
lamb center roast	LAMB LEG CENTER ROAST
lamb leg chop lamb steak leg steak lamb steak—leg	LAMB LEG CENTER SLICE
frenched lamb leg	LAMB LEG FRENCHED STYLE ROAST
(shank bone exposed 2 inches, makes for easier carving)	
american leg (full leg with shank bone removed)	LAMB LEG AMERICAN STYLE ROAST
leg of lamb boneless for shish kebab	LAMB CUBES FOR KABOBS
(shoulder as well as leg yields suitable lean for kabobs)	
lamb stew lamb for stew	LAMB FOR STEW
(shoulder as well as leg yields suitable lean for stew)	
lamb cube steaks cube lamb steaks	LAMB CUBED STEAK

Marks of quality. The round mark of federal inspection—U.S. Inspected and Passed—tells you that the lamb you buy came from a healthy animal, that it was processed under sanitary conditions, and that it has been honestly labeled. All lamb is inspected either by the federal government or by an adequate state inspection system that meets the federal standards.

Quality grading is, as with all foods, optional, and not all lamb is stamped with the USDA grade shield indicating Prime, Choice, Good, Utility, or Cull lamb. However, as packers know that consumers look for and respect the grade shield, many that process high-quality meats do have them graded. Some packers use their own brand names instead of grades to represent the quality levels of their products—indeed, a single packer may sell meat under several brand names, each representing a different level of quality.

Take into consideration the appearance of the lamb, especially when there is no grade stamp. Meat from high-quality young lamb has pink, firm, fine-textured lean. Cross sections of bone appear red, moist, and porous. The lean of older high-quality lambs is light red; the bones appear drier, harder, and less red than those of younger lambs.

In all cases, external fat should be firm. Color of the fat, however, is not an indication of quality—color varies with the breed and age of the animal, as well as with the type of feed on which it has been fattened.

Regardless of the cut (or the cost), lamb furnishes high-quality protein in the diet; it is also rich in iron and the B vitamins. Today's lamb, thanks to improved breeding and feeding, has more protein, less fat, and furnishes fewer calories than that of a decade or more ago.

LAMB IN YOUR KITCHEN

Most of the federally graded lamb you will find in the market is USDA Prime or USDA Choice. As you should with everything you buy, take a good look at lamb to make certain it appears fresh, has a mild and agreeable odor, and that if it is packaged, the package is not wet or sticky.

how to buy: Unless you plan to freeze it, buy only the amount of lamb you can use within 3 days. From one pound of fresh lamb as purchased, count on 3 to 3½ 3-ounce servings of ground, boneless leg, boneless shoulder, and stewing lamb; bone-in legs and shoulder roasts should give 2½ to 3 3-ounce servings per pound. These figures assume that most of the visible fat is trimmed before the meat is eaten.

how to store: Store raw fresh lamb, loosely wrapped, in the coldest part of the refrigerator up to 5 days for roasts, chops, and steaks. Stewing lamb and ground lamb may be stored 1 or 2 days, as may lamb variety meats. Store cooked lamb in the refrigerator, closely covered, up to 3 days; store gravy or broth separately, 1 or 2 days.

nutritive value: There is some variation in nutritive values, depending on the age of the lamb, proportion of fat to lean, and somewhat on how the meat was cooked. A sound basis for family meal planning, when combined with foods from the other three of the basic food groups, lamb is the heart of a

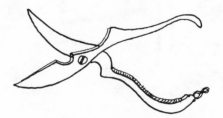

well-balanced menu. Considered in servings of 3 ounces of cooked lean meat, lamb furnishes between 230 and 240 calories, and:

protein	21.5 grams
fat	16.1 grams
calcium	9 milligrams
phosphorus	177 milligrams
iron	1.4 milligrams
sodium	53 milligrams
potassium	241 milligrams
thiamin	.13 milligram
riboflavin	.23 milligram
niacin	4.7 milligrams

Lamb has no carbohydrate, no vitamins A and C.

Tips on preparing, cooking. All lamb is sufficiently tender so that even the cuts usually braised are ready to eat in a much shorter time than, say, the less tender cuts of beef.

Wherever there is room for a difference of opinion, you can count on one to occur: there is considerable controversy among lovers of lamb as to whether the meat should be served rare, medium, or well done. There are fewer advocates of bloody-rare lamb than there are of beef in the same condition, but most knowing lamb eaters cook or order the meat "pink"—medium, that is. Cook leg, loin, and shoulder roasts rare in a 300 to 325°F. oven to an internal (meat thermometer) temperature of 140°; the meat is medium—the desirable pink—at 160°, and well done at 175°. If the roast is frozen it need not be thawed, but one-third to one-half again the roasting time will be required.

Like beef, lamb roasts will be juicier and more flavorful and will carve better if allowed to "rest" for 15 to 20 minutes after being removed from the oven. The parchmentlike fell, which covers the outer fat on lamb, should be left in place on roasts (it helps retain the juices) but removed from other cuts.

Lamb chops an inch or more thick can be broiled; those less than an inch are better panbroiled. This holds true for rib, loin, shoulder, sirloin, and leg chops—the last two often called steaks. These, too, can be served rare, medium, or well done, although shoulder chops—more often braised, though they can be broiled or panfried—are generally served well done.

Because it is both tender and juicy, lamb lends itself well to cookouts. Boned and rolled legs and shoulders are ideal for spit-roasting, while thick chops and ground-lamb patties cook beautifully on the grill. A butterflied leg—boned, but not rolled—grill-cooks in a brief time; baste with lemon butter or with a combination of oil, dry vermouth, and summer savory. Cubes of boneless leg or shoulder, marinated in garlic-flavored oil and lemon juice, make great kabobs. Skewer with mushroom caps, cherry tomatoes, and squares of green pepper, and cook on the grill (or under the broiler).

Freezing lamb. All cuts of fresh lamb freeze well; follow instructions in the special feature, PUTTING FOOD BY. Ground lamb may be stored at 0°F. or lower up to 4 months, other cuts up to 9 months.

Some perfect partners. Lamb and fruit go well together. A boneless lamb shoulder can be stuffed with a combination of rice, prunes, and dried apricots, and flavored with celery and onion, for a very superior dish indeed. If you prefer a bread stuffing for the shoulder or for a boned leg or breast, season it liberally with rosemary or marjoram.

A plain leg of lamb is a delightful dish, but if you take the time to make a number of shallow cuts and put into each one a sliver of garlic and a tiny piece of lemon peel, you will be amply rewarded; fresh young green peas are a perfect accompaniment. Serve braised shanks Greek style, with a dilled lemon (avgolemono) sauce; braised cucumbers are a deliciously unusual vegetable side dish.

Stuff eggplant or zucchini with a mixture of ground lamb and bread crumbs, with onion and celery in the thyme-seasoned stuffing. Or serve broiled eggplant with broiled lamb chops: season butter with garlic juice and spread on the eggplant slices as if you were buttering bread; broil until tender and browned on both sides, 5 to 7 minutes a side, depending on the thickness of the slices. Those who like sweet relishes with their meat opt for mint or currant jelly with lamb. Those who don't prefer a tart mint sauce. Or try this savory mixture: melt a 10-ounce glass of currant jelly over low heat; stir in 2 tablespoons vinegar, 1 teaspoon dijon-style mustard, and 1 teaspoon grated orange peel.

A crown roast of lamb is a handsome and succulent main dish for a company-coming meal. The butcher will prepare it for you by tying two or more racks of lamb (depending on how many you are going to serve) into a circular, crown shape. Stuff the center with a mixture of ground lamb, onion, brown rice, and pine nuts, or omit the onion and add chopped mint leaves and a little grated lemon peel. Pad the ends of the bones with small pieces of foil to prevent their charring in the oven. Before serving the roast, replace the foil with a preserved kumquat on each bone. For a truly memorable dinner, begin the meal with hot clam broth; surround the lamb with an edible garnish of broiled tomatoes and broiled mushroom caps, and serve hot herb/parmesan rolls and italian green beans; follow with a salad of young spinach leaves and ripe olives; complete the occasion with a cold lemon soufflé.

From the other side of the world. In many markets, frozen lamb from down-under—particularly from New Zealand—is available in the familiar cuts. Defrost in the refrigerator, allowing about 24 hours.

The New Zealand temperature is mild enough so that weaned lambs can graze outdoors in any season, busily converting the forage into high-quality protein. On the two main islands that make up New Zealand, there are in the neighborhood of three million people—but there are about a hundred million sheep and lambs. Since the seasons in the south temperate zone are the reverse of ours, this imported lamb comes to our markets at times when our own supplies are short. It is inspected and processed in modern plants, shipped to the United States in freezer ships to maintain high quality. See also GROUND MEATS, KID, and MUTTON.

LAMB'S WOOL

A favorite drink in Samuel Pepys' time—he mentions it, as what doesn't he, in his diary—lamb's wool is made by baking peeled and cored apples, combining the pulp with ale, sweetening the mixture to taste with sugar, and spicing it to taste with nutmeg and ginger. Just the thing on the kind of dank and foggy night when the cold seems to eat into your bones. Actually, it's very good indeed, and would be fine to serve (to adults, mind you) on Halloween, especially with fresh-from-the-kettle doughnuts.

LANCETTE: see PASTA

LAND JAEGER: see SAUSAGES

LANGUAGE OF FOOD

Those who pride themselves on calling a spade a spade must be sometimes discombobulated by the many names we have for the same food. It is not surprising—or, at least, it ought not to be—to find that a favorite food has another name in a foreign language. But in English, how does it happen that, for instance, round griddle-cooked breakfast breads can be flapjacks, hotcakes, griddle cakes, flannel cakes, pancakes, and more, including wheat cakes and simply "a stack, please"?

Besides the legitimate multiple nomenclature, there are slang terms to be coped with, as well—hen fruit and cackleberries, moo juice and slugamoo, slumgullion and bucket o' nuttin', rotgut and white lightning. Food language is further complicated by those whose sensitive natures prevent them from calling a spade a damned shovel, prompting them to refer to liver, kidneys, and the like as inmeats or lights, testicles as fries or mountain oysters, pigs' feet as trotters. It gives one pause.

Our kitchens have been infiltrated by a great number of foreign terms, the majority of them French words for which we never bothered to work up English equivalents: mousse, hors d'oeuvre, purée, soufflé, crepe, pâté, menu, café, canapé, consommé, bouillon, table d'hôte, carte du jour, and dozens more. Besides those, there is another set of cooking terms for which we do have English equivalents; however, the equivalents are used less often than the foreign terms, such as pâte à choux. Then there are terms that are a linguistic mishmash, such as pizza pie.

Sometimes foreign-language words creep into our kitchens in disguise, having been somehow transmogrified in the passage. Bacon, for example—a word from the Old French —meant pork, both fresh and cured. It crossed the channel to England, where it had the same meaning for many years, through the reign of Elizabeth I. Little by little it lost its other meanings until only what we now call bacon remained. Meanwhile, what we call bacon has become "lard" in French, and a strip—rasher—of bacon is a "tranche de lard."

We can hardly consider English a foreign language, but if you were suddenly dropped into a British kitchen the conversation might well surprise you. English English and American English can vary widely. If your hostess in that British kitchen asks you to hand her the treacle, pass the molasses. If she says there's gammon for dinner, that's ham. If she plans to serve vegetable marrow with it, she intends to have squash (but if, on the other hand, she mentions squash, she's talking about a soft drink). She may glaze the ham with made mustard and demerara—prepared mustard and dark brown sugar. (But castor sugar—granulated white—or loaf sugar— lump sugar—will be used to fill the sugar basin—sugar bowl.) For dessert, she might make a bramble shape—a molded blackberry pudding.

More: greased paper = wax paper, swedes = rutabagas, crisps = potato chips, chips = french fries, groundnuts = peanuts, courgettes = zucchini, endive = chicory, biscuits = cookies (corrupted from the Dutch *koekjes*), mince = hash, dried currants = raisins, corn = wheat, maize = corn, and there are dozens more.

If you assist your British hostess in her cooking, be careful not to be tripped up by differences in measurements:

English	American
1 teaspoon	1½ teaspoons
1 dessertspoon	1 tablespoon
1 tablespoon	2 tablespoons
1 teacup	½ cup + 2 tablespoons
1 breakfast cup	1¼ cups

Having worked your way through the problems of the recipe, you still have the regulo of the gas range to contend with. This is a dial, somewhat like the thermostat dial on our own gas ranges but with different markings. If the recipe directs you to bake a cake for 25 minutes at Mark 4, that's

350°F. To blaze a trail through a British cookbook for you, here are all the marks of the regulo:

mark	degrees F.
½	250
1	275
2	315
3	325
4	350
5	375
6	400
7	425
8	450
9	475
10	500
11	525
12	550

So, as you go about your appointed rounds in your own American kitchen today, making an English mince out of French reliefs (leftovers), give a thought to a wide world of kitchen-bound women who are likewise giving a thought to you, wondering why on earth you call the foods you cook by such outlandish names.

LARD

Rendered hogs' fat, lard makes up nearly one-sixth of the weight of hogs raised in this country, a matter of some three billion pounds. Contrary to widespread belief, lard is highly digestible—as much so as butter. It makes excellent pastries and hot breads, and can be used for deep-fat frying, although its smoking point is rather low. For some reason lard fell into disfavor with American cooks several decades ago, but it is making a comeback today.

Although it might seem that lard is lard, there are several distinct commercial varieties, differentiated by the type of fat used and the kind of rendering process employed:

- *kettle-rendered leaf lard:* Made from the leaf fat (internal abdominal hog fat, excluding that which clings to the intestines), rendered in a steam-jacketed open kettle; produces lard light in color, slightly grainy, firm textured; mild flavor; keeps well.
- *kettle-rendered lard:* Made from both leaf and back fat, rendered as above at a slightly higher temperature; somewhat darker in color than leaf lard, slightly grainy; pleasing flavor; keeps well.
- *prime steam lard:* Made from killing and cutting fats, rendered in direct contact with steam under pressure, then rapidly cooled; very smooth texture, almost white, somewhat stronger flavor than the above two and costs less; accounts for about 80 percent of lard used in this country; keeps satisfactorily.

- *hydrogenated lard:* A more recent development, this aerating of lard firms the consistency, changes the flavor somewhat, and considerably improves keeping qualities.

Rendering lard at home. Although a relatively small number of us, other than some who farm, slaughter and butcher hogs and so give ourselves occasion for rendering lard, the back-to-the-earth movement among young people has produced a new segment in our population. Many of these "natural life" advocates bring with them courage, goodwill, determination—and, unfortunately, not a great deal more to equip them for a way of living quite unlike the one they are used to. Because hogs are easier to raise and are more quickly brought to slaughtering condition than other farm animals, many of these young people buy a pig or two to rear for meat. For them, some advice.

a) Don't make friends with the pig you propose to eat. Consider it meat on the hoof, not a pet, or when its day of reckoning comes you (and especially children) won't be able to cope with the trauma of slaughtering and butchering.

b) If you have never slaughtered an animal, don't try it alone the first time. Get a knowledgeable local farmer to show you how and to help you, or take it to a plant to be slaughtered. The process requires skill, determination, and a strong stomach.

c) As long as you are committed to the project, don't let any of the carcass go to waste. Cure whatever of the meat you wish, can or freeze whatever remains that can't be eaten fresh within a few days (see special feature: PUTTING FOOD BY). Then render the lard for a winter's worth of cooking fat like this:

1. Remove the fat promptly, wash and chill at once.
2. Grind the fat or cut it into small pieces for easier handling.
3. Place a part of the fat in a large, heavy kettle; cook slowly, stirring gently. When that fat begins to melt, gradually add more. But do not fill the kettle—a boil-over can be very dangerous.
4. Continue to cook slowly, stirring frequently to prevent scorching. As water evaporates from the fat, the temperature will rise slowly; do not let it rise above 255°F. During the cooking, small brown bits—these are cracklings—will rise to the surface and float; when the rendering is almost complete, the cracklings will sink to the bottom of the kettle. Be very careful at this point that they do not stick to the bottom and burn.
5. Remove the lard from the heat and allow it to cool slightly. Dip carefully (a lard burn is both painful and dangerous) into 5- or 10-pound containers. Remove cracklings, press excess fat out of them, and refrigerate or freeze. Strain lard through triple-thickness

cheesecloth into containers in which it will remain. Chill, then freeze immediately—quick chilling produces a fine-grained lard.

6. Store tightly covered in a dark, cool place or, preferably, the freezer. If you wish, you can improve the storage time of the lard by adding an antioxidant (most locker plants sell it) or, if that is against your natural-living precepts, prolong storage life by adding 3 pounds of hydrogenated vegetable shortening to every 50 pounds of lard as it is cooling.

Lard can be freezer-stored up to 12 months. Remove small amounts to refrigerator storage up to 40 days for cooking use. Keep closely covered. Some commercial lards can be stored at room temperature—be guided by the label.

LARDING

This procedure accounts for the fact that pot roasts in France are so much better—more juicily succulent—than they are in this country. Inserting long strips of fat into meat across the grain is called larding, a ploy that almost immeasurably increases the flavor, tenderness, and juiciness of the meat.

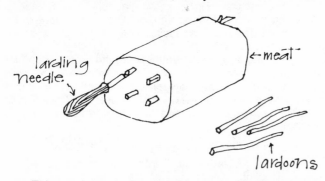

This requires a larding needle, obtainable at most hardware or housewares stores. It is a long metal device rather like a knitting needle, pointed at one end and with a gripper at the other to secure the lardoons—the long, thin strips of fat. Larding is not at all difficult to do, and once you've tried it, the improvement of the meat will be so great you'll kick yourself for not learning how long ago. Improve flavor even further by soaking the lardoons in brandy, then rolling them before using in a mixture of salt, pepper, finely chopped parsley, and a pinch of ground cloves.

LASAGNA

The word covers both the name for the noodle with which it is made and the dish itself. Lasagna noodles may be plain or ruffle-edged, are sometimes green—that is, colored and flavored with spinach juice. The dish is, at its simplest, layers of the noodles with meat-tomato sauce and ricotta and mozzarella cheeses, but it may also incorporate such goodies as sausages (Italian sweet or hot, or small smoked links) or meatballs. A glorious "white" lasagna layers a ricotta-spinach-egg mixture with the noodles and a sauce made with chicken broth and cream, along with chunks of chicken breast and flavorful tiny ground veal meatballs, with grated parmesan to top it all off. See also PASTA.

LEAF LETTUCE: see SALAD GREENS
AND PLANTS

LEAVENING AGENTS

Those things which make baked goods rise are leavening agents. Breads—loaves, rolls, sweet rolls, coffeecakes, and the like—are raised by yeast, an organism that grows through the action of liquid plus that of the gluten in flour. Quick breads—loaves, muffins, biscuits, scones, as well as griddle cakes and waffles and all their assorted relatives—are chemically leavened through the use of baking powder or baking soda, which produce gases in flour mixtures, causing them to rise. Air, beaten into egg whites, sometimes helped along by a small amount of cream of tartar (an ingredient in some baking powders), leavens certain foods, such as angel food and sponge cakes, and contributes to the leavening of a number of others that are in part chemically leavened.

Time changes leavening agents. The first baking powders put on the market years ago were "single-action," and recipes of a past era meant that ingredient when they called for baking powder. It has all but disappeared from the market by now, however. Here are some leavening updates.

single-action baking powder: Today's baking powder ("double-action") is not always reliable as a substitute in old recipes that call for the single-action kind. If you wish to try a recipe from an old-time cookbook, sift 2 tablespoons cream of tartar with 1 tablespoon each of baking soda and cornstarch. Use 1 teaspoon of the mixture for each teaspoon of single-action baking powder called for in the recipe.

double-action baking powder: This is available virtually everywhere, and is what is meant when a recipe in a modern cookbook calls for baking powder. Unless you do a great deal of baking, buy baking powder in small amounts; it keeps well, but will eventually lose its potency.

compressed yeast, in cakes: This product, too, disappeared from our markets some time ago, when active dry yeast became available. However, unlike single-action baking powder, yeast cakes have reappeared. Moist and easily crumbled, they come in .6- and 1-ounce sizes; use the .6-ounce size when the recipe calls for 1 cake of yeast, the 1-ounce when the recipe calls for 2 cakes. Also called "fresh" yeast, compressed yeast must be refrigerated and should be used within 2 weeks.

active dry yeast: This, yeast in granular form, comes in small sealed envelopes, each equal to a .6-ounce cake of compressed yeast. Recently, this product has also become available in 4-ounce jars for those who do a considerable amount of baking. Use 2¾ teaspoons for each envelope of active dry yeast or cake of fresh yeast called for in a recipe. Store in a cool, dry place until opened; after opening, cover tightly and refrigerate. Both envelopes and jars carry expiration dates—for good baking results, abide by those dates.

baking soda: This versatile product is also used as a leavening agent, but only in mixtures that have an acid ingredient —sour milk or cream, buttermilk, some fruit juices, molasses. Do not attempt to substitute it for baking powder, or disaster will ensue.

For more leavening information, see BAKING POWDER, BAKING SODA, BREADS, and YEAST.

LEEKS

When Caedwalla, King of Gwynedd (North Wales), sallied forth to meet Edwin, King of Northumbria, on the field of battle near Doncaster, he issued a ukase, to wit: each Welsh soldier must wear a leek fastened to his helmet so their leader could tell his men from the enemy. As all this happened in A.D. 633, not many details are available, but we do know that Edwin was slain, that Caedwalla and his men were victorious. To commemorate the victory, the leek was adopted as the national emblem of Wales, and remains so to this day. (The following year, Edwin's nephew, Oswald, avenged his uncle by killing Caedwalla, but that's another story, having nothing to do with leeks, the subject at hand.)

A member of the onion family—whose name is legion— the leek is grown for its thick stalk, which is always cooked before serving. Leeks have been called poor man's asparagus, and may be prepared in any of the ways used for that vegetable; they are, as well, an ingredient in several soups. Although they are grown, cooked, served, and loved all over Europe and the British Isles, they are not widely appreciated in this country and are, consequently, rather hard to come by and quite expensive compared to other kinds of ONIONS.

Preparing leeks for cooking. Cut off a portion of the green end so that about 5 inches remain; strip off the outside leaves and cut off the root end. Because the convolutions of leeks offer many hiding places for dirt and sand, they must be thoroughly washed, either under running water (turn them so that water runs into them) or in several changes of cold water.

Cooking leeks. To be served either hot or cold, leeks need only a relatively brief cooking time, 15 to 20 minutes. Cook in boiling salted water or braise in a small amount of chicken or beef stock or bouillon. Drain well and serve at once, or refrigerate to serve cold. Count on two to four leeks per serving, depending on their size.

Ways to serve. Hot leeks may be simply dressed with butter or lemon butter. Or braise the vegetable (on top of the stove or in the oven) in bouillon with a bay leaf and a little thyme, and serve with a sour-cream or a mushroom sauce, or with a liberal sprinkling of butter-browned bread crumbs. Or serve, as you might asparagus, with hollandaise sauce or a white sauce with hard-cooked eggs.

Leeks in soup. Flemish-style leek soup combines the vegetable with sorrel, chervil, and winter savory for flavoring, and with potatoes; the soup is cooked up to 3 hours, by which time the potatoes will have disintegrated into the water to form a thick, creamy mixture. French-style leek soup calls for cooking cut-up leeks slowly in hot butter, adding flour and hot milk; the whole business is puréed through a sieve, then cream is added and the soup reheated. Scotch-style leek soup, called Cock-a-leekie, cooks the leeks in chicken broth thickened with oatmeal. Welsh-style cooks cut-up leeks and an onion in butter, then adds them to partially cooked potatoes, and continues cooking until the potatoes are done; the mixture is sieved and then stirred into beaten egg yolks in a soup tureen, along with a small amount of heavy cream.

LEFTOVERS

You can learn a great deal about a woman's courage, moral fiber, and outlook on life by a close study of her attitude toward leftovers. Does she spurn them, scraping them hastily into the garbage pail and slapping the lid back on? (Wasteful, but honest.) Does she carefully transfer them to a plastic container, set the cover in place just so, and the next day take them out, look at them meditatively, then throw them away? (The road to hell is paved with good intentions.) Does she stuff them far back on a refrigerator shelf where, with luck, she won't find them again until they're too old to use? (Sneaky, and something of a coward.) Does she dump them into the refrigerator and then tomorrow dump them back on plates and call them dinner? (Aggressive, and lacking in imagination and sympathy.) Does she save and refrigerate them nicely and then, two days later, ask her family, "You don't want lima beans again, do you?" (No guts.) Does she always cook much too much of everything and then grimly store it, as grimly serve it again night after night until it's gone? (Filled with hostility, needs professional help.) Does she tend her leftovers well, freezing some for later use, serving the remainder in a new way after skipping a day on which she serves something entirely different? (A true kitchen gentlewoman, and a lovesome thing, God wot!)

Facing up to the challenge. Leftovers fall into two broad groups: a) planned on, such as a large piece of roast beef and its accompanying gravy, and b) accidental, such as a tablespoon of peas or a half cup of rice. With the a) group you must have had something in mind, so go ahead and do it. With the b) group you have two courses open to you: 1) toss it out and forget it, or 2) put it away for a purpose you determine before storing it, so that it will not go to waste.

planned-ons: When you knew all along that there would be half a chicken plus some gravy, or a tag end of corned beef, or a cupful of poached salmon, or some other substantial portion left after tonight's dinner, you have a planned-on leftover—or, as some coyly call it, a "planover." You had made up your mind in advance what other-meal purpose it was going to serve or, at the very least, you knew that it would make a contribution in one of several tasty forms. Perhaps you had a chicken pie planned, or chicken à la king to serve in frozen patty shells, plus a bonus of broth to be made from the rack and skin. You had counted on the corned beef for reuben sandwiches on Saturday, on the salmon for a pair of salmon timbales to serve yourself and the old friend you'd invited to lunch.

Planned-on roast beef leftovers can be turned into a crisply browned hash, with half as much potato as beef, liberally seasoned with onion and moistened with leftover gravy. Or a beef-mushroom pie with a flaky pastry topping. Roast lamb makes a graceful second appearance as a curry with apples and onions in the mixture and plain yogurt in the sauce, while the bones and scraps are freezer-hoarded as the basis of a hearty soup with plenty of vegetables and barley or vermicelli. Ham returns as a pineapple/mustard-glazed loaf, and the bone and scraps as the backbone of split pea soup. Tongue slices come back gelled in well-seasoned aspic, while the end piece—the schlung—flavors lentil soup excellently. Turkey reappears on toast points, with a mornay sauce.

There are hundreds of ways to go, so many that it generally pays to cook enough so that there will surely be leftovers for a second meal, sometimes a third. Extra-large amounts of many foods can be frozen, to put in their second-time-around appearance weeks or months later.

accidentals: These are the ones that, improvidently, we tend to consign to the dog's dinner or the garbage can. But virtually all are usable in one way or another—perhaps even those that you don't normally consider leftovers.

The cooking water of vegetables is an example. In the first place, vegetables should be cooked in as small as possible an amount of water. Nevertheless, there is always some left at the point where the recipe says, "drain and serve." That liquid has both flavor and nutrients to offer, so when you drain, don't do it down the sink. Instead, collect it to use as liquid in soup. Store, tightly covered, in the refrigerator up to 1 week or in the freezer up to 1 year, until you've accumulated enough to use. Meantime, you have—haven't you?—been collecting other soup materials, preferably in the freezer. Bones from roasts and chops. Small amounts of leftover meats, frozen separately in broth that can also go into the soup kettle. A stray mushroom or two. Rice. Vegetables in amounts too small to serve a second time. Even (undressed) salad greens.

Isn't there any way, other than in soup, to use up these dribs and drabs? Indeed. In casseroles. In those two excellent Chinese user-uppers, fried rice and egg foo yong. Scrambled with eggs for lunch or breakfast, depending on the nature of the leftover. Added to commercial soups for the children's lunch—and use vegetable cooking liquid in place of water to dilute the soup. Incorporated into stews and pot-pies and skillet dishes. Included in creamed, serve-on-toast dishes.

Freeze chicken and turkey livers and giblets until you've gathered enough for a meal. Cook poultry necks, wing tips, skin, and bones to make a rich chicken stock; refrigerate it, remove the fat that will rise to the surface, and freeze. You'll have it ready for soups and sauces, and also to use as a freezing medium for leftover poultry at some other time.

Breakfast takes on new meaning. There are often breakfast leftovers that can nicely serve another purpose. Freeze two muffins to accompany a salad some lunch time when you're alone. An extra rasher or two of cooked bacon can tastily garnish the vegetable or salad tonight or tomorrow. Cut leftover buttered toast in little squares and dry out in a 200°F. oven to use as a casserole topper or a salad ingredient, or to float in soup. Freeze waffles and pancakes to be oven- or toaster-heated another day. A spoonful of scrambled egg dressed up with finely chopped onion, celery, and green pepper makes an excellent sandwich filling. Refrigerate leftover cooked cereal; slice, dredge with flour, sauté to serve with butter and syrup for tomorrow's breakfast. Use leftover coffee in chocolate pie or pudding, in gelatin desserts, in lamb gravy.

Sweet set-asides. Baked apples and applesauce—other fruit sauces, too—freeze well and are especially useful in single-portion containers to pack in carried lunches. Slice sweet bread or boston brown bread thinly, sandwich with cream cheese, and freeze for lunch boxes. Ball or dice a leftover section of melon before it dies of old age, and freeze to add to fruit salads or cups; do the same with other ripe fruits before they start downhill. Freeze single slices of cake or packages of three or four cookies against the day when someone pines for a sweet snack.

A day in the life of a roast of pork. Suppose, one day as you browse the meat department, you spot a handsome fresh ham. It is love at first sight, and the per-pound price at which it's on sale makes it an excellent bargain. On the other hand, the darned thing weighs more than 13 pounds, and you are the home cook for a family of three. Dear Abby, what should you do?

Buy it. Right off, hand it back to the butcher and ask him to cut a 2-inch slice from the butt (big) end. When you get home, wrap the slice properly and stash it in the freezer to braise with apples and onions, serve with sauerkraut, for a later meal. At the same time, take out of the freezer the single layer of devil's food cake you cannily froze three weeks ago. Call up your sister and invite her and her husband to dinner. Put the pork on to roast. Cut the cake layer in two, fill and frost it, and set it aside. With the pork, plan on serving sautéed apple rings, mashed sweet potatoes with pork gravy, and panned cabbage; salad will be wedges of lettuce with roquefort dressing.

The dinner can't help but be a luscious success. But the kitchen is full of leftovers—now what? Cube some of the pork, enough for one meal, and freeze it to use later in pork curry or chop suey. Wrap the remains—which no longer look so formidable—in foil and refrigerate, along with the leftover cabbage and sweet potatoes. Tomorrow, stir a little orange juice and grated orange peel into the potatoes and reheat in the oven (topped with marshmallows, if you're really big on sweets); serve with braised shoulder lamb chops.

The following day, cook chopped onion, celery, and carrot; add to the pork gravy, which today you season with sage, along with cubes of the pork. Turn into a small casserole or large pie pan, top with mashed potato (from a package, if you wish), sprinkle with grated cheese and bake until heated through. Serve with scalloped leftover cabbage, which can go into the oven at the same time. Use the remaining pork to make a salad with celery, pecans, chopped raw apple, and white raisins; serve two nights later with mugs of hot tomato soup and hot biscuits—of either homemade or refrigerated dough. Meanwhile, put the bone on to cook in water with a sliced onion, two cut-up ribs of celery; season to taste with salt, pepper, and a little thyme. Simmer 2½ hours; remove the bone, scrape off any meat scraps and return them to the stock. Refrigerate, remove and discard fat that rises to the surface; freeze stock. Later, cook cut green beans, sliced carrots, and old-fashioned liver dumplings in it for a hearty whole-meal soup. You have now coped successfully with all those leftovers, have had three excellent dinners from the pork, and stowed the makings of two more plus stock for soup in the freezer, to say nothing of having paid back your sister and brother-in-law, to whom you owed a meal. It was, indeed, a bargain. And that's what's meant by planning.

LEMON PEEL

Grated, lemon peel (call it rind, if you prefer, or zest if you are a fancier of the just-right cooking term) is a delightful flavoring for a number of dishes, both sweet and savory. Candied, it has a place in fruitcakes, cookies, steamed puddings, and sweet breads. A twist is a proper garnish for a martini and other beverages, or for a cup of hot, dark espresso.

Grate lemon peel at home, or buy it ready-grated in small jars shelved with the spices at the supermarket. You can candy lemon peel at home if you like—a good cookbook will tell you how—or you can buy it, diced, in small cans or plastic tubs. See also HERBS AND SAVORY SEASONINGS.

LEMON SOLE: see FISH

LEMONADE

Legend has it that many years ago near Nishapur, Khurasan (the birthplace of Omar Khayyam), in the shadow of the Himalayas, a group of thirsty Arabs took a long, hard look at a lemon tree and invented lemonade. We've all been drinking it (with the possible exception of Omar who, if you recall, preferred a jug of wine) ever since. Paradise enow!

In hot weather, make lemonade with the juice of a big lemon, 1 to 3 tablespoons of sugar, and a cup of water. Mix well, pour over ice in a tall glass. If it's available, add a sprig of mint. Increase the amounts to make a pitcherful.

In cold weather, make lemonade the same way, but substitute honey for the sugar, hot water for the cold water and ice. Sip to soothe a sore throat, or simply to thaw you out. Mint is good in this hot version, too.

For an alcoholic cooler, add red wine half-and-half to the cold lemonade. Spike the hot lemonade with rum if you like.

When there's a thirsty crowd coming, or simply because you're a think-ahead kind of person, make lemonade base and store it in the refrigerator, ready to use in an instant refresher. This way: In a jar with a tight-fitting cover, combine 1 tablespoon grated lemon peel, 1½ cups sugar, and ½ cup boiling water; cover and shake until the sugar is dissolved. Add 1½ cups freshly squeezed lemon juice; cover tightly and refrigerate. To make lemonade, combine the base, ice, and water in a tall glass. Try ¼ cup of base to 1 cup of water plus plenty of ice, and adjust proportions if that is too strong or too weak to suit your taste.

LEMONS

The lemon tree, the song tells us, is good to look at and produces flowers of sweet aroma. "But the fruit of the poor lemon," it continues, "is impossible to eat."

Nothing could be farther from the truth. We use the fruit in dozens of ways in our kitchens, so often and so naturally that we do it without thinking. A wedge of lemon to squeeze into a comforting cup of hot tea. A little lemon to keep mushrooms and artichokes from darkening as they cook. Lemon replacing vinegar in mayonnaise or salad dressing for fish or fruit salads. Lemon butter for vegetables or seafood. Lemon filling for a layer cake. Lemon in beverages of all sorts. A squirt of juice to dress salad greens for waistline-watchers. Lemon sauce for puddings, for baked apples and apple dumplings. The juice to add flavor and retard darkening in fresh peach, apple, and avocado dishes. As a seasoning, replacing salt for low-salt dieters.

And, of course, there's lemon pie, refreshingly tart-sweet, handsome with it's mile-high meringue—second only to apple pie as America's favorite.

True, the fruit is impossible to eat in the way that we eat apples or bananas or pears or grapefruit. We once knew a small burro, Adelita—named after a camp follower of Pancho Villa—who relished whole lemons. She chomped away at them as horses will on apples, savoring every morsel, her velvety lips puckered from the tartness. Finished, she would kick up her little heels, gallop once around her corral, and come back to beg for another lemon, please. Adelita, however, was the exception. Most of us don't eat lemons whole. But we do use them, juice or peel, to make or to improve the flavor and the appearance of dozens of foods of every description from the beginning of the meal to the end of it.

The ubiquitous lemon. Nobody seems to be quite sure where the lemon was first used, who brought the fruit in from the wilds and planted the first lemon groves. We do know, however, that before those groves were planted lemon trees grew freely in India and Burma, perhaps as a mutation of the citron or the result of cross-breeding between the citron and the lime. The fruit was growing in Palestine when the Crusaders went there in the twelfth century, and they brought seeds back to Europe. At roughly the same time, Arabs carried lemons to Spain.

We are indebted to the Spanish explorers for introducing lemons to this country, as we are indebted to them for so many things. The fruit came to Hispaniola—Haiti today—with Columbus on his second voyage, one of his men having picked up some seedlings in the Canary Islands when the flotilla called there en route to the New World. Twenty years or so after that, later explorers carried the seeds to Florida.

Fr. Junipero Serra planted California's first lemons—and other fruits, including olives—near San Diego when he came north from Mexico in 1769 to establish missions. (What an indomitable little man that Franciscan must have been, stumping through the California desert wilderness on his game leg, sowing crops for the body on the one hand and for the soul on the other, founding churches and schools, teaching the Indians how to plant and harvest and read and write and serve the white man's God, then moving north to do it all over again and yet again, some dozen times.)

Florida led the country in lemon production until the big freeze of 1895 destroyed the state's citrus crop. At that point, California took over as chief producer. During the gold rush of 1849, lemons—as a preventative of scurvy—sold at one dollar each in the area of Sutter's Mill.

Today, the combined production of California and Arizona is greater than that of Italy and Spain, where Europe's large lemon crop is grown. Varieties cultivated in the United States are the eureka, lisbon, genoa, sicily, belair, and villafranca. Commercial production aside, one of the pleasures of living in California is being able to go out and pick lemons—and oranges and limes and grapefruit—from your backyard tree. A bonus of that happy arrangement is the heavenly fragrance of the citrus trees in bloom. There are even single trees that produce all kinds of citrus fruits at once.

LEMONS IN YOUR KITCHEN

Quality lemons—as is true of most fruit—are heavy for their size. The skin is richly yellow; paler or green-tinged fruit is very young and will be slightly higher in acidity. Very coarse or rough texture means that the skin is thick and, consequently, that the lemon will not yield as much juice as a thinner-skinned variety. Lemons should be firm to the touch.

how to buy: Avoid dark color and dryness—a fresh lemon has a sprightly look and its skin a lemon-oil gloss. Old lemons turn hard, or their skins shrivel. And, of course, pass by any fruit with soft spots, mold on the surface, or punctures in the skin—all signs of decay.

Unless you buy in quantity from a producer, lemons are generally sold by the piece in markets, at a per-lemon price.

how to store: Although they will keep up to 2 weeks at room temperature, the refrigerator crisper is the place to store them; they will last up to 6 weeks there, even longer if you put them in perforated plastic bags. Close cut pieces of leftover lemon in a tightly sealed plastic bag; use within 1 week.

nutritive value: Feel free to use lemon juice as you like, even on a weight-loss diet—a whole cup has only about 60 calories. A 1-cup measure of the juice furnishes:

protein	1.2	grams
fat	.5	gram
carbohydrate	19.5	grams
calcium	17	milligrams
phosphorus	24	milligrams
iron	.5	milligram
sodium	2	milligrams
potassium	344	milligrams
thiamin	.07	milligram
riboflavin	.02	milligram
niacin	.2	milligram
ascorbic acid	112	milligrams
vitamin A	50	international units

Freezing lemons. Don't freeze whole lemons. They don't freeze well and, even if they did, it would be a waste of freezer space, because lemons are available fresh all year around. However, if someone (or your backyard tree) has presented you with a large supply, squeeze them and freeze the juice in tightly closed containers. Grate the peel and freeze that, too, in small portions in tightly closed plastic containers or freezer bags.

Other ways, other forms. There is lemon all over the market, in many forms, to use as you wish.

in the produce section: Fresh lemons, of course; also bright yellow plastic lemons filled with fresh-squeezed juice, and bottled fresh juice.

on grocery shelves, in jars or bottles: Lemon juice, to

use as you would the fresh-squeezed variety. Store at room temperature until opened, in the refrigerator after opening. Also, pure lemon extract. And, in jars, lemon curd (a British specialty), a sharply lemon-flavored custard—use it as a filling in cakes, cookies, tarts—and lemon marmalade.

on grocery shelves, in packages: Lemon pie filling mix—add eggs and sugar, cook and use following label directions. Lemon instant pudding mix, too.

in grocery frozen-food section: Fresh-frozen lemon juice—use as you would fresh lemon juice; thaw and store in the refrigerator. Lemonade mix, sweetened—add water, following the label. If you (or your children) prefer, there's pink lemonade mix, too. Lemon pies, ready to thaw and serve.

A baker's dozen of lemon-use ideas. Any good, reliable cookbook should be able to supply you with dozens of lemon-use recipes. You will find, for example, ways to make several kinds of lemon pie—lemon meringue, lemon sour cream, lemon chiffon, French bake-in-the-crust lemon pie, lemon cheese pie in a gingersnap crust, the English two-crust variety filled with paper-thin lemon slices, and more. Lemon ice, too, and sherbet and ice cream. Lemon pound cake, the from-scratch way or made with cake and instant pudding mixes. Several kinds of lemon cookies. A beautiful, easy-make cold lemon soufflé.

But lemon isn't confined to desserts. Search out recipes for lemon-spiked sauces, main dishes, salad dressings. And try these lemon quick-trick ideas to get you started:

- sauté very thin veal (or chicken or turkey) cutlets briefly in butter, remove to a hot platter and keep warm; in the same pan, lightly brown an additional 2 tablespoons butter; add 2 tablespoons lemon juice and stir to incorporate browned bits; add 1 tablespoon drained capers; pour over cutlets
- freeze small strips of lemon peel in ice cubes to add flavor and glamour to beverages
- to juice half a lemon, stick a fork into it and twist—no reamer to wash
- if the recipe calls for sour milk or buttermilk and you have none on hand, place 1 tablespoon lemon juice in a measuring cup, add milk to the 1-cup measurement; let stand 5 minutes.
- for a few drops of lemon juice, roll a lemon until it's pliable, stick a food pick into it; remove pick, squeeze out juice; replace pick as a stopper and refrigerate the lemon until you need it again

- cut 3 skinned and boned chicken breasts into julienne strips; melt butter in a skillet, add chicken and sprinkle with flour, salt, and tarragon; sauté 5 minutes, stirring constantly; dissolve 1 chicken bouillon cube in 1 cup boiling water, add to chicken; add 1 thinly sliced lemon; cover, reduce heat, and simmer 5 minutes
- bring 3 cups chicken broth to a boil; add ¼ cup instant rice, cover and let stand 5 minutes off heat; bring again to a boil; slowly add, while stirring, 2 eggs beaten with 2 tablespoons lemon juice—almost-instant Greek avgolemono soup
- in blender container, place 3 egg yolks, 2 tablespoons lemon juice, dash of cayenne; turn blender on and off, just to combine; melt ¼ pound butter until it begins to foam; turn blender on high and add butter very slowly—quick, never-fail hollandaise
- combine grated peel of 2 lemons with ¾ cup superfine granulated sugar—use to sweeten iced tea, sprinkle over fruit, french toast, hot cooked cereal
- halve lemons lengthwise or crosswise and scrape shells clean; use as cups to hold individual servings of horseradish cream sauce, mayonnaise, relish
- in a saucepan, combine 1 tablespoon cornstarch, ½ cup sugar, 1 cup cold water; cook, stirring, until mixture bubbles; stir in 2 tablespoons lemon juice, 1 teaspoon grated lemon peel, 1 tablespoon butter—serve hot over cottage pudding or gingerbread
- mash one 3-ounce package cream cheese with 2 tablespoons grated lemon peel—use to stuff dates and prunes for salad or snacks
- in a saucepan, combine 1 tablespoon sugar, 2 tablespoons cornstarch, ½ cup lemon juice, 3 whole cloves, with liquid drained from 1-pound can of beets; cook, stirring, until mixture boils; remove cloves, stir in ⅛ teaspoon salt, 1 tablespoon butter, 2 teaspoons grated lemon peel; add beets, cook until heated through—serve hot, or omit butter and serve cold

Gizmo department. There are, on the market, several gadgets to help you cope with lemons—other citrus fruits as well—in your kitchen. Some are very useful. Some are rather silly, as gadgets often can be, but if you're a gizmo freak you'll love 'em all.

1) *citrus peeler:* made of plastic (lemon yellow or orange orange), it doesn't look as if it would peel anything, but it zips off citrus skins cleanly in no time flat
2) *zester:* metal object with a wooden or plastic handle and four holes at the business end; again, it doesn't look as if it would do a thing, but scrape it firmly down the side of a lemon and you'll get lovely fine shreds of the peel, with no membrane attached

3) *small-amount juicer:* this one looks as if it would work like the proverbial charm; it works, but not all that well —clear plastic gadget in hollow tube shape, with teeth at one end, a strainer and cover at the other; shove the toothed end into a lemon and squeeze, out comes strained lemon juice; leave gadget in place, snap cover shut, and refrigerate till next time

4) *citrus grater:* small grater with very sharp teeth, made of porcelain (a very pretty kitchen hang-up) or stainless metal; actually it's not absolutely necessary to have a separate grater for citrus if you remember to wash a regular grater very well after you've used it for onion or other strong flavors

5) *stripper:* as opposed to the peeler that gets the skin off citrus fruit so you can discard it, this metal knifelike gadget with a narrow opening in the blade peels off strips of peel of the kind to use as twists for drinks

Waste-not/want-not note. You've done everything you possibly can with a lemon. You've grated its peel to use in salad dressing. You've juiced it, and used part in veal piccata, part as a rinse for your freshly washed hair, and a little to bleach a stain out of your white linen blouse. You've helped your six-year-old plant the seeds for show-and-tell at school. You've rubbed the pulp on your hands to take away the odor of the garlic clove you just peeled. You dipped half the peel in salt, to polish your copper-bottom saucepan. Now what? Now you toss the remains in the garbage disposal, where it will keep that monster fresh and sweet-smelling. Farewell, good and faithful servant!

LENTILS

These are small annual legumes (plants that produce their fruit in pods) whose origins are lost in antiquity. Many authorities believe that the "mess of pottage" for which Esau sold his birthright was a dish of lentils, perhaps stewed with meat —probably lamb—and herbs. That transaction seems to fall under the head of carrying gourmandizing too far, but indeed a lentil dish is worth considerable as a hearty, flavorful, hunger-stemming food.

Although not used extensively in this country, lentils are a dietary staple in many places in Asia, the Middle East, North Africa, and those parts of Europe close to or bordering on the Mediterranean.

The chief contribution of lentils to the diet is vegetable protein, although they do furnish some B vitamins and iron. With the addition of a small amount of high-quality protein from meat or dairy products, their contribution to the nutritionally balanced diet is rounded out—drink milk with a meal in which lentils substitute for animal protein, or serve a creamed lentil-tomato soup, which will furnish some vitamin C for good measure. As for food energy, a cup of cooked lentils contributes about 105 calories.

Lentils need not be soaked before cooking, and they cook in a shorter time than their relatives, dried peas and beans. Most lentils to be found in our markets (in packages or bags) are brown in color, but the family has members that range from pale beige through a lovely salmon shade.

If you have never experimented with lentils, make a flavorful soup to try on the family. Add onion, a cut-up carrot, and a cut-up rib of celery, as well as a few sprigs of parsley for flavor, and base the mixture on a leftover ham bone, or a pair of ham hocks. If you prefer a thick, smooth soup, purée in a blender or press the lentil mixture through a sieve.

LETTUCE: see SALAD GREENS AND PLANTS

LICORICE

Used to flavor medicines, tobacco, cigars and cigarettes, soft drinks and alcoholic ones, as well as candy and chewing gum, licorice is an herb related to peas. It is raised commercially in Spain and Italy, and grows wild in some parts of both Europe and Asia. The dried root is the part used for flavoring, a love-it-or-hate-it taste. If you enjoyed licorice candy—blissfully gummy and tooth-staining—as a child you probably enjoy it today, but if your memory of the flavor is connected with childhood medicines, licorice-flavored sweets are more likely to turn you off.

LIEDERKRANZ: see CHEESE

LIGHT CREAM: see CREAM

LIMA BEAN FLOUR: see FLOUR

LIMA BEANS: see BEANS

LIMBURGER: see CHEESE

LIMES

Much that was said about lemons a little while back holds true for limes. Like lemons, limes are a flavoring/garnishing fruit, rather than one to eat out of hand.

Roughly the same shape as lemons, limes are smaller. The peel is thin and green, as is the flesh; a cut-open lime sends up one of the loveliest odors nature has to offer. The pulp is very juicy and eye-wateringly acid, but when the sharp acidity is overcome with sweetening, the fruit has delicious flavor.

The lime tree is sensitive to cold, so it can be grown only in tropical and subtropical climates. It grew wild for centuries in Asia, was brought back and domesticated by those peripatetic Spanish explorers, without whom all of us would probably be huddled today in some dank cave, tearing the flesh off a dinosaur bone with our teeth, and quarreling over whose right it was to sit nearest the fire.

The American supply of limes is raised in California, Florida, and Mexico. Most of these are the large, dark green variety called Persian. A smaller, paler, rounder kind, the Key lime, grows only in the Florida Keys, the long skein of islands extending from that state's southernmost tip. From these that excellent dessert, Key Lime Pie, is made, with a cornstarch-thickened filling flavored with lime juice and grated peel, topped with a delicately browned meringue. Somewhat different and equally luscious if not even more so, is Florida Lime Pie, an egg-sugar-heavy cream custard, again flavored with lime juice and grated peel; in this the crust is made of graham cracker crumbs, the topping is whipped cream decorated with grated lime peel. Although the limes themselves are deliciously green, the juice is rather pale; often recipes for dishes made with lime juice call for a few drops of green food coloring.

Choosing and using limes. Like lemons, limes are sold by the piece; buy them at a per-lime price—unless, of course, you have a sturdy, shrublike little lime tree in your backyard. (If you do, it will put out flowers of exquisite aroma to turn into chubby limes for you to pick at your leisure.) In the market, fresh limes are generally available from June to December. Choose firm ones, heavy for their size; store as you would lemons. Limes are slightly more perishable than lemons. Rich in vitamin C, lime juice is low in calories.

Other ways. Both sweetened and unsweetened lime juice are available, processed to be cupboard-stored until opened, refrigerator-stored after opening. There is also a lime-flavored gelatin dessert. Frozen concentrated lime juice, limeade, and lime-lemonade can be found in your market's frozen-food section, as well as a lime mix for daiquiri cocktails. Bottled fresh lime juice can be found in some produce departments.

Using limes in cooking and serving. A good cookbook will offer a number of delightful recipes using lime juice and peel—main dishes, salads, and desserts.

Meanwhile, here are some lime quick-tricks to try:

- peel and pit peaches, brush with lime juice for flavor and to prevent darkening; form cream cheese in small balls, roll in grated lime peel; put one ball in the pit-cavity of each peach half; serve as a salad, on lettuce leaves
- don't let honeydew melon go to the table without wedges of lime to squeeze over the fruit
- combine lime juice and honey in equal amounts; use as a dressing for fruit salad

- marinate halved, skinned, boned chicken breasts in lime juice seasoned with salt and a little cardamom for 2 hours; drain, reserving marinade; brush each chicken piece all over with cooking oil; place in a skillet, pour reserved marinade over; cover tightly and simmer until chicken is tender, about 45 minutes
- combine ½ cup superfine sugar with 1 tablespoon grated lime peel; sprinkle over fresh raspberries, blueberries, or strawberries
- in a saucepan, combine 2 slightly beaten eggs, 2 tablespoons cornstarch, ¾ cup sugar, ⅛ teaspoon salt, ⅓ cup each lime juice and water; cook, stirring, over low heat until mixture bubbles and thickens; stir in ⅓ cup dairy sour cream, 1 tablespoon grated lime peel —use as a sauce for any kind of fresh fruit or for pound cake
- into one 8-ounce tub whipped cream cheese, softened, fold 1 teaspoon grated lime peel, 2 teaspoons lime juice, and 2 tablespoons chopped candied ginger —serve on spice cake squares, or as a filling for thin-sliced orange-nut bread sandwiches
- in a blender container, place ½ cup fresh lime juice, ¾ cup fresh orange juice, ⅓ cup sugar, and 4 egg whites; process until very frothy; divide among 4 tall glasses, add ice, fill with club soda
- gin and tonic, refreshing warm-weather drink, isn't quite right without a wedge of lime to squeeze and drop into the glass

Since the days when British ships carried limes to prevent scurvy—that's why, to this day, British sailors are called "limeys"—the little green fruit has had a firm, if somewhat limited place in our kitchens. Its exquisite flavor should prompt us to make wider use of the lime, experiment with new ways to enjoy it and to enrich our family's diet with its generous amounts of vitamin C—one medium lime supplies over one-half of the U.S. RDA for ascorbic acid.

LIMESTONE LETTUCE: see SALAD GREENS AND PLANTS

LIMPA

This delicious rye bread, often shaped into a pudgy round loaf, is a Scandinavian specialty. Molasses sweetens it, grated orange peel contributes to its very special flavor.

LINE, TO: see page 447

LINGONBERRIES

Smaller European cousins of our cranberries, lingonberries are used in much the same way, made into a sauce or relish. The Scandinavian countries are particularly fond of lingonberries and make inventive use of them in a number of dishes. For example, Swedish plättar—small, thin, delicate pancakes—served with lingonberry preserve and sour cream make a memorable eating experience.

Lingonberries are not available fresh in markets in this country. Some few Scandinavian specialty food shops import the berries and make their own sauce or preserve; the imported preserve can also be found in jars in gourmet food shops.

LINGUINE: see PASTA

LIQUEURS

This is one of Alice's portmanteau words, covering a multitude of liquid delights including cordials, fruit-flavored brandies, and some esoteric concoctions whose formulae are among the world's best-kept secrets. All liqueurs are alcoholic, some mildly so, some having considerable of what grandpa liked to describe as "a kick." To determine the alcoholic content of an individual liqueur, examine the label for the "proof" of the product. That number represents exactly twice the percentage of alcohol by volume. That is, a 90-proof whiskey contains 45 percent alcohol, a 100-proof whiskey 50 percent alcohol. Most liqueurs (and wines, as well) are much lower in alcoholic content than are distilled spirits. A proof of 54—27 percent alcohol—is a reasonable example of liqueur proof, although some go considerably higher: green Chartreuse is 110 proof (55 percent alcohol) and yellow Chartreuse is 86 proof.

The sorcerer's solace, the monk's medication. Many of the liqueurs we know today had their origins in alchemists' laboratories or in monasteries and convents, fabricated not for enjoyment but as cures (or, at least, ameliorations) for the myriad ills the flesh is heir to. Other liqueurs were homemade curealls, known as ratafias, cordials, or digestifs, distilled downcellar by righteous ladies whose motto was: "Lips that touch liquor shall never touch mine." Comforted by the Bible's exhortation to "take a little wine for thy stomach's sake," rabidly prohibitionist housewives and those whose religion forbade alcoholic beverages nevertheless fermented and distilled concoctions of whatever suitable came to hand, and doled them out to family, friends, and neighbors when they fell ill. In some cases the cure was worse than the disease, but in most the result was delicious as well as stimulating. Many an Uncle Joe spent the winter fighting off chronic bronchitis ("Beats me why this danged cough hangs on so long!") with the help of many an Aunt Essie's famous cowslip cordial.

Updating the liqueur situation. The best way to appreciate the wide variety of liqueurs available is to look over the shelves devoted to them in a well-stocked liquor store. The number of kinds is staggering. So is the number of colors—many are clear, but there are also bright yellows, pale and dark greens, murky browns, purples, even blues. And lately some milky beverages (strawberry-milky, chocolate-milky,

and more) have been added that don't really fall into the liqueur category except that nobody seems to know what else to call a sweet, low-alcohol concoction that certainly isn't a wine.

A liqueur's chief function is to serve as a postprandial drink, generally with coffee, after—or in place of—dessert. (A number of restaurants have begun the pleasant custom of listing several sweet liqueurs with their desserts.) There are other uses as well for these richly flavored beverages. Chief among them is as sauces for ice creams and ices, or for simple cakes and puddings. A plain sponge or pound cake, pricked all over with a skewer or a long-tined fork, laved with liqueur—chocolate, coffee, or fruit—allowed to stand for a time, and then served as is or with a fluff of unsweetened whipped cream results in a dessert that is such stuff as dreams are made on. Liqueurs are also used as flavorings for various kinds of sweets, such as bavarian creams, chiffon pies, and the like. Some few—the less-sweet ones—have a place in nondessert dishes. And many are components of various mixed drinks, adding mellowing smoothness as well as distinctive flavor.

"What's that you're drinking?" It's not always possible to give a clear answer to that question, other than the name that's on the bottle. When we drink whiskey, we know it's made from grain; rum starts with sugarcane; wine comes from grapes. But liqueurs? Who knows! Many are manufactured from age-old secret recipes, closely guarded over the years. Even many of those whose names seem to give a straightforward indication of the bottle's contents are the results of intricate choosing and blending. One brand of blackberry brandy, for example, is made of seven different kinds of blackberries, with the addition of a few raspberries and loganberries to smooth and soften their flavor.

If not to the ingredients in all cases, the label will at least give some clues about the nature of the bottle's contents. Fruit-flavored brandies—which must be made with brandy; other liqueurs can be based on any spirit—are generally less sweet than others, and often higher in proof. These also allow you to make a reasonably accurate guess as to the taste. Liqueurs with the word "crème" in their names are likely to be mellow, smooth, and full-bodied; sometimes the names here, as well, give a good indication of flavor. Beyond those points, you're on your own—in many cases only the maker knows what's in the bottle, and he's not about to reveal the secret.

Some liqueurs are cloyingly sweet; some taste, to the

uneducated palate at least, rather more like cough medicine than anything else. But most are meltingly delectable.

Here are some of the most widely distributed—and widely enjoyed—of the many liqueurs available. Most range from 30 to 60 percent alcohol by volume; those outside those limits are noted.

liqueur	characteristics
Abricots, Crème d'	apricot liqueur, sweet and rich
Absinthe	now illegal in most countries; the original was 136 proof, anise flavored, and made with wormwood, a poison; there are several safer products on the market that resemble absinthe
Advocaat	Dutch; egg yolks, sugar, and spirits—rather like an eggnog; 40 proof
Almond, Crème d'	pink in color, almondlike in flavor; made with almonds and several kinds of fruit pits
Amaretto	flavor reminiscent of almonds; made of apricot pits
Anesone	flavored like anisette, but less sweet; may be as much as 100 proof
Anisette	flavored with anise, tasting somewhat like licorice; generally clear, but some are colored red
Apry	another apricot liqueur
B & B	Benedictine and brandy—the latter cutting somewhat the heavy sweetness of the former
Bananes, Crème de	quite sweet banana liqueur, generally reproducing the fruit flavor faithfully
Benedictine	based on cognac, made of a secret-formula combination of sugar, various herbs, and roots by Benedictine monks since the early part of the sixteenth century; D.O.M. on the label stands for Deo, Optimo, Maximo—"to God, the best, the greatest"—motto of the Benedictine order
Blackberry	available as a liqueur and as blackberry brandy, which is considerably less sweet than the liqueur; to confuse matters, there is also a totally nonsweet blackberry brandy that is not a liqueur at all
Brazilia	coffee-flavored Brazilian liqueur
C & C	Curaçao and cognac—which somewhat ameliorates the sweetness
Cacao, Crème de	vanilla-tinged chocolate flavor; sweet, and a chocoholic's delight; comes both clear—called white—and brown; with a float of cream on top it makes a lovely dessert substitute
Cacao Mit Nuss	reproduces (with added zing) the good candy and dessert flavor combination of chocolate with filberts
Café, Crème de	coffee liqueur; also good topped with a float of cream
Caramello	a late-comer to the ranks; could drive to drink anyone who loves caramels or caramel-flavored desserts
Cassis, Crème de	low-proof deep red liqueur made from French black currants; Cassis added to white wine results in kir, a mild and delicious aperitif
Cerise, Crème de	cherry liqueur of French origin
Chartreuse	made by monks of the Carthusian order since the beginning of the seventeenth century; the green is 110 proof, the yellow 86 proof; green chartreuse, considered by many the best of all liqueurs, is flavored with 130 herbs
Cheri-Suisse	the chocolate-plus-cherry flavor you get when you bite into a chocolate-covered cherry candy
Cherry	there are several cherry liqueurs and several cherry brandies; made of cherries and their pits, the flavor is pleasantly not-too-sweet
Chocla Menthe	American made, combining crème de menthe with chocolate
Chococo	combination of chocolate and coconut, for all the world like a candy bar with spirits spilled on it
Chokalu	Mexican; rather like crème de cacao
Ciao	Italian; rather fruity, but the formula is a secret
Claristine	herb-and-spice flavor; originally made by the Clarist nuns of Belgium before World War I, in which their convent was destroyed
Cointreau	orange flavored; very sweet
Cordial Medoc	French; oranges, cherries, brandy, and crème de cacao are in the blend; none is outstanding in the flavor
Curaçao	Dutch West Indies; made from the peel of small oranges grown there, along with spices; sometimes based on port wine, sometimes on rum; outstanding kinds come in handsome crockery bottles; may be orange, white, green, or an unfortunate blue

liqueur	characteristics
Drambuie	Scots; supposedly the recipe was a gift from Bonnie Prince Charlie to the family that is still making the liqueur from ten-year-old Scotch whisky with herbs and heather honey; the name derives from a Gaelic phrase *an dram buidheach,* which can be roughly translated as "a drink that satisfies"—to its admirers, truer words were never spoken
Expresso	made from the Italian dark-roast beans that produce espresso coffee
Fior di Alpi	Italian; herb-and-spice secret formula; in each bottle, a small branch on which sugar crystals grow
Fleur de Mocha	coffee again—this time a blend of Columbian and Javanese beans
Forbidden Fruit	grapefruit in a brandy base
Fraises, Crème de	strawberry—depending on brand, may be made of cultivated or wild berries
Framboise, Crème de	raspberry, faithful to the fresh-berry flavor; note that there is also Framboise without the "crème de"—a raspberry brandy, unsweetened
Galliano Liquore	Italian; mellow-smooth anise/vanilla flavor with a hint of spice
Gerbirgs Enzian	gentian root flavor—a love-it-or-leave-it taste
Ginger	there are several ginger-flavored brandies—good hot or cold
Glayva	Scots; honey, herbs, and anise for flavor
Goldwasser	since the end of the sixteenth century Danziger Goldwasser—to give it its full name—has been made of orange, coriander, caraway . . . and 22-carat gold leaf in small flecks throughout
Grand Marnier	French; orange flavor, cognac base; not as tooth-jarringly sweet as some of the orange liqueurs; a Soufflé Grand Marnier is a glorious dessert
Grasshopper	combines chocolate and mint; basis of the grasshopper cocktail
Herbsaint	one of the several nonlethal substitutes for absinthe
Honey	there are several honey-based liqueurs, faithful to the flavor; they make an excellent milk punch
Irish Mist	Irish whiskey and honey, a smooth and alluring combination
Kahlua	Mexican; another—and a very flavorful and mellow—coffee liqueur
Kirsch, Crème de	sweet white cherry liqueur; don't confuse it with Kirsch or Kirschwasser, unsweetened white cherry brandy so fine for macerating fresh fruit
Kümmel	flavored with caraway; usually white, but color differs with brand, so does sweetness
Mandarines, Crème de	French; interesting tangerine flavor
Maraschino	made of the small, black mascara cherry and its pits; if you wonder, tastes very little like preserved maraschino cherries, which is probably a blessing
Mastic or Mastika	Middle Eastern; agreeably nonsweet, high proof; a shrub, mastic, flavors it
Menthe, Crème de	mint flavored; tastes cool because of the menthol in the mint; colored green or white, sometimes pink or gold
Moka, Crème de	another coffee-flavored liqueur
Noyaux, Crème de	flavored with various fruit pits, the combination adds up to almond; pink in color
O-Cha	Japanese; made of green tea; the flavor is pleasant, but the aftertaste bitter
Ojen	Spanish; colorless, anise flavored—proof and sweetness vary from maker to maker
Ouzo	Greek; turns cloudy in the usual 4-to-1 water-ouzo mixture; high proof, usually 90 or above; somewhat licorice/anise flavor
Parfait Amour	purple is the color of "perfect love" but there are several flavor combinations, depending on the maker; considering the color, the kind made with violets makes the best sense
Pasha	another coffee liqueur, this one from Turkey
Pastis de Marseille	French; not-too-sweet licorice flavor
Peach	there are several of these, made of whole fresh fruit or a combination of fresh and dry steeped in brandy or neutral spirits
Peppermint Schnapps	like crème de menthe, but less sweet and higher proof

liqueur	characteristics
Pernod	anise flavored, a direct descendant of absinthe—but without the wormwood—made by the same old firm
Pimento Dram	Jamaican; based on rum, hot with pepper
Piña, Licor de	Caribbean or Hawaiian; faithful to the flavor of the pineapple from which it's made; nicely tart/sweet
Ponche Real	Spanish; orange flavor, based on brandy
Prunelle, Crème de	faithful to the flavor of its small, tart plums; some brands add figs or prunes
Raki	Middle Eastern; anise flavored, high proof
Rock and Rye	rye whiskey with rock-candy syrup and fruit juices; some brands have fruit in the bottle, some pieces of rock candy
Rose, Crème de	flavored with rose petals, along with vanilla and spices; exotic, perfumy
Rumona	Jamaican; vanilla-chocolate-coffee
Sabra	Israeli; combines chocolate and orange
Sambuca	Italian; flavor delicately aniselike
Sloe Gin	not gin at all, this liqueur is made of sloe plums, fruit of the blackthorn; deep rosy color, not particularly sweet; in the roaring twenties, a sloe gin fizz was the downfall of many a maiden who had never had a drink before
Southern Comfort	American; sweetened whiskey with peaches; 100 proof; used in mixed drinks
Strega	Italian; pale yellow; delicate, haunting flavor, result of a secret formula—strega means "witch"
Swedish Punch	the clears-the-sinuses potency of arak, an East-Indian rum, is tempered with tea, citrus juices, and spices
Tangerine	mildly spiced tangerine flavor
Tia Maria	Jamaican; coffee-with-spice flavor
Triple Sec	another of the many orange liqueurs; this one combines orange-flower water and orris root in a clear mixture
Tuaca	Italian; milk brandy, orange flavor with coconut undertones
Van der Hum	South African; tangerine peel and spices give it flavor
Vandermint	Dutch; nicely balanced flavor of chocolate and mint
Vieille Curé	French; monastery-made of brandy base with a blend of herbs
Violette, Crème de	violet petals flavor it, modified with a trace of vanilla
Wisniowka	Polish; the flavor is wild cherry
Zitronen Eis	refreshingly, if rather sweetly, flavored with lemon

And that is only a few of the liqueurs. One authority lists 260 kinds, then modestly adds that the list he offers is by no means complete.

Once liqueurs were served only one way—straight, in a small stemmed glass—with the exception of the crème de menthe frappé, scorned by two-fisted topers as "a ladies' drink." Today, the rigid do-things-right rules have been abandoned in favor of how-you-like-it enjoyment. Many liqueurs are given the frappé treatment: poured over shaved or crushed ice, served with a short straw. Or they are taken on the rocks. Either way, the addition of ice helps cut the heavy sweetness of a number of liqueurs to let the flavor shine through.

Available to use as a substitute for dessert are small chocolate cups in which to serve liqueurs. One drinks one's drink, then eats the cup in a routine that has Marx Brothersish possibilities. Very good though, especially with a not-too-sweet orange flavor such as Grand Marnier, or a liqueur made with mint—indeed any flavor that goes well with chocolate. Coffee served at the same time helps to temper the sweetness.

Liqueurs are available in pints, tenths (⅖ gallon), and fifths (⅘ gallon) as well as some oddball sizes—check the label. Some of the bottles are almost as attractive as their contents. Almost.

LIQUOR BOTTLES

The Treasury Department's Bureau of Alcohol, Tobacco and Firearms decreed early in 1977 that by January 1, 1980, all bottles of distilled spirits must be metric-sized. The official conversion factor is: 1 liter = 0.264172 U.S. gallon.

The new sizes have been slowly—and erratically—appearing in liquor stores ever since, causing considerable confusion (particularly when intermingled with bottles of the old sizes) to shopkeeper and customer alike. Because of the vast hoo-hah raised by Americans over metric ("Who *says*

409

we have to be like the rest of the world?"), at the time this is written the government appears to be easing up, if not backing off, concerning the conversion; it's anybody's guess what tomorrow will bring. Meanwhile, here are the relationships between the old and the new bottles:

metric size	fluid ounces	nearest equivalent present U.S. size	fluid ounces
1.75 liters	59.2	½ gallon	64
1 liter	33.8	1 quart	32
750 milliliters	25.4	⅘ quart (fifth)	25.6
500 milliliters	16.9	1 pint	16
375 milliliters	12.7	⅘ pint (tenth)	12.8
200 milliliters	6.8	½ pint	8
50 milliliters	1.7	miniature	1.6

To many people, unfortunately, drinking is a very serious business. All this hanky-panky may drive some to drink, others to take the pledge—though, as with all concerns, things will doubtless even themselves out in the long run.

LIQUORS

Although there are mixed drinks in wide variety, enough to fill thick bartenders' guides—to say nothing of the hundreds of specialties of the house that hosts love to serve and guests wish they wouldn't—the liquors on which all this frantic mixing is based are relatively few in number.

Whiskey, the leader. No matter how you spell the word (with the "e" here, without it in Canada and abroad), something in the neighborhood of four-fifths of all the hard liquor drunk in the United States is whiskey. All whiskeys are made of grain, which is not by any manner of means to say they all taste alike. Each depends for its individual flavor on the kind of grain used, the method the maker employs to distill his product, and the age of the liquor.

Bourbon, America's favorite whiskey by far, is made of a combination of grains that must be at least 51 percent corn; it is a straight whiskey (that is, not a blend of several distillations) and must be aged only in charred new oak barrels.

Rye whiskey must be made from a mixture of at least 51 percent rye grain. However, most of the whiskey loosely thought of as "rye" is blended, rather than straight rye. Wheat and barley are other grains used in the making of whiskey.

Blends of straight whiskey are combinations of two or more straight whiskeys, chosen with care—some for mellowness, some for flavor and aroma, some for strength—to create a happy marriage. Blended whiskey is something else again—one-third to one-fifth straight whiskey, the remainder neutral spirits.

Scotch whiskeys are, with a few exceptions, blends—often of as many as 30 straight whiskeys; the grains in them are barley, corn, and rye, and although they are easily distinguished from one another (by Scotch drinkers, at least), they all have a smoky flavor.

Canadian whiskey is light, mild of flavor, but not at all lacking in authority. Irish whiskey is hearty and heavy, with distinctive flavor and aroma, but with none of the smoky overtones that are characteristic of Scotch.

Gin, for what ails you. Franciscus de la Boë, a Dutch professor of medicine, distilled pure laboratory alcohol with the essence of juniper berries to create what he intended to be a blood cleanser, to be sold by apothecaries. Instead (to his pleasure or dismay, history does not tell us), he found he had a liquor whose popularity spread with eye-opening speed. He had invented gin—the word is a corruption of *genever,* Dutch for "juniper."

While whiskeys are most often drunk straight, or modified only by ice, water, or charged water, gin is a mixing liquor. Its flavor still derives from juniper, but various makers have added flavorings to distinguish their gin from others, among them cardamom, orange peel, coriander, and bitter almonds.

Because gin is relatively easy to make, it has often been —particularly during the disaster of Prohibition—a do-it-yourself project. Even the most verbal are struck dumb trying to describe the flavor of some of that era's bathtub gin. Many back-country stills today produce what is essentially gin (excuse it, please, legitimate distillers), although it is known by a wide variety of names, the most picturesque being "white lightning."

Except for the true Dutch gin—taken icy cold—the liquor is seldom drunk straight; it is, however, the base, the "kick," of innumerable mixed drinks in many parts of the world.

Vodka, "without distinctive character, aroma, or taste." The quotation is part of the government's definition of vodka. If that's true, why does anyone drink it? Because a) there are vast numbers of people who dislike the taste of alcoholic beverages but enjoy the effect they have, and b) because other vast numbers believe—erroneously—that vodka can't be smelled on the breath. Picture good old George Snapperworth, sneakily imbibing four vodka martinis at lunch, then hurrying back to the office, confident that no one will know he has been drinking. George, we have news for you. Everybody knows. And not because you tend to fall on your silly face on one of your several afternoon trips to the men's room—that only confirms what was already surmised.

Made of water, grain, and yeast, what flavor a particular vodka has—and they all have some flavor—depends on the individual distiller. But the differences are subtle.

Except by Russians, and by Scandinavians (who call it aquavit), vodka is seldom drunk straight. It takes the place of other liquors in some familiar mixed drinks, and also provides an alcoholic but tasteless base for drinks—bloody mary, bullshot, screwdriver, and such—in which a liquor flavor is not desirable but the effect is.

A bottle of yo-ho-ho. Rum is, according to one point of view, an absolutely splendid way to use up leftovers. When sugarcane is crushed and boiled down, a portion of the resulting liquid crystallizes—that's sugar. Part of the remainder is treated and sold as molasses. Part is fermented and distilled—and that, after aging, is rum. The youngest rums we import are about three years old, but aging can go on for ten years or even longer.

A great deal of the rum drunk in the United States once came from Cuba. At the time of Castro's revolution, Cuban rum-makers moved bag and baggage to Puerto Rico, where rum distilling was already going on to some extent. Light Puerto Rican rums, two to five years old and known as white label or carta blanca, are 80 proof and used in mixed drinks such as daiquiris and rum sours. Golden rums, five to eight years old, gold label or carta d'oro, also 80 proof, can be drunk as whiskeys are, in highballs or on the rocks; they are the right type for rum and cola or rum collins. These are the two most often encountered, but there are others.

Many rum distilleries offer a 151-proof product, too strong for all but the most devoted rum drinker, but excellent for cooking, especially in flambéed dishes—there's no difficulty setting *that* stuff afire. There are also the "black" kinds, molasses-tasting and somehow seeming thick, although they are not; by no means everyone's dish of rum, they are Jamaican (the darkest, most pungent), Demerara (slightly paler and lighter of body, but still assertive), and Barbados (midway between Jamaican and the lighter Puerto Rican kinds). Haitian rum is heavy in flavor, but smooth. Hawaiian rum is soft and light. Virgin Islands rum is light and dry, but its flavor is more reminiscent of molasses than that of the Puerto Ricans.

Finally, there is "ancient" rum, about fifteen years old, smooth and mellow. To use such a rum in a mixed drink is an insult. Like fine brandy it should be savored straight.

The Mexican connection. The maguey, a succulent plant—relative of cactus—grows in the foothills of the Sierra Madre. Its fruit (the stem of the plant, rather like an outsize pineapple) supplies Mexicans with two potables: *pulque,* a knock-your-head-off beerlike drink, and *tequila,* joy of the gringos who have fallen in love with the margarita cocktail. Some of the tequila found in the United States is imported raw by distillers, who age and bottle it at 80 to 100 proof.

Although it looks like gin or vodka—and the tequila you drink on a visit to Mexico is unaged, as our gins and vodkas are—tequila is really a kind of brandy if one abides by the definition that brandies are made of fruit.

Devotees of Dutch gin say tequila is much like it, and drink their tequila straight and icy cold. Others like it the Mexican way: suck a wedge of lime, toss down a shot of tequila, finish off with a lick of salt held in the hollow between thumb and forefinger. Most north-of-the-border tequila drinkers opt for the margarita, however, and some for tequila martinis or sours.

Very happy endings. Robert Hall, a Baptist clergyman of 150 years ago, exhorted his parishioners to "call things by their right names." Do not, he continued, in a place where spiritous liquors are sold, call for a glass of brandy, but "ask for a glass of liquid fire and distilled damnation." One gets the feeling that he spoke from experience.

On the other hand, the French, who also have had considerable experience of the subject, call brandy *eau de vie*—water of life. It is highly probable that more people follow the French thought on the subject than the Reverend Hall's.

Brandy, simply, is distilled wine. Who first got the notion of thus treating wine is lost in the murk of time, although there are assorted legends concerning it. Most of them agree that, one way or another, the first brandy was come by accidentally. Be that as it may, distillers have been making brandy on purpose for centuries, and doing very nicely, thank you.

Best of all brandies is that made in the Cognac region of France, and best of all cognacs is *fines champagne cognac,* made totally of grapes grown in the Grande Champagne area of the Cognac region.

Besides that designation, there are other things that a brandy bottle's label can tell you. Stars have little meaning—in fact, one of the great brandy firms dropped the stars from their label a decade ago. However, initial letters do have meaning: V.O. = very old; V.S.O.P. = very superior old pale (brandy twenty to twenty-five years old); V.V.S.O.P. = very, very superior old pale (about forty years old); X.O. = extra old, an assurance that the cognac in the bottle is well aged and of the finest quality.

These designations have meaning for brandy snobs, little significance for the ordinary brandy lover. In fact, no brandy imported into the United States may carry an age on its label. And it is true that for brandy, as for a beautiful woman, after age fifty, it's downhill all the way. If you come by a bottle of old brandy, rather than falling to your knees and knocking your head on the floor, drink it. It will never get any better. Brandy ages only in wooden casks; bottles do nothing for it.

We import brandies other than *fines champagnes* from France, and we also import German, Spanish, and Portuguese brandies, each with its individual characteristics.

Metaxa, Greek brandy, is made from muscat grapes and has a deep, rich, very pronounced flavor (but it is not resinous—don't confuse it with some Greek wines). Pisco is young brandy from Peru, tasting very little like brandy but with a charm of its own, drunk straight or in a pisco "sawer"—sour. And we make brandy here at home, in California, some of it very good indeed.

Many older-generation drinkers in the United States learned—with pleasure—to drink brandy both straight and in mixed drinks during World War II, when it was the easiest liquor to come by.

Besides those made from grapes, brandies are also made from other fruits. Apple brandy is applejack in this country, calvados in France. Pear brandies range all the way from pearjack (made by Uncle Oscar on the back porch by allowing pears to freeze and thaw alternately) to Switzerland's elegant version that has a whole pear in each bottle. Red raspberry brandy is framboise in France, himbeergeist in Germany. Plum brandy is mirabelle in France, slivovitz in several countries of central Europe—the latter is (unlike most fruit brandies) aged and tastes like something it would be quite safe to feed the baby right up to the point where it knocks you flat on your back.

For other bibulous topics, see ALE, BEER, BEVERAGES, BITTERS, COCKTAILS, HIGHBALL, JIGGER, JULEP, LAMB'S WOOL, LIQUEURS, and WINE.

LITER: see special feature: MEASURING UP TO METRIC

LITTLENECK CLAMS: see SHELLFISH

LIVER: see VARIETY MEATS

LIVER SAUSAGE, LIVERWURST: see COLD CUTS

LOBSTERS, LOBSTER TAILS: see SHELLFISH

LOGANBERRIES

The shape and size of blackberries, loganberries are red, taking on a purplish hue when fully ripe. Although not commercially grown to any great extent, you may be able to find loganberries in some markets in June and July. Canned loganberries are also available in limited distribution.

If loganberries grow wild near you, or if you have vines on your property, pick the fresh, plump berries. When fully ripe, the berry will come away, leaving its cap behind on the plant. Use within 3 days. They are more often eaten cooked—in pie, jam, and such—than fresh. Properly prepared, they may be frozen in syrup or dry-packed with or without sugar. (See special feature: PUTTING FOOD BY.) Use frozen or canned loganberries for pies and tarts, or to make a refreshing loganberry ice.

LOIN, LOIN CHOPS: see individual meat name, as LAMB, VEAL

LONDON BROIL: see BEEF

LONG ISLAND DUCKLING: see DUCK

LOQUATS

The fruit of a small ornamental evergreen tree that bears very fragrant white flowers, the loquat is small, with a fuzzy skin, yellow-to-orange flesh, and large black seeds. Very juicy, the fruit has a sweet/acid flavor and may be eaten raw or made into jam or preserves. A native of China, it is grown today in many tropical and subtropical regions, more often for the beauty of the tree than for its fruit. See also EXOTIC FRUIT.

LOW-CALORIE FOODS: see special feature: NUTRITION NOTEBOOK

LOWFAT MILK: see MILK

LOX: see page 452

LUMACHE: see PASTA

LUNCH

"We have breakfast and dinner on purpose," a teenager once said to us while munching potato chips, "but lunch is totally by accident."

You know what she meant. Unless we deck ourselves in finery and ceremoniously go out to lunch, the midday meal tends to take one of two forms: a sweep-the-kitchen event that uses up yesterday's leftovers, or a heated-up can of soup. We once knew a woman who served herself and her children scrambled-something for lunch day in and day out—whatever was in the refrigerator she threw into a skillet, broke two eggs over it, and scrambled the whole mess. Sometimes it was quite tasty, a frittatalike mixture of vegetables and/or scraps of meat; sometimes it was horrendous, as in the specialité de la maison, her baked apple and cold boiled potato scramble.

Workaday eating. Once lunch was a considerably more elaborate affair than it is today. When there was a large group of men who had spent the morning doing heavy work, as on a farm, the midday meal was dinner rather than lunch. But even city folk once gathered at the table—father home from work, the children from school—for a hearty lunch (which had been preceded by a hearty breakfast and would later be followed by a hearty dinner).

Nowadays, few men—or women, if the one at home is the househusband—come home for lunch. Most youngsters over the age of five have lunch at school. So the houseperson and perhaps very young children are the only at-home lunchers.

Women at home alone tend to eat on the fly, consuming whatever comes to hand, from a tomato and a piece of cheese—not at all a bad lunch—to those two chocolate eclairs that are going to go to waste if they aren't eaten—ghastly from a nutritional point of view, but pretty tasty from that of the guilt-ridden but happy eater. If there are small fry to be fed, mother's lunch may be a lot more wholesome because when she prepares lunch for them she's likely to include herself; however, if they're still in the baby food stage, it's back to those eclairs for her.

Brown-bagging it. Although fewer children carry lunch than was customary a number of years ago—many schools having taken it upon themselves to serve a nutritionally balanced noonday meal—many adult business people now bring lunch from home. There are several reasons. Except for expense-account fare, eating out costs a lot. Many women, some men, are dieting and find it hard to eat a suitable diet lunch in a restaurant. If the meal is quickly eaten in the office, lunch-hour time remains in which to do some shopping or run errands. And many simply prefer to avoid the noise, the waiting on line, the gulped food that are part of the lunch break, especially in big cities.

Carried lunches, for children or adults, can be wholesome and appealing. But there are some attendant hazards, chief among them the fact that many foods spoil very easily. Hot foods must be kept hot (140° or above) and cold foods cold (below 40°) for safety's sake. Large-mouth vacuum jars are helpful; preheat them with boiling water or precool with ice water before filling, and make certain they are well washed after each use. Frozen sandwiches will be thawed, but still quite safe to eat, by lunch time. Freeze small cans of fruit or vegetable juice before packing them; although they are safe at room temperature, they taste better cool and will help keep the rest of the lunch cold. Many foods, of course, don't require any special care—breads, cookies and cakes, raw fruits and vegetables (provided they have been well washed and dried) are some of the safe lunch-time bets.

The four-way lunch. Sandwiches are fine lunch-box fare for kids and adults alike, but they get tiresome after a while. Vary with a vacuum jar of stew, chili, hearty meal-in-one soup, a tasty dinner leftover, even rice or potatoes or pasta topped with meat or poultry or fish in gravy or sauce. Hard-cooked eggs are safest left in their shells—be sure to pack salt and pepper or seasoned salt.

Some businesses provide refrigerators in which perishable food can be safely stored, and microwave ovens or hot plates so that food can be heated or water boiled for such lunch items as make-in-a-cup soups.

However prepared or eaten, nourishing carried lunches should provide:

- a protein food—meat, poultry, fish, cheese, eggs, or that old brown-bag standby, peanut butter
- something crisp for contrast—strips of celery, carrot, green pepper, radishes, scallions, or a packed-in-a-leakproof-carton salad, with dressing carried separately to add at lunch time
- a hot or cold beverage, or hot or cold soup
- a treat of whatever kind the luncher enjoys—fruit, cookies, nuts, popcorn, chips

If the protein food is in a sandwich, no extra bread is needed; if not, provide a roll or crackers.

Bags versus boxes. So tacky they're chic, brown bags are a favored way to carry lunch. But not, the USDA says, the best way. The department is concerned about food poisoning, feels that many cases of "flu" and "guess I've got a bug of some kind" are in reality related to carried lunches. If your with-it reputation demands brown bags, buy them especially for lunch carrying; don't reuse grocery bags. But you'll be wise, USDA says, to choose an insulated lunch box for yourself or your lunch-carrying child. They hold food temperatures well, and are easy to keep clean.

Individual-portion canned foods, the experts continue, are truly safe lunch products. But a vacuum bottle is fine, provided the food is boiling hot or icy cold when put into a scrupulously clean container. To keep foods cold, pack a freezer gel device with the lunch, or freeze water in a small container, put it into a plastic bag to prevent moisture from reaching the food, and pack it in the lunch box. Until it's time to eat, store your lunch in the coolest available place, never on a radiator.

LUNCHEON MEATS: see COLD CUTS

LYCHEES: see EXOTIC FRUIT

A SHORT COURSE IN LABEL READING

Labels on today's food cans and packages can tell you everything you want—and need—to know about the contents, provided you understand where and how to look

Labeling has come a long, long way since the days when it was possible to purchase Uncle Elmer's World-Famous Snake Root Emulsion, guaranteed—right there on the label—to cure everything from hives to brain tumors, improve the appetite, dye the hair a glorious red, and prevent rust on the metal parts of buggy whips.

Monitoring food labels (drug labels, too) in today's market is a function of the Food and Drug Administration—the FDA. To help you be an aware buyer, an informed consumer, certain information is required to appear on the label. Other information is included at the option of the manufacturer or processor. A third type of information to be found on labels takes the form of symbols or codes or dates.

To assist consumers in finding out more about what they're getting in the products they buy, the *FDA Consumer,* that department's monthly voice, has brought together label facts and know-how. Here, straight from (if the FDA will excuse us) the horse's mouth, is a rundown of the information most often found on food labels, along with where to find it and what it means.

THE LABEL BASICS

Certain information is required on all food labels:

a) the name of the product
b) net contents or net weight (on canned food labels, weight includes liquid in which the product is packed, as water with vegetables, syrup with fruits)
c) name and place of business of manufacturer, packer, or distributor
d) with a few exceptions, ingredients must be listed

List of ingredients. The ingredient present in the largest amount—by weight—must be listed first, followed in descending order of weight by the other ingredients. Any additives used in the product must be listed, but colors and flavors do not have to be listed by name; the list of ingredients may simply say "artificial color" or "artificial flavor" or "natural flavor." If the flavors are artificial, this fact must be stated. Butter, cheese, and ice cream, however, are not required to state the presence of artificial color.

The only foods not required to list all ingredients are so-called standardized foods. FDA has set "standards of identity" for some foods. These standards require that all foods called by a particular name (catsup and mayonnaise are examples) contain certain mandatory ingredients. Under the law, the mandatory ingredients in standardized foods need not be listed on the label. Manufacturers may add optional ingredients, however, and at the time this is being written, the FDA is revising the food standards regulations to require that optional ingredients in standardized foods be listed on the product label.

NUTRITION INFORMATION REQUIREMENTS

Under FDA regulations, any food to which a nutrient has been added, or any food for which a nutritional claim is made, must have the nutritional content listed on the label. In addition, many manufacturers put nutrition information on products when not required to do so.

Nutrition labels tell you how many calories and how much protein, carbohydrate, and fat are in a serving of the product. They also tell the percentage of the U.S. Recommended Daily Allowances (U.S.RDAs) of protein and seven important vitamins and minerals that each serving of the product contains. Nutrition information can help you shop for more nutritious food and plan nutritionally balanced meals for your family. (For more detailed information on U.S.RDAs and other nutritional considerations, see the special feature: NUTRITION NOTEBOOK.)

How to read nutrition labels. Nutrition information is given on a per-serving basis. The label tells the size of a serving (for example: 1 cup, 2 ounces, 1 tablespoon), the number of servings in the container, the number of calories per serving, and the amounts (in grams) of protein, carbohydrate, and fat per serving.

Protein is listed twice on the label: in grams and as a percentage of the U.S.RDA.

Seven vitamins and minerals must be shown, in a specific order. The listing of 12 other vitamins and minerals, and of cholesterol, fatty acid, and sodium content, is optional.

What U.S. RDA means. The U.S. Recommended Daily Allowances (U.S.RDAs) are the approximate amounts of protein, vitamins, and minerals that an adult should eat every day to maintain good health. Nutrition labels list the U.S.RDA by percentage. For example, the label may state that one serving of the food contains 35 percent of the Recommended Daily Allowance of vitamin A and 25 percent of the Recommended Daily Allowance of iron. The total amount of food an individual eats in a day should supply the U.S. Recommended Daily Allowance of all essential nutrients.

Key to metric units. Nutrition labels show amounts in grams rather than ounces, because a gram is a small unit of measurement, and many food components are present in very small amounts. To help you read nutrition labels:

1 pound (lb.)	=	448 grams (g)
1 ounce (oz.)	=	28 grams (g)
1 gram (g)	=	1,000 milligrams (mg)
1 milligram (mg)	=	1,000 micrograms (mcg)

Nutrition quality. Many foods today are manufactured into products that are different from traditional foods. Some classes of these foods include frozen dinners, breakfast cereals, meal replacements, noncarbonated breakfast beverages fortified with vitamin C, and main dishes—such as macaroni and cheese, pizzas, stews, and casseroles.

FDA establishes voluntary nutritional guidelines for such foods, so consumers can be assured of getting a proper level and range of nutrients when using them. A product that complies with an FDA nutritional quality guideline may include on its label a statement that it meets the U.S. nutritional quality guideline for that particular class of food.

DOES "IMITATION" MEAN "BEWARE"?

Some foods are labeled as "imitations" of other foods. Under an FDA regulation, the word "imitation" must be used on the label when the product is not as nutritious as the product which it resembles and for which it is a substitute. If a product is similar to an existing one, and is just as nutritious, a new name can be given to it rather than calling it "imitation." For example, eggless products that are nutritionally equivalent to eggs have been given such names as Eggbeaters and Scramblers.

However, although products labeled "imitation" do not meet established nutritional standards, they are not necessarily inferior in other ways—indeed, they may be superior, depending on the points of view. Weight-loss dieters and those interested in maintaining their normal weight find such products as imitation mayonnaise and imitation cream cheese, for example, to be a two-fold blessing. These products offer good flavor and texture, but are lower in calories than the foods they imitate. Imitation mayonnaise has considerably less oil than regular mayonnaise; the fat content of imitation cream cheese is only about half that of regular cream cheese. Using them means lowered calorie content.

Aware that "imitation" is a dirty word in many people's minds, some manufacturers try to avoid it—calling, for example, their low-cholesterol imitation bacon by some name such as "breakfast strips" to avoid the term "imitation bacon." Others make capital of the lowered fat and/or calorie content, frankly and proudly extolling their products in print and on radio and TV as imitation, and pointing out their virtues. One brand of imitation mayonnaise, for example, tells consumers why the product must be so labeled, and concludes with the line, "We have to call it imitation, but you don't!"

CALLING IT BY ITS RIGHT NAME

Some foods may look from the label as though they are one thing and actually be another. To prevent deception of consumers, FDA has ruled that such foods must have a "common or usual" name that gives the consumer accurate information about what is in the package or container.

For example, a beverage that looks like orange juice but actually contains very little orange juice must use a name such as "diluted orange juice drink." The product also may be required to state on the label the percentage of the characterizing ingredient it contains. In this case, the common or usual name might be "diluted orange juice beverage, contains 10 percent orange juice." A noncarbonated beverage that appears to contain a fruit or vegetable juice but does not contain any juice must state on the label that it contains no fruit or vegetable juice.

Another special labeling requirement concerns packaged foods in which the main ingredient or component of a recipe is not included, as in the case of some "main dishes" or "dinners." On such foods, the common or usual name consists of the following:

a) the common name of each ingredient in descending order by weight—for example, "noodles and tomato sauce"

b) identification of the food to be prepared from the package—for example, "for preparation of chicken casserole"

c) a statement of ingredients that must be added to complete the recipe—for example, "you must add chicken to complete the recipe"

GRADES

Some food products carry a grade designation on the label, such as "U.S. Grade A." Grades are set by the U.S. Department of Agriculture, based on the quality levels inherent in a product—its taste, texture, and appearance. Department of Agriculture grades are not based on nutritional content.

Milk and milk products in most states carry a "Grade A" label. This grade is based on FDA recommended sanitary standards for the production and processing of milk and milk

CHICKEN 'N' NOODLE

FROZEN CASSEROLE
DINNER

Ingredients: chicken, egg noodles, nonfat dry milk, chicken fat, peas, pimientos, sodium chloride, leaf thyme

CR07780

NET WEIGHT 16 OZ. (435 GRAMS)

Goodbonnet Foods, Inc.
2344 Goodbonnet Lane
Chicago, Ill. 60666

INSPECTED
U.S. DEPARTMENT OF AGRICULTURE
P-42

1380010130

Nutrition Information (# per serving)
Serving size: 8 oz. Servings per container: 2

protein	28 g	fat	33 g
carbohydrate	43 g	sodium	830 mg

(Polyunsaturated fat: 2 g, saturated: 9 g)

Information on fat and cholesterol content is provided for individuals who on the advice of a physician are modifying their total dietary intake of fat and cholesterol.

Percentage of U.S. Recommended Daily Allowance (U.S. RDA)

protein	35	riboflavin	15
vitamin A	35	niacin	25
vitamin C	10	calcium	4
thiamin	15	iron	25

the net contents or net weight must be on all food labels

on products that have a long "shelf life" many companies use code dating

many manufacturers or processors include helpful nutrition information on their labels; such information is not mandatory unless a nutritional claim for the product is made

some manufacturers or processors voluntarily include helpful dietary information on their labels

many food labels carry a small block of parallel lines of various widths with accompanying numbers for computerized checkouts and inventories

the name and place of business of the manufacturer, packer, or distributor must be on all food labels

on most foods, the ingredients must be listed on the label

the name of the product must be on all food labels

416

products, which are regulated by the states. The grade is not based on nutritional values. However, FDA has established standards that require certain levels of vitamins A and D when they are added to milk.

For example, you might buy a carton labeled "Nonfat Milk, Vitamin A and D Added." On the nutrition label you would find the percentage of the U.S.RDA for those two vitamins that a 1-cup serving offers, along with the other RDA information.

OPEN DATING

To help consumers obtain food that is fresh and wholesome, many manufacturers date their product. Open dating, as this practice often is called, is not regulated by FDA.

Four kinds of open dating are commonly used.

pack date: This is the day the food was manufactured or processed or packaged. In other words, it tells how old the food is when you buy it. The importance of this information to consumers depends on how quickly the particular food normally spoils. Most canned and packaged foods have a long shelf life when stored under dry, cool conditions.

pull or sell date: This is the last date the product should be sold, assuming it has been stored and handled properly. The pull date allows for some storage time in the home refrigerator. Cold cuts, ice cream, milk, and refrigerated fresh dough products are examples of foods with pull dates.

expiration date: This is the last date the food should be eaten or used. Baby formula and yeast are examples of products that may carry expiration dates.

freshness date: This is similar to the expiration date but may allow for normal home storage. Some bakery products that have a freshness date are sold at a reduced price for a short time after the expiration date.

CODE DATING

Many companies use code dating on products that have a long "shelf life." This is usually for the company's information, rather than for the consumer's benefit. The code gives the manufacturer and the store precise information about where and when the product was packaged, so that if a recall should be required for any reason, the product can be identified quickly and withdrawn from the market.

UNIVERSAL PRODUCT CODE

Many food labels now include a small block of parallel lines of various widths, with accompanying numbers. This is the Universal Product Code (UPC). The code on a label is unique to that product. Some stores are equipped with computerized checkout equipment that can read the code and automatically ring up the sale.

In addition to making it possible for stores to automate part of their checkout work, the UPC, when used in conjunction with a computer, also can function as an automated inventory system. The computer can tell management how much of a specific item is on hand, how fast it is being sold, and when and how much to order.

For more information on UPC and how it works, see COMPUTERIZED SUPERMARKET CHECKOUT.

SYMBOLS ON FOOD LABELS

The symbol "R" on a label signifies that the trademark used on the label is registered with the U.S. Patent Office.

The symbol "C" indicates that the literary and artistic content of the label is protected against infringement under the copyright laws of the United States. Copies of such labels have been filed with the Copyright Office of the Library of Congress.

The symbol consisting of the letter "U" inside the letter "O" is one whose use is authorized by the Union of Orthodox Jewish Congregations of America, more familiarly known as the Orthodox Union, for use of foods that comply with Jewish dietary laws. The symbol consisting of the letter "K" inside the letter "O" is used to indicate that the food is "Kosher" —that is, it complies with the Jewish dietary laws, and its processing has been under the direction of a rabbi.

None of these symbols is required by, or is under the authority of, any of the labeling laws that are enforced by the Food and Drug Administration.

AND A LOT FOR FREE

Some manufacturers and processors of food go far beyond what is required of them in the matter of labeling, furnishing through their labels—and sometimes as adjuncts to the labels—a large quantity of useful information.

What to do with it now that you've bought it. Recipes are the chief extra that many food processors add to their labels. A complete food, such as a frozen main dish, probably will offer serving suggestions rather than recipes, but large numbers of foods, canned and packaged and frozen, offer recipes. A can of tomato sauce, for example, might give you instructions for making a meat loaf that uses part of the sauce as the liquid ingredient in the loaf, the remainder as a glaze for it. A can of salmon might tell you how to make a salmon soufflé; a can of green beans, how to turn the contents into green beans amandine; a package of noodles, how to make Fettucine Alfredo; a carton of eggs, how to produce a proper french omelet. Besides wanting to be of assistance to the consumer—and they really do want to help you—processors have in mind the fact that if you turn out a truly good dish using their product, you're more likely to buy it a second time, try the recipe on *that* label, and again come back for more, ad infinitum.

Large packages usually offer more than one recipe. A

package of biscuit mix, for example, will tell you how to make all the basics using the product—biscuits, waffles, pancakes, dumplings, shortcake, and more—as well as offering a special new recipe for a tasty and unusual use of it. The basics will be there, package after package, but the special recipes will be changed from time to time, to broaden your knowledge (and your use) of the product.

Cake mixes will give you basic preparation and baking instructions, will probably offer a couple of variations on the basic cake to be made from the mix, and some extras as well —perhaps how to use the mix for cookies, perhaps a frosting recipe or two. Cake flour packages will show you how to use the flour in a number of different cakes. Packages of ready-to-cook cereals will tell you how to prepare the breakfast version and perhaps how to make cookies or quick breads from the product as well. Cracker packages may offer you a number of dips and spreads, or use of the crushed crackers to make a pie shell or bread a cutlet. A canned ham label will certainly tell you how to heat the ham, will probably suggest some flavor-enhancing glazes, and may also give you some good ideas about using up leftovers.

At the very least, if the food in the can or package must be cooked, the label will tell you how. If it should be heated, the label will give you instructions. And if it must be combined with other foods to complete the dish (as with packaged "helper" main dishes, that must have meat added), the label will tell you how to go about this, and will probably offer some suggestions for variations as well.

Foods contained in large packages allow their manufacturers more space in which to woo you. Those who process foods in small containers sometimes, unfortunately, try to make up this deficit by printing extra information in such tiny type that they ought to furnish a magnifying glass with each package. Others go to the trouble (and the extra cost) of printing small leaflets that are attached to the can or package, containing the recipes and other information they want you to have—and hope that, having it, you will be induced to buy that brand again the next time, instead of trying another.

And more, besides. Sometimes labels carry free or low-cost offers—free recipe or special-use leaflets, for example, or a whole cookbook that cannot be obtained elsewhere, or is offered for a price lower than the book sells for in the stores. Generally these offers require you to send in a proof of purchase, most often the product's label or a specified portion of it. Some products make these offers so regularly that the labels are printed with a small seal or other device that can be cut off and used as proof of purchase. This is particularly true for offers that require more than one proof of purchase.

Premiums, too. Some labels offer premiums, anything from a set of soup mugs to a copper teakettle and dozens of others, at a price less than you'd pay for comparable merchandise in a store. These generally require proof of purchase to accompany the check or money order you send to pay for the merchandise, and warn you to allow a specified length of time—several weeks or sometimes months—before you can expect delivery.

There are ongoing premium offers, too. These usually take the form of sets that you can accumulate, a piece at a time, over a long period. Sets of cookware, for example, to accumulate a pot or pan at a time, or silverware or stainless steel tableware, to accumulate a place setting at a time. These, too, require proofs of purchase. Sometimes the offer is double-barreled—you may buy a piece or a part of a set for so much money plus so many proofs of purchase, or for less money and considerably more proofs of purchase.

In general these offers are entirely legitimate and the merchandise you get is of good quality, exactly as described on the label. There was a time when such offers turned out to be for shoddy merchandise; indeed, sometimes the merchandise never did turn up. But the government, acting on consumer complaints, took a hand and now keeps a watchful eye on such offers. In any case, reputable merchants know that if they cheat you they will be the losers in the long run. And it's true, although some prefer not to believe it, that reputable merchants don't want to cheat you, even if they could get away with it.

All in all, the labels on the food you buy can offer some interesting, and in most cases profitable, reading. No wonder so many of us are compulsive label readers, often to the point where we get to know by heart the information contained on the labels of foods we use every day.

THE ALERT CONSUMER

Shopping is one of those house-and-home chores that must be done. Some of us enjoy it, some hate it, but we all do it. And, as they say, anything worth doing is worth doing well. Learning to read—and be guided by—the labels on the food cans and packages we bring home comes high on the list of worth-doing-well facets of food shopping, along with checking and comparing prices and inspecting the packages to be sure they're intact. If we think of running our homes as a business and ourselves as business executives, rather than lumping the whole deal under the catchall "drudgery," food shopping takes on new significance.

MACADAMIA NUTS

Although we think of them as being Hawaiian, because most of the macadamias in our markets are imported from there, the nuts are native to Queensland and New South Wales, in Australia. But it is in Hawaii that the nuts are grown commercially. Now a few plantations are getting underway in California, where the tree has been grown as an ornamental for over fifty years.

The macadamia is a handsome tree, a subtropical evergreen that flourishes in any climate in which avocados and lemons thrive in well-drained and slightly acidic soil. However, it will grow and bear under conditions fairly far removed from those ideals, is resistant to the root rot that kills many avocados, and requires very little care. Ants seem to be its only enemies, and those are easily controlled. Smog does not affect it.

Where is all this horticultural information leading? To the fact that California is on the verge of starting a macadamia nut industry, because—although the nuts are priced in the luxury class—Hawaii cannot supply enough to meet the demand, despite the fact that a full-grown tree yields 100 pounds of nuts a year, some as much as 150 pounds.

Buying and using macadamias. At present the nuts are available shelled, in vacuum-pack cans, as whole nuts or pieces. They are nearly round and somewhat larger than a filbert; the flavor is vaguely reminiscent of almonds with overtones of coffee; the texture is rather mealy.

Macadamias are often served with drinks—by those who truly enjoy them, and also by those who realize that their guests will know how expensive the nuts are and be suitably impressed.

Not a great many recipes using the nuts have been originated to date, but macadamias can be substituted for pecans to make a delicious pie, and used sliced or chopped in nut bread and nut cake and cookie recipes. Store opened cans of the nuts in the refrigerator tightly covered.

Roughly 6½ ounces of macadamias will yield about 1½ cups when chopped. Like most nuts, they are high in fat; they also contain small amounts of protein, vitamins, and minerals. Depending on size—which varies considerably—6 to 10 of the nuts furnish about 100 calories.

MACARONI: see PASTA

MACARONI SALADS: see SALADS

MACAROONS

These are small, easy-to-make cookies with a meringue base. When baked to a delicate brown, they are crunchy on the outside, chewy within. Traditionally they are made with almond paste or ground almonds, but today flaked coconut is often substituted. Some desserts—an elaborate trifle is one of them—call for crumbled macaroons as an ingredient. Plan on using up the cookies within 2 days of making, or freeze them; they go stale, getting very hard, after that time.

MACE: see SPICES

MACEDOINE: see page 453

MACERATE: see MARINATE

MACKEREL

Classified as a fat fish, suitable for broiling, fresh mackerel is widely available in season in fish stores and supermarket fish departments (see FISH). Mackerel, with a pleasingly distinctive flavor, can also be found in 15-ounce cans shelved close to those other far more expensive canned fish, salmon and tuna, in your supermarket. Substitute canned mackerel in your favorite canned salmon and tuna recipes for tasty, low-budget main dishes. Unlike more delicate fish, mackerel's robust flavor will stand up to pungent seasonings such as garlic and onions.

MACROMINERALS: see special feature: NUTRITION NOTEBOOK

MADELEINES

When Marcel Proust dipped a madeleine into his tea and took a bite, a whole world of memories flooded his mind and heart, engendering his *Remembrance of Things Past*. There is no promise of such an experience for everyone in the eating of a madeleine, but the little sweets—halfway between a cupcake and a cookie—are a welcome addition to the home cook's repertoire, just right to serve for snacks, with a fruit dessert or, of course, with an afternoon cup of tea.

Not too sweet, nicely crumbly of texture, madeleines may be flavored with vanilla or almond or lemon, and are baked—to be authentic—in madeleine pans, which produce a fluted pattern on the baked cakes. Lacking the proper pans, you might bake the madeleine mixture in small cupcake or muffin tins, filling them no more than one-third full, so that the cakes will not be too thick. They should not be frosted, but dust them with a little confectioners sugar if you wish.

Madeleines are sometimes a specialty in good French bakeries, and are well worth seeking out.

MADRILENE

Consommé madrilène is a delicately flavored clear soup whose flavor is owed equally to meat stock and tomatoes; it is a handsome dark red. Served hot or cold—when cold, it is virtually always jellied—madrilène makes a delicious, not-too-filling first course. Hot madrilène most often comes to the table with a very thin slice of lemon floating on top. The cold, jellied variety may be accompanied by a wedge of lemon for the diner to squeeze over the soup, or it may be more substantially topped with a dab of sour cream, plain or sprinkled with chives.

Madrilène is available canned; shake the can well and store it in the refrigerator to gel in about 24 hours. Or open the can, add to the madrilène 1 tablespoon lemon juice, a dash of hot pepper sauce, and 1½ cups finely diced vegetables—celery, green onions, green pepper, cucumber—in proportions to taste. Spoon into the cups in which it will be served; refrigerate, covered, 24 hours. Rather like an easy-do, soft-gel gazpacho.

MAGNESIUM: see special feature: NUTRITION NOTEBOOK

MAIN DISHES

Planning menus, most home cooks decide on the main dish first and plan around it. (Some few start with the dessert and work backwards; they are doubtless the ones who were told, as children, "Finish all your nice meat and potatoes or you can't have any chocolate pudding.")

Most main dishes take one of two forms: 1) plain meats or fish or poultry, possibly to be served with sauce or gravy and a starchy food—potatoes, rice, pasta—plus a vegetable, a bread, and a salad; or 2) "made" dishes—casseroles, skillets, stews, hearty soups, and the like—which have some of those elements within them, needing only a salad and sometimes bread to complete the main portion of the meal. Often, for the sake of trimness, we streamline those patterns somewhat, eliminating either the bread or the starchy food, sometimes both, in favor of larger vegetable helpings or the addition of a second vegetable.

Main dishes can be double-batched, half to serve and half to freeze; the frozen ones are a busy-day blessing and great when you ask some other member of the family to start dinner before you will be home. Casseroles, stews, and such specialties as chili are only marginally more difficult to prepare in double batches. Or you can cook ahead especially for freezing. Many ambitious working women rise early on Saturday or Sunday mornings to cook and freeze the whole next week's worth of main dishes. See also CASSEROLES, GARNISHING, POTPIES, SOUPS, STEWS, and the special feature: NUTRITION NOTEBOOK.

MALT

Grain—most often barley—is malted by soaking it in water and allowing it to sprout. This results in maltose, from which malt is extracted for use in making beer and distilling whiskey. *Malt Extract* is a heavy syrup produced by soaking malt in water. *Malt Extract Barm* is a combination of malt extract and water, maintained at 70°F. as a medium for growing yeast. *Malt Liquor* describes beer, ale, stout, porter, and the related beverages in whose making malt is used. *Malt Whiskey* is distilled from mash containing not less than 51 percent rye or barley. *Malt Wine* is another name, a British one, for stout.

MALT VINEGAR: see VINEGARS

MALTED MILK

A powder made of dried milk mixed with wheat and malted-barley extracts. It has a distinctive flavor; mixed with milk, it makes a delicious and nourishing drink, and may be had plain or flavored with chocolate. Thick, soda-fountain type malted milks can be made at home in the blender with milk, ice cream, malted milk powder, and any desired flavoring.

MANDARIN ORANGES

Small, easy-peel citrus fruit, yellow to red-orange in color, the mandarin orange family includes tangerines, temple oranges, and Japanese satsuma oranges. Since most of the canned mandarin oranges we buy are imported from Japan, these are satsumas.

At least some of the members of the mandarin family are to be found in the market from November through May; the canned variety is, of course, available all year around.

Like other citrus fruit, the mandarin's chief nutritional contribution is vitamin C. A 3½-ounce serving furnishes in the neighborhood of 60 calories. Use the fruit, canned or fresh, in fruit salads, cups, and compotes, the fresh fruit for snacking or carried lunches. See also ORANGES.

MANGANESE: see special feature: NUTRITION NOTEBOOK

MANGOES

A tropical and subtropical fruit, with juicy, distinctively flavored orange flesh and a single large, flat pit, mangoes are believed to have originated in India. Today, our supply of them comes chiefly from Florida and Mexico; they appear in the market in late April and continue through August, with peak supplies—and the best prices—in June and July. The skin of the mango is green and often speckled, sometimes with a yellowish or rosy-red blush. Held between the palms of the hands, a ripe mango will yield a little to gentle pressure. Use ripe fruit within 3 days. Ripen underripe mangoes (two or more fare better than a single fruit) in a paper or plastic bag, not closed airtight, at room temperature.

Nutritionally, mangoes contribute vitamins A and C to the diet in generous supply, and some iron as well. One cup of the fruit, diced or sliced, furnishes less than 110 calories.

Tackling a mango. Your first experience with a mango can end in messy defeat if you don't go at it properly. The fruit is exceedingly juicy, and the pulp clings tenaciously to the big pit. With a sharp knife, cut just through the skin in several places and peel back—the skin comes away almost as readily as that of a banana. Then cut the flesh from the pit in chunks or long slices. To serve on the half shell, at breakfast or for dessert, slip a sharp knife into the fruit at the stem end; work the knife around the pit, first on one side, then on the other. Slit the skin all around and pull the fruit apart. Serve as is, to be eaten with a spoon. Or prepare the mango Hawaiian style by scoring the mango half lengthwise and crosswise almost to the skin; turn inside out and push up on the skin—the sections of fruit will stand up in an attractive pattern.

Serve mangoes plain with a wedge of lemon or lime to squeeze over it. Or combine with fresh pineapple and banana in a tropical fruit salad-dessert to dress with half-and-half lime juice and honey, and sprinkle with shredded coconut. Or purée the fruit in the blender with kirsch or any orange-flavor liqueur to use as a sauce for ice cream or lemon or lime ice.

Out of season, mangoes are available in cans. Or they may be canned or frozen—in water or medium-heavy syrup —at home. See also EXOTIC FRUIT.

MANGOSTEENS: see EXOTIC FRUIT

MANICOTTI: see PASTA

MAPLE

Thirteen kinds of maple trees grow in the United States, one sort or another flourishing in all parts of the country. Their naked branches make a handsome pattern against bleak winter skies; in spring they turn a tender green; in summer they offer cool shade; in autumn their leaves put on a great show, blazing yellow and flaming red.

But maple trees have more to offer than beauty, as the earliest settlers learned from the Indians, who showed their new neighbors how to tap the trees for their sweet sap and how to boil it down to make maple syrup and maple sugar. Although the sap of all maple trees is sweet (as is the sap of many other trees), only the sugar maple and the black maple are tapped. A stand of those trees is called a "sugar bush."

The collection of sap and the sugaring-off process remain virtually the same today as in those early days for some New Englanders to whom the making of maple syrup and sugar remains a time of festivity—and very hard work. In February, when the sap begins to run, a hole is bored in each tree of the sugar bush, a spout inserted, and a bucket hung on the spout to catch the sap. Collected and carried to "sugar camp," the sap is poured into huge kettles and boiled down. It requires thirty-five gallons of sap to produce one gallon of maple syrup, and the boiling to achieve that result takes many days and much arm-breaking stirring; further boiling and stirring reduces the syrup to maple sugar.

Today, except for those farms in New England that still follow this arduous process, maple syrup and sugar are produced through a modern process that taps the trees mechanically and supplants the long boiling with huge evaporator plants. Pure maple syrup and maple sugar—in blocks, or molded into small, decorative shapes as maple-sugar candy —are widely (and expensively) available. Much more common is maple-blended syrup—which is part maple, part sugar and corn syrup—and maple-flavored syrup—which is the sugar/corn syrup with maple flavoring added.

Maple or maple-blended or -flavored syrup can be used to make a number of delicious desserts: cookies, cakes, pies, and tarts—all of them with an old-fashioned aura. The most common use, however, is on waffles or pancakes.

Delicious to spread on hot toast or biscuits is maple butter, easily made by gradually creaming 1 cup of syrup into ½ cup of butter. Baked apples sweetened with maple sugar or syrup are a long-time favorite. So are baked beans with salt pork, in which maple syrup substitutes for the more usual molasses. Grandma's maple frosting is very easy: boil 2 cups maple syrup to 232°F.; gradually beat into 2 stiffly beaten, lightly salted egg whites; continue to beat until the mixture stands in soft peaks. Maple Frango is made the same way, except that the syrup is boiled to the soft-ball stage (238°); after it is beaten into the egg whites, it is folded into 1 cup of heavy cream that has been beaten until stiff, and the mixture is frozen—today, freeze in an ice cube tray.

Cautionary note: If you substitute pure maple sugar or syrup in your cooking, remember that it is considerably sweeter than the cane or beet sugar we generally use.

MARASCHINO CHERRIES: see CHERRIES

MARGARINE

In 1867, Napoleon III had what can be considered, depending on your point of view, a great or a terrible idea. He approached a French chemist, one Hypolite Mège-Mouries, with the offer of a valuable prize if he could, in the Emperor's words, "produce a cheap butter for the army, navy, and the needy classes of the population." After considerable experimentation, M. Mège-Mouries produced a solid white substance with a pearly gleam; he called it oleo-margarine, "oleo" from "oil" and "margarine" from the Greek word *margarites,* which means "pearly." To earn his emperor's prize, the chemist had melted and clarified suet (animal kidney fat), separated the softer fats—stearins—under pressure, mixed the remaining harder fats with milk, and churned the mass until it was solid.

A later, simpler method heated and pressed the fats, and the solid part that remained after pressing was sold as "butterine." Still later, vegetable fats—peanut oil and palm oil —were blended into the mixture to give it a melting point similar to butter's, and the margarine was hydrogenized to solidify it.

M. Mège-Mouries considered that he had invented not a substitute for butter but a less expensive form of the real thing—after all, both butter and his product were made from animal fat, *n'est-ce pas?* It developed that the dairy industry disagreed wholeheartedly. But at that early stage, the dairy industry had no inkling of the problem it would eventually have on its hands.

The chemist patented his margarine formula in both France and England in 1869, and in the United States in 1873. Margarine never really caught on in France, where the cuisine-conscious felt that the product was an insult to the good butter they had been using in their cooking for years. It fared better in England, but that country still uses far more butter than margarine, and margarine consumption is declining steadily there.

In the United States, however, it was a different story. The dairy industry fought the new product tooth and nail. Anti-margarine lobbying in Washington produced results: a tax on margarine, and a restriction on the sale of margarine colored yellow to resemble butter. But despite the facts that early margarines were no bargain in flavor (although they were much cheaper than butter, even after the tax was passed on to the consumer), and that they strongly resembled lard in the eyes of those used to nice, yellow butter, sales of the product boomed.

A capsule of yellow coloring was included with margarine so that the home cook could work it into the product to turn it a pleasant butter yellow. And manufacturers constantly improved the product, eliminating the somewhat off-putting flavor of M. Mège-Mouries' invention and the others that followed shortly after. A typical margarine of today is a blend of fine vegetable oil and nonfat milk that is fortified with vitamin A in quantities of 15,000 international units per pound. Other present-day margarines may still contain animal as well as vegetable fats, and the fats may be mixed with cream, milk, skim milk, or nonfat dry milk, singly or several combined. Other ingredients may be colorings, flavorings, preservatives, emulsifiers, and vitamin D. All margarine on the market is fortified with vitamin A, and by law the product must be 80 percent fat. Now, virtually all margarine is colored a gentle butter yellow, the federal restrictive taxes having been lifted in 1950, and the various state restrictions on the production of colored margarine removed thereafter.

If your standard, as it is most people's, is butter, margarines have been getting better and better—more butterlike— through the years. But most margarines can no longer be classified as "poor man's butter," for prices have risen too, until that of many brands is close to the price of butter, and that of a few premium brands equals it. The rationale behind using margarine rather than butter has changed radically, and at the same time so has the national attitude toward the product. Once many people bought margarine because it was cheap; they were ashamed of using it and kept it, insofar as they could, a secret. Now many people buy margarine because it is lower in saturated fats—very important to cholesterol watchers—and they boast about it as they discuss their diet. (By "diet," weight-loss is not meant—butter and margarine are equal in calories, 102 per tablespoon. However, for weight-loss dieters, lowered-fat imitation margarine is available, at about half that amount.)

Buying and using margarine. Buy where the turnover is rapid, store in the refrigerator. Unless you intend to freeze it, buy no more margarine than you can use in a week to 10 days' time; well refrigerated, it will keep up to 30 days, but like butter, it loses its fresh flavor as time goes by. Read the label for ingredients, remembering that they are listed in order of amount. If you are watching cholesterol, buy corn oil or safflower oil margarine, or at least avoid any of the brands containing animal fat.

Margarine is marketed in several forms. Regular margarines come in 1-pound packages, the contents divided into four quarter-pound sticks. Soft margarine (easy-spreading), diet (calorie-lowered), and whipped (also easy-spreading and presumably less fattening because the air whipped into it makes it go farther) margarines are sold in ½- and 1-pound plastic tubs with well-fitting covers that can be washed and reused as containers for storing other foods in the refrigerator (but not in the freezer). One company has recently added a "squeeze" margarine to its line—a thick liquid to use on such foods as waffles and hot vegetables, for basting and sautéing, and in recipes where melted butter or margarine is called for. This comes in a bottle, equivalent to a pound of regular margarine, has an easy-pour/easy-close top, and does not harden at refrigerator temperatures. See also OLEOMARGARINE.

MARINADES: see BARBECUE, KABOBS, and
    MEAT TENDERIZERS

MARINATE, MACERATE

To soak foods in a liquid to tenderize and/or flavor them. Meats (and poultry) are said to be marinated, fruits macerated. A usual marinade contains oil or other fat, seasonings of various kinds, and an acid—vinegar or wine or lemon juice —which is the tenderizing agent. Fruits are most often macerated in brandy, rum, wine, or a liqueur, sometimes in the juice of a fruit different from the one(s) being soaked. Maceration is for flavor enhancing only, not for tenderizing.

MARJORAM: see HERBS AND SAVORY
SEASONINGS

MARMALADES: see special feature:
PUTTING FOOD BY

MARRONS

The French term for CHESTNUTS, marrons—generally imported—may be purchased in jars, preserved in rum or brandy or in a vanilla syrup, and are used as a sauce for ice cream or other desserts. Marrons glacés are whole nuts covered with a thin, sweet coating—very expensive and very, very good.

MARROW

One of Queen Victoria's favorite dishes was baked marrow piled on fresh, hot toast, with a little lemon juice on the side. In her day, marrow bones were baked or steamed and sent to the table napkin wrapped, to be delved into by the individual diner using a special, long-handled marrow spoon—now a collector's item.

Marrow is the fatty center portion of beef bones. It is still popular in England, served as a savory—the nonsweet dish served after a sweet dessert to clear the palate for the sweet wine (port, madeira, or the like) that will follow. Rich and delicate of flavor, marrow is light and is one of the more easily digestible fats. It sometimes appears on the menus of English or pretend-to-be-English restaurants in this country.

Used in soup, marrow bones enrich the stock and provide a bonus of cooked marrow. Or buy the bones separately —they are available wherever beef is sold, although they are seldom on display because few people know what to do with them. Have the butcher cut the bones into short lengths; remove the marrow and poach it briefly in beef bouillon or bake the bones and remove the marrow afterwards. Serve it on toast as an unusual—and unusually delectable—appetizer. Marrow is also used in tiny dumplings cooked and served in clear soup as well as other ways. If you enjoy your first experiment with it, consult a good general cookbook for other uses to try.

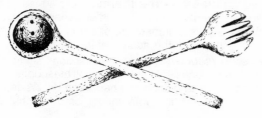

MARSHMALLOW CREAM (or CREME)

Sold in glass jars, marshmallow cream is marshmallow in an easy-to-use form for cooking. Perhaps its best-known use is in a no-fail fudge made with the cream plus sugar, evaporated milk, and semisweet chocolate bits. It's incredibly good —creamy and smooth, with excellent flavor—and sinfully calorie-laden. Find the recipe in some cookbooks or on the marshmallow cream or chocolate bits label.

There are other uses for the thick, sticky cream in desserts and confections. Stuff dates or prunes with it. Sandwich thin chocolate wafers with it. Layer it in serving dishes with chocolate or butterscotch pudding. Make frosting with it.

Children love the stuff, and many would blissfully eat spoonful after spoonful right out of the jar if allowed. They also welcome it in one of those sandwiches that horrify adults but leave kids crowing with delight: marshmallow cream, peanut butter, and sliced bananas on whole wheat bread.

MARSHMALLOWS

Puffy, pudgy pillows of candy, marshmallows are a favorite with children. Their chief ingredients are sugar, gelatin, and egg whites. Because such a large volume of air is incorporated during the making, they are a relatively low-calorie candy.

Marshmallows come in plastic bags of various sizes, plain white or in several pastel colors. There are also miniature marshmallows, chocolate-covered ones, and gloriously gooey caramel-coated marshmallows. Marshmallows are used to a limited extent in cooking: in rocky road fudge or frosting, as a variation from meringue on top of cream pies, in a sweet-but-good "forgotten fruit salad," which was very popular at ladies' luncheons in the thirties, and in a number of desserts.

MARZIPAN

A mixture of ground blanched almonds, sugar, and unbeaten egg whites, marzipan is a thick confectionary paste of exquisite flavor that can be molded into many shapes (by hand or in small wooden or metal or rubber molds); rolled into a sheet and used in place of or in addition to frosting on a cake; or cut into ribbons, bows, or any desired decoration with a sharp knife, and made into ornaments for the Christmas tree. In fact, it is at Christmas that marzipan comes into its own. At that season, handsome marzipan shapes can be purchased in many specialty food or confectionary shops, but it's pleasant and not too difficult to make your own marzipan and mold your own shapes from it. Turn the project into a whole-family affair that can become a Christmas tradition at your house.

Marzipan is supposed to have originated in the Near East—where both almonds and sugar were plentiful—and been brought back to Europe by the Crusaders. It eventually became one of the traditional Christmas sweets in many countries. Scandinavians in particular are fond of it, and in

Denmark a chubby little pink marzipan pig is considered a good-luck gift.

Easy to color (use liquid or paste food coloring) and easy to work with, marzipan can be prepared in advance and stored in the refrigerator for several weeks. Or it may be purchased, ready-prepared, in specialty food shops and confectionaries. Shapes made of the paste will also keep well, tightly covered—to prevent a crust forming on the outside—and refrigerated.

MASA: see CORN

MASA HARINA: see GRAINS

MASH, TO: see page 447

MASK, TO: see page 447

MATZOTH

This is the unleavened bread that Jews eat at Passover to commemorate the flight from Egypt, when their forefathers had to eat unleavened bread because there was no time to set yeast bread and wait for it to rise.

Flat, crisp, and crackerlike, matzoth are good snack food, or they can be used as a bread to accompany appetizer dips and spreads. Today, they are available plain, flavored with onion or cheese, or chocolate covered.

MAYONNAISE

Asked suddenly "What is mayonnaise?" you would probably reply, "It's a salad dressing." And so it is, so it is—but it's also a great deal more, a truly versatile sauce that can be varied in a dozen directions, served in or on or with dozens of foods. It can even be used as the shortening in baking, as touted in advertising campaigns of one mayonnaise manufacturer, although what the advantage is or why one would want to use it as such remains obscure.

Buy it, make it at home. Mayonnaise is available in virtually all markets, in a number of sizes. Store, unopened, on a cupboard shelf up to 4 months; refrigerate opened jars of mayonnaise, tightly covered, up to 6 months. Homemade mayonnaise must be refrigerated and should be kept no more than 1 week.

Commercial mayonnaises are not required to list ingredients on the label; they are one of those few foods that conform to a standard recipe. By that standard, mayonnaise must contain at least 65 percent oil by weight, acid ingredients such as vinegar or lemon juice, and an emulsifier—egg (yolk or whole), gelatin, starch paste, or edible gums. It may also contain salt, sweetening ingredients, monosodium glutamate, and a variety of other seasonings, provided they do not impart the color of egg yolk to the product; thus, in a mayonnaise lacking in eggs, it would be improper to add turmeric in a quantity that would color the product an egg-yolk yellow.

Some mayonnaises use some egg and some other emulsifier as well. If there is no egg whatever in the mixture, it must be labeled "salad dressing" rather than "mayonnaise."

Homemade mayonnaise is delicious and, contrary to horror stories bandied about, not at all difficult if you keep your wits about you. The secret lies in the oil—in both the amount used and the manner in which it is added. One egg yolk can emulsify no more than ¾ cup of oil; 3 yolks to 2 cups of oil is a better ratio and one that produces a fine mayonnaise. At the beginning, the oil must be added literally drop by drop, and you must not stop beating the mixture. Once the sauce has begun to "take," as grandma used to say, the oil can be added in a very thin stream as you continue to beat. But don't be impatient and dump in too much oil at one time or the mixture will break up into its component parts—"turning," that's called. Even if it turns, the damage can be repaired: in a clean bowl, beat 1 egg yolk until it is thick, then beat the turned mayonnaise into it (not the other way around) in very small amounts.

You can make mayonnaise by hand with a wire whip, or you can use a portable or stand-type electric mixer, a blender, or a food processor. In the blender or processor, use whole egg rather than yolks—with yolks alone, the sauce becomes too thick and won't beat properly. If it does become too thick, even with whole eggs, thin it with drop-by-drop warm water.

However you make it, the basic recipe is simple: egg plus oil plus acid plus seasoning. Beat the eggs until they are thick; beat in the seasonings and the acid; then add the oil very gradually, beating constantly. That is all there is to it—and the whole process takes no more than 5 minutes. Taste the sauce and adjust the seasonings if necessary. The acid can be lemon juice or vinegar, the seasoning salt and pepper (white or cayenne), plus dry or dijon-style prepared mustard, if you want to add bite. The oil can be olive or peanut or any light, virtually flavorless salad oil, depending on the taste you want.

You might make mayonnaise with wine vinegar and olive oil, seasoned with garlic and mustard, to serve with, say, cold ratatouille. Or make it with lemon juice and a light oil and fold in drained chopped capers, to dress a chicken salad. Once you have the basic mayonnaise, you can vary it in dozens of ways.

Ringing changes on the theme. Here are some of the best-liked mayonnaise variations. In all cases, start with 1½ cups of mayonnaise, homemade or commercial, and gently but thoroughly fold in the additional ingredients.

salsa verde (sauce vert): 1½ tablespoons finely minced parsley, 2 teaspoons minced chives, 2 teaspoons minced fresh tarragon, 1 teaspoon snipped fresh dill, ½ teaspoon minced fresh chervil; *use with* shrimp, crab, or lobster.

424

thousand island: 2 tablespoons chili sauce, 1 teaspoon minced green pepper, ½ teaspoon each minced pimiento and snipped chives; *use with* hearts of lettuce or any green salad, or sandwiches.

russian dressing: 2 tablespoons minced onion, 2 tablespoons minced green pepper, ¼ cup bottled chili sauce; use with lettuce wedges, sliced tomatoes, or on hamburgers.

tartar sauce: 1 mashed hard-cooked egg yolk; 3 minced shallots; 4 minced gherkins; 1 tablespoon each minced fresh tarragon, parsley, capers, onion, and chervil; 1 teaspoon each dijon-style mustard and lemon juice; sugar, salt, and pepper to taste; *use with* fish of any kind, hot or cold.

sauce rémoulade: 1 tablespoon minced gherkin; 1 teaspoon each dijon-style mustard, minced parsley, minced fresh tarragon, and minced fresh chervil; anchovy paste to taste; *use with* briefly cooked and chilled julienne strips of celery or celeriac, or artichoke hearts.

salsa daria: 2 chopped hard-cooked eggs, 2 tablespoons drained india relish, 1 tablespoon tomato paste, ½ teaspoon worcestershire sauce, 2 drops hot pepper sauce; *use with* hearts of lettuce or thickly sliced tomatoes.

sauce niçoise: 3 tablespoons tomato paste, 3 tablespoons minced green pepper, 1 teaspoon snipped chives; *use with* any cold fish or shellfish.

summer blessing: 1 cup dairy sour cream, 2 tablespoons lime juice; *use with* combined cantaloupe, honeydew, and watermelon balls; or any fresh fruit salad.

mustard mayonnaise: 2 tablespoons lemon juice, 2 tablespoons dijon-style mustard, 1 cup lightly whipped heavy cream; *use with* braised scallions, leeks, or belgian endive; or a mixed cooked-vegetable salad.

cumberland-style mayonnaise: melt and cool ¼ cup tart currant jelly; fold into mayonnaise with 2 tablespoons lemon juice and 1 tablespoon hot/sweet prepared mustard; *use with* cold pork or venison.

gold rush dressing: ⅓ cup thawed orange juice concentrate, 3 tablespoons honey, 2 tablespoons grated orange peel, 2 teaspoons grated lemon peel, ¼ teaspoon nutmeg; *use with* any fresh or canned fruit salad.

horseradish sauce: ¾ cup buttermilk, 3 tablespoons thinly sliced green onion, 2 tablespoons prepared horseradish; *use with* hot or cold beef, or sliced tomatoes and cucumbers, or thinly sliced bermuda onions.

west-coast blue: 1½ cups crumbled bleu cheese, ⅓ cup dry white wine or 2 tablespoons lemon juice, 2 tablespoons grated onion, hot pepper sauce to taste; *use with* hot cooked vegetables, tossed green salad, or as a savory dip.

Make all of these dressings an hour or two—or longer—in advance and refrigerate, tightly covered. That way, the flavors have ample opportunity to meld and mellow.

Some mayonnaise specials. Mayonnaise collée is simply plain mayonnaise given extra flavor and some backbone, so that it will stand up to its task—which is to mask (coat) cold meat, poultry, fish, eggs, or cooked vegetable salads. Sauce aïoli is a very garlicky olive-oil/lemon-juice mayonnaise served as a dip with crudités, with fish or cabbage soups, or as a dressing for cooked cabbage wedges or brussels sprouts or hot cooked little new potatoes in their jackets.

MEAL

Two meanings here: 1) grain not as finely ground as flour—cornmeal is an example, and 2) the sum of all the foods served at one sitting—breakfast, lunch, dinner, supper are all meals.

MEASURE, MEASUREMENTS: see special features:
THE HOME COOK'S NEW MATH and YOU CAN'T WORK WITHOUT TOOLS

MEASURING UP TO METRIC:
see page 33

MEAT

Meat supplies the major source of protein in our daily diet, and meat's fat supplies satiety value, the "staying power" that keeps you from being hungry again shortly after a meal. Even those who trim away all separable fat from the meat they eat get some fat—it is marbled through the meat and lends it juiciness and flavor. Fat is one of the essential nutrients in the diet, and is the carrier of fat-soluble vitamins, moving them through our bodies to the points where they are needed and used.

Meat of all kinds is easy to digest: the proteins are at least 97 percent digested, the fat 96 percent. And because there are enough cuts and kinds of beef, pork, veal, and lamb in our markets, the home cook could prepare a different meat dish every day of the year; thus we need never tire of meat and so cheat ourselves of the protein that our bodies require.

Meat shopping. With most of us, meat claims the largest share of the household food budget, so it pays to meat shop with a head's-up attitude. If you buy meat at a butcher shop, you can inspect it from all sides, but if you buy prepackaged meat at a supermarket, you are often hampered by the cardboard or plastic tray in which it rests. (New York and some other states' laws require that those trays be made of see-through plastic, a boon for meat shoppers.) Inspect the meat as well as you can—for example, never look merely at one end of a roast; one end can be very lean and handsome, but the other end may well be fatty and badly cut through with gristle. Estimate how much of what you'll pay for will be thrown out—pork chops with a heavy outer layer of fat are not a good buy, for example, because too much of the weight you pay for will be cut away and discarded.

If the meat has a pull date—the last day on which it can

be sold—be guided by that as an indication of how long the meat has been cut and out on the counter. Let your eyes guide you, too. Fresh meat *looks* fresh, and it smells fresh—that is, it has no particular odor. Old meat has an unpleasant off-odor, and in meat that is beginning to spoil that off-odor is very strong. Buy from a market where the quality is consistently good.

Some meat packers bypass government grading for their own system of name-grades; once you have learned what these indicate, corresponding roughly to the USDA's prime, choice, and good, you will find them a reliable guide. Although all meat is government inspected, not all is graded. But at a market whose foods and services you know and trust, you can expect to find USDA graded meat or the graded meats of a reliable packer. The USDA grades are:

beef	veal	lamb	pork
prime	prime	prime	U.S. No. 1
choice	choice	choice	U.S. No. 2
good	good	good	U.S. No. 3
standard	standard	utility	medium
commercial	utility	cull	cull
utility	cull		
cutter			
canner			

Prime and choice for the first three, and U.S. No. 1 for pork are the grades you will find in most supermarkets, although some began to carry "good" beef, which is less expensive, when customers complained about the high cost of the meat. Many carry only choice, and those that do stock prime carry very little of it, a kind of token for those of the customers who know and love excellent meat; most prime beef goes to restaurants. Some small and elegant meat markets, however, carry nothing but prime, although most such markets will offer both prime and choice as well as the first, possibly also the second, grade of pork. The lower grades go to canners and pet-food packers, except those that find their way to markets in poorer neighborhoods—particularly in areas where little English is spoken—and are often sold at the same or even higher prices than prime and choice grades in other neighborhoods.

Meat cooking. Tender cuts of meat (and some that have been tenderized) are cooked with dry heat: roasting, broiling, frying, panbroiling without added fat. Less tender cuts should be cooked with moist heat: braised or immersed in liquid. The less tender cuts are always cooked long and slowly; the tender cuts are ready in a relatively shorter time.

Although standard names for cuts of meat are becoming more widely used, some holdout shops still call their meats by names that give no indication of which part of the animal, or even which animal, it comes from. How do you know which way such meats should be cooked? Ask the butcher. Or if there is bone in the meat, inspect the bone. Study the bone chart below as a guide to tender and not-so-tender meats.

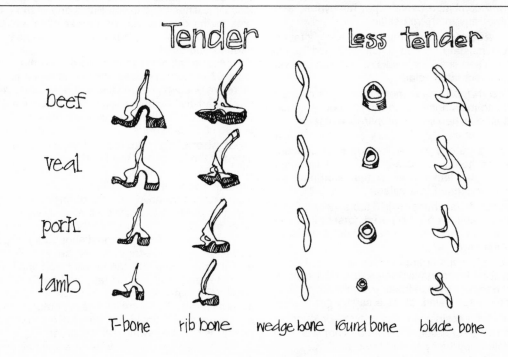

Tender   Less tender

beef   veal   pork   lamb

T-bone   rib bone   wedge bone   round bone   blade bone

Frozen meats. Most frozen meat can be cooked from the frozen state, and will take from half-again to twice as long to cook as an identical nonfrozen cut. Frozen steaks and chops to be broiled should be cooked at a lower temperature and farther from the source of heat, so that they will be cooked inside before they are too brown on the outside. To cook single servings without thawing, it's necessary to pack steaks and chops and ground meat patties for the freezer with pieces of plastic film separating them, or the entire package will have to be thawed in order to get the pieces apart.

The USDA says that up to six cents per retail pound of beef could be saved if the public would accept meat cut and packaged at warehouses rather than at retail stores. This meat would be frozen when purchased. One of the biggest problems to overcome, says the USDA, is consumer resistance to new marketing techniques such as this one. For some reason, the same consumers who readily buy frozen turkey are reluctant to buy frozen beef—even though, according to a department survey, 80 percent of shoppers who buy meat several days before cooking (those who do a week's shopping at one time) freeze meat after they bring it home.

Centralized cutting of both fresh and frozen beef provides greater total carcass use, the USDA points out, as well as greater product uniformity, improved sanitation, and reduced handling, packaging, and transportation costs. Frozen beef keeps better and shrinks less than fresh beef.

Agriculture predicts that consumer resistance will lessen and more frozen beef will be sold in years to come, especially in smaller retail stores where not enough meat is sold to justify maintaining a fresh meat counter.

For more about specific kinds and cuts of meat, nutritional contributions of meat to the diet, and meat storage, see BEEF, COLD CUTS, FORCEMEAT, GAME, HAM, HORSEMEAT, HUNG MEAT, INMEATS, JERKED MEAT, LAMB, MINCEMEAT, PORK, SAUSAGES, VARIETY MEATS, VEAL, FOOD STORAGE, and the special features: NUTRITION NOTEBOOK and WHAT'S IN A FOOD'S NAME?

MEAT TENDERIZERS

Ever since Mrs. Cavewife figured out that the crushed berries from that funny-looking plant over there would make it possible to chew the wild boar steak on tonight's menu, both home cooks and the meat industry have been looking for ways to make tough meat tender and therefore more palatable. By now, several foolproof ways have been developed, some mechanical, some chemical.

Mechanical tenderizers. In grandma's day, no kitchen was complete without a meat grinder, and to many of us that remains true today. Ground meat from whatever cut of whatever animal is tender because the tough fibers have been cut into tiny pieces—the meat is, in a sense, prechewed.

In most markets, ground meat of several kinds is available: beef of two or three sorts (depending on the cut and the amount of fat), lamb, veal, pork, ham, and—becoming more widely available every day, as home cooks learn its many uses—ground raw turkey. Some markets offer a combination beef-veal-pork meat loaf mixture, seasoned or not, with or without filler (bread or cracker crumbs, soy protein, and such); the label will tell you what's in the mix. Ham-loaf mixtures are also available in some markets. But unless you are a novice cook, you will probably want to buy ground meat of various kinds in the proportions you like for meat loaves, and season them in your own way.

Cube steaks, the fibers of which have been broken down by machine in a honeycomb pattern to tenderize them, are available in most markets, too. Also (these are usually frozen) "preformed" beef or ham or veal steaks or patties, the latter often breaded. These are made of chopped or ground meat formed into patty or steak shapes.

Mechanical tenderizers are available for home use, too. One is the meat mallet; it looks like a small sledgehammer made of wood, the two faces of its business end carved into a series of teeth. A second such gadget is made of metal with a round, toothed business end and a handle that fits easily into the hand. A third is made of sturdy plastic; at the bottom is a disk perforated with a number of holes, above each of which is positioned a sharp-pointed spike that comes down through the hole and into the meat by spring action when the top is pressed. Some home cooks simply use the edge of a heavy saucer or plate to perform the tenderizing function.

All of these may be used, as well as for tenderizing, to pound flour, seasoned or not, into the meat to help browning. Cautionary note: All the meat tenderizer tools should be washed as soon as you're through using them. They can be easily cleaned then, but if you let them sit around, getting the areas between those teeth clean is a chore you wouldn't wish on your worst enemy.

Chemical tenderizers. These fall into two classes, marinades and powdered commercial tenderizers.

Long ago, in times when no meat was really tender but some cuts only less tough than others, home cooks learned to soak meat in wine to give their family's teeth a fighting chance. Today we follow the same procedure, with a certain amount of refinement.

Marinades generally have three kinds of ingredients: an acid—wine, vinegar, or lemon juice—to attack and tenderize tough fibers, fat—oil or, less usually, melted butter—to make the meat juicy, and seasonings, which can range all the way from salt and pepper through herbs and spices of several kinds to garlic, onions, crushed juniper berries and more, to enhance the meat's flavor with their own. Sometimes the marinade is discarded after the meat has soaked in it; more often it is used to baste the meat as it cooks or, as a part of the braising liquid, it is heated and served as a sauce with the meat. Marinades are easily made at home; there are also preseasoned commercial marinade mixes available.

The other chemical tenderizer is a white crystalline powder, the chief ingredient of which is papain, an enzyme extracted from the papaya. Other ingredients are salt, sometimes dextrose—a type of sugar—and something, such as calcium stearate, to keep the mixture from caking. The surface of the meat is moistened with water, then sprinkled with the tenderizer in proportions of about ½ teaspoon per pound of meat, then pierced deeply all over with a kitchen fork. The meat is turned and the process is repeated on the other side. The meat can be cooked at once or, if it seems to be unconscionably tough, allowed to stand for half an hour or so before cooking. It can even be frozen, because it is the heat of cooking that activates the enzyme to do most of the work of tenderizing.

Papain tenderizers can be purchased unseasoned—except for salt—or seasoned with various herbs and spices. Unless you are a novice cook, you are better off buying the plain tenderizer and seasoning the meat to your family's liking. For example, onion or garlic juice can be added to the water used to moisten the meat; the act of puncturing it with a fork drives the seasoning into the meat. Also, be aware that tough cuts of meat are flavorful in themselves, and often you're better off allowing the meat's own good taste to stand alone. In any event, never salt any meat that has been tenderized—the tenderizer is sufficiently salty (sometimes too much so if you use it with a too-lavish hand) for any taste. See also KABOBS.

MELBA SAUCE: see special feature: SAUCE SORCERY

MELBA TOAST

Mme. Nellie Melba sang her way around the world in the late nineteenth century, the toast, as they say, of three continents. (Melba was her stage name; born in Australia, the diva borrowed it from the city of Melbourne.) She was very fond of a substantial and extravagant supper after her performance, and chefs wherever she went vied with one another to invent dishes in her honor. Many of these have been lost —perhaps deservedly, for good food tends to hang around a long time—but with us still are Pêche Melba and Melba toast. The dessert seems very Melbalike: a split fresh peach topped with vanilla ice cream, the whole bathed in a purée of fresh raspberries fortified with kirschwasser. But the toast? Was the singer perhaps suffering from indigestion on the occasion when the toast came into being, from too long a series of too-rich suppers? More likely she was on a diet after all that food so that her costumes would fit. Melba toast is very good, but very plain: bread sliced whisper-thin and baked to brown crispness.

To accompany a weight-loss dieter's meal, to use as a base for canapés or other appetizers, or simply to eat because it is so pleasantly simple and crunchy, melba toast is available, packaged, in a number of kinds—rye (with or without seeds), whole wheat, onion- or garlic-flavored among them.

If you prefer, make the toast at home—it's an excellent way to use up bread that threatens to go stale. Cut bread of any kind into ⅛-inch slices; if you freeze it, you'll be able to get the thinness you want very easily. Cut shapes from the slices with cookie cutters if you wish, or simply divide the slices in half. Place a rack on a baking sheet, spread out the bread pieces on the rack. Bake in a 250°F. oven until they are dry and the shade of golden brown that suits you. Thin slices of rolls or buns may also be used.

MELONS

Ripe and juicy and honey-sweet, melons somehow call up memories of hot, still August weather. Days when even the bees seemed to fly more slowly, and cicadas set up a ceaseless droning. Days when small boys sneaked away from chores with fishpoles over their shoulders and the dog for company, shuffling barefoot down the road to the catfish pond, leaving behind them knee-high clouds of talc-fine dust. Days when grandpa thumped his way around the watermelon patch, listening for just the right sound (a dull thud—if the sound was metallic, the melon wasn't yet ripe) to choose a melon to set away in the ice house for tomorrow's picnic. Days of lemonade and pressed chicken and the tag end of last year's peach conserve, deviled eggs and wilted lettuce with bacon, and pearl tapioca pudding. Days of . . . what were we talking about? Melons.

Perhaps the word conjures such recollections because melons require a long, hot growing season, and come ripe only when the summer nears its end, when you try not to think about winter but know that it must come, and soon.

No one is quite sure where melons originated, but they have been around forever—for human beings' forever, at least, and perhaps long before that. Drawings in Egyptian tombs, dated *circa* 2400 B.C., show muskmelons. The Assyrians grew them. So did the Greeks and the Chinese. They had been growing in Russia long before anyone thought to claim them as a local invention. They spread to Europe and when, finally, explorers and settlers brought them to this country, it was only to learn that they'd been growing here all the time. Watermelons originated in Africa, spread north and east and west from there.

Gourds that climbed high on the social ladder. Melons are members of the gourd family; squashes, pumpkins, and cucumbers are their cousins, as well as the inedible gourds grown as ornaments and the raw material for a wide assortment of vases, dishes, birdhouses, and the like. There are only two broad classes of edible melons. Watermelons (which Mark Twain called "what angels eat") come in various

428

shapes and sizes, from monsters to feed a big family to neat little cannonball shapes easily accommodated in an apartment refrigerator; their flesh may range from a rather light pink to deep red, with shiny dark seeds scattered throughout. All the remaining edible ones are muskmelons—a cantaloupe is a muskmelon, and so is a cranshaw, a persian, and all the rest, even though each has an appearance and flavor different from the others. They are muskmelons from "musk," the old Persian word for perfume, arising from the sweet, hot, somehow exotic scent that these melons have. All carry their pale seeds in a fiber-filled hollow in the center, where they are easy to scoop out and discard.

Choosing a just-right, just-ripe melon. When you go to buy a melon, you must understand the difference between a mature one and a fully ripe, ready-to-eat one. The sugar level in a mature melon has reached its optimum point. In three or four more days—at home, at room temperature—the melon will ripen to the right-for-eating stage, its sweetness and juices and flavors at their delicious best. But a melon picked before it is mature will never reach that final perfect stage, no matter how much you cosset it. Its flesh will be hard; its juice at a minimum; its flavor, if it has any at all, will resemble a cucumber's.

Here is the know-how you need to choose a fine melon.

Cantaloupe. *in the market:* June, July, and August; *shop for:* a melon with a smooth, nicely rounded, somewhat depressed scar at the stem end; beige to yellow to golden skin covered with a coarse, dry netting definably raised above the skin; about a 5-inch waistline, weighs in the neighborhood of 3 pounds; *beware of:* piece of stem clinging to the scar or any roughness of the scar; soft spots, cracks, mold, bruises; *when it's ripe:* rind gives slightly when pressed, seeds rattle somewhat (but not a great deal) when it's shaken; the smell is a rich spice-and-musk; flesh is orange, firm but yielding.

Casaba. *in the market:* September and October; *shop for:* an onion shape, tapering somewhat to a point at the stem end, where a part of the stem may still be attached; color range is pale green to golden yellow, with a tough/rough rind streaked with deep, lengthwise wrinkles; no noticeable aroma; diameter averages 6½ inches, the weight about 6 pounds; *beware of:* an all-green melon; bruises, soft spots; *when it's ripe:* skin is yellow to golden all over, and blossom end yields slightly to pressure; flesh is soft, creamy-white, very sweet, very juicy.

Christmas (Santa Claus) melon. *in the market:* end of September through December; *shop for:* shape like a miniature watermelon—a long oval; rind is mottled dark green to yellow; 5 to 6 inches around, 8 to 12 inches long; 4 to 6 pounds in weight; *beware of:* soft, off-color spots; bruises; cracks; *when it's ripe:* blossom end is slightly soft; flesh is pale green, soft and juicy, sweet—resembles that of a ripe honeydew.

Cranshaw. *in the market:* August and September; *shop for:* a melon longer than wide, rounded at blossom end, somewhat pointed at the other; rind is green/gold, lightly ribbed; diameter varies, weight is 7 to 9 pounds; rich, exotically spicy aroma; *beware of:* cracks; rough, heavy ribbing; bruises; *when it's ripe:* skin is golden; blossom end slightly softened; aroma very noticeable; flesh is orange to salmon, thick, richly juicy, mildly spicy.

Honeydew, Honeyball. *in the market:* June through October; *shop for:* rounded oval shape, cream-yellow color; yellow patches, giving the appearance that the white has rubbed off, indicate a good choice; average 7 inches diameter, weight 5 to 7 pounds; honeyball is smaller, round; *beware of:* all-white or green-white skin; bruises, soft spots, cracks; *when it's ripe:* it has a pleasant fragrance; exterior looks waxy and yellowish; gives slightly under pressure, particularly at the blossom end; flesh is pale green, thick, very juicy.

Persian. *in the market:* July to October; *shop for:* basketball shape, completely round; dark gray-green rind well covered with flat netting; 6 to 7½ inches in diameter, 6 to 7 pounds in weight; *beware of:* bruises—these melons bruise very easily; dry, sunken patches; white or pale tan areas of rind; round brown spots; mold; *when it's ripe:* under the netting, rind has turned lighter green or green/brown; gives slightly under pressure; pleasant, distinctive aroma has developed; flesh is deep orange or salmon, flavor is mild, not too sweet.

Spanish. *in the market:* from Spain (these are the best and sweetest), early November through early January; from South America, January to the middle of March; from California (limited numbers and distribution), August through October; *shop for:* dark green, rough, hard rind; elongated oval shape; about 6 inches in diameter, 6 to 7 pounds in weight; *beware of:* pale color, strong smell (a good melon of this kind has no aroma), bruises and soft spots, all-over softness; *when it's ripe:* it smells clean, but there is no melony aroma; unlike others, most spanish melons in market are already ripe; flesh is the color of pale honey, thick and juicy, richly flavorful, resembling the best honeydew you ever had.

Watermelon. *in the market:* long season, from May into September; *shop for:* long, rounded cylinders to almost-round shapes; rind can vary from allover medium-dark green to striped to mottled dark/light green to gray-green, but whatever the color, it should be somewhat velvety rather than brightly shiny; diameters vary, weight ranges from 16 to 30 pounds; large melons have more edible meat in proportion than smaller ones; *beware of:* a melon whose underside (where it has touched the ground) is pale green; out-of-shape, unsymmetrical melons; if buying cut pieces, pass by those with fibrous look or hard white streaks and lots of pale seeds; *when it's ripe:* yellowish to yellow on the ground side; rind has a waxlike bloom, but no high shine; flesh is deep pink to rosy red, seeds very dark brown or black; it's more difficult to choose a ready-to-eat watermelon than it is any other type of melon—rely on your dealer or buy cut portions if you're unlucky at choosing a good one.

Be aware that the "in the market" dates given above for all melons are averages in areas of four-season climates; melons may be shipped in to any area at any season, but will be more expensive than in-season locally grown ones. In warm, almost seasonless climates, where two- and three-crop farming is a way of life, there are melons of some kind available all year around.

Whether or not you enjoy an abundance of all kinds of melons at reasonable in-season and not-too-unreasonable out-of-season prices depends—unless you grow your own—on where you live. In a big east-coast city, all kinds of melons are available a good part of the year in elegant greengroceries at their-weight-in-gold prices; often, of whatever kind, they are cucumber-flavored because they were picked too soon in order to assure "safe" shipment. The exception is cantaloupes, which are sold at reasonable prices in season and out, although the out-of-season ones are often small and exceedingly strong in flavor. Honeydews are available in good supply as well, but they are seldom quite sweet enough or juicy enough, because they are seldom ripe enough.

As you move west, things pick up—more melons, better flavor. The whole Midwest raises melons, and in-season cantaloupe in particular is abundant and flavorful. Colorado grows large numbers of excellent melons, and ships them all over. When you reach the west, California in particular, you have arrived at melon-lovers' heaven. (All fruit lovers actually, indeed all food—except meat—lovers.)

MELONS IN YOUR KITCHEN

Plain, salted or salt-and-peppered, sugared, dressed with lemon or lime juice, spiked with kirsch or liqueur, in fruit cups and salads, half-shelled to hold a chicken or seafood salad, old-fashioned sundaed with vanilla ice cream and pineapple sauce—however you serve melons, in those or a dozen other ways, they are refreshingly delicious, add a flavor fillip to any meal.

how to buy: Consult the previous listings.

how to store: Unless they are fully ripe, store melons at room temperature until they reach their peak. Fully ripe melons are best served at room temperature, or only slightly chilled; if you must hold a ripe melon, refrigerate it but take it out a half hour or so before serving. Halves or sections of melons should be tightly enclosed in plastic bags—leave the seeds in place unless the fruit is slightly overripe—and stored in the refrigerator.

nutritional value: The water content of all melons is high (in the neighborhood of 90 percent), meaning that they are a boon to waistline-watchers as well as to everyone else. Because they vary so greatly in size, it's impossible to compare nutritive values of, say, halves or quarters of melons. So we'll compare servings of melon balls—20 balls to a serving, which is about a cupful—of several common kinds.

	cantaloupe	casaba	honeydew	watermelon	
food energy	48	46	56	42	calories
protein	1.1	2	1.4	.8	grams
fat	.2	trace	.5	.3	gram
carbohydrate	12	11.1	13.1	10.2	grams
calcium	22	24	24	11	milligrams
phosphorus	26	27	27	16	milligrams
iron	.6	.7	.7	.8	milligram
sodium	19	20	20	2	milligrams
potassium	402	427	427	160	milligrams
thiamin	.06	.07	.07	.05	milligram
riboflavin	.05	.05	.05	.05	milligram
niacin	1	1	1	.3	milligram
ascorbic acid	53	22	39	11	milligrams
vitamin A	5,440	50	70	940	international units

Tips on preparing. Virtually no preparation is required. Wash and dry the melon of whatever kind, and cut it—halves, wedges, diced pieces, balls. A melon baller is a useful gadget; metal, it has a cup-shaped business end with relatively sharp edges and a hole so that the juicy melon doesn't create a vacuum that would make the ball difficult to release. Some melon ballers have two cups of different sizes, others have a baller on one end and a butter curler or some other gadget on the other.

An attractive way to prepare melon, and one that makes eating with a fork simple and spatterless, is this. Cut a muskmelon of any kind into serving-size wedges and remove the seeds. With a sharp knife cut under the flesh, about ⅛ to ¼ inch up from the rind, from end to end of the wedge; this separates the meat from the rind. Now cut the meat across the wedge into mouthful-size pieces, at right angles to the first cut. Pull these cut pieces out to extend ½ inch or so over the edge, alternating so that one piece extends on the left, the next on the right. Serve on individual plates, with a wedge of lemon or lime to be squeezed over the melon; garnish with a sprig of mint. Or omit the lemon and sprinkle the melon with finely chopped candied ginger.

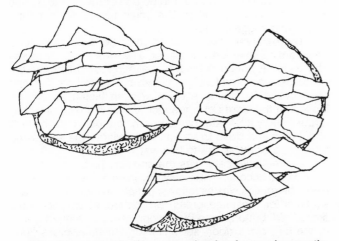

To give a melon half a sawtooth edge for serving, particularly if you are going to use the halves as holders for a mixed-fruit concoction or a salad of some sort, plunge a sharp knife into the equator of the melon all the way to the center, making the cut about an inch to an inch and a half long and at a 45-degree angle to the ends of the melon. Starting at the bottom of the first cut, make a second of the same size beside it, but with the angle in the opposite direction. Continue, alternating angles, all the way around. Gently pull the melon apart, scoop out the seeds—and, if you wish, most of the flesh—and fill with whatever you have in mind. Each half of a small melon—a cantaloupe, perhaps—can hold a single serving, but consider larger melon halves as dishes for several servings. If you cut a slice off the bottom of each half, it will stand less tippily on the plate.

Freezing melons. Diced or cut in balls, melons of all sorts freeze well, when properly prepared (see special feature: PUTTING FOOD BY) and stored at 0° or lower.

Other ways, other forms. In the produce department, you'll find whole melons and, in some, halves or wedges, their cut sides protected by transparent plastic film.

Other than fresh, melons are obtainable only frozen; usually these are melon balls, a single kind or a combination of several.

Some perfect partners. Melons go well with one another—a three-melon cup, balls of cantaloupe, honeydew, and watermelon, is very handsome and very good. They also partner well with bananas, pineapple, and oranges, and with berries—particularly fresh raspberries. Ginger points up melon flavor, so does mace.

Sometimes, let melon stand in for a vegetable in the main course, serving two or three thin peeled wedges with, for example, chicken, or with a cold veal loaf, or with lamb curry. Melon wedges of the same sort garnish and add substance to individual servings of chicken, turkey, or shellfish salad. Or toss cubes of cantaloupe or honeydew with a salad of mixed greens, along with cubes of mild cheese, and croutons for crisp contrast. And don't forget classic melon and prosciutto as an appetizer, varying it sometimes by substituting thin salami slices or bleu cheese chunks.

Dress all-melon or part-melon fruit salads with half-and-half honey and lime or lemon juice, or with sour cream sprinkled with cinnamon. Or make an old-fashioned "boiled" dressing, substituting orange and lemon juice for the vinegar the recipe calls for. Serve melon-ball cups—to start a meal or to finish it—laved with ginger ale or, if it's a party, with champagne. For breakfast, fill the hollow of half a cantaloupe with dry cereal, add sugar and milk or cream.

For dessert, offer dishes heaped with several kinds of melon balls rolled first in honey then in chopped nuts or coconut. Top melon sections with yogurt and sprinkle with mint, or with ice cream, ice, or frozen yogurt and offer several liqueurs to serve as sauces. For a very special cookout, plug a watermelon, slowly pour into it as much white-label rum as it will hold, put the plug back, and refrigerate overnight.

Those are only some ideas. Consult a good cookbook for more elaborate melon cookery—excellent soups, fine chutneys and relishes, melon ice creams and ices.

However you eat melons, enjoy their sweet summer goodness. But don't, like Catherine de' Medici, consume them with such a passion of delight that you make yourself sick. If you do, your mother-in-law may offer scathing remarks about those who make pigs of themselves—hers did.

MELT, TO: see page 447

MENU

In its simplest definition, this is the answer to the question that springs eternal: "What's for dinner?"

At home, the menu—technically the complete listing of all the foods to be served, or offered for service, at a meal—is sometimes an exceedingly informal tag-end of information carried around in the home cook's head. Slightly more formalized is the menu—or, more often, if she's well organized, a week's worth of them—written down by the home cook as an aid to her thinking and a help in making out her shopping lists. To the uninitiated, her notes might seem like random jottings in a foreign tongue, but to her it's very important and also perfectly clear: Sun, rst bf, m pot & g, gr bns, o-o sal, E's choc glop.

In a restaurant, the menu—or bill of fare—is a listing of all the various dishes available plus their prices, usually grouped as appetizers, soups, meats, poultry, fish and shellfish, salads, vegetables, desserts, beverages. In some cases it has been made up by an elf, so that appetizers appear as "to get you started," meats are "hot off the grill," and desserts "happy endings," but with a little luck you can fight your way through it.

For more on menus, see the special feature: NUTRITION NOTEBOOK to guide you to well-balanced meals.

MERINGUE PASTE: see PASTRY

MERINGUES

Egg whites and sugar are the chief ingredients of meringue; slow adding of the sugar plus adequate beating are the secrets of success.

Soft meringues: High-peaked, delicately browned toppings for cream-filling pies and such specialties as baked alaska.

Hard meringues: Baked slowly, then dried; usually they have a central depression to be filled later with ice cream, fruit, or a cream or bavarian-type filling.

Meringue kisses: drop cookies of flavored meringue, often with inclusions such as chopped nuts or glacéed fruit.

All of the above are made in basically the same way: egg whites, usually lightly salted, are beaten until foamy; beating is continued while sugar is added in one-tablespoon increments until the meringue is stiff and all sugar is dissolved. *Italian meringue* is made like a boiled frosting—a sugar/water syrup is cooked to 238–240°F. (soft-ball stage); egg whites are beaten until they hold stiff peaks, then the syrup is slowly beaten into them.

Soft meringues are baked only until lightly browned; usually they are swirled over the top of the pie or pudding in a pleasant random pattern, so that the peaks brown more deeply than the valleys. Meringue kisses are baked until crisp, usually a matter of about half an hour. Hard meringues and italian meringue desserts are baked in a very slow oven (200°F.) for as much as 2 hours; the heat is then turned off, and the meringues are left in the oven to dry and crisp for at least 3 hours, as much as overnight. Of whatever kind, except the soft variety, meringues must be baked on parchment cooking paper or unglazed brown paper lining a baking sheet —unless they are, getting them off the baking sheet is a nightmare struggle, which the meringues always win.

METRIC: see special feature: MEASURING
UP TO METRIC

METTWURST: see SAUSAGES

MICROWAVE COOKING

When you are in the food business—writing about food, testing it, originating recipes, editing cookbooks—you can be very lucky, as when someone sends you a whole country ham or a box of comice pears with a "thought you'd enjoy this" note. On the other hand, you can be very unlucky, as when the mail brings a letter saying, "You have, of course, heard of the new microwave ovens. We are sending you one, knowing that you would wish to be one of the first to try this wholly new cooking method. We would appreciate your comments and suggestions."

The early microwave ovens could be described with a one-word comment: Awful. Better, a two-word one: Unbelievably awful. A potato did indeed bake in record time, as the accompanying literature promised, but tasted as if it had been boiled for hours. A roast chicken tasted soggy and looked, in the words of a grandchild, "as if it died and they forgot to bury it." Water came briskly to a boil, but who was about to spend close to six hundred dollars—the suggested retail price at the time—to boil water briskly?

A three-layer cake was the crusher. To begin with, the oven would accommodate only one layer at a time. For each layer, the routine was as follows: put pan in oven, close door, set timer for 2 minutes, press "on" button; when timer rings, press "off" button, open oven door, give pan a quarter turn to the left, close door, set timer for 1 minute, press "on" button; when timer rings, press "off" button, open door, give pan another quarter turn, close door, set timer, press . . . but you must get the idea. And that was, you remember, only one layer. The same mystic rites had to be repeated for the other layers. When all was done, what did you have? Three deadwhite layers of reasonably acceptable although entirely different-from-usual texture, with a gummy, semicandied goo on top and, you guessed it, a boiled taste.

But the times they are a-changing, and microwave ovens have changed right along with them. Somehow they got rid of a lot of the drawbacks before they ever put the things on the market, and rapidly got rid of more soon afterward. It is no longer necessary to hover over the oven like a hen with one chick, although some foods still must be turned often, and some must be stirred regularly. Foods taste like themselves. Various methods of browning have gotten around the long-dead look. Some foods cook exceedingly well by microwave—better than by conventional methods. Unlike the first ones, present ovens range from "somewhat adjustable" (the lower-priced ones) to "as adjustable as you'd ever need them to be" (the more expensive ones).

Moist foods do very well—casseroles, chicken baked in cream or tomato juice, baked apples, poached and braised foods in general. But microwave-cooked baked goods—pies, cakes, breads, pastries, cookies—come off a poor second to their conventionally baked counterparts. Vegetables, fresh or frozen, cook very well in little water and have excellent flavor and texture. But rice and other grains and pastas cook just as rapidly by conventional methods, and the texture of all but rice is better. Lamb and veal stews fare better in the microwave than beef, because the rapid cooking doesn't get to beef stew meat's tough connective tissues as well as long, slow cooking does. Another point is that the excellent flavor of stews is a result of that slow cooking, and is enriched by evaporation of liquid during cooking time; this doesn't happen by microwave.

For picky jobs, the microwave method is great. Defrosting takes a relatively brief time. Reheating is far superior in a microwave than by conventional methods. Melting—chocolate, marshmallows, caramels, whatever—goes very well; so does dissolving gelatin. Crumb crusts do fine. So do steamed puddings—the time is amazingly short—and such desserts as cobblers, apple betty, and the like. So do puddings of the cornstarch-base variety, and those from a mix.

But don't ask for crisp frozen french fries or onion rings when you microwave them. As for breaded foods, the breading turns to mucilage.

The microwave growth cycle. Since the days when the only thing you could do to control what happened in your microwave oven was to turn it on or turn it off, there have been a lot of changes made. Variable cooking speeds made an early appearance, and today in some microwave ovens you can put a dish in and program the appliance like a computer to thaw the food, then cook it, then brown it, then hold it at a keep-warm temperature until you're ready to ring the dinner bell. Some have sensor-probes—somewhat the equivalent of using a meat thermometer in conventional cooking—that, when they are plunged into the food and a separate temperature control set, sense when it is done and tell the oven to shut itself off. Many have browning devices, either a special pan for the purpose or an electric grid in the top of the oven, like a conventional electric broiler, with a separate on/off switch.

Some microwave ovens have even turned the whole concept—fast cooking—upside down, with a *slow* setting, so that you can slow-cook such foods as pot roasts, soups, stews, and the like at a simmer, much as in a crockery slow-cooker.

Tricks of the trade. Despite all the giant technological leaps that microwave ovens have made, they still require some special handling. In conventional cooking, whether oven, broiler, or stovetop, heat attacks the food from the outside and moves inward. Microwave cooking is not by heat but by agitation: simplistically, microwaves excite the molecules in the food and that movement is what accomplishes the cooking.

It's necessary to give some thought to the arrangement of food before you put it in to cook by microwave. Insofar as possible, foods such as meat and vegetables should be cut in pieces of equal size, and arranged in a single layer. If some pieces are thinner or smaller than others, and particularly if they have bones, put them in the center with larger, thicker pieces around the outside—with a chicken, for example, put the wings in the center, thighs and drumsticks toward the outer rim. If one portion of a single piece will cook more quickly than another portion—as with asparagus, in which the tips cook faster than the stalks—arrange the food with the tender part toward the center of the dish, the tougher toward the outside. In some cases, to make certain microwaves penetrate the food all around, some foods should be rearranged in their cooking dish during the cooking process, others should be stirred—always from the outside toward the center—and for others the cooking utensil should be given a quarter turn occasionally during the cooking period.

Some cooking basics remain the same in the microwave as with conventional methods, although the total time will be shorter—frozen and refrigerated foods will take longer than those started at room temperature, large quantities take longer than small ones, liquids cook in a shorter time than solids. Foods overlapped or stacked take longer (and in this case, don't cook as well) than those in a single layer.

In microwave cooking, strive always for underdoneness —if the food is truly underdone, it can always go back into the microwave oven for a few seconds. But foods continue to cook after they are removed from the microwave oven, and that additional standing time must be taken into consideration to avoid overcooked food.

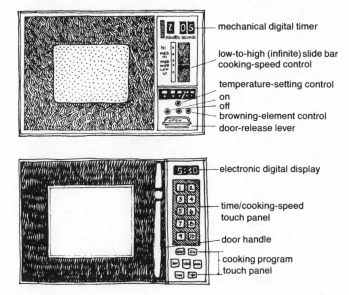

mechanical digital timer

low-to-high (infinite) slide bar cooking-speed control

temperature-setting control

on

off

browning-element control

door-release lever

electronic digital display

time/cooking-speed touch panel

door handle

cooking program touch panel

Pots and pans and such. In the early days of microwaves, you cooked in virtually any old thing that came to hand—a teacup, a paper plate, a piece of plastic wrap—as long as it was not made of metal and had no metal parts. It was difficult to treat with respect a food you had just cooked for one minute in a paper napkin. There was a certain unreality about the whole thing.

But all that has changed. Cookware manufacturers—as we all knew they would—brought out a wide array of pans made expressly for microwave ovens. No matter what you have in mind to cook, there's a vessel for exactly that purpose, attractively shaped and as spanking-clean white, most of them, as grandma's wash flapping on the clothesline on a sunny, breezy spring day. There is even a nice white muffin pan for those who would like some nice white boiled muffins for breakfast.

To sum it up. Today's microwave ovens are useful, worthwhile kitchen appliances. For those whose cooking/eating habits can best be described as "on the fly"—those who use many convenience foods, particularly frozen ones—and for those whose families seldom assemble at one time for formal mealtimes, they are a godsend. Even the most dedicated make-it-from-scratch cook will find a microwave oven a modern miracle worker in some areas. But microwaving is by no means the be-all and end-all of cookery. See also the special feature: YOU CAN'T WORK WITHOUT TOOLS.

MILK

In your mind's eye, picture a cow. As long as you're doing it you might as well picture a Brown Swiss, that most appealing of cows, whose hipbones do not stick up so unpaddedly and whose appearance is therefore more sweetly soignée than that of other breeds; whose enormous eyes are limpid brown pools surrounded by lashes so long and thick it's difficult to believe she doesn't get up extra early in the morning to put on her eye makeup before the farmer arrives to milk her; whose nose—which, when you scratch it, causes her to assume an engagingly contemplative expression—is made of the finest grade of taupe silk velvet; whose warm breath speaks of hot sun on buttercups and clover.

Got it? You are looking at the simplest and yet most intricately efficient factory in the world, neatly packaged in cowhide. From horns to udders, she's one big milk-production machine—a neat 11,000 pounds a year on the average—with, as is true of all well-run manufacturing plants, assorted no-waste by-products as a sideline.

The all-weather, all-purpose food. While you're engaged in looking, shift your eyes to the cow's chief product. A carton of milk is not as attractive as Bossy herself but it has its points, and good flavor and good nutrition are chief among them.

protein: The amino acids of protein help the body build new tissue, repair old; it's one of the blood builders, forms antibodies to fight infection, and supplies a share of energy—*two 8-ounce glasses of milk supply about 30 percent of an adult woman's RDA of protein, about 25 percent of an adult man's; children who drink the amounts recommended for them get an even larger share.*

calcium: This necessary mineral helps build and maintain bones and teeth, helps the heart and other muscles to contract and relax as they should, the nerves to transmit messages, and the blood to clot satisfactorily—*of all foods common in the United States, milk is the best source of calcium; two 8-ounce glasses daily supply nearly ¾ of the adult RDA.*

phosphorus: This mineral works in tandem with calcium to make teeth and bones strong and rigid; also helps to regulate many of the internal functions of the body *milk supplies a large share of the phosphorus RDA for children and adults.*

vitamin D: This, the "sunshine vitamin," helps the body absorb calcium, works with calcium and phosphorus to build strong bones—*most fluid milk is fortified with vitamin D; a quart contains sufficient for everyone's needs.*

riboflavin: This, sometimes called vitamin B_2, helps the body's cells to use oxygen, aids in keeping tissues healthy and vision clear, helps the body to make efficient use of protein—*two 8-ounce glasses of milk supply about 50 percent of an adult man's RDA of riboflavin, and about 66⅔ percent of a woman's.*

and more: Milk also supplies some vitamin A, some thiamin, and some of the substances from which the body manufactures niacin, as well as smaller amounts of other nutrients.

lactose, too: Lactose is the milk sugar that aids in the absorption of calcium, phosphorus, and other minerals. Science has indications that lactose also serves other functions in the body's workings, and is investigating those probabilities.

Milk beyond our remembering. Other than that it must have been well before 2000 B.C., no one really knows when milk was first used as a food by man, although it seems likely that goats, sheep, and possibly cattle were raised by primitive peoples before it was realized that their milk could nourish humans as well as the animals' own young.

It seems logical that the discovery was made to preserve the life of a baby whose mother had died. If the little animals thrived on their mothers' milk, might not a little human do so too? Some thinking person must have decided that it was worth a try, given an animal's milk to the starving infant, and watched with delight as the experiment succeeded. (Human milk is more digestible, but measure for measure, cows' has more than three times as much protein and almost four times as much calcium; it has fewer carbohydrates—only about half the amount in human milk—and a little less fat; the vitamins are divided—more of some in human milk, more of others in the milk of cows.)

Certainly after that first experiment, the lives of many infants who would otherwise have perished were preserved, exceedingly important in a day when the world was very big but human beings relatively few. From there it could only have been a small step to the incorporation of milk into the diet of older children and adults.

The choice is wide, and up to you. Today, when you select milk from your market's dairy case and grocery shelves, there are many kinds to choose among. The differences lie in the amount of milk fat—milk's natural fat content—and, dependent on the milk fat, the number of calories furnished. Also, you can take home fluid milk that is fresh or canned (evaporated or sweetened condensed) or dry (whole or nonfat) or flavored in several ways.

Here is what is available to you in markets everywhere:

whole milk: Contains at least 3½ percent milk fat; one 8-ounce glass furnishes about 150 calories.

lowfat (may also be labeled "2%") milk: Contains 2 percent milk fat; 8-ounce glass, about 120 calories.

99% fat-free milk: Contains 1 percent milk fat; 8-ounce glass, about 102 calories.

nonfat (may also be labeled "skim") milk: Contains less than ½ percent milk fat; 8-ounce glass, about 86 calories; often fortified with vitamins A and D to replace amounts lost in processing.

buttermilk: Made by adding special bacteria to lowfat or nonfat milk; 8-ounce glass furnishes about 99 calories if base is lowfat, 88 if base is nonfat; buttermilk was once the residue that remained after butter was churned—although all buttermilk is now cultured, some processors add tiny flecks of butter to their product to give it the old-fashioned look.

chocolate milk: Made by adding chocolate flavor to whole milk; 8-ounce glass, about 208 calories.

lowfat chocolate milk (may be labeled "chocolate dairy drink"): Made with lowfat rather than whole milk; 8-ounce glass furnishes about 180 calories.

nonfat dry milk: Skim milk with the water content removed; when reconstituted according to label directions has some fat content and furnishes same number of calories as nonfat fluid milk; it may or may not be fortified with vitamins A and D—check the label; the USDA has established grades for nonfat dry milk—the grade shield signifies that the product has been produced in a clean, sanitary plant and meets exacting quality standards; highest quality is U.S. Extra Grade.

dry whole milk: As above, but made from whole milk.

dry buttermilk: As above, but made from buttermilk.

evaporated milk: Whole milk with about 60 percent of the water content removed; product is canned; furnishes about 338 calories per cup, undiluted; evaporated skim milk is also available. (See EVAPORATED MILK.)

sweetened condensed milk: Evaporated milk with sugar added; product is canned; furnishes about 980 calories per cup, undiluted.

sweet acidophilus milk: A relative newcomer that may also be available in your dairy case, depending on the area in which you live.

Some authorities believe that in a few years this will be the most common milk used for drinking. A live bacterial culture, *lactobacillus acidophilus,* is added to the milk; unlike the cultures in yogurt, this one survives—indeed, it thrives—in the human digestive tract. The friendly acidophilus bacteria are present in milk as it comes from the cow but are unfortunately killed, along with various harmful bacteria, during pasteurization. For years science has been searching for a way to return the acidophilus bacteria to pasteurized milk without turning the milk sour. A number of years ago acidophilus milk appeared on the market along with a campaign urging people to drink it for their health's sake, but it was so unpleasantly sour that, health or not, few could manage to drink it, no one liked it, and it disappeared from the market.

Then in 1976, scientists at North Carolina State University found the answer: inoculate pasteurized milk with dormant acidophilus bacteria (4,000,000,000 per quart!), which will begin to grow only when they reach the digestive system. This produces *sweet* acidophilus milk, unchanged in consistency, taste, and color from regular pasteurized fluid milk. It can be used as you would use any milk, except that if you heat it above 110 degrees, the acidophilus bacteria will be destroyed.

You will not find health claims on the label of the new milk—if it carried them, it would have to be called a drug. But many authorities are exceedingly enthusiastic about sweet acidophilus, pointing out that modern food processing and handling plus our widespread exposure to antibiotics of various kinds have so upset the bacterial balance in our digestive tracts that we need the acidophilus culture to restore nature's balance to normalcy there.

At the time this is written, most sweet acidophilus milk on the market is lowfat, but some dairies are beginning to make it with whole milk as well.

Milk-based and like-milk products. As well as all the various kinds of "regular" milk available to you, there are certain other products related to milk about which it is difficult to make general statements because they are regulated by local or state laws. They are therefore not available in some places and where available may vary in composition.

solids-added: Although the United States Public Health Service regulates the amount of butterfat content (minimums and maximums) in fluid milk, milk solids other than fat, which do not change the fat content, may be added to lowfat or nonfat milk in some places. Such products will be labeled "containing added nonfat milk solids" or some such phrase.

The purpose is usually to make the flavor of the lowfat or nonfat product more closely resemble that of whole milk.

filled milk (or cream): This may be available fluid, frozen, evaporated, condensed, concentrated, or dried. It is milk or cream to which a fat other than butterfat has been added as well as, in some cases, artificial color and flavor; the resulting product resembles milk or cream. Filled milk can be legally sold within a number of states, but cannot be shipped interstate or in foreign commerce. It may be, and in some cases must be, labeled "imitation milk."

imitation milk: This, unlike filled milk, contains no complete milk ingredients—such as skim milk or nonfat dry milk—but nevertheless resembles milk in flavor and appearance. The formula for one imitation milk, as an example, includes sodium caseinate, vegetable fat, corn syrup or dextrose, emulsifiers, and artificial color and flavor. These products may or may not furnish the nutrients that we depend upon in cows' milk—read the label carefully. They may be, but are not required to be unless shipped interstate, labeled "imitation milk."

coffee lighteners: These, also called "coffee whiteners," are substitutes for milk or cream as normally used in coffee or other hot or cold beverages, and are available in jars as a dry powder, or frozen as a fluid. They are made in the same manner as imitation milk and usually contain, among other ingredients, sodium caseinate and vegetable oil.

There are also some other products that contain "real" milk, generally dry nonfat or whole. Among them are cocoa mixes made ready to serve by adding only water, and fancy coffee combinations—made of coffee and dry milk plus various flavors such as orange, coconut, almond, chocolate, as well as other ingredients—also made ready to serve by adding only hot water.

And, of course, there are many foods that are milk-rich, among them cheese, butter, and ice cream and other frozen desserts.

MILK IN YOUR KITCHEN

Most milk today is *pasteurized*—heat-processed to kill harmful bacteria. Whole milk once separated in the bottle, the cream rising to the top, but today most of it is *homogenized*—forced through a fine sievelike apparatus that breaks up the cream and produces a suspension in which the cream remains uniformly distributed throughout. Some milk is *fortified*—a process that adds vitamins (A or D or both) and minerals or returns to the milk those lost in the processing.

how to buy: In many places milk is dated, in some cases carrying the date on which it was bottled, in some a last-date-of-sale. In either case, the milk will remain sweet in your refrigerator for a number of days after the date on the carton. If milk is not dated in your area, buy from a busy store where turnover is rapid, meaning that fresh supplies are constantly brought in.

how to store: Refrigerate fluid milk as soon as possible after purchase. Reclose opened cartons securely. For best flavor use in 3 to 5 days. Evaporated and sweetened condensed milk cans can be stored unopened at room temperature (preferably under 75°) up to 6 months; after opening, refrigerate, covered, and use in 3 to 5 days. Dry milk (nonfat or whole) packages can be stored at room temperature; after opening the package, reclose securely or transfer contents to a tightly covered container—exposed to air, the milk may become lumpy and stale. Reconstituted dry milk must be refrigerated, tightly covered; use in 3 to 5 days.

nutritive value: Here are the nutritional yields for several types of fresh fluid milk—from these, values of other types (reconstituted, dry, diluted evaporated, and so on) can be extrapolated. Yields listed below are for one 8-ounce serving.

	whole 3.5% fat	nonfat (skim)	lowfat w/2% add'l milk solids	chocolate dr. made w/nonfat	
protein	8.5	8.8	10.3	8.3	grams
fat	8.5	.2	4.9	5.8	grams
carbohydrate	12	12.5	14.8	27.3	grams
calcium	288	296	352	270	milligrams
phosphorus	227	233	276	228	milligrams
iron	.1	.1	.1	.5	milligram
sodium	122	127	150	115	milligrams
potassium	351	355	431	255	milligrams
thiamin	.07	.09	.10	.1	milligram
riboflavin	.41	.44	.52	.4	milligram
niacin	.2	.2	.2	.3	milligram
ascorbic acid	2	2	2	3	milligrams
vitamin A	350	10*	200	210	international units

*nonfortified; if fortified with vitamin A, consult carton label for amount

Tips on preparing, cooking. What can you make with milk? "What can't you?" is an easier question to answer. Cream soups and bisques and chowders. Many kinds of custards and puddings, bavarians, cream pies, frozen desserts. Creamed meats, fish, and poultry to serve on toast, rice, or mashed potatoes. Milk shakes, malted milks, and other milk-rich beverages. Salads and dressings and sauces. And, of course, there is some milk in dozens of other things we make, from meat loaves to cookies. If you include other milk products—butter, cheese, cream, sour cream—there's very little that doesn't contain milk, and our hearts go out to those, relatively few, who are allergic to it.

Milk must be heated or cooked at low temperatures; heat slowly, and do not let it boil. At high temperatures, the protein in milk coagulates into a thin film on top and a coating on the sides of the pan. Prolonged milk temperatures produce off-flavors. Milk scorches easily, another reason for low temperatures and slow heating. Use moderate baking temperatures for casseroles that contain a high proportion of milk, and for such dishes as scalloped potatoes. Flour or cornstarch prevents the coagulation of protein, and mixtures made with them—sauces and the like—can be boiled, but must be stirred constantly to prevent lumping. In cooked or baked foods, dry milk may be reconstituted and used as a liquid or it may be sifted and added with the dry ingredients.

When the recipe calls for sour milk, use buttermilk or prepare sour milk by combining 1 tablespoon of vinegar or lemon juice with milk to measure 1 cup; let it stand 5 minutes before you use it. If the recipe calls for buttermilk, use that or the home-soured variety—the two are interchangeable.

Sweetened condensed milk is enjoyed by some as a "cream and sugar" combination for coffee. This type of milk should be used only in recipes particularly tailored for its use —sweetened condensed milk and evaporated milk are two entirely different products and cannot be used interchangeably in cooking.

Freezing milk. It doesn't work. Undiluted evaporated milk that is to be whipped can be freezer-chilled until ice crystals begin to form around the edges. Heavy cream that has been whipped can be frozen. If you wish to freeze a cream soup, freeze the base and add the milk when you thaw and heat the soup for serving. Casseroles bound with a thickened milk sauce can be frozen, but plain white sauce if frozen may separate on thawing and heating. The long and short of it is: don't try to freeze milk.

How much is enough? Mothers have been endlessly saying "Drink your milk!" since time immemorial. How much? Here are numbers of 8-fluid-ounce cups of milk per day recommended by nutritionists:

children under age 9	2 to 3 cups
children 9 to 12	3 or more cups
teenagers	4 or more cups
adults	2 or more cups
pregnant women over 19	3 or more cups
nursing mothers over 19	4 or more cups

A mother-to-be or nursing mother still in her teens needs more milk than other teenagers. The recommended daily amounts are based on the calcium that milk supplies, for it is difficult to get sufficient calcium for the body's needs without milk in some form in the daily diet.

To give each member of your family an adequate amount:

- serve milk as a beverage
- include milk-rich products, such as ice cream and cheese, in meals regularly
- use milk in preparing main dishes

The following amounts of milk products and milk-rich foods furnish about as much calcium as 1 cup of fresh whole milk:

- 1⅓ ounces natural cheddar cheese
- 1½ ounces process cheddar cheese
- 1⅓ cups creamed cottage cheese
- 1 ounce swiss cheese
- 1 cup cocoa made with milk
- 1 serving cup custard
- 1⅓ cups ice cream
- 1 cup soft-serve ice milk
- ¾ cup homemade macaroni and cheese
- 1 milk shake, made with ⅔ cup milk and ½ cup ice cream
- 1 cup oyster stew
- ⅕ of a 14-inch cheese-topped pizza
- 1 cup cornstarch pudding made with milk
- 1⅓ cups canned cream soup, made with equal volume of milk
- 1 8-ounce cup yogurt

Those who are allergic to cows' milk, take heart. Goats' milk is available for you and for others on various special diets. It can be purchased both fresh and canned, is slightly richer than cows' milk, and delicious. Other milks—ewes', camels', mares', and more—that people of other cultures drink or use in cooking aren't generally available here. But they're flavorful, wholesome, nutritious, and they'd do in a pinch. Milk is so good, so universally liked, so important to our diet, so versatile in its uses, we'd soon be raising herds of dairy camels or whatever if a catastrophe struck our Ayrshires and Guernseys and Jerseys and Brown Swisses. We couldn't get along without milk, and we wouldn't try to. See also CREAM, FILLED MILK, ICE MILK, IRRADIATED MILK, MALTED MILK, and YOGURT.

MILLET: see GRAINS

MINCE, TO: see page 447

MINCEMEAT

When grandma spoke of mincemeat she meant mince*meat* —the sweet, spicy mixture she made at home was based on minced, chopped, or ground beef and usually had beef suet in it, too. When beef wasn't available, or simply because grandpa liked it better, she often made the mincemeat with venison.

Although nothing but inertia prevents our making mincemeat—with meat or without it—at home today, many of us shortcut by buying the commercial product, moist in a jar or dry in a package. It has good flavor, and it can be made better with a little judicious dressing-up. To sufficient commercial mincemeat for a 9-inch pie, add 2 tablespoons chopped candied orange peel, one small peeled apple cut in large chunks, ¼ cup raisins, ½ cup chopped walnuts, ½ teaspoon cinnamon, 2 tablespoons each of molasses and brandy. Served hot (mince pie rewarms very well) with a large dollop of well-brandied hard sauce, it is indeed like grandma used to make, and no one misses the meat.

If you prefer, find a good mincemeat recipe in a reliable cookbook and make the filling from scratch. It's not at all difficult. Whichever way you go, the aroma that will fill your house while the pie bakes is exquisitely unlike any other.

MINERALS: see special feature:
NUTRITION NOTEBOOK

MINESTRONE: see page 453

MINT: see HERBS AND SAVORY SEASONINGS

MINUTE STEAK: see BEEF

MIREPOIX

A mixture of vegetables—a representative mirepoix might contain chopped carrots, onions, garlic, shallots, and celery, with a little thyme and a bay leaf—used to season stews, soups, meats, and some kinds of fish.

Spread a bed of mirepoix in a pan, set a roast of lamb on it in lieu of a rack, and roast in the usual manner. When it is done, set the meat aside, skim off the fat, take the bay leaf out of the mirepoix, and put the baked vegetables from the bottom of the pan into the blender with ¾ cup hot water. Purée until well blended, then return the mixture to the roasting pan along with 2 tablespoons of the fat. Set over medium heat and let it come to a boil, scraping the pan to loosen all the good brown essence. Thicken with 2 tablespoons of flour dissolved in ¾ cup of cold brewed coffee. Season to taste. Even the French duke who lent his name to mirepoix never tasted so exquisite a gravy.

MIXES

There are all sorts of mixes on the market, convenience items of ingredients precombined in proper proportions to produce foods of many kinds. Although mixes for baked goods are the most common, there are others as well.

Available are, among others, biscuit mix (sometimes labeled "baking mix" because its versatility goes far beyond biscuits), and mixes for cakes, coffeecakes, sweet breads, corn breads, and gingerbreads, as well as combinations to produce muffins, Irish soda bread, popovers, and many more good things. There are also mixes for various flavors of salad dressing, breading mixtures for chicken or fish or pork chops, instant and to-be-cooked pudding and pie filling mixes in a wide array of flavors, seasoning mixes for such foods as stews, chili, gravies, spaghetti and other sauces, mixes for pancake and waffle and crepe batters, for pie crust, for pie and cake fillings, and dozens of others.

The do-it-yourself route. All of these foods can, of course, be made from scratch without the aid of a mix. And many mixes can be made at home, by precombining some ingredients (usually dry ones, often shortening as well), ready to be measured and added to liquid or an egg/liquid combination. Here are some examples of made-at-home mixes.

pastry mix: In a large bowl, place 12 cups all-purpose flour, 2 tablespoons salt, and 5 cups solid white vegetable shortening. Mix—with your hands, a pastry blender, or two knives— until it is the consistency of coarse meal. Store tightly covered. To measure, stir mixture, then pack into measuring cup. Use 2 cups of the mixture plus about ¼ cup very cold water to make pastry for a 2-crust pie.

shake-up mix for chicken: Combine well 1 cup all-purpose flour, 1 cup fine dry bread crumbs, ¼ cup cornstarch, 1 tablespoon plus 1 teaspoon chicken-flavor instant bouillon granules, 1 tablespoon sugar, 2 teaspoons dried minced onion, 2 teaspoons salt, ½ teaspoon garlic powder, ¼ teaspoon white pepper; if you like the flavor of thyme and/or sage with chicken, add ½ teaspoon of either or ¼ teaspoon each of both. This amount will coat about 10 pounds of chicken parts. Brush each chicken piece on all sides with oil. Place mix (about ¼ of it for a 2½-pound chicken) in a plastic bag; shake chicken in mix 1 or 2 pieces at a time, and place in a single layer on a shallow baking pan. Bake at 400°F. for 20 minutes, turn and bake an additional 20 to 25 minutes, or until fork-tender.

Many other mixes can be made at home, including such things as granola-type cereal—which isn't a mix in the same sense, because once it is made nothing more needs to be done to it to prepare it for eating. The homemade mixes have two things going for them: they are considerably cheaper than the store-bought kinds and, for those who worry about such things, are totally lacking in additives and preservatives.

See also CAKE MIXES, BISCUIT MIXES, and COCKTAIL MIXES.

MOCHA

A delicious coffee/chocolate flavor, mocha comes into its own in all sorts of wonderful desserts. A simple one is a sundae of coffee ice cream with chocolate or hot fudge sauce. If you are fond of this combination of flavors, add a tablespoon of instant coffee powder to your favorite chocolate cake or frosting as you prepare it or a teaspoon to a 4-cup recipe of cocoa before you add the liquid.

MOCK CHICKEN LEGS

These, popular some thirty years ago, are a combination of seasoned ground veal and pork, molded into a chicken-drumstick shape and lightly breaded, with a skewer taking the place of the leg bone. This all took place, as you can imagine, when chicken was more expensive than veal, an unlikely occurrence these days. However, mock chicken legs still make unscheduled appearances in butcher shops now and then, when there are veal scraps to be used up. If you buy them, remember that they contain pork and so must be well cooked.

MOLASSES

One of the charms of visiting places where sugarcane grows is being presented with a piece of the stalk to taste. It is not all that much of a treat, but one makes a big thing of it because the presenter is usually a small boy with large, anxious eyes, who stands on one foot and holds his breath in anticipation of your verdict—and the accompanying coin, unless you are the all-time Unspeakable American Tourist. (The U.A.T.'s name, unfortunately, is legion. He starts half his sentences with "Why don't these people—." Why don't they feed their animals better, dress their children better, forbid their children to beg, clean up their sewers, clothe their women more modestly, smarten up their houses, and much more, often including, for heaven's sake, speak a civilized language.)

Back to sugarcane. It is sweet, and the closer to the ground, the sweeter the stalk. The cane is gathered by cutting, including as much as possible of the sugar-rich end, and hauled to mills, where the stalks are roughly torn up, passed through rollers, boiled, and the resulting gummy syrup put into drainers in which the liquid drips away, leaving raw sugar behind. The dripped-away liquid, by-product of sugar refining, is molasses: light molasses from the first boiling of the syrup, dark from the second, blackstrap (enjoyed by health-fooders and cattle alike) from the third.

Molasses was a necessity to the colonists, for sugar was very costly, maple sugar and honey scarce—and besides, molasses could be made into beer and rum, as well as used as a sweetener at table and in cooking. Columbus introduced sugarcane to the West Indies, and in time molasses became the backbone of colonial trade, as well as the sweetener most often used in the colonies because it was the most readily available.

Boston's famous baked beans were sweetened with molasses, and so were New England's Indian Pudding and a particularly delicious kind of doughnut. In Pennsylvania, the Amish and Mennonites made "wonderful good" shoofly pie with it, and poured it over hot-from-the-oven biscuits at breakfast. Molasses went into corn bread, and often pieces of that very American bread were laved with the sweet syrup or dipped into it. Hasty pudding—cornmeal mush—was the usual supper dish; if there was enough molasses so that you could have a little poured over it, supper was very special.

And, of course, there was grandma's remedy for the sweet lethargy that invades minds and limbs when spring chases winter away: to purify the blood and cleanse the system, sulfur-and-molasses was her homemade tonic, doled out in large and ghastly spoonfuls to the whole protesting family.

Buying and using molasses. Light molasses—sometimes still used as a table syrup as well as in cooking—and dark, for sturdier, spice-rich dishes, are available in bottles or jars almost everywhere. Health food stores sell blackstrap, if that is your pleasure. Another kind of molasses, sorghum, is also available; it is not made from sugarcane but from sorghum grains, which look a great deal like corn.

All molasses can be shelf-stored at room temperature up to 1 year until it is opened; after opening, refrigerate, tightly covered, up to 2 months. It will keep unrefrigerated but sometimes ferments. As it is with sugar, it is the flavor of molasses rather than its nutritive value that draws us to it; molasses, however—as sugar does not—furnishes a fair amount of both iron and calcium.

Today we emulate our ancestors in using molasses to make gingerbread and ginger waffles, to lend its good flavor to baked beans and barbecued limas. Molasses, prepared mustard, and cider vinegar, 1 cup of each, combine into an unusual, flavorful barbecue sauce with a special affinity for spareribs. Or heat togehter ½ cup molasses, 1 cup each of honey and corn syrup, ¼ cup butter, and a few grains of salt to make a delicious topping for pancakes. See also BLACKSTRAP MOLASSES.

MONOSODIUM GLUTAMATE

This, made from glutamic acid, one of the "building block" amino acids found in protein, is used as a flavor enhancer. MSG, as it is more easily referred to, has no flavor of its own but points up and intensifies the flavors of other foods, particularly meat, fish, poultry, and some vegetables. Many home cooks routinely use MSG, and so do many food processors.

Monosodium glutamate has held a place of esteem in Oriental cooking for generations. Because it is so widely used in Chinese and Japanese restaurants, some who seem to be particularly sensitive to the substance suffer from dizzy spells and shortness of breath after a meal there—indeed, those symptoms have come to be known as the "Chinese restaurant syndrome."

MONTEREY JACK: see JACK CHEESE and CHEESE

MOOSE: see GAME

MOSTACCIOLI: see PASTA

MOUNTAIN GOAT, SHEEP: see GAME

MOUSSE: see page 453

MOUSSELINE: see page 453

MOZZARELLA

A fresh (that is, not aged) white cooking cheese of mild flavor and, when heated, stringy consistency. Italian originally, mozzarella is now made here. In slices or grated, it is a must ingredient in many of those dishes that, although they are ethnically Italian, have become part of the American cuisine —lasagna, eggplant parmigiana, and pizza among them. Originally made of buffalos' milk, even in Italy, cows' milk is the source of mozzarella today. Buy the cheese only when you plan to use it within a day or two—each passing day turns some of the delicate flavor strong and defeats the purposes for which the cheese is made.

Mozzarella may also be eaten uncooked, out of hand— a perfect choice for those who are put off by the strong flavors of ripened cheeses. See also CHEESE.

MUD HEN: see GAME

MUENSTER: see CHEESE

MUFFINS

There are New Yorkers who cannot get the day started without one of the large, grainy-textured corn muffins peculiar to the area, split and toasted and buttered, and washed down with coffee. And some of those, if queried, would probably reply that those big, coarse favorites of theirs are the beginning and the end of the muffin story. They couldn't be more mistaken.

Quick-and-easy kinds. Muffins are QUICK BREADS (although there are a few yeast-raised kinds) baked as small, round, single servings in pans especially designed for the purpose, now known as muffin tins but once called, more attractively, gem pans. Next to the corn ones, blueberry muf-

fins—thickly studded with berries that purple-stain the batter surrounding them—are the best known. But there are many others: whole wheat, bran (usually with raisins), banana, walnut (or pecan or whatever nuts are available—they all make good muffins better), orange, cinnamon-apple, and a dozen more.

Accommodatingly, muffins will accept almost any inclusions you happen to have—cooked rice, cooked pumpkin or yam, corn kernels stripped off the cob, berries of most kinds and all sorts of mashed or cut-up fruit, grated cheddar or swiss cheese, spices, herbs, whatever. Surprise muffins are created by filling muffin tins about one-quarter full, adding a cube of cheese or a dab of jam or jelly or a sprinkling of streusel mixture, then covering with more batter.

The "muffin method of mixing," as home economics classes refer to it, is simple. Dry ingredients are combined. Liquid ingredients, eggs and shortening such as oil or melted butter, are separately combined, the wet dumped into the dry, and the mixture stirred just enough to moisten the dry ingredients. This produces a lumpy, rough-looking batter, into which the inclusions—if any—are gently folded. The whole point is to keep mixing to a minimum. Because they bake in half an hour or less, it's easily possible to throw together a batch of muffins for breakfast, the only problem being that if you do it once you'll never get any peace until you make it a habit.

And the other kinds. A large number of New Yorkers who do not start the day with a corn muffin do get it underway with "toasted english, please"—a split and toasted english muffin, eaten austerely plain or slathered with jam, jelly, honey, or marmalade. ENGLISH MUFFINS are leavened with yeast; not kneaded, after their first rising they are rolled out on a board sprinkled with cornmeal, cut in 3- to 4-inch rounds, set to rise again on a cornmeal-covered board, then stovetop-baked on an ungreased griddle. Available almost everywhere, in both restaurants and food markets, english muffins once came in only one kind—plain white—but there are now cornmeal english, sourdough, whole wheat, and raisin-studded bran, among others.

English muffins aren't the only yeast-raised ones. There are several kinds, baked conventionally in muffin tins in the oven, that are raised with yeast or sourdough. But those leavened with baking powder or soda—the quick-bread muffins of all kinds—are by far the more popular in this country. See also BREADS and REFRIGERATED DOUGH.

MULBERRIES

Seldom cultivated, never raised commercially, mulberries are the red or almost-black or almost-white fruit of the mulberry tree. They are edible—but, in the opinion of many, just barely. Slightly sour but otherwise virtually flavorless, mulberries are sometimes used in jams or jellies, or in old-fashioned mulberry wine.

MULL, TO: see page 447

MULLET: see FISH

MUSCATS: see RAISINS

MUSH: see HASTY PUDDING

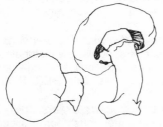

MUSHROOMS

The fellow who ate the first mushroom must indeed have been a) brave, b) stupid, or c) very, very hungry. Not, perhaps, quite as desperate as the one who sampled the first raw oyster, but all the same, pushed beyond the bounds of prudence. At any rate, whoever you were we are most grateful to you. To many of us, a cuisine without mushrooms would lose many of its delights.

There are more than forty thousand varieties of fleshy mushroomlike fungi, but only a few are edible. Even for those who are considered (or consider themselves) "experts," gathering wild mushrooms can be a very chancy business. Whole families have been wiped out by a dish of mushrooms mother and dad picked and brought home; those of us lacking the death wish buy our mushrooms (commercially raised, not wild ones) at the market. Old wives' tales—poisonous mushrooms turn a silver spoon black but nonpoisonous ones do not, and others equally nonsensical—are purely and simply superstition and not to be relied on.

Cultivation of the culinary delicacy has been known and practiced for a long time. Ancient Egyptians grew mushrooms, but only for their pharaohs—they were, as with many other foods of times long gone by, considered much too good for the common people. Food of the gods, the Romans called them, and fed their legionnaires mushrooms to give them strength and courage—after all they were magic, weren't they, coming up unplanted and then disappearing a short time later, only to reappear at another time and in another place?

Not surprisingly, the French developed mushroom cultivation, growing the delicacies in deep caves. The Swedes, no slouches as food experts themselves, brought cultivation above ground. Mushrooms have been used in good cooking in this country for generations—Martha Washington's cookbook offers several recipes containing "mushrumps." But they have been commercially grown in the United States only since the end of the nineteenth century. By now we raise nearly 170 million pounds—and mushrooms, remember, "weigh light," as grandma used to say. A small area in Pennsylvania is our national mushroom capital, although they are grown in many other places as well, not excluding home cellars and even under the beds of some do-it-yourselfers, along with such other light-shunning goodies as bean sprouts.

MUSHROOMS IN YOUR KITCHEN

Mushrooms with steak. Mushrooms with dill-seasoned sour cream sauce. Mushrooms with sherried cheese-bread crumb stuffing. Raw mushroom salad. Mushroom omelet. Cream of mushroom soup. Mushrooms à la grecque. Creamed oysters and mushrooms. Stir-fried beef with mushrooms and snow peas. Savory mushroom quiche. And literally dozens upon dozens more wonderful ways to enjoy mushrooms—by now, if you are one of the mushroom-enjoyers, you are doubtless drooling (in a genteel, well-bred manner, it goes without saying) and promising yourself mushrooms for dinner.

how to buy: Normal color is white to a pallid brown, depending on the area in which you live. Look for caps that are closed (not spread wide, with cracks marring the circumference), that are clean, that feel firm to light pressure. The gills—the flutings between cap and stem—should be free from the stem, and look crowded; in small mushrooms they are white, but range from pinkish to brown-black as size increases. The stem should be thick, solid, and smooth except for the fuzzy ring that marks the place where the mushroom pushed up out of the earth or other medium in which it was grown. Count on 1 pound of fresh mushrooms to furnish 4 cups sliced, raw; a pound will yield 20 to 24 medium-size caps, with a bonus of stems for soup and sauce.

Small mushrooms are least expensive—choose them for chopping and slicing. Those with long stems are usually cheaper than the shorter ones, because caps are more tender than stems. Medium-size mushrooms can be sliced for salads, for sautéing, to stuff for appetizer servings. The very big ones—3 inches or more in diameter—are just right to stuff as a main or side dish.

how to store: Mushrooms bought loose or in a paper carton can be stored in the refrigerator as is if you're going to use them on the day of purchase. If you wish to hold them up to 5 days, take a little more care: spread the mushrooms out on a nonmetal platter or tray in a single layer, cover with dampened paper towels and refrigerate. Store cooked mushrooms in a tightly covered container, in the refrigerator, up to 3 days.

nutritive value: A comfort to gourmet weight-loss dieters, mushrooms are one of a small number of elegant yet low-calorie foods. In 1 cup of diced or sliced mushrooms, there are only 20 calories; other nutrients supplied by the same measure of mushrooms are:

protein	1.9	grams
fat	.2	gram
carbohydrate	3.1	grams
calcium	4	milligrams
phosphorus	81	milligrams
iron	.6	milligram
sodium	11	milligrams
potassium	290	milligrams
thiamin	.07	milligram
riboflavin	.32	milligram
niacin	2.9	milligrams
ascorbic acid	2	milligrams
vitamin A	trace	international unit

Tips on preparing, cooking. Wipe mushrooms with a damp paper towel—never wash in a large amount of water, and never soak them in water. To remove stems, twist gently; if you leave stems in place, cut off and discard a thin slice from the bottoms. Cut stems off even with caps if the mushrooms are to be stuffed—that remaining stub of stem helps the mushroom hold its shape nicely during cooking. And never commit the heresy of peeling mushrooms; the thin skins hold a part of the flavor—and the nutrients—and help the mushrooms keep their shape in cooking. If you need further convincing, peeled mushrooms darken more easily than unpeeled ones.

In whatever way you cook mushrooms, make the cooking time brief. If you sauté them, sliced, 3 to 4 minutes is ample. To cook them to add to such dishes as casseroles, place in a pan with ¼ inch water. Cover pan and cook over medium-high heat 2 to 3 minutes, until the mushrooms have expressed their liquid; uncover and continue to cook until the liquid is somewhat evaporated, another 2 minutes or so. Use the liquid, full of good mushroom flavor, in making sauce. A little lemon juice added during cooking will keep the mushrooms from turning dark. See also DUXELLES.

Freezing mushrooms. Although mushrooms are available all year around, they are less plentiful—and so, more expensive—in the summer, making winter mushrooms a practical freezer item. Freeze small mushrooms whole, quarter larger ones. Steam-blanch 3 to 5 minutes, depending on size; chill, drain, pack, and freeze. Or sauté in butter 2 minutes; pack, pouring butter from the skillet over the mushrooms; freeze. Add lemon juice to the sautéed mushrooms, citric or ascorbic acid to the blanched ones, to prevent darkening.

Other ways, other forms. Although fresh mushrooms are virtually always to be had, other forms are available.

in grocery produce or "gourmet food" section: Dried mushrooms, black and rather off-putting to look at until you know their secret—superb flavor; rehydrate in warm water before using.

in grocery spice-and-seasoning section: Freeze-dried diced mushrooms in jars, not widely distributed; cooking rehydrates them without previous soaking—good flavor for cooked dishes and sauces. See HERBS AND SAVORY SEASONINGS.

on grocery shelves, in cans or jars: 3½-, 4-, 6-, and 8-ounce sizes of whole button mushrooms, slices, and pieces and stems—all in liquid; also "butter-broiled" mushrooms, more like fresh in flavor than other canned varieties.

in grocery frozen-food section: Whole or sliced frozen mushrooms, plain or in butter sauce; also mushroom combinations, as with peas or beans, plain or in butter sauce.

Elegance and—sometimes—magic. *Agaricus campestris* is the mushroom we buy fresh, in stores. But there are more exotic edible kinds, rarely encountered fresh, but sometimes to be found in specialty food shops. Morels are pixie-cap shaped with a pitted, put-off texture and appearance; these have incomparable flavor. Giant puffballs, shaggy manes, and sulphur shells are other edible mushrooms sometimes gathered in the wild, all with fine flavor and texture—provided the gatherer knows what he's about. Cèpes and chanterelles are available canned.

In 1977, enok mushrooms—full name enoki-dake—first appeared fresh in some markets. They are very small, cream-colored, with neat little ball-shape caps and long, thin stems. They are sold loose or, more often, in 3½-ounce bags. Popular in the northern part of Japan for centuries, they are now cultivated in California—in, should you care, a medium of sawdust, rice bran, and water.

Slightly sharper, slightly more acid-tasting than our old friend *Agaricus campestris,* enoks can be added raw to salads, lightly pickled in lemon juice, oil, and seasonings as an appetizer, very briefly sautéed in butter to serve with meats, or batter-dipped and tempura-fried. However accomplished, the cooking time must be very short—longer cooking turns them tough and bitter.

Inedible—at least in the what's-for-supper sense—is one member of the *Amanita* family (other members can bring death from a single mouthful) that is intoxicating in the falling-down-drunk meaning of the term. Some members of the *Psilocybe* family are the hallucogenic mushrooms sacred to Indians of Mexico and South America (as peyote—not a mushroom but a cactus "button"—is to some of the Indians of our own Southwest). From this mushroom, the eating of which produces "visions" that are believed to be religious experiences, a mind-altering drug of abuse, psilocybin, is obtained.

MUSKMELONS: see MELONS

MUSKRAT: see GAME

MUSSELS: see SHELLFISH

MUST: see WINE

MUSTARD

Those yellow-flowered, tall, thin plants that dot midwestern fields in summer are wild mustard. Long, long ago, in Europe and Asia, the plants were brought in from the fields and cultivated, to provide a yellow savory seasoning for a number of dishes of the peoples of many cultures.

It is available to us now as mustard seed. The name was conferred by the Romans, who for some obscure reason—we tried it, and it remains obscure—soaked the seeds in must, unfermented grape juice. We use the seed most often in pickles; dry mustard that we use as a savory seasoning is made from the ground mild-tasting, light-colored seeds; prepared mustard, a brown or yellow mixture sold in jars, ranges from mild to hot and is flavored with sugar, vinegar, or white wine. In its simplest forms, prepared mustard is slathered on millions of ball park, fairground, street vendor, and carnival hot dogs yearly by eager eaters of that all-American specialty. Hold the sauerkraut, please!

Make a cooked mustard sauce like a boiled salad dressing, but up the mustard content to 3 tablespoons of the yellow prepared kind, and add a little horseradish for zing. Or make the simplest mustard sauce of all, to serve cold: combine 1 cup dairy sour cream, 1 tablespoon lemon juice, 1 teaspoon sugar, and ¼ cup prepared mustard. Add a bit of mustard to baked beans, and perk up the mayonnaise for meat salads (ham in particular) with it.

Dry mustard is mild as mother's milk when it comes from the container. Ah, but add a little liquid, any kind at all, and things start happening. Make a very thin paste of 2 tablespoons dry mustard, ¼ teaspoon sugar, 1 teaspoon vinegar, and enough water for the consistency you want; use as a dip for tiny smoked cocktail sausages or miniature appetizer egg rolls. That recipe makes a very small amount? It does indeed, because a little goes a long, long way. See also DIJON MUSTARD, PREPARED MUSTARD, HERBS AND SAVORY SEASONINGS, SEEDS, and SPICES.

MUSTARD-SEED OIL: see OILS, SALAD AND COOKING

MUTTON

As explained by a man who enjoys it and finds it very difficult to buy in this country, mutton is lamb that had sense enough to go hide at slaughtering time, postponing its fate until next year. Indeed, some mutton is so strong of flavor, dark of color, and generally unacceptable, that one suspects the lamb of having hidden for a decade or so. But mutton from an animal between one and two years old is delicious. However, only a few "carriage trade" butcher shops have it on hand, although some others will order it for you. In England and the European continent, though, mutton is much appreciated, as it is in Near- and Middle-Eastern countries.

In New York City there used to be, of blessed memory, Keen's English Chop House. There, in a ramble of rooms where the low ceilings were made to seem lower by the many clay pipes—one for each regular, favored customer, with his/her name on it—that hung from them, "The Chop" was served, and had been since the days of Lily Langtry and Diamond Jim Brady. The Chop was mutton, curled around a lamb kidney, and was of such proportions that the waiter—somewhat male chauvinist, but demonstrably no pig—always offered to carve it for lady guests, who might be fatigued by such a chore. It was served medium-rare; you were not asked, it was simply assumed that if you had sense enough to eat at Keen's you wouldn't want it any other way. And so you wouldn't—the language simply is not adequate to describe the gustatorial splendors of that huge, sublimely flavorful, meltingly tender mutton chop.

Whatever became of those waiters? They had all started at Keen's as young bus boys, had grown gray in service—much too old to be turned loose on an unfeeling world by the time the restaurant closed. Who now serves mutton chops? Who eats them? What became of all those clay pipes? What occupies that space on Thirty-Sixth Street now—some tacky boutique? Some shop with plastic replicas of the Statue of Liberty with "souvenir of New York" across her navel? Oh François, you may indeed inquire, "Where are the snows of yester-year?" (Don't turn in your grave, Villon—some of us mourn lost ladies, some of us lost mutton chops.)

MYSOST: see CHEESE

WHAT DOES IT MEAN WHEN THE RECIPE SAYS . . . ?

Mini-dictionary of kitchen terms and methods of preparing and cooking food—to guide the tyro, encourage the experimenter, and confirm the old pro

When you bard a piece of beef do you write an ode to it? When you scallop cabbage, do you cut neatly rounded edges on each leaf? When you shirr eggs, do you do it by hand or use your sewing machine? When you stew lamb, does it end up inebriated? When you crush a cracker, is its ego permanently damaged?

The kitchen has a language all its own. Even old kitchen hands—those of us who read cookbooks for pleasure as others read novels, who clasp our hands on our bosoms in ecstasy at the sight of a perfect artichoke, swoon with joy if someone presents us with a brace of wild ducks—are brought up short every now and then by a food-related word. If you are one of those, give a thought to culinary newcomers, the Johnny-come-latelies to gastronomy who hear the siren song of the kitchen but can't join the chorus because they don't know the words.

Here, in brief definitions, are the lyrics to the tune—not all of them, because the world of cooking is a wide one, and whole books of cooking terms can be (and have been) compiled. But these are, as grandma was wont to say, enough to be getting on with; the common, usual terms used in the preparing and cooking of food, plus some of those often found in recipes, in food articles, on menus.

What you'll find here are definitions of the words that have to do with food and with assorted kitchen activities. What you won't find are the standard foods themselves—the meats, poultry, fish, vegetables, dairy products, nuts, fruits, and all the rest. These are listed and dealt with at length in the alphabetical sections of this book. Nor will you find utensils, pots, pans, appliances, and other cookery paraphernalia—for those, see the special feature: YOU CAN'T WORK WITHOUT TOOLS.

PREPARATION HOW-TO

Bard. Cover or wrap with fat; *purpose:* to ensure that meat or poultry will be juicy after cooking—as it cooks and melts, the fat bastes the roast or bird; *method:* drape and tuck very thin pieces of fat around the meat or poultry—they may or may not be tied in place.

Baste. Lave food with liquid as it cooks—can be fat, drippings or sauce; *purpose:* to keep food moist, juicy, add flavor; *method:* with a spoon, ladle, or bulb baster.

Beat. Mix a single food (as whole eggs, or whites or yolks) or a combination (as a cake batter) in a steady, sturdy motion; *purpose:* to combine ingredients or to incorporate air, or both; *method:* by hand with a spoon or whisk, or with an electric or mechanical mixer.

Bind. Add an ingredient to hold other ingredients together; *purpose:* to achieve a homogenous whole that will not separate; *method:* eggs (or yolks only) or thick sauces stirred or folded into mixtures of food act as binders—mayonnaise is used to bind salads (as potato, chicken, fish), cream sauce or béchamel to bind creamed chicken or vegetables or such.

Blanch. Plunge into hot, then cold water; *purpose:* a) to loosen skins, as of tomatoes and peaches, for easier peeling, b) to prepare certain foods for freezing (see special feature: PUTTING FOOD BY); *method:* have boiling water ready, plunge food (by the piece, or contained in a sieve or colander) into it, then plunge into cold water to stop the cooking action.

Bone. Remove bones. See the special feature: CARVING, BONING, AND OTHER KITCHEN TECHNIQUES.

Bread. Coat food with fine dry bread or cracker or other (such as cornflake) crumbs; *purpose:* to provide food with a crust when cooked; *method:* food (as meat, croquettes) is usually dipped in flour, then in beaten egg, then in crumbs, or it may be merely moistened, as by dipping in buttermilk, then coated with crumbs by rolling or dipping.

Brush. Coat food with a thin film of liquid; *purpose:* to protect the surface and/or to provide it with a glaze or the appearance of one; *method:* with a spoon or pastry brush. Fat, cream, egg, dorure (egg yolk-and-cream mixture for pastry), oil, even water (as for french bread) are used for brushing various foods.

Carve. Cut meat in slices or pieces; *purpose:* to ready it for serving; *method:* with a very sharp knife. See the special feature: CARVING, BONING, AND OTHER KITCHEN TECHNIQUES.

Chill. Make thoroughly cold; *purpose:* to prevent growth of bacteria, to cause to thicken (as gelatin, puddings), or simply because the food tastes better chilled; *method:* in the refrigerator or by immersing the food container in a bowl of ice or ice and water.

Chop. Cut into small pieces; *purpose:* to reduce to convenient size and shape, as chopped celery for a fish salad; *method:* with a knife on a board, with a multi-bladed chopper in a wooden bowl, or (sometimes, some foods) in a blender.

Coat. Cover with a thin layer of another food, such as sugar, flour, light batter (as fritters), or crumbs; *purpose:* to protect the food in cooking and/or provide a crisp crust on the cooked food; *method:* by shaking food pieces in a bag with, or by dipping them into, coating material.

Cool. Bring to a point where the food is no longer warm to the touch; *purpose:* preparatory to refrigeration or freezing, or because food is to be served that way; *method:* let stand at room temperature (chancy for most foods for more than 20 minutes) or refrigerate.

Correct. Change the taste of a mixture by adding seasoning; *purpose:* to improve the flavor; *method:* taste the mixture, then add a small amount of salt (or pepper or herb or whatever), stir to combine, taste again, add more if necessary.

Cream. Bring a food (or two or several in combination) to a soft, very malleable, heavy creamlike consistency; *purpose:* for ease of later combining thoroughly with other ingredients or ease of spreading (as butter or other mixtures to spread on bread); *method:* in a bowl or other container with a (preferably slotted) spoon, or at low speed with an electric mixer. Most often said of combining butter and sugar in making cake.

Crimp. Work edge of pastry into a pattern; *purpose:* largely decorative, but also in some cases to provide a barrier edge to contain juices during cooking; *method:* turn edge of pie crust under along pie plate rim for single crust, top crust under bottom for double-crust pie, then press into decorative edging with fingers or press with tines of a fork.

Crush. Reduce to a pulp, paste, or powder; *purpose:* for ease of combining with other ingredients or to ensure even distribution throughout the mixture to which it will be added; *method:* in a heavy vessel with the back of a spoon, or with a mortar and pestle, or with a rolling pin on a board, or with a special tool, such as a garlic press.

Cube. Cut into pieces that are small, but larger than either chopped or diced foods; *purpose:* for ease of combining with other ingredients and/or simply for good looks; *method:* with a knife on a board. Cubes are about ½ inch on all sides. Most often said of meat or cheese.

Cut In. Combine flour and shortening (butter, margarine, lard, hydrogenated shortening) in making pastry; *purpose:* to reduce the mixture to tiny flour-coated particles of fat; *method:* with two knives in a crisscross motion, or with a special tool called a pastry blender. Recipe will specify the size of particles, as "consistency of cornmeal."

Deglaze. Take up cooked-on juices and browned bits in a pan in which meat or poultry has been cooked; *purpose:* to provide juices to serve with the meat (au jus) or material to use in making sauce or gravy; *method:* pour off fat, add a small amount of water (or stock or wine) to pan, cook over low heat, stirring and scraping to get up all the cooked-to-the-pan goodness.

Devil. Combine with one or several hot ingredients, such as mustard, hot pepper sauce, or worcestershire; *purpose:* to enhance (sometimes to change entirely) the flavor; *method:* combine with the food (as with the yolks in deviled eggs) or coat it (as in deviled beef bones) so that deviling ingredients will permeate the food in cooking.

Dice. Cut into small cubes, roughly ¼ inch on all sides. See also Chop, Cube.

Dilute. Make thinner or less strong; *purpose:* to achieve the consistency and/or flavor required; *method:* add water, milk, or other liquid until desired consistency/strength is reached.

Dissolve. Combine a dry ingredient with a liquid one until the dry loses its identity; *purpose:* for desired texture in the finished product; *method:* stir with a spoon, or use an electric mixer or blender as the recipe directs. Most often said of sugar and gelatin.

Dot. Scatter (usually butter or other fat) over the surface of a mixture, such as a casserole dish; *purpose:* so that in cooking the scattered ingredient will melt and blend into the mixture; *method:* cut butter or other ingredient into small pieces, place on surface of mixture at reasonably equal intervals.

Drain. Remove liquid or fat; *purpose:* to prepare food for serving or for the addition of other ingredients; *method:* a) pour off liquid or fat from pan in which food has been browned or cooked, b) drain liquid from vegetables by pouring into a colander or sieve, or c) place fat-cooked foods (as bacon, croquettes) on absorbent paper to soak up excess fat.

Dredge. Cover with (plain or seasoned) flour or (less usually) sugar; *purpose:* to help in browning and/or to keep juices in, or (sugar) to garnish and/or add sweetness; *method:* shake food in a bag containing the dredging flour or mixture or dip food in it, turning to coat on all sides.

Drizzle. Top one food with another of a thin consistency; *purpose:* to enhance flavor in cooking or before serving; *method:* pour, spoon, or ladle melted butter or other fat, or marinade or other liquid, over food in a light, thin stream. An ingredient that is drizzled over a food is generally of a rather small quantity, as butter is drizzled over the crumbed surface of a casserole dish before baking, for example.

Dust. Coat lightly (usually incompletely) with flour or sugar; *purpose:* to enhance flavor or appearance; *method:* sprinkle food with dusting ingredient. Often said of a plain cake— "dust with confectioners sugar."

Eviscerate. Remove the entrails; *purpose:* to prepare fowl or game for cooking; *method:* with a knife suited to the size of the bird or animal being prepared, plus the fingers. Fortunately for those of us with delicate sensibilities, the butcher takes care of this little chore these days, unless you are called upon to deal with a hunter's bag. Even then, it is properly the hunter's province—not only because he has had the pleasure of bagging the game but, more importantly, because game should be eviscerated very shortly after it is shot, for reasons of flavor and to retard spoilage. Other terms are "draw" and, less delicately, "gut."

Flake. Break gently into thin, flat pieces; *purpose:* a) of fish, to ready it for adding to a salad or creamed mixture, or b) also of fish, to determine whether it is sufficiently cooked; *method:* use fingers or a fork or two forks, pulling food apart gently at the natural breaks in its structure.

Flour. Cover or dust with flour; *purpose:* a) to aid in browning when food is cooked, b) to prevent foods from sticking together, as with raisins or other fruit to be incorporated into a batter, or c) to keep food from sticking to a surface, as bread to be kneaded, cookies or biscuits to be rolled out; *method:* sprinkle surface of food or board lightly with flour, spread gently with fingertips. Boards on which certain pastries are rolled are sometimes "floured" with sugar.

Flute. See Crimp.

Fold. a) Incorporate one ingredient gently into another, or b) bring one portion of a food, such as pastry, over the remaining portion, as in making a turnover; *purpose:* to combine ingredients more gently than by stirring or beating, or to provide a top covering for a filling; *method:* a) pour or spoon ingredient to be folded in (such as egg whites) on top of prepared mixture (such as cake batter) in a bowl, and incorporate into the prepared mixture by cutting down, gently scraping across, then cutting up to the top again with a flat whisk or rubber spatula—gently is the watchword; b) carefully, with fingers, lift one half of rolled or patted-out dough over the remaining half, often to cover a sweet or savory filling—if recipe directs, close edges by pressing with fingers or tines of a fork. Omelets are also folded before serving, whether or not they incorporate a filling—with a spatula, lift one side to cover the remaining side; slip gently out of the pan and onto a serving plate.

Glaze. Cover the surface of a food with a thin substance; *purpose:* to create a shine and/or to add flavor and/or enhance appearance; *method:* apply with a brush (as on cookies, pastries) or pour or spoon over (as on ham, cakes).

Grate. Reduce to fine, usually granular, particles; *purpose:* to bring the grated material to a state in which it will melt easily, or may be readily sprinkled over or incorporated into another food; *method:* use the fine openings of a several-sided grater, or a fine, single-sided one.

Grease. Coat a cooking surface with fat; *purpose:* to keep the food from sticking to the surface and (secondarily) to help produce a well-browned appearance; *method:* using a brush, piece of paper, or fingers, coat the pan surface liberally with an unsalted fat (sweet butter, unsalted margarine, hydrogenated shortening).

Grease and Flour. Grease as above; sprinkle pan with flour, turn so that the flour adheres to the grease over the entire surface; turn pan upside down and tap to shake out the excess flour.

Grind. Reduce to very small particles; *purpose:* to produce meat, poultry, fish, and other foods of a consistency to be used in patties, loaves, fritters, mousses, and the like; *method:* put through a food grinder, electric or hand operated, or (some foods) process in a blender.

Hull. Remove leaves and stems from berries; *purpose:* to prepare them for serving or to use in cooking; *method:* gently, with the fingers—for the more delicate-minded, there's a small pincerslike device known as a huller. Berries should not be hulled until just before they are to be used, and generally should be washed before hulling.

Husk. Remove outside protective leaves from ears of corn; *purpose:* to prepare corn for cooking; *method:* with the hands, strip the husks down and off, starting at the top of the ear (where the tassel of corn silk shows). Strip silk away also before cooking—with fingers, or (gently) a small, dry vegetable brush.

Infuse. See Steep. Prepared coffee and tea are both infusions. So is the resulting liquid, used for flavoring and seasoning, when herbs are soaked in hot water.

Julienne. Cut into long, thin, matchstick pieces; *purpose:* to produce attractive, convenient-size segments of meat, cheese, vegetables, and other foods, chiefly for use in salads or as a garnish; *method:* on a board, with a sharp, pointed knife.

Knead. Work with dough to change its texture; *purpose:* to make dough smooth and elastic and, sometimes, to ensure even distribution of ingredients; *method:* on a floured board, with the hands, by folding dough toward you with the fingers, pressing it away with the heel of the hand, and repeating. Most often said of yeast doughs.

Lard. Thread thin strips of, or insert cubes of, fat through meat; *purpose:* to ensure that the cooked meat will be moist and juicy; *method:* a) with a special tool, a larding needle—rather like a giant darning needle, or b) by making incisions with a sharp knife and tucking in cubes of fat. The pieces of fat are called lardoons.

Leaven. Add baking powder, baking soda, or yeast to mixture; *purpose:* to make the mixture rise when baked (baking powder) or partially before baking (yeast); *method:* a) baking powder and soda are often sifted/added with dry ingredients, or soda may be dissolved in a liquid (water, sour milk or cream, buttermilk, molasses) before adding; b) yeast is dissolved in warm water or, in specially adapted recipes, combined with dry ingredients to which warm liquid is added.

Line. Cover sides and/or bottom of a pan with paper or thinly sliced fat or other food; *purpose:* a) to keep a mixture to be baked from sticking during the cooking process, b) to provide a reasonably sturdy surrounding for a delicate mixture, or c) to add flavor or substance; *method:* a) grease pan or not as recipe directs, then smooth paper onto greased surface, or b) position slices of food on bottom and around sides of pan. Baking sheets on which macaroons or meringues are baked are often lined with parchment paper, jelly roll pans with wax paper; casserole dishes to be frozen are often lined with foil. Pans or molds for refrigerator desserts are often lined with split ladyfingers or thin slices of sponge cake. Pâté molds (for baked pâtés) are often lined with thin slices of blanched bacon.

Macerate. Let stand in a liquid, such as wine or brandy; *purpose:* to infuse the food, usually fruit, with the flavor of the liquid; *method:* prepare fruit, pour wine or other liquid (often kirsch or rum) over it and let stand—at room temperature or refrigerated—as directed by recipe.

Marinate. Soak foods in an acid and/or oil-based liquid; *purpose:* to tenderize the food (meat) and/or permeate it with flavor; *method:* place liquid ingredients and seasonings in a deep dish, so that meat (or, less often, other foods) will be covered by liquid, or in a tightly closed plastic bag. Foods are marinated short term (an hour or so) at room temperature, long term (several hours or overnight) in the refrigerator.

Mash. Reduce to a smooth, even-textured mass; *purpose:* a) of vegetables, one of the accepted methods of serving (often with butter, cream, and seasonings added), as mashed potatoes and mashed turnips, b) of seasonings, such as garlic, to ensure even distribution and/or no discernible pieces, in the food to which they are added; *method:* a) vegetables, with a potato masher or by putting through a food ricer, b) seasonings, with back of spoon, in mortar and pestle, or in special small press.

Mask. Cover or coat with a stiffened sauce or gelatin mixture; *purpose:* most often to enhance appearance while improving texture and/or flavor; *method:* a sauce, such as chaud-froid (see special feature: SAUCE SORCERY), or a partially congealed aspic, is spooned over a food such as cold poached fish or chicken breasts, cold sliced rare beef. Masking material is generally added in several thin layers; each layer is allowed to congeal before another is added.

Melt. Change (usually fat or chocolate) from a solid to a liquid; *purpose:* to use as a sauce, or to facilitate incorporation into other ingredients; *method:* a) of butter or other fat, in a small pan over low heat, b) of chocolate, in a double boiler, in a small vessel set into simmering water, or in a small pan over low heat with other ingredients, such as butter, milk, or water.

Mince. Reduce to very fine pieces. See Chop; minced foods are even finer. Most often said of meat.

Mull. Heat a liquid—generally a beverage—with other ingredients; *purpose:* to infuse the liquid with the flavors of the other ingredients, which are generally herbs or spices; *method:* place liquid in a saucepan or pot, add herbs or spices, heat gently—may simmer, but should not boil—as recipe directs. Wine and cider are the most common mulled beverages.

Oil. Coat a pan or mold with cooking oil (see Grease). Oil is not always an acceptable substitute for solid fats in preparing pans for cooking—if there are spaces between the foods, as with cookies on a baking sheet, the oil will cook to a difficult-to-remove gum. Molds for gelatin desserts or salads may be coated with a very thin film of oil to facilitate later unmolding.

Pare. Remove skin or rind; *purpose:* when skin or rind is inedible or is not wanted for the dish being prepared; *method:* with a sharp, thin-bladed knife or a swivel-bladed vegetable parer.

Peel. Remove skin or rind. See Pare. Most often said of fruits whose skins come off readily, such as oranges. Some people distinguish "peeling" fruits and "paring" vegetables, but the two words are interchangeable.

Pipe. Border or top one food with another, using a pastry bag and tube; *purpose:* for decoration—to add a sweet or savory edible garnish; *method:* food must be of suitable consistency to force through the pastry tube. Egg-enriched mashed potatoes (duchesse) are often piped as a border around planked steaks, or into nests which, when baked, are filled with peas or other vegetables. Frosting or whipped cream is piped on the (frosted or not) surface of cakes and other desserts.

Pit. Take out seeds or stones; *purpose:* when seeds are inedible or not wanted for the dish being prepared; *method:* with sharp-pointed knife and fingers, or with special devices, such as a cherry pitter.

Plump. Soak in liquid, most often said of dried fruit; *purpose:* to restore moisture and render fruit softer and more inviting; *method:* place fruit in a container, pour water or other liquid over and let stand, soaking, 15 to 30 minutes, then drain. Prunes are often "cooked" by plumping in hot water—see label of prune package for directions. Sometimes fruits are plumped in a portion of the liquid from the dish into which they are to be incorporated—in this case, do not drain, follow recipe directions for amount of liquid.

447

Pound. Beat food—generally meat—with a heavy object to break down tissue structure; *purpose:* primarily to tenderize, but also at the same time to flatten and, sometimes, to incorporate seasoned flour into the meat to enhance flavor and facilitate browning; *method:* place meat (floured or not, as recipe directs) between two slices of wax paper or on a board and strike with a meat mallet (wooden or metal hammer with toothed face), or with the edge of a heavy saucer or small plate. Beef round is often pounded for chicken-fried or swiss steak; veal cutlet (leg slices) is pounded for scallopini.

Preheat. Bring oven, broiler, or sometimes cooking pan to required temperature before food is put in to cook; *purpose:* so that leavened foods will rise properly, so that broiled meats will sear and brown immediately, sealing in juices; *method:* turn on the oven or other cooking device about 10 minutes in advance of putting in food, or follow manufacturer's instructions. Skillets (electric skillets, too) are preheated before meat is added for the same reason, and so that foods will brown in fat rather than boiling in it while the fat and the pan come up to the required temperature. Some broilers do not require preheating—read the use and care booklet that came with your stove or countertop broiler. Energy-watchers suggest that we save energy by not preheating ovens, and it is true that preheating is not required for unleavened foods and those not required to brown, such as casseroles or chicken baked in a sauce. However, preheating is essential for usable results with cakes and breads.

Prick. Make small holes in the surface of a food; *purpose:* to let air in or out; *method:* lightly puncture surface with the tines of a fork. Most often said of pastry for a single-crust pie shell to be baked without filling—pricking all over with a fork helps prevent bubbles and risen sections. See BAKE BLIND.

Proof. Start the rekindling of life in yeast; *purpose:* to ready the yeast for use as leavening in various kinds of breads; *method:* dissolve the yeast in warm liquid (80 to 90°F. for compressed, 105 to 115°F. for active dry yeast) without stirring for 5 to 10 minutes, the longer time for compressed yeast. Sometimes a small pinch of sugar is added to help the yeast "work." Some methods do not call for the preliminary dissolving of active dry yeast.

Purée. Reduce to a mushy, thick semiliquid; *purpose:* to use the food (as with fruit) as a sauce or coating, or to facilitate incorporation with other ingredients, or to feed infants or those with digestive problems; *method:* process in blender, or put through a fine sieve or food mill.

Reduce. Make the volume of a liquid less; *purpose:* to concentrate flavor and/or thicken the liquid slightly; *method:* over heat, by boiling or simmering uncovered—reduction is effected by evaporation.

Render. Separate fat, as a liquid, from surrounding or interspersed tissue; *purpose:* to get rid of the fat or, alternatively, to turn it into a usable form; *method:* in a heavy pan, over low heat. Rendered fat that is to be used, as for frying, should be strained to remove browned particles.

Roll. Shape dough or pastry into a sheet; *purpose:* a) to prepare pastry for fitting into pie or tart pans, or b) to ready bread doughs (as biscuits, scones, snails) or cookies for cutting and shaping; *method:* with a rolling pin, on a floured board—the rolling pin may have a stockinette "slipcover," the board a stretched canvas topping, both of which allow you to roll without incorporating as much extra flour into the dough as with plain pin and board. Some doughs are patted rather than rolled out—follow recipe directions.

Score. Cut part way through fat or meat; *purpose:* a) to keep edges from curling, as with fat on edges of steak, b) to keep fat from shrinking and pulling meat out of shape, as with scoring the top of a ham (this also provides a usable surface for a decorative glaze), or c) to tenderize by cutting long muscle, as with the crisscross scoring on a flank steak. Other foods are—infrequently—scored, as with the crisscross scoring on some kinds of Mexican pan dulce (sweet bread).

Shred. Cut in small, thin, strung-out pieces; *purpose:* to facilitate melting or incorporation with other ingredients, or to create a garnish, or to reduce to desired form—as with shredded cabbage for coleslaw; *method:* a) for vegetables, a mandoline shredder, b) for cheese, a grater with fairly large openings. Or use a food processor.

Sift. Put dry ingredients through a fine-mesh screen; *purpose:* to loosen and lighten texture by incorporating air, and to remove lumps; *method:* shake or otherwise move through a sieve or a special tool, a sifter, operated by a small crank or by a shuttle moved across the mesh by an opening and closing motion of the handle (for the effete, battery-operated sifters are available—grandma would turn in her grave!). Flours and sugars are the substances most often sifted, sometimes with other dry ingredients such as leavenings, spices, and salt. Do not sift unless the recipe directs—sifting whole wheat flour, for example, removes the bran.

Slice. Cut in thin, flat pieces; *purpose:* to prepare the food for cooking or for serving; *method:* on a board or other sturdy surface, with a sharp, long, thin-bladed knife (meats) or a knife with a serrated blade (as bread, tomatoes).

Sliver. See Julienne—but in this case the pieces are usually slightly smaller, less uniformly shaped.

Soak. Let stand, covered in liquid; *purpose:* to remove salt, to tenderize, or otherwise prepare for cooking; *method:* place food in a large, deep pan or dish, cover with water, let stand as recipe directs, often overnight. Said of country ham, which must be soaked to remove some of the salt, and of dried peas and beans, which must be soaked to soften somewhat by rehydration before cooking. See BEANS for alternate soaking method.

Sprinkle. Distribute an ingredient or combination over the surface of a food; *purpose:* generally, to provide an edible, flavor-enhancing garnish; *method:* ingredient to be sprinkled must be in fairly small pieces, as shredded cheese, chopped nuts, or chopped parsley—distribute, with fingers or from a spoon, evenly or in a pattern on surface of food.

Steep. Immerse dry food in a liquid for a period of time; *purpose:* to create an infusion, permeating the liquid with the flavor of the dry ingredient, as in making tea; *method:* pour freshly boiled water over the tea, herbs, or other dry ingredient from which the infusion is to be made, let stand about 5 minutes, then strain or drain off liquid.

Stir. Mix gently with a round-and-round motion; *purpose:* to combine ingredients, or to keep cooking food from sticking or scorching; *method:* with a spoon, in a circular pattern—a less forceful action than beating. (Some old wives—some new ones, too—claim that you must not reverse your movement from clockwise to counterclockwise or vice versa, or you'll somehow damage the mixture. Not true.)

Strain. Drain liquids from solids: *purpose:* to separate the two, sometimes in order to discard one or the other; *method:* pour through a strainer, colander, or sieve (if the liquid is to be saved, place over a bowl)—liquids drain through, solids are held in the strainer.

Stud. Press seasonings (sometimes edible garnish) into the surface of a food; *purpose:* to enhance the flavor and/or appearance; *method:* press directly into food, or cut a small slit with the point of a sharp knife and press seasoning into slit. Hams are sometimes studded with whole cloves, roasts of lamb with garlic slivers, and poached pears with blanched almonds.

Stuff. Fill the natural or man-made cavity of a food with a savory mixture; *purpose:* to enhance the flavor of the finished dish and add another dimension to the meal; *method:* usually based on a starch (most often bread of some variety, sometimes rice or wild rice), moistened and well seasoned, the stuffing is spooned lightly into the natural cavity of poultry, halved vegetables such as peppers or squash, or into a cavity made at home or by the butcher in such meats as breast of veal. Some meats are flattened, stuffing is spread on the surface, and the meat is rolled—beef roulade, veal birds, boned leg of lamb, for example.

Thicken. Add starch to liquid to make it denser; *purpose:* to produce a sauce or gravy that will cling to food, rather than running, as a liquid does—also, sometimes, in doing so to incorporate other ingredients such as butter or cream to enrich the sauce; *method:* a) combine flour, cornstarch, arrowroot, or other thickening agent with cold liquid (water, broth, milk, cream), add gradually to hot soup, stew, or sauce, stirring constantly, b) knead together equal amounts of butter and flour, add in bits to hot mixture while stirring (this is beurre

manié), or c) melt fat, stir in flour, and cook briefly before adding liquid (this is a roux).

Toss. Mix two or more ingredients gently, not combining them completely; *purpose:* to distribute ingredients evenly for flavor or texture, as in tossing pasta with butter and/or cheese, or tossing a green salad; *method:* with two forks or a fork and a spoon, in a lifting motion—and with a light hand.

Truss. Tie, lace, or sew meat or poultry; *purpose:* to retain original shape after food is cooked, and to prevent stuffing from leaking into the cooking pan; *method:* use white kitchen string to tie to retain shape, or string plus small skewers, or a large needle and heavy white thread to close cavity openings of stuffed poultry. Whole stuffed fish to be baked should be gently tied with white string around the body, as the flesh is so delicate that lacing or sewing would pull away during cooking.

Try Out. Another term for Render.

Whip. Beat rapidly; *purpose:* to incorporate air, thereby increasing volume; *method:* with a flat or balloon whisk, or with an electric mixer at high speed. Said most often of egg whites and heavy cream.

COOKING HOW-TO

Bake. Cook, in an oven or ovenlike device, by means of dry heat. Also, less frequently, to bake on a griddle—as pancakes, english muffins, crumpets.

Barbecue. Cook meat on a grill or spit over hot coals, basted with a savory, highly seasoned sauce—by extension, the same process in an oven.

Boil. Bring liquid to 212°F., the point at which bubbles rise and break on the surface; to cook in a boiling liquid.

Braise. Brown meat or other food in fat; drain fat, add small amount of liquid. Cover and cook over low heat.

Broil. Cook on a grill (over heat source) or in an oven broiler (under heat source) by direct, dry heat. Most grills and broilers broil one side of the food at a time, but some electric broiler appliances cook both sides simultaneously. Only tender—or tenderized—meats may be broiled. Often a vegetable—such as halved tomatoes, slices of precooked potato or squash—is broiled with the meat.

Caramelize. Heat sugar in a heavy pan, stirring constantly, until it melts into a golden brown syrup. Less often, a sugar-water mixture is cooked until it turns into such a syrup.

Clarify. a) Make stock or broth clear (remove cloudiness) by cooking with egg white and/or egg shells, then straining; b) melt butter, pour off clear liquid, leaving milky residue behind.

Coddle. Cook in liquid, hot but below boiling point. Eggs (in shell) are coddled—and are more deliciously tender than when boiled.

Crisp. Warm, usually in an oven, until the food becomes crisp—or until crispness is restored, as with somewhat stale crackers or cookies.

Deep Fry. Cook in hot, deep fat or oil until crisp, browned, and cooked through. Fat must be hot enough so that it cooks the food without soaking into it.

Flambé. Pour warm brandy or other spirits over a food and set afire. Beautiful, but be careful!

French Fry. Same as Deep Fry.

Fricassee. Brown a food in fat, drain fat, add a liquid or sauce. Cook, covered, over low heat until done. Most often said of chicken, but veal or pork may also be fricasseed.

Frizzle. Cook thinly sliced meat over high heat until the edges curl. Very thin bacon is frizzled, so is dried beef.

Fry. Cook in a skillet in a moderate amount of fat until browned and cooked through. The word implies more fat than Sauté, less than Deep Fry.

Grill. Cook on a grill. See Broil.

Panbroil. Cook meats in an ungreased or very lightly greased skillet over high heat, pouring off drippings as they accumulate.

Panfry. Cook meats in a skillet in a small amount of fat. See Sauté.

Parboil. Cook in liquid until about half done, in preparation for some other method of cooking (usually a brief one—that is, the food would not be cooked through if not first parboiled).

Plank. Broil on a seasoned hardwood plank. Steaks, sometimes chops, are planked. Often other foods are added for part of the broiling time—halved tomatoes or other vegetables, a piped border of duchesse potatoes.

Poach. Cook gently in a (sometimes seasoned) liquid that simmers but is not allowed to boil.

Pot Roast. Large (usually not a tender) cut of meat, browned and then cooked, covered, in a moderate amount of liquid until tender. Often vegetables are cooked with it.

Pressure Cook. Cook food in a special pot, a pressure cooker, which immerses the food in superheated steam under pressure. Pressure cooking is brief and sometimes tenderizing; however, some foods—particularly meats—tend to taste boiled. Many kinds of home canning and preserving are also done in a pressure cooker (see special feature: PUTTING FOOD BY).

Roast. Cook in the oven, by dry heat. Tender meats and poultry are roasted.

Sauté. Cook quickly in a skillet, in a small amount of fat. Fat should be hot, and the food must be dry (pat with absorbent paper if necessary) when placed in the fat.

Scald. Cook liquid (most often milk) over direct heat until small bubbles appear around the edge; liquid must not be allowed to boil.

Scallop. Bake in a casserole foods such as vegetables in alternating layers with crumbs or flour and milk or a thin white sauce.

Scramble. Cook gently, in fat over low heat, lifting portions of the food as it cooks to allow uncooked portions to flow beneath. Most often said of eggs and egg mixtures.

Sear. Brown meat quickly, without added fat, using high heat—in a skillet, under a broiler, in the oven.

Shirr. Bake seasoned whole eggs with cream (and sometimes crumbs) in individual serving dishes.

Simmer. Cook in liquid that is kept just below the boiling point; liquid moves gently, but only a few small bubbles are allowed to appear.

Skim. Remove fat or foam (scum) that has risen to the surface of a cooking liquid or food cooked in liquid, with an almost-flat, usually perforated tool called a skimmer, or with a spoon, a bulb baster, or a device called a fat mop.

Spit-Roast. Cook food on a revolving metal rod over fire or hot coals; spits are turned by hand, by a wind-up device, or electrically. Spit-roasted foods are usually basted with fat or a savory sauce.

Steam. Cook, covered, over a small amount of boiling water so that steam generated by the water circulates around/through the food. Food may be placed on a rack or in a metal french steamer basket above the water, or a specially designed utensil—called, logically, a steamer—may be used.

Stew. Cook food (usually meat or meat-vegetable combinations) in gently boiling liquid—a long, slow process, generally.

Stir Fry. Sauté briefly in a skillet or wok, stirring constantly and briskly. Vegetables are cooked tender-crisp by this Chinese method.

Toast. Brown by exposing to direct heat. Most often said of breads.

NOT HOW-TO, BUT WHAT-IS

Here is a miscellany of words that you might find in recipes or on menus. Food terms are multilingual; some of them have come into English usage in translation, some directly from their mother tongue.

A la. In the manner or style of. (Tripes à la mode de Caen is tripe as it is cooked in Caen, in the Normandy section of France—long, in a savory sauce.) By extension, we cook or serve many things "à la"—Chicken à la King, for example, two English words surrounding a French phrase. And we relish à la mode desserts—pie or cake topped with ice cream —that are not in the manner of anything in particular, but in a manner in which we enjoy them.

Agneau. French for lamb.

Al Dente. In Italian, "to the tooth"—said of pasta properly cooked to Italian standards: tender but not mushy, retaining firmness against the teeth when chewed.

Albondigas. Spanish word for meatballs. Sopa de Albondigas is meatball soup.

Amandine. Food garnished or sauced with almonds, usually toasted or butter-browned, as green beans amandine.

Antipasto. In Italian, "before the pasta"—that is, served before the main part of the meal. Appetizers, usually spicy or well-seasoned, such as pickled mushrooms, various cheeses, salami, marinated artichoke hearts.

Aperitif. French; an alcoholic beverage—cocktail or wine —served before the meal to whet the appetite.

Appetizer. Any food—hors d'oeuvres, canapés, antipasto —served before the main part of the meal (in the living room, with drinks, or at the table). Appetizers are supposed to pique the appetite, not overwhelm it.

Aspic. Meat or vegetable jelly, stiffened (meat) with its own gel or with commercial gelatin, or both. Used for coating and garnishing cold foods or by itself (tomato aspic) as a salad or appetizer.

Au Gratin. Creamy or cream-sauced food topped with crumbs and/or cheese, browned in the oven or under the broiler.

Au Jus. Served with its own (unthickened) pan juices— usually said of a roast of beef.

Au Lait. Beverage made with hot milk and coffee—café au lait. Sometimes, a beverage of chocolate or coffee/chocolate and hot milk. Café au lait is the favored French breakfast drink; with croissants, butter, and jam, it makes up a continental breakfast, a *café complet*.

Aubergine. French for eggplant. The term is used in the British Isles as well.

Baba. Round, rich yeast-dough cake soaked in syrup or rum.

Baguette. French; the long, slender, crisp-crusted loaf that we call french bread.

Bar-le-duc. Elegant French preserve of whole red or white currants suspended in a thick, sweet syrup.

Beignets. French for fritters; delicate deep-fried dough or pastry, or deep-fried batter-dipped foods of many kinds— beef, bananas, cheese, pears, eggplant, what you will.

Beurre. French for butter; BEURRE NOIR—browned (literally black) butter.

Beurre Manie. Equal amounts of butter and flour kneaded together; stirred, a small piece at a time, into boiling liquid to thicken it.

Bisque. Rich cream soup, usually fish- or shellfish-based.

Blanquette. A white (the meat is unbrowned) stew, generally made of veal—blanquette de veau; the gravy is enriched with cream and eggs, seasoned with lemon juice.

Boeuf. French for beef.

Bombe. Layer-within-layer dessert, made in a mold of two or more ice creams, frozen mousses, or sherbets, or a combination of these.

Borscht. A hearty soup based on beef stock, incorporating beets, onions, and sometimes other vegetables, such as carrots and celery. Served hot or cold, the lovely rosy-red soup is often garnished with a dollop of sour cream or a small whole boiled potato.

Bouillabaisse. French soup-stew, rich and hearty, based on fish and shellfish. That of the French port city of Marseilles is considered to be the authentic bouillabaisse.

Brochette. French word for skewer—food served "en brochette" has been cooked on a skewer or small spit.

Canapé. An appetizer—a savory, well-seasoned food (meat, fish, cheese, or a mixture) served on a small, crisp cracker or shape of toast or sautéed bread.

Chantilly. Whipped cream of a soft, not stiff texture, sometimes sweetened—named for the French village where once the royal dairy produced a particularly fine cream.

Chapon. Cube of bread soaked in garlic-flavored oil, tossed with a green salad to give a delicate taste of garlic— removed before the salad is served.

Charlotte. Dessert, usually a mold lined with ladyfingers and filled with a gelatin-whipped cream mixture—Charlotte Russe is this kind, but Apple Charlotte is made with buttered bread, filled with apple purée, and baked.

Chaud-Froid. Literally, hot-cold—a gelatin-stiffened white sauce (hot when cooked, cold when served) used to coat or mask foods, such as poached chicken breasts.

Chowder. A thick, hearty soup, substantial enough for a main dish—often based on fish or shellfish. The conflict still rages over whether the white (potato-onion-milk) New England or the red (tomato) Manhattan is the "proper" clam chowder.

Cioppino. America's answer to the bouillabaisse of France, this is a hearty soup/stew made of fish and shellfish —whatever is locally available goes into the pot—and often fortified with red wine. Served in large soup bowls, accompanied by crusty bread to sop up the flavorful liquid.

Cobbler. Deep-dish fruit pie with a top crust made sometimes of rich pastry, sometimes of biscuit dough. No bottom crust.

Compote. Sweetened cooked fruit, fresh or dried, served hot or chilled with its cooking syrup. Sometimes spiked with spirits.

Court Bouillon. Medium for poaching fish—a well-seasoned broth, often made with fish bones and heads, sometimes with white wine as part of the liquid.

Couscous. Staple food in North Africa—a kind of porridge of semolina wheat. It is steamed in a perforated pan, called a couscousier, placed over a kettle of the stew or soup with which it is later served, accompanied by a hot pepper sauce.

Cracklings. The small, crisp browned bits that remain when pork fat is rendered for lard, often incorporated into a corn bread—cracklin' bread.

Crème Pâtissière. A thick custard, cream enriched, used as a filling for pastries such as éclairs and napoleons.

Crepe. Thin, pliable pancake made of a rich batter, usually rolled or folded around a savory filling as a main dish, or served with a sweet sauce (sometimes a filling, also) as a dessert.

Croquette. Chopped meat, fish, or poultry or, less commonly, vegetables, well seasoned and bound with a thick white sauce. The mixture is chilled, shaped into a cone or patty, crumbed, and deep fried.

Croustade. A large or small case, made of bread that has been hollowed out, buttered, and toasted or baked. Used to contain a savory sauced mixture to be served as a main dish.

Croutons. Small squares or cubes of bread, sautéed in fat or dried and browned in the oven.

Cutlet. Small, thin, boneless piece of meat, most often veal.

Dacquoise. Almond meringue layers filled with buttercream.

Demitasse. In French, "half cup"—small cup used for hot, strong, black after-dinner coffee.

Drawn Butter. Clarified butter. Often served as a sauce, particularly with shellfish.

Duchesse. Mashed potatoes enriched with egg yolk and butter, piped through a pastry tube around meat, fish, or poultry, and oven-browned.

Dumplings. Balls or spoonfuls of dough, simmered in soups or steamed atop stews.

Duxelles. Combination of finely chopped mushrooms and shallots, sautéed. Used as a stuffing, sauce, or garnish.

Eclair. Finger-shaped dessert of PATE A CHOUX filled with CREME PATISSIERE or, less commonly, ice cream. Served frosted or sauced.

Enchiladas. Tortillas rolled around a meat or vegetable filling, served with a fiery tomato/hot pepper sauce (salsa).

Entrée. Once the course served before the meat, now the main course.

Entremets. Side dishes.

Escargot. French for snails—we import many edible snails from France.

Espresso. Dark, hearty Italian-roast coffee, brewed by steam extraction—usually served (here, but not in Italy) with a twist of lemon peel.

Fell. Thin membrane covering lamb or mutton—we see it chiefly on leg of lamb. If meat is young, leave in place to hold shape and juices; if old, remove—it becomes very tough when cooked.

Filet Mignon. A thick slice cut from the beef tenderloin, served as an individual steak.

Fillet. Thin, boneless piece of meat or fish.

Florentine. Dishes served in the manner of Florence, Italy—on a bed of spinach, napped with a cheese sauce, oven-browned. Not everything in Florence is served this way, of course, but many delightful egg and fish dishes are.

Fondant. A kneaded, sugar-syrup confection, used for bonbons and the centers of chocolate creams.

Fondue. Swiss specialty—melted cheese (emmenthal) with white wine and kirschwasser, eaten by dipping in cubes of crusty bread speared on a fork. By extension, other dip-and-eat dishes: fondue bourguignonne—raw steak dip-cooked in hot oil, served with dipping sauces—and chocolate fondue—melted chocolate, sometimes with liqueur, into which cubes of cake and pieces of fruit are dipped.

Frappé. Drink or dessert, like a water ice but frozen only to a mushy, not solid, consistency.

Fritter. Batter-coated food—whole or a mixture—deep fried.

Fromage. The French word for cheese.

Giblets. Heart, liver, and gizzard of any kind of poultry.

Goulash. A stew, flavored with paprika. From the Hungarian, where the word is *gulyás*.

Granité. Water ice, soft- rather than solid-frozen. Granité is often sold on the streets or at fairs, in paper cups, called "Italian ice."

Grenadine. Deep red, sweet syrup made from pomegranates, used in drinks and sometimes in desserts.

Gumbo. Thick, hearty soup-stew, based on shellfish or poultry, sometimes with ham, always with tomatoes and okra and often—as flavoring and thickening—filé powder, made of sassafras leaves. A Creole dish.

Hors d'Oeuvres. Bite-size, usually finger-food (often hot), appetizers.

Lox. Smoked salmon, a delicacy served as an appetizer or with cream cheese and bagels. The finest kind—best, most delicate flavor—is known as "Nova Scotia." Kin to this is lax, Scandinavian salmon used as an appetizer; gravad lax is preserved by being pickled with dill rather than smoked.

Macédoine. A combination of neatly, evenly cut fruits (or, less often, vegetables) in a pleasing combination of colors and flavors. Fruits are usually macerated in liqueur before serving.

Madrilène. Tomato-flavored consommé; served hot, but more often chilled and softly jelled.

Marron. French for chestnut; marrons glacés are candied chestnuts.

Marzipan. Almond-paste confection, sweetened and bound with egg white. Most often colored and molded into fruit and vegetable shapes—although a small pink marzipan pig is a traditional gift for a Scandinavian child at Christmas.

Meringue. Stiffly beaten mixture of egg whites and sugar. Traditional topping for certain pies; baked (often with nuts or chocolate) into small sweets called kisses; serves as the "crust" for angel pies; a component of blitz and other tortes.

Minestrone. A hearty vegetable soup of Italian origin. Grated parmesan or romano cheese is sprinkled over his portion by each diner.

Mocha. A mixture of coffee and chocolate—as a beverage or as a flavoring for desserts.

Mousse. Light, airy mixture, sweet or savory. Made with gelatin, it is chilled; made with eggs, it is baked. A fish-based mousse makes an excellent summer main dish. Chocolate mousse is a dessert favorite translated from the French by almost everyone.

Mousseline. A sauce to which whipped cream has been added—hollandaise and maltaise (orange-juice hollandaise) are the most usual ones.

Newburg. Sauce, enriched with sherry, cream, and egg yolks, for fish or shellfish—Lobster Newburg is the best known.

Niçoise. A dish with tomatoes, garlic, and ripe olives, with an olive oil-based sauce or dressing—food in the style of Nice, France. Salade Nicoise (tuna, anchovies, potatoes, green beans, and the above ingredients) is a lovely summer dish.

Paella. One-dish meal from Spain—chicken and shellfish combined with vegetables and rice, seasoned with garlic and saffron.

Parfait. Dessert layered in a tall, slender glass, alternating ice cream with fruit and/or sweet sauces topped with whipped cream, sometimes nut-sprinkled.

Pasta. The Italian portmanteau word for all the many varieties of macaroni, spaghetti, and noodles.

Pâté. A smooth, rich, deliciously seasoned mixture of minced or ground meats, almost always at least part liver. Pâté de foie gras is the epitome of the genre—a meltingly smooth mixture of goose livers, studded with truffles.

Pâte à Chou (or Choux). PASTRY from which shells for cream puffs, éclairs, and certain appetizers are made.

Petits Fours. Little sweets—cakes or cookies—elaborately iced.

Pilaf. Rice cooked in broth, often with minced or chopped vegetables, meat, fish, or poultry, plus herbs and other savory seasonings.

Poisson. French for fish.

Polenta. Cornmeal mush, Italian style—cooled, cubed, sauced, and baked; often cheese is stirred into the cooking cornmeal, or the finished dish is liberally cheese sprinkled.

Pollo. Both Spanish and Italian for chicken.

Popover. A crisp, light quick bread that is virtually all crust—the center is hollow. The secret of perfection is to have the batter cold, and the oven temperature and the heavy, well-greased pans very hot. Popovers are best eaten freshly baked, while still hot. Yorkshire Pudding, a British must with roast beef, is a kind of popover.

Porc. French for pork.

Potpie. Thickened stew, meat- or poultry-based, baked with biscuit or pastry crust in individual-serving casseroles.

Puff Paste. Pastry that, when baked, consists of many thin, airy layers; called *mille feuille*—"thousands of layers"—by the French, it is the pastry of which napoleons are made.

Quenelles. Small dumplings, delicate of flavor and texture. They are based on veal, chicken, or fish, poached in broth, served with an equally delicate sauce.

Quiche. A savory, open-faced pie, made with cheese and cream along with any of a variety of other foods—ham, bacon, onions, tomatoes, spinach, what you will.

Rissole. Two meanings—small deep-fried appetizer turnovers with a savory filling; partially cooked potatoes browned in hot fat to finish their cooking.

Riz. French for rice.

Roe. Fish eggs—caviar (sturgeon, salmon, or less authentically originated); shad roe is a late-winter delicacy, lightly sautéed and served with lemon, sometimes with bacon.

Rognons. French for kidneys.

Roux. Fat-and-flour mixture used to thicken sauces—as when you start white sauce by melting butter, then stirring in flour to make a smooth paste.

Smörgåsbord. Swedish appetizer buffet or, by extension, a whole meal of Scandinavian dishes served buffet style. Herring in various guises, many salads, stuffed eggs, cheeses—in the full-meal smörgåsbord, meatballs, brown beans, and many other goodies are added. A nosher's heaven.

Smørrebrød. Danish open-face sandwiches, as beautiful in their bounty as they are delicious. They preface a meal or, more reasonably, are a meal.

Soufflé. Main-dish or dessert mixture lightened and raised high with stiffly beaten egg whites. Main-dish soufflés are baked, must be served immediately after they are taken from the oven; dessert soufflés may be hot or cold.

Stock. Richly flavored, strong broth resulting from cooking meat, poultry, or fish at length in liquid with appropriate seasonings, sometimes with vegetables.

Taco. Crisp TORTILLA holding meat, shredded lettuce, cheese, chopped tomato; usually topped with a hot sauce.

Tamale. Soft cornmeal paste surrounding a savory filling, wrapped in cornhusk to retain its shape; usually served with a sauce.

Tart. Small individual pie, most often fruit filled.

Terrine. A kind of cooked pâté, made of ground meats layered with strips of ham or poultry or pieces of truffle. By extension, the earthenware dish in which it is baked is called the same name.

Timbale. Milk-and-egg custard incorporating minced fish, meat, or poultry. After baking, it is usually unmolded, served with a sauce.

Torte. Rich cake, sometimes layer-on-layer high. Ground nuts or sifted crumbs often take the place of all or part of the flour. Vienna is the (at least spiritual) home of tortes—sinfully rich chocolate Sacher Torte, heavenly meringue Spanisher Windtorte, Blitz Torte layered with rich custard, seven-layer Dobosch, dozens more.

Tortilla. Thin round griddle cake. Mexican bread, made of masa harina (see CORN) or wheat flour.

Tripe. The edible first and second stomach of various ruminants, most commonly beef cattle. A love-it-or-hate-it food, tripe is rich in protein, requires slow and very long cooking to reduce it to a state in which it is possible to masticate it.

Truffle. Fungus, black or white, that grows underground (usually beneath oak trees), is searched out by specially trained pigs (in France) or dogs (in Italy). Scarce and costly, truffles are at their best when fresh and also at their most expensive—fresh Italian white truffles sold in their 1977 season in New York City for $384.00 a pound. They are also available in miniature cans. Used in pâtés, sauces, pastas.

Tutti-frutti. Mixture of small-cut fruit, often in brandy or rum. Used as dessert sauce on ice cream, puddings, plain cake or, less often, as a condiment with meats.

Veau. French for veal—Ris de veau, French for sweetbreads.

Vichyssoise. Creation of French chef Louis Diat, this is a purée of leeks and potatoes, finished with cream and served cold. The soup usually comes to the table garnished with snipped chives.

Vinaigrette. Oil-and-vinegar sauce, well seasoned; served on cold vegetables, less commonly on cold meats or fish.

Zest. The oily, colored-part-only of the peel of citrus fruit.

Zuppa Inglese. Italian, literally "English soup"—meringue-topped, ricotta-plus-fruit-and-chocolate filled, soaked-in-rum cake.

NAPOLEONS

Familiar French pastries, napoleons are made with several layers of pâte feuilletée—puff pastry—filled with crème pâtissière—the thick custard filling we call pastry cream—cut into rectangles and frosted. Traditionally the frosting is white; bittersweet chocolate is dribbled over it in thin stripes and a knife is drawn through the chocolate before it sets to form a familiar, decorative pattern.

If you've a mind to make napoleons at home, give the matter mature thought. Unless you're an expert baker, a good French bakery can do the job better: the custard filling is relatively simple, but the puff pastry is rather difficult to work with. Look up a recipe for it in a good cookbook and you'll see what we mean. Or shortcut by buying frozen phyllo leaves to use for the pastry, making only the filling and frosting and completing the napoleons yourself.

NASTURTIUMS

You may think of this only as a cheerful, old-fashioned flower, bright with its orange/yellow/red colors, one that is exceedingly attractive to small black bugs but which, in spite of them, will take over the whole garden if you don't keep it in check.

But the nasturtium has more to offer. When the plant is young, pick small leaves to add to mixed green salads. They are peppery of flavor and tender-crisp of texture, and altogether a delightful—and pretty—salad green.

Later, when the plant has set seeds (they are more portly than most flower seeds, so you'll have no trouble finding them) pickle them for caperlike goodness—better than capers, many devotees staunchly maintain. It's easy: Gather the seeds while they are green and spread them out in the sun for a few days to dry. Then let them stand for 24 to 48 hours in cold vinegar. Bring fresh vinegar to a boil; drain the seeds, add them to the fresh vinegar, and boil for 10 minutes. Pour seeds and vinegar into small clean jars, cover tightly. Store in a cool place, where they will keep up to 6 months. Use in salads and sauces, with fish and eggs—indeed, in any recipe that calls for capers.

NATURAL FOODS

In our vocabulary there are four words pertaining to food that are misunderstood, misused, and maligned on all sides, by everyone from those known as food "nuts" to concerned home cooks trying to make their way through a barrage of verbiage on the subject of what's good, what's safe, what's nutritious to eat. The words are: organic, chemical, natural, and health—all perfectly good words whose perfectly good meanings have somehow become twisted out of shape.

Those words come up whenever food is discussed. In a fuzzy sort of way, people tend to think of "natural" foods as those that are eaten as they grow—that is, a pear or apple picked off the tree, a carrot or onion pulled from the ground. Wrong, others hasten to correct them—suppose those foods have been grown with the aid of inorganic, chemical fertilizers and/or disease and pest controls? Then they can no longer be called "natural," can they?

All right, how about "health" foods? Those are the ones, aren't they, that have been organically grown and have not, in their processing, been treated with anything synthetic—preservatives, hormones, antibiotics, additives of any description? True, others chime in, but that's not all—health foods are those that are not processed in any way.

Hold it. To begin with, processing is anything you do to a food. Peel it, and your natural pear has been processed; cook it, it's been further processed. Indeed, eat it, and by chewing and mingling it with the chemicals of your saliva, you are processing it still more.

Organic versus inorganic. The crux of the whole natural/health/organic food problem seems to lie in the definition of organic. What does the word signify—not depending on which "authority" you consult, but the true meaning?

As a service to consumers, who had bombarded the Department with questions on the subject, the USDA set one of its science advisors from the Agricultural Research Service the task of coming up with answers that would satisfy and be understandable to the concerned people anxious to eat—and to feed their children—a proper diet. The material that follows here is paraphrased from that research.

definitions of terms: All organic materials are complex combinations of chemicals, and all contain one chemical element in common: carbon. But although all organic materials are made up of chemicals, the reverse is not true—not all chemicals occur in the form of organic materials. However, all of our usual food supply is in organic form, because it has come from plant or animal sources.

The chief concerns today about things organic versus things chemical relates to how foods are grown and processed. There are no precise, official definitions, but some explanations have been proposed for legal use that can serve as guidelines:

"The term 'organically grown food' means food which

has not been subjected to pesticides or artificial fertilizers, and which has been grown in soil whose humus content has been increased by the addition of organic matter."

A further definition says, "The term 'organically processed food' means organically grown food which in its processing has not been treated with preservatives, hormones, antibiotics, or synthetic additives of any kind."

This helps to make clear the fact that people who complain of processed foods are actually complaining of foods not organically processed, that those who complain of chemicals are really complaining of synthetic additives.

"Organic" fertilizers.
Organic material or humus used in growing the plants we eat or the plants that are fed to the animals we eat, include manures, plant composts, and other plant residues such as peat moss and aged sawdust. These are all made by the living cells in animal or plant tissues. They contain the nutrients nitrogen, phosphorus, potassium, sulfur, magnesium, and other essential minerals in complex combinations with carbon, hydrogen, and—usually—oxygen.

Inorganic fertilizers—synthetic, commercial, whatever you want to call them—contain the same nutrients and the same chemicals, but they are in simpler forms and they are not always in combination with carbon. However, it is inaccurate to refer to inorganic fertilizers as "artificial." A plant is not aware of the type of fertilizer, organic or inorganic, that furnishes the chemicals necessary to its growth. But the plant does demand that these building blocks for its nutrients be in the *in*organic form. Cells of the plant itself synthesize the complex materials needed for growth, rather than absorbing them ready-made from the soil.

In other words, the plant does not directly "eat" the fertilizer given it, whether organic or inorganic—instead, it manufactures the nutrients it requires from the fertilizer. The only difference between the plant's use of organic and inorganic fertilizer is that when organic fertilizers are used, they must first be decomposed by microorganisms in the soil to convert them to the inorganic form in which they can be used by the plant.

This applies to animals, as well.
Organically raised animals are fed on organically grown feed and browse in organically grown pastures. They are given no growth stimulants, antibiotics, or synthetic materials of any kind. However, it is unlikely that an animal's cells, busily converting food into materials necessary for its body's growth and repair, are aware of whether the growth essentials are being furnished by feed in the organic or the inorganic form.

Good-sense growing.
All good gardening and farming practices call for the addition of organic matter (humus) to the soil. Soils rich in humus absorb and hold water better and are easier to till than soils with little organic content. Using organic materials is also a practical way to recycle naturally occurring materials that are valuable for plant growth.

But—and this is the big but that organic gardeners like to sweep under the rug—using only organic fertilizers will perpetuate any soil deficiencies that may occur in the organic material. Soil deficiencies can seriously reduce crop yields. Such yields are dramatically increased when the specific necessary components that are missing or in short supply are added to the soil in inorganic form. For example, adding iron to the soil in the western states or phosphorus to that in the states of the southeastern seaboard increases both quantity and quality of crops by eliminating soil deficiencies.

The pesticide problem.
Foods organically grown in the strict meaning of the term must not be treated with pesticides. Thus, organic food advocates point out, one of the benefits of organic farming would be to reduce pollution of our environment.

Unfortunately, organically grown food is not necessarily free of pesticides. Chemical residues from pesticides may remain in the soil for years after their use is discontinued. Also, pesticides sprayed on one crop may drift through the air onto another field. So, as it turns out, foods and feeds grown by usual commercial practices may contain no more chemical residue than those grown organically. In a test made in a state laboratory of fifty-five foods labeled as being organically grown, 35 percent contained pesticide residues, in contrast to only 20 percent of foods, tested at the same time, that had been grown by regular commercial methods. Unless or until commercial pesticides are banned, those who want organic foods cannot, unfortunately, be certain that they are getting what they want.

"Health" and "natural" foods—definitions again.
By common locution, foods referred to as "natural" are those in the same form as they were when harvested, having come from their growing place to the consumer without any man-made alterations or treatments. They are unprocessed. Fresh fruits and vegetables, for example, are "natural," but canned or frozen ones are processed. The big point to keep in mind is that natural foods are not necessarily organically grown foods. And investigation shows that many natural foods for which organic growing is claimed—and for which premium prices are charged—actually come from large commercial producing operations. That is a trap into which many advocates of natural/organic foods fall. It is impossible to tell by looking at an apple whether or not it was organically grown, and you certainly can't ask it. You can only rely on the word of the merchant, who in turn can only rely on the word of his supplier. In many cases the word is good. But in some cases merchant or processor or both have decided to make a bundle by bilking health-food buyers.

The term "health food" is particularly confusing. Every food that offers the body something it needs contributes to its health. It's a term used chiefly by enthusiastic but untrained persons to refer to foods that are claimed to have some special virtues in preventing, treating, or curing disease, or in some way contributing to a superior condition of health. FDA regulations do not permit such claims to be stated on food labels. (Why? Because they are not true.) Therefore, most of the claims are made in special articles or pamphlets used to advertise the "health" food.

How does it look, how does it taste? Many factors contribute to the appearance and the flavor of any given food: the variety; the nutrients supplied through the soil and air; how well or poorly it was tended; the temperature, light, and moisture available to it during its growing season; and the care used in harvesting, transporting, storing, and retailing it. All of these have far more influence on the appearance and flavor of a food than the kind of fertilizer or the kind of processing used.

Organically grown food often rates high in appearance and flavor. On the other hand, it is sometimes undersized and/or shriveled, harbors insects, deteriorates rapidly—and yet is priced higher than perfect-specimen examples of the same food commercially grown. But, the health-food advocates insist, even though it may not look as good, it's better for you.

Is it? There is no scientific evidence that plants grown with only organic fertilizer or meat from animals raised only on organically fertilized feed have greater nutritive value than food produced by the usual agricultural methods. Indeed, if the soil or fertilizer was lacking in some of the elements commercial methods provide, the food may be nutritionally inferior. Simply making a statement in no way guarantees that the statement is true. You can, if you wish, state that you are Queen Victoria, but it's unlikely that it will cause anyone to drop you a curtsy.

The bottom line—at the checkout counter. Generally, organic foods cost considerably more than the same items produced by commercial methods. Growing, harvesting, and transporting organically grown foods are usually not accomplished by the mass-production methods used for most of our food supply. Also, organic and "natural" foods cannot be stored as long as regular foods. Often, packaging materials and methods used for these foods are inferior.

To make a legitimate price comparison, the USDA sent out shoppers to buy fifty-five common food items at a chain supermarket and at a "natural" food store in the same day. Processed foods in the natural-food store averaged 190 per-

cent of the cost of the same items in the supermarket—almost twice as much. Unprocessed "natural" foods averaged 164 percent of their supermarket cost, virtually two-thirds more. The total cost of the "market basket" on that day was $22.11 less at the supermarket than at the natural-food store.

Some of the separate items are worth examining for price comparison. The following items cost at least twice as much at the natural-food store:

> canned applesauce, tomatoes, tomato juice
> grape jelly
> dried apples, raisins
> frozen corn
> cream of rice cereal
> whole wheat bread
> beef liver, chicken breast, chicken leg
> fresh grapefruit, oranges, cabbage, celery, cucumbers,
>   white potatoes

Possible alternatives. In order to alleviate this budget-busting cost factor, a number of health food cooperatives have sprung up. Prices are still higher than at supermarkets, but lower than at commercial health-food stores, because co-op members reduce costs by buying foods in large quantities and repackaging them in household amounts.

That seems, at first blush, if not to solve the problem at least to ameliorate it somewhat. Not true, however. Unless professional-grade care is taken in the handling and repackaging of the foods, they may easily become contaminated and unsafe to eat. Indeed, in some localities, repackaging food for sale at the retail level is against food sanitation regulations.

Trying to find your way through the maze. Although it once was difficult to find outlets that sold health foods, this is no longer the case. Such stores have proliferated amazingly. In fact, there are a great many present indications that much more food is being sold as organic or natural than is being produced in ways that can honestly earn them those labels. This means that there are unscrupulous marketers engaged in deceiving consumers—and reaping a tidy unearned increment thereby.

The unfortunate problem is that there is no way to distinguish between organic/natural foods and those produced by modern agricultural practices. Ethical producers and handlers of such foods are distressed about the possibilities for fraud and deceit inherent in their business. There are certain safeguards—FDA labeling restrictions, for example—but violations of these are not always apparent simply on examination of a food or a food package. The best safeguards are the buyer's caution and common sense.

The "different strokes" rationale. As health/organic/natural-food stores have proliferated, so have the reasons of those who patronize them. The return-to-nature idea has prompted many to enjoy foods in a more natural state—some, for example, find that whole-grain products have delightful flavor not present in a same grain highly milled (it is the processing here, however, not the organic or inorganic growing of the grain that accounts for the flavor). Some, dissatisfied or bored with their lives, feel they can give them more meaning by changing their food habits—although a little mind/spirit-searching might produce the desired long-term results. Some, particularly the young who are in revolt against convention, express their turning aside from established culture by exploring new food sources and eating habits. Munching on granola will not do away with the capitalist system, the Republican party, or pollution, but it expresses displeasure to a certain degree.

Extremists, convinced by silver-tongued food evangelists that rose-hip jam and alfalfa sprouts and garlic can cure all the ills the flesh is heir to, are another segment of the population to patronize health food stores. And that is unfortunate. So delicious and nutritionally sound a food as alfalfa sprouts can kill you—not in and of itself, but when substituted for proper medication and professional care for a life-threatening disease or condition.

All of these, and all the others who for one reason or another have turned to organic/natural/health foods, should be aware that they must:

- find markets where they can feel sure that the foods come from ethical suppliers and are what they are claimed to be
- be able and willing to pay more for this food than for comparable food bought at a supermarket
- not expect the higher cost of these special foods to buy additional nutritive value
- not neglect total nutritional requirements for good health by restricting food choices to only a limited variety of "health" foods

Those of us who understand the importance of a nutritionally adequate and balanced diet, who deplore conspicuous waste, who detest those who prey on the innocent or frightened, tend to want to shake all-out health-food freaks until their teeth rattle, or cajole them as if they were not quite bright. But this is an approach that solves nothing. The best we can hope for is that they will read this and the many other bodies of information on such foods available, and learn to take care and to tread warily once inside the health food store.

For more information on other facets of the natural/organic/health-food movement, see HEALTH FOODS and the special feature: NUTRITION NOTEBOOK.

NAVEL ORANGES: see ORANGES

NAVY BEANS: see BEANS

NECTAR

A Greek word, nectar was the beverage of the gods who lived on Mount Olympus. Hebe, goddess of youth, was the official cupbearer who meted out nectar to the other gods. The poet Homer described the drink rather unimaginatively as being like red wine—although it is not recorded where he sampled nectar or from whom he got his information about it.

Nectar is also the sweet liquid that occurs in flowers—what the bee brings home to the hive to be transformed into honey.

And there is a third, come-lately meaning: fruit juice with pulp of the fruit suspended in it. All sorts of fruit nectars are available in cans—peach, pear, strawberry, and apricot are most familiar—as well as combinations, such as strawberry-coconut. They are deliciously like drinking the liquified fruit, and are a more substantial beverage than merely the juice of the fruit. An even more substantial, highly nutritious drink that children love and adults are likely to repeat once they've tried it is made by whirling any flavor of fruit nectar in the blender with vanilla ice cream.

Chill nectars in the refrigerator, shake well before opening, and serve as a breakfast beverage or as a pleasant dinner appetizer. Or pour over ice cubes, top with a scoop of fruit ice in the same or a compatible flavor, garnish with a sprig of mint, and serve as a refreshing cooler on a hot day.

Nectars may also be used as a base for alcoholic beverages—"lady drinks" that mask the flavor of the liquor.

NECTARINES

If faced with the necessity for a technical definition of a nectarine, one might hesitate. Is it an off-beat peach, a very peachlike plum, or a fruit in its own right, related to neither? Nature herself seems unable to decide: sometimes, when you plant a peach pit, you get a nectarine tree and sometimes it happens the other way around. Indeed, sometimes you'll get a fruit that is half nectarine, half peach. Walking through an orchard when there is no fruit on the trees, you would be hard put to it to tell which will appear, so alike are the blossoms and the foliage.

An old cookbook says that nectarines, "peaches without fuzz," are dry of flesh, are rather sour and sometimes bitter of flavor, and are "poor cookers." That was, obviously, before the time of modern-day nectarines, which are in truth fuzzless, but when fully ripe are very juicy, have firm but almost melt-in-your-mouth flesh, and a flavor that, although vaguely peachlike, is—its advocates contend, at least—far superior to its fuzzy relative. And they are handsome! If this was indeed, as some suggest, the "apple" that Eve gave Adam, no wonder he could not resist its blandishments. (It would be nice if they could make up their minds, but at this late date it is doubtful that we'll ever know what fruit the old setters-down of myths had in mind. The only thing today's "experts" seem sure of is that it was *not* an apple.)

Nectarines are golden as the summer sunlight both outside and in, and the skin is often richly red-blushed. They are perfect for out-of-hand eating, sliced for breakfast alone or with cereals, combined with other summer fruit in cups and salads, or made into a fresh nectarine shortcake to crown any meal. And if yesterday's nectarines were poor cookers, today's certainly are not—make them into pies and tarts, cobblers and dumplings and roly-polys. Before the season ends, be sure to put some away for winter days as jams and conserves or as pickled or brandied nectarines, a great accompaniment for pork or chicken or duck. Putting up nectarines is almost like capturing summer sun in a jar.

NECTARINES IN YOUR KITCHEN

Most of the nectarine crop of the United States is grown in California. Fruit is in the market during summer and early fall, with the peak season—the most and best fruit and the lowest prices—in June and July.

how to buy: Choose nectarines that are ready to eat, or almost so—hard, green fruit will shrivel and rot rather than ripen at home. However, mature but not-quite-ready nectarines will ripen at room temperature in a loosely closed brown paper bag. Select plump fruit, firm but not hard. Cradle a nectarine in your hands and press very lightly with your thumbs along the "seam"—a little give, a slight softness, indicates fruit at its peak of perfection. Avoid bruises and soft spots. Nectarines are generally sold by the pound, less usually by the dozen.

how to store: In the refrigerator, loose or in a ventilated plastic bag, is the proper storage for fully ripe nectarines. Store mature but not fully ripe ones in a bag, as above, at room temperature. Or, for no more than a day or two, place nectarines in a fruit bowl at room temperature to tempt passersby to snack.

nutritive value: One raw nectarine, about 2½ inches in diameter, furnishes between 85 and 90 calories—a dessert equally good for dieter and nondieter. It also yields:

protein	.8	gram
fat	trace	gram
carbohydrate	23.6	grams
calcium	6	milligrams
phosphorus	33	milligrams
iron	.7	milligram
sodium	8	milligrams
potassium	406	milligrams
thiamin	trace	milligram
riboflavin	trace	milligram
niacin	trace	milligram
ascorbic acid	18	milligrams
vitamin A	2,280	international units

Tips on preparing, cooking. The beautiful and delicious nectarine of today has been "constructed" since World War II by selective breeding. As with peaches, there are both freestone and clingstone varieties. Those two words perfectly describe the condition: in the freestone, the pit is relatively loose from the flesh and easily removed; in the clingstone, the pit clings obstinately to the flesh and requires considerable prying to wrest it away. To pit fresh clingstone nectarines for use in recipes, slide a grapefruit knife in at the stem end and, proceeding cautiously, cut all the way around the stone. Pulling gently, lift it out. Then halve or otherwise cut up the fruit as the recipe requires.

Skins of most nectarines are tender; the fruit need not be peeled unless you are using it in a recipe that directs you to do so. The skin of eaten-out-of-hand fruit contributes to the daily fiber intake. But if you must peel, dip the nectarines briefly into boiling water and the skins will be easy to remove. The peel of a perfectly ripe nectarine—peach, too—doesn't require this treatment. Simply nick it, catch the flap with a knife and pull gently; the skin will come away easily.

Like peaches, although not quite so determinedly, the flesh of peeled and/or sliced nectarines will darken on exposure to air. To prevent this, brush with lemon juice or drop pieces into a solution of 1 tablespoon of white vinegar to 2 cups of water; or use a commercial (ascorbic acid) preparation, following the label.

Freezing nectarines. Properly prepared (see special feature: PUTTING FOOD BY), nectarines may be freezer-stored at 0°F. as peaches are.

Other ways, other forms. Summer-sweet nectarines are particularly precious, because they are available—commercially at least—only as fresh fruit. But they may be frozen or canned or pickled or brandied at home, made into jams, conserves, and chutneys to put by.

Some perfect partners. Make lightly honey-sweetened nectarine slices into a super summer shortcake. Sauté quartered fruit gently in butter to serve with fish; sprinkle the sautéed fruit lightly with sugar and mace, cook a couple of minutes longer to glaze, and serve with pork or poultry. Halve nectarines, brush with lemon juice, fill the pit cavities with ham salad or curry-flavored chicken salad, and serve as an appetizer. Combine nectarines and pitted fresh sweet cherries in orange juice or ginger ale for a special fruit cup. Slice and alternate with layers of strawberries in a glass fruit bowl; serve with custard sauce. Chop nectarines coarsely, add

lemon juice, brown sugar (or molasses), golden raisins, and broken pecans in proportions that please your taste; let stand at least an hour, and serve as a quick/easy chutney with curries or with roast duck or goose. Make nectarine-orange marmalade, brightened with slivers of maraschino cherries.

NESSELRODE

Once upon a time there was a noble Russian statesman who was very fond indeed of high living, his definition of which included exquisite state dinners produced by his French chef. An inventive fellow, the chef concocted a number of new and delectable dishes, many of which he named after his employer, Count Nesselrode. Some, such as a pair of excellent game soups, are still with us. Some of them no longer appear on even the most elegant of tables—roasted thrushes, for example, the tiny birds stuffed with foie gras and garnished with truffles.

But it was in the field of desserts that the chef really shone, and we are grateful to him for elegant, classic Nesselrode Pudding, and for today's nesselrode sauce and nesselrode pie, collateral relatives of the Count's favorite. The pudding is a sinfully rich molded concoction made of sweet cream thickened with egg yolks and combined with chestnut purée, flavored with malaga wine and maraschino liqueur, and liberally bejeweled with candied orange peel and cherries, currants, and raisins. Frozen, it is brought to the table decorated with glacéed cherries and chestnuts, and is guaranteed to draw gasps of admiration on sight and little whimpers of sheer joy as it is consumed by those fortunate enough to be invited to share it.

Today, such a pudding is generally stiffened with gelatin rather than being frozen, often flavored with rum, and is not quite so lavish. A similar combination is used for a high, light pie filling, generally topped with whipped cream and decorated with shaved chocolate. Nesselrode sauce—preserved fruit in syrup, flavored with rum or sherry—is served over ice cream or plain cake or pudding.

NEUFCHATEL (NEUCHATEL): see
CHEESE

NEW POTATOES: see POTATOES

NEWBURG

This is a rich cream-and-egg sauce—usually flavored with sherry or madeira but sometimes with brandy—in which seafood is served. Lobster Newburg was one of the specialties of Delmonico's, a New York restaurant dedicated to fine food and gracious service in the high-living latter part of the nineteenth century.

Lobster—or crab or shrimp or a combination—Newburg still appears on menus of good restaurants on occasion, and makes a delicious and impressive dish to serve at home, from a chafing dish, over toast points.

NIACIN: see special feature: NUTRITION
NOTEBOOK

NICOISE: see SALADS

NONDAIRY CREAMER

A white substance, sold as a powder in jars or as a frozen liquid, used to "whiten" coffee or other beverages in place of cream. It contains no dairy products. See also CREAM and MILK.

NONDAIRY TOPPING

Also a white substance, sold as a packaged powder to be reconstituted or as a thaw-and-serve product in plastic tubs, to be used wherever whipped cream would be used—as a dessert topping, in dishes comparable to chiffons, bavarians, and so on. It has a mild, lightly sweet flavor, with a hint of vanilla. It contains no dairy products. See also TOPPINGS.

NOODLES: see CHINESE NOODLES,
CELLOPHANE NOODLES, and PASTA

NUT BUTTERS

Spreads made from finely ground nuts—peanut butter is the most familiar—nut butters can be made of almonds, cashews, and filberts, or of almost any kind of nut.

The butters may be made at home in a blender, food processor, or a "peanut butterer"—a gadget that reduces the nuts to a pulp. Homemade nut butters must be stored in the refrigerator, where they will keep about two weeks. Commercial butters of this sort, except those from health food stores, contain preservatives which retard spoilage, and so can be shelf stored.

NUTMEG: see SPICES

NUTRITION NOTEBOOK:
see page 177

NUTS

Nuts are dried fruits, occurring most usually as a kernel encased in a shell, a woody outer covering. The shells of many kinds of nuts are in turn encased in burrs or husks, but we seldom see those unless we are fortunate enough to live near growing nut trees.

Nuts are sold in many ways: in the shell, shelled, shelled and blanched (the thin brown skin that encases the kernel removed), roasted dry or with oil, toasted, deep-fried, salted, sugared, spiced, and with such seasonings as smoke or garlic. In the shell, find them in specialty shops or in the produce department of a supermarket; or buy shelled nuts in tins or plastic bags in the same shops and shelved near spices or confections in supermarkets.

For further information on specific types of nuts, see each under its own name, as ALMONDS, CASHEWS, PEANUTS, WALNUTS.

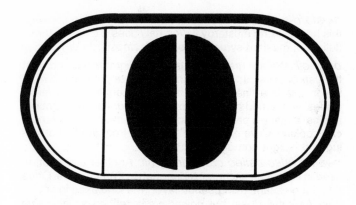

OATMEAL, OATS

Oats are one of the types of grasses from which we derive the cereals we use in food. Like the others, the grain is made up of a soft inner portion covered by an outer husk that is removed before we eat the grain. (Horses and cattle, however, munch the entire grain, husk and all, and seem to enjoy it. But their choices are not as wide as ours—who knows if Dobbin and Bossy consume oats philosophically while secretly longing for apple pie or a nice, juicy nutburger.)

Oats of two kinds, common and red, grew profusely in Europe long ago, were brought in from the wild state—as other grains were—and eventually bred into the oats we know today: the most nutritious of all the cereal grains and, other than rye, the most easily cultivated. Those wild oats, incidentally, were not the same as the ones sown by young men frittering away their youth in idle dissipation; those are useless weeds that resemble oats, so that the wild-oat sowing that grandma so heartily condemned would be comparable to the planting of a worthless crop.

Cold does not bother oats—they can be grown as far north as the Arctic Circle; they flourish in Alaska's fertile Mantanuska Valley, for example—and they thrive in a damp climate, explaining why Ireland and Scotland grow so many oats to use in so many ways.

Oats into meal. To prepare oats for human use, the grain is cleaned, sized, and dried to loosen the hulls—this also develops the nutlike flavor many people prize in the cereal. After a second cleaning, the hulls are removed by machine.

Rolled oats—the familiar flat flakes—are produced by putting the prepared grain through a series of heated rollers. Oatmeal is made by grinding the cleaned and hulled grain; it is produced in three steel-cut grinds—three sizes of pieces, from coarse to extra-fine—to be used as a cereal, and may be even more finely ground to produce oat flour.

At these stages, oats are not particularly inviting, although until modern means of transportation made other foods readily available, people in many northern countries where oats grew used the grain as a diet staple in porridge and griddle- or hearth-baked flat, rough breads. King Alfred, if you remember, allowed the baking oat cakes to burn, proving that he must indeed be the person he said he was, for only so grand a fellow as a king could be so unconcerned with scarce and precious food as to let it burn.

Various types of processing have brought oats from King Alfred's day to this one through a number of felicitous changes that have improved flavor, texture, and cooking time.

Buying and using oat products. Rolled oats, in both regular and quick-cooking varieties, are widely available for making hot breakfast cereal and such delights as old-fashioned oatmeal cookies, raisin studded or with a date-nut filling. Scotch and Irish oatmeal, both more roughly cut than the varieties found in this country and requiring long, slow cooking, are sold in specialty food shops, as is oat flour. (Because oat protein does not occur in the form of gluten, the flour must be combined with wheat flours, which are glutenous, in order to make yeast-leavened oat bread.)

There are a number of oat or oat-combination cereals available—dry ones that are puffed or flaked, both dry and to-be-cooked kinds plain or flavored with maple and/or fortified with wheat germ or soy protein. Store these at room temperature, plan on using within 3 months. Cooked oat cereals must be refrigerated, covered; use within 4 days.

To cook oat cereals, follow the package directions—they are pre-prepared in so many different ways that it's impossible to give useful general directions.

If you enjoy the nutty flavor and stick-to-the-ribs quality of oatmeal for breakfast, you are also doing yourself a nutritional favor. Although the nutritional values of the various oat cereals vary considerably (read the labels), base your calculations on these yields for plain oatmeal, made from rolled oats according to package directions. One cup of this cereal furnishes 132 calories (that's without such additions as sugar and milk), as well as:

protein	4.8	grams
fat	2.4	grams
carbohydrate	23.3	grams
calcium	22	milligrams
phosphorus	137	milligrams
iron	1.4	milligrams
sodium*	523	milligrams
potassium	146	milligrams
thiamin	19	milligrams
riboflavin	.05	milligram
niacin	.2	milligram

*if prepared by package directions; if no salt is added during cooking, the cereal contains only a trace of sodium; oatmeal has no vitamins A or C

Serve hot oatmeal with milk or cream and brown or white

sugar, or with a pat of butter melting over the top. Vary it sometimes with maple syrup, with chopped nuts, with chocolate or carob bits. Or as the Scots do, provide a bowl of cold milk and dip each spoonful of the hot cereal into it before eating. Or make Cream Crowdie by toasting oats until brown and crispy and combining with whipped heavy cream and brown sugar to taste. And if you want luck in the coming year, griddle-bake a bannock—an unleavened oat bread—on New Year's Eve. See also FLOUR.

OIL, TO: see page 447

OILS, SALAD AND COOKING

If you are old enough—and that's quite old—you may remember cod liver or halibut liver oil, rich in vitamins A and D, being given you (given is too mild a word—poured down your throat is better) when you were a child; it had a taste so incredibly awful that once experienced it cannot be entirely put out of mind by the passing years. There are other animal oils, too—whale oil, for lamps, is an example. But the oils we use in foods are all mild vegetable products, removed from plant materials by pressing or melting.

To be technical about it, oil is a substance of viscous (slippery/sticky) texture, fluid at room temperature, insoluble in water. In the kitchen we use oil for:

- rich texture and/or flavor, as in salad dressings
- a cooking medium, as in sautéing, shallow or deep-fat frying
- shortening, the tenderizer in cakes, pastries, quick breads

Such edible oils, common in American kitchens, are obtained from corn, cottonseed, olives, and soybeans, among other plants. And there are many more. Some come readily to hand, others fall under the heading of culinary exotica.

Here are a few of the better-known edible oils used around the world.

almond oil: Faintly sweet, used in the making of confectionary of many kinds; it is the "essential oil" from which almond flavoring extract is made.

coconut oil: Used in Africa and southeast Asia for cooking; here, we are more likely to encounter it in cosmetic products, such as soaps and shampoos.

corn oil: This is one of our most commonly used cooking oils; it is completely tasteless. Because it does not smoke at usual frying temperatures, it is excellent for deep-fat frying.

cottonseed oil: As a straight cooking oil, this is used mostly by East Indians; it is a component of a number of our vegetable shortenings and some margarines.

grape-seed oil: Not widely available here, it is a fine salad oil, with excellent odor and flavor.

mustard-seed oil: Also much used in East Indian cookery, this has a strong mustardy flavor; Italy uses it to flavor those delightful mustard-syrup pickled fruits, mostarda di frutta.

olive oil: We are grateful to Italian immigrants who brought the use of olive oil to this country; delicate but distinctive of flavor, this is a fine salad oil and is essential to the many dishes we learned how to prepare from our Italian neighbors and have made a part of the glorious mishmash that is American cooking. Olive oil labeled "virgin" is from the first pressing and is light and delicate of flavor.

peanut (also called groundnut) oil: Another that is often used in American kitchens, more often in French ones. Once it had a pleasant, mild peanut flavor (the kind used in southeast Asia still does) but nowadays is refined so as to be tasteless.

rape (also called colza) oil: The second most widely used oil of the Mediterranean area, it is seldom available here.

safflower oil: Made from the seeds of the false saffron, native to Asia but now grown here; light and virtually tasteless (there is a slightly nutty overtone), the oil has found a place in American kitchens since the time, a number of years ago, when its use was urged in a diet book that became a best seller. (Don't be misled into thinking it is lower in calories than other oils. It is not; its "low" is saturated fat, also true of corn and some other kitchen oils, all of them useful on low-cholesterol diets.)

sesame-seed oil: This one is flavorful, with a rich and robust, somewhat nutlike taste. Prized in Oriental cookery, it often is used as a flavoring or to mask strong fish flavors.

soybean oil: One of the seemingly innumerable products of the versatile soybean, this is much used in American kitchens. If your cooking/salad oil is not prominently labeled with the source—such as "pure corn oil" or "pure safflower oil"—a diligent search of the label will probably show you that it is soybean oil, something processors seem reluctant to tout.

sunflower oil: Light, with a mildly nutlike flavor, this is neither widely available nor widely used in American kitchens.

walnut oil: The salad-dressing oil of choice for French cooks; except in the walnut-growing areas of France it is so expensive that it is usually hoarded for special-occasion salads.

There are others, as well. Many "essential oils" (see almond oil, above) have only one or two uses; some of these are the oils from which pure flavoring extracts are made.

There was once a line drawn—sharper in cooks' minds than in necessary practice—between oils used as a medium in which to cook foods and those used as a food ingredient, and a further one between those used "raw"—as in salad dressing—and those used in cooked foods. Those lines have virtually disappeared. All of the common oils (you will have noticed that they are no longer labeled "salad" or "cooking" oil, but simply "oil") can be used interchangeably in cooking and as a cooking medium, with the single exception of olive oil. That fine oil lends its exquisite flavor to certain dressings and in certain kinds of cooking, but is wrong elsewhere—a chiffon cake made with olive oil would be a culinary error, for instance. But most of the oils in ordinary use are bland, mild, and virtually flavorless.

Do not, however, attempt to substitute oil for solid shortening in baking—for butter, margarine, lard, or white hydrogenated shortening, that is. Recipes using oil are especially tailored for it because oil adds more liquid to a product than the solid shortenings—indiscriminate substitution can cause baking failures. But when recipes call for oil, by all means use it—and learn to produce airy, delightfully flavored and textured chiffon cakes, "pound" cakes made with cake mixes, a particularly tender and flaky pastry, and certain specialty cookies and breads.

Buying and using oil. Unless you use a good deal of oil in your kitchen, don't buy in large amounts. Although it keeps relatively well, oil does eventually get rancid—that is, it decomposes and acquires an unpleasant odor and flavor. Although this may not occur for 2 or 3 months, rancidity may develop sooner if the oil is exposed to moisture or light; it can also pick up, undesirably, the flavors of other foods if not kept tightly covered. Store on a kitchen shelf, in cool darkness. If you must for some reason store oil for a long period, put it —again, tightly covered—in the refrigerator; it will become cloudy and thicker than it originally was, but be usable. The exception to this is olive oil, which will solidify at refrigerator temperatures over a long period.

Oil is available in pint and quart bottles, as well as quart, gallon, and sometimes even larger, cans. Olive oil can be bought in smaller sizes in both bottles and cans.

Pure oil is pure fat—it contains no other nutrients. A tablespoon of oil furnishes in the neighborhood of 120 calories, a cup slightly under 2,000.

OKRA

Slave traders, venturing to Abyssinia and the Sudan long ago, brought back to the Arab countries along with their poor human goods one of the captives' favorite foods, a seed-bearing green pod—actually a fruit, but used as a vegetable —that the Arabs called *bâmiya,* and that we call okra. Moors carried the vegetable to Spain, it is believed, and from there it moved to France. No one seems quite sure how it arrived in the New World—brought by black slaves from Africa, where okra flourishes, is one theory, but it seems highly unlikely that unfortunate men and women would think to or want to or be allowed to gather plants or seeds at a time when they didn't know why they had been captured or where they might be headed. More reasonable is the idea that French or Span-

ish colonists brought okra here, particularly to the region that is now Louisiana, where okra grows abundantly today and is used in many savory ways in the Creole cuisine.

Gumbo, an African-dialect word, is another term for okra, and the word is also used for the savory Cajun-country soup/stews of which okra is a chief ingredient.

OKRA IN YOUR KITCHEN

Cross-breeding has by now produced okra of several kinds —almost-white as well as deep green, smooth pods as well as ridged ones, long, svelte ballerina types and short, girthy ones. But the most usual okra remains green, ridged, of medium length and diameter. The vegetable is grown and used widely in our southern states, as well as in India and throughout most of South America. Available here the year around in the South, okra comes to market in the North in late April and can be found through November.

how to buy: Look for fresh-colored pods that spring back to the touch, that have an air of youth and crispness; they should be no more than 4 inches in length. Snap one—it should snap easily, and its seeds should be fairly firm but yielding, in no way hard. Avoid shriveled, limp pods, dull color, soft spots.

how to store: Store okra in the refrigerator, in a covered container or in the crisper, up to 4 days; cooked okra, in a tightly covered container, can be refrigerated for the same period.

nutritive value: One cup of cooked crosscut slices of okra —product of ten to sixteen pods, depending on size—furnishes 46 calories; the same cooked amount yields:

protein	3.2 grams
fat	.5 gram
carbohydrate	9.6 grams
calcium	147 milligrams
phosphorus	66 milligrams
iron	.8 milligram
sodium	3 milligrams
potassium	278 milligrams
thiamin	.21 milligram
riboflavin	.29 milligram
niacin	1.4 milligrams
ascorbic acid	32 milligrams
vitamin A	780 international units

Tips on preparing, cooking. Other than washing and nipping off the stems, okra needs little preparation. Sometimes—in some varieties—there is a fringe around the top where the cap meets the pod, rather like a thin beard; if it's there, cut that off, too. Pods, if small and tender, may be left whole. Larger pods can be cut in crosswise slices.

Cook, covered, in very little boiling water until just tender —10 to no more than 15 minutes. Beyond that time the tenderness will become toughness, and the mucilaginous quality prized by makers of gumbo will become unhappily overwhelming. Or thick slices or whole young pods may be dipped in egg, then in crumbs or cornmeal, and fried—in shallow or deep fat—again, very briefly. And, of course, okra may be added to several kinds of soups and stews, but heed the same advice and add near to the end of cooking time to avoid a gummy mess.

Freezing okra. Properly prepared (see special feature: PUTTING FOOD BY), okra can be freezer-stored up to 12 months at 0°F. or below.

Other ways, other forms. As well as fresh okra, your supermarket or specialty food store should supply you with okra in a limited number of forms.

on grocery shelves, in cans or jars: Canned okra, plain or in seasoned tomato sauce; crisp little baby okra pickles.

in grocery frozen-food section: Plain frozen okra, fine to have when the fresh is out of season, as whole pods or slices.

Some perfect partners. Okra and corn go well together. So do okra and onions or tomatoes or lima beans—or go all out and combine all of these in a delicious vegetable mélange, flavored or not with bacon or salt pork as you choose. Or, for a delightful and unusual salad, serve cooked and chilled okra vinaigrette, as you would asparagus.

If you have never tried okra, it is worth your experimenting. The flavor is mild and delicious, not so unusual that it comes as a shock to the palate unused to it. It's easy to prepare, easy to cook—what's holding you back? It certainly serves as a fine answer to those who complain, "We always have the same old thing!"

OLEOMARGARINE

The word comes from "oleo," a term for rendered beef fat, the principal fat used by the French chemist who invented oleomargarine. At the behest of his emperor, he combined beef fat, milk, and water in a 10 : 4 : 3 ratio to produce "poor man's butter." The product has, fortunately for those who use it, come a long way since those days. For more information, see MARGARINE, the term by which the spread is generally known today.

OLIVE OIL: see OILS, SALAD AND
COOKING

OLIVES

One of the world's great al fresco meals is also one of the simplest: crusty bread to be torn off in chunks, a big wedge of good cheese, a handful of olives, and red wine with which to wash it all down. If you happen to take your lunch under a peach or apricot tree, where you can reach up and pick dessert, so much the better.

Unlike other orchardists, the grower of olives cannot wander among his trees sampling the fruit, for olives must be treated before they can be eaten—fresh-picked ones are inedibly bitter. That being so, how did man come by the knowledge of how to prepare the fruit for eating? It's easy to understand that olives fallen to the ground and trodden upon would show that the fruit contained a useful oil. But who was the curious, persistent fellow who worked out the complicated lye-and-brine treatment the fruit must have to make it palatable?

Six thousand years ago olives were cultivated in Israel and Syria. Olive orchards spread slowly west until they reached Italy some six centuries B.C. Throughout the warm and sunny Mediterranean area of that time, olives, wheat bread, figs, and grapes were the basic foods. Olives provided the fat essential to a diet in which dairy foods were absent.

Modest in size, the olive tree (a gift, the legend goes, from Athena to the ancient Greeks) is gnarled of trunk with soft gray-green, blow-in-the-breeze foliage somewhat like that of a willow. It bears its fruit abundantly or not at all. Often olive trees planted by nature lovers in their backyards will not bear—not because they are of the wrong variety, not because they have been improperly polinated, not because the climate is unsuitable for them, but simply, it seems, because they are sulking. Perhaps they are lonely—perhaps the sun is not quite warm enough, perhaps the songs we sing are the wrong songs, in the wrong language. Or perhaps they consider us come-lately upstarts, for whom it is not worth making an effort—after all, the trees planted by the Phoenicians in Spain in 600 B.C. are still growing, still bearing fruit.

Olive trees came to this country with Catholic missionaries, first to Mexico, then with Father Junipero Serra to California—planted by him along with oranges, lemons, and the Word—where they now flourish.

Olives from tree to table. Olive trees begin to bear their small, pale green, hard-stoned fruit when they are about eight years old. The fruit is picked when green to produce all the various kinds of green olives we enjoy. Straw-colored olives are green-ripe and are marketed (in cans only) thus labeled —the least widely available kind and the least purchased and used but, to some olive fanciers, the best of all. Ripe olives are dark when picked, but not as purple/black as they are when we eat them; part of that color is due to the processing. Those are the three wide general classes of eating olives. Those destined for oil are allowed to remain even longer on the tree, until they are virtually black and rich with fully developed oil. (Some of these are eaten, too; salt-cured, they are small and somewhat shriveled, and have entrancing flavor.) The first pressing of cold olives produces the fine virgin olive oil. They are heated for a second pressing, yielding a less fancy grade of oil, darker of color and stronger of flavor.

Eating olives are cured by soaking in a lye solution, then

(after washing) in brine. Spanish-style green olives are kept in the brine up to 12 months; there they ferment, and sugar is added from time to time to keep fermentation continuous. Green-ripe and ripe olives are heated, lye-soaked, exposed to air—which develops their color—then washed and packed in brine without going through the fermentation process.

The olives called Greek or Italian—depending on where you buy them and to whom you are speaking—are mixed with salt, which removes some of the bitterness and most of the moisture. They may be dry packed or in oil; often the dry-packed ones are dipped in oil by knowledgeable olive-eaters before they are popped into the anticipatory mouth. Such olives may be bought in bulk at ethnic groceries and specialty food shops, but other olives in this country come in jars (green) or cans (green-ripe or ripe). Olive salad, sometimes called olive condite, is available—broken small green olives with pimientos, in oil. So is olive butter, a spread of finely chopped green olives; it makes a delicious sandwich with cream cheese, or a fine addition to the yolk mixture for deviled eggs. Ripe olives are available sliced and chopped in small cans, and in spreads, combined with cream cheese or with process cheese food.

Buying and using olives. In cans or jars, store olives unopened up to several years on kitchen shelves; after opening, refrigerate up to 3 or 4 weeks. If refrigerated olives develop a white scum, rinse them before serving; do not use olives that have turned soft.

Olives are graded by size—the larger the size, the fewer the olives per jar or can, and the higher the price. Green-ripe olives are virtually always as they come from the tree, retaining their pits. Green olives may be pitted or unpitted, the pitted ones plain or stuffed with (usually) pieces of pimiento, or with capers, anchovies, almonds, onions, or other exotica. Ripe olives are also available pitted or unpitted, but are seldom stuffed—you can stuff the big ones yourself for excellent appetizers.

As well as using them as condiments or appetizers, experiment with olives in cooked dishes. Add to lemon butter to serve with fish. Slice and include in meat loaves, or use a small olive to center a "surprise" meatball. Add small whole stuffed olives to a tomato-onion-garlic-parsley sauce in which to bake chicken Mediterranean style. Include slices of pitted ripe olive in cream sauce for chicken or crab. Stir small cubes of mild cheese and lots of sliced ripe olives into scrambled eggs just before they are done. Include pieces of pimiento-stuffed green olives in burgers, and in meat sauce for pasta.

Nutritionally, olives contribute very little—they do contain some of the essential nutrients, but in quantities so small you could eat olives all day and not nearly approach any RDA. They do, as does everything but water, furnish calories —about 4 calories each for medium-size green olives, 5 calories each for ripe olives of the same size.

Pass the super-colossals, please. As most green olives are sold in glass jars, you have only to look to determine the size of the individual olives that the jar contains. Ripe olives, however, are most often sold canned, ranging in size from small to super colossal through a list of size names that verges on the hilarious. Fortunately, the label also shows you a picture of the size of the olives within—a "large" ripe olive, for example, is not what many people would consider very big. Here are the sizes, as agreed to—and adhered to—by olive processors:

size	average number per pound
small	135 olives
medium	113 olives
large	98 olives
extra large	82 olives
mammoth	70 olives
giant	53 to 60 olives
jumbo	46 to 50 olives
colossal	36 to 40 olives
super colossal	no more—often fewer—than 32

Since the dove brought back to Noah an olive branch indicating that the flood waters were receding, olives have had a place in our orchards and our kitchens, although for those of us not raised where the fruit is a part of the daily cuisine, they are generally an acquired taste.

OMELETS

There are two broad classifications of omelets (or omelettes, as you'll find them spelled in old cookbooks): french and puffy. And there are two equally broad, but sharply divided, schools of thought on the subject: those who quail at the very mention of making a french omelet, and those who wouldn't be caught dead making—or serving—a puffy one. True of both kinds is the fact that omelets are not difficult to make, assorted cookbooks, grandmothers, and old wives notwithstanding. Any gutsy home cook who can follow directions can make a perfect omelet, french or puffy, on the first try.

Both kinds are, of course, made of eggs. There are no inclusions other than seasonings and, in some cases, a little water. Either type may be served plain or with one of a wide variety of sauces. There the likeness ceases and the diversity begins.

Puffy omelets. These take rather more time to make and to cook than french omelets. The egg yolks are beaten until thick and pale, the egg whites beaten separately until stiff but not dry, and the yolks folded into the whites. The mixture is poured into an ovenproof skillet in which butter or other shortening has been melted, and set over a low flame to cook—without stirring—until the bottom is brown and set and the whole omelet is puffed, a matter of 8 to 10 minutes. Cooking is finished in the oven, perhaps another 10 minutes. (Advice:

serve with a sauce; without a good one, a bite of puffy omelet tends to taste like a rather dry mouthful of nothing—which clues you concerning which school of omelet-thought we belong to.)

French omelets. These are so quickly made that it is possible to prepare and serve individual ones to a whole tableful of eager eaters.

Remember the old children's trick of patting your head and rubbing your stomach at the same time? If you can do that, you can whip up french omelets by the dozens—you'll see why in a minute. The eggs are not separated, but are beaten briefly with a fork, only enough to combine whites and yolks without creating any foam or beating in air. Butter is melted in an omelet pan or any small, slope-sided skillet over high heat until it foams and sizzles—this is the only egg dish that violates the low-heat precept. Pour in the eggs. Immediately, stir with the fork—hold so the tines are parallel to the bottom of the pan—and at the same time, draw the pan back and forth over the heat. (Pat your head, rub your stomach.) Stop stirring when the fork leaves a clean path in the pan, a matter of a minute or so. Cook 1 minute longer, still shaking the pan. That's it.

Puffy omelets may be made to serve 4 to 8, depending on the size of the skillet—and the number of eggs, of course. French omelets are best made individually—each takes only about 3 minutes, start to finish—or, at most, to serve no more than 2 people.

Folding the omelet. Puffy or french, omelets are usually folded, although a large puffy omelet may, alternatively, be cut in wedges for serving. To fold a puffy omelet, make a shallow cut in the top, parallel to the skillet handle, dividing the omelet into ⅓/⅔ sections. Fold the ⅓ over the ⅔ gently, then slide the entire omelet out on a warm serving plate. Fold a french omelet by slipping a spatula under the half nearest the handle and easing it over the other half; or fold ⅓ toward the center, the far ⅓ in to overlap it slightly. Slide out onto a warm serving platter or individual serving plate.

Saucing and otherwise dressing-up. French omelets may have all sorts of inclusions, such as finely chopped vegetables—but then they are really Italian frittata, not french omelets. They may be sprinkled, just before folding, with grated cheese, bacon bits, finely sliced scallions, snipped chives, snipped parsley, whatever suits your fancy. Or a piece of something may be placed on one side before the second side is folded over it—thin frizzled ham, a meltable cheese, a (ah, heaven!) slice of foie gras. (See also FILLINGS.)

Puffy omelets, too, may have inclusions—such as grated cheddar, in which case they are more soufflé than omelet. Like french omelets, they may be sprinkled with almost anything your heart desires before serving, but bear in mind that they are delicate, and any heavy sprinklings will destroy the puffiness.

Best, serve a savory sauce with either kind of omelet. Spanish or other tomato sauce. Sour cream. A cheese sauce zippy with cayenne. Ham-mustard sauce. A Sauce Soubise —a purée of long-cooked onions. Almost anything—well, other than hard-cooked eggs—in a white or cream sauce.

A quick-to-make french omelet can be served on almost any occasion and, because there are few kitchens without eggs, can be a lifesaver when you'd like to ask droppers-in to share a meal with you (they don't deserve it, but that's beside the point). If you happen to have a jar of caviar, top the omelets with a little, plus sour cream.

Press french omelets into service as a hearty dessert to end a light meal or, again, to serve to unexpected callers. Offer them with lightly sweetened fruit or berries, with or without whipped or sour cream or, in a pinch, with preserves or jelly topped with sour cream, or just with a sprinkling of confectioners sugar.

ON FEEDING YOUNGSTERS: see page 474

ONIONS

You will remember that the Pardoner (a seller of civic and political indulgences), perhaps the least attractive of the pilgrims gathered together by Chaucer, "well loved the garlic, onions, aye and leeks," which may give a clue to his unpopularity. He fulminated against the sins of Gluttony, Drunkenness, Gambling, and Swearing with a breath tainted by his favorite foods.

But aside from their unfortunate effect on the breath of the eater—a matter that the careful can easily remedy—the members of the onion family are as well-loved by the general run of us as by that particular Canterbury Pilgrim. Indeed, a great many of the foods we prize and relish would be much the worse, not worth the prizing and relishing, if it were not for the contribution made to them by the onion and its assorted relatives.

Bearing that in mind, perhaps the children of Israel, on the flight from Egypt, can be forgiven that they "fell a-lusting," and wept, and cried, "Who shall give us flesh to eat? We remember the fish which we did eat in Egypt freely; the cucumbers, and the melons, and the leeks, and the onions, and the garlick: but now our soul is dried away; there is nothing at all, beside this manna, before our eyes." (On the other hand, who can blame Moses for crying out, at this point, "Wherefore hast thou afflicted thy servant . . . that thou layest the burden of this people upon me?" And, indeed, who can blame the Lord for smiting them with a plague? There they were, finally out of the land of Egypt, finally free of the house of bondage, and they were complaining about the menu!)

Onions and lilies, scallions and hyacinths. All of those are parts of the same family, the lilies and hyacinths with their beauty and their entrancing aroma, the homely onions and their cousins with their own pervasive odor. Peel back a lily bulb and you will find that it is constructed in the familiar onion pattern, layer on neat, closely wrapped layer of stored food from which a plant will rise and burgeon. But we take onions, in all their many forms, before they can nourish the plants for which they were intended and use them to flavor our food. If you lose track of an onion in your kitchen vegetable bin, you'll see what we mean—it will do the thing nature intended it to do: sprout spindly yellow-green shoots, trying its best to be a plant.

Onions come in several sizes and shapes and colors, all blessed—if that is the word—with a pungent, volatile oil, one of whose components is sulphur, from which the strongly distinctive flavor and odor arise. Members of the onion family commonly available for kitchen use include:

- domestic *dry* onions, available all year and generally used in cooked foods, are medium size and globular, with brown, white, or—less commonly—red skins; although the brown-skinned ones are really a pretty shade of tan, they are usually known as "yellow" onions; of this group, the white are mildest

- bigger and milder are the flat rounds of *spanish, bermuda,* and *italian* onions—the spanish have brown or yellow skins, the bermudas white or brown, the italians red; generally used raw (in salads, for example), one or another of these mild onions is in the market at all seasons

- GREEN ONIONS—also called spring onions and scallions—are relatively delicate in flavor for use in salads or eating as is, or braised to be served in the manner of asparagus; available all year around

- LEEKS look rather like monster green onions; for cooking uses in soups and stews or separately as a vegetable; limited availability the year around

- *shallots* are small, rather out-of-round bulbs with light-brown skins; for cooking, they have an onion plus garlic flavor much admired by discriminating cooks; available in small-quantity packages—mesh bags or open-top boxes—all year

- *chives* are the onions whose tops, rather than bulbs, have many kitchen uses, both cooked and raw; available the year around in small bunches, or growing in small pots—or grow your own, on a light, sunny kitchen windowsill

ONIONS IN YOUR KITCHEN

It is difficult to imagine any kitchen, even the smallest two-burner hot plate kind, without onions in some form, if only onion powder or freeze-dried ones in a jar. Any self-respecting kitchen where regular cooking is done is likely to house onions in several forms so that the home cook can lay hands on them whenever they are needed—which is often.

how to buy: Dry onions are most often sold by the pound; the big ones, such as bermudas, may be sold by the pound or the piece, shallots by the bag or the box, green onions and leeks by the bunch, chives by the bunch or pot. Also available, particularly around the holiday season, may be very small white onions, often labeled "boiling onions," by the bag or box, to be served as a vegetable side dish.

Choose dry onions, of whatever size or color, that are bright looking and absolutely solid, without any softness; softness and/or dark color, particularly at the root end, indicate oncoming spoilage. Fresh onions—green, leeks, chives—should be clean and green of foliage, with no wet/slippery texture, no turning-yellow color.

how to store: Dry onions need a cool, well-ventilated place, spread in a single layer, where moisture will not get to them; they need not be refrigerated, and may be stored up to 4 weeks under optimum conditions. Trim the tops (only the wilted ends) and roots of leeks and scallions; enclose tightly in a plastic bag and refrigerate up to 3 weeks. Place cut chives in a small water-filled glass, as if they were a bouquet, and enclose glass and all in an airtight plastic bag; refrigerate up to 2 weeks. Refrigerate cooked onions of all kinds in a tightly covered container up to 5 days.

nutritive value: One cup of chopped dry onions, raw, furnishes 65 calories; the same measure of sliced raw green onions, including all edible parts of the green tops, furnishes 36 calories. Other nutritive values:

	dry	green	
protein	2.6	1.5	grams
fat	.2	.2	gram
carbohydrate	14.8	8.2	grams
calcium	46	51	milligrams
phosphorus	61	39	milligrams
iron	.9	1	milligram
sodium	17	5	milligrams
potassium	267	231	milligrams
thiamin	.05	.05	milligram
riboflavin	.07	.05	milligram
niacin	.3	.4	milligram
ascorbic acid	17	32	milligrams
vitamin A	70	2,000*	international units

*for bulb plus entire green top, in which the vitamin A is contained; value for bulb alone is only a trace

467

Tips on preparing, cooking. Onion skins are tough in the fresh varieties, papery in the dry kinds; either variety of onion must be peeled before it is used. Remove only the skin —the outer layer—however. All that lies beneath is good food that should not be wasted. Covered in boiling water for a minute or so, then drained, onions will peel more easily. To mitigate the tediousness of peeling small boiling onions, cut a cross in the root end of each; cover with boiling water, cook 5 minutes, and drain. The skins will then slip off easily, and cooking can be continued.

How to peel raw onions without weeping has been the subject of many a spirited discussion as well as assorted solemn magazine and cookbook articles, and there are almost as many old wives' tales on the subject as there are old wives. The consensus seems to be that what works for one will not necessarily work for everyone—or even anyone— else. Some people seem not to be much affected by the fumes. Others, courageous or masochistic as the case may be, simply go to it, grimly peeling and bitterly weeping until the job is done. Some mendaciously allow the youngsters to help mommy by peeling the onions for her. Some, tossing liberation to the winds, cajole their husbands into doing the dirty work with the old you're-so-strong-and-I'm-so-weak ploy, one unlikely to cut much ice after the honeymoon stage.

For what they are worth, here are some of the assorted onion-peeling helps that cooks have worked out; one or another of them may be just what you need:

> chew gum vigorously
> smoke a strong cigar (a somewhat damned-if-you-do/
>   damned-if-you-don't solution)
> peel under running water (works for many)
> peel under standing water (same difference)
> hold a large crust of bread in your mouth as you peel
> start at the root end
> start at the stem end
> start in the middle and work both ways
> constantly dip your knife into water with lemon juice or
>   vinegar added to it
> peel by an open window, with a fan behind you
> peel directly beneath the kitchen exhaust fan (requires
>   a ladder for short women with high-placed fans)
> peel close to a solid room deodorizer
> light a candle (romantic but iffy)

Whatever, as the kids say, turns you on—or whatever, in this case, turns off your tears.

Freezing onions. Freeze small onions whole, larger ones chopped or sliced or diced, and chives snipped, in containers of convenient one-use size or in bags from which a portion can be removed and the remainder (promptly) returned to the freezer. But freeze only for the sake of convenience—since onions are available in all seasons it's unwise to waste freezer space and energy on large amounts. Properly prepared for freezing (see special feature: PUTTING FOOD BY), they can be stored at 0°F. or below up to 1 year.

Other ways, other forms. Fresh and dry onions are available throughout the year in produce markets, but there are a number of other ways in which onions can make a kitchen appearance.

on grocery shelves, in cans, jars, or packages: Whole canned boiled onions, to cream or add to soups or stews or casseroles; canned or dry-mix onion soup; pickled little pearl onions; onion bouillon cubes or powder; in spice-and-herb department: freeze-dried sliced green onions and snipped chives, onion powder, onion salt, sliced or diced or flaked dehydrated onions. See also PEARL ONIONS and HERBS AND SAVORY SEASONINGS.

in grocery frozen-food section: Chopped and small whole onions in bags; snipped chives in small tubs; small onions combined with peas, plain or creamed; creamed small whole onions.

Some onion-use tips and tricks. Until you come to the sweet part of the meals, there's a use for one or another of the onion family in virtually all kinds of dishes.

One of the great vegetables, fine with steaks and a splendid change from deep-fried onion rings, goes like this: Slice bermuda onions thin—at least twice as many as you think you'll need, as they lose a good deal of bulk in cooking and this is a seconds-please dish. In a skillet, melt butter to a depth of ¼ inch. Add onions, ¼ cup of water, and a sprinkling of salt; cover and cook over high heat 5 minutes. Uncover, lower heat, and cook until the liquid has evaporated and the onions are tender, but do not allow them to brown.

Instead of creaming small boiled onions, drain them, turn into a skillet with melted butter and a liberal sprinkling of sugar or a drizzle of honey, and cook over medium heat until they are lightly browned and beautifully glazed.

Parboil whole peeled bermuda or spanish onions until they just begin to soften. Drain; scoop out the centers, leaving an undamaged shell. Mix the scooped-out portion with butter-browned bread crumbs, a little cream, salt and white pepper to taste, and return to the onion shells, topping with more of the bread crumbs. Bake until tender. Virtually anything you'd like to use may be added to the filling—leftover cooked meat, chicken, or fish, other cooked vegetables, chopped mushrooms, whatever.

If your family is fond of onion soup, as a change from the French style try cream of onion—send it to the table liberally topped with grated sharp cheddar.

For a delicious onion quiche, fill a 9-inch unbaked pie shell with sliced onions that have been cooked in butter until limp but not browned. Season with salt and white pepper, sprinkle with snipped parsley. Pour over them 3 eggs beaten with 1½ cups of milk or light cream, and bake at 375°F. until a knife inserted in the center comes out clean. Here, too, inclusions can be made—slivers of ham, crumbled bacon, leftover cooked vegetables, grated cheddar or swiss cheese.

Make a salad of peeled, sliced oranges and rings of red-skinned onions on a bed of lettuce; pass french dressing. Or make peasant sandwiches of heavily buttered dark bread with piled-up thin slices of mild onion between them. Bake sliced onions and apples together, sprinkled with brown sugar and dotted with butter, to serve as a relish with roast pork. For the best of onion rings, cut mild ones into ¼-inch slices, soak at least an hour in milk; drain, dip into flour, and fry in deep fat.

Finally, some minor kitchen wizardry. If you need the mildness of bermuda or spanish onions, but only strong yellow ones are available, slice the yellow onions thinly into a pan and pour boiling water over them. Let stand for a minute or two, then drain well and refrigerate for several hours. They will be crisp and mild of flavor.

Onions are so delicious, use them often and in many ways—any good cookbook will offer dozens of recipes of many kinds. They're even worth weeping over, in case none of the without-tears peeling methods suggested above works for you.

OOLONG TEA: see TEA

OPEN DATING

In the last dozen years, dates have appeared on all sorts of canned, frozen, and packaged goods in the stores and supermarkets, and on a number of fresh foods as well. These dates are to guide you in choosing and using the foods you buy, and some of them serve that purpose very well. Dated milk (it is not dated in all areas) may carry a statement such as "pasteurized and bottled before midnight of June 30, 1978," or, less fulsomely, "June 30, '78" or "6/30/78," but however dated, we know that milk is a fresh food, that it has a relatively short life, and we buy accordingly—no more than we can use up within a few days after the date it carries.

Other fresh foods are similarly dated. We know we have a right to complain if yeast labeled "guaranteed if used before June 20, 1978" does not behave properly, provided we use it before the date specified. We bake and serve refrigerated-dough biscuits and rolls and the like before the date on the end of the container. We check the date on the fresh meat label before we buy.

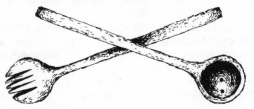

But open dating on some foods is not as clearly understandable as those examples are. Worse, there are several types of open dating in use. Still worse, a recent USDA survey shows that most consumers don't know how to read the dates. Worst of all, according to that same survey, many are not explained by the food manufacturer or processor.

What do those numbers mean? There are four types of open dating in wide general use at the present time, some of them reasonably clear, some unreasonably obscure.

pull date: This is the last recommended day of sale of the product in the retail store—if you buy on that date, you can still expect reasonable shelf or refrigerator time in which to use up the product. Used most often on dairy foods.

expiration date: This is the last date on which the product should be used if you expect it to be at top quality—actually, the date on which the product's useful life ends. Often you'll find the phrase "do not use after" followed by the date.

pack date: This is the date on which the product was packaged and/or given its final processing. It may not even look like a date, but rather a string of numbers such as "44630827," which translate to "44" as the branch of the processor in which that particular package was produced, "6308" as shorthand for the date June 30, 1978, and "27" the formula—recipe—by which the contents was made. Such dates generally appear on long-life foods such as canned goods, and are more useful to the USDA or FDA in case of necessity for a recall of the product than they are to the consumer on a food shopping trip.

quality-assurance date: This is a sort of end-of-the-best, a date after which the product, although still edible, begins to lose quality. Often you'll find the phrase "best when used before" followed by the date. Most often used on foods that, although not highly perishable, begin to go stale after a time —breakfast cereals are an example.

One of the oversights in the web of regulations covering food package labeling is that processors, other than those packing meat, poultry, and fish under federal inspection, do not have to explain open dating methods to the consumer. See also the special feature: A SHORT COURSE IN LABEL READING.

OPPOSUM: see GAME

ORANGE PEEL: see HERBS AND SAVORY SEASONINGS

ORANGES

At one time, not all that long ago, an orange was a very special once-a-year treat found in the toe of a Christmas stocking. It was cherished—its globular golden beauty admired, its exotic aroma enjoyed—for a day or two, and finally eaten both sybaritically and thriftily, with slow savoring that allowed no drop of juice or capsule of flesh to go to waste.

Today oranges are plentifully piled in big, handsome pyramids in the supermarkets, so that we can eat the fruit out of hand, have juice for breakfast, orangeade as a cooling and refreshing drink, oranges in cups and salads and desserts whenever we wish.

The fruit's beginnings are lost in the mists of time, so far back do they go. Was it the "apple" that Eve offered Adam? Was it the "golden apple" of the Hesperides, fruit of the tree that grew to mark the marriage of Juno and Jove? Where did the Chaldeans and the Babylonians get the orange seeds they planted so many years before the birth of Christ—from an even older civilization in the Indus Valley, the ancient city of Mohenjo-Davo, flourishing (brick houses with bathrooms, an underground sewage system, vast cultivated fields and gardens, flocks and herds) in 4000 B.C.? In China, where oranges are mentioned in writings of two centuries B.C. and where, by a little more than a century A.D., a horticulturalist made neat lists of the many kinds of oranges growing in his immediate area, including one seedless variety?

No one can be sure. But it is certain that by the first century A.D. there were a few oranges growing in Italy. The fruit must have been spread by the usual routes—the Arab spice trade, the Chinese silk trade, the proselytizing Muslims, the Roman conquerors, the Crusaders returning home. (It was they, it is believed, who accounted for oranges in many paintings of the Last Supper—Crusaders told of oranges growing in Israel, and painters assumed that they must have grown there at the time of Christ.)

We do know for certain how the fruit came to the New World. On his second voyage, Columbus stopped at the Canary Islands. There one of his men gathered orange slips—lemons, too—and brought them along to plant on Hispaniola, the island now divided between the republics of Haiti and Santo Domingo. From there they spread to Florida and later to Arizona and California.

Harvesting and marketing. Oranges must be fully mature, their color, flavor, and juiciness developed, before they are picked—unlike some fruit, their quality does not improve after they are harvested. Oranges change in color slowly from green to orange as they ripen. An expert can tell when they are ready to pick, but more reliable are tests for juice volume/fruit sugar/fruit acid made by big growers to make assurance doubly sure. Some oranges, having turned the pleasant orange of ripeness, lose some of their color to a returning green. This is because orange trees are continuous-bearing—on one tree at one time there may be buds, blossoms, immature oranges, and ripe ones. As the tree produces chlorophyll to feed the leaves and immature fruit, some of it is reflected in a new blush of green on the mature fruit. Some ripe Florida oranges subject to this "regreening" are treated with a harmless gas and food dye to restore the orange color that consumers look for when they buy. Such oranges must be stamped "color added."

Orange harvesting is still a by-hand operation; pickers, wearing gloves to avoid injuring the peel, clip the fruit from the stems. Taken to the packing house, the oranges are inspected, cleaned, washed, and dried—and sometimes waxed and polished, as well. Then they are babied on their way, shipped under refrigeration when the weather is warm, in heated carriers when it is cold.

Oranges around the world. There are three species of oranges: *Citrus sinensis,* the sweet or common orange with which we are most familiar; *Citrus reticulata,* the mandarin orange and its relatives, the various other slip-skin oranges; and *Citrus aurantium,* the sour or bitter orange.

sweet oranges: The most widely grown commercial varieties are valencia—the one we most often use as a juice orange—and navel—the orange of choice for eating out of hand or in fruit cups and salads. Valencias have thin, reddish-yellow skins and may have few or no seeds or a large number, depending on the kind. Early valencias come from Florida, later-season ones from Arizona and California. Some of the popular juice oranges are hamlin, parson brown, and pineapple.

navel oranges: Called that, not from a connection with the seagoing branch of the armed forces but because of a round, puckery area at the stem end that bears a striking resemblance to the human navel, these have a bright, true-orange color. Somewhat thick skinned, they are easy to peel and are seedless. Most navel oranges come from Arizona and California, although a few are commercially raised in Florida.

mandarin oranges: There are a number of kinds, all characterized by relatively small size and loose, easy-peel skins. Fresh mandarins are seldom found in markets in the United States except in those near where the oranges are grown. Close relatives of mandarins are temple and king oranges, with thick, rough-surfaced but easily peeled skins. The small murcott orange is another of this group, as are tangerines, with their neat, bite-size segments and dark-orange skins that fit so loosely they appear to have recently lost weight and have not yet had time to get their clothes taken in. Another member of this group is the tangelo, a cross between the tangerine and the grapefruit with characteristics of both. See MANDARIN ORANGES.

bitter oranges: Low in sugar and high in acid, these are seville oranges, grown principally in Spain. Too sour for use as juice or eating fruit, they go into marmalades, liqueurs, and various kinds of natural orange flavorings, and one variety is used in the perfume industry.

visitors from overseas: Thick-skinned JAFFA ORANGES, grown in the Mediterranean region, appear in our markets around the holidays; they are big, juicy, virtually seedless, and easy to segment. Blood oranges can also sometimes be found in our markets, but so infrequently that they are a curiosity; small and juicy, their flesh is red or red-streaked.

ORANGES IN YOUR KITCHEN

There are those who feel that the entire day will go somehow awry if they don't have their orange juice in the morning with breakfast or, often, instead of it. And they have good nutrition on their side. A medium-size orange or an 8-ounce glass of orange juice supplies the entire adult RDA of vitamin C. So when you go to purchase oranges, you're buying goodness of several kinds.

how to buy: As with other citrus fruit, choose oranges that are heavy for their size and unblemished—any break in the skin, however small, allows molds to enter. Fresh oranges of one kind or another are available in markets the year around, sold loose or in netting bags by weight, or—the fancier kinds —by the piece.

how to store: If the oranges you buy will be used up within a few days, they can be safely stored at room temperature. To keep them longer, up to 2 months, refrigerate them.

nutritive value: Besides its generous helping of vitamin C, the orange has other nutritional contributions to make. Although various kinds differ somewhat in nutritional value, the following table approximates values throughout the whole orange family.

	whole medium-size navel	whole medium-size valencia	8 ounces juice	
food energy	71	62	112	calories
protein	1.8	1.4	1.7	grams
fat	.1	.4	.5	gram
carbohydrate	17.8	15	25.8	grams
calcium	56	48	27	milligrams
phosphorus	31	27	42	milligrams
iron	.6	1	.5	milligram
sodium	1	1	2	milligrams
potassium	272	230	496	milligrams
thiamin	.14	.12	.22	milligram
riboflavin	.06	.05	.07	milligram
niacin	.6	.5	1	milligram
ascorbic acid	85	59	124	milligrams
vitamin A	280	240	500	international units

Tips on preparing, serving. Wash oranges before eating, and from there go in any direction. Peel if you like—fingers work well, or there is a sturdy plastic orange-peeler that zips skins off in no time. Gently break into segments, or slice with a sharp knife. Or section for fruit cups and salads by holding the peeled orange over a bowl (to catch juice) and cutting with a small, sharp knife between segments, from outside to center; once a segment is cut on each side, a flip of the knife will free it to drop, membraneless, into the bowl. Or leave the peel in place, cut the orange in half from end to end and each half into thirds, and eat directly from the skin —it's a bit messy but fun, and you get all the juice and, if you wish it (a lot of us delight in it), the chewy, bitter white membrane. In many California restaurants, this kind of skin-on orange section takes the place of the omnipresent parsley to garnish anything from breakfast eggs to dinner steak.

For juicing, cut oranges in half around the equator, and juice on a hand or electric reamer.

From the time oranges arrived in Florida, the Seminole Indians of that area were enchanted with them. You might like to try the fruit in the Seminole way: cut the top off an orange and gently plunge a knife down into the meat in several places; drizzle honey, as much as it will take, into the orange and set it aside for an hour or so, then eat from the shell with a spoon.

Or try them in one of the dozens of California ways. To make a delicious dessert, a lifesaver in a dessertless emergency: peel oranges and cut in thin slices; arrange four of five slices overlapping in a circle on an individual serving plate, sprinkle with brown sugar, top with sour cream, and sprinkle the cream very lightly with cinnamon.

Or combine two fruits, in the Brazilian manner: top a slice of fresh pineapple with a thick, peeled orange slice or two, and eat with a knife and fork.

Freezing oranges. Sectioned oranges, alone or in combination with grapefruit or pineapple, and orange juice—these freeze well but, because the fresh fruit is always available, are one of those items that should be passed by, to save valuable freezer space, unless you have an orange tree whose produce you wish to save. Even so, share the fruit with friends and neighbors, or make jelly or conserve or marmalade, rather than freezing it. It's much better fresh, and commercial frozen orange juice concentrate is better—and cheaper—than the home-frozen variety.

Other ways, other forms. Oranges are at their best when fresh, both for eating and cooking. But there are other forms available in most markets.

on grocery shelves, in cans or jars: Canned segments, alone or combined with grapefruit segments; canned juice, plain or in other fruit combinations; marmalade, cranberry-orange relish, orange jelly, heavenly orange-blossom honey; orange-flavored drinks, bottled or as powdered concentrate; candied orange peel; and in the spice section: grated orange peel in small jars, orange extract, orange-flower water, orange bitters.

in grocery frozen-food section: Orange juice concentrate, orangeade concentrate, orange-grapefruit juice concentrate; tangerine juice concentrate; combined orange and grapefruit segments.

in grocery dairy case: Fresh orange juice in cartons or bottles, orange juice and other fruit combinations, reconstituted orange juice concentrate in cartons, orangeade, containers of orange segments combined with other fruits for cups or salads.

Some perfect partners. Orange, fruit or juice, is a widely enjoyed flavor, and there are literally hundreds of ways to delight orange lovers. Cook rice in half-and-half orange juice and water with grated orange peel to reinforce the flavor, add chopped mint leaves to serve with lamb, thyme to serve with veal or chicken. Put through the food grinder a pound of raw cranberries and two large oranges, peel and all; measure, and add half the measure of coarsely chopped walnuts, and a teaspoon of chopped candied ginger for each ½ cup of fruit mixture. To the liquid from a can of sliced beets add 2 tablespoons thawed but undiluted frozen orange juice concentrate, 1 tablespoon lemon juice, 1 tablespoon cornstarch, ⅛ teaspoon ground cardamom; combine well and stir over medium heat until thickened and bubbly, then add the beets and heat through.

Browse in a good general cookbook for all kinds of with-orange recipes—dressings for salads, relishes for main dishes, gelatin and other salads, cakes and pies and tarts and cookies, puddings and bavarians, quick breads and muffins, frozen desserts, marmalades and candied orange peel and chocolate-coated orange peel. A big, wide, flavorful world of recipes, waiting for you to try them.

If you live where orange trees grow, or are lucky enough to have your own orange tree in your backyard, you know why orange blossoms are associated with weddings—the flowers are pure beauty and the scent glorious. And being that lucky, you may well have excess oranges to convert into pomanders, those old-fashioned treasures to hang in clothes or linen closets to scent delightfully everything within.

To make pomanders, stud whole fresh oranges with whole cloves—stick them into the peel in a random pattern. Buy powdered orrisroot at the drug store and make a half-and-half mixture of the orrisroot and ground cinnamon. Put a heaping teaspoon of the mixture in a small bag, add a clove-stuck orange, and shake gently until the fruit is well covered. Set aside in a cool, dry place until the orange dries, a matter of 2 to 3 weeks. Cradle each orange in a square of nylon netting, tie at the top with cord or ribbon—enough to serve as a hanger. Scent your own closets and drawers with pomanders, or give them as delightful small gifts.

OREGANO: see HERBS AND SAVORY SEASONINGS

ORGANIC FOODS: see HEALTH FOODS and NATURAL FOODS, and the special feature: NUTRITION NOTEBOOK

ORGEAT

A syrup of almonds in orange-flower water, sweetened. It makes a refreshing drink mixed with water and served over ice, and is called for in the recipes for certain alcoholic beverages. You'll find it, in bottles, in specialty or gourmet food shops.

OVEN

A heated chamber in which to cook food. It seems to us today somewhat ridiculous to define an oven. Everyone who does any amount of cooking has one, either as a part of an electric- or gas-heated kitchen range or wall-mounted away from the stovetop burner cooking area. But in the days farther back in time than those of the old-fashioned coal- or wood-fired kitchen stove, the oven in the form we know it now didn't exist.

How did they bake and roast in those days? Baking and roasting then were separated functions; baking—of bread, cakes, pies, and so on—was done in an oven built into the fireplace chimney (that was before the days of central heating, as well), and roasting was accomplished in front of or over an open fire, the meat resting on a grill or impaled on a spit.

Many villages and towns, in the days when the kitchen fireplace was the only available cookstove, built community outdoor ovens to be shared by all. Women took their bread to bake in them; large quantities of meat, for a celebration in which all residents had a part, were roasted in them. Most often beehive-shaped, these community ovens were large enough to accommodate dozens of loaves of bread—or pies or whatever—which were slid into the oven's interior on long-handled wooden paddles. There was a firepit beneath to supply heat; those who kept it fueled were often small boys who, in the way of small boys, wandered off and left the fire to die down. Retribution was swift, but sometimes too late to save the bread.

Another sort of old-time cooking chamber, the dutch oven, is still with us—a large, heavy pot with a tight-fitting cover, which was used to cook over an open fire or, nowadays, on the stovetop. Pot-roasting is one of the chief uses of the dutch oven, but soups and stews can be made in it as well, and in a pinch it can be pressed into service for baking bread or biscuits or puddings such as roly-poly or deep-dish pie. Another old-timer, the reflector oven, is used by us today only in campfire cooking. It is open on one side—the side facing the fire—and lined with highly polished, shiny material that reflects the fire's heat all around the food placed within it. A new kind of reflector oven, using the heat of the sun, is being worked on, but these solar ovens are not yet perfected for widespread use.

Today there are toaster ovens, heated by electricity, that use less energy for baking small amounts of food than the range oven does. The really important newcomer is the microwave oven (see MICROWAVE COOKING).

Optimum ovenmanship. Timing and temperature control are the two keys to successful oven cooking. The thermostat on a modern electric or gas range controls temperature, but should be checked for accuracy regularly against an independent oven thermometer, particularly if foods do not bake properly.

Determining whether the oven had reached the proper temperature was once a chancy proposition, accomplished by grandma by sticking her hand into the hot oven and counting—the number she reached before the heat compelled her to snatch her hand out told her what temperature the oven had "come up to."

Accurate timing can be assured if you set a timer, either an independent one or the one that comes as standard equipment on most of today's ranges. Some timers give only a brief ding! to remind you, so that you must stay within reach of their voices; others persistently buzz, demanding your attention, until they are shut off.

Recipes in modern cookbooks tell you at what temperature to set the oven control and how long to bake that particular food, making time- and temperature-control problems virtually nonexistent. However, if you have an old and cherished cookbook whose recipes you'd like to try, here are present-day equivalents of the oven specifications in such recipes:

very slow	250°F.
slow	300°F.
moderately slow	325°F.
moderate	350°F.
moderately hot	375°F.
hot	400 to 425°F.
very hot	450 to 500°F.

The preheating controversy. We are told not to preheat our ovens these days, as one of the many ways to save electricity or gas. That is, in many cases, a penny-wise/pound-foolish instruction to follow. For leavened foods—breads, cakes, some kinds of cookies—the oven *must* be preheated (ten minutes usually does it) to the temperature the recipe specifies or you will have a baking failure. Pies should also go into a preheated oven, or their crusts will not be crisply browned. For roasts, casseroles, and the like, preheating is not necessary. However, unless the cooking time is quite long, you may have to add that 10 minutes to the end of the cooking time, so nothing is saved.

OXTAILS

The tails of beef cattle, very flavorful, although not very meaty. Purchased in sections or slices, oxtails may be braised—with or without vegetables—or used as the basis of a savory, hearty soup. See also BEEF.

OYSTER PLANT: see UNUSUAL VEGETABLES

OYSTERS: see SHELLFISH

ON FEEDING YOUNGSTERS

Comes the millenium, kids will eat no more, no less, no differently from the sensible norm; until then there are options open to despairing parents—but equating food with love is not one of them

"Drink your milk," mothers say to their young in tones ranging from those appropriate to the asking of alms to those suitable to the issuing of a papal fiat. Or, "Eat your green beans," sometimes adding, totally inexcusably, "for Mommy." The entirely reasonable response to that is if Mommy wants green beans, let her eat them herself.

Or, equally ridiculous, in the manner of the nurse who inquires, "Shall we have our bath?" Mommy says, "Shall we eat our nice green beans?" Unless you have a separate dish of green beans of your own that you intend to attack as the child attacks his, or unless you intend that you and he shall eat the one dish of green beans in concert, so to speak, a spoon for you, then a spoon for him, you are making a fool of yourself. This is a condition children are amazingly quick to detect.

Part of the child-feeding problem is that there really is no such problem, unless/until it is created in the minds of parents, urged on by grandparents and certain collateral relatives, largely female. Less than a problem, it is a legitimatized matter for discussion, for snap-at, worry-at coffee hour debate by women who feel that discussing the eating or noneating of their children in all its phases makes morning and afternoon gossip sessions worthy, credible, even somehow noble, as discussions of new hairdos and the physical attributes of the box boy at the A & P can in no way be construed to be.

One big contribution to the child-feeding nonproblem is made by mothers—even, sometimes especially, those who in other circumstances brag of their offspring's breathtaking intellectual capacity—who seem to forget, the moment they pick up a spoon, how bright kids really are. How perceptive. How much aware of the signals their parents send out, the nuances of tone, the smallest displays of body language. How imitative they are, and enjoy being. How—yes, it's quite true—subtle they can be.

So . . . if you say, "Let's eat our nice green beans," and get a "You like 'em so much, eat 'em yourself" reply, you have no right to be either surprised or offended. You brought it on yourself.

DEFINING THE PROBLEM OR LACK OF SAME

One top-priority item for mothers and other feeders of the young to understand and believe is this: Your child will not starve, nor will he be overcome by assorted deficiency diseases, if he "eats like a bird" or "just picks at his food" or "doesn't eat enough to keep a kitten mewing" or any of the other more-picturesque-than-accurate old sayings. The other side of the coin: If you demonstrate by word or deed or even thought (they've all got built-in crystal balls) that you are worried or upset by this noneating behavior, the problem will at once grow and enlarge itself spectacularly, following this sequence:

1. I have not been eating (perhaps as an attention-getting device or because I just wasn't feeling particularly hungry).
2. This has thrown Mommy into a tizzy.
3. I can't imagine why the tizzy, but all this *sturm und drang* certainly is exciting and gratifying!
4. Now therefore I will eat even less, and the excitement will increase arithmetically (I don't know about geometrically yet, but give me time!).

It is not necessary for you to believe us on this subject. Ask your pediatrician. If the picks-at-his-food behavior goes on longer than your nervous system can bear, take the child in for a checkup. The doctor may have some good advice. But the gist of it will be a more polite version of "shut up and back off," and he will charge you never to force, beg, or bribe a child to eat. All three are foolish and futile. As with most childhood problems, it will right itself; if it does not, it should be the cause that is sought for. A cure is no good, even if it appears for a time to work, if you've cured the wrong mal- or dysfunction. In other words, find and treat the inward problem if there is one (and there need not necessarily be one at all), not just the symptoms.

CORRUPTION IN SMALL PLACES

Get-'em-to-eat ploys are, one and all, foolishly unacceptable. "You can't have your dessert unless you eat your meat and potatoes" is shameless bribery; far worse, it sets up in a child's mind the idea that sweet things are in some way superior to savory ones, and therefore more highly desirable. "Eat it for Mommy" is shameless groveling, putting you in an untenable position. (If he says no, he's denying you, not the food—and he knows it.) "Eat it or go to your room!" only proves which of you is the bigger physically and the smaller emotionally. "Eat or you can't go to Grandma's tomorrow" is a ridiculous threat—what has the one to do with the other?

But the other extreme is wrong too. The mother who throws up her hands and says, in effect, "All right, don't eat —see if I care!" can have her actions and statements interpreted as "I don't care about you," a concept not only untrue but potentially damaging.

That is not to say that food and love have an equivalence relationship. Unless there is something so wrong in your family relationship that it needs psychiatric sorting out, your child does not refrain from eating because he hates you. And the other side of the controversy should be equally true: you do not force food down your child's protesting gullet as a sign of your love for him.

In between those two absurdities lie all sorts of traps for the unwary. When a child's eating habits change drastically, he is probably telling you something. You must learn to attune yourself to the signals and cope with the causes that set them in motion. We are generally realistic about a child's lack of appetite when he is ill. But what if food loses its appeal when he is well?

The thing not to do is to set up a general court martial. "What's wrong with you? Why aren't you eating?" may well be questions to which he doesn't know the answers. Or he may know that something is wrong but not make the connection between it and his lack of appetite. Or he may make the connection but have no intention of telling you, at least not as a bald answer to a bald question.

To begin with, think about yourself and your own approaches to food. Are you always equally hungry when mealtime rolls around? Isn't it true that sometimes, for no particular reason at which you can point a finger, you're a little off your feed? The same can be true of a child. If he misses a part or all of a meal, he's not going to starve. Indeed, he won't starve if he misses part or all of many meals, but if he's normally a good eater there is probably something wrong. It can range all the way from coming down with a cold through a row with one of his friends or siblings to a (reasonable or not) feeling that his teacher is "down on him." Whatever, you need to find the cause. And whatever the cause, jumping all over him with questions and cajolings and/or threats is not the road to success.

"Sometimes I'm not hungry, either," will usually break the ice. Follow it with, "When I was your age, your Aunt Dorothy and I used to get into some big arguments. That always spoiled my appetite." Or, "Daddy told me that when he was in the third grade he used to have a teacher who got mad at him because he made a lot of noise and caused problems." Or, "When I get a headache I don't feel like eating much of anything." You're usually able to make an educated guess about what might be wrong, one that will guide your comments. If you can't, simply take easygoing, no-panic shots in the dark until one of them finds the mark. But the point is, don't talk *at* a child, talk *to* him, which generally leads to being able to talk *with* him. And be sure to give him time to make up his mind to respond. Keep in mind, as in the all-too-true old joke, the difference between mother and smother, the difference between warm and swarm.

PARANOID PARENTHOOD

We've all known the kind of woman who isn't truly contented with her lot unless she has something to complain about. If she has a child, he's often the subject of her complaints and his eating habits come in for a large share of the carping. According to your nature, you may be annoyed or saddened or moved to laughter by her statement that her sturdy little boy or girl, the picture of glowing good health, full of energy and outgoing of disposition, "doesn't eat enough to keep a bird alive."

That makes an important point: children's eating problems, so universally a matter for lament among mothers, often exist only in those mothers' minds. Or they are, at best, a gross exaggeration. There are some points that ought not to need making, but of which many people lose sight:

1. Children are smaller than adults; ergo, they quite naturally and normally eat less than adults.

2. Most of us enjoy some foods and dislike others; to this rule, children are no exception.

3. We, as adults, would be highly indignant, and would find some way of protesting, if someone four times our size stood over us and forced us to eat when we didn't feel like eating—why should children be any different?

4. If a child has asked for and been given a substantial snack shortly before a meal, his appetite for that meal will be diminished, just as yours would be.

5. An occasional day, or few days, of "eating like a bird" is not cause for panic; corollary to that, if you allow it to panic you, your child may find the excitement more satisfying than food, and keep it up.

Most important of all, if your child's eating habits are truly bad of either quality or quantity, all the harping and/or begging in the world is not going to remedy the situation one iota. Football players may indeed go out and win one for their injured comrade, but no right-minded kid is going to eat to make his momma happy. In desperation, perhaps, to shut her up—but not to make her happy.

Children are exceedingly pragmatic. A child fails to understand—quite sensibly—why *his* eating or ignoring of *his* food, because of *his* hunger or lack of it, should make his mother dazzlingly happy or reduce her to tears. Similarly, when his mother speaks of all the starving children in the world, and what a crime it is to waste good food, he may not work through the steps, but his mind makes the quantum leap: His discarded half a peanut butter sandwich won't stem the tide of starvation. Besides, he has simple logic on his side: If his mother's so worried about starving children, why doesn't she send them that half a sandwich and stop bugging him about it?

Common sense is on the child's side. It is undeniably true that the amount of food we waste is criminal. But it is equally true that there is no possible way to get that half sandwich into the hands of a child who needs it, however desperately. So work out a system of overall food-saving in your household by all means, but as for that sandwich, quit while you're still ahead, while you still have some tatters of dignity and sense left to you.

DON'T DO AS I DO, DO AS I TELL YOU

Until he ventures out into the big world of school, most of a child's knowledge, plus his likes and dislikes, and the setting of his good or bad habits, are all acquired by osmosis, from the example of his parents.

Is it fair to say that it's hard to convince a child that the best possible dessert is a pear—at the same time that you are wolfing down an éclair? Is it logical to assume that a child will believe that his well-balanced lunch is good for him—while you lunch on a cup of tea because you're on a crash diet? Is it reasonable to expect a child to welcome "these lovely carrots" while his father is at that very moment saying "no, thanks" as the carrots are passed to him, particularly if dad's tone is as of one who has just refused a helping of arsenic? Is it wise to expect a child to lap up his milk with gurgles of glee when not fifteen minutes ago he heard you tell your friend how much you hate the stuff? Is it sensible to try to establish a good-eating regimen for a young child when he sees his older siblings get away with lunching on a bag of potato chips and a cola?

If you want your child to eat a well-balanced diet, you have to give more than lip service to the idea. The rest of the family must set him a good example by eating—and not complaining about—that same well-balanced diet. You must start out in the right direction; there's small hope of reclaiming an infant food junkie once the habit is established.

And you should not let the food be overwhelming. Portions of a size suitable for a professional strong man make a child turn away in disgust. And food pieces too big for small hands and small mouths pose problems that are all too easy to solve by simply giving up. A portion of a disliked food that must be eaten before enjoyed foods are allowed simply tempts a child to skip the whole meal.

Child-size plates and utensils, cups and glasses, are musts. So are child-size portions, distributed on the plate so that there is no suggestion of a mountain of food to be somehow gotten through. Eye-appeal helps, too—the bright green

of peas, the glow of orange fruit gelatin, the shined-up cheeks of a red apple with a couple of neat little golden cubes of mild cheddar cheese. Give the cottage cheese a sprinkle of paprika, cut a sandwich into four little triangles for childish fingers to cope with. Offer finger foods—carrot and celery sticks, finger-shapes of buttered whole wheat bread or roasted meats. If cooked vegetables are rejected, try raw ones. If eggs are rejected, bake them into a custard. It takes some doing—but what useful was ever easy? Offer a choice —a flat-out "we're going to have carrots" courts a refusal, but "would you like carrots or peas?" implies, without laying down the law, that there's going to be one or the other, but allows the child to choose; anything he chooses he is also very likely to eat, if only on the dance-with-the-guy-what-brung-you principle.

Without in any way implying that mommy has extended herself to make the food tempting, go ahead and do so. Pour out pancake batter into the griddle in odd shapes, and let the child think up a name for the shape. Use cookie cutters to produce sandwiches or bread slices in fancy shapes. Use tiny canape cutters to shape pieces of vegetable invitingly. Cut meat into julienne strips and pile them into a "fence." Paint a food-color face on a hard-cooked egg.

Although this is by no means universally true, most children like plain foods. No fancy sauces, no tricky combinations, no sneaking a disliked food inside a liked one. Some kids, indeed, mix everything on their plates into an appalling (to us) mess before attacking it. Swallow your comment— good eating comes first, good table manners come later.

"I CAN DO IT MYSELF!"

In feeding youngsters, patience is indeed a virtue. Fortitude likewise. Stamina too. You will never be called upon to display these virtues to a greater extent than at the time your youngster determines that he will feed himself. This is a most eventful period for the child, a time of discovery and of ego building, but also one of frustration. Be prepared to mop up both spilled food and tears of rage, and to do both with an encouraging smile, an it-doesn't-matter attitude. And patience, patience.

Your part is to prepare the food in ways easy for the child to handle—bite-size bits, easy-hold pieces. Then back off. Be ready to help if you're called upon to do so, but unless or until, keep your distance. Don't hover. Don't bark out directions like a drill instructor. Don't charge off in hot pursuit of every errant pea that escapes. Don't moan, rage, or call on heaven to help you when the milk niagaras to the floor for the umpteenth time. Preserve your cool. This is a learning process, and learning takes time and practice and the slow development of the necessary skills. If by word or deed you indicate to your child that he's a klutz, that you feel he'll never get the hang of it, he may give up. Wouldn't you? If he asks for your help, give it with a smile. But if he doesn't, keep your hands in your pockets and button your lip. Bear in mind that you no longer rummage around in your plate with your fingers to search out an elusive nubbin of carrot. If you could learn, so will he, given time.

Another facet of the do-it-myself desire manifests itself a little later, and is often a lifesaver in getting a picky eater to sit up and take nourishment. He wants to dish up his own cereal, pour milk over it himself, scramble his own egg, make his own sandwich, mix his own in-a-cup soup for lunch. Let him, as long as you're there to keep an eye on the proceedings when such potential dangers as stoves and knives are involved. You'll find that a child seldom leaves behind on his plate food he's prepared himself.

THE BUDDY SYSTEM

The world of a small child is a kind of benevolent dictatorship, with mommy as the petty tyrant. It is she who decrees naptime, bedtime, mealtime. It is she who decides what the youngster will wear, how he will spend his time, what he will be allowed to touch and explore. A team effort, with mother making some concessions and child making some decisions, works a whole lot better. Give him choices, and you'll help him develop his decision-making process.

Wide choices don't work for the very young—they confuse the child and drive mommy up the wall. But a choice between two offerings makes him feel he's a part of the group, not just putty in his mother's hands. The blue suit with the bunnies or the yellow one with the big pocket? Vanilla ice cream or strawberry? Pea soup or cream of celery? Scrambled egg or soft-boiled? Winnie-the-Pooh or Pinocchio?

Too much trouble? Not really, if the choices are narrow and you approach the making of them matter of factly. If you assume that he will make the choice readily, he will. If you vascilate, so will he. Your attitude sets the mood, but the choices are his. A child rarely refuses to eat what he has chosen. It even works well with many children for that other household bugabear, bedtime. The choice: go to bed now or in half an hour? Never mind that he always chooses the half hour later—agree, set a timer, and when the bell rings, off to bed. It was his choice.

There can be narrower choices, too. Suppose that he doesn't like cauliflower. Tell him, "Daddy and I like our cauliflower this way, with browned butter on it. But you can have it with cheese on top. Which way would you like it?" This offers a choice—not between eating or not eating cauli-flower, but between eating it one way or another—and usually works like a charm.

OVERBOARD IN THE OTHER DIRECTION

Some youngsters, far from being picky, are dedicated eaters of everything not nailed down. This is a horrid habit to allow a child to acquire, because up ahead lies obesity. If you pile your child's plate high, allowing or even encouraging him to eat far beyond his daily requirements, stop and ask yourself why. Are you demonstrating your love for him with food? Are you buying his love for you with food? Or are you merely the victim of an old habit of your own and of your parents before you? Here is an ugly truth: The earlier a child becomes fat and the fatter he becomes early, the fatter—and the unhappier about it—he's going to be all his life. And another: If you tell yourself it's just baby fat, that it's cute, and besides he'll outgrow it, you've really got your eyes shut and your fingers stuck in your ears trying to avoid reality.

Even if you face up to the fact that your child is overweight, you may argue that this is childhood, when you're supposed to do what you want to, supposed to have a good time. Eating is his good time. (He's lucky, and so are you, if it isn't his only one—fat kids usually don't participate in sports; they take a lot of kidding and have a rougher time of it generally than slim ones.) Anyway, you tell yourself, let him do as he pleases now. Later on, when it will really matter, he can diet off that excess poundage.

True, he can. But not easily. And not permanently. Fat kids grow up to be fat adults—or thin adults whose lives are doggedly, grimly devoted to staying that way. The number of a body's fat cells is set in youth, and remains constant. Determined dieting may (usually temporarily) remove the fat, but the cells remain, ready to fill up with fat at the drop of a chocolate cream. The struggle against fat can be lifelong if poor eating—overeating—habits are established when you're young.

That's not to say that a child's life should be a long series of Spartan meals, with never any treats, any goodies. That child will grow up thin, but he'll also grow up with a personality warp of some sort. There is a very good, well-known Hollywood actress who grew up with a tendency to put on pounds, because she came from a "fat family," where everyone ate with reckless abandon. The camera's eye sees a person as fifteen to twenty pounds heavier than he really is so that, in order to look pleasantly slender to the camera, the actress —all actresses and actors—must be that much underweight. For some it's easy. They seem to get along fine on a diet of nervous tension and cottage cheese. But for some it's a bitter, unceasing hardship. The actress we have in mind had a beautiful home in Beverly Hills, with a handsome kitchen stocked only with coffee, tea, diet soda, hard-cooked eggs, cottage cheese, carrots, celery, and an occasional melon. And big bottles of vitamin-mineral supplements. Taken out to lunch, she would burst into tears as the pastry cart was

477

trundled past her table. Once, on the set, she went into hysterics as a grip came by munching a candy bar. Finally, one particularly hungry day, she brought it all to an end. She began to eat. Now, although she's still young, she plays character parts. She put back the underweight twenty pounds and perhaps another six or seven. She doesn't eat excessively, but she does consume a balanced, full-of-flavor diet. And when she wishes, she treats herself to an ice cream soda. And she's happy.

The point? Common sense. Practicality. Moderation. Those should govern the feeding of children as well as of actresses.

RULES AND BOUNDARIES

The feeding of a family, adults and children alike, should be in no way a catch-as-catch-can affair if the adults want the children to absorb good eating habits as they grow. Meals—nutritionally balanced ones—should be served on time in a pleasant atmosphere. Children should be expected to be on time for meals, in an acceptably clean state of hands and face, an acceptable condition of disposition.

That which is served must also be that which is eaten. Any mother who replies, "I'll fix you an egg," to the complaint, "I don't feel like meat loaf tonight," is worse than a sucker; she's doing damage to the complainer's personality—as much as, perhaps more than, if she says, "You eat every speck of that meat loaf or you can't go to the movies on Saturday!" Mother should never be a short-order cook, nor should anyone else be allowed to cater to the complainer's protest, including the complainer himself.

There should certainly be no hard and fast rule that everything, like it or not, must be eaten. But any new food should be tried—and that *should* be a hard and fast rule. Any child who looks at a new food and says, "I don't like it," is being allowed to make a fool of himself. He need not be required to eat it, but he should be required to try it.

When children are young, it's more practical to dish the plates in the kitchen for family meals, rather than passing food at the table. That way, the young/smaller eaters can be given servings of appropriate size and so can the older/bigger eaters. Not as much food is wasted that way, and nobody feels overwhelmed—although some, notably teenage boys who have appetites suitable for an entire family of fifteen, may feel a bit underwhelmed. But for them, there are always seconds. Thirds. Who's counting? The average teenage boy burns up his food so fast he could gobble up a whole barbecued ox, ask anxiously, "What's for dessert?" and never gain an ounce.

Teenage girls err in the other direction, on the side of fad diets, crash diets, anything to take off a few pounds that, for most of them, are completely unnecessary to shed. A girl at this precariously balanced stage can look in the mirror at her too-skinny image and wail, "I'm so *fat!*" Uncertainty is the plague of the teen years, in which young people bewilderedly ask themselves who they are, where they are headed, what's wrong with them, will they ever be taller, prettier, able to cope, popular—indeed, will anything, ever, be right for them? That they weigh too much, whether it is true or completely false, is a convenient scapegoat, because they feel it is something they can control. If I were thinner, they decide, all would be well, all my troubles would disappear. And they go on a diet.

A truly tragic aftermath of this habit of dangerously cut-down dieting by teenage girls is that very often they later produce puny, sickly, sometimes deformed, sometimes mentally retarded, babies. Such girls have done themselves harm in their foolish, offbeat dieting, and harmed the next generation as well. This is most often a product of the junk-food diet—the girl who keeps her figure on an intake of colas and chips or other taste-good/low-nutrition food. At the formative time of the teen years, a good, well-balanced diet is particularly important, not only for the present but also for the future.

How can you prevent this? Unfortunately, it's not easy. Sweet reason will not prevail. But if you start young, your daughter is unlikely to fall into this trap. Youngsters who know from the time they are old enough to understand what's good for them and what isn't, who have been taught to be proud of their well-nourished but not overweight bodies, of their good health—the glowing skin, the shining hair, the sense of well-being that a nutritionally balanced diet brings over the years—are better oriented in the teen world, better able to cope with its uncertainties, than their less fortunate friends. They have a more rational view of their bodies, a sense of their own worth that helps them weather the storms. They look so good, feel so good, that they don't have to grope for contacts, pray for popularity, wonder grimly if things will ever get better.

THE STRUCTURED WAY

As a parent who can ask no more for a child than that he grow into happy, healthy adulthood, the way is clear and there are plenty of guideposts. From the very beginning:

- treat mealtime as one of the many routine events of the day, no more or less special, set apart, than any other of the day's activities
- neither order nor plead with a child to eat—simply expect him to, and show him that you do with a pleasant, no-big-deal attitude
- establish food-related behavior boundaries, so that he is well aware of what is acceptable and what is not
- if a preschool child is a very picky eater, try six very small meals a day instead of three larger ones
- if he virtually stops eating, try to find out the reason, but without a heavy-handed cross-examination and

without showing him that he has upset you; if the condition persists, take him to the doctor to make certain there is no physical cause, then be warm and supportive but not overanxious—under such circumstances the problem will right itself or it will surface so that you can deal with it

- temper your expectations of the amount a child should eat with common sense; serve small portions
- set good eating habits and attitudes toward food for the imitative youngster to observe and use as patterns for himself
- get him in the habit of good-for-him snacks, simply by the assumption that there is no other kind and making sure no other kind is available

If you start off by following these guidelines, your youngster should grow up with a right-minded attitude toward food so much a part of him that by the time he reaches an age where he chooses food for himself, his choices will automatically be reasonable ones. This is not to say, of course, that there are never any treats, never any slipping from the straight and narrow. A child who doesn't eat himself sick on junk at the circus, who is never allowed a hamburger and french fries, who is totally forbidden candy, whose birthday cake is a loaf of sprouted-wheat bread, is a deprived child. He who hasn't sampled childhood's delights is a cheated child. But he can be made to understand that these are special-occasion treats, not a way of life.

And take it easy. Don't be a dragon who breathes fire at the first sign of a fall from grace. Take good, wholesome food in your stride, as a perfectly natural part of living, and so will your child. Above all, remember: Food is not a reward. Food is not a punishment. Food is neither love nor hate.

Food is only something to eat. That's all.

PACKAGE SIZES: see CAN, JAR, AND PACKAGE SIZES

PACKAGED FOODS: see CANNED AND PACKAGED FOODS

PAELLA: see JAMBALAYA

PANBROIL, TO: see page 450

PANCAKES

And wheat cakes, griddle cakes, whatever else you want to call them. They are the joy of the hearty American breakfaster, the bane of the would-be hearty one whose scales tell him no, while his stomach cries out, "Oh, please!"

Wholesome, rib-sticking, and delicious, any of the wide variety of griddle-baked breakfast cakes makes a superb way to start the day. Serve with butter and syrup (maple, elderberry, blueberry, whatever takes your fancy), or with a spicy fruit topping such as peach or apricot, or well buttered and sprinkled liberally with brown or—luxury!—maple sugar. Accompany them with links or patties of sausage, or crisp bacon, or ham in any manner from thin frizzled to big slabs of country-style. Nobody should need more than juice and a beverage to round out such a meal, but there are some breakfast insatiables who clamor for eggs, as well.

Long before we had griddles and waffle irons that plugged into a wall socket and winked a red light at us when the utensil was hot enough, griddles and irons were heated, and the food cooked in them over flame and coals in an open fireplace, later over a burner of an old-fashioned coal stove, still later on a gas or electric stove. Many of today's griddles and waffle irons are covered with a nonstick coating, a cleanup boon but, some say, not as productive of perfectly browned cakes as the old-fashioned kind. Electric utensils may be equipped with a timer dial and/or an adjustable gizmo to produce pale, medium, or dark brown cakes.

Grandma had her own nonstick griddle, a utensil that has virtually disappeared except at such places as flea markets and stores that specialize in good-old-days' foodstuffs and cooking utensils. It was made of soapstone. It cooked evenly, thoroughly, beautifully, turning out stack after stack of handsome buckwheat or sourdough or whatever kind of griddle cake was on the breakfast menu that morning. It did not require greasing, and it was, all in all, a joy.

Without little red warning lights, how did the cook know when the griddle was at the proper stage of hotness? She sprinkled a few drops of water on it. If they simply lay there, slowly boiling away, the griddle was not hot enough. If they disappeared in steam as soon as they touched the surface, the griddle was too hot. But if they skipped about in a merry dance, the griddle was ready to receive the first cakes. See also BREADS, FLAPJACKS, QUICK BREADS, WAFFLES.

PANFRY, TO: see page 450

PANS, POTS: see special features: THE HOME COOK'S NEW MATH and YOU CAN'T WORK WITHOUT TOOLS

PAPAYAS: see EXOTIC FRUIT

PAPRIKA: see SPICES and HERBS AND SAVORY SEASONINGS

PARAFFIN

A waxy substance, clear when melted but opaque white when hardened, used most often in home kitchens as an airtight preservative coating to top containers of homemade jelly. Paraffin is the wax that coats commercial wax paper. Crafters use paraffin in candlemaking. Commercially, it is often used in cosmetics and in some pharmaceuticals.

Small boys and girls of a couple of generations ago who lived in homes where there was much "putting up" of jelly enjoyed chewing paraffin, as one would chew gum. Flaky, chippy, hard to get started, it was sooned warmed by the mouth into a chewy mass, flavorless but great exercise for the mandibles. Are there still paraffin chewers anywhere? Or is this generation too protected, too sensible?

PARBOIL, TO: see page 450

PARCHMENT

In the cooking definition, a special kind of paper, useful for lining pans because many foods—meringues are an example—that stick to pans merely greased come away easily and intact from cooking parchment. The paper is also used for cooking *en papillote:* the food—meat, poultry, fish, is encased in parchment paper with appropriate seasonings, cooked in the paper casing and served from it, the point being to hold in the juices to surround the food as it cooks. Today, heavy-duty aluminum foil often takes the place of parchment paper for this kind of cooking—it is less expensive, molds better in taking the shape of the food, and closes more readily to make an airtight seal.

PARE, TO: see page 447

PARFAITS

A several-layered gooey delight, the parfait is a richly delicious dessert. It always contains ice cream of some sort—those desserts that substitute pudding for ice cream are not the real McCoy—sometimes of several sorts, layered with various sauces and other delights. Gild the dish by topping with whipped cream, a sprinkling of nuts, and, if you must, the ubiquitous maraschino cherry.

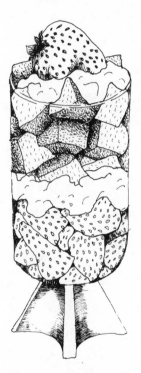

Parfaits are served most often in specially-for-them containers called, not surprisingly, parfait glasses. Lack of them need not hold you back; use any glass (glass because the dessert is so pretty seen through the transparency) you have at hand—wine glasses, footed tumblers, even juice or old-fashioned glasses.

Anything goes, but here are some ideas to get you started. Layer so that the sauce or other non-ice cream ingredient comes out on top, and be generous with the sauce:

chocolate ice cream, marshmallow creme
chocolate-almond ice cream, crushed almond macaroons, white crème de cacao
orange ice, chocolate ice cream, green crème de menthe, slivered almonds

coffee ice cream, chocolate sauce, chopped peanuts
vanilla ice cream, crushed fresh papaya
vanilla ice cream, crushed fresh strawberries
strawberry ice cream, raspberry sauce
banana ice cream, pineapple-rum sauce, macadamia nuts
vanilla ice cream, highly spiced applesauce
butter pecan ice cream, caramella liqueur
vanilla ice cream, maple-blend syrup thick with slivered, toasted almonds
vanilla ice cream, pear slices, fudge sauce
pineapple ice, orange ice, tutti-frutti sauce
cherry-vanilla ice cream, hot fudge sauce

By now you must get the idea; you're on your own.

PARMESAN: see CHEESE

PARSLEY

What's the best thing to do with the little frill of parsley without which a restaurant-served dinner plate feels naked? Eat it—it's loaded with vitamins and has fine, zippy flavor.

What's the best thing to do with those frills of parsley with which you intended to garnish dinner plates at home? Fry them, for new flavor, new texture, an entirely new change on an old theme. Wash the parsley and dry it very well—any clinging water will make the fat spatter unpleasantly. Heat fat or oil to 375°F. Drop small clusters of parsley into hot fat. Fry only until the parsley rises to the surface of the fat and becomes crisp, a matter of seconds. Take it out and drain on absorbent paper, then use as a garnish. See also HERBS AND SAVORY SEASONINGS.

PARSNIPS

Early colonists in New England were fond of parsnips, waiting eagerly for the first heavy frost so they could pull and cook the first batch of the season—because, as everyone knew of course, parsnips were poisonous until they had been frozen.

Although they didn't cultivate them—there was an abundant supply growing wild—early Greeks and Romans loved parsnips. In fact, the emperor Tiberius so doted on the vegetable he had it imported for him from Germany, where an especially sweet and flavorful species grew along the banks of the river Rhone.

The old wives' tale of poison was long ago dispelled, but we still leave parsnips in the ground at least until after the first frost, sometimes all winter, because the deep cold improves their flavor, turns their starch into sugar. From such parsnips, those same colonists made a gingered wine, used of course only for medicinal purposes, and said to have been most comforting to travelers on a cold evening.

PARSNIPS IN YOUR KITCHEN

Or don't you—shop for parsnips, that is, and serve them to

481

your family? The world is full of people who shamelessly say, "I don't like parsnips," when actually they've never sampled them. A great change in winter, when fresh vegetables are not summer-abundant, parsnips are delicious. To many, they are better of both flavor and texture than carrots.

Sneaking up on parsnips. If you are one of those who has never even tried parsnips, fie! Remedy the situation at once.

how to buy: Carrot shape, carrot size, but creamy white to pale tan in color, parsnips are in season all year around, but they are most abundant in the market in late autumn and winter. They are usually sold by the pound, sometimes, like carrots, by the plastic bag. Choose firm roots, not misshapen, of small to medium size. Big roots are often woody. Flabby parsnips will have unpleasant texture when cooked. And, of course, avoid mold, soft spots, brown spots.

how to store: Parsnips enjoy moisture. Store them in a plastic bag in your refrigerator's crisper up to 3 weeks. If they are cooked, cover and refrigerate up to 3 days.

nutritive value: One cup of diced, cooked parsnips will supply slightly over 100 calories; the same measure, prepared the same way, yields these nutritive values:

protein	2.3	grams
fat	.8	gram
carbohydrate	23.1	grams
calcium	70	milligrams
phosphorus	96	milligrams
iron	.9	milligram
sodium	12	milligrams
potassium	587	milligrams
thiamin	.11	milligram
riboflavin	.12	milligram
niacin	.2	milligram
ascorbic acid	16	milligrams
vitamin A	50	international units

Tips on preparing, cooking. Treat a parsnip as you would a carrot. If it's somewhat long in the tooth, peel it. If it's young (not as likely as with carrots because of that stay-in-the-ground-till-frost ploy), scrape it or simply scrub it well. Cut off root and leaf ends. Small parsnips may be left whole, or the vegetable may be quartered lengthwise and the resulting pieces halved. Or dice, or cut into cartwheel slices, as with carrots. Cook in a small amount of boiling (salted) water until tender—perhaps 25 minutes for whole parsnips, 10 to 15 minutes for cut pieces. Or they may be baked in a covered dish in a 350°F. oven until tender, 30 to 40 minutes. Serve with butter or lemon butter, or with the cooking liquid thickened lightly with cornstarch to use as a sauce. Or, if you prefer, mash the parsnips, season with butter and a little nutmeg or mace. Or cook until barely tender, sauté in butter over medium heat until brown, adding a little sugar or not, as

you choose. Or make parsnips, along with potatoes and salt pork, into a Boston-style hot-milk chowder.

Freezing parsnips. Properly prepared, in the manner of carrots (see special feature: PUTTING FOOD BY), parsnips may be freezer-stored at 0°F. or below up to 12 months.

Other ways, other forms. Parsnips show up fresh only, in the produce section of your market. You may also find them in bags, fresh or frozen, of mixed vegetables for soups and stews.

Some perfect partners. Parsnips and pork go very nicely together, and the vegetable partners chicken equally well.

Some good vegetable medleys include parsnips in combination with green peas, with green beans, and with mustard or collard greens. Garnish a dish of boiled or sautéed parsnips with chopped pecans or peanuts, or sieved hard-cooked egg, or bits of crisp bacon.

Nice-to-know note: Parsnips were one of the gifts we made to the native Americans living here when we came to colonize. The Indians did so much to save the white settlers from starvation, to share their life-sustaining secrets, it's pleasant to think that we brought at least one food the natives took to and enjoyed.

PARTRIDGE: see GAME

PASCAL CELERY: see CELERY

PASSION FRUIT: see EXOTIC FRUIT

PASTA

The word is an Italian one, meaning "paste," that we have adopted and made a part of English as well. "Alimentary paste," teachers of home economics used to call it. Although there are, at least according to one authority, more than 160 accepted kinds of pasta obtainable, they are all essentially the same: a paste of flour and water, shaped and dried. Only the size and the shape differentiates one kind from another. The exception is egg noodles, which also are available in a number of shapes and sizes: these contain 5.5 percent egg solids. Most pasta—including the egg noodle varieties—is enriched with B vitamins and iron, in these proportions:

nutrient:	milligrams added per pound of flour:
thiamin	4 to 5
riboflavin	1.7 to 2.2
niacin	27 to 34
iron	13 to 16.5

The flour of choice for all pasta is semolina, milled from hard red durum wheat grown in various parts of the world. It is temperamental about its soil and climate—in the United States, durum is most successfully grown in the "durum triangle," the northeastern part of North Dakota, but it is also produced in South Dakota, Minnesota, Montana, and in parts of Canada adjacent to those states where, if conditions are just right, the crop (it is spring-planted) is good.

Making a batch of pasta. In pasta factories, all the many sorts are machine produced. Simply, the process is this:

1. Fine semolina flour arrives at the factory. It is either already enriched, or is enriched at this point or in the dough stage.
2. The flour is mixed in carefully measured portions with water to make a stiff dough. Enrichment, if it has not taken place before, occurs now. Any other additions are made at this point—spinach juice for green macaroni products, beet juice for less well known red ones, and eggs for all the various shapes and sizes of egg noodles.
3. The dough is forced through dies under pressure; the shape of each die determines the shape of the pasta. Some dies are simply holes of assorted sizes. Others are more complicated, with needled centers so that the finished pasta will be hollow. Some have curved centers to make "elbow" macaroni and spaghetti. Some have patterned edges to ridge the pasta. Some are more complicated—to produce such shapes as shells. And some, such as alphabets that kids so love in soup, are all pattern.
4. After shaping, the pasta is slowly dried—spread out on flat screens or (the "long goods," such as spaghetti and spaghettini) draped over wooden rods. Egg noodle dough is rolled to the desired thickness and cut to the desired width before drying.

5. When it is completely dried, the "long goods" is cut to exact package length; it and all the other pastas are weighed, packaged, and sealed, as a part of a continuous, around-the-clock automated process.

PASTA IN YOUR KITCHEN

Some say that a long-forgotten Italian cook "invented" pasta, others that Marco Polo brought some home with him from his adventures in the Orient. How the food came to the United States is more certain, even to the year: Thomas Jefferson brought macaroni here from France in 1786. (Generally, *macaroni* is used to designate tubular pastas—those with a central hole—and *spaghetti* for flat, rodlike pasta without holes. Spaghetti is long and thin, spaghettini thinner, vermicelli thinnest of all.)

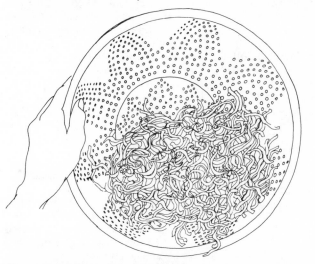

The pasta parade. Italian of origin or not, pasta is now all-American. What red-blooded local youngster would scorn macaroni and cheese, spaghetti with meat sauce, tuna-noodle casserole, lasagna? When you go shopping with pasta on your list, you can bring home one of literally dozens of shapes, all virtually interchangeable, your choice depending on your family's favorites or the use to which you're going to put the pasta, or merely on your whim of the moment.

Some of the shapes are delightful, their translated-from-the-Italian names even more so, and aptly descriptive as well. Here are only a few of the many kinds available:

amorini	little cupids
canneloni	tubes; large, ridged, they are served stuffed and sauced
capeletti d'angelo	angels' hair
capelli de prete	priests' hats
capelli pagliaccio	clowns' hats

conchiglie	seashells; large ones are stuffed and sauced
ditali	thimbles, ditalini are little thimbles; often labeled more prosaically "salad mac" as this size is perfect for macaroni salads
farfalle	bow ties; farfalline are little bows
farfalloni	big butterflies
fettucine	thin, flat noodles—fettucine Alfredo is a specialty of some restaurants
fusilli	spindles; twisted spaghetti, the theory being that the twists help the sauce to cling
lancette	little spears
lasagna	broad, flat noodles; some are ruffle-edged; some are green
linguine	little tongues
linguine de passero	sparrows' tongues
lumache	snails—lumachine are small snails, lumacone, large ones
manicotti	large, hollow tubes with plain surface; always served stuffed
mostaccioli	little mugs
occhi di lupo	wolves' eyes
ravioli	little pillows of pasta dough with a cheese or meat filling
ricciolina	little curls
rigatoni	fluted ones—macaroni with fine lengthwise ridges
rotelle	spirals; sometimes labeled corkscrews or, rather dismally, curlies
stelle	stars
stivaletti	little boots
vermicelli	little worms
ziti	bridegrooms

There are several sorts of pasta used mainly for soups. These include alphabet shapes, favorites with children everywhere; stellette, or little stars; quadriccini, little squares; conchiglietti, tiny seashells; semini, little seeds.

So . . . when you go out to buy pasta, feel free. Try new shapes and sizes. Most pastas can be substituted one for another in recipes. If you're making the substitution of uncooked pasta, do it by weight for most accurate amounts—8 ounces of this for 8 ounces of that. If the pasta is already cooked, substitute it cup for cup, as the recipe requires.

how to buy: Make certain the packages, whether cardboard boxes or plastic bags, are intact, with no breaks or open places. Choose fresh-looking packages.

how to store: If you're going to use the product within a few weeks, store in its original package on a cool, dark pantry shelf. For good, fresh flavor beyond that period, store pasta in a tightly closed metal or glass container up to 1 year, noodles up to 6 months. Some of the fancy shapes add to kitchen decor when stored in cork- or screw-topped glass bottles or jars. Cooked pasta will keep, tightly covered, in the refrigerator up to 4 days. For best second-time-around use, cool the leftover pasta, store it in cold water in the refrigerator, tightly covered. Or rinse, then toss with a little oil before storing to prevent sticking.

nutritive value: An 8-ounce (½-pound) package of pasta offers 838 calories—bear in mind before you faint dead away that this is a lot of pasta, about 4⅖ cups, sufficient for 4 to 6 people, depending on how you intend to serve it. The same amount of enriched pasta cooked, before saucing or other preparation, yields:

protein	28.4	grams
fat	2.7	grams
carbohydrate	170.7	grams
calcium	61	milligrams
phosphorus	368	milligrams
iron	6.5	milligrams
sodium	5	milligrams
potassium	447	milligrams
thiamin	1.03	milligrams
riboflavin	.57	milligram
niacin	8	milligrams

In its plain state, pasta contains no vitamins A or C.

Tips on preparing, cooking. Pasta of any kind should be cooked in a large amount of water, and the bigger the individual pieces of pasta (lasagna, manicotti, canelloni), the more water you'll need in proportion to the dry pasta. A rule of thumb is 2½ to 3 quarts of rapidly boiling water, with 1 tablespoon of salt, for 8 ounces of pasta. Add the pasta gradually so that the water will not stop boiling. Cook to the "al dente" stage—firm, but with no starchy taste remaining—or to any stage of softness your family prefers, somewhere between 7 and 10 minutes for pasta of medium size. For a cooked-again use, such as in a casserole, undercook a little so that the pasta of the finished product won't be mushy. Spaghetti and spaghettini should be cooked whole—that is, don't break the dry pasta—even though too long for the pot to handle. Put in one end, gradually push the sticking-out pieces down as the lower parts soften.

Some cooks like to add oil—about a tablespoon per quart—to the cooking water to keep the pasta from sticking together and the rapidly boiling water from splashing. However, high-quality pasta properly cooked should not stick. Stir with a fork when added to the water, several times again during cooking. Cook all pasta uncovered; covering makes the pasta sticky, and you'll have a horrendous boil-over problem. Drain pasta as soon as it is done, and serve immediately. Unless the product is to be served in a salad, or held for later use, do not rinse it.

Freezing pasta. There's no point—if at all possible, plain pasta, the kind that is sauced, should be served immediately after it is cooked. However, casseroles and other combination dishes made with almost any kind of pasta freeze well and are great to have on hand for emergencies. The pasta itself can be kept, frozen, up to 1 year, but be guided as to storage time by the other ingredients in a combination dish.

Other ways, other forms. Although pasta is so easy it's the home cook's delight, there are a number of pasta-plus dishes available in your market.

on grocery shelves, in cans or jars: Circular and regular-type spaghetti in tomato sauce, macaroni and cheese, macaroni salad, ravioli in plain or meat sauce, chicken and noodles in gravy.

in grocery frozen-food section: Various pasta-based main course dishes, ready to heat and serve, such as tuna-noodle casserole, stuffed seashells, lasagna. Also—ready to cook and serve—ravioli, tortellini, and other stuffed pastas.

Some perfect partners. Think hard—can you come up with anything that isn't good with pasta, other than desserts and other sweets? (There are sweet noodle pudding desserts, so even the sweets ban is not entirely true.)

Although virtually no one eats pasta as it comes naked from the cooking pot, preparation for serving ranges all the way from the very simple to the very elaborate. As a side dish, try the hot pasta well buttered, with or without a sprinkling of parsley and/or parmesan, or in a favorite Italian way, with olive oil and crushed garlic, with a dish of freshly grated parmesan or romano on the side. Or beat an egg with a little cream, toss the pasta in this along with a liberal amount of cheese. Make this one heartier by adding bits of crisp-cooked bacon or slivers of ham, and/or sliced ripe or stuffed green olives.

A good general cookbook will lead you to literally dozens of ways to use pastas in casseroles and skillet dishes. While experimenting with those, don't neglect plain boiled spaghetti or spaghettini topped with:

red clam sauce
white clam sauce
butter and shredded jack cheese
canned tomato spaghetti sauce with lots of added green chilies
mushroom sauce—fresh mushrooms, if possible
tomato sauce with leftover chicken or turkey
slices of leftover chicken or turkey, the whole topped with mornay sauce

very soft scrambled eggs, bacon pieces—for a most superior brunch; or top with soft-poached eggs and hollandaise
tomato sauce with diced leftover roast beef or lamb or veal or pork
chunks of fish poached in well-seasoned water/white wine, the poaching medium thickened with egg to sauce the dish
or any one of a dozen other quick/easy sauces

If you are faced with six to eight starving teenagers (or adults) and have nothing on hand, try this pantry-shelf spaghetti for a memorable meal. Into a large saucepot place two large jars of tomato sauce—the thick kind. Add ½ teaspoon garlic juice, ¼ cup instant dried onion, ¼ cup parsley flakes, ¾ teaspoon sugar, ½ cup dry red wine, ½ pound canned mushrooms (two or three cans, depending on size, liquid and all). Combine, place over low heat. Drain and flake two 6½- or 7-ounce cans of solid white tuna, or one 8-ounce can of flaked ham and one 8-ounce can of boned chicken, or thinly slice two cans of Vienna sausage, or cook ½ pound of bacon and break into bite-size pieces. Put on water to boil for 1 pound of spaghetti or spaghettini. Let the sauce simmer 10 minutes. Add the pasta to the boiling water, and the meat or fish to the sauce. Let the sauce simmer, stirring occasionally, until the spaghetti is done. Drain the pasta, place on a large platter, pour the sauce over. Serve with grated parmesan or romano, a tossed green salad, and packaged bread sticks.

Some informational odds and ends. Most people like their pasta al dente—cooked through, but still firm. However, here's an odd-but-true fact you might like to know: The longer you cook pasta, the lower in calories it becomes. That's because more of the carbohydrate is leached out in the longer cooking. For example, 3½ ounces of elbow macaroni cooked al dente yield about 150 calories; the same amount cooked until quite soft yields only about 115 calories.

One package (6 or 7 ounces) of macaroni measures about 2 cups before cooking and increases to 4 cups when cooked—4 to 6 servings, depending on the manner of service. The same is true of spaghetti—a 7- or 8-ounce package measures about 4 cups of the cooked product, or 4 to 6 servings. Egg noodles, however, do not expand in this manner. Roughly 2 ounces uncooked—measuring about 1 cup—yields only 1 cup when cooked, or one generous or two skimpy servings.

Available all year around at relatively low prices that do not fluctuate seasonally, universally liked, easy to cook, a perfect stretcher for meat, fish, and poultry—what more could you ask of a product? Let's hear it for pasta! See also LASAGNA.

PASTEURIZATION

The process by which foods are heated for a sufficient length of time and to a sufficient temperature to kill bacteria and to make the food safe for human consumption. Most often applied to milk, some other foods, such as fruit juices, are also pasteurized. The process was discovered by Louis Pasteur, a French scientist whose chief interest was in the improvement of wines. Pasteurization was first applied to wine and beer.

PASTRAMI

Beef that is cured, smoked, and treated to an elaborate coating of pepper and spices before cooking. Pastrami can be served cold but is much better hot. At its very best, it is thin-sliced, the slices piled high on dark pumpernickel bread or a kaiser roll, with mustard and a fresh dill pickle on the side. When we first came to seek our fortune in New York from a place where there was no such thing as a Jewish delicatessen, dinner for the first eight nights in a row consisted of just such a sandwich washed down with a glass of milk (which outraged the kosher soul of the delicatessen owner), followed by a large, flat almond macaroon. Then we discovered blintzes, and were off on a new tack.

Pastrami is available sliced or by the whole piece in many specialty food shops and delicatessens, and sliced in packages in many large supermarkets.

PASTRY

A dough (one of several kinds), pastry in pie-shell or tart-shell form is used as a container for both sweet and savory foods. The kinds of things that can be cooked in and/or served in pastry shells almost defy counting.

Basic pie-crust pastry for a 2-crust pie calls for 2 cups flour, 1 teaspoon salt, ¾ cup shortening, 5 to 6 tablespoons cold water. The salt and flour are combined, the shortening cut in with a pastry blender or two knives used scissors-fashion until the mixture resembles coarse crumbs, and water added a tablespoon at a time until the mixture just holds together. When you roll it out (it may be rolled immediately, but is easier to handle if chilled for an hour first), treat it with respect. Don't slam it around or roll it as if you were laying an asphalt road, or stretch it unduly. And don't skimp —there is no way that a pastry for an 8-inch pie pan will fit a 9-inch, or a 9-inch one fit a 10-inch. That way lie holes, leaks, and like disasters.

Broadening horizons. The above is your plain, basic, all-weather/all-purpose pie crust, and it hardly scratches the surface of the extensive subject of pastries and pastry-making. There are also basic tools—a rolling pin is essential, a flat area for rolling a must. Preferably, the flat area is wooden, and is not used for such things as chopping onions, but is reserved for pastry-making. Stockinette sleeves can be had to slip onto the rolling pins, muslin cloths (sometimes marked with 8-, 9-, and 10-inch circles) to cover the roll-out surface, both of which help in keeping the dough from sticking, meaning it's minimumly handled and the more tender for it.

Beyond those basics there are dozens more tools to be had: pastry wheels to cut crimp-edged dough; specially marked rolling pins to form patterns in the pastry and rolling pins of various special kinds, such as a hollow glass one to be filled with ice water before using; marble slab work surfaces; pans of every size and description, from throw-away heavy foil ones through glass, tin, pottery, and aluminum; brushes of several kinds for brushing away excess flour and/ or applying glaze to the top crust; charming little "pie birds" to stick in the center of juicy fruit pies to keep the filling from boiling over onto the oven floor. But these are not musts— only a rolling pin and a flat surface are essential.

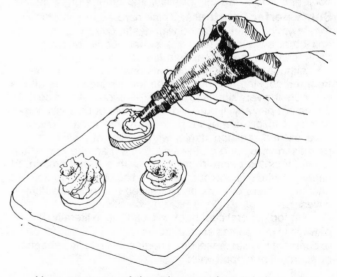

Here are some of the other pastries:

pâte brisée: Flour, salt, butter, shortening, ice water—use as any other pie crust.

pâte sucrée: Flour, confectioners sugar, butter, egg—use for any sweet pie or tart.

cream-cheese pastry: Butter, cream cheese, milk, flour, salt—use in any pie or tart recipe, or roll out and sprinkle with cheese or with sugar and cinnamon for small treats.

flour-paste pie dough: Flour and water stirred together to a smooth paste, shortening cut into more salted flour, the two mixtures combined.

hot-water pie crust: Shortening (often lard) and hot water combined, beaten together until cool; then flour, baking powder, and salt added (this crust is mealy rather than flaky).

no-roll crust: Made like basic pie-crust pastry, but patted and fitted into the pan, rather than being rolled out; not as good as rolled, but satisfactory if you pay attention to what you're doing and get the dough patted to an even thickness.

oil pie dough: This, too, is patted into the pan rather than rolled, but is much more satisfactory than the dough just above; made of flour and salt into which a mixture of cooking oil and cold milk, beaten until creamy, is added—again, a crumbly rather than flaky result.

mürbeteig: First cousin of pâte sucrée, but not as sweet; contains flour, granulated sugar, salt, softened butter, egg yolk, vanilla, and lemon juice—use primarily for fruit-filled pies and tarts.

pâte à pâté: At one time—as you might guess from the name of this—all pâtés were enclosed in pastry, the dish was known as pâté en croute; this pastry combines flour, butter, lard, egg yolks, and ice water; it is generally painted with an egg wash (dorure) and decorated with leaf cutouts made of the pastry.

flaky pastry (quick puff paste): The method rather than the ingredients make this unlike the others; made of flour, salt, butter, lard, lemon juice, and ice water, it is rolled into a rectangle, ⅓ of the rectangle is dotted with bits of butter or butter-plus-lard, it is folded and rolled (this is called a turn), then chilled; the dotting, folding, rolling, and chilling are repeated for four turns in all.

puff paste (pâte feuilletée): The principle here is the same as for the flaky pastry, but a great deal more butter is used in the fold-roll-chill steps of the turns; the butter is slightly softened, rolled between sheets of wax paper into a rectangle, and this chilled rectangle rolled into the chilled pastry, making four turns in all, during which one must be careful not to roll the edges so that air is expelled from the pastry; it is a temperamental and difficult pastry—depending not only on your skill but also on the weather—but worth the effort.

danish pastry: This pastry (which the Danes modestly call Viennese) is made with yeast, flour, eggs, milk, sugar, butter, and salt, and generally flavored with vanilla or cardamom; it is chilled rather than set to rise like most yeast doughs, and then rolled out, dotted with butter, folded and rolled and chilled for a total of four turns, as for puff pastry.

pâte à chou: This is the pastry of éclairs and cream puffs; it is made by melting butter in water, adding flour, and then, off the heat, beating in eggs one at a time; contrary to rumor, it is not at all difficult to make.

strudel dough: This one requires the stretching of the dough (flour, egg, salt, water or milk, melted butter, vinegar) from a relatively small ball to a monster tissue-thin sheet, which in turn requires the patience of a saint and the skill of a pool shark—unless you happen to combine these virtues, forget it and buy your strudel ready-made or buy phyllo (quite similar) and go on from there.

phyllo: The pastry of the Middle East, used for both sweet and savory dishes; the making requires even greater patience and skill than strudel, and it's something that those of us born elsewhere can't ever seem quite to master; buy phyllo (filo), generally frozen, and do your thing with it.

meringue paste: Made from egg whites and sugar, this is not really pastry at all, but is often used as pastry is to make a pie shell (angel pie) crisp layers (schaumtorten), individual tart shells to fill with ice cream or ice and sauce (meringues glacés), and other pastrylike sweets.

Dressing up the already-dressy. You can, if you wish, make additions to the plainer pie crusts, such as pâte brisée—indeed, to commercial pie crust mixes, some of which are very good. Depending on the filling you are going to use in the pie or tart, try one or another of these next time you bake:

poppy seeds, 1 to 3 teaspoons
caraway seeds, same amount
nuts chopped very fine, ¼ to ½ cup
one tablespoon peanut butter—great for chocolate or
  vanilla cream pie
grated sharp cheese, such as cheddar, ¼ to ½ cup
spice of any flavor compatible with the filling (cinnamon,
  nutmeg, mace, cardamom, allspice), about ½ teaspoon
for a chocolate-flavor crust, 2 tablespoons cocoa
for savory pies (quiches, onion-tomato tarts, and the
  like), about ½ teaspoon of any dried herb compatible
  with the filling flavor, such as thyme, basil, sage
grated lemon or orange peel, about 1 teaspoon

Other ways to go. You will find exact recipes for all the various kinds of pastry we've listed here in a good, general cookbook. Such a cookbook will also lead you to various substitute-for-pastry pie crusts: crusts made with graham or other cracker crumbs, with dry toasted bread or cake crumbs, with rusk or zwieback crumbs or cookie crumbs, with crumbs made by crushing or rolling various kinds of dry cereals, with finely chopped nuts, with toasted coconut and butter—perhaps the easiest of all. Or you can press slightly softened ice cream into a pie plate, refreeze it, and use this "crust" to hold a fresh fruit mélange or a fruit-plus-sauce or -custard filling. See also BAKE BLIND, CHOU(X) PASTE, DOUGHNUTS, FRANGIPANE, KOLACHKY, NAPOLEONS, PATTYCASES, PIES, REFRIGERATED DOUGH, TIMBALES, TURNOVERS, and VOL-AU-VENT.

PASTRY MIXES: see MIXES

PATE A CHOU: see CHOU(X) PASTE and PASTRY

PATES

Basically, even if this sounds like heresy, a pâté is a meat loaf. The greatest of meat loaves, the superlative in meat loaves, but meat loaf all the same.

Pâtés range all the way from simple, unbaked ones to those in pastry jackets (pâté en croute) or in aspic (en gelée) made with stock and wine. Most pâtés are made of ingredients very finely ground or puréed, although there are country pâtés (pâté de campagne) of rougher texture. Pâtés may be plain (if that is the right word to describe anything so ineluctably smooth, so almost insupportably delicious) or have inclusions such as pistachio or pine nuts (pignolias) or, most elegantly, truffles. Many are brandy flavored and well seasoned —but gently, so that the brandy and/or seasoning is a subtle touch, not an overpowering one. Some have thin slices of meat—tongue, ham, chicken, or such exotica as stuffed breasts of quail—in the pâté, surrounded by the forcemeat. Even the homely hard-cooked egg sometimes appears in the center of a pâté.

These delights need little embellishment. Serve in slices or in cubes, with good crusty bread and sour pickles—tiny French cornichons are ideal.

Pâtés may be made of livers of all sorts, of forcemeat— finely chopped or puréed filling—of chicken, pork, veal, ham (often with bacon), duck, flavorful fish such as salmon, and even our old friend, canned tuna, or a combination of several ingredients. See also FOIE GRAS and FORCEMEAT.

PATISSERIE

Pastry—pies, tarts, and tartlettes. A patissier is a pastry cook, one of the batallion of chefs in the kitchen of a large French hotel or inn or restaurant.

PATTYCASES, PATTY SHELLS

These are cup-shaped nonsweet pastries used to hold mixtures such as creamed chicken, lobster newburg, and the like —a more elegant way of serving such foods than simply on toast. If you are not in a baking mood, many bakeries sell pattycases, and there is one brand of frozen puff-paste pattycase that is reliable and bakes (provided you follow directions) into handsome, crisp, light-as-a-feather cases. These can also be thawed, rolled, and used as crusts for deep-dish pies or to wrap a beef wellington.

PATTYPAN SQUASH: see SQUASH

PEACHES

Everything that has been said about NECTARINES is also true of peaches: availability, how to buy and store, preparation, food values. In addition, unlike nectarines, peaches may be found other than fresh at your market: in cans as halves or slices in light, medium-heavy syrup, extra-heavy syrup, or water-packed; in frozen-food cases, sliced; on grocery shelves, dried. Diced, they can be had in small, easy-open cans for lunch boxes. Spiced and/or brandied peaches are available in jars. In recipes, peaches and nectarines are totally interchangeable, and their seasons are the same.

"The fruit provokes lust," an English herbalist wrote of peaches two centuries ago, "this tree belongs to Venus." "Peach house" was once an English slang term for a house of prostitution. And for a long time and to this day, a pretty girl is described as "a peach."

PEANUT BUTTER: see PEANUTS and NUT BUTTERS

PEANUT FLOUR: see FLOUR

PEANUT OIL: see OILS, SALAD AND COOKING

PEANUTS

When George Washington Carver worked out three hundred uses for peanuts, it created quite a stir. When Jimmy Carter was elected President, peanuts had a brief resurgence of fame. In between, we've steadily eaten and enjoyed peanuts and their best-known products, peanut butter and peanut oil. Often we call them goobers, unknowingly using the name for them brought here by slaves from Africa, a corruption of the word "nguba." The nuts made a roundabout journey to our tables. Pre-Incas of South America, the peanut's home, buried the nuts with their dead to nourish them on their final long journey. Spanish explorers took them back to Spain. From there they spread through Africa and Asia, and were finally brought to this country by settlers of Virginia.

Peanuts are cultivated throughout the South as food for both humans and livestock. There are two major kinds: the virginia, a long, large nut of oval shape, and the spanish, smaller and more nearly round. Both kinds have established themselves as important crops, and as well-loved foods, particularly as snacks. How could you have a baseball game without peanuts? How could you feed a hungry kid without the peanut butter sandwich? How could you watch television without a bowl of peanuts, salted or not, dry- or oil-roasted? And it is a deprived child who has never carefully pried apart the halves of a virginia peanut to expose the little old troll with the long mustache who hides inside.

But snacks and sandwiches are by no means the end of the peanut repertoire. We use peanut oil in cooking and salads and the nuts themselves in a wide variety of dishes.

Putting peanuts to work in the kitchen. When you buy the nuts in the shell, look for clean, unblemished, unbroken shells; avoid those that have a loose, dry rattle—they are probably stale. Peanuts in the shell may be kept for several weeks in a cool, dry place, but preserve their best quality when stored in the refrigerator; roasted peanuts do not keep as long or as well as fresh ones. To obtain 1 pound of shelled nut meats—about 3½ cups—you'll need 1⅓ pounds of peanuts in the shell.

Peanut butter, to the wonder and delight of all, was introduced in 1890 and has been a household staple ever since —there is a jar of the wholesome, flavorful spread in four out of five American homes today; something close to 250,000 tons of it is consumed here each year. If you wish, you can make peanut butter at home. Indeed, there's a gadget just for the purpose, but such specialization isn't necessary. Use your blender, into which place 1 cup roasted peanuts and 1½ tablespoons peanut oil and—if the nuts are not already salted—½ teaspoon salt. Add more oil if necessary. Process until the consistency you want is obtained, anything from a chunky mix to a smooth purée.

The trouble with peanuts, as most of us know, is not in eating them but in bringing ourselves to stop eating them once started. To guide you along such a hazardous course, keep in mind that ten virginia peanuts or twenty spanish peanuts, roasted and salted, contain 53 calories (and what's ten or even twenty peanuts to a devoted peanut nut?). But don't despair—there are nutritive values to be had. Those same ten or twenty peanuts yield:

protein	2.3 grams
fat	4.5 grams
carbohydrate	1.7 grams
calcium	7 milligrams
phosphorus	36 milligrams
iron	.2 milligram
sodium	38 milligrams
potassium	61 milligrams
thiamin	.03 milligram
riboflavin	.01 milligram
niacin	1.5 milligrams

Peanuts contain no vitamins A or C.

Cooking with peanuts. There are dozens of ways in which to use peanuts in cooking. Cautionary note: Their flavor is strong; they are not one of the some-is-good/more-is-better ingredients. Here are some ideas—look for recipes in a good general cookbook.

    ham-peanut canapé spread (for a truly superb flavor,
        spread it on quarters of fresh peaches instead of on
        crackers or toast)
    peanut or cream of peanut soup
    ham loaf with peanuts
    pork kabobs with peanut butter marinade/dipping sauce
    mustard-peanut sauce for ham
    African stew with peanuts and coconut milk
    peanut stuffing for poultry
    honey-sweetened peanut butter cookies

    crookneck squash sautéed with peanuts
    butternut squash with bacon-peanut stuffing
    pumpkin soufflé with peanuts
    peanut butter salad dressing for fruit
    peanut-date muffins
    peanut brittle
    layer cake with peanut butter filling, peanut frosting
    peanut-maple syrup pie
    celery stuffed with bleu cheese and peanuts
    peanut butter-stuffed baked apples
    glazed carrots with chopped peanuts
    chocolate-peanut pudding pie
    sweet potato-peanut casserole
    banana-peanut salad

And there are dozens more, enough to satisfy the most ardent fan of the ubiquitous goober.

PEARL BARLEY: see BARLEY and GRAINS

PEARL ONIONS

Very tiny onions, most often pickled. They are authoritative in sandwiches and in small appetizer kabobs, and there are those who feel that a martini is not a martini without a pearl onion. See also ONIONS.

PEARS

Those who love pears will be happy—and not surprised—to know that they are reasonably close relatives of roses. More prosaically, they are an even closer relative of apples; they grew wild in eastern Asia since before man worked out a way to record his history. By 300 B.C., pear orchards were common in Greece. The many kinds of pears we know at present are hybrids, result of botanical tinkering with those wild pears.

Today, pears are grown commercially in both the eastern and western parts of the United States, and in between, many a farm or suburban household has a pear tree or two to furnish fruit for home consumption.

Pears are one of those fruits that are picked before they are fully ripe—in fact, if allowed to ripen on the tree, the flesh becomes mealy or gritty. Commercially, the immature pears are placed in refrigerated storage, from which they can emerge and ripen as needed—which accounts for the long season in which fresh pears are available in the market.

PEARS IN YOUR KITCHEN

Most of the pears you encounter in the market will not be ripe, but can be ripened at home. They are eating-ripe when the flesh at the stem end gives readily when pressed.

how to buy: Avoid blemishes and bruises, and particularly breaks in the skin. Skin color differs so greatly (see adjacent chart) that it is not a reliable indicator. Be sure the pears are not getting soft at the blossom end—they will probably have started to rot at the core.

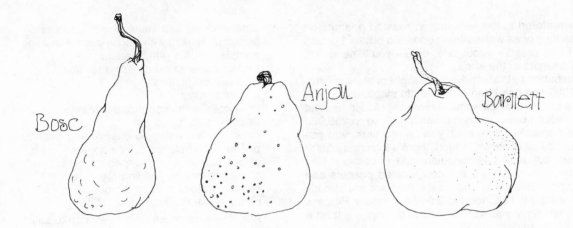

COMMON FRESH PEAR VARIETIES

kind	season	size/shape/color	flavor/texture	use for
anjou	October–April	large, plump; short neck; yellow-green thin skin	rich, spicy—almost winy—smooth texture	eating, cooking, and canning
bartlett	July–October	medium size; bell-shaped; creamy yellow, often with red blush	fine-grained; juicy, mild	eating out of hand or in salads and desserts
bosc	October–February	large; long, tapering neck; underlying yellow with all-over russet tone	mildly acid, slightly grainy	eating; good for baking and broiling
clapp favorite	August and September	large; yellow with some russeting and sometimes red blush	sweet; sometimes rather dry	eating; excellent for canning
comice	October–January	large, portly; short neck; greenish yellow with red blush	at its best, the sweetest and juciest, with excellent flavor	eating and in salads and desserts; fine with cheese
seckel	September–December	small; long neck; yellow with deep russet overlay	spicy; smooth, buttery flesh	eating, canning, pickling
winter nelis	February–May	medium size; short neck; yellow-green skin with russet markings	sweet; sometimes grainy	eating, cooking, canning

how to store: Refrigerate fully ripe pears up to 1 week. Those that you wish to bring to ripeness, store in a loosely closed paper bag and check often.

nutritive value: A pear of medium size, about 2½ inches in diameter and 3 inches tall (averaging 3 pears per pound), contains about 85 calories. Other yields for that same pear:

protein	1 gram
fat	.6 gram
carbohydrate	21.6 grams
calcium	11 milligrams
phosphorus	16 milligrams
iron	.4 milligram
sodium	3 milligrams
potassium	183 milligrams
thiamin	.03 milligram
riboflavin	.06 milligram
niacin	.1 milligram
ascorbic acid	6 milligrams
vitamin A	30 international units

Tips on preparing, cooking. If you are going to eat a pear out of hand, as a snack, eat the skin too unless it's exceptionally tough—it supplies fiber necessary to the diet, and the relatively high cellulose content of the fruit supplies more.

For cooking—approach the project gently—pears may be cored with an apple corer, or you may use one of those core-and-slice gadgets that look like miniature wagon wheels. Pears to be used raw, as in a salad, must be treated with lemon juice or a commercial (ascorbic acid) mixture to keep them from turning dark after peeling.

Freezing pears. Don't try. It doesn't work well enough to be worthwhile.

Other ways, other forms. Pears are available, in a limited number of forms, to serve the year around, when fresh ones are out of season.

on grocery shelves, in cans or jars: Pear halves or slices in cans or jars of several sizes, in light, medium, or heavy syrup, or water-packed for weight-loss dieters. Green minted pears and red cinnamon-flavored pears to be served as relishes.

on grocery shelves, in packages or bags: Dried pears, to be stewed or baked alone or in combination with other dried fruit.

Some perfect partners. Raw pears, cored and their cores stuffed with cream cheese combined with chopped peanuts, walnuts, or pecans, make a delicious salad. Cook sliced slightly underripe pears in sweetened/spiced water or water/white wine to make a sauce, or whole (peeled) in cranberry juice and spices to make a delicious serve-with-meat relish. Brandy pears for a different relish. Pear pie is a festive dessert; pear betty, made like its more familiar apple cousin, is delicious. Try an upside-down pear cake. Poires Hélène is a classic dessert—the pears are baked and served with ice cream and chocolate sauce. For an unusual appetizer, spread pear wedges with a bleu cheese-nut mixture. And serve pears and cheese—brie, fontina, for example—as the perfect finishing touch for a meal.

The flavor of pears is distinctive yet delicate. Fresh, canned, or dried, they add variety to any course of the meal.

PEAS

Nature is a very neat packager of foods and peas are one of her better efforts. Zip the pods open, flick a thumbnail, and out tumble the handsome green peas, clean and ready to use. Or, if you prefer, there are the thick-but-tender pods of the peas the French call mange-tout—eat it all—and the snow peas or Chinese pea pods that can be eaten contents, package, and all. As for the peas themselves, looks can be deceiving: the slightly wrinkled peas are generally more tender and flavorful than the plumply smooth ones.

We grow two large general classes of the vegetable, garden peas—the green ones we eat—and field peas, which are fed—plant, pod, and all—to livestock, and from which the yellow split peas of which we make soup are obtained. They like cool moisture, and so are planted in the early spring in the North, in the fall in the South. California supplies about 60 percent of the peas that come to market in this country.

As a staple food, peas have been with us a long time, since biblical days. Early Greeks and Romans knew and enjoyed them, but they did not spread to western Europe until the early sixteenth century.

PEAS IN YOUR KITCHEN

Grandma was very concerned with the pea patch that was a part of her kitchen garden. She watched the plants grow, put out their pretty flowers (smaller, but very like the beautiful and fragrant sweet peas that climbed the back fence), and develop pods that gradually plumped out. One morning, guided by her foodstuffs sixth sense, she would announce, "It's time for the first mess of peas," to the pleasure of the whole family.

Today only a few of us can gather peas from our own gardens, but we can go to market when they come in season —in March, April, and May and again, a second crop, starting in August and finishing in November.

how to buy: Choose velvety, nearly unblemished pods, well-filled but not looking as if they were about to burst. The peas should not rattle in their pods—if they do, they're old and tough. Color should be bright green and, of course, avoid damp or slimy peas, and those with damaged pods. One pound of fresh peas will yield 1 cup after shelling.

how to store: Do not shell peas until shortly before you are going to cook them. Store, unshelled, in the refrigerator up to 5 days. After cooking, refrigerate in a covered container up to 5 days. Store uncooked split dried peas on a cool, dry kitchen shelf up to 8 months.

nutritive values: One cup of shelled, cooked fresh peas contains 114 calories; the same amount of cooked split dried peas, 230. Other values for the same amount, cooked:

	fresh peas	dried peas	
protein	8.6	16	grams
fat	.6	.6	gram
carbohydrate	19.4	41.6	grams
calcium	37	32	milligrams
phosphorus	158	178	milligrams
iron	2.9	3.4	milligrams
sodium	2	26	milligrams
potassium	314	592	milligrams
thiamin	.45	.30	milligram
riboflavin	.18	.18	milligram
niacin	3.7	1.8	milligrams
ascorbic acid	32	trace	milligrams
vitamin A	860	80	international units

As you can see, when peas are dried they lose a little here, gain a little there, in the translation.

Tips on preparing, cooking. Shell peas shortly before cooking. If the pods were intact, the peas will not need washing. Cook in 1 inch of boiling salted water 8 to 12 minutes, until barely tender. Or cook fresh peas in the French manner: Place 1 tablespoon butter in a skillet with a tight-fitting cover. Wash 2 or 3 large outside lettuce leaves, leaving some water clinging to them. Spread out in the skillet. Add the peas, cover with more damp lettuce leaves. Cover skillet, cook over high heat until bubbling, then lower heat and steam until peas are just tender, about 15 minutes. Discard lettuce, season peas to taste.

Split dried peas may or may not need soaking—consult the package. If they are soaked, cook them in the soaking water to save the nutrients leached out by soaking, following package directions.

Freezing peas. Properly prepared for freezing (see special feature: PUTTING FOOD BY), peas may be stored at 0° or below up to 1 year.

Other ways, other forms. Peas appear in a number of ways in your market, making it easy to serve them all year.

on grocery shelves, in cans or jars: Canned peas in several can sizes, marked "sweet" (meaning small, wrinkled, very tender) or "early" or "June" (slightly larger, slightly less tender). Also peas and carrots canned together, and a diet pack that is low-sodium. Dried peas in packages or plastic bags or, less often, in bulk, both yellow and green.

in grocery frozen-food section: Peas frozen alone or with carrots, with mushrooms, with tiny onions (plain or creamed), and in butter sauce. Whole edible-pod peas, frozen alone or with water chestnuts.

Some perfect partners. Peas are at their best when young, cooked and served alone, lightly seasoned with salt, white pepper, and butter. But a dish of little new potatoes and fresh peas creamed together is certainly not to be sneezed at. Neither is one of peas and carrots, or peas and tiny onions, either one creamed or simply dressed with butter, salt, and pepper. And don't neglect the delectable pea-mushroom combination, or peas and green beans, or peas with little flecks of pimiento to give color and flavor. Use leftover peas in creamed dishes or cold in salads.

With dried peas, yellow or green, make pea soup—the pease porridge of the old nursery rhyme. A ham bone or a couple of ham hocks gives the soup flavor.

One of the great summer dishes—and one of the easiest to prepare—is a very special, very easy cold pea soup. In the container of a blender break up a package of uncooked frozen peas. Add two large lettuce leaves and 1 cup chicken broth. Season with ½ teaspoon salt, ¼ teaspoon white pepper, and a dash of ground cardamom; process into a smooth purée. Add 1 cup half-and-half, process ½ minute. That's it. Chill until serving time. Serves 4.

PECANS

Pecans are native American nuts, indigenous to the southern part of the United States. They are grown commercially as far north as Indiana and Virginia, but are a major crop in Texas and Oklahoma, and have been for many years.

The American Indians were using the nuts as food when the first Spanish explorers arrived. But it was when settlers came into the pecan's growing area that inventive cooks began to work out the many pecan dishes that are now a part of "Southern cooking."

The nuts are medium-to-large, with a smooth shell of a handsome brown. Inside, the nut is richly brown, too, with a distinctive, slightly sweet flavor and a somewhat crumbly texture. Peak season is from September through November, but the nuts are in the market all year long. Buy them in the shell, by the pound, or shelled as halves, chopped nuts, broken pieces, or ground—the perfect halves being, reasonably, the most expensive. For cooking or snacking, purchase them roasted, salted or not, in vacuum tins or glass jars or plastic bags.

Putting pecans to work in your kitchen. When you buy pecans in the shell, look for unblemished shells and check to see that the nuts inside do not rattle freely—a sign of old age. Store in a cool, dry place up to 6 months, even longer in the refrigerator. Shelled nuts in vacuum cans or jars will keep almost indefinitely until opened, when they should be refrigerated; those in ordinary cans and bags should also be refrigerated after opening.

Pecans marry well with both savory and sweet foods. Use them in appetizers and in confections, and almost anywhere in the meal between those two extremes. Chop and add to chicken hash, for example, or to stuffing for turkey, duck, or goose. Strew them over candied sweet potatoes or yams. Finely chopped, add them to pie crust. And, of course, make pecan pie—that incredibly rich, incredibly good Southern specialty—or pralines, almost equally known and loved. Use them in nut breads and cookies of many kinds, or make a three-layers-high pecan cake and lavish it with chocolate frosting. And those are only a few of dozens of pecan dishes. However you use them, they will repay you with incomparable flavor and texture.

PECTIN

Colorless and flavorless, pectin is a carbohydrate found in a number of plants, but particularly in apples and crab apples, currants and plums. It has a property that makes other fruits gel and for that reason is used in the making of fruit jellies. It is available as a liquid in bottles or in granular form in packages. See also the special feature: PUTTING FOOD BY.

PEEL, TO: see page 447

PEKOE: see TEA

PEPPER: see HERBS AND SAVORY
SEASONINGS

PEPPERMINT: see HERBS AND SAVORY
SEASONINGS

PEPPERONI: see SAUSAGES

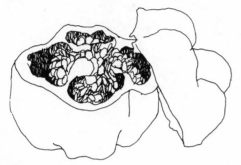

PEPPERS

First, differentiate between peppers, fruits (but we use them like vegetables), and pepper, the bitey spice we use, along with salt, to add flavor and zest to foods.

Peppers come in assorted shapes and sizes, various colors, and many degrees on the sweet-to-hot scale. Sweet peppers are green when mature—the condition in which we usually find them in the market—and turn red as they continue to age. Some are long, pointed, and slim, but the most familiar are the chunky bell or bullnose (very apt—look at a pepper in that light next time you handle one). One is heart-shaped, the sweet pimiento, and more often canned than eaten fresh in home-prepared dishes.

The hotter—pungent is the word—peppers are also often green when purchased, although they may be a lovely shade of yellow-green or they may be red. It is in the red stage that they are commonly used. Often these peppers are strung and dried for out-of-season use, or they may be purchased dried or as crushed hot pepper flakes, or ground as, depending on the variety, paprika or cayenne.

Like pecans, peppers are a native American food—this time the place of origin was South America, where the Indians were using them long before the early explorers put in an appearance. They are believed to have been cultivated by pre-Incan tribes as long as 2,000 years ago.

PEPPERS IN YOUR KITCHEN

Chinese pepper steak and stuffed peppers are two of the more popular ways peppers (in both cases the green, bell variety) are served in American homes. But they have many other uses.

how to buy: The pepper should look fresh, be of the proper color for its kind, and have no soft or pale spots, which tell you that decay is setting in. Limp or shriveled peppers should be avoided, as should badly misshapen ones. They are available all year around, but the peak season is June through September.

how to store: Refrigerate, covered or in a plastic bag, up to 5 days; cooked, refrigerate in a covered container 1 or 2 days.

nutritive value: Peppers of the various kinds do not differ widely in caloric value or nutritive content. As an example, 1 cup of diced sweet green bell pepper contains 33 calories, and yields these nutritive contributions to the diet:

protein	1.8	grams
fat	.3	gram
carbohydrate	7.2	grams
calcium	14	milligrams
phosphorus	33	milligrams
iron	1.1	milligrams
sodium	20	milligrams
potassium	320	milligrams
thiamin	.12	milligram
riboflavin	.12	milligram
niacin	.8	milligram
ascorbic acid	192	milligrams
vitamin A	630	international units

Tips on preparing, serving. Cut off both ends, then trim out the inner ribs and the seeds. Be sure to get all the seeds —in even the mildest peppers, the seeds have quite a bite. Then cut into halves, rings, julienne strips, or dice, depending on the use you are going to make of them. If you are going to stuff the peppers, parboil them 5 minutes, drain, then stuff with your favorite filling and bake. Peppers may be stuffed with another vegetable or vegetable combination (corn, succotash, peas and carrots, and so on) to use as a side dish, or with a meat, fish, or poultry combination for main-dish service.

Freezing peppers. Properly prepared (see special feature: PUTTING FOOD BY), peppers may be stored at 0°F. up to 12 months. They may also be frozen without blanching. Freeze in quarters, in strips, or diced, with seeds and ribs removed. Frozen peppers lose their crispness, so are best used in cooked dishes. Pimientos must be peeled before freezing—char in a 400°F. oven 3 or 4 minutes, then rub the skins off.

Other ways, other forms. Peppers are available in the market in several ways.

on grocery shelves, in cans, jars, or bottles: Halves or chopped sweet pimientos; red or green hot pepper sauce, and the fiery tabasco; whole or sliced or diced peppers—from mild to very hot; pepper relishes of several sorts; freeze-dried nubbins of sweet green bell pepper to be rehydrated and used as fresh pepper is used; flakes of hot red pepper includ-

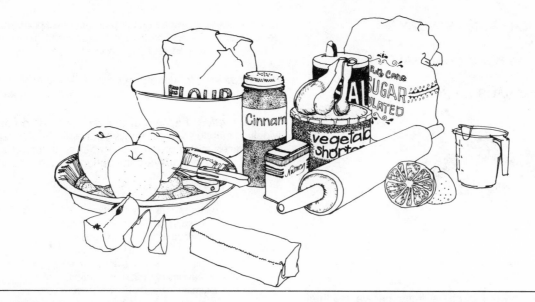

ing the even hotter yellow seeds; paprika; cayenne—the last four shelved with spices and herbs.

in grocery frozen-food section: Little tubs of frozen chopped sweet green peppers, stuffed pepper main dishes and other main dishes in which peppers play a large role, such as pepper steak.

Pepper color adds variety to meals; pepper flavor adds distinctiveness. If you aren't in the habit of using peppers, or if you only use the sweet green bells, it wouldn't hurt a bit to broaden your horizons. See also CHILIES, HERBS AND SAVORY SEASONINGS, and JALAPENO PEPPERS.

PERCH: see FISH

PERCOLATOR GRIND: see COFFEE

PERIWINKLE: see SHELLFISH

PERSIAN MELONS: see MELONS

PERSIMMONS: see EXOTIC FRUIT

PESTICIDES: see NATURAL FOODS

PETIT SUISSE: see CHEESE

PETITS FOURS: see page 453

PHEASANT: see GAME

PHOSPHORUS: see MILK and the special feature: NUTRITION NOTEBOOK

PHYLLO: see PASTRY

PICKLES AND RELISHES: see special feature: PUTTING FOOD BY

PICKLING SPICE: see SPICES

PICNIC HAM: see HAM

PIE CRUSTS: see PASTRY

PIE PLANT: see RHUBARB

PIES

Somewhere, perhaps in the back country of Australia or among certain isolated tribes of Eskimos, there must be somebody who doesn't like pie. But pie-haters are indeed few and far between.

There are dozens of kinds. Many fruit pies. Ditto berries. The oddball dessert pies, such as fudge, and chess, and pecan, peanut, and brown sugar. Meringue pies. Ice cream pies. Bottom-crustless deep-dish pies. Cream pies. And more, more.

Not to mention the main-dish pies, ranging all the way from a wide assortment of quiches through out-of-hand little goodies such as Cornish pasties, to Britain's sturdy steak-and-kidney and our own good beef and chicken pies, a clam pie that makes unparalleled eating, Shepherd's Pie. And still more.

And there are turnovers, too. And tarts. And Southern fried pies. The whole wide and wonderful field of pies challenges the senses and stuns the imagination.

Discretion is the better part. "Pie's fattening," some cooks say flatly in answer to their families' clamor for their favorite dessert. Well, true. So is lettuce. It's all relative—and depends on how much you eat. Anyone who sits down and consumes a full pie at one sitting deserves the Ima Hogg award for the current year. But even if you have a whole family of unfortunate overweights, pie now and then is a deserved reward after all those fruit cups and low-cal gelatin desserts.

How do you know just how many calories you're doling out to your family when you serve them pie? Consult the list below. It gives the calorie count for *whole* ready-to-eat 9-inch pies. Do the simple division by 4 or 5 or 6 or 7 or 8, depending on the size of the cuts you serve, and you'll know how many calories in each slice of whatever kind. The whole-pie counts admittedly take one's breath away, but the divided-by-6 or whatever counts aren't all that bad. In a whole, 9-inch pie, you'll find:

pie	calories	pie	calories
apple	2,419	mince	2,561
banana custard	2,011	peach	2,410
blackberry	2,296	pecan	3,449
blueberry	2,287	pineapple	2,391
butterscotch	2,430	pineapple	
cherry	2,466	chiffon	1,866
chocolate chiffon	2,125	pineapple	
chocolate cream		custard	2,002
meringue	2,293	pumpkin	1,920
coconut custard	2,139	raisin	2,552
custard	1,984	rhubarb	2,391
lemon chiffon	2,028	strawberry	1,469
lemon meringue	2,142	sweet potato	1,938

That's not the entire, broad spectrum of the pie field, of course. But it'll give you a good general idea. Did you find some surprises in the list, comparing one kind of pie to another? Did you find to your chagrin that your own favorite was the most calorie-loaded of all? C'est la vie. See also MERINGUES, PASTRY, POTPIES, and QUICHES.

PIGEON: see GAME

PIGNOLIAS: see PINE NUTS

PIGS' FEET

Known by the somewhat more beguiling name of "trotters" in Britain, these are just what the label says—the feet of pigs. Sometimes your market will have fresh ones, in which case you can cook them in well-seasoned water and enjoy the good flavor and the contest between you and the trotter to get all the savory little bits and pieces of meat that cling to the bones. Or add a foot or two to soup or stock if you wish the stock to gel—pigs' feet are loaded with natural gelatin.

Find them also pickled, in jars—a tasty addition to the cocktail appetizer spread, or great for snacking. See PORK.

PIGS IN BLANKETS

A pig in a blanket is a sausage—any one of several kinds—with an outer wrapper (the blanket), which may also be one of several kinds. For your first try at pigs in blankets you might use the small, fully cooked, ready-to-eat smoked sausages available at delicatessen counters, giving them overcoats of pie-crust pastry—from a mix, if you like. Bake until golden brown. From there, branch out.

A pork sausage of the breakfast sort wrapped in a pancake is also a pig in a blanket. So is a fat Italian sausage, sweet or hot, in a manicotti or canelloni tube, lightly stovetop browned. Perhaps best of all are small pork sausages of the breakfast type wrapped in puff pastry; for this, use commercial frozen patty shells, thawed and rolled to about a ⅛-inch thickness. In any case, be sure the sausages—almost all of which are at least part pork—are fully cooked before you wrap them. The brief time in the oven required to cook the pastry is not sufficient to cook the sausages.

PIKE: see FISH

PILAF, PILAU (or PILAW, PILAV, PELLO)

However you spell it, it's a rice dish indigenous to the entire Near East. Generally the rice is first sautéed, then boiled, and may be only well-seasoned with herbs and spices, or may have such inclusions as bits of meat, fish, poultry, vegetables, or whatever comes to hand. And if even rice doesn't come to hand, make a pilaf of barley or cracked wheat.

PIMIENTOS (PIMENTOS): see PEPPERS

PINE NUTS (or PIGNOLIAS, PINONS, PINOCCHIOS)

These are the only nuts that are used more often in cooking than as an appetizer or snack food. The edible seed from the cones of certain kinds of pine trees, pine nuts range from off-white to palest yellow, are small, and have a somewhat soft texture.

Most pine nuts are sold shelled and blanched and loose by the pound or in small plastic bags. They have a mild but like-nothing-else flavor, not at all "piney."

Pine nuts are used in sauces and stuffings for duck,

goose, chicken, turkey, and game. Their flavor combines beautifully with that of poultry, ham, pork, lamb, and veal. Besides excellent flavor, they contribute an unusual soft-crunch texture that is very appealing. For increased flavor and crispness, roast the nuts in the oven, spread in a single layer on an ungreased baking sheet, at 375°F. about 15 minutes, stirring frequently.

Store in a cool, dark place in the kitchen, in a covered container, where they will keep for several months, or in the refrigerator, covered, where they will keep even longer. Although at one time they were not, pine nuts can now be found almost everywhere—if not in supermarkets, then in specialty food or health food shops.

Pesto alla genovese is one of the classic uses for pine nuts; it is made of the nuts crushed and mixed with garlic, fresh basil, grated parmesan or romano, and olive oil. Use it as a sauce for pasta, or to give flavor to soups.

PINEAPPLE CHEESE: see CHEESE

PINEAPPLES

When Columbus came to the West Indies he found that some of the natives had whole pineapples or pineapple tops near the entrances to their huts, placed there to tell visitors they were welcome. The fruit had migrated to the islands from pre-Incan Peru. The Spanish explorers gave them a new name, piña—from the fruit's resemblance to a pine cone—and adopted the custom of using them as a sign of hospitality. The custom spread to England, then back to the New World with the settlers. In beautiful restored Williamsburg, Virginia, many of the houses have carved pineapples above the front door or on the gate posts, and when the town is decorated for Christmas, fresh pineapples, along with apples and oranges, have a traditional part in the festivities.

The wide-roving Spanish explorers introduced the pineapple to Hawaii, where it now grows in abundance as an important commercial crop, although it first was treated as a weed and rooted out of gardens and farms. By 1892 the first cannery was established, and now Hawaii exports more than three-quarters of a billion pounds of canned fruit and juice. The state also exports the fresh fruit, but most of the fresh pineapple in our markets comes from Puerto Rico and Mexico. The fruit comes in all sizes, from 1 to 20 pounds, but those in our markets usually weigh between 3 and 6 pounds.

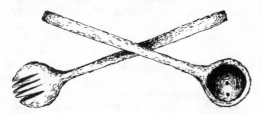

PINEAPPLES IN YOUR KITCHEN

There is fresh pineapple in the market all year around, the peak of the season being March through June.

how to buy: Choose pineapples heavy for their size. In color they should be deep golden yellow with little green showing —a pineapple almost entirely green is under-mature. A ripe pineapple gives just slightly when the skin is pressed, but be on your guard against soft spots, particularly soft brownness at the base of the fruit, which indicates decay.

how to store: Fully ripe, store covered in the refrigerator, to be used as soon as possible, up to 3 days. Let underripe pineapples mature at room temperature, but not in direct sunlight. Cooked or opened canned pineapple can be refrigerated, covered, up to 5 days.

nutritive value: A cup of diced fresh pineapple furnishes between 85 and 88 calories; the same amount yields:

protein	.6	gram
fat	.3	gram
carbohydrate	21.2	grams
calcium	26	milligrams
phosphorus	12	milligrams
iron	.8	milligram
sodium	2	milligrams
potassium	226	milligrams
thiamin	.14	milligram
riboflavin	.05	milligram
niacin	.3	milligram
ascorbic acid	26	milligrams
vitamin A	110	international units

Tips on preparing, cooking. There are several ways to attack a pineapple, each requiring a large, sharp knife or a gizmo called a pineapple parer. This latter looks like the gadget that cores apples and cuts them into wedges. However, because of the unevenness of the depth of a pineapple's "eyes," this sometimes wastes too much good pineapple, and other times leaves you with a lot of hand trimming to do anyway.

The basic approach is to cut off the top and leaves, then the bottom, then slice the fruit, then pare each slice separately. If you wish, remove the core—some people think it's the best part—and cut each slice into chunks of a size appropriate to the way you intend to serve the pineapple.

Alternatively, cut off the top and bottom, then the skin, leaving the whole-but-naked pineapple to do with what you will. Or leave bottom and leaves in place, cut the pineapple in half lengthwise. Take out the meat with a small, sharp knife. Mix with other fruit—pineapple is a very good mixer— or with the ingredients for a pineapple-meat or -poultry or -fish salad, and pile the salad back in the fruit shells for serving.

Freezing pineapple. Properly prepared (see special feature: PUTTING FOOD BY), pineapple may be stored at 0°F. or below up to 12 months. Pineapple may be frozen or canned in syrup or sugar, or simply in water, or in pineapple juice.

Other ways, other forms. No one ever need lack for pineapple—in various packs, it's all over the market.

on grocery shelves, in cans, jars, or bottles: Canned pineapple as slices, chunks, tidbits, spears, or crushed, in heavy or light syrup or in pineapple juice; as the basis of a canned or bottled piña colada drink mix; diet-packed slices or tidbits in water; ice cream topping in bottles; canned juice, plain or with orange or grapefruit juice. Candied pineapple slices or pieces.

in grocery frozen-food section: Plain pineapple or pineapple-orange or -grapefruit combinations, as a concentrate to be diluted into a refreshing drink; frozen tidbits.

Some perfect partners. Almost any fruit goes well with pineapple, but it has a special affinity for those that grow in its own climate—bananas, papayas, and avocados are examples. Or mix with celery, a touch of onion, and cubed chicken or turkey, drained and flaked tuna, poached salmon or slivers of smoked salmon, any white-fleshed fish, lamb, veal—almost anything. Bind with mayonnaise or salad dressing, and pile back into the shells. Or cut the shells in quarters and fill with sherbet, sauce with liqueur. A finger-shape of pineapple makes a tasty, edible stirrer for a fruit or alcoholic beverage.

PIPE, TO: see page 447

PISTACHIO NUTS

It is said that pistachios grew in the garden of Eden—and tasting them, even just looking at them, makes such a claim easy to believe. The trees on which they grow live as long as a thousand years, linking the past to the present as few things do. They are native to Asia Minor, where they have grown since the beginning of recorded time, were taken to Italy in the first century A.D., and have flourished there since. Now they grow in California, too, although the major nut supply comes from Turkey and Afghanistan.

Growing in clusters, like grapes, each pistachio is encased in a rough outer burr that encloses a hard, ivorylike shell that splits open as the nuts mature. Gathered by hand in late summer, they are relieved of their burrs, then washed and spread in the sun to dry. They are then sorted—a by-hand process, because no one has been able to devise a machine that can separate the open nuts from the closed ones. They are exported to this country in their raw state, then roasted and salted (and sometimes tinted red with vegetable dye, which for some reason the processors think makes them more attractive) here before they go to market. Some-times instead of dye they are given a white coating of salt.

A part of the culinary delight of pistachios lies in the handsome green color of the kernels. But the flavor is also a strong contributing factor—it is out of the ordinary, exotic, not capable of comparison with anything else. The nuts are widely used throughout the world, not as well known or as variously used here as in some other countries.

Buy pistachios in bulk or in moistureproof cans or plastic bags of several sizes. The largest nuts come from Iran; the smallest from Afghanistan; the highest-quality, darkest-green ones from Italy. Shelled pistachios are also available, although not as widely distributed. Store the nuts, shelled or not, in the refrigerator, tightly covered, for best and longest keeping qualities.

Because they are slightly sweet (but no more so than pecans), pistachios are seldom used in appetizers. The exception is pâtés, to which they add as much elegance (as well as lovely color) as truffles, that other good pâté inclusion. The nuts are also used in meat and poultry stuffings, pilafs, in many kinds of desserts, dessert sauces, and confections and—chopped—to decorate cakes and cookies of various sorts.

One ounce of pistachios yields slightly over 200 calories. There are 700 of the smallest nuts in a pound, 350 of the largest ones. They are in the market the year around.

PIT, TO: see page 447

PITA: see POCKET BREADS

PIZZAS

Round or square, thin crust or thick, by the cut or by the whole pie, just tomato sauce and cheese or topped "with everything, please," we devour pizza as if there were going to be a law passed later this evening banishing it from the face of the earth.

The pizza idea hasn't been with us all that long, but once started it spread like chicken pox through the third grade. There are few places in these United States where you aren't in easy reach of a pizza "parlor," and although the food is Italian in origin, nowadays every-ethnic-body makes and sells pizza. A few years ago, a prominent New York magazine conducted a massive, tongue-in-cheek survey to find the very best pie in the whole five boroughs of the city. A gentleman named Goldberg won—which must prove something, although we're not quite sure what.

A pizza, in case you've been in hiding for the past twenty years, consists of a yeast-raised crust—it can be thick (Sicilian) or thin, but is always chewy—with savory toppings. These invariably include tomato sauce and mozzarella cheese, but from there anything goes. Hot or sweet Italian sausage, pepperoni, onions, garlic, peppers, mushrooms, anchovies, other cheeses, and ripe olives are a few of the more common ones. But you can get a pizza topped with anything your hungry imagination dreams up—sardines, ground beef, strips of barbecued pork, chunks of chicken, spinach and egg —you name it.

On the home ground: It isn't necessary to go out or send out for pizzas. They can be made at home from scratch (any general cookbook will tell you how), from a mix, from a pizza crust brought home from the supermarket to top and bake as you wish. Or pull out and bake a ready-made frozen pizza from the supermarket. All are good—the last is usually better if the somewhat skimpy topping is enhanced before you stick it in to bake.

There are, as there always are with something popular, some far-out variations. Sweet fruit pizzas for dessert, for example. Or pizza with a ground meat "crust." Make and eat them if you like—they can be very good—but don't call them pizza. To deserve that name, only the real thing will do.

PLANK, TO: see page 450

PLANT PROTEIN: see TEXTURED PLANT PROTEIN

PLANTAINS: see EXOTIC FRUIT

PLASTICS

How we ever managed to run our kitchens successfully before plastics were discovered remains a mystery. Where do you put fresh vegetables if you don't have a plastic bag? What do you do with leftovers lacking a plastic container with a snug cover? How do you wrap a sandwich if not in a plastic sandwich bag or a small, sandwich-shape plastic box?

Not that plastics are entirely without drawbacks. Plastic mixing bowls can be a trap—they don't get grease-free clean, even those that can be run through the dishwasher. Some swear by plastic wrap, others at it—it seems to behave well for the former and badly for the latter, so where there are problems they may lie in the nature of the user.

But most of the many kinds of plastic we use are amenable and admirable—and we'd be sore pressed if someone came along and took them away from us at this late date.

PLUMP, TO: see page 447

PLUMS

Long before Little Jack Horner stuck his thumb into the Christmas pie and pulled out a plum, the fruit had been widely known and used. Plums are indigenous almost everywhere throughout the world, so that although they were brought in from the wild and improved with hybridization, they did not need to be carried anywhere by settlers or explorers—wherever the newcomers went, plums were already there, waiting.

The plum is an ornamental tree, attractive in shape and foliage and putting out, in the spring, beautiful flowers that have a heavenly aroma. Early settlers in this country were delighted to find plums—even though the fruit was small and not very sweet—with which to vary their monotonous diet. In Virginia, some ingenious cook whose name is lost to fame invented greengage plum ice cream, and it is still offered on the menu of the King's Arms Inn at Colonial Williamsburg. Damson plums (that they were named after the city of Damascus tells you how long they have been around) were the most generally cultivated in this country before 1850, but they are now used almost exclusively for jam and jelly, rather than as an eat-out-of-hand fruit.

It was in the late nineteenth and early twentieth century that plums really came into their own. Hybridizing, Luther Burbank produced more than sixty varieties, including some superior kinds of prune plum. These, called prunes both before and after they are dried, are unique in that they will dry without fermenting, and that they are freestone—all other plums are clingstone. In all, throughout the world, there are more than two thousand varieties of plums to choose among. Some of the best known in this country are damson, italian prune, el capitan, kelsey, ace, greengage, santa rosa, queen ann, mariposa, el dorado, and the wonderfully named elephant heart.

PLUMS IN YOUR KITCHEN

Depending on their variety, plums come into the market from June through October; sometimes varieties imported from Latin America are available January through March.

how to buy: Choose plums that are firm but not hard—truly hard ones will not ripen. They should give just slightly to gentle pressure between the palms of the hands. Avoid soft and/or brown spots, and plums with cracked skin.

how to store: Store ripe fruit, covered, in the refrigerator up to 1 week. Ripen under-mature fruit in a paper bag at room temperature until ready to eat, then refrigerate. Refrigerate, covered, cooked plums or opened canned ones up to 5 days.

nutritive value: Although plums differ in values somewhat according to type, an average can be struck. As an example, take a whole plum, 2½ inches in diameter. Such a plum contains between 30 and 35 calories, and yields:

protein	3	grams
fat	.1	gram
carbohydrate	8.1	grams
calcium	8	milligrams
phosphorus	12	milligrams
iron	.3	milligram
sodium	1	milligram
potassium	112	milligrams
thiamin	.02	milligram
riboflavin	.02	milligram
niacin	.3	milligram
ascorbic acid	4	milligrams
vitamin A	160	international units

Tips on preparing, cooking. For plums at their best, no preparation other than washing is needed. Eat them out of hand for a snack, alone or with mild cheese for dessert. Unless you have some kind of digestive disorder, eat them skins and all—that's fiber added to your diet.

Plum sauce—plums cooked in a little water until their skins burst and sweetened if necessary—is delicious. Some kinds, such as our native wild beach plums, are too hard and sour to eat raw, but are exceptional for jam and jelly. An upside-down plum cake makes a happy ending for a meal. So does plum bread pudding. A deep-dish plum cobbler is a treat, especially when gilded with a scoop of vanilla ice cream. Plums are great in salads, too, either combined with other fresh fruit of the season or sparklingly encased in a crown of gelatin. Plum pie, with a lattice or streusel topping, is as good as it is pretty.

Freezing plums. Properly prepared (see special feature: PUTTING FOOD BY), plums may be stored at 0°F. or lower up to 1 year.

Other ways, other forms. There are no frozen plums, no plum juice on the market.

on grocery shelves, in cans or jars: Whole plums of several kinds in syrup, plum preserves and jelly (both domesticated and wild beach-plum kinds), plum butter, Oriental plum dipping sauce.

For a special treat, make a plum-garlic sauce to baste chicken or kabobs on the barbecue, or to serve with miniature egg rolls as an appetizer. Cook ½ pound of pitted fresh prune plums in water to cover until tender. Drain, reserving liquid. Purée in the blender along with 3 cloves of minced garlic and salt and pepper to taste. Stir in enough of the reserved liquid to achieve the consistency of thick cream. Return to pan, bring to a boil, reduce heat, and simmer 5 minutes.

See also BEACH PLUMS and PRUNES.

POACH, TO: see page 450

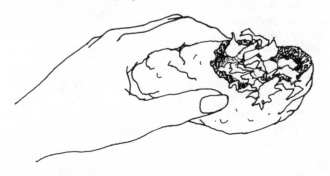

POCKET BREADS

These breads are an importation from the Near East, where they are eaten abundantly. They are white or whole or cracked wheat, essentially round, and can be partially split to form a pocket into which all sorts of good things can be crammed, making a wonderful no-drip sandwich.

To acquire pocket breads used to be quite chancy. For instance, living in Manhattan, getting hold of pita—as they are most often called—required a safari into the wilds of Brooklyn, to an Arabic neighborhood. Then all of a sudden pocket breads began to turn up in supermarkets, in plastic bags, and we've all been able to enjoy them ever since.

POISSON: see page 453

POLENTA: see page 453

POLLO: see page 453

POLYUNSATURATED FATS: see FATS

POMEGRANATES: see EXOTIC FRUIT

POMPANO: see FISH

PONT L'EVEQUE: see CHEESE

POONA: see CHEESE

POPCORN

Not all corn will pop, but when you've popped the variety reserved especially for this delicacy, you have made a snack worthy of kings and princes. The smell of hot buttered popcorn is almost better than the taste. Unfortunately, like peanuts, popcorn is a nobody-can-eat-only-one food. True aficionados, taking in the movies, can finish their first bag before the coming attractions have finished, and must go back for a second supply to carry them through the main feature.

There's nothing new about popcorn. Some early arrivals in this country found native Americans both using it as a food and wearing it as a decoration.

Favorite dressing for popcorn is melted butter and salt. But the kernels can be sprinkled with cheese, mixed with caramel or a melted marshmallow mixture. And if you don't eat it, string popcorn as one of the trimmings for a truly old-fashioned Christmas tree. Final idea—if you are going to mail or otherwise ship any kind of delicate object any distance, pack it in liberal amounts of popcorn. It's safer than any other packing. See also CORN.

POPOVER: see page 453

POPPY SEEDS: see SEEDS

PORC: see page 453

PORK

Unfortunately, most of the butcher-shop or meat-counter customers who buy pork think in terms of BACON and pork loin, the latter as either chops or roasts. But a hog is by no means all pork chops. There are pork steaks and pork tenderloins. There are fresh leg and shoulder of pork (often also sold cured and/or smoked, as hams and picnics; see HAM), which make great family-size roasts. There are pork cube steaks and blade steaks and chops and arm steaks, pork for stew and ground pork. There are spareribs—both the meatier country-style kind and the succulent regular ribs—which should be by no means confined to a cookout. There are pork hocks and pigs' feet and neck bones and liver for savory low-budget meals. And there are little pork sausages and sausage roll for patties. You can feed your family several delectable pork meals a week and not run out of ideas.

If you're thinking that pork is hard to digest, forget it. That's another old wives' tale with no foundation in fact. Nor is pork excessively calorie laden. Today's porkers are raised to be less fat-burdened than yesterday's portly hogs.

Shopping for pork. All pork is federally inspected for wholesomeness—you can be sure that the animal was slaughtered and processed under sanitary conditions. Pork is not graded as beef is—that is, not as Prime, Choice, and so on. It is graded 1, 2, 3, and 4, but you will not find these grade numbers on the retail cuts you buy.

In common with beef, lamb, and veal, the ICMISC (the Industrywide Cooperative Meat Identification Standards Committee) has come up with a list of recommended standard names for pork cuts. (For a detailed discussion see BEEF.) It is their hope that retailers will follow these guidelines and that consumers will learn them, so that the home cook will always know what she is buying through consistent labeling.

Below are the primal (wholesale carcass) cuts and the recommended retail names.

PRIMAL CUT: FRESH PORK SHOULDER

common name	recommended name
new york style shoulder fresh shoulder fresh pork shoulder	PORK SHOULDER WHOLE
new york style shoulder bnls fresh shoulder bnls fresh pork shoulder bnls	PORK SHOULDER RST BONELESS
fresh picnic picnic whole fresh picnic pork picnic shoulder	PORK SHOULDER ARM PICNIC
boneless fresh picnic butt half picnic bnls fresh pork picnic roast fresh picnic bnls	PORK SHOULDER ARM PICNIC BNLS

common name	recommended name
pork arm roast fresh pork arm roast	PORK SHOULDER ARM ROAST
arm steak picnic steak fresh picnic steak	PORK SHOULDER ARM STEAK
fresh pork butt pork boston shoulder pork butt roast pork boston butt roast boston style butt	PORK SHOULDER BLADE BOSTON ROAST
boneless pork butt pork boston shoulder bnls boneless pork butt roast bnls rolled butt roast bnls boston roast	PORK SHOULDER BLADE BOSTON RST BNLS
blade pork steak pork loin 7-rib cut pork steak	PORK SHOULDER BLADE STEAK
boneless porklets porklets pork cube steak (cubed steaks are made from any boneless pieces of pork, put through a cubing machine)	PORK CUBED STEAK
boneless cubed pork pork cubes	PORK CUBES FOR KABOBS
fresh hock pork hock pork shank fresh pork hock	PORK HOCK

PRIMAL CUT: FRESH PORK LOIN

common name	recommended name
pork loin 7-rib roast pork loin 5-rib roast rib end roast rib pork roast pork loin rib end	PORK LOIN BLADE ROAST
blade pork chops pork loin blade steaks pork chops end cut	PORK LOIN BLADE CHOPS
country-style spareribs country ribs blade end country spareribs	PORK LOIN COUNTRY-STYLE RIBS
pork backribs loin backribs country back bones pork ribs for barbecue	PORK LOIN BACK RIBS

Pork Chart

Retail Cuts of Pork—Where They Come from and How to Cook Them

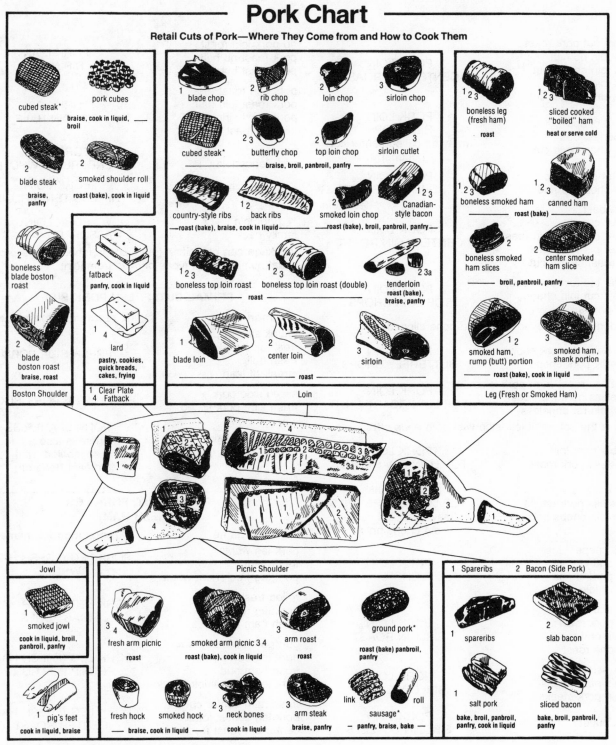

cubed steak*   pork cubes

braise, cook in liquid, broil

blade steak   smoked shoulder roll

braise, panfry   roast (bake), cook in liquid

boneless blade boston roast

blade boston roast
braise, roast

Boston Shoulder

fatback
panfry, cook in liquid

lard
pastry, cookies, quick breads, cakes, frying

1 Clear Plate
4 Fatback

blade chop   rib chop   loin chop   sirloin chop

cubed steak*   butterfly chop   top loin chop   sirloin cutlet

braise, broil, panbroil, panfry

country-style ribs   back ribs   smoked loin chop   Canadian-style bacon

roast (bake), braise, cook in liquid   roast (bake), broil, panbroil, panfry

boneless top loin roast   boneless top loin roast (double)   tenderloin
roast (bake), braise, panfry

roast

blade loin   center loin   sirloin

roast

Loin

boneless leg (fresh ham)   sliced cooked "boiled" ham
roast   heat or serve cold

boneless smoked ham   canned ham
roast (bake)

boneless smoked ham slices   center smoked ham slice
broil, panbroil, panfry

smoked ham, rump (butt) portion   smoked ham, shank portion
roast (bake), cook in liquid

Leg (Fresh or Smoked Ham)

Jowl

smoked jowl
cook in liquid, broil, panbroil, panfry

pig's feet
cook in liquid, braise

Picnic Shoulder

fresh arm picnic   smoked arm picnic 3 4   arm roast   ground pork*
roast   roast (bake), cook in liquid   roast   roast (bake) panbroil, panfry

fresh hock   smoked hock   neck bones   arm steak   link   roll   sausage*
braise, cook in liquid   cook in liquid   braise, panfry   panfry, braise, bake

1 Spareribs   2 Bacon (Side Pork)

spareribs   slab bacon

salt pork   sliced bacon
bake, broil, panbroil, panfry, cook in liquid   bake, broil, panbroil, panfry

*May be made from Boston shoulder, picnic shoulder, loin, or leg

501

center cut pork roast pork loin rib half pork loin center cut pork loin roast loin roast center cut	PORK LOIN CENTER RIB ROAST	rib pork loin roast pork roast rib half pork roast blade half	PORK LOIN RIB HALF
rib cut chops rib pork chops pork chops end cut	PORK LOIN RIB CHOPS (may be called center cut chops)	pork loin roast pork roast loin half pork roast sirloin half loin cut roast	PORK LOIN SIRLOIN HALF
pocket pork chops pork chops stuffed	PORK LOIN RIB CHOPS FOR STUFFING	pork tender pork tenderloin	PORK LOIN TENDERLOIN WHOLE
pork roast center cut center cut pork loin roast center cut loin roast loin roast center cut	PORK LOIN CENTER LOIN ROAST	pork tipless tenderloin	PORK LOIN TIPLESS TENDERLOIN

center cut loin pork chops
center cut loin chops   PORK LOIN
strip chops   TOP LOIN CHOPS

(tenderloin is removed and chine bone clipped)

¼ pork loin   PORK LOIN
family pack   ASSORTED CHOPS

(package can contain 7 to 11 chops, should have proportional number of all types derived from loin)

bnls butterfly pork chops   PORK LOIN
butterfly pork chops   BUTTERFLY CHOPS

PRIMAL CUT: FRESH PORK SIDE

common name	recommended name
chunk side of pork fresh side pork fresh belly streak of lean	FRESH SIDE PORK
sliced side pork fresh side pork sliced	FRESH SIDE PORK SLICED
fresh spareribs pork spareribs fresh	PORK SPARERIBS (there is also a cut, so labeled, with breast bone off)

boneless roast from pork loin
boneless pork loin roast   PORK LOIN
pork loin rst boneless   TOP LOIN ROAST BNLS

(this is the boneless loin strip with both ends off)

double pork loin   PORK LOIN
boneless pork roast   TOP LOIN ROAST BNLS

boneless pork chops   PORK LOIN
strip loin chops bnls   TOP LOIN CHOPS BNLS
     (may be called center
     cut chops bnls)

PRIMAL CUT: PORK LEG
(FRESH HAM)

common name	recommended name
pork leg whole fresh ham pork leg fresh ham whole	PORK LEG (FRESH HAM) WHOLE
rolled fresh ham pork leg roast bnls fresh ham boneless	PORK LEG (FRESH HAM) ROAST BNLS
butt portion fresh ham pork leg butt portion fresh ham butt pork leg roast sirloin portion	PORK LEG (FRESH HAM) RUMP PORTION
fresh ham center cut roast pork leg center roast center cut roast fresh ham	PORK LEG (FRESH HAM) CENTER ROAST

pork chops
loin end chops   PORK LOIN
loin pork chops   CHOPS
center loin chops

loin end roast
loin pork roast   PORK LOIN
sirloin end roast   SIRLOIN ROAST
hipbone roast

pork sirloin chops
sirloin pork chops   PORK LOIN
sirloin pork steaks   SIRLOIN CHOPS

pork cutlets   PORK LOIN
     SIRLOIN CUTLETS

fresh ham center slices
center fresh ham slices
fresh pork leg steak
leg of pork steak
fresh ham center cut

PORK LEG (FRESH HAM)
CENTER SLICE

pork leg shank portion
fresh ham shank portion
pork leg roast shank portion

PORK LEG (FRESH HAM)
SHANK PORTION

butt half fresh ham
pork leg sirloin half
pork leg roast sirloin half
fresh ham butt half

PORK LEG (FRESH HAM)
RUMP HALF

shank half fresh ham
pork leg shank half
pork leg roast sirloin half
fresh ham shank half

PORK LEG (FRESH HAM)
SHANK HALF

pork tenderettes
fresh ham cube steak
pork cube steak
porklets

PORK CUBED STEAK

Dividing up the wholesale pork. When they talk about "going whole hog," it is not the meat counter they have in mind. There's a great deal of the whole hog that never gets that far.

Suppose the hog weighs 210 pounds. When butchered and dressed, 60 pounds of that weight have been lost in skin and other waste and trimmings, leaving a 150-pound carcass to go to market. But when that carcass is divided into retail cuts, 30 additional pounds are lost to fat (rendered into lard), bones, and other waste, leaving salable retail cuts totalling 120 pounds. Even so, another 16.8 pounds of that getting-smaller total goes for the lesser cuts such as jowl, feet, tail, neckbones, and trimmings to be used in sausage. And a whopping 23.7 pounds of that "salable retail cuts" carcass is fat to be rendered for lard.

Bringing home the bacon and all the rest. The lean meat of young pork is grayish-pink, that of older animals a delicate rose color. The lean meat of both is fine-grained, firm, nicely marbled, and surrounded by firm white fat. Bones are porous and pinkish.

how to store: Pork should be stored in the coldest part of the refrigerator, where the temperature falls just short of freezing. Plan on keeping fresh pork no more than 2 days before you cook it—it is the most perishable of the meats. Store in its wrappings if the meat was prepackaged, loosely in wax paper or foil if not. Cooked pork should be wrapped or covered and refrigerated in the coldest area up to 3 days. To calculate the number of servings, count on ⅓ pound per serving for boneless cuts, ½ pound for cuts with a moderate

amount of bone, and 1 pound per serving for cuts heavy with bone.

nutritive value: Pork contains all the "perfect" amino acids that are necessary for body building and repair, as do other kinds in the meat category of the four food groups essential to a well-balanced diet. It is also rich in the B vitamins. Pork contains no carbohydrates, no vitamins A and C. In available space, it's impossible to give nutritive values for all the many pork cuts, but consider a 3-ounce serving of roasted fresh ham, trimmed of visible fat, as an example. Such a serving contains 184 calories, and yields these essential nutrients:

protein	25.2 grams
fat	8.5 grams
calcium	11 milligrams
phosphorus	262 milligrams
iron	3.2 milligrams
sodium	62 milligrams
potassium	282 milligrams
thiamin	.52 milligram
riboflavin	.25 milligram
niacin	4.8 milligrams

Pork, ounce for ounce, is the food richest in the B vitamin niacin, and it is also a good source of iron.

Freezing and thawing pork. Freeze fresh pork from the market as soon and as rapidly as possible, properly wrapped, labeled, and dated for freezing. Before you put it in the freezer, cut into portion or recipe sizes, separating chops and ground-pork patties from one another so that they can be easily parted while still frozen. Wrap well, pressing out all air. Roasts, chops, and patties can be cooked from the frozen state, provided you allow sufficient time for thorough cooking, bearing in mind that pork must never be served in any condition other than well done. Store pork in the freezer at 0° or lower up to 9 months—pork does not keep for as long a time as other frozen meats; the fat tends to turn rancid after that maximum 9-month period.

Thaw pork in its original wrapper in the refrigerator, never at room temperature. A roast will take somewhere between 12 and 24 hours, smaller pieces a proportionately shorter time.

Cooking pork. Present-day pork has been bred to have less fat and to be cooked to an internal temperature of 170°F. rather than the 185° that used to be recommended—at this new temperature it is safe, juicier, and more flavorful. Also, less cooking time means less shrinkage. Insert the thermometer into the meat in the thickest part of the flesh, but well away from the bone. If you do not use a thermometer, allow 25 minutes per pound, plus an additional 25 minutes, all at an oven temperature of 350°F. Meat cooked by methods other than roasting is done when it is completely fork-tender.

Some perfect partners. Pork and fruit have carried on so long-lived a love affair it's practically a scandal. Pork and oranges. Pork and plums. Pork and apples. Pork and cranberries. Pork partners beautifully with sauces, jellies, herbs and spices and seeds, as well as applesauce (a good dash of cinnamon won't hurt a bit), cranberry or cranberry-orange or cranberry-raisin-walnut relish, cranberry or orange or currant jelly, curry, sage, caraway, anise, ginger, chili. And onions and garlic—pork's richly good flavor can take a lot of either, or of the two in combination.

Fill a crown roast of pork or a pork loin—either between individual chops or between the loin meat (it's easy to cut a pocket) and the ribs with a savory stuffing. Or heap individual chops or chops with a pocket cut in them with a stuffing, too —perhaps one boasting a liberal helping of chopped peanuts. Barbecue spareribs with a tomato-onion-molasses baste for an unbeatable treat.

Because pork gravy is so good, plan on something— mashed or riced potatoes, a simple pilaf, plain or caraway noodles, yams or sweet potatoes—that will complement it. And serve a vegetable that is particularly pork-happy, such as parsnips, sauerkraut, lightly panned cabbage, glazed onions or creamed onions and peas, egg-sauced creamed spinach, carrots in the Vichy style, turnips and rutabagas. Coleslaw makes a good pork go-with salad, so does carrot-and-raisin-and-nut, so does regular waldorf or pear-pecan waldorf. Apple or pumpkin desserts are particularly appropriate—but not if you've served apples or yams in the main part of the meal.

However and whenever you serve pork, count on it for high nutritional value and a warm welcome from family and guests. See also GROUND MEATS, LARD, MOCK CHICKEN LEGS, and PIGS' FEET.

PORK SAUSAGES: see SAUSAGES

PORT DU SALUT: see CHEESE

PORTERHOUSE: see BEEF

POT CHEESE: see CHEESE

POT ROAST: see page 450

POTASSIUM: see special feature: NUTRITION NOTEBOOK

POTATO CHIPS: see CHIPS

POTATO FLOUR: see FLOUR

POTATO SALADS: see SALADS

POTATOES

As a nice change of pace, nobody claims that the potato was the "apple" with which Eve tempted Adam in the Garden of Eden. But the potato has something in common with the apple: an average boiled potato, skin and all, contains no more calories than the average raw apple, which appears regularly on weight-loss diet menus. Something to think about—something to salivate over if you're a pudgy potato lover.

There are very few of us who don't like potatoes. And they have a lot going for them. They're always, in spite of fluctuations in prices, a low-cost food item. And a nutritionally sound one. A dollar spent on potatoes provides more thiamin than a dollar spent on any other food. Potatoes are second (after citrus fruits) in vitamin C—ascorbic acid—second in niacin, and second in iron for every food dollar spent.

Kinds and classifications. There are two types of potatoes, mealy and waxy, and the home potato cook should learn which type is best for the purpose she has in mind. Mealy potatoes cook up fluffy and light. Use them for baking and mashing and frying. Use waxy potatoes where you wish them to hold their shape—sliced, diced, cubed, as in casseroles and scalloped potatoes, or for boiling whole. They mash badly and fry poorly.

Potatoes of four kinds are available:

- *russets* are the big, long ovals with a somewhat rough, netted-appearing surface; bake these, or use for french frying—they are mealy (Idaho or Maine)
- all-purpose *whites* can be long or round, waxy or mealy or in-between; some are for baking, some for other uses, and only trial and error will make you potato-wise about the local types in your area (Eastern, Long Island)
- *red* potatoes may be long or round, but all are waxy; use for boiling and in salads
- *new* potatoes are "new" because they are shipped from field to market directly after being dug, with no storage period in between; usually waxy, use them in salads, or cook and serve whole, unpeeled

Whenever you can, serve potatoes with their jackets still in place, and encourage your family to eat the skins—nutrients lurk there, and the skins provide diet-necessary fiber.

POTATOES IN YOUR KITCHEN

Some families feel that a meal is not a meal without potatoes. To others, potatoes are sometimes things, appearing on the table only now and again. The first probably are suffering from lack of variety, and need such things as rice, pasta, grits, or groats to relieve the monotony. The second are missing a lot of tasty, wholesome, budget-easy eating.

how to buy: To calculate servings: 3 medium baking potatoes = 1 pound; 1 pound potatoes = 4 servings mashed, 4 to 5 servings french fried, 2 cups cubes or slices. Choose potatoes that are reasonably clean, that are firm and smooth, with regular shape so there won't be too much lost in peeling. Avoid those with wilted, wrinkled skin, soft dark areas, cuts in the skin, and those that have begun to sprout. Never buy potatoes with a green tinge—they may be bitter, and some people are allergic to the chemical that produces the green color.

how to store: Potatoes should not be refrigerated. On the other hand, their best keeping temperature is between 45 and 50 degrees, and few of our kitchens are that cold. Store in the coolest possible place—a sheltered but unheated back entryway is ideal. If you have no such storage place, don't buy more potatoes than you'll use in a week's time. Avoid long exposure to light—that's what gives them the green tinge.

nutritive value: Low in sodium, virtually fat free, easy to digest, potatoes are acceptable in almost any diet. One long-shaped potato whose dimensions are about 2½ inches in diameter and 4¾ inches in length contains 146 calories; one round potato 2½ inches in diameter contains 88 calories. As well, potatoes of these dimensions, peeled and boiled, yield:

	long	round	
protein	4.3	2.6	grams
fat	.2	.1	gram
carbohydrate	32.6	19.6	grams
calcium	14	8	milligrams
phosphorus	95	57	milligrams
iron	1.1	.7	milligrams
sodium	5	3	milligrams
potassium	641	385	milligrams
thiamin	.20	.12	milligram
riboflavin	.08	.05	milligram
niacin	2.7	1.6	milligrams
vitamin A	trace	trace	international units

Tips on preparing, cooking. Scrub the vegetable gently under running water with a vegetable brush or kitchen sponge. Leave the skins on if you can; if you peel, use a swivel-blade vegetable parer to remove the thinnest possible amount of the skin. Peeled potatoes turn dark if not cooked immediately; put the pieces, as you peel them, into the water you will use for cooking. Cooked whole, potatoes retain maximum nutrients; however, if a shorter cooking time is wanted or if the recipe you are using requires it, slice, dice, or cube the potatoes.

- to *boil,* use a heavy saucepan with a tight-fitting lid; cook in about 1 inch of (salted) water until tender, which should be 35 to 40 minutes for whole potatoes, 20 to 25 minutes for cut-up ones
- to *steam* (an excellent method of cooking potatoes), place a wire rack in the bottom of a kettle or large saucepan, add water to just below the level of the rack; bring to a boil, add potatoes, cook tightly covered until tender, which should take 30 to 45 minutes for whole potatoes, 20 to 30 for cut-up ones; if a rack is not available, improvise with crumpled foil in the bottom of the pan
- to *rice,* prepare boiled or steamed potatoes, drain and peel; force through a vegetable ricer or food mill; toss with melted butter before or after ricing, and season to taste
- to *mash,* prepare boiled or steamed potatoes, drain and peel; using a potato masher, electric mixer, or ricer, mash potatoes; gradually add heated milk, salt and white pepper to taste, and butter if you wish; beat until potatoes are smooth and fluffy
- to *pan roast,* prepare boiled or steamed potatoes, but cook only 10 minutes, drain and peel; arrange in a shallow baking pan, brush with melted butter or salad oil; bake, uncovered, at 400°F., about 45 minutes, or until fork-tender, turning occasionally; or arrange around meat in roasting pan, turn and baste with meat drippings frequently
- to *bake,* use an oven temperature of 400° F. if you are not baking anything else, but if you have another dish to bake, potatoes will tolerate any temperature from 325 to 450—simply adjust the time to suit (at 400 the time should be about 45 minutes); pierce each potato several times with the tines of a fork before baking, to allow steam to escape and ensure that the potatoes won't burst; do not wrap in foil—that steams them, instead of baking
- to *fry,* cut potatoes into thin finger shapes and toss into a bowl of ice and water as you cut, then dry them on absorbent paper; meanwhile, heat about 4 inches of cooking oil to 385 to 390°F. in a deep fryer or large, heavy saucepan; place a layer of potato strips in a wire basket or a few at a time directly into the oil and cook until golden and tender, about 5 minutes; drain on absorbent paper, salt lightly, and keep warm in a low oven; leftover boiled or steamed or baked potatoes may be fried in a small amount of hot butter (add onion if you wish) for a second-time-around dish

Freezing potatoes. Don't do it—it doesn't work in home freezers. True, there are many potato dishes in the freezer at the market, but these are frozen by means not possible at home. Some precooked potato dishes can be frozen at home, but they will not be as good as when you add the potatoes just before serving.

Other ways, other forms. There are many kinds of ready-to-eat or easy-to-fix potato dishes in your market.

on grocery shelves, in cans or packages: Precooked potatoes, slices or small whole, in cans; potato chips, plain or flavored, in bags or tubes; dry flakes or granules to turn into mashed potatoes, in packages; packaged potato side dishes with all the trimmings included—au gratin, with sour cream and chives, and such—to which you add water, sometimes butter, before baking.

in grocery frozen-food section: Heat-and-serve baked potatoes with cheese or sour cream and chives; heat-and-serve or cook-and-serve french fries, hashed browns, potatoes o'brien, shoestrings, country-style or cottage-style fries; potatoes with other vegetables in bags of frozen for-stew and for-soup ingredients; potatoes in other combination dishes, such as beef or chicken pies; scalloped and au gratin potatoes ready to bake.

Some perfect partners. It's easier to list what doesn't go with potatoes than what does. Little new potatoes creamed with fresh new peas is a treat. Potatoes scalloped with ham makes a hearty winter meal. So does peasanty potato soup, with bacon and lots of onions. Bake potatoes in the oven along with meat loaf and serve both with a good tomato sauce. Have mashed or riced potatoes whenever the meat of the meal produces gravy, then use the leftovers to make potato cakes for another meal. Pan roast potatoes with leg or shoulder of lamb. Dress up a simple meal of hamburgers or wieners with a pan of potatoes au gratin. For Sunday brunch, make a farmer's omelet—diced boiled potatoes, bacon or slivered ham, and onions, scrambled with eggs. Find cookbook recipes for offbeat ways to use up leftover mashed potatoes—delectable biscuits, old-fashioned potato doughnuts, potato bread, steamed potato pudding with citrus sauce, and many more.

A long time, a lot of potatoes. The Incas of Peru were cultivating potatoes by 200 B.C. Unlike many other foods the Spanish explorers carried back to Europe, potatoes were not welcomed—indeed, in many places they were considered totally unacceptable. Because they were not mentioned in the Bible, some said, potatoes were unfit for human consumption. They were the cause of all sorts of dread diseases, others claimed.

But time took care of that problem, as it does with so many things, and potatoes became universally accepted, a major part of the diet of many peoples worldwide. See also SWEET POTATOES and YAMS.

POTPIES

Savory main-dish pies, with two crusts or only a top one, potpies are made of cut-up meat, poultry, or fish, with a sauce or gravy, and usually with vegetables.

There are several kinds of individual-serving potpies in your market's freezer. And if you have leftover roast or poultry, plus gravy, making potpies—individuals or one large one—to stash in the freezer is a good way to use them up. Add vegetables (but not potatoes) and top with a crust—thawed and rolled-out frozen pattycases are great for this purpose.

POTS, PANS: see special features: THE HOME COOK'S NEW MATH and YOU CAN'T WORK WITHOUT TOOLS

POULTRY: see CHICKEN, CORNISH GAME HEN, DUCK, SQUAB, and TURKEY

POULTRY SEASONING: see SPICES

POUND, TO: see page 448

POUND CAKES: see CAKES

POWDERED MILK: see MILK

POWDERED SUGAR: see SUGAR

PRAIRIE CHICKEN: see GAME

PRALINE

A cookie-size, cookie-shape confection made famous in the French Quarter of New Orleans. It is rich with brown sugar, butter, and cream, studded with pecans, and tastes like more.

PRAWNS

A kind of shellfish, kin to shrimp. Although you may find prawns on menus, in this country they are likely to be simply very large shrimp—prawns are not widely available here. Those of the British Isles, particularly Ireland, are famous. See SHELLFISH.

PREHEAT, TO: see page 448

PREPARED HORSERADISH

Usually bottled, found in the dairy case, prepared horseradish is a combination of ground horseradish root and white vinegar. Refrigerate it at home, too. The flavor is very hot when fresh; it gradually loses its oomph as it grows older. Some prepared horseradish has grated beets added, turning it a rosy red. Find dried ground horseradish on the spice shelves at the market, to be mixed at home. (This is not in wide distribution.)

PREPARED MUSTARD

Most often in glass jars but sometimes in chubby little pottery ones, prepared mustard is made of ground mustard seeds.

It may be bright yellow or dark brown or any number of in-between shades. Vinegar, white wine, and various spices give distinction to the many brands, and the flavor can range from very hot to quite mild.

It is a must on many kinds of sandwiches (where would a hot dog be without mustard—they'd have to call the ball game!). Mustard is also used as a condiment with several kinds of meat and as a component in sauces.

PRESERVATIVES: see ADDITIVES AND PRESERVATIVES

PRESERVE, PRESERVING: see special feature: PUTTING FOOD BY

PRESSURE COOK, TO: see page 450

PRETZELS

If you have ever eaten your way through the Pennsylvania Dutch country—a not-to-be-missed gustatory experience—you know how attached those wonderful people are to pretzels. They are everywhere: soft ones and hard, mammoth to miniscule, plain and rough salted and—honest!—chocolate- or butterscotch-dipped.

Pretzels are fine for snacking, a great addition to the cocktail hour collection of nibbles. Your supermarket will have them in several sizes and shapes, ready to serve. In New York City and environs and in a few other areas, hot soft pretzels are sold by street vendors.

PRICK, TO: see page 448

PRICKLY PEARS: see EXOTIC FRUIT

PRIME, PRIME RIBS: see BEEF

PRIMOST: see CHEESE

PROCESS CHEESE, PROCESS CHEESE FOOD: see CHEESE

PROCESSING FOOD: see FOOD PROCESSING

PROOF, TO: see page 448

PROSCIUTTO

A kind of Italian HAM, cured, air-dried, spiced. Its flavor is delicious, but it can be overpowering—serve sliced very thin. Wonderful as an appetizer with melon, figs, pears, or peaches.

PROTEIN: see MILK, TEXTURED PLANT PROTEIN, and the special feature: NUTRITION NOTEBOOK

PROVOLONE: see CHEESE

PRUNES, PRUNE JUICE

Prunes are dried plums—a special prune-plum variety that has the remarkable property of drying without fermenting.

The dried fruit is available in boxes for home preparation (very simple—follow the label) or in jars, ready-prepared, for nonkitchen types. One pound of dried prunes yields 4 cups cooked prunes with pits, 3 cups pitted.

Prune juice, available bottled or canned, is the liquid obtained when the prunes are cooked. Both prunes and the juice have a considerable laxative property.

PUDDINGS AND CUSTARDS

When we say "pudding" we think first of dessert, but there are savory puddings and savory custards, too. Some are main dishes, some side dishes; all add delectable variety to meals.

Pudding patterns. One of the simple ways to classify puddings—aside from whether they are sweet or savory—is by the way they are cooked.

steamed puddings: These are cooked (often in a decorative mold) on a rack over boiling water, a process that generally requires several hours. Steamed puddings have a firm texture, rather like cake, and many can be turned out of the mold whole to be admired by diners before they are served. Many savory and almost all sweet steamed puddings are served with a sauce. Examples are Christmas plum pudding, cheese-corn pudding, steamed chocolate pudding.

baked puddings: These cook in the oven, generally in a considerably shorter time than a steamed pudding requires. They may be either firm or soft in texture, but few are firm enough to turn out as a mold. Examples are spoon bread, yorkshire pudding to serve with roast beef, blueberry cottage pudding, bread pudding, rice pudding.

Another baked sweet is the pudding cake. For this, a cakelike batter is spread in the baking pan and sprinkled with a dry mixture. Then hot water is poured over (but not stirred in) and the pudding is baked. Done, it forms into two layers —a cakelike, but very moist one, plus a sauce. Favorites are chocolate and lemon.

stovetop puddings: These are cooked either in a heavy saucepan or a double boiler. They include those thickened with egg and cornstarch, and tapioca puddings. They may be chocolate, vanilla, or butterscotch flavored, and tapioca puddings are often made with fruit. All are soft, sweet, and must be spooned into individual dishes for serving.

refrigerator puddings: These are made of layers of split ladyfingers or thin-sliced pound or sponge or angel food cake with a custard or whipped cream filling, sometimes gelatin-stiffened. They require 8 hours or more in the refrigerator to mellow and thicken. Some can be turned out, others must be dished. Chocolate and various fruit and berry flavors are favorites. Bavarians and spanish creams—without the cake— fall into this category, too.

convenience puddings: These are of two kinds, those that

must be cooked and those that are simply beaten with liquid, requiring no cooking. All are sweet. To-cook varieties include old standby vanilla, chocolate, lemon, and butterscotch, and some specials such as butter pecan, pistachio, coconut cream, banana cream. Instant puddings have less body than the to-be-cooked ones; they come in roughly the same spectrum of flavors. A good cookbook will give you many convenience pudding variation recipes. Other convenience puddings are junket—to be mixed with warm milk—and various fruit-flavored gelatins, to be dissolved in hot water, then refrigerated until thickened.

Custards and their relatives. Custards can also be either sweet or savory, can be baked in the oven or stovetop-cooked in either a heavy saucepan or a double boiler.

baked custards: Most of the savory ones are vegetable based, such as corn custard, the other ingredients being milk and eggs and appropriate seasonings. Sweet custards are combinations of milk, eggs, sugar, flavored with—usually—vanilla and/or nutmeg. Some of these are made with the yolks of the eggs only (freeze the whites for later use), which results in a somewhat firmer, more dense custard, and some with evaporated milk, which gives an excellent consistency. To tell when a baked custard is done, test it with the blade of a table knife halfway between the center and the edge—if the blade comes out clean, the custard can be removed from the oven even if the center looks a bit shaky; it will finish cooking as it cools.

Custard may be baked in one several-servings dish or in individual custard cups. In either case, the baking dish(es) are set in a pan of hot water for the cooking period.

A delicious version of such custard is crème brulée—baked custard that is, after baking, sprinkled with brown sugar and run under the broiler. Keep an eye on it—it burns very readily.

stovetop custards: These are flour (or cornstarch)-sugar-milk mixtures, cooked until thickened and bubbly. Then a portion of the mixture is stirred into beaten eggs, and the eggs added to the cooked mixture. The custard continues to cook until it is thickened once more, but must not be allowed to boil after the eggs are added. "Soft" or English custard, or custard sauce, is a much less thick version, which is cooked only until the mixture coats a metal spoon.

See also BAVARIAN CREAM, GELATIN, HASTY PUDDING, INDIAN PUDDING, JUNKET, and YORKSHIRE PUDDING.

PUFF PASTE: see PASTRY

PUFFED CEREALS: see CEREALS

PUMPKIN

Pumpkin is so good, it ought not to be reserved only for jack o'lanterns and Thanksgiving pies.

The pumpkin is a gourd, close kin to cucumbers and squash. Native Americans were using pumpkins when the first settlers arrived, and generously shared this good food, as well as the seeds and cultivation instructions, with the newcomers. In New England, the first pumpkin "pie" was made by cutting off the top of a pumpkin, taking out the seeds, filling the cavity with milk, spices, and a natural sweetener such as maple syrup or honey, then baking the whole thing. Sounds pretty good.

Fresh pumpkins are available in the fall and into the winter; canned pumpkin may be had the year around. Frozen pumpkin pies, for noncooks, can be found in the market's frozen food case and, of course, bakeries make the pies, especially around the holidays.

But pie is only the beginning. Consult a good cookbook and try pumpkin custard, pumpkin soup, savory pumpkin soufflé, pumpkin pound cake, pumpkin bread and rolls, pumpkin chiffon cake, pumpkin ice cream, pumpkin spice cookies, gingered pumpkin waffles, and a dozen more.

A word about fresh pumpkin. If you're a back-to-nature freak, by all means try fresh pumpkin. Choose pumpkins that are bright orange, heavy for their size, and without blemish. Small ones are more tender than the giants. Boil or bake, then mash or whirl in the blender to produce the pumpkin purée most recipes call for.

Cautionary note. Fresh pumpkins may be stringy, too strong of flavor or almost flavorless. Unless you're dead set on experimenting, use the canned variety—one of the few foods better canned than fresh. But unless you're not much of a cook, buy the purée rather then the ready-to-bake pumpkin pie mix, and flavor your pie to your own liking.

Although pumpkin itself is not high-calorie, some of the goodies we make from it are. Only 33 calories in 3½ ounces of pumpkin purée. Pumpkin seeds are another story—dried, roasted, and salted, 3½ ounces yields 553 calories.

PUMPKIN-PIE SPICE: see SPICES

PUNCH: see BEVERAGES

PUREE, TO: see page 448

PUTTING FOOD BY: see page 337

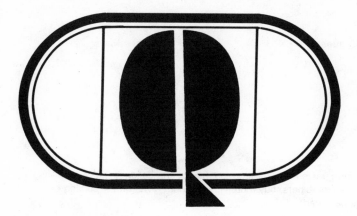

QUADRICCINI: see PASTA

QUAIL: see GAME

QUANTITY COOKERY

How do you feed a crowd—not just six extra people at Thanksgiving, but a *big* crowd? The youngsters of the graduating class, for instance, and their parents. A meet-your-candidate rally. The church couples' club. Wedding guests at the subsequent reception. How do you cope?

In the first place, despite the jokes about the disasters attendant on accomplishing anything by committee, you need a committee. Don't even for a moment consider attacking such a project solo. You'll be in deep trouble long before the big day arrives.

Getting things going. Well in advance of the date of the party—and this means weeks, not days—the committee should meet and decide:

1. on a menu
2. how to serve—at tables, or as a buffet
3. who is going to be responsible for what

the menu: Take the available facilities into consideration. If the function is to take place in a church hall or school with a fully equipped kitchen, you need be restrained only by your capabilities. But if the festivities are scheduled for a private home, the kitchen will have only one stovetop, two ovens at best and one at worst. These might be augmented by a couple of hot plates and a big electric roaster oven, but remember that space will be restricted, too—a lot of ladies madly cooking and bumping bottoms in a small area can be very nervous-making. Confine your menu largely to foods that can be made in other people's homes and carried to the party, where they will be served cold or must only be heated just before serving.

Remember, too, that hot foods turn into lukewarm ones all too readily. If the meal is a dinner, you're likely to be able to get everyone eating before the food cools, but if it's a come-and-go affair, such as a reception, most of the food—other than something to be served from a chafing dish—should be cold, and meant to be in that condition.

For a reception, the best menu is small, delicious sandwiches that are made elsewhere and carried to the party, plus champagne or champagne punch, a nonalcoholic punch for those who don't imbibe, plus wedding cake—which, if you want an elaborate one, you'll sensibly order from a good bakery. The groom's cake (usually fruitcake) could be home-made if there's a very good baker on the committee.

If you want to be a bit more fancy—and hearty—add to the menu a make-ahead, such as lobster newberg or curried chicken, kept warm in a chafing dish and served in small pastry cases or patty shells. Again, save yourselves work by ordering the cases or patty shells in advance from a good bakery. Same thing applies if you're going to use tiny french rolls for one of the kinds of sandwiches.

Even if it's a sit-down dinner and you have full kitchen facilities, as in a church, confine yourself to simple-but-good foods: a not-too-elaborate casserole, or roast turkey or (if the budget can stand it) ham or beef. Pot roast can be delightful, but choose to accompany it with easy-do buttered, poppy seed, or parslied noodles rather than, for example, dumplings, which must be made at the last minute and are difficult to turn out in large quantities.

For dessert: everybody likes ice cream, but everybody also serves it, and it does tend to melt into puddles if service isn't all that quick. Offer cake instead, two each made at home by the good bakers on the committee. Or fresh fruit in season with cheese or with made-ahead cookies, such as shortbread. Or coeur à la crème with fresh seasonal berries or peaches—another make-ahead. In between the two extremes, plan on frozen vegetables to save a lot of preparation time, good bread from a bakery or home-baked and frozen in advance by members, either a gelatin salad or mixed greens doused at the last minute with made-ahead dressing. Coffee can be set up early—most kitchen-equipped churches have large coffee makers.

If you're having potatoes, bake them—saves all that peeling and mashing wear and tear. On the tables put bowls of sour cream with chives and whipped butter, and let each diner dress his own.

how to serve: If it's an iffy decision, opt in favor of buffet. It is possible to get the food to the diners a little faster with table service, and if you have a bevy of teenage girls volunteering to be waitresses, go that way. But a buffet table is handsome, easy to arrange, and diners can choose what they want—a larger helping of this, only a little bit of that. For any kind of party other than a dinner, buffet service is the only solution. If you like, you can have someone at the buffet table —if it's large enough—or at another table, to dispense coffee and punch. Or tea, if this is an old-fashioned/back-in-style tea party.

food	quantity to feed 100 guests
BEVERAGES	
fruit juice	10 46-ounce cans
instant coffee	2 10-ounce jars
ground coffee	3 pounds
coffee cream	3 quarts
cube sugar	2½ pounds
granulated sugar	2 pounds
wine (3-ounce serving)	10 quarts (but unless the guests are wine-knowing, buy by the gallon or half gallon—jug wine; if the guests are wine-bibers, buy more—this amount gives only 1 serving each; there are 32 ounces per quart)
MAIN DISHES	
ground beef	35 pounds
bone-in ham	65 pounds
frankfurters	28 pounds (or count them individually, allowing for seconds in some cases)
chickens, turkeys	80 to 85 pounds
beef (roasts, pot roasts, boneless)	30 pounds (¼-pound servings plus some extras)
VEGETABLES	10 2½-pound packages or 40 10-ounce packages
SALAD MAKINGS	
hearts of lettuce	30 medium heads
lettuce leaves	15 medium heads
salad dressing (french or other thin type)	12 cups (3 quarts)
potato salad	3½ gallons
STARCHES	
spaghetti, noodles	17 pounds
regular rice	11 pounds
quick-cooking rice	7 to 8 28-ounce packages
potatoes	count by the piece—anywhere from 100 big (baking) potatoes to 300 (small new) ones
CONDIMENTS AND RELISHES	
cranberry sauce	15 1-pound cans
spiced apple rings	20 1-pound jars
olives and pickles	5 quarts
mustard	2½ quarts
catsup	7 to 8 14-ounce bottles
BREADS	
french bread	8 18-inch loaves
rolls	10 dozen—that's 1 roll each plus 2 dozen extra
butter or margarine	4 pounds (unless you buy it "hotel cut," in which case there are 92—rather meager—pats per pound)
DESSERT	
ice cream	5 gallons or 22 1-quart bricks
cake	count by the piece—1 slice per person (100 slices) + 2 extra cakes
cookies	3 per serving (300—24½ dozen)
cupcakes	100 plus 2 dozen extras

who does what: Decide early—and write it all down—who will be responsible for each of the various aspects of the party. Someone—or two, at most—will have to do the shopping and ordering, if this is to be a dinner cooked mostly in such facilities as a church or school kitchen. Then there are the actual cooks, who will have to turn up early on the day of the event. Decide in advance which of those cooks will be responsible for each part of the menu, from start to finish. Even if the dinner is to be served buffet style, tables should be set in advance, with napkins and tableware, glasses, cups and saucers, and condiments—pickles, olives, relishes, sauces—in place. Don't forget the salt and pepper. If you are serving rolls, they can be buttered and heated and placed on the buffet table, or bread or hard rolls of a type that do not need heating can be on the table, along with butter. Liquids, from ice water to wine, should be placed on the tables just before the crowd is called to dinner. Diners can pick up their own dessert and coffee, or it can be served to them. In either case, tables must be cleared first.

Churches and schools generally have their own dishes, glasses, and flatware. If not, or for other parties taking place in less equipped circumstances, everything—including big tablecloths and napkins—can be rented.

For a wedding or anniversary reception or any kind of similar gathering where a full meal will not be served, tables other than the buffet are not required. Just be careful not to serve anything that can't be eaten with fingers, small forks, or food picks. You will, of course, need small plates, napkins, forks, cups and saucers if you're serving coffee or tea, and/or wine glasses or punch cups. And a decision will have to be made as to who will set the buffet table and keep the platters and trays supplied from the kitchen.

For a party to which members of the committee will bring most of the food, ready to serve, let each one do her own shopping, keeping track of her expenditures if this is a for-profit affair or if one person is going to bear all the costs.

If there is to be a centerpiece on the buffet table or on sit-down diners' tables, it should be decided who will buy, arrange, and put it (them) in place. The same is true of any other decorations there may be.

cautionary note: In all cases, let the food be suitable for the occasion. For a morning meet-your-candidate gathering, just coffee and coffeecake or danish pastries; for an afternoon one, just tea and coffee and plain cake. For a church or club dinner (unless it's a "gourmet dining" club), delicious, well-cooked food, but on the simple side—food that everyone will eat and enjoy. For a wedding or anniversary reception or the like, a certain elegance is in order in both the food and the way it is served.

How much will serve how many? It's all a matter of multiplication. Suppose you're going to serve soup in cups.

The usual soup or coffee cup holds 6 ounces, which is ¾ of the standard measuring cup. So you'll need, for 100 people, ¾ of 100 measuring cups, or 75 standard measuring cups of soup. That's a little more than 6 gallons.

That's all right for soup—nobody is likely to ask for seconds, and it would be served at the table, not buffet style, so no one will help himself to more than he should and mess up the calculations. But there are other considerations, other variables, for most foods. Men eat more than women, as a rule of thumb—if you are serving a men's club dinner, count on more food, larger helpings, than for a ladies' bridge tournament luncheon. If something irresistibly good is being served, such as homemade bread, allow two servings a person. Some will eat only one, but that will leave extras for the pig-of-himself who eats three or four.

The chart opposite gives you an idea of how much will have to be bought. These are for 100 people, and are sufficiently generous amounts to allow for some seconds. Don't forget to buy herbs, spices, or any special seasonings needed in cooking.

Some last words. In calculating amounts of food, don't forget the kitchen and dining room committees—they have to eat, too. And don't neglect cleanup. All those pots and pans (should be done while guests are eating), all those plates and glasses and cutlery and serving dishes must be washed. If at all possible, this should be a separate group that can attack the problem while the kitchen and dining room committees are eating.

Don't work too hard, and have a good party!

QUARK

For a delicious snack with a cup of coffee or tea (and a less calorie-laden one than cakes or pastries) try quark, served with thin-sliced whole wheat toast or french bread, and a selection of condiments to sprinkle on.

To make enough to serve 4, place 1 pint large-curd cottage cheese and ½ teaspoon salt in the blender. Process, starting and stopping often to push the cheese down into the blades, until the mixture is smooth and creamy.

As to the condiments, offer anything you like. Some suggestions: strawberry or seedless raspberry jam, thin-sliced scallions, and/or radishes, caraway or poppy seeds, alfalfa or bean sprouts, snipped chives or parsley, crumbled crisp bacon.

QUENELLES

Little egg-shaped dumplings, usually formed with two spoons, quenelles are made of fine-ground meat or fish or poultry, nicely seasoned. They are cooked by poaching gently in liquid—water, beef or chicken broth, or water/white wine.

QUICHES

A savory pie, with a bottom but not a top crust, a quiche can be made of any taste-great-together vegetables in a custardy egg-milk base, usually with grated cheese. To get you started, try onions (sauté until soft but not brown before placing them in the pastry shell) with jack cheese, tomatoes with cheddar and crumbled crisp bacon, mushrooms with gruyère, slivered ham and cooked, sliced leeks. There are dozens. See also ONIONS.

QUICK BREADS

These are called "quick" because they are relatively so, as compared with yeast-raised breads, which take several hours in the making and baking. Leavened with baking powder or soda, they range from all kinds of biscuits and muffins through nut breads and fruit breads to pancakes and waffles. See BISCUITS, BREADS, MUFFINS, PANCAKES, REFRIGERATED DOUGH, and WAFFLES.

QUINCES: see EXOTIC FRUIT

SAUCE SORCERY

Crowning glory of *haute cuisine,* the number, variety, and complications of the classic French sauces paralyze the mind and the creativity of the everyday cook—ah, but there are other ways!

In cooking—and this is true in many other disciplines, as well—the experts tend to make their subject so abstruse, to surround it with such an air of mystery, such an aura of complexity, and to couch their instructions in terms so circumlocutory and overabundant (rather like this sentence?) that ordinary mortals quail and take to their heels.

One of America's best cooks—and writers—in her first cookbook was apparently so fearful of being misunderstood that she fell into this trap. Each recipe ranged over page after page, offering instructions in minutest detail, so that directions for the most simple process made that process appear to be complicated beyond belief, certainly far beyond the capabilities of any but the most talented home cook. The result was to drive novices to despair of ever being able to boil water properly—and other good cooks to want to shake her until her teeth rattled. Fortunately, over the years (decades, by now) she has relaxed.

But for complication, she was a mere amateur compared to many of the great French chefs who, when they decide to set down their techniques, set them down in unimaginably involved detail, spelling out every possible variation and ramification. They are guilty in all culinary areas, but the urge to explicate truly overwhelms them when they reach those exquisite ornaments of their native cuisine, sauces.

Although the Russians may have invented all else that makes life worthwhile, France—to hear the chefs tell it—invented sauces. And to a great extent they're right. Until the heyday of French cooking began, assorted barbarians may have poured a little melted yak butter or berry juice over food and called it sauce, but it wasn't Sauce.

Of the subject, Antonin Carême—he who was called "the cook of kings and the king of cooks"—pointed out in his *L'Art de la Cuisine* that French sauces are the best it is possible to make, virtually the entire collection being of French invention with the exception of the few "gallicised" Italian, Dutch, and Russian ones. He adds: "Be assured that no foreign sauce is comparable to those of our great cuisine. I have made comparisons; I have visited England, Russia, Germany, and Italy, and I have met, everywhere, our cooks occupying the highest posts in foreign courts."

More mildly, *Larousse Gastronomique,* the bible of French cookery, points out that by the word "sauce" is meant in a general way "every kind of liquid seasoning for food."

There are, it continues, in the French culinary scheme of things "almost two hundred recipes for sauces, brown and white, hot and cold (not including variations)."

French variations on a Dutch theme. Consider, for example, *hollandaise,* that superlative butter-lemon-egg yolk sauce that has come to all of us from Holland by way of France. Everyone knows what hollandaise is. If you have not made it at home, you have certainly encountered it in a restaurant or at the table of a cook more courageous than you are. Perhaps the word should be curious, rather than courageous—it does not take courage to make hollandaise. If you can read you can follow the simple directions in a simple, well-written cookbook. It's easy—Scout's honor. But such an enormous hoo-haw has been made over hollandaise, how difficult it is to prepare, how often it will fail, how complicated the whole process, it's a wonder anyone short of a French chef ever had the intestinal fortitude to attempt it. But you can. Just avoid the kind of cookbook written in the manner of the directions for putting a child's toy together, and you'll get along fine.

Hollandaise illustrates a second point about sauces: how versatile, how open to variation, a good sauce can be. Hollandaise is not one but many sauces, a whole family of them.

The basic sauce is made by gently heating flavored egg yolks, very gradually adding butter to them, seasoning with lemon juice, salt, and sometimes cayenne. The process is accomplished over very low direct heat, or in a double boiler. (And if even that seems too complicated—it takes no more than 5 or 6 minutes—hollandaise that is absolutely failure-proof can be made in the blender.) If the sauce is too thick for your purpose, thin it with a little hot water. If you have leftover hollandaise, refrigerate it or freeze it. It is not difficult—and the product is a lovely yellow, supremely rich, ineluctably smooth masterpiece of the culinary art.

So there you are, with the basic sauce. You can vary it in many ways by altering the ingredients somewhat or by making additions to the straight, basic hollandaise. You can:

- add to it minced parsley or chives or tarragon or a combination, or minced and sautéed mushrooms, or about 2 tablespoons of any puréed vegetable

- lighten it (and make it go farther) by folding in stiffly beaten egg whites
- both lighten and enrich it by folding in stiffly beaten heavy cream (the result is *Sauce Mousseline*)
- make it with browned butter (*Sauce Noisette*)
- vary its flavor by making it with orange juice, rather than lemon, and adding grated orange peel *(Sauce Maltaise)*
- make it with a white-wine fish fumet (reduced fish stock) rather than lemon juice for flavoring; vary it further by making it with heavy cream, as well
- flavor the basic sauce heavily with mustard *(Sauce Moutarde)*
- flavor it with a reduction of wine, vinegar, shallots, and tarragon in place of lemon juice *(Sauce Béarnaise);* you can vary this variation by adding tomato paste

You have made hollandaise, you know how to vary it. What do you do with it? Many, many things, some few of which are:

- use basic hollandaise on fish (poached salmon, for one), on asparagus or artichokes (make them even more of a flavor experience by serving as a separate course), on eggs benedict
- serve basic hollandaise plus minced herbs over poached fish, or with almost any egg dish, or on whole cooked cauliflower
- serve basic hollandaise plus mushrooms on briefly sautéed veal scallops or turkey breast cutlets on toast points, or with shrimp
- bring Sauce Mousseline to the table with a delicate fish soufflé or mousse
- dress asparagus or broccoli with Sauce Maltaise
- serve fish dishes of all sorts, particularly poached sole or sole roulades with shrimp, with the version of hollandaise made with fish fumet
- Sauce Béarnaise is traditional with steak, but try it on broiled chicken or fried fish; the tomato-paste variation is fine with steaks, too, and a nice change of pace with lamb steaks or chops

Use hollandaise leftovers to enrich cream or velouté sauces or spread lightly on dense dark bread to top with smoked salmon or hard-cooked eggs and capers. And that is truly not half the hollandaise story.

As you can see, sauces not only have virtues on their own, but also challenge a cook's curiosity and inventiveness. Many sauces lend themselves to this sort of change-ringing, among them MAYONNAISE, which we tend in this country to think of as a dressing for salads, but which has many other uses and many variations that expand its horizons.

Another sauce with unlimited possibilities is what we often call french dressing—sauce *vinaigrette*. It is a simple combination of oil and vinegar, seasoned to taste, and varied in as many ways as there are variation thinkers-up. The oil may be a mild and tasteless one, or fine olive oil. The vinegar may be red or white wine vinegar, or a garlic- or herb-flavored kind, or part lemon juice may be substituted, or the vinaigrette may be made with lemon juice entirely, no vinegar. The usual proportions are 3 parts oil to 1 part vinegar, but you can vary these too as your taste dictates. The usual seasonings are salt and freshly ground black pepper, with perhaps a bit of mustard. But you can add almost any salad-good herb, onion or garlic juice, curry powder, tomato purée, bleu or parmesan cheese—even sugar, if you've a mind to, although keep that bit of heresy to yourself if you ever have an opportunity to discuss vinaigrette with a French chef.

Make vinaigrette shortly before you intend to use it, either right in the bottom of the salad bowl before you add the greens, or in a separate container. There's no point in making it in advance—it's so easy, it might as well be fresh, too.

Here are a few vinaigrette ideas to spark your own:

- marinate cold cooked asparagus, or braised leeks, scallions, or endive in peppery lemon vinaigrette; garnish with chopped hard-cooked egg and pimiento
- add chopped capers and minced scallions, parsley, tarragon, and chervil to make *Sauce Ravigote;* serve on hot or cold boiled beef, chicken, or fish
- make red-wine/olive-oil vinaigrette well seasoned with garlic juice and 2 mashed anchovies for each ½ cup of the sauce; serve on a salad of sturdy greens with halved black olives and crumbled feta cheese
- beat dijon-type prepared mustard to taste into vinaigrette to serve with a cold-meat platter
- season vinaigrette liberally with slivered fresh basil and cracked black peppercorns to serve over thickly sliced tomatoes
- layer hot sliced potatoes with vinaigrette and lots of sliced scallions, salt, and pepper; chill, then fold in just enough sour cream to bind, and garnish with capers —one of the great potato salads

The basic sauces. These are the ones, in French cuisine, on which other sauces are based and/or on which other sauces ring (almost innumerable) changes. There is *Sauce Espagnole,* the basic brown sauce made of brown stock with a MIREPOIX, and cooked down to a rich essence. On this are based tomato sauces and the compound brown sauces (*Sauces Composées*). Basic white sauces are *Sauce Béchamel*—your old friend, white sauce, made with a butter-flour roux and milk—and *Sauce Velouté*, made with white stock (chicken or veal) substituting for the milk. Velouté may also be made with fish stock. Again, these are the bases on which many compound sauces are built. And there are, of course, some sauces in the vast repertoire that are not based on either brown or white sauces.

Sauces may be unthickened, but most of them are thickened in some manner. They are reduced—cooked down—until the ingredients become thick through evaporation of liquid, as in many tomato-based sauces and in some containing heavy cream, which thickens lightly when reduced. Many are made with a roux—melted butter or other fat into which flour is stirred until smooth; a roux may be white or brown, brownness achieved by browning the butter or the flour or both. Some are thickened with beurre manié—kneaded butter—in which butter and flour are combined (best accomplished with the fingers) into a smooth paste and added in small bits to boiling liquid. Some replace flour with cornstarch or, less often, potato starch or arrowroot or rice flour, or mashed hard-cooked egg yolks as the thickening agent. Some are thickened with fine, soft bread crumbs.

There are sauces to be served hot and those to be served cold; there are savory sauces for the main portions of the meal, and sweet sauces with which to lily-gild dozens of desserts. If you really want to get into sauce-making, consult a French cookbook—in the original, in translation, or one of the several very good ones written in English but following the French tradition. To accord sauces their rightful place, most French cookbooks open with instructions for sauce-making, on the theory that if you don't know sauces you won't be able to cook in the French manner.

Meanwhile, here are some few of the better-known sauces—a sampling which barely dents the surface of this vast culinary area. But they will give you an idea of the length and breadth of the genre, clue you when ordering from a French menu, and lead you to seek recipes for those that titillate your imagination.

BRIEF LEXICON OF SAVORY SAUCES

aigre-douce (French) or agro-dolce (Italian): Sweet-sour sauce; the French version is made of caramelized sugar, wine vinegar, white wine, shallots, and raisins, along with meat juices; the Italian is made of brown sugar, currants, chocolate, candied fruit peel, capers, vinegar, and meat juices, often with almonds or pine nuts added. Served with rabbit or hare, or with braised meats of various sorts. Pork or chicken in sweet-sour sauce in the Chinese manner is a favorite with Americans who patronize Chinese restaurants.

aïoli: The richly garlicky mayonnaise of the countries near the Mediterranean—one of the sauces for which everyone has his favorite recipe. Used with everything from raw vegetables to cabbage soup.

albert: Horseradish sauce spiked with mustard and vinegar, often thickened with bread crumbs. Served with beef.

allemande: One of the classic French sauces, although its name acknowledges its origin. Velouté enriched with eggs.

almond: Many kinds, most made with crushed almonds and bread crumbs, some with melted butter with sliced almonds. The former are used with fish and poultry, the latter with vegetables.

anchovy: Here, too, everyone has his own recipe. Generally the basic sauce incorporates wine, with chopped or mashed anchovies or anchovy paste added.

apple: Reduced apple purée, variously seasoned with spices and/or herbs, to be served with pork.

aurore: French classic—béchamel lightly flavored (and colored) with tomato purée.

barbecue: Strictly American, this one—most often a brown/tomato sauce, highly seasoned, used to baste grill-cooked meats from beef or pork ribs to chicken.

bâtarde: French classic—rather like Sauce Allemande except that in this case the eggs enrich béchamel.

bavaroise: Hot sauce for fish or shellfish—wine vinegar/butter combination, seasoned with horseradish and nutmeg.

bercy: Velouté made with reduced fish stock and white wine, seasoned with shallots and parsley.

beurre noir: Butter, not black but nut-brown, served as is or flavored in several ways—capers or lemon juice, for example—to serve with fish, asparagus, the cabbage family, sometimes with meat as well.

bigarade: Juices expressed during the cooking of duck, combined with orange (and sometimes lemon) juice and julienne strips of orange peel, sometimes with mashed duck liver.

bolognese: Classic Italian tomato-based sauce with wine and herbs, most often served with pasta.

bordelaise: Meat essence and red wine, with shallots, pepper, and parsley, sometimes other herbs as well—generally served with grilled meats.

bourguignonne: Mushrooms (or mushroom trimmings, in the manner of the thrifty French) cooked with shallots, parsley, and bay leaf in red wine, thickened with beurre manié—served with meats.

bread: The British serve bread sauce with poultry—bread crumbs cooked in milk, seasoned with onion and sometimes with lemon juice, parsley, and diced ham as well.

cambridge: British sauce for mutton—mayonnaise with added hard-cooked egg yolks, anchovies, capers, mustard.

caper: Everybody has his favorite sauce using these flavorful little pickled buds, adding them to browned butter, to mayonnaise, to various other sauces, to serve with lamb or salmon or poultry primarily, but with other meats and fish as well.

chasseur: The hunter's sauce, to serve with rabbit, game, sometimes with domestic meats; made with white wine, chopped mushrooms, shallots, meat essence, parsley.

chaud-froid: May be white or brown, used to mask (coat) cold foods. The brown one is made with reduced brown sauce to which Madeira and truffles are added, given body with gelatin. The white is velouté stiffened with gelatin.

demiglaze: Basic brown sauce reduced with meat stock until it is one-tenth its original volume; flavored with sherry.

diable: Used primarily to devil meat or turkey bones, but it also has other uses—meat stock, tomato, wine, black and red pepper.

diplomat: French classic—Sauce Normande (below) enriched with lobster butter, flavored with brandy; for fish.

financière: Madeira sauce (below) with truffles, chicken livers added.

gribiche: This is one of those that begins with hard-cooked egg yolks—to them are added seasonings, oil and vinegar, and chopped gherkins and capers; served with cold fish and shellfish.

laguipière: Sauce Normande (below) to which truffles soaked in Madeira are added; served with fish.

lyonnaise: Purée of onions cooked with white wine and vinegar, combined with demiglaze; served with meats.

madeira: Reduced brown sauce and brown stock with Madeira wine; served with roasted or braised meats.

matelote: Demiglaze combined with fish stock, red wine, and mushrooms; served with fish.

mint: One of the sauces of which there are many variations —the most basic is vinegar combined with chopped mint, seasoned, sometimes sweetened; served chiefly with lamb.

mornay: Béchamel with grated cheese, usually gruyère (swiss) but sometimes parmesan, or a combination of the two.

nantua: Fish velouté enriched with crayfish butter (sometimes lobster butter is substituted), with tomato purée, white wine, and brandy added; served with shellfish.

newburg: Béchamel made with cream, enriched with egg yolks, seasoned with paprika, flavored with sherry. Served chiefly with lobster, sometimes with other shellfish.

normande: Velouté made with reduced fish stock, the liquor from mussels or oysters (sometimes, in error, clam juice), and mushroom stock, enriched with egg yolks and cream; served with fish.

parsley: Everybody's easy sauce for fish—melted butter with chopped parsley, sometimes with lemon juice as well.

périgueux: One of the French classics—truffles and Madeira added to demiglaze.

piquante: Basic brown sauce with capers, shallots, and white wine; the mixture is puréed, liberally seasoned with pepper.

poivrade: Basic brown sauce with wine vinegar and white wine and, of course, peppercorns; various minced vegetables and herbs season the mixture, according to the chef's fancy. Served with meat, sometimes with game.

poulette: Béchamel enriched with egg yolks and cream, flavored with mushrooms and shallots; served with poultry.

provencale: Reduced tomatoes, oil, substantial seasoning —particularly garlic; sometimes with mushrooms added. Served with meats and fish, or with vegetables.

ravigote, cold: Mayonnaise with chopped capers and hard-cooked eggs; served with cold fish, vegetables.

ravigote, hot: Béchamel made with white wine, seasoned chiefly with chervil and tarragon; served with poultry, liver, kidneys.

réforme: Half-and-half poivrade and demiglaze, with chopped or julienned hard-cooked egg whites, tongue, truffles, mushrooms, gherkins.

remoulade: Mustardy mayonnaise with capers, gherkins, herbs, and mashed anchovy or anchovy paste. Celeri remoulade is the classic, but the sauce may be served with other foods.

robert: Onions slow-cooked in white wine are added to a Sauce Espagnole that is sharply seasoned with mustard and pepper; served with steaks, other meats.

soubise: Béchamel combined with onion purée, seasoned delicately with nutmeg. Served with eggs, chicken, or pork— or, in Europe, with mutton.

suprême: Velouté enriched with cream; served with poultry, in particular with boned and skinned chicken breasts.

tartar: Hard-cooked egg yolks, oil, and vinegar, with snipped chives and chopped onions; or it may be (more usually) mayonnaise with chives, capers, gherkins. Served with fish, hot or cold, or cold chicken.

verte: Green mayonnaise, made that color by adding puréed blanched herbs (parsley, tarragon, sometimes basil); sometimes spinach and/or watercress deepens the green color.

vin blanc: Velouté made with fish stock, enriched with egg yolks, with softened butter added just before serving. For fish. (Many sauces are "finished" in this manner—for a not quite so authentic but less rich sauce, omit the butter finish.)

ROUNDUP OF SWEET SAUCES

Most common of the dessert sauces is *Crème Chantilly*—whipped cream. Another easy and simple—and very good—sweet sauce is made with fruit juice thickened with cornstarch, sweetened if desired, sometimes spiked with lemon juice to point up the flavor, sometimes with berries or cut-up fruit added. Another, even simpler, is cut-up or crushed fruit alone, sweetened if necessary.

Hard sauce is made by creaming together butter and confectioners sugar; it can be flavored with anything from rum or brandy to fruit juice or purée. LIQUEURS in their infinite variety make excellent dessert sauces. Custard sauce—variously known also as English custard or Crème Anglaise or soft custard—sweetly and mildly sauces such desserts as plain cake or cake topped with sliced or crushed fruit or berries. And plain cream—heavy, but not whipped—is the best of sauces for such down-home desserts as apple betty, fruit dumplings, or cobblers.

Melba sauce, designed for peach melba but most acceptable elsewhere, combines puréed raspberries with currant jelly for lovely color and piquant flavor. Try it on briefly baked bananas, or over baked custards turned out of their cups. Wine custard—Bavarian Weinschaum—or Italian Zabaglione are richly delicious variations on the custard theme. Spicy cider sauce dresses up a bland pudding or a plain cake.

Buttery brown sugar sauce, honey sauce, caramel sauce, butterscotch sauce, maple sugar sauce—these are all cousins, all delicious on ice cream, plain cake, dessert waffles, blancmange-type puddings.

And then, of course, there is chocolate sauce in many versions—thin and bittersweet, richly fudgy to be served hot, chocolate custard, chocolate-mint, the great mocha flavor of chocolate-coffee. Serve on ice cream, plain cake, or pudding, and dress them further if you wish with such crisp sprinkle-on additions as chopped or slivered nuts or crushed candies, or top with brandied fruit.

Many sweet sauces (and some savory ones) can be bought ready-made in bottles or jars, their quality, depending on brand, ranging all the way from awful to superb. A little judicious shopping and sampling (not a difficult chore for anyone with a sweet tooth) will certainly turn up a brand to suit your taste. As a general conclusion, the canned or bottled sweet sauces are better than any but the tomato savory ones.

KIND WORDS FOR THE HOME SAUCER

One is tempted to cheer novice sauce cooks on with a rah-rah pep talk. It can, however, be boiled down to one simple sentence: You can do it. Choose a reliable cookbook, one that does not make you feel as if you ought to salaam before approaching the sauce chapter. Read each recipe you want

to try all the way through to make sure you understand it before you start to cook—as well as making certain, of course, that you have all the ingredients on hand.

At least until you work your way out of the novice class, don't substitute or cut corners. Consider the recipe inviolable until you can make that sauce with your eyes shut and one hand tied behind your back—after you've reached that point, feel free.

As well as your common sense plus the ability to read and follow directions, you will need a few basic tools:

- wire whisks, balloon-type for deep pots, flat type for shallow pots; brisk stirring with these prevents lumping, a favorite pastime of sauces
- a very heavy saucepan and, for some, a double boiler
- a mortar and pestle for crushed ingredients—fun to use, but lacking such equipment, substitute a small bowl and the back of a heavy spoon
- a good strainer is necessary, one that can be lined with wet muslin or cheesecloth—many sauces must be strained
- a sturdy sieve or foodmill
- a rotary-drum grater and a small, flat hand-grater—many sauce components must be grated
- not absolutely necessary, but a pleasure, is a wooden sauce spoon, heavily durable, with a pointed bottom at one side of the bowl—this helps you get into the very edges of the pan as you stir

And, finally, some bits and pieces of advice—the know-how that gives you confidence as you take saucepot in hand:

- give a roux ample time to cook before going on to the next step—if not, the sauce will have a raw, floury taste that the best ingredients in the world can't mask
- make additions to a sauce gradually, stirring as you go, rather than dumping all of the next ingredient in at once; this is particularly true when you add cold ingredients to a hot sauce
- neither overmix nor overcook sauces thickened with cornstarch—they may suddenly become thin again
- when you add eggs to sauce (raw eggs, that is), stir some of the hot mixture into the eggs to warm them,

then turn the eggs into the hot mixture; this prevents the cold eggs from cooking in shreds—like egg-drop soup—rather than melding in smoothly as they should

- stir, *stir,* STIR—sauce-making is not terribly difficult, but it does require the patience to stand at the stove, stirring constantly, while the sauce cooks
- don't attempt to hurry things along by turning up the heat—you'll get lumps at best, burned sauce at worst; many sauces will curdle if allowed to boil

Last words. Don't sauce everything in sight. One savory sauce (other than dressing for salad) and one sweet one is the absolute maximum. Don't skimp—if either your budget or your waistline or both can't cope with all that butter and cream, seek out an alternative rather than trying to make a sauce with fewer or lesser ingredients. And remember that you learned the lesson of honesty at your mother's knee: if you must make a sauce from a packaged mix, by all means do so. But don't try to pass it off as homemade hollandaise or whatever. Someone will know—if no one else, you will.

For more ways in which sauces are used, see DECO-RATING and GARNISHING.

RABBIT

To some people the idea of eating rabbit is anathema. A bunny? Not me! But when you come right down to it, what's the difference between a rabbit and a chicken? Or a duck or goose or lamb or pig—or even a steer? The difference lies, really, in whether or not the animal or bird was a friend. Particularly when there are children in the family, eating a pet is a horror. But impersonal meat, brought home from the market no longer looking at all as the living animal did, should cause no such problems.

A few markets sell fresh rabbit, a great many of them the frozen kind. Young rabbit may be chicken-fried, older ones made into stews, ragouts, hasenpfeffer. The meat is mild but flavorful, rather like chicken. See also GAME.

RABBIT, WELSH: see RAREBIT

RACCOON: see GAME

RACLETTE

A Swiss specialty, raclette is cheese melted and served with little boiled potatoes and a glass of white wine. The face of a whole large piece of cheese such as swiss, gruyère, or emmenthaler is exposed to the heat, then a serving scraped off onto a diner's plate and the cheese returned to the heat —which should be, properly, an open fire.

RADISHES

Peppery-flavored vegetables, radishes may be round and red or long and white; there are even some exotic purple, yellow, and black ones. They find their place on a tray of raw relishes or sliced in a salad or, more unusually, served whole as an appetizer with unsalted butter. Or they can be a part of an array of crudités offered with a dip. The name comes from the Latin *radix,* meaning root. Radishes are available all year around, in bunches with the leaves and stems still in place or, leaves removed, in small plastic bags. Pinch them gently to make sure they are solid, not pithy; they should be well formed and plump-looking. At home, remove roots, stems,

and leaves, wash well, and refrigerate in the crisper up to 1 week. Low in calories, a medium-size radish contains only 8.

RAIL: see GAME

RAISE: see BAKING POWDER, BAKING SODA, LEAVENING AGENTS, and YEAST

RAISINS

These are grapes, dried either naturally—in the sun—or by means of artificial heat. It is believed to be the Egyptians who first remarked that grapes left on the vine grew dry and wrinkled and sweeter, and that when picked they kept well.

Raisin bread is much loved by many, and so are plump, raisin-studded cookies. Raisins make a sweetly rich pie, and mincemeat and fruitcake would be lost without them. Rich in vitamins and iron, they are a fine snack for youngsters.

From grape to raisin. Nearly 4 pounds of grapes produce 1 pound of raisins, and not all grapes are suitable—some are for eating out of hand, some for wine-making, some for grape juice and jelly, and only a few for drying into raisins.

dark seedless: These are made from thompson seedless grapes, the little amber-green, seed-free ones we like to eat out of hand. They are sundried on sheets of paper spread between the grapevines, and are then washed and stemmed before packing.

golden seedless: Surprisingly, these are made from the same grapes, which are treated with sulphur dioxide to retain their original color, then dried in artificial heat.

muscats: Large, dark, and very sweet, these are made from muscat grapes. They may be purchased with the seeds still in place or seeded, and they are quite scarce.

zantes: Also called zante currants, these are very tiny. They are made from the zante corinth grape and have a distinctive flavor, quite different from other raisins.

Keeping and cooking raisins. Raisins will keep reasonably well at kitchen-shelf temperatures, but very well—up to 15 months—at 40°F.; that means in the refrigerator, unless you wear earmuffs and mittens while you cook.

For good distribution throughout a batter, dust the raisins with a little of the flour called for in the recipe, then fold them in, flour and all, making sure they are well scattered. If the recipe requires "plumped" raisins, soak them for 5 minutes in hot water, or overnight in fruit juice or liquor in the refrigerator. Drain well before adding.

RAMBUTANS: see EXOTIC FRUIT

RAPE OIL: see OILS, SALAD AND COOKING

RARE

In cooking, the opposite of well done—indeed, what seems to some to be impossibly underdone. The term is most often applied to beef steaks and roasts, and means that the meat is brown on the outside, but red and running red juices within.

RAREBIT

A concoction of sharp cheese, most often cheddar, melted in milk or beer. Seasoned with mustard, worcestershire, and sometimes onion juice, it is served over toast or toasted crackers. A heartier version calls for sliced tomatoes on the toast before the rarebit is poured over and bacon or frizzled ham to top it all off. Pickles are virtually a necessity with rarebits. The name is often corrupted to "rabbit."

RASPBERRIES

Though they have a wonderfully delicate flavor all their own that makes them the favorite fruit of many, and a handsome array of colors ranging from red through purple and amber to black, raspberries also have drawbacks. They are exceedingly perishable, and often it's impossible—particularly in a market in a large city—to find a box of raspberries worth taking home. And because they are so perishable, they're also exceedingly expensive, much more so than most other fruits.

You can solve those problems by finding a raspberry patch in the woods, for they still grow wild in many places. Or you can plant the prickly touch-me-not canes in your backyard or garden for summertime berry feasts—provided only that the birds, who also love them, don't beat you to it.

RASPBERRIES IN YOUR KITCHEN

Raspberry devotées like their berries plain or with cream and sugar. But you can also make several kinds of delectable pies, tarts, puddings, bavarians, cold soufflés, and icebox cakes with the berries. Or serve them with coeur à la crème.

how to buy: Be wary. Take a good, long look at the box of raspberries, both on top and underneath. They may look great at first glance, but a wet, stained box bottom indicates that only the top layer of berries will be worth eating. Choose berries that are firm, bright in color, not misshapen. They are in season from June through November, at their peak in July.

how to store: Sort the berries, removing any bad ones. Spread out on a tray or plate and refrigerate. The sooner they are used the better, but very fresh ones will store up to 2 days. Never wash raspberries until just before you use them.

nutritive value: The two most familiar raspberries, the black and the red, differ somewhat in nutritional values. One cup of the raw, black raspberries contains 70 calories, of the red, 85; the same amount of each also yields:

	black	red	
protein	1.5	1.7	grams
fat	.6	.2	gram
carbohydrate	16.7	21.4	grams
calcium	27	36	milligrams
phosphorus	27	36	milligrams
iron	1.1	1.5	milligrams
sodium	1	2	milligrams
potassium	207	277	milligrams
thiamin	.04	.02	milligram
riboflavin	.11	.1	milligram
niacin	2.9	1.2	milligrams
ascorbic acid	31	22	milligrams
vitamin A	160	220	international units

Freezing raspberries. Frozen in sugar or syrup (see special feature: PUTTING FOOD BY), raspberries may be stored at 0°F. or lower up to 1 year. The berries may also be washed—briefly and carefully—in ice water, spread out on a tray or baking sheet, and frozen until firm; working swiftly, transfer to freezer container, cover, and return to freezer at once.

Other ways, other forms. One type or another of good raspberry flavor is available all year around.

on grocery shelves, in cans or jars: Canned raspberries in syrup; raspberry jam (some seedless) and jelly; apple-raspberry sauce.

in grocery frozen-food section: Raspberries with juice in metal-ended cardboard containers and quick-frozen in plastic bags.

RATATOUILLE

A vegetable mélange whose ingredients may vary somewhat from cook to cook. Generally contains onions, garlic, eggplant, mushrooms, zucchini or crookneck squash, tomatoes, added to the pot in the order in which they will be done. Olive oil is the cooking medium. May be served hot as a vegetable, cold as an appetizer.

RAVIOLI: see PASTA

RED CABBAGE: see CABBAGE

RED PEPPERS: see HERBS AND SAVORY SEASONINGS and PEPPERS

RED POTATOES: see POTATOES

RED SNAPPER: see FISH

RED WINE VINEGAR: see VINEGAR

REDUCE, TO: see page 448

REFRIGERATED DOUGH

Not to be confused with frozen products, these are the biscuits, rolls, and other breads and pastries usually in tubes, generally shelved near the dairy case or in a special refrigerated case of their own. There are biscuits of several kinds: crescent rolls, danish-type sweet rolls, muffins, small bread loaves, turnovers, cookies. All are ready to bake and serve. Baked according to package directions, all of these are acceptably good hot breads—as good as, perhaps better than—the average home cook can make from scratch. (The breads that is—the cookies aren't up to truly good homemades, the turnovers tend to be more crust than filling, and the muffins are only so-so.)

That's not all. With a little ingenuity and hardly any expenditure of time and effort, these good breads can be turned into any number of I-made-them-myself treats. For example, open two tubes of biscuits, tear each biscuit in half. Dip each piece in melted butter, then in cinnamon-sugar. Pile helter-skelter in a 9-inch tube pan and bake. Result: delicious cinnamon pullaparts for breakfast or brunch.

The crescent rolls can be lightly spread with any sweet —jam or marmalade, for instance, with a sprinkle of chopped nuts—or savory—anchovy-lemon butter, melted butter and grated cheese—before rolling, to turn them into very welcome snacks or appetizers. Or the dough may be unrolled, the perforations pinched together, and the whole sheet of dough sprinkled or spread with cheese, or butter and cinnamon-sugar and cut into strips. Or use the whole sheet as the crust for a meat or poultry potpie.

A good general cookbook will give you recipes.

RELISHES: see special feature: PUTTING FOOD BY

RENDER, TO: see page 448

RENNET

This is a natural enzyme obtained from the fourth stomach of a calf. Its particularly valuable property is that it causes milk to coagulate. This makes it invaluable in cheesemaking.

Easy to digest, rennet is also used in making delicate milk-based desserts, suitable for children and invalids but also liked by many who fall into neither category, and in some ice creams. Commercially, it is available in tablet form and as a flavored powder to which warm milk is added to make a mild, custardy pudding.

RHUBARB

This is a plant that offers a number of contradictions. Although technically a vegetable, it is used by cooks as a fruit. It is not the root or leaves that we eat, as with most plants, but the stems. (Cautionary note: The pretty, frilly, pale yellow-green leaves are poisonous.) A hardy perennial, rhubarb grows in most climates. Our grandmothers, setting out a row of goodies to cool on the kitchen windowsill, called it pieplant. Its first uses were medicinal—in fact, Chinese writings tell us that the plant was being used for that purpose as early as 2700 B.C.

Plain rhubarb is low in calories, a fact that does us little good because it must be heavily sweetened to be palatable. It is in season from February through June, and can be used to make old-fashioned sauce and several kinds of pies and puddings. It is also used in jams and conserves, to make a delicious sherbet and an ice cream equally so. Strawberries and rhubarb have a special·affinity and are often combined in pies.

RIB ROAST, STEAK: see BEEF

RIBOFLAVIN: see MILK

RICCIOLINA: see PASTA

RICE

To more than half the world's population, rice is the staff of life, the principal source of nourishment—not, unfortunately, because it is so nutritionally rich, but because it is relatively easy to grow, can be successfully cultivated where other grains cannot, and yields a larger volume per acre than wheat or corn. It is inexpensive to process, cheap to buy, and—of first importance in economically deprived areas—it is filling.

The Oriental peoples are traditionally the largest users of rice. From the Indus Valley, in what is now Pakistan, the Chinese acquired their first rice as much as 5,000 years ago. Confucius commended to his followers the polished white rice—a dictum that fortunately all did not follow, for many of those that did died of beriberi. In the eighth century A.D., Moslems introduced rice to Spain, and seven centuries later the Spanish carried it to Italy.

In this country, Dr. Henry Woodward of North Carolina planted in his garden in 1671 a small amount brought him as a gift from a port in East Africa by a sea captain friend. For a time the plant was only a curiosity, but eventually it became for many years the state's principal crop.

In the United States and in other parts of the world where rice is not the primary dietary staple, it is used mainly as a side dish—an alternative to potatoes or pasta—or as a good, inexpensive extender for meat, fish, and poultry main dishes, or in desserts.

White rice or brown? White and brown rice are variations of the same grain. At the mill, the rice—which is the seed of an annual cereal grass—is cleaned and dried. Then the outer husk is removed, leaving behind a coating of bran that gives brown rice its color and contains much of the nutritive value. Brown rice accounts for only about one percent of that purchased in this country, but it is brown rice that is used mainly by those who rely on rice as the mainstay of their diet.

Milling away the layer of bran results in white, or polished, rice—the other 99 percent of the grain consumed in the United States. This milling also removes the thiamin, niacin, and iron that the bran contains. Food value of white rice is often beefed up by spraying the grains with a solution of these nutrients—an example of a beneficial, acceptable food additive. If the amount of nutrients restored meets. federal standards, the label will tell you that the rice is "enriched," as most of the rice for sale in this country is.

Choosing the rice to suit your purpose. Stores and markets have rice for sale in various forms. Which kind you choose and which form is a matter of taste and the use to which you are going to put it. Brown rice has a rather nutty flavor, a chewy texture; white rice is blander and softer.

long-grain, medium-grain, short-grain: Both brown and white rice are available as long-grain or short-grain and, less generally, medium-grain. The names are descriptive of the length of the individual grain of rice, and virtually all the grains in a package labeled in any of these three ways should reflect the label. A grain of long-grain rice is four to five times as long as it is wide, medium-grain is about twice as long as wide, and short-grain is virtually round. In some areas, packages of rice in which broken particles are mixed with whole grains are available at a considerable saving, useful where economy is an important factor.

Unless the package states otherwise, the rice you buy will probably be short-grain—long- and medium-grain rices are almost always so labeled. Long-grain rice, properly prepared, will maintain the identity of each grain after cooking, standing up in a light, fluffy mound. Medium- and short-grain rice tends to be more tender and moist, and the grains will cling together in a more cohesive mass. Long-grain cooks a bit more quickly than medium- or short-grain, and the finished product is drier. Although all three forms can be used interchangeably, long-grain rice is best liked as a side dish or in combination with meat, fish, or poultry in hot or salad-type main dishes. Medium- or short-grain rice is most often used for croquettes and molds, and for puddings, because of its soft, cohesive quality.

parboiled (converted) rice: Parboiled rice (often labeled "converted") may be either white or brown, although white is by far the more popular. Packages will be labeled "converted white rice" or "converted brown rice." This rice has been treated, during the milling process, to force some of the nutrients in the bran layer to penetrate the grain. It is parboiled, steamed, and dried before packaging.

precooked (instant) rice: As the name indicates, this is rice (white or brown) that has been cooked after milling, and the moisture removed before packaging. It requires only a brief period of heating/cooking before serving.

RICE IN YOUR KITCHEN

Uncooked rice measures 2¼ cups per pound—1 cup of rice weighs about 6¾ ounces, a heaping half cup weighs about ¼ pound. Volume increases a little more than three times when the rice is cooked.

A cup of raw rice will yield three to six servings, depending on whether it is to be used as a side dish or will be the basis of a main dish. One-half cup of cooked rice is considered a serving, although if the rice is a major part of the meal, ⅔ to ¾ cup per person is a more reasonable measure.

To guide you:

1 cup regular white rice	=	3 cups cooked
1 cup parboiled (converted) rice	=	4 cups cooked
1 cup regular brown rice	=	4 cups cooked
1 cup precooked (instant) rice	=	2 cups cooked

how to buy: Regular white and brown rice is available in 1- and 2-pound packages and, chiefly in neighborhoods where many of the people consider rice a diet staple, in 5-, 10-, and even 25-pound bags.

how to store: The shelf life of rice is a year or longer, although unless your family is very fond of rice, the 1- and 2-pound sizes are generally most practical for the average family. Keep in the original package until opened, then transfer to a container with a screw-top or other tight-fitting lid, as rice is one of the household products subject to invasion by that pantry pest, the weevil. Store in a dark place (a closed cupboard is fine) and keep dry.

nutritive value: Cooked enriched long-grain white rice and brown rice are almost identical in number of calories per cup of the cooked product—white 223, brown 232. Neither form has vitamins A or C. Other yields for 1 cup hot cooked rice:

	brown	white	
protein	4.9	4.1	grams
fat	1.2	.2	grams
carbohydrate	49.7	49.6	grams
calcium	23	21	milligrams
phosphorus	142	57	milligrams
iron	1	1.8	milligrams
sodium	550	767	milligrams
potassium	137	57	milligrams
thiamin	.18	.23	milligram
riboflavin	.04	.02	milligram
niacin	2.7	2.1	milligrams

Tips on preparing, cooking. Except for brands labeled "coated" (see below), rice need not—indeed, should not, because nutrients can be leached away—be washed before using. Follow the package directions for proportions of rice to water, which vary somewhat between long- and short-grain varieties, and considerably between regular and con-

522

verted or precooked forms. Package directions call for the addition of salt (use it—unless you are on a low-sodium diet —to alleviate the bland, flat taste) and some call for the addition of butter or other fat, which helps to keep the grains from sticking together in the cooked product. Timing is important. Again, follow package directions—undercooking results in grains with an unpleasantly hard "core" or a rubbery texture, overcooking in a gluey mass. Well-cooked rice is soft but not mushy; each grain should be discernibly separate from all the rest. Brown rice takes longer to cook than white.

Cooked rice may be kept warm for a short period in a colander or strainer over hot water or, lightly covered, in a low oven. Reheat leftovers in the buttered top of a double boiler, or use in puddings or casserole dishes, or as an addition to soups.

a special caution concerning coated rice: In brief, don't use it. Federal regulations allow the coating of rice if the label bears the information "coated with talc and glucose; wash before using." The coating is for cosmetic purposes—it makes the raw rice look better, but pretty uncooked rice is hardly a necessity—and must be washed off before the rice is used. Unfortunately, many of the nutrients go down the drain with the washing water, but that is not the chief objection to this form of rice. Talc, a part of the coating, is often contaminated with asbestos, and it is believed that inhaled or ingested asbestos may cause cancer. Read the label carefully; avoid coated rice.

From the point of view of nutrition, rice is not the best of the "starchy" side dishes, one or another of which forms a major part of the main meal of many people. A medium baked potato, including its skin, has fewer calories and offers a somewhat higher percentage of nutrients, as well as 44 percent of the RDA of vitamin C. Enriched spaghetti, with fewer calories, does not contain vitamin C, but does offer an appreciably higher percentage of nutrients, and enriched egg noodles are even better from the nutritional point of view. Kidney beans, at 149 calories in a serving, offer for example, 21.2 percent of the RDA of protein, 16.7 percent of iron, 21.9 percent of phosphorus, 5.9 percent of calcium, 23.4 percent of magnesium, 6.3 percent of riboflavin, and 6.7 percent of niacin.

But, looked at from a slightly different point of view, rice is very low in both fat and sodium, and is therefore important to those on either low-cholesterol or low-sodium diets. It is also relatively inexpensive to use as a side dish or as an extender in meat, fish, poultry, or vegetable main dishes. And plain white rice is very easy to digest—important on bland/low-fiber diets.

Brown rice contains a slightly larger amount of fiber than white, but not an amount sufficient to influence your choice between the two, and neither brown nor white offers sufficient fiber to play a significant role in a high-fiber diet.

Freezing rice. Rice freezes reasonably well, but there is really no point to freezing plain boiled rice—it's one of those items that takes up useful space and gets kicked around in the freezer till it is lost. You can, however, freeze "made" dishes containing rice, such as casseroles.

Other ways, other forms. Rice in varying forms can be found in several sections of the market.

on grocery shelves, in packages or cans: Ready-to-eat breakfast cereal—puffed, flaked, crisp little nuggets; ready-to-cook rice cereal, finely milled; in cans or jars: rice-chicken main dishes, spanish rice, rice pudding; in packages: dry rice mixes, using regular or instant rice, for spanish, saffron, herb, and others, and seasoned rice-vermicelli combinations.

in grocery frozen-food section: Rice-vegetable combinations, such as suitably seasoned white rice with mushrooms or peas; Chinese-style fried rice.

Some perfect partners. If economy is important to you, use regular rather than precooked (instant) rice, and avoid the many varieties of flavored rice mixes. You can duplicate these readily and much less expensively, and ring changes on them to suit your own taste, by starting with plain white or brown rice and adding whatever you wish. Such made-at-home dishes cost only about half as much as the prepared rice mixes.

Cook the rice as the package directs, either in water or an equal amount of broth or bouillon, or add bouillon cubes to the water. Or cook in tomato juice for Spanish- or Italian-style dishes, or in half-and-half water and orange juice for a delightful flavor with veal. Spices and herbs can be added as you like. Try thyme and/or sage in rice to be served with pork or poultry, oregano or basil in rice to be used in or with tomato-flavored dishes. Turmeric imparts excellent flavor and also the attractive deep-yellow color of much more expensive saffron.

Rice can be combined with sautéed onion, mushrooms, celery, and pepper, singly or in any combination, to add flavor. Lemon juice, lemon pepper, and seasoned salt all alleviate the blandness. Or combine rice with almost any leftover to extend the leftover and improve the flavor of the rice. Peanuts, for example, add crunch as well as flavor, and they raise the protein level of the dish. Parslied rice, in proportions of three-quarters white or brown rice to one-quarter chopped

parsley, makes an excellent meat accompaniment; it also provides a bonus of the vitamins and minerals in which parsley is rich.

Add small dabs of leftover rice to canned soups as you heat them or scramble with egg (and with any leftover vegetables the refrigerator has to offer) for a hearty luncheon dish. Finally, to impart greater flavor to the rice, it may be toasted before cooking—spread on a baking sheet, place in a 400° F. oven until golden brown—or lightly sautéed in butter, margarine, oil, or bacon fat to add a nutlike taste.

WILD RICE, considered a culinary delicacy, is not a true rice but the seed of a grass of another sort. Brown or white rice may be mixed with wild rice, half and half, for a dish with wild rice flavor at only half the cost. Each kind should be separately cooked and combined before serving.

Rice is one of the always-on-hand staples in many kitchens. See also PILAF.

RICE FLOUR

Chiefly used in the diets of those allergic to wheat or other grain products, rice flour can be found in specialty food shops. Don't try to use it interchangeably with other flours—recipes especially developed for the product are necessary. See also FLOUR.

RICOTTA: see CHEESE

RIGATONI: see PASTA

RISSOLE: see page 453

RIZ: see page 453

ROAST, TO: see page 450

ROCK CORNISH HEN: see CHICKEN and CORNISH GAME HEN

ROCK LOBSTER: see SHELLFISH

ROCK SALT

Large-grained, sometimes containing impurities such as dirt and stones, rock salt is used chiefly in making ice cream in an old-fashioned freezer or as a bed for oysters Rockefeller.

ROE

Eggs, still enclosed in the thin membrane in which they occur in the female fish, are called roe. The roe of many kinds of fish is sold—limited availability—in various fish markets, but the most familiar kinds are the roe of sturgeon, shad, and salmon. Sturgeon roe is CAVIAR; salmon roe—much larger and colored red-orange—is called salmon caviar and is usually sold in small jars, to be used as an appetizer, often in combination with sour cream. Shad roe is generally lightly sautéed, served with bacon or just a wedge of lemon, but may be deviled or, suitably seasoned, used as a filling for small, elegant reception- or tea party-type sandwiches.

ROGNONS: see page 453

ROLL, TO: see page 448

ROLLED ROAST: see meat entries: BEEF, LAMB, PORK, VEAL

ROLLS: see BREAD

ROMADUR: see CHEESE

ROMAINE: see SALAD GREENS AND PLANTS

ROMANO: see CHEESE

ROQUEFORT: see CHEESE

ROSE: see WINE

ROSE PETALS: see CANDIED FLOWERS

ROSEMARY: see HERBS AND SAVORY SEASONINGS

ROSETTES

These are small fried sweets made of a thin batter, and cooked in deep fat. A rosette iron is needed—a contraption with a heatproof handle and a business end onto which can be fastened various metal rosette shapes such as butterflies, flowers, and abstract designs; some have a timbale form for small, tartlike shells in which to serve a savory or sweet filling.

Learning to use a rosette iron is a bit tricky, but the whole secret lies in dipping the iron into the batter only about three-quarters of the way up the side. If the batter comes up over the top of the form, the rosette will be difficult to remove from the iron.

Drain rosettes on absorbent paper, store in an airtight jar. They may be sprinkled with confectioners sugar just before serving.

ROSEWATER

Not many American kitchens count a bottle of rosewater among the staples, but in Europe, and especially in the Near East, this lovely essence of rose petals—with the odor and flavor of roses—is used regularly as a flavoring.

ROTELLE: see PASTA

ROUGHAGE: see FIBER

ROUND, ROUND STEAK: see BEEF

ROUX

A flour-and-fat mixture, used for thickening sauces and gravies. Fat (butter, or fat from cooked meat) is heated, flour stirred in until a smooth, bubbling mixture is obtained. Then liquid—water, milk, broth, tomato juice, whatever—is added gradually and the mixture stirred constantly until it bubbles and becomes thickened to the desired consistency. See also the special feature: SAUCE SORCERY.

ROYAL ICING

A thick frosting, better known for its usefulness than for its delicacy or flavor. This is the icing used with a pastry bag and tube to make the elaborate flower, leaf, and other designs with which fancy cakes are decorated. Unless properly made, it can reach a tooth-crunching hardness—watch it!

RUM: see LIQUORS

RUM CAKES

A divinely heady dessert of Italian extraction. In its epitome it consists of rum-soaked cake layers put together with a ricotta-candied fruits-chunks of chocolate filling and topped with meringue. Beggars the imagination unless you've tried it. An Italian-restaurant specialty, or make it at home.

RUM EXTRACT: see FLAVORING
EXTRACTS

RUMTOPF

This is one of the Provident Cook's specialties—it is made in summer, but anxious eaters must wait until winter before it can be consumed. But when winter comes, there will be rumtopf sundaes, plain cake with rumtopf, rumtopf pudding, rumtopf apple pie, rumtopf-roasted duck, rumtopf served as a relish with all kinds of meat dishes, dozens more.

You will need a large receptable (no point going into this in a small way). One gallon or two is a good size, and the jar must be made of ceramic, crockery, or glass and have a cover. Other than that, have on hand granulated sugar and light rum, the 60-proof kind. And fruit:

- strawberries—wash and dry them, cut the large ones in half
- peaches and apricots—dip in boiling water 1 minute, zip off skins; pit; halve apricots, slice peaches
- melons—halve, seed, cut into balls or thin slices
- raspberries—sort carefully; do not wash
- plums—wash, dry, peel if you like, slice
- seedless grapes—wash, halve
- pineapple—peel, cut in chunks

Do not use blackberries or apples or any grape other than the seedless. You may use blueberries if you wish, but they will give the mixture a dark color.

Getting it together. Mix equal amounts—cup for cup—of fruit and sugar in a large bowl, let stand 1 hour. Transfer to your rumtopf crock. Pour in rum so that it comes a generous half inch above the fruit. Place a saucer or small plate on the fruit and weight it—the fruit must be at all times totally submerged in the rum. Cover the crock. If the cover doesn't fit snugly, put a layer of plastic film between crock and cover. Let the crock stand undisturbed at room temperature.

You may add equal amounts of fruit and sugar as fruits come into season; add more rum as necessary. Do not stir.

In two to three months after the last fruit is added, the rumtopf will be ready. Stir well before using.

Cautionary note: If you have an Uncle Lushwell, hide the rumtopf when he's coming to visit. Stronger men than he have been known to burst into tears at the very mention of the word.

RUSSETS: see POTATOES

RUSSIAN DRESSING: see MAYONNAISE

RUTABAGAS

Known in parts of Europe as Swedes or Swedish turnips, rutabagas are not turnips at all, but another member of the cabbage family. Big, golden fleshed, and globular, they usually arrive at the market with a coating of wax that keeps them from spoiling. This, and the rutabaga's skin, must be peeled away before cooking.

Thomas Jefferson, as he did with a number of other foods, introduced the rutabaga to America. This was not one of his more successful ventures—the rutabaga may well take the dubious honor of being our unfavorite vegetable, although brussels sprouts are a very close second, being elbowed for position by kohlrabi. Too bad, because in the winter, when there are not as many fresh vegetables in the market and the out-of-season ones are expensive, rutabagas can add variety to meals.

They can be sliced, boiled, and buttered. Or mashed (sometimes half-and-half with potatoes). Or made into a soufflé, or creamed, or used in soup. You can even make a rutabaga pie, à la pumpkin. Or candy them, à la sweet potatoes.

Choose solid, unblemished rutabagas, with no soft spots or cuts. Store in a cool place or in the refrigerator up to 1 month. Rutabagas may be frozen, but there is little point to it—they are in the market and reasonably priced all winter.

RYE

This is a cereal grass, one that is closely related to wheat—so closely that an amateur cannot distinguish between the two when they are growing in fields.

The grain is used to make rye flour—which in turn is used, combined with wheat flour, to make rye bread, all-rye pumpernickel, and certain kinds of flat breads, as well as whiskey, gin, and malt liquors. Because it can withstand colder temperatures than wheat, rye is a staple in northern Europe and in Russia, and early settlers in New England found that they could grow rye more successfully than wheat.

Rye flour can be had in some supermarkets, as well as in specialty and health food shops. All-rye and rye-combination flours must be refrigerated. Rye cereals, both dry and to-be-cooked are widely available, as is rye bread—light and dark, with caraway seeds or without—and pumpernickel.

Nutritionally, rye flour—which is not enriched, as is usually true of wheat flour—is a source of carbohydrate, with small amounts of protein, potassium, and the B vitamins.

The word rye is also used as the name of a category of whiskey, not as popular as it once was. See LIQUORS. See also RYE FLOUR.

SACCHARIN

When, in 1977, the FDA proposed to ban saccharin as a possible cancer-causing agent, a wave of protest went up. It came in part from diabetics, to whom such a ban would mean no sweets whatever in their already considerably restricted diets. And it came in part from weight-loss dieters and those who keep themselves on somewhat restricted diets to control their weight. To these it meant, for the most part, no more low- or no-calorie soft drinks, one of the staples of those diets.

Reprieve came with a postponement of the ban. However, after February 20, 1978, all packages of saccharin were required to carry on the label the warning that the contents may be cancer-causing. Meanwhile, the FDA held new hearings on cyclamate, an artificial sweetener taken off the market in 1969, but concluded that the ban must remain in force. Aspartame and Neo-DHC are being investigated as this is written. The former is an artificial sweetener for which its proponents claim 200 times the sweetness of sugar and only ⅛ calorie per teaspoon. Neo-DHC, derived from a substance in grapefruit peel, is being worked on by two companies along with the USDA. See also ADDITIVES AND PRESERVATIVES.

SADDLE

A cut of meat—lamb, pork, or beef—that includes the two hind legs and the portion of the back below the last rib.

SAFFLOWER OIL: see OILS, SALAD AND COOKING

SAFFRON: see SPICES and HERBS AND SAVORY SEASONINGS

SAGE: see CHEESE and HERBS AND SAVORY SEASONINGS

SAGO

This is a kind of flour, red to brown in color, obtained from the pith in the trunks of the sago and other tropical palm trees. It is an easily digested form of starch and is a diet staple of many countries in the areas in which the palms grow.

SAINT JOHN'S BREAD: see CAROB

SALAD DRESSINGS

The two chief dressings for salad are sauce vinaigrette—french dressing—and mayonnaise, but there are others. There are, to begin with, many changes to be rung on those two old standbys. Then there is sour cream, which can be varied in a dozen ways for a dozen kinds of salads. There are old-fashioned boiled dressings for both savory and fruit salads. For fruit, there is honey, its sticky sweetness cut by combining it with liberal amounts of citrus fruit juice.

Vinaigrette and variations. Basic french dressing is a combination of oil and vinegar, with salt and black pepper as seasonings. The oil may be one of the virtually flavorless kitchen OILS that we use for both salad and cooking or olive oil. The vinegar may be the ordinary white or cider type, or it may be red or white wine vinegar, which are available plain or flavored with garlic, tarragon, or some other herb, or the vinegar may be omitted entirely and lemon juice substituted for it.

To the plain french dressing, by whatever combination of vinegars and oils you concoct, certain additions can be made. Here are some of the many possible variations.

chiffonade dressing: To basic french dressing, add chopped hard-cooked egg, pickled beets, and green olives, as well as minced parsley and grated onion.

mustard dressing: Add dry or dijon-style prepared mustard for sharpness.

herb-mustard dressing: To the mustard dressing add minced parsley, tarragon, chervil, and chives.

garlic dressing: Crush garlic and salt to a paste, add the vinegar and oil as for basic french dressing.

french dressing for meat salads: Make garlic dressing, add a few drops worcestershire sauce plus pan juices from roasted meat.

curry dressing: To basic french, add minced shallot, curry powder.

anchovy dressing: To basic french, add anchovy paste to taste.

cream french: Combine heavy cream, lemon juice, salt, white pepper, and olive oil.

avocado dressing: Beat together half-and-half basic french, mashed avocado; adjust seasonings.

roquefort french: To cream french, add crumbled roquefort cheese.

lorenzo dressing: Combine chili sauce, salt, pepper, minced watercress leaves, and oil.

Mayonnaise and variations: see MAYONNAISE

Old-fashioned boiled dressings. These are what grandma used to make, and we still make and enjoy. The basic ingredients for the savory type are eggs (or just yolks), flour, vinegar, milk or cream, sugar, mustard, salt and pepper. Grated onion may be added. So may minced garlic or garlic juice, or virtually any other flavor-changer that suits your fancy. The amount of sugar controls the sweetness, so that the dressing can be just as sweet or as tart as your family likes it. Many recipes call for butter to be stirred in at the end of the cooking period; this makes a richer dressing, but is not absolutely necessary, and its omission can be a boon to those with an eye on their waistlines.

Use this dressing on coleslaw, potato or macaroni salad. Cook bacon and heat the dressing with some of the bacon fat for Pennsylvania Dutch-style wilted lettuce. Fairly sweet, it's excellent with a mixed fruit salad. Or for fruit, make a variation of boiled dressing, the basic ingredients of which are eggs, sugar, flour, concentrate for orange juice, water, salt, and nutmeg, with cream stirred in at the end of the cooking period.

Sour cream dressings. Use dairy sour cream and, depending on the salad you have in mind and the flavors you like, add any combination of these: lemon juice, sugar, salt, white pepper, paprika, minced chives or parsley, mustard, anchovy paste, poppy or toasted sesame seeds, chopped nuts, minced fresh dill, tarragon or basil, crumbled crisp bacon, garlic or onion juice, chopped pimiento, chopped stuffed or ripe olives, minced watercress or nasturtium leaves. For variety (and fewer calories) add any of these ingredients to unflavored yogurt rather than sour cream.

Honey-based dressings. To your taste, cut the sweet thickness of the honey with lime (for choice) or lemon or grapefruit juice. Use as is, or add any or a combination of these: grated orange peel, finely chopped nuts, poppy or toasted sesame seeds, ground nutmeg, cinnamon, cardamom, curry powder, or crumbled rosemary or marjoram.

Besides the homemade kinds, you have your choice of a wide variety of bottled dressings, some very good indeed.

SALAD GREENS AND PLANTS

A head of iceberg lettuce doth not a salad make. If you're in that rut, it's high time you got out of it and looked around you at the big garden of salad makings. Not only are there other kinds of salad greens, but there are many vegetables—some of which we tend to think of only in their cooked state—that make salads sit up and sing. Here are some of the greens:

belgian endive	cos lettuce
bibb lettuce	dandelion greens
boston (or butter) lettuce	curly endive
chicory	escarole

leaf lettuce (best known kinds are redhead and salad bowl)	nasturtium leaves
	romaine (same as cos)
	spinach
limestone lettuce	watercress

And don't forget iceberg, as long as you vary it with other greens, or use a mixture in a tossed green salad—it keeps well, and adds chewy crispness to a bowl of salad.

When you go to buy salad makings, be on the lookout for young and tender greens, free of dirt. (But dirt is by nature a part of some—often there's a muddy clump at the very heart of a head of boston lettuce, for example.) Yellow, dry, or wilted leaves or those with brown edges proclaim that the green has outlived its usefulness. Store in separate plastic bags in the refrigerator's crisper.

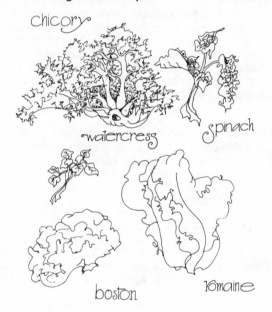

Most cookbooks advocate washing the lettuce before storing it, but we feel it's better simply to pick off any discolored leaves and store without washing. It's exceedingly difficult to get off every drop of water, and moisture encourages rust and rot. Instead, wash the leaves and dry them as thoroughly as possible shortly before you are going to use them. If you're making green salad for a large group, wash and dry the greens a couple of hours before the party and add whatever else (except dressing) is going into the salad. Lay out a very large plastic bag and place a spread-out towel inside. Pile the salad on the towel, close the bag with a twister tie or pipe cleaner, and carefully, gently put the whole thing into the refrigerator, towel side down, until you're ready to dress the salad.

528

And the other vegetables. We know, of course, that we make slaw from cabbage. But thin-shredded cabbage, red or green—chinese cabbage, too—makes an attractive and crunchy addition to a mixed green salad. So do these other vegetables, for variety's sake:

hearts of palm (canned)
white, kidney, or ceci beans (canned)
artichoke hearts (cooked)
sliced cucumber
sliced water chestnuts or bamboo shoots
thin-sliced raw turnip
thin onion rings
chopped celery stalks and leaves

raw carrot (shredded or (thin-sliced)
bean or alfalfa sprouts
sliced radishes
sliced mushrooms
thin-sliced raw zucchini
strips of green pepper
sliced finocchio
tomatoes (big ones seeded, little ones halved)

Some fruits go well in a tossed green salad, too—slices of avocado, sections of orange or grapefruit, chunks of apple or fresh pear, whole or halved (seeded) grapes, slices of fresh peach. Indeed, almost anything goes.

SALAD OILS: see OILS, SALAD AND COOKING

SALADS

There are so many kinds of salads, both side-dish and main-dish, that one never ought to have to stop and ponder what kind to serve. A mixed green salad is right with just about anything, and there are dozens of ways to garnish it. Here are some tasty ones:

cubes or slivers of cheese
small pretzel sticks
plain or flavored croutons
bite-size dry cereal
nuts—plain, salted, and/or toasted
fried chinese noodles (canned or packaged)

broken cheese crackers
coconut chips (packaged)
pickle slices or chunks
chopped or sliced hard-cooked eggs

And there are, believe us, others. Prepare salad, dress it, sprinkle on one of the above, and toss lightly again. And that barely scratches the surface of the tossed salad subject. Vary the greens, vary the vegetable additions, vary the kinds of dressings, vary the garnishing additions, and you have literally hundreds of different salads.

Side-dish salads. Tossed green salad is not the only one. When you bog down, change the pace with one of these:

waldorf: Apple chunks (don't peel them), diced celery, walnuts; another time, try pear chunks and pecans. (See WALDORF SALAD.)

sweet carrot: ⅔ coarsely grated carrot, ⅓ raisins.

slaw: Make it with green or napa or red or chinese cabbage; add pineapple chunks or seedless grapes or chopped peanuts or minced onion or grated carrot or slivered green pepper or thin radish slices. (See COLESLAW.)

russian—or call it french or italian: Nobody's quite sure of the rightful claimant's name, but it's mixed cooked vegetables with plenty of minced garlic and chopped celery; dress it with mayonnaise or boiled dressing.

spinach: Cartwheels of hard-cooked eggs and thin rings of red onion enliven the spinach; use hot bacon dressing.

hearts of lettuce: Sometimes the simple one is the best; top with roquefort or russian dressing.

stuffed endive: Pale spears of belgian endive stuffed with cream cheese with chives, served on lettuce leaves. (See BELGIAN ENDIVE.)

white bean: ½ drained (canned) white beans, ½ a combination of chopped celery, sliced scallions; season well, toss with olive oil and white wine vinegar.

beets and red dutch eggs: Beet and onion slices in a dressing of oil and vinegar and a dash of cloves, with part of the beet liquid; immerse peeled hard-cooked eggs in the liquid, let stand 24 hours.

pawnbrokers' special: Balls of three kinds of melon—honeydew, watermelon, and cantaloupe—with honey-lime dressing or half-and-half sour cream and mayonnaise.

avocado/grapefruit: Sections of each alternating in a wheel on leaves of boston lettuce.

fodder: Alfalfa sprouts, pine nuts, and shredded lettuce.

caesar: Romaine, croutons, cut-up anchovy fillets, with its own special dressing of a raw or coddled egg, garlic-flavored olive oil, lemon juice, salt, pepper, and mustard, the whole deal sprinkled with parmesan.

asparagus vinaigrette: That's it—cold cooked asparagus marinated for several hours in french dressing.

scallion or leek: Same thing with cooked scallions or leeks.

artichoke: Cold cooked artichoke with french dressing into which to dip the leaves; or cook, cool, and marinate artichoke hearts.

green bean: Cold cooked green beans, lorenzo dressing.

cucumber: Thin-sliced cucumbers in plain yogurt with chives.

tomato: Sliced beefsteak tomatoes liberally sprinkled with minced fresh basil, salt, and lots of coarse black pepper, dressed with french dressing with a speck of sugar.

There are many more—these happen to be our favorites. And don't forget gelatin salads and fruit salads of various kinds to enliven other meals. (See FRUIT COCKTAILS.)

Main-dish salads. These go on picnics, of course. And they are just the thing for a summer luncheon or supper, or to take their place on a buffet table for a crowd. Here are some of the classics, both elegant and homely:

sausage and kraut: Slice the sausage (kielbasa is good), combine with the kraut; season and dress with vinaigrette.

beef: Julienne strips of rare roast beef, paper-thin onion rings, strips of dill pickle; olive oil and red wine vinegar combine for the dressing.

jambon persilée (parslied ham): ⅔ ham chunks, ⅓ snipped parsley in a delicate, lemony white-wine gelatin.

chicken: There are dozens of versions—with celery and minced onion, with fresh pineapple, with seedless grapes, with chopped walnuts, with capers and lemon mayonnaise, with roquefort-stuffed pitted fresh cherries are only a few.

potato: Here, too, there are many—hot, with bacon dressing; cold made of ½ potatoes and half hard-cooked egg, or with lots of chopped dill pickle, or with onion and celery and slivers of ham, or with apples and curry dressing, and many, many more.

niçoise: Bed of greens on a platter; arranged on it in separate heaps are vinaigrette-marinated cooked potatoes and green beans, tomatoes, tunafish; decorated with anchovy fillets.

chef's: Bed of mixed greens on which julienne strips of ham, chicken, and cheese, slices of hard-cooked egg, and wedges of tomato are laid in an attractive pattern.

macaroni: Start out with cold, well-drained elbow macaroni or small seashells or any other chunky pasta you fancy; add all or some of these: chopped celery, chopped onion, sliced green olives, cheddar cheese cubes, ham slivers, pickle slices, chunks of hard-cooked egg, shredded red cabbage.

shrimp: Plain or with celery and a bit of onion, dressed with green mayonnaise with plenty of lemon juice, or with lots of capers and plain lemon mayonnaise.

salmon: Cold poached or canned salmon with celery, chives, cucumber, slices of sweet pickle.

tomato surprise: Making these for the first time, one home cook who was not a tomato lover was heard to say, "I'll be surprised if anyone eats them!"—but they're very good. Hollow out medium-size tomatoes and set upside down to drain; salt lightly, then fill with chicken, shrimp, or russian salad.

avocado half-shells: Halve ripe avocados, fill the cavities with crabmeat, shrimp, or chicken salad—chicken with a curry dressing is a particularly good choice.

And there are many more, of course. Every household has its favorites, asked for again and again.

A commonsense plea. No matter what anybody says, wash your salad bowl! It's true, some very prestigious cooking experts advocate using a wooden salad bowl and never washing it, simply wiping it out with absorbent paper after use. Stop and think a minute. Old oil gets rancid. And the smell and flavor of rancid oil are disgusting. Would you wipe off the dishes with a paper towel after dinner and consider them ready for the next meal?

A wooden salad bowl, attractive as it may be, is a very

poor choice. If the inside of the bowl has a finish, mandatory washing will wear the finish away. If it is not finished, oil and vinegar and onion and garlic and anchovies and all the other high smells/flavors of salad ingredients will sink into the wood and become impossible to remove. Handsome glass and ceramic bowls are available in a wide variety of shapes and sizes, and are a far more sensible—and hygienic—choice. Don't decide on a metal one, though. It will wash well, but it will give a metallic flavor to the salad. See also GARNISHING and GELATIN.

SALAMI: see SAUSAGES

SALMI

Unless you're an expert cook, you're unlikely to make a salmi, but it doesn't hurt to know what it is. A game bird is partially roasted, then carved and cooked in a chafing dish with truffles and mushrooms in a white-wine sauce. It is served on sautéed bread spread with pâté de foie gras. Beautiful, beautiful—but hardly the thing you run up when unexpected guests drop in.

SALMON: see FISH

SALMON, CANNED

This used to be a pantry staple. It was always easy to make a salmon loaf or salad, or cream the fish to serve on toast, when your inventiveness about what to have for dinner failed you. But in recent years canned salmon has become so expensive we all think twice before we buy it, again before we use it.

SALSIFY: see UNUSUAL VEGETABLES

SALT

Would you be surprised to learn that only 5 percent, at most, of this country's salt supply is for table use? It's true. The rest goes into commercial projects—everything from preserving pickles to melting ice on the highways.

Grandma would have been lost without her old wooden salt box, hung conveniently near the stove where she could reach in for a pinch whenever she needed it. And if she spilled a little in transit, she threw a few grains over her left shoulder to ward off bad luck.

Most of the salt we use comes from rock salt mines or from brine wells—the water from these is commercially evaporated, leaving the salt behind. A third source is the natural evaporation of sea water, which results in larger, "saltier" crystals, generally crushed for table use in a salt grinder. Much of the salt we buy has a small amount of iodine in it (goiter has been almost wiped out since this practice was begun), plus an agent to help it flow freely, but it is almost pure sodium chloride. A substitute, made with potassium chloride, is marketed for those on low-salt diets. (There can be no such thing as a salt-free diet, because sodium chloride occurs, in varying quantities, in just about everything we eat.) The human body is, in fact, about 2 percent salt, necessary to keep us in good health—it aids digestion, and maintains the delicate balance of fluids.

There are salts available other than the table salt we buy. Kosher salt, prepared under religious supervision, is somewhat coarser than common table salt, and has no additives. There are various seasoned salts, some with butter flavoring, some with herbs and spices. And there is rock salt, not for eating but for such purposes as use in an ice cream freezer of the old-fashioned kind and for sprinkling on the slippery front steps to melt the ice and keep the mailman from going rump over teakettle. (He has enough trouble with the neighborhood dogs.) See also ROCK SALT.

SALT PORK: see BACON

SAMBALS: see CURRY

SAMSOE: see CHEESE

SANDWICHES

Ever since the Earl of Sandwich, not wishing to leave the gaming tables, slapped a hunk of meat between two slices of bread and called it dinner, we've been a world of sandwich eaters. Elegant sandwiches with such fillings as shad roe, caviar, or foie gras for a wedding reception. Peanut butter and jelly for the kids' lunches. Watercress or cucumber for a refined English tea. Reuben—corned beef, swiss cheese, and sauerkraut—or rare roast beef or piled-high pastrami for starving trenchermen. Grilled hamburgers and hot dogs on buns for a satisfying cookout. Ham and cheese for a picnic. Egg salad on toast for a quick drugstore-counter lunch. Mile-high and two-miles-long heroes to fill the bottomless pit that is a teenage boy's stomach. The tag end of last night's tuna-fish salad in a sandwich for mom's lunch. Bagels with lox and cream cheese for a New York breakfast. Tacos for a Tex-Mex snack. Pita stuffed with roast lamb and onions and peppers for an eat-on-the-street snack. The wonderful, mouth-watering array of a platter of Danish smørrebrød. Grilled cheese with bacon and tomato for lunch on the run. Fried-pie empañadas to munch at a fiesta. Italian sausages, sweet or hot, with a glass of red wine at the street fair.

Don't let anyone try to say that we don't eat sandwiches. Or that we don't relish them, or that we could do without them. Hungry, just from reading the list? Make yourself a sandwich. See also FILLINGS and GARNISHING.

SAPODILLAS: see EXOTIC FRUIT

SAPSAGO: see CHEESE

SARDINES

"Sardine" is not the name of a kind of fish, but indicates the kind of treatment the fish has been given. Herring, alewife, pilchard, brisling, sprat—all can be sardines if caught when they are small and immature. The fishermen scale and salt the fish aboard their boats, take them to the cannery when the trip is over. There the fish are washed, cooked, canned —in brine or oil, mustard or tomato sauce—sealed, and cooked again. Some sardines are canned whole—that is, with heads and tails and bones still in place, and can be eaten that way, as the bones are very soft. Others have heads and tails removed, but bones are left. Still others have heads and tails removed, as well as skin and bones.

Sardines in sauce can be served on toast. Or make sardine sandwiches or canapés, or mash and season for an appetizer spread. And there are those who dote on the little fish as a satisfying, right-out-of-the-can snack, or with scrambled eggs for breakfast.

One sardine about 2⅔ inches long (16 to 20 in a can) contains 10 calories. The fish supply high-quality protein, as well as calcium, phosphorus, sodium, and potassium.

SARDO: see CHEESE

SARSAPARILLA

This is a soft drink. Its distinctive flavor is derived from the roots of a South American vine related to the lily. If you've never seen a Western in which the men belly up to the bar and one by one order whiskey, and then the hero—tall, dark, handsome, and wearing a white hat—asks for a sarsaparilla, you haven't lived.

SAUCE SORCERY: see page 513

SAUCES: see CHILE SAUCE, HOLLANDAISE SAUCE, HOT PEPPER SAUCE, MAYONNAISE, NEWBURG, SOY SAUCE, STEAK SAUCE, WHITE SAUCE, WORCESTERSHIRE SAUCE

SAUERKRAUT

While the British were giving their sailors lime or lemon juice to prevent scurvy, that scourge of long sea voyages, the Dutch were accomplishing the same thing with *zourkool*— sauerkraut. Kraut is an excellent source of ascorbic acid— vitamin C—and of some of the B vitamins and needed minerals as well.

Although we don't seem to know what they called it (sauerkraut is a German word, meaning sour cabbage), the Chinese were eating it some 2,000 years ago. The laborers who built the Great Wall of China were kept fit by the sauerkraut that was served them along with their daily ration of rice. Genghis Khan—who managed to sack China in spite of the Great Wall—took the pickled cabbage back home, along with everything else he could lay hand on, and later carried it into Europe. There the Germans fell on it with shouts of joy.

That early cabbage was pickled in wine, but some thrifty German discovered that just as good results could be had by fermenting the cabbage in salt, and that's the way it's been done ever since.

Kraut in America. The taste and know-how for sauerkraut came to this country with German and Dutch settlers. Their descendants, today's Pennsylvania Dutch, have a great fondness for it. They are a people observant of nature's ways. At Christmas they serve poultry with sauerkraut, at New Year's, sauerkraut with pork—because the chicken scratches backward, signifying the end of the old year, but the pig roots forward, looking to the new one.

Buying, storing, serving. In great grandma's day, kraut was made at home in a barrel stashed in the basement or cold cellar, thrifty use-up of the extras from the family cabbage patch. In early grocery stores, the sauerkraut barrel and the dill pickle barrel stood side by side. But today, sauerkraut is sold in cans to be found on grocery shelves all year around, and as "fresh" kraut, in jars in the refrigerated section of the market.

Although it is pickled, sauerkraut is by no means indestuctible. Store cans on cool, dark shelves, and plan to use within 6 months; it does not have as long a shelf life as many others of the canned vegetables. Store jars of fresh kraut in the refrigerator, to be used within 5 days. As a general rule, fresh kraut has a milder flavor than the canned variety.

After opening, rinse sauerkraut in a colander or sieve under cold running water. Simmer 10 to 15 minutes in unsalted water; long cooking makes it strong and dark-colored. If you enjoy the flavor, add caraway seeds to the kraut as it cooks. Drain, dress with butter, and serve. Or, if you are having roast pork—one of sauerkraut's favorite partners— drain a little of the pork drippings into a skillet and sauté the kraut briefly, until it begins to brown and takes on some of the good pork flavor. Or casserole sauerkraut with apple wedges to serve with pork or game. Or add minced onion to cooled kraut, dress with homestyle boiled dressing, and serve as a salad. A reliable general cookbook will guide you to a dozen other ways to serve this good, good-flavored vegetable.

One cup of sauerkraut furnishes only 42 calories; it is rich in essential vitamins and minerals—and very high in sodium, making it forbidden to those on low-salt diets.

Canned sauerkraut juice is also available. Chilled, it is a tart waker-upper, a tangy appetizer.

SAUSAGES

It should be no surprise that sausage comes so close to sauerkraut in the alphabetical scheme of things. The two are old friends, and have gotten together for many a good meal. One of their great partnerships is in the hot dog with sauerkraut on a bun that's been slathered with mustard—which somehow always tastes much better when bought from a street vendor than when made at home.

In 1900, the slang for the frankfurter was dachshund sausage—nobody had ever heard of a hot dog. On a chilly day in April of that year, one Harry Mozley, president of the catering firm that furnished snacks at the Polo Grounds where the old New York Giants used to play, was painfully aware that in this weather his cold drinks and ice cream were finding few customers. Then inspiration came to him. He sent his men out to scour the neighborhood for all the dachshund sausages and rolls they could find. It wasn't long before the vendors were roaming the Polo Grounds stands crying, "They're red hot! Get your dachshund sausages while they're red hot!"

But it was Tad Dorgan, the well-known cartoonist, who gave the new treat its name. He drew a now-famous cartoon of the sausages in buns barking at one another. The problem was, he hadn't the foggiest notion of how to spell "dachshund." Finally, in his caption, he simply called the sausage "hot dog" and the name has stuck ever since.

Harry Mozley is dead. But it's nice to know that his granddaughter is married to a scion of one of the biggest mustard-making family firms. A hot dog simply isn't a hot dog without mustard.

Every shape, size, and flavor. Sausages can be classified in several ways. Cook-before-eating sausages are made of fresh meat, neither cured nor smoked; they must be refrigerated and should be stored only up to 2 days, as they are very perishable; as they are all, or at least in part, fresh pork, they must be thoroughly cooked. Ready-to-serve sausages may be made of uncured or cured meats; they are perishable, and may be refrigerated up to 1 week. Fully cooked, they can be served cold or heated. Cooked sausages may be refrigerated up to 1 week; they are fully cooked, and some are smoked after cooking. Semidry sausages also need no cooking; less than 20 percent of the natural moisture content has been removed; they can be stored in the refrigerator up to 2 weeks. Dry sausages have had more than 20 percent of the moisture removed, and will also keep up to 2 weeks under refrigeration. They are of two kinds, salamis and cervelats, the former more heavily seasoned.

There are, in all, perhaps 250 kinds of sausages to be had. Here are some of the types that seem to be sausage-fanciers' favorites.

alessandri: Salami, but of American rather than Italian origin. The same applies to *alpino.*

arles: Salami of French origin, but very like the Italian.

berliner-style: Coarsely ground cured pork plus some mildly cured finely chopped beef. Unseasoned, but smoked and cooked.

blood sausage (blutwurst): Cooked, diced pork fat, finely ground meat, beef blood, and gelatin, well seasoned. Ready to eat.

bockwurst: Large part veal, smaller part pork, with milk, chives, eggs, and chopped parsley. Must be thoroughly cooked.

bologna: The big favorite next to frankfurters. Finely ground cured beef and pork combination that can be had in a ring shape, large rounds, or square sandwich shape. Ready to eat.

bratwurst: Pork or pork with veal, flavored with sage and lemon. Comes in links like frankfurters. Cook before eating.

braunschweiger: Smoked liver sausage, ready to eat. Sometimes studded with pistachio nuts.

cappicola: Air-dried sausage of pork seasoned with hot pepper and given a mild cure. Ready to eat.

cervelat: Name of a number of much-alike sausages, dry and mildly seasoned. Ready to eat.

chorizos: Hotly spicy Spanish-type sausage, made of coarsely cut pork. Cook before eating.

farmer cervelat: Half-and-half beef and pork, coarsely cut, mildly seasoned, cured and dried. Cook before eating.

frankfurters: Or call them franks, or wieners, or hot dogs— by whatever name, they are far and away America's favorite sausage. Serve hot or cold, but in either case cook before eating. Buy them as big dinner franks or regular, in-a-bun size, or long "Texas Style" at fairs or carnivals, or little cocktail types. See also HOT DOGS.

headcheese: Made of the (cooked) hog's head with natural gelatin, nicely seasoned. Ready to eat.

kielbasa (Polish sausage): Coarsely ground pork with some beef, garlic added. In long, small diameter links. Cook before eating.

knockwurst (knoblauch): Like frankfurters, but with garlic as one of the seasonings. Cook before eating.

land jaeger: Dry, smoked Swiss sausage, pressed into squared shape. Ready to eat.

liver sausage (liverwurst): Puréed livers and pork, spiced and onion seasoned. Ready to eat.

mettwurst: Largely cured beef, with some pork, flavored with pepper and coriander. Cook before eating.

pepperoni: Dry, Italian-type sausage of pork with some beef, red-pepper seasoned. The sausage of choice for pizza. Ready to eat.

pork sausage (fresh): Made of high-quality pork, gently

seasoned—often with sage. Can be had as small links, a long coil, or patties—sometimes in bulk. Cook thoroughly.

salami: Generic name for Italian-type sausage, dry and highly seasoned. May be labeled Cotto, Genoa, Milano, Sicilian, as well as German-type and Hungarian-type, both heavily smoked. Moistened with wine or grape juice. Ready to eat. See also ITALIAN SAUSAGE.

souse: Like headcheese, except for sweet-sour flavor.

summer sausage: A mildly seasoned, soft cervelat. Ready to eat.

thuringer-style sausage: Like fresh pork sausage, but sometimes with veal and beef; sage is not used. Cook before eating.

If frankfurters are the beginning and end of your sausage experience, it's time you branched out. Try that homely but delicious British dish, bangers 'n' mashed: fluffy mashed potatoes with precooked little fresh pork sausage links half buried in them, a little of the sausage fat dribbled over before reheating in the oven. Simmer a ring bologna until heated through, serve with little new potatoes and glazed onions. Let a kielbasa take the place of corned beef for a different boiled dinner. Thickly slice liver sausage, dredge with flour, brown lightly—often entices kids and husbands who "can't stand liver." And there are dozens more ways with sausage. See also PIGS IN BLANKET.

SAUTE, TO: see page 450

SAVORY, SUMMER AND WINTER: see
    HERBS AND SAVORY SEASONINGS

SAVOY CABBAGE: see CABBAGE

SAVVY COOK, THE: see page 599

SBRINZ: see CHEESE

SCALD, TO: see page 450

SCALLIONS: see ONIONS

SCALLOP: see SQUASH

SCALLOP, TO: see page 450

SCALLOPS: see SHELLFISH

SCAMPI

Often, on menus, you see the offering "Shrimp Scampi." But scampi is not a way of preparing shrimp, although shrimp is often prepared in the same manner as scampi. These are a delicate, tender shellfish resembling shrimp but with a different—many say much better—flavor. They are found in the Adriatic Sea. Italians grill them with oil and garlic. We sometimes do this with shrimp—but that in no way makes the two the same.

SCORE, TO: see page 448

SCOTCH: see LIQUORS

SCOTCH EGGS

Hard-cooked eggs given an overcoat of bulk fresh pork sausage before they are deep-fat fried. May be eaten hot or cold. They are a good brunch dish, fine for taking on a picnic.

SCRAMBLE, TO: see page 450

SCRAPPLE

Pennsylvania is scrapple country, both in Philadelphia and in the Pennsylvania Dutch area that surrounds Lancaster. Scrapple is yellow cornmeal cooked in pork broth, with bits of finely chopped pork incorporated. The mixture is poured into a loaf pan to cool and congeal, then sliced and fried.

Canned scrapple can sometimes be found in supermarkets, but it is in very limited distribution—you'll have to hunt for it.

SEA BASS: see FISH

SEA SALT: see SALT

SEAFOOD: see FISH and SHELLFISH

SEAR, TO: see page 450

SEASON

Two meanings: 1) to add salt, pepper, herbs, or spices to a food to enhance its flavor; 2) when any given food is at its best and most abundant, that food is "in season."

SEASONINGS: see HERBS AND SAVORY
    SEASONINGS, SALT, SEEDS, and SPICES

SEEDS

Some of the various seasonings we use in cooking are made from the ground seeds of certain plants. But often we use the seeds themselves, to add both flavor and texture to many foods. For some foods the seeds are ground (in the blender), for some they are left whole. It's a matter of choice—whole they are in smaller pieces than chopped nuts; if you like the crunch, don't grind them. Here are some of the common seasoning seeds and their uses:

anise: In butter, on crackers; in cabbage soup and many cream soups; in coffeecakes and the breads for tea sandwiches; stirred into cottage cheese; to flavor stews, particularly lamb and veal; in butter, on carrots; in cookies, such as springerle and others, and in anise cake; as a flavoring for many kinds of candy.

caraway: In liptauer CHEESE; in cabbage soup and clam chowder; in rye bread and as a sprinkled-on topping for rolls; mixed with cheddar or gorgonzola as an appetizer spread; in deviled eggs; to season pork, liver, kidneys, and in goulash; mixed into turnips, sauerkraut, rice, and the batter for potato pancakes; sprinkled over beets or in the beet-pickling liquid; in coleslaw; as the flavoring for seed cake, a British tea-time favorite; to season baked apples or pears; in candy.

cardamom: To flavor fruit cups; in pea soup; in danish pastry, coffeecakes, and sweet rolls; in anything made with orange or orange flavored; in cookies; to season baked apples; to give special flair to demitasse; in jellies, honey, pickles.

celery seed: In appetizer spreads and dips; in almost any soup; in stews—fish, meat, or poultry; to season stuffings; stirred into scrambled eggs; in meat loaves; in stewed tomatoes; to flavor aspics and fish or potato salads; in salad dressings.

coriander: In some soups, notably pea; in buns, breads, and biscuits; mixed into cream or cheddar cheese; to season pork roasts and sausages; in stuffings; to season rice and fried potatoes; in tossed green salads; as seasoning for gingerbread, various cakes, cookies; in applesauce and pie and baked apples; to season stewed pears; in rice pudding; in pickles; in candy.

cumin: In appetizer cheese spreads; to flavor chicken, pea, and bean soup; in various breads; in deviled eggs; in many Mexican dishes; to season chili con carne; to season sauerkraut and cabbage; to season chicken dishes; to flavor rice; in sugar cookies; in fruit pies.

dill: To season any kind of fish cocktail; in avocado dishes; to flavor borscht, tomato, and bean soups; with most kinds of fish, in poaching liquid and/or sauce; in cottage cheese; to flavor lamb stew, creamed chicken; to season sauerkraut, green and wax beans, beets; in coleslaw, potato, cucumber, and avocado salads; in apple pie; in pickles; to season sour cream.

fennel: To season seed crackers; in cream soups; to top rolls; to season halibut and codfish; in omelets; to season liver and pork dishes; in sauerkraut, lentils, and pickled beets; in fish and mixed green salads; in seed cake, cookies, and apple pie; to season baked fruit and puddings; in pickles; in candy.

mustard: In many kinds of appetizers; in potato soup; as a garnish for scalloped fish, scalloped eggs; with any cheese; to season steaks and chops, ham and cold cuts; to flavor baked beans, green beans; in macaroni dishes; in coleslaw and tossed salads, and to flavor salad dressings; folded into mayonnaise, béarnaise and cheese sauces; in pickles. (See MUSTARD.)

poppy: In cheese spreads for appetizers; in various breads and rolls, in the dough or as a filling; in salad dressings; to flavor noodles, mashed potatoes; in several kinds of cakes and cookies; with pears.

sesame: In dips and spreads for appetizers; as a soup garnish; topping for rolls; in fillings for tea sandwiches; as a topping for casseroles; in hashed brown potatoes; mixed with or topping noodles; in potato salads, as a garnish for other salads; in various cookies and cakes; as a substitute for nuts in anything; in several kinds of candy; as a decoration for icings.

And these are only some of the uses to be made of the great flavor and crunchy texture of the several kinds of seeds. See also HERBS AND SAVORY SEASONINGS, SPICES, and SUNFLOWER SEEDS.

SELENIUM: see special feature: NUTRITION NOTEBOOK

SEMOLINA: see PASTA

SESAME: see SEEDS

SESAME-SEED OIL: see OILS, SALAD AND COOKING

SEVILLE ORANGES: see ORANGES

SHAD ROE: see ROE

SHALLOTS: see ONIONS

SHELLFISH

For those long-ago peoples who were lucky enough to live by the water, shellfish were an important source of food. Unlike the finny fish, they did not have to be caught, only gathered.

There are both saltwater and freshwater shellfish. All have these characteristics in common:

- most are hatched from eggs, and when they hatch are creatures quite different from what they'll be as adults
- they have a shell, but unlike fish, no fins, skull, or vertebrae; shells may be single (univalves) or two-part (bivalves)
- they are an excellent source of high-quality protein, are rich in the essential minerals, and contain the vitamins, other than vitamin C, needed in the diet; they are all low-calorie and low-sodium, making them useful in diets with those requirements
- they are easily digestible; most are very tender

Before modern freezing methods and rapid freezer or refrigerator transportation, shellfish could be enjoyed in abundance only by those living close to their home. But now these delicious foods can be enjoyed by everyone, no matter where they live.

Types and kinds. There are two basic kinds of shellfish, mollusks and crustaceans. Mollusks have a soft body fully or partially enclosed in a univalve or bivalve shell. Abalone, conch, and periwinkle are univalve mollusks; clam, cockle, mussel, oyster, and scallop are bivalves. The second type, crustaceans, have elongated and segmented bodies, eyes

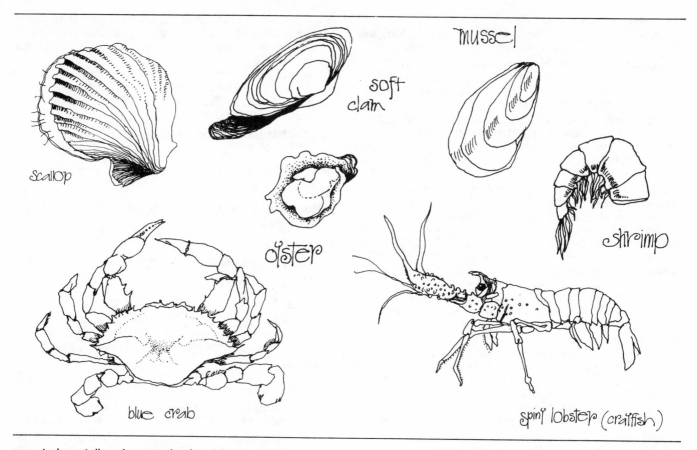

scallop

soft clam

mussel

oyster

shrimp

blue crab

spiny lobster (crayfish)

mounted on stalks, claws, and softer, jointed shells. Lobster, crab, and shrimp are of this group.

Choosing and buying shellfish. Use your eyes, but also your nose and your fingers when making your purchase of fresh shellfish. Lobster and crab should show signs of life —movement, wriggling of claws—or don't buy; if they are dead, it's impossible to determine how long they've been dead. Crab and lobster are also sold cooked, in which condition they are red in color. Smell them—there should be no high, unpleasant odor. You can also buy crab and lobster "picked"—the meat removed from the shell. Oysters, hard-shell clams, and scallops should all close their shells when tapped with a finger; if they don't, they are not alive. However, all of these are also sold shucked—removed from their shells —and in this case your sense of smell should guide you. Shrimp are sold headless; they can be "green"—shell in place, not cooked—cooked but not shelled, or cooked, shelled, and with the central back vein removed. Each process done by the fish market raises the per-pound price of the shrimp, but take into consideration that when they are

shelled you are not paying for the weight of the shell. Here, too, let your nose guide your purchases. Shrimp occur in a number of sizes, from very small to very large.

Shellfish of most kinds are also available frozen, in shell or out, cooked or uncooked. They can also be had canned, in which case they are always shelled; they may be vacuum-packed or in brine or their own juices. Look for the USDA inspection shield on canned and frozen products.

Keeping and cooking shellfish. All of these creatures are very perishable indeed, and speed must be the watchword. Cook live shellfish as soon as you get them home; refrigerate the meat and use it as soon as possible. It's best to buy shellfish the same day that you are going to eat them. For storage longer than the second day, freeze them. Shuck oysters, clams, and scallops before freezing; plan on using within 3 months. Cook lobster and crab; use within 1 month. Uncooked shrimp, shelled or not, can be freezer stored up to 3 months. Plan on using commercial, packaged frozen shellfish within 4 months.

Most shellfish are tender, and overcooking toughens

them. Mollusks in shell are done when the shells open—if the shell does not, the mollusk was dead before cooking, and must be discarded. Out of shell, they are cooked when the edges of the meat curl, a matter of a very few minutes.

Crustaceans are done when they turn pink or red—from 2 to 4 minutes for shrimp to 10 or 15 or even 20 for lobster, depending on size.

Mollusks such as clams, oysters, scallops, can be eaten raw; all shellfish may be boiled, steamed, broiled, baked, or fried. Consult a general or seafood cookbook for many good ways to cook and serve each kind.

A mollusk and crustacean rundown. Each kind of shellfish is different from every other kind, and it's these differences that make them such interesting, delicious menu items.

abalone: Fresh, obtainable only near the coast—canned and frozen elsewhere; a kind of marine snail, only the foot of which is eaten; tough, must be tenderized before cooking.

clam: Among the kinds are hardshell, softshell, surf, butter, littleneck, geoduck, and pismo clams, all bivalves; they burrow deep in the sand, were difficult to gather until a special dredge was invented; can be eaten raw or cooked—who doesn't love a clambake?—but the geoduck (long-necked and not very pretty) is used only for chowder.

cockle: To be found in salt water both here and in Europe; eaten raw or cooked, as with clams; they have never caught on in this country.

conch: We see the beautiful spiral shell more often than the creature that inhabits it; lives in waters of the Caribbean and off the Florida coast; excellent flavor, but tough and must be tenderized before cooking.

crab: Common types are king (very big), dungeness, stone, snow, and blue; crab is eaten cooked, either hot or cold; the meat is difficult to pick out in the smaller kinds, but worth the effort.

crayfish: In looks and taste, like a lobster, but usually much smaller; there are both freshwater (small) and saltwater varieties, the latter often called spiny or rock lobster.

lobster: The maine or northern lobster is, to lobster lovers, the only true one—spiny lobsters, of which only the tail is edible (they have tiny claws) are found in warmer waters than the maine variety; cook in shell.

mussel: Only the saltwater variety is eaten; more often consumed by gourmets in restaurants than by the general public at home.

oyster: Found in salt water along both the east and west coasts, classified as eastern, pacific, and olympia; eastern are of various medium sizes; pacific are very large; olympic are tiny, no larger than a thumbnail, and exquisitely flavored; oysters are "farmed" to keep them in ample supply.

periwinkle: Found in both fresh and salt water here and in Europe; not popular here, but beloved in the British Isles.

scallop: We eat the "eye," or large muscle of these; bay scallops are tiny and sweet, sea scallops larger; beware of unscrupulous fish dealers, who sometimes stamp rounds of "sea scallops" out of less expensive flat fish.

shrimp: best-loved (or, at least, most-often-eaten) shellfish in this country, they come in many sizes; shrimp should be cooked in the shell, may be served hot or cold.

Vary home menus with shellfish—they are quick/easy to cook, delicious plain or in salads, casseroles, or sauced dishes. See also PRAWNS and SCAMPI.

SHERBET

Not as rich as ice cream but with a bit more substance than ice—it is made with milk rather than water—sherbet is the perfect light dessert after a heavy meal.

Sherbets are almost always made with fruit; a few are flavored with wine or liqueur; all may be served plain, or made a bit more festive with liqueur spooned over to serve as a sauce. Orange sherbet is perhaps the best known, but almost any fruit can be used—pineapple, cranberry, lemon, and lime are familiar ones, but nectarines and peaches, strawberries and plums may be used.

The chief ingredients are fruit, sugar, milk, and often egg whites. Some sherbet recipes call for gelatin. Marshmallows melted in the milk make an exquisitely smooth chiffon sherbet. The dessert may be frozen in refrigerator trays—in which case it must be taken out and beaten once or twice during the freezing period—or in an old-fashioned freezer.

SHERRY: see WINE IN COOKING and XERES

SHIRR, TO: see page 450

SHORT COURSE IN LABEL READING, A:
see page 414

SHORTCAKES

These may be desserts or main dishes. In all cases, they consist of two pieces of a breadlike or cakelike substance, with a sauce between and on top. A rich, sweet biscuit, split, filled, and topped with sliced strawberries and drenched in heavy cream made up the first shortcake. As good ideas often do, this one took off in all directions. First other fruits were substituted—raspberries, blackberries, peaches, bananas, or any fruit that came to hand. Some cooks substituted cakes for biscuits. Some ignored the fruit and sandwiched devil's food or pound cake with ice cream, topping the combination with chocolate or butterscotch sauce. Finally, an inventive home cook tried sandwiching biscuits or squares of corn bread with creamed chicken or ham or shellfish and the savory shortcake was born.

SHORTENING: see FATS

SHRED, TO: see page 448

SHRIMP: see SHELLFISH

SIDE DISHES

These should be chosen to complement and enhance the star of the meal, the main dish. When planning a menu, take into consideration contrast of colors and textures and flavors. Taste-alike dishes and those with a sameness of color should be avoided so that the meal is never boring to eye or palate.

Side dishes include the starches—potatoes or rice or pasta, or a less common sort such as grits or kasha—one or two vegetables, and a salad to be served either to begin the meal, to accompany the main dish, or as a separate course following it. Gravies and sauces, savory jellies, relishes, pickles, and olives are also among the side dishes, or can be considered as garnishes.

SIFT, TO: see page 448

SIMMER, TO: see page 450

SIMPLE SYRUP: see SYRUPS

SKIM, TO: see page 450

SKIM MILK: see MILK

SLAW: see COLESLAW and SALADS

SLICE, TO: see page 448

SLIVER, TO: see page 448

SLOW COOKERS: see special feature:
YOU CAN'T WORK WITHOUT TOOLS

SMITHFIELD HAM: see HAM

SMOKING: see special feature: PUTTING
FOOD BY

SMORGASBORD

Once considered a substantial array of appetizers, to be followed by a full meal, in this country at least smörgåsbord is more often treated as the dinner itself. And well it might be —a more eye-filling, mouth-watering, outlandishly delectable spread of foods would be hard to find.

The thing to remember about smörgåsbord dining is not to panic. Don't be lured on and on by a feeling of, "I want some of that—oh, and that, and that, and that, too!" Don't pile your plate high with a mixture of foods that don't live well with one another. You're expected to go back to the table several times. (The unofficial record was set by a hollow-legged teenage boy in a New York restaurant, who made nineteen trips to the table, cheered on by waiters, busboys, other diners, even the manager.)

Start with fish. There will be herring prepared in several ways, crayfish or lobster, shrimp, smoked fish of a number of kinds, black or salmon caviar, and many fish salads. For the second plateful, collect cold meats, deviled eggs, and salads other than fish—wilted cucumbers, for example, and good coleslaw, tossed greens, and that wonderful beet-apple combination. For the third, take hot dishes—most often meatballs, chicken of some sort, rice, those delicious Swedish brown beans—and a sampling of the large number of cheeses. Dessert and coffee may be served to you, or you may make a final trip.

A smörgåsbord is a wonderful way to entertain at home, particularly if you know a good Scandinavian delicatessen where some of the specialties can be purchased. Others you can make at home. Except in places where there is a large number of Swedish folk there are few smörgåsbords, and such a buffet will delight guests, particularly the solid trenchermen among them.

SMØRREBRØD

Think of all the different kinds of sandwiches, all the manifold combinations and permutations, all the kinds of breads and fillings and garnishes. Imagine them all laid out, open-face, on a table. That's Danish smørrebrød.

SNACKS

To define the word simply: anything eaten other than at regular mealtimes. At home or away, there are morning snacks—coffee breaks—of coffee alone or with a danish pastry or a cut of coffeecake. There are afternoon snacks—a cup of tea with perhaps two or three little tea sandwiches, or a slice of plain cake. There are after-school snacks—a glass of milk and some cookies. There are cocktail-time snacks—all the wide array of hot and cold appetizers. There are TV snacks—bowls of peanuts or popcorn or small, savory crackers. And there are bedtime snacks—a glass of warm milk, or another cup of coffee for those it doesn't keep awake, and perhaps a cracker or cookie or two. There are dozens of variations on these, anything from a Dagwood-type sandwich that rates as a snack only because it's eaten between meals to a chaste glass of diet soda.

SNAILS

Fresh snails, which are bought live, are a considerable nuisance to prepare, but worth every moment of it and then some, snail-lovers say. Soak them first, for 1 hour, in a brine made of 3 tablespoons of salt to a quart of water. Then wash well under running water, scrubbing the shells with a stiff brush. In lightly salted water, boil 30 minutes, then remove from their shells as soon as they are cool enough to handle. Cut off the operculum, the hard bottom part that the snail uses as a door to its shell. Put a little garlic-herb butter into each shell, and put the snails back in. Cover with more of the butter and bake in a 350°F. oven until the butter sizzles. Or follow any snail recipe that strikes your fancy.

Canned snails are less of a challenge. You can buy shells separately, or some are put up in a two-part can with snails in one end, shells in the other. But do have shells—snails are something of a letdown, somehow don't taste right, without them. These need only the butter-and-bake treatment. Frozen snails, in their shells and already buttered, are also available. They need only heating until the butter sizzles. Or, if the whole idea doesn't please you, order snails in a restaurant—usually "escargot" on the menu. They'll be served in a special dish with tongs to hold the hot shells and a small fork with which to draw the meat from the shell.

SNAPBEANS: see BEANS

SNOW PEAS: see PEAS

SOAK, TO: see page 448

SODA: see BAKING SODA and CLUB SODA

SODA POP: see SOFT DRINKS

SODAS: see ICE CREAM

SODIUM: see SALT and the special feature: NUTRITION NOTEBOOK

SOFT DRINKS

This appellation applies generally to all nonalcoholic beverages, but is usually thought of as meaning only those "sodas" that are carbonated and come in bottles or cans. There are 100 billion bottles and cans of soft drinks sold each year. That's 500 containers per capita—and if you're not consuming your share, someone else is making up for you. See also BEVERAGES and COLA.

SOLE: see FISH

SORBITOL

One of the banned artificial sweeteners.

SORGHUM: see MOLASSES

SORREL

Known for centuries—indeed, since 3000 B.C.—this is a perennial herb with a bitey, acid flavor. When young, sorrel can be used in salads; older leaves may be cooked in the manner of spinach or used in soups and sauces as a flavoring. Sorrel soup—"schav" in Jewish cuisine—is very good.

SOUFFLE: see page 454

SOUL FOOD

If you feel that soul food is all watermelon and hog jowl, you live in a very circumscribed world. The term includes all the inventive dishes created by (usually Southern) cooks, both black and white, whose genius was seemingly not at all hampered by low budgets. Soul food is a subject to which whole books could be—and have been—devoted. Lay hands on one, browse and experiment, broaden your horizons and your menus.

SOUPS

Hot and hearty or cool and refreshing, soup can start the meal or—with salad and bread—it can *be* the meal.

Stock is the heart and soul of many soups. Once on the back of every stove in France—and in other countries as well—the stockpot simmered away, tasty bones and scraps added to it as they became available. Nowadays, we tend to get our stock—beef broth, chicken broth—from a can. Although connoisseurs may feel that the best of soup was lost with the passing of the stockpot, we still make and serve some very creditable ones.

Every country of the world has its favorites. The Russians favor cabbage, or beef-and-beet borscht. The French make a delicate lettuce soup and are great hands with cream soups—chicken, mushroom, celery, many others. Italian stracciatella and minestrone have traveled to many other countries. The British are fond of oxtail soups with vegetables and curried soups borrowed from their years in India. The Chinese (who have their soup at the end of the meal rather than the beginning) make wonton, egg drop, and sizzling rice soups, among others. Greek avgolemono is lemony chicken broth with rice and airy strands of egg. You'll find peanuts in African soups, meatballs in Mexican. It's a wide soup world.

Waste not, want not—make soup! Here we tend toward opening a can rather than making soup from scratch, and that's too bad. A lot of wonderful leftovers get lost in the shuffle rather than finding a home in the soup pot. With a few bits of meat clinging to it, the bone of any meat, the carcass of any poultry should say "soup" to you. Simmer a lamb bone with bay leaf, add carrots and barley. A ham bone (or a tag end of bacon) flavors pea, bean, or lentil whole-meal soups. Slow-cook a beef bone, add celery and lima beans and onion. Make broth with a chicken carcass, add snipped watercress leaves, cook little dumplings in it just before serving. Bone-based soups are all the better for being made the day before serving. Refrigerate, then take off the congealed fat that will have risen to the surface before reheating.

There are plenty of soups to be made when no meat bone is available—avocado, potato, cream of mushroom, cream of almost any vegetable, gazpacho, onion, and many more, including those half stew/half soup fish concoctions, bouillabaisse and cioppino. Don't forget sturdy fish and shellfish and other chowders, and cold soups—plain or jellied—when warm weather comes. When fresh tomatoes are at their most abundant (and least expensive), make concentrated tomato soup base, freeze it, thin with milk or light cream when you heat and eat.

Finishing-touch dress-ups. Don't let the soup go to the table naked. Sprinkle on a garnish that will make it even more delicious. Croutons, packaged or homemade. A drift of snipped parsley, watercress, or chives. A dab of sour cream or unsweetened whipped cream. Popcorn, plain or cheesed. Pretzel sticks. Tiny cheese crackers. Thin lemon slices. Little meat, fish, or sausage balls. Small puffs of choux paste. Thin sausage slices. Grated cheese. Toasted sesame seeds. And that's not half of the possibles.

If soup is to be the main part of the meal, serve a salad with it, a substantial one if the soup is light, a simple one if the soup is hearty. And a bread, as well—anything from crackers of assorted kinds through french bread, cheese or garlic bread, toasted sourdough, split and toasted french rolls, and rusks to big rounds of ship's biscuit. See also BOUILLON, GARNISHING, GAZPACHO, GUMBO, LEEKS, MADRILENE, ONIONS, and XAVIER.

SOUR CREAM: see CREAM and SALAD DRESSINGS

SOURDOUGH: see BREADS

SOURSOPS: see EXOTIC FRUIT

SOUSE: see SAUSAGES

SOY FLOUR: see FLOUR

SOY FOOD EXTENDER: see TEXTURED PLANT PROTEIN

SOY SAUCE

An Oriental sauce, made of fermented soybeans and other ingredients. Salty, it is used to season many Oriental dishes, in the cooking or at the table. A buy-it, not a make-at-home item.

SOYBEAN OIL: see OILS, SALAD AND COOKING

SOYBEANS: see BEANS

SPAGHETTI: see PASTA

SPANISH MELONS: see MELONS

SPANISH ONIONS: see ONIONS

SPARERIBS: see PORK

SPEARMINT: see HERBS AND SAVORY SEASONINGS

SPICES

When you make for a port from which spices are shipped, they say, you can smell the hot, heavy, somehow mysterious aroma while you are still far out at sea. John Milton said it more elegantly when he spoke of the "Sabean odours from the spicy shore of Araby the Blest," in *Paradise Lost*. And are there any of us so pressed for time or so unappreciative of the kitchen's joys that we do not stop long enough to take a deeply satisfying whiff of whatever spice we are adding to the food we are cooking? They are the stuff, surely, that dreams are made on.

Back to earth, here are the common spices in every kitchen, and some of their uses.

allspice: The evergreen tree, member of the myrtle family, on which the allspice berries grow is a native of the western hemisphere. Early explorers took the tree back home with them; it grew, but it did not bear. Nor has anyone ever been able to induce the allspice to bear its fruit anywhere but in its Caribbean home in Jamaica, Guatemala, Honduras, and Mexico. The name was given to the spice because its aroma is suggestive of three other spices, cloves, cinnamon, and nutmeg; *forms and uses:* When dried, the allspice berry resembles a large peppercorn. It can be bought whole or ground. Use to flavor meat broths and gravies, in pickles and relishes and preserves, and in fruitcakes and pies.

anise: A member of the parsley family, anise is the small, gray-brown seed with the unmistakable flavor of licorice. Known for centuries, anise has been used as a medicine, a digestive, a charm to ward off the evil eye, as well as a flavoring for a variety of foods. Our supply today comes from Turkey, Spain, and Syria; *forms and uses:* Most often sold as the whole seed, anise is also available ground in limited supply. It gives flavor to anisette and other liqueurs and is used in fruit cups and compotes, chicken, duck, and veal dishes, as well as in cookies, candies, and confections.

cardamom: This is a precious spice, second in cost only to saffron. It is the dried fruit of a member of the ginger family, yields only 250 pounds an acre, and must be hand-gathered by snipping the fruit off the plant with scissors. Of that poundage, a good deal is taken up by the pod that contains the seed that is the spice itself. Vikings discovered the plant on a voyage to its native India, which accounts for the many uses of the spice made in all the Scandinavian countries. That elusive and wonderful flavor in true danish pastry is cardamom; *forms and uses:* Can be had in green (unbleached) or white (bleached) pods, or as a ground spice. Use in sweet rolls and breads, sparingly in pea soup, and in pumpkin and apple pies.

cinnamon: Now it spices many of the foods we love best, but once cinnamon was a choice perfume, burned as incense and used to scent the baths of wealthy Romans; in medieval times it was a basic ingredient of love potions. It is the aromatic dried bark of certain evergreen trees, and has been with us a long time—Egyptians were importing it in 200 B.C.; *forms and uses:* We can buy cinnamon ground or in quills—sticks of curled, dried bark. Our favorite baking spice, it is used in all sorts of cakes, breads, cookies, and pies. The flavor has a particular affinity for chocolate. Stick cinnamon spices pickles and beverages.

cloves: A clove tree—a kind of evergreen—is a beautiful sight when in bloom, but commercial trees are never allowed to come into flower. The unopened flower buds, when dried, are the cloves so familiar in our kitchens. Once cloves were among the most costly of spices. Wars were fought in Europe and between Europeans and those native to the islands where the cloves grew over exclusive rights to the clove trade. In the Moluccas, where the spice was discovered, parents plant a clove tree when each child is born. We import cloves today from the Malagasy Republic (once Madagascar) and Tanzania (once Zanzibar); *forms and uses:* Cloves are available both whole and ground. The whole ones we use in studding ham and other pork, in pickling fruit, and (stuck in an onion) in stews. Ground cloves spice all sorts of baked goods and various desserts—particularly chocolate ones—and vegetables, such as beets, onions, sweet potatoes, and squash, with a sweet flavor.

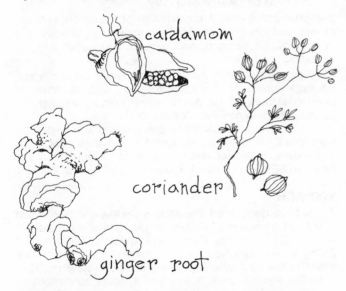

cardamom

coriander

ginger root

coriander: In the Bible, in the book of Exodus, manna is described as being, "like coriander seed, white." Persians raised coriander 3,000 years ago, and its pervasive fragrance helped to perfume the hanging gardens of Babylon. The leaves of this plant of the parsley family are widely used; they go by the names of "cilantro" and "Chinese parsley." The small, white to yellowish-brown ridged seed, which is the

spice itself, we import from Morocco, Rumania, Argentina, and France; *forms and uses:* Coriander is available as whole seeds or ground spice. The flavor is what makes frankfurters taste the way they do, is necessary in every curry powder formula, and is an important part of mixed pickling spice. In its ground form, we use it to flavor buns, pastry, cookies, cakes.

cumin: Looked at under a magnifier, cumin seed resembles a tiny ear of corn. Its odor reveals its kinship with caraway. A number of superstitions once surrounded cumin—it was thought to be the symbol of a miser, that happiness lay ahead for the bride and groom who carried the spice through the wedding ceremony, that if the seed were cursed during sowing, it would produce a bountiful crop. Cumin is a native of Egypt; today we import it from Iran, Morocco, Lebanon, and Syria; *forms and uses:* The spice is available as whole seed or in ground form. It is an important ingredient of both curry and chili powders. German cooks use it to flavor pork and sauerkraut, the Dutch enjoy it in cheese, and it appears in various Near Eastern and Latin American dishes.

ginger: Once ginger was the rich man's spice, rivaling black pepper in cost. Almost 5,000 years ago, the Greeks were making a kind of gingerbread. The spice was brought to England before the Norman Conquest and to the Caribbean shortly after the New World was discovered. It is the rhizome—root—of the ginger plant, which grows in the tropics, that is used as the familiar spice. We import it from Nigeria, Sierra Leone, Jamaica, and India; *forms and uses:* We can buy ginger whole, cracked (broken into small bits), and ground; crystallized (candied) and preserved ginger are also available. We use it in pickling, in all kinds of baked goods, in fruit desserts, and—sparingly—in meat, fish, and poultry dishes of some kinds. (See GINGER.)

mace: See *nutmeg,* below.

mustard: There are a great many people who enjoy mustard—it takes an annual crop of more than 400 million pounds to satisfy the world's demands. It has been known as a lively spice since prehistoric times. Two main types are grown to be used as spices, white and yellow, with a couple of subspecies, brown and oriental mustard. We grow a large amount in this country, and also import from Canada, Denmark, and the United Kingdom; *forms and uses:* Prepared mustard is available in many flavors and degrees of hotness, but as a spice we buy it as whole seeds or ground. We use the former in pickling, cooked with beets, cabbage, and cauliflower, or as a salad garnish. Ground mustard we use to flavor dozens of meat, fish, poultry, egg, and cheese dishes, in sauces and in dressings. (See MUSTARD.)

nutmeg and mace: Not even the Arabs, those great spice traders, discovered nutmeg until about A.D. 600; the evergreen tree with its peachlike fruit in those times grew only in the Moluccas, those faraway spice islands. Nutmeg and mace must necessarily be gathered simultaneously; the nutmeg is the pit of the tree's fruit, and mace is the thin, bright red, lacy network—called an aril—that surrounds it. Today the nutmeg grows in many places other than the Moluccas. We import most of both the nutmeg and mace we use from Indonesia and the West Indies; *forms and uses:* We buy mace ground or as "blades"—not widely available, and difficult to use in cooking—and nutmeg whole and in ground form. (Special grinders for nutmeg, like small pepper mills, can be bought.) Mace is the spice of choice for pound cakes, cherry pie, and fish sauces, among other uses. Nutmeg is more widely popular, and is used in all sorts of baked goods, puddings, sauces, vegetables, and beverages (could we have New Year's eggnog without it?).

paprika: Hungarians three centuries ago fell in love with paprika—they called it Turkish Pepper—and invented a whole array of "paprikash" dishes. The spice is relatively mild (relative to cayenne, for example), is made from the pods of certain mild, sweet peppers, and is a brilliant red, which fades to brownish red as the spice ages. Depending on the kind, the spice's flavor ranges from almost flavorless to rather nippy. If it is labeled simply "paprika," it will be the mild, sweet type. Other kinds are available in specialty shops. We grow large quantities of the paprika peppers in California, and also import the spice from Spain, Hungary, Yugoslavia, Morocco, and Bulgaria; *forms and uses:* Paprika is available ground. It is our great garnishing spice, used to give color to many pale dishes. Sprinkled on the top of casseroles, it will help them attain a handsome brown appearance. And we make a number of the paprikashes that got paprika started.

saffron: This is the spice that has the distinction of being the world's most expensive. Fortunately, a little goes a long way. The "threads" of saffron are the dried stigmas of a certain kind of crocus—there are only three in each flower, and they must be picked by hand; 225,000 stigmas go to make up a pound of the spice. It is native to the Mediterranean; we import most of ours from Spain, some from Portugal; *forms and uses:* Saffron is available ground and as the whole dried stigmas. It is steeped in hot water and the liquid added to color and flavor breads and rolls. Saffron has a particular affinity for rice and is used in many rice-combination dishes —particularly with chicken or fish—both in this country and abroad.

Spice blends, allied seasonings. Processors of spices have made things easy for hesitant cooks by combining a number of spices (herbs, as well) into mixtures just right for certain common flavoring purposes. Here are the most widely used.

apple-pie spice: Blended sweet baking spices, cinnamon predominating, along with cloves, nutmeg or mace, allspice, and ginger. Need not be confined to apple pie—it's a good spice for many dishes, other fruit pies and pastries.

barbecue spice: A blend of chili peppers with cumin, garlic, cloves, paprika, salt, and sugar. Flavors barbecue sauce; used in salad dressings, casseroles, egg and cheese dishes.

chili powder: Starts with chili pepper, adds cumin, oregano, garlic, salt, cloves, allspice, sometimes onion. For Tex-Mex cooking, in sauces for shellfish cocktails, and in hamburgers, egg dishes, stews, and gravies.

cinnamon-sugar: Sugar well-flavored with cinnamon. Makes cinnamon toast, tops many kinds of baked goods, fried apple rings, and such. Easily prepared in the home kitchen.

curry powder: From sixteen to twenty spices and herbs combined to give the flavor of East Indian curries. That is its chief use, but try it also in salad dressings, deviled eggs, scalloped tomatoes, fish chowders, split pea soup—but take it easy!

mixed pickling spice: Combines mustard seed, bay leaf, black and white peppercorns, dill seed, red peppers, ginger, cinnamon, mace, allspice, coriander. Used, of course, for pickling, but also good in certain soups and stews.

poultry seasoning: A combination of thyme and sage in ⅔ to ⅓ proportions. Some makers add onion powder, some celery powder as well. Used in stuffing and in dredging mix for poultry to be pan- or oven-fried.

pumpkin-pie spice: A combination of cinnamon, nutmeg, cloves, and ginger—just right for pumpkin pie, but use also in cookies, gingerbread, and pastries and sweet rolls for breakfast.

Spice processors put out many other blends; some package dozens of very specific ones—such as those for ham, roast beef, salads, pastas, eggs, even a particular one for mashed potatoes—and others only a few.

There are other allied products shelved with spices, as well. You'll find dried grated lemon and orange peel, meat tenderizers, cream of tartar, and monosodium glutamate. See also SEEDS and HERBS AND SAVORY SEASONINGS.

SPINACH

As we have discovered, the ancient Greeks and Romans in their heyday knew of a great many good things to eat that we enjoy today. But they didn't have spinach. A number of youngsters—adults, too, for that matter—will say that they weren't missing much. There is a considerable amount of prejudice against spinach; much of it stems from improper cleaning, cooking, and serving.

Just where and when spinach first made its culinary appearance is a mystery. The first written record of the vegetable is by the Chinese, in the middle of the seventh century A.D. Moors brought spinach to Spain a century later, and from there it spread throughout Europe and finally to the New World.

SPINACH IN YOUR KITCHEN

The vegetable is classified as an herb. It is available throughout the year, raised in the South during the winter and in most other parts of the country in the spring and fall.

how to buy: Fresh spinach can be bought in bulk, by the pound, or—washed and trimmed—in plastic bags. In either case, the leaves should not be yellowed but have a freshly dark green look, and may be of the flat-leaf or crinkled variety. Wilt, decay, crushed leaves, and signs of insect damage should indicate to you spinach not worth your trouble.

how to store: In the refrigerator, in a plastic bag, raw spinach can be stored up to 5 days. Cooked spinach, in a covered container, can be refrigerated up to 5 days as well.

nutritive value: One cup of cooked, fresh spinach—calorie-low and vitamin-rich—contains only 41 calories and yields:

protein	5.4	grams
fat	.5	gram
carbohydrate	6.5	grams
calcium	167	milligrams
phosphorus	68	milligrams
iron	4	milligrams
sodium	90	milligrams
potassium	583	milligrams
thiamin	.13	milligram
riboflavin	.25	milligram
niacin	.9	milligram
ascorbic acid	50	milligrams
vitamin A	14,580	international units

Tips on preparing, cooking. The chief drawback of spinach is that it harbors inordinate amounts of sand. If it is not totally removed, those who aren't all that crazy about the vegetable anyway will raise howls of protest and have right on their side.

Packaged spinach is supposed to be ready-washed, but inspect it to make sure as you go through picking away any wilted leaves and the heavy stems. Do the same picking over for bulk raw spinach. Then immerse in warm water, which tends to seek out the sand and send it to the bottom of the sink. Lift off the spinach, then wash again in cold running water until you're certain all the sand is removed.

Cook in the water that clings to the leaves, in a covered pan, for 3 to 7 minutes or until just tender, turning often with a fork. Drain and season. That pesky sand, plus overcooking —which gives spinach a strong and disagreeable flavor— account for most people's objections to the vegetable.

Freezing spinach. Properly prepared (see special feature: PUTTING FOOD BY), spinach may be freezer-stored at 0°F. or below up to 1 year.

Other ways, other forms. There are a number of convenience forms other than fresh in which you can find spinach in your market.

on grocery shelves, in cans: Canned spinach comes in a variety of sizes. However, the process of canning somewhat discolors the spinach and gives it a rather strong flavor. You may prefer the fresh or the frozen varieties.

in grocery frozen-food section: Frozen spinach in leaf or chopped forms; creamed spinach; ready-to-bake spinach soufflé.

Some perfect partners. Something tart goes well with spinach. Usually it's lemon juice, although some people prefer a little vinegar. Eggs go well with the vegetable—in fact, topped with creamed eggs, spinach is appealing to many who don't like it simply seasoned with salt, pepper, and perhaps lemon juice. Or spread fish fillets with a well-seasoned spinach mixture, roll and bake. Or make a Greek spinach pie —easy when you buy the frozen phyllo pastry. Or season chopped spinach with salt, white pepper, and a speck of nutmeg; stir in just enough sour cream to barely coat the spinach, and heat, but do not boil. Or, for brunch, put a layer of well-seasoned spinach in the bottom of baking dishes, top with raw eggs, sprinkle with grated swiss cheese, and bake until the eggs are done to your liking. There are a number of Italian-origin dishes that feature spinach; "Florentine" in the recipe title gives you the clue.

Spinach is so good and so good for you, and can be served in so many guises that there's no need to let your family fall into the "I hate spinach" trap.

SPIT-ROAST, TO: see page 450

SPONGE CAKES: see CAKES

SPOON BREAD

Made with white or yellow cornmeal, and with eggs, milk, and shortening, spoon bread is baked to a puddinglike texture and must be served with a spoon—hence the name. Serve as the "starch" part of the meal, in place of potatoes, pasta, or rice. It's particularly good with pork, chicken, or game. See also PUDDINGS AND CUSTARDS.

SPRING ONIONS: see ONIONS

SPRINKLE, TO: see page 449

SPROUTS

Are you a part of the big sprouts revolution? Until a few years ago, few of us ever saw sprouts much less ate them, except as part of an occasional meal in a Chinese restaurant. Then the health-food buffs discovered how delicious and nutritious sprouts were, and soon we began to find them in the produce section of our supermarkets. Now everyone's sprout-happy.

How do you use sprouts? In soups, as a just-before-serving garnish. In salads of just about every description. In sandwiches, replacing lettuce or other greens. In main dishes such as meat loaves and hamburgers and those stir-fry mixtures that are so good and so easy-do.

Why would you want to use sprouts? They're good—crunchy and crispy, with fine flavor. And they're vitamin-loaded. When beans and seeds sprout, a great vitamin-producing transformation takes place. For example, the vitamin C content of soybeans increases more than 500 percent by the third day of sprouting. Most sprouts are five times more nutritious in the sprouted than in the dry form.

Sprout-it-yourself techniques. Even if the idea of gardening turns you off, you can sprout seeds and beans at home, indoors, with a minimal effort and outlay. You'll find it fascinating and satisfying, and it's a great fun/educational project for youngsters.

the jar method: Start with alfalfa seeds or mung beans, both available at your supermarket or, if not, at a health food store. Put seeds in a quart jar, cover with warm water and soak 8 hours or overnight. Place cheesecloth or nylon net over the top of the jar and secure with a rubber band or canning-jar ring. Drain off excess water. Put the jar on its side in a warm, dark place. Two or three times a day add some water, swish it around to rinse the seeds, and drain well; put the jar back in place on its side.

The sprout crop will be ready in three or four days. Place the jar on a windowsill and let the sprouts have light for one day, to begin making chlorophyll. Now they're ready to use and enjoy. Refrigerate those you're not going to eat at once; use within 2 or 3 days to enjoy optimum flavor and nutrition.

the pan method: Soak the seeds as above; drain. Line the bottom of a shallow glass or ceramic pan with cheesecloth or absorbent paper. Spread a solid layer of seeds or beans on the lining. Add water enough to wet the liner, but not so much that the seeds soak in it. Add more water as necessary

to keep the cheesecloth wet—but no more than that, or the seeds will rot. Cover the pan with clear plastic wrap. Store in a dim place until sprouting is well along, then put into the light for greening. Snip or pull off sprouts when ready, and refrigerate up to 3 days.

Sprouts are ready to eat when they reach these sizes:

alfalfa	1 inch
chick-peas	½ to ¾ inch
flaxseed	¾ inch
lentils	1 inch
mung	1½ to 2½ inches
soybeans	½ inch

Home-grown sprouts, besides being fun to produce, are economical. The cost of the seeds is only about one-quarter the cost of the ready-to-eat sprouts you buy in the store. Just be sure to use whole, solid beans or seeds, discarding any that have split or look shriveled, and you'll raise a great crop.

SPUN SUGAR

This is a sugar-and-water syrup, boiled to the thread stage. The threads are then strung out between two sticks or poles, allowed to cool and dry. The mixture can be colored (before cooking) with any shade of food coloring. The result is used to decorate cakes and ice creams. It's a rather messy procedure, but the results are very pretty. If you'd like to try—and if you're skillful with your hands—consult a good general cookbook.

SQUAB

An elegant bird, considered a great delicacy, a squab is a young pigeon that has not been allowed to fly. Fresh or frozen, they are available in specialty markets or gourmet food stores, and may be roasted (stuffed), broiled, or sautéed. They are served well done. Each bird is a single serving.

SQUASH

This is another of the foods unknown until the New World—the western hemisphere—was discovered. A member of the vine-growing gourd family, squash was called "askutasquash" (meaning "eat it uncooked") by the native Americans, and is believed to have been grown in Peru, where many of the foods we enjoy originated, as much as 2,000 years ago. The squash of the old days had more seeds than meat, and many were raised primarily for the seeds, which are not only edible but tasty.

Inevitably, squash found its way to the Old World—early explorers delighted in taking home with them all the evidence possible that the New World was really new. The vegetable was well liked, especially in Italy, and hybridizers began to "invent" new forms of old favorites. Zucchini, for example, is an Italian development.

There are two main squash types, winter and summer,

and a number of varieties of each. Both are cultivated as annuals where the winters are cold, but are perennial where there is no harsh winter season. Summer squash are harvested shortly after they firm up, before skin and seeds have a chance to toughen. Winter squash are allowed to remain on the vine, to mature fully, until the first frost is expected.

Summer squash. There are a number of kinds of summer squash—enough so that no one kind need become tiresome.

caserta: Striped light and dark green, the caserta is shaped like the cocozelle, but thicker. Best when 6 or 7 inches long and 1 to 1½ inches thick.

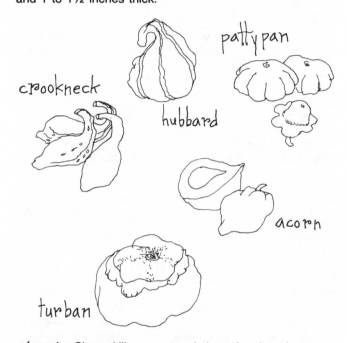

chayote: Shaped like a pear and about the size of an acorn squash, the chayote is pale green and, unlike other squash, has only one central seed, which is edible. Its flavor is very delicate. Do not peel.

cocozelle: A smooth or slightly ribbed cylindrical squash striped dark green and yellow, with a flavor rather like zucchini. Best when 6 to 8 inches long, 2 inches in diameter.

cymling (also called scallop or pattypan): Skin may be smooth or somewhat bumpy; pale green when young, it turns white as the squash matures. The vegetable is shaped like a dish and has a scalloped edge. Best when 3 to 4 inches across.

yellow crookneck and straightneck: Yellow, somewhat bumpy skin that grows deeper in color as the vegetable matures. At their best when about half mature, while skin is still soft enough so that the squash does not need to be peeled.

The crookneck can grow to 10 inches in length, the straightneck to 20, but they are much preferable before they reach maturity.

zucchini: Cylindrical, but often somewhat larger at the base; the skin has wide dark green stripes alternating with narrow pale green ones. Can grow to 12 inches in length, but best when less mature—4 to 5 inches long.

Winter squash. All are green or orange in color, with a hard, tough skin. These are the common varieties:

acorn (also known as table queen and des moines): Deeply ribbed dark green skin that may turn orange in storage. Orange flesh. Grows 5 to 8 inches in length, 4 to 5 inches thick.

buttercup: Rises to a turban-shaped mound at the blossom end. Skin is dark green with marks and some stripes of pale gray. Flesh is dry but sweet, orange in color. Grows 4 to 5 inches long, 6 to 8 inches thick, with a 2- to 3-inch turban.

butternut: Cylindrical, tapering to a bulbous end. Skin is smooth, generally buff colored. Flesh is orange, sweet, moist. Grows to 12 inches in length, up to 5 inches thick at the bulb.

hubbard: Globe shaped with a tapered neck, grows up to 12 inches in length. The warty skin is varied—a dusty blue-gray, a deep green, an orange that leans toward red. The flesh is sweet, usually moist, and yellow-orange.

turban: Shaped like a drum, with a turban like buttercup. Bumpy skin of the squash proper is orange with stripes at the blossom end, of the turban blue-green. Grows to 10 inches in length, 15 in diameter.

SQUASH IN YOUR KITCHEN

Some of the summer squash—zucchini is an example—are in the market all year long; others are available May through July, although you may find them at other seasons, shipped in from warm climates. Winter squash's peak season is October, but it is in the market from August through December; exceptions are butternut and acorn, which are available the year around.

how to buy: Make certain that the squash is solid, without soft spots, that it is of proper size and color for its kind. Avoid squash with cuts or other breaks in the skin. Summer varieties should be young, have tender skins. Both summer and winter squash should be heavy for their size.

how to store: Store raw summer squash in the refrigerator up to 2 weeks; winter squash should not be refrigerated, but stored in a dry, well-ventilated place, at a temperature between 50 and 55°F. for 1 to 4 weeks—shorter time if the storage place is warmer. Store both types, cooked, in the refrigerator in a covered container, up to 5 days.

nutritive value: The many types of squash vary in nutritive values, but not greatly. Calorie counts for a 3½-ounce serving of summer varieties boiled, without butter, range from 13

545

to 16 calories. Also low in sodium, they are excellent on both weight-loss and low-sodium diets. A 3½-ounce serving of winter varieties ranges from 34 to 68 calories. Summer squash has appreciable amounts of vitamins A and C and niacin. Winter varieties are high in vitamin A and have appreciable amounts of vitamin C, riboflavin, and iron.

Tips on preparing, cooking. Both kinds of squash may be boiled; both should be seeded and cut up, but only the winter varieties peeled. Peel summer kinds only if past their prime. Unpeeled squash should be scrubbed—they are sometimes quite dirty.

Summer squash, if they're as young as they ought to be, can be panned in a covered skillet with butter and a small amount of water. Salt and white pepper season them well, with the pan liquid reduced and poured over them. Or if you like, use a little nutmeg or cinnamon in place of the pepper. Or casserole summer squash with other vegetables. Onions pair well with their flavor and so do tomatoes.

Peel winter types for boiling. Or halve acorn and butternut types, seed and put face down in a pan with about ½ inch of water. Bake until tender, 45 to 65 minutes. Acorn squash take very well to stuffing with a meat-rice or a vegetable mixture. Turn butternut cut side up, salt lightly, and put butter and brown sugar or maple syrup in the cavity. The bigger squash (peel left on) should be cut into serving-size pieces to bake. Season and dot with butter. Place in a covered dish, or wrap each piece in foil.

Freezing squash. Properly prepared (see special feature: PUTTING FOOD BY), both summer and winter squash can be stored at 0°F. or below up to 1 year.

Other ways, other forms. Although most squash is sold and eaten fresh, there are a few other forms to be found.

on grocery shelves, in cans: Squash (winter in the form of a purée) and sliced zucchini in tomato sauce.

in grocery frozen-food section: Zucchini, and frozen puréed winter squash.

In most of our kitchens, squash of one kind or another is an old friend. It usually pays to experiment with something new—try a variety of squash with which your family is not familiar.

SQUIRREL: see GAME

STABILIZERS: see ADDITIVES AND PRESERVATIVES

STAINLESS STEEL KITCHEN UTENSILS: see special feature: YOU CAN'T WORK WITHOUT TOOLS

STANDING RIB: see BEEF

STEAK: see individual meat name: BEEF, LAMB, PORK, VEAL

STEAK SAUCE

A rather thick, dark red-brown commercial product, bottled, that many people enjoy with steak. It is made with a multitude of ingredients and is useful, for those who like its flavor, as a pep-up for stews and casseroles as well.

STEAM, TO: see page 450

STEEP, TO: see page 449

STELLE: see PASTA

STEW, TO: see page 450

STEWS

As generally recognized, the term means a concoction of small pieces of meat or poultry or fish plus vegetables in a savory gravy. Most stews are long-cooking foods, because they are generally made of the more economical but less tender cuts of meat and the long cooking period is necessary to make them tender.

In some cases, the meat is browned in fat before liquid is added. Flavoring vegetables—such as onion (often stuck with three or four cloves) and celery—are added at the beginning of the cooking period; vegetables to be eaten as part of the stew and other ingredients—pasta, for example—are added toward the end of the cooking period, so that they will be just done but not overcooked when the stew is served. Or these ingredients may be cooked separately and incorporated into the stew just before serving. This is often done with carrots or parsnips or turnips by people who don't like the sweet taste they impart to the stew when cooked in it.

Almost any vegetable is proper material for a stew other than beets, which turn the mixture a sickly pink. Some stews traditionally call only for certain vegetables—but feel free to break with tradition if the fancy moves you.

Beef stews. These are generally hearty, cold-weather fare. Although no law (community or culinary) says you must brown the meat, the stew will be both more flavorful and better looking if you do. Kidneys are traditional with beef stews; include them if your family enjoys them. After browning, add liquid—generally water, sometimes tomato juice or stock for fine flavor, just to cover the meat. Tuck in an onion studded with three cloves, a bay leaf if you like the flavor. Toward the end of cooking time, add vegetables in any combination you like: carrots, tomatoes, small whole onions, green beans, lima beans, potatoes. Check seasoning and correct it if necessary and—the choice is yours—thicken with flour-water paste if you wish.

Lamb stews. Here the flavor will be less affected by browning or not browning the meat. Again, add an onion for flavoring along with the liquid. Thyme, marjoram, or rosemary are delicious with lamb. Or you may flavor your stew with curry powder near the end of cooking time. Appropriate additions: potatoes, peas, tomatoes, eggplant, turnips, celery, small onions. Onions and potatoes only are traditional in Irish stew. Rice, tomatoes, and green peppers go into a Spanish lamb stew.

Veal stews. The best-known is blanquette de veau, in which the meat is not browned. Small white onions and mushroom caps are the vegetables; the gravy is flavored with lemon juice, thickened with eggs and cream. Garnish with parsley, serve with noodles for an entrancing meal. There are other veal stews as well, but however you use the veal, do not brown it or brown only very lightly. Sour cream is delicious added to a veal stew gravy. Peas, parsnips, carrots, celery, and snow peas are appropriate.

Pork stews. The most-often-served pork stew in this country is American chop suey, a blend of cut-up pork (browned or not) with celery and onions, sometimes water chestnuts, bean sprouts and/or bamboo shoots. But flavorful pork can find a place in a stew with sweet potatoes or yams and corn, with lima beans and carrots, or with almost any combination of vegetables you wish.

Chicken stews. Old-fashioned fricassee is a favorite, cooked—without browning the fowl—in water or chicken stock, with mushrooms, small onions, and sometimes peas added. The gravy is enriched with milk or cream and thickened, and the stew is served with rice or noodles or in the down-home way over flaky baking powder biscuits. Brunswick stew adds to the cooking chicken onions, tomatoes, lima beans, corn cut from the cob, and okra. Chicken lives well with carrots, parsnips, and turnips, too. Sliced stuffed green or ripe olives are a nice addition.

Fish stews. These, the only stews that cook in a short time, we also miscall chowders, sometimes bisques. But the stews are not thickened. Oyster stew, for example—oysters and their liquor, with a bit of onion for seasoning, in an un-thickened milk gravy, sprinkled with parsley or paprika before serving. Clams can make a stew as well. So can lobsters, and crabs—the meat, no shells—or any of the finny fish. Don't season these stews too highly, because fish flavors are delicate. And don't overpower them with lots of vegetables. Fish and shellfish stews are simple and very good.

Some stew notions. Meat stews are at their best when made one day, reheated and served the next. The flavors

have a chance to meld into a delicious whole by this method, and you can easily remove excess fat. Chicken stews also reheat well, but if there is cream or eggs or both in the gravy, don't boil or you'll have a curdled mess on your hands. Fish stews are best served immediately.

Rice, mashed potatoes (if there are no potatoes in the dish), and dumplings are all good stew accompaniments. So is crusty bread. There should be something with which to eat that savory gravy, for some the best part of the stew.

Every country has its favorites. And there are all sorts of dishes that really classify as stews: cassoulet, for example, with its white beans, loin of pork, lamb shoulder, ham shank, sausage, and sometimes duck. Mexican stews are usually hot with peppers. In Africa, you'll find fruit or peanuts or both in the stewpot. Some stew gravies are fortified with wine, some few with beer. Chinese stews are cooked in part soy sauce, and include scallions, ginger, and sherry (or rice wine, if you are being authentic). Often, after meats are browned and the excess fat drained away, the meat is returned to the pot to cook on a bed of MIREPOIX.

Satisfying, stick-to-the-ribs fare, stews are economical—at least relatively so. They make excellent family meals and some are perfect for guests as well. See also GOULASH.

STILTON: see CHEESE

STIR, TO: see page 449

STIR FRY, TO: see page 450

STIVALETTI: see PASTA

STOCK: see BROWN STOCK, WHITE STOCK, and HERBS AND SAVORY SEASONINGS

STORING FOOD: see FOOD STORAGE

STRAIGHTNECK: see SQUASH

STRAIN, TO: see page 449

STRAWBERRIES

To many people, particularly those who live in climates where the winter is long and cold, the first shipped-in strawberries that come on the market in February are the true harbingers of spring.

There are several versions of how the strawberry got its name—none, certainly, derived from its color or appearance. One says that the name describes the characteristic strewed appearance of the plant stems and runners. Another version attributes the name to the straw used as a mulch between the plant rows to keep the berries clean and to protect them during the winter months. A third says that in the days when strawberries had a very short season and were not grown in any quantity, they were brought to market strung on straws.

Ranging in price from very reasonable for in-season local berries to exorbitant when they are the tiny wild *fraises*

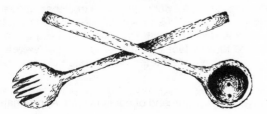

des bois flown in from France in their brief season to a few fancy-food purveyors (to be eaten with equally costly crème fraîche), strawberries are loved for their delightful flavor and plump crimson good looks. Served simply with cream and sugar (or deliciously but less familiarly with sour cream and brown sugar), or layered with ice cream in a parfait or crowning our own American strawberry shortcake, or handsomely glazed on a strawberry cream pie, they are a favorite on American tables throughout the country.

When the berries are ripe, growers can often be found who throw open their fields to local people on a pick-your-own basis. Picking strawberries can be a family affair, a pleasant day in the sunshine, and yield enough berries—at a much lower cost than if they were bought at the store—for preserves, for jam and jelly to put away the flavor of spring and summer to relish when winter comes. Strawberry picking is often a source of pocket money for youngsters, too.

STRAWBERRIES IN YOUR KITCHEN

Although there are processed strawberries of several kinds in the market, once the fresh berries appear, all thought of any other kind flees our minds, replaced by visions of short-cakes.

Buying and keeping the berries. Strawberries are most generally sold in pint baskets. Large size is not necessarily a sign of a top-quality berry. Flavor depends on variety, not size. You'll get larger volume—often a better bargain—when you buy small or medium-size berries. Choose large ones if appearance matters—if they are to be used as a garnish, for example. Look for fully ripe berries, richly and brightly red; very dark color indicates that the berries are old and beginning to deteriorate. The berry should have a natural shine; the cap should be green and fresh looking. Pick up the basket and look at the bottom. Red stains and leaking juice indicate crushed or deteriorated berries under that inviting top layer. Plan on using strawberries the day, or at most the day after, you buy them. If for some reason strawberries are not used soon after purchase, cook them before they go to waste—make sauce to serve over ice cream or cake, or a combination of the two if you're feeling lavish, or over a simple pudding. Or bake a pie. Or make a jar of preserves.

Do not wash strawberries until just before you serve them or use them in a cooked dish. As soon as you get them home, remove the berries from their basket, leave the caps on, and spread the berries out on a baking sheet or other shallow container. Refrigerate immediately. Washing and capping berries before refrigeration causes loss of food value and hurries spoilage. Pick the berries over, discarding soft ones, cutting away any signs of spoilage—bad strawberries have a particularly dreadful taste.

Getting them ready. Leaving the caps in place, wash the berries quickly in a colander or strainer in cold water. Never soak them. For the cook who wants to have everything, there is available a gadget called a strawberry huller (also useful back in the dear, dead days when chickens had pinfeathers), which is shaped rather like a large, blunt pair of tweezers with finger grips. Such specialization is unnecessary—use the point of a sharp knife to remove the strawberry caps or, even better, the rounded point of your potato peeler. Leave the berries whole, slice or crush, depending on the use you are going to make of them; sweeten or not as you prefer.

Sweetened berries may stand 30 minutes to develop flavor and juice, but not much longer. Serve as soon as practical after preparation is complete.

A pint basket contains about 12 ounces of fruit, or about 3¼ cups of whole, 2¼ cups of sliced, or 1⅔ cups of crushed strawberries. Count on about ¾ of a cup of berries per serving, a bit less if they're sliced or crushed, rather more for strawberryholics, whose name is legion. There are even some who cheerfully endure the manifestation of strawberry allergy, a siege of hives, when the season comes around.

Contributions to nutrition. We are admonished by nutritionists to get an adequate amount of vitamin C, and strawberries are a wonderful way to achieve that desideratum. One cup of the berries contains 89 milligrams of ascorbic acid—nearly four-fifths of the RDA of the vitamin, as well as smaller amounts of vitamin A, calcium, riboflavin, and niacin. The amount of vitamin C, however, varies with the variety of berry as well as with the climate in which it's grown, the weather, and the condition of harvesting. If yours are berries the sun has shown on intensely, their vitamin C content will be high. The vitamin is quickly lost when the caps are removed or the berries punctured, exposing their flesh to the air.

A lovely luxury for a weight-loss diet, strawberries provide only 55 calories per cup—sugarless and creamless, of course.

Other ways to go. When fresh strawberries are not available, or when the price has soared out of reach, turn away from the produce department to the grocery shelves and freezer cases.

canned: In cans, strawberries are packed in both light and heavy syrup, in 8- and 16- or 17-ounce sizes; they are generally whole small- to medium-size berries. The flavor is somewhat different from that of raw or cooked-at-home berries, and sometimes the berries lose some of their rosy color in the canning process. Serve these as is; or with cream, whipped cream, or topping, as dessert; or use in dishes, measure for measure, calling for fresh berries. Drain the canned berries if the recipe does not call for juice, and be sure to make allowance for the fact that these berries are sweeter than unsugared fresh ones. Refrigerate canned berries, covered, after opening.

frozen: Whole or sliced, in syrup/juice or not, sweetened or not, frozen strawberries can be had in 1-pound bags and

10-ounce packages. They are more akin to fresh berries than are the canned ones, and can be served in any manner that you'd serve the fresh berries, or used in any recipe. Refrigerate leftovers—but, like fresh berries, frozen ones should be used up quickly. Thaw just before serving—in fact, they are delicious if a few ice crystals remain when they come to the table. Strawberries are easily home-frozen (they were one of the first commercially frozen foods to appear on the market); they need not be sweetened, or they may be frozen by sugar-pack or syrup-pack methods.

Jams, jellies, preserves. These sweet treats can be found in jars and glasses (sometimes in cans) of varying sizes. Buy the size that suits your family needs—that is, a size that can be used up in a week or, at most, two. Although none of these will spoil in a much longer time than that, they do lose some flavor with long storage after they are opened. Strawberry jam is thick, with plenty of cut-up fruit (broken or crushed in those at the low end of the price scale). Jelly is, of course, clear (some fancy sorts may sport a strawberry leaf suspended in the richly red gel). Preserve has larger chunks of fruit or whole small berries, and the syrup in which they occur is usually somewhat thinner than that of jam. Jam may also be somewhat sweeter than preserve. Make strawberry jam, jelly, or preserve easily at home, during the peak of your local strawberry season. Any good general or canning-and-preserving cookbook will offer you an appealing variety of recipes.

STREUSEL

A combination of sugar—most often brown—butter, flour, and often spices used as a topping.

STRINGBEANS: see BEANS

STRUDEL: see PASTRY

STUD, TO: see page 449

STUFF, TO: see page 449

STUFFINGS

In our kitchen, wherever there is a possibility for stuffing, we go ahead and stuff. In meats, fish, poultry, vegetables, stuffing adds substance to the meal, in many cases is a welcome replacement for potatoes or rice or pasta, and is an economical way to extend the main dish. But best of all, stuffing is delicious, flavorful, a culinary joy. It is, as the Pennsylvania Dutch (who are very big on stuffing) say, "wonderful good."

Although bread-based stuffings are the most common, both rice and mashed potatoes also make a good starting point. And there are many variations on each theme, plus other good stuffings with more limited uses.

Some ideas to get you into the stuffing habit. Split frankfurters, spread with mustard, spoon sweet relish down the centers, top with American cheese and bake until the

cheese melts. Cut pockets in pork chops (or have the butcher do it) and fill with bread stuffing seasoned with thyme. Stuff a pocketed veal breast with a mixture of cooked rice, pine nuts, onion, and parsley. Spoon sage-flavored bread stuffing with plenty of celery and onion and chestnuts into chicken or turkey. Stuff a goose with well-seasoned mashed potatoes, a duck with orange sections and sauerkraut, game hens with a wild-rice mixture, wild duck with a bread stuffing made of pumpernickel with apple chunks and onion.

Stuff big mushroom caps with the chopped stems sautéed with onion and bread crumbs. Stuff acorn squash with ground beef and rice. Fill eggplant shells with the pulp of the vegetable combined with tomatoes, season with garlic. Parboil green bell peppers for five minutes, halve and seed, stuff with chopped leftover chicken and cooked rice, season with turmeric. Fill hollowed-out tomatoes with butter-browned bread crumbs and parmesan. Roll flat-pounded boned chicken breasts around a stick of cold herb-flavored butter or a finger of cheddar before cooking. Spread veal cutlets with marjoram-seasoned bread stuffing, roll and tie to make veal birds. Make beef birds with a stuffing of a dill pickle strip, a piece of swiss cheese, a sprinkling of dry bread crumbs seasoned with oregano.

You do get the idea, don't you? A good general cookbook will give you the recipes for these, and more. See also FILLINGS.

SUBSTITUTIONS: see special feature: THE HOME COOK'S NEW MATH

SUCCOTASH

In our present terms, a side dish that combines corn and beans—lima or green. Once, however, it incorporated other vegetables and often bits of bacon or salt pork, and was virtually a meal in itself. This is another American Indian dish shared with the early settlers who came to this country.

SUCKLING PIG: see BARBECUE

SUCROSE: see GLUCOSE and SUGAR

SUET

This is the white, crumbly-textured fat that surrounds the kidneys in beef cattle. At one time it was an ingredient in many dishes, but gave way to such later discoveries as butter, margarine, oils, and solidified shortenings. It is still an excellent fat (melted) to use for shallow frying. It has virtually

no odor or flavor. Suet puddings—boiled in a bag and heavy as lead—were once very much beloved in England and New England, where they still make suet puddings and use the fat in pastry.

Today, most of us in this country use suet only for barding or in winter to put out as an offering for the cold and hungry birds.

SUGAR

In 1890 the per capita consumption of sugar was 25 pounds. By 1977 it had reached nearly 100 pounds. Considering that many of us in no way eat up our full allotment, this gives a startling idea of how much sugar some others are eating to make up the quota. That's virtually 2 pounds of sugar a week, and the USDA estimates that another pound of other kinds of sugars—corn syrup, honey, fruit—is consumed by each and every one of us. In just plain white sugar alone we take in 500 carbohydrate calories a day; of the 525 pounds of food that the average person does away with in a year's time, more than 20 percent is sugar.

We are not alone with our mammoth sweet tooth. In fact, we are well down the list. England, Scotland, Ireland, and the Netherlands consume well over 100 pounds of sugar per capita annually, in an orgy of sweet eating.

On the brighter side. There are several kinds of sugar. The word is a general term for sucrose (in white and brown sugar, maple syrup, and molasses), glucose or dextrose (corn syrup and honey), fructose (fruits and honey), and lactose (milk). The body utilizes the various sugars in different ways. Some people can have difficulty with one type but be able to tolerate one or more of the others. For example, diabetics utilize both lactose and fructose more easily than sucrose.

Sugar is a natural food, taken from sugarcane and sugar beets. It is a carbohydrate, manufactured in green plants by a process known as photosynthesis. It has been used by man for a long time, originating in the South Pacific some 8,000 years ago, gradually traveling to Southeast Asia and India, then to China, and finally to Europe, where it was first treated as a rare luxury. Columbus brought sugarcane to the New World on his second voyage. In colonial times, white sugar (afforded only by the well-to-do) was imported from the West Indies in compact cones wrapped in blue paper and had to be grated for table and cooking purposes.

Health-food buffs feel that raw (unrefined) sugar is better than the refined kinds. However, the FDA prohibits the sale of raw sugar because of the impurities it contains. Some semirefined sugars are for sale, but they are nevertheless about 97 percent sucrose—and that's sugar, raw or refined.

Sugar in the diet. Sugar can be divided into two groups: the pure or refined forms (sucrose, glucose) used in candies, pastries, beverages, and other high-calorie but low-nutrient foods; and the forms (fructose, lactose) that are naturally present in foods that also contain essential vitamins and minerals. It is only sucrose and glucose that are frowned upon by nutritionists as empty, but obesity-contributing, calories. Honey, molasses, and brown sugar do contain some vitamins and iron, but in such small amounts that they are no better nutritionally than white sugar.

The biggest users of sugar in the United States today are the manufacturers of beverages—soft drinks, wines, cordials, liquors (rum), and beers. Next are makers of bakery products, closely followed by producers of confections and chewing gum. Sugar is also used, in small amounts as a seasoning, in all sorts of foods where one would not expect it. In the curing of hams, for example. In canned soups, many breads, catsup, relishes, salad dressings, and many more everyday foods.

Nutritionists do not agree to a man that sugar is bad for us. For example, two eminent Harvard specialists are at odds on the subject. Dr. Jean Mayer is wholeheartedly against pure sugar, feeling that the less we ingest of it the better off we are. But Dr. Frederick Stare has said that up to 25 percent of our calories can come from sugar as long as nutritional needs are met. (To be practical about it, it would be difficult to take in 25 percent of our daily diet as sugar, meet all our nutritional needs, and not get very fat indeed. And obesity is, all nutritionists agree, to be avoided.)

Kinds and forms of sugar. Today we can buy sugar of a number of types in markets of any size.

granulated sugar: The pure white sugar we use at table and for much of our cooking; comes in 1-pound packages and 5- and 10-pound and larger bags.

superfine: Very fine granulated white sugar that dissolves readily, is used in beverages, on fruit, and in special baking; 1 cup granulated equals 1 cup superfine; sold in 1-pound packages.

confectioners: Granulated sugar that has been crushed into a soft powder (cornstarch is added to prevent caking); used in frostings, confections, and for dusting foods such as unfrosted cake; 1¾ cups confectioners equals 1 cup granulated (but do not substitute one for the other in cooking); sold in 1-pound packages.

brown sugar: Fine crystals of sugar coated with molasses; light and dark (sometimes called old-fashioned) brown sugars are widely available, sometimes also a medium brown; 1 cup packed brown sugar equals 1 cup granulated; light brown

is used in baking, frostings, and candies; dark brown is used in such foods as gingerbread, mincemeat, and in some cookies and cakes; granulated brown sugar (called "brownulated" by its processor), which pours freely and does not cake, is available but less widely used—follow table on package for substitution in recipes; a liquid form is also available, but not widely—use only in specially formulated recipes; brown sugar is sold in 1-pound packages or bags.

maple sugar: Sold loose or in cakes or decorative forms; expensive; see also MAPLE.

colored sugars: Made with vegetable colors, to be used for sprinkling on cookies and in other decorative ways; sold in small jars.

cinnamon-sugar: Mixture of granulated sugar and cinnamon, for sprinkling on buttered toast, cookies, and such; sold in small jars.

Store all sugars, after opening, in airtight jars or cannisters to prevent caking. Sugar keeps indefinitely. See also INVERT SUGAR, SPUN SUGAR, and XYLITOL.

SULPHUR: see special feature: NUTRITION NOTEBOOK

SUMMER SAUSAGE: see SAUSAGES

SUMMER SQUASH: see SQUASH

SUNCHOKE: see ARTICHOKES, JERUSALEM

SUNFLOWER OIL: see OILS, SALAD AND COOKING

SUNFLOWER SEEDS

Roasted and salted, sunflower seeds are virtually as much a no-one-can-eat-only-one snack as peanuts. One cup of the hulled kernels (the hard outer husk must be removed) provides 257 calories. Many birds also enjoy sunflower seeds, and will obligingly do the husking themselves in return for a handout. If you are a bird lover, it pays to plant a few sunflowers—they grow rapidly, virtually untended—in your yard each summer to give yourself a bird-food supply for the coming winter.

SUPREME

Although recipes for many dishes call themselves "suprême" of this or that, in cooking, a suprême is the boned half of a chicken breast, encountered among the entrées on French menus as "suprême de volaille."

SWEET BREADS: see BREADS

SWEET CORN: see CORN

SWEET POTATOES

A close relative of the morning glory but not related to our common white potato, sweet potatoes are the root of a tropical vine, used by us as a vegetable. They are another of the foods that originated in the western hemisphere, that were cultivated and enjoyed long before we come-lately folk got here. Early Spanish explorers dutifully trotted them back to Europe, and Europeans introduced them to the Far East and North America.

Because of the by-products that are made from them (alcohol, starch, animal feed), sweet potatoes are an important commercial crop in many countries, though less for their contribution to the diet than for their contribution to commerce. In the United States they rank among the top ten vegetables grown.

Sweet potatoes must be cured before they can be marketed. After the harvest, they are stored under conditions of high temperature and high humidity for 7 to 10 days, then at 50 to 55°F. until they go to market. This procedure postpones deterioration and decay.

Kinds in the market. There are many varieties of sweet potatoes but two types predominate in this country's markets. One has a light yellow to pale orange-brown skin, and yellow flesh. The second, often erroneously called "yam," has an orange to coppery brown skin and bright- to red-orange flesh; it is sweeter and more moist than the first variety. (See YAMS.)

SWEET POTATOES IN YOUR KITCHEN

The vegetable is grown in the southern states and in California, and some varieties are grown on the Atlantic seacoast as far north as New Jersey. They are most plentiful in the market in the fall and early winter, but in many places they can be had all year around.

how to buy: Choose potatoes of good shape—and uniform size if you are going to bake them—without blemishes, pleasingly plump, clean and dry.

how to store: Refrigerate up to 1 month, or store in a cool dry place for a somewhat lesser time. Cooked, refrigerate in a covered container up to 5 days.

nutritive value: One sweet potato—uncooked dimensions 5 inches in length, 2 in diameter—when cooked yields 161 calories. Other nutritive values for that same potato are:

protein	2.4	grams
fat	.6	gram
carbohydrate	37	grams
calcium	46	milligrams
phosphorus	66	milligrams
iron	1	gram
sodium	14	milligrams
potassium	342	milligrams
thiamin	.1	milligram
riboflavin	.08	milligram
niacin	.8	milligram
ascorbic acid	25	milligrams
vitamin A	9,230	international units

Tips on preparing, cooking. Wash potatoes, trim off any woody or bruised parts, but do not peel before cooking. Boil in salted water until tender, a matter of 20 to 30 minutes. They can then be mashed, or sliced for such dishes as candied sweet potatoes. Or grease the skins and bake at 400°F. 30 to 40 minutes. (The greased skins peel more readily.) Sweet potatoes may also be french fried. Boil for 10 minutes, then peel and cut into finger shapes and fry.

Freezing sweet potatoes. Properly prepared for freezing (see special feature: PUTTING FOOD BY), sweet potatoes may be stored at 0°F. or lower up to 1 year.

Other ways, other forms. Although they are generally available fresh, there are sweet potatoes in other guises in the market.

on grocery shelves, in cans or packages: Canned in its juices or with pineapple; in packages, dried.

in grocery frozen-food section: Frozen candied sweet potatoes.

Some perfect partners. Sweet potatoes pair well with many foods, are particularly good with pork, ham, and poultry. They make tasty skillet dishes with pork chops or sausage, a savory soufflé to use as a side dish. They may be scalloped with apples or in orange juice with orange slices or with cranberries, or with nuts—chestnuts and peanuts are particularly good. And, of course, kids would be desolated without candied sweet potatoes with marshmallows. You can even

make a cream of sweet potato soup or a sweet potato pie much like pumpkin for dessert, as well as waffles, puddings, and doughnuts.

SWEETBREADS: see VARIETY MEATS

SWEETENED CONDENSED MILK: see MILK

SWEETSOPS: see EXOTIC FRUIT

SWEET-SOUR

A flavor combination that, properly done, exactly balances the sweet and the tart elements so that one does not overpower the other, but both can be detected. Most often the sweet-sour element is a sauce, but sometimes simply a seasoning. The Chinese make wonderful sweet-sour pork dishes. The Germans love sweet-sour red cabbage. And the distinctive flavor is used in many meat, poultry, and fish dishes and with vegetables throughout the world.

SWISS CHARD: see UNUSUAL VEGETABLES

SWISS CHEESE: see CHEESE

SWORDFISH: see FISH

SYRUPS

Sweet liquids, thin to very thick, syrups are pourable and generally sticky. Some are simply solutions of sugar and water, and are used for sweetening—in drinks in which dry sugar will not readily dissolve, to use in freezing fruits, and so on. Among the common syrups (sometimes spelled "sirup") are these:

- *simple syrup*—sugar and water, boiled until the sugar dissolves; may be flavored or not; used for sweetening and preserving, and in candies and some frostings
- *natural syrups*—molasses, sorghum syrup, maple syrup, corn syrup (light and dark), maple-flavored cane syrup, and honey; used in many ways in cooking and as a sauce for such foods as pancakes and waffles
- *commercial syrups*—sugar solutions that are flavored, as with chocolate or various fruits and/or spices; used as sauces for ice cream, plain cakes, waffles

Syrups may be stored in a cool, dark spot. Many of them will congeal into sugar if refrigerated. See also GOLDEN SYRUP, HEAVY SYRUP, HONEY, MAPLE, and MOLASSES.

YOU CAN'T WORK WITHOUT TOOLS

When something new for the kitchen comes on the market, some home cooks pine until they have it for their own—others can turn out a seven-course meal with just a paring knife and a saucepan

The food processor was put on sale a few years ago. Immediately hundreds of women read the ads, swooned with joy and, when they recovered, rushed out to buy this newest in a long line of electrical and mechanical kitchen helpers. For weeks, the family ate nothing but those things that could be ground, sliced, grated, kneaded, or otherwise attended to by the processor.

Then, for some of them at least, light began to dawn. Wasn't it rather silly to use the processor—and wash it afterwards—to get a tablespoon of minced onion, when a knife and a cutting board could do the job? Wasn't it rather sad to watch the processor knead its little gray nubbin of bread dough, when kneading dough by hand is such a great and therapeutic experience? So many of the processors were shoved aside, to line up with the seldom-used drink mixer, the cordless rechargeable electric flour sifter, the cordless electric peppermill, the electric peeling wand, and other "investments," and brought out again only when its wonders could be truly useful.

The same thing happened to mama when the blender came on the market quite a while back. She found that it didn't need to be used for everything it could do, and there were some things it couldn't do. (Grind nuts, for example. Neither can the food processor. In both cases they come out oily and gummy. For proper ground nuts to use in, say, a torte, one needs a drum-type Mouli grater. But before you rush out to buy one, ask yourself: How often do I make torte? How often do I grind nuts for any purpose? Have I ever made anything that called for ground nuts?)

WHAT KIND OF COOK ARE YOU?

There are cooks and cooks. Some seldom serve anything except convenience foods and items from the delicatessen or the fast-food takeout places—but these are not cooks at all, in the true sense, and we can ignore them. There are the competent cooks, who turn out three meals a day for the family, but accomplish the feat with little joy. There are the oh-boy! cooks who cut out millions of recipes, descend on the kitchen like Attila the Hun (and get the place into the same sort of ravaged mess), turn out culinary extravaganzas without regard for the likes and dislikes of the people who are

going to eat them, lay the recipe aside, and never repeat themselves. And there are the good cooks, who move about the kitchen with efficient speed, humming as they go, and produce a succession of inspired meals, whether the main dish is frankfurters or squab, hamburger or rack of lamb.

Oddly, it's the competent but joyless cook who needs the most support in the way of kitchen utensils and appliances—anything to cheer the task. Good cooks can get by with basics, although some of them delight in every truly useful gadget and gizmo that comes along. But they know the difference between useful and useless and between need and want. They don't throw away the old grapefruit knife when a newly designed one comes on the market. They don't buy a pasta maker when they know they're never going to make pasta, preferring to buy it fresh-made from the Italian market down the street. But they do have all the tools they need, and every one of them is of good quality. (Ticky-tacky tools are worse than none.) And, because no two cooks, good or so-so, are alike, each one's list of essentials differs from everyone else's.

THE KITCHEN ITSELF

We all know that the Big 3 are essential—stove, sink, refrigerator. Beyond those lies—what?

microwave oven: If you can, try before you buy, in the home of a friend who has one. And ask other good-cook friends how often they use the oven, and for what. There are thousands of kitchens today harboring microwave ovens (some stoves now come with two ovens, one conventional and one microwave). In many of those kitchens, the microwave oven is in almost constant use. In others, it's used only for thawing and warming up—not enough for so expensive an appliance.

dishwasher: If you hate the clean-up process, it can be a blessing. Even if you're a wash-as-you-go cook, a dishwasher can be a joy after dinner—stack the dishes in the washer, turn it on, and go join the family. It's wasteful to use the washer unless you have a full load. That means, however, that cooked-on foods must be cleaned off before the dishes and pots are put into the washer, unless it has a rinse-and-hold cycle, a mechanical blessing that does the rinsing for you. (You must remove large scraps, such as bones and uneaten chunks of food, however.) Most of today's dishwashers can cope with cooked-on food and other hard-to-clean messes if they are fresh, but don't do the job thoroughly if the messes have sat around overnight, waiting for the dishwasher to be fully loaded. Dishwashers come in built-in and free-standing models. If you are energy-conscious, shut off the dishwasher when it reaches the "dry" cycle and let the dishes air dry.

garbage disposal: A mixed blessing. You must keep in mind what can (most garbage, such as peelings, dish scrapings, and so on) and what cannot (large bones, anything metal) be put into it. And you need to keep a sharp eye on young children, who in their eagerness to get back to TV scrape everything off plates into the disposal, including the cutlery. And on helpful visiting friends, who tend to throw out the baby with the bathwater, particularly if they don't have a disposal of their own.

trash compactors: These are great for neatly and easily getting rid of the accumulation of junk that piles up in every home until you sometimes wonder if the neighbors don't sneak their castoffs into your kitchen in the dead of night.

As for the room itself, a kitchen should be arranged to save steps—all the elements for baking in one place, for example, the pots and pans near the stove, the spices and herbs neatly in a rack where you can lay hands easily on what you want. Good lighting is essential, including small strip lights in some places if necessary so you never work in your own shadow. There should be a place right beside the stove on which to rest hot pans, made of a material heat won't damage. And a place beside the refrigerator to put down foods you want to store in it while you get them into proper storage containers. (See KITCHEN.)

Counter materials should be nonstain and easy to keep clean. Appliances that stand out on counters but are not in constant use should have covers so that they don't have to be washed when you do want to use them. A built-in cutting board is not all that kitchen designers would like you to believe. If you chop onions, for example, a cutting board needs thorough cleansing; if you cut raw meat on the board, it must not only be scrubbed but disinfected with a bleach solution we are now told. All that scrubbing is lots easier to do at the sink than when the board is in a fixed position.

STORAGE AND OTHER NONCOOKING FUNCTIONS

Cannister sets marked Flour, Sugar, Coffee, and Tea can be very gay and decorative. But if no one in your home drinks tea, what do you put in the tea cannister? And what do you do with all the other staples that should be transferred to airtight containers once they're opened? Cornmeal, corn-

starch, cake flour, brown sugar, confectioners sugar, and all the rest—where do you stash them?

Much more practical are a number of unmarked wide-mouthed glass jars with airtight screw-on covers. They come in several sizes to accommodate items bought in large and in small quantities. Because they're see-through, they do not need labeling.

For refrigerator storage, plastic freezer containers with their tight-fitting covers are the most practical. Again, they come in several sizes. And—even if you've never done any canning and don't plan to—widemouthed, screw-top quart- and pint-size canning jars are useful for both refrigerator and dry storage.

Unless your kitchen boasts a metal-lined built-in bread drawer, a bread box is not essential but very useful. Especially in a family with children, where lots of bread is used, it's good to have a designated place where the bread lives. If the youngsters make themselves sandwiches, it's much easier to get them to put the bread away if it has a home of its own.

Again, a spice rack, separate from the kitchen shelves, is virtually a must, particularly if you keep a large number of spices, herbs, and other seasonings on hand.

If your cupboard space is limited, dish-storage racks are very useful. In a well-designed one you can store a whole service for eight in the space that one or two stacks of plates would normally occupy. Cup hooks are fine for keeping the cups off shelves—and for saving handles, which often get broken when cups are stacked. If you have a lot of glass stemware, think more than once about a wooden gadget that hangs stemware under a shelf, out of harm's way. If you have space—and space can almost always be made if you stop and give the matter thought—include two open-top, ventilated-side bins, one for root vegetables, one for fruit that is not refrigerator stored.

Little things that loom large. If you've ever wondered how we got along before plastic bags were invented, you are not alone. The bags—sandwich, medium, and large sizes—are essential for storing vegetables, fruit, any odd-shaped object such as a whole chicken or a partly-used roast, small dribs and drabs of leftovers that take up too much refrigerator space if put into containers. Close the bags with pipe cleaners—they can be reused many times and, unlike the paper-covered twister ties, the metal does not come away and tear the bag.

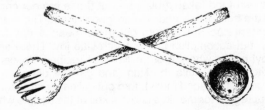

Other wrappings for storage and a dozen other uses are needed—absorbent paper, wax paper, plastic film, foil (both regular and heavy-duty), and dispensers for them. Cheese-cloth has a number of kitchen uses as well, as you'll find if you keep a bolt of it on hand.

FOOD PREPARATION HELPERS

Some of these are essential if you do any amount of cooking at all, some are nonessential to some cooks, absolute musts to others. Only you can decide which fall into each category.

- *mixing bowls*—a set of them, graduated in size from 3-cup to 4-quart; they may be glass or ceramic or metal, but not plastic (even in the dishwasher, all grease does not come off plastic bowls; it can lurk there to keep egg mixtures from beating properly)

- *metal dry measures*—a set, in 1-, ½-, ⅓-, and ¼-cup sizes; fill to the brim, level off with a spatula or the blunt side of a knife

- *glass liquid measures*—1-cup size, marked on the see-through side in fractions of a cup, some nowadays with regular measure on one side, metric on the other; 2-cup and 4-cup sizes can be very useful, too

- *measuring spoons*—metal, in 1-tablespoon, 1-tea-spoon, ½- and ¼-teaspoon sizes; some sets add ½-tablespoon and ⅛-teaspoon sizes; two sets are useful—it's annoying to have to wash the vanilla off a spoon before you can measure the salt

- *rubber- or plastic-bladed spatulas*—one each of the wide-blade and the narrow-blade kinds—use to push food into the blades of the blender, get the last drop of cake batter out of the bowl, fold in dry ingredients, and a dozen other uses

- *cutting boards*—a large one and a small; choose be-tween wooden—more difficult to keep clean—and plastic (some of which stain in spite of what the label says)

- *knives*—at least 2 paring knives (sharp!) so you don't have to endlessly wash one; a 5-inch general utility knife; a carver; a slicer; a grapefruit knife; an 8-inch French chef's (chopping) knife

- *other cutting devices*—a pair of kitchen shears; a swiv-el-blade peeler; 2 can openers, 1 regular (electric or hand-turned) and 1 beer-opener type; a standup, 4-faced grater; egg slicer

- *spoons and stirrers*—2 metal spoons, 1 solid-bowl, 1 slotted; 2 wooden spoons, large and small, and a wooden spatula (gets in the corners and edges when you stir); 1 medium-size wire whisk (but a set of 4 in graduated sizes is even better); 4-tined mixing fork; rotary beater, hand or electric

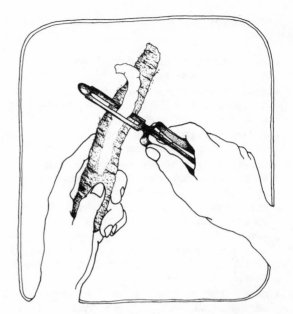

- *if you're a baker*—pastry blender; rolling pin (with a stockinette cover for ease of use and less sticking); pastry board and/or pastry cloth; pastry wheel for cut-ting; pastry brush; flour sifter; cookie cutters

- *washing, draining*—vegetable brush; colander (drain-ing, washing fruits); 2 strainers, 1 large, 1 small

- *fairly essential oddments*—meat thermometer, toaster, skewers, string, corkscrew, bottle opener, knife sharpener, juicer or reamer, electric blender

- *not-so-essential oddments*—candy and deep-fat ther-mometers, cookie press, cake-decorating set, garlic press, meat grinder, food mill, funnels, ring and other shape molds, ice cream spade, kitchen scales, apple corer

TOP-OF-STOVE COOKERY

You can go overboard in the pots and pans department, buying each item in every possible size and shape, or you can —if there is such a term—go underboard, and confine your-self to one measly saucepan and one skillet that always seems to be too large or too small for the task at hand, and make the table silver do double duty as kitchen forks and spoons. In the first instance you'll doubtless wonder shortly if you can't knock out a wall to give yourself more kitchen storage space. In the second, you'll be forever washing the pans in order to get on to the next task—and, doubtless, cursing yourself regularly for being so parsimonious.

As with all other areas of kitchen tools, you are the best

judge of what you need and want. But here are some of the essentials.

- *saucepans:* a 1-quart, a 2-quart, and a 3-quart size, each with its own cover
- *pots for large amounts:* a 5- or 6-quart dutch oven, heavy duty, or a 6-quart kettle—preferably both—each with its own cover
- *skillets:* a 10-inch and a 7-inch; the 10-inch one, at least, should have a cover
- *double boiler:* a pot-within-a-pot that keeps delicate foods from sticking and/or boiling; either can be used separately—one cover fits both pans
- *coffee maker:* either a stovetop model—drip, percolator or vacuum—or an electric one
- *small oddments:* a turner, metal (and a wooden or nylon one if you use pots and pans with nonstick finish); a ladle; 2-tined fork with a long handle and a smaller one; a timer
- *nice, but not essential except to some:* electric frying pan, teakettle, tea pot, chicken fryer, griddle, potato masher, tongs, omelet pan, crepe pan

OVEN COOKERY

We once moved into an apartment in which the kitchen stove had suffered a dichotic trauma. The stovetop looked as if it had lived through the Hundred Years' War and been on the losing side, but the oven had never been used. How had she managed, that woman? She had never made a pie or a cake or cookies or biscuits, nor had she even baked the ready-made kind—the frozen pies, the refrigerated dough biscuits and cookies. She had never roasted meat, baked a casserole. What on earth did those people eat—and, a corollary, what did they look like? Unfortunately, we never found out.

There are large numbers of use-in-the-oven pans in all shapes and sizes. Turn a devoted baker loose in a housewares store and she'll buy one of each. Such proliferation isn't necessary, but the right pan for the task is more a requirement in the oven than on top of the stove. Here are some common ones.

- *cake pans:* 2 or 3 round layer cake pans, 8 or 9 inches in diameter by 1 inch deep; a 9- × 9- × 2-inch square; an 8- × 8- × 2-inch square; a 9- or 10-inch tube pan; a 9- × 13- × 2-inch baking pan
- *loaf or bread pan:* 9- × 5- × 2¾ inches
- *pie plates:* 8- and 9-inch sizes
- *casserole dishes:* come in many sizes, from 1- to 6-quart; choose 2 of appropriate size for your family and when you have guests

- *other necessities:* 2 baking sheets; muffin pans—for cupcakes, too; custard cups; open roaster with a rack; cake racks (for cooling)
- *nice but not essential:* jelly roll pan; shallow baking dish (sometimes called a pudding pan), 1½-quart size; springform pan; soufflé dish; covered roaster

WHAT ARE POTS AND PANS MADE OF?

When you buy a cooking utensil, you can't tell a great deal by looking at it, except whether or not it is attractive. Beauty is certainly not essential, but it cheers the cook. The important questions to ask, however, are these:

1. *What is it made of?* Ask the salesperson, and read carefully the manufacturer's tag. How about the handle—is it heat resistant? (Plastic and wooden handles are, but they burn or melt in the oven, so consider the use you'll make of this particular pan.)
2. *How heavy is it?* Lightweight pans have very limited use—foods in them stick and burn readily. A heavier pan, that will heat slowly and evenly, is a better choice for general purposes. A very heavy pan—a large cast-iron dutch oven, for example—is fine for limited use, but may be too heavy for everyday use.
3. *Is it well made?* Does it sit flat on its bottom? Does it refrain from tipping, even when empty? Does the handle feel comfortable in your hand? Does the cover fit snugly?

As a rule, it's not a good idea to buy a large matched set of cooking utensils. They will all be made of the same material and the same weight of material, and no one weight or material is right for all kinds of cooking. Buy each pan separately, according to use.

The most-used materials. These are the common materials for cookware, along with some idea of price, ease of care, and durability.

copper: Very good to look at, and conducts heat well. The copper should be at least ⅛ inch thick. Copper pans have a tin lining, which will wear away after considerable time; the pan must be retinned before further use. Copperware is very expensive, and must be kept polished—a chore.

aluminum: Durable, and a good heat conductor. Here weight is important—the thicker the aluminum, the more evenly it cooks. Aluminum is moderately priced, easy to clean, and durable—but it has some drawbacks. It will discolor certain foods. To cook eggs, or foods made with wine, lemon juice, or vinegar, use a pot of another material. Aluminum will also become stained, but the stains can be removed by boiling vinegar in the pot.

stainless steel: More expensive than aluminum, but durable (if thick) and easy to clean. Stainless steel is a poor conductor of heat, but this is overcome in good-quality cookware by a layer of copper or aluminum, either on the outside bottom or sandwiched between two layers of the steel on the bottom of the pan.

cast iron, enameled cast iron: Heavy, but very durable; heats slowly and evenly, and holds the heat well. Moderate in price. Much cast iron must be seasoned before use—follow the manufacturer's directions. To hold the seasoning, use soap—not detergent—to clean, and do not scrub with steel wool. Dry pans thoroughly; this material rusts. Cast iron will discolor some foods. Enameled cast iron, although more expensive than the plain, has all the advantages and none of the disadvantages. It does not require seasoning, is easy to clean, will not discolor food. And it's very good to look at.

enamelware: These have an enameled surface over a lighter material than cast iron—often too light to be useful. Easy to clean, but a poor conductor of heat. Chips easily. Prices range from cheap to expensive, depending on weight. Must be discarded when the enamel surface begins to deteriorate—chemical reactions can occur in the chipped or cracked spots.

glass and pottery: Check tags—some pieces of these materials can be used on top of the stove, others only in the oven. Prices are moderate. Heat unevenly, but hold heat well. One advantage is that dishes of these materials can come directly from oven to table. Break fairly readily, especially when subjected to sudden changes of temperature.

glass ceramic: Heats somewhat unevenly, but holds heat well. Attractive, it can go from stovetop or oven to the table. (Some have snap-on handles that can be removed for table service.) Withstands extreme changes of temperature—can go directly from freezer to stove. Rather heavy, easy to clean.

Given complete freedom to choose as we'd like, we'd have a selection of stainless steel, enameled cast iron, and glass ceramic pots and pans for both oven and stovetop use, with glass soufflé dishes and pottery casseroles.

A word about nonstick finishes. Home cooks seem either to love or hate these, with no so-so in the middle. The finishes are applied to the inner surface of the pan, and do not alter the heat-conducting properties of the material from which the pan is made. Food does not stick to the surfaces and, in theory, no fat is needed in cooking. However, baked goods cooked in nonstick-finish pans will not brown nicely unless the pans are greased. Plastic or nylon utensils—turners, spoons, and such—must be used so that the surface will not be marred, although shallow scratches will not affect the pan's usefulness. Wash—they clean quite easily—in hot, soapy water; do not scour. Surface may discolor (usually from overheating; the pans cannot withstand high heat), but this also does not affect the usefulness of the pan.

A word about cookware in microwave ovens. Metal pots and pans cause the oven to arc. Use cookware especially designed for the microwave oven—there's a wide variety available—or glass, pottery, or chinaware (if it has no metal-band trimming). For quick reheating, a paper cup (not waxed) or plate, or even a paper napkin will serve.

YOU CAN'T CUT WITHOUT CUTLERY

A dull knife is the number-one cook frustrater. Besides, it's dangerous. Dull knives cause slippages, and slippages cause cuts—not in the food, but in the user. On the other hand, a sharp knife, and the right one for the purpose, is a joy. It cuts swiftly and neatly through hard foods and soft. If your budget is limited, better to have two or three good knives than a whole array of poor ones.

Shopping for quality. It is not true in many cases, but in this one it is: Generally, the more expensive the knife, the better it will be. That's because it costs the manufacturer to build quality into a knife. Here are the criteria for judging.

the blade: Good quality or poor, all knife blades are made of steel and carbon; in some cases chromium is a component, which turns the knife into stainless steel. Blades of carbon steel have an excellent cutting edge that sharpens well when sharpening is needed, but they rust and quickly acquire stains that cannot be removed any more easily than that "damned spot" on Lady MacBeth's hand.

High-quality, high-carbon stainless steel is the best choice. It will give you an excellent cutting edge (which poor quality stainless steel does not), and will resist rust and stains. Ask the salesperson about the knife you wish to buy, and also read the manufacturer's tags, before you make up your mind.

the business edge: The use that will (or should) be made of it determines the kind of cutting edge each knife has. Serrated or scallop-edged knives cut bread well, are perfect for achieving neat, even slices of tomato. But if you attack a roast with such a knife you'll have hash in no time. The rocker blade and straight, fine edge of a French chef's knife is just right for chopping and slicing vegetables, but it will turn a loaf of bread back into dough. The long, narrow, sharp blade of a slicer is just right for achieving thin, well-shaped slices of ham, but too long and not tough enough for cutting up raw meat. A knife of any kind does well only what it was designed to do. Whack away at bones with a cleaver and you'll get somewhere, but do the same with your chef's knife and you can kiss it goodbye.

the handle: The material from which a handle is made is important, but the way it is joined to the blade is much more so. Handles may be made of wood—maple, rosewood, walnut are common choices. Or they may be made of plastic-impregnated wood, which is very durable. Other possible handle materials are plastic, bone, and ivory, or a combination of two.

The blade has two parts, formed from the same piece of metal, the cutting part and the tang, which is the portion that fits into the handle. The longer the tang, the stronger and more durable the knife. In the best knives, the tang extends the full length of the handle, which is made of two pieces of wood or other material, placed one on each side of the tang and secured to it by rivets. Be sure the rivets are flush with the handle—protruding, they will make use uncomfortable; sunken, they will collect dirt. Beware of a knife in which the tang is only slipped into a hollow in the handle instead of being riveted—it will come apart in no time.

the heft: Pick up the knife and hold it in a ready-for-use position. It should feel comfortable, neither too heavy nor too big for the size of your hand. Where the weight is distributed is related to the use for which the knife was made. Small knives, such as parers, are weightier in the handle, heavy duty knives, such as chef's, are weightier in the blade.

Treat it well, it will serve you well. Dull knives must be sharpened. All knives must be stored so that their blades will not be damaged.

sharpening: Unless it's very dull (and how did that happen?), a knife needs only a few licks on a sharpening steel to put it back into operating condition. The steel is that long, round, pointed object you've doubtless seen the butcher use at the market. Hold the steel by its handle, horizontally and pointed away from you, in your left hand, unless you're a southpaw. With your other hand, pick up the knife by its handle and position it with the back end of the blade near the point of the steel. With light pressure, draw the blade toward you, letting the whole length of the blade contact the steel. Turn the knife over and repeat. Three or four repeats on each side should be sufficient. Sharpen knives both before and after each use.

Abused knives can be brought back to life with a whetstone. Moisten the stone with a few drops of light oil. Holding the blade at a 20-degree angle to the stone, draw the blade from the back end to the point across the stone. Do this, alternating sides of the blade, ten or twelve times.

Electric sharpeners and mechanical ones are also available. They can work well, provided you follow the manufacturer's directions to the letter. Don't use on knives with serrated or scalloped blades.

storing: Wooden knife holsters, wall-hung or freestanding, or magnetized strips, wall-hung, both designed to keep knives out of harm's way, are best for storage. Don't pile knives helter-skelter into a drawer. The edges can be dulled or nicked by such abuse.

caring for: Wash, rinse, and dry knives shortly after using them. Never put them to soak. Always slice or chop on a cutting board—you can ruin both the knife and the counter surface if you use that to cut on. Never use a knife for any purpose other than the one for which it was made—it is not a screwdriver, bottle opener, or paper cutter.

Even though directions say a knife is dishwasher safe, you'll keep your knives longer and in better condition if you wash and dry them by hand and put them safely away immediately. A good knife is a long-term investment.

SMALL ELECTRICAL APPLIANCES

Their name is legion: slow cookers, toaster ovens, waffle irons, grills, mixers (stand or hand-held), blenders, food processors, knives, crepe makers, corn poppers, fondue pots, bag sealers, toasters, doughnut makers, steam cookers, deep fryers, frying pans, woks, pizza makers, griddles, coffee makers, broilers, and a dozen more, all the way down to such effete gadgets as electric flour sifters. And there is a wide selection of models. So how do you choose the appliance that is right for you?

Look and read. Look for the symbol of Underwriters' Laboratories. If an electrical appliance carries the UL seal, it means that it has been tested and listed by the Laboratories as meeting their—very stringent—safety and performance standards.

Inspect the appliance closely. Does it appear to be well made? Are the handles and base insulated for safe table and countertop use? If it has a cover, does it fit well? Has it a removable control, and is it marked "immersible" or "dishwasher safe" so that the business part of the appliance can be easily cleaned? Does it sit evenly, without rocking, on a flat surface?

Read the guarantee. What is the extent and length provided against electrical and mechanical defects of both workmanship and materials? Is a listing of the manufacturer's authorized service and repair stations included?

Look at the use-and-care booklet. Is it adequate, giving explicit instructions? When you get the appliance home, read that use-and-care booklet from cover to cover, and then put it in a safe spot, where you can find and refer to it. If you should misplace it, write to the manufacturer for another, giving the model number and a full description.

Safe use at home. Position any appliance on a level surface so there can be no possibility of tipping. Use it at a safe distance from water and from the kitchen range. Connect it to a 110–120 volt AC electrical outlet only. Always use the cord and heat control supplied with the appliance. Be guided by the use-and-care booklet regarding the use of extension cords. Be sure that the appliance cord is positioned so that it cannot be pulled out of either appliance or outlet, and so that it cannot be tripped over.

When connecting an appliance, hold the heat control (never the cord) in one hand, and insert into the appliance.

Then plug the cord into an outlet. To disconnect, remove the plug from the outlet, allow the appliance to cool, then detach the heat control.

Take care when using liquids in the appliance. A sudden addition of cold water can cause a burst of steam that can be dangerous. Never cover an appliance in which you are heating cooking oil. Do not carry an appliance from place to place when it contains hot liquid or oil.

Energy factors. As a general rule, appliances use less energy than is used by a conventional range. It is more economical, for instance, to bake potatoes in a toaster oven than in the range oven. But if you are baking several dishes at once, add the potatoes to the conventional oven rather than using the toaster oven solely for them.

Rule of thumb: Heat-producing appliances (such as frypans, toasters) cost more to run than motor-operated ones, such as a blender. The operating wattage will also clue you —the higher the wattage figure, the more it costs to run the appliance. And, of course, the length of time you use the appliance and the frequency of use are both factors as well.

Operating wattages of some common small and large appliances are listed below. You can also use this listing (third column) to determine how much the appliance costs to run for a year's time. For this, you need to know the number of kilowatt-hours per year the appliance uses (third column), and the rate per kilowatt-hour that your local electric company charges (sometimes listed on the electric bill; if not, call the company and ask). The kilowatt-hours per year listed below are national averages—you may, of course, use a particular appliance more or less than those averages.

small appliance	average operating wattage	killowatt-hours per year
blender	300	1
broiler	1,143	85
can opener	102	.03
coffee maker		
brew cycle	593	90
warm cycle	80	48
corn popper	570	9
fondue pot	794	7
frypan	9,190	100
griddle	1,207	46
knife	95	.08
mixer		
hand held	68	1
on stand	150	2
roaster	1,335	58
sandwich grill	1,161	35
toaster	1,146	39
waffle iron	1,200	19

large appliance	average operating wattage	killowatt-hours per year
dishwasher	1,200	360
freezer (15 cubic feet)	341	1,195
microwave oven	1,450	190
range (including oven)	12,200	704
self-cleaning oven	12,200	730
refrigerator-freezer		
14 cubic feet	326	1,137
same, frost-free	615	1,829

If you do your math homework on those, you may come to a better understanding of your electric bill. And before you throw yourself into a panic, remember we're talking about costs per *year*.

EXTRA PAIRS OF HANDS

If you are like the average cook, you have some pots and pans and small appliances in your kitchen that you have tucked away and seldom or never use, others that you feel you simply could not do without. And it's interesting to know that some of the ones you never bother with are those that your neighbor uses every day, some of the ones you swear by are the very ones she ignores.

Here are some of the most commonly used kitchen helpers and their usual functions.

electric mixers: There are stand and hand-held models, most often used for mixing cake batters and whipping eggs and cream. Better the stand than the hand-held model—the former can perform all the services of the smaller machine, but the latter can't replace the stand model in many of its functions.

toasters: An electric toaster is not the only way to make toast, but since it was invented many years ago we've happily discarded all the old ways. A must in most kitchens. See also TOAST.

waffle irons: A necessity in waffle-nut households—there is no alternative—but seldom used in homes where waffles are not a regular breakfast item. Since the advent of the frozen waffle, which children can heat for themselves in the toaster, they are less often used than before. A pity, because there are all sorts (see WAFFLES), not only for breakfast but throughout the day, including excellent dessert waffles.

electric skillets: The alternative is a skillet on the stovetop, but the electric variety does not have to be as constantly monitored. Heat is controlled and maintained by a thermostat dial with a number of settings. They are good for both frying and braising, but seldom used for the auxilary purposes the use-and-care booklets list, such as cooking large roasts, baking cakes and biscuits. Most models have high dome covers, usually with steam vents.

blenders: Some home cooks keep their blenders in constant use for all functions, such as crumbing bread, grating cheese, chopping nuts, and such. Others use theirs only when they want to produce a smoother, more completely blended consistency than electric mixers can, as in reducing various fruits and vegetables to a purée, making blender hollandaise and béarnaise and thick-shake ice cream drinks.

griddles: If you inherited your great-grandmother's old soapstone griddle, you may well still be using it, although many of today's kitchens number electric griddles among their batteries of appliances. However, most electric griddle functions can be accomplished in stovetop or electric skillets, and often are. In large families, electric griddles can be helpful because they offer big cooking surfaces.

food processors: These are so new—and expensive—that there are relatively few of them in use. Modern recipes that mention the appliance at all always offer an alternative, as "in food processor or blender" (which may give you a clue as to whether or not you want or need one). The processors chop, slice, shred, and mix as their chief functions—if you already have tools and/or appliances that perform these functions, you may not need (but on the other hand you may want) a processor. There are many American and foreign ones on the market. Be certain that the one you choose will perform the functions you wish. For example, although it is claimed for them that they will crush ice and grind coffee beans, many do not do an adequate job of either. Again, although you can beat egg whites or whip cream in most processors, the volume achieved is not as great as with a mixer or hand beater. On many, the feeding tube is too small to accommodate some of the foods—cucumbers, zucchini—you would like to slice. So if you decide to add a food processor to your collection of kitchen helpers, be an informed shopper. Some who own one swear by it, some swear at it.

slow cookers: With a slow cooker you can, if you wish, leave the house in the morning, come home at dinner time to a cooked meal. Ranging in capacity from 3½ to 8 quarts, slow cookers are what their name implies—they cook slowly, at low temperatures, foods that are braised or cooked in liquid. (However, some newer models of these appliances also roast and bake and even deepfry, but the function of most of them is to slow cook.) All have temperature-control thermostats regulated by dials. Most are large covered pots set on or in separate heating units, but some of the latest models have wraparound heating units. Cooking times vary; beef stew, for example, is ready to serve in from 5 to 10 hours, depending on the make of the appliance. When you shop for a slow cooker, be aware that for safety's sake the appliance must reach a temperature of 125°F. within 3 hours of being turned on, and must then move quickly to 165°F.—this is necessary to destroy bacteria that can cause the food to spoil.

woks: In contrast, woks are fast rather than slow cookers. They can be had as stovetop or electric models, the electric having the advantage of allowing you to cook at the table. Although it is true that you can accomplish any cooking function of the wok by using other pans or appliances, the wok often does the job better, more rapidly—and it's attractive and fun to use. Stir-frying, which produces quickly cooked meats, poultry, and fish, along with tender-crisp vegetables—all with matchless flavor—is the wok's first function; tempura-style deep frying is its second. But you can use the appliance for American-type cooking—sautéing, deep frying and simmering—as well, producing anything from a poached fish to scrambled eggs to french fries. Electric woks stand on attached feet; stovetop ones sit in a detachable ring placed over the burner. All have covers; some have removable shelves to keep cooked foods hot while others are still cooking; some have steamer attachments. With all, read the use-and-care booklet carefully and abide by it—woks concentrate their heat in the center of the pan, necessitating somewhat different cooking techniques from those used with other types of pans.

SOMEBODY'S LISTENING

Time was when everything was made to fit the average person. If you were much taller than average, you had to make your own clothes or have them made. If you were very small, although a grown woman, you had to go to the girls' department to find something to fit you. If your feet were outside the normal range of shoe sizes, you had your shoes handmade or wore the only thing available, grandma's arch preservers. If your feet were extraordinarily small, you had to patronize an outlet for manufacturers' samples and be content with whatever they had.

But all that has changed. Now there are tall clothes and tiny clothes, big shoes and little ones. And a change has come in the kitchen, too. Once, even if you were a single person living alone, if you wanted an appliance you bought the family size or did without. And if you were handicapped, it never occurred to manufacturers that you needed extra help.

Small wonders. Do you live alone? Or are you, at most, a family of two—roommates, or a husband and wife whose children have grown and moved away? Then you know that cooking for one or two isn't easy. Perhaps you've wanted to french fry, but didn't like to heat enough oil for an army. Or you've yearned for a small grill-griddle, a miniature slow cooker.

All at once, your desires have been granted. Now, in the last few years, all sorts of mini-appliances have come on the market. There's a french fryer that takes only 2 cups of oil—several of them, in fact, some with plastic covers like those that come with coffee cans, so that the oil can be covered and stored right in the fryer. There are small pressure cookers, just the right size for a feed-one-or-two meal. They operate just like the big ones, but have only a 1-quart capacity. There's a speedy 1-cup coffee maker, and several with capacities of 1 to 4 cups. There are little doughnut machines, turning out two at a time. There are small skillets, round or square, immersible and with thermostatic controls. There are little multi-purpose grills that cook up one hamburger (some will do two) in a very brief time, can also be used to cook frankfurters, to toast english muffins and, when laid flat, cook eggs, pancakes, or french toast.

All of these scaled-down little wonders work well and accomplish what they are advertised to accomplish. It's a mini-revolution for which thousands of loners and duos are grateful.

Kitchen help for the blind and visually impaired.
How can a person who can't see cook? Lots of them have been doing it for years. Some appliances have always had raised numbers and letters on their dials—although they are only slightly raised, skilled fingers can feel them and "read" them. But those appliances were only a few, and difficult for the blind to work with anyway.

Now appliance manufacturers have come to the rescue with raised-numeral dials, braille cookbooks, and braille or cassette-tape use-and-care manuals. Three electric-range manufacturers have brought out raised-letter controls on their stoves. If you have a gas oven, you can remove the temperature control dial, return it to the manufacturer, and they will send it back with the low-temp setting, and the 300-, 400-, and 500-degree settings marked so the blind can use it to control both oven and broiler.

Braille controls and a braille cookbook are available from the manufacturer of at least one microwave oven. Braille use-instructions and a cookbook can be had for at least one slow cooker, which also prints its cookbooks in large type for the vision-impaired. One pressure cooker marks the weight so the blind can set it by feel, and offers a braille cooking chart. At least two blender makers offer raised settings marks and braille cookbooks. Coded dials can be ordered free of charge for one maker's washers and dryers, and another maker will send you for the asking braille control panels to slip over the regular ones.

The American Foundation for the Blind, 15 West 16th Street, New York, New York 10011, can give you information on where to buy these products or who manufactures them, and also offers "Aids and Appliances," a catalog of many kinds of appliances, tools, and other materials—everything from clocks to calculators—for the use of the blind and the vision-impaired.

What does your kitchen need? Whatever it is, it's out there waiting for you. Appliances large and small, to perform virtually any kitchen function. Tools and utensils in such profusion it's almost embarrassing. Cookbooks by the hundreds, dedicated to the general or to the specific. Restaurant pots and pans and utensils for the devoted cook—even restaurant ranges and refrigerators.

Prices range from moderate to blow-your-head-off, but whatever you want, it's there, waiting.

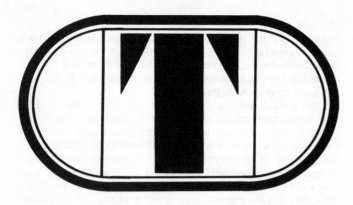

TABASCO: see HOT PEPPER SAUCE

TACOS, TACO SHELLS

The very tasty Mexican answer to the Earl of Sandwich's invention, tacos are crisped corn tortillas bent while still flexible into U-shapes and filled with all manner of good things, including shredded lettuce, chili peppers, ground or chopped meat, grated cheese, avocado slices or guacamole, and chopped tomato, and topped off with a spicy sauce.

If you're not up on tortillas, buy them ready-made—fresh on the west coast, frozen elsewhere. Bend into taco-shape to hold the good filling, and crisp briefly in hot oil. A taco holder is an inexpensive investment if you're fond of the delicious snacks, because a taco's only drawback is that it wants to lie down when you want it to stand up.

Ready-shaped, ready-crisped taco shells are available in packages, leaving only the choice of filling for you to cope with. Treat the package carefully—the shells, very light and crisp, are easily broken.

TAKE-OUT FOODS: see FAST FOODS

TAMALES

Another Mexican contribution to good eating, tamales are made of a spicy meat filling surrounded by a soft cornmeal casing, the whole held together in a cornhusk wrapper. Make them at home, or buy canned or from a Tex-Mex food outlet. Serve with a sauce of chili con carne, with or without beans. And don't forget to remove the cornhusk.

TANGELOES: see EXOTIC FRUIT

TANGERINES

Members of the mandarin family (see ORANGES), tangerines are oranges that are somewhat flattened on both the blossom and stem ends. They have easily removed deep-orange skins; the segments within come apart readily, and are a convenient mouthful size.

When you buy tangerines, choose those heavy for their size with deep-colored skins. In the market, they are at their peak during the holiday season, a good fruit with which to carry out the tradition of tucking an orange into the toe of a child's Christmas stocking.

A medium-size tangerine provides 40 calories; the fruit is a good source of vitamin C and offers small amounts of vitamins A and B and minerals. Refrigerated in a plastic bag or the crisper section, the fruit will stay fresh for several weeks. Frozen tangerine juice concentrate is available. See also MANDARIN ORANGES.

TAPAS

One of the current "in" words for an array of appetizers, rapidly taking the place of hors d'oeuvres—perhaps because everyone got tired of trying to spell the term. In Spain, where the word comes from, every bar of any size has an eye-dazzling, taste-tempting array of tapas to encourage the customers to eat, drink, and be merry.

TAPIOCA

The manioc is one of the principal plants used for food in tropical countries. When the starch in the roots of the plant is heated until the grains burst, small, odd-shaped masses result. These are baked, removing all moisture, to produce flake tapioca, which is ground to make the granulated form of the food—the quick-cooking tapioca we find in packages at the market. Or the damp starch is forced through sieves to make the round pellets grandma knew as pearl tapioca, but which we seldom see these days unless we visit specialty food shops.

Pearl tapioca appears almost exclusively in desserts, but the granulated, quick-cooking type is used to thicken gravies and soups, in place of bread crumbs in ground-meat mixtures, as well as in making an array of puddings and as the thickening agent in fruit pies, to keep the juices under control. (See FLOUR.)

Mostly carbohydrate, tapioca is easily digested, and is sometimes used in bland diets. A 3½-ounce measure of raw tapioca, either type, yields about 350 calories.

TARRAGON: see HERBS AND SAVORY SEASONINGS

TARRAGON VINEGAR: see VINEGARS

TART: see page 454

TARTAR SAUCE: see MAYONNAISE and the special feature: SAUCE SORCERY

T-BONE STEAK: see BEEF

TEA

Water was the first beverage. Then, probably by accident, wine was discovered. Next came tea, with coffee and other drinkables following along as come-lately upstarts.

The Chinese—we still associate them with tea in our minds—were the first to enjoy the delicious, stimulating brew, and they introduced it to the rest of the world. But they managed to keep it to themselves until the seventeenth century, although they had been cultivating tea plants since more than three centuries B.C.

The origins of tea are lost, but there are many myths and legends surrounding its discovery. One such story has it that the beverage was the gift to his people of the emperor Shen Nung, called the Divine Cultivator because he is supposed to have been the first to till the soil. Another attributes tea to the Indian sage Bodhidharma, who, annoyed at having fallen asleep while meditating, cut off his eyelids and flung them away. On the spot where they landed a plant grew with leaves that had the power, when brewed and drunk, of warding off sleep.

Tea travels around the world. First the plants grew wild in China, until finally demand induced farmers to cultivate it. When missionaries came, they carried the word to their homelands. The Dutch were the first traders to import tea, which—at the equivalent of a hundred dollars per pound—became the fashionable beverage of the very rich. Finally, the powerful British East India Company opened up the tea trade on a large scale, brought prices down, and changed the habits of its countrymen. The English began drinking tea—and they are still at it—in the morning as an eye opener, in the afternoon, along with delicious little sandwiches, hot scones with jam, and slices of seed cake to stave off starvation until dinner.

English colonists brought their favorite beverage to America. But when the colonists, believers in free trade, clashed with the East India Company, which wanted a monopoly on the tea trade with the New World, tons of tea were dumped into Boston Harbor by outraged citizens.

Who drinks tea? Nearly every country has at least some tea drinkers, with the British leading the way. They consume about eight pounds per capita annually, three times as much as the Japanese, ten times as much as Americans.

Tea is not only a beverage but a ceremony in Japan, arising from the precepts of purity, harmony, and respect of Zen Buddhism. The English drink their tea black, or with milk and sometimes sugar. Moroccans like theirs exceedingly sweet, adding large quantities of both sugar and honey. In Russia, the tea is very strong and is served in glasses with metal holders rather like our old-fashioned soda fountain glasses; the drinkers sweeten the beverage with jam or sugar taken into the mouth before the tea is drunk; they will tolerate lemon, but never milk. Here in America, those of us who drink tea at all will have lemon or sugar or both, but seldom milk.

Tea from plant to pot. Warm temperature plus rich, well-drained soil and plenty of rain are conditions under which the tea plant thrives. The best tea is cultivated at altitudes of over 5,000 feet, where the plants grow in the shade of taller trees. When tender new leaves and buds appear on the bushes, the tea harvest begins. On how and what the harvesters pick depends the nature and characteristics of the various kinds of teas that will be sent to market. Each worker gathers only one kind, making sure to choose leaves all of one size to assure an even brew when the tea is prepared for drinking.

- *fine pluck*—only the youngest and most tender leaves (which are also the fewest) to produce a superior tea
- *normal pluck*—young buds and leaves, to produce an average or better-than-average tea
- *coarse pluck*—this includes some of the older leaves, to produce an average or less-than-average tea

Processing follows the harvest. What happens to the tea during the course of manufacture has a great influence on the quality of the finished product. Processing turns the tea leaves into black, green, or oolong.

black tea: This is the kind most Americans drink—those that drink tea at all. When brewed, it has a memorable aroma, a rich amber color, and a pungent flavor. These are the result of processing, in which the tea leaves are first spread on racks to dry, then bruised to release the juices. For several hours the tea is allowed to ferment, then the fermentation process is stopped by a second drying. It is the chemical change that takes place in the tea during fermentation that accounts for the flavor, body, and color. India and Sri Lanka are famous for their black teas.

green tea: When brewed, it has a green-gold color and a mellow, subtle flavor. This is the favorite tea of Orientals. To process it, the leaves are steamed, lightly bruised to release juices, then heat-dried to preserve them. There is no fermentation period. Green tea more closely resembles in both color and flavor the fresh-plucked leaves than black tea does. Green teas are processed in China, Japan, and Taiwan.

oolong tea: When brewed, oolong is a rich golden color, with the odor of black tea and somewhat the flavor of green. The flavor is smoother than black and has more authority than green. It is processed as black tea is, but the fermentation time is much shorter. China, Japan, and Taiwan produce oolong teas.

Within each type of tea there can be vast differences of quality, depending on such factors as the growing region, the amount of sunshine and shade, the altitude at which the tea was grown, the type of pluck, the care given it in processing. Teas are graded by a very old and very complicated system. For example, black tea grades denote size of leaf, not quality —"orange pekoe," a term most tea drinkers know or have at least heard, simply means that the leaves before processing were large, and says nothing about the quality. Green teas are graded by age and size of leaf, and here grades do reflect quality. In oolongs, age and size do not count; these teas are graded on a basis of quality alone.

The consumer's friend—the tea taster. To protect both consumer and importer, tea tasters inspect and sample teas that come into the country. Here, they work for the FDA; in the United Kingdom, for the customs service. They are on the lookout for substandard, tainted teas and such sneaky devices as dyed leaves. Importers also employ tea tasters to choose and blend fine teas.

A tea taster looks first at the size, shape, and color of the dried leaf. He sniffs it, noting the aroma. Then he adds boiling water to the dry tea and watches carefully to see the rate at which the leaves uncurl, how quickly or slowly a drinkable infusion is reached, and if the aroma is characteristic of that particular tea. Finally, he tastes the brew for flavor, pungency, and strength. All these are factors in judging the quality of any given tea.

Fine blends of tea are created based on the tea tasters' verdicts. There are only three types of tea, but there are as many as 3,000 different blends on the market. A straight—unblended—green, black, or oolong tea is called by tasters a "self-drinker."

Names, origins, and characteristics of the more familiar teas are shown in the chart below.

SELECTIONS FOR THE HOME TEA TASTER

type	common name	origin	characteristics
black	keemun	China	unblended, this is known as "english breakfast tea"; full-bodied, rich, fine aroma
black	hunan	China	imported to this country only in the past few years; delicate flavor and aroma
black	lapsang souchong	China	tea from the south of China, with a distinctive smoky flavor that is either much enjoyed or heartily disliked—no middle course
black	china blacks	China	large number of teas—some blends, some self-drinkers—marketed under this name; most are good but not great
green	moyunes	China	the ne plus ultra of Chinese green teas
green	tienkais	China	very good, but not quite as good as moyunes; has all the characteristics of fine green tea
green	gyokuro	Japan	subtle but sparkling aroma and flavor; very little is imported in this country
green	mattcha	Japan	the tea of the Japanese tea ceremony; comes in powdered form; strong, slightly bitter
green	sencha	Japan	a large class of green teas; considered common, but some are quite good
green	bancha	Japan	the least of the green teas; caffeine is lower than in other greens
black	assam	India	a self-drinker; strong and full-bodied
black	darjeeling	India	splendid color, aroma, and flavor; self-drinker
black	lapsang souchong	Taiwan	smoky of flavor and aroma, like its Chinese counterpart
green and oolong	pouchong	Taiwan	very lightly fermented; light-bodied, with the aroma of jasmine
oolong	formosa oolong	Taiwan	the best of all teas, many experts believe; amber color, magnificent flavor
black	ceylon	Sri Lanka (Ceylon)	among the world's top teas—light but with body, fine aroma, delicate but substantial flavor

Brewing tea for ultimate flavor. If you have drunk only tea made from a tea bag in a cup, you have not experienced the true delights of this fine beverage. Not only does tea have great aroma and flavor, but it also gives you a lift—not as great as coffee's, with only about half of coffee's caffeine, but very satisfying.

hot tea: Use a pot of any material other than metal, which gives the beverage an off-flavor. Run fresh, cold tap water. (Soft water makes the best tea. If you live in a hard-water area, you may want to use bottled water.) Set the water on the range and wait until it comes to a full, rolling boil.

Warm the pot by filling it with boiling water, then throwing out the water. Measure tea into the heated pot, one teaspoon for each cup (tea cups hold 5¾ or 6 ounces) and "one for the pot." If you wish, you may use high-quality tea bags; put one for each cup into the pot. Pour the proper amount of boiling water—measured—over the tea. Stir, cover, and let stand (the process is called steeping) for 3 to 5 minutes; time is needed to release the full flavor. But know the characteristics of the tea you are using. Some, when steeped, become almost black; others remain pale throughout the steeping period. Strain, pour, and enjoy. Tea fanciers prefer theirs with nothing added, but milk can be poured in—the British way—or the tea may be sugared and/or given a squirt of lemon juice.

iced tea: Since iced tea was first served at the 1904 world's fair in St. Louis, it has been an American favorite, drunk even by those who don't like hot tea. Brew as for hot tea, but make it extra strong. Cool, but don't refrigerate—that makes the beverage cloudy. Pour over ice cubes in a tall glass to serve. Add sugar and/or lemon if you wish; milk is not used in iced tea.

Buying and keeping tea. Even though tea prices have risen, along with those of everything else, it is a much less expensive beverage than coffee. At the time this is written, a cup of coffee, brewed from ground roast, costs about 7 cents. A cup of tea, brewed from loose tea, costs only about 2 cents. One pound of tea will make between 200 and 230 cups.

Tea can be purchased loose from a tea merchant, loose in packages at supermarkets and specialty food shops, in tea bags, as powdered "instant" tea—some kinds are presugared and lemon flavored—or ready-prepared in cans, like soft drinks. There is also a tea specially prepared to use in electric drip coffee makers.

Because it is delicate and quick to absorb odors and flavors from other foods, transfer tea after opening to a container with an airtight lid. It will keep for 6 months.

"Scented" teas for a change of pace. If you like to experiment, try various flavors in your tea. You might enjoy a wedge of lime or orange instead of lemon. Or a clove or two or a piece of cinnamon stick brewed with the tea. Or mint leaves—we often use them in iced tea, but they are fine in the hot brew, too. Or grated orange peel or a small piece of candied ginger brewed with the tea. All are delicious.

If you prefer, there are a number of flavored teas on the market. Try orange peel with spice, cinnamon flavored, Irish tea (a blend of ⅓ Ceylon, ⅔ Assam), jasmine, Chinese restaurant (½ oolong, ¼ green, ¼ jasmine), lemon with spice, mint flavored, or tea with hibiscus blossoms and rose hips. You'll probably find that you like some, dislike others, but each has a loyal following of tea buffs. See also JASMINE TEA.

TENDERIZERS: see MEAT TENDERIZERS

TEQUILA: see LIQUORS

TERRINE: see page 454

TEXTURED PLANT PROTEIN, TEXTURED VEGETABLE PROTEIN

Foods that resemble forms of meat, poultry, and other animal products have been sold in the United States for many years—it's just that the average shopper and/or diner has paid no attention. Eaten mostly by vegetarians and sold only in specialty food shops (at prices comparable to or higher than the animal foods whose place in the diet they were supposed to take), only a small percentage of the population knew they existed until a short time ago.

Until 1973, the only meat analogs to be found in a supermarket were "bacon-flavored pieces," which got a mixed reception. As long as meat was relatively inexpensive, no one but vegetarians had much interest in these meat substitutes. Then, when meat prices soared, consumers quickly discovered the combination of ground beef and textured plant protein some supermarkets began to offer at several cents per pound less than regular ground beef. And ever since, many more products made from plant protein sources that can be combined with or substituted for more expensive animal products have continued to appear on the market.

According to the *FDA Consumer,* chances are good that today one or more products in the average family's weekly grocery supply contains some sort of plant protein product.

And chances are even better that tomorrow's markets will carry many more foods made partially or completely from plant protein.

To combat rising food costs, many institutions—hospitals, colleges, restaurants—are serving vegetable protein products. The USDA has approved them for the nation's school lunch program, and millions of school children have happily consumed meat loaf, sloppy joes, chili, and similar dishes "extended" with some form of plant protein; more is being used each year.

The general public has also begun to accept—and buy—foods made partly or entirely of the plant protein. Food companies have put on the market "sausage" links and patties, "hamburgers," "ham" slices, "fish" fillets, and a number of other nonmeat foods, offering a variety of new choices to the consumer.

How pseudo-meat is made. Protein is extracted from cereal grains, legumes, and other vegetable sources. The plant may be used at various stages of refinement—the greater the refinement, the more protein the product contains. Soybeans, wheat, peanuts, or cottonseed are some of the sources. Soybeans are a good source of protein and extracts made from them have been staples in the diet of Oriental peoples for thousands of years. Research on the use of soybeans for human consumption has been going on for many years in the United States, and more protein products are made from soy here at present than from any other source. Protein isolate is the most highly refined product, containing at least 90 percent protein.

Different manufacturing methods are used to create the varying textures of foods—chips, flakes, chunks, whatever. Various flavorings, colorings, binders, emulsifiers, fat, and other nutrients are combined with the plant protein and fabricated into frozen, canned, or dried products that closely resemble the taste, texture, and appearance of the foods they duplicate.

Label reading is important in the use of these products, and manufacturers' directions for the preparation of them should be followed faithfully. Some, for example, are dried and require rehydration, which will increase the volume of the food to a considerable extent. These have a good shelf life when dry, but after rehydration must be treated like any other perishable product. Frozen products must be refrigerated after thawing and used within a day or two. Some of these new foods become dry or tough under high or prolonged heat. Again, it's important to read and follow the label.

Foods made with or of textured plant protein offer advantages to some dieters, disadvantages to others. Some contain fewer calories than the foods they simulate. All contain little or no cholesterol and are low in saturated fats. But those who must limit their carbohydrate intake—diabetics, for example—must be aware that some of these foods contain carbohydrate that is not present in the food they imitate. Also, some of these products contain more sodium than the natural food.

Sample and judge. The idea of "fake" sausages or whatever is repugnant to some. But it's best not to be like the child who takes a look at a food he's never had before and immediately says, "I don't like it." As we urge children to do, we urge the skeptical also: Taste and see, don't reject out of hand.

THIAMIN: see special feature: NUTRITION NOTEBOOK

THICKEN, TO: see page 449

THOUSAND ISLAND DRESSING: see MAYONNAISE

THYME: see HERBS AND SAVORY SEASONINGS

TI LEAVES

Pronounced "tea," these leaves are used, in their South Pacific homes, as wrappers to hold food while it is being cooked, and often as plates on which food is later served. If you've ever been to a Hawaiian luau, you've encountered ti leaves.

TILSIT: see CHEESE

TIMBALES

Shells made of puff pastry (see PASTRY), generally deeper than a pie shell, filled with a meat, poultry, fish, or vegetable mixture. Timbales may also be made of a fritterlike batter into which a special utensil, a timbale iron, is dipped, then immersed in hot deep fat until cooked.

The word is also used for a baking dish, shaped like a pastry shell, in which foods are cooked. Custard cups can be substituted, and the finely textured mixture cooked in them turned out and served with a sauce.

TIMERS, TIMING

In cooking, as in law, time is of the essence. Each food has its own optimum cooking time, the moment when it is just properly done, neither over- nor under-cooked.

To achieve this desirable state, you need a good kitchen timer—unless you prefer to waste time, hovering over the food and keeping an eagle eye on it until it reaches just the required state of doneness. Timers are mechanical, need only to be set for the proper number of minutes. Go about your business, and the timer will ring, reminding you that the food is done. Many stoves are equipped with timers; so are other kitchen appliances, such as some electric mixers. One-hour timers are relatively inexpensive. Those that can be set for longer periods—some up to 7 hours—are also available. Considerably more expensive, they are nevertheless useful to cooks, especially forgetful ones, when a large piece of meat is being roasted, a large custard baked, and so on. See also DONENESS.

TOAST

Bread (preferably beginning to stale) browned, in an electric toaster or under the oven broiler, is toast. But that is barely the beginning of this delicious, versatile food.

When you were sick as a child, were you fed milk toast? Remember how it steamed, how the toast's butter melted into little rivulets? It's still just as good as it was then— feed it to the family as a surprise breakfast treat some day soon.

Still on the subject of breakfast, have you made french toast recently? Try it with a peach topping made by boiling the syrup from a can of peaches with a piece of stick cinnamon, a few cloves, and a sprinkle of nutmeg. Add the peach slices, and serve hot. Or how about cinnamon toast? Bake the bread in your waffle iron for a change of looks and texture, butter well, and sprinkle liberally with cinnamon-sugar. To spruce up a soup-and-salad supper, try monkey toast: trim the crusts from a loaf of unsliced bread, then pull the bread apart into irregularly shaped pieces with two forks. Bake in a 300°F. oven until it's dry and a light golden brown.

Creamed or other sauced foods are good served on toast, better served in toast cups: cut crusts from bread slices, spread with soft butter, and press, butter-side down, into muffin cups; brush top sides with melted butter and brown in the broiler.

Just toast, all by itself except for a slathering of butter, is very good indeed. But if you use one of these sweet or savory butters to spread on it, toast is even better.

With ½ pound of butter, combine well:

- 2 tablespoons confectioners sugar, ½ teaspoon maple extract
- ¼ cup of honey
- 3 tablespoons toasted sesame seeds, 2 peeled and crushed garlic cloves
- ½ teaspoon onion powder, 1 teaspoon lemon juice, and 1½ teaspoons prepared horseradish
- ¼ cup packed brown sugar, 2 teaspoons grated orange peel, and 2 teaspoons orange juice
- 3 tablespoons finely chopped salted pecans
- ¼ cup minced capers
- 2 teaspoons lemon juice, ½ teaspoon grated lemon peel, and 1 tablespoon minced parsley
- 1 teaspoon lemon juice, 2 teaspoons anchovy paste
- 3 tablespoons minced chives
- 1 teaspoon onion juice, 2 tablespoons prepared mustard
- 3 tablespoons chopped stuffed green olives, 1 teaspoon onion juice

- ¼ cup packed brown sugar, ½ teaspoon ground cardamom
- ¼ cup orange marmalade, ¼ teaspoon nutmeg
- ¼ cup apricot preserve, 2 tablespoons finely chopped walnuts
- ½ cup grated sharp cheddar, dash of cayenne
- 1 tablespoon tomato paste, ¼ cup grated parmesan, ½ teaspoon basil

If you let your imagination range freely among the tastes and textures you really enjoy, you'll probably be able to come up with a dozen more such butters.

See also MELBA TOAST.

TOAST, TO: see page 450

TOASTERS: see special feature: YOU CAN'T WORK WITHOUT TOOLS

TOFU

Bean curd, a white, cheeselike substance with mild flavor. It is rich in protein. Use to garnish soups and in stir-fry dishes of all sorts. Sold in Chinese or Japanese food shops or in supermarkets in places where there is a large Oriental population. Tofu is perishable—refrigerate it.

TOMALLEY AND CORAL

Tomalley is the liver of a lobster, the green substance within the body. Coral is roe of a lobster. The color of coral, it can often be found in the body of a cooked female lobster. Use in sauce to serve with the shellfish.

TOMATILLOES

A small yellow-green fruit (sometimes it may be red, as well) that looks like a very small tomato. It is used to make jam or preserves, or is made into a sauce to serve with meats. The tomatillo is sold fresh in places where there is a Mexican community, in cans elsewhere.

TOMATOES

Did you have your 65 pounds of tomatoes last year? Are you going to consume your quota this year? That's the amount eaten per capita annually in the United States.

The tomato—a fruit that we treat as a vegetable—is another of the western hemisphere's contributions to the world's diet. It grows on vines that sprawl if allowed, but can be trained to climb neatly on a stake or a hollow tube of wire or other support if it is provided for them. Although we are most familiar with the red tomato, the vegetable also has off-white, yellow, green, and striped variations, may be smooth-skinned or ridged, round or flattened or pear-shaped, and ranges in size from the big beefsteaks to the small, round cherry tomato.

Pre-Incan civilizations of Peru and Ecuador found

tomatoes growing wild. As these peoples migrated north to Central America and Mexico, they carried the tomato with them. Explorers of Mexico took the "tomatl" back to Europe. The Spanish and Italians made them into sauces, but the rest of Europe considered them attractive ornamental plants and certainly nothing that anyone sensible would eat. Indeed, they were believed by some to be poisonous, by others to be an aphrodisiac—the latter, presumably, overcame their prejudice and ate them. *Pomme d'amour* they were called—love apples.

By the latter part of the eighteenth century, tomatoes had been brought back to the New World, and they were being eaten by many people, both here and in Europe. But it wasn't until the end of the nineteenth century, when the tomato canning industry got underway, that the fruit became a common, widely used food.

TOMATOES IN YOUR KITCHEN

A semitropical plant, tomatoes are grown only in the warm season when there is no danger of frost, or in areas where there is no cold period. The fruit that is sold fresh comes largely from Texas, California, Florida, New Jersey, New York, and Maryland. Different varieties are grown for processing in California, Indiana, Maryland, New Jersey, Ohio, and Pennsylvania.

Growing and harvesting. Fresh tomatoes are available everywhere throughout the year, shipped in from warmer climates to cold-weather areas in winter. The fruit can be picked when mature but still green, and will ripen in transit or while warehoused. Vine-ripened tomatoes, however, have better flavor. Some tomatoes are grown hydroponically, in large tanks that are periodically flooded with water to which nutrients have been added. This growing method is more costly, but the crop is considerably greater than that harvested from tomato plants conventionally grown in soil.

how to buy: If they are to be used immediately, select fully ripe tomatoes. They should be plump, without soft spots, have bright color. The very best tomatoes are the home-grown ones. If you don't have a garden, buy when you can from farmers' markets or roadside stands, where you will find locally grown, vine-ripened fruit. When buying, keep in mind the use you are going to make of the tomato—big ones for stuffing, medium to large for slicing and salads, smaller fruit for cooking.

how to store: If fully ripe, store in the vegetable crisper of the refrigerator. If mature but not ripe, store at room temperature—60 to 70 degrees—until ripe. Do not try to ripen tomatoes in sunlight, which inhibits color and flavor development. The best method is to put several together in a paper bag. Don't close it tightly—and don't forget about them! Ripe tomatoes will keep, refrigerated, up to 5 days.

nutritive value: The values given here are year-around averages, because they fluctuate somewhat with the season. Vine-ripened summer local tomatoes, for example, have considerably more vitamin C than shipped-in, transit-ripened winter tomatoes. One whole tomato, about 3 inches in diameter, yields 39 calories and provides these nutrients:

protein	1.9	grams
fat	.4	gram
carbohydrate	8.3	grams
calcium	23	milligrams
phosphorus	48	milligrams
iron	.9	milligram
sodium	5	milligrams
potassium	429	milligrams
thiamin	.11	milligram
riboflavin	.07	milligram
niacin	1.2	milligrams
ascorbic acid	40	milligrams
vitamin A	1,580	international units

Tips on preparing, cooking. To remove the skins from fresh tomatoes, impale on the tines of a fork at the stem end, immerse in boiling water for ½ minute, then dip in cold water. With the point of a sharp knife, peel the tomato—the skin will slip off easily and neatly. Another method: rotate the impaled tomato over an open flame until the skin wrinkles; it will then peel readily. Sometimes it's necessary to peel tomatoes, but don't do it unless it's required—that skin supplies "roughage," the fiber needed in a balanced diet.

Stuffed tomatoes, raw or cooked, seem to be well liked by almost everyone. Stuff the raw ones with a salad mixture of vegetables, chicken, shrimp, tuna, or any other you'd like to use. Tomatoes are an accommodatingly compatible flavor with almost any other food. If you want to serve more salad than the slightly hollowed-out tomato will hold, cut the tomato into 6 to 8 petals, slicing through the skin to within ½ inch of the bottom; spread the petals, and you'll have a larger area to stuff. In either case, first invert the tomatoes on absorbent paper to drain. Cooked stuffed tomatoes may be filled with another vegetable or a mixture, with creamed foods, or with the removed pulp combined with chopped mushrooms and butter-sautéed bread crumbs.

Sliced beefsteak tomatoes (cut with a knife that has a serrated or scalloped blade) are delicious sprinkled with oil and vinegar; then with a mixture of ½ salt, ¼ sugar, and ¼ coarsely ground black pepper; then with coarsely chopped fresh basil. Or slice and serve as individual salads on beds of watercress, with mayonnaise on the side; let each diner season his own portion.

Broiled tomatoes are excellent with any kind of broiled meat or poultry. Halve the tomatoes, then make a number of shallow slits on each cut surface. Season with salt and pepper, top liberally with a mixture of melted butter, bread or cracker crumbs, and grated cheddar or parmesan. Broil until lightly browned.

The BLT is a favorite sandwich, but thin slices of tomato go well in many other sandwiches, too. Or slice them thickly, sprinkle well with salt and pepper, and sandwich between two slices of mayonnaise-spread sprouted wheat bread.

Fried tomatoes, green ones or ripe, are a farm-style favorite. Cut in ½-inch slices. Dip green tomatoes into seasoned flour and cook slowly in hot fat. Dip ripe ones into beaten egg, then into dry bread or cracker crumbs, cook quickly in hot fat. Bacon drippings are a very good fat in which to fry tomatoes. Season the slices after cooking.

Freezing tomatoes. Raw tomatoes, because of their high water content, cannot be frozen. (But they may be canned; see special feature: PUTTING FOOD BY.) However, cooked tomato mixtures, tomato sauce or dishes that are cooked in the sauce or have tomatoes as an ingredient, may be freezer stored at 0°F. or below. In determining the freezer storage time, be guided by other ingredients in the dish—chicken, beef, and so on.

Other ways, other forms. You'll find a wide variety of tomato products in your market.

on grocery shelves, in cans, jars, or bottles: Canned tomatoes, in their own juice or sometimes with tomato paste added—whole, in neat slices, or in pieces; canned stewed tomatoes with onion, celery, and green pepper; canned tomato sauce, plain or with herbs or onions or bits of tomato, or with meat or mushrooms for pasta; canned tomato paste or purée (the paste is the thicker of the two); canned or bottled tomato juice and tomato-based mixed vegetable juice; in bottles, tomato catsup—regular or several specially seasoned kinds—and chili sauce.

in grocery frozen-food section: No frozen tomatoes as such, but a wide variety of dishes that use tomatoes or tomato sauce as one of the ingredients; frozen tomato pasta sauces.

Some perfect partners. Basil, thyme, rosemary, summer savory, and marjoram all complement the flavor of both raw and cooked tomatoes. Bacon, mushrooms, shrimp, chicken, eggplant, and beans are all naturals with the fruit. And in any cooked tomato dish, remember always to add a very small amount of sugar, which cuts the acid taste and mellows the flavor.

Whether you raise your own or buy them fresh or canned, tomatoes without a doubt play an important part in the meals you serve family and guests all year around.

TONGUE: see VARIETY MEATS

TOOTHPICKS: see FOOD PICKS

TOPPINGS, DESSERT

Dessert toppings may be found in your market freezer case, ready to thaw and use, or as a powder on the grocery shelves to be whipped with liquid before using. These are nondairy products, but may be used in place of whipped cream in a variety of delicious—and considerably lower-calorie—dishes, such as chiffon pies, soufflés, and bavarians.

Or you may (less expensively) make a good whipped topping at home, to use in place of whipped cream on or in many desserts. Start by putting the large electric mixer bowl and the beaters in the refrigerator to be thoroughly chilled. When they are ready, put 4 teaspoons cold water in a cup and sprinkle over it 1 envelope unflavored gelatin; let stand until softened. Add ⅓ cup boiling water and stir until the gelatin is dissolved; cool to room temperature. In the chilled bowl, combine 1 cup ice water with 1⅓ cups nonfat dry milk. Beat at high speed until soft peaks form, about 5 minutes. As you continue to beat, gradually add 6 tablespoons sugar. Scrape down the sides of the bowl and, continuing to beat, gradually add ⅓ cup salad oil, 1 teaspoon vanilla, 2 teaspoons lemon juice, and the gelatin mixture. Scrape down the sides of the bowl again and continue to beat 1 minute longer. Makes about 6 cups.

To use as a topping, place in a rigid container, cover, and refrigerate or freeze. Or use as an ingredient in desserts. A good general cookbook will have a number of recipes using whipped topping, either the commercial or homemade kind.

TORTE: see page 454

TORTILLA: see page 454

TOSS, TO: see page 449

TRACE ELEMENTS: see special feature: NUTRITION NOTEBOOK

TRAPPIST: see CHEESE

TRASH COMPACTORS: see special feature: YOU CAN'T WORK WITHOUT TOOLS

TRIPE: see VARIETY MEATS

TRITICALE

A hybrid grain—part wheat, part rye, with a higher amount and a more complete protein than either of them—triticale is rapidly gaining supporters, particularly among whole-grain enthusiasts. It got its name from a combination of *triticum,* Latin for wheat, and *secale,* for rye.

The grain has been around for a long time—it was discovered in 1875—but no one paid much attention until about twenty years ago. Now there are many acres under cultivation, for both commercial and experimental purposes. Not only has triticale a higher (17 to 18 percent, compared to wheat's 13 to 14) and higher-quality protein content, but it will grow in areas where wheat will not, in arid lands of Asia and North Africa, for example. Oddly, in the great wheat-growing areas of our own country, triticale yields per acre are relatively low.

Available as whole grain—called berries—or as flakes—flattened kernels—and as flour, triticale is low in gluten, the protein that gives bread doughs their elasticity; without gluten, breads will not rise well. In bread-making, up to 50 percent triticale may be used, substituting for half the wheat flour. Be aware, though, that the bread will not rise as high and handsomely as that made entirely from wheat flour. The flakes may also be used in breads, as wheat germ is, to give a crunchy texture. It is at its best in coarse-textured breads, such as pumpernickel, sweetened with honey or molasses. In making such breads, always add the wheat flour first, which gives the gluten ample time to develop.

Triticale berries may be cooked and used hot for a side-dish pilaf or as a breakfast cereal, as rice is, or cold, in ricelike salads. The grain has a somewhat chewy texture and a nut-like flavor.

You may be able to find triticale in your supermarket, but are more likely to be able to buy it in shops that specialize in whole-grain cereals, or in health food stores.

TROUT: see FISH

TRUFFLES

If you don't care for the flavor of truffles you are, according to epicures, very peculiar. But you are also very lucky. Among foods, only caviar is more expensive.

The truffle is a fungus, composed largely of water (but most foods are), high in protein and exceedingly low in calories. The French truffle is black as a lump of coal, with a nubbled skin; inside it is black, too, with veins, like the marbling in quality steaks, of gray. Italian truffles (which the French sniff at) are white.

Fortunately the truffle flavor is strong, and a little goes a long way. A few thin slices can turn cream-scrambled eggs into a production. A whole truffle, nestled into the center of a bloc of foie gras, lifts diners to gastronomic heaven. A poularde demi-deuil (chicken in half-mourning) has half a truffle, in thin slices, slid under the breast skin, with the other half saved to perfume the sauce espagñole with madeira that accompanies it.

The market for truffles could accommodate 250 tons of the strange fungus a year, but supply seldom goes as high as demand. The problem is, no one knows much about truffles—not even, really, what they are or how they grow or why they grow. They may be small as beans, big as baking potatoes. The season in which they are harvested ("hunted" might be a better term) runs from late November to early March. But because they grow underground and are not—cannot be—cultivated, nobody knows until the hunt is underway whether any given season will be a good or a poor one. The season in which this is being written was rather a poor one. French farmers were getting about three hundred francs—roughly sixty dollars—for a kilo, 2.2 pounds. By the time they are processed, they will be selling at retail for twice that amount.

The truffle trade. Truffles are searched out by pigs or (less often) dogs on leashes. They root about in the ground where truffles are known to appear, under oak trees, sometimes under hazels, beeches, or junipers; it is believed that there is some kind of symbiotic relationship between truffle and tree. The pigs are specially trained, and have a remarkably keen sense of smell. Piggy snuffles around until she smells a truffle, then begins to dig. Her master pulls her away, gives her a potato for solace, and digs up the truffle. If the master is kind and the day's take is good, he may give the pig the smallest truffle at the end of the day to keep up her spirits.

At market, one day a week during the season, the truffles are sold to wholesalers, who clean, sort, and prepare them for the retail trade. They are sold fresh or canned, or buried deep in FOIE GRAS—some of the truffle wholesalers are in the foie gras business as well.

The problem with truffles is that where many grew this year, few or none may grow next year. Or ever again, as a matter of fact. But where none grew before, a handsome crop may suddenly appear. And nobody has even been able to discover why. If the pigs know, they aren't telling.

After cleaning, the truffles are pressure-cooked. Some to be sold at retail are peeled, some are not. The processing must take place within 5 days of gathering; meanwhile, the truffles are refrigerated at 41°F. while they wait. Those with the best shape, the most attractive marbling, are peeled with a special knife and sold as "Truffles du Perigord, Peeled Extra." Next best are the unpeeled "Brushed Extra" variety, followed by "Peeled First Choice" and "Brushed First Choice." Pieces and peelings are also sold—no tiny part of a truffle ever goes to waste.

TRUSS, TO: see page 449

TRY OUT, TO: see page 449

TUNA, CANNED

Cans of tuna on the pantry shelf, even though considerably more expensive than they used to be, are a home cook's ace in the hole for emergencies. The fish may be served creamed or à la king (stashed-away frozen patty shells are fine with these), or in any one of a number of casserole and skillet dishes and salads that can be put together quickly and with little fuss.

There are several species of tuna. Only albacore may be labeled "white meat"—the others (such as bluefin and skipjack) are labeled "light meat." Three packs are available; the differences lie in the size of the pieces of fish, and do not relate to quality.

- *solid pack*—contains 3 or 4 large pieces of fish; the most expensive of the canned tunas, it is ideal for cold plates, or in any recipe where appearance is important
- *chunk pack*—convenient size pieces for mixed salads and casseroles; moderately priced
- *flake pack*—pieces smaller than the chunk style; good for sandwich spreads and for appetizers where the fish is blended with other ingredients; lowest in price

Packed in water or oil, tuna can be had in 3¼-, 3½-, 6-, 6½-, 7-, 9¼-, 12½-, and 13-ounce cans.

TUNAFISH: see FISH

TURBAN: see SQUASH

TURKEY

Some hunters contend that the most succulent bird of all is the wild turkey, properly cooked. And it was, of course, the wild turkey that attended our early Thanksgiving gatherings.

But now we have domesticated fowl, pampered, well fed, not allowed to exercise, so that they will be juicy and tender. These commercially raised birds have meaty legs, thighs, and wings, and bosoms of a size to put any showgirl to shame. They have fine flavor and they are relatively inexpensive, making them the perfect choice for large company-coming meals. And now, if the small family wants to enjoy turkey, parts are available: thighs, drumsticks, wings, breasts, and thin, boneless breast slices that can be treated like boned half chicken breasts, as well as standing in for expensive veal scallops in many recipes we now avoid because of their cost.

TURKEY IN YOUR KITCHEN

Since it is unlikely, these days, that father is going a-hunting to bring home a bird, you'll have to buy yours at the market. You'll find frozen birds all year around, fresh ones at the holiday season and often at other times as well.

how to buy: In a fresh bird, look for creamy yellow skin color—not blue—without any breaks in the skin. For its weight, the bird should be short; it should be plump and broad-breasted. In a frozen bird, check these same points; also, make certain that the turkey has not begun to thaw and that there are no breaks in the plastic bag in which it is packed.

how to store: Refrigerate a fresh bird, loosely covered, up to 6 days. A frozen bird will keep up to 6 months at 0°F. or below in the freezer; after thawing, refrigerate for no more than 2 days.

how much to buy: Large turkeys yield more servings per pound than small ones, because the ratio of bone to meat is less in the big birds. Here are some guidelines for buying whole, unstuffed turkey:

ready-to-cook weight:	number of servings:
6 to 12 pounds	6 to 12
12 to 16 pounds	12 to 20
16 to 20 pounds	20 to 28
20 to 24 pounds	28 to 32

If it is a frozen, stuffed turkey, allow 1½ pounds per serving; if boneless turkey roll or roast, allow ⅓ to ½ pound per serving; if turkey parts, allow ½ pound per serving.

nutritive value: Turkey is a good source of high-quality protein, with less fat than most meats. A serving consisting of 1 piece of white meat (4 inches long, 2 inches wide, ¼ inch thick) plus 2 pieces of dark meat (each 2½ inches long, 1⅝ inches wide, and ¼ inch thick) yields 162 calories, and provides these nutrients:

protein	26.8	grams
fat	5.2	grams
calcium	7	milligrams
phosphorus	210	milligrams
iron	1.5	milligrams
sodium	111	milligrams
potassium	312	milligrams
thiamin	.04	milligram
riboflavin	.15	milligram
niacin	6.5	milligrams

Turkey contains no carbohydrate or vitamins A or C.

Tips on preparing, cooking. Unless it is an already stuffed, frozen bird (which must be cooked from the frozen state), the frozen turkey must be thawed. You can go any of three ways:

1. Leave in original wrappings; place on a tray in the refrigerator for 2 to 3 days, letting it thaw at its own pace.
2. Leave in original wrappings; place in a sink or deep pan filled with cold water and change water frequently (warm water will cause the outside of the bird to thaw too quickly, and can cause the proliferation of bacteria).
3. Leave in original wrappings, but remove any metal fasteners; place in a shallow nonmetal baking dish breast side up; place in a microwave oven at medium-low setting for 30 minutes; give a quarter turn, and repeat as long as necessary, covering any parts that begin to brown; let stand 30 minutes at room temperature, then roast immediately.

To prepare a fresh or thawed turkey for roasting, remove wrappings, free legs and tail. Take the giblets from the cavity and pull out the tucked-in neck skin. Rinse, pat dry with absorbent paper. Rub cavities with salt if desired. Refrigerate. Stuffing may be made and refrigerated separately, but do not stuff the turkey until just before you put it in the oven.

When ready to cook, spoon some stuffing into the neck cavity; pull the neck skin to the back and fasten with a small skewer. Spoon more stuffing lightly into the body cavity. Do not pack it in. If there is a band of skin across the tail, tuck drumstick ends into it, or tie the legs to the tail. Twist the wing tips back, behind the shoulder joints. If you don't wish to stuff the bird, put onions and celery in the cavity for flavor.

roasting the turkey: There are several ways to roast the bird, relatively equal in effectiveness. The choice is up to you:

1. *Whole bird:* Preheat oven to 325°F.; place fresh or thawed bird on a rack in a shallow roasting pan, breast side up. Brush with melted butter or cooking oil; cover with a loose foil tent, touching the bird only at the drumsticks and neck. When two-thirds done, cut skin or string holding drumsticks and remove foil tent; baste with pan drippings, continue to roast until the thickest part of the drumstick is very soft and leg moves easily in its socket, or until meat thermometer inserted in the center of the inside thigh muscle (it must not touch bone) registers 185°F.
2. *Covered roaster:* Preheat oven to 350°F.; place turkey breast side up on a rack on pan, brush with oil or butter and insert meat thermometer; do not add water. Place cover on roaster until last half hour of cooking, at which point remove cover and baste; continue cooking, uncovered, until done.

3. *Roasting foil-wrapped:* Preheat oven to 450°F.; place turkey in the center of a piece of greased wide heavy-duty foil, bringing the ends up over the bird, overlapping them and pressing the foil against the ends of the turkey. Place in a shallow roasting pan (no rack); open foil for the last 20 minutes of cooking so that bird will brown.
4. *Roasting in cloth:* Cook giblets and neck in advance in water with 1 small onion and 1 rib of celery. Remove giblets and reserve, discard onion and celery; in broth melt ½ cup butter. Preheat oven to 325°F.; place turkey on a rack in a shallow roasting pan. Dip an old, clean dish towel or a triple layer of cheesecloth into the hot broth-butter mixture and lay over turkey; roast, redipping the cloth at 30-minute intervals until 45 minutes before the bird will be done; remove cloth and allow to brown.
5. *Roasting turkey pieces:* Preheat oven to 325°F.; place turkey pieces skin side up on a rack in a shallow roasting pan, and brush with cooking oil. Insert meat thermometer; roast uncovered until thermometer registers 185°F.
6. *Roasting halves and quarters:* Preheat oven to 325°F.; place turkey skin side up on a rack in a shallow roasting pan. Brush with cooking oil; insert meat thermometer; tent loosely with foil. Remove foil 45 minutes before end of cooking time and roast uncovered until thermometer registers 185°F.

Although various conditions affect the cooking time of turkey, here is a rough timetable to help you in your dinner planning:

weight	roasting time
6 to 8 pounds	3½ to 4 hours
8 to 12 pounds	4 to 4½ hours
12 to 16 pounds	4½ to 5½ hours
16 to 20 pounds	5½ to 6½ hours
20 to 24 pounds	6½ to 7½ hours

These times are for whole, foil-tented turkeys. Foil-wrapped turkeys will cook in about half the above times at 450°F. But bear this in mind—the foil-wrapped turkey does not have as good a flavor as the cloth- or tent-roasted one; it has a somewhat steamed, rather than a roasted taste.

stuffing the turkey: Turkey will roast equally well stuffed or unstuffed. Stuffing, however, adds another dimension to the meal.

Allow ¾ to 1 cup of stuffing for each pound that the bird weighs. Here are some suggestions:

• *bread stuffing*—in a skillet, combine butter, minced onion, salt, pepper, chopped celery; season with thyme and sage and cook 5 minutes; combine with soft day-old bread crumbs, moistened with broth

- *oyster stuffing*—add drained, chopped oysters to the butter mixture
- *nut stuffing*—add cooked and peeled chestnuts, chopped, or broken pecan pieces to butter mixture
- *corn bread stuffing*—substitute crumbled cold unsweetened corn bread for half of bread crumbs
- *egg stuffing*—beat eggs slightly, add with crumbs
- *rice stuffing*—omit crumbs, substitute rice that has been cooked until nearly tender

Freezing turkey. Wrap and freeze giblets separately. Tie whole turkey legs and wings close to the body, wrap and freeze; may be freezer stored at 0°F. or below up to 6 months. To freeze cooked turkey, remove meat from bones. Package in meal-size portions, either in a rigid container in broth, or wrapped in heavy-duty foil; freezer-store up to 3 months. Freeze leftover gravy separately if you wish. Do not freeze stuffing.

Cautionary notes. Stuff the turkey just before you are going to put it in the oven. Never partially cook a turkey one day and complete roasting the next. Cook commercially stuffed frozen turkeys without thawing—bacteria that could cause food poisoning can grow readily if you do not take these precautions. Refrigerate cooked turkey, gravy, and stuffing, all separate from one another, up to 4 days.

Other ways, other forms. Besides fresh turkey and turkey parts, the market offers turkey in several other forms.

on grocery shelves, in cans or jars: Turkey gravy, with or without giblets; boned turkey, turkey à la king, turkey soups; baby-food turkey dinners.

in grocery frozen-food section: Whole frozen turkey, stuffed or not; frozen turkey parts; turkey plate dinners; turkey slices in gravy; turkey pie; boned and rolled turkey roasts.

Smoked turkey is also available, whole or breasts. Read the label carefully—some smoked turkey is ready to eat, other kinds require further cooking.

Ground fresh turkey, to be used in the same manner—and in many of the same dishes—as ground beef is available at some supermarket fresh-meat counters. It is lower in fat content and less expensive than ground beef.

Some perfect partners. Most families have traditional Christmas and Thanksgiving menus from which they don't—and don't want to—stray. To complement the turkey they include a number of dishes such as these: mashed potatoes with giblet gravy, scalloped oysters, candied sweet potatoes, peas with mushrooms, creamed onions, candied carrots, brussels sprouts with chestnuts, rutabaga soufflé, cranberry sauce or cranberry-orange relish or cranberry sherbet, relishes (such as radishes, stuffed celery, scallions, green and ripe olives, a variety of pickles), corn bread or parker house rolls, mince pie with hard sauce, plum pudding with hard or lemon sauce or both, pumpkin pie or pecan pie with whipped cream.

Pushing back from the table, somebody's sure to say, "I won't eat again for a week." A few hours later, that same somebody will ask plaintively, "Aren't we going to have any supper?"

TURMERIC: see HERBS AND SAVORY SEASONINGS

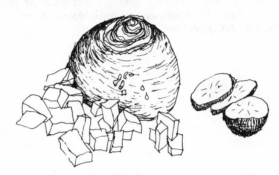

TURNIPS, TURNIP GREENS

Turnips are by no means everybody's favorite vegetable and turnip greens have about an equal place in diners' affections. But at least they hold their own—turnips have been cultivated and eaten for some 4,000 years and they're still with us.

A cool-weather root vegetable, the turnip finds considerable acceptance in Great Britain and the northerly countries of Europe; here, both turnips and their greens are most used and appreciated in our southern states.

Buying and keeping. Available in bunches with the leaves still in place, or as turnips and turnip greens sold separately, the vegetable is in the market all year around, with the peak season October to March.

Choose solid, unblemished turnips, heavy for their size, and fresh, young-looking greens. You'll find both white turnips and a variety that shades to a handsome purple at the leaf end. Store in a cool place (about 55°F.) or in the refrigerator up to 1 month. Cooked turnips can be refrigerated up to 3 days. Turnips themselves are a moderate source of vitamin C; the greens provide excellent amounts of vitamins A and C and are a good source of calcium, iron, and riboflavin.

To cook, wash the turnips, peel them, and slice or dice. Cook in boiling (salted) water about 15 minutes, until tender. The greens, if they are young, may be cooked briefly, like spinach. They are often cooked for a long time, with pieces of ham or bacon, in the South. Or the greens and small dices of the vegetable itself may be cooked together. Serve simply with butter, salt, and pepper, or with a little cream, salt, and a light sprinkling of ground ginger.

Or cook turnips in consommé and mash. Or grate raw turnip for an excellent crunchy turnip slaw; dress with well-seasoned sour cream or old-fashioned boiled dressing. Or include very thin slices of raw turnips in a platter of crudités. Both turnips and their greens may be frozen.

TURNOVERS

Pastries, triangular or semicircular in shape, with a sweet or savory filling. Tiny turnovers, with a filling such as mushrooms, shrimp, or chicken livers, make delicious and substantial hot hors d'oeuvres. Larger ones, with meat, chicken, or fish filling in a well-seasoned sauce can be served as a main dish. Dessert turnovers are usually fruit filled.

TUTTI-FRUTTI

A combination of preserved fruits, Italian in origin, used as a sauce for ice cream or plain cake. (For method of preparation, see FRUIT.) Tutti-frutti flavored ice cream used to be very popular in the United States, but has somehow disappeared from the scene. Even those places that boast a large number of ice cream flavors no longer include tutti-frutti.

UGLI FRUIT: see EXOTIC FRUIT

UNBLEACHED FLOUR: see FLOUR

UNIT PRICING

Most foods we buy in our markets today are unit priced—that is, they are priced not only by the piece, package, or whatever, but also by the ounce or pound. Unit pricing was mandated to help the shopper compare sizes within a single brand of a product and between various brands of the same product.

Unit prices may appear on the package or on the price tag on the front of the shelf where the product is for sale.

It pays to check unit prices as you shop. Sometimes the large, economy size is less a bargain than you think—when you compare its per-ounce price with the per-ounce price of a smaller size, you may find that the smaller size actually, by the unit, is no more than, or the same as, or even less than the larger size. Larger sizes are a convenience when the product is something—a detergent, say—that will not spoil or grow stale. But if it is, for example, a dry breakfast cereal, the large size is not necessarily economical for a small family that will not consume the entire contents before it begins to stale. And if the unit price for a smaller package is less than or equal to the large package, the small one is an even better buy. Food that goes to waste is no bargain at any price.

UNITED STATES DEPARTMENT OF AGRICULTURE

The USDA, taking into consideration research conducted by its own laboratories and by commercial food processors, and comments from the general public and concerned groups such as consumer organizations, sets standards for various foods that must be adhered to by processors who market them.

The Department also maintains a mandatory food inspection system and a discretionary food grading system to guide consumers in buying and to assure that the food they buy is wholesome and has been processed under sanitary conditions. See the special feature: YOUR PARTNER IN THE KITCHEN.

UNIVERSAL PRODUCT CODE: see COMPUTERIZED SUPERMARKET CHECKOUT and the special feature: A SHORT COURSE IN LABEL READING

UNLEAVENED

When the Hebrews fled from Egypt, "out of the house of bondage," they ate unleavened bread because there was no time to set leavened bread and wait for it to rise. The only leavening agent in those days was a form of yeast. The familiar matzoth of the present time commemorate that unleavened bread.

Today there are several kinds of leavening. YEAST, BAKING POWDER, and BAKING SODA—in conjunction with an acid—are all leavening agents. They cause breads, quick breads, cakes, and some cookies to become light and to rise high in the baking.

But we still have a number of unleavened foods, besides matzoth, that we enjoy. Many kinds of crackers are unleavened. Quite a few cookie recipes do not call for a leavening agent, and this is true of cookies that we buy, as well. There are all sorts of flat breads, our own and imports, that are made only of flour (white, rye, various whole grains), salt, and sometimes flavorings.

UNSWEETENED CHOCOLATE, COCOA: see CHOCOLATE AND COCOA

UNUSUAL VEGETABLES

It's no wonder that our ancient ancestors were devoted meat-eaters, turning to vegetables only when there was nothing else to put in the communal cookpot. Most wild vegetables were tough, stringy, woody, or bitter. Even when brought in from the wild and cultivated, they often retained some of their unpleasant characteristics. Not all that long ago vegetables were still more good for you than good, and when hybridizers who had gone to work to improve matters produced what seemed like a masterpiece, those lucky enough to try it were overcome with joy. Small, early peas—*petit pois*—were introduced to the court of Louis XIV and became such a sensation that they turned into a secret vice. Courtiers would retire to their chambers to eat a dish of peas sneaked to them by a loyal retainer.

Today our produce markets are piled high with an eye-dazzling and salivation-causing array of fresh vegetables, and when the particular one we fancy is not in season, we can find it canned or frozen. But there are still some vegetables that we don't bring home because we don't recognize their names or know their characteristics or their uses. Here are some of them.

cardoon: A relative of the globe artichoke, the roots and stems of the cardoon are cooked, then most often chilled and served as a salad. May also be sautéed in butter or brought to the table in a béchamel sauce. Delicate, agreeable flavor.

celeriac (celery root, knob celery): With a celerylike flavor, this is a knob-rooted form of the same vegetable, may be cooked or served raw. Raw julienne strips can be served with a mustard sauce as a salad or appetizer, or grated and dressed with vinegar and salt as a kind of slaw. Or cooked and served hot with butter, pepper, and salt, or chilled with vinaigrette. Also called celeri-rave.

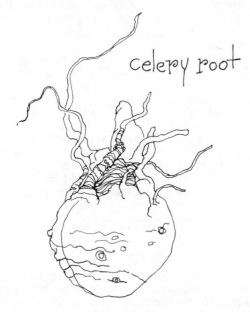

celery root

chard: A leafy green—prepare and cook it in the manner of spinach, in only the water that clings to the leaves. The stems are also edible, may be cut fine and cooked with the leaves, or separately in larger pieces. Some chard is all green, some has handsome red stalks, the color bleeding over into the leaves. Also called swiss chard.

chayote (christophine): A form of squash, pear-shaped and pale green, unusual in that it has only one seed, which is edible. The tender skin of the young chayote is also edible. Bake or boil, as with other squash, or batter-dip and french fry. The flavor is elusive, very delicate.

dasheen: This is the taro that is a dietary staple in many tropical countries. It is a starchy tuber, a relative of the calla lily, which may weigh as much as 5 or 6 pounds; it has a white flesh covered by a fibrous brown skin. Prepare and use as you would potatoes in any form other than mashed. Like the potato, the dasheen's flavor is mild.

jicama: A large bulbous turnip-shaped root from Mexico, with a brown skin and crisp, juicy white flesh of mild flavor. May be cut in julienne strips or thin slices and served raw with a dip or dressing, or mixed with other vegetables in a salad. Cooked, the jicama retains its crispness, can be used wherever you might use water chestnuts.

kohlrabi: A type of cabbage, raised for its bulbous stem rather than its head, although the leaves when young may be used as a green vegetable. Dice the stem and cook as you would turnip, or cook whole, hollow out, and stuff with a savory filling made with rice or bread crumbs and meat, poultry, or fish. Turniplike taste, but delicate. (See KOHLRABI.)

salsify (oyster plant): A root vegetable, carrot-shaped but smaller, with a delicate flavor reminiscent of oysters, some say, or of parsnips. Peel and cook as you would carrots.

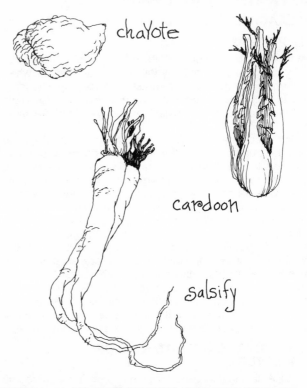

chayote

cardoon

salsify

USDA: see UNITED STATES DEPARTMENT OF AGRICULTURE

U.S. RDA: see special feature: NUTRITION NOTEBOOK and A SHORT COURSE IN LABEL READING

UTENSILS: see special feature: YOU CAN'T WORK WITHOUT TOOLS

VACHERIN: see CHEESE

VALENCIA ORANGES: see ORANGES

VANILLA

Orchids are for admiring, with breathtaken oohs and aaahs, at the orchid show. Or for wearing by women on their shoulders or wrists or in their hair—an out-of-style fancy that still has considerable merit. Or for raising, as a hobby. Or for flavoring tonight's tapioca pudding or chocolate-frosted cake.

Vanilla, that kitchen staple, comes from an orchid plant. It grows as a long pod filled with small beans, and we use both the pod, called the vanilla bean, and the essence taken from it, vanilla extract, in so many ways we'd be hard put to do without it. The pod is green (odorless) when fresh, dark brown when we buy it dried; the extract is dark brown. Both have a heavenly, pungent aroma and unmistakable flavor.

Spanish explorers first encountered vanilla in Mexico and carried the beans back home, where cooks soon found dozens of uses for them, and merchants even flavored tobacco with the excellent new aromatic. The orchid still grows in Mexico and we get some of our vanilla from there, but most of the large amount we use is today imported from the Malagasy Republic, an island off the east coast of Africa.

In the United States we use more extract than beans, but in Europe the opposite is true. The flavor enhances many others—it does wonders for chocolate for example, or if you want a pistachio flavor, add ½ teaspoon each of vanilla and almond extract to the food you are preparing.

Many good cooks wouldn't feel quite complete without a jar of vanilla sugar handy. There are two ways to go about preparing it:

1. In a container with a tight lid, bury a vanilla bean in sugar, either granulated or confectioners.
2. Place the dried bean (it may have been used previously once or twice for flavoring) in a blender with 1 cup granulated sugar; blend at high speed until the bean is pulverized. Strain through a fine sieve, store in a covered jar.

You can also, if you wish to experiment, make your own vanilla extract. Add 2 split vanilla beans to 1 cup vodka (which is flavorless); cover and let stand for 1 month.

Use vanilla sugar to sweeten fresh fruits, in whipped cream, on cinnamon toast, replacing part of the plain sugar called for in custards and puddings, cakes and other sweets—anywhere both vanilla and sugar are called for, or would point up the flavor of a food. See also FLAVORING EXTRACTS.

VANILLIN

A name you will see often on food labels. You can also buy vanillin as an extract. An artificial vanilla flavor that, the manufacturers say, tastes just like the real thing. Don't believe them.

VARIETY MEATS

Heart, liver, kidneys, sweetbreads, tongue, brains, and tripe—these are the variety meats, obtained from all four of our major meat sources, beef, lamb, pork, and veal. All are nutritious (some more so than others), relatively inexpensive, and can—when properly prepared—furnish delicious family meals as well as a number of tempting gourmet-fare dishes.

About heart. Hearts from beef, lamb, pork, and veal are available. Because none of the hearts is tender meat, they require long, slow cooking, and should be cooked in liquid or braised. The flavor is excellent plain, but can be augmented by cooking the meat with tomatoes or other vegetables.

Wash heart and cut off hard parts. If the meat is to be braised, it can be stuffed with any bread or rice combination that you would use to stuff poultry.

to cook in liquid: Cover with water to which 1 teaspoon salt for each quart has been added. Cover tightly and cook slowly until tender—beef hearts will require 3 to 3½ hours, pork, lamb, and veal 2 to 2½ hours. If you wish, you may bake in a 300°F. oven rather than cooking on top of the stove.

to braise: Brown heart on all sides in a small amount of fat. Add ½ cup (or a little more for beef) liquid, cover tightly, and cook at low temperature—in the oven or over a burner—until tender. This will require about the same amount of time as heart cooked in liquid.

Thinly sliced cooked heart makes delicious sandwiches, or it may be ground and combined with other ingredients for a spread, or chopped or diced as the basis of a hearty salad.

About liver. This is probably the best-known of the variety meats. For generations, home cooks have been coaxing their children and husbands to "Eat all your nice liver, dear." Actually, no one should need coaxing. Liver is delicious, can be prepared in so many ways that no one need ever tire of it. And it's loaded with nutrients.

Beef, pork, lamb, and veal are all available. None needs scalding as old-fashioned cookbooks used to direct, although some cooks like to soak beef liver—it has the strongest flavor of the four—in milk before cooking. Beef and pork liver may be braised or panfried; lamb and veal liver may be panfried or broiled; all four may be deep-fat fried. For braising you may want to buy a whole liver or a large piece, rather than slices.

to braise, whole or large piece: Dredge with seasoned flour, brown in fat. If desired, add vegetables such as onions and carrots. Add ½ cup liquid, cover tightly, and cook over low heat, allowing 30 minutes per pound.

to braise slices: Follow above directions, but use only ¼ cup liquid, allow 20 minutes total cooking time.

to broil: Use slices ½ to ¾ inch thick. Dip in melted bacon drippings or butter. Broil at moderate temperature just long enough to brown lightly, about 3 minutes each side.

to panfry: Dredge in seasoned flour, brown on both sides in small amount of cooking fat. Liver should be sufficiently cooked when brown—overdone liver is tough.

to deep-fat fry: Have liver cut in long, thin strips. Dredge in seasoned flour; fry in deep fat at 350°F. until nicely browned. If desired, the liver strips may be dipped in beaten egg, then in crumbs, before frying.

Liver that is to be used for a loaf, a pâté, or such must be ground. Don't attempt to grind raw liver. Partially cook it first—about 5 minutes on each side in cooking fat.

About kidneys. You can buy veal and lamb chops cut with a portion of kidney included, in the British manner. In fact, the British are very fond of kidneys, especially broiled with bacon for breakfast, and in their great beefsteak and kidney pie.

Beef kidneys are less tender and stronger in flavor than those of pork, veal, and lamb, all of which are available. Before cooking, cut away hard parts and remove membrane. Slice or cut in pieces as you like. Lamb kidneys, because of their small size, are halved or left whole. (See KIDNEYS.)

to cook in liquid: Cover with liquid; cover pot tightly and cook slowly until tender, about 1 hour.

to braise: Dredge in seasoned flour, brown in cooking fat. Add a small amount of liquid and cook slowly until tender.

to broil: Marinate in french dressing for 1 hour, or brush with melted butter before cooking. Broil about 5 minutes on each side. May also be wrapped in bacon slices before broiling, or broiled en brochette with other foods.

About sweetbreads (the thymus gland). These are a delicacy, adaptable to many delicious dishes to serve family or guests. They are very perishable and should be precooked as soon as you get them home, unless you intend to braise or panfry them at once. Wash sweetbreads before cooking, remove the membrane before or after cooking.

to precook: Simmer 20 minutes in water to which 1 teaspoon salt, 1 tablespoon lemon juice or vinegar (and any other desired seasonings) have been added for each quart of water. The acid helps to keep the sweetbreads white and firm.

After precooking, sweetbreads should be refrigerated if not used at once. Precooked sweetbreads may be broken into pieces for salads or to scramble with eggs, reheated in a cream sauce alone or with ham or veal, dipped in egg and crumbs and fried in shallow or deep fat until browned, made into croquettes, or dipped into melted butter and broiled.

to braise (without precooking): Wash and remove membrane. Dredge in flour or roll in crumbs and brown in a small amount of fat; cover and cook slowly about 20 minutes.

to panfry (without precooking): Prepare and cook as for braising, but do not cover. Cook, turning occasionally, 20 minutes.

About tongue. Beef and veal tongues are generally available uncooked. Those of lamb and pork are small, and are most often sold ready to serve. Tongue may be fresh, pickled (corned), or smoked when you buy it—consult the label. Soak smoked or pickled tongue in cold water to cover for 3 hours before cooking.

to cook: Place tongue in a large pot and cover with water. Add 1 teaspoon salt for each quart of water if tongue is fresh; omit salt with pickled or smoked meat. Spices or vegetables may be added to the cooking water as you like. Cover tightly and cook until tender, 3 to 4 hours.

Remove skin and cut away roots—plunging into cold water will help to loosen the skin. If the tongue is to be served cold, it will be more juicy if allowed to cool, in the refrigerator, in the liquid in which it was cooked. Don't throw away the root end—the schlung. It makes a great flavoring for lentil or pea soup.

Serve tongue sliced in sandwiches or ground for a spread. Or serve sliced hot, with a spicy raisin sauce. Or sliced cold, in aspic. Or hot in a casserole, cold in a salad.

About brains. Like sweetbreads, brains are delicate and perishable. Unless they are going to be used at once, precook brains to firm them and improve their keeping qualities. They are tender, mild in flavor, and can be used in a number of savory dishes. Wash before cooking, remove membranes before or after.

to precook: Follow directions for precooking sweetbreads, above.

to braise (without precooking): Wash, remove membranes. Flour or roll in crumbs. Brown in a small amount of fat, then cover and cook slowly for 20 minutes.

578

to panfry (without precooking): Follow directions for braising, but do not cover; cook 20 minutes, turning occasionally.

Scramble precooked brains with eggs, serve them à la king, or in any of the ways suggested for sweetbreads.

About tripe (stomach lining of beef cattle). The French are particularly fond of tripe, and have worked out many delightful ways to serve it; à la mode de Caen, for example, brings tripe to the table in a savory sauce based on tomatoes.

Tripe is available fresh, pickled, or canned. If you buy fresh tripe, it will most likely be partially cooked. However, it is necessary to give it further precooking before using.

to precook: Simmer tripe for 2 hours in water to which 1 teaspoon salt has been added for each quart of water.

Tripe may be served with a well-seasoned tomato or Creole sauce. Or it may be brushed with melted butter and broiled until lightly browned. Or pieces may be dipped in fritter batter and deep-fat fried. Or served in a cream sauce. Or spread with dressing and baked. Tripe is also used in Philadelphia Pepper Pot, a delicious soup.

Don't be afraid to experiment. All of these variety meats can be served in many wonderful ways. Don't pass them by because you're certain your family won't like them —how do you know until you've tried? Any good cookbook will give you recipes for serving according to the suggestions given above, and in many other ways. Don't be timid!

Nutritive values of variety meats. In limited space, it is impossible to list nutritive values for the beef, lamb, pork, and veal kinds of each of the variety meats. But we can express an average among the four kinds in terms of percentage of RDA—the Recommended Daily Allowance (see special feature: NUTRITION NOTEBOOK). These are the percentages of the RDA of a 3½-ounce serving, for a young man:

nutrient	liver	kidney	heart	brains	sweet-breads	tongue	tripe
protein	55	50	55	22	53	40	33
calories	8	8	7	4	6	8	3
calcium	2	2	1	16	26	2	16
iron	176	130	51	21	31	18	16
phosphorus	66	31	21	41	52	14	17
magnesium	7	—	7	—	—	—	trace
vitamin A	876	23	2	—	—	—	—
ascorbic acid	68	27	trace	42	42	46	—
thiamin	22	34	16	7	4	4	trace
riboflavin	248	268	75	12	9	16	8
niacin	111	59	40	17	16	19	6

Get into the habit of serving variety meats at least once a week—for the nutrition, change of pace, and great flavor that they have to contribute to your meals. See also GIBLETS and INMEATS.

VEAL

Tender, delicate, and delicious, true veal—not the older calf that is the only excuse for veal offered by some markets—is gray to pink when uncooked. Admittedly expensive, it has become a special-treat or special-occasion meat. And because of that it is even more important than with other meats to know what you're buying and how to cope with it when you get it home.

Young beef that is 4 to 14 weeks old, veal is available all year around, most abundant in late winter and spring. The color of the raw lean becomes more pink—less gray—with increased age in the animal from which it is taken. Veal has little fat; what fat is present should be firm and creamy white. The meat has a velvety texture, without marbling. A large portion of the total veal carcass is tender enough to be cooked by dry-heat methods; only neck slices, riblets, and fore shanks require braising or cooking in liquid. The breast, which is often stuffed, may be roasted or braised. In any case, braised portions of veal require a much shorter cooking time to make them tender than similar cuts of beef.

Calling it by its right name. As with other meats, the meat industry's ICMISC—Industrywide Cooperative Meat Identification Standards Committee—has arrived at a master list of recommended names for cuts of veal, to aid the consumer in purchasing. If retailers adhere to these names in labeling their veal, the home cook will always know what she is buying wherever she buys it. (See BEEF for an in-depth explanation.)

Veal Chart

Retail Cuts of Veal—Where They Come from and How to Cook Them

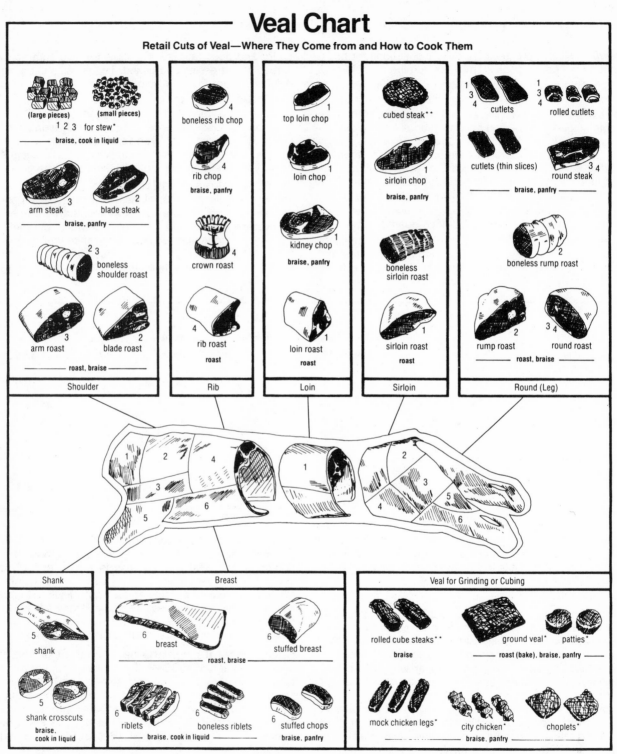

Shoulder

(large pieces) (small pieces)
1 2 3 for stew*
— braise, cook in liquid —

arm steak 3 blade steak 2
— braise, panfry —

boneless 2 3
shoulder roast

arm roast 3 blade roast 2
— roast, braise —

Rib

boneless rib chop 4

rib chop 4
braise, panfry

crown roast 4

rib roast 4
roast

Loin

top loin chop 1

loin chop 1

kidney chop 1
braise, panfry

loin roast 1
roast

Sirloin

cubed steak**

sirloin chop 1
braise, panfry

boneless 1
sirloin roast

sirloin roast 1
roast

Round (Leg)

cutlets 1 3 4 rolled cutlets 1 3 4

cutlets (thin slices) 1 round steak 3 4
— braise, panfry —

boneless rump roast 2

rump roast 2 round roast 3 4
— roast, braise —

Shank

shank 5

shank crosscuts 5
braise, cook in liquid

Breast

breast 6 stuffed breast 6
— roast, braise —

riblets 6 boneless riblets 6 stuffed chops 6
— braise, cook in liquid — braise, panfry

Veal for Grinding or Cubing

rolled cube steaks** ground veal patties*
braise — roast (bake), braise, panfry —

mock chicken legs* city chicken* choplets*
— braise, panfry —

*Veal for stew or grinding may be made from any cut.
**Cube steaks may be made from any thick solid piece of boneless veal.

PRIMAL CUT: VEAL SHOULDER

common name	recommended name
veal shoulder roast veal round bone roast	VEAL SHOULDER ARM ROAST
veal round bone steak veal shoulder steak shoulder veal chop round bone round bone veal chops	VEAL SHOULDER ARM STEAK
veal shoulder roast veal blade roast	VEAL SHOULDER BLADE ROAST
veal shoulder steak shoulder veal chops	VEAL SHOULDER BLADE STEAK
rolled veal shoulder veal shoulder boneless veal rolled roast	VEAL SHOULDER RST BNLS
stew veal veal stew (large pieces) veal stew (small pieces) veal stew boneless	VEAL FOR STEW

PRIMAL CUT: VEAL FORESHANK AND BREAST

common name	recommended name
breast-of-veal veal breast	VEAL BREAST
veal riblets	VEAL BREAST RIBLETS
veal shank cross-cut shank	VEAL SHANK CROSS CUTS

PRIMAL CUT: VEAL RIB

common name	recommended name
veal rib roast rib veal roast	VEAL RIB ROAST
veal chops veal rib chops rib veal chop	VEAL RIB CHOPS
veal crown roast veal crown rib roast	VEAL RIB CROWN ROAST

PRIMAL CUT: VEAL LOIN

common name	recommended name
veal loin roast	VEAL LOIN ROAST
rolled veal loin roast bnls veal loin roast	VEAL LOIN ROAST BNLS
veal kidney chops kidney veal chops	VEAL LOIN KIDNEY CHOPS
veal chops veal loin chops loin veal chops	VEAL LOIN CHOPS
veal chops bnls veal chops	VEAL LOIN TOP LOIN CHOPS

PRIMAL CUT: VEAL LEG

common name	recommended name
veal sirloin roast	VEAL LEG SIRLOIN ROAST
veal steak veal sirloin steak sirloin veal chop	VEAL LEG SIRLOIN STEAK
rolled double sirloin roast boneless sirloin roast	VEAL LEG SIRLOIN ROAST BNLS
veal leg roast leg of veal	VEAL LEG ROUND ROAST
veal scallopini veal steak veal steakettes	VEAL LEG ROUND STEAK
veal rump roast rump of veal	VEAL LEG RUMP ROAST
rolled rump roast veal roast boneless rump of veal bnls	VEAL LEG RUMP ROAST BNLS
veal heel roast	VEAL LEG HEEL ROAST
veal cubed steak cubed veal steak	VEAL CUBED STEAK

(The entire leg yields suitable lean for cubed steak.)

veal kabobs veal stew veal city chicken	VEAL CUBES FOR KABOBS
veal cutlets	VEAL CUTLETS

VEAL IN YOUR KITCHEN

Veal is so delicate—and so much appreciated—that even a veal stew can be an elegant dish for guests. A blanquette de veau is such a dish, a white veal stew with mushrooms, its gravy thickened with eggs and cream. Veal round steak or cubed steak can be offered as veal birds—stuffed, rolled, and braised in a savory liquid. A veal crown roast, something of a budget buster, is a handsome and delicious main dish. Veal has so little fat that it is never broiled.

Coping with veal. Because it is expensive, be cautious when you buy veal, careful when you cook it.

how to buy: Be guided by the label, but also by your eyes and nose. Fresh veal has virtually no odor, and has a clean, fresh look. The best veal may be labeled "milk-fed," indicating that it came from a very young animal, and will be gray in color. As the age of the animal increases, the color tends more and more toward pink. Deep pink or red color indicates that the meat is not veal, but should be labeled "calf." If the veal is packaged, be certain that the package is not damp or dripping.

how to store: Loosen or remove market wrapping; store loosely wrapped in the coldest part of the refrigerator. Ground veal may be refrigerated up to 2 days, other forms to 3. Refrigerate cooked veal, covered, up to 4 days.

nutritive value: In limited space it is impossible to give values for all cuts of veal. However, to guide you, a serving of roasted veal, consisting of two slices, each 4½ inches long, 2¼ inches wide, and ¼ inch thick, yields 229 calories and provides these nutrients:

protein	23.1	grams
fat	14.4	grams
calcium	10	milligrams
phosphorus	211	milligrams
iron	2.9	milligrams
sodium	57	milligrams
potassium	259	milligrams
thiamin	.14	milligram
riboflavin	.34	milligram
niacin	6.6	milligrams

Veal contains no carbohydrate, no vitamins A or C.

Tips on preparing, cooking. Veal requires coddling. Cook it slowly and gently, whether by dry or moist heat. Roast veal at 300 to 325°F. (the lower temperature is preferable) until its interior temperature reaches 170°F. on a meat thermometer. If you braise veal or cook it in liquid, it will require a considerably shorter time than other meats. It is done when fork-tender—don't cook it to death.

Cook stewing veal in liquid with a bay leaf (remove after 30 minutes), an onion stuck with three whole cloves, two diced ribs of celery, one whole sliced carrot, and a veal knuckle bone (ask the butcher). When it is very tender, remove veal and bone, strain stock and boil it down until it is reduced by half. Shred the cooked veal into a loaf pan and pour the stock over, just to cover the meat. Cover, weight, and refrigerate—tomorrow, pressed veal for dinner.

Or stuff a breast of veal with well-seasoned cooked rice and peas; roast or braise. Or cook a veal roast; when cold, slice in ½-inch cuts, spread each slice with DUXELLES, then a thick purée of cooked onions; reassemble the roast—it is now Veal Prince Orloff—for serving.

Or make some of these famous veal dishes: Osso Buco, Paprikash, City Chicken, Wiener Schnitzel, Vitello Tonnato. You'll find recipes in a good general cookbook.

Freezing veal. Properly wrapped, all raw veal other than ground can be freezer-stored at 0°F. or lower up to 7 months; ground, up to 3 months. Cooked veal in a sauce or gravy may be freezer-stored up to 3 months.

Other ways, other forms. In the market's freezer section, raw boneless roasts and small steaks or cubed steaks are sometimes available. Cooked veal cutlet dinners are also to be had. The only other form of veal—except fresh, at the meat counter—is strained or chopped baby food and junior food, both with and without vegetables. See also GROUND MEATS.

VEAU: see page 454

VEGETABLE GARDENS: see special
feature: THE GROW-IT-YOURSELF BOOM

VEGETABLE JUICES

Certain vegetable juices—such as carrot, celery, sauerkraut—are available canned in supermarkets and fresh-made, to be drunk on the spot or carried home in cartons, at health food stores.

VEGETABLE OIL: see OILS, SALAD AND COOKING

VEGETABLE PROTEIN: see TEXTURED PLANT PROTEIN

VEGETABLES: see individual vegetable entries, as BEANS, CARROTS, PEAS, RATATOUILLE, SUCCOTASH, and UNUSUAL VEGETABLES

VEGETARIANISM

We tend to think that the other guy, if he's not just exactly like us, is just a little bit (or sometimes very) peculiar. In line with this, those of us who are carnivorous look askance at vegetarians. But we can't afford to. More and more young people are turning to vegetarianism of one sort or another, and we may at any moment be asked to provide meals for a son or daughter who has decided to eschew meat.

Classes of vegetarians. All vegetarians refrain from eating meat (and poultry and fish), but beyond that salient rule they divide into four groups.

vegans: These are the strict vegetarians. They eat no food whatever that comes from animal sources—no meat, fish, poultry, milk, eggs, or cheese.

lacto-ovo vegetarians: These abstain from meat, but do eat eggs, milk, and milk products.

lacto-vegetarians: These allow themselves milk and milk products, but no eggs.

ovo-vegetarians: These eat eggs, but allow themselves no milk or milk products.

Motivations, sensible and not so. Religious, cultural, ethnic, and moral reasons motivated vegetarians in the past, reasons that the rest of the world, even if not understanding, could respect. Present-day vegetarianism is inspired by those reasons and, in some, simply by compassion for the animals, our brothers.

But others are following what they believe to be the teachings of various Eastern philosophies, which they understand only vaguely and tend to misinterpret. Still others have read biochemical misinformation on food, which they do not understand at all.

A third group has a very simple motivation: the continually rising cost of food—a vegetarian diet costs less than a carnivorous one, and they adopt it for that reason.

Nutritional considerations. No matter what its motivation, a lacto-ovo vegetarian diet can be nutritious and satisfying—and can reduce food bills, if that is the reason for adhering to it. Such a regimen increases fiber in the diet and reduces the fat and cholesterol in which most carnivorous diets are too high. Another benefit is weight control—most adult vegetarians weigh 10 to 20 pounds less than those of the same age and condition in life who eat meat.

On the other hand the strict vegetarians, the vegans, have a very real threat of malnutrition hanging over them. The effects will not necessarily become apparent for a number of years, as many as twelve to fifteen, when signs of irreversible nerve damage—the destruction of certain nerve fibers—show up. This is caused by a lack of vitamin B_{12}, of which there is no adequate source in a strictly vegetable diet. Although B_{12} is available as a medication, and if taken faithfully will prevent nerve damage, it will not cure the condition once it has taken place and the damage is done.

The vegan diet is also lacking in calcium, and calcium taken as a medication is not as efficiently utilized as when the mineral is acquired from food. Such a lack is especially dangerous for infants and growing children, and for pregnant and lactating women. Other deficiencies in such a diet are iron and iodine and vitamin D. Cod liver and other fish-liver oils supply vitamin D, and so does milk fortified with the vitamin —but vegans are not allowed milk. Iodine is available in salt, iron as a medication. Fortunately, long-term strict vegetarians are rare.

The macrobiotic diet, an Eastern cultist regimen that gradually eliminates all foods other than brown rice from the diet, is a self-evident disaster. It leads to serious malnutrition and, if adhered to over a long period, to death.

What do vegetarians eat? Lacto-ovo vegetarians can, if they give a bit of thought to the subject, have some delicious and nutritionally balanced meals. That they can be wholesome and healthful is evidenced by some of the people who are vegetarians, including Candice Bergen, Dennis Weaver, and David Carradine, actors; Cesar Chavez, the labor leader; Yehudi Menuhin, the famous violinist; and author Isaac Bashevis Singer.

Consider these mouth-watering vegetarian dinners:

Cheese-stuffed manicotti with marinara sauce
Italian green beans
Tossed green salad with french dressing
Strawberry shortcake

———————————

Creamed eggs and celery on whole wheat toast
Steamed spinach
Caramel custard with chopped pecans

———————————

Cabbage rolls with walnut-rice stuffing, tomato sauce
Corn on the cob
Sliced bananas in orange juice
Chocolate cookies

———————————

Fettucine alfredo
Buttered broccoli
Three-bean salad
Crisp bread sticks
Vanilla pudding

As you can see, vegetarians—at least the lacto-ovo ones—are not exactly starving. And although meals may take a bit more skillful planning than those with a wider variety of foods for selection, they can be nutritionally balanced and delicious.

VENISON: see GAME

VERMICELLI: see PASTA

VICHYSSOISE: see page 454

VINAIGRETTE: see SALAD DRESSINGS
and the special feature: SAUCE SORCERY

VINEGARS

The origin of the word, from the Latin *vinum*—wine—and *aigre*—sour—reminds us that the first vinegars were wines that had fermented. The use of such "spoiled" wine was probably one of those serendipitous discoveries that sometimes occur.

Today we define vinegar as a sour liquid that is produced by fermenting a dilute distilled alcohol with acetic acid bacteria. Apple cider is the most commonly used of the fermentable liquids that can be made into vinegar, but the distilled alcohol from grains and wines are also widely used.

Vinegar was once mainly a preservative when combined with salt brine or a medicine prescribed in the treatment of scurvy and to hasten the healing of wounds. And, interestingly, it was also used as a thirst-quencher, a beverage for which a small amount of vinegar was mixed with water.

Great-grandma made her own vinegar in her kitchen, and perpetuated the fermentation process by saving the "mother of vinegar"—the growth of acetic acid bacteria that forms on the surface of fermenting liquids—from one batch and adding it to the next. This is essentially the same process that commercial manufacturers of vinegar use today on a much larger scale. Present-day vinegars are pasteurized, however, so that the "mother" is rarely formed in vinegar we buy.

Vinegar varieties. The three principal types of vinegar available to us in our markets are cider, distilled, and wine. A fourth, malt vinegar, is not as widely used, but seems to be gaining in popularity—perhaps with the increasing popularity of fish and chips, which are properly eaten sprinkled with malt vinegar. Flavored vinegars can be made by adding various taste-enhancing elements to any of these vinegars.

cider vinegar: This type is the most commonly used. It is made by fermenting apple cider, and has an acetic acid content of from 5 to 6 percent. A pale gold-brown in color, it has a flavor that speaks of the apples used in its making.

distilled vinegar: This is the one we refer to—and recipes call for—as white vinegar. It contains 5 to 12 percent acetic acid, is made by fermenting a dilute solution of alcohol distilled from grain mash. Colorless, it has no flavor of the grain from which it was made, which is eliminated in the distillation.

wine vinegar: This can be made from any of the three broad classifications of wine—red, white, or rosé. Like cider vinegar, its acetic acid content is 5 to 6 percent. The color and flavor reflect the type of wine used.

malt vinegar: This is made from barley malt and, like good wines, is aged before it is put on the market. Russet-brown in color, it is definitely aromatic and has a distinctive flavor that some enjoy, others feel is too assertive.

flavored vinegars: The most common additives used to flavor vinegar—most often wine vinegar—are tarragon, basil, and garlic. Such flavored vinegars can be made at home. Crush the garlic clove or bruise the herbs and add to a bottle of red or white wine vinegar. Let stand for three days, then strain the vinegar and return it to its bottle.

A wide variety of salad dressings and sauces depend on vinegar for their delightful flavor. We use it in smaller amounts to perk up the flavors of many foods, as well as a preservative in relishes and all sorts of pickled foods.

VIOLETS, CANDIED: see CANDIED
FLOWERS

VIRGINIA HAM: see HAM

VITAMINS: see MILK and the special feature:
NUTRITION NOTEBOOK

VODKA: see LIQUORS

VOL-AU-VENT

A hollow shell made of puff paste (see PASTRY), a vol-au-vent looks like a very much overgrown patty shell. All sorts of savory mixtures in sauces are served in it. Although patty shells often come to the table without the small, round cover that hides the hollow, a vol-au-vent always wears its pastry hat.

FASHIONS IN FOOD

If, as they say, we are what we eat, we must indeed be a rather peculiar lot—particularly if we subscribe to the dozens of come-and-go food fads

As every woman knows, if you keep clothes long enough—particularly old favorites, reluctantly set aside when they went out of style—some of them will once again become the very latest thing. Not true, of course—and fortunately—of all fashions. It's doubtful that there will be a second time around for bustles, and if zoot suits (and their concomitant DA haircut) come into style again, we may all take to the hills. On the other hand, men's spats are sure of a rerun (it will be at least the fourth) because they are good-looking, and cozy in cold climates. Ladies' floating printed chiffon dresses (you are always a lady, never a woman or a girl or, heaven forbid, a dame or a broad when you wear chiffon) went out, came back, left the scene again, but will doubtless return, because they are pretty, comfortable, becoming, and make a female *feel* like a lady.

Food, too, has its ins and outs, especially among people who like to entertain a lot and want to be classed as movers and shakers at the dinner table. Considerations other than what's the latest thing govern most of us in our kitchens, budget being the first one and ability to cope the second.

In the days of a bevy of servants—or, at the very least, a three-dollar-a-week "hired girl" plus the woman who "came in to oblige" on special occasions—coping was less of a problem. Dinner parties were always sit-down affairs that rambled through many courses before the ladies adjourned to the drawing room, leaving the gentlemen to their port, cigars, and discussions of politics or off-color jokes or both.

WAY-BACK-WHEN FADS AND FANCIES

In 1905 the first lady of good cooking, Fannie Merritt Farmer, whose landmark *Boston Cooking School Cook Book* had been in print for nine years, published her *A Book Of Good Dinners For My Friend, Or, What To Have For Dinner*. In it she offered menus for family meals, holiday occasions, and formal dinner parties, along with the appropriate recipes. Here, to give you an idea of why it was necessary to have a staff in the kitchen, is one menu Fannie suggests for a formal dinner:

Oyster Cocktail   Saltines
Mushrooms and Sago Soup   Dinner Braids
Lobster Chops   Cucumber Boats   Sauce Tartare
Swedish Timbales with Calf's Brains
Larded Fillet of Beef with Truffles

Brown Mushroom Sauce
Potato Rings   Flageolets   Buttered Carrots
Asparagus with Mousseline Sauce
Dressed Lettuce   Cheese Fingers
Apricot and Wine Jelly with Pistachio Bisque
Ice Cream
Cream Sponge Balls
Salted Almonds   Bonbons
Water Thins   Neufchatel Cheese
Café Noir

Even family dinners at that point were nothing to sneeze at. One typical menu Fannie Farmer suggests starts with Chicken Soup (cream of chicken) with Imperial Crusts, a version of melba toast. It goes on to Shoulder of Braised Veal, Parched Rice with Tomato Sauce, and Succotash. California Salad with Mayonnaise followed—on consultation with the recipes, this turns out to be a crabmeat concoction of the kind we think of as a main-dish salad today. The meal was rounded out with Strawberry Short Cake and Café Noir. Obviously, no one left the table hungry. Another family menu calls for Boiled Haddock with Hot Sauce Tartare, French Fried Potatoes, Devilled Chicken Fricasse [sic], Chestnut Balls, Artichokes with Hollandaise Sauce, Dressed Lettuce, Cream Cheese with Bar-le-duc and Wafers, Custard Pudding, and the inevitable Café Noir. If the lady of the house had to produce this all by herself, it's just as well she didn't also have to chauffeur Johnny to Little League and Suzie to ballet lessons in the afternoon and attend a PTA meeting that evening. If the children came home after school and wanted to know "What's for dinner?" just telling them must have encroached considerably on their homework time.

Fortunately for mom's sanity and everybody's waistline, dinner menus, both company and family, have undergone radical changes since Fannie's day. We no longer stuff our loved ones into an early grave. And when we entertain, we no longer try to one-up our friends by serving ever more elaborate (and expensive) multi-course meals. But in our way, we kowtow to fashion just the same. Waves of "in" dishes sweep the country like a plague, so that if you're invited out to dinner six nights in a row you may well have to contend with the same menu on six successive evenings, varied only by the expertise of the home cook.

There was, for example, the Beef Wellington madness.

585

A proper Beef Wellington is a thing of beauty and a joy to the palate, with its beautifully rare whole fillet of beef encased in meltingly smooth pâté and flavorful duxelles, and wearing a handsomely browned pastry overcoat. But even the very best Beef Wellington encountered over and over again wears out its welcome, and many of those Wellingtons that turned up on the dinner party circuit in the 1960s were a long way from perfect.

As almost always happens with something good, Beef Wellington had lots of imitations. Using eye of round instead of tenderloin was one trap a lot of economy-minded hostesses fell into. There is nothing wrong with eye of round. It is a respectable cut of beef, delicious when properly cooked and served. But tenderloin it isn't. As for the mock wellingtons made of ground beef, liverwurst, and canned mushrooms, bundled into a wrapping made from biscuit mix—it's best to draw a veil of obscurity over those monstrosities, and be on our way.

YOU WIN SOME, YOU LOSE SOME

In spite of both cooks who couldn't hack it and sorry imitations, Beef Wellington made it to the dinner party circuit and stayed several years. In fact, it's still there—but you can be fairly safe in assuming that if you're invited out to dinner today, the main dish will not inevitably be a wellington.

Fondue made it, too. There's an informality, a camaraderie, about gathering around the fondue pot that caught on instantly. Following simple directions and using good ingredients, fondue is both easy to prepare and delicious. And almost everyone likes it. As good ideas do, this one proliferated in all directions. Fondue bourguignonne came next—beef cooked in a communal pot in oil (or in beef broth, perhaps not quite as delectable, but easier on the calorie-conscious), with a selection of savory sauces in which to dip the just-cooked morsel of meat. If beef, someone thought, why not chicken? Why not shrimp? Why not almost anything that won't fall apart when speared on a fork and dip-cooked? So we have fondues of all sorts, including the somewhat dubious (and even sloppier to carry from pot to mouth than other fondues, none of which are exactly tidy) chocolate fondue—milk or bittersweet chocolate melted with one or another kind of liqueur, with cake cubes and fruit pieces for dipping and sometimes chopped nuts or coconut to roll the goodie in. Messy, but a joy to chocolate-lovers and dessert-devourers of every stripe.

One good idea generally sparks another. The fondue success moved in two directions: to the steamboat, a handsome oriental brass contrivance for cooking meat and vegetables in hot broth—and, by extension, the food cooked in it—and to raclette, another (like fondue) Swiss specialty. Hostesses soon discovered that steamboat could be cooked in the fondue pot or even the electric skillet that they already owned, and the steamboat utensil, exceedingly costly, wasn't

necessary. So steamboat food—such an array as veal kidneys, boneless steak, chicken breast, slivers of pork loin, pieces of red snapper fillet, shrimp, celery, snow peas, scallions, spinach, and eggs to poach in the broth, which is drunk at the end of the meal—is comforting diners everywhere, but not many such spreads are cooked in authentic steamboats. As for raclette, an eating ceremony in which cheese is warmed before an open fire and the soft part scraped off onto diners' plates on which boiled potatoes and pickles already reside—well, many a living room carpet has never been the same since a raclette party, and anyway, the meal isn't all that appealing. So raclette really never caught on. (Appliance manufacturers put a raclette warmer on the market—but then, they'd come up with a device for throwing the baby out with the bath water if they thought it had the remotest chance of becoming popular.)

There have been other such losers—foods that looked as if they were going to spread like wildfire, but sputtered out before they really got started. Carpetbag Steak was one. This Australian specialty consists of a thick sirloin steak stuffed with oysters, marinated in oil and lemon juice seasoned with onion, cooked to taste, and sauced with the marinade fortified with sherry. Sounds good? Lots of other people thought so too, tried it, and didn't like it. They went back to serving their oysters on the half shell and grilling their sirloins unstuffed.

Veal Prince Orloff was another that didn't make the dinner-party circuit, this time not because of the flavor or texture. The recipe called for a delicate boneless leg of veal, roasted to perfection, thinly sliced, the slices spread with duxelles (sautéed chopped mushrooms) and soubise (purée of cooked onions) and the whole thing put back together again. A thing of beauty. An unparalleled pleasure on which to dine. The only trouble was, just about the time home cooks were catching on to the idea of an Orloff as the mainstay of their company dinner, veal shot up in price to the point where you had to mortgage the house and sell the children into bondage in order to purchase a large veal roast. The prince had to abdicate, and made no more public appearances.

THE GREAT OUTDOORS

Suckling pig suffered the same fate for a different reason. A young, whole little pig is one of the great taste experiences —crispy, meltingly tender, exquisitely flavored. Unfortunately, an uncooked suckling pig bears an appalling resemblance to a dead child, and when it is spitted and roasted the situation isn't all that much improved. There are those among us who pooh-pooh this idea, to whom a suckling pig is the height of cookout elegance—but the rest of us (in the majority) can't bear to buy, much less spit and cook one.

While we're on the subject of cookouts we're on the subject of a fashion that seems to be here to stay. But a couple of generations ago, a cookout was a crazy notion.

Haul all that food outdoors, and then have to fight the flies and ants for it, only to haul all the dirty dishes back inside? Oh, sure, a picnic was nice once in a while, as long as it didn't happen too often. And some people, we understood, went out in the woods and cooked their food over an open fire. Sheer madness!

Then a generation ago, some pioneers (some nuts, a lot of us tended to think of them) began grilling hamburgers and hot dogs in the backyard. The idea caught on, and we've never looked back. We grill and kettle-cook and spit-roast everything in sight and guzzle it all with joyous abandon, the sauce running down our chins.

BRUNCH AND SIMILAR CONSIDERATIONS

Once, if you had suggested inviting people over for breakfast, you would have got such a look from mama as would pin you to the wall. Oh certainly, if you entertained guests overnight you had, unfortunately, to feed them something in the morning. But turn the first meal of the day into a social occasion? As the saying of the times had it, perish forbid!

Now brunch is, as one enthusiastic if ungrammatical cookbook author puts it, an entertaining occasion. And a great idea, too. Sunday is most often brunch day, and Sunday brunch makes an infinitely preferable party to Sunday evening dinner, on whose heels Monday morning work follows all too closely. In fact, the Saturday night cookout in warm weather, the Sunday brunch in cold, have become suburban rituals, warm and friendly and informal ways to relax between two work weeks.

There are often football games to watch on Sundays. The brunch meal is over with by the time the game begins, and the party can break up into watchers and nonwatchers, each with company in their preference and—the nonwatchers—someone to talk to. If the game takes place near home, the brunch metamorphoses into a tailgate picnic, just as easy and perhaps even more fun. And here the home nonwatchers can get in their licks, asking when the quarterback is coming up to bat and what position the water boy plays.

Brunch has other things in its favor. The meal can be both good and hearty without shooting the week's food budget, for appropriate brunch food tends to be less expensive (and less elaborate, a plus for the cook) than dinner food. Drinks are likely to be fewer and less lethal by day than by night. Women are more inclined to pitch in and help clean up after brunch (while the kids and the ball game bunch disappear) than after dinner. A good deal all around, brunch.

FOREIGN INTRIGUE

For entertaining, Italian food is in, and has been for a long time, ever since we started entertaining less elaborately—and less expensively. Big platters or casseroles based on pasta have everything going for them—they're make-ahead easy, they're tasty and filling, and they don't cost an arm and a leg. Spanish paella is in, too, for all the same reasons and another one—it makes a great change from all that pasta. Cioppino is in as well—most people think of it as Spanish or Italian, in spite of its San Francisco origin. North African couscous—made of tiny pellets of semolina, called faufal—got onto the entertainment circuit unchanged, but the stews it accompanies have been modified in many cases. (Americans, especially men, tend to feel that such things as yams, bananas, dried apricots, and peanuts don't belong in stews.) A wave of Mexican food, or its close relative, Tex-Mex, swept the country not long ago. We've had chili with us for a long time as an economical-but-acceptable way to feed a crowd, guacamole less long as an appetizer, and every once in a while some adventurous cook would feed her guests Turkey Molé, mostly so she could say, "You know, there's chocolate in the sauce—can you imagine!" But since the mid-1970s nachos have multiplied, enchiladas have proliferated, tacos have abounded, burritos have expanded their horizons, until now, at any party, it's here a buñuelo, there a natilla, and everywhere, *everywhere,* a margarita.

The Indonesian rijsttafel—translated as "rice table" but actually a mind-boggling array of foods—has not fared as floridly, but it's getting there. It has in its favor that although there are many dishes, most of them can be prepared in advance, many are very inexpensive, and, particularly, that you don't meet it coming and going at everyone's party.

Curries, too, are widely accepted and acceptable for much the same reasons. Besides being exceedingly good, a curry dinner is exceedingly pretty, particularly served buffet style with all those little bowls of sambals—accompaniments—in their endless variety of flavors and textures and colors, surrounding the golden curry and white rice. Another thing going for it is that beer is the proper drink with curry, and we all know that it is a relatively inexpensive beverage.

In the appetizer department, particularly cocktail-party snacks, we've had (French) hors d'oeuvres around so long we no longer think of them as "foreign food." (Spanish) tapas are less familiar, though rapidly coming into their own at our parties. However, (Russian) zazuski—except for caviar—haven't yet made it big, but may well be the next wave of munches and nibbles.

British pub fare is gaining momentum, especially such good eat-out-of-hand food as cornish pasties and scotch eggs. Other than at breakfast time—English breakfasts are fabulous—our overseas cousins aren't all that great as cooks. (There are many fine restaurants in Britain, but their food tends to be French or that catchall term, Continental.) At a less elegant level, though, pubs offer hearty slabs of roast beef, for which they are famous, as well as other good, sturdy food. They make (excuse it, cut—in Britain one cuts, not makes, a sandwich) stupendous ham sandwiches as well as fine ones of that great beef between two slices of good country bread. Steak-and-kidney pie is another pub treat. It all started in this country with fish and chips, from which humble, newspaper-wrapped beginnings the desire to eat British has expanded mightily.

Japanese food is another area of ethnicity we took to our hearts. We learned how to eat in the Nipponese manner when Japanese restaurants sprang up in the fifties and sixties. (Funny, we'd had Chinese restaurants lots longer than that, and although many of us learned to cook—and love—Chinese food, it never became the fad that Japanese cooking has.) When the wok appeared on the scene, we began to stir-fry in droves, found that raw fish tasted better than it sounded, learned the difference between sushi and sashi, and started to serve Japanese party meals.

SOME LUCKY HUNCHES

For years, many of us had—off and on, as the mood seized us—been making crepes. We made them, without fuss, in 7-inch skillets, although a few of us owned French crepe pans given to us by Aunt Clothilde eight Christmases ago. But it didn't occur to us to make crepes all day every day, nor to stuff them down the gullet of every poor soul we invited to break bread with us. Then someone said to himself, "I'll bet the time is ripe for crepes—and to that end I will invent a gadgety crepe pan and make a mint." It was, and he did. Now, nothing edible is de rigueur unless it lurks inside a crepe. All over America, women are dipping what looks like the bottoms of crepe pans into batter, placing them over the heat, and uttering little yelps of joy as the finished crepe is added to the mile-high stack she is readying for the freezer. Crepe mixes came on the market, ditto frozen crepe batter. And more new crepe pans—stovetop and plug-in electric. Crepes are good. Properly made, crepes are delectable. Served at reasonable intervals, they make a welcome change. But enough, already!

Or take sourdough. There's something about those little crocks of sourdough starter that drives women wild. Sourdough bread, rolls, waffles, pancakes, muffins, sourdough white, whole wheat, rye—they're all exceedingly good and, like all homemade breads, provide a delightful treat. But sourdough, unlike regular yeast breads, is an assertive flavor. A strong, lingering taste. You wouldn't like it if you were required to eat even your very favorite food—rare roast beef, say, or chocolate mousse, or green beans amandine, or whatever is your pleasure—day in and day out. With sourdough, it's the same difference. Like any other good thing, it should be approached with restraint. Try to say, "I think I'll make some sourdough bread today," not because you haven't made any since yesterday, but because you haven't made any since last month.

Or wine and cheese. Two great epicurean delights, wine and cheese, separately or together. A wine-and-cheese party now and then is a splendid way to entertain. But if you have

a set of friends you entertain frequently, and you entertain them frequently with wine and cheese instead of the meal they have every right to expect when they're invited for dinner, and they entertain you in the same fashion, you're all going to run through several sets of friends with amazing rapidity.

End of sermon—the text of which was, in case you overlooked it, "Thou shalt exercise ordinary common sense in the kitchen."

TURNING BACK THE SANDS OF TIME

At one time, all bread was made at home. (But not always baked at home—community ovens have been used by many peoples, through many stages of civilization.) Then for a time, in this country at least, virtually no bread was made at home, except on more remote farms. Now we've swung back to a happy in-between. More and more women—men, too—are experiencing the enormous satisfaction of making bread at home, and their families and friends are learning the pleasures of eating the homemade loaves and buns and rolls and sweet breads. Where once the home cook might have dug her toe in the dirt and admitted she made her own bread, now she brings it to the table with her head high, exuding justifiable pride from every pore. All over America, the air is filled with the incomparable aroma of baking. Once again, fashion has come full circle—or, more accurately, what was once necessity has today become the thing to do. It couldn't have happened to a finer food.

The back-to-the-good-old-days trend is spreading in other directions, too. Women's magazines that once pushed galantine of duck or saddle of lamb printaniere for dinner parties are now extolling the virtues of homemade sausage and baked beans with brown bread. Cheered by their success with breads and the sense of accomplishment breadmaking gives them, women who had never baked before are trying their hands at from-scratch cakes and pies, hot biscuits, doughnuts, tender waffles, dozens of other delights they had no idea could be so wonderfully good.

Home (or community) gardens have become popular, too, with a multitude of direct and collateral benefits. Fresh produce is the chief one, of course—you haven't lived until you've cut your own tender young asparagus and rushed it to pot and then to table. To use up all those lettuces and radishes and tomatoes and cucumbers, families everywhere are adopting the West Coast custom of starting the meal with salad, a double-dose benefit—vitamins in their optimum form plus the fact that a salad starter tempers the appetite for heavier, richer foods, and so helps weight control.

The rash of produce from those gardens is leading to another revival, home preserving—canning, freezing, drying, pickling—which, when properly done, not only provides food for the months ahead, but a kind of family pride rarely experienced. As for collateral benefits from the garden, there's all that fresh air and sunshine, as well as the cleansing experience of working with your hands that many of us have never known before.

Who can tell—at the rate we're going backward into the old-now-new ways of living, tomorrow's chicken in every pot may come from the coop in every backyard. Whether or not that happens, whether or not we reverse the trend and it becomes again the fashion to spend as little time as possible in the kitchen and no time at all in the garden, we have learned a wonderful thing to know: that it's not the costliness of food that makes it impressive, but a combination of the best possible ingredients with roll-up-your-sleeves work and the seasoning of love that makes a dish great, a meal an accomplishment.

WAFER PAPER

A very thin, crisp, paperlike material. Edible, it is made of fine flour and water, lightly sweetened and flavored. It is sometimes used as a base for very light, delicate, and airy desserts, making them more stable for serving.

WAFERS

When concerned with eating, the word has two allied meanings: 1) a thin, round, crisp cookie and 2) a small, flat candy. Cookie wafers often accompany a dessert such as ice cream, mousse, or pudding to the table. Candy wafers—most often flavored with peppermint, sometimes with fruit juices—may be plain or chocolate-covered, and are served as an after-dinner sweet or a snack.

WAFFLE IRONS: see special feature: YOU CAN'T WORK WITHOUT TOOLS

WAFFLES

Quick breads that gain their honeycombed appearance from the utensil in which they are baked, waffles are served—with butter and maple or fruit syrup—at breakfast or brunch, as a base for main-dish foods in cream or other sauces, and—often with whipped cream and/or fruit—as a dessert. Most often made with white flour, they may have whole grains or cornmeal in the batter as well, be sprinkled with nuts or sesame seeds or crumbled crisp bacon before being baked. Chocolate or chocolate chip waffles, a dessert or snack item, are most often served with ice cream, gingerbread waffles with lemon sauce and/or sour cream or softened cream cheese.

Each European country has its particular kind of waffle. The Belgian waffle, for example, served with strawberries and whipped cream, has been a favorite in this country since the 1963 World's Fair in New York, where they were served. French waffles—gaufres—are very light and crisp. Swiss ones—bricelets—are made in the form of a small ball that flattens in the special waffle iron as it cooks. Scandinavians love waffles. In Sweden a special day, March 25, is dedicated to them, and the delicious Scandinavian waffles—they are heart-shaped—are served at one or more of the meals on that day.

When you make waffles, follow the recipe in a good cookbook or in the recipe leaflet that came with your waffle maker. Leftover batter can be refrigerated, or bake it and freeze the resulting waffles for a later breakfast or to serve as a base for a quickly creamed food (dried beef, leftover chicken, pork or veal, tuna or salmon) for a busy-day supper. See also PANCAKES.

WALDORF SALAD

Created by the chef of the Waldorf-Astoria for the hotel's opening late in the nineteenth century, waldorf salad is made of diced apples and celery and chopped walnuts, bound with mayonnaise. Today there are many variations, created by compatible additions such as chicken, tunafish, pineapple, seeded or seedless grapes, raisins, miniature marshmallows, dates, mandarin orange sections.

WALNUT OIL: see OILS, SALAD AND COOKING

WALNUTS

There are two kinds of walnuts, the native American black walnut and the more familiar English—actually Persian in origin—walnut.

Black walnuts. The tree on which these grow is handsome—a native American nut tree—and its wood as well as its fruit is much sought after. The flavor of the black walnut is richly exotic, and so strong and persistent that its uses in cooking are limited. Its love-it-or-leave-it taste is delicious to some, off-putting to others. Various other nuts lend subtle flavor to foods in which they are incorporated, but the flavor of black walnuts is overpowering, disguising any other with which it is combined.

Difficult to shell—unlike their English cousins—black walnuts are usually sold shelled, in cans or, more often, in small plastic bags. Because the inside of the shell is an intricate arrangement of small chambers, undamaged halves cannot be obtained, so black walnuts are always sold as bits and pieces.

The nuts have been known in this country for over a thousand years, as evidence found in prehistoric Indian mounds in Ohio proves. The tree grows in the eastern part of the country from Maine to Florida, and as far west as Minnesota. The nuts were widely used and very much appreciated by the country's early settlers.

Like pine nuts, black walnuts are seldom eaten out of hand. Use them to flavor cakes and cookies, in the stuffing for such strong-flavored birds as wild duck and guinea hen, and in a delicious confection for lovers of the flavor, black walnut brittle. Store in a covered container in the refrigerator and buy no more than you will use in a short time—they are oily, and the oil turns rancid more rapidly than is true of other nuts.

One cup, or slightly less, of the nutmeats can be had from ⅓ pound of the nuts in shell. One ounce yields about 195 calories.

English walnuts. Almost every habitable portion of the world has walnut trees of one kind or another. It is believed they have been growing some nine thousand years; evidence in the remains of Swiss lake dwellings, dating to 7000 B.C., shows that the nuts formed a part of the food of those early peoples.

The Romans enjoyed the nuts and, considering them a gift from the gods, felt that they brought good luck, good health, and general well-being to those who ate them. In those times the best walnuts came from Persia. The Romans carried them to England, where the Old English word for "foreign" was combined with the word for "nut" to give them their name, corrupted now to "walnut." The English had a high regard for them, and sent them with settlers to be planted in all their colonies.

Growing wild, walnuts are small, difficult to crack, and often contain bitterly unpalatable meat. But they were bred long ago for size and flavor. Today's english walnuts are comparatively large, not hard to crack, and each contains two handsome, intricately lobed meats. Although there is a thin inner skin, walnuts are seldom blanched. The skin is very difficult to remove, and does not in any way affect the flavor.

Walnuts are eaten as they come from the shell, or may be toasted or salted. They are used broken or chopped in many kinds of foods from appetizers to sweets. Grated or ground, the nuts substitute for flour in many tortes. Pickled walnuts and walnut catsup are two condiments made from the nuts. Walnut oil is considered by many cooks, especially the French, as the greatest of the salad oils.

California, with more than 100,000 acres of walnut trees, produces the world's largest crop. The nuts may be purchased in bulk in the shell, or shelled in cans or jars or large and small plastic bags. They can be had as whole halves, or chopped, or as broken bits and pieces—the least expensive. In buying walnuts in the shell, shake them—if they rattle very freely, they may be old and dry. Store shelled nuts, closely covered, in the refrigerator. One pound of walnuts in the shell will yield about ½ pound of nutmeats, measuring about 2 cups. One ounce of english walnut meats provides about 192 calories.

WATER

We seldom consider water as an ingredient or as a nutrient, but it is both. Indeed, our bodies are made up preponderantly of water, as are most of the foods we eat. To give you an idea of foods' water content, here are some examples:

food	water content
ground chuck	53 percent
butter	15.5 percent
whole wheat bread	36.4 percent
sweet corn	72.4 percent
cucumbers	95.1 percent
orange, sliced	86.4 percent
rice, cooked	70.3 percent
macaroni, cooked	64.1 percent
tuna salad	69.8 percent
plums, whole	86.6 percent

Those figures give you a rough understanding of the part water plays in our everyday diet. There are few foods whose water content is low. See also the special feature: NUTRITION NOTEBOOK

WATER CHESTNUTS

Used as a vegetable, the water chestnut is in reality the bulb of an Asian water-growing plant. About the size of walnuts, water chestnuts have a rough brown outer skin and a crunchy white, mildly sweet meat. Available canned or fresh (the fresh usually only in Oriental neighborhoods), water chestnuts can be used in all sorts of Chinese and Japanese dishes, and in many of our own favorites, too. Wherever nuts are appropriate, water chestnuts are as well. Try them slivered, in place of almonds, in dishes that call for those nuts. Fresh ones must be peeled—somewhat difficult—and can be stored in a bowl of water in the refrigerator up to 4 days. Canned water chestnuts keep well on cupboard shelves; after opening, store as you would fresh ones.

Water chestnuts provide very small amounts of vitamins and minerals; there are 25 calories in four of the nuts. Water chestnut flour, available only in Oriental markets, is used to thicken sauces in Chinese cooking.

WATER JACKET

A pan into which other, smaller pans filled with food are placed. Water is poured into the outer pan, and the whole business placed in the oven to cook. Because the water jacket provides steam, the food in the smaller containers remains moist. Custards and other custardlike dishes are always baked in a water jacket. In French cooking, the water jacket is a *bain marie*.

WATERCRESS: see SALAD GREENS AND PLANTS

WATERFOWL: see GAME

WATERMELONS: see MELONS

WAX BEANS: see BEANS

WAX PAPER

Thin paper coated on both sides with paraffin. It is used to cover dishes to be refrigerated and to line baking pans. It is not as much used today as it was before foil came on the market.

WEDDING CAKES

At one time there were two cakes at every wedding reception of any size. There was the towering bride's cake, made of a white batter and suitably frosted and decorated, and the groom's cake, made of a spice-molasses batter with fruit, often with rolled-out almond paste in lieu of frosting. Guests ate the bride's cake, were given pieces of the groom's in small, decorative boxes to take home and "sleep on for good luck."

Today, the groom's cake seems to have fallen into disfavor at most weddings. Now there is only the big white cake, called not the bride's, but the wedding cake. Bride and groom together cut the first slice. Once both cakes were made at home, but nowadays the single cake is usually ordered from a caterer or bakery.

WEIGH, WEIGHTS

If you were a European home cook, you could not function without a kitchen scale, as most recipe proportions are expressed as weights. Here, usually it is only meats for which weight is given in recipes, because we buy them by weight. (See also special features: MEASURING UP TO METRIC and THE HOME COOK'S NEW MATH.) If you or any member of your family is on a weight-loss or other diet you may need a scale, as diet portions of food are often called for by weight rather than measure.

WELL

Sometimes a recipe will direct you to place the sifted or otherwise combined ingredients into a bowl or on a pastry board, then "make a well in the dry ingredients." What the recipe is asking for is a hole: push the dry ingredients away from the middle of the pile, so that you create a depression in the center of them. Then into this depression place the eggs or liquid ingredients or whatever the recipe calls for. By this method it is easier to combine the dry ingredients with the liquid and/or eggs, a little at a time, than if you simply dumped them on top.

WELSH RAREBIT (RABBIT): see RAREBIT

WESTPHALIAN HAM

A German air-dried ham, spiced and with an assertive flavor, much resembling the Italian prosciutto. Cut in very thin slices. Sometimes ready-sliced westphalian ham can be found, packed in plastic bags, in supermarket cold-cut cases. It can be served, as prosciutto is, with fruit such as melon or figs, as an appetizer.

WHALES

During World War II, when food was rationed, whale meat appeared in some butcher shops and markets. It is still available frozen, but not widely distributed, for those who developed a taste for it. Not many people did, strangely, even those who enjoy wild game. The meat, which is tough, must be cooked in liquid or braised, and even so requires a long cooking period for tenderizing.

WHAT DOES IT MEAN WHEN THE RECIPE SAYS...?: see page 444

WHAT'S IN A FOOD'S NAME: see page 259

WHEAT

Grown originally in the fertile Euphrates valley thousands of years ago, wheat was probably the first grain to be brought in from the wilds and cultivated. It is now grown throughout the world, and is the most important grain everywhere except in the Far Eastern countries. Demeter, Greek goddess of the fields and fertility, is often depicted holding a sheaf of wheat.

In this country, early colonists brought wheat with them, but found that the eastern seaboard was far better suited to the growing of native corn. When the frontier was opened, however, pioneers learned that the wide plains of the Midwest were ideal for wheat-growing. See also CEREALS, GRAINS, and FLOUR.

WHEAT GERM: see FLOUR

WHEY

By-product of cheesemaking, whey is the thin part of the milk remaining after the curds, the thicker part, have been removed. Some whey CHEESE is also manufactured. Most whey, however, is further separated, the fattier parts being used in the making of butter, the remainder fed to livestock.

You may have noticed in milk that has soured that the separation of curds, rising to the top of the container, and whey, the watery material at the bottom, takes place without human intervention, although it is accomplished mechanically in cheese factories. We have it on the best authority, that of Ms. Muffet, that a dish of home-separated curds and whey was once considered a delicacy.

WHIP, TO: see page 449

WHIPPED BUTTER: see BUTTER

WHIPPED TOPPINGS: see TOPPINGS, DESSERT

WHIPPING CREAM: see CREAM

WHISKEYS: see LIQUORS

WHITE BEANS: see BEANS

WHITE BREADS: see BREADS

WHITE PEPPER: see HERBS AND SAVORY SEASONINGS

WHITE POTATOES: see POTATOES

WHITE SAUCE

A simple sauce of many uses, made of fat (usually butter), flour, and milk. Neither butter nor flour is browned. Although the term "white sauce" covers other blond sauces, such as velouté (made in part with stock), the term specifically means the sauce we all make so regularly that we can do it with our eyes shut. If it makes you any happier, you may call this sauce béchamel, although a good chef traditionally makes his béchamel with at least part cream; simple white sauce is made with milk.

The offhand cook makes white sauce by melting butter, stirring in flour (using a whisk) and letting it bubble, then gradually adding cold milk, whisking madly throughout. The less-experienced cook will make the butter-flour ROUX and gradually add hot milk, whisking as she goes. The hot milk prevents lumping so long as brisk stirring takes place while it is added. The Nervous Nellie cook makes white sauce in a double boiler as an added precaution.

If you have problems. White sauce is not delicate and can take a fair amount of monkeying with. If it's too thick, thin with more milk, added a little at a time. If lumpy, strain it. If too thin, thicken with beurre manié (see BUTTER). If it must wait awhile, place over hot water; do not cover, but float a little milk or melted butter on top to keep a skin from forming. If it must wait a long time, cool, then refrigerate; if it is to wait a very long time, freeze it. It's not a fussy sauce.

Three-ways good. Versatile white sauce has many uses. *Thin* white sauce is used in making cream soups. *Medium* white sauce is used to cream foods—meat, fish, poultry, vegetables. *Thick* white sauce is the hold-it-together ingredient in croquettes and soufflés. These are the standard proportions for the three kinds:

type	fat	flour	liquid
thin	1 tablespoon	1 tablespoon	1 cup
medium	2 tablespoons	2 tablespoons	1 cup
thick	3 tablespoons	3 tablespoons	1 cup

If you are following a recipe that calls for 4 tablespoons of flour and 4 of fat in the thick sauce, use them—some foods require the addition of considerable backbone to make them stand up and behave properly.

All white sauces are seasoned with salt and white pepper—black pepper shows up as little "dirty" specks. In addition, a wide variety of seasonings can be incorporated, depending on the use to which the sauce will be put: onion or garlic juice, snipped parsley, chives, herbs of several sorts.

WHITE STOCK

The stockpot, simmering forever on the back of the stove, is a thing of the past—except, perhaps, in restaurants in France, where the chef will not allow himself to be weaned from the ways that were good enough for grandpa. Nevertheless, fine recipes insistently call for stock, rather than broth or consommé from a can, the substitutes many of us use today.

Some of us, some of the time, still make stock when we want a special-occasion food to be just as it ought to be. Against such a day, we stockpile bones and carcasses and discarded parts in our freezer, ready to be used when the mood seizes us.

Making white stock. This may be made with veal bones or chicken parts. In a large pot place 4 pounds of veal knuckle bones or 4 pounds of poultry backs, necks, wings, and feet. Cover with cold water; bring to a boil. Drain off and discard the water. Add 4 quarts of fresh cold water and bring slowly to a boil; reduce the heat and simmer, uncovered, 30 minutes. Add 8 white peppercorns, 6 whole cloves, 1 bay leaf, 1 teaspoon thyme, 6 sprigs of parsley, 1 diced medium-size onion, 3 diced ribs of celery, and 1 diced medium-size carrot. Skim the stock and continue to simmer for 3 hours, partially covered. At that point the liquid should be reduced by half. Strain, cool uncovered and, if you are not going to use

it immediately, cover and refrigerate. If you are a plan-ahead cook, the stock may be frozen, preferably in rigid, pint-size containers with well-fitting covers.

Making fish stock (fumet). Use this flavorful fish stock as a base for soups and chowders, or in sauces and aspics. In a pan place 2½ cups cold water, ½ cup chopped onion, ¼ cup chopped carrot, ½ cup chopped celery, 6 white peppercorns, 3 whole cloves, a BOUQUET GARNI, ½ cup dry white wine or 3 tablespoons lemon juice, and 1½ pounds lean fish bones, skins, tails, trimmings, and heads (remove gills). If you have thriftily put away shrimp, lobster and/or crab shells against this occasion, add them. Heat until the liquid begins to simmer; continue simmering, uncovered, 15 minutes—no longer, or bitter flavors may develop. Skim, strain, and refrigerate, covered, unless it is to be used immediately. Or the fumet may be frozen.

WHITE VINEGAR: see VINEGARS

WHITEFISH: see FISH

WHOLE MILK: see MILK

WHOLE WHEAT: see FLOUR

WILD DUCK: see GAME

WILD GOOSE: see GAME

WILD RICE

This is one cereal grass that is used for food but has never been domesticated. Not related to the regular rice, white or brown, that we commonly use, it grows in wet areas near the Great Lakes, just as it has for centuries and—also as it has been for centuries—is harvested by local Indian tribes. They go into the rice swamps in boats, bending over the tall grasses to shake off the ripe kernels into the boat bottom.

Because it is in short supply and because it is difficult to gather, wild rice has always—except to the Indians—been a luxury food. It has an assertive flavor, much liked by some, heartily disliked by others. Fortunately, considering the price at which wild rice sells, it comes close to tripling in volume when it is cooked.

Flavorful, versatile. Plain—that is with butter, pepper, and salt—or seasoned with such herbs as sage or thyme, wild rice is an interesting and unusual side dish to serve in place of white or brown rice, potatoes or noodles with pork, chicken, duck, or any kind of wild game. It is also delicious with shellfish. For flavor variation, stir in sautéed mushrooms and/or onion and green pepper before serving.

Wild rice can be made into a poultry stuffing, into quick breads such as pancakes and muffins. If you wish to tame the flavor—or to economize—combine wild rice half-and-half with white or brown rice; use as you would the unmixed wild rice.

Tips on preparing, cooking. There are often stones and small clumps of dirt and chaff in wild rice, which means it must be well washed. For 2¼ cups of the finished product, wash ¾ cup wild rice in 3 or 4 changes of cold water; remove any foreign matter you see as you wash. Bring 3 cups water and 1 teaspoon salt to a boil. Add wild rice gradually, so boiling will not be stopped. Cover and simmer, stirring occasionally, for 30 to 45 minutes, or until tender and all water is absorbed.

Wild rice is available in packages and bags, uncooked or precooked (instant) and combined with white rice. Store in a covered container in a cool, dry place. Keeps indefinitely. Refrigerate cooked wild rice, covered, up to 5 days.

WILD TURKEY: see GAME

WINE, WINE IN COOKING

We have no record of when or where wine was first made, nor of that inspired soul who first thought, "I'll bet if I added some wine to this sauce it would improve it no end."

Although concoctions have been made for centuries from such unlikely bases as rhubarb, dandelion greens, and mulberries, and dubbed "wine" by their proud makers, wine is made from the grape, the fruit of the vine that carries inside its neat skin all that is necessary for wine-making. Nothing—no yeast, no sugar—needs to be added. Just grapes, crushed and allowed to ferment on their own.

Wines are red, white, or rosé, depending on the grapes from which each is made; they are sparkling or still, depending on the method of making. There are fortified wines, to which brandy (also fruit of the vine) has been added. There are aperitif wines to be drunk before the meal (infinitely more civilized than cocktails, connoisseurs insist), sweet wines to accompany desserts, and many kinds of varying dryness (nonsweetness) to be enjoyed with each of the courses in between. And there are after-dinner wines to be served, in the old-fashioned way, to the gentlemen who remain at the dinner table to discuss business and women after the ladies have retired to the drawing room to discuss business, clothes, men, and other women not present.

Are there special wines to be used in cooking? No. It is not necessary to use the venerable bottles left you by great-uncle Simon in his will, but the rule on cooking with wine is this: do not add to food any wine you would not be willing to drink.

In cooking, wine is a flavoring. If you are not timid about using herbs, onions, garlic, and flavoring extracts, there is no reason for you to be timid about flavoring with wine. And don't be afraid that if you use wine in cooking your guests will stagger away from the table and fall asleep on the living room sofa. Wine in cooking is used with discretion, and besides, most of the alcohol evaporates during the cooking process, leaving only a residue of elegant flavor behind.

You will find on supermarket grocery shelves—not in the alcoholic beverages department—wines processed especially for cooking: dry white, dry red, and sherry. These, however, bear little resemblance to ordinary drinking wine. They have inclusions to keep them from spoiling after they are opened, and they are salted. They will not do for your culinary efforts what plain, unadulterated drinking wine will.

If you begin to use wine in your cooking and fall in love with the improvements it creates, don't let the affair get out of hand. A dinner of pea soup with sherry, beef and mushrooms in burgundy accompanied by cabbage panned in rosé, a salad of pears in white wine gelatin, followed by marsala-flavored custard for dessert is overdoing things to the point of nausea. Wine-cooked dishes are special because they differ distinctly and distinctively from the other foods served at that particular meal.

What goes with what? The old rule is that red wines go with red meats, pork, and game, white wines with fish, poultry, and veal. But that is rapidly being cast aside, along with a number of other worn-out shibboleths. How about coq au vin, for example, that delectable dish of chicken cooked, against the rule, in red wine? Use your judgment and common sense, or follow tried-and-true recipes as a guide for your wine cookery.

Here are some generalizations about cooking with wine to help you get into the swing of things:

- when cooking with wine, bring the dish to the boiling point, and do not cover—this allows the spirits to evaporate, leaving the essential flavor behind; but do not boil

- when you marinate meat in wine (for flavor and/or as a tenderizer), dry the meat well before cooking or it will not brown; this applies even if, later, you will use the wine marinade as a basting sauce

- meats that will eventually have wine added to their cooking sauce should be well browned at the start of their cooking period, before wine is added

- white wine is best with fish—the only part of the old rule that should be adhered to; red wine is too assertive a flavor, and will also stain the flesh of the fish an unpleasant color

- delicate dishes (fillet of sole, for example) can take only a little wine, while more robust ones can stand more (cioppino, beef en daube)

- if a recipe does not call for wine, but you would like to substitute some for part of the liquid, add only a very little at a time, tasting as you go

- be sparing with sherry, which has a strong flavor; make certain what you use is dry sherry, not one of the sweet varieties; soup is the exception, where cream sherry may be used

- when you are making a very tart or a very highly, spicily seasoned dish, omit wine

- taste as you cook—never add so much wine that it drowns out the flavor of the dish's chief ingredient; in dishes with very salty ingredients, add salt to season only at the end of cooking time, if needed

- if you have seasoned a dish with wine and plan on drinking wine at dinner with it, make certain the two are the same wine or at least highly compatible

Laying in supplies. Wine comes in bottles of a surprising number of sizes. The contents—in fluid ounces—of some of these is useful to know, and of some of the others eye-opening. You'll probably never go out to buy a nebuchadnezzar of champagne, for example, unless you plan on throwing a considerable bash.

Bear in mind when you buy wine that the larger bottles are more economical than the smaller ones, provided you will use their contents in a reasonable time. Such a time is, for table or dinner wines, up to 10 days, tightly covered and refrigerated. Sparkling wines, however, will not retain their sparkle longer than a few hours after opening. As a rule, red wines keep better than the white varieties; fortified wines, with their higher alcoholic content (14 to 23 percent), are the best keepers after opening.

Here are the bottle sizes and their capacities:

size	fluid ounces
split (2/5 pint)	6.4
tenth (4/5 pint)	12.8
pint	16
fifth (4/5 quart)	24
quart	32
half gallon	64
gallon	128

Champagne producers have a set of sizes all their own, most of them with fanciful, Bible-oriented names. The government does not allow the largest sizes to be imported. Champagne is bottled in these sizes, with their singing appellations:

size	fluid ounces
split or nip	6 ounces
half-bottle	12.5 ounces
fifth (4/5 quart)	24 ounces
champagne quart	26 ounces
magnum	52 ounces
jeroboam	104 ounces

From vine to bottle. Growing wine grapes and transforming them into wine is a chancy business from start to finish. The grapes will grow in soil that will support very little else, but that is the only easy part. If there is too little rain the vines must be irrigated, but too much rain prevents the grapes from ripening properly because they soak up too much moisture, which results in lowered sugar content. There must be enough sun to develop the natural sugar content, but too much sun causes too-early ripening. Harvest of the grapes is delayed as long as possible to allow for further sugar development, but a too-early or too-late harvest results in an inferior wine. Viticulturists—wine-grape growers—and vintners —wine-makers—need a crystal ball and a great measure of good luck in their very iffy vocation.

Selecting the proper day for the harvest is the most nerve-racking part of the long series of choices the viticulturist must make. The skins of the grapes must be covered with the microscopic yeast organisms, *saccharomyces,* that settle on the grapes as they ripen. If it rains, these are washed away and the harvest must be delayed until a new coating of the yeast settles on the grapes; but with delay comes the risk of frost.

After the grapes are picked, they are hurried to the press. In California, hydraulic presses are used, but in many parts of Europe old hand-presses are still in use. And feet. In Spain, special shoes are supplied to those who trample out the grape juices, but in Italy they cling to the old barefoot method.

The mass of skins, pulp, and juices is known as *must.* In the must, natural fermentation, which converts the natural sugars to alcohol, begins under carefully controlled temperatures to prevent too-rapid or too-slow progress. The period may last from a few days to a few weeks. Then the wine is separated from the lees—the hulls and pulp—and stored in wooden casks for some months. At the end of that time, a second fermentation occurs and any solid particles that remain drop to the bottom of the cask. If necessary, the wine is cleared by dropping a film of egg whites, charcoal, or any of several other substances on the top of the wine; the film sinks gradually to the bottom of the cask, taking impurities with it. Finally, after a briefer period of cool storage, the wine is bottled. And everybody heaves a provisional sigh of relief —provisional because the wine must remain in the bottle for a time before it is possible to say just how good (or not-so-good) it is.

This long and nervous-making process is true only of fine wines. Ordinary wines, jug types and inexpensive bottles, do not receive nearly so much care in the making.

Entertaining via the wine route. A party at which you serve only wine—no "hard" liquor—can be a mellow, enjoyable, and not too costly one. Of course, you have to be a bit choosy about your guests, omitting the fellow who reserves Saturday night as his time to throw as many martinis as possible into himself, pinch a few females in the early stages, proposition a few in the later ones, and finally fall flat on his face and require carrying home or putting away in the host's guest room. Instead, invite only those who will enjoy wine from the beginning of the evening to the end of it, before, during, and after the meal.

Or you may decide to have a wine-tasting party, and skip the meal entirely. Offer guests two or three or four wines that have something in common; they can choose the one they prefer, or put an order-of-cost evaluation on all, or simply enjoy them and forget the pretensions to expertise. You might offer wines from several places, but made from the same grape—reislings from Alsace and California, for example—or differing brands from the same region, or several of the same kind, but from different vintages (years). Put out a pitcher of water, breadsticks, thin slices of french bread, and some hard but not strong cheese to nibble (clear the palate, professional wine-tasters would say) between tastings. If you wish to, offer a buffet supper after the tastings are complete, or simply allow people to go their own way in search of dinner, as after a cocktail party.

Or entertain friends with a wine and cheese party, offering only one or two kinds of wine and an assortment of cheeses with the necessary bread and crackers.

WINE JELLY

A gel, stiffened with gelatin or pectin, made of white or red wine, often flavored with herbs. To be served as a garnish or condiment with meats and poultry.

WINE VINEGAR: see VINEGARS

WINTER MELONS

A kind of squash, much used in the Chinese cuisine. It is large, white of skin and yellow of seed. The Chinese make it into winter melon soup, and incorporate chunks of it in various mixed dishes. It can also be pickled.

WINTER SQUASH: see SQUASH

WOKS: see special feature: YOU CAN'T WORK WITHOUT TOOLS

WOODCHUCK: see GAME

WOODCOCK: see GAME

WOODRUFF

A sweet herb used, in Europe, to flavor fruit and wine combinations. Its most familiar use is in May Wine, a young German white wine in which the herb has been macerated.

WORCESTERSHIRE SAUCE

Once in this country the private preserve of one company, but now made by several, worcestershire sauce is thin, spicy, dark brown. Its flavor comes from its "secret blend" of ingredients, which may include anchovies, onions, soy sauce, garlic, molasses, and a dozen more. It is served with meats and used to flavor stews, meat pies, soups, and various sauces and dressings.

XAVIER

A delectable clear, unthickened soup, named to honor Count Xavier of Saxony. Little cheese dumplings always garnish it.

XENIUM

A gift of fine food and/or wine, presented to a guest or stranger in one's home. (Perhaps, turned around, the forerunner of the hostess present often brought by guests today?) In other times, the gift was a freewill offering, but in the medieval era the giving of such a gift was compulsory.

XERES

The French word for sherry, derived from the Spanish town, Jerez, where sherry wine originated. The Xeres cocktail—sherry served with orange bitters and ice—makes a pleasant preprandial drink for those who prefer something not too heavily alcoholic before the meal.

XXXX

Appears on the label of boxes of confectioners sugar. XXX was used on powdered sugar, not as finely pulverized as confectioners. Now the powdered type is seldom available, and confectioners takes its place in most recipes (see SUGAR).

XYLITOL

This is a sugar substitute. Although most sugar substitutes have as one of their attributes a far lower calorie count than sugar, this is not true of xylitol, which provides the same number of calories—and the same sweetness—as sugar. However, it is claimed that unlike sugar, xylitol will not cause tooth decay. It is still under investigation as this is written.

YAMS

A tuber that grows beneath the soil at the root of a tropical vine. Although yams and sweet potatoes are different, and come from two distinct plants, the flavors are very much alike and, when the two are cooked, it is almost impossible to tell one from the other. Yams can be as small as a white potato, or they may be as much as 8 feet long and weigh up to 100 pounds—not exactly the vegetable that one brings home from the market for tonight's dinner.

Yams are a diet staple in many tropical countries. Here they can be bought only in some markets in Spanish-speaking neighborhoods. What many of us call and buy as yams are really a kind of sweet potato, one with a moist orange flesh and a dark rose-brown skin. See also SWEET POTATOES.

YEAST

A unicellular microorganism used as a leavening agent in baked foods, particularly various breads, and in beer. It is available as compressed cakes or in the dry, granular form originally developed for the armed services so that fresh bread could be baked wherever the men went. For a lengthy discussion of yeast and its properties and uses, see BREADS and LEAVENING AGENTS.

YELLOW CROOKNECK: see SQUASH

YELLOW-EYED PEAS: see BEANS

YIELD

The number of individual portions a recipe makes. Once cookbooks did not offer the home cook this useful piece of information, but virtually all published today give yields for each recipe. See the special feature: THE HOME COOK'S NEW MATH.

YOGURT

Also spelled yoghurt, yoghourt, yagourt, yogoort, and in a variety of other ways, yogurt is fermented milk of a custard-like consistency. Here it is made of whole or partially skimmed cows' milk, but in the various countries that knew the product long before we did, it may be made of the milk of sheep, goats, camels, or water buffalo.

The food has been known in countries of the Middle East for hundreds of years; it is only since 1940 that we have used it here. The culture responsible for yogurt's flavor and consistency was isolated by the head of the Pasteur Institute in France at the beginning of the twentieth century; he was awarded a Nobel prize for his discovery. Until that point, yogurt making was a hit-or-miss proposition, achieved by adding a bit of leftover yogurt to fresh milk and waiting to see what would happen. Now, however, it can be precisely made.

A good source of calcium, yogurt contains the same nutrients as the milk from which it is made. Yogurt is much like dairy sour cream, because both are cultured, but it contains fewer calories. Plain yogurt made with skim milk yields 125 to 150 calories per cup as opposed to sour cream's approximately 485, and is often used—by those who are watching their weight as well as those who enjoy its flavor—

in dishes where sour cream is called for. Fruit-flavored yogurts, often used as dessert or in making various desserts, provide from 260 to 350 calories per cup.

Yogurt is easily digested and its lactic acid content helps in the digestion of other foods. Use the tangy product as a sauce for fruit and vegetables, in salad dressings, and in many cooked dishes—curries, for example. As is true of sour cream, yogurt requires a brief cooking time at low heat or it will separate. It is also used in baking—consult a good general cookbook for pies, cakes, and other desserts made with yogurt. Or simply have a cup of wholesome, nutritious yogurt in place of lunch.

If you wish, you can make yogurt at home. Use a little of the commercial product as a starter, or a package of yogurt culture, which is available at health food stores. For accuracy —and accuracy is necessary for satisfactory results—you will also need a thermometer. The milk you use may be as lean as skim or as rich as half-and-half. Heat a pint of it to 180° F. on the thermometer. Cool it to between 105 and 110°F. Stir into it very thoroughly 3 tablespoons plain, unflavored yogurt or a package of yogurt culture. Place in jars, and put the jars into an oven preheated to 100°F. Cover the jars immediately. Milk mixed with yogurt should reach the desirable consistency in 3 to 4 hours, but that mixed with yogurt culture may take 7 to 8 hours. Check every 30 minutes or so.

Electrical yogurt makers with temperature control are available, and you may want to buy one if you become enchanted with making your own. If you wish fruit in the yogurt, have it ready—sweetened and slightly warmed, in the bottom of the jars before you add the milk. And don't forget each time you make a batch to save a little of the yogurt to use as starter for the next batch.

YORKSHIRE PUDDING

Made of a batter very like that used for popovers, yorkshire pudding is Britain's traditional accompaniment for roast beef. It may be poured over the meat drippings in the roasting pan, into a pan in which some of the meat drippings have been placed, or baked separately in custard cups—in which case the batter usually has some meat drippings beaten into it for flavor.

Cut in squares or as individual servings, serve yorkshire pudding piping hot, with roast beef and its gravy. With such a meal, no potatoes, pasta, or rice are required.

YOU CAN'T WORK WITHOUT TOOLS: see page 553

YOUR PARTNER IN THE KITCHEN: see page 92

ZABAGLIONE

Of Italian origin, this is a custard beaten over hot water until it is thickened; it is sweetened with sugar, flavored with wine —most often marsala. Serve as a dessert or a dessert sauce.

ZANTES: see RAISINS

ZEST

The thin, outer peel of citrus fruit, which contains the oils of the fruit and its sharpest flavor. Remove from the fruit in small pieces with a very sharp knife, taking only the very outer surface. Or use a zester, a small gadget with a wooden handle and a business end that has little holes in it. Drawn over the skin of the orange, lemon, or lime, it removes only the zest, leaving the rest of the peel behind.

ZIEGEL: see CHEESE

ZITI: see PASTA

ZINC: see special feature: NUTRITION NOTEBOOK

ZUCCHINI: see SQUASH

ZUPPA INGLESE: see page 454

ZWIEBACK

A slice of twice-baked bread, crisp and slightly sweet. The dough, yeast-raised, sweetened, and flavored with a little lemon and a little cinnamon, is baked as a loaf, cooled, and sliced. The slices are returned to the oven and baked at a low temperature until they dry out and take on a light golden brown color.

THE SAVVY COOK

There are tricks in this, as in every trade—here are new and better ways, bright-easy ideas, make-do tips and tidbits of insiders' know-how to lend you a hand in the kitchen

If you are in the food business—raising it, selling it, cooking it, writing about it—you are asked a great many questions, and you are expected to consult the index file in your head and come up with the answers on the spur of the moment.

At the meat counter: Why is some of this ground beef brown and some, in other packages, bright red? On the phone: I was making homemade mayonnaise according to your recipe and it curdled—now what? In the market, in front of the shelves holding coffee: Coffee is so high these days, isn't there any way to make it go farther without making it weaker? At the greengrocer's: How do you tell when a peach or a nectarine is ripe? And from a small boy who has just learned what the word "cannibal" means: Have you got a recipe for cooking humans?

After a while it dawns on you, quite reasonably, that if one person seeks an answer, there are bound to be others plagued by the same question. So here is a random batch of kitchen Qs, with their appropriate As.

But first, before we lose track of them, let's deal with the questions above.

ground beef: Check the last-day-of-sale date on the packages. If the brown package's date is today, and the red's the day after tomorrow, the brown is a bit elderly. But if both dates are the same, it's likely that the brown package was exposed to air longer before wrapping than the red one.

mayonnaise: Beat in a tablespoon of boiling water. If that doesn't work, beat an egg yolk in a separate bowl, then very slowly beat the curdled mayonnaise into it.

coffee: Chemistry uses a process called "sequential extraction" that works for coffee brewing. Into the filter of an automatic drip coffee maker, measure 6 coffee measures (or 12 level tablespoons) of coffee. Pour in 18 ounces of boiling water and allow it to run through completely. Repeat with 18 ounces more boiling water. When that has run through completely, pour in 12 ounces of boiling water. Now, in the carafe, you have 8 cups (coffee cups, that is, not measuring cups) of the beverage, brewed with the amount of coffee that will make only 6 cups by the usual method. The 8 cups will be equally as strong as the 6. Glass measuring cups are marked in fluid ounces—use a large one to measure the water.

peaches and nectarines: Press gently with the ball of your thumb on either side of the "seam"—the crease that runs down one face of the fruit from stem- to blossom-end. If there is a little give, a slight softness, the fruit is ripe.

humans: No. A flat, unequivocal no. (Restrain the impulse to make a funny, such as "Braised with onions might be good," or "Had you thought of spit-roasting?" You never can tell what a kid, particularly a boy kid, has in mind.)

ON THE THRIFTY SIDE

Our family loves veal, but the price is out of sight. Do you know any recipes that make a little veal go a long way?

Stews, ragouts, and goulashes—any meat-plus-vegetable dish—stretch the meat. If you're speaking of veal cutlets or scallops, there's no way to stretch these other than giving everyone a very small helping. But there's a good substitute. Halves of a boned chicken breast or slices of turkey breast (they come ready-sliced and packaged as "cutlets") can be used in any recipe calling for veal cutlets or scallops. Place on a board between two sheets of wax paper and pound very thin with a meat mallet.

We all love cheese, but it's getting more and more expensive. How can I save money on it?

Don't buy packaged slices or, worse, singly wrapped slices. Buy whole pieces and, using a wire cheese cutter, slice it yourself. If your youngsters are devoted to American cheese, as many are, buy the pasteurized process cheese spread in loaves, rather than regular American. It works well in grilled cheese sandwiches, and also in that excellent meatless main dish, cheese strata. (Pep up the egg-milk mixture with onion powder, mustard, and worcestershire.)

Even tuna, which our family enjoys and which I use often for economy meals, is going up in price. Any suggestions?

Buy chunk light rather than solid-pack white for casserole dishes—same nutrients, same flavor, lower price. For sandwiches, use the flaked kind. Have you thought of trying canned mackerel on your family? The flavor is excellent—use it in place of tuna, or substitute it for half the tuna a recipe calls for.

Heavy cream is very costly, and very high-calorie, too. My family enjoys whipped-cream desserts and none of them but me has to worry about gaining weight. How about whipped evaporated milk? I know it's cheaper, but how is it from the calorie standpoint?

You'll save on both counts. Evaporated milk costs only about half as much as heavy cream, and the calorie cost is even lower—only about one-eighth as much as heavy cream, ounce for ounce.

I have a family of milk drinkers. There are seven of us, so you can imagine what the milk bills are. I do use reconstituted nonfat dry milk for cooking, but the children and my husband refuse to drink it. Is there any way to improve the flavor?

Mix the two—half reconstituted nonfat dry milk, half regular homogenized milk. They shouldn't be able to tell the difference. Once you have them drinking this, cut down the homogenized milk little by little. If you do it very gradually, you'll soon be able to serve a beverage as low as one-fourth homogenized. And you won't be cheating them of nutrients. Only the fat is missing from the dry milk, and we all ingest entirely too much fat, anyway.

Ham is our whole family's favorite meat, but we simply can't afford it more often than once in a great while. Are there any alternatives that might satisfy our ham cravings?

Picnic butt and shoulder rolls are considerably cheaper than ham and have equally good flavor. Also, shop carefully at the meat counter among the boned hams, which are the most expensive of all. Several packing companies now put out "preformed" hams that look very much like the expensive boneless ones. They are made of ham pieces pressed into the familiar shape, and are considerably less expensive but retain that good ham flavor. In the canned meats section, look for small, tuna-size cans of chopped ham, excellent for ham-salad sandwiches or for stirring into scrambled eggs, or in casseroles. At the refrigerated meats counter, you may find packages of thin ham "steaks" (these, too, are preformed ham) put out by one packer. The flavor is very good. Finally, in the same section, look for refrigerated canned ham patties, ready to brown and serve.

Can you tell me any good way to stretch wild rice? We all love it, but it costs an arm and a leg.

You can stretch it with brown rice, ¾ brown to ¼ wild, this way: Melt two tablespoons butter in a skillet. Add the brown rice and sauté in the butter until it turns browner—but watch it, as it burns easily. Then cook the brown rice and the wild rice separately, as the packages direct. Combine the two when both are cooked. Without the browning process, you can use half brown rice and half wild for a satisfactory combination. Adding sautéed onions and mushrooms will stretch such a dish even more, and improve it as well.

We all enjoy morning orange juice, but don't like the frozen kind nearly as well as fresh-squeezed. However, isn't the frozen concentrate cheaper? Also, why do oranges seem less juicy now than they did when I was a child?

Frozen concentrate is considerably cheaper than squeezing oranges yourself. In fact, it's cheaper than the canned or bottled juice, too. Try reconstituting the frozen concentrate in your blender, using refrigerated water rather than that from the tap. The combination of the chilled beverage and the added air the blender beats in improves the taste enormously. As for those juicy oranges from your childhood, they probably had not been refrigerated. Take oranges—all citrus fruit—out of the refrigerator about an hour, or even more, before serving. For the absolute maximum of juice, boil the oranges or other citrus fruits for one minute before squeezing them.

Does it pay to bake bread at home? I'm not crazy about the idea, but I'd do it if it saved money.

It saves a lot. More than half, as a matter of fact. Try baking some to see whether or not you enjoy making it. It's not difficult, and although the process stretches out over a long period, much of that time is taken up with rising, which you don't have to supervise. However, if you find that making bread is a bore or a chore, find other ways to save.

DOWN AT THE GREENGROCERY

I always peel carrots, but the other day I remembered that my grandmother used to scrape them. Which is best?

The point is to remove as little of the carrot as possible. If you peel them with a knife, you're cutting away too much; peel with a swivel-blade vegetable parer, taking off as thin as possible an amount. If grandmother scraped with a knife, she probably got too much, too. To scrape, use a wire brush or a clean metal pot sponge; once over lightly does it. Scraping by this method usually removes the least amount of carrot.

What's the best way to remove corn kernels from the cob for such dishes as fritters and custards?

There's a gadget for this, called a corn stripper, that works very well. Lacking that, stand the ear of corn on a plate, stem (flat) end down. For whole kernels, simply slice them off with a sharp knife. For the milky interior, without the skin, draw the point of a sharp paring knife down the center of each row of kernels; then, with the dull side of the knife, scrape them off the cob.

I've seen a big, knobby brown root called a jimaca, or something like that, in the produce market. What is it?

It's a jicama, a root vegetable from Mexico that grows in semitropical climates. Peel it, cut it into small finger-shaped pieces, and serve it raw with a dip or a rémoulade sauce, or cut it into smaller pieces to include in a tossed green salad. It's very crisp, and has a pleasant, mild flavor. It can also be cooked and mashed, like potatoes.

Are snow peas and Chinese pea pods the same thing? How should they be cooked—both the fresh and the frozen kinds?

They are the same thing, and you can find them frozen (alone or with water chestnuts) all year around, and fresh in produce markets and Chinese specialty food shops during the summer. However you cook them, fresh or frozen, make it brief. Place in a skillet with ¼ inch boiling water and a little butter, return to a boil and simmer no more than 2 minutes. Serve hot with butter or hollandaise sauce, or chill and add to salads. Or add, uncooked, to stir-fry dishes 2 or 3 minutes before the dish is finished.

Recipes often say to peel and seed cucumbers, which is a big nuisance. Now I've come across a recipe tht tells me to peel and seed tomatoes. How?

First the cucumber. Cut off both ends, then take off the thinnest possible layer of skin with a swivel-blade vegetable peeler. Cut in half lengthwise. Now your tool is a teaspoon. Slip the tip under the seed mass at one end and push, zipping the seeds out all at once in no time.

Spear a tomato with a long-handled fork at the stem end. Hold over the lighted burner of a gas stove until the skin sputters and cracks, at which point you can easily peel it off in big pieces. Or drop into boiling water for one minute, then peel the same way—and as easily. With a sharp knife, cut out the stem and core in a cone-shaped piece. With your hands, squeeze out seeds and the juice that surrounds them. There is no way to keep a tomato intact and shapely and completely seed it at the same time.

A recipe I'd like to try calls for onion juice. How on earth do you juice an onion?

As with an orange, cut it in half and ream it on a juicer. (Give the juicer a thorough bath afterwards.) You can also buy onion juice in small bottles, handy where the flavor without the texture is desirable.

When I buy a big melon, a casaba or a honeydew, we can eat only half of it at a time. I enclose the remaining half in foil or a plastic bag and refrigerate it. But it always worries me— should I take the seeds out of the stored half? Or doesn't it matter?

It matters. Leave the seeds in place to help keep the melon juicy and fresh-tasting. However, unless the melon is very ripe, or unless you're going to keep it for more than a day or two, don't refrigerate it. Just store in a cool place.

The other evening, in a natural-foods restaurant, we had a delicious cold soup that I think was made with raw peas. I asked the waiter, but he said he didn't know how it was made. Any ideas?

In a blender, place 2 cups shelled fresh peas or 1 package frozen peas, unthawed but broken up. Add ½ teaspoon salt, ⅛ teaspoon white pepper, ⅛ teaspoon ground cardamom, 1 teaspoon onion juice, 1 large lettuce leaf torn in pieces, and 1 cup chicken broth. Purée. Stir in 1 cup of half-and-half—or, for a richer soup, heavy cream.

How should mushrooms be washed? In an old cookbook, I read something about saving mushroom peelings to add to soup. I've never peeled mushrooms—should I?

Mushrooms are seldom very dirty, but if they are, dunk them briefly in cool, not cold, water. Otherwise, wipe them off with a damp cloth or paper towel. Never peel them—peeling wastes a part of the goodness.

Why does cauliflower turn gray? Am I cooking it too long? It seems to be about the right texture when I cook it.

Are you using an aluminum pan? Cauliflower can turn gray when cooked in aluminum. Switch to a stainless steel or enamel-coated one. Be sure, when you buy cauliflower, that it is nice and white, and that the curd—the white part—is hard. Cook only until tender-crisp, in a proportion of ⅓ milk to ⅔ water for snowy whiteness.

We like stuffed tomato salads, but juice always leaks out of the tomato and makes the salad watery. What should I do?

Prepare the tomatoes in advance. Skin them or not as you prefer; with a sharp knife, cut out a portion of the interior from the stem end. Salt the tomatoes lightly and turn them upside down on several thicknesses of paper towel to drain. Put the salad filling into the tomatoes just before you serve them.

I have recently moved from the east to the west coast. All the mushrooms here look old. I'm used to those nice white mushrooms back home. Here they're brown and sort of shaggy looking. What's wrong with them?

Nothing's wrong. They're simply a different kind of mushroom. The western variety does need a rather more careful scrutiny when you buy them, to make sure they're good. The brown mushrooms—golden cream is their name, but it doesn't describe them very well—are a newer variety. However, western markets do carry the familiar white mushrooms in small containers, like berry boxes. If you don't take to the brown ones, buy the white—there is little if any difference in price.

Can pears be ripened at home? The ones in the store always seem to be green and too hard to eat. And why can't I find frozen pears?

Yes, pears ripen well at home. Put them in a bowl or other open container, or in a bag that is not airtight, and leave them at room temperature until they yield to gentle pressure when you cradle them between your hands. Like all fruit, pears ripen better if there are several, rather than just one.

You can't find frozen pears because there aren't any. Pears do not freeze well—in fact, they don't freeze, period. But they're available fresh almost all year.

I saw some apples in the market labeled "granny smith." My father and grandfather were both apple growers, but I never heard of a fruit by that name. Where do they come from?

Medium-size, green-skinned granny smith apples are shipped from New Zealand to the United States. They are excellent all-purpose apples with crisp white flesh, and they are particularly welcome in our markets because they begin arriving here in May and continue all summer. That's because New Zealand is in the south temperate zone—south of the equator—and when it's winter here, it's summer there.

I know that if you cover fruits with lemon juice they won't turn dark, but is there any other way to keep them from darkening? All that sour lemon juice turns me off.

It isn't necessary to use all that much lemon juice. Dilute the juice of one lemon with one cup water for a solution that will prevent darkening. Or use orange or lime or grapefruit juice if you prefer one of those flavors. Hard fruit, such as apples, can be slipped into a bowl of lightly salted plain water as you cut them up. Or resort to one of the commercial browning inhibitors. They are largely ascorbic acid (vitamin C) and do the job well. Find them shelved near the pectin and other canning products in your market, and follow label directions.

I'm sure my mother used to ripen green tomatoes by setting them on the windowsill, but when I do it they rot before they ripen. What am I doing wrong?

You're doing wrong the same thing your mother did—you're putting them on the windowsill. (You've probably forgotten that besides putting them on the windowsill she also often said, "Pshaw! These tomatoes are no good.") Put them in a bag to ripen. As with other fruit, several will ripen more readily than a single fruit. A plastic bag is fine, but don't put it into direct light, and don't close it airtight. The USDA suggests that the best way of all is to give tomatoes—and peaches, pears, and any other fruit you need to ripen—a friend to help them: a very ripe apple. Ripe apples give off ethylene, a gas that helps unripe fruit to ripen. Be sure that the container or bag is not tightly closed, because that will cause a too-high concentration of carbon dioxide, and retard ripening; also, it may cause too high a humidity, which will encourage spoilage. If you wish tomatoes to ripen very slowly, refrigerate them in their air-circulating bag, without the apple.

Is it true that leaving the avocado pit in an avocado mixture, such as guacamole or cream of avocado soup, will keep the mixture from turning dark?

It won't prevent discoloration, but it will slow it down somewhat. So will the addition of lemon juice to the mixture. But unless you favor avocado so lemon-laden that the lemon is all you can taste, plan on serving avocado mixtures no more than four hours after making them. Even at that point, they will have begun to darken, lemon or not, pit or not.

I made my mother-in-law's lentil soup, and it was done almost three hours before the recipe said it would be. Was there something wrong with the lentils, or was it me?

It was the lentils, not you. But there was nothing wrong with them, either. You probably soaked them, as an old-fashioned recipe would direct. Today's lentils—and this is true of dried peas and beans as well—generally do not need soaking. Read the label on the box or bag and be guided by it.

My little boy, it turns out, is allergic to pumpkin. We all like traditional pumpkin pie for Thanksgiving. Is there any substitute that I can use instead of pumpkin?

Yes, you can use the cooked and mashed flesh of any of the winter squashes—hubbard, banana, butternut, and even acorn. You can also use cooked and mashed sweet potatoes or yams (look up a recipe for the latter two; a slightly different balance of ingredients is needed). But you can substitute the squash measure for measure in your favorite pumpkin pie recipe. However, a warning—pumpkin and squash are very close relatives. If your son is allergic to one he may also be allergic to the other.

Everybody in our family loves green spring onions—scallions, I guess you'd call them. Is there any way to serve them other than just as is, raw, with salt?

Yes, you can braise them in water or chicken broth and serve them hot or cold. (And you can call them spring onions or green onions or scallions—they answer to all three.) Cut off the roots and the ends of the green tops, leaving all the top that is not dried or slimy. Tear off a piece of aluminum foil long enough to fit across the bottom and up the sides of a large skillet with some to spare at each end. Fold the foil in half lengthwise; with a kitchen fork, pierce the foil in a number of places. Fit it into the skillet. Add the scallions, placing them across the foil. Add water or chicken broth to the depth of ¾ inch. Salt lightly if you wish. Bring to a boil; turn down the heat, cover the skillet, and cook until the onions are tender—as much as 30 minutes if they're not all that young. Lift the foil by the ends, holding over the skillet to drain. (This is a good trick with asparagus, too.) Serve the scallions hot with butter or lemon butter, or cold with lemon juice and white pepper, or with vinaigrette.

Sometimes the limes I buy are dark green, sometimes so pale a green they are almost yellow. Are they different kinds?

Not necessarily. As they age, after picking, limes go from dark green to light green to yellow. Actually, the older—yellower—ones will yield more juice than freshly picked limes.

FOWL, FLESH, AND GOOD RED HERRING

I know that liver is good for us, and I'd like to serve it to my family, but they rebel. Any suggestions? Also, in the course of trying to find a way everyone would eat it, I made liver dumplings. They called for ground liver, and I ground it myself. What a mess! Where did I go wrong?

You can make liver very tender and also less strong in flavor by covering the slices with milk and letting them stand (in the refrigerator) up to three hours. Pat the slices dry, dip into flour seasoned with salt, pepper, and a little thyme. Sauté very briefly—the longer you cook liver the tougher and stronger it gets. You're on the right track with liver dumplings. Also a meat loaf or meatballs, substituting ground liver for part of the meat, may be acceptable. Try the family on chicken livers, too; they are the most delicately flavored.

Now, the grinding. We assume you ground it raw. It can't be done that way without reducing the liver to a sort of bloody pudding. Parboil the liver before you grind it—two or three minutes is long enough to firm it up—or sauté it very briefly.

We love anchovies, but sometimes they're very salty. Is there anything I can do to reduce the salt and let the flavor through?

You can soak them in lukewarm water or, even better, in milk. Ten to twenty minutes will do it. Dry well between paper towels.

When I broil sole or similar fish fillets, they always break when I turn them to cook the second side. Even when I use a big, flat pancake turner they break as I flip them over. What am I doing wrong? I try to be very careful.

What you are doing wrong is turning them at all. Broiled fish fillets do not need turning. They will cook through when broiled only on one side. They are done when they lose their translucency and flake easily. Using your big pancake turner, ease them off the broiler pan onto a warm platter or individual plates. Incidentally, broiling is not the best way to cook sole or other lean fillets—they dry out too much by this method, unless you baste constantly. Try poaching them instead, and reserve broiling for steaks of salmon or swordfish, or other fat fish. See FISH for details.

The other night, a friend served us the best pot roast I have ever tasted. It was cooked in foil. I don't know her well enough to ask for the recipe. Can you tell me how?

The foil is the trick. This method of pot-roasting is easy and produces tender meat and the most flavorful gravy imaginable. Brown a 4- to 5-pound pot roast on all sides in a skillet or under the broiler. While it browns, chop 2 small onions, 1 carrot, and a rib of celery. Tear off a piece of heavy-duty foil large enough to encase the meat completely and a bit more to make a double-fold seal. Place the browned meat in the center of the foil and bring up the foil around it, but do not seal. Sprinkle the chopped vegetables over the meat. Add a bay leaf, and sprinkle well with salt and pepper. Now add ½ cup of liquid—water, tomato juice or sauce, dry red wine. Or you can skip the liquid entirely—don't worry, the meat will absolutely not dry out.

Seal the foil airtight around the meat by making a double (drugstore) fold where the two ends of foil meet, and then turn up the sides snugly. Bake in a 275°F. oven for 3½ hours. Don't open the foil to peek during cooking. Pour the accumulated juices into a saucepan, skim off excess fat, and thicken for gravy. An even simpler version, and very good indeed, calls for placing the unbrowned meat on the foil, sprinkling with a package of dry onion soup mix, and proceeding as above. Either way produces a most savory pot roast indeed.

What is that dry, thin, papery covering on a leg of lamb? Should I cut it off or leave it in place?

That parchmentlike membrane is called the "fell." It covers the exterior fat on all cuts of lamb, but is usually removed from all but the leg before the lamb is sold at retail. The fell protects the meat, keeping the wholesale cuts fresh. The flavor of the lamb is not affected whether the fell is left in place or removed. However, if you are going to marinate the leg of lamb, it is best to cut away the fell or it will keep the marinade ingredients from penetrating the meat.

I don't like the idea of leaving bacon at room temperature until it is warm enough so the slices can be separated. Is there any other way to get the slices apart neatly?

Large numbers of slices separate more readily than singles. Count the number of slices you need and separate from the remainder; place the slices to be used into the pan in a block. The heat will make it easy to separate the slices in a few moments. Or separate the slices one by one when they are cold by using a rubber spatula—it takes longer, but it's the way to go if you want only a slice or two.

We like stir-fry beef dishes, and also stroganoff, both of which call for thin slices of raw beef. I use a very sharp knife, but it's still difficult to get uniform slices as thin as I'd like them. Is there a trick to it?

There is. Freeze the meat before you cut it. It does not have to be frozen solid—even partially frozen beef cuts much more easily than meat at room or refrigerator temperature.

My husband is particularly fond of breaded cutlets, both veal and chicken. But my breading always seems to fall off, at least partially, during cooking. Is there a way to prevent this?

Refrigerating the cutlets between breading and cooking will help keep the breading in place. It's also a time saver—bread the meat in the morning instead of just before dinner. Also, make certain that each of the elements of the breading—flour, then egg, then cracker or fine bread crumbs—covers the meat completely, sides as well as top and bottom, before you go on to the next step. Place the breaded cutlets on plate or platter in one layer for refrigeration; don't pile them on top of one another.

I like to sauté some meats in butter, but I'm never sure when the butter is hot enough but not too hot. How can I tell?

Butter goes through three stages in heating—it melts, then foams, then browns. Place the butter in the pan, let it melt and foam. Then add the food immediately after the foam starts to subside and before browning begins. Adding a little cooking oil—one part to three or four parts of butter—helps to slow down the browning of the butter.

The shrimp I cook are often tough, although I cook them only six or seven minutes. What am I doing wrong?

Six minutes should be all right for shrimp in their shell. If you shell them first (which is easier and less messy) place the shelled shrimp in a saucepan, and cover them with boiling water. Put the cover on the pan. Exactly five minutes later, drain the shrimp. They will be cooked to perfection.

Is there any way to cook bacon without standing over it, constantly turning the pieces and pouring off the fat?

Bake it. Place the slices on a rack in a shallow pan. Bake in a preheated 450°F. oven for 10 to 15 minutes. No turning. No pouring off fat—it drains through the rack into the pan.

SWEET AND LOVELY

How long should ice cream store well in a home freezer—ice cream from the market, that is? Ours seems to get grainy after as little as a week or ten days.

In a separate freezer, one that maintains a constant temperature of 0°F. or lower, you can store ice cream about four weeks. Do you have children who are allowed to help themselves? Give them these tips: 1) Get the ice cream out of the freezer and back into it as rapidly as possible. Ice cream that has begun to thaw will refreeze to a grainy texture and develop ice crystals. 2) When some ice cream is removed from a container, stuff the resulting empty space with wax paper or plastic wrap before returning it to the freezer. 3) Always make sure the cover is replaced securely before returning the container to the freezer.

When the fruit is in season, we like to make homemade fresh peach ice cream. I'd like to put bigger chunks of peach in, but the one time we tried it the pieces of peach froze into hard, unpleasant lumps. Is there any way to prevent this?

There is—if you like the flavor of kirsch and don't object to its alcoholic content. Cut up the peaches several hours before you will use them, and pour kirsch over them to cover; let stand. (The kirsch will also prevent the peaches from turning brown.) Drain the peaches and add to the ice cream mixture. Alcohol does not freeze, and it helps to keep the fruit from freezing.

My baked custards turn watery when they cool. What am I doing wrong? Also, I like the flavor of nutmeg in custard, but not the little specks of it. Is there a nutmeg extract?

If you are following all other recipe directions to the letter, it must be that you are cooking the custard too long. Test for doneness with a silver or stainless steel knife blade inserted into the custard about 1 to 1½ inches from the edge of the baking dish. If the knife comes out clean, the custard is done —it will continue cooking for a bit from its own heat, and will firm up when refrigerated. Incidentally, custard made with egg yolks only, rather than whole eggs, will be firmer. And custard made with evaporated milk will be more stable. Dilute with one part water to three parts milk. Yes, there is a nutmeg extract available. You will probably find it only at a specialty foods shop. Use it sparingly.

My mother-in-law calls all cakes "tortes." Isn't there a difference between a cake and a torte?

Cakes are made with flour. In place of all or part of the flour, ground nuts or sifted fine dry bread or cracker crumbs are substituted in tortes. Bonafide tortes call for no flour, but some modern recipes use part flour. However, a cake made with all flour is a cake, Mama.

Why do my cakes, whether made from scratch or a mix, develop a mound like a young mountain in the middle as they bake?

It's possible that the from-scratch cakes have too much flour. This is not possible with mixes, however, so the second diagnosis must be the right one: your oven is too hot. If you are baking the cakes at the temperature the recipe directs, your oven thermostat may be out of kilter. Check it with a separate oven thermometer, or call the electric or gas company or the dealer from whom you bought the stove to send someone to check it.

There are just two in our family. We both like layer cake, but can't get through a whole one before it gets stale. Can I divide the cake and freeze half?

Easily. But do it before you frost it. Freeze one whole layer; cut the second layer in half and fill, stack and frost it just as if it were a whole cake. Thaw the other half and do the same for it up to four months later.

My puddings develop a thick, gummy layer on top when refrigerated, even though I cover them tightly. What's wrong?

We assume you mean egg-and-milk puddings, thickened with flour or cornstarch, and cooked on top of the stove. Covering this sort of pudding isn't enough. While the pudding is hot, press a layer of plastic wrap or a plastic storage bag on the top surface of the pudding, making sure it touches the entire surface, especially all around the sides.

My family likes muffins and quick breads such as orange-raisin or apple-pecan. Mine have good flavor, but the texture is coarse and has a lot of holes. What am I doing wrong?

You're being too good to them, probably—beating them too much. In fact, don't beat them at all. Stir, and then only until the dry ingredients are completely moistened. The batter will look lumpy but the texture of the finished product will be good.

How can I keep the bottom crust of a pie, such as custard or pumpkin, from getting soggy during baking?

There are several ways, none of them perfect. Each good cook swears by her own method—and will go right on swearing by it even if, at the moment, you are eating a piece of her soggy-crust pie. 1) Make the pastry several hours in advance of the filling; roll and fill the pie pan, then chill at least 2 hours. Preheat the oven to 450°F. Bake the pie shell "blind" (see BAKE BLIND) for 7 minutes. Remove, cool completely, pour in the filling, and bake according to recipe directions. 2) As you break the eggs for the filling, save about ¼ of one of the egg whites. Gently rub (with your fingers) all over the bottom and sides of the unbaked pie shell. Add the filling and bake as usual. 3) Bake the pie shell and the filling separately, using pie pans of identical size and depth. Cool separately, then slip the cooked custard into the cooked crust. Though in this way, we hasten to assure you, lies madness.

Why does chocolate turn a nasty gray when stored over a long period—or even, sometimes, a short period? Can it still be used?

That's the fat content (cocoa butter) rising to the surface, which it does when the chocolate is stored in too warm a place, or in summer when every place is warm. The flavor will not be affected unless the chocolate is old as well as having "bloom"—that's what the gray film is called. Use it in any recipe in which the chocolate must be melted, and the bloom will disappear as the chocolate melts.

I usually don't have too much difficulty unmolding gelatin desserts and salads, but I do have trouble getting the food centered on the serving plate, and it resists being moved.

Rinse the serving plate with cold water before unmolding the mixture. Then, if the food is off-center, you can give it a gentle shove and it will slide into place. Rinsing the mold with cold water before you fill it helps gelatin dishes to unmold more easily. So does coating it with a *very thin* film of cooking oil before you fill it.

It would be nice to be able to whip cream several hours before using it to top a dessert, but it always separates. I like to have my whole dinner finished ahead of time when I have company. How can I make the whipped cream hold up?

When you beat the cream, add 1 teaspoon of white corn syrup for each cup of cream (measured before beating). It should hold up for at least three hours. To stabilize it for a longer period (and to use if you wish to pipe whipped cream decorations through a pastry bag), try this. Soften 1 teaspoon unflavored gelatin in 2 tablespoons of cold water. Measure 1 cup of heavy cream; remove 3 tablespoons of the measured cream and scald it. Add to the softened gelatin, stirring until the gelatin is completely dissolved; refrigerate until thickened but not set. Beat until frothy. Beat the remaining cream, adding a few grains of salt, 2 tablespoons confectioners sugar and ½ teaspoon vanilla extract. Fold in the gelatin mixture. If you'd like chocolate whipped cream, melt 1 (6-ounce) bag of semisweet chocolate bits; cool slightly, fold into the finished stabilized whipped cream.

How do professional cooks section oranges and grapefruit so neatly, without including any of the white membrane?

Cover the fruit with boiling water and let stand 5 minutes. Then peel—use a sharp knife, not your fingers. The outer membrane will come away with the peel. Hold the peeled fruit over a bowl. With the knife, cut down to the center along the edge of each membrane that separates the sections, turning the knife slightly at the end of each cut after the first to push out the section so it will drop into the bowl.

BITS OF THIS AND DATA

My poached eggs are never neat. The whites spread all over the pan and stick to the bottom, and the yolks don't get a film over them unless they're overcooked. What's the right way?

In the first place, eggs to be poached must be very fresh. The white of a fresh egg is thick and holds together; the yolk stands high and is well rounded. The chef's way is to poach eggs one at a time in a small saucepan in which a whirlpool is created by stirring the water. This is not, however, very practical when there's a family waiting for breakfast. So try it this way: Spray a skillet with nonstick pan spray. Place water to a depth of 1 inch in the skillet. Add 1 tablespoon white vinegar and 1 teaspoon salt. Bring the water to a simmer. Break each egg into a saucer and slide it into the water. As the eggs cook, baste the yolks gently with the water to form the film over them. Remove with a perforated skimmer, so water will drain away.

I'm not much of a one for gadgets, such as separate choppers for nuts, onions, etc. But there must be a better way to chop an onion than to cut it into slices and then cut each slice into pieces. Is there? How about other vegetables?

There is. Peel an onion and cut it in half lengthwise. Place it on a chopping board cut-side down, with the root end to your left, holding it in place with your left hand. With a sharp knife, cut several slices parallel to the board from tip to, but not through, the root end. Now make several cuts, to but not through the root end, at right angles to the cutting board and to the previous cuts. Now slice the half onion at the root, and neat pieces will fall in front of your knife. For minced onions, make all cuts as close together as possible. For chopped or diced, make the cuts proportionately farther apart.

Cut celery, seeded cucumber, green pepper, and carrots into long, thin strips. Hold a bundle of strips with your left hand. Cut across the strips into small pieces, regulating the size by whether the recipe calls for the vegetable to be minced, diced, or chopped.

Bonus: To acquire a small amount—a tablespoon or two —of parsley, watercress, or chives, hold a bundle of sprigs in your left hand, snip off bits of the vegetable with kitchen scissors.

I had always thought that my peanut-butter-loving kids were stuffing themselves with empty calories, but now I've learned that peanuts are rich in protein. Can you suggest some ways to use them in family meals?

Add chopped peanuts to coleslaw, and to the stuffing for pork chops or chicken. Sprinkle over hot cereal in the morning and over ice cream or puddings at dinner time. Brown halves lightly in butter to dress green beans, broccoli, spinach, or brussels sprouts. Stir into pancake or waffle batter. Stuff celery with a mixture of cream cheese and chopped peanuts. Add to creamed leftover ham or chicken; serve over corn bread. Add to bran muffin or plain cupcake batter. Make a sandwich filling of chopped peanuts, grated cheddar, and crumbled crisp bacon.

Is there a better way to make stale bread and rolls seem fresh than warming them in the oven?

The oven is the right way, but perhaps you're going about it the wrong way. Breads warmed in the oven on a baking sheet or in foil will get warm, but you need dampness to refresh the bread. For biscuits and rolls, dampen a brown paper bag well and put them inside it. For bread, sprinkle the loaf (or part of a loaf) lightly with water, then put it into a brown paper bag. Either way, twist the end of the bag closed and place in a 300°F. oven, 5 to 7 minutes for biscuits or rolls, 15 minutes for bread.

I've joined the great crepes movement, along with everyone else—love to make them, love to eat them, love to serve them to guests. But my platter of ready-to-serve crepes isn't all that appetizing. They taste great, but they're rather tacky looking and tend to come unfolded. Any hints?

Don't try to put too much filling into each crepe, or it's bound to bulge out like a size twenty female in a size twelve dress. Fill a crepe, then position it on the platter or serving dish before you fill another, bucking them snugly against one another for support.

There are several ways to fold crepes. Settle on one that works for you. (See illustrations under main entry: CREPES.) For the *basic fold,* spread the filling on the crepe, then fold each side to the center. For the *envelope fold,* make the basic fold and then turn up the two ends. For the *roll,* spread filling evenly, roll up the crepe jelly-roll fashion. For the *quarter fold,* spread on filling, fold in half, then in half again. For *torte style,* spread each crepe with filling and stack them like a layer cake; cut in wedges to serve.

Is there anything you can do—other than throwing it out—with brown sugar that has hardened into a brick?

If it is really brick hard, grate it as you would cheese on an upright grater, using the medium openings. Or place it in a saucepan, pour over it ¼ cup boiling water for a pound of sugar, and cook over low heat until it is reduced to a syrup. Add more hot water to make it the consistency you like for pancakes or waffles, or add 1 teaspoon vanilla extract and ½ cup heavy cream, and use the resulting sauce for ice cream or plain cake. Next time, store the brown sugar in a metal container with an airtight lid—this will keep it soft.

We're a family of dumpling-eaters—in soups and stews, and sweet ones cooked in a fruit sauce. Is there any way to get the dumpling batter to fall off the spoon in neat, even pieces?

Easy. Before spooning out each dumpling, dip the spoon into the hot liquid—the soup or stew or fruit syrup.

Is it possible to store and reheat leftover pasta so that it seems like fresh-cooked?

Store, covered, in a bowl of cold water, in the refrigerator (up to four days). The water keeps the pasta from hardening and sticking together. When you're ready to use it the second time, drain well, place in a pan, and pour boiling water over it, covering completely. Place over high heat for one minute. Drain and serve. It will not taste exactly like fresh-cooked, because it is not, but it will be acceptable. Or add leftover pasta, which has been stored as above and drained, to casserole or skillet dishes, or (five minutes before the dish is done) to soups and stews.

I like to make casserole dishes in advance, cook them until they are almost done, then refrigerate them to be warmed up at dinner time. But I've lost two good glass casserole dishes by doing this—they cracked when I put them in the oven. Is there a safe way?

Don't preheat the oven. Set the casserole in the oven, then turn it on. As the oven warms up, it will gradually warm the dish as well. It's the sudden change from refrigerator to hot oven that sometimes makes glass crack. In any case, it is never necessary to preheat the oven for casserole and other baked dishes, either to cook them or to warm them. However, despite the information given by energy-savers who don't understand cooking, it is absolutely necessary to preheat the oven for any food that is leavened with baking powder, soda, or yeast. Also preheat for pies, to prevent the crust from becoming soggy.

How do you cut up sticky things, such as dates and prunes? And how about marshmallows for fruit salad?

Put dates into the freezer for a short time. Partially frozen, they cut easily. Dip knife or kitchen scissors (easier with scissors) in hot water as you cut up prunes, in cold water to cut up marshmallows, dipping as often as necessary.

I make a date-nut cake that is rich enough so that it doesn't need frosting. To dress it up, I like to sprinkle it with confectioners sugar. However, the sugar turns gray, as it doesn't on bundt cake, for instance. Why?

That happens because the date-nut cake is very moist. Sprinkle the cake with sugar just before you bring it to the table. Or give the cake a thin glaze instead of using sugar.

FILE IT SO YOU CAN FORGET IT

These are a few—only a very few—of the food-related shortcuts and how-to ideas that are helpful to the home cook.

Unless you have the kind of mind that catalogs this sort of information and presents it when needed, like a data-retrieval system, make yourself a file. Get a 3 × 5 file box with cards and alphabetical dividers, and whenever you come across a bit of information you'll want to use later, file it away. It's maddening to recall that there is a better way, but not to remember the better way itself. Get it down on paper.

THE COOK'S GENERAL REFERENCE LIBRARY

A visit to a bookstore will quickly demonstrate how many hundreds of cookbooks there are in existence, many of them general, all-purpose guides for the home cook, many of them exceedingly specialized. In spite of this great proliferation of how-to-cook literature, it would be entirely possible to do a lifetime's food preparation with the help of only one good, general cookbook. There are a number of such basic books available. Among the best is:

Joy of Cooking by Irma S. Rombauer and Marion Rombauer Becker (Indianapolis and New York: Bobbs-Merrill Company, Inc.). First published in 1931 and regularly updated ever since, it contains more than 4,500 recipes, and is the one book most often recommended to amateurs by experts in the cooking field.

Here are others, all basic, all crammed with recipes and how-to information sufficient to keep the average home cook busy through thousands of meals:

American Home All-Purpose Cook Book by Frances M. Crawford and the Food Staff of *American Home* (New York: M. Evans and Company, Inc.).

The Family Circle Cookbook by the Food Editors of *Family Circle* and Jean Anderson (New York: Family Circle, Inc.).

The Doubleday Cookbook (2 vols.) by Jean Anderson and Elaine Hanna (New York: Doubleday & Company, Inc.).

The Redbook Cookbook, edited by Ruth Fairchild Pomeroy (New York: The McCall Publishing Company).

And there are several more equally as good, including a volume utilized by cooking craftsmen and experts:

Larousse Gastronomique. The Encyclopedia of Food, Wine, & Cooking by Prosper Montagne. Edited by Charlotte Turgeon and Nina Froud (New York: Crown Publishers, Inc.).

Rather more specialized, filled with recipes and information to delight the somewhat more established home cook, are any of the several cookbooks written by America's three great cooking specialists: James Beard, Craig Claibourne, and Julia Child. There are, as well, literally hundreds that deal well with a particular phase of cooking—meats, fish, poultry, breads, salads, and all the others; and there are many devoted to one particular food, such as mushrooms, nuts, chicken, cheese, whatever. Ethnic cookbooks abound, enticing you to experiment with the glorious culinary specialties of all the countries of the world. And there are books dealing with all the uses of a certain utensil, such as the slow cooker, the wok, the toaster oven, the food processor, and all the rest. Finally, if you or any member of your family is on a diet of any kind—weight-loss, diabetic, low-sodium, low-cholesterol—there are cookbooks to guide you in producing properly prepared (and attractive and delicious) foods within the range allowed by the diet.

There are many of us who spend a large part of our working lives helping you become a good home cook. A leisurely browse through the shelves of a bookstore will lead you to exactly the right guidance you need to show you the way to being the kind of cook you want to be.